ESSENTIAL WORLD ATLAS

CONTENTS

Copyright © 1996 Reed International Books Limited

George Philip Limited,
an imprint of Reed Books,
Michelin House, 81 Fulham Road, London SW3 6RB,
and Auckland, Melbourne, Singapore and Toronto

Cartography by Philip's

Published in North America by
Oxford University Press, Inc.,
198 Madison Avenue,
New York, N.Y. 10016, U.S.A.

Oxford is a registered trademark of Oxford University Press

Library of Congress Cataloging-in-Publication Data

Essential world atlas
   p. cm.
   Includes index.
   ISBN 0–19–521267–3 (alk. paper)
   1. Atlases.
   G1021.E88   1996 <G&M>
   912—dc20   96–3062
                     CIP
                     MAP

ISBN 0–19–521267–3   (Pbk.)

Printing (last digit):
9 8 7 6 5 4 3 2 1

Printed in Hong Kong

WORLD MAPS

World Statistics: Countries

This alphabetical list includes all the countries and territories of the world. If a territory is not completely independent, then the country it is associated with is named. The area figures give the total area of land, inland water and ice. The population figures are 1995 estimates. The annual income is the Gross National Product per capita in US dollars. The figures are the latest available, usually 1994.

Country/Territory	Area km² Thousands	Area miles² Thousands	Population Thousands	Capital	Annual Income US $
Adélie Land (Fr.)	432	167	0.03	–	–
Afghanistan	652	252	19,509	Kabul	220
Albania	28.8	11.1	3,458	Tirana	340
Algeria	2,382	920	25,012	Algiers	1,650
American Samoa (US)	0.20	0.08	58	Pago Pago	2,600
Andorra	0.45	0.17	65	Andorra La Vella	14,000
Angola	1,247	481	10,020	Luanda	600
Anguilla (UK)	0.1	0.04	8	The Valley	6,800
Antigua & Barbuda	0.44	0.17	67	St John's	6,390
Argentina	2,767	1,068	34,663	Buenos Aires	7,290
Armenia	29.8	11.5	3,603	Yerevan	660
Aruba (Neths)	0.19	0.07	71	Oranjestad	17,500
Ascension Is. (UK)	0.09	0.03	1.5	Georgetown	–
Australia	7,687	2,968	18,107	Canberra	17,510
Austria	83.9	32.4	8,004	Vienna	23,120
Azerbaijan	86.6	33.4	7,559	Baku	730
Azores (Port.)	2.2	0.87	238	Ponta Delgada	–
Bahamas	13.9	5.4	277	Nassau	11,500
Bahrain	0.68	0.26	558	Manama	7,870
Bangladesh	144	56	118,342	Dhaka	220
Barbados	0.43	0.17	263	Bridgetown	6,240
Belarus	207.6	80.1	10,500	Minsk	2,930
Belgium	30.5	11.8	10,140	Brussels	21,210
Belize	23	8.9	216	Belmopan	2,440
Benin	113	43	5,381	Porto-Novo	420
Bermuda (UK)	0.05	0.02	64	Hamilton	27,000
Bhutan	47	18.1	1,639	Thimphu	170
Bolivia	1,099	424	7,900	La Paz/Sucre	770
Bosnia-Herzegovina	51	20	3,800	Sarajevo	2,500
Botswana	582	225	1,481	Gaborone	2,590
Brazil	8,512	3,286	161,416	Brasília	3,020
British Indian Ocean Terr. (UK)	0.08	0.03	0	–	–
Brunei	5.8	2.2	284	Bandar Seri Begawan	9,000
Bulgaria	111	43	8,771	Sofia	1,160
Burkina Faso	274	106	10,326	Ouagadougou	300
Burma (Myanmar)	677	261	46,580	Rangoon	950
Burundi	27.8	10.7	6,412	Bujumbura	180
Cambodia	181	70	10,452	Phnom Penh	600
Cameroon	475	184	13,232	Yaoundé	770
Canada	9,976	3,852	29,972	Ottawa	20,670
Canary Is. (Spain)	7.3	2.8	1,494	Las Palmas/Santa Cruz	–
Cape Verde Is.	4	1.6	386	Praia	870
Cayman Is. (UK)	0.26	0.10	31	George Town	20,000
Central African Republic	623	241	3,294	Bangui	390
Chad	1,284	496	6,314	Ndjaména	200
Chatham Is. (NZ)	0.96	0.37	0.05	Waitangi	–
Chile	757	292	14,271	Santiago	3,070
China	9,597	3,705	1,226,944	Beijing	490
Christmas Is. (Aus.)	0.14	0.05	2	The Settlement	–
Cocos (Keeling) Is. (Aus.)	0.01	0.005	0.6	West Island	–
Colombia	1,139	440	34,948	Bogotá	1,400
Comoros	2.2	0.86	654	Moroni	520
Congo	342	132	2,593	Brazzaville	920
Cook Is. (NZ)	0.24	0.09	19	Avarua	900
Costa Rica	51.1	19.7	3,436	San José	2,160
Croatia	56.5	21.8	4,900	Zagreb	4,500
Cuba	111	43	11,050	Havana	1,250
Cyprus	9.3	3.6	742	Nicosia	10,380
Czech Republic	78.9	30.4	10,500	Prague	2,730
Denmark	43.1	16.6	5,229	Copenhagen	26,510
Djibouti	23.2	9	603	Djibouti	780
Dominica	0.75	0.29	89	Roseau	2,680
Dominican Republic	48.7	18.8	7,818	Santo Domingo	1,080
Ecuador	284	109	11,384	Quito	1,170
Egypt	1,001	387	64,100	Cairo	660
El Salvador	21	8.1	5,743	San Salvador	1,320
Equatorial Guinea	28.1	10.8	400	Malabo	360
Eritrea	94	36	3,850	Asmara	500
Estonia	44.7	17.3	1,531	Tallinn	3,040
Ethiopia	1,128	436	51,600	Addis Ababa	100
Falkland Is. (UK)	12.2	4.7	2	Stanley	–
Faroe Is. (Den.)	1.4	0.54	47	Tórshavn	23,660
Fiji	18.3	7.1	773	Suva	2,140
Finland	338	131	5,125	Helsinki	18,970
France	552	213	58,286	Paris	22,360
French Guiana (Fr.)	90	34.7	154	Cayenne	5,000
French Polynesia (Fr.)	4	1.5	217	Papeete	7,000
Gabon	268	103	1,316	Libreville	4,050
Gambia, The	11.3	4.4	1,144	Banjul	360
Georgia	69.7	26.9	5,448	Tbilisi	560
Germany	357	138	82,000	Berlin/Bonn	23,560
Ghana	239	92	17,462	Accra	430
Gibraltar (UK)	0.007	0.003	28	Gibraltar Town	5,000
Greece	132	51	10,510	Athens	7,390
Greenland (Den.)	2,176	840	59	Godthåb (Nuuk)	9,000
Grenada	0.34	0.13	94	St George's	2,410
Guadeloupe (Fr.)	1.7	0.66	443	Basse-Terre	9,000
Guam (US)	0.55	0.21	155	Agana	6,000
Guatemala	109	42	10,624	Guatemala City	1,110
Guinea	246	95	6,702	Conakry	510
Guinea-Bissau	36.1	13.9	1,073	Bissau	220
Guyana	215	83	832	Georgetown	350
Haiti	27.8	10.7	7,180	Port-au-Prince	800
Honduras	112	43	5,940	Tegucigalpa	580
Hong Kong (UK)	1.1	0.40	6,000	–	17,860
Hungary	93	35.9	10,500	Budapest	3,330
Iceland	103	40	269	Reykjavik	23,620
India	3,288	1,269	942,989	New Delhi	290
Indonesia	1,905	735	198,644	Jakarta	730
Iran	1,648	636	68,885	Tehran	4,750
Iraq	438	169	20,184	Baghdad	2,000
Ireland	70.3	27.1	3,589	Dublin	12,580
Israel	27	10.3	5,696	Jerusalem	13,760
Italy	301	116	57,181	Rome	19,620
Ivory Coast	322	125	14,271	Yamoussoukro	630
Jamaica	11	4.2	2,700	Kingston	1,390
Jan Mayen Is. (Nor.)	0.38	0.15	0.06	–	–
Japan	378	146	125,156	Tokyo	31,450
Johnston Is. (US)	0.002	0.0009	1	–	–
Jordan	89.2	34.4	5,547	Amman	1,190
Kazakstan	2,717	1,049	17,099	Alma-Ata	1,540
Kenya	580	224	28,240	Nairobi	270
Kerguelen Is. (Fr.)	7.2	2.8	0.7	–	–
Kermadec Is. (NZ)	0.03	0.01	0.1	–	–
Kiribati	0.72	0.28	80	Tarawa	710
Korea, North	121	47	23,931	Pyŏngyang	1,100
Korea, South	99	38.2	45,088	Seoul	7,670
Kuwait	17.8	6.9	1,668	Kuwait City	23,350
Kyrgyzstan	198.5	76.6	4,738	Bishkek	830
Laos	237	91	4,906	Vientiane	290
Latvia	65	25	2,558	Riga	2,030
Lebanon	10.4	4	2,971	Beirut	1,750
Lesotho	30.4	11.7	2,064	Maseru	660
Liberia	111	43	3,092	Monrovia	800
Libya	1,760	679	5,410	Tripoli	6,500
Liechtenstein	0.16	0.06	31	Vaduz	33,510
Lithuania	65.2	25.2	3,735	Vilnius	1,310
Luxembourg	2.6	1	408	Luxembourg	35,850
Macau (Port.)	0.02	0.006	490	Macau	7,500
Macedonia	25.7	9.9	2,173	Skopje	730
Madagascar	587	227	15,206	Antananarivo	240
Madeira (Port.)	0.81	0.31	253	Funchal	–
Malawi	118	46	9,800	Lilongwe	220
Malaysia	330	127	20,174	Kuala Lumpur	3,160
Maldives	0.30	0.12	254	Malé	820
Mali	1,240	479	10,700	Bamako	300
Malta	0.32	0.12	367	Valletta	6,800
Marshall Is.	0.18	0.07	55	Dalap-Uliga-Darrit	1,500
Martinique (Fr.)	1.1	0.42	384	Fort-de-France	3,500
Mauritania	1,025	396	2,268	Nouakchott	510
Mauritius	2.0	0.72	1,112	Port Louis	2,980
Mayotte (Fr.)	0.37	0.14	101	Mamoundzou	1,430
Mexico	1,958	756	93,342	Mexico City	3,750
Micronesia, Fed. States of	0.70	0.27	125	Palikir	1,560
Midway Is. (US)	0.005	0.002	2	–	–
Moldova	33.7	13	4,434	Chişinău	1,180
Monaco	0.002	0.0001	32	Monaco	16,000
Mongolia	1,567	605	2,408	Ulan Bator	400
Montserrat (UK)	0.10	0.04	11	Plymouth	4,500
Morocco	447	172	26,857	Rabat	1,030
Mozambique	802	309	17,800	Maputo	80
Namibia	825	318	1,610	Windhoek	1,660
Nauru	0.02	0.008	12	Yaren District	10,000
Nepal	141	54	21,953	Katmandu	160
Netherlands	41.5	16	15,495	Amsterdam/The Hague	20,710
Neths Antilles (Neths)	0.99	0.38	199	Willemstad	9,700
New Caledonia (Fr.)	19	7.3	181	Nouméa	6,000
New Zealand	269	104	3,567	Wellington	12,900
Nicaragua	130	50	4,544	Managua	360
Niger	1,267	489	9,149	Niamey	270
Nigeria	924	357	88,515	Abuja	310
Niue (NZ)	0.26	0.10	2	Alofi	–
Norfolk Is. (Aus.)	0.03	0.01	2	Kingston	–
Northern Mariana Is. (US)	0.48	0.18	47	Saipan	11,500
Norway	324	125	4,361	Oslo	26,340
Oman	212	82	2,252	Muscat	5,600
Pakistan	796	307	143,595	Islamabad	430
Palau	0.46	0.18	17	Koror	2,260
Panama	77.1	29.8	2,629	Panama City	2,580
Papua New Guinea	463	179	4,292	Port Moresby	1,120
Paraguay	407	157	4,979	Asunción	1,500
Peru	1,285	496	23,588	Lima	1,490
Philippines	300	116	67,167	Manila	830
Pitcairn Is. (UK)	0.03	0.01	0.06	Adamstown	–
Poland	313	121	38,587	Warsaw	2,270
Portugal	92.4	35.7	10,600	Lisbon	7,890
Puerto Rico (US)	9	3.5	3,689	San Juan	7,020
Qatar	11	4.2	594	Doha	15,140
Queen Maud Land (Nor.)	2,800	1,081	0	–	–
Réunion (Fr.)	2.5	0.97	655	Saint-Denis	3,900
Romania	238	92	22,863	Bucharest	1,120
Russia	17,075	6,592	148,385	Moscow	2,350
Rwanda	26.3	10.2	7,899	Kigali	200
St Helena (UK)	0.12	0.05	6	Jamestown	–
St Kitts & Nevis	0.36	0.14	45	Basseterre	4,470
St Lucia	0.62	0.24	147	Castries	3,040
St Pierre & Miquelon (Fr.)	0.24	0.09	6	Saint Pierre	–
St Vincent & Grenadines	0.39	0.15	111	Kingstown	1,730
San Marino	0.06	0.02	26	San Marino	20,000
São Tomé & Príncipe	0.96	0.37	133	São Tomé	330
Saudi Arabia	2,150	830	18,395	Riyadh	8,000
Senegal	197	76	8,308	Dakar	730
Seychelles	0.46	0.18	75	Victoria	6,370
Sierra Leone	71.7	27.7	4,467	Freetown	140
Singapore	0.62	0.24	2,990	Singapore	19,310
Slovak Republic	49	18.9	5,400	Bratislava	1,900
Slovenia	20.3	7.8	2,000	Ljubljana	6,310
Solomon Is.	28.9	11.2	378	Honiara	750
Somalia	638	246	9,180	Mogadishu	500
South Africa	1,220	471	44,000	C. Town/Pretoria/Bloem.	2,900
South Georgia (UK)	3.8	1.4	0.05	–	–
Spain	505	195	39,664	Madrid	13,650
Sri Lanka	65.6	25.3	18,359	Colombo	600
Sudan	2,506	967	29,980	Khartoum	750
Surinam	163	63	421	Paramaribo	1,210
Svalbard (Nor.)	62.9	24.3	4	Longyearbyen	–
Swaziland	17.4	6.7	849	Mbabane	1,050
Sweden	450	174	8,893	Stockholm	24,830
Switzerland	41.3	15.9	7,268	Bern	36,410
Syria	185	71	14,614	Damascus	5,700
Taiwan	36	13.9	21,100	Taipei	11,000
Tajikistan	143.1	55.2	6,102	Dushanbe	470
Tanzania	945	365	29,710	Dodoma	100
Thailand	513	198	58,432	Bangkok	2,040
Togo	56.8	21.9	4,140	Lomé	330
Tokelau (NZ)	0.01	0.005	2	Nukunonu	–
Tonga	0.75	0.29	107	Nuku'alofa	1,610
Trinidad & Tobago	5.1	2	1,295	Port of Spain	3,730
Tristan da Cunha (UK)	0.11	0.04	0.33	Edinburgh	–
Tunisia	164	63	8,906	Tunis	1,780
Turkey	779	301	61,303	Ankara	2,120
Turkmenistan	488.1	188.5	4,100	Ashkhabad	1,400
Turks & Caicos Is. (UK)	0.43	0.17	15	Cockburn Town	5,000
Tuvalu	0.03	0.01	10	Fongafale	600
Uganda	236	91	21,466	Kampala	190
Ukraine	603.7	233.1	52,027	Kiev	1,910
United Arab Emirates	83.6	32.3	2,800	Abu Dhabi	22,470
United Kingdom	243.3	94	58,306	London	17,970
United States of America	9,373	3,619	263,563	Washington, DC	24,750
Uruguay	177	68	3,186	Montevideo	3,910
Uzbekistan	447.4	172.7	22,833	Tashkent	960
Vanuatu	12.2	4.7	167	Port-Vila	1,230
Vatican City	0.0004	0.0002	1	–	–
Venezuela	912	352	21,800	Caracas	2,840
Vietnam	332	127	74,580	Hanoi	170
Virgin Is. (UK)	0.15	0.06	20	Road Town	–
Virgin Is. (US)	0.34	0.13	105	Charlotte Amalie	12,000
Wake Is.	0.008	0.003	0.30	–	–
Wallis & Futuna Is. (Fr.)	0.20	0.08	13	Mata-Utu	–
Western Sahara	266	103	220	El Aaiún	300
Western Samoa	2.8	1.1	169	Apia	980
Yemen	528	204	14,609	Sana	800
Yugoslavia	102.3	39.5	10,881	Belgrade	1,000
Zaire	2,345	905	44,504	Kinshasa	500
Zambia	753	291	9,500	Lusaka	370
Zimbabwe	391	151	11,453	Harare	540

World Statistics: Physical Dimensions

Each topic list is divided into continents and within a continent the items are listed in order of size. The order of the continents is as in the atlas. The bottom part of many of the lists is selective in order to give examples from as many different countries as possible. The figures are rounded as appropriate, and both metric and imperial measurements are given.

World, Continents, Oceans

	km^2	$miles^2$	%
The World	509,450,000	196,672,000	–
Land	149,450,000	57,688,000	29.3
Water	360,000,000	138,984,000	70.7
Asia	44,500,000	17,177,000	29.8
Africa	30,302,000	11,697,000	20.3
North America	24,241,000	9,357,000	16.2
South America	17,793,000	6,868,000	11.9
Antarctica	14,100,000	5,443,000	9.4
Europe	9,957,000	3,843,000	6.7
Australia & Oceania	8,557,000	3,303,000	5.7
Pacific Ocean	179,679,000	69,356,000	49.9
Atlantic Ocean	92,373,000	35,657,000	25.7
Indian Ocean	73,917,000	28,532,000	20.5
Arctic Ocean	14,090,000	5,439,000	3.9

Ocean Depths

Atlantic Ocean	m	ft
Puerto Rico (Milwaukee) Deep	9,220	30,249
Cayman Trench	7,680	25,197
Gulf of Mexico	5,203	17,070
Mediterranean Sea	5,121	16,801
Black Sea	2,211	7,254
North Sea	660	2,165

Indian Ocean	m	ft
Java Trench	7,450	24,442
Red Sea	2,635	8,454

Pacific Ocean	m	ft
Mariana Trench	11,022	36,161
Tonga Trench	10,882	35,702
Japan Trench	10,554	34,626
Kuril Trench	10,542	34,587

Arctic Ocean	m	ft
Molloy Deep	5,608	18,399

Mountains

Europe		m	ft
Mont Blanc	*France/Italy*	4,807	15,771
Monte Rosa	*Italy/Switzerland*	4,634	15,203
Dom	*Switzerland*	4,545	14,911
Liskamm	*Switzerland*	4,527	14,852
Weisshorn	*Switzerland*	4,505	14,780
Taschorn	*Switzerland*	4,490	14,730
Matterhorn/Cervino	*Italy/Switzerland*	4,478	14,691
Mont Maudit	*France/Italy*	4,465	14,649
Dent Blanche	*Switzerland*	4,356	14,291
Nadelhorn	*Switzerland*	4,327	14,196
Grandes Jorasses	*France/Italy*	4,208	13,806
Jungfrau	*Switzerland*	4,158	13,642
Grossglockner	*Austria*	3,797	12,457
Mulhacén	*Spain*	3,478	11,411
Zugspitze	*Germany*	2,962	9,718
Olympus	*Greece*	2,917	9,570
Triglav	*Slovenia*	2,863	9,393
Gerlachovka	*Slovak Republic*	2,655	8,711
Galdhöpiggen	*Norway*	2,468	8,100
Kebnekaise	*Sweden*	2,117	6,946
Ben Nevis	*UK*	1,343	4,406

Asia		m	ft
Everest	*China/Nepal*	8,848	29,029
K2 (Godwin Austen)	*China/Kashmir*	8,611	28,251
Kanchenjunga	*India/Nepal*	8,598	28,208
Lhotse	*China/Nepal*	8,516	27,939
Makalu	*China/Nepal*	8,481	27,824
Cho Oyu	*China/Nepal*	8,201	26,906
Dhaulagiri	*Nepal*	8,172	26,811
Manaslu	*Nepal*	8,156	26,758
Nanga Parbat	*Kashmir*	8,126	26,660
Annapurna	*Nepal*	8,078	26,502
Gasherbrum	*China/Kashmir*	8,068	26,469
Broad Peak	*China/Kashmir*	8,051	26,414
Xixabangma	*China*	8,012	26,286
Kangbachen	*India/Nepal*	7,902	25,925
Trivor	*Pakistan*	7,720	25,328
Pik Kommunizma	*Tajikistan*	7,495	24,590
Elbrus	*Russia*	5,642	18,510
Demavend	*Iran*	5,604	18,386
Ararat	*Turkey*	5,165	16,945
Gunong Kinabalu	*Malaysia (Borneo)*	4,101	13,455
Fuji-San	*Japan*	3,776	12,388

Africa		m	ft
Kilimanjaro	*Tanzania*	5,895	19,340
Mt Kenya	*Kenya*	5,199	17,057
Ruwenzori (Margherita)	*Uganda/Zaïre*	5,109	16,762
Ras Dashan	*Ethiopia*	4,620	15,157
Meru	*Tanzania*	4,565	14,977
Karisimbi	*Rwanda/Zaïre*	4,507	14,787
Mt Elgon	*Kenya/Uganda*	4,321	14,176
Batu	*Ethiopia*	4,307	14,130
Toubkal	*Morocco*	4,165	13,665
Mt Cameroon	*Cameroon*	4,070	13,353

Oceania		m	ft
Puncak Jaya	*Indonesia*	5,029	16,499
Puncak Trikora	*Indonesia*	4,750	15,584
Puncak Mandala	*Indonesia*	4,702	15,427
Mt Wilhelm	*Papua New Guinea*	4,508	14,790
Mauna Kea	*USA (Hawaii)*	4,205	13,796
Mauna Loa	*USA (Hawaii)*	4,170	13,681
Mt Cook	*New Zealand*	3,753	12,313
Mt Kosciusko	*Australia*	2,237	7,339

North America		m	ft
Mt McKinley (Denali)	*USA (Alaska)*	6,194	20,321
Mt Logan	*Canada*	5,959	19,551
Citlaltepetl	*Mexico*	5,700	18,701
Mt St Elias	*USA/Canada*	5,489	18,008
Popocatepetl	*Mexico*	5,452	17,887
Mt Foraker	*USA (Alaska)*	5,304	17,401
Ixtaccihuatl	*Mexico*	5,286	17,342
Lucania	*Canada*	5,227	17,149
Mt Steele	*Canada*	5,073	16,644
Mt Bona	*USA (Alaska)*	5,005	16,420
Mt Whitney	*USA*	4,418	14,495
Tajumulco	*Guatemala*	4,220	13,845
Chirripó Grande	*Costa Rica*	3,837	12,589
Pico Duarte	*Dominican Rep.*	3,175	10,417

South America		m	ft
Aconcagua	*Argentina*	6,960	22,834
Bonete	*Argentina*	6,872	22,546
Ojos del Salado	*Argentina/Chile*	6,863	22,516
Pissis	*Argentina*	6,779	22,241
Mercedario	*Argentina/Chile*	6,770	22,211
Huascaran	*Peru*	6,768	22,204
Llullaillaco	*Argentina/Chile*	6,723	22,057
Nudo de Cachi	*Argentina*	6,720	22,047
Yerupaja	*Peru*	6,632	21,758
Sajama	*Bolivia*	6,542	21,463
Chimborazo	*Ecuador*	6,267	20,561
Pico Colon	*Colombia*	5,800	19,029
Pico Bolivar	*Venezuela*	5,007	16,427

Antarctica		m	ft
Vinson Massif		4,897	16,066
Mt Kirkpatrick		4,528	14,855

Rivers

Europe		km	miles
Volga	*Caspian Sea*	3,700	2,300
Danube	*Black Sea*	2,850	1,770
Ural	*Caspian Sea*	2,535	1,575
Dnepr (Dnipro)	*Volga*	2,285	1,420
Kama	*Volga*	2,030	1,260
Don	*Volga*	1,990	1,240
Petchora	*Arctic Ocean*	1,790	1,110
Oka	*Volga*	1,480	920
Dnister (Dniester)	*Black Sea*	1,400	870
Vyatka	*Kama*	1,370	850
Rhine	*North Sea*	1,320	820
N. Dvina	*Arctic Ocean*	1,290	800
Elbe	*North Sea*	1,145	710

Asia		km	miles
Yangtze	*Pacific Ocean*	6,380	3,960
Yenisey–Angara	*Arctic Ocean*	5,550	3,445
Huang He	*Pacific Ocean*	5,464	3,395
Ob–Irtysh	*Arctic Ocean*	5,410	3,360
Mekong	*Pacific Ocean*	4,500	2,795
Amur	*Pacific Ocean*	4,400	2,730
Lena	*Arctic Ocean*	4,400	2,730
Irtysh	*Ob*	4,250	2,640
Yenisey	*Arctic Ocean*	4,090	2,540
Ob	*Arctic Ocean*	3,680	2,285
Indus	*Indian Ocean*	3,100	1,925
Brahmaputra	*Indian Ocean*	2,900	1,800
Syrdarya	*Aral Sea*	2,860	1,775
Salween	*Indian Ocean*	2,800	1,740
Euphrates	*Indian Ocean*	2,700	1,675
Amudarya	*Aral Sea*	2,540	1,575

Africa		km	miles
Nile	*Mediterranean*	6,670	4,140
Zaïre/Congo	*Atlantic Ocean*	4,670	2,900
Niger	*Atlantic Ocean*	4,180	2,595
Zambezi	*Indian Ocean*	3,540	2,200
Oubangi/Uele	*Zaïre*	2,250	1,400
Kasai	*Zaïre*	1,950	1,210
Shaballe	*Indian Ocean*	1,930	1,200
Orange	*Atlantic Ocean*	1,860	1,155
Cubango	*Okavango Swamps*	1,800	1,120
Limpopo	*Indian Ocean*	1,600	995
Senegal	*Atlantic Ocean*	1,600	995

Australia		km	miles
Murray–Darling	*Indian Ocean*	3,750	2,330
Darling	*Murray*	3,070	1,905
Murray	*Indian Ocean*	2,575	1,600
Murrumbidgee	*Murray*	1,690	1,050

North America		km	miles
Mississippi–Missouri	*Gulf of Mexico*	6,020	3,740
Mackenzie	*Arctic Ocean*	4,240	2,630
Mississippi	*Gulf of Mexico*	3,780	2,350
Missouri	*Mississippi*	3,780	2,350
Yukon	*Pacific Ocean*	3,185	1,980
Rio Grande	*Gulf of Mexico*	3,030	1,880
Arkansas	*Mississippi*	2,340	1,450
Colorado	*Pacific Ocean*	2,330	1,445
Red	*Mississippi*	2,040	1,270
Columbia	*Pacific Ocean*	1,950	1,210
Saskatchewan	*Lake Winnipeg*	1,940	1,205

South America		km	miles
Amazon	*Atlantic Ocean*	6,450	4,010
Paraná–Plate	*Atlantic Ocean*	4,500	2,800
Purus	*Amazon*	3,350	2,080
Madeira	*Amazon*	3,200	1,990
São Francisco	*Atlantic Ocean*	2,900	1,800
Paraná	*Plate*	2,800	1,740
Tocantins	*Atlantic Ocean*	2,750	1,710
Paraguay	*Paraná*	2,550	1,580
Orinoco	*Atlantic Ocean*	2,500	1,550
Pilcomayo	*Paraná*	2,500	1,550
Araguaia	*Tocantins*	2,250	1,400

Lakes

Europe		km^2	$miles^2$
Lake Ladoga	*Russia*	17,700	6,800
Lake Onega	*Russia*	9,700	3,700
Saimaa system	*Finland*	8,000	3,100
Vänern	*Sweden*	5,500	2,100

Asia		km^2	$miles^2$
Caspian Sea	*Asia*	371,800	143,550
Aral Sea	*Kazakstan/Uzbekistan*	33,640	13,000
Lake Baykal	*Russia*	30,500	11,780
Tonlé Sap	*Cambodia*	20,000	7,700
Lake Balqash	*Kazakstan*	18,500	7,100

Africa		km^2	$miles^2$
Lake Victoria	*East Africa*	68,000	26,000
Lake Tanganyika	*Central Africa*	33,000	13,000
Lake Malawi/Nyasa	*East Africa*	29,600	11,430
Lake Chad	*Central Africa*	25,000	9,700
Lake Turkana	*Ethiopia/Kenya*	8,500	3,300
Lake Volta	*Ghana*	8,500	3,300

Australia		km^2	$miles^2$
Lake Eyre	*Australia*	8,900	3,400
Lake Torrens	*Australia*	5,800	2,200
Lake Gairdner	*Australia*	4,800	1,900

North America		km^2	$miles^2$
Lake Superior	*Canada/USA*	82,350	31,800
Lake Huron	*Canada/USA*	59,600	23,010
Lake Michigan	*USA*	58,000	22,400
Great Bear Lake	*Canada*	31,800	12,280
Great Slave Lake	*Canada*	28,500	11,000
Lake Erie	*Canada/USA*	25,700	9,900
Lake Winnipeg	*Canada*	24,400	9,400
Lake Ontario	*Canada/USA*	19,500	7,500
Lake Nicaragua	*Nicaragua*	8,200	3,200

South America		km^2	$miles^2$
Lake Titicaca	*Bolivia/Peru*	8,300	3,200
Lake Poopo	*Peru*	2,800	1,100

Islands

Europe		km^2	$miles^2$
Great Britain	*UK*	229,880	88,700
Iceland	*Atlantic Ocean*	103,000	39,800
Ireland	*Ireland/UK*	84,400	32,600
Novaya Zemlya (N.)	*Russia*	48,200	18,600
Sicily	*Italy*	25,500	9,800
Corsica	*France*	8,700	3,400

Asia		km^2	$miles^2$
Borneo	*South-east Asia*	744,360	287,400
Sumatra	*Indonesia*	473,600	182,860
Honshu	*Japan*	230,500	88,980
Celebes	*Indonesia*	189,000	73,000
Java	*Indonesia*	126,700	48,900
Luzon	*Philippines*	104,700	40,400
Hokkaido	*Japan*	78,400	30,300

Africa		km^2	$miles^2$
Madagascar	*Indian Ocean*	587,040	226,660
Socotra	*Indian Ocean*	3,600	1,400
Réunion	*Indian Ocean*	2,500	965

Oceania		km^2	$miles^2$
New Guinea	*Indonesia/Papua NG*	821,030	317,000
New Zealand (S.)	*Pacific Ocean*	150,500	58,100
New Zealand (N.)	*Pacific Ocean*	114,700	44,300
Tasmania	*Australia*	67,800	26,200
Hawaii	*Pacific Ocean*	10,450	4,000

North America		km^2	$miles^2$
Greenland	*Atlantic Ocean*	2,175,600	839,800
Baffin Is.	*Canada*	508,000	196,100
Victoria Is.	*Canada*	212,200	81,900
Ellesmere Is.	*Canada*	212,000	81,800
Cuba	*Caribbean Sea*	110,860	42,800
Hispaniola	*Dominican Rep./Haiti*	76,200	29,400
Jamaica	*Caribbean Sea*	11,400	4,400
Puerto Rico	*Atlantic Ocean*	8,900	3,400

South America		km^2	$miles^2$
Tierra del Fuego	*Argentina/Chile*	47,000	18,100
Falkland Is. (E.)	*Atlantic Ocean*	6,800	2,600

MAP PROJECTIONS

MAP PROJECTIONS

A map projection is the systematic depiction on a plane surface of the imaginary lines of latitude or longitude from a globe of the earth. This network of lines is called the graticule and forms the framework upon which an accurate depiction of the earth is made. The map graticule, which is the basis of any map, is constructed sometimes by graphical means, but often by using mathematical formulae to give the intersections of the graticule plotted as x and y co-ordinates. The choice between projections is based upon which properties the cartographer wishes the map to possess, the map scale and also the extent of the area to be mapped. Since the globe is three dimensional, it is not possible to depict its surface on a two dimensional plane without distortion. Preservation of one of the basic properties listed below can only be secured at the expense of the others and the choice of projection is often a compromise solution.

Correct Area

In these projections the areas from the globe are to scale on the map. For example, if you look at the diagram at the top right, areas of 10° x 10° are shown from the equator to the poles. The proportion of this area at the extremities are approximately 11:1. An equal area projection will retain that proportion in its portrayal of those areas. This is particularly useful in the mapping of densities and distributions. Projections with this property are termed **Equal Area, Equivalent or Homolographic.**

Correct Distance

In these projections the scale is correct along the meridians, or in the case of the Azimuthal Equidistant scale is true along any line drawn from the centre of the projection. They are called **Equidistant.**

Correct Shape

This property can only be true within small areas as it is achieved only by having a uniform scale distortion along both x and y axes of the projection. The projections are called **Conformal or Orthomorphic.**

In order to minimise the distortions at the edges of some projections, central portions of them are often selected for atlas maps. Below are listed some of the major types of projection.

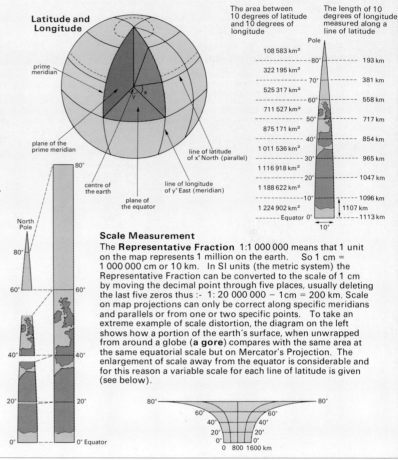

Latitude and Longitude

prime meridian

plane of the prime meridian

centre of the earth

plane of the equator

line of latitude of x° North (parallel)

line of longitude of y° East (meridian)

The area between 10 degrees of latitude and 10 degrees of longitude

Pole	
108 583 km²	—80°— 193 km
322 195 km²	—70°— 381 km
525 317 km²	—60°— 558 km
711 527 km²	—50°— 717 km
875 171 km²	—40°— 854 km
1 011 536 km²	—30°— 965 km
1 116 918 km²	—20°— 1047 km
1 188 622 km²	—10°— 1096 km
1 224 902 km²	1107 km
Equator 0°	1113 km

The length of 10 degrees of longitude measured along a line of latitude

Scale Measurement

The **Representative Fraction** 1:1 000 000 means that 1 unit on the map represents 1 million on the earth. So 1 cm = 1 000 000 cm or 10 km. In SI units (the metric system) the Representative Fraction can be converted to the scale of 1 cm by moving the decimal point through five places, usually deleting the last five zeros thus :- 1: 20 000 000 – 1cm = 200 km. Scale on map projections can only be correct along specific meridians and parallels or from one or two specific points. To take an extreme example of scale distortion, the diagram on the left shows how a portion of the earth's surface, when unwrapped from around a globe (**a gore**) compares with the same area at the same equatorial scale but on Mercator's Projection. The enlargement of scale away from the equator is considerable and for this reason a variable scale for each line of latitude is given (see below).

0 800 1600 km

AZIMUTHAL OR ZENITHAL PROJECTIONS

These are constructed by the projection of part of the graticule from the globe onto a plane tangential to any single point on it. This plane may be tangential to the equator (**equatorial case**), the poles (**polar case**) or any other point (**oblique case**). Any straight line drawn from the point at which the plane touches the globe is the shortest distance from that point and is known as a **great circle**. In its **Gnomonic** construction *any* straight line on the map is a great circle, but there is great exaggeration towards the edges and this reduces its general uses. There are five different ways of transferring the graticule onto the plane and these are shown on the right. The central diagram below shows how the graticules vary, using the polar case as the example.

Equidistant | Equal-Area | Orthographic | Gnomonic | Stereographic (conformal)

Oblique Case

The plane touches the globe at any point between the equator and poles. The oblique orthographic uses the distortion in azimuthal projections away from the centre to give a graphic depiction of the earth as seen from any desired point in space. It can also be used in both Polar and Equatorial cases. It is used not only for the earth but also for the moon and planets.

Polar Case

The polar case is the simplest to construct and the diagram below shows the differing effects of all five methods of construction comparing their coverage, distortion etc., using North America as the example.

Equatorial Case

The example shown here is Lambert's Equivalent Azimuthal. It is the only projection which is both equal area and where bearing is true from the centre.

Stereographic

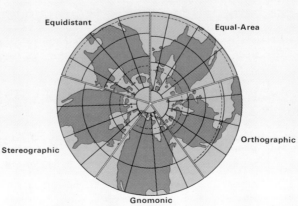

Equidistant

Equal-Area

Orthographic

Gnomonic

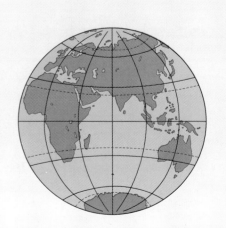

CONICAL PROJECTIONS

These use the projection of the graticule from the globe onto a cone which is tangential to a line of latitude (termed the **standard parallel**). This line is always an arc and scale is always true along it. Because of its method of construction it is used mainly for depicting the temperate latitudes around the standard parallel i.e. where there is least distortion. To reduce the distortion and include a larger range of latitudes, the projection may be constructed with the cone bisecting the surface of the globe so that there are two standard parallels each of which is true to scale. The distortion is thus spread more evenly between the two chosen parallels.

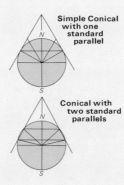

Simple Conical with one standard parallel

Conical with two standard parallels

Bonne

This is a modification of the simple conic whereby the true scale along the meridians is sacrificed to enable the accurate representation of areas. However scale is true along each parallel but shapes are distorted at the edges.

Simple Conic

Scale is correct not only along the standard parallel but also along all meridians. The selection of the standard parallel used is crucial because of the distortion away from it. The projection is usually used to portray regions or continents at small scales.

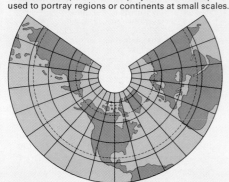

Lambert's Conformal Conic

This projection uses two standard parallels but instead of being equal area as Albers, it is Conformal. Because it has comparatively small distortion, direction and distances can be readily measured and it is therefore used for some navigational charts.

Albers Conical Equal Area

This projection uses two standard parallels and once again the selection of the two specific ones relative to the land area to be mapped is very important. It is equal area and is especially useful for large land masses oriented East-West, for example the U.S.A.

CYLINDRICAL AND OTHER WORLD PROJECTIONS

This group of projections are those which permit the whole of the Earth's surface to be depicted on one map. They are a very large group of projections and the following are only a few of them. Cylindrical projections are constructed by the projection of the graticule from the globe onto a cylinder tangential to the globe. In the examples shown here the cylinder touches the equator, but it can be moved through 90° so it touches the poles - this is called the **Transverse Aspect**. If the cylinder is twisted so that it touches anywhere between the equator and poles it is called the **Oblique Aspect**. Although cylindrical projections can depict all the main land masses, there is considerable distortion of shape and area towards the poles. One cylindrical projection, **Mercator** overcomes this shortcoming by possessing the unique navigational property that any straight drawn on it is a line of constant bearing (**loxodrome**), i.e. a straight line route on the globe crosses the parallels and meridians on the map at the same angles as on the globe. It is used for maps and charts between 15° either side of the equator. Beyond this enlargement of area is a serious drawback, although it is used for navigational charts at all latitudes.

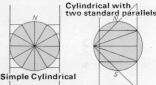

Cylindrical with two standard parallels

Simple Cylindrical

Mercator

Mollweide

Sanson-Flamsteed

Mollweide and Sanson-Flamsteed

Both of these projections are termed **pseudo-cylindrical**. They are basically cylindrical projections where parallels have been progressively shortened and drawn to scale towards the poles. This allows them to overcome the gross distortions exhibited by the ordinary cylindrical projections and they are in fact Equal Area, Mollweide's giving a slightly better shape. To improve the shape of the continents still further they, like some other projections can be **Interrupted** as can be seen below, but this is at the expense of contiguous sea areas. These projections can have any central meridian and so can be 'centred' on the Atlantic, Pacific, Asia, America etc. In this form both projections are suitable for any form of mapping statistical distributions.

Hammer

This is not a cylindrical projection, but is developed from the Lambert Azimuthal Equal Area by doubling all the East-West distances along the parallels from the central meridian. Like both Sanson–Flamsteed and Mollweide it is distorted towards its edges but has curved parallels to lessen the distortion.

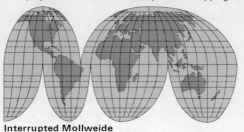

Interrupted Mollweide

Interrupted Sanson-Flamsteed

User Guide

Organization of the atlas

Prepared in accordance with the highest standards of international cartography to provide accurate and detailed representation of the earth, the atlas is made up of four separate sections and is organized with ease of use in mind.

The first section of the atlas consists of up-to-date world geographical and demographical statistics, graphics on map projections intended to help the reader understand how cartographers create and use map projections, and this user guide.

The second section of the atlas, the 32-page United States Maps section, has blue page borders and offers comprehensive coverage of the United States and its outlying areas, with climate and agricultural maps, politically colored maps with some topographical detail, maps of major urban areas, and a 16-page index with longitude and latitude coordinates.

The third section of the atlas, the 32-page Introduction to World Geography section, consists of thematic maps, graphs, and charts on a range of geographical and demographical topics, and a subject index.

The fourth and final section of the atlas, the 96-page World Maps section, has gray page borders and covers the earth continent by continent in the classic sequence adopted by cartographers since the 16th century. This section begins with Europe, then Asia, Africa, Australia and Oceania, North America, and South America. For each continent, there are maps at a variety of scales: first, physical relief maps and political maps of the whole continent, then large scale maps of the most important or densely populated areas.

The governing principle is that by turning the pages of the World Maps section, the reader moves steadily from north to south through each continent, with each map overlapping its neighbors. Immediately following the maps in the World Maps section is the comprehensive index to the maps, which contains 44,000 entries of both place names and geographical features. The index provides the latitude and longitude coordinates as well as letters and numbers, so that locating any site can be accomplished with speed and accuracy.

Map presentation

All of the maps in the atlas are drawn with north at the top (except for the map of the Arctic Ocean and the map of Antarctica). The maps in the United States Maps section and the World Maps section contain the following information in their borders: the map title; the scale; the projection used; the degrees of latitude and longitude; and on the physical relief maps, a height and depth reference panel identifying the colors used for each layer of contouring. In addition to this information, the maps in the World Maps section also contain locator diagrams which show the area covered, the page numbers for adjacent maps, and the letters and numbers used in the index for locating place names and geographical features.

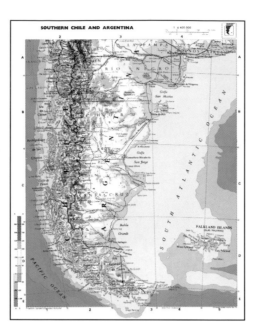

Map symbols

Each map contains a vast amount of detail which is conveyed clearly and accurately by the use of symbols. Points and circles of varying sizes locate and identify the relative importance of towns and cities; different styles of type are employed for administrative, geographical and regional place names. A variety of pictorial symbols denote landscape features such as glaciers, marshes and reefs, and man-made structures including roads, railroads, airports, canals and dams. International borders are shown by red lines. Where neighboring countries are in dispute, the maps show the *de facto* boundary between nations, regardless of the legal or historical situation. The symbols are explained on the first page of each of the map sections.

Map scales

The scale of each map is given in the numerical form known as the representative fraction. The first figure is always one, signifying one unit of distance on the map; the second figure, usually in millions, is the number by which the map unit must be multiplied to give the equivalent distance on

LARGE SCALE		
1: 1 000 000	1 cm = 10 km	1 inch = 16 miles
1: 2 500 000	1 cm = 25 km	1 inch = 39.5 miles
1: 5 000 000	1 cm = 50 km	1 inch = 79 miles
1: 6 000 000	1 cm = 60 km	1 inch = 95 miles
1: 8 000 000	1 cm = 80 km	1 inch = 126 miles
1: 10 000 000	1 cm = 100 km	1 inch = 158 miles
1: 15 000 000	1 cm = 150 km	1 inch = 237 miles
1: 20 000 000	1 cm = 200 km	1 inch = 316 miles
1: 50 000 000	1 cm = 500 km	1 inch = 790 miles
SMALL SCALE		

the earth's surface. Calculations can easily be made in centimeters and kilometers, by dividing the earth units figure by 100 000 (i.e. deleting the last five 0s). Thus 1:1 000 000 means l cm = 10 km. The calculation for inches and miles is more laborious, but 1 000 000

divided by 63 360 (the number of inches in a mile) shows that 1:1 000 000 means approximately 1 inch = 16 miles. The table shown provides distance equivalents for scales down to 1:50 000 000.

Measuring distances

Although each map is accompanied by a scale bar, distances cannot always be measured with confidence because of the distortions involved in portraying the curved surface of the earth on a flat page. As a general rule, the larger the map scale (i.e. the lower the number of earth units in the representative fraction), the more accurate and reliable will be the distance measured. On small scale maps such as those of the world and of entire continents, measurement may only be accurate along the standard parallels, or central axes, and should not be attempted without considering the map projection.

Latitude and longitude

Accurate positioning of individual points on the earth's surface is made possible by reference to the geometrical system of latitude and longitude. Latitude parallels are drawn west–east around the earth and numbered by degrees north and south of the Equator, which is designated 0° of latitude. Longitude meridians are drawn north–south and numbered by degrees east and west of the prime meridian, 0° of longitude, which passes through Greenwich in England. By referring to these coordinates and their subdivisions of minutes (1/60th of a degree) and seconds (1/60th of a minute), any place on earth can be located to within a few hundred yards. Latitude and longitude are indicated by blue lines on the maps; they are straight or curved according to the projection employed. Reference to these lines is the easiest way of determining the relative positions of places on different large scale maps, and for plotting compass directions.

Name forms

For ease of reference, both English and local name forms appear in the atlas. Oceans, seas and countries are shown in English throughout the atlas; country names may be abbreviated to their commonly accepted form (e.g. Germany, not The Federal Republic of Germany). Conventional English forms are also used for place names on the smaller scale maps of the continents. However, local name forms are used on all large scale and regional maps, with the English form given in brackets only for important cities – the large scale map of Eastern Europe and Turkey thus shows Moskva (Moscow). For countries which do not use a Roman script, place names have been transcribed according to the systems adopted by the British and US Geographic Names Authorities. For China, the Pin Yin system has been used, with some more widely known forms appearing in brackets, as with Beijing (Peking). Both English and local names appear in the index to the world maps.

UNITED STATES MAPS

SETTLEMENTS

◌ WASHINGTON D.C.　■ Tampa　◉ Fresno　◉ Waterloo　◎ Ventura　⊙ Barstow　○ Blythe　○ Hope

Settlement symbols and type styles vary according to the scale of each map and indicate the importance of towns on the map rather than specific population figures

ADMINISTRATION

——— International Boundaries

········· Internal Boundaries

⬚ National Parks, Recreation Areas and Monuments

Country Names
CANADA

Administrative Area Names
MICHIGAN

COMMUNICATIONS

═══ Major Highways

⌒ Other Principal Roads

≍ Passes

✈+✧ Airports and Airfields

⌒ Principal Railroads

-··- Railroads Under Construction

⌒ Other Railroads

╤---╘ Railroad Tunnels

⸺ Principal Canals

PHYSICAL FEATURES

⌒ Perennial Streams

······ Intermittent Streams

⬭ Perennial Lakes and Reservoirs

⬭ Intermittent Lakes and Salt Flats

Swamps and Marshes

▱ Permanent Ice and Glaciers

▲ 8848 Elevations in meters

▼ 8050 Sea Depths in meters

1134 Height of Lake Surface Above Sea Level in meters

1 meter is approx. 3.3 feet

CITY MAPS

In addition to, or instead of, the symbols explained above, the following symbols are used on the city maps between pages 20-29

◢ Urban Areas

⌒ Limited Access Roads

⌒ Aqueducts

Woodland and Parks

⌒ Secondary Roads

········ Ferry Routes

⌒ State Boundaries

✕ Airports

⌒ Canals

⌒ County Boundaries

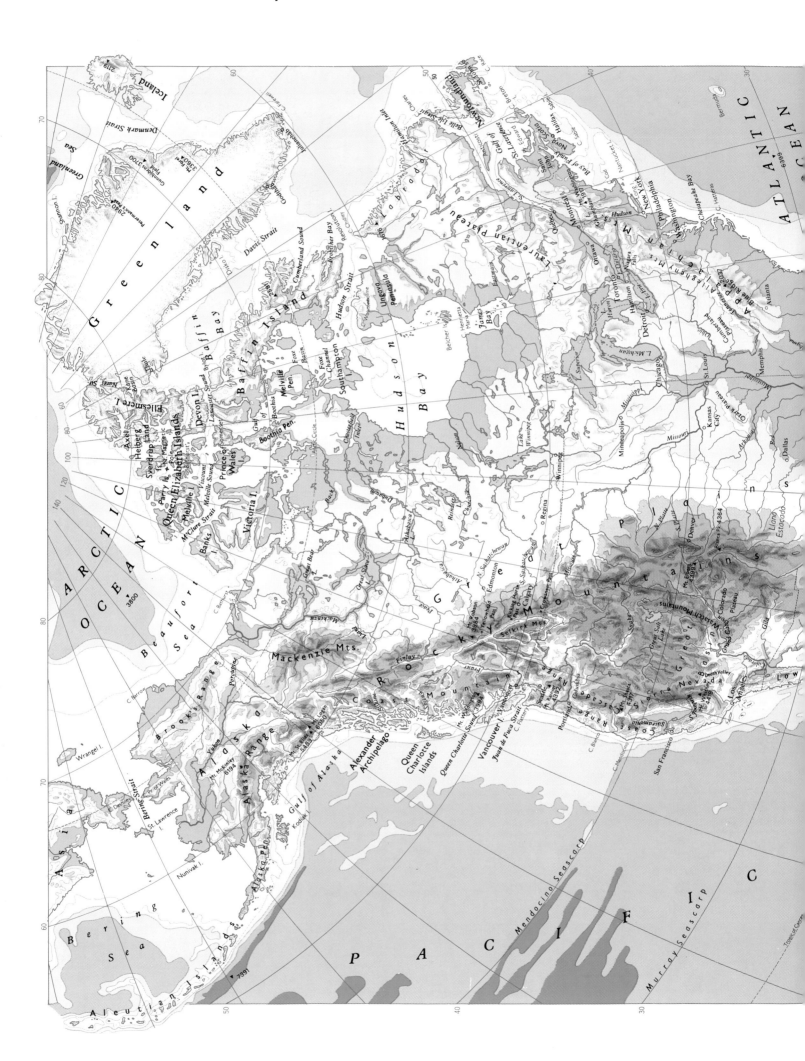

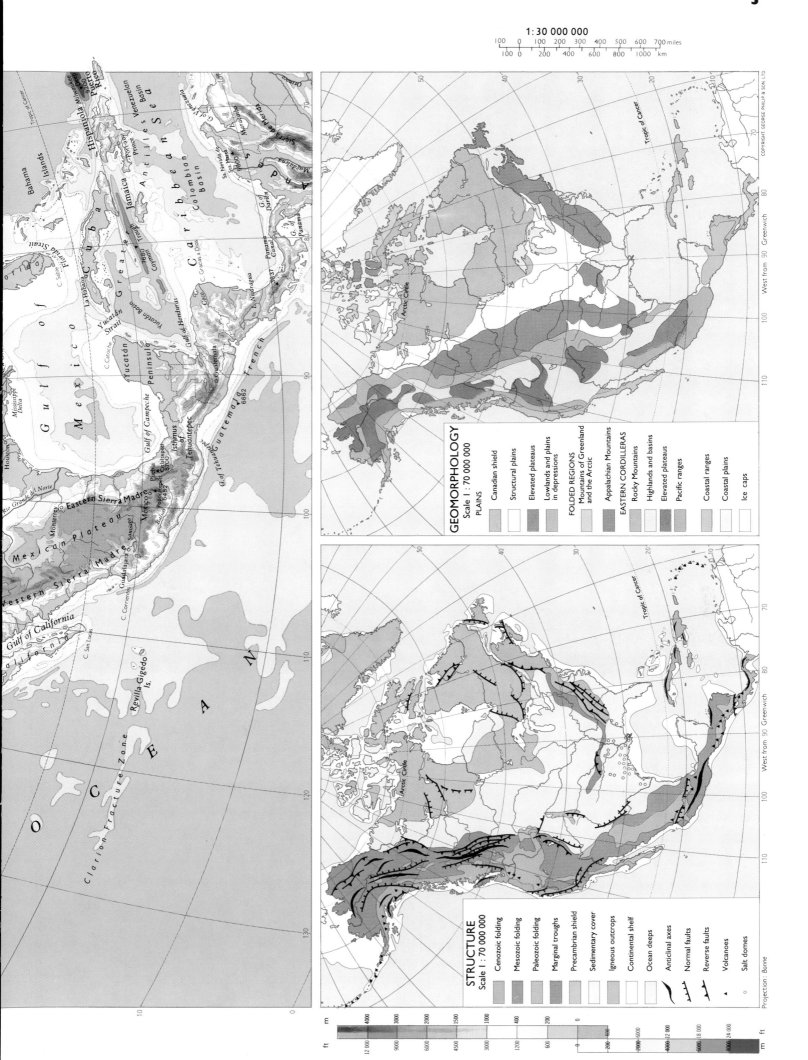

1:30 000 000

100   0   100   200   300   400   500   600   700 miles

100   0   200   400   600   800   1000   km

GEOMORPHOLOGY
Scale 1 : 70 000 000

PLAINS
Canadian shield
Structural plains
Elevated plateaus
Lowlands and plains in depressions

FOLDED REGIONS
Mountains of Greenland and the Arctic
Appalachian Mountains

EASTERN CORDILLERAS
Rocky Mountains
Highlands and basins
Elevated plateaus
Pacific ranges
Coastal ranges
Coastal plains
Ice caps

STRUCTURE
Scale 1 : 70 000 000

Cenozoic folding
Mesozoic folding
Paleozoic folding
Marginal troughs
Precambrian shield
Sedimentary cover
Igneous outcrops
Continental shelf
Ocean deeps
Anticlinal axes
Normal faults
Reverse faults
Volcanoes
Salt domes

Projection: Bonne

West from 90 Greenwich

West from 90 Greenwich

Arctic Circle

Tropic of Cancer

Tropic of Cancer

Gulf of Mexico

Caribbean Sea

Greater Antilles

Bahama Islands

Cuba

Jamaica

Hispaniola

Puerto Rico

Mexican Plateau

Western Sierra Madre

Eastern Sierra Madre

Gulf of California

Clarion Fracture Zone

PACIFIC OCEAN

Yucatán Peninsula

Isthmus of Tehuantepec

Guatemala Trench

Venezuelan Basin

Colombian Basin

Revilla Gigedo Is.

m
4000
3000
2000
1500
1000
400
200
0

ft
12 000
9000
6000
4500
3000
1200
600
0
200
6000
12 000
18 000
24 000
ft   m

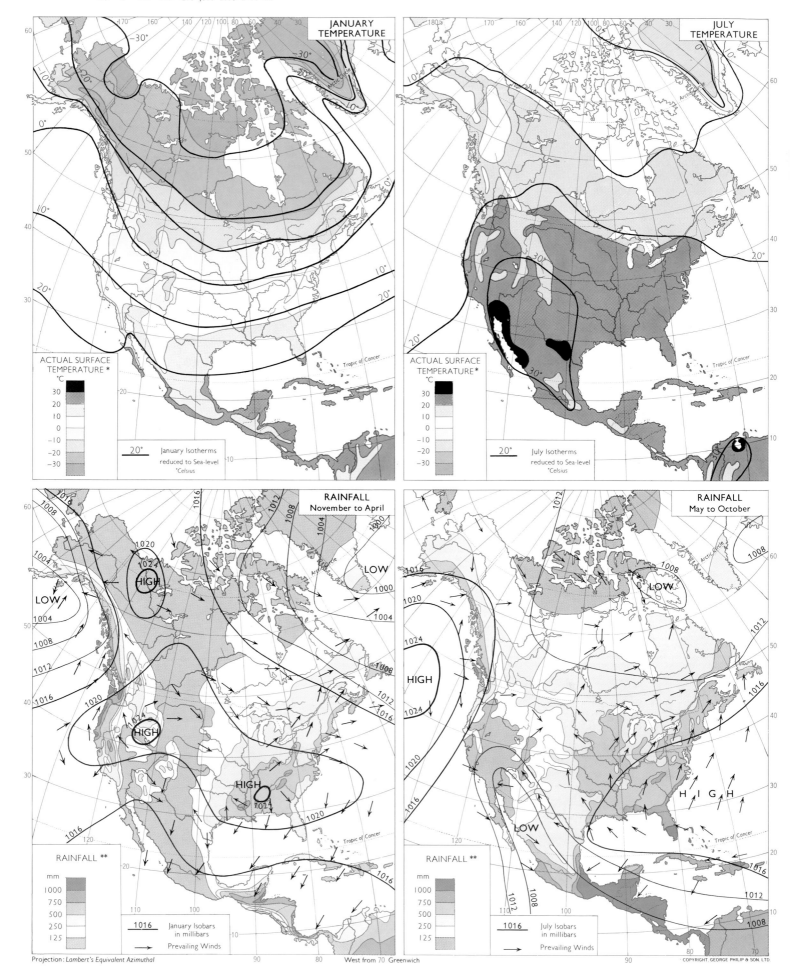

1:70 000 000

JANUARY
TEMPERATURE

ACTUAL SURFACE
TEMPERATURE *
°C
30
20
10
0
-10
-20
-30

_20°_ January Isotherms
reduced to Sea-level
°Celsius

JULY
TEMPERATURE

ACTUAL SURFACE
TEMPERATURE *
°C
30
20
10
0
-10
-20
-30

_20°_ July Isotherms
reduced to Sea-level
°Celsius

RAINFALL
November to April

RAINFALL **
mm
1000
750
500
250
125

_1016_ January Isobars
in millibars
→ Prevailing Winds

RAINFALL
May to October

RAINFALL **
mm
1000
750
500
250
125

_1016_ July Isobars
in millibars
→ Prevailing Winds

Projection : Lambert's Equivalent Azimuthal   West from 70 Greenwich   COPYRIGHT. GEORGE PHILIP & SON. LTD

*To convert °C to °F, multiply by 1.8, then add 32   **1 in equals 25.4mm

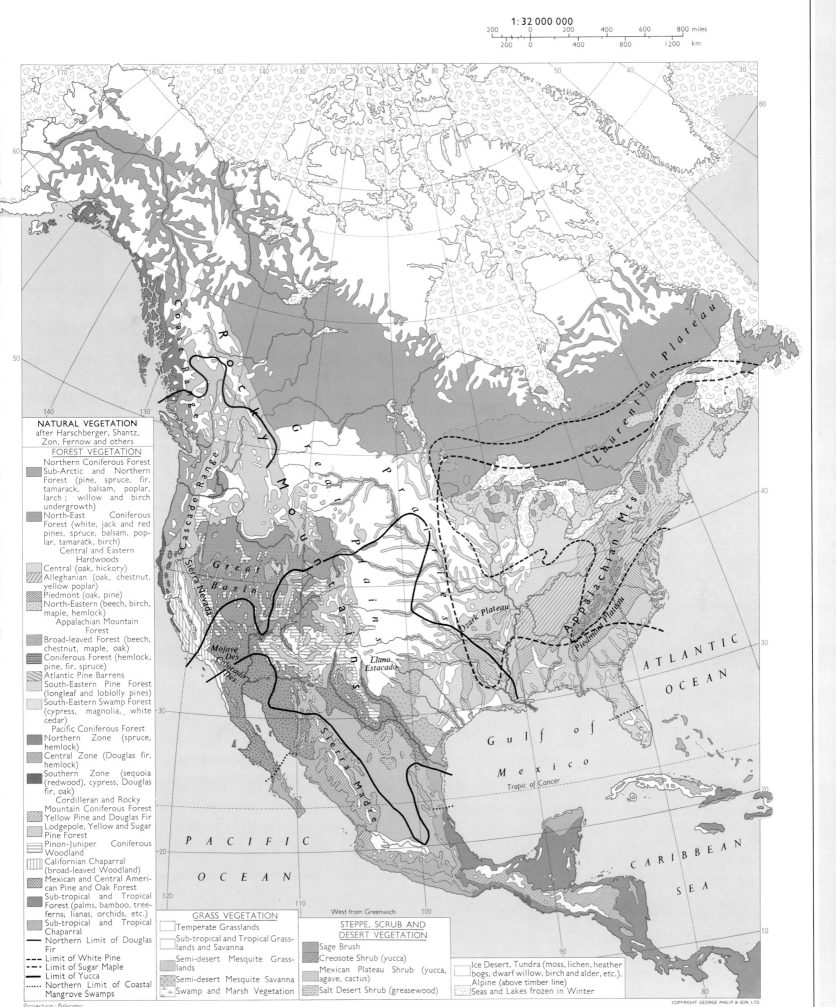

1 : 32 000 000

Projection: Polyconic

NATURAL VEGETATION
after Harschberger, Shantz, Zon, Fernow and others

FOREST VEGETATION

Northern Coniferous Forest
Sub-Arctic and Northern Forest (pine, spruce, fir, tamarack, balsam, poplar, larch; willow and birch undergrowth)

North-East Coniferous Forest (white, jack and red pines, spruce, balsam, poplar, tamarack, birch)

Central and Eastern Hardwoods

Central (oak, hickory)

Alleghanian (oak, chestnut, yellow poplar)

Piedmont (oak, pine)

North-Eastern (beech, birch, maple, hemlock)

Appalachian Mountain Forest

Broad-leaved Forest (beech, chestnut, maple, oak)

Coniferous Forest (hemlock, pine, fir, spruce)

Atlantic Pine Barrens

South-Eastern Pine Forest (longleaf and loblolly pines)

South-Eastern Swamp Forest (cypress, magnolia, white cedar)

Pacific Coniferous Forest

Northern Zone (spruce, hemlock)

Central Zone (Douglas fir, hemlock)

Southern Zone (sequoia (redwood), cypress, Douglas fir, oak)

Cordilleran and Rocky Mountain Coniferous Forest

Yellow Pine and Douglas Fir

Lodgepole, Yellow and Sugar Pine Forest

Pinon-Juniper Coniferous Woodland

Californian Chaparral (broad-leaved Woodland)

Mexican and Central American Pine and Oak Forest

Sub-tropical and Tropical Forest (palms, bamboo, tree-ferns, lianas, orchids, etc.)

Sub-tropical and Tropical Chaparral

—— Northern Limit of Douglas Fir

‒ ‒ ‒ Limit of White Pine

‒·‒·‒ Limit of Sugar Maple

—— Limit of Yucca

········ Northern Limit of Coastal Mangrove Swamps

GRASS VEGETATION

Temperate Grasslands

Sub-tropical and Tropical Grasslands and Savanna

Semi-desert Mesquite Grasslands

Semi-desert Mesquite Savanna

Swamp and Marsh Vegetation

STEPPE, SCRUB AND DESERT VEGETATION

Sage Brush

Creosote Shrub (yucca)

Mexican Plateau Shrub (yucca, agave, cactus)

Salt Desert Shrub (greasewood)

Ice Desert, Tundra (moss, lichen, heather bogs, dwarf willow, birch and alder, etc.). Alpine (above timber line)

Seas and Lakes frozen in Winter

PACIFIC OCEAN

ATLANTIC OCEAN

Gulf of Mexico

CARIBBEAN SEA

Tropic of Cancer

West from Greenwich

Coast Range

Rocky Mountains

Cascade Range

Sierra Nevada

Great Basin

Mojave Des.

Colorado Des.

Sierra Madre

Great Plains

Prairies

Llano Estacado

Ozark Plateau

Appalachian Mts

Piedmont Plateau

Laurentian Plateau

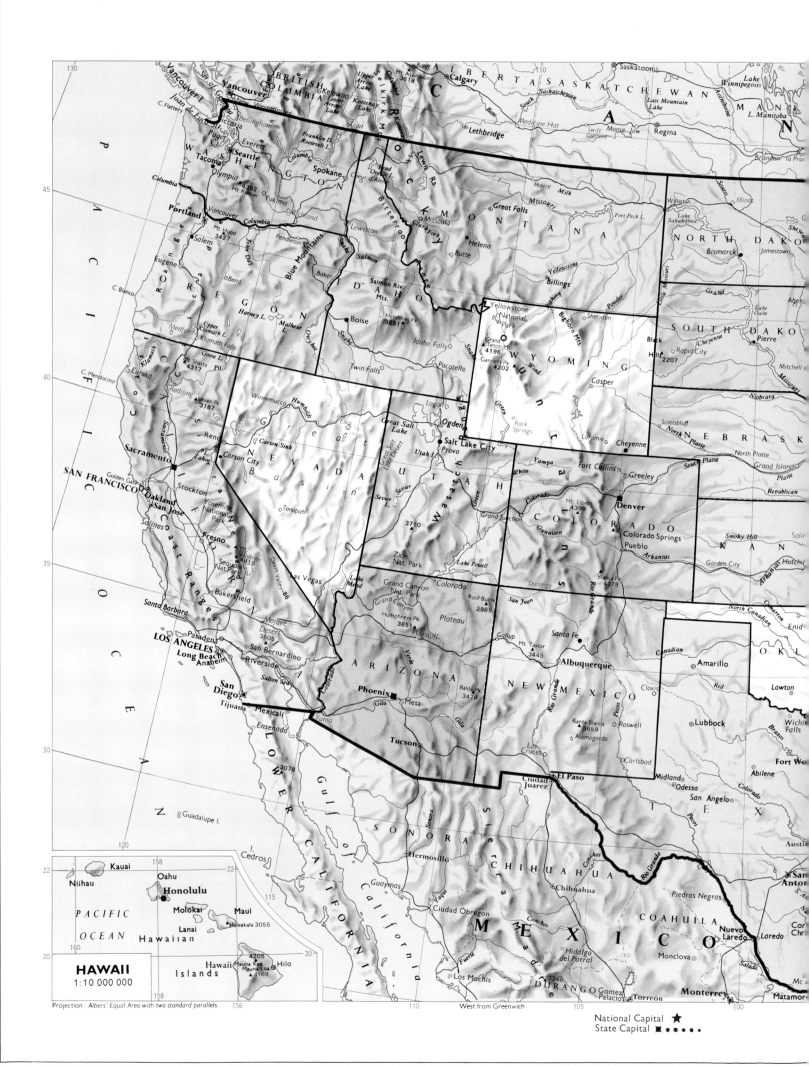

National Capital ★
State Capital ■ ● ● ● ●

HAWAII
1:10 000 000

Projection: Albers' Equal Area with two standard parallels

1:12 000 000

50   0   50   100   150   200   250   300 miles
50   0   50 100 150 200 250 300 350 400 450 km

Lake Winnipeg

O   N   T   A   R   I   O

Winnipeg
Lake of
the Woods

MINNESOTA   Duluth

WISCONSIN

Minneapolis
St. Paul

Rochester

IOWA

Des Moines

MISSOURI

Kansas City   St. Louis

Springfield

OKLAHOMA
Oklahoma City
Fort Smith

ARKANSAS
Little Rock

Tulsa

Dallas

Shreveport

Houston

LOUISIANA
Baton Rouge
New Orleans

Delta of the
Mississippi

Lake Superior

Thunder Bay

Sault Ste. Marie

MICHIGAN

Milwaukee

CHICAGO

ILLINOIS   INDIANA

Indianapolis

Cincinnati

KENTUCKY

Nashville

Memphis

Chattanooga

TENNESSEE

MISSISSIPPI   ALABAMA

Birmingham

Jackson

Montgomery

GEORGIA

Atlanta

Columbus

Lake Huron

DETROIT

Cleveland

OHIO

Columbus

WEST VIRGINIA

Charleston

NORTH CAROLINA

Charlotte

Greenville

SOUTH CAROLINA

Columbia

Savannah

Jacksonville

FLORIDA

Tampa
St. Petersburg

Orlando

Miami

MONTREAL

Ottawa

MAINE

NEW BRUNSWICK

Quebec

TORONTO

Buffalo

NEW YORK

PENNSYLVANIA

Pittsburgh

PHILADELPHIA

Baltimore
Washington D.C.

VIRGINIA

Richmond

Norfolk

Boston

NEW YORK

Atlantic City

ATLANTIC   OCEAN

BAHAMAS

Nassau

GULF   OF   MEXICO

COPYRIGHT. GEORGE PHILIP & SON. LTD.

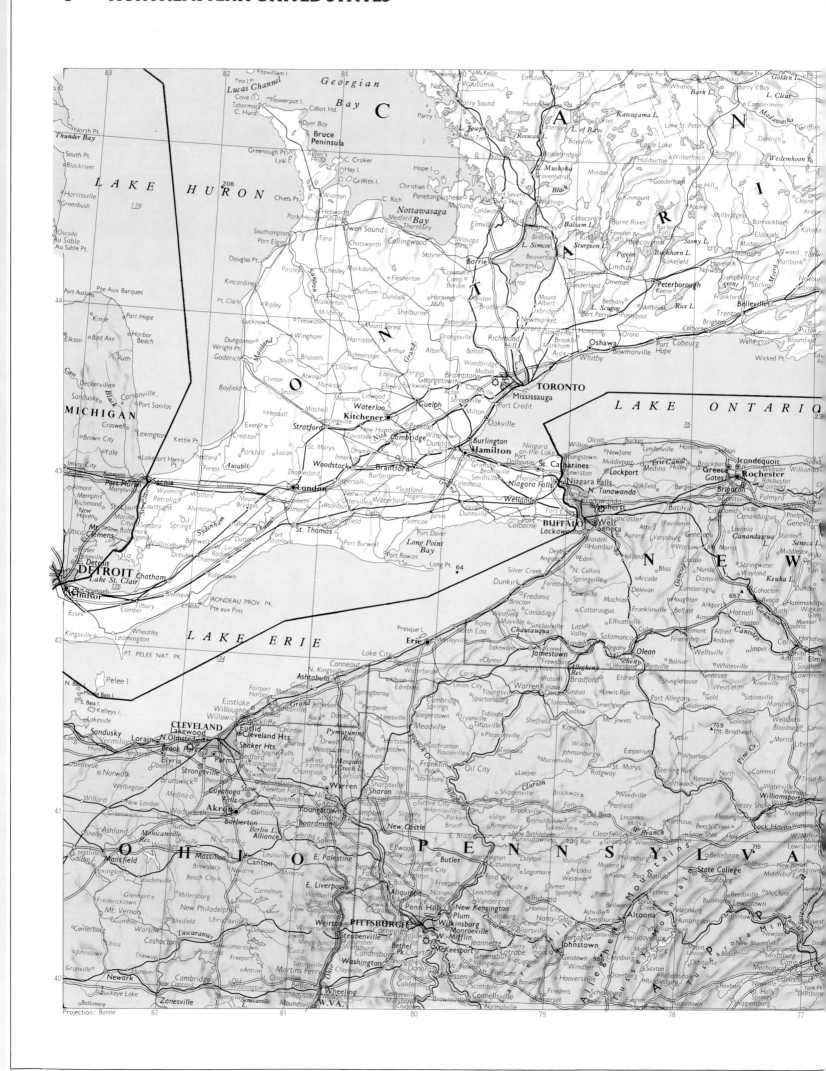

Projection: Bonne

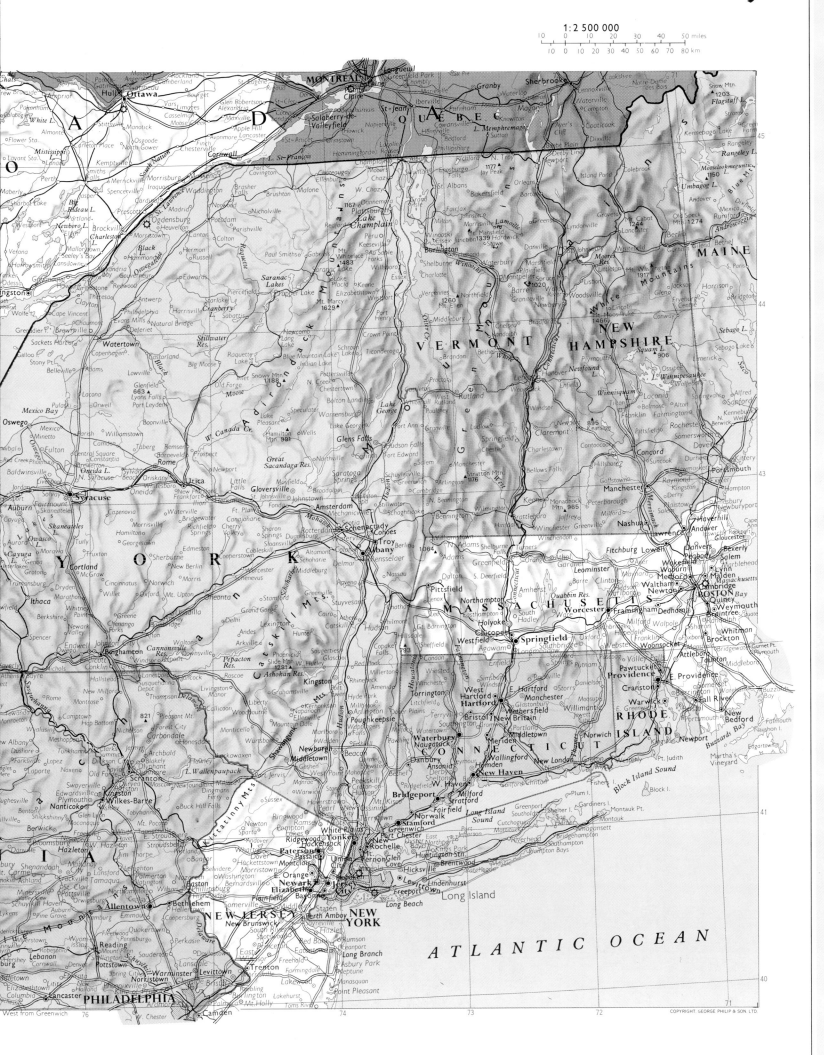

1:2 500 000

ATLANTIC OCEAN

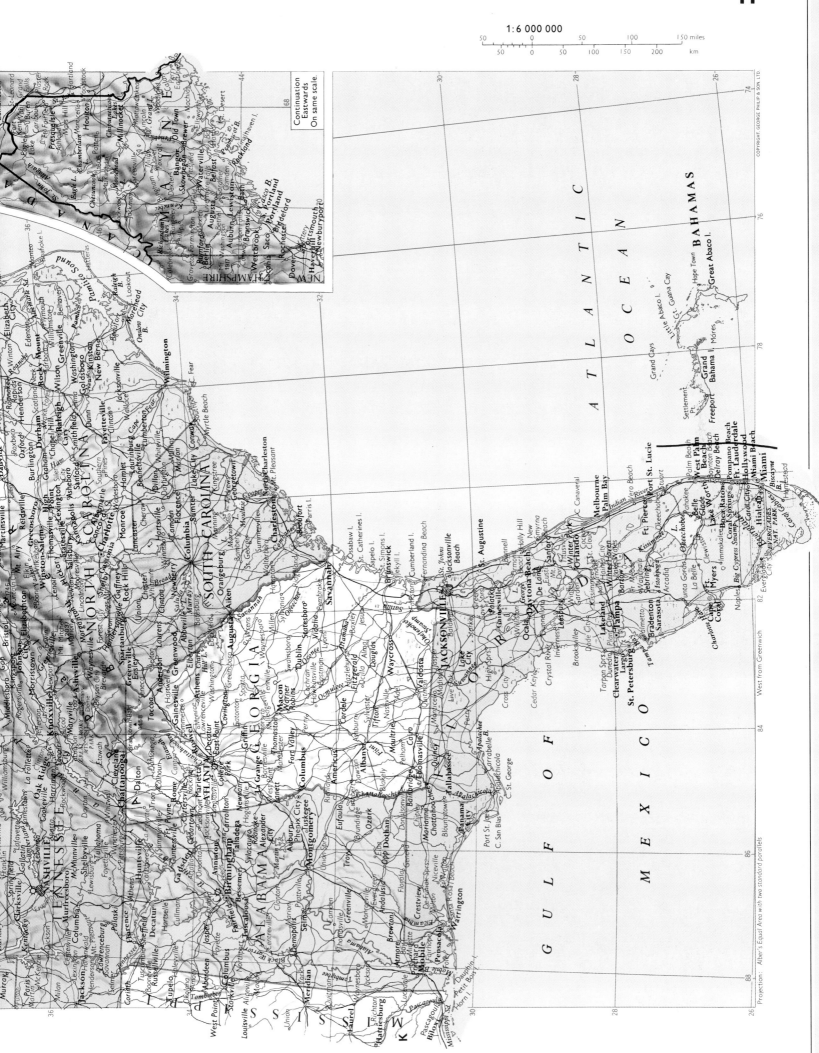

1:6 000 000

50   0   50   100   150 miles

50   0   50   100   150   200   km

Continuation
Eastwards
On same scale.

ATLANTIC

OCEAN

BAHAMAS

Hope Town
Great Abaco I.
Little Abaco I.
Gt. Guana Cay
Grand Cays
Grand
Bahama I.
Settlement
Pt.
Freeport

GULF   OF

MEXICO

Projection: Alber's Equal Area with two standard parallels

West from Greenwich

COPYRIGHT GEORGE PHILIP & SON LTD.

1:6 000 000

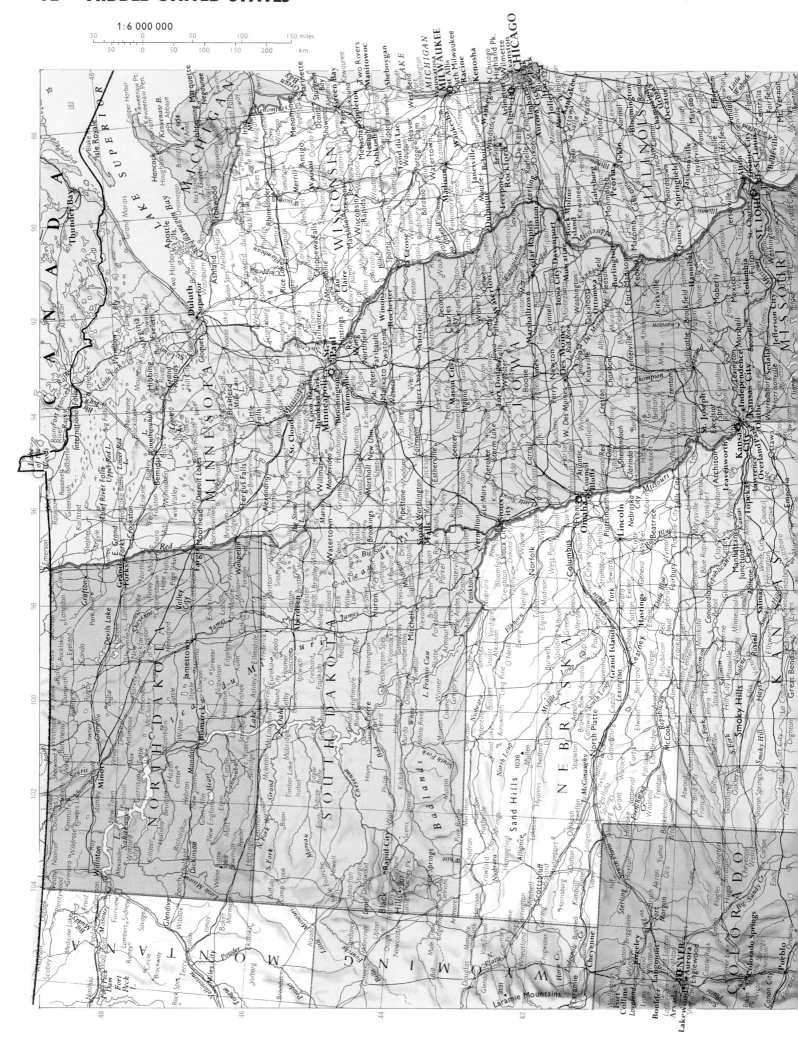

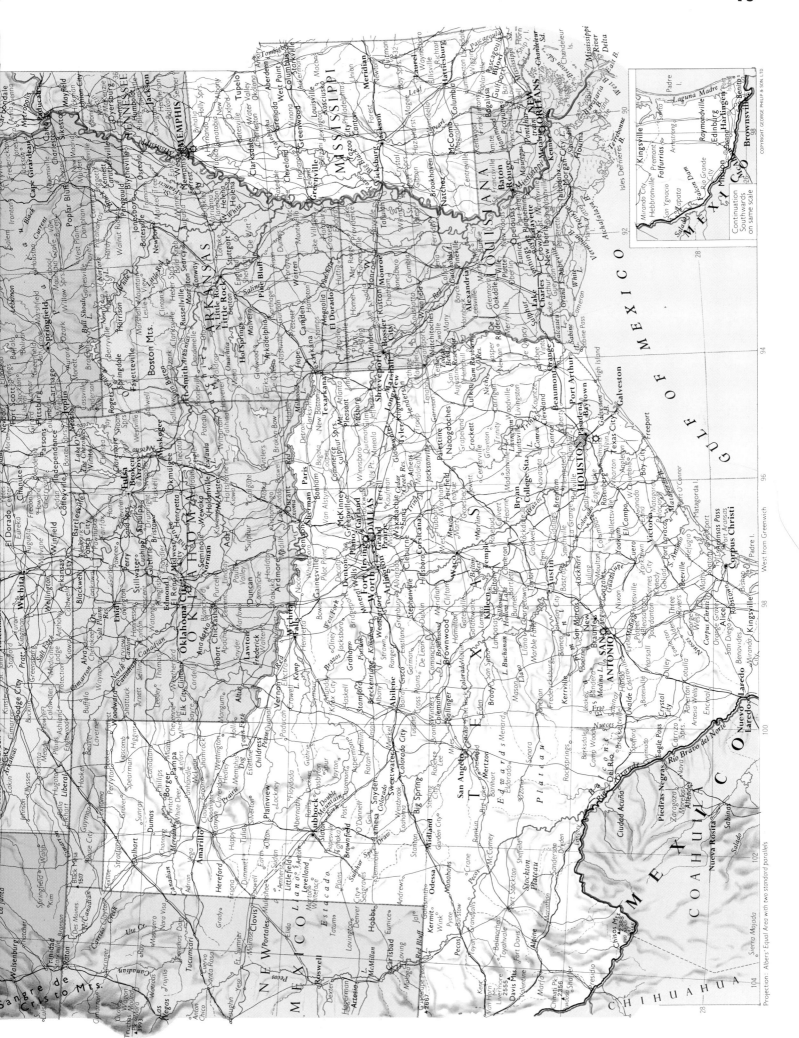

Projection: Albers' Equal Area with two standard parallels

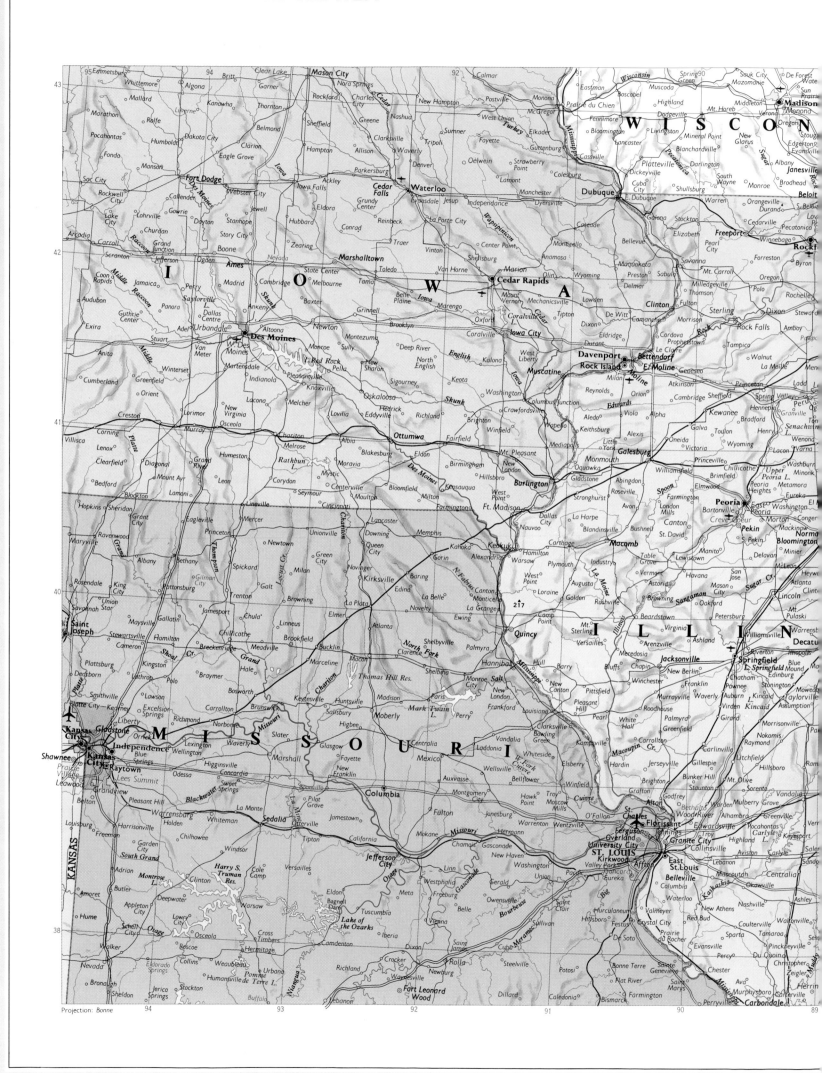

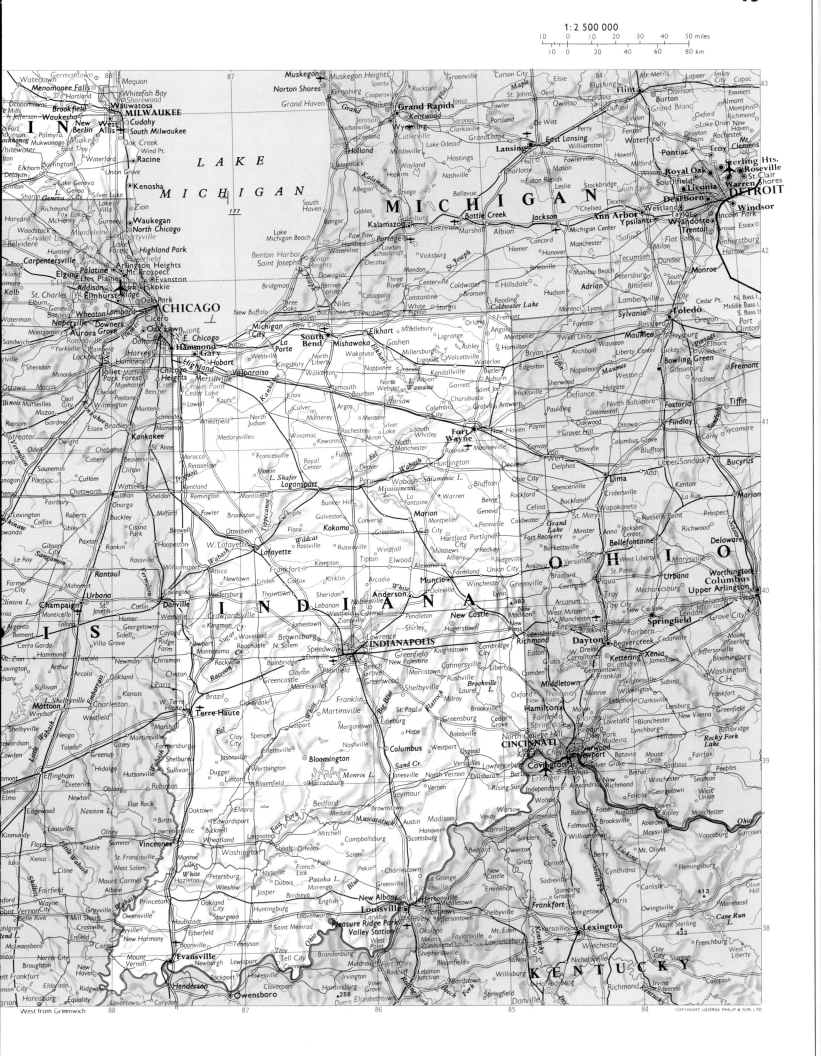

1:2 500 000

10 0 10 20 30 40 50 miles
10 0   20   40   60   80 km

LAKE

MICHIGAN

177

MILWAUKEE

MICHIGAN

DETROIT

Windsor

CHICAGO

OHIO

INDIANA

Fort
Wayne

Toledo

Lima

Columbus
Upper Arlington

Indianapolis

Springfield

Dayton

Terre Haute

Bloomington

Cincinnati

Newport
Covington

Louisville

Frankfort

Lexington

Evansville

Owensboro

Henderson

KENTUCKY

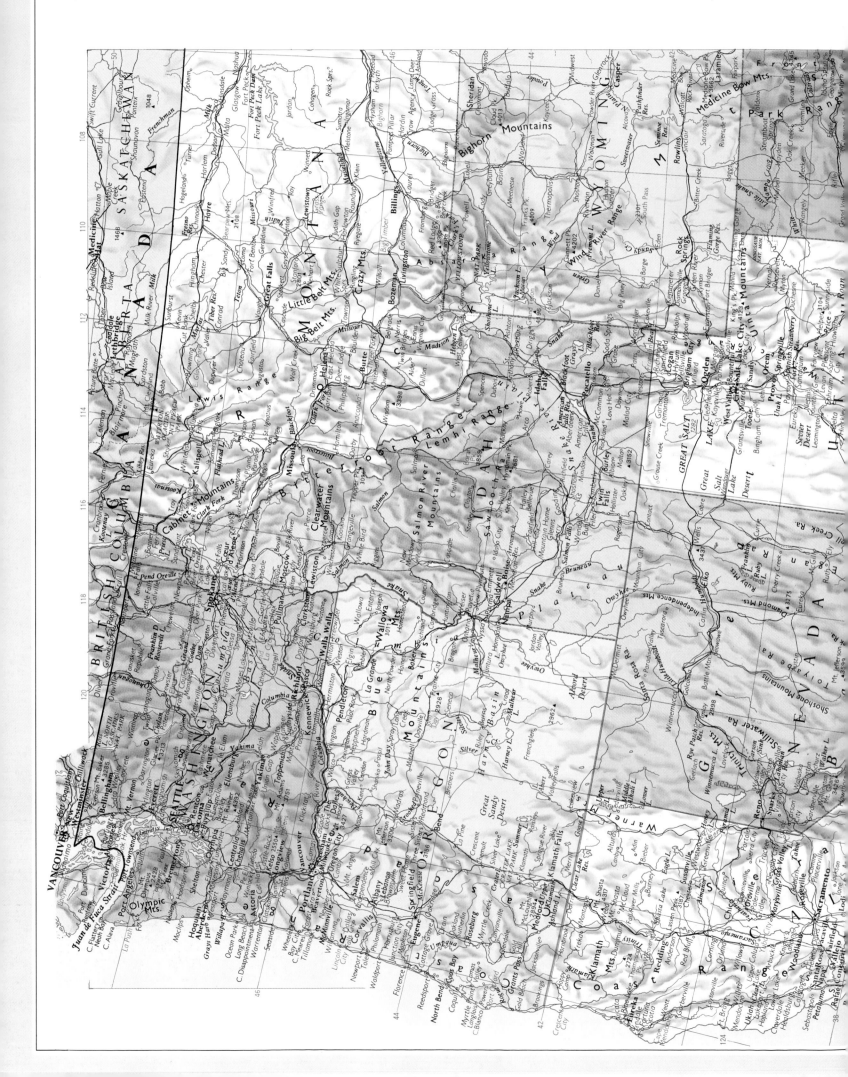

1:6 000 000

50 0 50 100 miles

50 0 50 100 150 km

Projection: Albers' Equal Area with two standard parallels

West from Greenwich

COPYRIGHT GEORGE PHILIP & SON, LTD

SEATTLE-PORTLAND
REGION
On same scale

1 : 2 500 000

10 0 10 20 30 40 50 miles

10 0 10 20 30 40 50 60 70 80 km

Projection Bonne

COPYRIGHT GEORGE PHILIP & SON LTD.

West from Greenwich

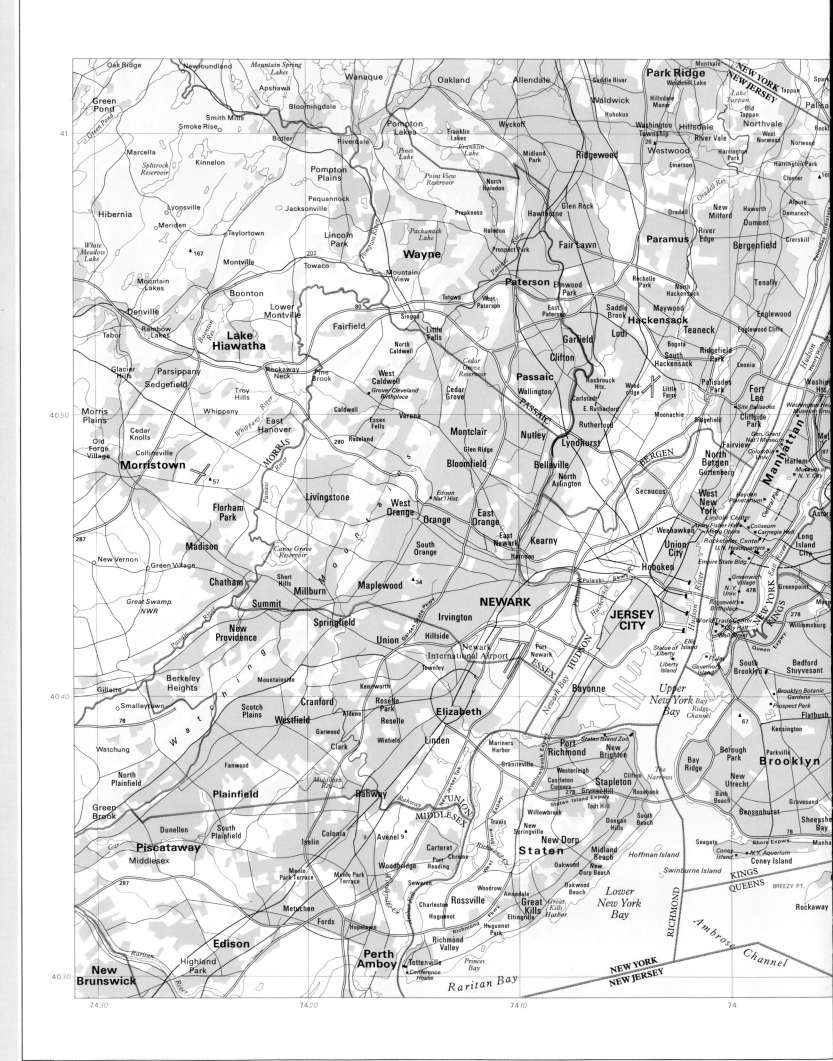

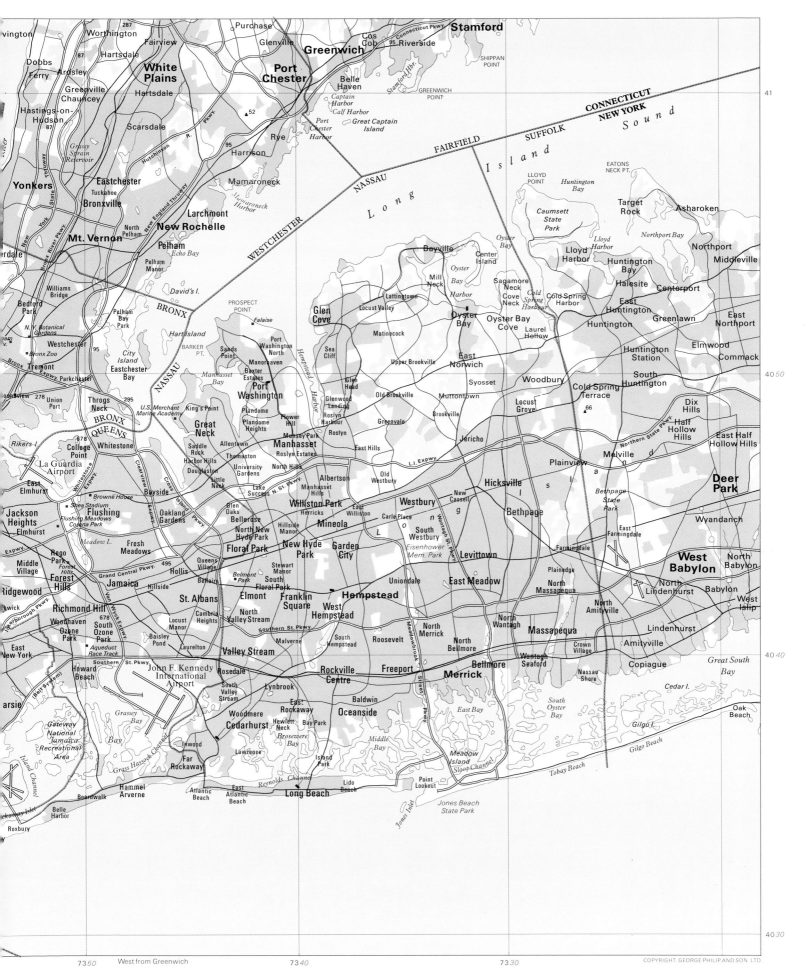

1: 250 000

West from Greenwich

COPYRIGHT GEORGE PHILIP AND SON. LTD

1: 250 000

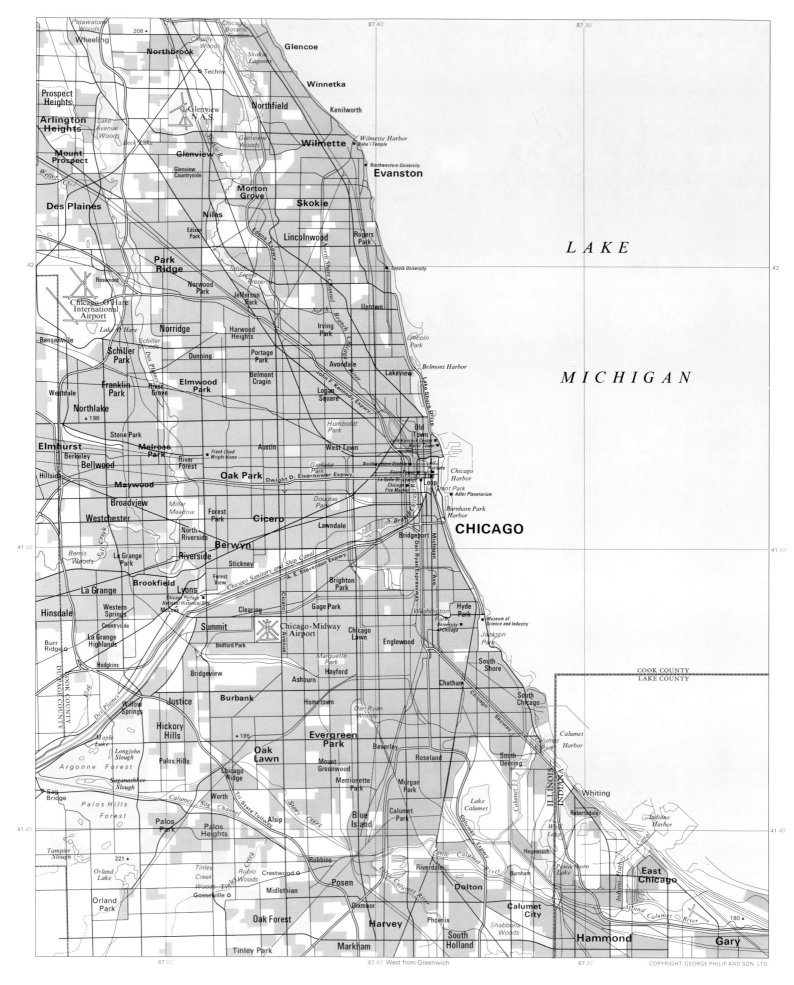

LAKE

MICHIGAN

CHICAGO

COPYRIGHT GEORGE PHILIP AND SON LTD.

87°50'   87°40' West from Greenwich   87°30'

1: 250 000

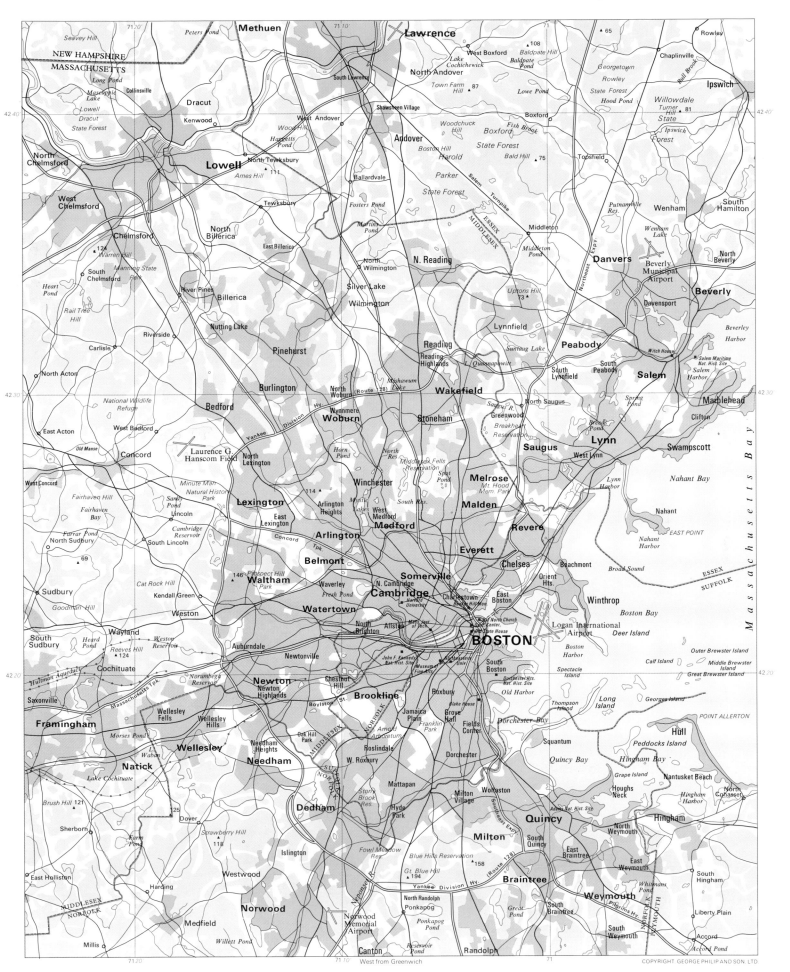

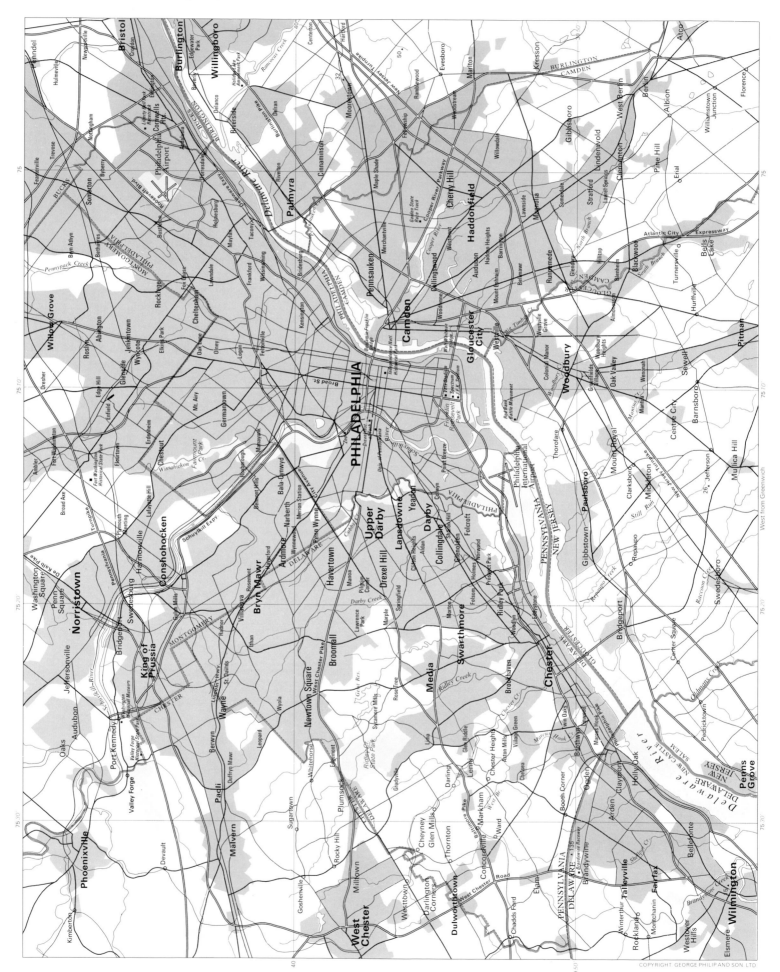

1 : 250 000

1: 250 000

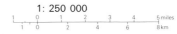

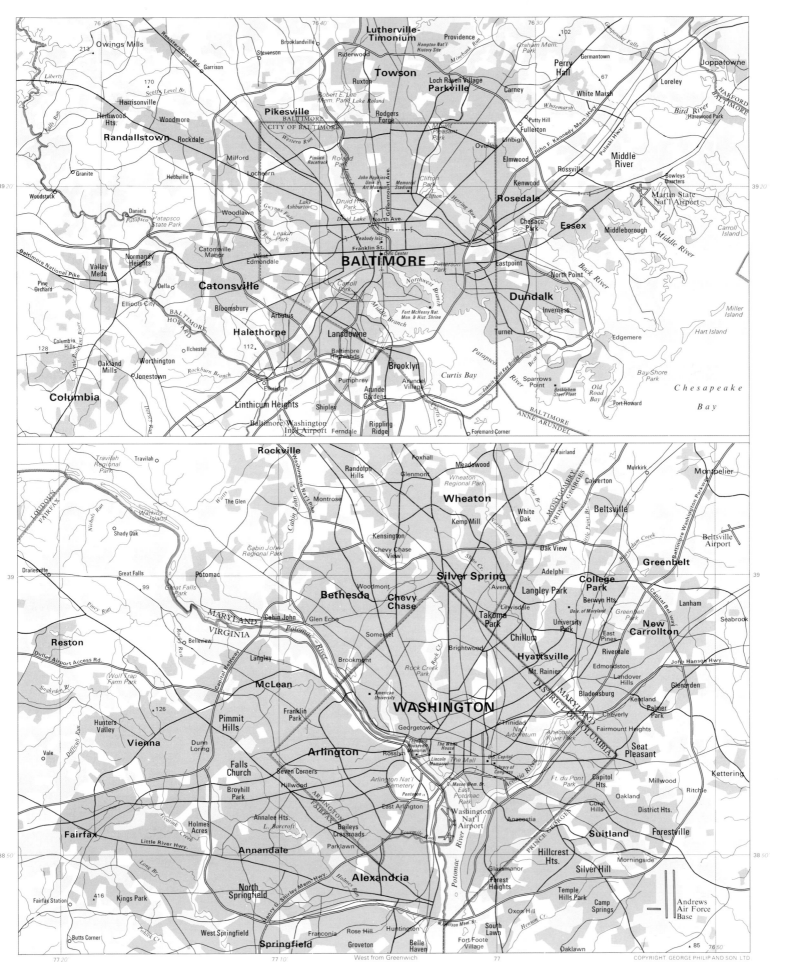

West from Greenwich

1: 250 000

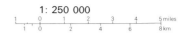

1 : 250 000

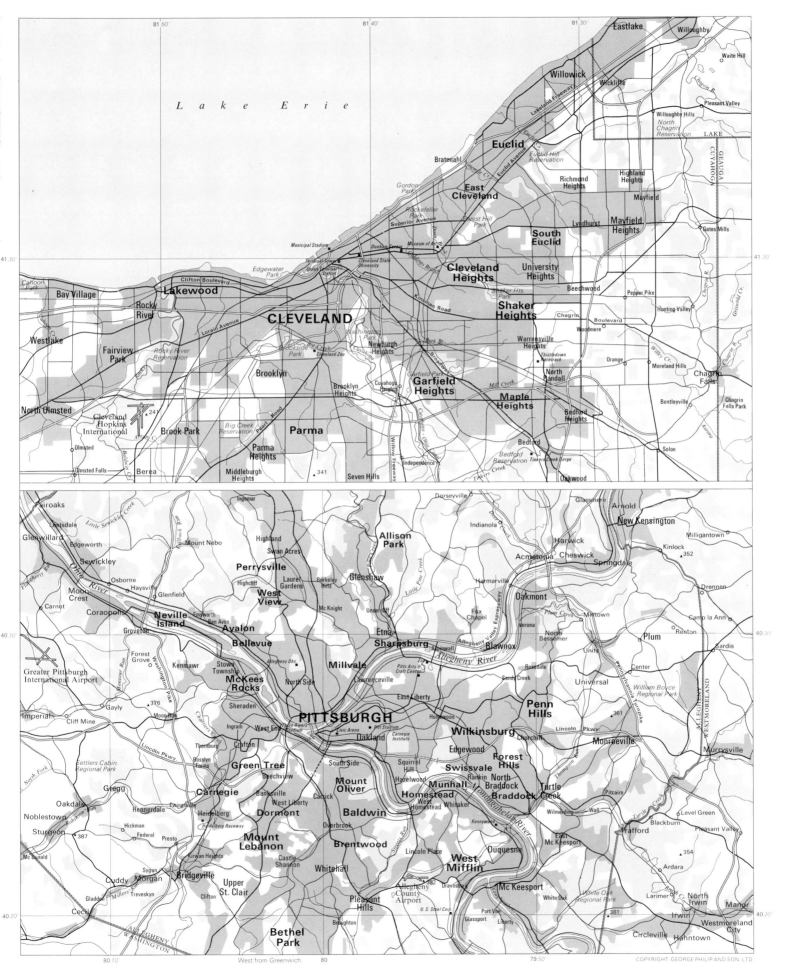

CLEVELAND

Lake Erie

Eastlake
Willoughby
Waite Hill
Willowick
Wickliffe
Pleasant Valley
Willoughby Hills
North Chagrin Reservation
LAKE
GEAUGA CUYAHOGA
Bratenahl
Euclid
Euclid Hill Reservation
Highland Heights
Richmond Heights
Mayfield
Gordon Park
East Cleveland
Gates Mills
Rockefeller Park
Forest Hill Park
South Euclid
Lyndhurst
Mayfield Heights
Superior Avenue
Municipal Stadium
Dunham Tavern
Museum of Art
Terminal Tower
Cleveland State University
Union Station
Edgewater Park
Cleveland Heights
University Heights
Beechwood
Clifton Boulevard
Pepper Pike
Bay Village
Lakewood
Shaker Hts.
Hunting Valley
Rocky River
Kinsman Road
Shaker Heights
Chagrin
Boulevard
Westlake
CLEVELAND
Woodmere
Washington Park
Burk Br.
Warrensville Heights
Fairview Park
Rocky River Reservation
Brookside Park
Big Creek
Cleveland Zoo
Newburgh Heights
Broadway
Thistledown Racetrack
Orange
Moreland Hills
North Olmsted
Brooklyn
Garfield Park
Garfield Heights
North Randall
Mill Creek
Chagrin Falls
Brooklyn Heights
Cuyahoga Heights
Bentleyville
Chagrin Falls Park
Maple Heights
Bedford Heights
Cleveland Hopkins International
Brook Park
Big Creek Reservation
Pearl Road
Parma
Willow Freeway
Independence
Bedford
Solon
Olmsted
Parma Heights
Bedford Reservation
Tinkers Creek Gorge
Olmsted Falls
Berea
Middleburgh Heights
341
Seven Hills
Tinkers Creek
Oakwood

PITTSBURGH

Fairoaks
Dorseyville
Glassmere
Arnold
Ingomar
New Kensington
Glenwillard
Leetsdale
Little Sewickley Creek
Milligantown
Indianola
Edgeworth
Mount Nebo
Highland
Allison Park
Harwick
Kinlock
Sewickley
Swan Acres
Cheswick
352
Acmetonia
Springdale
Osborne
Haysville
Perrysville
Highcliff
Laurel Gardens
Berkeley Hills
Glenshaw
Harmarville
Drennen
Moon Crest
Glenfield
West View
Little Pine Creek
Oakmont
Carnot
McKnight
Undercliff
Fox Chapel
Camp la Ann
Coraopolis
Emsworth
Neville Island
Ben Avon
Avalon
Etna
Verona
Renton
Groveton
Sharpsburg
Aspinwall
North Bessemer
Plum
Sardis
Forest Grove
Bellevue
Allegheny Obs.
Pitts Arts & Craft Center
Blawnox
Allegheny River
Unity
Center
Greater Pittsburgh International Airport
Kenmawr
Stowe Township
Millvale
Universal
Universal
William Boyce Regional Park
McKees Rocks
North Side
Lawrenceville
Sandy Creek
Rosedale
376
Gayly
Sheraden
East Liberty
361
Imperial
Moon Run
Ingram
West End
PITTSBURGH
Homewood
Penn Hills
Cliff Mine
Crafton
Civic Arena
Oakland
Carnegie Institute
Wilkinsburg
Lincoln Pkwy
Monroeville
Thornburg
Churchill
Murrysville
Settlers Cabin Regional Park
Rosslyn Farms
Green Tree
South Side
Squirrel Hill
Edgewood
Forest Hills
Gregg
Beechview
Hazelwood
Swissvale
Carnegie
Banksville
West Liberty
Munhall
Rankin
North Braddock
Turtle Creek
Oakdale
Dormont
Mount Oliver
Carrick
Homestead
Braddock
Pitcairn
Noblestown
Heidelberg
Heidelberg Raceway
Baldwin
West Homestead
Whitaker
Wilmerding
Level Green
Sturgeon
Hickman
Federal
Presto
Overbrook
Wall
Blackburn
Pleasant Valley
387
Mount Lebanon
Brentwood
Lincoln Place
Kennywood
East McKeesport
Trafford
McDonald
Sygan
Bridgeville
Whitehall
Duquesne
354
Cuddy
Morgan
Upper St. Clair
Ardara
Gladden
Millers Run
Treveskyn
Castle Shannon
West Mifflin
McKeesport
North Irwin
Cecil
Kirwan Heights
Clifton
Allegheny County Airport
White Oak
White Oak Regional Park
Larimer
Irwin
Manor
Pleasant Hills
U.S. Steel Corp.
Westmoreland City
Bethel Park
Broughton
Glassport
Port Vue
Liberty
381
Circleville
Hahntown

1: 250 000

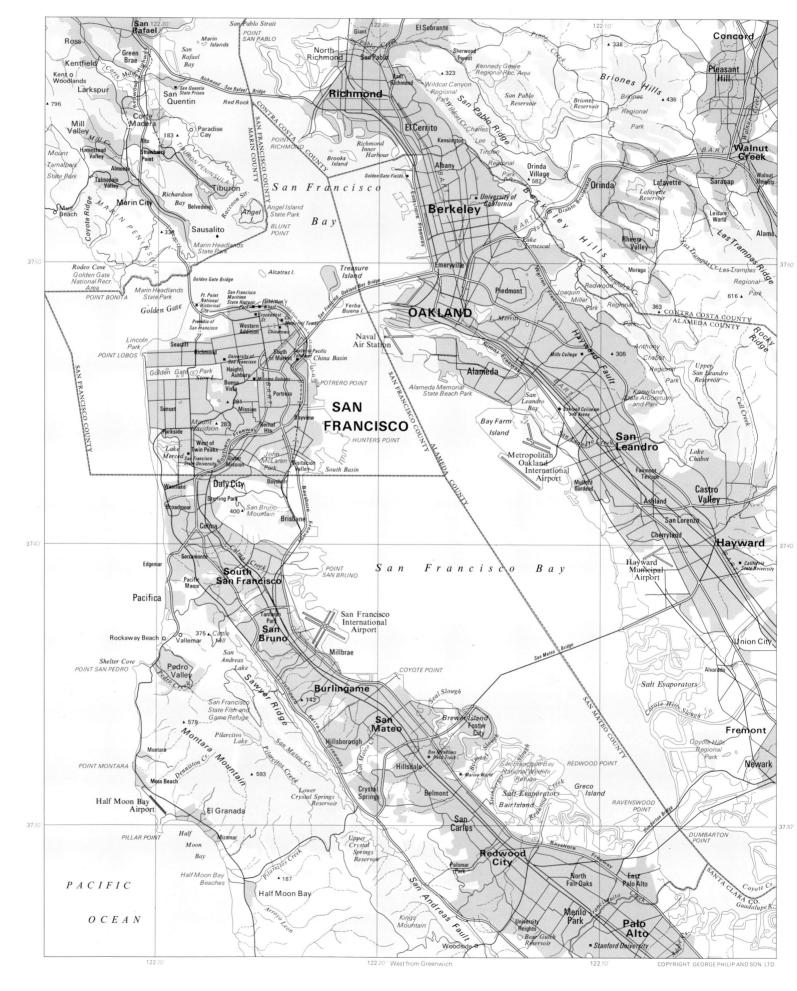

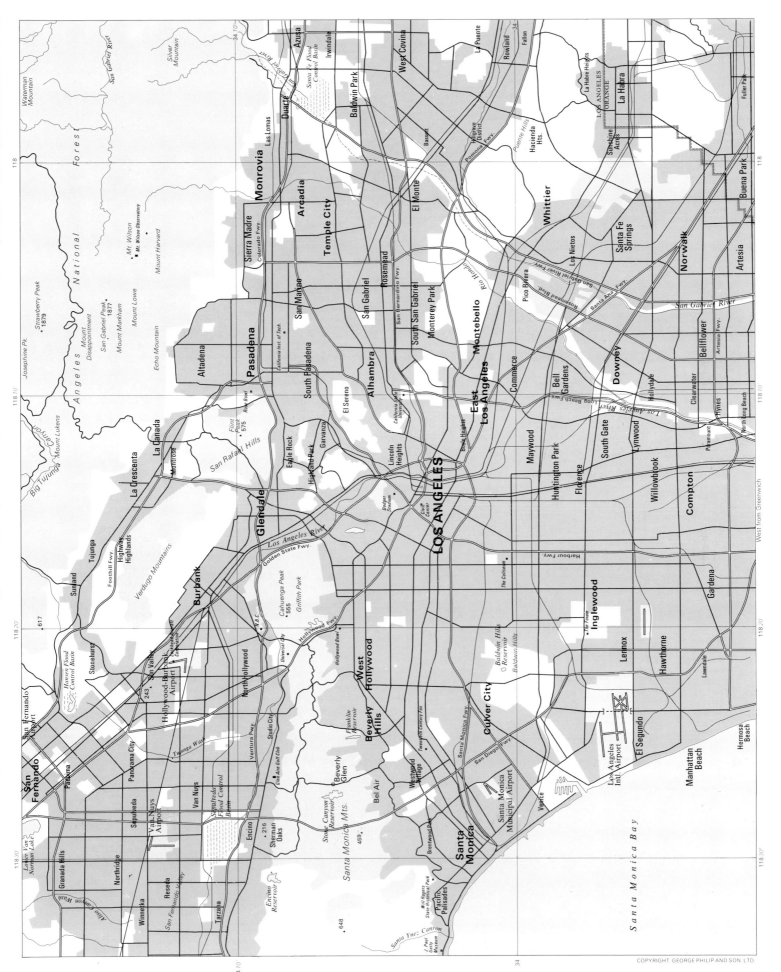

1 : 250 000

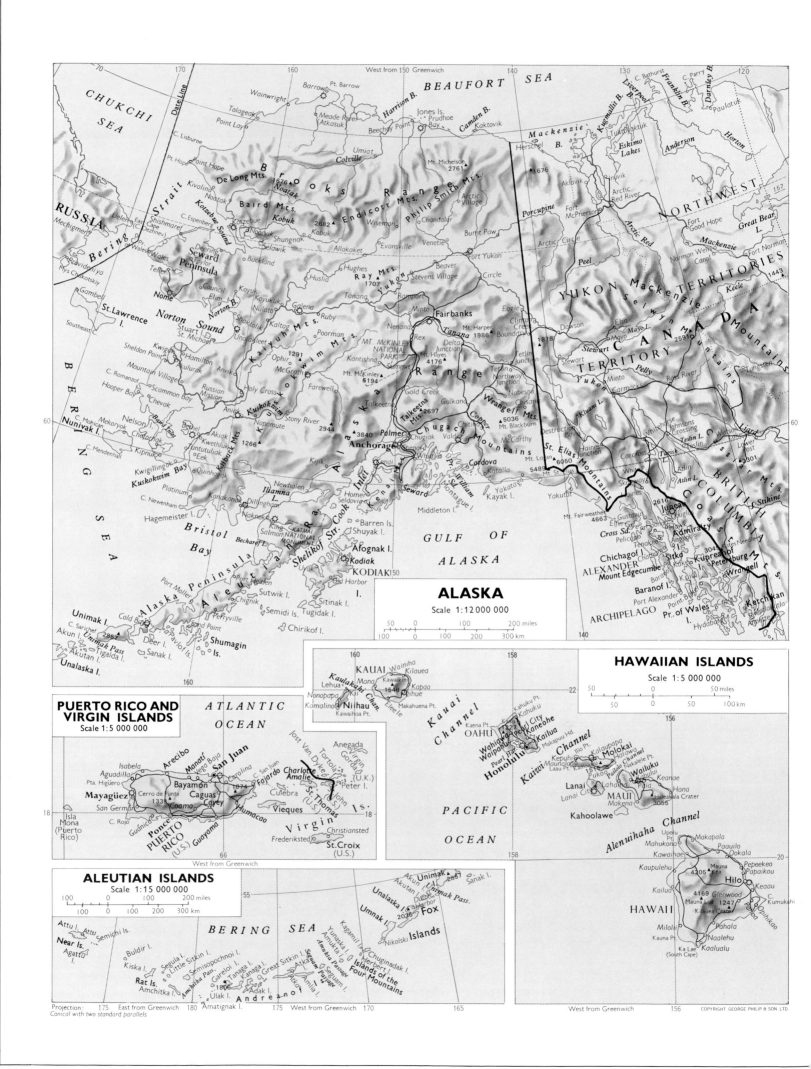

ALASKA
Scale 1:12 000 000

HAWAIIAN ISLANDS
Scale 1:5 000 000

PUERTO RICO AND VIRGIN ISLANDS
Scale 1:5 000 000

ALEUTIAN ISLANDS
Scale 1:15 000 000

Projection: Conical with two standard parallels

COPYRIGHT. GEORGE PHILIP & SON. LTD.

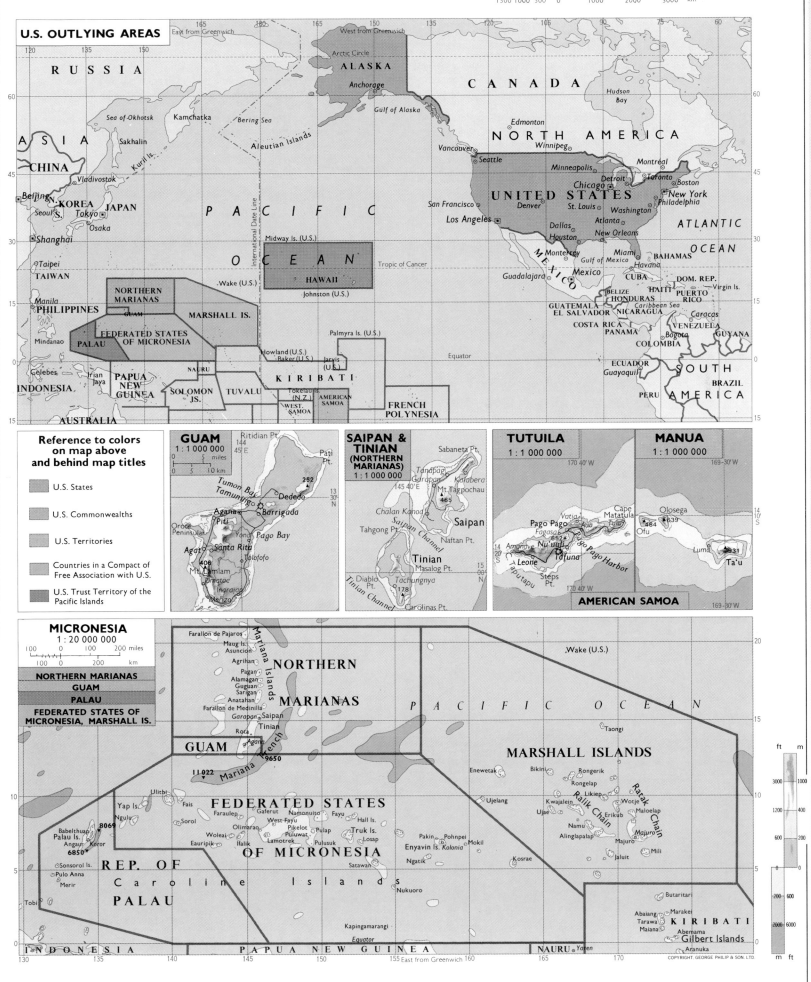

1 : 110 000 000

U.S. OUTLYING AREAS

RUSSIA

ASIA

CHINA

Sea of Okhotsk
Kamchatka
Sakhalin
Kuril Is.
Vladivostok
Beijing
N. KOREA
JAPAN
Seoul S.
Tokyo
Osaka
Shanghai
Taipei
TAIWAN
Manila
PHILIPPINES
Mindanao
Celebes
Irian Jaya
INDONESIA
PAPUA NEW GUINEA
AUSTRALIA

Bering Sea
Aleutian Islands
ALASKA
Anchorage
Gulf of Alaska
Arctic Circle

CANADA
Hudson Bay
Edmonton
NORTH AMERICA
Vancouver
Seattle
Winnipeg
Minneapolis
Montreal
Toronto
Detroit
Boston
Chicago
New York
UNITED STATES
Denver
St. Louis
Washington
Philadelphia
San Francisco
Los Angeles
Dallas
Atlanta
Houston
New Orleans
ATLANTIC OCEAN
Monterrey
Miami
BAHAMAS
Gulf of Mexico
Havana
Guadalajara
MEXICO
Mexico
CUBA
DOM. REP.
Virgin Is.
HAITI
PUERTO RICO
GUATEMALA
BELIZE
HONDURAS
Caribbean Sea
Caracas
EL SALVADOR
NICARAGUA
Caracas
COSTA RICA
PANAMA
VENEZUELA
GUYANA
Bogota
COLOMBIA
ECUADOR
Guayaquil
SOUTH AMERICA
BRAZIL
PERU

PACIFIC OCEAN
International Date Line
Midway Is. (U.S.)
Tropic of Cancer
HAWAII
Johnston (U.S.)
Wake (U.S.)
NORTHERN MARIANAS
GUAM
MARSHALL IS.
FEDERATED STATES OF MICRONESIA
PALAU
Palmyra Is. (U.S.)
Howland (U.S.)
Baker (U.S.)
Jarvis (U.S.)
NAURU
KIRIBATI
Equator
SOLOMON JS.
TUVALU
Tokelau Is. (N.Z.)
WEST SAMOA
AMERICAN SAMOA
FRENCH POLYNESIA

Reference to colors on map above and behind map titles

- U.S. States
- U.S. Commonwealths
- U.S. Territories
- Countries in a Compact of Free Association with U.S.
- U.S. Trust Territory of the Pacific Islands

GUAM
1 : 1 000 000

Ritidian Pt.
144 45'E
Pati Pt.
252
Tumon Bay
Tamuning
Dededo
13 30' N
Agana
Barrigada
Piti
Orote Peninsula
Yona
Pago Bay
Agat
Santa Rita
Talofofo
Mt. Lamlam
406
Inarajan
Umatac
Merizo

SAIPAN & TINIAN (NORTHERN MARIANAS)
1 : 1 000 000

Sabaneta Pt.
Tanapag
145 40'E
Garapan
Kalabera
Mt. Tagpochau
465
Chalan Kanoa
Saipan
Saipan Channel
Tahgong Pt.
Naftan Pt.
Tinian
Masalog Pt.
15 00' N
Diablo Pt.
Tachungnya
178
Tinian Channel
Carolinas Pt.

TUTUILA
1 : 1 000 000
170 40' W

Vatia
Cape Matatula
Pago Pago
Aua
Tula
Fagasa
652
Nu'uuli
Amanave
Tafuna
14 20' S
Leone
Pago Pago Harbor
Aputapu
Steps Pt.
170 40' W

MANUA
1 : 1 000 000
169 30' W

Olosega
484
639
Ofu
Luma
931
Ta'u
14 10' S

AMERICAN SAMOA
169 30' W

MICRONESIA
1 : 20 000 000
100   0   100   200 miles
100   0   200   km

- NORTHERN MARIANAS
- GUAM
- PALAU
- FEDERATED STATES OF MICRONESIA, MARSHALL IS.

Farallon de Pajaros
Maug Is.
Asuncion
Agrihan
Pagan
Alamagan
Guguan
Sarigan
Anatahan
Farallon de Medinilla
Garapan
Saipan
Rota
Tinian
NORTHERN MARIANAS
Mariana Islands
GUAM
Agana
11 022
Mariana Trench
9650

PACIFIC OCEAN
Wake (U.S.)
Taongi
MARSHALL ISLANDS
Enewetak
Bikini
Rongerik
Rongelap
Rarak Chain
Ujelang
Kwajalein
Wotje
Likiep
Maloelap
Ralik Chain
Ujae
Erikub
Namu
Alinglapalap
Majuro
Mili
Jaluit

 bikini
Ulithi
Fais
Yap Is.
Ngulu
8069
Babelthuap
Palau Is.
6850
Angaur
Koror
Sonsorol Is.
Pulo Anna
Merir
Tobi
REP. OF PALAU

Sorol
Faraulep
Gaferut
Namonuito
Fayu
Hall Is.
West Fayu
Pikelot
Pulap
Truk Is.
Olimarao
Puluwat
Losap
Woleai
Ifalik
Lamotrek
Pulusuk
Eauripik
Satawan
Ngatik
Nukuoro
FEDERATED STATES OF MICRONESIA
Caroline Islands
Pakin
Pohnpei
Mokil
Enyavin Is.
Kolonia
Kosrae

Kapingamarangi
Equator

INDONESIA
PAPUA NEW GUINEA
NAURU
Yaren
KIRIBATI
Butaritari
Abaiang
Marakei
Tarawa
Maiana
Abemama
Gilbert Islands
Aranuka

East from Greenwich

ft   m
3000   1000
1200   400
600   200
0
200   600
2000   6000
m   ft

INDEX

UNITED STATES & OUTLYING AREAS

This index lists all the place names which appear on the large scale maps of the United States and outlying areas (pages which precede this index). Place names for the rest of the world can be found in the World Maps Index at the end of the atlas.

The number in dark type which follows each name in the index refers to the page number on which the place or feature is located. The geographical coordinates which follow the page number give the latitude and longitude of each place. The first coordinate indicates the latitude – the distance north or south of the Equator. The second coordinate indicates the longitude – the distance east or west of the Greenwich Meridian. Both latitude and longitude are

measured in degrees and minutes (there are 60 minutes in a degree). Rivers are indexed to their mouths or confluences. A solid square ■ follows the name of a country, while an open square □ signifies that the name is a state. An arrow → follows the name of a river.

The alphabetic order of names composed of two or more words is governed by the first word and then by the second. Names composed of a proper name (Alaska) and a description (Gulf of) are positioned alphabetically by the proper name. All names beginning St. are alphabetized under Saint and those beginning Mc under Mac.

Abbreviations used in the index

Ala. — Alabama	Ill. — Illinois	N.J. — New Jersey	Res. — Reserve, Reservoir,
Amer. — America, American	Ind. — Indiana	N. Mex. — New Mexico	Reservation
Ariz. — Arizona	Kans. — Kansas	N.Y. — New York	S.C. — South Carolina
Ark. — Arkansas	Ky. — Kentucky	Nat. Mon. — National Monument	S. Dak. — South Dakota
B. — Bay	L. — Lake	Nat. Park — National Park	Sa. — Serra, Sierra
C. — Cape	La. — Louisiana	Nat. Rec. Area. — National	Sd. — Sound
Calif. — California	Ld. — Land	Recreation Area	St. — Saint
Chan. — Channel	Mass. — Massachusetts	Nebr. — Nebraska	Ste. — Sainte
Colo. — Colorado	Md. — Maryland	Nev. — Nevada	Str. — Strait
Conn. — Connecticut	Mich. — Michigan	Okla. — Oklahoma	Tenn. — Tennessee
Cr. — Creek	Minn. — Minnesota	Oreg. — Oregon	Tex. — Texas
D.C. — District of Columbia	Miss. — Mississippi	Pa. — Pennsylvania	U.S.A. — United States of America
Del. — Delaware	Mo. — Missouri	Pac. Oc. — Pacific Ocean	Va. — Virginia
Dist. — District	Mont. — Montana	Pass. — Passage	Vt. — Vermont
E. — East, Eastern	Mt.(s) — Mountain(s)	Pen. — Peninsula	Wash. — Washington
Fla. — Florida	N. — North, Northern	Pk. — Peak	W. — West, Western
G. — Gulf	N.B. — New Brunswick	Pt. — Point	W. Va. — West Virginia
Ga. — Georgia	N.C. — North Carolina	R. — Rio, River	Wis. — Wisconsin
Gt. — Great	N. Dak. — North Dakota	R.I. — Rhode Island	Wyo. — Wyoming
I.(s) — Island(s)	N.H. — New Hampshire	Ra.(s) — Range(s)	

A

Abbaye, Pt., Mich. **10** 46 58N 88 8W
Abbeville, La. **13** 29 58N 92 8W
Abbeville, S.C. **11** 34 11N 82 23W
Abbotsford, Wis. **12** 44 57N 90 19W
Aberdeen, Ala. **11** 33 49N 88 33W
Aberdeen, Idaho **16** 42 57N 112 50W
Aberdeen, S. Dak. **12** 45 28N 98 29W
Aberdeen, Wash. **18** 46 59N 123 50W
Abernathy, Tex. **13** 33 50N 101 51W
Abert, L., Oreg. **16** 42 38N 120 14W
Abilene, Kans. **12** 38 55N 97 13W
Abilene, Tex. **13** 32 28N 99 43W
Abingdon, Ill. **14** 40 48N 90 24W
Abingdon, Va. **11** 36 43N 81 59W
Absaroka Range, Wyo. . **16** 44 45N 109 50W
Accomac, Va. **10** 37 43N 75 40W
Ackerman, Miss. **13** 33 19N 89 11W
Ada, Minn. **12** 47 18N 96 31W
Ada, Okla. **13** 34 46N 96 41W
Adams, Mass. **9** 42 38N 73 7W
Adams, N.Y. **9** 43 49N 76 1W
Adams, Wis. **12** 43 57N 89 49W
Adams Mt., Wash. **18** 46 12N 121 30W
Adel, Ga. **11** 31 8N 83 25W
Adelanto, Calif. **19** 34 35N 117 22W
Adin, Calif. **16** 41 12N 120 57W
Adirondack Mts., N.Y. . **9** 44 0N 74 0W
Admiralty I., Alaska **30** 57 30N 134 30W
Admiralty Inlet, Wash. . **16** 48 8N 122 58W
Adrian, Mich. **15** 41 54N 84 2W
Adrian, Tex. **13** 35 16N 102 40W
Affton, Miss. **14** 38 33N 90 20W
Afognak I., Alaska **30** 58 15N 152 30W
Afton, N.Y. **9** 42 14N 75 32W
Agana, Guam .... **31** 13 28N 144 45 E
Agattu I., Alaska ..... **30** 52 25N 172 30 E
Agua Caliente Springs,
  Calif. **19** 32 56N 116 19W
Aguadilla, Puerto Rico . **30** 18 26N 67 10W
Aguanga, Calif. **19** 33 27N 116 51W
Aiken, S.C. **11** 33 34N 81 43W
Ainsworth, Nebr. **12** 42 33N 99 52W
Aitkin, Minn. **12** 46 32N 93 42W
Ajo, Ariz. **17** 32 22N 112 52W
Akiak, Alaska **30** 60 55N 161 13W
Akron, Colo. **12** 40 10N 103 13W
Akron, Ohio **8** 41 5N 81 31W
Akulurak, Alaska **30** 62 40N 164 35W
Akun I., Alaska **30** 54 11N 165 32W

Akutan I., Alaska **30** 54 7N 165 55W
Alabama □ **11** 33 0N 87 0W
Alabama →, Ala. **11** 31 8N 87 57W
Alameda, Calif. **28** 37 46N 122 15W
Alameda, N. Mex. **17** 35 11N 106 37W
Alameda County, Calif. . **28** 37 40N 122 10W
Alamo, Nev. **19** 36 21N 115 10W
Alamogordo, N. Mex. . **17** 32 54N 105 57W
Alamosa, Colo. **17** 37 28N 105 52W
Alaska □ **30** 64 0N 154 0W
Alaska, G. of, Pac. Oc. . **30** 58 0N 145 0W
Alaska Peninsula, Alaska **30** 56 0N 159 0W
Alaska Range, Alaska . **30** 62 50N 151 0W
Alava, C., Wash. **16** 48 10N 124 44W
Albany, Ga. **11** 31 35N 84 10W
Albany, Minn. **12** 45 38N 94 34W
Albany, N.Y. **9** 42 39N 73 45W
Albany, Oreg. **16** 44 38N 123 6W
Albany, Tex. **13** 32 44N 99 18W
Albemarle, N.C. **11** 35 21N 80 11W
Albemarle Sd., N.C. ... **11** 36 5N 76 0W
Albert Lea, Minn. **12** 43 39N 93 22W
Albia, Iowa **14** 41 2N 92 48W
Albion, Idaho **16** 42 25N 113 35W
Albion, Mich. **15** 42 15N 84 45W
Albion, Nebr. **12** 41 42N 98 0W
Albuquerque, N. Mex. . **17** 35 5N 106 39W
Alcatraz I., Calif. **28** 37 49N 122 25W
Alcoa, Tenn. **11** 35 48N 83 59W
Alcova, Wyo. **16** 42 34N 106 43W
Alder, Mont. **16** 45 19N 112 6W
Alder Pk., Calif. **18** 35 53N 121 22W
Aledo, Ill. **14** 41 12N 90 45W
Alenuihaha Channel,
  Hawaii **30** 20 30N 156 0W
Aleutian Is., Pac. Oc. . **30** 52 0N 175 0W
Aleutian Ra., Alaska . **30** 55 0N 155 0W
Alexander, N. Dak. **12** 47 51N 103 39W
Alexander Arch., Alaska **30** 56 0N 136 0W
Alexander City, Ala. ... **11** 32 56N 85 58W
Alexandria, Ind. **15** 40 16N 85 41W
Alexandria, La. **13** 31 18N 92 27W
Alexandria, Minn. **12** 45 53N 95 22W
Alexandria, S. Dak. ... **12** 43 39N 97 47W
Alexandria, Va. **25** 38 49N 77 6W
Alexandria Bay, N.Y. .. **9** 44 20N 75 55W
Alfred, Maine **9** 43 29N 70 43W
Algoma, Wis. **10** 44 36N 87 26W
Algona, Iowa **14** 43 4N 94 14W
Alhambra, Calif. **29** 34 5N 118 9W
Alice, Tex. **13** 27 45N 98 5W
Aliceville, Ala. **11** 33 8N 88 9W

Aliquippa, Pa. **8** 40 37N 80 15W
All American Canal,
  Calif. **17** 32 45N 115 15W
Allakaket, Alaska **30** 66 34N 152 39W
Allegan, Mich. **15** 42 32N 85 51W
Allegheny →, Pa. **8** 40 27N 80 1W
Allegheny Plateau, Va. . **10** 38 0N 80 0W
Allen Park, Mich. **26** 42 14N 83 12W
Allentown, Pa. **9** 40 37N 75 29W
Alliance, Nebr. **12** 42 6N 102 52W
Alliance, Ohio **8** 40 55N 81 6W
Allison Park, Pa. **27** 40 33N 79 56W
Alma, Ga. **11** 31 33N 82 28W
Alma, Kans. **12** 39 1N 96 17W
Alma, Mich. **10** 43 23N 84 39W
Alma, Nebr. **12** 40 6N 99 22W
Alma, Wis. **12** 44 20N 91 55W
Almanor, L., Calif. ... **16** 40 14N 121 9W
Alpaugh, Calif. **18** 35 53N 119 29W
Alpena, Mich. **10** 45 4N 83 27W
Alpine, Ariz. **17** 33 51N 109 9W
Alpine, Calif. **19** 32 50N 116 46W
Alpine, Tex. **13** 30 22N 103 40W
Alta Sierra, Calif. **19** 35 42N 118 33W
Altadena, Calif. **29** 34 11N 118 8W
Altamaha →, Ga. **11** 31 20N 81 20W
Altamont, N.Y. **9** 42 43N 74 3W
Altavista, Va. **10** 37 6N 79 17W
Alton, Ill. **14** 38 53N 90 11W
Altoona, Pa. **8** 40 31N 78 24W
Alturas, Calif. **16** 41 29N 120 32W
Altus, Okla. **13** 34 38N 99 20W
Alva, Okla. **13** 36 48N 98 40W
Alvarado, Tex. **13** 32 24N 97 13W
Alvin, Tex. **13** 29 26N 95 15W
Alzada, Mont. **12** 45 2N 104 25W
Amargosa →, Calif. .. **19** 36 14N 116 51W
Amargosa Range, Calif. **19** 36 20N 116 45W
Amarillo, Tex. **13** 35 13N 101 50W
Amatignak I., Alaska . **30** 51 16N 179 6W
Amboy, Calif. **19** 34 33N 115 45W
Amchitka I., Alaska .. **30** 51 32N 179 0 E
Amchitka Pass., Alaska **30** 51 30N 179 0W
American Falls, Idaho . **16** 42 47N 112 51W
American Falls
  Reservoir, Idaho **16** 42 47N 112 52W
American Samoa ■,
  Pac. Oc. **31** 14 20S 170 40W
Americus, Ga. **11** 32 4N 84 14W
Ames, Iowa **14** 42 2N 93 37W
Amesbury, Mass. **9** 42 51N 70 56W
Amherst, Mass. **9** 42 23N 72 31W

Amherst, Tex. **13** 34 1N 102 25W
Amite, La. **13** 30 44N 90 30W
Amlia I., Alaska **30** 52 4N 173 30W
Amory, Miss. **11** 33 59N 88 29W
Amsterdam, N.Y. **9** 42 56N 74 11W
Amukta I., Alaska **30** 52 30N 171 16W
Anaconda, Mont. **16** 46 8N 112 57W
Anacortes, Wash. **18** 48 30N 122 37W
Anadarko, Okla. **13** 35 4N 98 15W
Anaheim, Calif. **19** 33 50N 117 55W
Anamoose, N. Dak. ... **12** 47 53N 100 15W
Anamosa, Iowa **14** 42 7N 91 17W
Anatone, Wash. **16** 46 8N 117 8W
Anchorage, Alaska ... **30** 61 13N 149 54W
Andalusia, Ala. **11** 31 18N 86 29W
Anderson, Calif. **16** 40 27N 122 18W
Anderson, Ind. **15** 40 10N 85 41W
Anderson, Mo. **13** 36 39N 94 27W
Anderson, S.C. **11** 34 31N 82 39W
Andover, Mass. **23** 42 39N 71 7W
Andreanof Is., Alaska . **30** 52 0N 178 0W
Andrews, S.C. **11** 33 27N 79 34W
Andrews, Tex. **13** 32 19N 102 33W
Andrews Air Force Base,
  Md. **25** 38 48N 76 52W
Anegada I., Virgin Is. . **30** 18 45N 64 20W
Angeles National Forest,
  Calif. **29** 34 15N 118 5W
Angels Camp, Calif. .. **18** 38 4N 120 32W
Angleton, Tex. **13** 29 10N 95 26W
Angola, Ind. **15** 41 38N 85 0W
Angoon, Alaska **30** 57 30N 134 35W
Aniak, Alaska **30** 61 35N 159 32W
Animas, N. Mex. **17** 31 57N 108 48W
Ann, C., Mass. **9** 42 38N 70 35W
Ann Arbor, Mich. **15** 42 17N 83 45W
Anna, Ill. **13** 37 28N 89 15W
Annandale, Va. **25** 38 50N 77 12W
Annapolis, Md. **10** 38 59N 76 30W
Annette, Alaska **30** 55 2N 131 35W
Anniston, Ala. **11** 33 39N 85 50W
Annville, Pa. **9** 40 20N 76 31W
Anoka, Minn. **12** 45 12N 93 23W
Ansley, Nebr. **12** 41 18N 99 23W
Anson, Tex. **13** 32 45N 99 54W
Ansonia, Conn. **9** 41 21N 73 5W
Antero, Mt., Colo. ... **17** 38 41N 106 15W
Anthony, Kans. **13** 37 9N 98 2W
Anthony, N. Mex. **17** 32 0N 106 36W
Antigo, Wis. **12** 45 9N 89 9W
Antimony, Utah **17** 38 7N 112 0W
Antioch, Calif. **18** 38 1N 121 48W

Blackfoot River Reservoir

Blackfoot River Reservoir, Idaho 16 43 0N 111 43W
Blacksburg, Va. 10 37 14N 80 25W
Blackstone, Va. 10 37 4N 78 0W
Blackwell, Okla. 13 36 48N 97 17W
Blackwells Corner, Calif. 19 35 37N 119 47W
Blackwood, N.J. 24 39 48N 75 4W
Blaine, Wash. 18 48 59N 122 45W
Blair, Nebr. 12 41 33N 96 8W
Blake Pt., Mich. 12 48 11N 88 25W
Blakely, Ga. 11 31 23N 84 56W
Blanca Peak, Colo. 17 37 35N 105 29W
Blanchard, Okla. 13 35 8N 97 39W
Blanco, Tex. 13 30 6N 98 25W
Blanco, C., Oreg. 16 42 51N 124 34W
Blanding, Utah 17 37 37N 109 29W
Block I., R.I. 9 41 11N 71 35W
Bloomer, Wis. 12 45 6N 91 29W
Bloomfield, Iowa 14 40 45N 92 25W
Bloomfield, N.J. 20 40 48N 74 12W
Bloomfield, N. Mex. 17 36 43N 107 59W
Bloomfield, Nebr. 12 42 36N 97 39W
Bloomingdale, N.J. 20 41 0N 74 15W
Bloomington, Ill. 14 40 28N 89 0W
Bloomington, Ind. 15 39 10N 86 32W
Bloomsburg, Pa. 9 41 0N 76 27W
Blossburg, Pa. 8 41 41N 77 4W
Blountstown, Fla. 11 30 27N 85 3W
Blue Island, Ill. 10 41 40N 87 40W
Blue Island, Ill. 22 41 40N 87 40W
Blue Lake, Calif. 16 40 53N 123 59W
Blue Mesa Reservoir, Colo. 17 38 28N 107 20W
Blue Mts., Oreg. 16 45 15N 119 0W
Blue Mts., Pa. 9 40 30N 76 30W
Blue Rapids, Kans. 12 39 41N 96 39W
Blue Ridge Mts., N.C. 11 36 30N 80 15W
Bluefield, Va. 10 37 15N 81 17W
Bluff, Utah 17 37 17N 109 33W
Bluffton, Ind. 15 40 44N 85 11W
Blunt, S. Dak. 12 44 31N 99 59W
Bly, Oreg. 16 42 24N 121 3W
Blythe, Calif. 19 33 37N 114 36W
Boca Raton, Fla. 11 26 21N 80 5W
Boerne, Tex. 13 29 47N 98 44W
Bogalusa, La. 13 30 47N 89 52W
Bogata, Tex. 13 33 28N 95 13W
Boise, Idaho 16 43 37N 116 13W
Boise City, Okla. 13 36 44N 102 31W
Bolivar, Mo. 13 37 37N 93 25W
Bolivar, Tenn. 13 35 12N 89 0W
Bonham, Tex. 13 33 35N 96 11W
Bonne Terre, Mo. 14 37 55N 90 33W
Bonners Ferry, Idaho 16 48 42N 116 19W
Bonsall, Calif. 19 33 16N 117 14W
Booker, Tex. 13 36 27N 100 32W
Boone, Iowa 14 42 4N 93 53W
Boone, N.C. 11 36 13N 81 41W
Booneville, Ark. 13 35 8N 93 55W
Booneville, Miss. 11 34 39N 88 34W
Boonville, Ind. 15 38 3N 87 16W
Boonville, Mo. 14 38 58N 92 44W
Boonville, N.Y. 9 43 29N 75 20W
Borah Peak, Idaho 16 44 8N 113 47W
Borger, Tex. 13 35 39N 101 24W
Boron, Calif. 19 35 0N 117 39W
Borrego Springs, Calif. 19 33 15N 116 23W
Bossier City, La. 13 32 31N 93 44W
Boston, Mass. 23 42 21N 71 3W
Boswell, Okla. 13 34 2N 95 52W
Bottineau, N. Dak. 12 48 50N 100 27W
Boulder, Colo. 12 40 1N 105 17W
Boulder, Mont. 16 46 14N 112 7W
Boulder City, Nev. 19 35 59N 114 50W
Boulder Creek, Calif. 18 37 7N 122 7W
Boulder Dam = Hoover Dam, Ariz. 19 36 1N 114 44W
Boundary, Alaska 30 64 4N 141 6W
Boundary Peak, Nev. 18 37 51N 118 21W
Bountiful, Utah 16 40 53N 111 53W
Bovill, Idaho 16 46 51N 116 24W
Bowbells, N. Dak. 12 48 48N 102 15W
Bowdle, S. Dak. 12 45 27N 99 39W
Bowie, Ariz. 17 32 19N 109 29W
Bowie, Tex. 13 33 34N 97 51W
Bowling Green, Ky. 10 36 59N 86 27W
Bowling Green, Ohio 15 41 23N 83 39W
Bowman, N. Dak. 12 46 11N 103 24W
Boyce, La. 13 31 23N 92 40W
Boyne City, Mich. 10 45 13N 85 1W
Boynton Beach, Fla. 11 26 32N 80 4W
Bozeman, Mont. 16 45 41N 111 2W
Brackettville, Tex. 13 29 19N 100 25W
Braddock, Pa. 27 40 24N 79 51W
Bradenton, Fla. 11 27 30N 82 34W
Bradford, Pa. 8 41 58N 78 38W
Bradley, Ark. 13 33 6N 93 39W
Bradley, Calif. 18 35 52N 120 48W
Bradley, S. Dak. 12 45 5N 97 39W
Brady, Tex. 13 31 9N 99 20W
Brainerd, Minn. 12 46 22N 94 12W
Braintree, Mass. 23 42 12N 71 0W
Brandywine, Del. 24 39 49N 75 32W
Branford, Conn. 9 41 17N 72 49W
Branson, Colo. 13 37 1N 103 53W
Branson, Mo. 13 36 39N 93 13W
Brasstown Bald, Ga. 11 34 53N 83 49W
Brattleboro, Vt. 9 42 51N 72 34W
Brawley, Calif. 19 32 59N 115 31W
Brazil, Ind. 15 39 32N 87 8W
Brazos →, Tex. 13 28 53N 95 23W
Breckenridge, Colo. 16 39 29N 106 3W
Breckenridge, Minn. 12 46 16N 96 35W
Breckenridge, Tex. 13 32 45N 98 54W
Bremerton, Wash. 18 47 34N 122 38W
Brenham, Tex. 13 30 10N 96 24W
Brentwood, Pa. 27 40 22N 79 59W
Breton Sd., La. 13 29 35N 89 15W
Brevard, N.C. 11 35 14N 82 44W
Brewer, Maine 11 44 48N 68 46W
Brewer, Mt., Calif. 18 36 44N 118 28W
Brewster, N.Y. 9 41 23N 73 37W
Brewster, Wash. 16 48 6N 119 47W
Brewton, Ala. 11 31 7N 87 4W
Bridgehampton, N.Y. 9 40 56N 72 19W
Bridgeport, Calif. 18 38 15N 119 14W
Bridgeport, Conn. 9 41 11N 73 12W
Bridgeport, Nebr. 12 41 40N 103 6W
Bridgeport, Pa. 24 39 48N 75 21W
Bridgeport, Tex. 13 33 13N 97 45W
Bridger, Mont. 16 45 18N 108 55W
Bridgeton, N.J. 10 39 26N 75 14W
Bridgeville, Pa. 27 21 0N 80 6W
Bridgewater, Mass. 9 41 59N 70 58W
Bridgewater, S. Dak. 12 43 33N 97 30W
Briggsdale, Colo. 12 40 38N 104 20W
Brigham City, Utah 16 41 31N 112 1W
Brighton, Colo. 12 39 59N 104 49W
Brinkley, Ark. 13 34 53N 91 12W
Bristol, Conn. 9 41 40N 72 57W
Bristol, Pa. 24 40 6N 74 53W
Bristol, R.I. 9 41 40N 71 16W
Bristol, S. Dak. 12 45 21N 97 45W
Bristol, Tenn. 11 36 36N 82 11W
Bristol B., Alaska 30 58 0N 160 0W
Bristol L., Calif. 17 34 23N 116 50W
Bristow, Okla. 13 35 50N 96 23W
Britton, S. Dak. 12 45 48N 97 45W
Broad →, S.C. 11 34 1N 81 4W
Broadus, Mont. 12 45 27N 105 25W
Broadview, Ill. 22 41 51N 87 52W
Brockport, N.Y. 8 43 13N 77 56W
Brockton, Mass. 9 42 5N 71 1W
Brockway, Mont. 12 47 18N 105 45W
Brogan, Oreg. 16 44 15N 117 31W
Broken Bow, Nebr. 12 41 24N 99 38W
Broken Bow, Okla. 13 34 2N 94 44W
Bronte, Tex. 13 31 53N 100 18W
Bronx, N.Y. 21 40 50N 73 52W
Bronxville, N.Y. 21 40 56N 73 49W
Brook Park, Ohio 27 41 24N 81 48W
Brookfield, Ill. 22 41 48N 87 50W
Brookfield, Mo. 14 39 47N 93 4W
Brookhaven, Miss. 13 31 35N 90 26W
Brookings, Oreg. 16 42 3N 124 17W
Brookings, S. Dak. 12 44 19N 96 48W
Brookline, Mass. 23 42 19N 71 7W
Brooklyn, Md. 25 39 13N 76 35W
Brooklyn, N.Y. 20 40 37N 73 57W
Brooklyn, Ohio 27 41 26N 81 44W
Brooks Ra., Alaska 30 68 40N 147 0W
Brooksville, Fla. 11 28 33N 82 23W
Brookville, Ind. 15 39 25N 85 1W
Broomall, Pa. 24 39 58N 75 22W
Brothers, Oreg. 16 43 49N 120 36W
Browerville, Minn. 12 46 5N 94 52W
Brownfield, Tex. 13 33 11N 102 17W
Browning, Mont. 16 48 34N 113 1W
Brownsville, Oreg. 16 44 24N 122 59W
Brownsville, Tenn. 13 35 36N 89 16W
Brownsville, Tex. 13 25 54N 97 30W
Brownwood, Tex. 13 31 43N 98 59W
Brownwood, L., Tex. 13 31 51N 98 35W
Brundidge, Ala. 11 31 43N 85 49W
Bruneau, Idaho 16 42 53N 115 48W
Bruneau →, Idaho 16 42 56N 115 57W
Brunswick, Ga. 11 31 10N 81 30W
Brunswick, Maine 11 43 55N 69 58W
Brunswick, Md. 10 39 19N 77 38W
Brunswick, Mo. 14 39 26N 93 8W
Brush, Colo. 12 40 15N 103 37W
Bryan, Ohio 15 41 28N 84 33W
Bryan, Tex. 13 30 40N 96 22W
Bryant, S. Dak. 12 44 35N 97 28W
Bryn Mawr, Pa. 24 40 1N 75 19W
Bryson City, N.C. 11 35 26N 83 27W
Buchanan, L., Tex. 13 30 45N 98 25W
Buchon, Pt., Calif. 18 35 15N 120 54W
Buckeye, Ariz. 17 33 22N 112 35W
Buckhannon, W. Va. 10 39 0N 80 8W
Buckland, Alaska 30 65 59N 161 8W
Buckley, Wash. 16 47 10N 122 2W
Bucklin, Kans. 13 37 33N 99 38W
Bucyrus, Ohio 15 40 48N 82 59W
Buellton, Calif. 19 34 37N 120 12W
Buena Park, Calif. 29 33 51N 118 1W
Buena Vista, Colo. 17 38 51N 106 8W
Buena Vista, Va. 10 37 44N 79 21W
Buena Vista L., Calif. 19 35 12N 119 18W
Buffalo, Mo. 14 37 39N 93 6W
Buffalo, N.Y. 8 42 53N 78 53W
Buffalo, Okla. 13 36 50N 99 38W
Buffalo, S. Dak. 12 45 35N 103 33W
Buffalo, Wyo. 16 44 21N 106 42W
Buford, Ga. 11 34 10N 84 0W
Buhl, Idaho 16 42 36N 114 46W
Buhl, Minn. 12 47 30N 92 46W
Buldir I., Alaska 30 52 21N 175 56 E
Bull Shoals L., Ark. 13 36 22N 92 35W
Bunker Hill Monument, Mass. 23 42 21N 71 3W
Bunkie, La. 13 30 57N 92 11W
Bunnell, Fla. 11 29 28N 81 16W
Buras, La. 13 29 22N 89 32W
Burbank, Calif. 29 34 11N 118 18W
Burbank, Ill. 22 41 44N 87 47W
Burkburnett, Tex. 13 34 6N 98 34W
Burke, Idaho 16 47 31N 115 49W
Burley, Idaho 16 42 32N 113 48W
Burlingame, Calif. 28 37 35N 122 22W
Burlington, Colo. 12 39 18N 102 16W
Burlington, Iowa 14 40 49N 91 14W
Burlington, Kans. 12 38 12N 95 45W
Burlington, Mass. 23 42 30N 71 13W
Burlington, N.C. 11 36 6N 79 26W
Burlington, N.J. 24 40 4N 74 54W
Burlington, Vt. 9 44 29N 73 12W
Burlington, Wash. 18 48 28N 122 20W
Burlington, Wis. 10 42 41N 88 17W
Burnet, Tex. 13 30 45N 98 14W
Burney, Calif. 16 40 53N 121 40W
Burns, Oreg. 16 43 35N 119 3W
Burns, Wyo. 12 41 12N 104 21W
Burnt Paw, Alaska 30 67 2N 142 43W
Burwell, Nebr. 12 41 47N 99 8W
Bushnell, Ill. 12 40 33N 90 31W
Bushnell, Nebr. 12 41 14N 103 54W
Butler, Mo. 14 38 16N 94 20W
Butler, Pa. 8 40 52N 79 54W
Butte, Mont. 16 46 0N 112 32W
Butte, Nebr. 12 42 58N 98 51W
Buttonwillow, Calif. 19 35 24N 119 28W
Buzzards Bay, Mass. 9 41 45N 70 37W
Byers, Colo. 12 39 43N 104 14W
Byhalia, Miss. 13 34 52N 89 41W
Bylas, Ariz. 17 33 8N 110 7W

C

Cabazon, Calif. 19 33 55N 116 47W
Cabinet Mts., Mont. 16 48 0N 115 30W
Cabool, Mo. 13 37 7N 92 6W
Caddo, Okla. 13 34 7N 96 16W
Cadillac, Mich. 10 44 15N 85 24W
Caguas, Puerto Rico 30 18 14N 66 2W
Cairo, Ga. 11 30 52N 84 13W
Cairo, Ill. 13 37 0N 89 11W
Calais, Maine 11 45 11N 67 17W
Calcasieu L., La. 13 29 55N 93 18W
Caldwell, Idaho 16 43 40N 116 41W
Caldwell, Kans. 13 37 2N 97 37W
Caldwell, Tex. 13 30 32N 96 42W
Calexico, Calif. 19 32 40N 115 30W
Calhoun, Ga. 11 34 30N 84 57W
Caliente, Nev. 17 37 37N 114 31W
California, Mo. 14 38 38N 92 34W
California □ 17 37 30N 119 30W
California, University of, Calif. 28 37 52N 122 15W
California City, Calif. 19 35 10N 117 55W
California Hot Springs, Calif. 19 35 51N 118 41W
Calipatria, Calif. 19 33 8N 115 31W
Calistoga, Calif. 18 38 35N 122 35W
Callaway, Nebr. 12 41 18N 99 56W
Calumet, Mich. 10 47 14N 88 27W
Calumet City, Ill. 22 41 37N 87 32W
Calvert, Tex. 13 30 59N 96 40W
Calwa, Calif. 18 36 42N 119 46W
Camanche Reservoir, Calif. 18 38 14N 121 1W
Camarillo, Calif. 19 34 13N 119 2W
Camas, Wash. 18 45 35N 122 24W
Camas Valley, Oreg. 16 43 2N 123 40W
Cambria, Calif. 18 35 34N 121 5W
Cambridge, Idaho 16 44 34N 116 41W
Cambridge, Mass. 23 42 22N 71 6W
Cambridge, Md. 10 38 34N 76 5W
Cambridge, Minn. 12 45 34N 93 13W
Cambridge, N.Y. 9 43 2N 73 22W
Cambridge, Nebr. 12 40 17N 100 10W
Cambridge, Ohio 8 40 2N 81 35W
Camden, Ala. 11 31 59N 87 17W
Camden, Ark. 13 33 35N 92 50W
Camden, Maine 11 44 13N 69 4W
Camden, N.J. 24 39 56N 75 7W
Camden, S.C. 11 34 16N 80 36W
Camden, B., Alaska 30 70 30N 145 0W
Camdenton, Mo. 14 38 1N 92 45W
Cameron, Ariz. 17 35 53N 111 25W
Cameron, La. 13 29 48N 93 20W
Cameron, Mo. 14 39 44N 94 14W
Cameron, Tex. 13 30 51N 96 59W
Camino, Calif. 18 38 44N 120 41W
Camp Crook, S. Dak. 12 45 33N 103 59W
Camp Nelson, Calif. 19 36 8N 118 39W
Camp Wood, Tex. 13 29 40N 100 1W
Campbell, Calif. 18 37 17N 121 57W
Campbellsville, Ky. 10 37 21N 85 20W
Canadian, Tex. 13 35 55N 100 23W
Canadian →, Okla. 13 35 28N 95 3W
Canandaigua, N.Y. 8 42 54N 77 17W
Canarsie, N.Y. 21 40 38N 73 53W
Canaveral, C., Fla. 11 28 27N 80 32W
Canby, Calif. 16 41 27N 120 52W
Canby, Minn. 12 44 43N 96 16W
Canby, Oreg. 18 45 16N 122 42W
Cando, N. Dak. 12 48 32N 99 12W
Cannon Ball →, N. Dak. 12 46 20N 100 38W
Canon City, Colo. 12 38 27N 105 14W
Cantil, Calif. 19 35 18N 117 58W
Canton, Ga. 11 34 14N 84 29W
Canton, Ill. 14 40 33N 90 2W
Canton, Miss. 13 32 37N 90 2W
Canton, Mo. 14 40 8N 91 32W
Canton, N.Y. 9 44 36N 75 10W
Canton, Ohio 8 40 48N 81 23W
Canton, Okla. 13 36 3N 98 35W
Canton, S. Dak. 12 43 18N 96 35W
Canton L., Okla. 13 36 6N 98 35W
Canutillo, Tex. 17 31 55N 106 36W
Canyon, Tex. 13 34 59N 101 55W
Canyon, Wyo. 16 44 43N 110 36W
Canyonlands National Park, Utah 17 38 15N 110 0W
Canyonville, Oreg. 16 42 56N 123 17W
Cape Charles, Va. 10 37 16N 76 1W
Cape Fear →, N.C. 11 33 53N 78 1W
Cape Girardeau, Mo. 13 37 19N 89 32W
Cape May, N.J. 10 38 56N 74 56W
Capitan, N. Mex. 17 33 35N 105 35W
Capitola, Calif. 18 36 59N 121 57W
Carbondale, Colo. 16 39 24N 107 13W
Carbondale, Ill. 14 37 44N 89 13W
Carbondale, Pa. 9 41 35N 75 30W
Cardiff-by-the-Sea, Calif. 19 33 1N 117 17W
Carey, Idaho 16 43 19N 113 57W
Carey, Ohio 15 40 57N 83 23W
Caribou, Maine 11 46 52N 68 1W
Carlin, Nev. 16 40 43N 116 7W
Carlinville, Ill. 14 39 17N 89 53W
Carlisle, Pa. 8 40 12N 77 12W
Carlsbad, Calif. 19 33 10N 117 21W
Carlsbad, N. Mex. 13 32 25N 104 14W
Carlyle, Ill. 12 38 37N 89 22W
Carmel, N.Y. 9 41 26N 73 41W
Carmel-by-the-Sea, Calif. 18 36 33N 121 55W
Carmel Valley, Calif. 18 36 29N 121 43W
Carmi, Ill. 15 38 5N 88 10W
Carmichael, Calif. 18 38 38N 121 19W
Carnegie, Pa. 27 40 24N 80 5W
Caro, Mich. 10 43 29N 83 24W
Carol City, Fla. 11 25 56N 80 16W
Caroline Is., Pac. Oc. 31 8 0N 150 0 E
Carpinteria, Calif. 19 34 24N 119 31W
Carrabelle, Fla. 11 29 51N 84 40W
Carrington, N. Dak. 12 47 27N 99 8W
Carrizo Cr. →, N. Mex. 13 36 55N 103 55W
Carrizo Springs, Tex. 13 28 31N 99 52W
Carrizozo, N. Mex. 17 33 38N 105 53W
Carroll, Iowa 14 42 4N 94 52W
Carrollton, Ga. 11 33 35N 85 5W
Carrollton, Ill. 12 39 18N 90 24W
Carrollton, Ky. 15 38 41N 85 11W
Carrollton, Mo. 14 39 22N 93 30W
Carson, N. Dak. 12 46 25N 101 34W
Carson City, Nev. 18 39 10N 119 46W
Carson Sink, Nev. 16 39 50N 118 25W
Cartersville, Ga. 11 34 10N 84 48W
Carthage, Ark. 13 34 4N 92 33W
Carthage, Ill. 14 40 25N 91 8W
Carthage, Mo. 13 37 11N 94 19W
Carthage, S. Dak. 12 44 10N 97 43W
Carthage, Tex. 13 32 9N 94 20W
Caruthersville, Mo. 13 36 11N 89 39W
Casa Grande, Ariz. 17 32 53N 111 45W
Cascade, Idaho 16 44 31N 116 2W
Cascade, Mont. 16 47 16N 111 42W
Cascade Locks, Oreg. 18 45 40N 121 54W
Cascade Ra., Wash. 18 47 0N 121 30W
Cashmere, Wash. 16 47 31N 120 28W
Casmalia, Calif. 19 34 50N 120 32W
Casper, Wyo. 16 42 51N 106 19W
Cass City, Mich. 10 43 36N 83 11W
Cass Lake, Minn. 12 47 23N 94 37W
Casselton, N. Dak. 12 46 54N 97 13W
Cassville, Mo. 13 36 41N 93 52W
Castaic, Calif. 19 34 30N 118 38W
Castle Dale, Utah 16 39 13N 111 1W
Castle Rock, Colo. 12 39 22N 104 51W
Castle Rock, Wash. 18 46 17N 122 54W
Castro Valley, Calif. 28 37 42N 122 4W
Castroville, Calif. 18 36 46N 121 45W
Castroville, Tex. 13 29 21N 98 53W
Cat I., Miss. 13 30 14N 89 6W
Catahoula L., La. 13 31 31N 92 7W
Cathlamet, Wash. 18 46 12N 123 23W
Catlettsburg, Ky. 10 38 25N 82 36W
Catonsville, Md. 25 39 16N 76 43W
Catskill, N.Y. 9 42 14N 73 52W
Catskill Mts., N.Y. 9 42 10N 74 25W
Cavalier, N. Dak. 12 48 48N 97 37W
Cave City, Ky. 10 37 8N 85 58W
Cayey, Puerto Rico 30 18 7N 66 10W
Cayuga L., N.Y. 9 42 41N 76 41W
Cedar →, Iowa 14 41 17N 91 21W
Cedar City, Utah 17 37 41N 113 4W
Cedar Creek Reservoir, Tex. 13 32 11N 96 4W

Creston

Creston, *Calif.* **18** 35 32N 120 33W
Creston, *Iowa* **14** 41 4N 94 22W
Creston, *Wash.* **16** 47 46N 118 31W
Crestview, *Calif.* **18** 37 46N 118 58W
Crestview, *Fla.* **11** 30 46N 86 34W
Crete, *Nebr.* **12** 40 38N 96 58W
Crockett, *Tex.* **13** 31 19N 95 27W
Crooked →, *Oreg.* **16** 44 32N 121 16W
Crookston, *Minn.* **12** 47 47N 96 37W
Crookston, *Nebr.* **12** 42 56N 100 45W
Crooksville, *Ohio* **10** 39 46N 82 6W
Crosby, *Minn.* **12** 46 29N 93 58W
Crosbyton, *Tex.* **13** 33 40N 101 14W
Cross City, *Fla.* **11** 29 38N 83 7W
Cross Plains, *Tex.* **13** 32 8N 99 11W
Cross Sound, *Alaska* **30** 58 0N 135 0W
Crossett, *Ark.* **13** 33 8N 91 58W
Croton-on-Hudson, *N.Y.* **9** 41 12N 73 55W
Crow Agency, *Mont.* **16** 45 36N 107 28W
Crowell, *Tex.* **13** 33 59N 99 43W
Crowley, *La.* **13** 30 13N 92 22W
Crowley, L., *Calif.* **18** 37 35N 118 42W
Crown Point, *Ind.* **15** 41 25N 87 22W
Crows Landing, *Calif.* **18** 37 23N 121 6W
Crystal City, *Mo.* **14** 38 13N 90 23W
Crystal City, *Tex.* **13** 28 41N 99 50W
Crystal Falls, *Mich.* **10** 46 5N 88 20W
Crystal River, *Fla.* **11** 28 54N 82 35W
Crystal Springs, *Miss.* **13** 31 59N 90 21W
Cuba, *N. Mex.* **17** 36 1N 107 4W
Cudahy, *Wis.* **15** 42 58N 87 52W
Cuero, *Tex.* **13** 29 6N 97 17W
Cuervo, *N. Mex.* **13** 35 2N 104 25W
Culbertson, *Mont.* **12** 48 9N 104 31W
Culebra, Isla de, *Puerto Rico* **30** 18 19N 65 18W
Cullman, *Ala.* **11** 34 11N 86 51W
Culpeper, *Va.* **10** 38 30N 78 0W
Culver City, *Calif.* **29** 34 1N 118 23W
Cumberland, *Md.* **10** 39 39N 78 46W
Cumberland, *Wis.* **12** 45 32N 92 1W
Cumberland →, *Tenn.* **11** 36 15N 87 0W
Cumberland I., *Ga.* **11** 30 50N 81 25W
Cumberland Plateau, *Tenn.* **11** 36 0N 85 0W
Cummings Mt., *Calif.* **19** 35 2N 118 34W
Currant, *Nev.* **16** 38 51N 115 32W
Current →, *Ark.* **13** 36 15N 90 55W
Currie, *Nev.* **16** 40 16N 114 45W
Currituck Sd., *N.C.* **11** 36 20N 75 52W
Curtis, *Nebr.* **12** 40 38N 100 31W
Cushing, *Okla.* **13** 35 59N 96 46W
Custer, *S. Dak.* **12** 43 46N 103 36W
Cut Bank, *Mont.* **16** 48 38N 112 20W
Cuthbert, *Ga.* **11** 31 46N 84 48W
Cutler, *Calif.* **18** 36 31N 119 17W
Cuyahoga Falls, *Ohio* **8** 41 8N 81 29W
Cynthiana, *Ky.* **15** 38 23N 84 18W

D

Dade City, *Fla.* **11** 28 22N 82 11W
Daggett, *Calif.* **19** 34 52N 116 52W
Dahlonega, *Ga.* **11** 34 32N 83 59W
Dakota City, *Nebr.* **12** 42 25N 96 25W
Dalhart, *Tex.* **13** 36 4N 102 31W
Dallas, *Oreg.* **16** 44 55N 123 19W
Dallas, *Tex.* **13** 32 47N 96 49W
Dalton, *Ga.* **11** 34 46N 84 58W
Dalton, *Mass.* **9** 42 28N 73 11W
Dalton, *Nebr.* **12** 41 25N 102 58W
Daly City, *Calif.* **28** 37 42N 122 26W
Dana, Mt., *Calif.* **18** 37 54N 119 12W
Danbury, *Conn.* **9** 41 24N 73 28W
Danby L., *Calif.* **17** 34 13N 115 5W
Danforth, *Maine* **11** 45 40N 67 52W
Daniel, *Wyo.* **16** 42 52N 110 4W
Danielson, *Conn.* **9** 41 48N 71 53W
Dannemora, *N.Y.* **9** 44 43N 73 44W
Dansville, *N.Y.* **8** 42 34N 77 42W
Danvers, *Mass.* **23** 42 34N 70 56W
Danville, *Ill.* **15** 40 8N 87 37W
Danville, *Ky.* **15** 37 39N 84 46W
Danville, *Va.* **11** 36 36N 79 23W
Darby, *Mont.* **16** 46 1N 114 11W
Darby, *Pa.* **24** 39 55N 75 16W
Dardanelle, *Ark.* **13** 35 13N 93 9W
Dardanelle, *Calif.* **18** 38 20N 119 50W
Darlington, *S.C.* **11** 34 18N 79 52W
Darlington, *Wis.* **14** 42 41N 90 7W
Darrington, *Wash.* **16** 48 15N 121 36W
Darwin, *Calif.* **19** 36 15N 117 35W
Dauphin I., *Ala.* **11** 30 15N 88 11W
Davenport, *Calif.* **18** 37 1N 122 12W
Davenport, *Iowa* **14** 41 32N 90 35W
Davenport, *Wash.* **16** 47 39N 118 9W
David City, *Nebr.* **12** 41 15N 97 8W
Davis, *Calif.* **18** 38 33N 121 44W
Davis Dam, *Ariz.* **19** 35 11N 114 34W
Davis Mts., *Tex.* **13** 30 50N 103 55W
Dawson, *Ga.* **11** 31 46N 84 27W
Dawson, *N. Dak.* **12** 46 52N 99 45W
Dayton, *Ohio* **10** 39 45N 84 12W
Dayton, *Tenn.* **11** 35 30N 85 1W
Dayton, *Wash.* **16** 46 19N 117 59W
Daytona Beach, *Fla.* **11** 29 13N 81 1W
Dayville, *Oreg.* **16** 44 28N 119 32W
De Funiak Springs, *Fla.* **11** 30 43N 86 7W
De Kalb, *Ill.* **15** 41 56N 88 46W
De Land, *Fla.* **11** 29 2N 81 18W
De Leon, *Tex.* **13** 32 7N 98 32W
De Long Mts., *Alaska* **30** 68 30N 163 0W
De Pere, *Wis.* **10** 44 27N 88 4W
De Queen, *Ark.* **13** 34 2N 94 21W
De Quincy, *La.* **13** 30 27N 93 26W
De Ridder, *La.* **13** 30 51N 93 17W
De Smet, *S. Dak.* **12** 44 23N 97 33W
De Soto, *Mo.* **14** 38 8N 90 34W
De Tour Village, *Mich.* **10** 46 0N 83 56W
De Witt, *Ark.* **13** 34 18N 91 20W
Deadwood, *S. Dak.* **12** 44 23N 103 44W
Dearborn, *Mich.* **26** 42 19N 83 10W
Dearborn Heights, *Mich.* **26** 42 20N 83 17W
Death Valley, *Calif.* **19** 36 15N 116 50W
Death Valley Junction, *Calif.* **19** 36 20N 116 25W
Death Valley National Monument, *Calif.* **19** 36 45N 117 15W
Decatur, *Ala.* **11** 34 36N 86 59W
Decatur, *Ga.* **11** 33 47N 84 18W
Decatur, *Ill.* **14** 39 51N 88 57W
Decatur, *Ind.* **15** 40 50N 84 56W
Decatur, *Tex.* **13** 33 14N 97 35W
Decorah, *Iowa* **12** 43 18N 91 48W
Dedham, *Mass.* **23** 42 15N 71 10W
Deer I., *Alaska* **30** 54 55N 162 18W
Deer Lodge, *Mont.* **16** 46 24N 112 44W
Deer Park, *N.Y.* **21** 40 46N 73 19W
Deer Park, *Wash.* **16** 47 57N 117 28W
Deer River, *Minn.* **12** 47 20N 93 48W
Deering, *Alaska* **30** 66 4N 162 42W
Defiance, *Ohio* **15** 41 17N 84 22W
Del Mar, *Calif.* **19** 32 58N 117 16W
Del Norte, *Colo.* **17** 37 41N 106 21W
Del Rio, *Tex.* **13** 29 22N 100 54W
Delano, *Calif.* **19** 35 46N 119 15W
Delavan, *Wis.* **15** 42 38N 88 39W
Delaware, *Ohio* **15** 40 18N 83 4W
Delaware □ **10** 39 0N 75 20W
Delaware →, *Del.* **10** 39 15N 75 20W
Delhi, *N.Y.* **9** 42 17N 74 55W
Dell City, *Tex.* **17** 31 56N 105 12W
Dell Rapids, *S. Dak.* **12** 43 50N 96 43W
Delphi, *Ind.* **15** 40 36N 86 41W
Delphos, *Ohio* **15** 40 51N 84 21W
Delray Beach, *Fla.* **11** 26 28N 80 4W
Delta, *Colo.* **17** 38 44N 108 4W
Delta, *Utah* **16** 39 21N 112 35W
Deming, *N. Mex.* **17** 32 16N 107 46W
Demopolis, *Ala.* **11** 32 31N 87 50W
Denair, *Calif.* **18** 37 32N 120 48W
Denison, *Iowa* **12** 42 1N 95 21W
Denison, *Tex.* **13** 33 45N 96 33W
Denton, *Mont.* **16** 47 19N 109 57W
Denton, *Tex.* **13** 33 13N 97 8W
Denver, *Colo.* **12** 39 44N 104 59W
Denver City, *Tex.* **13** 32 58N 102 50W
Deposit, *N.Y.* **9** 42 4N 75 25W
Derby, *Conn.* **9** 41 19N 73 5W
Dernieres, Isles, *La.* **13** 29 2N 90 50W
Des Moines, *Iowa* **14** 41 35N 93 37W
Des Moines, *N. Mex.* **13** 36 46N 103 50W
Des Moines →, *Iowa* **12** 40 23N 91 25W
Des Plaines, *Ill.* **22** 42 2N 87 54W
Deschutes →, *Oreg.* **16** 45 38N 120 55W
Desert Center, *Calif.* **19** 33 43N 115 24W
Desert Hot Springs, *Calif.* **19** 33 58N 116 30W
Detour, Pt., *Mich.* **10** 45 40N 86 40W
Detroit, *Mich.* **26** 42 20N 83 2W
Detroit, *Tex.* **13** 33 40N 95 16W
Detroit City Airport, *Mich.* **26** 42 24N 83 0W
Detroit Lakes, *Minn.* **12** 46 49N 95 51W
Detroit-Wayne Airport, *Mich.* **26** 42 13N 83 20W
Devils Den, *Calif.* **18** 35 46N 119 58W
Devils Lake, *N. Dak.* **12** 48 7N 98 52W
Dexter, *Mo.* **13** 36 48N 89 57W
Dexter, *N. Mex.* **13** 33 12N 104 22W
Diablo, Mt., *Calif.* **18** 37 53N 121 56W
Diablo Range, *Calif.* **18** 37 20N 121 25W
Diamond Mts., *Nev.* **16** 39 50N 115 30W
Diamond Springs, *Calif.* **18** 38 42N 120 49W
Diamondville, *Wyo.* **16** 41 47N 110 32W
Dickinson, *N. Dak.* **12** 46 53N 102 47W
Dickson, *Tenn.* **11** 36 5N 87 23W
Dickson City, *Pa.* **9** 41 29N 75 40W
Dierks, *Ark.* **13** 34 7N 94 1W
Dighton, *Kans.* **12** 38 29N 100 28W
Dilley, *Tex.* **13** 28 40N 99 10W
Dillingham, *Alaska* **30** 59 3N 158 28W
Dillon, *Mont.* **16** 45 13N 112 38W
Dillon, *S.C.* **11** 34 25N 79 22W
Dimmitt, *Tex.* **13** 34 33N 102 19W
Dingmans Ferry, *Pa.* **9** 41 13N 74 55W
Dinosaur National Monument, *Colo.* **16** 40 30N 108 45W
Dinuba, *Calif.* **18** 36 32N 119 23W
Disappointment, C., *Wash.* **16** 46 18N 124 5W
Divide, *Mont.* **16** 45 45N 112 45W
Dixon, *Calif.* **18** 38 27N 121 49W
Dixon, *Ill.* **14** 41 50N 89 29W
Dixon, *Mont.* **16** 47 19N 114 19W
Dixon, *N. Mex.* **17** 36 12N 105 53W
Dodge Center, *Minn.* **12** 44 2N 92 52W
Dodge City, *Kans.* **13** 37 45N 100 1W
Dodgeville, *Wis.* **14** 42 58N 90 8W
Dodson, *Mont.* **16** 48 24N 108 15W
Doland, *S. Dak.* **12** 44 54N 98 6W
Dolores, *Colo.* **17** 37 28N 108 30W
Dolores →, *Utah* **17** 38 49N 109 17W
Dolton, *Ill.* **22** 41 37N 87 35W
Donaldsonville, *La.* **13** 30 6N 90 59W
Donalsonville, *Ga.* **11** 31 3N 84 53W
Doniphan, *Mo.* **13** 36 37N 90 50W
Donna, *Tex.* **13** 26 9N 98 4W
Dormont, *Pa.* **27** 40 23N 80 2W
Dorris, *Calif.* **16** 41 58N 121 55W
Dos Palos, *Calif.* **18** 36 59N 120 37W
Dothan, *Ala.* **11** 31 13N 85 24W
Douglas, *Alaska* **30** 58 17N 134 24W
Douglas, *Ariz.* **17** 31 21N 109 33W
Douglas, *Ga.* **11** 31 31N 82 51W
Douglas, *Wyo.* **12** 42 45N 105 24W
Douglasville, *Ga.* **11** 33 45N 84 45W
Dove Creek, *Colo.* **17** 37 46N 108 54W
Dover, *Del.* **10** 39 10N 75 32W
Dover, *N.H.* **9** 43 12N 70 56W
Dover, *N.J.* **9** 40 53N 74 34W
Dover, *Ohio* **8** 40 32N 81 29W
Dover-Foxcroft, *Maine* **11** 45 11N 69 13W
Dover Plains, *N.Y.* **9** 41 43N 73 35W
Dowagiac, *Mich.* **15** 41 59N 86 6W
Downey, *Calif.* **29** 33 56N 118 8W
Downey, *Idaho* **16** 42 26N 112 7W
Downieville, *Calif.* **18** 39 34N 120 50W
Doylestown, *Pa.* **9** 40 21N 75 10W
Drain, *Oreg.* **16** 43 40N 123 19W
Drake, *N. Dak.* **12** 47 55N 100 23W
Drexel Hill, *Pa.* **24** 39 56N 75 18W
Driggs, *Idaho* **16** 43 44N 111 6W
Drummond, *Mont.* **16** 46 40N 113 9W
Drumright, *Okla.* **13** 35 59N 96 36W
Dryden, *Tex.* **13** 30 3N 102 7W
Du Bois, *Pa.* **8** 41 8N 78 46W
Du Quoin, *Ill.* **14** 38 1N 89 14W
Duanesburg, *N.Y.* **9** 42 45N 74 11W
Duarte, *Calif.* **29** 34 8N 117 57W
Dublin, *Ga.* **11** 32 32N 82 54W
Dublin, *Tex.* **13** 32 5N 98 21W
Dubois, *Idaho* **16** 44 10N 112 14W
Dubuque, *Iowa* **14** 42 30N 90 41W
Duchesne, *Utah* **16** 40 10N 110 24W
Duckwall, Mt., *Calif.* **18** 37 58N 120 7W
Duluth, *Minn.* **12** 46 47N 92 6W
Dulworthtown, *Pa.* **24** 39 54N 75 33W
Dumas, *Ark.* **13** 33 53N 91 29W
Dumas, *Tex.* **13** 35 52N 101 58W
Duncan, *Ariz.* **17** 32 43N 109 6W
Duncan, *Okla.* **13** 34 30N 97 57W
Dundalk, *Md.* **25** 39 16N 76 30W
Dunedin, *Fla.* **11** 28 1N 82 47W
Dunkirk, *N.Y.* **8** 42 29N 79 20W
Dunlap, *Iowa* **12** 41 51N 95 36W
Dunmore, *Pa.* **9** 41 25N 75 38W
Dunn, *N.C.* **11** 35 19N 78 37W
Dunnellon, *Fla.* **11** 29 3N 82 28W
Dunning, *Nebr.* **12** 41 50N 100 6W
Dunseith, *N. Dak.* **12** 48 50N 100 3W
Dunsmuir, *Calif.* **16** 41 13N 122 16W
Dupree, *S. Dak.* **12** 45 4N 101 35W
Dupuyer, *Mont.* **16** 48 13N 112 30W
Duquesne, *Pa.* **27** 40 22N 79 52W
Durand, *Mich.* **15** 42 55N 83 59W
Durango, *Colo.* **17** 37 16N 107 53W
Durant, *Okla.* **13** 33 59N 96 25W
Durham, *N.C.* **11** 35 59N 78 54W
Duryea, *Pa.* **9** 41 20N 75 45W
Dutch Harbor, *Alaska* **30** 53 53N 166 32W
Dwight, *Ill.* **15** 41 5N 88 26W
Dyersburg, *Tenn.* **13** 36 3N 89 23W

E

Eads, *Colo.* **12** 38 29N 102 47W
Eagle, *Alaska* **30** 64 47N 141 12W
Eagle, *Colo.* **16** 39 39N 106 50W
Eagle Butte, *S. Dak.* **12** 45 0N 101 10W
Eagle Grove, *Iowa* **14** 42 40N 93 54W
Eagle L., *Calif.* **16** 40 39N 120 45W
Eagle L., *Maine* **11** 46 20N 69 22W
Eagle Lake, *Tex.* **13** 29 35N 96 20W
Eagle Nest, *N. Mex.* **17** 36 33N 105 16W
Eagle Pass, *Tex.* **13** 28 43N 100 30W
Eagle Pk., *Calif.* **18** 38 10N 119 25W
Eagle River, *Wis.* **12** 45 55N 89 15W
Earle, *Ark.* **13** 35 16N 90 28W
Earlimart, *Calif.* **19** 35 53N 119 16W
Earth, *Tex.* **13** 34 14N 102 24W
Easley, *S.C.* **11** 34 50N 82 36W
East B., *La.* **13** 29 0N 89 15W
East Chicago, *Ind.* **22** 41 38N 87 26W
East Cleveland, *Ohio* **27** 41 32N 81 35W
East Detroit, *Mich.* **26** 42 27N 82 58W
East Grand Forks, *Minn.* **12** 47 56N 97 1W
East Greenwich, *R.I.* **9** 41 40N 71 27W
East Hartford, *Conn.* **9** 41 46N 72 39W
East Helena, *Mont.* **16** 46 35N 111 56W
East Jordan, *Mich.* **10** 45 10N 85 7W
East Lansing, *Mich.* **15** 42 44N 84 29W
East Liverpool, *Ohio* **8** 40 37N 80 35W
East Los Angeles, *Calif.* **29** 34 1N 118 10W
East Meadow, *N.Y.* **21** 40 42N 73 31W
East Orange, *N.J.* **20** 40 46N 74 11W
East Point, *Ga.* **11** 33 41N 84 27W
East Providence, *R.I.* **9** 41 49N 71 23W
East St. Louis, *Ill.* **14** 38 37N 90 9W
East Stroudsburg, *Pa.* **9** 41 1N 75 11W
East Tawas, *Mich.* **10** 44 17N 83 29W
East Walker →, *Nev.* **18** 38 52N 119 10W
Eastchester, *N.Y.* **21** 40 57N 73 49W
Eastlake, *Ohio* **27** 41 38N 81 28W
Eastland, *Tex.* **13** 32 24N 98 49W
Eastman, *Ga.* **11** 32 12N 83 11W
Easton, *Md.* **10** 38 47N 76 5W
Easton, *Pa.* **9** 40 41N 75 13W
Easton, *Wash.* **18** 47 14N 121 11W
Eastport, *Maine* **11** 44 56N 67 0W
Eaton, *Colo.* **12** 40 32N 104 42W
Eatonton, *Ga.* **11** 33 20N 83 23W
Eatontown, *N.J.* **9** 40 19N 74 4W
Eau Claire, *Wis.* **12** 44 49N 91 30W
Eden, *N.C.* **11** 36 29N 79 53W
Eden, *Tex.* **13** 31 13N 99 51W
Eden, *Wyo.* **16** 42 3N 109 26W
Edenton, *N.C.* **11** 36 4N 76 39W
Edgar, *Nebr.* **12** 40 22N 97 58W
Edgartown, *Mass.* **9** 41 23N 70 31W
Edgefield, *S.C.* **11** 33 47N 81 56W
Edgeley, *N. Dak.* **12** 46 22N 98 43W
Edgemont, *S. Dak.* **12** 43 18N 103 50W
Edina, *Mo.* **14** 40 10N 92 11W
Edinburg, *Tex.* **13** 26 18N 98 10W
Edison, *N.J.* **20** 40 31N 74 22W
Edmeston, *N.Y.* **9** 42 42N 75 15W
Edmond, *Okla.* **13** 35 39N 97 29W
Edmonds, *Wash.* **18** 47 49N 122 23W
Edna, *Tex.* **13** 28 59N 96 39W
Edwards, *Calif.* **19** 34 55N 117 51W
Edwards Plateau, *Tex.* **13** 30 45N 101 20W
Edwardsville, *Pa.* **9** 41 15N 75 56W
Eek, *Alaska* **30** 60 14N 162 2W
Effingham, *Ill.* **15** 39 7N 88 33W
Egeland, *N. Dak.* **12** 48 38N 99 6W
Ekalaka, *Mont.* **12** 45 53N 104 33W
El Cajon, *Calif.* **19** 32 48N 116 58W
El Campo, *Tex.* **13** 29 12N 96 16W
El Centro, *Calif.* **19** 32 48N 115 34W
El Cerrito, *Calif.* **28** 37 54N 122 18W
El Dorado, *Ark.* **13** 33 12N 92 40W
El Dorado, *Kans.* **13** 37 49N 96 52W
El Granada, *Calif.* **28** 37 30N 122 28W
El Monte, *Calif.* **29** 34 3N 118 1W
El Paso, *Tex.* **17** 31 45N 106 29W
El Paso Robles, *Calif.* **18** 35 38N 120 41W
El Portal, *Calif.* **18** 37 41N 119 47W
El Reno, *Okla.* **13** 35 32N 97 57W
El Rio, *Calif.* **19** 34 14N 119 10W
El Segundo, *Calif.* **29** 33 55N 118 24W
Elba, *Ala.* **11** 31 25N 86 4W
Elbert, Mt., *Colo.* **17** 39 7N 106 27W
Elberta, *Mich.* **10** 44 37N 86 14W
Elberton, *Ga.* **11** 34 7N 82 52W
Eldon, *Mo.* **14** 38 21N 92 35W
Eldora, *Iowa* **14** 42 22N 93 5W
Eldorado, *Ill.* **15** 37 49N 88 26W
Eldorado, *Tex.* **13** 30 52N 100 36W
Eldorado Springs, *Mo.* **14** 37 52N 94 1W
Electra, *Tex.* **13** 34 2N 98 55W
Eleele, *Hawaii* **30** 21 54N 159 35W
Elephant Butte Reservoir, *N. Mex.* **17** 33 9N 107 11W
Elfin Cove, *Alaska* **30** 58 12N 136 22W
Elgin, *Ill.* **15** 42 2N 88 17W
Elgin, *N. Dak.* **12** 46 24N 101 51W
Elgin, *Nebr.* **12** 41 59N 98 5W
Elgin, *Nev.* **17** 37 21N 114 32W
Elgin, *Oreg.* **16** 45 34N 117 55W
Elgin, *Tex.* **13** 30 21N 97 22W
Elida, *N. Mex.* **13** 33 57N 103 39W
Elim, *Alaska* **30** 64 37N 162 15W
Elizabeth, *N.J.* **20** 40 39N 74 12W
Elizabeth City, *N.C.* **11** 36 18N 76 14W
Elizabethton, *Tenn.* **11** 36 21N 82 13W
Elizabethtown, *Ky.* **10** 37 42N 85 52W
Elizabethtown, *Pa.* **9** 40 9N 76 36W
Elk City, *Okla.* **13** 35 25N 99 25W
Elk Grove, *Calif.* **18** 38 25N 121 22W
Elk River, *Idaho* **16** 46 47N 116 11W
Elk River, *Minn.* **12** 45 18N 93 35W
Elkhart, *Ind.* **15** 41 41N 85 58W
Elkhart, *Kans.* **13** 37 0N 101 54W
Elkhorn →, *Nebr.* **12** 41 8N 96 19W
Elkin, *N.C.* **11** 36 15N 80 51W
Elkins, *W. Va.* **10** 38 55N 79 51W
Elko, *Nev.* **16** 40 50N 115 46W
Ellendale, *N. Dak.* **12** 46 0N 98 32W
Ellensburg, *Wash.* **16** 46 59N 120 34W
Ellenville, *N.Y.* **9** 41 43N 74 24W
Ellinwood, *Kans.* **12** 38 21N 98 35W
Ellis, *Kans.* **12** 38 56N 99 34W
Ellisville, *Miss.* **13** 31 36N 89 12W
Ellsworth, *Kans.* **12** 38 44N 98 14W
Ellwood City, *Pa.* **8** 40 52N 80 17W
Elma, *Wash.* **18** 47 0N 123 25W

Georgetown

Elmhurst, *Ill.* **22** 41 53N 87 55W
Elmira, *N.Y.* **8** 42 6N 76 48W
Elmont, *N.Y.* **21** 40 42N 73 42W
Elmwood Park, *Ill.* **22** 41 55N 87 48W
Eloy, *Ariz.* **17** 32 45N 111 33W
Elsinore, *Utah* **17** 38 41N 112 9W
Elwood, *Ind.* **15** 40 17N 85 50W
Elwood, *Nebr.* **12** 40 36N 99 52W
Ely, *Minn.* **12** 47 55N 91 51W
Ely, *Nev.* **16** 39 15N 114 54W
Elyria, *Ohio* **8** 41 22N 82 7W
Emery, *Utah* **17** 38 55N 111 15W
Emmetsburg, *Iowa* **14** 43 7N 94 41W
Emmett, *Idaho* **16** 43 52N 116 30W
Empire State Building, *N.Y.* **20** 40 44N 73 59W
Emporia, *Kans.* **12** 38 25N 96 11W
Emporia, *Va.* **11** 36 42N 77 32W
Emporium, *Pa.* **8** 41 31N 78 14W
Encinal, *Tex.* **13** 28 2N 99 21W
Encinitas, *Calif.* **19** 33 3N 117 17W
Encino, *N. Mex.* **17** 34 39N 105 28W
Enderlin, *N. Dak.* **12** 46 38N 97 36W
Endicott, *N.Y.* **9** 42 6N 76 4W
Endicott, *Wash.* **16** 46 56N 117 41W
Endicott Mts., *Alaska* **30** 68 0N 152 0W
England, *Ark.* **13** 34 33N 91 58W
Englewood, *Colo.* **12** 39 39N 104 59W
Englewood, *Kans.* **13** 37 2N 99 59W
Enid, *Okla.* **13** 36 24N 97 53W
Ennis, *Mont.* **16** 45 21N 111 44W
Ennis, *Tex.* **13** 32 20N 96 38W
Enterprise, *Oreg.* **16** 45 25N 117 17W
Enterprise, *Utah* **17** 37 34N 113 43W
Enumclaw, *Wash.* **18** 47 12N 121 59W
Ephraim, *Utah* **16** 39 22N 111 35W
Ephrata, *Wash.* **16** 47 19N 119 33W
Erie, *Pa.* **8** 42 8N 80 5W
Erie, L., *N. Amer.* **8** 42 15N 81 0W
Erskine, *Minn.* **12** 47 40N 96 0W
Erwin, *Tenn.* **11** 36 9N 82 25W
Escalante, *Utah* **17** 37 47N 111 36W
Escalante →, *Utah* **17** 37 24N 110 57W
Escambia →, *Fla.* **11** 30 32N 87 11W
Escanaba, *Mich.* **10** 45 45N 87 4W
Escondido, *Calif.* **19** 33 7N 117 5W
Espenberg, C., *Alaska* **30** 66 33N 163 36W
Essex, *Md.* **25** 39 18N 76 28W
Estancia, *N. Mex.* **17** 34 46N 106 4W
Estelline, *S. Dak.* **12** 44 35N 96 54W
Estelline, *Tex.* **13** 34 33N 100 26W
Estherville, *Iowa* **12** 43 24N 94 50W
Etawah →, *Ga.* **11** 34 20N 84 15W
Etowah, *Tenn.* **11** 35 20N 84 32W
Euclid, *Ohio* **27** 41 34N 81 33W
Eudora, *Ark.* **13** 33 7N 91 16W
Eufaula, *Ala.* **11** 31 54N 85 9W
Eufaula, *Okla.* **13** 35 17N 95 35W
Eufaula L., *Okla.* **13** 35 18N 95 21W
Eugene, *Oreg.* **16** 44 5N 123 4W
Eunice, *La.* **13** 30 30N 92 25W
Eunice, *N. Mex.* **13** 32 26N 103 10W
Eureka, *Calif.* **16** 40 47N 124 9W
Eureka, *Kans.* **13** 37 49N 96 17W
Eureka, *Mont.* **16** 48 53N 115 3W
Eureka, *Nev.* **16** 39 31N 115 58W
Eureka, *S. Dak.* **12** 45 46N 99 38W
Eureka, *Utah* **16** 39 58N 112 7W
Eustis, *Fla.* **11** 28 51N 81 41W
Evans, *Colo.* **12** 40 23N 104 41W
Evanston, *Ill.* **22** 42 3N 87 41W
Evanston, *Wyo.* **16** 41 16N 110 58W
Evansville, *Ind.* **15** 37 58N 87 35W
Evansville, *Wis.* **14** 42 47N 89 18W
Eveleth, *Minn.* **12** 47 28N 92 32W
Everett, *Mass.* **23** 42 24N 71 3W
Everett, *Wash.* **18** 47 59N 122 12W
Everglades, The, *Fla.* **11** 25 50N 81 0W
Everglades City, *Fla.* **11** 25 52N 81 23W
Everglades National Park, *Fla.* **11** 25 30N 81 0W
Evergreen, *Ala.* **11** 31 26N 86 57W
Evergreen Park, *Ill.* **22** 41 43N 87 42W
Everson, *Wash.* **16** 48 57N 122 22W
Evesboro, *N.J.* **24** 39 54N 74 56W
Ewing, *Nebr.* **12** 42 16N 98 21W
Excelsior Springs, *Mo.* **14** 39 20N 94 13W
Exeter, *Calif.* **18** 36 18N 119 9W
Exeter, *N.H.* **9** 42 59N 70 57W
Exeter, *Nebr.* **12** 40 39N 97 27W

F

Fabens, *Tex.* **17** 31 30N 106 10W
Fagatogo, *Amer. Samoa* **31** 14 17S 170 41W
Fair Lawn, *N.J.* **20** 40 56N 74 7W
Fair Oaks, *Calif.* **18** 38 39N 121 16W
Fairbank, *Ariz.* **17** 31 43N 110 11W
Fairbanks, *Alaska* **30** 64 51N 147 43W
Fairbury, *Nebr.* **12** 40 8N 97 11W
Fairfax, *Del.* **24** 39 47N 75 32W
Fairfax, *Okla.* **13** 36 34N 96 42W
Fairfax, *Va.* **25** 38 50N 77 19W
Fairfield, *Ala.* **11** 33 29N 86 55W
Fairfield, *Calif.* **18** 38 15N 122 3W
Fairfield, *Conn.* **9** 41 9N 73 16W
Fairfield, *Idaho* **16** 43 21N 114 44W
Fairfield, *Ill.* **15** 38 23N 88 22W
Fairfield, *Iowa* **14** 40 56N 91 57W
Fairfield, *Mont.* **16** 47 37N 111 59W
Fairfield, *Tex.* **13** 31 44N 96 10W
Fairhope, *Ala.* **11** 30 31N 87 54W
Fairmead, *Calif.* **18** 37 5N 120 10W
Fairmont, *Minn.* **12** 43 39N 94 28W
Fairmont, *W. Va.* **10** 39 29N 80 9W
Fairmount, *Calif.* **19** 34 45N 118 26W
Fairplay, *Colo.* **17** 39 15N 106 2W
Fairport, *N.Y.* **8** 43 6N 77 27W
Fairview, *Mont.* **12** 47 51N 104 3W
Fairview, *Okla.* **13** 36 16N 98 29W
Fairview, *Utah* **16** 39 50N 111 0W
Fairview Park, *Ohio* **27** 41 26N 81 52W
Fairweather, Mt., *Alaska* **30** 58 55N 137 32W
Faith, *S. Dak.* **12** 45 2N 102 2W
Fajardo, *Puerto Rico* **30** 18 20N 65 39W
Falcon Dam, *Tex.* **13** 26 50N 99 20W
Falfurrias, *Tex.* **13** 27 14N 98 9W
Fall River, *Mass.* **9** 41 43N 71 10W
Fall River Mills, *Calif.* **16** 41 3N 121 26W
Fallbrook, *Calif.* **17** 33 25N 117 12W
Fallon, *Mont.* **12** 46 50N 105 8W
Fallon, *Nev.* **16** 39 28N 118 47W
Falls Church, *Va.* **25** 38 53N 77 11W
Falls City, *Nebr.* **12** 40 3N 95 36W
Falls City, *Oreg.* **16** 44 52N 123 26W
Falmouth, *Ky.* **15** 38 41N 84 20W
Famoso, *Calif.* **19** 35 37N 119 12W
Farewell, *Alaska* **30** 62 31N 153 54W
Fargo, *N. Dak.* **12** 46 53N 96 48W
Faribault, *Minn.* **12** 44 18N 93 16W
Farmerville, *La.* **13** 32 47N 92 24W
Farmington, *Calif.* **18** 37 55N 120 59W
Farmington, *Mich.* **26** 42 26N 83 22W
Farmington, *N. Mex.* **17** 36 44N 108 12W
Farmington, *Utah* **16** 41 0N 111 12W
Farmington →, *Conn.* **9** 41 51N 72 38W
Farmington Hills, *Mich.* **26** 42 29N 83 23W
Farmville, *Va.* **10** 37 18N 78 24W
Farrell, *Pa.* **8** 41 13N 80 30W
Farwell, *Tex.* **13** 34 23N 103 2W
Faulkton, *S. Dak.* **12** 45 2N 99 8W
Fawnskin, *Calif.* **19** 34 16N 116 56W
Fayette, *Ala.* **11** 33 41N 87 50W
Fayette, *Mo.* **14** 39 9N 92 41W
Fayetteville, *Ark.* **13** 36 4N 94 10W
Fayetteville, *N.C.* **11** 35 3N 78 53W
Fayetteville, *Tenn.* **11** 35 9N 86 34W
Fear, C., *N.C.* **11** 33 50N 77 58W
Feather →, *Calif.* **16** 38 47N 121 36W
Felton, *Calif.* **18** 37 3N 122 4W
Fennimore, *Wis.* **14** 42 59N 90 39W
Fenton, *Mich.* **15** 42 48N 83 42W
Fergus Falls, *Minn.* **12** 46 17N 96 4W
Fernandina Beach, *Fla.* **11** 30 40N 81 27W
Ferndale, *Calif.* **16** 40 35N 124 16W
Ferndale, *Mich.* **26** 42 27N 83 7W
Ferndale, *Wash.* **18** 48 51N 122 36W
Fernley, *Nev.* **16** 39 36N 119 15W
Ferriday, *La.* **13** 31 38N 91 33W
Ferron, *Utah* **17** 39 5N 111 8W
Fertile, *Minn.* **12** 47 32N 96 17W
Fessenden, *N. Dak.* **12** 47 39N 99 38W
Filer, *Idaho* **16** 42 34N 114 37W
Fillmore, *Calif.* **19** 34 24N 118 55W
Fillmore, *Utah* **17** 38 58N 112 20W
Findlay, *Ohio* **15** 41 2N 83 39W
Finley, *N. Dak.* **12** 47 31N 97 50W
Firebaugh, *Calif.* **18** 36 52N 120 27W
Fitchburg, *Mass.* **9** 42 35N 71 48W
Fitzgerald, *Ga.* **11** 31 43N 83 15W
Five Points, *Calif.* **18** 36 26N 120 6W
Flagler, *Colo.* **12** 39 18N 103 4W
Flagstaff, *Ariz.* **17** 35 12N 111 39W
Flambeau →, *Wis.* **12** 45 18N 91 14W
Flaming Gorge Dam, *Utah* **16** 40 55N 109 25W
Flaming Gorge Reservoir, *Wyo.* **16** 41 10N 109 25W
Flandreau, *S. Dak.* **12** 44 3N 96 36W
Flat River, *Mo.* **13** 37 51N 90 31W
Flathead L., *Mont.* **16** 47 51N 114 8W
Flattery, C., *Wash.* **18** 48 23N 124 29W
Flaxton, *N. Dak.* **12** 48 54N 102 24W
Flint, *Mich.* **15** 43 1N 83 41W
Flint →, *Ga.* **11** 30 57N 84 34W
Floodwood, *Minn.* **12** 46 55N 92 55W
Flora, *Ill.* **10** 38 40N 88 29W
Floral Park, *N.Y.* **21** 40 43N 73 42W
Florala, *Ala.* **11** 31 0N 86 20W
Florence, *Ala.* **11** 34 48N 87 41W
Florence, *Ariz.* **17** 33 2N 111 23W
Florence, *Calif.* **29** 33 57N 118 13W
Florence, *Colo.* **12** 38 23N 105 8W
Florence, *Oreg.* **16** 43 58N 124 7W
Florence, *S.C.* **11** 34 12N 79 46W
Floresville, *Tex.* **13** 29 8N 98 10W
Florham Park, *N.J.* **20** 40 46N 74 23W
Florida □ **11** 28 0N 82 0W
Floydada, *Tex.* **13** 33 59N 101 20W
Flushing, *N.Y.* **21** 40 45N 73 49W
Folkston, *Ga.* **11** 30 50N 82 0W
Follett, *Tex.* **13** 36 26N 100 8W
Fond du Lac, *Wis.* **12** 43 47N 88 27W
Ford City, *Calif.* **19** 35 9N 119 27W
Fordyce, *Ark.* **13** 33 49N 92 25W
Forest, *Miss.* **13** 32 22N 89 29W
Forest City, *Iowa* **12** 43 16N 93 39W
Forest City, *N.C.* **11** 35 20N 81 52W
Forest Grove, *Oreg.* **18** 45 31N 123 7W
Forest Hills, *N.Y.* **21** 40 42N 73 51W
Forest Hills, *Pa.* **27** 40 25N 79 51W
Forestville, *Md.* **25** 38 50N 76 52W
Forestville, *Wis.* **10** 44 41N 87 29W
Forks, *Wash.* **18** 47 57N 124 23W
Forman, *N. Dak.* **12** 46 7N 97 38W
Forrest City, *Ark.* **13** 35 1N 90 47W
Forsyth, *Ga.* **11** 33 2N 83 56W
Forsyth, *Mont.* **16** 46 16N 106 41W
Fort Apache, *Ariz.* **17** 33 50N 110 0W
Fort Benton, *Mont.* **16** 47 49N 110 40W
Fort Bragg, *Calif.* **16** 39 26N 123 48W
Fort Bridger, *Wyo.* **16** 41 19N 110 23W
Fort Collins, *Colo.* **12** 40 35N 105 5W
Fort Davis, *Tex.* **13** 30 35N 103 54W
Fort Defiance, *Ariz.* **17** 35 45N 109 5W
Fort Dodge, *Iowa* **12** 42 30N 94 11W
Fort Garland, *Colo.* **17** 37 26N 105 26W
Fort Hancock, *Tex.* **17** 31 18N 105 51W
Fort Irwin, *Calif.* **19** 35 16N 116 34W
Fort Kent, *Maine* **11** 47 15N 68 36W
Fort Klamath, *Oreg.* **16** 42 42N 122 0W
Fort Laramie, *Wyo.* **12** 42 13N 104 31W
Fort Lauderdale, *Fla.* **11** 26 7N 80 8W
Fort Lee, *N.J.* **20** 40 50N 73 58W
Fort Lupton, *Colo.* **12** 40 5N 104 49W
Fort Madison, *Iowa* **14** 40 38N 91 27W
Fort Meade, *Fla.* **11** 27 45N 81 48W
Fort Morgan, *Colo.* **12** 40 15N 103 48W
Fort Myers, *Fla.* **11** 26 39N 81 52W
Fort Payne, *Ala.* **11** 34 26N 85 43W
Fort Peck, *Mont.* **16** 48 1N 106 27W
Fort Peck Dam, *Mont.* **16** 48 0N 106 26W
Fort Peck L., *Mont.* **16** 48 0N 106 26W
Fort Pierce, *Fla.* **11** 27 27N 80 20W
Fort Pierre, *S. Dak.* **12** 44 21N 100 22W
Fort Scott, *Kans.* **13** 37 50N 94 42W
Fort Smith, *Ark.* **13** 35 23N 94 25W
Fort Stanton, *N. Mex.* **17** 33 30N 105 31W
Fort Stockton, *Tex.* **13** 30 53N 102 53W
Fort Sumner, *N. Mex.* **13** 34 28N 104 15W
Fort Valley, *Ga.* **11** 32 33N 83 53W
Fort Walton Beach, *Fla.* **11** 30 25N 86 36W
Fort Wayne, *Ind.* **15** 41 4N 85 9W
Fort Worth, *Tex.* **13** 32 45N 97 18W
Fort Yates, *N. Dak.* **12** 46 5N 100 38W
Fort Yukon, *Alaska* **30** 66 34N 145 16W
Fortuna, *Calif.* **16** 40 36N 124 9W
Fortuna, *N. Dak.* **12** 48 55N 103 47W
Fossil, *Oreg.* **16** 45 0N 120 9W
Fosston, *Minn.* **12** 47 35N 95 45W
Fostoria, *Ohio* **15** 41 10N 83 25W
Fountain, *Colo.* **12** 38 41N 104 42W
Fountain, *Utah* **16** 39 41N 111 37W
Fountain Springs, *Calif.* **19** 35 54N 118 51W
Four Mountains, Is. of, *Alaska* **30** 53 0N 170 0W
Fowler, *Calif.* **18** 36 38N 119 41W
Fowler, *Colo.* **12** 38 8N 104 2W
Fowler, *Kans.* **13** 37 23N 100 12W
Fowlerton, *Tex.* **13** 28 28N 98 48W
Fox Is., *Alaska* **30** 52 30N 166 0W
Foxpark, *Wyo.* **16** 41 5N 106 9W
Frackville, *Pa.* **9** 40 47N 76 14W
Framingham, *Mass.* **23** 42 18N 71 23W
Frankfort, *Ind.* **15** 40 17N 86 31W
Frankfort, *Kans.* **12** 39 42N 96 25W
Frankfort, *Ky.* **15** 38 12N 84 52W
Frankfort, *Mich.* **10** 44 38N 86 14W
Franklin, *Ky.* **11** 36 43N 86 35W
Franklin, *La.* **13** 29 48N 91 30W
Franklin, *Mass.* **9** 42 5N 71 24W
Franklin, *N.H.* **9** 43 27N 71 39W
Franklin, *Nebr.* **12** 40 6N 98 57W
Franklin, *Pa.* **8** 41 24N 79 50W
Franklin, *Tenn.* **11** 35 55N 86 52W
Franklin, *Va.* **11** 36 41N 76 56W
Franklin, *W. Va.* **10** 38 39N 79 20W
Franklin D. Roosevelt L., *Wash.* **16** 48 18N 118 9W
Franklin L., *Nev.* **16** 40 25N 115 22W
Franklin Park, *Ill.* **22** 41 55N 87 52W
Franklin Square, *N.Y.* **21** 40 41N 73 40W
Franklinton, *La.* **13** 30 51N 90 9W
Franks Pk., *Wyo.* **16** 43 58N 109 18W
Frederick, *Md.* **10** 39 25N 77 25W
Frederick, *Okla.* **13** 34 23N 99 1W
Frederick, *S. Dak.* **12** 45 50N 98 31W
Fredericksburg, *Tex.* **13** 30 16N 98 52W
Fredericksburg, *Va.* **10** 38 18N 77 28W
Fredericktown, *Mo.* **13** 37 34N 90 18W
Fredonia, *Ariz.* **17** 36 57N 112 32W
Fredonia, *Kans.* **13** 37 32N 95 49W
Fredonia, *N.Y.* **8** 42 26N 79 20W
Freehold, *N.J.* **9** 40 16N 74 17W
Freel Peak, *Nev.* **18** 38 52N 119 54W
Freeland, *Pa.* **9** 41 1N 75 54W
Freeman, *Calif.* **19** 35 35N 117 53W
Freeman, *S. Dak.* **12** 43 21N 97 26W
Freeport, *Ill.* **14** 42 17N 89 36W
Freeport, *N.Y.* **21** 40 39N 73 35W
Freeport, *Tex.* **13** 28 57N 95 21W
Fremont, *Calif.* **28** 37 33N 122 2W
Fremont, *Mich.* **10** 43 28N 85 57W
Fremont, *Nebr.* **12** 41 26N 96 30W
Fremont, *Ohio* **15** 41 21N 83 7W
Fremont →, *Utah* **17** 38 24N 110 42W
Fremont L., *Wyo.* **16** 42 57N 109 48W
French Camp, *Calif.* **18** 37 53N 121 16W
French Creek →, *Pa.* **8** 41 24N 79 50W
Frenchglen, *Oreg.* **16** 42 50N 118 55W
Frenchman Cr. →, *Mont.* **16** 48 31N 107 10W
Frenchman Cr. →, *Nebr.* **12** 40 14N 100 50W
Fresno, *Calif.* **18** 36 44N 119 47W
Fresno Reservoir, *Mont.* **16** 48 36N 109 57W
Friant, *Calif.* **18** 36 59N 119 43W
Frio →, *Tex.* **13** 28 26N 98 11W
Friona, *Tex.* **13** 34 38N 102 43W
Fritch, *Tex.* **13** 35 38N 101 36W
Froid, *Mont.* **12** 48 20N 104 30W
Fromberg, *Mont.* **16** 45 24N 108 54W
Front Range, *Colo.* **16** 40 25N 105 45W
Front Royal, *Va.* **10** 38 55N 78 12W
Frostburg, *Md.* **10** 39 39N 78 56W
Fullerton, *Calif.* **19** 33 53N 117 56W
Fullerton, *Nebr.* **12** 41 22N 97 58W
Fulton, *Mo.* **14** 38 52N 91 57W
Fulton, *N.Y.* **9** 43 19N 76 25W
Fulton, *Tenn.* **11** 36 31N 88 53W

G

Gadsden, *Ala.* **11** 34 1N 86 1W
Gadsden, *Ariz.* **17** 32 33N 114 47W
Gaffney, *S.C.* **11** 35 5N 81 39W
Gail, *Tex.* **13** 32 46N 101 27W
Gainesville, *Fla.* **11** 29 40N 82 20W
Gainesville, *Ga.* **11** 34 18N 83 50W
Gainesville, *Mo.* **13** 36 36N 92 26W
Gainesville, *Tex.* **13** 33 38N 97 8W
Galax, *Va.* **11** 36 40N 80 56W
Galena, *Alaska* **30** 64 44N 156 56W
Galesburg, *Ill.* **14** 40 57N 90 22W
Galiuro Mts., *Ariz.* **17** 32 30N 110 20W
Gallatin, *Tenn.* **11** 36 24N 86 27W
Gallipolis, *Ohio* **10** 38 49N 82 12W
Gallup, *N. Mex.* **17** 35 32N 108 45W
Galt, *Calif.* **18** 38 15N 121 18W
Galva, *Ill.* **14** 41 10N 90 3W
Galveston, *Tex.* **13** 29 18N 94 48W
Galveston B., *Tex.* **13** 29 36N 94 50W
Gambell, *Alaska* **30** 63 47N 171 45W
Gamerco, *N. Mex.* **17** 35 34N 108 46W
Ganado, *Ariz.* **17** 35 43N 109 33W
Ganado, *Tex.* **13** 29 2N 96 31W
Gannett Peak, *Wyo.* **16** 43 11N 109 39W
Gannvalley, *S. Dak.* **12** 44 2N 98 59W
Garapan, *Pac. Oc.* **31** 15 12N 145 53 E
Garber, *Okla.* **13** 36 26N 97 35W
Garberville, *Calif.* **16** 40 6N 123 48W
Garden City, *Kans.* **13** 37 58N 100 53W
Garden City, *Mich.* **26** 42 20N 83 20W
Garden City, *N.Y.* **21** 40 43N 73 38W
Garden City, *Tex.* **13** 31 52N 101 29W
Garden Grove, *Calif.* **19** 33 47N 117 55W
Gardena, *Calif.* **29** 33 53N 118 17W
Gardiner, *Mont.* **16** 45 2N 110 22W
Gardiners I., *N.Y.* **9** 41 6N 72 6W
Gardner, *Mass.* **9** 42 34N 71 59W
Gardnerville, *Nev.* **18** 38 56N 119 45W
Gareloi I., *Alaska* **30** 51 48N 178 48W
Garey, *Calif.* **19** 34 53N 120 19W
Garfield, *N.J.* **20** 40 52N 74 6W
Garfield, *Wash.* **16** 47 1N 117 9W
Garfield Heights, *Ohio* **27** 41 25N 81 37W
Garland, *Utah* **16** 41 47N 112 10W
Garner, *Iowa* **14** 43 6N 93 36W
Garnett, *Kans.* **12** 38 17N 95 14W
Garrison, *Mont.* **16** 46 31N 112 49W
Garrison, *N. Dak.* **12** 47 40N 101 25W
Garrison, *Tex.* **13** 31 49N 94 30W
Garrison Res. = Sakakawea, L., *N. Dak.* **12** 47 30N 101 25W
Gary, *Ind.* **22** 41 35N 87 23W
Gassaway, *W. Va.* **10** 38 41N 80 47W
Gastonia, *N.C.* **11** 35 16N 81 11W
Gatesville, *Tex.* **13** 31 26N 97 45W
Gaviota, *Calif.* **19** 34 29N 120 13W
Gaylord, *Mich.* **10** 45 2N 84 41W
Genesee, *Idaho* **16** 46 33N 116 56W
Genesee →, *N.Y.* **8** 43 16N 77 36W
Geneseo, *Ill.* **14** 41 27N 90 9W
Geneseo, *Kans.* **12** 38 31N 98 10W
Geneva, *Ala.* **11** 31 2N 85 52W
Geneva, *N.Y.* **8** 42 52N 76 59W
Geneva, *Nebr.* **12** 40 32N 97 36W
Geneva, *Ohio* **8** 41 48N 80 57W
Geneva, L., *Wis.* **15** 42 38N 88 30W
Genoa, *N.Y.* **9** 42 40N 76 32W
Genoa, *Nebr.* **12** 41 27N 97 44W
George, L., *Fla.* **11** 29 17N 81 36W
George, L., *N.Y.* **9** 43 37N 73 33W
George West, *Tex.* **13** 28 20N 98 7W
Georgetown, *Colo.* **16** 39 42N 105 42W
Georgetown, *D.C.* **25** 38 54N 77 3W
Georgetown, *Ky.* **10** 38 13N 84 33W

Georgetown

Georgetown, S.C. 11 33 23N 79 17W
Georgetown, Tex. 13 30 38N 97 41W
Georgia □ 11 32 50N 83 15W
Geraldine, Mont. 16 47 36N 110 16W
Gering, Nebr. 12 41 50N 103 40W
Gerlach, Nev. 16 40 39N 119 21W
Gettysburg, Pa. 10 39 50N 77 14W
Gettysburg, S. Dak. 12 45 1N 99 57W
Geyser, Mont. 16 47 16N 110 30W
Giant Forest, Calif. 18 36 36N 118 43W
Gibbon, Nebr. 12 40 45N 98 51W
Giddings, Tex. 13 30 11N 96 56W
Gila →, Ariz. 17 32 43N 114 33W
Gila Bend, Ariz. 17 32 57N 112 43W
Gila Bend Mts., Ariz. 17 33 10N 113 0W
Gillette, Wyo. 12 44 18N 105 30W
Gilmer, Tex. 13 32 44N 94 57W
Gilroy, Calif. 18 37 1N 121 34W
Girard, Kans. 13 37 31N 94 51W
Glacier Park, Mont. 16 48 30N 113 18W
Glacier Peak, Wash. 16 48 7N 121 7W
Gladewater, Tex. 13 32 33N 94 56W
Gladstone, Mich. 10 45 51N 87 1W
Gladwin, Mich. 10 43 59N 84 29W
Glasco, Kans. 12 39 22N 97 50W
Glasco, N.Y. 9 42 3N 73 57W
Glasgow, Ky. 10 37 0N 85 55W
Glasgow, Mont. 16 48 12N 106 38W
Glastonbury, Conn. 9 41 43N 72 37W
Glen Canyon Dam, Ariz. 17 36 57N 111 29W
Glen Canyon National Recreation Area, Utah 17 37 15N 111 0W
Glen Cove, N.Y. 21 40 52N 73 38W
Glen Lyon, Pa. 9 41 10N 76 5W
Glen Ullin, N. Dak. 12 46 49N 101 50W
Glencoe, Ill. 22 42 7N 87 44W
Glencoe, Minn. 12 44 46N 94 9W
Glendale, Ariz. 17 33 32N 112 11W
Glendale, Calif. 29 34 9N 118 14W
Glendale, Oreg. 16 42 44N 123 26W
Glendive, Mont. 12 47 7N 104 43W
Glendo, Wyo. 12 42 30N 105 2W
Glenmora, La. 13 30 59N 92 35W
Glenns Ferry, Idaho 16 42 57N 115 18W
Glenrock, Wyo. 16 42 52N 105 52W
Glens Falls, N.Y. 9 43 19N 73 39W
Glenshaw, Pa. 27 40 32N 79 58W
Glenview, Ill. 22 42 4N 87 48W
Glenville, W. Va. 10 38 56N 80 50W
Glenwood, Ark. 13 34 20N 93 33W
Glenwood, Hawaii 30 19 29N 155 9W
Glenwood, Iowa 12 41 3N 95 45W
Glenwood, Minn. 12 45 39N 95 23W
Glenwood Springs, Colo. 16 39 33N 107 19W
Globe, Ariz. 17 33 24N 110 47W
Gloucester, Mass. 9 42 37N 70 40W
Gloucester City, N.J. 24 39 53N 75 7W
Gloversville, N.Y. 9 43 3N 74 21W
Gogebic, L., Mich. 12 46 30N 89 35W
Golconda, Nev. 16 40 58N 117 30W
Gold Beach, Oreg. 16 42 25N 124 25W
Gold Creek, Alaska 30 62 46N 149 41W
Gold Hill, Oreg. 16 42 26N 123 3W
Golden, Colo. 12 39 42N 105 15W
Golden Gate, Calif. 16 37 54N 122 30W
Golden Gate, Calif. 28 37 48N 122 30W
Golden Gate Bridge, Calif. 28 37 49N 122 28W
Goldendale, Wash. 16 45 49N 120 50W
Goldfield, Nev. 17 37 42N 117 14W
Goldsboro, N.C. 11 35 23N 77 59W
Goldsmith, Tex. 13 31 59N 102 37W
Goldthwaite, Tex. 13 31 27N 98 34W
Goleta, Calif. 19 34 27N 119 50W
Goliad, Tex. 13 28 40N 97 23W
Gonzales, Calif. 18 36 30N 121 26W
Gonzales, Tex. 13 29 30N 97 27W
Gooding, Idaho 16 42 56N 114 43W
Goodland, Kans. 12 39 21N 101 43W
Goodnight, Tex. 13 35 2N 101 11W
Goodsprings, Nev. 17 35 50N 115 26W
Goose L., Calif. 16 41 56N 120 26W
Gorda, Calif. 18 35 53N 121 26W
Gordon, Nebr. 12 42 48N 102 12W
Gorman, Calif. 19 34 47N 118 51W
Gorman, Tex. 13 32 12N 98 41W
Goshen, Calif. 18 36 21N 119 25W
Goshen, Ind. 15 41 35N 85 50W
Goshen, N.Y. 9 41 24N 74 20W
Gothenburg, Nebr. 12 40 56N 100 10W
Gowanda, N.Y. 8 42 28N 78 56W
Grace, Idaho 16 42 35N 111 44W
Graceville, Minn. 12 45 34N 96 26W
Grady, N. Mex. 13 34 49N 103 19W
Grafton, N. Dak. 12 48 25N 97 25W
Graham, N.C. 11 36 5N 79 25W
Graham, Tex. 13 33 6N 98 35W
Graham, Mt., Ariz. 17 32 42N 109 52W
Granada, Colo. 13 38 4N 102 19W
Granbury, Tex. 13 32 27N 97 47W
Grand →, Mo. 14 39 23N 93 7W
Grand →, S. Dak. 12 45 40N 100 45W
Grand Canyon, Ariz. 17 36 3N 112 9W
Grand Canyon National Park, Ariz. 17 36 15N 112 30W
Grand Coulee, Wash. 16 47 57N 119 0W
Grand Coulee Dam, Wash. 16 47 57N 118 59W
Grand Forks, N. Dak. 12 47 55N 97 3W
Grand Haven, Mich. 15 43 4N 86 13W
Grand I., Mich. 10 46 31N 86 40W
Grand Island, Nebr. 12 40 55N 98 21W
Grand Isle, La. 13 29 14N 90 0W
Grand Junction, Colo. 17 39 4N 108 33W
Grand L., La. 13 29 55N 92 47W
Grand Lake, Colo. 16 40 15N 105 49W
Grand Marais, Mich. 10 46 40N 85 59W
Grand Rapids, Mich. 15 42 58N 85 40W
Grand Rapids, Minn. 12 47 14N 93 31W
Grand Teton, Idaho 16 43 54N 111 50W
Grand Valley, Colo. 16 39 27N 108 3W
Grande, Rio →, Tex. 13 25 58N 97 9W
Grandfalls, Tex. 13 31 20N 102 51W
Grandview, Wash. 16 46 15N 119 54W
Granger, Wash. 16 46 21N 120 11W
Granger, Wyo. 16 41 35N 109 58W
Grangeville, Idaho 16 45 56N 116 7W
Granite City, Ill. 14 38 42N 90 9W
Granite Falls, Minn. 12 44 49N 95 33W
Granite Mt., Calif. 19 33 5N 116 28W
Granite Peak, Mont. 16 45 10N 109 48W
Grant, Nebr. 12 40 53N 101 42W
Grant, Mt., Nev. 16 38 34N 118 48W
Grant City, Mo. 14 40 29N 94 25W
Grant Range, Nev. 17 38 30N 115 25W
Grants, N. Mex. 17 35 9N 107 52W
Grants Pass, Oreg. 16 42 26N 123 19W
Grantsburg, Wis. 12 45 47N 92 41W
Grantsville, Utah 16 40 36N 112 28W
Granville, N. Dak. 12 48 16N 100 47W
Granville, N.Y. 10 43 24N 73 16W
Grapeland, Tex. 13 31 30N 95 29W
Grass Range, Mont. 16 47 0N 109 0W
Grass Valley, Calif. 18 39 13N 121 4W
Grass Valley, Oreg. 16 45 22N 120 47W
Grayling, Mich. 10 44 40N 84 43W
Grays Harbor, Wash. 16 46 59N 124 1W
Grays L., Idaho 16 43 4N 111 26W
Great Barrington, Mass. 9 42 12N 73 22W
Great Basin, Nev. 16 40 0N 117 0W
Great Bend, Kans. 12 38 22N 98 46W
Great Bend, Pa. 9 41 58N 75 45W
Great Falls, Mont. 16 47 30N 111 17W
Great Kills, N.Y. 20 40 32N 74 9W
Great Neck, N.Y. 21 40 48N 73 44W
Great Plains, N. Amer. 2 47 0N 105 0W
Great Salt L., Utah 16 41 15N 112 40W
Great Salt Lake Desert, Utah 16 40 50N 113 30W
Great Salt Plains L., Okla. 13 36 45N 98 8W
Great Sitkin I., Alaska 30 52 3N 176 6W
Great Smoky Mts. Nat. Pk., Tenn. 11 35 40N 83 40W
Greater Pittsburgh International Airport, Pa. 27 40 29N 80 13W
Greeley, Colo. 12 40 25N 104 42W
Greeley, Nebr. 12 41 33N 98 32W
Green →, Ky. 10 37 54N 87 30W
Green →, Utah 17 38 11N 109 53W
Green B., Wis. 10 45 0N 87 30W
Green Bay, Wis. 10 44 31N 88 0W
Green Cove Springs, Fla. 11 29 59N 81 42W
Green River, Utah 17 38 59N 110 10W
Green Tree, Pa. 27 40 25N 80 4W
Greenbelt, Md. 25 39 0N 76 52W
Greenbush, Minn. 12 48 42N 96 11W
Greencastle, Ind. 15 39 38N 86 52W
Greene, N.Y. 9 42 20N 75 46W
Greenfield, Calif. 18 36 19N 121 15W
Greenfield, Calif. 19 35 15N 119 0W
Greenfield, Ind. 15 39 47N 85 46W
Greenfield, Iowa 14 41 18N 94 28W
Greenfield, Mass. 9 42 35N 72 36W
Greenfield, Mo. 13 37 25N 93 51W
Greenport, N.Y. 9 41 6N 72 22W
Greensboro, Ga. 11 33 35N 83 11W
Greensboro, N.C. 11 36 4N 79 48W
Greensburg, Ind. 15 39 20N 85 29W
Greensburg, Kans. 13 37 36N 99 18W
Greensburg, Pa. 8 40 18N 79 33W
Greenville, Ala. 11 31 50N 86 38W
Greenville, Calif. 18 40 8N 120 57W
Greenville, Ill. 14 38 53N 89 25W
Greenville, Maine 11 45 28N 69 35W
Greenville, Mich. 15 43 11N 85 15W
Greenville, Miss. 13 33 24N 91 4W
Greenville, N.C. 11 35 37N 77 23W
Greenville, Ohio 15 40 6N 84 38W
Greenville, Pa. 8 41 24N 80 23W
Greenville, S.C. 11 34 51N 82 24W
Greenville, Tenn. 11 36 13N 82 51W
Greenville, Tex. 13 33 8N 96 7W
Greenwich, Conn. 21 41 1N 73 38W
Greenwich, N.Y. 9 43 5N 73 30W
Greenwood, Miss. 13 33 31N 90 11W
Greenwood, S.C. 11 34 12N 82 10W
Gregory, S. Dak. 12 43 14N 99 20W
Grenada, Miss. 13 33 47N 89 49W
Grenora, N. Dak. 12 48 37N 103 56W
Gresham, Oreg. 18 45 30N 122 26W
Greybull, Wyo. 16 44 30N 108 3W
Gridley, Calif. 18 39 22N 121 42W
Griffin, Ga. 11 33 15N 84 16W
Grinnell, Iowa 14 41 45N 92 43W
Groesbeck, Tex. 13 30 48N 96 31W
Groom, Tex. 13 35 12N 101 6W
Grosse Pointe, Mich. 26 42 23N 82 54W
Groton, Conn. 9 41 21N 72 5W
Groton, S. Dak. 12 45 27N 98 6W
Grouse Creek, Utah 16 41 42N 113 53W
Groveland, Calif. 18 37 50N 120 14W
Grover City, Calif. 19 35 7N 120 37W
Groveton, N.H. 9 44 36N 71 31W
Groveton, Tex. 13 31 4N 95 8W
Grundy Center, Iowa 14 42 22N 92 47W
Gruver, Tex. 13 36 16N 101 24W
Guadalupe, Calif. 19 34 59N 120 33W
Guadalupe →, Tex. 13 28 27N 96 47W
Guadalupe Peak, Tex. 17 31 50N 104 52W
Guam ■, Pac. Oc. 31 13 27N 144 45 E
Guánica, Puerto Rico 30 17 58N 66 55W
Guayama, Puerto Rico 30 17 59N 66 7W
Guernsey, Wyo. 12 42 19N 104 45W
Gueydan, La. 13 30 2N 92 31W
Guilford, Maine 11 45 10N 69 23W
Gulfport, Miss. 13 30 22N 89 6W
Gulkana, Alaska 30 62 16N 145 23W
Gunnison, Colo. 17 38 33N 106 56W
Gunnison, Utah 16 39 9N 111 49W
Gunnison →, Colo. 17 39 4N 108 35W
Guntersville, Ala. 11 34 21N 86 18W
Gurdon, Ark. 13 33 55N 93 9W
Gustavus, Alaska 30 58 25N 135 44W
Gustine, Calif. 18 37 16N 121 0W
Guthrie, Okla. 13 35 53N 97 25W
Guttenberg, Iowa 14 42 47N 91 6W
Guymon, Okla. 13 36 41N 101 29W
Gwinn, Mich. 10 46 19N 87 27W

H

Hackensack, N.J. 20 40 53N 74 3W
Haddonfield, N.J. 24 39 53N 75 2W
Hagemeister I., Alaska 30 58 39N 160 54W
Hagerman, N. Mex. 13 33 7N 104 20W
Hagerstown, Md. 10 39 39N 77 43W
Hailey, Idaho 16 43 31N 114 19W
Haines, Alaska 30 59 14N 135 26W
Haines, Oreg. 16 44 55N 117 56W
Haines City, Fla. 11 28 7N 81 38W
Halawa, Hawaii 30 21 9N 156 47W
Haleakala Crater, Hawaii 30 20 43N 156 16W
Halethorpe, Md. 25 39 14N 76 41W
Haleyville, Ala. 11 34 14N 87 37W
Half Moon B., Calif. 28 37 29N 122 28W
Half Moon Bay, Calif. 28 37 27N 122 25W
Hallettsville, Tex. 13 29 27N 96 57W
Halliday, N. Dak. 12 47 21N 102 20W
Hallstead, Pa. 9 41 58N 75 45W
Halstad, Minn. 12 47 21N 96 50W
Hamburg, Ark. 13 33 14N 91 48W
Hamburg, Iowa 12 40 36N 95 39W
Hamburg, Pa. 9 40 33N 75 59W
Hamden, Conn. 9 41 23N 72 54W
Hamilton, Alaska 30 62 54N 163 53W
Hamilton, Mo. 12 39 45N 93 59W
Hamilton, Mont. 16 46 15N 114 10W
Hamilton, N.Y. 9 42 50N 75 33W
Hamilton, Ohio 15 39 24N 84 34W
Hamilton, Tex. 13 31 42N 98 7W
Hamlet, N.C. 11 34 53N 79 42W
Hamlin, Tex. 13 32 53N 100 8W
Hammond, Ind. 22 41 35N 87 29W
Hammond, La. 13 30 30N 90 28W
Hammonton, N.J. 10 39 39N 74 48W
Hampton, Ark. 13 33 32N 92 28W
Hampton, Iowa 14 42 45N 93 13W
Hampton, N.H. 9 42 57N 70 50W
Hampton, S.C. 11 32 52N 81 7W
Hampton, Va. 10 37 2N 76 21W
Hamtramck, Mich. 26 42 23N 83 4W
Hana, Hawaii 30 20 45N 155 59W
Hancock, Mich. 12 47 8N 88 35W
Hancock, Minn. 12 45 30N 95 48W
Hancock, N.Y. 9 41 57N 75 17W
Hanford, Calif. 18 36 20N 119 39W
Hankinson, N. Dak. 12 46 4N 96 54W
Hanksville, Utah 17 38 22N 110 43W
Hannaford, N. Dak. 12 47 19N 98 11W
Hannah, N. Dak. 12 48 58N 98 42W
Hannibal, Mo. 14 39 42N 91 22W
Hanover, N.H. 9 43 42N 72 17W
Hanover, Pa. 10 39 48N 76 59W
Happy, Tex. 13 34 45N 101 52W
Happy Camp, Calif. 16 41 48N 123 23W
Harbor Beach, Mich. 10 43 51N 82 39W
Harbor Springs, Mich. 10 45 26N 85 0W
Hardin, Mont. 16 45 44N 107 37W
Hardman, Oreg. 16 45 10N 119 41W
Hardy, Ark. 13 36 19N 91 29W
Harlan, Iowa 12 41 39N 95 19W
Harlan, Ky. 11 36 51N 83 19W
Harlem, Mont. 16 48 32N 108 47W
Harlem, N.Y. 20 40 48N 73 56W
Harlingen, Tex. 13 26 12N 97 42W
Harlowton, Mont. 16 46 26N 109 50W
Harney Basin, Oreg. 16 43 30N 119 0W
Harney L., Oreg. 16 43 14N 119 8W
Harney Peak, S. Dak. 12 43 52N 103 32W
Harper, Mt., Alaska 30 64 14N 143 51W
Harper Woods, Mich. 26 42 26N 82 56W
Harriman, Tenn. 11 35 56N 84 33W
Harrisburg, Ill. 15 37 44N 88 32W
Harrisburg, Nebr. 12 41 33N 103 44W
Harrisburg, Oreg. 16 44 16N 123 10W
Harrisburg, Pa. 8 40 16N 76 53W
Harrison, Ark. 13 36 14N 93 7W
Harrison, Idaho 16 47 27N 116 47W
Harrison, Nebr. 12 42 41N 103 53W
Harrison Bay, Alaska 30 70 40N 151 0W
Harrisonburg, Va. 10 38 27N 78 52W
Harrisonville, Mo. 14 38 39N 94 21W
Harrisville, Mich. 8 44 39N 83 17W
Hart, Mich. 10 43 42N 86 22W
Hartford, Conn. 9 41 46N 72 41W
Hartford, Ky. 10 37 27N 86 55W
Hartford, S. Dak. 12 43 38N 96 57W
Hartford, Wis. 12 43 19N 88 22W
Hartford City, Ind. 15 40 27N 85 22W
Hartselle, Ala. 11 34 27N 86 56W
Hartshorne, Okla. 13 34 51N 95 34W
Hartsville, S.C. 11 34 23N 80 4W
Hartwell, Ga. 11 34 21N 82 56W
Harvard University, Mass. 23 42 22N 71 7W
Harvey, Ill. 22 41 36N 87 39W
Harvey, N. Dak. 12 47 47N 99 56W
Harwood Heights, Ill. 22 41 57N 87 47W
Haskell, Okla. 13 35 50N 95 40W
Haskell, Tex. 13 33 10N 99 44W
Hastings, Mich. 15 42 39N 85 17W
Hastings, Minn. 12 44 44N 92 51W
Hastings, Nebr. 12 40 35N 98 23W
Hatch, N. Mex. 17 32 40N 107 9W
Hatteras, C., N.C. 11 35 14N 75 32W
Hattiesburg, Miss. 13 31 20N 89 17W
Havana, Ill. 14 40 18N 90 4W
Havasu, L., Ariz. 19 34 18N 114 28W
Haverhill, Mass. 9 42 47N 71 5W
Haverstraw, N.Y. 9 41 12N 73 58W
Havertown, Pa. 24 39 58N 75 18W
Havre, Mont. 16 48 33N 109 41W
Haw →, N.C. 11 35 36N 79 3W
Hawaii □ 30 19 30N 156 30W
Hawaii I., Pac. Oc. 30 20 0N 155 0W
Hawaiian Is., Pac. Oc. 30 20 30N 156 0W
Hawarden, Iowa 12 43 0N 96 29W
Hawkinsville, Ga. 11 32 17N 83 28W
Hawley, Minn. 12 46 53N 96 19W
Hawthorne, Calif. 29 33 54N 118 21W
Hawthorne, Nev. 16 38 32N 118 38W
Haxtun, Colo. 12 40 39N 102 38W
Hay Springs, Nebr. 12 42 41N 102 41W
Hayden, Ariz. 17 33 0N 110 47W
Hayden, Colo. 16 40 30N 107 16W
Hayes, S. Dak. 12 44 23N 101 1W
Haynesville, La. 13 32 58N 93 8W
Hays, Kans. 12 38 53N 99 20W
Hayward, Calif. 28 37 40N 122 4W
Hayward, Wis. 12 46 1N 91 29W
Hazard, Ky. 10 37 15N 83 12W
Hazel Park, Mich. 26 42 28N 83 5W
Hazelton, N. Dak. 12 46 29N 100 17W
Hazen, N. Dak. 12 47 18N 101 38W
Hazen, Nev. 16 39 34N 119 3W
Hazlehurst, Ga. 11 31 52N 82 36W
Hazlehurst, Miss. 13 31 52N 90 24W
Hazleton, Pa. 9 40 57N 75 59W
Healdsburg, Calif. 18 38 37N 122 52W
Healdton, Okla. 13 34 14N 97 29W
Hearne, Tex. 13 30 53N 96 36W
Heart →, N. Dak. 12 46 46N 100 50W
Heavener, Okla. 13 34 53N 94 36W
Hebbronville, Tex. 13 27 18N 98 41W
Heber Springs, Ark. 13 35 30N 92 2W
Hebgen L., Mont. 16 44 52N 111 20W
Hebron, N. Dak. 12 46 54N 102 3W
Hebron, Nebr. 12 40 10N 97 35W
Hecla, S. Dak. 12 45 53N 98 9W
Hedley, Tex. 13 34 52N 100 39W
Helena, Ark. 13 34 32N 90 36W
Helena, Mont. 16 46 36N 112 2W
Helendale, Calif. 19 34 44N 117 19W
Helper, Utah 16 39 41N 110 51W
Hemet, Calif. 19 33 45N 116 58W
Hemingford, Nebr. 12 42 19N 103 4W
Hemphill, Tex. 13 31 20N 93 51W
Hempstead, N.Y. 21 40 42N 73 37W
Hempstead, Tex. 13 30 6N 96 5W
Henderson, Ky. 15 37 50N 87 35W
Henderson, N.C. 11 36 20N 78 25W
Henderson, Nev. 19 36 2N 114 59W
Henderson, Tenn. 11 35 26N 88 38W
Henderson, Tex. 13 32 9N 94 48W
Hendersonville, N.C. 11 35 19N 82 28W
Henlopen, C., Del. 10 38 48N 75 6W
Hennessey, Okla. 13 36 6N 97 54W
Henrietta, Tex. 13 33 49N 98 12W
Henry, Ill. 14 41 7N 89 22W
Henryetta, Okla. 13 35 27N 95 59W
Heppner, Oreg. 16 45 21N 119 33W
Herbert I., Alaska 30 52 45N 170 7W
Hereford, Tex. 13 34 49N 102 24W
Herington, Kans. 12 38 40N 96 57W
Herkimer, N.Y. 9 43 0N 74 59W
Herman, Minn. 12 45 49N 96 9W
Hermann, Mo. 12 38 42N 91 27W
Hermiston, Oreg. 16 45 51N 119 17W

Keewatin

Hernandez, Calif. **18** 36 24N 120 46W
Hernando, Miss. **13** 34 50N 90 0W
Herreid, S. Dak. **12** 45 50N 100 4W
Herrin, Ill. **14** 37 48N 89 2W
Hesperia, Calif. **19** 34 25N 117 18W
Hetch Hetchy Aqueduct, Calif. **18** 37 29N 122 19W
Hettinger, N. Dak. **12** 46 0N 102 42W
Hi Vista, Calif. **19** 34 45N 117 46W
Hialeah, Fla. **11** 25 50N 80 17W
Hiawatha, Kans. **12** 39 51N 95 32W
Hiawatha, Utah **16** 39 29N 111 1W
Hibbing, Minn. **12** 47 25N 92 56W
Hickory, N.C. **11** 35 44N 81 21W
Hickory Hills, Ill. **22** 41 43N 87 50W
Hicksville, N.Y. **21** 40 46N 73 30W
Higgins, Tex. **13** 36 7N 100 2W
High Island, Tex. **13** 29 34N 94 24W
High Point, N.C. **11** 35 57N 80 0W
High Springs, Fla. **11** 29 50N 82 36W
Highland Park, Ill. **15** 42 11N 87 48W
Highland Park, Mich. **26** 42 24N 83 6W
Highmore, S. Dak. **12** 44 31N 99 27W
Hiko, Nev. **18** 37 32N 115 14W
Hill City, Idaho **16** 43 18N 115 3W
Hill City, Kans. **12** 39 22N 99 51W
Hill City, Minn. **12** 46 59N 93 36W
Hill City, S. Dak. **12** 43 56N 103 35W
Hillcrest Heights, Md. **25** 38 50N 76 57W
Hillman, Mich. **10** 45 4N 83 54W
Hillsboro, Kans. **12** 38 21N 97 12W
Hillsboro, N. Dak. **12** 47 26N 97 3W
Hillsboro, N.H. **9** 43 7N 71 54W
Hillsboro, N. Mex. **17** 32 55N 107 34W
Hillsboro, Oreg. **18** 45 31N 122 59W
Hillsboro, Tex. **13** 32 1N 97 8W
Hillsdale, Mich. **15** 41 56N 84 38W
Hillsdale, N.J. **20** 41 0N 74 2W
Hillsdale, N.Y. **9** 42 11N 73 30W
Hilo, Hawaii **30** 19 44N 155 5W
Hinckley, Utah **16** 39 20N 112 40W
Hingham, Mass. **23** 42 14N 70 54W
Hingham, Mont. **16** 48 33N 110 25W
Hinsdale, Ill. **22** 41 47N 87 56W
Hinsdale, Mont. **16** 48 24N 107 5W
Hinton, W. Va. **10** 37 40N 80 54W
Hobart, Okla. **13** 35 1N 99 6W
Hobbs, N. Mex. **13** 32 42N 103 8W
Hoboken, N.J. **20** 40 44N 74 3W
Hogansville, Ga. **11** 33 10N 84 55W
Hogeland, Mont. **16** 48 51N 108 40W
Hohenwald, Tenn. **11** 35 33N 87 33W
Hoisington, Kans. **12** 38 31N 98 47W
Holbrook, Ariz. **17** 34 54N 110 10W
Holden, Utah **16** 39 6N 112 16W
Holdenville, Okla. **13** 35 5N 96 24W
Holdrege, Nebr. **12** 40 26N 99 23W
Holland, Mich. **15** 42 47N 86 7W
Hollidaysburg, Pa. **8** 40 26N 78 24W
Hollis, Okla. **13** 34 41N 99 55W
Hollister, Calif. **18** 36 51N 121 24W
Hollister, Idaho **16** 42 21N 114 35W
Holly, Colo. **12** 38 3N 102 7W
Holly Hill, Fla. **11** 29 16N 81 3W
Holly Springs, Miss. **13** 34 46N 89 27W
Hollywood, Calif. **17** 34 7N 118 25W
Hollywood, Fla. **11** 26 1N 80 9W
Holton, Kans. **12** 39 28N 95 44W
Holtville, Calif. **19** 32 49N 115 23W
Holy Cross, Alaska **30** 62 12N 159 46W
Holyoke, Colo. **12** 40 35N 102 18W
Holyoke, Mass. **9** 42 12N 72 37W
Homedale, Idaho **16** 43 37N 116 56W
Homer, Alaska **30** 59 39N 151 33W
Homer, La. **13** 32 48N 93 4W
Homestead, Fla. **11** 25 28N 80 29W
Homestead, Oreg. **16** 45 2N 116 51W
Homestead, Pa. **27** 40 24N 79 55W
Hominy, Okla. **13** 36 25N 96 24W
Hondo, Tex. **13** 29 21N 99 9W
Honey L., Calif. **18** 40 15N 120 19W
Honolulu, Hawaii **30** 21 19N 157 52W
Hood, Mt., Oreg. **16** 45 23N 121 42W
Hood River, Oreg. **16** 45 43N 121 31W
Hoodsport, Wash. **18** 47 24N 123 9W
Hooker, Okla. **13** 36 52N 101 13W
Hoonah, Alaska **30** 58 7N 135 27W
Hooper Bay, Alaska **30** 61 32N 166 6W
Hoopeston, Ill. **15** 40 28N 87 40W
Hoover Dam, Ariz. **19** 36 1N 114 44W
Hop Bottom, Pa. **9** 41 42N 75 46W
Hope, Ark. **13** 33 40N 93 36W
Hope, N. Dak. **12** 47 19N 97 43W
Hope, Pt., Alaska **30** 68 20N 166 50W
Hopkins, Mo. **14** 40 33N 94 49W
Hopkinsville, Ky. **11** 36 52N 87 29W
Hopland, Calif. **18** 38 58N 123 7W
Hoquiam, Wash. **18** 46 59N 123 53W
Horn I., Miss. **11** 30 14N 88 39W
Hornbeck, La. **13** 31 20N 93 24W
Hornbrook, Calif. **16** 41 55N 122 33W
Hornell, N.Y. **8** 42 20N 77 40W
Hornitos, Calif. **18** 37 30N 120 14W
Horse Creek, Wyo. **12** 41 57N 105 10W
Horton, Kans. **12** 39 40N 95 32W
Hosmer, S. Dak. **12** 45 34N 99 28W
Hot Creek Range, Nev. **16** 38 40N 116 20W
Hot Springs, Ark. **13** 34 31N 93 3W
Hot Springs, S. Dak. **12** 43 26N 103 29W
Hotchkiss, Colo. **17** 38 48N 107 43W
Houck, Ariz. **17** 35 20N 109 10W
Houghton, Mich. **12** 47 7N 88 34W
Houghton L., Mich. **10** 44 21N 84 44W
Houlton, Maine **11** 46 8N 67 51W
Houma, La. **13** 29 36N 90 43W
Houston, Mo. **13** 37 22N 91 58W
Houston, Tex. **13** 29 46N 95 22W
Howard, Kans. **13** 37 28N 96 16W
Howard, S. Dak. **12** 44 1N 97 32W
Howe, Idaho **16** 43 48N 113 0W
Howell, Mich. **15** 42 36N 83 56W
Hualapai Peak, Ariz. **17** 35 5N 113 54W
Huasna, Calif. **19** 35 6N 120 24W
Hubbard, Tex. **13** 31 51N 96 48W
Hudson, Mich. **15** 41 51N 84 21W
Hudson, N.Y. **9** 42 15N 73 46W
Hudson, Wis. **12** 44 58N 92 45W
Hudson, Wyo. **16** 42 54N 108 35W
Hudson →, N.Y. **9** 40 42N 74 2W
Hudson Falls, N.Y. **9** 43 18N 73 35W
Hughes, Alaska **30** 66 3N 154 15W
Hugo, Colo. **12** 39 8N 103 28W
Hugoton, Kans. **13** 37 11N 101 21W
Hull, Mass. **23** 42 18N 70 54W
Humacao, Puerto Rico **30** 18 9N 65 50W
Humble, Tex. **13** 29 59N 93 18W
Humboldt, Iowa **14** 42 44N 94 13W
Humboldt, Tenn. **13** 35 50N 88 55W
Humboldt →, Nev. **16** 39 59N 118 36W
Hume, Calif. **18** 36 48N 118 54W
Humphreys, Mt., Calif. **18** 37 17N 118 40W
Humphreys Peak, Ariz. **17** 35 21N 111 41W
Hunter, N. Dak. **12** 47 12N 97 13W
Hunter, N.Y. **9** 42 13N 74 13W
Huntingburg, Ind. **15** 38 18N 86 57W
Huntingdon, Pa. **8** 40 30N 78 1W
Huntington, Ind. **15** 40 53N 85 30W
Huntington, N.Y. **21** 40 52N 73 25W
Huntington, Oreg. **16** 44 21N 117 16W
Huntington, Utah **16** 39 20N 110 58W
Huntington, W. Va. **10** 38 25N 82 27W
Huntington Beach, Calif. **19** 33 40N 118 5W
Huntington Park, Calif. **29** 33 58N 118 13W
Huntington Woods, Mich. **26** 42 28N 83 10W
Huntsville, Ala. **11** 34 44N 86 35W
Huntsville, Tex. **13** 30 43N 95 33W
Hurley, N. Mex. **17** 32 42N 108 8W
Hurley, Wis. **12** 46 27N 90 11W
Huron, Calif. **18** 36 12N 120 6W
Huron, S. Dak. **12** 44 22N 98 13W
Huron, L., Mich. **8** 44 30N 82 40W
Hurricane, Utah **17** 37 11N 113 17W
Huslia, Alaska **30** 65 41N 156 24W
Hutchinson, Kans. **13** 38 5N 97 56W
Hutchinson, Minn. **12** 44 54N 94 22W
Huttig, Ark. **13** 33 2N 92 11W
Hyannis, Nebr. **12** 42 0N 101 46W
Hyattsville, Md. **25** 38 57N 76 58W
Hydaburg, Alaska **30** 55 12N 132 50W
Hyndman Peak, Idaho **16** 43 45N 114 8W
Hyrum, Utah **16** 41 38N 111 51W
Hysham, Mont. **16** 46 18N 107 14W

I

Ida Grove, Iowa **12** 42 21N 95 28W
Idabel, Okla. **13** 33 54N 94 50W
Idaho □ **16** 45 0N 115 0W
Idaho City, Idaho **16** 43 50N 115 50W
Idaho Falls, Idaho **16** 43 30N 112 2W
Idaho Springs, Colo. **16** 39 45N 105 31W
Idria, Calif. **18** 36 25N 120 41W
Iliamna L., Alaska **30** 59 30N 155 0W
Iliff, Colo. **12** 40 45N 103 4W
Ilio Pt., Hawaii **30** 21 13N 157 16W
Ilion, N.Y. **9** 43 1N 75 2W
Illinois □ **14** 40 15N 89 30W
Illinois →, Ill. **14** 38 58N 90 28W
Imbler, Oreg. **16** 45 28N 117 58W
Imlay, Nev. **16** 40 40N 118 9W
Immokalee, Fla. **11** 26 25N 81 25W
Imperial, Calif. **19** 32 51N 115 34W
Imperial, Nebr. **12** 40 31N 101 39W
Imperial Beach, Calif. **19** 32 35N 117 8W
Imperial Dam, Ariz. **19** 32 55N 114 25W
Independence, Calif. **18** 36 48N 118 12W
Independence, Iowa **14** 42 28N 91 54W
Independence, Kans. **13** 37 14N 95 42W
Independence, Mo. **14** 39 6N 94 25W
Independence, Oreg. **16** 44 51N 123 11W
Independence Mts., Nev. **16** 41 20N 116 0W
Indian →, Fla. **11** 27 59N 80 34W
Indiana, Pa. **8** 40 37N 79 9W
Indiana □ **15** 40 0N 86 0W
Indianapolis, Ind. **15** 39 46N 86 9W
Indianola, Iowa **14** 41 22N 93 34W
Indianola, Miss. **13** 33 27N 90 39W
Indio, Calif. **19** 33 43N 116 13W
Inglewood, Calif. **29** 33 57N 118 19W
Ingomar, Mont. **16** 46 35N 107 23W
Inkom, Idaho **16** 42 48N 112 15W
Inkster, Mich. **26** 42 17N 83 16W
Interior, S. Dak. **12** 43 44N 101 59W
International Falls, Minn. **12** 48 36N 93 25W
Inverness, Fla. **11** 28 50N 82 20W
Inyo Mts., Calif. **17** 36 40N 118 0W
Inyokern, Calif. **19** 35 39N 117 49W
Iola, Kans. **13** 37 55N 95 24W
Ione, Calif. **18** 38 21N 120 56W
Ione, Wash. **16** 48 45N 117 25W
Ionia, Mich. **15** 42 59N 85 4W
Iowa □ **12** 42 18N 93 30W
Iowa City, Iowa **14** 41 40N 91 32W
Iowa Falls, Iowa **14** 42 31N 93 16W
Ipswich, Mass. **23** 42 41N 70 50W
Ipswich, S. Dak. **12** 45 27N 99 2W
Iron Mountain, Mich. **10** 45 49N 88 4W
Iron River, Mich. **12** 46 6N 88 39W
Ironton, Mo. **13** 37 36N 90 38W
Ironton, Ohio **10** 38 32N 82 41W
Ironwood, Mich. **12** 46 27N 90 9W
Irvine, Ky. **15** 37 42N 83 58W
Irvington, N.Y. **20** 40 42N 74 13W
Isabel, S. Dak. **12** 45 24N 101 26W
Isabela, Puerto Rico **30** 18 30N 67 2W
Ishpeming, Mich. **10** 46 29N 87 40W
Isla Vista, Calif. **19** 34 25N 119 53W
Island Falls, Maine **11** 46 1N 68 16W
Island Pond, Vt. **9** 44 49N 71 53W
Isle Royale, Mich. **12** 48 0N 88 54W
Isleta, N. Mex. **17** 34 55N 106 42W
Isleton, Calif. **18** 38 10N 121 37W
Ismay, Mont. **12** 46 30N 104 48W
Istokpoga, L., Fla. **11** 27 23N 81 17W
Ithaca, N.Y. **9** 42 27N 76 30W
Ivanhoe, Calif. **18** 36 23N 119 13W

J

Jackman, Maine **11** 45 35N 70 17W
Jacksboro, Tex. **13** 33 14N 98 15W
Jackson, Ala. **11** 31 31N 87 53W
Jackson, Calif. **18** 38 21N 120 46W
Jackson, Ky. **10** 37 33N 83 23W
Jackson, Mich. **15** 42 15N 84 24W
Jackson, Minn. **12** 43 37N 95 1W
Jackson, Miss. **13** 32 18N 90 12W
Jackson, Mo. **13** 37 23N 89 40W
Jackson, Ohio **10** 39 3N 82 39W
Jackson, Tenn. **11** 35 37N 88 49W
Jackson, Wyo. **16** 43 29N 110 46W
Jackson Heights, N.Y. **21** 40 44N 73 53W
Jackson L., Wyo. **16** 43 52N 110 36W
Jacksonville, Ala. **11** 33 49N 85 46W
Jacksonville, Calif. **18** 37 52N 120 24W
Jacksonville, Fla. **11** 30 20N 81 39W
Jacksonville, Ill. **14** 39 44N 90 14W
Jacksonville, N.C. **11** 34 45N 77 26W
Jacksonville, Oreg. **16** 42 19N 122 57W
Jacksonville, Tex. **13** 31 58N 95 17W
Jacksonville Beach, Fla. **11** 30 17N 81 24W
Jacob Lake, Ariz. **17** 36 43N 112 13W
Jal, N. Mex. **13** 32 7N 103 12W
Jalama, Calif. **19** 34 29N 120 29W
Jaluit I., Pac. Oc. **31** 6 0N 169 30 E
Jamaica, N.Y. **21** 40 42N 73 48W
James →, S. Dak. **12** 42 52N 97 18W
Jamestown, Ky. **10** 36 59N 85 4W
Jamestown, N. Dak. **12** 46 54N 98 42W
Jamestown, N.Y. **8** 42 6N 79 14W
Jamestown, Tenn. **11** 36 26N 84 56W
Janesville, Wis. **14** 42 41N 89 1W
Jasper, Ala. **11** 33 50N 87 17W
Jasper, Fla. **11** 30 31N 82 57W
Jasper, Minn. **12** 43 51N 96 24W
Jasper, Tex. **13** 30 56N 94 1W
Jay, Okla. **13** 36 25N 94 48W
Jayton, Tex. **13** 33 15N 100 34W
Jean, Nev. **19** 35 47N 115 20W
Jeanerette, La. **13** 29 55N 91 40W
Jefferson, Iowa **14** 42 1N 94 23W
Jefferson, Tex. **13** 32 46N 94 21W
Jefferson, Wis. **15** 43 0N 88 48W
Jefferson, Mt., Nev. **16** 38 51N 117 0W
Jefferson, Mt., Oreg. **16** 44 41N 121 48W
Jefferson City, Mo. **14** 38 34N 92 10W
Jefferson City, Tenn. **11** 36 7N 83 30W
Jeffersonville, Ind. **15** 38 17N 85 44W
Jena, La. **13** 31 41N 92 8W
Jenkins, Ky. **10** 37 10N 82 38W
Jennings, La. **13** 30 13N 92 40W
Jermyn, Pa. **9** 41 31N 75 31W
Jerome, Ariz. **17** 34 45N 112 7W
Jersey City, N.J. **20** 40 42N 74 4W
Jersey Shore, Pa. **8** 41 12N 77 15W
Jerseyville, Ill. **14** 39 7N 90 20W
Jesup, Ga. **11** 31 36N 81 53W
Jetmore, Kans. **13** 38 4N 99 54W
Jewett, Tex. **13** 31 22N 96 9W
Jewett City, Conn. **9** 41 36N 72 0W
Johannesburg, Calif. **19** 35 22N 117 38W
John Day, Oreg. **16** 44 25N 118 57W
John Day →, Oreg. **16** 45 44N 120 39W
John F.Kennedy International Airport, N.Y. **21** 40 38N 73 46W
John H. Kerr Reservoir, N.C. **11** 36 36N 78 18W
Johnson, Kans. **13** 37 34N 101 45W
Johnson City, N.Y. **9** 42 7N 75 58W
Johnson City, Tenn. **11** 36 19N 82 21W
Johnson City, Tex. **13** 30 17N 98 25W
Johnsondale, Calif. **19** 35 58N 118 32W
Johnstown, N.Y. **9** 43 0N 74 22W
Johnstown, Pa. **8** 40 20N 78 55W
Joliet, Ill. **15** 41 32N 88 5W
Jolon, Calif. **18** 35 58N 121 9W
Jonesboro, Ark. **13** 35 50N 90 42W
Jonesboro, Ill. **13** 37 27N 89 16W
Jonesboro, La. **13** 32 15N 92 43W
Jonesport, Maine **11** 44 32N 67 37W
Joplin, Mo. **13** 37 6N 94 31W
Joppatowne, Md. **25** 39 24N 76 21W
Jordan, Mont. **16** 47 19N 106 55W
Jordan Valley, Oreg. **16** 42 59N 117 3W
Joseph, Oreg. **16** 45 21N 117 14W
Joseph City, Ariz. **17** 34 57N 110 20W
Joshua Tree, Calif. **19** 34 8N 116 19W
Joshua Tree National Monument, Calif. **19** 33 55N 116 0W
Jourdanton, Tex. **13** 28 55N 98 33W
Judith →, Mont. **16** 47 44N 109 39W
Judith, Pt., R.I. **9** 41 22N 71 29W
Judith Gap, Mont. **16** 46 41N 109 45W
Julesburg, Colo. **12** 40 59N 102 16W
Julian, Calif. **19** 33 4N 116 38W
Junction, Tex. **13** 30 29N 99 46W
Junction, Utah **17** 38 14N 112 13W
Junction City, Kans. **12** 39 2N 96 50W
Junction City, Oreg. **16** 44 13N 123 12W
Juneau, Alaska **30** 58 18N 134 25W
Juniata →, Pa. **8** 40 30N 77 40W
Juntura, Oreg. **16** 43 45N 118 5W
Justice, Ill. **22** 41 44N 87 49W

K

Ka Lae, Hawaii **30** 18 55N 155 41W
Kaala, Hawaii **30** 21 31N 158 9W
Kadoka, S. Dak. **12** 43 50N 101 31W
Kaena Pt., Hawaii **30** 21 35N 158 17W
Kagamil I., Alaska **30** 53 0N 169 43W
Kahoka, Mo. **14** 40 25N 91 44W
Kahoolawe, Hawaii **30** 20 33N 156 37W
Kahuku Pt., Hawaii **30** 21 43N 157 59W
Kahului, Hawaii **30** 20 54N 156 28W
Kailua Kona, Hawaii **30** 19 39N 155 59W
Kaiwi Channel, Hawaii **30** 21 15N 157 30W
Kaiyuh Mts., Alaska **30** 64 30N 158 0W
Kake, Alaska **30** 56 59N 133 57W
Kaktovik, Alaska **30** 70 8N 143 38W
Kalama, Wash. **18** 46 1N 122 51W
Kalamazoo, Mich. **15** 42 17N 85 35W
Kalamazoo →, Mich. **15** 42 40N 86 10W
Kalaupapa, Hawaii **30** 21 12N 156 59W
Kalispell, Mont. **16** 48 12N 114 19W
Kalkaska, Mich. **10** 44 44N 85 11W
Kamalino, Hawaii **30** 21 50N 160 14W
Kamiah, Idaho **16** 46 14N 116 2W
Kanab, Utah **17** 37 3N 112 32W
Kanab →, Ariz. **17** 36 24N 112 38W
Kanaga I., Alaska **30** 51 45N 177 22W
Kanakanak, Alaska **30** 59 0N 158 58W
Kanarraville, Utah **17** 37 32N 113 11W
Kanawha →, W. Va. **10** 38 50N 82 9W
Kane, Pa. **8** 41 40N 78 49W
Kaneohe, Hawaii **30** 21 25N 157 48W
Kankakee, Ill. **15** 41 7N 87 52W
Kankakee →, Ill. **15** 41 23N 88 15W
Kannapolis, N.C. **11** 35 30N 80 37W
Kansas □ **12** 38 30N 99 0W
Kansas →, Kans. **12** 39 7N 94 37W
Kansas City, Kans. **14** 39 7N 94 38W
Kansas City, Mo. **14** 39 6N 94 35W
Kantishna, Alaska **30** 63 31N 151 5W
Kapaa, Hawaii **30** 22 5N 159 19W
Karlstad, Minn. **12** 48 35N 96 31W
Karnes City, Tex. **13** 28 53N 97 54W
Kaskaskia →, Ill. **14** 37 58N 89 57W
Katalla, Alaska **30** 60 12N 144 31W
Katmai National Park, Alaska **30** 58 20N 155 0W
Kauai, Hawaii **30** 22 3N 159 30W
Kauai Channel, Hawaii **30** 21 45N 158 50W
Kaufman, Tex. **13** 32 35N 96 19W
Kaukauna, Wis. **10** 44 17N 88 17W
Kaupulehu, Hawaii **30** 19 43N 155 53W
Kawaihae, Hawaii **30** 20 3N 155 50W
Kawaihoa Pt., Hawaii **30** 21 47N 160 12W
Kawaikimi, Hawaii **30** 22 5N 159 29W
Kayak I., Alaska **30** 59 56N 144 23W
Kaycee, Wyo. **16** 43 43N 106 38W
Kayenta, Ariz. **17** 36 44N 110 15W
Kaysville, Utah **16** 41 2N 111 56W
Keaau, Hawaii **30** 19 37N 155 2W
Keams Canyon, Ariz. **17** 35 49N 110 12W
Keanae, Hawaii **30** 20 52N 156 9W
Kearney, Nebr. **12** 40 42N 99 5W
Kearny, N.J. **20** 40 45N 74 9W
Keeler, Calif. **18** 36 29N 117 52W
Keene, Calif. **19** 35 13N 118 33W
Keene, N.H. **9** 42 56N 72 17W
Keewatin, Minn. **12** 47 24N 93 5W

Keller

Keller, *Wash.* **16** 48 5N 118 41W
Kellogg, *Idaho* **16** 47 32N 116 7W
Kelso, *Wash.* **18** 46 9N 122 54W
Kemmerer, *Wyo.* **16** 41 48N 110 32W
Kemp, L., *Tex.* **13** 33 46N 99 9W
Kenai, *Alaska* **30** 60 33N 151 16W
Kenai Mts., *Alaska* **30** 60 0N 150 0W
Kendallville, *Ind.* **15** 41 27N 85 16W
Kendrick, *Idaho* **16** 46 37N 116 39W
Kenedy, *Tex.* **13** 28 49N 97 51W
Kenmare, *N. Dak.* **12** 48 41N 102 5W
Kennebec, *S. Dak.* **12** 43 54N 99 52W
Kennett, *Mo.* **13** 36 14N 90 3W
Kennewick, *Wash.* **16** 46 12N 119 7W
Kenosha, *Wis.* **15** 42 35N 87 49W
Kensington, *Kans.* **12** 39 46N 99 2W
Kent, *Ohio* **8** 41 9N 81 22W
Kent, *Oreg.* **16** 45 12N 120 42W
Kent, *Tex.* **13** 31 4N 104 13W
Kentfield, *Calif.* **28** 37 57N 122 33W
Kentland, *Ind.* **15** 40 46N 87 27W
Kenton, *Ohio* **15** 40 39N 83 37W
Kentucky □ **10** 37 0N 84 0W
Kentucky →, *Ky.* **15** 38 41N 85 11W
Kentucky L., *Ky.* **11** 37 1N 88 16W
Kentwood, *La.* **13** 31 0N 90 30W
Kentwood, *La.* **13** 30 56N 90 31W
Keokuk, *Iowa* **14** 40 24N 91 24W
Kepuhi, *Hawaii* **30** 21 10N 157 10W
Kerman, *Calif.* **18** 36 43N 120 4W
Kermit, *Tex.* **13** 31 52N 103 6W
Kern →, *Calif.* **19** 35 16N 119 18W
Kernville, *Calif.* **19** 35 45N 118 26W
Kerrville, *Tex.* **13** 30 3N 99 8W
Ketchikan, *Alaska* **30** 55 21N 131 39W
Ketchum, *Idaho* **16** 43 41N 114 22W
Kettle Falls, *Wash.* **16** 48 37N 118 3W
Kettleman City, *Calif.* **18** 36 1N 119 58W
Kevin, *Mont.* **16** 48 45N 111 58W
Kewanee, *Ill.* **14** 41 14N 89 56W
Kewaunee, *Wis.* **10** 44 27N 87 31W
Keweenaw B., *Mich.* **10** 47 0N 88 15W
Keweenaw Pen., *Mich.* **10** 47 30N 88 0W
Keweenaw Pt., *Mich.* **10** 47 25N 87 43W
Keyser, *W. Va.* **10** 39 26N 78 59W
Keystone, *S. Dak.* **12** 43 54N 103 25W
Kijik, *Alaska* **30** 60 20N 154 20W
Kilauea, *Hawaii* **30** 22 13N 159 25W
Kilauea Crater, *Hawaii* **30** 19 25N 155 17W
Kilbuck Mts., *Alaska* **30** 60 30N 160 0W
Kilgore, *Tex.* **13** 32 23N 94 53W
Killdeer, *N. Dak.* **12** 47 26N 102 48W
Killeen, *Tex.* **13** 31 7N 97 44W
Kim, *Colo.* **13** 37 15N 103 21W
Kimball, *Nebr.* **12** 41 14N 103 40W
Kimball, *S. Dak.* **12** 43 45N 98 57W
Kimberly, *Idaho* **16** 42 32N 114 22W
King City, *Calif.* **18** 36 13N 121 8W
King of Prussia, *Pa.* **24** 40 5N 75 22W
Kingfisher, *Okla.* **13** 35 52N 97 56W
Kingman, *Ariz.* **19** 35 12N 114 4W
Kingman, *Kans.* **13** 37 39N 98 7W
Kings →, *Calif.* **18** 36 3N 119 50W
Kings Canyon National Park, *Calif.* **18** 36 50N 118 40W
Kings Mountain, *N.C.* **11** 35 15N 81 20W
King's Peak, *Utah* **16** 40 46N 110 27W
Kingsburg, *Calif.* **18** 36 31N 119 33W
Kingsley, *Iowa* **12** 42 35N 95 58W
Kingsport, *Tenn.* **11** 36 33N 82 33W
Kingston, *N.Y.* **9** 41 56N 73 59W
Kingston, *Pa.* **9** 41 16N 75 54W
Kingston, *R.I.* **9** 41 29N 71 30W
Kingstree, *S.C.* **11** 33 40N 79 50W
Kingsville, *Tex.* **13** 27 31N 97 52W
Kinsley, *Kans.* **13** 37 55N 99 25W
Kinston, *N.C.* **11** 35 16N 77 35W
Kiowa, *Kans.* **13** 37 1N 98 29W
Kiowa, *Okla.* **13** 34 43N 95 54W
Kipnuk, *Alaska* **30** 59 56N 164 3W
Kirkland, *Ariz.* **17** 34 25N 112 43W
Kirksville, *Mo.* **14** 40 12N 92 35W
Kiska I., *Alaska* **30** 51 59N 177 30 E
Kissimmee, *Fla.* **11** 28 18N 81 24W
Kissimmee →, *Fla.* **11** 27 9N 80 52W
Kit Carson, *Colo.* **12** 38 46N 102 48W
Kittanning, *Pa.* **8** 40 49N 79 31W
Kittatinny Mts., *N.J.* **9** 41 0N 75 0W
Kittery, *Maine* **11** 43 5N 70 45W
Kivalina, *Alaska* **30** 67 44N 164 33W
Klamath →, *Calif.* **16** 41 33N 124 5W
Klamath Falls, *Oreg.* **16** 42 13N 121 46W
Klamath Mts., *Calif.* **16** 41 20N 123 0W
Klein, *Mont.* **16** 46 24N 108 33W
Klickitat, *Wash.* **16** 45 49N 121 9W
Knights Ferry, *Calif.* **18** 37 50N 120 40W
Knights Landing, *Calif.* **18** 38 48N 121 43W
Knox, *Ind.* **15** 41 18N 86 37W
Knox City, *Tex.* **13** 33 25N 99 49W
Knoxville, *Iowa* **14** 41 19N 93 6W
Knoxville, *Tenn.* **11** 35 58N 83 55W
Kobuk, *Alaska* **30** 66 55N 156 52W
Kobuk →, *Alaska* **30** 66 55N 157 0W
Kodiak, *Alaska* **30** 57 47N 152 24W
Kodiak I., *Alaska* **30** 57 30N 152 45W
Kokomo, *Ind.* **15** 40 29N 86 8W
Konawa, *Okla.* **13** 34 58N 96 45W
Kooskia, *Idaho* **16** 46 9N 115 59W
Koror, *Pac. Oc.* **31** 7 20N 134 28 E
Kosciusko, *Miss.* **13** 33 4N 89 35W
Kotzebue, *Alaska* **30** 66 53N 162 39W
Kotzebue Sound, *Alaska* **30** 66 20N 163 0W
Kountze, *Tex.* **13** 30 22N 94 19W
Koyuk, *Alaska* **30** 64 56N 161 9W
Koyukuk →, *Alaska* **30** 64 55N 157 32W
Kremmling, *Colo.* **16** 40 4N 106 24W
Kualakahi Chan, *Hawaii* **30** 22 2N 159 53W
Kuiu I., *Alaska* **30** 57 45N 134 10W
Kulm, *N. Dak.* **12** 46 18N 98 57W
Kumukahi, C., *Hawaii* **30** 19 31N 154 49W
Kupreanof I., *Alaska* **30** 56 50N 133 30W
Kuskokwim →, *Alaska* **30** 60 5N 162 25W
Kuskokwim B., *Alaska* **30** 59 45N 162 25W
Kuskokwim Mts., *Alaska* **30** 62 30N 156 0W
Kwethluk, *Alaska* **30** 60 49N 161 26W
Kwigillingok, *Alaska* **30** 59 51N 163 8W
Kwiguk, *Alaska* **30** 62 46N 164 30W
Kyburz, *Calif.* **18** 38 47N 120 18W

L

La Barge, *Wyo.* **16** 42 16N 110 12W
La Belle, *Fla.* **11** 26 46N 81 26W
La Canada, *Calif.* **29** 34 12N 118 12W
La Conner, *Wash.* **16** 48 23N 122 30W
La Crescenta, *Calif.* **29** 34 13N 118 14W
La Crosse, *Kans.* **12** 38 32N 99 18W
La Crosse, *Wis.* **12** 43 48N 91 15W
La Fayette, *Ga.* **11** 34 42N 85 17W
La Follette, *Tenn.* **11** 36 23N 84 7W
La Grande, *Oreg.* **16** 45 20N 118 5W
La Grange, *Calif.* **18** 37 42N 120 27W
La Grange, *Ga.* **11** 33 2N 85 2W
La Grange, *Ill.* **22** 41 48N 87 53W
La Grange, *Ky.* **10** 38 25N 85 23W
La Grange, *Tex.* **13** 29 54N 96 52W
La Guardia Airport, *N.Y.* **21** 40 46N 73 52W
La Habra, *Calif.* **29** 33 56N 117 57W
La Harpe, *Ill.* **14** 40 35N 90 58W
La Jara, *Colo.* **17** 37 16N 105 58W
La Junta, *Colo.* **13** 37 59N 103 33W
La Mesa, *Calif.* **19** 32 46N 117 3W
La Mesa, *N. Mex.* **17** 32 7N 106 42W
La Moure, *N. Dak.* **12** 46 21N 98 18W
La Pine, *Oreg.* **16** 43 40N 121 30W
La Plant, *S. Dak.* **12** 45 9N 100 39W
La Porte, *Ind.* **15** 41 36N 86 43W
La Push, *Wash.* **18** 47 55N 124 38W
La Salle, *Ill.* **14** 41 20N 89 6W
La Selva Beach, *Calif.* **18** 36 56N 121 51W
Laau Pt., *Hawaii* **30** 21 6N 157 19W
Lac du Flambeau, *Wis.* **12** 45 58N 89 53W
Lackawanna, *N.Y.* **8** 42 50N 78 50W
Lacona, *N.Y.* **9** 43 39N 76 10W
Laconia, *N.H.* **9** 43 32N 71 28W
Lacrosse, *Wash.* **16** 46 51N 117 58W
Ladysmith, *Wis.* **12** 45 28N 91 12W
Lafayette, *Colo.* **12** 39 58N 105 12W
Lafayette, *Ind.* **15** 40 25N 86 54W
Lafayette, *La.* **13** 30 14N 92 1W
Lafayette, *Tenn.* **11** 36 31N 86 2W
Laguna, *N. Mex.* **17** 35 2N 107 25W
Laguna Beach, *Calif.* **19** 33 33N 117 47W
Lahaina, *Hawaii* **30** 20 53N 156 41W
Lahontan Reservoir, *Nev.* **16** 39 28N 119 4W
Lake Alpine, *Calif.* **18** 38 29N 120 0W
Lake Andes, *S. Dak.* **12** 43 9N 98 32W
Lake Anse, *Mich.* **10** 46 42N 88 25W
Lake Arthur, *La.* **13** 30 5N 92 41W
Lake Charles, *La.* **13** 30 14N 93 13W
Lake City, *Colo.* **17** 38 2N 107 19W
Lake City, *Fla.* **11** 30 11N 82 38W
Lake City, *Iowa* **14** 42 16N 94 44W
Lake City, *Mich.* **10** 44 20N 85 13W
Lake City, *Minn.* **12** 44 27N 92 16W
Lake City, *S.C.* **11** 33 52N 79 45W
Lake George, *N.Y.* **9** 43 26N 73 43W
Lake Havasu City, *Ariz.* **19** 34 27N 114 22W
Lake Hiawatha, *N.J.* **20** 40 52N 74 22W
Lake Hughes, *Calif.* **19** 34 41N 118 26W
Lake Isabella, *Calif.* **19** 35 38N 118 28W
Lake Mead National Recreation Area, *Ariz.* **19** 36 15N 114 30W
Lake Mills, *Iowa* **12** 43 25N 93 32W
Lake Providence, *La.* **13** 32 48N 91 10W
Lake Village, *Ark.* **13** 33 20N 91 17W
Lake Wales, *Fla.* **11** 27 54N 81 35W
Lake Worth, *Fla.* **11** 26 37N 80 3W
Lakeland, *Fla.* **11** 28 3N 81 57W
Lakeside, *Ariz.* **17** 34 9N 109 58W
Lakeside, *Calif.* **19** 32 52N 116 55W
Lakeside, *Nebr.* **12** 42 3N 102 26W
Lakeview, *Oreg.* **16** 42 11N 120 21W
Lakewood, *Colo.* **12** 39 44N 105 5W
Lakewood, *N.J.* **9** 40 6N 74 13W
Lakewood, *Ohio* **27** 41 29N 81 49W
Lakin, *Kans.* **13** 37 57N 101 15W
Lakota, *N. Dak.* **12** 48 2N 98 21W
Lamar, *Colo.* **12** 38 5N 102 37W
Lamar, *Mo.* **13** 37 30N 94 16W
Lambert, *Mont.* **12** 47 41N 104 37W
Lame Deer, *Mont.* **16** 45 37N 106 40W
Lamesa, *Tex.* **13** 32 44N 101 58W
Lamont, *Calif.* **19** 35 15N 118 55W
Lampasas, *Tex.* **13** 31 4N 98 11W
Lamy, *N. Mex.* **17** 35 29N 105 53W
Lanai City, *Hawaii* **30** 20 50N 156 55W
Lanai I., *Hawaii* **30** 20 50N 156 55W
Lancaster, *Calif.* **19** 34 42N 118 8W
Lancaster, *Ky.* **10** 37 37N 84 35W
Lancaster, *N.H.* **9** 44 29N 71 34W
Lancaster, *Pa.* **9** 40 2N 76 19W
Lancaster, *S.C.* **11** 34 43N 80 46W
Lancaster, *Wis.* **14** 42 51N 90 43W
Lander, *Wyo.* **16** 42 50N 108 44W
Lanesboro, *Pa.* **9** 41 57N 75 34W
Lanett, *Ala.* **11** 32 52N 85 12W
Langdon, *N. Dak.* **12** 48 45N 98 22W
Langley Park, *Md.* **25** 38 59N 76 58W
Langlois, *Oreg.* **16** 42 56N 124 27W
Langtry, *Tex.* **13** 29 49N 101 34W
Lansdale, *Pa.* **9** 40 14N 75 17W
Lansdowne, *Md.* **25** 39 14N 76 39W
Lansdowne, *Pa.* **24** 39 56N 75 15W
Lansford, *Pa.* **9** 40 50N 75 53W
Lansing, *Mich.* **15** 42 44N 84 33W
Laona, *Wis.* **10** 45 34N 88 40W
Lapeer, *Mich.* **15** 43 3N 83 19W
Laporte, *Pa.* **9** 41 25N 76 30W
Laramie, *Wyo.* **12** 41 19N 105 35W
Laramie Mts., *Wyo.* **12** 42 0N 105 30W
Larchmont, *N.Y.* **21** 40 55N 73 44W
Laredo, *Tex.* **13** 27 30N 99 30W
Larimore, *N. Dak.* **12** 47 54N 97 38W
Larkspur, *Calif.* **28** 37 56N 122 32W
Larned, *Kans.* **12** 38 11N 99 6W
Las Animas, *Colo.* **12** 38 4N 103 13W
Las Cruces, *N. Mex.* **17** 32 19N 106 47W
Las Vegas, *N. Mex.* **17** 35 36N 105 13W
Las Vegas, *Nev.* **19** 36 10N 115 9W
Lassen Pk., *Wash.* **16** 40 29N 121 31W
Lathrop Wells, *Nev.* **19** 36 39N 116 24W
Laton, *Calif.* **18** 36 26N 119 41W
Laurel, *Miss.* **13** 31 41N 89 8W
Laurel, *Mont.* **16** 45 40N 108 46W
Laurens, *S.C.* **11** 34 30N 82 1W
Laurinburg, *N.C.* **11** 34 47N 79 28W
Laurium, *Mich.* **10** 47 14N 88 27W
Lava Hot Springs, *Idaho* **16** 42 37N 112 1W
Laverne, *Okla.* **13** 36 43N 99 54W
Lawrence, *Kans.* **12** 38 58N 95 14W
Lawrence, *Mass.* **23** 42 43N 71 7W
Lawrenceburg, *Ind.* **15** 39 6N 84 52W
Lawrenceburg, *Tenn.* **11** 35 14N 87 20W
Lawrenceville, *Ga.* **11** 33 57N 83 59W
Laws, *Calif.* **18** 37 24N 118 20W
Lawton, *Okla.* **13** 34 37N 98 25W
Laytonville, *Calif.* **16** 39 41N 123 29W
Le Mars, *Iowa* **12** 42 47N 96 10W
Le Roy, *Kans.* **13** 38 5N 95 38W
Le Sueur, *Minn.* **12** 44 28N 93 55W
Lead, *S. Dak.* **12** 44 21N 103 46W
Leadville, *Colo.* **17** 39 15N 106 18W
Leaf →, *Miss.* **13** 30 59N 88 44W
Leakey, *Tex.* **13** 29 44N 99 46W
Leamington, *Utah* **16** 39 32N 112 17W
Leavenworth, *Kans.* **12** 39 19N 94 55W
Leavenworth, *Wash.* **16** 47 36N 120 40W
Lebanon, *Ind.* **15** 40 3N 86 28W
Lebanon, *Kans.* **12** 39 49N 98 33W
Lebanon, *Ky.* **10** 37 34N 85 15W
Lebanon, *Mo.* **14** 37 41N 92 40W
Lebanon, *Oreg.* **16** 44 32N 122 55W
Lebanon, *Pa.* **9** 40 20N 76 26W
Lebanon, *Tenn.* **11** 36 12N 86 18W
Lebec, *Calif.* **19** 34 50N 118 52W
Lee Vining, *Calif.* **18** 37 58N 119 7W
Leech L., *Minn.* **12** 47 10N 94 24W
Leedey, *Okla.* **13** 35 52N 99 21W
Leeds, *Ala.* **11** 33 33N 86 33W
Leesburg, *Fla.* **11** 28 49N 81 53W
Leesville, *La.* **13** 31 9N 93 16W
Lefors, *Tex.* **13** 35 26N 100 48W
Lehi, *Utah* **16** 40 24N 111 51W
Lehighton, *Pa.* **9** 40 50N 75 43W
Lehua I., *Hawaii* **30** 22 1N 160 6W
Leland, *Miss.* **13** 33 24N 90 54W
Lemhi Ra., *Idaho* **16** 44 30N 113 30W
Lemmon, *S. Dak.* **12** 45 57N 102 10W
Lemon Grove, *Calif.* **19** 32 45N 117 2W
Lemoore, *Calif.* **18** 36 18N 119 46W
Lennox, *Calif.* **29** 33 56N 118 21W
Lenoir, *N.C.* **11** 35 55N 81 32W
Lenoir City, *Tenn.* **11** 35 48N 84 16W
Lenora, *Kans.* **12** 39 37N 100 0W
Lenox, *Mass.* **9** 42 22N 73 17W
Lenwood, *Calif.* **19** 34 53N 117 7W
Leola, *S. Dak.* **12** 45 43N 98 56W
Leominster, *Mass.* **9** 42 32N 71 46W
Leon, *Iowa* **14** 40 44N 93 45W
Leonardtown, *Md.* **10** 38 17N 76 38W
Leoti, *Kans.* **12** 38 29N 101 21W
Leslie, *Ark.* **13** 35 50N 92 34W
Leucadia, *Calif.* **19** 33 4N 117 18W
Levan, *Utah* **16** 39 33N 111 52W
Levelland, *Tex.* **13** 33 35N 102 23W
Levittown, *N.Y.* **21** 40 43N 73 31W
Levittown, *Pa.* **9** 40 9N 74 51W
Lewellen, *Nebr.* **12** 41 20N 102 9W
Lewes, *Del.* **10** 38 46N 75 9W
Lewis Range, *Mont.* **16** 48 5N 113 5W
Lewisburg, *Pa.* **8** 40 58N 76 54W
Lewisburg, *Tenn.* **11** 35 27N 86 48W
Lewiston, *Idaho* **16** 46 25N 117 1W
Lewiston, *Maine* **11** 44 6N 70 13W
Lewistown, *Mont.* **16** 47 4N 109 26W
Lewistown, *Pa.* **8** 40 36N 77 34W
Lexington, *Ill.* **15** 40 39N 88 47W
Lexington, *Ky.* **15** 38 3N 84 30W
Lexington, *Mass.* **23** 42 26N 71 13W
Lexington, *Miss.* **13** 33 7N 90 3W
Lexington, *Mo.* **14** 39 11N 93 52W
Lexington, *N.C.* **11** 35 49N 80 15W
Lexington, *Nebr.* **12** 40 47N 99 45W
Lexington, *Oreg.* **16** 45 27N 119 42W
Lexington, *Tenn.* **11** 35 39N 88 24W
Lexington Park, *Md.* **10** 38 16N 76 27W
Libby, *Mont.* **16** 48 23N 115 33W
Liberal, *Kans.* **13** 37 3N 100 55W
Liberal, *Mo.* **13** 37 34N 94 31W
Liberty, *Mo.* **14** 39 15N 94 25W
Liberty, *Tex.* **13** 30 3N 94 48W
Lida, *Nev.* **17** 37 28N 117 30W
Lihue, *Hawaii* **30** 21 59N 159 23W
Lima, *Mont.* **16** 44 38N 112 36W
Lima, *Ohio* **15** 40 44N 84 6W
Limon, *Colo.* **12** 39 16N 103 41W
Lincoln, *Ill.* **14** 40 9N 89 22W
Lincoln, *Kans.* **12** 39 3N 98 9W
Lincoln, *Maine* **11** 45 22N 68 30W
Lincoln, *N. Mex.* **17** 33 30N 105 23W
Lincoln, *Nebr.* **12** 40 49N 96 41W
Lincoln Park, *Mich.* **26** 42 14N 83 9W
Lincolnton, *N.C.* **11** 35 29N 81 16W
Lincolnwood, *Ill.* **22** 42 1N 87 45W
Lind, *Wash.* **16** 46 58N 118 37W
Linden, *Calif.* **18** 38 1N 121 5W
Linden, *N.J.* **20** 40 38N 74 14W
Linden, *Tex.* **13** 33 1N 94 22W
Lindsay, *Calif.* **18** 36 12N 119 5W
Lindsay, *Okla.* **13** 34 50N 97 38W
Lindsborg, *Kans.* **12** 38 35N 97 40W
Lingle, *Wyo.* **12** 42 8N 104 21W
Linthicum Heights, *Md.* **25** 39 12N 76 41W
Linton, *Ind.* **15** 39 2N 87 10W
Linton, *N. Dak.* **12** 46 16N 100 14W
Lipscomb, *Tex.* **13** 36 14N 100 16W
Lisbon, *N. Dak.* **12** 46 27N 97 41W
Lisburne, C., *Alaska* **30** 68 53N 166 13W
Litchfield, *Conn.* **9** 41 45N 73 11W
Litchfield, *Ill.* **14** 39 11N 89 39W
Litchfield, *Minn.* **12** 45 8N 94 32W
Little Belt Mts., *Mont.* **16** 46 40N 110 45W
Little Blue →, *Kans.* **12** 39 42N 96 41W
Little Colorado →, *Ariz.* **17** 36 12N 111 48W
Little Falls, *Minn.* **12** 45 59N 94 22W
Little Falls, *N.Y.* **9** 43 3N 74 51W
Little Fork →, *Minn.* **12** 48 31N 93 35W
Little Humboldt →, *Nev.* **16** 41 1N 117 43W
Little Lake, *Calif.* **19** 35 56N 117 55W
Little Missouri →, *N. Dak.* **12** 47 36N 102 25W
Little Red →, *Ark.* **13** 35 11N 91 27W
Little Rock, *Ark.* **13** 34 45N 92 17W
Little Sable Pt., *Mich.* **10** 43 38N 86 33W
Little Sioux →, *Iowa* **12** 41 48N 96 4W
Little Snake →, *Colo.* **16** 40 27N 108 26W
Little Wabash →, *Ill.* **15** 37 55N 88 5W
Littlefield, *Tex.* **13** 33 55N 102 20W
Littlefork, *Minn.* **12** 48 24N 93 34W
Littleton, *N.H.* **9** 44 18N 71 46W
Live Oak, *Fla.* **11** 30 18N 82 59W
Livermore, *Calif.* **18** 37 41N 121 47W
Livermore, Mt., *Tex.* **13** 30 38N 104 11W
Livingston, *Calif.* **18** 37 23N 120 43W
Livingston, *Mont.* **16** 45 40N 110 34W
Livingston, *N.J.* **20** 40 47N 74 18W
Livingston, *Tex.* **13** 30 43N 94 56W
Livonia, *Mich.* **26** 42 24N 83 22W
Llano, *Tex.* **13** 30 45N 98 41W
Llano →, *Tex.* **13** 30 39N 98 26W
Llano Estacado, *Tex.* **13** 33 30N 103 0W
Loa, *Utah* **17** 38 24N 111 39W
Lock Haven, *Pa.* **8** 41 8N 77 28W
Lockeford, *Calif.* **18** 38 10N 121 9W
Lockhart, *Tex.* **13** 29 53N 97 40W
Lockney, *Tex.* **13** 34 7N 101 27W
Lockport, *N.Y.* **8** 43 10N 78 42W
Lodge Grass, *Mont.* **16** 45 19N 107 22W
Lodgepole, *Nebr.* **12** 41 9N 102 38W
Lodgepole Cr. →, *Wyo.* **12** 41 20N 104 30W
Lodi, *Calif.* **18** 38 8N 121 16W
Lodi, *N.J.* **20** 40 52N 74 5W
Logan, *Kans.* **12** 39 40N 99 34W
Logan, *Ohio* **10** 39 32N 82 25W
Logan, *Utah* **16** 41 44N 111 50W
Logan, *W. Va.* **10** 37 51N 81 59W
Logan International Airport, *Mass.* **23** 42 21N 71 0W
Logansport, *Ind.* **15** 40 45N 86 22W
Logansport, *La.* **13** 31 58N 94 0W
Lolo, *Mont.* **16** 46 45N 114 5W
Loma, *Mont.* **16** 47 56N 110 30W
Loma Linda, *Calif.* **19** 34 3N 117 16W
Lometa, *Tex.* **13** 31 13N 98 24W
Lompoc, *Calif.* **19** 34 38N 120 28W
London, *Ky.* **10** 37 8N 84 5W
London, *Ohio* **15** 39 53N 83 27W
Lone Pine, *Calif.* **18** 36 36N 118 4W
Long Beach, *Calif.* **19** 33 47N 118 11W
Long Beach, *N.Y.* **21** 40 35N 73 40W
Long Beach, *Wash.* **18** 46 21N 124 3W

Long Branch, *N.J.* **9** 40 18N 74 0W
Long Creek, *Oreg.* **16** 44 43N 119 6W
Long I., *N.Y.* **9** 40 45N 73 30W
Long Island Sd., *N.Y.* **9** 41 10N 73 0W
Long Pine, *Nebr.* **12** 42 32N 99 42W
Longmont, *Colo.* **12** 40 10N 105 6W
Longview, *Tex.* **13** 32 30N 94 44W
Longview, *Wash.* **18** 46 8N 122 57W
Lonoke, *Ark.* **13** 34 47N 91 54W
Lookout, C., *N.C.* **11** 34 35N 76 32W
Lorain, *Ohio* **8** 41 28N 82 11W
Lordsburg, *N. Mex.* **17** 32 21N 108 43W
Los Alamos, *Calif.* **19** 34 44N 120 17W
Los Alamos, *N. Mex.* **17** 35 53N 106 19W
Los Altos, *Calif.* **18** 37 23N 122 7W
Los Angeles, *Calif.* **29** 34 3N 118 13W
Los Angeles Aqueduct, *Calif.* **19** 35 22N 118 5W
Los Angeles International Airport, *Calif.* **29** 33 56N 118 23W
Los Banos, *Calif.* **18** 37 4N 120 51W
Los Lunas, *N. Mex.* **17** 34 48N 106 44W
Los Olivos, *Calif.* **19** 34 40N 120 7W
Loudon, *Tenn.* **11** 35 45N 84 20W
Louisa, *Ky.* **10** 38 7N 82 36W
Louisiana, *Mo.* **14** 39 27N 91 3W
Louisiana □ **13** 30 50N 92 0W
Louisville, *Ky.* **15** 38 15N 85 46W
Louisville, *Miss.* **13** 33 7N 89 3W
Loup City, *Nebr.* **12** 41 17N 98 58W
Loveland, *Colo.* **12** 40 24N 105 5W
Lovell, *Wyo.* **16** 44 50N 108 24W
Lovelock, *Nev.* **16** 40 11N 118 28W
Loving, *N. Mex.* **13** 32 17N 104 6W
Lovington, *N. Mex.* **13** 32 57N 103 21W
Lowell, *Mass.* **23** 42 38N 71 16W
Lower L., *Calif.* **16** 41 16N 120 2W
Lower Lake, *Calif.* **18** 38 55N 122 37W
Lower Red L., *Minn.* **12** 47 58N 95 0W
Lowville, *N.Y.* **9** 43 47N 75 29W
Lubbock, *Tex.* **13** 33 35N 101 51W
Lucedale, *Miss.* **11** 30 56N 88 35W
Lucerne Valley, *Calif.* **19** 34 27N 116 57W
Ludington, *Mich.* **10** 43 57N 86 27W
Ludlow, *Calif.* **19** 34 43N 116 10W
Ludlow, *Vt.* **9** 43 24N 72 42W
Lufkin, *Tex.* **13** 31 21N 94 44W
Luling, *Tex.* **13** 29 41N 97 39W
Luma, *Amer. Samoa* **31** 14 15S 169 32W
Lumberton, *Miss.* **13** 31 0N 89 27W
Lumberton, *N.C.* **11** 34 37N 79 0W
Lumberton, *N. Mex.* **17** 36 56N 106 56W
Lund, *Nev.* **16** 38 52N 115 0W
Luning, *Nev.* **16** 38 30N 118 11W
Luray, *Va.* **10** 38 40N 78 28W
Lusk, *Wyo.* **12** 42 46N 104 27W
Lutherville-Timonium, *Md.* **25** 39 25N 76 36W
Luverne, *Minn.* **12** 43 39N 96 13W
Lyman, *Wyo.* **16** 41 20N 110 18W
Lynchburg, *Va.* **10** 37 25N 79 9W
Lynden, *Wash.* **18** 48 57N 122 27W
Lyndhurst, *N.J.* **20** 40 49N 74 8W
Lynn, *Mass.* **23** 42 28N 70 57W
Lynwood, *Calif.* **29** 33 55N 118 12W
Lyons, *Colo.* **12** 40 14N 105 16W
Lyons, *Ga.* **11** 32 12N 82 19W
Lyons, *Ill.* **22** 41 48N 87 49W
Lyons, *Kans.* **12** 38 21N 98 12W
Lyons, *N.Y.* **8** 43 5N 77 0W
Lytle, *Tex.* **13** 29 14N 98 48W

M

Mabton, *Wash.* **16** 46 13N 120 0W
McAlester, *Okla.* **13** 34 56N 95 46W
McAllen, *Tex.* **13** 26 12N 98 14W
McCall, *Idaho* **16** 44 55N 116 6W
McCamey, *Tex.* **13** 31 8N 102 14W
McCammon, *Idaho* **16** 42 39N 112 12W
McCarthy, *Alaska* **30** 61 26N 142 56W
McCloud, *Calif.* **16** 41 15N 122 8W
McClure, L., *Calif.* **18** 37 35N 120 16W
McClusky, *N. Dak.* **12** 47 29N 100 27W
McComb, *Miss.* **13** 31 15N 90 27W
McConaughy, L., *Nebr.* **12** 41 14N 101 40W
McCook, *Nebr.* **12** 40 12N 100 38W
McDermitt, *Nev.* **16** 41 59N 117 43W
McFarland, *Calif.* **19** 35 41N 119 14W
McGehee, *Ark.* **13** 33 38N 91 24W
McGill, *Nev.* **16** 39 23N 114 47W
McGregor, *Iowa* **14** 43 1N 91 11W
Machias, *Maine* **11** 44 43N 67 28W
McIntosh, *S. Dak.* **12** 45 55N 101 21W
Mackay, *Idaho* **16** 43 55N 113 37W
McKees Rocks, *Pa.* **27** 40 28N 80 3W
McKeesport, *Pa.* **27** 40 21N 79 51W
McKenzie, *Tenn.* **11** 36 8N 88 31W
McKenzie →, *Oreg.* **16** 44 7N 123 6W
Mackinaw City, *Mich.* **10** 45 47N 84 44W
McKinley, Mt., *Alaska* **30** 63 4N 151 0W
McKinney, *Tex.* **13** 33 12N 96 37W
McLaughlin, *S. Dak.* **12** 45 49N 100 49W
McLean, *Tex.* **13** 35 14N 100 36W
McLean, *Va.* **25** 38 56N 77 10W
McLeansboro, *Ill.* **15** 38 6N 88 32W
McLoughlin, Mt., *Oreg.* **16** 42 27N 122 19W
McMillan, L., *N. Mex.* **13** 32 36N 104 21W
McMinnville, *Oreg.* **16** 45 13N 123 12W
McMinnville, *Tenn.* **11** 35 41N 85 46W
McNary, *Ariz.* **17** 34 4N 109 51W
Macomb, *Ill.* **14** 40 27N 90 40W
Macon, *Ga.* **11** 32 51N 83 38W
Macon, *Miss.* **11** 33 7N 88 34W
Macon, *Mo.* **14** 39 44N 92 28W
McPherson, *Kans.* **12** 38 22N 97 40W
McPherson Pk., *Calif.* **19** 34 53N 119 53W
McVille, *N. Dak.* **12** 47 46N 98 11W
Madera, *Calif.* **18** 36 57N 120 3W
Madill, *Okla.* **13** 34 6N 96 46W
Madison, *Fla.* **11** 30 28N 83 25W
Madison, *Ind.* **15** 38 44N 85 23W
Madison, *N.J.* **20** 40 45N 74 25W
Madison, *Nebr.* **12** 41 50N 97 27W
Madison, *S. Dak.* **12** 44 0N 97 7W
Madison, *Wis.* **14** 43 4N 89 24W
Madison →, *Mont.* **16** 45 56N 111 31W
Madison Heights, *Mich.* **26** 42 29N 83 6W
Madisonville, *Ky.* **10** 37 20N 87 30W
Madisonville, *Tex.* **13** 30 57N 95 55W
Madras, *Oreg.* **16** 44 38N 121 8W
Madre, Laguna, *Tex.* **13** 27 0N 97 30W
Magdalena, *N. Mex.* **17** 34 7N 107 15W
Magee, *Miss.* **13** 31 52N 89 44W
Magnolia, *Ark.* **13** 33 16N 93 14W
Magnolia, *Miss.* **13** 31 9N 90 28W
Mahanoy City, *Pa.* **9** 40 49N 76 9W
Mahnomen, *Minn.* **12** 47 19N 95 58W
Mahukona, *Hawaii* **30** 20 11N 155 52W
Maine □ **11** 45 20N 69 0W
Makapuu Hd., *Hawaii* **30** 21 19N 157 39W
Makena, *Hawaii* **30** 20 39N 156 27W
Malad City, *Idaho* **16** 42 12N 112 15W
Malaga, *N. Mex.* **13** 32 14N 104 4W
Malakoff, *Tex.* **13** 32 10N 96 1W
Malden, *Mass.* **23** 42 26N 71 3W
Malden, *Mo.* **13** 36 34N 89 57W
Malheur →, *Oreg.* **16** 44 4N 116 59W
Malheur L., *Oreg.* **16** 43 20N 118 48W
Malibu, *Calif.* **19** 34 2N 118 41W
Malone, *N.Y.* **9** 44 51N 74 18W
Malta, *Idaho* **16** 42 18N 113 22W
Malta, *Mont.* **16** 48 21N 107 52W
Malvern, *Ark.* **13** 34 22N 92 49W
Malvern, *Pa.* **24** 40 2N 75 31W
Mammoth, *Ariz.* **17** 32 43N 110 39W
Mana, *Hawaii* **30** 22 2N 159 47W
Manasquan, *N.J.* **9** 40 8N 74 3W
Manassa, *Colo.* **17** 37 11N 105 56W
Manatí, *Puerto Rico* **30** 18 26N 66 29W
Mancelona, *Mich.* **10** 44 54N 85 4W
Manchester, *Conn.* **9** 41 47N 72 31W
Manchester, *Ga.* **11** 32 51N 84 37W
Manchester, *Iowa* **14** 42 29N 91 27W
Manchester, *Ky.* **10** 37 9N 83 46W
Manchester, *N.H.* **9** 42 59N 71 28W
Mandan, *N. Dak.* **12** 46 50N 100 54W
Mangum, *Okla.* **13** 34 53N 99 30W
Manhasset, *N.Y.* **21** 40 47N 73 39W
Manhattan, *Kans.* **12** 39 11N 96 35W
Manhattan, *N.Y.* **20** 40 48N 73 57W
Manhattan Beach, *Calif.* **29** 33 53N 118 25W
Manila, *Utah* **16** 40 59N 109 43W
Manistee, *Mich.* **10** 44 15N 86 19W
Manistee →, *Mich.* **10** 44 15N 86 21W
Manistique, *Mich.* **10** 45 57N 86 15W
Manitou Is., *Mich.* **10** 45 8N 86 0W
Manitou Springs, *Colo.* **12** 38 52N 104 55W
Manitowoc, *Wis.* **10** 44 5N 87 40W
Mankato, *Kans.* **12** 39 47N 98 13W
Mankato, *Minn.* **12** 44 10N 94 0W
Manning, *S.C.* **11** 33 42N 80 13W
Mannington, *W. Va.* **10** 39 32N 80 21W
Mansfield, *La.* **13** 32 2N 93 43W
Mansfield, *Mass.* **9** 42 2N 71 13W
Mansfield, *Ohio* **8** 40 45N 82 31W
Mansfield, *Pa.* **8** 41 48N 77 5W
Mansfield, *Wash.* **16** 47 49N 119 38W
Manteca, *Calif.* **18** 37 48N 121 13W
Manteo, *N.C.* **11** 35 55N 75 40W
Manti, *Utah* **16** 39 16N 111 38W
Manton, *Mich.* **10** 44 25N 85 24W
Manua Is., *Amer. Samoa* **31** 14 13S 169 35W
Manville, *Wyo.* **12** 42 47N 104 37W
Many, *La.* **13** 31 34N 93 29W
Manzano Mts., *N. Mex.* **17** 34 40N 106 20W
Maple Heights, *Ohio* **27** 41 25N 81 33W
Mapleton, *Oreg.* **16** 44 2N 123 52W
Maplewood, *N.J.* **20** 40 43N 74 16W
Maquoketa, *Iowa* **14** 42 4N 90 40W
Marana, *Ariz.* **17** 32 27N 111 13W
Marathon, *N.Y.* **9** 42 27N 76 2W
Marathon, *Tex.* **13** 30 12N 103 15W
Marble Falls, *Tex.* **13** 30 35N 98 16W
Marblehead, *Mass.* **23** 42 29N 70 51W
Marengo, *Iowa* **14** 41 48N 92 4W
Marfa, *Tex.* **13** 30 19N 104 1W
Mariana Trench, *Pac. Oc.* **31** 13 0N 145 0 E
Marianna, *Ark.* **13** 34 46N 90 46W
Marianna, *Fla.* **11** 30 46N 85 14W
Marias →, *Mont.* **16** 47 56N 110 30W
Maricopa, *Ariz.* **17** 33 4N 112 3W
Maricopa, *Calif.* **19** 35 4N 119 24W
Marietta, *Ga.* **11** 33 57N 84 33W
Marietta, *Ohio* **10** 39 25N 81 27W
Marin City, *Calif.* **28** 37 52N 122 30W
Marina, *Calif.* **18** 36 41N 121 48W
Marine City, *Mich.* **10** 42 43N 82 30W
Marinette, *Wis.* **10** 45 6N 87 38W
Marion, *Ala.* **11** 32 38N 87 19W
Marion, *Ill.* **14** 37 44N 88 56W
Marion, *Ind.* **15** 40 32N 85 40W
Marion, *Iowa* **14** 42 2N 91 36W
Marion, *Kans.* **12** 38 21N 97 1W
Marion, *Mich.* **10** 44 6N 85 9W
Marion, *N.C.* **11** 35 41N 82 1W
Marion, *Ohio* **15** 40 35N 83 8W
Marion, *S.C.* **11** 34 11N 79 24W
Marion, *Va.* **11** 36 50N 81 31W
Marion, L., *S.C.* **11** 33 28N 80 10W
Mariposa, *Calif.* **18** 37 29N 119 58W
Marked Tree, *Ark.* **13** 35 32N 90 25W
Markham, *Ill.* **22** 41 35N 87 41W
Markleeville, *Calif.* **18** 38 42N 119 47W
Marksville, *La.* **13** 31 8N 92 4W
Marlboro, *Mass.* **9** 42 19N 71 33W
Marlin, *Tex.* **13** 31 18N 96 54W
Marlow, *Okla.* **13** 34 39N 97 58W
Marmarth, *N. Dak.* **12** 46 18N 103 54W
Marple, *Pa.* **24** 39 56N 75 21W
Marquette, *Mich.* **10** 46 33N 87 24W
Marsh I., *La.* **13** 29 34N 91 53W
Marsh L., *Minn.* **12** 45 5N 96 0W
Marshall, *Ark.* **13** 35 55N 92 38W
Marshall, *Mich.* **15** 42 16N 84 58W
Marshall, *Minn.* **12** 44 25N 95 45W
Marshall, *Mo.* **14** 39 7N 93 12W
Marshall, *Tex.* **13** 32 33N 94 23W
Marshall Is. ■, *Pac. Oc.* **31** 9 0N 171 0 E
Marshalltown, *Iowa* **14** 42 3N 92 55W
Marshfield, *Mo.* **13** 37 15N 92 54W
Marshfield, *Wis.* **12** 44 40N 90 10W
Mart, *Tex.* **13** 31 33N 96 50W
Martha's Vineyard, *Mass.* **9** 41 25N 70 38W
Martin, *S. Dak.* **12** 43 11N 101 44W
Martin, *Tenn.* **13** 36 21N 88 51W
Martin L., *Ala.* **11** 32 41N 85 55W
Martin State National Airport, *Md.* **25** 39 19N 76 25W
Martinez, *Calif.* **18** 38 1N 122 8W
Martinsburg, *W. Va.* **10** 39 27N 77 58W
Martinsville, *Ind.* **15** 39 26N 86 25W
Martinsville, *Va.* **11** 36 41N 79 52W
Maryland □ **10** 39 0N 76 30W
Marysvale, *Utah* **17** 38 27N 112 14W
Marysville, *Calif.* **18** 39 9N 121 35W
Marysville, *Kans.* **12** 39 51N 96 39W
Marysville, *Ohio* **15** 40 14N 83 22W
Maryville, *Tenn.* **11** 35 46N 83 58W
Mason, *Nev.* **18** 38 56N 119 8W
Mason, *Tex.* **13** 30 45N 99 14W
Mason City, *Iowa* **14** 43 9N 93 12W
Massachusetts □ **9** 42 30N 72 0W
Massachusetts B., *Mass.* **9** 42 20N 70 50W
Massapequa, *N.Y.* **21** 40 41N 73 28W
Massena, *N.Y.* **9** 44 56N 74 54W
Massillon, *Ohio* **8** 40 48N 81 32W
Matagorda, *Tex.* **13** 28 42N 95 58W
Matagorda B., *Tex.* **13** 28 40N 96 0W
Matagorda I., *Tex.* **13** 28 15N 96 30W
Mathis, *Tex.* **13** 28 6N 97 50W
Mattawamkeag, *Maine* **11** 45 32N 68 21W
Mattituck, *N.Y.* **9** 40 59N 72 32W
Maui, *Hawaii* **30** 20 48N 156 20W
Maumee, *Ohio* **15** 41 34N 83 39W
Maumee →, *Ohio* **15** 41 42N 83 28W
Mauna Kea, *Hawaii* **30** 19 50N 155 28W
Mauna Loa, *Hawaii* **30** 19 30N 155 35W
Maupin, *Oreg.* **16** 45 11N 121 5W
Maurepas, L., *La.* **13** 30 15N 90 30W
Mauston, *Wis.* **12** 43 48N 90 5W
Max, *N. Dak.* **12** 47 49N 101 18W
Mayagüez, *Puerto Rico* **30** 18 12N 67 9W
Maybell, *Colo.* **16** 40 31N 108 5W
Mayer, *Ariz.* **17** 34 24N 112 14W
Mayfield, *Ky.* **11** 36 44N 88 38W
Mayfield Heights, *Ohio* **27** 41 31N 81 28W
Mayhill, *N. Mex.* **17** 32 53N 105 29W
Maysville, *Ky.* **15** 38 39N 83 46W
Mayville, *N. Dak.* **12** 47 30N 97 20W
Maywood, *Calif.* **29** 33 59N 118 12W
Maywood, *Ill.* **22** 41 52N 87 52W
McGrath, *Alaska* **30** 62 58N 155 40W
Mead, L., *Ariz.* **19** 36 1N 114 44W
Meade, *Kans.* **13** 37 17N 100 20W
Meade River = Atkasuk, *Alaska* **30** 70 30N 157 20W
Meadow Valley Wash →, *Nev.* **19** 36 40N 114 34W
Meadville, *Pa.* **8** 41 39N 80 9W
Meares, C., *Oreg.* **16** 45 37N 124 0W
Mecca, *Calif.* **19** 33 34N 116 5W
Mechanicsburg, *Pa.* **8** 40 13N 77 1W
Mechanicville, *N.Y.* **9** 42 54N 73 41W
Medford, *Mass.* **23** 42 25N 71 7W
Medford, *Oreg.* **16** 42 19N 122 52W
Medford, *Wis.* **12** 45 9N 90 20W
Media, *Pa.* **24** 39 55N 75 23W
Medical Lake, *Wash.* **16** 47 34N 117 41W
Medicine Bow, *Wyo.* **16** 41 54N 106 12W
Medicine Bow Pk., *Wyo.* **16** 41 21N 106 19W
Medicine Bow Ra., *Wyo.* **16** 41 10N 106 25W
Medicine Lake, *Mont.* **12** 48 30N 104 30W
Medicine Lodge, *Kans.* **13** 37 17N 98 35W
Medina, *N. Dak.* **12** 46 54N 99 18W
Medina, *N.Y.* **8** 43 13N 78 23W
Medina, *Ohio* **8** 41 8N 81 52W
Medina →, *Tex.* **13** 29 16N 98 29W
Medina L., *Tex.* **13** 29 32N 98 56W
Meeker, *Colo.* **16** 40 2N 107 55W
Meeteetse, *Wyo.* **16** 44 9N 108 52W
Mekoryok, *Alaska* **30** 60 20N 166 20W
Melbourne, *Fla.* **11** 28 5N 80 37W
Mellen, *Wis.* **12** 46 20N 90 40W
Mellette, *S. Dak.* **12** 45 9N 98 30W
Melrose, *Mass.* **23** 42 27N 71 2W
Melrose, *N. Mex.* **13** 34 26N 103 38W
Melrose Park, *Ill.* **22** 41 53N 87 53W
Melstone, *Mont.* **16** 46 36N 107 52W
Memphis, *Tenn.* **13** 35 8N 90 3W
Memphis, *Tex.* **13** 34 44N 100 33W
Mena, *Ark.* **13** 34 35N 94 15W
Menard, *Tex.* **13** 30 55N 99 47W
Menasha, *Wis.* **10** 44 13N 88 26W
Mendenhall, C., *Alaska* **30** 59 45N 166 10W
Mendocino, *Calif.* **16** 39 19N 123 48W
Mendocino, C., *Calif.* **16** 40 26N 124 25W
Mendota, *Calif.* **18** 36 45N 120 23W
Mendota, *Ill.* **14** 41 33N 89 7W
Menlo Park, *Calif.* **28** 37 26N 122 11W
Menominee, *Mich.* **10** 45 6N 87 37W
Menominee →, *Wis.* **10** 45 6N 87 36W
Menomonie, *Wis.* **12** 44 53N 91 55W
Mer Rouge, *La.* **13** 32 47N 91 48W
Merced, *Calif.* **18** 37 18N 120 29W
Merced Pk., *Calif.* **18** 37 36N 119 24W
Meredith, L., *Tex.* **13** 35 43N 101 33W
Meriden, *Conn.* **9** 41 32N 72 48W
Meridian, *Idaho* **16** 43 37N 116 24W
Meridian, *Miss.* **11** 32 22N 88 42W
Meridian, *Tex.* **13** 31 56N 97 39W
Merkel, *Tex.* **13** 32 28N 100 1W
Merrick, *N.Y.* **21** 40 39N 73 32W
Merrill, *Oreg.* **16** 42 1N 121 36W
Merrill, *Wis.* **12** 45 11N 89 41W
Merriman, *Nebr.* **12** 42 55N 101 42W
Merryville, *La.* **13** 30 45N 93 33W
Mertzon, *Tex.* **13** 31 16N 100 49W
Mesa, *Ariz.* **17** 33 25N 111 50W
Meshoppen, *Pa.* **9** 41 36N 76 3W
Mesick, *Mich.* **10** 44 24N 85 43W
Mesilla, *N. Mex.* **17** 32 16N 106 48W
Mesquite, *Nev.* **17** 36 47N 114 6W
Metairie, *La.* **13** 29 58N 90 10W
Metaline Falls, *Wash.* **16** 48 52N 117 22W
Methuen, *Mass.* **23** 42 43N 71 12W
Metlakatla, *Alaska* **30** 55 8N 131 35W
Metropolis, *Ill.* **13** 37 9N 88 44W
Metropolitan Oakland International Airport, *Calif.* **28** 37 43N 122 13W
Mexia, *Tex.* **13** 31 41N 96 29W
Mexico, *Mo.* **14** 39 10N 91 53W
Miami, *Ariz.* **17** 33 24N 110 52W
Miami, *Fla.* **11** 25 47N 80 11W
Miami, *Tex.* **13** 35 42N 100 38W
Miami →, *Ohio* **10** 39 20N 84 40W
Miami Beach, *Fla.* **11** 25 47N 80 8W
Miamisburg, *Ohio* **15** 39 38N 84 17W
Michelson, Mt., *Alaska* **30** 69 20N 144 20W
Michigan □ **10** 44 0N 85 0W
Michigan, L., *Mich.* **10** 44 0N 87 0W
Michigan City, *Ind.* **15** 41 43N 86 54W
Micronesia, Federated States of ■, *Pac. Oc.* **31** 11 0N 160 0 E
Middle Alkali L., *Calif.* **16** 41 27N 120 5W
Middle Loup →, *Nebr.* **12** 41 17N 98 24W
Middle River, *Md.* **25** 39 21N 76 26W
Middleburg, *N.Y.* **9** 42 36N 74 20W
Middleport, *Ohio* **10** 39 0N 82 3W
Middlesboro, *Ky.* **11** 36 36N 83 43W
Middlesex, *N.J.* **9** 40 36N 74 30W
Middleton I., *Alaska* **30** 59 26N 146 20W
Middletown, *Conn.* **9** 41 34N 72 39W
Middletown, *N.Y.* **9** 41 27N 74 25W
Middletown, *Ohio* **15** 39 31N 84 24W
Middletown, *Pa.* **9** 40 12N 76 44W
Midland, *Mich.* **10** 43 37N 84 14W
Midland, *Tex.* **13** 32 0N 102 3W
Midlothian, *Tex.* **13** 32 30N 97 0W
Midwest, *Wyo.* **16** 43 25N 106 16W
Milaca, *Minn.* **12** 45 45N 93 39W
Milan, *Mo.* **14** 40 12N 93 7W
Milan, *Tenn.* **11** 35 55N 88 46W
Milbank, *S. Dak.* **12** 45 13N 96 38W
Miles, *Tex.* **13** 31 36N 100 11W
Miles City, *Mont.* **12** 46 25N 105 51W
Milford, *Conn.* **9** 41 14N 73 3W
Milford, *Del.* **10** 38 55N 75 26W
Milford, *Mass.* **9** 42 8N 71 31W
Milford, *Pa.* **9** 41 19N 74 48W
Milford, *Utah* **17** 38 24N 113 1W
Milk →, *Mont.* **16** 48 4N 106 19W
Mill City, *Oreg.* **16** 44 45N 122 29W
Mill Valley, *Calif.* **28** 37 54N 122 32W
Millburn, *N.J.* **20** 40 43N 74 19W
Mille Lacs L., *Minn.* **12** 46 15N 93 39W
Milledgeville, *Ga.* **11** 33 5N 83 14W
Millen, *Ga.* **11** 32 48N 81 57W
Miller, *S. Dak.* **12** 44 31N 98 59W
Millersburg, *Pa.* **8** 40 32N 76 58W
Millerton, *N.Y.* **9** 41 57N 73 31W

Millerton L.

Millerton L., *Calif.* **18** 37 1N 119 41W
Millinocket, *Maine* **11** 45 39N 68 43W
Milltown, *Pa.* **24** 39 57N 75 32W
Millvale, *Pa.* **27** 40 28N 79 59W
Millville, *N.J.* **10** 39 24N 75 2W
Millwood L., *Ark.* **13** 33 42N 93 58W
Milnor, *N. Dak.* **12** 46 16N 97 27W
Milolii, *Hawaii* **30** 19 11N 155 55W
Milton, *Calif.* **18** 38 3N 120 51W
Milton, *Fla.* **11** 30 38N 87 3W
Milton, *Mass.* **23** 42 14N 71 2W
Milton, *Pa.* **8** 41 1N 76 51W
Milton-Freewater, *Oreg.* **16** 45 56N 118 23W
Milwaukee, *Wis.* **15** 43 2N 87 55W
Milwaukie, *Oreg.* **18** 45 27N 122 38W
Mina, *Nev.* **17** 38 24N 118 7W
Minden, *La.* **13** 32 37N 93 17W
Mineola, *N.Y.* **21** 40 44N 73 38W
Mineola, *Tex.* **13** 32 40N 95 29W
Mineral King, *Calif.* **18** 36 27N 118 36W
Mineral Wells, *Tex.* **13** 32 48N 98 7W
Minersville, *Pa.* **9** 40 41N 76 16W
Minersville, *Utah* **17** 38 13N 112 56W
Minetto, *N.Y.* **9** 43 24N 76 28W
Minidoka, *Idaho* **16** 42 45N 113 29W
Minneapolis, *Kans.* **12** 39 8N 97 42W
Minneapolis, *Minn.* **12** 44 59N 93 16W
Minnesota □ **12** 46 0N 94 15W
Minot, *N. Dak.* **12** 48 14N 101 18W
Minto, *Alaska* **30** 64 53N 149 11W
Minturn, *Colo.* **16** 39 35N 106 26W
Mirando City, *Tex.* **13** 27 26N 99 0W
Mishawaka, *Ind.* **15** 41 40N 86 11W
Mission, *S. Dak.* **12** 43 18N 100 39W
Mission, *Tex.* **13** 26 13N 98 20W
Mississippi □ **13** 33 0N 90 0W
Mississippi →, *La.* **13** 29 9N 89 15W
Mississippi River Delta, *La.* **13** 29 10N 89 15W
Mississippi Sd., *Miss.* **13** 30 20N 89 0W
Missoula, *Mont.* **16** 46 52N 114 1W
Missouri □ **12** 38 25N 92 30W
Missouri →, *Mo.* **12** 38 49N 90 7W
Missouri Valley, *Iowa* **12** 41 34N 95 53W
Mitchell, *Ind.* **15** 38 44N 86 28W
Mitchell, *Nebr.* **12** 41 57N 103 49W
Mitchell, *Oreg.* **16** 44 34N 120 9W
Mitchell, *S. Dak.* **12** 43 43N 98 2W
Mitchell, Mt., *N.C.* **11** 35 46N 82 16W
Moab, *Utah* **17** 38 35N 109 33W
Moberly, *Mo.* **14** 39 25N 92 26W
Mobile, *Ala.* **11** 30 41N 88 3W
Mobile B., *Ala.* **11** 30 30N 88 0W
Mobridge, *S. Dak.* **12** 45 32N 100 26W
Moclips, *Wash.* **18** 47 14N 124 13W
Modena, *Utah* **17** 37 48N 113 56W
Modesto, *Calif.* **18** 37 39N 121 0W
Mohall, *N. Dak.* **12** 48 46N 101 31W
Mohawk →, *N.Y.* **9** 42 47N 73 41W
Mohican, C., *Alaska* **30** 60 12N 167 25W
Mojave, *Calif.* **19** 35 3N 118 10W
Mojave Desert, *Calif.* **19** 35 0N 116 30W
Mokelumne →, *Calif.* **18** 38 13N 121 28W
Mokelumne Hill, *Calif.* **18** 38 18N 120 43W
Moline, *Ill.* **14** 41 30N 90 31W
Molokai, *Hawaii* **30** 21 8N 157 0W
Monahans, *Tex.* **13** 31 36N 102 54W
Mondovi, *Wis.* **12** 44 34N 91 40W
Monessen, *Pa.* **8** 40 9N 79 54W
Monett, *Mo.* **13** 36 55N 93 55W
Monmouth, *Ill.* **14** 40 55N 90 39W
Mono L., *Calif.* **18** 38 1N 119 1W
Monolith, *Calif.* **19** 35 7N 118 22W
Monroe, *Ga.* **11** 33 47N 83 43W
Monroe, *La.* **13** 32 30N 92 7W
Monroe, *Mich.* **15** 41 55N 83 24W
Monroe, *N.C.* **11** 34 59N 80 33W
Monroe, *Utah* **17** 38 38N 112 7W
Monroe, *Wis.* **14** 42 36N 89 38W
Monroe City, *Mo.* **14** 39 39N 91 44W
Monroeville, *Ala.* **11** 31 31N 87 20W
Monroeville, *Pa.* **27** 40 26N 79 46W
Monrovia, *Calif.* **29** 34 9N 118 1W
Montague, *Calif.* **16** 41 44N 122 32W
Montague I., *Alaska* **30** 60 0N 147 30W
Montalvo, *Calif.* **19** 34 15N 119 12W
Montana □ **16** 47 0N 110 0W
Montauk, *N.Y.* **9** 41 3N 71 57W
Montauk Pt., *N.Y.* **9** 41 4N 71 52W
Montclair, *N.J.* **20** 40 49N 74 12W
Monte Vista, *Colo.* **17** 37 35N 106 9W
Montebello, *Calif.* **29** 34 1N 118 8W
Montecito, *Calif.* **19** 34 26N 119 40W
Montello, *Wis.* **12** 43 48N 89 20W
Monterey, *Calif.* **18** 36 37N 121 55W
Monterey B., *Calif.* **18** 36 45N 122 0W
Monterey Park, *Calif.* **29** 34 3N 118 7W
Montesano, *Wash.* **18** 46 59N 123 36W
Montevideo, *Minn.* **12** 44 57N 95 43W
Montezuma, *Iowa* **14** 41 35N 92 32W
Montgomery, *Ala.* **11** 32 23N 86 19W
Montgomery, *W. Va.* **10** 38 11N 81 19W
Monticello, *Ark.* **13** 33 38N 91 47W
Monticello, *Fla.* **11** 30 33N 83 52W
Monticello, *Ind.* **15** 40 45N 86 46W
Monticello, *Iowa* **14** 42 15N 91 12W
Monticello, *Ky.* **11** 36 50N 84 51W
Monticello, *Minn.* **12** 45 18N 93 48W
Monticello, *Miss.* **13** 31 33N 90 7W
Monticello, *N.Y.* **9** 41 39N 74 42W
Monticello, *Utah* **17** 37 52N 109 21W
Montour Falls, *N.Y.* **8** 42 21N 76 51W
Montpelier, *Idaho* **16** 42 19N 111 18W
Montpelier, *Md.* **25** 39 3N 76 50W
Montpelier, *Ohio* **15** 41 35N 84 37W
Montpelier, *Vt.* **9** 44 16N 72 35W
Montrose, *Colo.* **17** 38 29N 107 53W
Montrose, *Pa.* **9** 41 50N 75 53W
Moorcroft, *Wyo.* **12** 44 16N 104 57W
Moorefield, *W. Va.* **10** 39 5N 78 59W
Mooresville, *N.C.* **11** 35 35N 80 48W
Moorhead, *Minn.* **12** 46 53N 96 45W
Moorpark, *Calif.* **19** 34 17N 118 53W
Moose Lake, *Minn.* **12** 46 27N 92 46W
Moosehead L., *Maine* **11** 45 38N 69 40W
Moosup, *Conn.* **9** 41 43N 71 53W
Mora, *Minn.* **12** 45 53N 93 18W
Mora, *N. Mex.* **17** 35 58N 105 20W
Moran, *Kans.* **13** 37 55N 95 10W
Moran, *Wyo.* **16** 43 53N 110 37W
Moravia, *Iowa* **14** 40 53N 92 49W
Moreau →, *S. Dak.* **12** 45 18N 100 43W
Morehead, *Ky.* **15** 38 11N 83 26W
Morehead City, *N.C.* **11** 34 43N 76 43W
Morenci, *Ariz.* **17** 33 5N 109 22W
Morgan, *Utah* **16** 41 2N 111 41W
Morgan City, *La.* **13** 29 42N 91 12W
Morgan Hill, *Calif.* **18** 37 8N 121 39W
Morganfield, *Ky.* **10** 37 41N 87 55W
Morganton, *N.C.* **11** 35 45N 81 41W
Morgantown, *W. Va.* **10** 39 38N 79 57W
Morongo Valley, *Calif.* **19** 34 3N 116 37W
Morrilton, *Ark.* **13** 35 9N 92 44W
Morris, *Ill.* **15** 41 22N 88 26W
Morris, *Minn.* **12** 45 35N 95 55W
Morrison, *Ill.* **14** 41 49N 89 58W
Morristown, *Ariz.* **17** 33 51N 112 37W
Morristown, *N.J.* **20** 40 48N 74 26W
Morristown, *S. Dak.* **12** 45 56N 101 43W
Morristown, *Tenn.* **11** 36 13N 83 18W
Morro Bay, *Calif.* **18** 35 22N 120 51W
Morton, *Tex.* **13** 33 44N 102 46W
Morton, *Wash.* **18** 46 34N 122 17W
Morton Grove, *Ill.* **22** 42 2N 87 45W
Moscow, *Idaho* **16** 46 44N 117 0W
Moses Lake, *Wash.* **16** 47 8N 119 17W
Mosquero, *N. Mex.* **13** 35 47N 103 58W
Mott, *N. Dak.* **12** 46 23N 102 20W
Moulton, *Tex.* **13** 29 35N 97 9W
Moultrie, *Ga.* **11** 31 11N 83 47W
Moultrie, L., *S.C.* **11** 33 20N 80 5W
Mound City, *Mo.* **12** 40 7N 95 14W
Mound City, *S. Dak.* **12** 45 44N 100 4W
Moundsville, *W. Va.* **8** 39 55N 80 44W
Mount Airy, *N.C.* **11** 36 31N 80 37W
Mount Angel, *Oreg.* **16** 45 4N 122 48W
Mount Carmel, *Ill.* **15** 38 25N 87 46W
Mount Clemens, *Mich.* **8** 42 35N 82 53W
Mount Clemens, *Mich.* **26** 42 35N 82 53W
Mount Desert I., *Maine* **11** 44 21N 68 20W
Mount Dora, *Fla.* **11** 28 48N 81 38W
Mount Edgecumbe, *Alaska* **30** 57 3N 135 21W
Mount Hope, *W. Va.* **10** 37 54N 81 10W
Mount Horeb, *Wis.* **14** 43 1N 89 44W
Mount Laguna, *Calif.* **19** 32 52N 116 25W
Mount Lebanon, *Pa.* **27** 40 22N 80 2W
Mount McKinley National Park, *Alaska* **30** 63 30N 150 0W
Mount Morris, *N.Y.* **8** 42 44N 77 52W
Mount Oliver, *Pa.* **27** 40 24N 79 59W
Mount Pleasant, *Iowa* **14** 40 58N 91 33W
Mount Pleasant, *Mich.* **10** 43 36N 84 46W
Mount Pleasant, *S.C.* **11** 32 47N 79 52W
Mount Pleasant, *Tenn.* **11** 35 32N 87 12W
Mount Pleasant, *Tex.* **13** 33 9N 94 58W
Mount Pleasant, *Utah* **16** 39 33N 111 27W
Mount Pocono, *Pa.* **9** 41 7N 75 22W
Mount Prospect, *Ill.* **22** 42 3N 87 55W
Mount Rainier National Park, *Wash.* **18** 46 55N 121 50W
Mount Royal, *N.J.* **24** 39 48N 75 13W
Mount Shasta, *Calif.* **16** 41 19N 122 19W
Mount Sterling, *Ill.* **14** 39 59N 90 45W
Mount Sterling, *Ky.* **15** 38 4N 83 56W
Mount Vernon, *Ind.* **15** 38 17N 88 57W
Mount Vernon, *N.Y.* **21** 40 54N 73 49W
Mount Vernon, *Ohio* **8** 40 23N 82 29W
Mount Vernon, *Wash.* **18** 48 25N 122 20W
Mount Wilson Observatory, *Calif.* **29** 34 13N 118 4W
Mountain Center, *Calif.* **19** 33 42N 116 44W
Mountain City, *Nev.* **16** 41 50N 115 58W
Mountain City, *Tenn.* **11** 36 29N 81 48W
Mountain Grove, *Mo.* **13** 37 8N 92 16W
Mountain Home, *Ark.* **13** 36 20N 92 23W
Mountain Home, *Idaho* **16** 43 8N 115 41W
Mountain Iron, *Minn.* **12** 47 32N 92 37W
Mountain View, *Ark.* **13** 35 52N 92 7W
Mountain View, *Calif.* **18** 37 23N 122 5W
Mountain Village, *Alaska* **30** 62 5N 163 43W
Mountainair, *N. Mex.* **17** 34 31N 106 15W
Muddy Cr. →, *Utah* **17** 38 24N 110 42W
Mule Creek, *Wyo.* **12** 43 19N 104 8W
Muleshoe, *Tex.* **13** 34 13N 102 43W
Mullen, *Nebr.* **12** 42 3N 101 1W
Mullens, *W. Va.* **10** 37 35N 81 23W
Mullin, *Tex.* **13** 31 33N 98 40W
Mullins, *S.C.* **11** 34 12N 79 15W
Mulvane, *Kans.* **13** 37 29N 97 15W
Muncie, *Ind.* **15** 40 12N 85 23W
Munday, *Tex.* **13** 33 27N 99 38W
Munhall, *Pa.* **27** 40 24N 79 54W
Munising, *Mich.* **10** 46 25N 86 40W
Murdo, *S. Dak.* **12** 43 53N 100 43W
Murfreesboro, *Tenn.* **11** 35 51N 86 24W
Murphy, *Idaho* **16** 43 13N 116 33W
Murphys, *Calif.* **18** 38 8N 120 28W
Murphysboro, *Ill.* **14** 37 46N 89 20W
Murray, *Ky.* **11** 36 37N 88 19W
Murray, *Utah* **16** 40 40N 111 53W
Murray, L., *S.C.* **11** 34 3N 81 13W
Murrieta, *Calif.* **19** 33 33N 117 13W
Murrysville, *Pa.* **27** 40 25N 79 41W
Muscatine, *Iowa* **14** 41 25N 91 3W
Muskegon, *Mich.* **15** 43 14N 86 16W
Muskegon →, *Mich.* **10** 43 14N 86 21W
Muskegon Heights, *Mich.* **15** 43 12N 86 16W
Muskogee, *Okla.* **13** 35 45N 95 22W
Musselshell →, *Mont.* **16** 47 21N 107 57W
Myerstown, *Pa.* **9** 40 22N 76 19W
Myrtle Beach, *S.C.* **11** 33 42N 78 53W
Myrtle Creek, *Oreg.* **16** 43 1N 123 17W
Myrtle Point, *Oreg.* **16** 43 4N 124 8W
Mystic, *Conn.* **9** 41 21N 71 58W
Myton, *Utah* **16** 40 12N 110 4W

N

Naalehu, *Hawaii* **30** 19 4N 155 35W
Nabesna, *Alaska* **30** 62 22N 143 0W
Naches, *Wash.* **16** 46 44N 120 42W
Nacimiento Reservoir, *Calif.* **18** 35 46N 120 53W
Naco, *Ariz.* **17** 31 20N 109 57W
Nacogdoches, *Tex.* **13** 31 36N 94 39W
Nakalele Pt., *Hawaii* **30** 21 2N 156 35W
Naknek, *Alaska* **30** 58 44N 157 1W
Nampa, *Idaho* **16** 43 34N 116 34W
Nanticoke, *Pa.* **9** 41 12N 76 0W
Napa, *Calif.* **18** 38 18N 122 17W
Napa →, *Calif.* **18** 38 10N 122 19W
Napamute, *Alaska* **30** 61 30N 158 45W
Napanoch, *N.Y.* **9** 41 44N 74 22W
Naples, *Fla.* **11** 26 8N 81 48W
Napoleon, *N. Dak.* **12** 46 30N 99 46W
Napoleon, *Ohio* **15** 41 23N 84 8W
Nara Visa, *N. Mex.* **13** 35 37N 103 6W
Narrows, The, *N.Y.* **20** 40 37N 74 3W
Nashua, *Iowa* **14** 42 57N 92 32W
Nashua, *Mont.* **16** 48 8N 106 22W
Nashua, *N.H.* **9** 42 45N 71 28W
Nashville, *Ark.* **13** 33 57N 93 51W
Nashville, *Ga.* **11** 31 12N 83 15W
Nashville, *Tenn.* **11** 36 10N 86 47W
Nassau, *N.Y.* **9** 42 31N 73 37W
Natchez, *Miss.* **13** 31 34N 91 24W
Natchitoches, *La.* **13** 31 46N 93 5W
Natick, *Mass.* **23** 42 16N 71 21W
National City, *Calif.* **19** 32 41N 117 6W
Natoma, *Kans.* **12** 39 11N 99 2W
Navajo Reservoir, *N. Mex.* **17** 36 48N 107 36W
Navasota, *Tex.* **13** 30 23N 96 5W
Neah Bay, *Wash.* **18** 48 22N 124 37W
Near Is., *Alaska* **30** 53 0N 172 0 E
Nebraska □ **12** 41 30N 99 30W
Nebraska City, *Nebr.* **12** 40 41N 95 52W
Necedah, *Wis.* **12** 44 2N 90 4W
Neches →, *Tex.* **13** 29 58N 93 51W
Needham, *Mass.* **23** 42 16N 71 13W
Needles, *Calif.* **19** 34 51N 114 37W
Neenah, *Wis.* **10** 44 11N 88 28W
Negaunee, *Mich.* **10** 46 30N 87 36W
Neihart, *Mont.* **16** 47 0N 110 44W
Neilton, *Wash.* **16** 47 25N 123 53W
Neligh, *Nebr.* **12** 42 8N 98 2W
Nelson, *Ariz.* **17** 35 31N 113 19W
Nelson I., *Alaska* **30** 60 40N 164 40W
Nenana, *Alaska* **30** 64 34N 149 5W
Neodesha, *Kans.* **13** 37 25N 95 41W
Neosho, *Mo.* **13** 36 52N 94 22W
Neosho →, *Okla.* **13** 36 48N 95 18W
Nephi, *Utah* **16** 39 43N 111 50W
Neptune, *N.J.* **9** 40 13N 74 2W
Neuse →, *N.C.* **11** 35 6N 76 29W
Nevada, *Mo.* **14** 37 51N 94 22W
Nevada □ **16** 39 0N 117 0W
Nevada, Sierra, *Calif.* **16** 39 0N 120 30W
Nevada City, *Calif.* **18** 39 16N 121 1W
Neville Island, *Pa.* **27** 40 30N 80 6W
New Albany, *Ind.* **15** 38 18N 85 49W
New Albany, *Miss.* **13** 34 29N 89 0W
New Albany, *Pa.* **9** 41 36N 76 27W
New Bedford, *Mass.* **9** 41 38N 70 56W
New Bern, *N.C.* **11** 35 7N 77 3W
New Boston, *Tex.* **13** 33 28N 94 25W
New Braunfels, *Tex.* **13** 29 42N 98 8W
New Britain, *Conn.* **9** 41 40N 72 47W
New Brunswick, *N.J.* **9** 40 30N 74 27W
New Carrollton, *Md.* **25** 38 58N 76 53W
New Castle, *Ind.* **15** 39 55N 85 22W
New Castle, *Pa.* **8** 41 0N 80 21W
New City, *N.Y.* **9** 41 9N 73 59W
New Cuyama, *Calif.* **19** 34 57N 119 38W
New Don Pedro Reservoir, *Calif.* **18** 37 43N 120 24W
New Dorp, *N.Y.* **20** 40 34N 74 8W
New England, *N. Dak.* **12** 46 32N 102 52W
New Hampshire □ **9** 44 0N 71 30W
New Hampton, *Iowa* **14** 43 3N 92 19W
New Haven, *Conn.* **9** 41 18N 72 55W
New Hyde Park, *N.Y.* **21** 40 43N 73 39W
New Iberia, *La.* **13** 30 1N 91 49W
New Jersey □ **9** 40 0N 74 30W
New Kensington, *Pa.* **8** 40 34N 79 46W
New Kensington, *Pa.* **27** 40 34N 79 46W
New Lexington, *Ohio* **10** 39 43N 82 13W
New London, *Conn.* **9** 41 22N 72 6W
New London, *Minn.* **12** 45 18N 94 56W
New London, *Wis.* **12** 44 23N 88 45W
New Madrid, *Mo.* **13** 36 36N 89 32W
New Meadows, *Idaho* **16** 44 58N 116 18W
New Melones L., *Calif.* **18** 37 57N 120 31W
New Mexico □ **17** 34 30N 106 0W
New Milford, *Conn.* **9** 41 35N 73 25W
New Milford, *Pa.* **9** 41 52N 75 44W
New Orleans, *La.* **13** 29 58N 90 4W
New Philadelphia, *Ohio* **8** 40 30N 81 27W
New Plymouth, *Idaho* **16** 43 58N 116 49W
New Providence, *N.J.* **20** 40 42N 74 23W
New Richmond, *Wis.* **12** 45 7N 92 32W
New Roads, *La.* **13** 30 42N 91 26W
New Rochelle, *N.Y.* **21** 40 55N 73 45W
New Rockford, *N. Dak.* **12** 47 41N 99 8W
New Salem, *N. Dak.* **12** 46 51N 101 25W
New Smyrna Beach, *Fla.* **11** 29 1N 80 56W
New Town, *N. Dak.* **12** 47 59N 102 30W
New Ulm, *Minn.* **12** 44 19N 94 28W
New York, *N.Y.* **20** 40 42N 74 0W
New York □ **9** 43 0N 75 0W
Newark, *Del.* **10** 39 41N 75 46W
Newark, *N.J.* **20** 40 43N 74 10W
Newark, *N.Y.* **8** 43 3N 77 6W
Newark, *Ohio* **8** 40 3N 82 24W
Newark International Airport, *N.J.* **20** 40 41N 74 10W
Newaygo, *Mich.* **10** 43 25N 85 48W
Newberg, *Oreg.* **16** 45 18N 122 58W
Newberry, *Mich.* **10** 46 21N 85 30W
Newberry, *S.C.* **11** 34 17N 81 37W
Newberry Springs, *Calif.* **19** 34 50N 116 41W
Newburgh, *N.Y.* **9** 41 30N 74 1W
Newburyport, *Mass.* **9** 42 49N 70 53W
Newcastle, *Wyo.* **12** 43 50N 104 11W
Newell, *S. Dak.* **12** 44 43N 103 25W
Newenham, C., *Alaska* **30** 58 39N 162 11W
Newhalen, *Alaska* **30** 59 43N 154 54W
Newhall, *Calif.* **19** 34 23N 118 32W
Newkirk, *Okla.* **13** 36 53N 97 3W
Newman, *Calif.* **18** 37 19N 121 1W
Newmarket, *N.H.* **9** 43 5N 70 56W
Newnan, *Ga.* **11** 33 23N 84 48W
Newport, *Ark.* **13** 35 37N 91 16W
Newport, *Ky.* **15** 39 5N 84 30W
Newport, *N.H.* **9** 43 22N 72 10W
Newport, *Oreg.* **16** 44 39N 124 3W
Newport, *R.I.* **9** 41 29N 71 19W
Newport, *Tenn.* **11** 35 58N 83 11W
Newport, *Vt.* **9** 44 56N 72 13W
Newport, *Wash.* **16** 48 11N 117 3W
Newport Beach, *Calif.* **19** 33 37N 117 56W
Newport News, *Va.* **10** 36 59N 76 25W
Newton, *Iowa* **14** 41 42N 93 3W
Newton, *Mass.* **23** 42 19N 71 13W
Newton, *Miss.* **13** 32 19N 89 10W
Newton, *N.C.* **11** 35 40N 81 13W
Newton, *N.J.* **9** 41 3N 74 45W
Newton, *Tex.* **13** 30 51N 93 46W
Newtown Square, *Pa.* **24** 39 59N 75 24W
Nezperce, *Idaho* **16** 46 14N 116 14W
Niagara, *Mich.* **10** 45 45N 88 0W
Niagara Falls, *N.Y.* **8** 43 5N 79 4W
Niceville, *Fla.* **11** 30 31N 86 30W
Nicholasville, *Ky.* **15** 37 53N 84 34W
Nichols, *N.Y.* **9** 42 1N 76 22W
Nicholson, *Pa.* **9** 41 37N 75 47W
Niihau, *Hawaii* **30** 21 54N 160 9W
Nikolski, *Alaska* **30** 52 56N 168 52W
Niland, *Calif.* **19** 33 14N 115 31W
Niles, *Ill.* **22** 42 1N 87 48W
Niles, *Ohio* **8** 41 11N 80 46W
Niobrara, *Nebr.* **12** 42 45N 98 2W
Niobrara →, *Nebr.* **12** 42 46N 98 3W
Nipomo, *Calif.* **19** 35 3N 120 29W
Nixon, *Tex.* **13** 29 16N 97 46W
Noatak, *Alaska* **30** 67 34N 162 58W
Noatak →, *Alaska* **30** 68 0N 161 0W
Noblesville, *Ind.* **15** 40 3N 86 1W
Nocona, *Tex.* **13** 33 47N 97 44W
Noel, *Mo.* **13** 36 33N 94 29W
Nogales, *Ariz.* **17** 31 20N 110 56W
Nome, *Alaska* **30** 64 30N 165 25W
Nonopapa, *Hawaii* **30** 21 50N 160 15W
Noonan, *N. Dak.* **12** 48 54N 103 1W
Noorvik, *Alaska* **30** 66 50N 161 3W
Norco, *Calif.* **19** 33 56N 117 33W
Norfolk, *Nebr.* **12** 42 2N 97 25W
Norfolk, *Va.* **10** 36 51N 76 17W
Norfork Res., *Ark.* **13** 36 13N 92 15W
Normal, *Ill.* **14** 40 31N 88 59W
Norman, *Okla.* **13** 35 13N 97 26W
Norridge, *Ill.* **22** 41 57N 87 49W

Perry

Norris, Mont. 16 45 34N 111 41W
Norristown, Pa. 24 40 7N 75 20W
North Adams, Mass. 9 42 42N 73 7W
North Bend, Oreg. 16 43 24N 124 14W
North Bergen, N.J. 20 40 48N 74 0W
North Berwick, Maine 9 43 18N 70 44W
North Billerica, Mass. 23 42 35N 71 16W
North Braddock, Pa. 27 40 25N 79 51W
North Canadian →, Okla. 13 35 16N 95 31W
North Carolina □ 11 35 30N 80 0W
North Chelmsford, Mass. 23 42 38N 71 23W
North Chicago, Ill. 15 42 19N 87 51W
North Dakota □ 12 47 30N 100 15W
North Fork, Calif. 18 37 14N 119 21W
North Las Vegas, Nev. 19 36 12N 115 7W
North Loup →, Nebr. 12 41 17N 98 24W
North Olmsted, Ohio 27 41 24N 81 55W
North Palisade, Calif. 18 37 6N 118 31W
North Platte, Nebr. 12 41 8N 100 46W
North Platte →, Nebr. 12 41 7N 100 42W
North Powder, Oreg. 16 45 2N 117 55W
North Reading, Mass. 23 42 34N 71 5W
North Richmond, Calif. 28 37 57N 122 22W
North Springfield, Va. 25 38 48N 77 12W
North Tonawanda, N.Y. 8 43 2N 78 53W
North Truchas Pk., N. Mex. 17 36 0N 105 30W
North Vernon, Ind. 15 39 0N 85 38W
Northampton, Mass. 9 42 19N 72 38W
Northampton, Pa. 9 40 41N 75 30W
Northbridge, Mass. 9 42 9N 71 39W
Northbrook, Ill. 22 42 7N 87 53W
Northern Marianas ■, Pac. Oc. 31 17 0N 145 0 E
Northfield, Ill. 22 42 5N 87 44W
Northfield, Minn. 12 44 27N 93 9W
Northlake, Ill. 22 41 54N 87 53W
Northome, Minn. 12 47 52N 94 17W
Northport, Ala. 11 33 14N 87 35W
Northport, Mich. 10 45 8N 85 37W
Northport, Wash. 16 48 55N 117 48W
Northway, Alaska 30 62 58N 141 56W
Northwood, Iowa 12 43 27N 93 13W
Northwood, N. Dak. 12 47 44N 97 34W
Norton, Kans. 12 39 50N 99 53W
Norton B., Alaska 30 64 45N 161 15W
Norton Sd., Alaska 30 63 50N 164 0W
Norwalk, Calif. 29 33 54N 118 4W
Norwalk, Conn. 9 41 7N 73 22W
Norwalk, Ohio 8 41 15N 82 37W
Norway, Mich. 10 45 47N 87 55W
Norwich, Conn. 9 41 31N 72 5W
Norwich, N.Y. 9 42 32N 75 32W
Norwood, Mass. 23 42 11N 71 13W
Nottoway →, Va. 10 36 33N 76 55W
Novato, Calif. 18 38 6N 122 35W
Noxen, Pa. 9 41 25N 76 4W
Noxon, Mont. 16 48 0N 115 43W
Nueces →, Tex. 13 27 51N 97 30W
Nulato, Alaska 30 64 43N 158 6W
Nunivak I., Alaska 30 60 10N 166 30W
Nutley, N.J. 20 40 49N 74 9W
Nyack, N.Y. 9 41 5N 73 55W
Nyssa, Oreg. 16 43 53N 117 0W

O

Oacoma, S. Dak. 12 43 48N 99 24W
Oahe, L., S. Dak. 12 44 27N 100 24W
Oahe Dam, S. Dak. 12 44 27N 100 24W
Oahu, Hawaii 30 21 28N 157 58W
Oak Creek, Colo. 16 40 16N 106 57W
Oak Forest, Ill. 22 41 36N 87 44W
Oak Harbor, Wash. 18 48 18N 122 39W
Oak Hill, W. Va. 10 37 59N 81 9W
Oak Lawn, Ill. 22 41 42N 87 44W
Oak Park, Ill. 22 41 52N 87 46W
Oak Park, Mich. 26 42 27N 83 11W
Oak Ridge, Tenn. 11 36 1N 84 16W
Oak View, Calif. 19 34 24N 119 18W
Oakdale, Calif. 18 37 46N 120 51W
Oakdale, La. 13 30 49N 92 40W
Oakes, N. Dak. 12 46 8N 98 6W
Oakesdale, Wash. 16 47 8N 117 15W
Oakhurst, Calif. 18 37 19N 119 40W
Oakland, Calif. 28 37 48N 122 17W
Oakland, N.J. 20 41 2N 74 13W
Oakland, Oreg. 16 43 25N 123 18W
Oakland City, Ind. 15 38 20N 87 21W
Oakland Pontiac Airport, Mich. 26 42 40N 83 24W
Oakley, Idaho 16 42 15N 113 53W
Oakley, Kans. 12 39 8N 100 51W
Oakmont, Pa. 27 40 31N 79 50W
Oakridge, Oreg. 16 43 45N 122 28W
Oasis, Calif. 19 33 28N 116 6W
Oasis, Nev. 18 37 29N 117 55W
Oatman, Ariz. 19 35 1N 114 19W
Oberlin, Kans. 12 39 49N 100 32W
Oberlin, La. 13 30 37N 92 46W
Ocala, Fla. 11 29 11N 82 8W
Oconomowoc, Wis. 12 43 7N 88 30W
Ocate, N. Mex. 13 36 11N 105 3W
Ocean City, N.J. 10 39 17N 74 35W
Ocean Park, Wash. 18 46 30N 124 3W
Oceano, Calif. 19 35 6N 120 37W
Oceanside, Calif. 19 33 12N 117 23W
Oceanside, N.Y. 21 40 38N 73 37W
Ocilla, Ga. 11 31 36N 83 15W
Ocmulgee →, Ga. 11 31 58N 82 33W
Oconee →, Ga. 11 31 58N 82 33W
Oconto, Wis. 10 44 53N 87 52W
Oconto Falls, Wis. 10 44 52N 88 9W
Octave, Ariz. 17 34 10N 112 43W
Odessa, Tex. 13 31 52N 102 23W
Odessa, Wash. 16 47 20N 118 41W
O'Donnell, Tex. 13 32 58N 101 50W
Oelrichs, S. Dak. 12 43 11N 103 14W
Oelwein, Iowa 12 42 41N 91 55W
Ofu, Amer. Samoa 31 14 11S 169 41W
Ogallala, Nebr. 12 41 8N 101 43W
Ogden, Iowa 14 42 2N 94 2W
Ogden, Utah 16 41 13N 111 58W
Ogdensburg, N.Y. 9 44 42N 75 30W
Ogeechee →, Ga. 11 31 50N 81 3W
Ohio □ 10 40 15N 82 45W
Ohio →, Ohio 10 36 59N 89 8W
Oil City, Pa. 8 41 26N 79 42W
Oildale, Calif. 19 35 25N 119 1W
Ojai, Calif. 19 34 27N 119 15W
Okanogan, Wash. 16 48 22N 119 35W
Okanogan →, Wash. 16 48 6N 119 44W
Okeechobee, Fla. 11 27 15N 80 50W
Okeechobee, L., Fla. 11 27 0N 80 50W
Okefenokee Swamp, Ga. 11 30 40N 82 20W
Oklahoma □ 13 35 20N 97 30W
Oklahoma City, Okla. 13 35 30N 97 30W
Okmulgee, Okla. 13 35 37N 95 58W
Okolona, Miss. 13 34 0N 88 45W
Ola, Ark. 13 35 2N 93 13W
Olancha, Calif. 19 36 17N 118 1W
Olancha Pk., Calif. 19 36 15N 118 7W
Olathe, Kans. 12 38 53N 94 49W
Old Baldy Pk. = San Antonio, Mt., Calif. 19 34 17N 117 38W
Old Dale, Calif. 19 34 8N 115 47W
Old Forge, N.Y. 9 43 43N 74 58W
Old Forge, Pa. 9 41 22N 75 45W
Old Harbor, Alaska 30 57 12N 153 18W
Old Town, Maine 11 44 56N 68 39W
Olean, N.Y. 8 42 5N 78 26W
Olema, Calif. 18 38 3N 122 47W
Olney, Ill. 15 38 44N 88 5W
Olney, Tex. 13 33 22N 98 45W
Olosega, Amer. Samoa 31 14 11S 169 38W
Olton, Tex. 13 34 11N 102 8W
Olympia, Wash. 18 47 3N 122 53W
Olympic Mts., Wash. 18 47 55N 123 45W
Olympic Nat. Park, Wash. 18 47 48N 123 30W
Olympus, Mt., Wash. 18 47 48N 123 43W
Omaha, Nebr. 12 41 17N 95 58W
Omak, Wash. 16 48 25N 119 31W
Onaga, Kans. 12 39 29N 96 10W
Onalaska, Wis. 12 43 53N 91 14W
Onamia, Minn. 12 46 4N 93 40W
Onancock, Va. 10 37 43N 75 45W
Onawa, Iowa 12 42 2N 96 6W
Onaway, Mich. 10 45 21N 84 14W
Oneida, N.Y. 9 43 6N 75 39W
Oneida L., N.Y. 9 43 12N 75 54W
O'Neill, Nebr. 12 42 27N 98 39W
Oneonta, Ala. 11 33 57N 86 28W
Oneonta, N.Y. 9 42 27N 75 4W
Onida, S. Dak. 12 44 42N 100 4W
Onslow B., N.C. 11 34 20N 77 15W
Ontario, Calif. 19 34 4N 117 39W
Ontario, Oreg. 16 44 2N 116 58W
Ontario, L., N. Amer. 8 43 20N 78 0W
Ontonagon, Mich. 12 46 52N 89 19W
Onyx, Calif. 19 35 41N 118 14W
Ookala, Hawaii 30 20 1N 155 17W
Opelousas, La. 13 30 32N 92 5W
Opheim, Mont. 16 48 51N 106 24W
Ophir, Alaska 30 63 10N 156 31W
Opp, Ala. 11 31 17N 86 16W
Oracle, Ariz. 17 32 37N 110 46W
Orange, Calif. 19 33 47N 117 51W
Orange, Mass. 9 42 35N 72 19W
Orange, N.J. 20 40 46N 74 13W
Orange, Tex. 13 30 6N 93 44W
Orange, Va. 10 38 15N 78 7W
Orange Cove, Calif. 18 36 38N 119 19W
Orange Grove, Tex. 13 27 58N 97 56W
Orangeburg, S.C. 11 33 30N 80 52W
Orcutt, Calif. 19 34 52N 120 27W
Orderville, Utah 17 37 17N 112 38W
Ordway, Colo. 12 38 13N 103 46W
Oregon, Ill. 14 42 1N 89 20W
Oregon □ 16 44 0N 121 0W
Oregon City, Oreg. 18 45 21N 122 36W
Orem, Utah 16 40 19N 111 42W
Orinda, Calif. 28 37 52N 122 10W
Orland, Calif. 18 39 45N 122 12W
Orland Park, Ill. 22 41 37N 87 52W
Orlando, Fla. 11 28 33N 81 23W
Ormond Beach, Fla. 11 29 17N 81 3W
Oro Grande, Calif. 19 34 36N 117 20W
Orogrande, N. Mex. 17 32 24N 106 5W
Oroville, Calif. 18 39 31N 121 33W
Oroville, Wash. 16 48 56N 119 26W
Osage, Iowa 12 43 17N 92 49W
Osage, Wyo. 12 43 59N 104 25W
Osage →, Mo. 14 38 35N 91 57W
Osage City, Kans. 12 38 38N 95 50W
Osawatomie, Kans. 12 38 31N 94 57W
Osborne, Kans. 12 39 26N 98 42W
Osceola, Ark. 13 35 42N 89 58W
Osceola, Iowa 14 41 2N 93 46W
Oscoda, Mich. 8 44 26N 83 20W
Oshkosh, Nebr. 12 41 24N 102 21W
Oshkosh, Wis. 12 44 1N 88 33W
Oskaloosa, Iowa 14 41 18N 92 39W
Ossabaw I., Ga. 11 31 50N 81 5W
Ossining, N.Y. 9 41 10N 73 55W
Oswego, N.Y. 9 43 27N 76 31W
Othello, Wash. 16 46 50N 119 10W
Otis, Colo. 12 40 9N 102 58W
Ottawa, Ill. 15 41 21N 88 51W
Ottawa, Kans. 12 38 37N 95 16W
Ottumwa, Iowa 14 41 1N 92 25W
Ouachita →, La. 13 31 38N 91 49W
Ouachita, L., Ark. 13 34 34N 93 12W
Ouachita Mts., Ark. 13 34 40N 94 25W
Ouray, Colo. 17 38 1N 107 40W
Outlook, Mont. 12 48 53N 104 47W
Overlea, Md. 25 39 21N 76 33W
Overton, Nev. 19 36 33N 114 27W
Ovid, Colo. 12 40 58N 102 23W
Owatonna, Minn. 12 44 5N 93 14W
Owego, N.Y. 9 42 6N 76 16W
Owens →, Calif. 18 36 32N 117 59W
Owens L., Calif. 19 36 26N 117 57W
Owensboro, Ky. 15 37 46N 87 7W
Owensville, Mo. 14 38 21N 91 30W
Owings Mills, Md. 25 39 25N 76 48W
Owosso, Mich. 15 43 0N 84 10W
Owyhee, Nev. 16 41 57N 116 6W
Owyhee →, Oreg. 16 43 49N 117 2W
Owyhee, L., Oreg. 16 43 38N 117 14W
Oxford, Miss. 13 34 22N 89 31W
Oxford, N.C. 11 36 19N 78 35W
Oxford, Ohio 15 39 31N 84 45W
Oxnard, Calif. 19 34 12N 119 11W
Oyster Bay, N.Y. 21 40 52N 73 31W
Ozark, Ala. 11 31 28N 85 39W
Ozark, Ark. 13 35 29N 93 50W
Ozark, Mo. 13 37 1N 93 12W
Ozark Plateau, Mo. 13 37 20N 91 40W
Ozarks, L. of the, Mo. 14 38 12N 92 38W
Ozona, Tex. 13 30 43N 101 12W

P

Paauilo, Hawaii 30 20 2N 155 22W
Pacific Grove, Calif. 18 36 38N 121 56W
Pacifica, Calif. 28 37 38N 122 29W
Padre I., Tex. 13 27 10N 97 25W
Paducah, Ky. 10 37 5N 88 37W
Paducah, Tex. 13 34 1N 100 18W
Page, Ariz. 17 36 57N 111 27W
Page, N. Dak. 12 47 10N 97 34W
Pago Pago, Amer. Samoa 31 14 16S 170 43W
Pagosa Springs, Colo. 17 37 16N 107 1W
Pahala, Hawaii 30 19 12N 155 29W
Pahoa, Hawaii 30 19 30N 154 57W
Pahokee, Fla. 11 26 50N 80 40W
Pahrump, Nev. 19 36 12N 115 59W
Pahute Mesa, Nev. 18 37 20N 116 45W
Paia, Hawaii 30 20 54N 156 22W
Paicines, Calif. 18 36 44N 121 17W
Pailolo Channel, Hawaii 30 21 0N 156 40W
Painesville, Ohio 8 41 43N 81 15W
Paint Rock, Tex. 13 31 31N 99 55W
Painted Desert, Ariz. 17 36 0N 111 0W
Paintsville, Ky. 10 37 49N 82 48W
Paisley, Oreg. 16 42 42N 120 32W
Pala, Calif. 19 33 22N 117 5W
Palacios, Tex. 13 28 42N 96 13W
Palatka, Fla. 11 29 39N 81 38W
Palau ■, Pac. Oc. 31 7 30N 134 30 E
Palermo, Calif. 16 39 26N 121 33W
Palestine, Tex. 13 31 46N 95 38W
Palisade, Nebr. 12 40 21N 101 7W
Palisades, N.Y. 20 41 1N 73 55W
Palm Beach, Fla. 11 26 43N 80 2W
Palm Desert, Calif. 19 33 43N 116 22W
Palm Springs, Calif. 19 33 50N 116 33W
Palmdale, Calif. 19 34 35N 118 7W
Palmer, Alaska 30 61 36N 149 7W
Palmer Lake, Colo. 12 39 7N 104 55W
Palmerton, Pa. 9 40 48N 75 37W
Palmetto, Fla. 11 27 31N 82 34W
Palmyra, Mo. 14 39 48N 91 32W
Palmyra, N.J. 24 40 0N 75 1W
Palo Alto, Calif. 28 37 26N 122 8W
Palos Heights, Ill. 22 41 40N 87 47W
Palos Hills Forest, Ill. 22 41 40N 87 52W
Palos Verdes, Calif. 19 33 48N 118 23W
Palos Verdes, Pt., Calif. 19 33 43N 118 26W
Palouse, Wash. 16 46 55N 117 4W
Pamlico →, N.C. 11 35 20N 76 28W
Pamlico Sd., N.C. 11 35 20N 76 0W
Pampa, Tex. 13 35 32N 100 58W
Pana, Ill. 14 39 23N 89 5W
Panaca, Nev. 17 37 47N 114 23W
Panama City, Fla. 11 30 10N 85 40W
Panamint Range, Calif. 19 36 20N 117 20W
Panamint Springs, Calif. 19 36 20N 117 28W
Pancake Range, Nev. 17 38 30N 115 50W
Panguitch, Utah 17 37 50N 112 26W
Panhandle, Tex. 13 35 21N 101 23W
Paola, Kans. 12 38 35N 94 53W
Paoli, Pa. 24 40 2N 75 28W
Paonia, Colo. 17 38 52N 107 36W
Papaikou, Hawaii 30 19 47N 155 6W
Paradise, Mont. 16 47 23N 114 48W
Paradise Valley, Nev. 16 41 30N 117 32W
Paragould, Ark. 13 36 3N 90 29W
Paramus, N.J. 20 40 56N 74 2W
Paris, Idaho 16 42 14N 111 24W
Paris, Ky. 15 38 13N 84 15W
Paris, Tenn. 11 36 18N 88 19W
Paris, Tex. 13 33 40N 95 33W
Parish, N.Y. 9 43 25N 76 8W
Park City, Utah 16 40 39N 111 30W
Park Falls, Wis. 12 45 56N 90 27W
Park Range, Colo. 16 40 0N 106 30W
Park Rapids, Minn. 12 46 55N 95 4W
Park Ridge, Ill. 22 42 0N 87 50W
Park Ridge, N.J. 20 41 2N 74 2W
Park River, N. Dak. 12 48 24N 97 45W
Parker, Ariz. 19 34 9N 114 17W
Parker, S. Dak. 12 43 24N 97 8W
Parker Dam, Ariz. 19 34 18N 114 8W
Parkersburg, W. Va. 10 39 16N 81 34W
Parkfield, Calif. 18 35 54N 120 26W
Parkston, S. Dak. 12 43 24N 97 59W
Parkville, Md. 25 39 23N 76 34W
Parma, Idaho 16 43 47N 116 57W
Parma, Ohio 27 41 24N 81 43W
Parma Heights, Ohio 27 41 23N 81 45W
Parowan, Utah 17 37 51N 112 50W
Parris I., S.C. 11 32 20N 80 41W
Parshall, N. Dak. 12 47 57N 102 8W
Parsons, Kans. 13 37 20N 95 16W
Pasadena, Calif. 29 34 9N 118 8W
Pasadena, Tex. 13 29 43N 95 13W
Pascagoula, Miss. 13 30 21N 88 33W
Pascagoula →, Miss. 13 30 23N 88 37W
Pasco, Wash. 16 46 14N 119 6W
Paso Robles, Calif. 16 35 38N 120 41W
Passaic, N.J. 20 40 51N 74 9W
Patagonia, Ariz. 17 31 33N 110 45W
Patchogue, N.Y. 9 40 46N 73 1W
Pateros, Wash. 16 48 3N 119 54W
Paterson, N.J. 20 40 54N 74 10W
Pathfinder Reservoir, Wyo. 16 42 28N 106 51W
Patten, Maine 11 46 0N 68 38W
Patterson, Calif. 18 37 28N 121 8W
Patterson, La. 13 29 42N 91 18W
Patterson, Mt., Calif. 18 38 29N 119 20W
Paullina, Iowa 12 42 59N 95 41W
Pauls Valley, Okla. 13 34 44N 97 13W
Paulsboro, N.J. 24 39 49N 75 14W
Pauma Valley, Calif. 19 33 16N 116 58W
Pavlof Is., Alaska 30 55 30N 161 30W
Pawhuska, Okla. 13 36 40N 96 20W
Pawling, N.Y. 9 41 34N 73 36W
Pawnee, Okla. 13 36 20N 96 48W
Pawnee City, Nebr. 12 40 7N 96 9W
Pawtucket, R.I. 9 41 53N 71 23W
Paxton, Ill. 15 40 27N 88 6W
Paxton, Nebr. 12 41 7N 101 21W
Payette, Idaho 16 44 5N 116 56W
Paynesville, Minn. 12 45 23N 94 43W
Payson, Ariz. 17 34 14N 111 20W
Payson, Utah 16 40 3N 111 44W
Pe Ell, Wash. 18 46 34N 123 18W
Peabody, Mass. 23 42 32N 70 57W
Peach Springs, Ariz. 17 35 32N 113 25W
Peale, Mt., Utah 17 38 26N 109 14W
Pearblossom, Calif. 19 34 30N 117 55W
Pearl →, Miss. 13 30 11N 89 32W
Pearl City, Hawaii 30 21 24N 157 59W
Pearl Harbor, Hawaii 30 21 21N 157 57W
Pearsall, Tex. 13 28 54N 99 6W
Pease →, Tex. 13 34 12N 99 2W
Pebble Beach, Calif. 18 36 34N 121 57W
Pecos, Tex. 13 31 26N 103 30W
Pecos →, Tex. 13 29 42N 101 22W
Pedro Valley, Calif. 28 37 35N 122 28W
Peekskill, N.Y. 9 41 17N 73 55W
Pekin, Ill. 14 40 35N 89 40W
Pelham, Ga. 11 31 8N 84 9W
Pelham, N.Y. 21 40 54N 73 46W
Pelican, Alaska 30 57 58N 136 14W
Pella, Iowa 14 41 25N 92 55W
Pembina, N. Dak. 12 48 58N 97 15W
Pembine, Wis. 10 45 38N 87 59W
Pembroke, Ga. 11 32 8N 81 37W
Pend Oreille →, Wash. 16 49 4N 117 37W
Pend Oreille L., Idaho 16 48 10N 116 21W
Pendleton, Calif. 19 33 16N 117 23W
Pendleton, Oreg. 16 45 40N 118 47W
Penn Hills, Pa. 27 40 27N 79 50W
Penn Yan, N.Y. 8 42 40N 77 3W
Pennsauken, N.J. 24 39 57N 75 5W
Pennsylvania □ 10 40 45N 77 30W
Pensacola, Fla. 11 30 25N 87 13W
Peoria, Ariz. 17 33 35N 112 14W
Peoria, Ill. 14 40 42N 89 36W
Perham, Minn. 12 46 36N 95 34W
Perris, Calif. 19 33 47N 117 14W
Perry, Fla. 11 30 7N 83 35W
Perry, Ga. 11 32 28N 83 44W
Perry, Iowa 14 41 51N 94 6W

Selma

Riverside, *Ill.* **22** 41 49N 87 48W
Riverside, *N.J.* **24** 40 2N 74 58W
Riverside, *Wyo.* **16** 41 13N 106 47W
Riverton, *Wyo.* **16** 43 2N 108 23W
Riverview, *Mich.* **26** 42 10N 83 11W
Roanoke, *Ala.* **11** 33 9N 85 22W
Roanoke, *Va.* **10** 37 16N 79 56W
Roanoke →, *N.C.* **11** 35 57N 76 42W
Roanoke I., *Ala.* **11** 35 55N 75 40W
Roanoke Rapids, *N.C.* **11** 36 28N 77 40W
Robert Lee, *Tex.* **13** 31 54N 100 29W
Roberts, *Idaho* **16** 43 43N 112 8W
Robstown, *Tex.* **13** 27 47N 97 40W
Rochelle, *Ill.* **14** 41 56N 89 4W
Rochester, *Ind.* **15** 41 4N 86 13W
Rochester, *Minn.* **12** 44 1N 92 28W
Rochester, *N.H.* **9** 43 18N 70 59W
Rochester, *N.Y.* **8** 43 10N 77 37W
Rock Hill, *S.C.* **11** 34 56N 81 1W
Rock Island, *Ill.* **14** 41 30N 90 34W
Rock Rapids, *Iowa* **12** 43 26N 96 10W
Rock River, *Wyo.* **16** 41 44N 105 58W
Rock Springs, *Mont.* **16** 46 49N 106 15W
Rock Springs, *Wyo.* **16** 41 35N 109 14W
Rock Valley, *Iowa* **12** 43 12N 96 18W
Rockdale, *Tex.* **13** 30 39N 97 0W
Rockford, *Ill.* **14** 42 16N 89 6W
Rocklake, *N. Dak.* **12** 48 47N 99 15W
Rockland, *Idaho* **16** 42 34N 112 53W
Rockland, *Maine* **11** 44 6N 69 7W
Rockland, *Mich.* **12** 46 44N 89 11W
Rockmart, *Ga.* **11** 34 0N 85 3W
Rockport, *Mo.* **12** 40 25N 95 31W
Rockport, *Tex.* **13** 28 2N 97 3W
Rocksprings, *Tex.* **13** 30 1N 100 13W
Rockville, *Conn.* **9** 41 52N 72 28W
Rockville, *Md.* **25** 39 4N 77 9W
Rockville Center, *N.Y.* **21** 40 39N 73 38W
Rockwall, *Tex.* **13** 32 56N 96 28W
Rockwell City, *Iowa* **14** 42 24N 94 38W
Rockwood, *Tenn.* **11** 35 52N 84 41W
Rocky Ford, *Colo.* **12** 38 3N 103 43W
Rocky Mount, *N.C.* **11** 35 57N 77 48W
Rocky Mts., *N. Amer.* **2** 39 0N 106 0W
Rocky River, *Ohio* **27** 41 28N 81 50W
Roebling, *N.J.* **9** 40 7N 74 47W
Rogers, *Ark.* **13** 36 20N 94 7W
Rogers City, *Mich.* **10** 45 25N 83 49W
Rogerson, *Idaho* **16** 42 13N 114 36W
Rogersville, *Tenn.* **11** 36 24N 83 1W
Rogue →, *Oreg.* **16** 42 26N 124 26W
Rohnert Park, *Calif.* **18** 38 16N 122 40W
Rojo, Cabo, *Puerto Rico* **30** 17 56N 67 12W
Rolette, *N. Dak.* **12** 48 40N 99 51W
Rolla, *Kans.* **13** 37 7N 101 38W
Rolla, *Mo.* **14** 37 57N 91 46W
Rolla, *N. Dak.* **12** 48 52N 99 37W
Romanzof C., *Alaska* **30** 61 49N 166 6W
Rome, *Ga.* **11** 34 15N 85 10W
Rome, *N.Y.* **9** 43 13N 75 27W
Romney, *W. Va.* **10** 39 21N 78 45W
Romulus, *Mich.* **26** 42 13N 83 23W
Ronan, *Mont.* **16** 47 32N 114 6W
Ronceverte, *W. Va.* **10** 37 45N 80 28W
Roof Butte, *Ariz.* **17** 36 28N 109 5W
Roosevelt, *Minn.* **12** 48 48N 95 6W
Roosevelt, *Utah* **16** 40 18N 109 59W
Roosevelt Res., *Ariz.* **17** 33 46N 111 0W
Ropesville, *Tex.* **13** 33 26N 102 9W
Rosalia, *Wash.* **16** 47 14N 117 22W
Rosamond, *Calif.* **19** 34 52N 118 10W
Roscoe, *S. Dak.* **12** 45 27N 99 20W
Roscommon, *Mich.* **10** 44 30N 84 35W
Roseau, *Minn.* **12** 48 51N 95 46W
Rosebud, *Tex.* **13** 31 4N 96 59W
Roseburg, *Oreg.* **16** 43 13N 123 20W
Rosedale, *Md.* **25** 39 19N 76 32W
Rosedale, *Miss.* **13** 33 51N 91 2W
Rosemead, *Calif.* **29** 34 4N 118 4W
Rosenberg, *Tex.* **13** 29 34N 95 49W
Roseville, *Calif.* **18** 38 45N 121 17W
Roseville, *Mich.* **26** 42 30N 82 57W
Ross, *Calif.* **28** 37 58N 122 33W
Ross L., *Wash.* **16** 48 44N 121 4W
Rossville, *N.Y.* **20** 40 32N 74 12W
Roswell, *N. Mex.* **13** 33 24N 104 32W
Rotan, *Tex.* **13** 32 51N 100 28W
Round Mountain, *Nev.* **16** 38 43N 117 4W
Roundup, *Mont.* **16** 46 27N 108 33W
Rouses Point, *N.Y.* **9** 44 59N 73 22W
Roxboro, *N.C.* **11** 36 24N 78 59W
Roy, *Mont.* **16** 47 20N 108 58W
Roy, *N. Mex.* **13** 35 57N 104 12W
Royal Oak, *Mich.* **26** 42 30N 83 9W
Ruby, *Alaska* **30** 64 45N 155 30W
Ruby L., *Nev.* **16** 40 10N 115 28W
Ruby Mts., *Nev.* **16** 40 30N 115 20W
Rudyard, *Mich.* **10** 46 14N 84 36W
Rugby, *N. Dak.* **12** 48 22N 100 0W
Ruidosa, *Tex.* **13** 29 59N 104 41W
Ruidoso, *N. Mex.* **17** 33 20N 105 41W
Rumford, *Maine* **9** 44 33N 70 33W
Rushford, *Minn.* **12** 43 49N 91 46W
Rushville, *Ill.* **14** 40 7N 90 34W
Rushville, *Ind.* **15** 39 37N 85 27W
Rushville, *Nebr.* **12** 42 43N 102 28W
Russell, *Kans.* **12** 38 54N 98 52W
Russellville, *Ala.* **11** 34 30N 87 44W
Russellville, *Ark.* **13** 35 17N 93 8W
Russellville, *Ky.* **11** 36 51N 86 53W
Russian Mission, *Alaska* **30** 61 47N 161 19W
Ruston, *La.* **13** 32 32N 92 38W
Ruth, *Nev.* **16** 39 17N 114 59W
Rye Patch Reservoir, *Nev.* **16** 40 28N 118 19W
Ryegate, *Mont.* **16** 46 18N 109 15W

S

Sabinal, *Tex.* **13** 29 19N 99 28W
Sabine →, *La.* **13** 29 59N 93 47W
Sabine L., *La.* **13** 29 53N 93 51W
Sabine Pass, *Tex.* **13** 29 44N 93 54W
Sac City, *Iowa* **14** 42 25N 95 0W
Saco, *Maine* **11** 43 30N 70 27W
Saco, *Mont.* **16** 48 28N 107 21W
Sacramento, *Calif.* **18** 38 35N 121 29W
Sacramento →, *Calif.* **18** 38 3N 121 56W
Sacramento Mts., *N. Mex.* **17** 32 30N 105 30W
Safford, *Ariz.* **17** 32 50N 109 43W
Sag Harbor, *N.Y.* **9** 41 0N 72 18W
Saginaw, *Mich.* **10** 43 26N 83 56W
Saginaw B., *Mich.* **10** 43 50N 83 40W
Saguache, *Colo.* **17** 38 5N 106 8W
Sahuarita, *Ariz.* **17** 31 57N 110 58W
St. Albans, *N.Y.* **21** 40 42N 73 44W
St. Albans, *Vt.* **9** 44 49N 73 5W
St. Albans, *W. Va.* **10** 38 23N 81 50W
St. Anthony, *Idaho* **16** 43 58N 111 41W
St. Augustine, *Fla.* **11** 29 54N 81 19W
St. Catherines I., *Ga.* **11** 31 40N 81 10W
St. Charles, *Ill.* **15** 41 54N 88 19W
St. Charles, *Mo.* **14** 38 47N 90 29W
St. Clair, *Pa.* **9** 40 43N 76 12W
St. Clair Shores, *Mich.* **26** 42 29N 82 54W
St. Cloud, *Fla.* **11** 28 15N 81 17W
St. Cloud, *Minn.* **12** 45 34N 94 10W
St. Croix, *Virgin Is.* **30** 17 45N 64 45W
St. Croix →, *Wis.* **12** 44 45N 92 48W
St. Croix Falls, *Wis.* **12** 45 24N 92 38W
St. Elias, Mt., *Alaska* **30** 60 18N 140 56W
St. Francis, *Kans.* **12** 39 47N 101 48W
St. Francis →, *Ark.* **13** 34 38N 90 36W
St. Francisville, *La.* **13** 30 47N 91 23W
St. George, *S.C.* **11** 33 11N 80 35W
St. George, *Utah* **17** 37 6N 113 35W
St. George, C., *Fla.* **11** 29 40N 85 5W
St. Helena, *Calif.* **16** 38 30N 122 28W
St. Helens, *Oreg.* **18** 45 52N 122 48W
St. Ignace, *Mich.* **10** 45 52N 84 44W
St. Ignatius, *Mont.* **16** 47 19N 114 6W
St. James, *Minn.* **12** 43 59N 94 38W
St. John, *Kans.* **13** 38 0N 98 46W
St. John, *N. Dak.* **12** 48 57N 99 43W
St. John →, *Maine* **11** 45 12N 66 5W
St. John I., *Virgin Is.* **30** 18 20N 64 42W
St. Johns, *Ariz.* **17** 34 30N 109 22W
St. Johns, *Mich.* **15** 43 0N 84 33W
St. Johns →, *Fla.* **11** 30 24N 81 24W
St. Johnsbury, *Vt.* **9** 44 25N 72 1W
St. Johnsville, *N.Y.* **9** 43 0N 74 43W
St. Joseph, *La.* **13** 31 55N 91 14W
St. Joseph, *Mich.* **15** 42 6N 86 29W
St. Joseph, *Mo.* **14** 39 46N 94 50W
St. Joseph →, *Mich.* **15** 42 7N 86 29W
St. Lawrence I., *Alaska* **30** 63 30N 170 30W
St. Louis, *Mich.* **10** 43 25N 84 36W
St. Louis, *Mo.* **14** 38 37N 90 12W
St. Louis →, *Minn.* **12** 47 15N 92 45W
St. Maries, *Idaho* **16** 47 19N 116 35W
St. Martinville, *La.* **13** 30 7N 91 50W
St. Marys, *Pa.* **8** 41 26N 78 34W
St. Michael, *Alaska* **30** 63 29N 162 2W
St. Paul, *Minn.* **12** 44 57N 93 6W
St. Paul, *Nebr.* **12** 41 13N 98 27W
St. Peter, *Minn.* **12** 44 20N 93 57W
St. Petersburg, *Fla.* **11** 27 46N 82 39W
St. Regis, *Mont.* **16** 47 18N 115 6W
St. Thomas I., *Virgin Is.* **30** 18 20N 64 55W
Ste. Genevieve, *Mo.* **14** 37 59N 90 2W
Saipan, *Pac. Oc.* **31** 15 12N 145 45 E
Sakakawea, L., *N. Dak.* **12** 47 30N 101 25W
Salamanca, *N.Y.* **8** 42 10N 78 43W
Salem, *Ind.* **15** 38 36N 86 6W
Salem, *Mass.* **23** 42 30N 70 55W
Salem, *Mo.* **13** 37 39N 91 32W
Salem, *N.J.* **10** 39 34N 75 28W
Salem, *Ohio* **8** 40 54N 80 52W
Salem, *Oreg.* **16** 44 56N 123 2W
Salem, *S. Dak.* **12** 43 44N 97 23W
Salem, *Va.* **10** 37 18N 80 3W
Salina, *Kans.* **12** 38 50N 97 37W
Salinas, *Calif.* **18** 36 40N 121 39W
Salinas →, *Calif.* **18** 36 45N 121 48W
Saline →, *Ark.* **13** 33 10N 92 8W
Saline →, *Kans.* **12** 38 52N 97 30W
Salisbury, *Md.* **10** 38 22N 75 36W
Salisbury, *N.C.* **11** 35 40N 80 29W
Sallisaw, *Okla.* **13** 35 28N 94 47W
Salmon, *Idaho* **16** 45 11N 113 54W
Salmon →, *Idaho* **16** 45 51N 116 47W
Salmon Falls, *Idaho* **16** 42 48N 114 59W
Salmon River Mts., *Idaho* **16** 45 0N 114 30W
Salome, *Ariz.* **19** 33 47N 113 37W
Salt →, *Ariz.* **17** 33 23N 112 19W
Salt Fork Arkansas →, *Okla.* **13** 36 36N 97 3W
Salt Lake City, *Utah* **16** 40 45N 111 53W
Salton City, *Calif.* **19** 33 29N 115 51W
Salton Sea, *Calif.* **19** 33 15N 115 45W
Saltville, *Va.* **10** 36 53N 81 46W
Saluda →, *S.C.* **11** 34 1N 81 4W
Salvador, L., *La.* **13** 29 43N 90 15W
Salyersville, *Ky.* **10** 37 45N 83 4W
Sam Rayburn Reservoir, *Tex.* **13** 31 4N 94 5W
San Andreas, *Calif.* **18** 38 12N 120 41W
San Andres Mts., *N. Mex.* **17** 33 0N 106 30W
San Angelo, *Tex.* **13** 31 28N 100 26W
San Anselmo, *Calif.* **18** 37 59N 122 34W
San Antonio, *N. Mex.* **17** 33 55N 106 52W
San Antonio, *Tex.* **13** 29 25N 98 30W
San Antonio →, *Tex.* **13** 28 30N 96 54W
San Antonio, Mt., *Calif.* **19** 34 17N 117 38W
San Ardo, *Calif.* **18** 36 1N 120 54W
San Augustine, *Tex.* **13** 31 30N 94 7W
San Benito, *Tex.* **13** 26 8N 97 38W
San Benito →, *Calif.* **18** 36 53N 121 34W
San Benito Mt., *Calif.* **18** 36 22N 120 37W
San Bernardino, *Calif.* **19** 34 7N 117 19W
San Blas, C., *Fla.* **11** 29 40N 85 21W
San Bruno, *Calif.* **28** 37 37N 122 24W
San Carlos, *Ariz.* **17** 33 21N 110 27W
San Carlos, *Calif.* **28** 37 30N 122 16W
San Carlos L., *Ariz.* **17** 33 11N 110 32W
San Clemente, *Calif.* **19** 33 26N 117 37W
San Clemente I., *Calif.* **19** 32 53N 118 29W
San Diego, *Calif.* **19** 32 43N 117 9W
San Diego, *Tex.* **13** 27 46N 98 14W
San Felipe →, *Calif.* **19** 33 12N 115 49W
San Fernando, *Calif.* **29** 34 17N 118 26W
San Francisco, *Calif.* **28** 37 46N 122 25W
San Francisco →, *Ariz.* **17** 32 59N 109 22W
San Francisco Bay, *Calif.* **28** 37 40N 122 15W
San Francisco International Airport, *Calif.* **28** 37 37N 122 22W
San Gabriel, *Calif.* **29** 34 5N 118 5W
San Germán, *Puerto Rico* **30** 18 5N 67 3W
San Gorgonio Mt., *Calif.* **19** 34 7N 116 51W
San Gregorio, *Calif.* **18** 37 20N 122 23W
San Jacinto, *Calif.* **19** 33 47N 116 57W
San Joaquin, *Calif.* **18** 36 36N 120 11W
San Joaquin →, *Calif.* **18** 38 4N 121 51W
San Joaquin Valley, *Calif.* **18** 37 20N 121 0W
San Jose, *Calif.* **18** 37 20N 121 53W
San Jose →, *N. Mex.* **17** 34 25N 106 45W
San Juan, *Dom. Rep.* **30** 18 49N 71 12W
San Juan, *Puerto Rico* **30** 18 28N 66 7W
San Juan →, *Utah* **17** 37 16N 110 26W
San Juan, C., *Puerto Rico* **30** 18 23N 65 37W
San Juan Bautista, *Calif.* **18** 36 51N 121 32W
San Juan Capistrano, *Calif.* **19** 33 30N 117 40W
San Juan Cr. →, *Calif.* **18** 35 40N 120 22W
San Juan Mts., *Colo.* **17** 37 30N 107 0W
San Leandro, *Calif.* **28** 37 44N 122 9W
San Lucas, *Calif.* **18** 36 8N 121 1W
San Luis, *Colo.* **17** 37 12N 105 25W
San Luis Obispo, *Calif.* **19** 35 17N 120 40W
San Luis Reservoir, *Calif.* **18** 37 4N 121 5W
San Marcos, *Tex.* **13** 29 53N 97 56W
San Marino, *Calif.* **29** 34 7N 118 5W
San Mateo, *Calif.* **28** 37 34N 122 20W
San Mateo Bridge, *Calif.* **28** 37 36N 122 11W
San Mateo County, *Calif.* **28** 37 30N 122 20W
San Miguel, *Calif.* **18** 35 45N 120 42W
San Miguel I., *Calif.* **19** 34 2N 120 23W
San Nicolas I., *Calif.* **19** 33 15N 119 30W
San Onofre, *Calif.* **19** 33 22N 117 34W
San Pedro →, *Ariz.* **17** 32 59N 110 47W
San Pedro Channel, *Calif.* **19** 33 30N 118 25W
San Quentin, *Calif.* **28** 37 56N 122 29W
San Rafael, *Calif.* **28** 37 58N 122 31W
San Rafael, *N. Mex.* **17** 35 7N 107 53W
San Rafael Mt., *Calif.* **19** 34 41N 119 52W
San Saba, *Tex.* **13** 31 12N 98 43W
San Simeon, *Calif.* **18** 35 39N 121 11W
San Simon, *Ariz.* **17** 32 16N 109 14W
San Ygnacio, *Tex.* **13** 27 3N 99 26W
Sanak I., *Alaska* **30** 54 25N 162 40W
Sand Point, *Alaska* **30** 55 20N 160 30W
Sand Springs, *Okla.* **13** 36 9N 96 7W
Sanders, *Ariz.* **17** 35 13N 109 20W
Sanderson, *Tex.* **13** 30 9N 102 24W
Sandpoint, *Idaho* **16** 48 17N 116 33W
Sandusky, *Mich.* **8** 43 25N 82 50W
Sandusky, *Ohio* **8** 41 27N 82 42W
Sandy Cr. →, *Wyo.* **16** 41 51N 109 47W
Sanford, *Fla.* **11** 28 48N 81 16W
Sanford, *Maine* **9** 43 27N 70 47W
Sanford, *N.C.* **11** 35 29N 79 10W
Sanger, *Calif.* **18** 36 42N 119 33W
Sangre de Cristo Mts., *N. Mex.* **13** 37 0N 105 0W
Santa Ana, *Calif.* **19** 33 46N 117 52W
Santa Barbara, *Calif.* **19** 34 25N 119 42W
Santa Barbara Channel, *Calif.* **19** 34 15N 120 0W
Santa Barbara I., *Calif.* **19** 33 29N 119 2W
Santa Catalina, Gulf of, *Calif.* **19** 33 10N 117 50W
Santa Catalina I., *Calif.* **19** 33 23N 118 25W
Santa Clara, *Calif.* **18** 37 21N 121 57W
Santa Clara, *Utah* **17** 37 8N 113 39W
Santa Cruz, *Calif.* **18** 36 58N 122 1W
Santa Cruz I., *Calif.* **19** 34 1N 119 43W
Santa Fe, *N. Mex.* **17** 35 41N 105 57W
Santa Fe Springs, *Calif.* **29** 33 56N 118 3W
Santa Lucia Range, *Calif.* **18** 36 0N 121 20W
Santa Margarita, *Calif.* **18** 35 23N 120 37W
Santa Margarita →, *Calif.* **19** 33 13N 117 23W
Santa Maria, *Calif.* **19** 34 57N 120 26W
Santa Monica, *Calif.* **29** 34 1N 118 29W
Santa Rita, *N. Mex.* **17** 32 48N 108 4W
Santa Rosa, *Calif.* **18** 38 26N 122 43W
Santa Rosa, *N. Mex.* **13** 34 57N 104 41W
Santa Rosa I., *Calif.* **19** 33 58N 120 6W
Santa Rosa I., *Fla.* **11** 30 20N 86 50W
Santa Rosa Range, *Nev.* **16** 41 45N 117 40W
Santa Ynez →, *Calif.* **19** 35 41N 120 36W
Santa Ynez Mts., *Calif.* **19** 34 30N 120 0W
Santa Ysabel, *Calif.* **19** 33 7N 116 40W
Santaquin, *Utah* **16** 39 59N 111 47W
Sapelo I., *Ga.* **11** 31 25N 81 12W
Sapulpa, *Okla.* **13** 35 59N 96 5W
Saranac Lake, *N.Y.* **9** 44 20N 74 8W
Sarasota, *Fla.* **11** 27 20N 82 32W
Saratoga, *Calif.* **18** 37 16N 122 2W
Saratoga, *Wyo.* **16** 41 27N 106 49W
Saratoga Springs, *N.Y.* **9** 43 5N 73 47W
Sargent, *Nebr.* **12** 41 39N 99 22W
Sarichef C., *Alaska* **30** 54 38N 164 59W
Sarita, *Tex.* **13** 27 13N 97 47W
Sarles, *N. Dak.* **12** 48 58N 99 0W
Satanta, *Kans.* **13** 37 26N 100 59W
Satilla →, *Ga.* **11** 30 59N 81 29W
Saugerties, *N.Y.* **9** 42 5N 73 57W
Saugus, *Mass.* **23** 42 28N 71 0W
Sauk Centre, *Minn.* **12** 45 44N 94 57W
Sauk Rapids, *Minn.* **12** 45 35N 94 10W
Sault Ste. Marie, *Mich.* **10** 46 30N 84 21W
Sausalito, *Calif.* **28** 37 51N 122 28W
Savage, *Mont.* **12** 47 27N 104 21W
Savanna, *Ill.* **14** 42 5N 90 8W
Savannah, *Ga.* **11** 32 5N 81 6W
Savannah, *Mo.* **14** 39 56N 94 50W
Savannah, *Tenn.* **11** 35 14N 88 15W
Savannah →, *Ga.* **11** 32 2N 80 53W
Sawatch Mts., *Colo.* **17** 38 30N 106 30W
Sayre, *Okla.* **13** 35 18N 99 38W
Sayre, *Pa.* **9** 41 59N 76 32W
Scammon Bay, *Alaska* **30** 61 51N 165 35W
Scenic, *S. Dak.* **12** 43 47N 102 33W
Schell Creek Ra., *Nev.* **16** 39 15N 114 30W
Schenectady, *N.Y.* **9** 42 49N 73 57W
Schiller Park, *Ill.* **22** 41 56N 87 52W
Schofield, *Wis.* **12** 44 54N 89 36W
Schurz, *Nev.* **16** 38 57N 118 49W
Schuyler, *Nebr.* **12** 41 27N 97 4W
Schuylkill Haven, *Pa.* **9** 40 37N 76 11W
Scioto →, *Ohio* **10** 38 44N 83 1W
Scobey, *Mont.* **12** 48 47N 105 25W
Scotia, *Calif.* **16** 40 29N 124 6W
Scotia, *N.Y.* **9** 42 50N 73 58W
Scotland, *S. Dak.* **12** 43 9N 97 43W
Scotland Neck, *N.C.* **11** 36 8N 77 25W
Scott City, *Kans.* **12** 38 29N 100 54W
Scottsbluff, *Nebr.* **12** 41 52N 103 40W
Scottsboro, *Ala.* **11** 34 40N 86 2W
Scottsburg, *Ind.* **15** 38 41N 85 47W
Scottsville, *Ky.* **11** 36 45N 86 11W
Scottville, *Mich.* **10** 43 58N 86 17W
Scranton, *Pa.* **9** 41 25N 75 40W
Seaford, *Del.* **10** 38 39N 75 37W
Seagraves, *Tex.* **13** 32 57N 102 34W
Sealy, *Tex.* **13** 29 47N 96 9W
Searchlight, *Nev.* **19** 35 28N 114 55W
Searcy, *Ark.* **13** 35 15N 91 44W
Searles L., *Calif.* **19** 35 44N 117 21W
Sears Tower, *Ill.* **22** 41 52N 87 37W
Seaside, *Calif.* **18** 36 37N 121 50W
Seaside, *Oreg.* **18** 46 0N 123 56W
Seat Pleasant, *Md.* **25** 38 53N 76 53W
Seattle, *Wash.* **18** 47 36N 122 20W
Sebastopol, *Calif.* **18** 38 24N 122 49W
Sebewaing, *Mich.* **10** 43 44N 83 27W
Sebring, *Fla.* **11** 27 30N 81 27W
Sedalia, *Mo.* **14** 38 42N 93 14W
Sedan, *Kans.* **13** 37 8N 96 11W
Sedro-Woolley, *Wash.* **18** 48 30N 122 14W
Seguam I., *Alaska* **30** 52 19N 172 30W
Seguam Pass, *Alaska* **30** 52 0N 172 30W
Seguin, *Tex.* **13** 29 34N 97 58W
Segula I., *Alaska* **30** 52 0N 177 50 E
Seiling, *Okla.* **13** 36 9N 98 56W
Selah, *Wash.* **16** 46 39N 120 32W
Selawik, *Alaska* **30** 66 36N 160 0W
Selby, *S. Dak.* **12** 45 31N 100 2W
Selden, *Kans.* **12** 39 33N 100 34W
Seldovia, *Alaska* **30** 59 26N 151 43W
Selfridge, *N. Dak.* **12** 46 2N 100 56W
Seligman, *Ariz.* **17** 35 20N 112 53W
Sells, *Ariz.* **17** 31 55N 111 53W
Selma, *Ala.* **11** 32 25N 87 1W
Selma, *Calif.* **18** 36 34N 119 37W
Selma, *N.C.* **11** 35 32N 78 17W

Selmer

Selmer, *Tenn.* **11** 35 10N 88 36W
Seminoe Reservoir, *Wyo.* **16** 42 9N 106 55W
Seminole, *Okla.* **13** 35 14N 96 41W
Seminole, *Tex.* **13** 32 43N 102 39W
Semisopochnoi I., *Alaska* **30** 51 55N 179 36 E
Senatobia, *Miss.* **13** 34 37N 89 58W
Seneca, *Oreg.* **16** 44 8N 118 58W
Seneca, *S.C.* **11** 34 41N 82 57W
Seneca Falls, *N.Y.* **9** 42 55N 76 48W
Seneca L., *N.Y.* **8** 42 40N 76 54W
Sentinel, *Ariz.* **17** 32 52N 113 13W
Sequim, *Wash.* **18** 48 5N 123 6W
Sequoia National Park, *Calif.* **18** 36 30N 118 30W
Settlement Pt., *Bahamas* **11** 26 40N 79 0W
Sevier, *Utah* **17** 38 39N 112 11W
Sevier →, *Utah* **17** 39 4N 113 6W
Sevier L., *Utah* **16** 38 54N 113 9W
Seward, *Alaska* **30** 60 7N 149 27W
Seward, *Nebr.* **12** 40 55N 97 6W
Seward Pen., *Alaska* **30** 65 0N 164 0W
Seymour, *Conn.* **9** 41 24N 73 4W
Seymour, *Ind.* **15** 38 58N 85 53W
Seymour, *Tex.* **13** 33 35N 99 16W
Seymour, *Wis.* **10** 44 31N 88 20W
Shafter, *Calif.* **19** 35 30N 119 16W
Shafter, *Tex.* **13** 29 49N 104 18W
Shaker Heights, *Ohio* **27** 41 28N 81 33W
Shakopee, *Minn.* **12** 44 48N 93 32W
Shaktolik, *Alaska* **30** 64 30N 161 15W
Shamokin, *Pa.* **9** 40 47N 76 34W
Shamrock, *Tex.* **13** 35 13N 100 15W
Shandon, *Calif.* **18** 35 39N 120 23W
Shaniko, *Oreg.* **16** 45 0N 120 45W
Sharon, *Mass.* **9** 42 7N 71 11W
Sharon, *Pa.* **8** 41 14N 80 31W
Sharon Springs, *Kans.* **12** 38 54N 101 45W
Sharpsburg, *Pa.* **27** 40 29N 79 56W
Shasta, Mt., *Calif.* **16** 41 25N 122 12W
Shasta L., *Calif.* **16** 40 43N 122 25W
Shattuck, *Okla.* **13** 36 16N 99 53W
Shaver L., *Calif.* **18** 37 9N 119 18W
Shawano, *Wis.* **10** 44 47N 88 36W
Shawnee, *Okla.* **13** 35 20N 96 55W
Sheboygan, *Wis.* **10** 43 46N 87 45W
Sheffield, *Ala.* **11** 34 46N 87 41W
Sheffield, *Mass.* **9** 42 5N 73 21W
Sheffield, *Tex.* **13** 30 41N 101 49W
Shelburne Falls, *Mass.* **9** 42 36N 72 45W
Shelby, *Mich.* **10** 43 37N 86 22W
Shelby, *Mont.* **16** 48 30N 111 51W
Shelby, *N.C.* **11** 35 17N 81 32W
Shelbyville, *Ill.* **15** 39 24N 88 48W
Shelbyville, *Ind.* **15** 39 31N 85 47W
Shelbyville, *Tenn.* **11** 35 29N 86 28W
Sheldon, *Iowa* **12** 43 11N 95 51W
Sheldon Point, *Alaska* **30** 62 32N 164 52W
Shelikof Strait, *Alaska* **30** 57 30N 155 0W
Shelton, *Conn.* **9** 41 19N 73 5W
Shelton, *Wash.* **18** 47 13N 123 6W
Shenandoah, *Iowa* **12** 40 46N 95 22W
Shenandoah, *Pa.* **9** 40 49N 76 12W
Shenandoah, *Va.* **10** 38 29N 78 37W
Shenandoah →, *Va.* **10** 39 19N 77 44W
Sheridan, *Ark.* **13** 34 19N 92 24W
Sheridan, *Wyo.* **16** 44 48N 106 58W
Sherman, *Tex.* **13** 33 40N 96 35W
Sherwood, *N. Dak.* **12** 48 57N 101 38W
Sherwood, *Tex.* **13** 31 18N 100 45W
Sheyenne, *N. Dak.* **12** 47 50N 99 7W
Sheyenne →, *N. Dak.* **12** 47 2N 96 50W
Ship I., *Miss.* **13** 30 13N 88 55W
Shippensburg, *Pa.* **8** 40 3N 77 31W
Shiprock, *N. Mex.* **17** 36 47N 108 41W
Shishmaref, *Alaska* **30** 66 15N 166 4W
Shoshone, *Calif.* **19** 35 58N 116 16W
Shoshone, *Idaho* **16** 42 56N 114 25W
Shoshone L., *Wyo.* **16** 44 22N 110 43W
Shoshone Mts., *Nev.* **16** 39 20N 117 25W
Shoshoni, *Wyo.* **16** 43 14N 108 7W
Show Low, *Ariz.* **17** 34 15N 110 2W
Shreveport, *La.* **13** 32 31N 93 45W
Shumagin Is., *Alaska* **30** 55 7N 159 45W
Shungnak, *Alaska* **30** 66 52N 157 9W
Shuyak I., *Alaska* **30** 58 31N 152 30W
Sibley, *Iowa* **12** 43 24N 95 45W
Sibley, *La.* **13** 32 33N 93 18W
Sidney, *Mont.* **12** 47 43N 104 9W
Sidney, *N.Y.* **9** 42 19N 75 24W
Sidney, *Nebr.* **12** 41 8N 102 59W
Sidney, *Ohio* **15** 40 17N 84 9W
Sierra Blanca, *Tex.* **17** 31 11N 105 22W
Sierra Blanca Peak, *N. Mex.* **17** 33 23N 105 49W
Sierra City, *Calif.* **18** 39 34N 120 38W
Sierra Madre, *Calif.* **29** 34 9N 118 3W
Sigurd, *Utah* **17** 38 50N 111 58W
Sikeston, *Mo.* **13** 36 53N 89 35W
Siler City, *N.C.* **11** 35 44N 79 28W
Siloam Springs, *Ark.* **13** 36 11N 94 32W
Silsbee, *Tex.* **13** 30 21N 94 11W
Silver City, *N. Mex.* **17** 32 46N 108 17W
Silver City, *Nev.* **16** 39 15N 119 48W
Silver Cr. →, *Oreg.* **16** 43 16N 119 13W
Silver Creek, *N.Y.* **8** 42 33N 79 10W
Silver Hill, *Md.* **25** 38 49N 76 55W
Silver L., *Calif.* **18** 38 39N 120 6W
Silver L., *Calif.* **19** 35 21N 116 7W
Silver Lake, *Oreg.* **16** 43 8N 121 3W
Silver Spring, *Md.* **25** 39 0N 77 1W
Silverton, *Colo.* **17** 37 49N 107 40W
Silverton, *Tex.* **13** 34 28N 101 19W
Silvies →, *Oreg.* **16** 43 34N 119 2W
Simi Valley, *Calif.* **19** 34 16N 118 47W
Simmler, *Calif.* **19** 35 21N 119 59W
Sinclair, *Wyo.* **16** 41 47N 107 7W
Sinton, *Tex.* **13** 28 2N 97 31W
Sioux City, *Iowa* **12** 42 30N 96 24W
Sioux Falls, *S. Dak.* **12** 43 33N 96 44W
Sirretta Pk., *Calif.* **19** 35 56N 118 19W
Sisseton, *S. Dak.* **12** 45 40N 97 3W
Sisters, *Oreg.* **16** 44 18N 121 33W
Sitka, *Alaska* **30** 57 3N 135 20W
Skagway, *Alaska* **30** 59 28N 135 19W
Skokie, *Ill.* **22** 42 2N 87 42W
Skowhegan, *Maine* **11** 44 46N 69 43W
Skunk →, *Iowa* **14** 40 42N 91 7W
Skykomish, *Wash.* **16** 47 42N 121 22W
Slaton, *Tex.* **13** 33 26N 101 39W
Sleepy Eye, *Minn.* **12** 44 18N 94 43W
Slidell, *La.* **13** 30 17N 89 47W
Sloansville, *N.Y.* **9** 42 45N 74 22W
Sloughhouse, *Calif.* **18** 38 26N 121 12W
Smith Center, *Kans.* **12** 39 47N 98 47W
Smithfield, *N.C.* **11** 35 31N 78 21W
Smithfield, *Utah* **16** 41 50N 111 50W
Smithville, *Tex.* **13** 30 1N 97 10W
Smoky Hill →, *Kans.* **12** 39 4N 96 48W
Snake →, *Wash.* **16** 46 12N 119 2W
Snake Range, *Nev.* **16** 39 0N 114 20W
Snake River Plain, *Idaho* **16** 42 50N 114 0W
Snelling, *Calif.* **18** 37 31N 120 26W
Snohomish, *Wash.* **18** 47 55N 122 6W
Snow Hill, *Md.* **10** 38 11N 75 24W
Snowflake, *Ariz.* **17** 34 30N 110 5W
Snowshoe Pk., *Mont.* **16** 48 13N 115 41W
Snowville, *Utah* **16** 41 58N 112 43W
Snyder, *Okla.* **13** 34 40N 98 57W
Snyder, *Tex.* **13** 32 44N 100 55W
Soap Lake, *Wash.* **16** 47 23N 119 29W
Socorro, *N. Mex.* **17** 34 4N 106 54W
Soda L., *Calif.* **17** 35 10N 116 4W
Soda Springs, *Idaho* **16** 42 39N 111 36W
Sodus, *N.Y.* **8** 43 14N 77 4W
Soledad, *Calif.* **18** 36 26N 121 20W
Solomon, N. Fork →, *Kans.* **12** 39 29N 98 26W
Solomon, S. Fork →, *Kans.* **12** 39 25N 99 12W
Solon Springs, *Wis.* **12** 46 22N 91 49W
Solvang, *Calif.* **19** 34 36N 120 8W
Solvay, *N.Y.* **9** 43 3N 76 13W
Somers, *Mont.* **16** 48 5N 114 13W
Somerset, *Colo.* **17** 38 56N 107 28W
Somerset, *Ky.* **10** 37 5N 84 36W
Somerset, *Mass.* **9** 41 47N 71 8W
Somerton, *Ariz.* **17** 32 36N 114 43W
Somerville, *Mass.* **23** 42 23N 71 5W
Somerville, *N.J.* **9** 40 35N 74 38W
Sonora, *Calif.* **18** 37 59N 120 23W
Sonora, *Tex.* **13** 30 34N 100 39W
South Baldy, *N. Mex.* **17** 33 59N 107 11W
South Bend, *Ind.* **15** 41 41N 86 15W
South Bend, *Wash.* **18** 46 40N 123 48W
South Boston, *Va.* **11** 36 42N 78 54W
South C. = Ka Lae, *Hawaii* **30** 18 55N 155 41W
South Cape, *Hawaii* **30** 18 58N 155 24 E
South Carolina □ **11** 34 0N 81 0W
South Charleston, *W. Va.* **10** 38 22N 81 44W
South Dakota □ **12** 44 15N 100 0W
South Euclid, *Ohio* **27** 41 31N 81 32W
South Fork →, *Mont.* **16** 47 54N 113 15W
South Fork, American →, *Calif.* **18** 38 45N 121 5W
South Gate, *Calif.* **29** 33 56N 118 12W
South Haven, *Mich.* **15** 42 24N 86 16W
South Holland, *Ill.* **22** 41 36N 87 36W
South Loup →, *Nebr.* **12** 41 4N 98 39W
South Milwaukee, *Wis.* **15** 42 55N 87 52W
South Pasadena, *Calif.* **29** 34 7N 118 8W
South Pass, *Wyo.* **16** 42 20N 108 58W
South Pittsburg, *Tenn.* **11** 35 1N 85 42W
South Platte →, *Nebr.* **12** 41 7N 100 42W
South River, *N.J.* **9** 40 27N 74 23W
South San Francisco, *Calif.* **28** 37 39N 122 24W
South Sioux City, *Nebr.* **12** 42 28N 96 24W
Southampton, *N.Y.* **9** 40 53N 72 23W
Southbridge, *Mass.* **9** 42 5N 72 2W
Southeast C., *Alaska* **30** 62 56N 169 39W
Southern Pines, *N.C.* **11** 35 11N 79 24W
Southfield, *Mich.* **26** 42 28N 83 15W
Southgate, *Mich.* **26** 42 11N 83 12W
Southington, *Conn.* **9** 41 36N 72 53W
Southold, *N.Y.* **9** 41 4N 72 26W
Southport, *N.C.* **11** 33 55N 78 1W
Spalding, *Nebr.* **12** 41 42N 98 22W
Spanish Fork, *Utah* **16** 40 7N 111 39W
Sparks, *Nev.* **18** 39 32N 119 45W
Sparta, *Ga.* **11** 33 17N 82 58W
Sparta, *Wis.* **12** 43 56N 90 49W
Spartanburg, *S.C.* **11** 34 56N 81 57W
Spearfish, *S. Dak.* **12** 44 30N 103 52W
Spearman, *Tex.* **13** 36 12N 101 12W
Spenard, *Alaska* **30** 61 11N 149 55W
Spencer, *Idaho* **16** 44 22N 112 11W
Spencer, *Iowa* **12** 43 9N 95 9W
Spencer, *N.Y.* **9** 42 13N 76 30W
Spencer, *Nebr.* **12** 42 53N 98 42W
Spencer, *W. Va.* **10** 38 48N 81 21W
Spirit Lake, *Idaho* **16** 47 58N 116 52W
Spofford, *Tex.* **13** 29 10N 100 25W
Spokane, *Wash.* **16** 47 40N 117 24W
Spooner, *Wis.* **12** 45 50N 91 53W
Sprague, *Wash.* **16** 47 18N 117 59W
Sprague River, *Oreg.* **16** 42 27N 121 30W
Spray, *Oreg.* **16** 44 50N 119 48W
Spring City, *Utah* **16** 39 29N 111 30W
Spring Mts., *Nev.* **17** 36 0N 115 45W
Spring Valley, *Minn.* **12** 43 41N 92 23W
Springdale, *Ark.* **13** 36 11N 94 8W
Springdale, *Wash.* **16** 48 4N 117 45W
Springer, *N. Mex.* **13** 36 22N 104 36W
Springerville, *Ariz.* **17** 34 8N 109 17W
Springfield, *Colo.* **13** 37 24N 102 37W
Springfield, *Ill.* **14** 39 48N 89 39W
Springfield, *Mass.* **9** 42 6N 72 35W
Springfield, *Mo.* **13** 37 13N 93 17W
Springfield, *N.J.* **20** 40 42N 74 18W
Springfield, *Ohio* **15** 39 55N 83 49W
Springfield, *Oreg.* **16** 44 3N 123 1W
Springfield, *Tenn.* **11** 36 31N 86 53W
Springfield, *Va.* **25** 38 46N 77 10W
Springfield, *Vt.* **9** 43 18N 72 29W
Springvale, *Maine* **9** 43 28N 70 48W
Springville, *Calif.* **18** 36 8N 118 49W
Springville, *N.Y.* **8** 42 31N 78 40W
Springville, *Utah* **16** 40 10N 111 37W
Spur, *Tex.* **13** 33 28N 100 52W
Stafford, *Kans.* **13** 37 58N 98 36W
Stafford Springs, *Conn.* **9** 41 57N 72 18W
Stamford, *Conn.* **9** 41 3N 73 32W
Stamford, *Tex.* **13** 32 57N 99 48W
Stamps, *Ark.* **13** 33 22N 93 30W
Stanberry, *Mo.* **12** 40 13N 94 35W
Standish, *Mich.* **10** 43 59N 83 57W
Stanford, *Mont.* **16** 47 9N 110 13W
Stanislaus →, *Calif.* **18** 37 40N 121 14W
Stanley, *Idaho* **16** 44 13N 114 56W
Stanley, *N. Dak.* **12** 48 19N 102 23W
Stanley, *Wis.* **12** 44 58N 90 56W
Stanton, *Tex.* **13** 32 8N 101 48W
Staples, *Minn.* **12** 46 21N 94 48W
Stapleton, *N.Y.* **20** 40 36N 74 5W
Stapleton, *Nebr.* **12** 41 29N 100 31W
Starke, *Fla.* **11** 29 57N 82 7W
Starkville, *Colo.* **13** 37 8N 104 30W
Starkville, *Miss.* **11** 33 28N 88 49W
State College, *Pa.* **8** 40 48N 77 52W
Staten Island, *N.Y.* **20** 40 34N 74 9W
Statesboro, *Ga.* **11** 32 27N 81 47W
Statesville, *N.C.* **11** 35 47N 80 53W
Statue of Liberty, *N.J.* **20** 40 41N 74 2W
Stauffer, *Calif.* **19** 34 45N 119 3W
Staunton, *Ill.* **14** 39 1N 89 47W
Staunton, *Va.* **10** 38 9N 79 4W
Steamboat Springs, *Colo.* **16** 40 29N 106 50W
Steele, *N. Dak.* **12** 46 51N 99 55W
Steelton, *Pa.* **8** 40 14N 76 50W
Steelville, *Mo.* **14** 37 58N 91 22W
Stephen, *Minn.* **12** 48 27N 96 53W
Stephenville, *Tex.* **13** 32 13N 98 12W
Sterling, *Colo.* **12** 40 37N 103 13W
Sterling, *Ill.* **14** 41 48N 89 42W
Sterling, *Kans.* **12** 38 13N 98 12W
Sterling City, *Tex.* **13** 31 51N 101 0W
Sterling Heights, *Mich.* **26** 42 35N 83 3W
Steubenville, *Ohio* **8** 40 22N 80 37W
Stevens Point, *Wis.* **12** 44 31N 89 34W
Stevens Village, *Alaska* **30** 66 1N 149 6W
Stigler, *Okla.* **13** 35 15N 95 8W
Stillwater, *Minn.* **12** 45 3N 92 49W
Stillwater, *N.Y.* **9** 42 55N 73 41W
Stillwater, *Okla.* **13** 36 7N 97 4W
Stillwater Range, *Nev.* **16** 39 50N 118 5W
Stilwell, *Okla.* **13** 35 49N 94 38W
Stockett, *Mont.* **16** 47 21N 111 10W
Stockton, *Calif.* **18** 37 58N 121 17W
Stockton, *Kans.* **12** 39 26N 99 16W
Stockton, *Mo.* **14** 37 42N 93 48W
Stoneham, *Mass.* **23** 42 29N 71 5W
Stony River, *Alaska* **30** 61 47N 156 35W
Storm Lake, *Iowa* **12** 42 39N 95 13W
Stove Pipe Wells Village, *Calif.* **19** 36 35N 117 11W
Strasburg, *N. Dak.* **12** 46 8N 100 10W
Stratford, *Calif.* **18** 36 11N 119 49W
Stratford, *Conn.* **9** 41 12N 73 8W
Stratford, *Tex.* **13** 36 20N 102 4W
Strathmore, *Calif.* **18** 36 9N 119 4W
Stratton, *Colo.* **12** 39 19N 102 36W
Strawberry Reservoir, *Utah* **16** 40 8N 111 9W
Strawn, *Tex.* **13** 32 33N 98 30W
Streator, *Ill.* **15** 41 8N 88 50W
Streeter, *N. Dak.* **12** 46 39N 99 21W
Stromsburg, *Iowa* **12** 41 7N 97 36W
Stroudsburg, *Pa.* **9** 40 59N 75 12W
Struthers, *Ohio* **8** 41 4N 80 39W
Stryker, *Mont.* **16** 48 41N 114 46W
Stuart, *Fla.* **11** 27 12N 80 15W
Stuart, *Nebr.* **12** 42 36N 99 8W
Stuart I., *Alaska* **30** 63 55N 164 50W
Sturgeon Bay, *Wis.* **10** 44 50N 87 23W
Sturgis, *Mich.* **15** 41 48N 85 25W
Sturgis, *S. Dak.* **12** 44 25N 103 31W
Stuttgart, *Ark.* **13** 34 30N 91 33W
Stuyvesant, *N.Y.* **9** 42 23N 73 45W
Sudan, *Tex.* **13** 34 4N 102 32W
Suffolk, *Va.* **10** 36 44N 76 35W
Sugar City, *Colo.* **12** 38 14N 103 40W
Suitland, *Md.* **25** 38 50N 76 55W
Sullivan, *Ill.* **15** 39 36N 88 37W
Sullivan, *Ind.* **15** 39 6N 87 24W
Sullivan, *Mo.* **14** 38 13N 91 10W
Sulphur, *La.* **13** 30 14N 93 23W
Sulphur, *Okla.* **13** 34 31N 96 58W
Sulphur Springs, *Tex.* **13** 33 8N 95 36W
Sulphur Springs Draw →, *Tex.* **13** 32 12N 101 36W
Sumatra, *Mont.* **16** 46 37N 107 33W
Summer L., *Oreg.* **16** 42 50N 120 45W
Summerville, *Ga.* **11** 34 29N 85 21W
Summerville, *S.C.* **11** 33 1N 80 11W
Summit, *Alaska* **30** 63 20N 149 7W
Summit, *Ill.* **22** 41 47N 87 47W
Summit, *N.J.* **20** 40 43N 74 21W
Summit Peak, *Colo.* **17** 37 21N 106 42W
Sumner, *Iowa* **14** 42 51N 92 6W
Sumter, *S.C.* **11** 33 55N 80 21W
Sun City, *Ariz.* **17** 33 36N 112 17W
Sun City, *Calif.* **19** 33 42N 117 11W
Sunburst, *Mont.* **16** 48 53N 111 55W
Sunbury, *Pa.* **9** 40 52N 76 48W
Suncook, *N.H.* **9** 43 8N 71 27W
Sundance, *Wyo.* **12** 44 24N 104 23W
Sunnyside, *Utah* **16** 39 34N 110 23W
Sunnyside, *Wash.* **16** 46 20N 120 0W
Sunnyvale, *Calif.* **18** 37 23N 122 2W
Sunray, *Tex.* **13** 36 1N 101 49W
Sunshine Acres, *Calif.* **29** 33 56N 117 59W
Supai, *Ariz.* **17** 36 15N 112 41W
Superior, *Ariz.* **17** 33 18N 111 6W
Superior, *Mont.* **16** 47 12N 114 53W
Superior, *Nebr.* **12** 40 1N 98 4W
Superior, *Wis.* **12** 46 44N 92 6W
Superior, L., *N. Amer.* **10** 47 0N 87 0W
Sur, Pt., *Calif.* **18** 36 18N 121 54W
Surf, *Calif.* **19** 34 41N 120 36W
Susanville, *Calif.* **16** 40 25N 120 39W
Susquehanna →, *Pa.* **9** 39 33N 76 5W
Susquehanna Depot, *Pa.* **9** 41 57N 75 36W
Sussex, *N.J.* **9** 41 13N 74 37W
Sutherland, *Nebr.* **12** 41 10N 101 8W
Sutherlin, *Oreg.* **16** 43 23N 123 19W
Sutter Creek, *Calif.* **18** 38 24N 120 48W
Sutton, *Nebr.* **12** 40 36N 97 52W
Sutwik I., *Alaska* **30** 56 34N 157 12W
Suwannee →, *Fla.* **11** 29 17N 83 10W
Swainsboro, *Ga.* **11** 32 36N 82 20W
Swampscott, *Mass.* **23** 42 28N 70 53W
Swarthmore, *Pa.* **24** 39 54N 75 20W
Sweet Home, *Oreg.* **16** 44 24N 122 44W
Sweetwater, *Nev.* **18** 38 27N 119 9W
Sweetwater, *Tex.* **13** 32 28N 100 25W
Sweetwater →, *Wyo.* **16** 42 31N 107 2W
Swissvale, *Pa.* **27** 40 25N 79 52W
Sylacauga, *Ala.* **11** 33 10N 86 15W
Sylvania, *Ga.* **11** 32 45N 81 38W
Sylvester, *Ga.* **11** 31 32N 83 50W
Syracuse, *Kans.* **13** 37 59N 101 45W
Syracuse, *N.Y.* **9** 43 3N 76 9W

T

Tacoma, *Wash.* **18** 47 14N 122 26W
Taft, *Calif.* **19** 35 8N 119 28W
Taft, *Tex.* **13** 27 59N 97 24W
Tahoe, L., *Nev.* **18** 39 6N 120 2W
Tahoe City, *Calif.* **18** 39 10N 120 9W
Takoma Park, *Md.* **25** 38 58N 77 0W
Talihina, *Okla.* **13** 34 45N 95 3W
Talkeetna, *Alaska* **30** 62 20N 150 6W
Talkeetna Mts., *Alaska* **30** 62 20N 149 0W
Talladega, *Ala.* **11** 33 26N 86 6W
Tallahassee, *Fla.* **11** 30 27N 84 17W
Talleyville, *Del.* **24** 39 48N 75 32W
Tallulah, *La.* **13** 32 25N 91 11W
Tama, *Iowa* **14** 41 58N 92 35W
Tamaqua, *Pa.* **9** 40 48N 75 58W
Tampa, *Fla.* **11** 27 57N 82 27W
Tampa B., *Fla.* **11** 27 50N 82 30W
Tanana, *Alaska* **30** 65 10N 152 4W
Tanana →, *Alaska* **30** 65 10N 151 58W
Taos, *N. Mex.* **17** 36 24N 105 35W
Tappahannock, *Va.* **10** 37 56N 76 52W
Tarboro, *N.C.* **11** 35 54N 77 32W
Tarpon Springs, *Fla.* **11** 28 9N 82 45W
Tarrytown, *N.Y.* **9** 41 4N 73 52W
Tatum, *N. Mex.* **13** 33 16N 103 19W
Tau, *W. Samoa* **31** 14 15S 169 30W
Taunton, *Mass.* **9** 41 54N 71 6W
Tawas City, *Mich.* **10** 44 16N 83 31W
Taylor, *Alaska* **30** 65 40N 164 50W
Taylor, *Mich.* **26** 42 13N 83 15W
Taylor, *Nebr.* **12** 41 46N 99 23W
Taylor, *Pa.* **9** 41 23N 75 43W
Taylor, *Tex.* **13** 30 34N 97 25W
Taylor, Mt., *N. Mex.* **17** 35 14N 107 37W
Taylortown, *N.J.* **20** 40 56N 74 23W
Taylorville, *Ill.* **14** 39 33N 89 18W
Teague, *Tex.* **13** 31 38N 96 17W

Washington

Washington, *N.J.* **9** 40 46N 74 59W
Washington, *Pa.* **8** 40 10N 80 15W
Washington, *Utah* **17** 37 8N 113 31W
Washington □ **16** 47 30N 120 30W
Washington, Mt., *N.H.* **9** 44 16N 71 18W
Washington Heights, *N.Y.* **20** 40 50N 73 55W
Washington I., *Wis.* **10** 45 23N 86 54W
Washington National Airport, *D.C.* **25** 38 51N 77 2W
Watching Mountains, *N.J.* **20** 40 42N 74 20W
Water Valley, *Miss.* **13** 34 10N 89 38W
Waterbury, *Conn.* **9** 41 33N 73 3W
Waterford, *Calif.* **18** 37 38N 120 46W
Waterloo, *Ill.* **14** 38 20N 90 9W
Waterloo, *Iowa* **14** 42 30N 92 21W
Waterloo, *N.Y.* **8** 42 54N 76 52W
Watersmeet, *Mich.* **12** 46 16N 89 11W
Waterton-Glacier International Peace Park, *Mont.* **16** 48 45N 115 0W
Watertown, *Conn.* **9** 41 36N 73 7W
Watertown, *Mass.* **23** 42 22N 71 10W
Watertown, *N.Y.* **9** 43 59N 75 55W
Watertown, *S. Dak.* **12** 44 54N 97 7W
Watertown, *Wis.* **15** 43 12N 88 43W
Waterville, *Maine* **11** 44 33N 69 38W
Waterville, *N.Y.* **9** 42 56N 75 23W
Waterville, *Wash.* **16** 47 39N 120 4W
Watervliet, *N.Y.* **9** 42 44N 73 42W
Watford City, *N. Dak.* **12** 47 48N 103 17W
Watkins Glen, *N.Y.* **8** 42 23N 76 52W
Watonga, *Okla.* **13** 35 51N 98 25W
Watrous, *N. Mex.* **13** 35 48N 104 59W
Watseka, *Ill.* **15** 40 47N 87 44W
Watsonville, *Calif.* **18** 36 55N 121 45W
Waubay, *S. Dak.* **12** 45 20N 97 18W
Wauchula, *Fla.* **11** 27 33N 81 49W
Waukegan, *Ill.* **15** 42 22N 87 50W
Waukesha, *Wis.* **15** 43 1N 88 14W
Waukon, *Iowa* **12** 43 16N 91 29W
Wauneta, *Nebr.* **12** 40 25N 101 23W
Waupaca, *Wis.* **12** 44 21N 89 5W
Waupun, *Wis.* **12** 43 38N 88 44W
Waurika, *Okla.* **13** 34 10N 98 0W
Wausau, *Wis.* **12** 44 58N 89 38W
Wautoma, *Wis.* **12** 44 4N 89 18W
Wauwatosa, *Wis.* **15** 43 3N 88 0W
Waverly, *Iowa* **14** 42 44N 92 29W
Waverly, *N.Y.* **9** 42 1N 76 32W
Wawona, *Calif.* **18** 37 32N 119 39W
Waxahachie, *Tex.* **13** 32 24N 96 51W
Waycross, *Ga.* **11** 31 13N 82 21W
Wayland, *Mass.* **23** 42 21N 71 20W
Wayne, *Mich.* **26** 42 16N 83 22W
Wayne, *N.J.* **20** 40 55N 74 14W
Wayne, *Nebr.* **12** 42 14N 97 1W
Wayne, *Pa.* **24** 40 2N 75 24W
Wayne, *W. Va.* **10** 38 13N 82 27W
Waynesboro, *Ga.* **11** 33 6N 82 1W
Waynesboro, *Miss.* **11** 31 40N 88 39W
Waynesboro, *Pa.* **10** 39 45N 77 35W
Waynesboro, *Va.* **10** 38 4N 78 53W
Waynesburg, *Pa.* **10** 39 54N 80 11W
Waynesville, *N.C.* **11** 35 28N 82 58W
Waynoka, *Okla.* **13** 36 35N 98 53W
Weatherford, *Okla.* **13** 35 32N 98 43W
Weatherford, *Tex.* **13** 32 46N 97 48W
Weaverville, *Calif.* **16** 40 44N 122 56W
Webb City, *Mo.* **13** 37 9N 94 28W
Webster, *Mass.* **9** 42 3N 71 53W
Webster, *S. Dak.* **12** 45 20N 97 31W
Webster, *Wis.* **12** 45 53N 92 22W
Webster City, *Iowa* **14** 42 28N 93 49W
Webster Green, *Mo.* **12** 38 38N 90 20W
Webster Springs, *W. Va.* **10** 38 29N 80 25W
Weed, *Calif.* **16** 41 25N 122 23W
Weedsport, *N.Y.* **9** 43 3N 76 35W
Weiser, *Idaho* **16** 44 10N 117 0W
Welch, *W. Va.* **10** 37 26N 81 35W
Wellesley, *Mass.* **23** 42 17N 71 17W
Wellington, *Colo.* **12** 40 42N 105 0W
Wellington, *Kans.* **13** 37 16N 97 24W
Wellington, *Nev.* **18** 38 45N 119 23W
Wellington, *Tex.* **13** 34 51N 100 13W
Wells, *Maine* **9** 43 20N 70 35W
Wells, *Minn.* **12** 43 45N 93 44W
Wells, *Nev.* **16** 41 7N 114 58W
Wellsboro, *Pa.* **8** 41 45N 77 18W
Wellsville, *Mo.* **14** 39 4N 91 34W
Wellsville, *N.Y.* **8** 42 7N 77 57W
Wellsville, *Ohio* **8** 40 36N 80 39W
Wellsville, *Utah* **16** 41 38N 111 56W
Wellton, *Ariz.* **17** 32 40N 114 8W
Wenatchee, *Wash.* **16** 47 25N 120 19W
Wendell, *Idaho* **16** 42 47N 114 42W
Wendover, *Utah* **16** 40 44N 114 2W
Weott, *Calif.* **16** 40 20N 123 55W
Wesley Vale, *N. Mex.* **17** 35 3N 106 2W
Wessington, *S. Dak.* **12** 44 27N 98 42W
Wessington Springs, *S. Dak.* **12** 44 5N 98 34W
West, *Tex.* **13** 31 48N 97 6W
West B., *La.* **13** 29 3N 89 22W
West Babylon, *N.Y.* **21** 40 43N 73 21W
West Bend, *Wis.* **10** 43 25N 88 11W
West Branch, *Mich.* **10** 44 17N 84 14W
West Chelmsford, *Mass.* **23** 42 36N 71 22W
West Chester, *Pa.* **10** 39 58N 75 36W
West Chester, *Pa.* **24** 39 57N 75 35W
West Columbia, *Tex.* **13** 29 9N 95 39W
West Covina, *Calif.* **29** 34 4N 117 55W
West Des Moines, *Iowa* **14** 41 35N 93 43W
West Frankfort, *Ill.* **14** 37 54N 88 55W
West Hartford, *Conn.* **9** 41 45N 72 44W
West Haven, *Conn.* **9** 41 17N 72 57W
West Helena, *Ark.* **13** 34 33N 90 38W
West Hempstead, *N.Y.* **21** 40 41N 73 38W
West Hollywood, *Calif.* **29** 34 5N 118 21W
West Memphis, *Ark.* **13** 35 9N 90 11W
West Mifflin, *Pa.* **27** 40 21N 79 53W
West Monroe, *La.* **13** 32 31N 92 9W
West New York, *N.J.* **20** 40 46N 74 0W
West Orange, *N.J.* **20** 40 46N 74 15W
West Palm Beach, *Fla.* **11** 26 43N 80 3W
West Plains, *Mo.* **13** 36 44N 91 51W
West Point, *Ga.* **11** 32 53N 85 11W
West Point, *Miss.* **11** 33 36N 88 39W
West Point, *Nebr.* **12** 41 51N 96 43W
West Point, *Va.* **10** 37 32N 76 48W
West Rutland, *Vt.* **9** 43 38N 73 5W
West View, *Pa.* **27** 40 31N 80 2W
West Virginia □ **10** 38 45N 80 30W
West Walker →, *Nev.* **18** 38 54N 119 9W
West Yellowstone, *Mont.* **16** 44 40N 111 6W
Westbrook, *Maine* **11** 43 41N 70 22W
Westbrook, *Tex.* **13** 32 21N 101 1W
Westbury, *N.Y.* **21** 40 45N 73 35W
Westby, *Mont.* **12** 48 52N 104 3W
Westchester, *Ill.* **22** 41 51N 87 53W
Westend, *Calif.* **19** 35 42N 117 24W
Westernport, *Md.* **10** 39 29N 79 3W
Westfield, *Mass.* **9** 42 7N 72 45W
Westfield, *N.J.* **20** 40 39N 74 20W
Westhope, *N. Dak.* **12** 48 55N 101 1W
Westlake, *Ohio* **27** 41 27N 81 54W
Westland, *Mich.* **26** 42 19N 83 22W
Westminster, *Md.* **10** 39 34N 76 59W
Westmorland, *Calif.* **17** 33 2N 115 37W
Weston, *Mass.* **23** 42 22N 71 17W
Weston, *Oreg.* **16** 45 49N 118 26W
Weston, *W. Va.* **10** 39 2N 80 28W
Westport, *Wash.* **16** 46 53N 124 6W
Westville, *Ill.* **15** 40 2N 87 38W
Westville, *Okla.* **13** 35 58N 94 40W
Westwood, *Calif.* **16** 40 18N 121 0W
Westwood, *Mass.* **23** 42 12N 71 13W
Wethersfield, *Conn.* **9** 41 42N 72 40W
Wewoka, *Okla.* **13** 35 9N 96 30W
Weymouth, *Mass.* **23** 42 12N 70 57W
Wharton, *N.J.* **9** 40 54N 74 35W
Wharton, *Tex.* **13** 29 19N 96 6W
Wheatland, *Wyo.* **12** 42 3N 104 58W
Wheaton, *Md.* **25** 39 2N 77 1W
Wheaton, *Minn.* **12** 45 48N 96 30W
Wheeler, *Oreg.* **16** 45 41N 123 53W
Wheeler, *Tex.* **13** 35 27N 100 16W
Wheeler Pk., *N. Mex.* **17** 36 34N 105 25W
Wheeler Pk., *Nev.* **17** 38 57N 114 15W
Wheeler Ridge, *Calif.* **19** 35 0N 118 57W
Wheeling, *W. Va.* **8** 40 4N 80 43W
White →, *Ark.* **13** 33 57N 91 5W
White →, *Ind.* **15** 38 25N 87 45W
White →, *S. Dak.* **12** 43 42N 99 27W
White →, *Utah* **16** 40 4N 109 41W
White Bird, *Idaho* **16** 45 46N 116 18W
White Butte, *N. Dak.* **12** 46 23N 103 18W
White City, *Kans.* **12** 38 48N 96 44W
White Deer, *Tex.* **13** 35 26N 101 10W
White Hall, *Ill.* **14** 39 26N 90 24W
White Haven, *Pa.* **9** 41 4N 75 47W
White House, The, *D.C.* **25** 38 53N 77 2W
White L., *La.* **13** 29 44N 92 30W
White Mts., *Calif.* **18** 37 30N 118 15W
White Mts., *N.H.* **9** 44 15N 71 15W
White Plains, *N.Y.* **21** 41 0N 73 46W
White River, *S. Dak.* **12** 43 34N 100 45W
White Sulphur Springs, *Mont.* **16** 46 33N 110 54W
White Sulphur Springs, *W. Va.* **10** 37 48N 80 18W
Whiteface, *Tex.* **13** 33 36N 102 37W
Whitefish, *Mont.* **16** 48 25N 114 20W
Whitefish Point, *Mich.* **10** 46 45N 84 59W
Whitehall, *Mich.* **10** 43 24N 86 21W
Whitehall, *Mont.* **16** 45 52N 112 6W
Whitehall, *N.Y.* **9** 43 33N 73 24W
Whitehall, *Pa.* **27** 40 21N 80 0W
Whitehall, *Wis.* **12** 44 22N 91 19W
Whitesboro, *N.Y.* **9** 43 7N 75 18W
Whitesboro, *Tex.* **13** 33 39N 96 54W
Whitetail, *Mont.* **12** 48 54N 105 10W
Whiteville, *N.C.* **11** 34 20N 78 42W
Whitewater, *Wis.* **15** 42 50N 88 44W
Whitewater Baldy, *N. Mex.* **17** 33 20N 108 39W
Whiting, *Ind.* **22** 41 41N 87 30W
Whitman, *Mass.* **9** 42 5N 70 56W
Whitmire, *S.C.* **11** 34 30N 81 37W
Whitney, Mt., *Calif.* **18** 36 35N 118 18W
Whitney Point, *N.Y.* **9** 42 20N 75 58W
Whittier, *Alaska* **30** 60 47N 148 41W
Whittier, *Calif.* **29** 33 58N 118 2W
Whitwell, *Tenn.* **11** 35 12N 85 31W
Wibaux, *Mont.* **12** 46 59N 104 11W
Wichita, *Kans.* **13** 37 42N 97 20W
Wichita Falls, *Tex.* **13** 33 54N 98 30W
Wickenburg, *Ariz.* **17** 33 58N 112 44W
Wiggins, *Colo.* **12** 40 14N 104 4W
Wiggins, *Miss.* **13** 30 51N 89 8W
Wilber, *Nebr.* **12** 40 29N 96 58W
Wilburton, *Okla.* **13** 34 55N 95 19W
Wildrose, *Calif.* **19** 36 14N 117 11W
Wildrose, *N. Dak.* **12** 48 38N 103 11W
Wildwood, *N.J.* **10** 38 59N 74 50W
Wilkes-Barre, *Pa.* **9** 41 15N 75 53W
Wilkesboro, *N.C.* **11** 36 9N 81 10W
Wilkinsburg, *Pa.* **27** 40 26N 79 52W
Willamina, *Oreg.* **16** 45 5N 123 29W
Willapa B., *Wash.* **16** 46 40N 124 0W
Willard, *N. Mex.* **17** 34 36N 106 2W
Willard, *Utah* **16** 41 25N 112 2W
Willcox, *Ariz.* **17** 32 15N 109 50W
Williams, *Ariz.* **17** 35 15N 112 11W
Williamsburg, *Ky.* **11** 36 44N 84 10W
Williamsburg, *Va.* **10** 37 17N 76 44W
Williamson, *W. Va.* **10** 37 41N 82 17W
Williamsport, *Pa.* **8** 41 15N 77 0W
Williamston, *N.C.* **11** 35 51N 77 4W
Williamstown, *N.Y.* **9** 43 26N 75 53W
Williamsville, *Mo.* **13** 36 58N 90 33W
Willimantic, *Conn.* **9** 41 43N 72 13W
Willingboro, *N.J.* **24** 40 3N 74 54W
Williston, *Fla.* **11** 29 23N 82 27W
Williston, *N. Dak.* **12** 48 9N 103 37W
Williston Park, *N.Y.* **21** 40 45N 73 39W
Willits, *Calif.* **16** 39 25N 123 21W
Willmar, *Minn.* **12** 45 7N 95 3W
Willow Brook, *Calif.* **29** 33 55N 118 13W
Willow Grove, *Pa.* **24** 40 8N 75 7W
Willow Lake, *S. Dak.* **12** 44 38N 97 38W
Willow Springs, *Mo.* **13** 37 0N 91 58W
Willowick, *Ohio* **27** 41 36N 81 30W
Willows, *Calif.* **18** 39 31N 122 12W
Wills Point, *Tex.* **13** 32 43N 96 1W
Wilmette, *Ill.* **10** 42 5N 87 42W
Wilmette, *Ill.* **22** 42 4N 87 42W
Wilmington, *Del.* **10** 39 45N 75 33W
Wilmington, *Del.* **24** 39 44N 75 32W
Wilmington, *Ill.* **15** 41 18N 88 9W
Wilmington, *N.C.* **11** 34 14N 77 55W
Wilmington, *Ohio* **15** 39 27N 83 50W
Wilsall, *Mont.* **16** 45 59N 110 38W
Wilson, *N.C.* **11** 35 44N 77 55W
Wilton, *N. Dak.* **12** 47 10N 100 47W
Winchendon, *Mass.* **9** 42 41N 72 3W
Winchester, *Conn.* **9** 41 53N 73 9W
Winchester, *Idaho* **16** 46 14N 116 38W
Winchester, *Ind.* **15** 40 10N 84 59W
Winchester, *Ky.* **15** 38 0N 84 11W
Winchester, *Mass.* **23** 42 26N 71 8W
Winchester, *N.H.* **9** 42 46N 72 23W
Winchester, *Tenn.* **11** 35 11N 86 7W
Winchester, *Va.* **10** 39 11N 78 10W
Wind →, *Wyo.* **16** 43 12N 108 12W
Wind River Range, *Wyo.* **16** 43 0N 109 30W
Windber, *Pa.* **8** 40 14N 78 50W
Windom, *Minn.* **12** 43 52N 95 7W
Window Rock, *Ariz.* **17** 35 41N 109 3W
Windsor, *Colo.* **12** 40 29N 104 54W
Windsor, *Conn.* **9** 41 50N 72 39W
Windsor, *Mich.* **26** 42 18N 83 0W
Windsor, *Mo.* **14** 38 32N 93 31W
Windsor, *N.Y.* **9** 42 5N 75 37W
Windsor, *Vt.* **9** 43 29N 72 24W
Windsor Airport, *Mich.* **26** 42 16N 82 57W
Winfield, *Kans.* **13** 37 15N 96 59W
Winifred, *Mont.* **16** 47 34N 109 23W
Wink, *Tex.* **13** 31 45N 103 9W
Winlock, *Wash.* **18** 46 30N 122 56W
Winnebago, *Minn.* **12** 43 46N 94 10W
Winnebago, L., *Wis.* **10** 44 0N 88 26W
Winnemucca, *Nev.* **16** 40 58N 117 44W
Winnemucca L., *Nev.* **16** 40 7N 119 21W
Winner, *S. Dak.* **12** 43 22N 99 52W
Winnetka, *Ill.* **22** 42 6N 87 43W
Winnett, *Mont.* **16** 47 0N 108 21W
Winnfield, *La.* **13** 31 56N 92 38W
Winnibigoshish, L., *Minn.* **12** 47 27N 94 13W
Winnipesaukee, L., *N.H.* **9** 43 38N 71 21W
Winnsboro, *La.* **13** 32 10N 91 43W
Winnsboro, *S.C.* **11** 34 23N 81 5W
Winnsboro, *Tex.* **13** 32 58N 95 17W
Winona, *Minn.* **12** 44 3N 91 39W
Winona, *Miss.* **13** 33 29N 89 44W
Winooski, *Vt.* **9** 44 29N 73 11W
Winslow, *Ariz.* **17** 35 2N 110 42W
Winsted, *Conn.* **9** 41 55N 73 4W
Winston-Salem, *N.C.* **11** 36 6N 80 15W
Winter Garden, *Fla.* **11** 28 34N 81 35W
Winter Haven, *Fla.* **11** 28 1N 81 44W
Winter Park, *Fla.* **11** 28 36N 81 20W
Winters, *Tex.* **13** 31 58N 99 58W
Winterset, *Iowa* **14** 41 20N 94 1W
Winthrop, *Mass.* **23** 42 22N 70 58W
Winthrop, *Minn.* **12** 44 32N 94 22W
Winthrop, *Wash.* **16** 48 28N 120 10W
Winton, *N.C.* **11** 36 24N 76 56W
Wisconsin □ **12** 44 45N 89 30W
Wisconsin →, *Wis.* **12** 43 0N 91 15W
Wisconsin Dells, *Wis.* **12** 43 38N 89 46W
Wisconsin Rapids, *Wis.* **12** 44 23N 89 49W
Wisdom, *Mont.* **16** 45 37N 113 27W
Wiseman, *Alaska* **30** 67 25N 150 6W
Wishek, *N. Dak.* **12** 46 16N 99 33W
Wisner, *Nebr.* **12** 41 59N 96 55W
Woburn, *Mass.* **23** 42 29N 71 10W
Wolf Creek, *Mont.* **16** 47 0N 112 4W
Wolf Point, *Mont.* **12** 48 5N 105 39W
Wood Lake, *Nebr.* **12** 42 38N 100 14W
Woodbury, *N.J.* **24** 39 50N 75 9W
Woodbury, *N.Y.* **21** 40 49N 73 27W
Woodfords, *Calif.* **18** 38 47N 119 50W
Woodlake, *Calif.* **18** 36 25N 119 6W
Woodland, *Calif.* **18** 38 41N 121 46W
Woodlawn, *Md.* **25** 39 19N 76 44W
Woodruff, *Ariz.* **17** 34 51N 110 1W
Woodruff, *Utah* **16** 41 31N 111 10W
Woodstock, *Ill.* **15** 42 19N 88 27W
Woodstock, *Vt.* **9** 43 37N 72 31W
Woodsville, *N.H.* **9** 44 9N 72 2W
Woodville, *Tex.* **13** 30 47N 94 25W
Woodward, *Okla.* **13** 36 26N 99 24W
Woody, *Calif.* **19** 35 42N 118 50W
Woonsocket, *R.I.* **9** 42 0N 71 31W
Woonsocket, *S. Dak.* **12** 44 3N 98 17W
Wooster, *Ohio* **8** 40 48N 81 56W
Worcester, *Mass.* **9** 42 16N 71 48W
Worcester, *N.Y.* **9** 42 36N 74 45W
Worland, *Wyo.* **16** 44 1N 107 57W
Wortham, *Tex.* **13** 31 47N 96 28W
Worthington, *Minn.* **12** 43 37N 95 36W
Wrangell, *Alaska* **30** 56 28N 132 23W
Wrangell Mts., *Alaska* **30** 61 30N 142 0W
Wray, *Colo.* **12** 40 5N 102 13W
Wrens, *Ga.* **11** 33 12N 82 23W
Wrightson Mt., *Ariz.* **17** 31 42N 110 51W
Wrightwood, *Calif.* **19** 34 21N 117 38W
Wyalusing, *Pa.* **9** 41 40N 76 16W
Wyandotte, *Mich.* **26** 42 12N 83 9W
Wymore, *Nebr.* **12** 40 7N 96 40W
Wyndmere, *N. Dak.* **12** 46 16N 97 8W
Wynne, *Ark.* **13** 35 14N 90 47W
Wyoming □ **16** 43 0N 107 30W
Wytheville, *Va.* **10** 36 57N 81 5W

X

Xenia, *Ohio* **15** 39 41N 83 56W

Y

Yadkin →, *N.C.* **11** 35 29N 80 9W
Yakataga, *Alaska* **30** 60 5N 142 32W
Yakima, *Wash.* **16** 46 36N 120 31W
Yakima →, *Wash.* **16** 47 0N 120 30W
Yakutat, *Alaska* **30** 59 33N 139 44W
Yalobusha →, *Miss.* **13** 33 33N 90 10W
Yampa →, *Colo.* **16** 40 32N 108 59W
Yankton, *S. Dak.* **12** 42 53N 97 23W
Yap Is., *U.S. Pac. Is. Trust Terr.* **31** 9 30N 138 10 E
Yates Center, *Kans.* **13** 37 53N 95 44W
Yazoo →, *Miss.* **13** 32 22N 90 54W
Yazoo City, *Miss.* **13** 32 51N 90 25W
Yellowstone →, *Mont.* **12** 47 59N 103 59W
Yellowstone L., *Wyo.* **16** 44 27N 110 22W
Yellowstone National Park, *Wyo.* **16** 44 40N 110 30W
Yellowtail Res., *Wyo.* **16** 45 6N 108 8W
Yermo, *Calif.* **19** 34 54N 116 50W
Yeso, *N. Mex.* **13** 34 26N 104 37W
Yoakum, *Tex.* **13** 29 17N 97 9W
Yonkers, *N.Y.* **21** 40 57N 73 52W
York, *Ala.* **11** 32 29N 88 18W
York, *Nebr.* **12** 40 52N 97 36W
York, *Pa.* **10** 39 58N 76 44W
Yorktown, *Tex.* **13** 28 59N 97 30W
Yorkville, *Ill.* **15** 41 38N 88 27W
Yosemite National Park, *Calif.* **18** 37 45N 119 40W
Yosemite Village, *Calif.* **18** 37 45N 119 35W
Youngstown, *N.Y.* **8** 43 15N 79 3W
Youngstown, *Ohio* **8** 41 6N 80 39W
Ypsilanti, *Mich.* **15** 42 14N 83 37W
Yreka, *Calif.* **16** 41 44N 122 38W
Ysleta, *N. Mex.* **17** 31 45N 106 24W
Yuba City, *Calif.* **18** 39 8N 121 37W
Yucca, *Ariz.* **19** 34 52N 114 9W
Yucca Valley, *Calif.* **19** 34 8N 116 27W
Yukon →, *Alaska* **30** 62 32N 163 54W
Yuma, *Ariz.* **19** 32 43N 114 37W
Yuma, *Colo.* **12** 40 8N 102 43W
Yunaska I., *Alaska* **30** 52 38N 170 40W

Z

Zanesville, *Ohio* **8** 39 56N 82 1W
Zapata, *Tex.* **13** 26 55N 99 16W
Zion National Park, *Utah* **17** 37 15N 113 5W
Zrenton, *Mich.* **26** 42 8N 83 12W
Zuni, *N. Mex.* **17** 35 4N 108 51W
Zwolle, *La.* **13** 31 38N 93 39W

WORLD MAPS

SETTLEMENTS

◖ **PARIS** ■ **Berne** ◉ **Livorno** ◉ **Brugge** ◎ *Algeciras* ⊙ *Frèjus* ○ *Oberammergau* ○ *Thira*

Settlement symbols and type styles vary according to the scale of each map and indicate the importance
of towns on the map rather than specific population figures

∴ Ruins or Archæological Sites   ˅ Wells in Desert

ADMINISTRATION

_____ International Boundaries

_ _ _ International Boundaries
(Undefined or Disputed)

▬▬▬··· Internal Boundaries

National Parks

Country Names

NICARAGUA

Administrative
Area Names

K E N T

CALABRIA

International boundaries show the *de facto* situation where there are rival claims to territory

---

COMMUNICATIONS

_____ Principal Roads

‿‿ Other Roads

-·-·-· Trails and Seasonal Roads

≍ Passes

✿ Airfields

‿‿ Principal Railroads

-·-·- Railroads
Under Construction

‿‿ Other Railroads

⌐---⌐ Railroad Tunnels

⸺⸺ Principal Canals

PHYSICAL FEATURES

‿‿ Perennial Streams

-·-·-· Intermittent Streams

◯ Perennial Lakes

⬭ Intermittent Lakes

Swamps and Marshes

Permanent Ice
and Glaciers

▲ 8848 Elevations (m)

▼ 8050 Sea Depths (m)

1134 Height of Lake Surface
Above Sea Level (m)

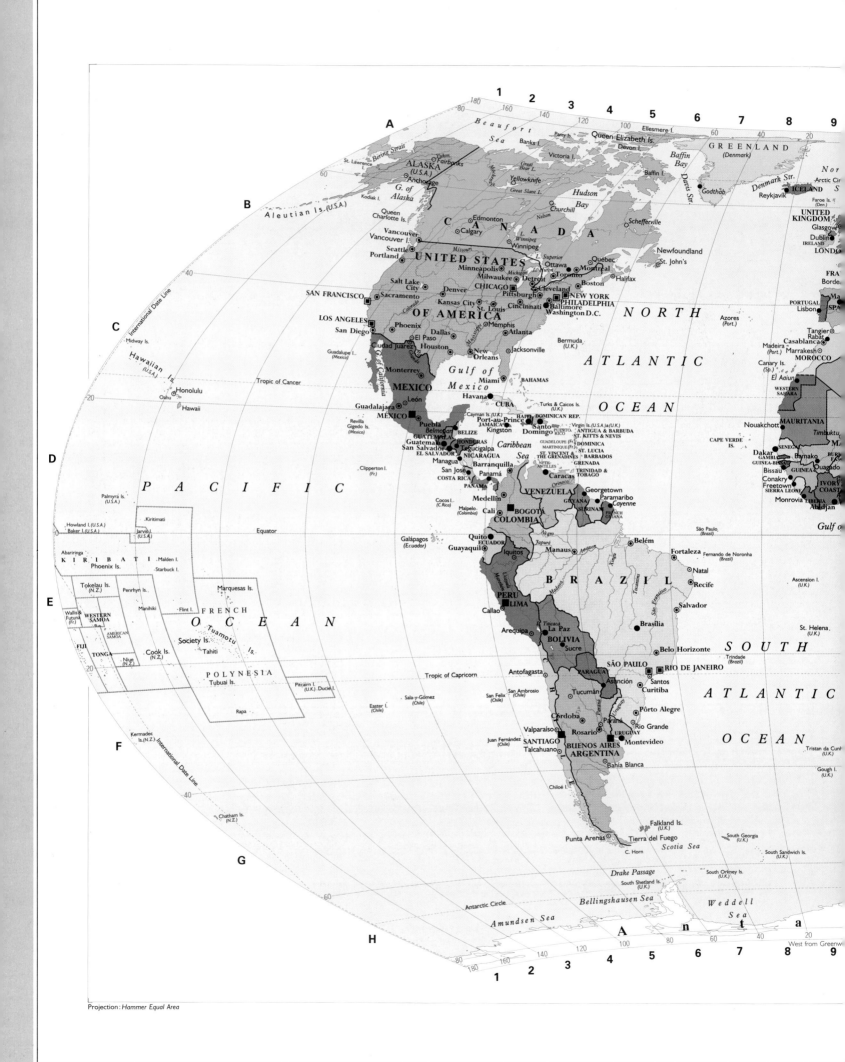

Projection: Hammer Equal Area

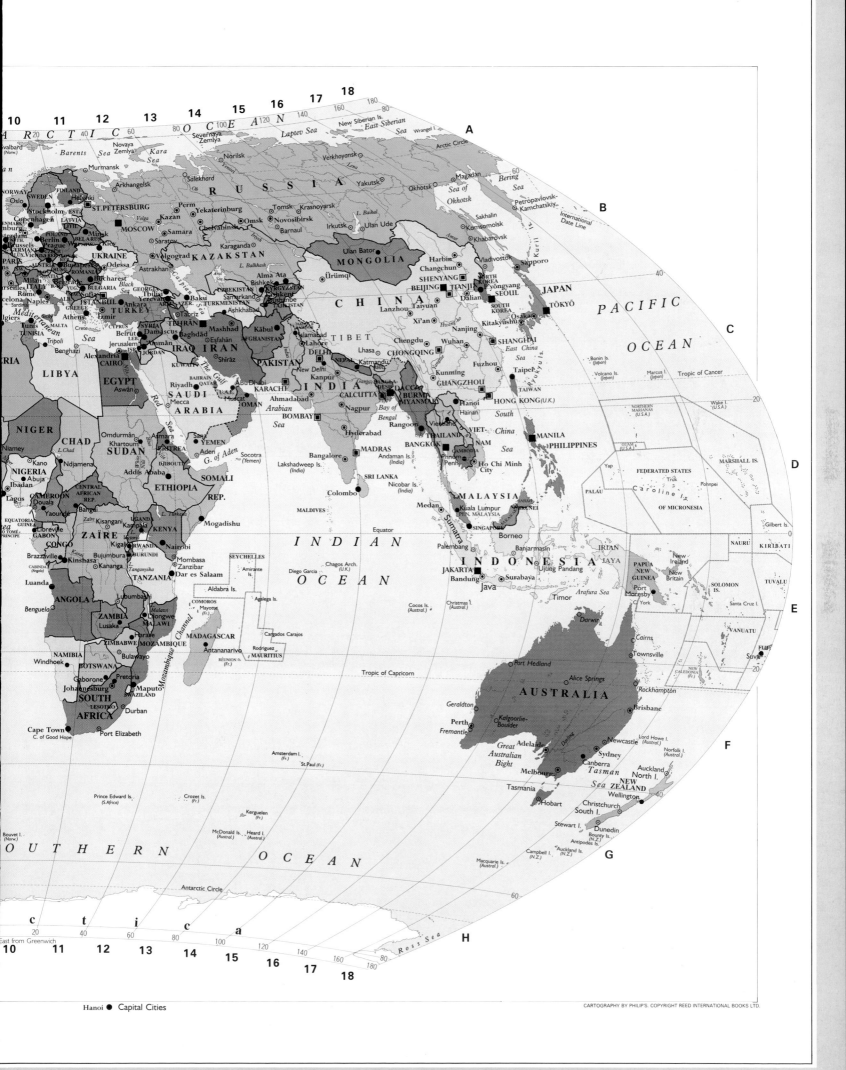

Hanoi ● Capital Cities

1:35 000 000

200 100 0   200   400   600 miles
400 200 0   400   800   1200 km

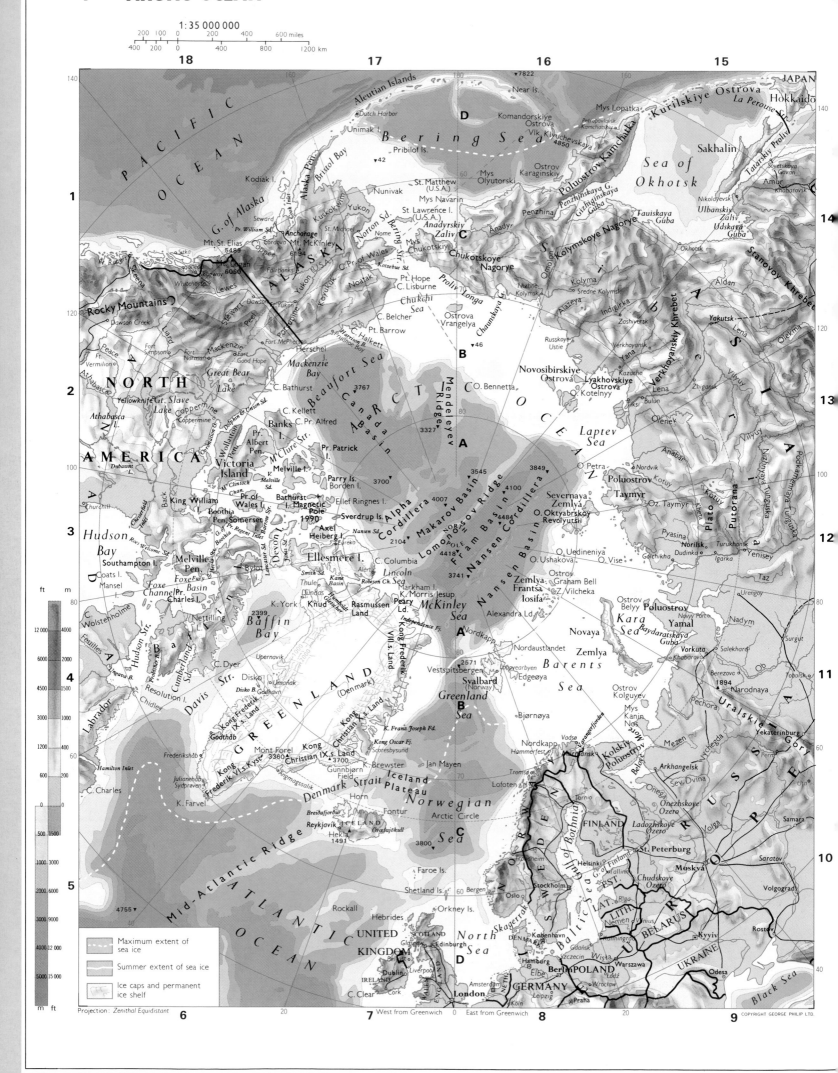

Maximum extent of
sea ice

Summer extent of sea ice

Ice caps and permanent
ice shelf

Projection: Zenithal Equidistant

COPYRIGHT GEORGE PHILIP LTD.

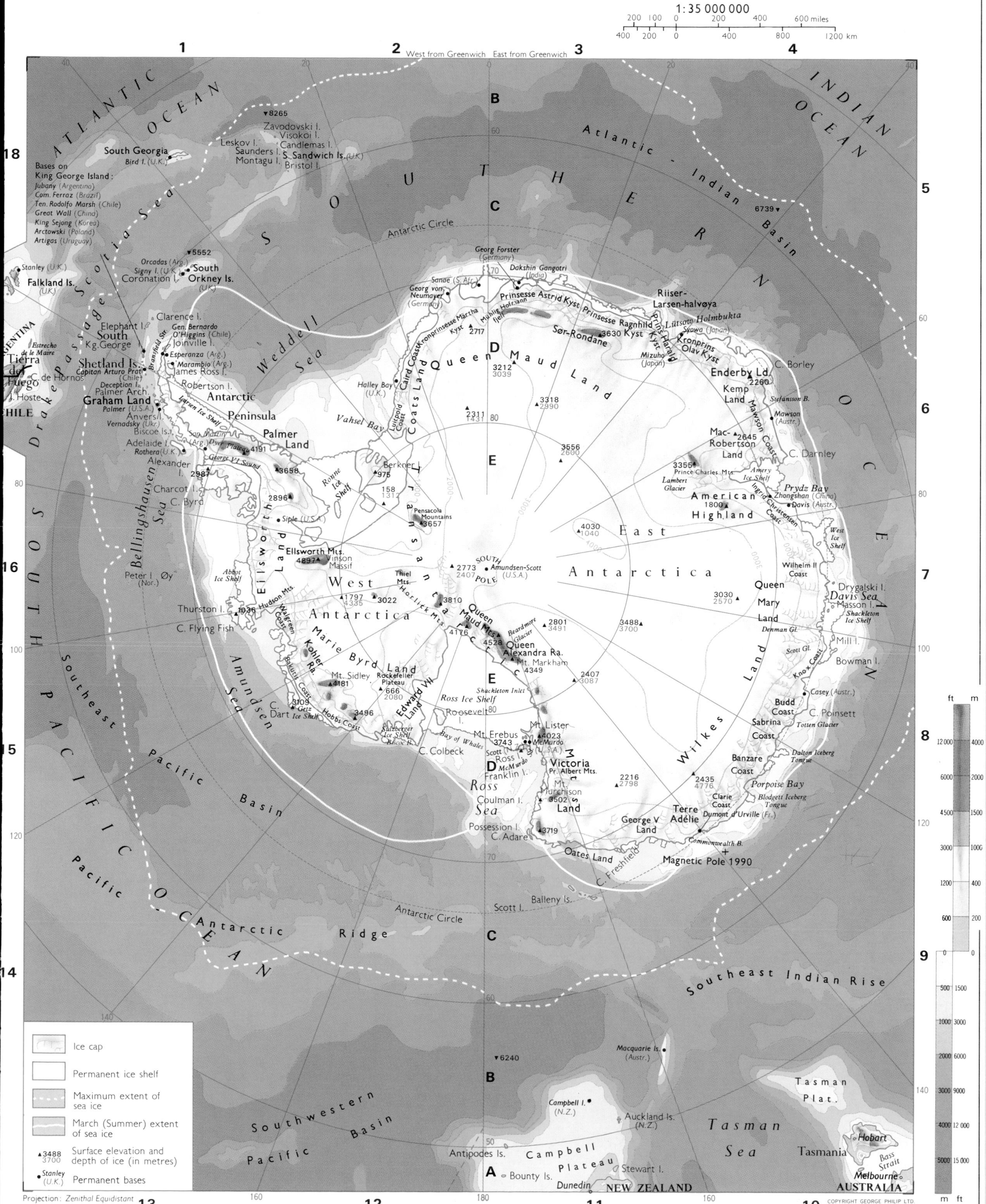

1:35 000 000

400 200 100 0 200 400 600 miles
400 200 0 400 800 1200 km

1 2 3 4

West from Greenwich East from Greenwich

ATLANTIC OCEAN

INDIAN OCEAN

SOUTHERN

Atlantic - Indian Basin

B

Antarctic Circle

C

6739▼

5

▼8265
Zavodovski I.
Leskov I. Visokoi I.
Saunders I. Candlemas I.
Montagu I. S. Sandwich Is. (U.K.)
Bristol I.

South Georgia
Bird I. (U.K.)

Bases on King George Island:
Jubany (Argentina)
Com. Ferraz (Brazil)
Ten. Rodolfo Marsh (Chile)
Great Wall (China)
King Sejong (Korea)
Arctowski (Poland)
Artigas (Uruguay)

Stanley (U.K.)
Falkland Is. (U.K.)

▼5552
Orcadas (Arg.)
Signy I. (U.K.) South
Coronation I. Orkney Is.

Scotia Sea

Weddell Sea

Georg Forster (Germany)
Sanae (S.Afr.) Dakshin Gangotri (India)
Georg von Neumayer (Germany)
Prinsesse Astrid Kyst Prinsesse Ragnhild Kyst
Mühlig Hofmann fjell
Insesse Martha Kyst 2717 Sør-Rondane ▲3630
3212 3039

Riiser-Larsen-halvøya
Lützow Holmbukta
Kronprins Olav Kyst
Syowa (Japan)
Mizuho (Japan)

D Queen Maud Land

Enderby Ld.
C. Borley
Kemp Land
2260
Stefansson B.
Mawson (Austr.)

6

Clarence I.
Elephant I.
South Kg.George
Gen. Bernardo O'Higgins (Chile)
Joinville I.
Esperanza (Arg.)
Marambio (Arg.)
James Ross I.
Robertson I.
Antarctic

ARGENTINA
Tierra del Fuego
de la Maire
C. de Hornos
I. Hoste
CHILE

Shetland Is.
Capitan Arturo Prat (Chile)
Deception I.
Palmer Arch.
Graham Land
Palmer (U.S.A.)
Anvers I.
Vernadsky (Ukr.)
Adelaide I.
Rothera (U.K.)
Alexander I.
Charcot I.
C. Byrd
Peter I. Øy (Nor.)
Thurston I.
C. Flying Fish

Drake Passage

Bellingshausen Sea

SOUTH

Palmer Land

Halley Bay (U.K.)

Vahsel Bay

Ronne Ice Shelf

975
Berkner I.

3658
2987
2896
Siple (U.S.A.)

Ellsworth Land

Ellsworth Mts.
4897
Vinson Massif

Abbot Ice Shelf

Hudson Mts.

West Antarctica

Marie Byrd Land

Kohler Ra.

Mt. Sidley 4181

Rockefeller Plateau 666

Getz Ice Shelf
Hobbs Coast 3496

C. Dart

Dart Ice Shelf 3709

Amundsen Sea

PACIFIC

Pacific Basin

SOUTHEAST

Pacific Ocean

Antarctic Ridge

Caird Coast
Coats Land
Luitpold Coast

2311 80
1731

Pensacola Mountains
3657

2773
2407

4797 4335
3022
1036

158 1317

Transantarctic

Thiel Mts.

3810

Horlick Mts.

Queen Maud Mts.

4116

4524

Beardmore Glacier

South Pole
Amundsen-Scott (U.S.A.)

3318 2990

3556 2800

3355 2600
Prince Charles Mts.
Lambert Glacier

Mac-Robertson Land
2645

Amery Ice Shelf

American Highland

4030 1040

East Antarctica

2801 3491

3488 3700

Beardmore Glacier

Mt. Markham 4349

Queen Alexandra Ra.

Shackleton Inlet

2407 3087

E

3030 2570

Queen Mary Land

Mawson Coast
Prydz Bay
Zhongshan (China)
1800
Davis (Austr.)

Ingrid Christensen Coast

West Ice Shelf

Wilhelm II Coast

Drygalski I.
Davis Sea
Masson I. (Austr.)
Shackleton Ice Shelf

Mill I.
Bowman I.

Knox Coast

Casey (Austr.)

Budd Coast
Sabrina Coast
Banzare Coast

Wilkes Land

7

Totten Glacier

C. Poinsett

Dalton Iceberg Tongue

Porpoise Bay

8

Ross Ice Shelf

Roosevelt I.

Edward VII Land

Schulberger Ice Shelf
Biscoe I.
Bay of Whales

Mt. Erebus 3743 4023
McMurdo
Scott (N.Z.) McMurdo (U.S.A.)
Ross I.

Mt. Lister 4023

Victoria
Pr. Albert Mts.

Franklin I.

Ross Sea

Coulman I.

Possession I.

C. Adare 3719

George V Land

Mt. Murchison 3502
2216 2798

2435 4776

Clarie Coast
Blodgett Iceberg Tongue
Dumont d'Urville (Fr.)
Terre Adélie

Commonwealth B.
C. Freshfield
Magnetic Pole 1990

Balleny Is.

Scott I.

Antarctic Circle

C

Oates Land

Southeast Indian Rise

Macquarie Is. (Austr.)

▼6240

B

Campbell I. (N.Z.)

Auckland Is. (N.Z.)

Tasman Plat.

Tasman Sea

Tasmania

Southwestern Pacific Basin

Antipodes Is.
Campbell Plateau
Bounty Is.

A

Stewart I.
Dunedin
NEW ZEALAND

Hobart
Bass Strait
Melbourne
AUSTRALIA

Legend:
- Ice cap
- Permanent ice shelf
- Maximum extent of sea ice
- March (Summer) extent of sea ice
- ▲3488 3700 Surface elevation and depth of ice (in metres)
- ● Stanley (U.K.) Permanent bases

Projection: Zenithal Equidistant

COPYRIGHT GEORGE PHILIP LTD.

The Antarctic Treaty was signed in Washington in 1959 so that scientific and technical research could continue unhampered by international politics.

All territorial claims covering land areas south of latitude 60°S have been suspended. Those claims were:

Norwegian claim	45°E – 20°W	
Australian claims {	45°E – 136°E	
	142°E – 160°E	
French claim	136°E – 142°E	
New Zealand claim	160°E – 150°W	
Chilean claim	90°W – 53°W	
British claim	80°W – 20°W	
Argentine claim	74°W – 53°W	

ft m
12 000 4000
6000 2000
4500 1500
3000 1000
1200 400
600 200
0 0
500 1500
1000 3000
2000 6000
3000 9000
4000 12 000
5000 15 000
m ft

1:20 000 000

100　0　100　200　300　400　miles
100　0　100　200　300　400　500　600　km

ATLANTIC OCEAN

Norwegian Sea

North Sea

Baltic Sea

White Sea

Barents Sea

Mediterranean Sea

Black Sea

Caspian Sea

Adriatic Sea

Ionian Sea

Aegean Sea

Tyrrhenian Sea

Ligurian Sea

Sea of Azov

Celtic Sea

Irish Sea

English Channel

Bay of Biscay

Gulf of Lions

Kattegat

Skagerrak

G. of Finland

G. of Bothnia

G. of Riga

Ural Mountains

Caucasus

Alps

Pyrenees

Apennines

Carpathians

Balkans

Dinaric Alps

Pindus

Scandinavia

Lapland

Finland

Iceland

Great Britain

Ireland

British Isles

Iberian Peninsula

Anatolia (Asia Minor)

Mesopotamia

Ukraine

Central Russian Uplands

Caspian Depression

Obshchi Syrt

Volga Hts.

Plain of Hungary

Wallachia

Transylvanian Alps

Plateau of the Shotts

Africa

Caspian Sea

Volga

Don

Dnieper

Dniester

Danube

Rhine

Elbe

Oder

Vistula

Ebro

Crete

Cyprus

Rhodes

Sardinia

Corsica

Sicily

Balearic Is.

Faroe Is.

Shetland Is.

Orkney Is.

Hebrides

Gotland

Öland

Bornholm

Åland

Saaremaa

CARTOGRAPHY BY PHILIP'S. COPYRIGHT REED INTERNATIONAL BOOKS LTD.

Projection: Bonne

West from Greenwich　0　East from Greenwich

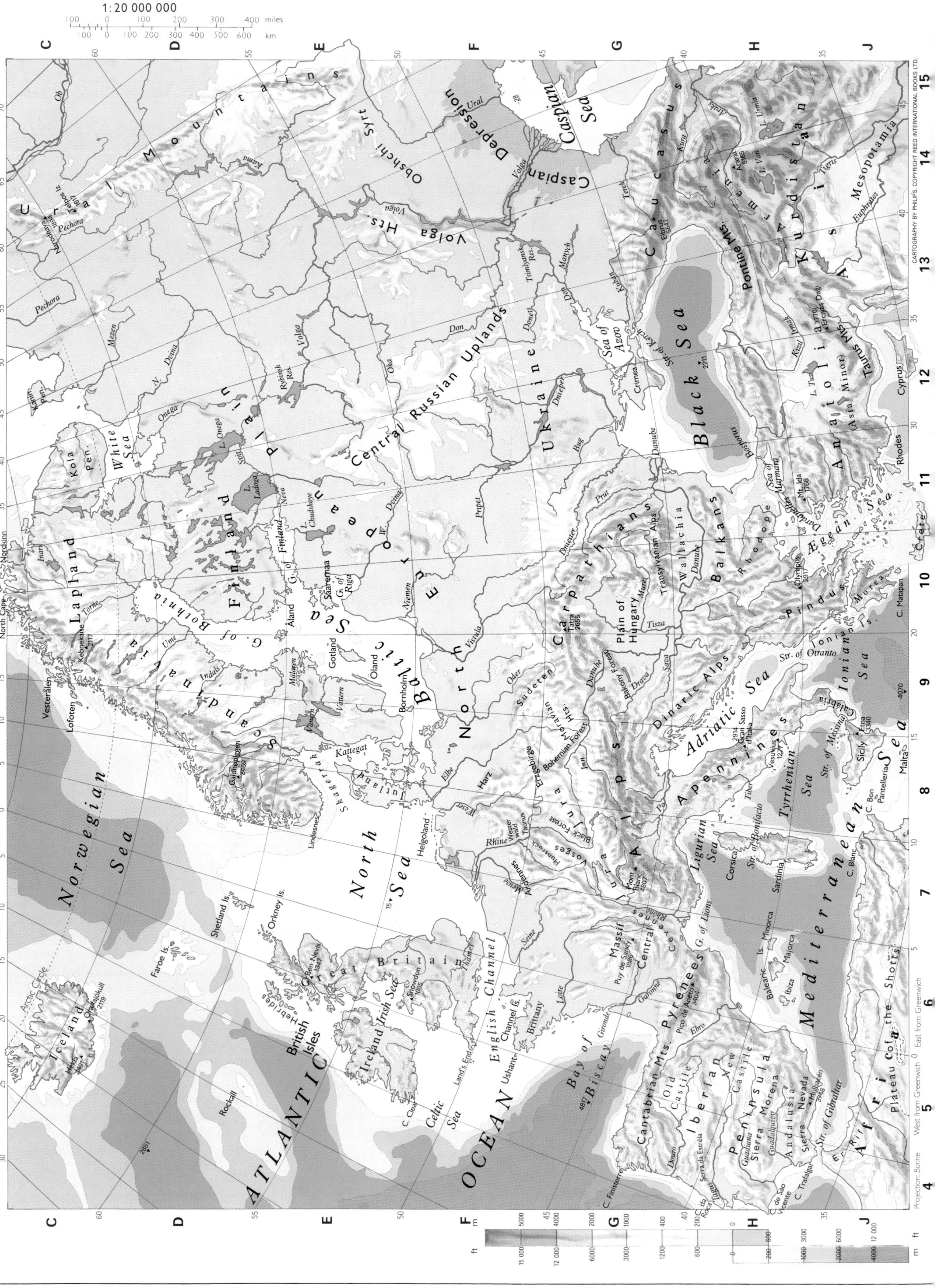

1 : 20 000 000

100 0 100 200 300 400 miles
100 0 100 200 300 400 500 600 km

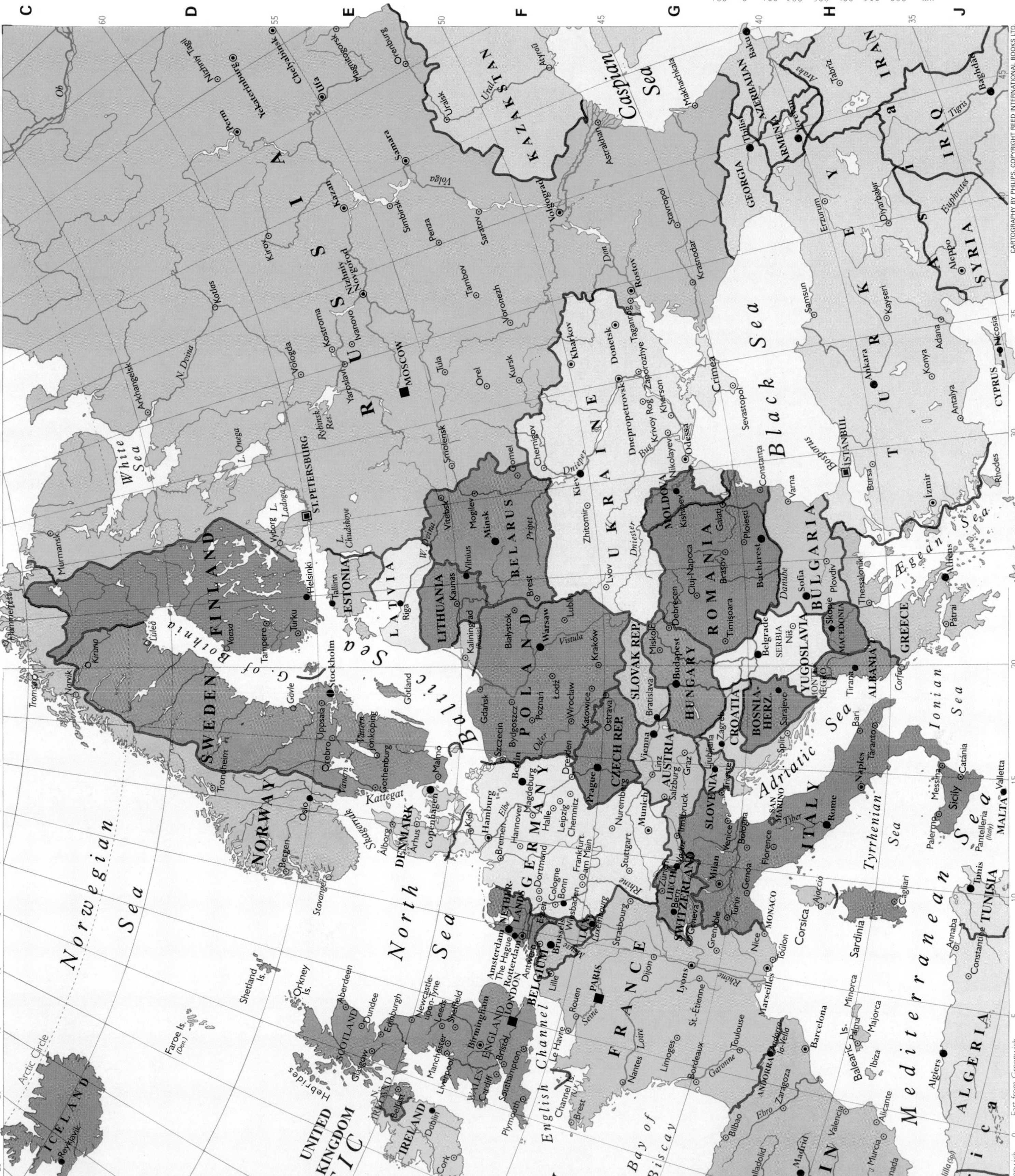

■ LONDON Capital Cities 9

Projection: Bonne   West from Greenwich   0   East from Greenwich

CARTOGRAPHY BY PHILIPS. COPYRIGHT REED INTERNATIONAL BOOKS LTD.

ICELAND
Reykjavik

ATLANTIC OCEAN

Norwegian Sea

NORWAY
Tromsø
Narvik
Bodø
Trondheim
Bergen
Stavanger
Oslo

SWEDEN
Kiruna
Luleå
Umeå
Östersund
Gävle
Uppsala
Stockholm
Göteborg
Jönköping
Norrköping
Malmö
Gothenburg

FINLAND
Helsinki
Tampere
Turku
Vaasa
Oulu

DENMARK
Copenhagen
Ålborg
Århus
Odense

Kattegat
Skagerrak
North Sea
Baltic Sea
G. of Bothnia

White Sea
Murmansk
Arkhangelsk

R U S S I A
MOSCOW
ST. PETERSBURG
Novgorod
Smolensk
Tula
Orel
Kursk
Voronezh
Tambov
Penza
Saratov
Samara
Volgograd
Astrakhan
Rostov
Krasnodar
Stavropol
Kazan
Nizhniy Novgorod
Ivanovo
Yaroslavl
Vologda
Kostroma
Kirov
Ufa
Magnitogorsk
Chelyabinsk
Yekaterinburg
Nizhniy Tagil
Perm
Orenburg

KAZAKHSTAN
Ural
Uralsk

Caspian Sea
Baku
Makhachkala

UNITED KINGDOM
ENGLAND
WALES
SCOTLAND
Glasgow
Edinburgh
Dundee
Aberdeen
Newcastle-upon-Tyne
Leeds
Sheffield
Manchester
Liverpool
Birmingham
Bristol
Cardiff
Southampton
Plymouth
LONDON

IRELAND
Dublin
Belfast
Cork

Shetland Is.
Orkney Is.
Hebrides
Faroe Is. (Den.)

ESTONIA
Tallinn
LATVIA
Riga
LITHUANIA
Vilnius
Kaunas
Kaliningrad

BELARUS
Minsk
Vitebsk
Mogilev
Gomel

POLAND
Warsaw
Gdańsk
Szczecin
Poznań
Łódź
Wrocław
Kraków
Katowice
Białystok
Bydgoszcz

GERMANY
Berlin
Hamburg
Bremen
Hannover
Magdeburg
Leipzig
Dresden
Cologne
Bonn
Frankfurt-am-Main
Stuttgart
Munich
Nuremberg
Dortmund
Essen
Düsseldorf

NETHERLANDS
Amsterdam
The Hague
Rotterdam

BELGIUM
Brussels
Antwerp

LUX.
Luxembourg

FRANCE
PARIS
Lille
Le Havre
Rouen
Nantes
Dijon
Strasbourg
Lyons
St.-Etienne
Grenoble
Bordeaux
Toulouse
Nice
Marseilles
Limoges

SWITZERLAND
Bern
Zürich
Geneva

AUSTRIA
Vienna
Salzburg
Graz
Linz
Innsbruck

CZECH REP.
Prague
Brno

SLOVAK REP.
Bratislava

HUNGARY
Budapest
Debrecen
Miskolc

SLOVENIA
Ljubljana

CROATIA
Zagreb
Split

BOSNIA-HERZ.
Sarajevo

YUGOSLAVIA
Belgrade
SERBIA
MONTENEGRO
Niš

MACEDONIA
Skopje

ALBANIA
Tirana

ROMANIA
Bucharest
Cluj-Napoca
Timişoara
Braşov
Galaţi
Constanţa
Ploieşti

MOLDOVA
Kishinev

BULGARIA
Sofia
Plovdiv
Varna

UKRAINE
Kiev
Kharkov
Donetsk
Dnepropetrovsk
Odessa
Zaporozhye
Lvov
Zhitomir
Nikolayev
Kherson
Sevastopol
Crimea

ITALY
Rome
Milan
Turin
Genoa
Venice
Bologna
Florence
Naples
Bari
Taranto
Palermo
Messina
Catánia

Sicily
Sardinia
Corsica

SAN MARINO
MONACO
LIECHTENSTEIN

MALTA
Valletta

SPAIN
Madrid
Barcelona
Valencia
Seville
Zaragoza
Málaga
Murcia
Bilbao
Córdoba
Granada
Valladolid
Alicante
La Coruña
Vigo

PORTUGAL
Lisbon
Porto

ANDORRA

GREECE
Athens
Thessaloniki
Patras

TURKEY
Istanbul
Ankara
Izmir
Bursa
Konya
Adana
Antalya
Kayseri
Erzurum
Diyarbakır
Samsun

CYPRUS
Nicosia

Crete
Rhodes

GEORGIA
Tbilisi
ARMENIA
Yerevan
AZERBAIJAN
Baku

IRAN
Tabriz

IRAQ
Baghdad
Mosul

SYRIA
Aleppo

MOROCCO
ALGERIA
Algiers
Constantine
Oran
Annaba

TUNISIA
Tunis

Mediterranean Sea
Adriatic Sea
Aegean Sea
Ionian Sea
Tyrrhenian Sea
Black Sea
Bay of Biscay
English Channel

Arctic Circle

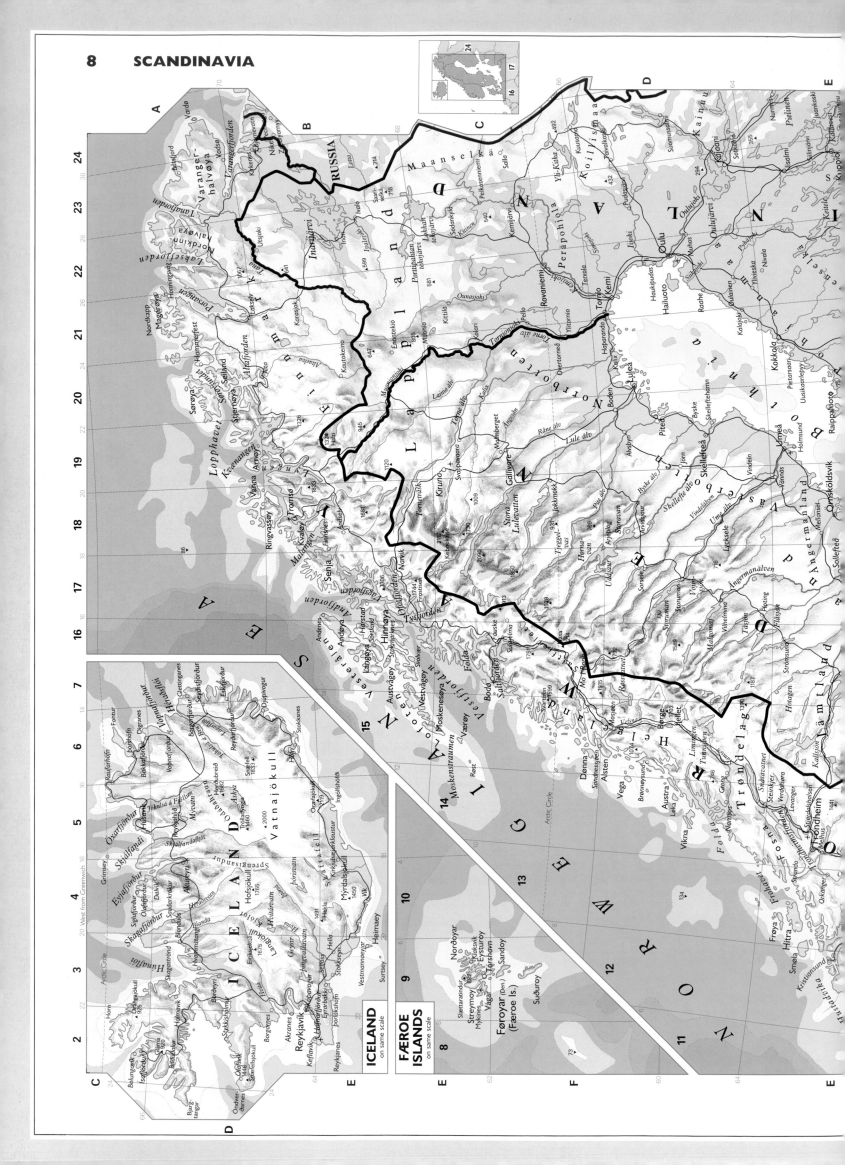

ICELAND
on same scale

FÆROE ISLANDS
on same scale

Føroyar (Den.)
(Færoe Is.)

RUSSIA

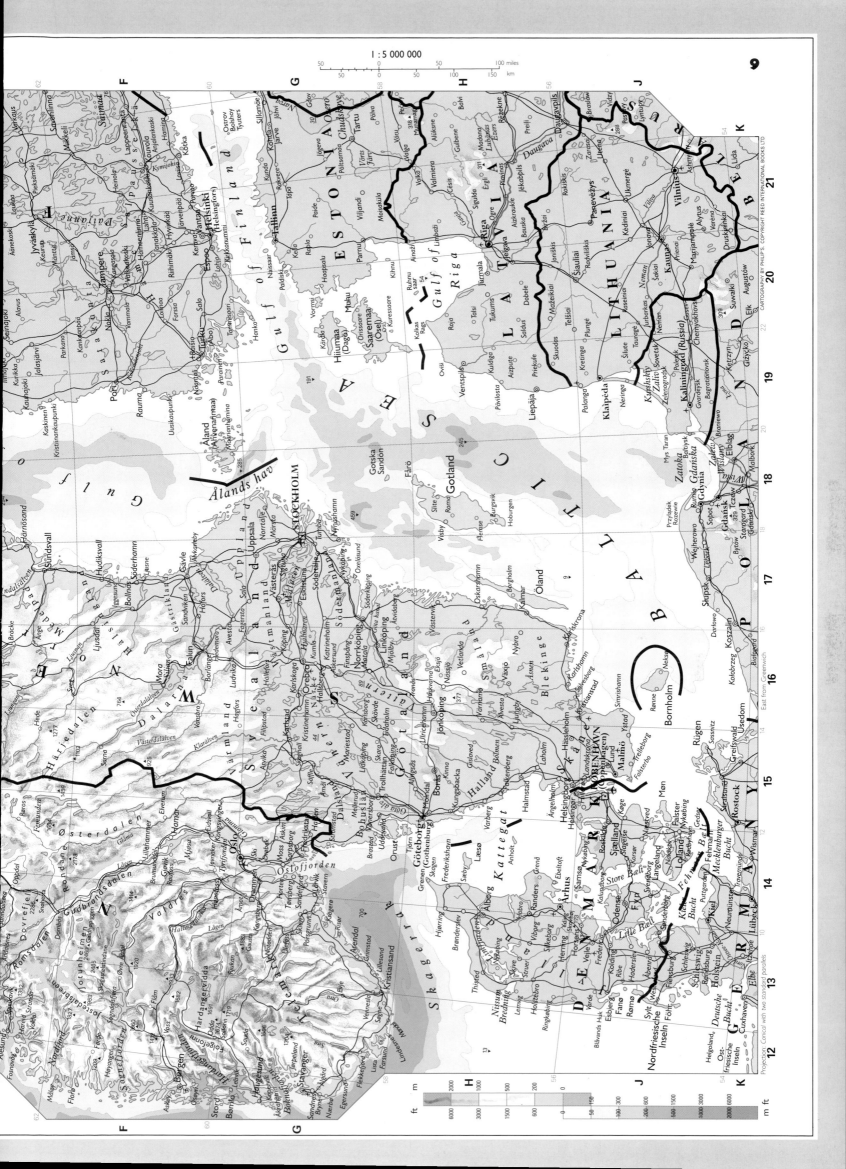

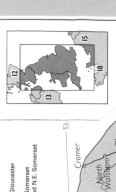

English Unitary Authorities
(from April 1996)

12. Hartlepool
13. Stockton-on-Tees
14. Middlesbrough
15. Redcar and Cleveland
16. Kingston upon Hull
17. York

18. South Gloucester
19. Bristol
20. North Somerset
21. Bath and N.E. Somerset

Welsh Unitary Authorities
(from April 1996)

1. Neath Port Talbot
2. Rhondda Cynon Taff
3. Bridgend
4. Merthyr Tydfil
5. Vale of Glamorgan
6. Caerphilly
7. Cardiff
8. Blaenau Gwent
9. Torfaen
10. Newport
11. Monmouthshire

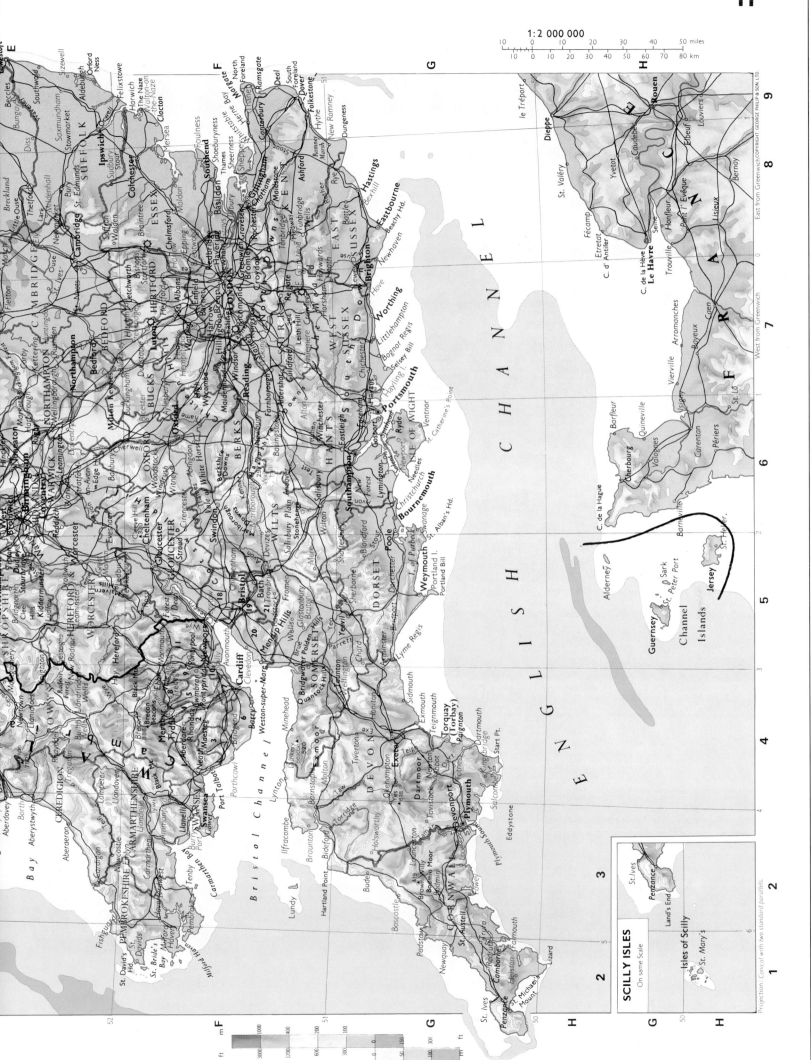

12 SCOTLAND

1:2 000 000

Scale bars: 10 0 10 20 30 40 50 miles / 10 0 10 20 30 40 50 60 70 80 km

Scottish Local Authorities
(From April 1996)

1. City of Aberdeen
2. Dundee City
3. West Dunbartonshire
4. East Dunbartonshire
5. City of Glasgow
6. Inverclyde
7. Renfrewshire
8. East Renfrewshire
9. North Lanarkshire
10. Falkirk
11. Clackmannan
12. West Lothian
13. City of Edinburgh
14. Midlothian

ORKNEY IS.
On same scale

Westray, Rousay, Eday, Sanday, Stronsay, Shapinsay, ORKNEY, Mainland, Stromness, Kirkwall, Scapa Flow, Hoy, South Ronaldsay, North Ronaldsay, Pentland Firth, Dunnet Hd., John o'Groats

SHETLAND IS.
On same scale

Unst, Yell, Yell Sound, Fetlar, Foula, SHETLAND, Mainland, Scalloway, Whalsay, Bressay, Lerwick, Sumburgh Hd.

Map labels

ATLANTIC OCEAN

NORTH SEA

Butt of Lewis, Flannan Is., Stornoway, Broad Bay, Eye Pen., LEWIS, WESTERN ISLES, L. Langavat, Tarbert, Harris, Sound of Harris, North Uist, Lochmaddy, Monach Is., Benbecula, South Uist, Lochboisdale, Sound of Barra, Barra, Barra Hd.

C. Wrath, Durness, Faraid Hd., Balnakeil, Strathy Pt., Dounreay, Thurso, Dunnet Hd., John o'Groats, Pentland Firth, Noss Hd., Wick, Lybster, Ord of Caithness, Helmsdale, Brora, Golspie, Dornoch, Dornoch Firth, Tarbat Ness, Tain, Invergordon, Cromarty, Moray Firth, Lossiemouth, Cullen, Portsoy, Banff, Macduff, Kinnaird's Head, Fraserburgh, Rattray Head, Peterhead, Buchan Ness

Tongue, Ben Hope 927, Halladale, Naver, L. Laxford, Reay Forest, Eddrachillis Bay, Lochinver, Assynt, B. More Assynt, Enard Bay, L. Shin, Lairg, Oykel, Ullapool, L. Broom, Loch Fannich, Ben Wyvis 1045, Dingwall, Strathpeffer, Conon, Beauly, Nairn, Forres, Elgin, Keith, Huntly, Turriff, Elon, Inverurie, Don

B. Dearg 1081, HIGHLAND, Ben Attow, Glen Affric, Glen Moriston, Fort Augustus, L. Oich, Newtonmore, MORAY, Grantown-on-Spey, Dufftown, Tomintoul, Aviemore, Monadhliath Mts., Kingussie, Cairn Gorm, Cairngorm Mts. 1245, Cairn Toul 1291, Ben Macdhui 1311, Braemar, Ballater, Aboyne, Banchory, ABERDEENSHIRE, Aberdeen, Girdle Ness

Gairloch, Torridon, Roraa, Raasay, Portree, Trotternish, Stromeferry, Kyle of Lochalsh, Cuillin Hills, Dornie, Glen Garry, L. Hourn, Mallaig, Morar, Arisaig, Glenfinnan, Fort William, Ben Nevis 1343, Ardgour, Glen Spean, Forest of Atholl, Blair Atholl, Pass of Killiecrankie, Pitlochry, Braes of Angus, Brechin, Montrose

Cuillin Sound, Canna, Rhum, Eigg, Muck, L. Moidart, Coll, Pt. of Ardnamurchan, Tobermory, MORVERN, Staffa, Mull, Ben More 966, Iona, Tiree, Loch Sunart, Ballachulish, L. Linnhe, Loch Leven, Oban, ARGYLL, Inveraray, L. Awe, Ben Cruachan 1124, L. Etive, Loch Fyne, Crinan, BUTE, Lochgilphead, Helensburgh, JURA, Sound of Jura, Islay, Bowmore, Gigha, Port Ellen, Rubha a' Mhail, Campbeltown, Mull of Kintyre, KINTYRE, Tarbert, Rothesay, Port Glasgow, Greenock, Dunoon, Dumbarton, Clydebank

Rannoch Moor, L. Rannoch, L. Tummel, Aberfeldy, Tay, Dunkeld, Blairgowrie, Alyth, Kirriemuir, Forfar, ANGUS, Arbroath, PERTH, Crieff, Ben Lawers 1214, Breadalbane, L. Earn, Comrie, Perth, Scone, Dundee, Firth of Tay, Tayport, Broughty Ferry, Carnoustie, St. Andrews, Fife Ness, Anstruther, KINROSS, Loch Leven, Glenrothes, Kirkcaldy, Leven, Buckhaven, Firth of Forth, North Berwick, Dunbar, St. Abb's Hd., Eyemouth, Berwick-upon-Tweed, Holy I.

Ben Vorlich 983, Ben More 1174, L. Katrine, Trossachs, Callander, STIRLING, Dunblane, Bridge of Allan, Allan, Alloa, Clackmannan, Bannockburn, Stirling, Grangemouth, Falkirk, Linlithgow, Livingston, Bathgate, LOTHIAN, Musselburgh, Edinburgh, Leith, Rosyth, Dunfermline, Haddington, Lammermuir Hills, Penicuik, Pentland Hills, Moorfoot Hills, Peebles, Tweed, Galashiels, Melrose, Selkirk, Coldstream, Kelso, Jedburgh, The Cheviot 816, Cheviot Hills, Hawick, Langholm, BORDERS

GLASGOW, Paisley, Johnstone, Rutherglen, E. Kilbride, Hamilton, Motherwell, Wishaw, Airdrie, Coatbridge, Cumbernauld, Carstairs, SOUTH LANARKSHIRE, Biggar, Broad Law 840, Moffat, SOUTHERN UPLANDS, Lockerbie, Gretna, Annan, DUMFRIES AND GALLOWAY, Dumfries, Thornhill, Sanquhar, Leadhills, Cumnock, Ayr, Prestwick, Troon, Irvine, Kilmarnock, Saltcoats, Ardrossan, NORTH AYRSHIRE, EAST AYRSHIRE, SOUTH AYRSHIRE, Maybole, Girvan, Ailsa Craig, Dalmellington, Merrick 843, Ken, L. Doon, Newton Stewart, Stranraer, Portpatrick, Luce Bay, Wigtown, Whithorn, Mull of Galloway, Solway Firth, Castle Douglas, Kirkcudbright, Dalbeattie, Gatehouse of Fleet, GALLOWAY, L. Ryan

Arran, Goat Fell 874, Brodick, Firth of Clyde, Ardrossan

NORTHERN IRELAND, Belfast, Belfast Lough, Bangor, Newtownards, Ballymena, Larne, Ballycastle, Rathlin, Fair Hd., Trostan 554, North Channel

ENGLAND, Carlisle, Workington, Penrith, Cumbrian Mts., Skiddaw 931, Cross Fell 893, Derwent, Ullswater, Alston, Hexham, Hadrian's Wall, N. Tyne, S. Tyne, Wear, Tees, Barnard Castle, Holy I.

Projection: Conical with two standard parallels.

West from Greenwich

COPYRIGHT GEORGE PHILIP & SON, LTD.

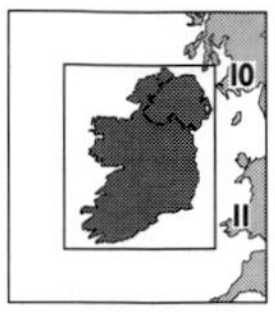

1:2 000 000

10 0 10 20 30 40 50 miles
10 0 10 20 30 40 50 60 70 80 km

A

Kintyre
Campbeltown
Arran
Ailsa Craig
Mull of Kintyre
North Channel
Malin Hd.
Giant's Causeway
Rathlin I.
Fair Hd.
Portrush
Lough Swilly
Carndonagh
Ballycastle
Inishowen Pen.
Moville
Buncrana
Stranraer
Tory I. Horn Hd.
Sheep Haven
Bloody Foreland
Coleraine
Ballymoney
554
Gweedore
Errigal 752
Aran I.
Letterkenny
Londonderry
Limavady
Trostan
Ballymena
Larne
I. Magee
Portpatrick

B

Gweebarra B.
DONEGAL
Sperrin Mts.
Strabane
Magherafelt
Antrim
Carrickfergus
Belfast L.
Glenties
Bluestack 676
Lifford
Finn
Sawel 683
Cookstown
NORTHERN IRELAND
ULSTER
Nephin
Belfast
Donaghadee
Loughros More B.
Rossan Pt.
Rathlin O Birne I.
Killybegs
Donegal
Omagh
Neagh
Lisburn
Bangor
Newtownards
Ards Pen.
Broad Haven
Erris Hd.
Belmullet
Mullet Peninsula
Donegal Bay
Bundoran
Ballyshannon
Lower L. Erne
Irvinestown
Enniskillen
Dungannon
Portadown
Lough
Armagh
Banbridge
Strangford
Downpatrick Hd.
Killala B.
Downpatrick
Dundrum
Slieve Donard 852
Newcastle
Mourne Mts.
Dundrum Bay

C

Achill Hd.
Achill I.
Achill
Conn 800
Clare I.
Clew Bay
Croagh Patrick 765
Westport
Castlebar
Claremorris
Roscommon
Sligo B.
Sligo
Collooney
Ballina
L. Allen
Arrow
Leitrim
Carrick-on-Shannon
Boyle
CAVAN
Belturbet
Annalee
Cootehill
Castleblayney
MONAGHAN
Carrickmacross
LOUTH
Dundalk
Dundalk Bay
Greenore
Carlingford L.
Warrenpoint
ROSCOMMON
Castlerea
Granard
Longford
Oldcastle
Ceanannas Mor (Kells)
Gowna
L. Sheelin
Kingscourt
Ardee
Drogheda
Balbriggan
CONNACHT
Inishbofin
Twelve Pins
Mweelrea 819
Killary Harbour
L. Mask
Ballinrobe
Robe
Tuam
Corrib
LONGFORD
Roscommon
L. Ree
Athlone
MEATH
An Uaimh (Navan)
Trim
Boyne
Swords
Lambay I.
Slyne Hd.
Clifden
Connemara
GALWAY
Ballinasloe
WESTMEATH
Mullingar
Maynooth
DUBLIN
Ireland's Eye
Howth Head
Slieve Aughty
IRELAND
Clara
Edenderry
Celbridge
Dublin (Baile Atha Cliath)
Dublin Bay

D

Galway
Athenry
Loughrea
Galway Bay
Inishmore
Aran Is.
Gort
Portumna
Shannon
OFFALY
Tullamore
Birr
Daingean
Mountmellick
Port Laoise
KILDARE
Kildare
Naas
Dun Laoghaire
Bray
Kippure 754
Poulaphouca Res.
Hags Hd.
Liscannor Bay
Ennistymon
L. Derg
Roscrea
LEIX LAOIS
Athy
WICKLOW
Mal Bay
CLARE
Ennis
Nenagh
Mizen Hd.
Miltown Malbay
Killaloe
Ballina
Keeper 694
Templemore
Nore
Carlow
Tullow
Shillelagh
Arklow
Kilkee
Kilrush
Ardnacrusha
Thurles
Kilkenny
CARLOW
Muine Bheag
Mt. Leinster 796
Gorey
Loop Hd.
Foynes
Rathkeale
LIMERICK
Limerick
TIPPERARY
Cashel
Callan
KILKENNY
Enniscorthy
Cahore Pt.
R. Shannon
Listowel
Newcastle
Golden Vale
Tipperary
Slievenamon 722
Carrick-on-Suir
Clonmel
WEXFORD
New Ross
Kerry Hd.
Fenit
Brandon Bay
Tralee Bay
Tralee
Rathluirc (Charleville)
Galtymore 920
Galty Mts.
Aherlow
Knockmealdown Mts.
Comeragh Mts.
Waterford
Wexford
Rosslare
Wexford Harbour
Greenore Pt.

E

Gt. Blasket I.
Brandon Mt. 953
Dingle
Sl. Mish
Maine
MUNSTER
Newmarket
Mitchelstown
WATERFORD
Tramore
Tuscar Rock
Carnsore Pt.
Dunmore Hd.
Dingle Bay
KERRY
Killarney
Laune
Blackwater
Kanturk
Mallow
Fermoy
Lismore
Dungarvan
Dungarvan Bay
Hook Hd.
Waterford Harbour
Saltee Is.
Valentia Harbour
Macgillycuddy's Reeks
Carrauntoohill 1040
Lakes of Killarney
CORK
Boggeragh Mts.
Macroom
Lee
Blarney
Cork
Youghal
Midleton
Youghal Harbour
St. David's Hd.
Valencia I.
Skellig Rocks
Kenmare
Caha Mts.
Glengarriff
Bantry
Passage West
Cobh
Cork Harbour
Crosshaven
Kinsale
Castletown Bearhaven
Bear I.
Bantry Bay
Bandon
Ballinskelligs B.
Crow Hd.
Dunmanus Bay
Skull
Clonakilty
Skibbereen
Clonakilty Bay
Old Head of Kinsale
Mizen Hd.
Fastnet Rock
Baltimore
Clear I.
C. Clear
Galley Hd.

ATLANTIC OCEAN

IRISH SEA

St. George's Channel

Towns underlined in Northern Ireland give their
names to the Districts in which they stand

The remaining Districts are:—
1 Fermanagh
2 Moyle
3 Newtownabbey
4 North Down
5 Castlereagh
6 Ards
7 Down
8 Newry & Mourne

ft m
3000 1000
1200 400
600 200
300 100
0 0
100 300
200 600
m ft

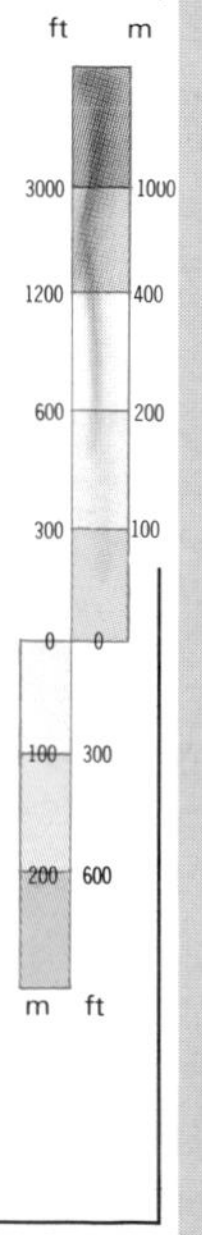

Projection: Conical with two standard parallels.

8 West from Greenwich

COPYRIGHT. GEORGE PHILIP & SON. LTD.

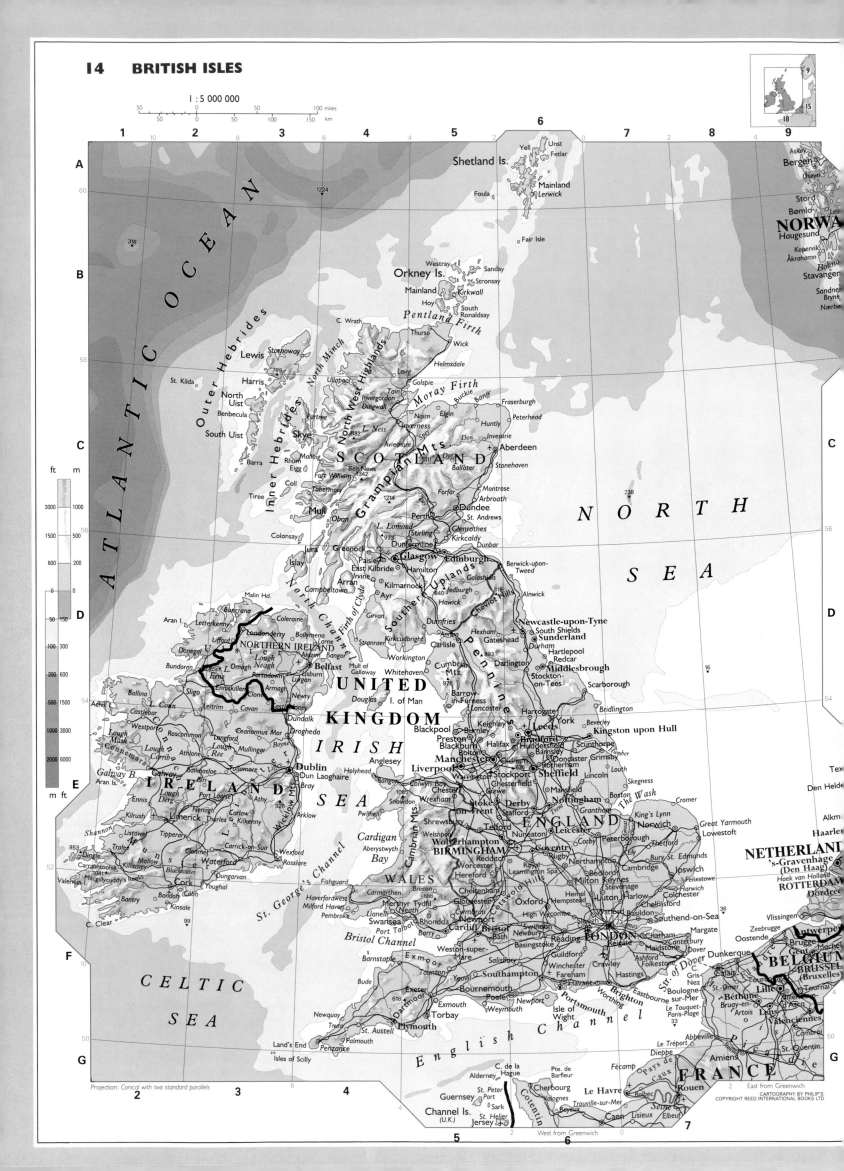

1 : 5 000 000

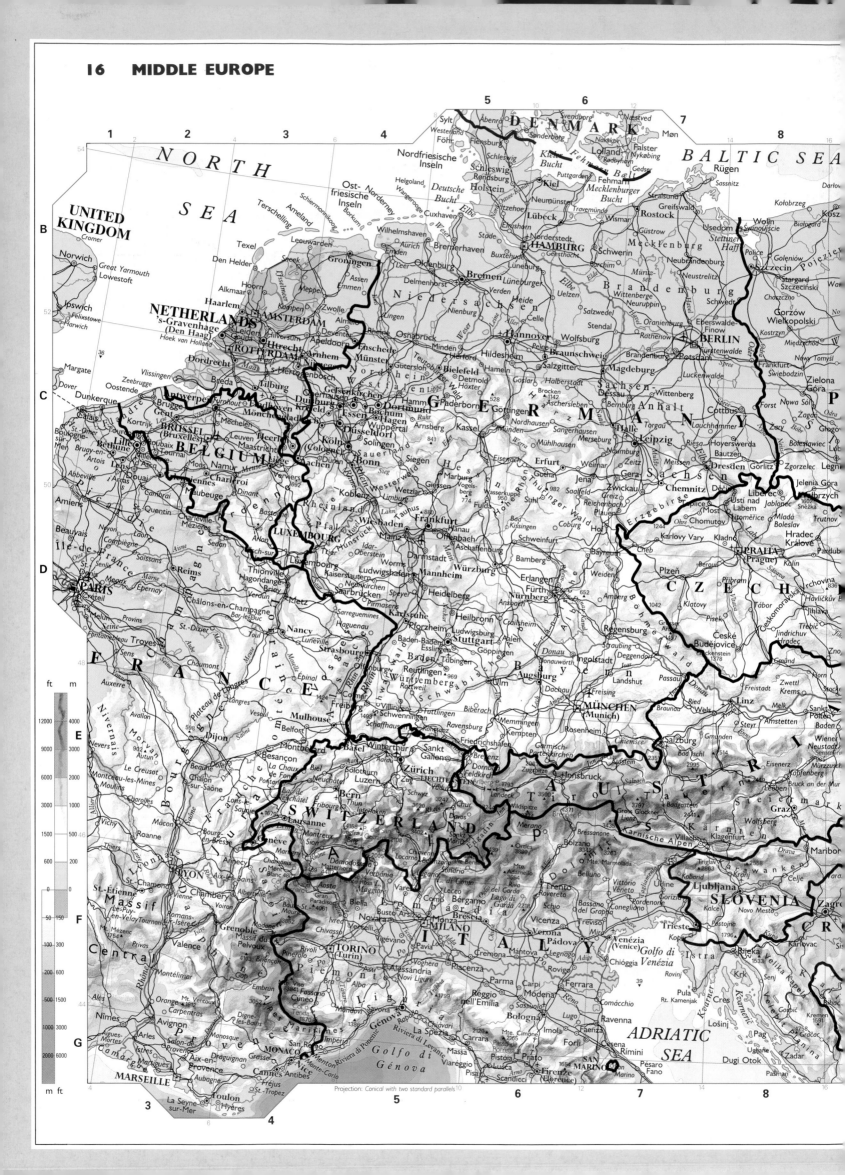

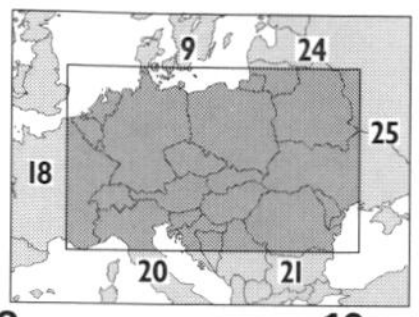

1:5 000 000

50 0 50 100 miles

50 0 50 100 150 km

LITHUANIA

BELARUS

MÍNSK

POLAND

WARSZAWA (Warsaw)

UKRAINE

KYÏV (Kiev)

Lviv (Lvov)

SLOVAK REP.

Bratislava

HUNGARY

BUDAPEST

ROMANIA

BUCUREŞTI (Bucharest)

MOLDOVA

Chişinău

YUGOSLAVIA

BEOGRAD (Belgrade)

BOSNIA-HERZEGOVINA

SARAJEVO

BULGARIA

East from Greenwich

CARTOGRAPHY BY PHILIP'S. COPYRIGHT REED INTERNATIONAL BOOKS LTD

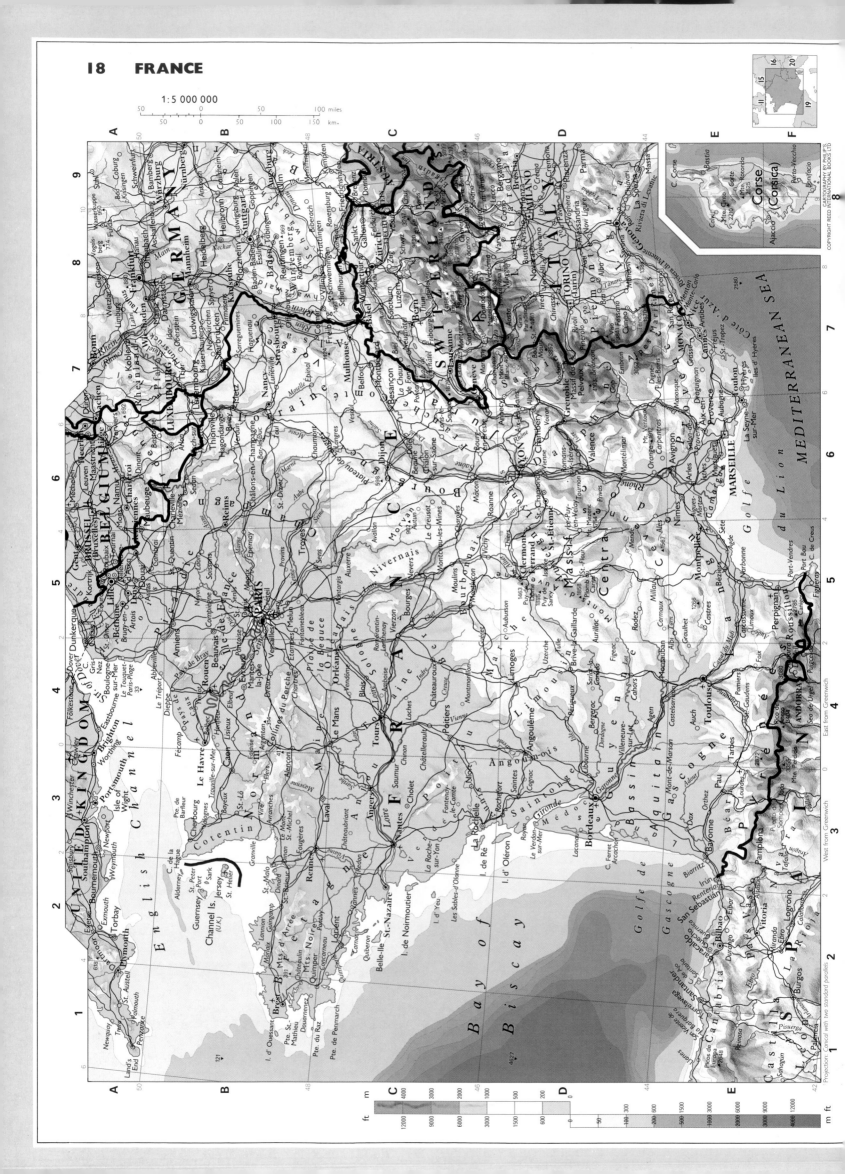

1 : 5 000 000

MEDITERRANEAN SEA

Corse (Corsica)

Projection: Conical with two standard parallels

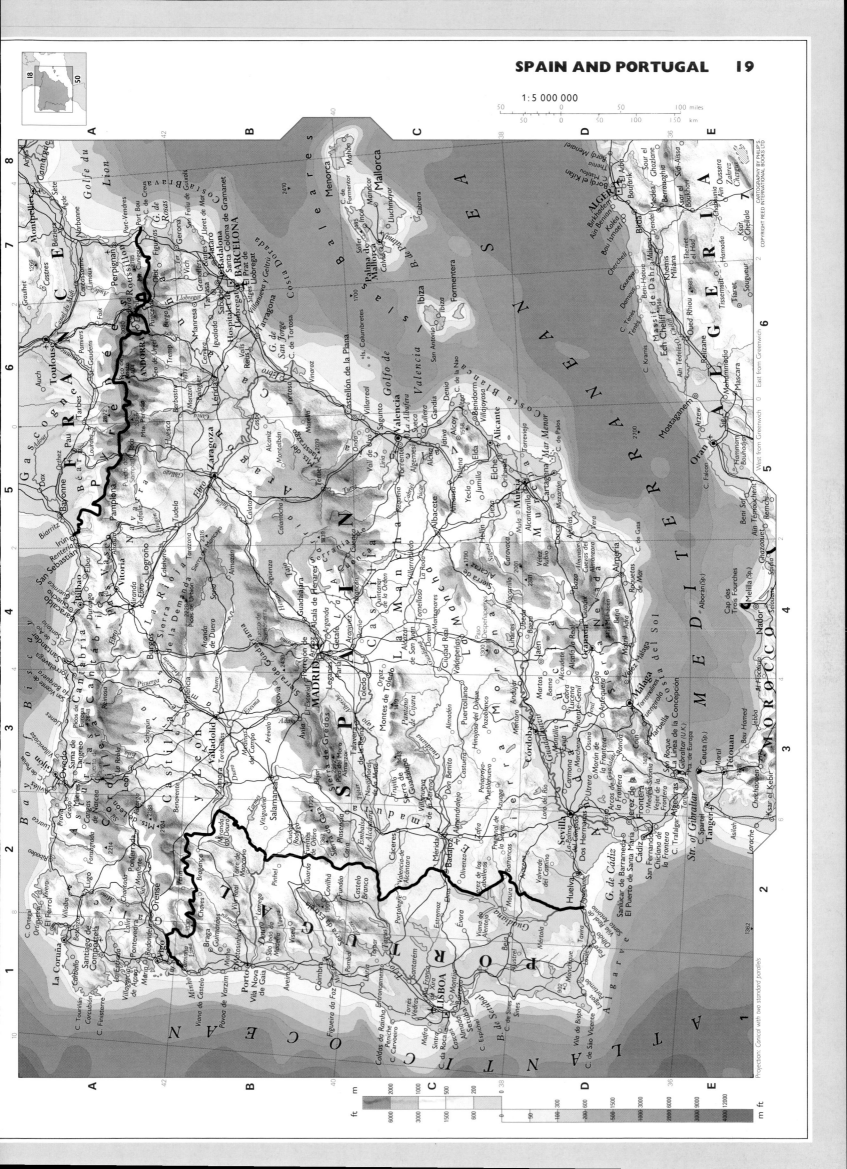

1:5 000 000

Projection: Conical with two standard parallels

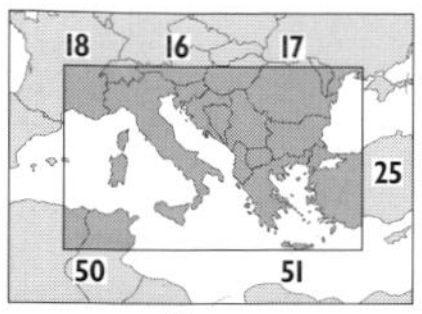

1 : 5 000 000

50 0 50 100 miles
50 0 100 150 km

HUNGARY
ROMANIA
Transilvania
Carpaţi Meridionali
UKRAINE
UKRAINE

Szeged
Makó
Arad
Timişoara
Deva
Alba-Iulia
Sibiu
Făgăraş
Braşov
Galaţi
Sulina

Subotica
Vojvodina
Novi Sad
Lugoj
Hunedoara
Petroşani
Câmpulung
Tecuci
Brăila

YUGOSLAVIA
BEOGRAD
(Belgrade)
Tîrgu-Jiu
Rîmnicu
Vîlcea
Piteşti
Ploieşti
Buzău
Tulcea

Smederevo
Dunăv
Danube
BUCUREŞTI
(Bucharest)
Constanţa

SERBIA
Craiova
Slatina
Silistra
Dobrich
Varna

Niš
Vidin
Lom
Turnu
Măgurele
Ruse
Razgrad
Šumen

SOFIYA
BULGARIA
Pleven
Veliko Tŭrnovo
Gabrovo
Sliven
Burgas

BLACK
SEA

MONTENEGRO
Podgorica
Kosovo
Priština
Pernik
Stara
Zagora
Yambol

Skopje
Kyustendil
Plovdiv
Asenovgrad
Khaskovo
Dimitrovgrad

MACEDONIA
Rhodopi Planina
Kŭrdzhali
Edirne
ISTANBUL

ALBANIA
Tirana
Durrësi
Elbasani
Prilep
Bitola
Drama
Xánthi
Komotini
Thrace

GREECE
Thessaloniki
Kaválla
Thásos
Samothráki
Gökçeada
Marmara
Denizi
Bursa

Ioánnina
Lárisa
Vólos
Límnos
Lésvos
TURKEY
İzmir
(Smyrna)

IONIAN
SEA

PATRAI
ATHÍNAI
(Athens)
Pelopónnisos
Khíos
Sámos
Kuşadası

AEGEAN SEA

Tripolis
Kíthira
Náxos
Dhodhekánisos
Ródhos
(Rhodes)

MEDITERRANEAN SEA

Krítí
Khaniá
Iráklion
Kárpathos

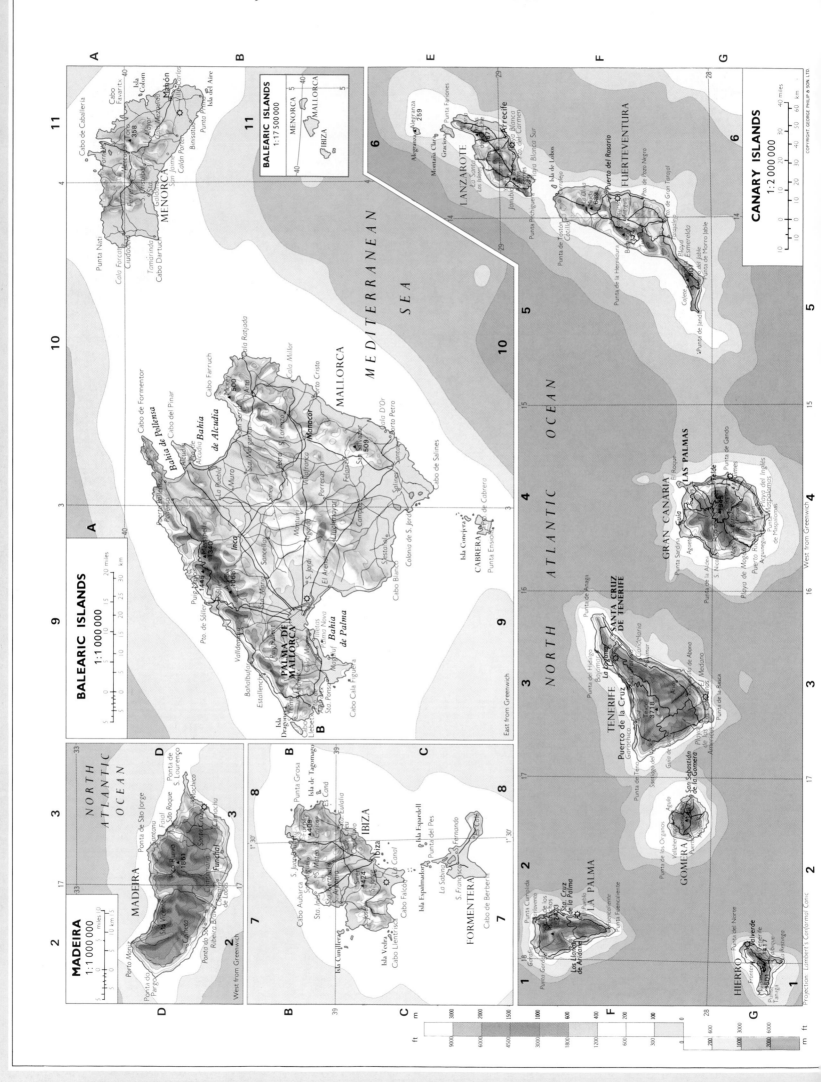

BALEARIC ISLANDS
1:1 000 000

MADEIRA
1:1 000 000

CANARY ISLANDS
1:2 000 000

BALEARIC ISLANDS
1:17 500 000

MENORCA

MALLORCA

IBIZA

MEDITERRANEAN SEA

MENORCA

Cabo de Caballería
Punta Nati
Ciudadela
Cala Forcat
Tamarindo
Cabo Dartuch
Punta Prima
Isla del Aire
San Jaime
Colón Porter
Binisalem
Mahón
Isla Colom
Cabo Favantx
Toro 358
Alayor
Mercadal

MALLORCA

Cabo de Formentor
Cabo de Pollensa
Bahía de Pollensa
Pollensa
Puerto Pollensa
Cabo del Pinar
Alcudia
Bahía de Alcudia
Cabo Farruch
Muro 500
San Servera
Cala Ratjada
Cala Millor
Porto Cristo
Lo Puebla
Sta. Margarita
La Muro
Inca 1340
Sineu
Petra
S. Lorenzo
Manacor
Puig Mayor 1445
1408
Sóller
Pto. de Sóller
Valldemosa
Estellencs
Banalbufar
Bunola
Puig puñent
Santa María
Marratxi
PALMA DE MALLORCA
Algaida
Montuiri
Porreras
Felanitx
Santany
Cala D'Or
Porto Petro
San Salvador 509
Cala S. Jordi
Cabo Blanco
Bahía de Palma
Isla Dragonera
Andraitx
Sta. Ponsa
Magaluf
Palma Nova
El Arenal
Llucmayor
Campos
Cabo de Salines
Salinas
Colonia de S. Jordi
Isla Conejera
CABRERA
Pto. de Cabrera
Punta Ensiola

IBIZA

Punta Grosa
Punta de Tagomago
Isla de Tagomago
S. Carlos
Sta. Eulalia
S. Juan
Portinatx
Puerto S. Miguel
S. Antonio
S. Agustín
S. Jordi
Salinas
Cabo Aubarca
Sta. Inés
IBIZA
Cabo Llentrisca
Isla Espalmador
Isla Vedra
La Sabina
S. Francisco
Cabo de Berberia
FORMENTERA
Punta del Pes
Isla Espardell
S. Fernando
Punta de la Gavina
Isla Cunillera

MADEIRA

NORTH ATLANTIC OCEAN
Porto Moniz
Ponta do Pargo
Punta de Tristão
Ponta de São Jorge
Ponta de S. Lourenço
Ponta de São Lourenço
São Vicente
Santana
Faial
São Roque
Machico
Santa Cruz
Caniçal
Caniço
FUNCHAL
Ribeira Brava
Câmara de Lobos
Pico Ruivo 1861
Calheta

CANARY ISLANDS

LANZAROTE
Alegranza 259
Montaña Clara
Graciosa
Punta Fariones
La Santa
Los Valles
Arrecife
Playa Blanca
Pto. del Carmen
Jameos
Punta Pechiguera
Isla de Lobos
FUERTEVENTURA
La Oliva 688
Corralejo
Puerto del Rosario
Punta de Toston
Cotillo
Betancuria
Punta de la Hermandad
Pto. de Pozo Negro
Pajara
Cofete
Playa de Jandía
Morro Esmerelda 807
Punta del Jable
Punta de Morro Jable
Punta de Jandía

GRAN CANARIA
El Roque
LAS PALMAS
Galdar
Guia
Agaete
Telde
Punta Sardina
Punta de Gando
S. Nicolás
Punta de la Aldea
Aguaguara
Playa del Inglés
Mogán
Puerto Rico
Playa de Mogán
Punta de Maspalomas
Maspalomas

TENERIFE
Punta de Anaga
SANTA CRUZ DE TENERIFE
La Laguna
Candelaria
Guimar
Punta del Hidalgo
Bajamar
Pico de Teide 3718
Puerto de la Cruz
Güimar
Icod
Garachico
Punta de Teno
Guia de Isora
Playa de las Americas
Medano
Punta de la Rasca

GOMERA
San Sebastián de la Gomera
Agulo
Vallehermoso
Hermigua
Punta de los Organos

LA PALMA
Punta Cumplida
Barlovento
Los Sauces
Sta. Cruz de la Palma
Pico de la Cruz 2400
Puntallana
Los Llanos de Aridane
Tazacorte
El Paso
Fuencaliente
Punta Fuencaliente

HIERRO
Punta del Norte
Valverde
Frontera
Golfo 1417
Restinga

NORTH ATLANTIC OCEAN

Projection: Lambert's Conformal Conic

West from Greenwich
East from Greenwich

m / ft scale legend:
ft 9000 6000 4500 3000 1800 1200 600 300 0
m 3000 2000 1500 1000 600 400 200 100 0
m 6000 3000 2000 1000 600 200 0 ft

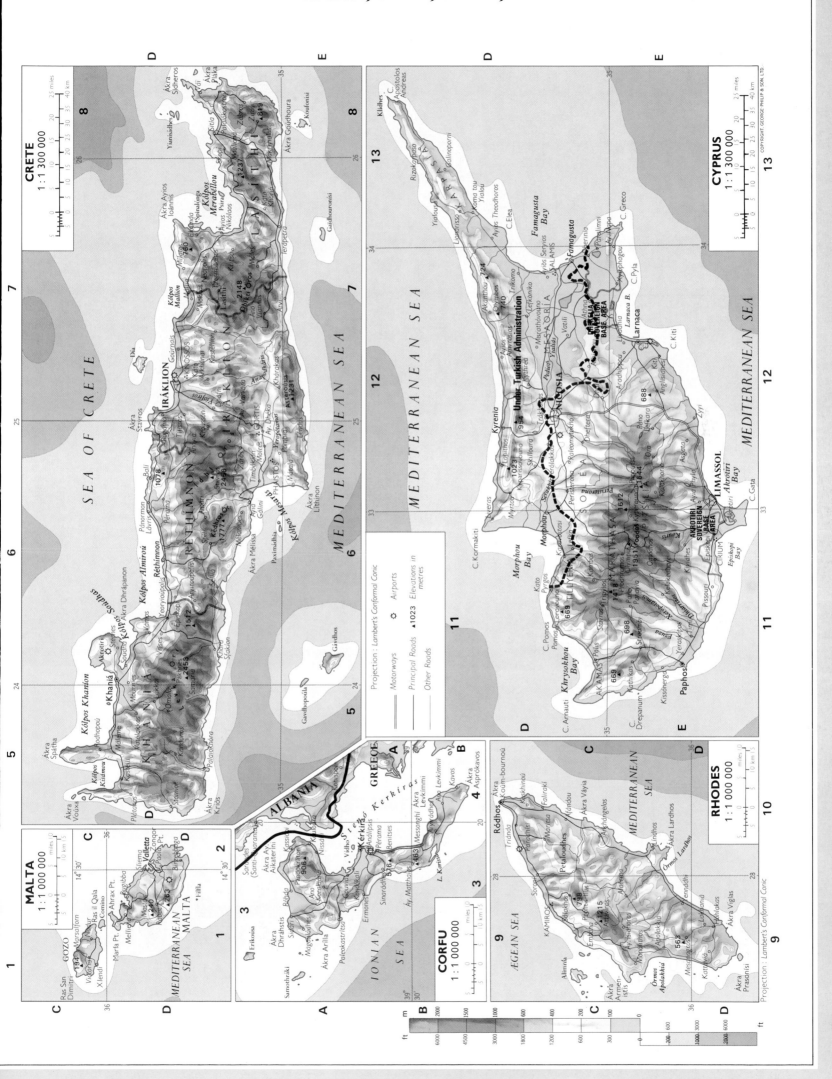

CRETE
1:1 300 000

MALTA
1:1 000 000

CORFU
1:1 000 000

RHODES
1:1 000 000

CYPRUS
1:1 300 000

Projection: Lambert's Conformal Conic

Motorways
Airports
Principal Roads   ▲1023   Elevations in metres
Other Roads

COPYRIGHT GEORGE PHILIP & SON LTD.

Projection: Lambert's Conformal Conic

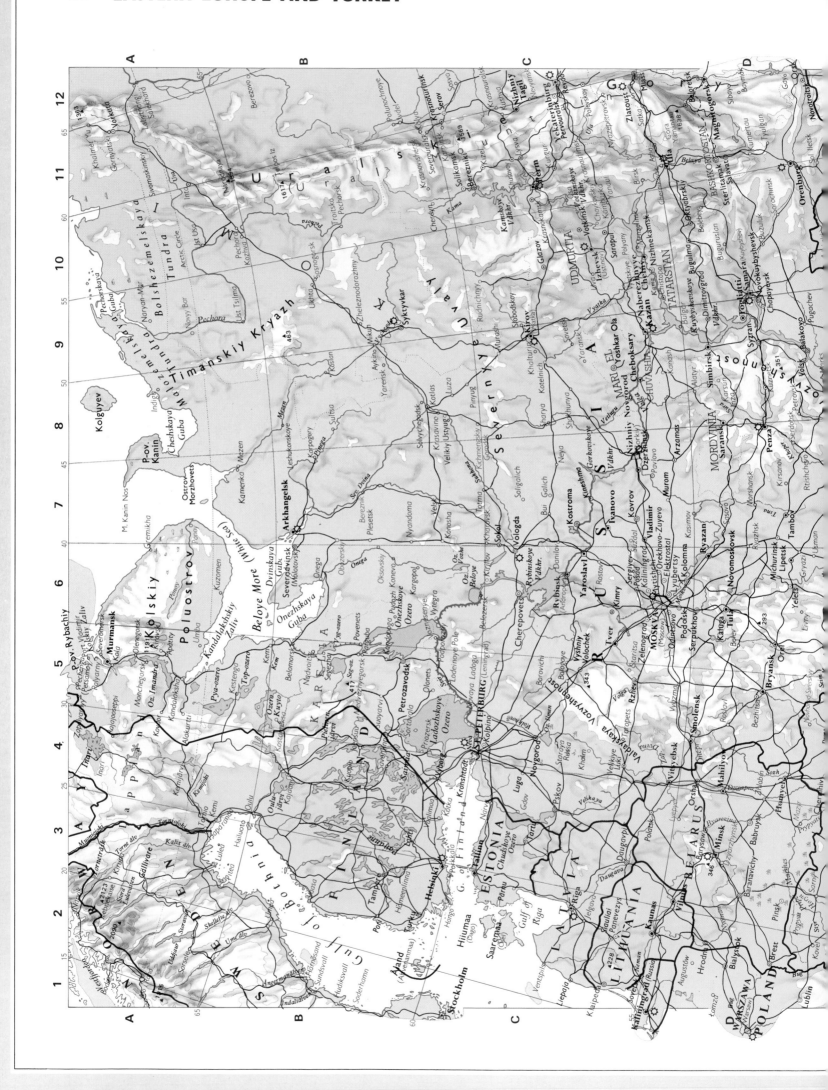

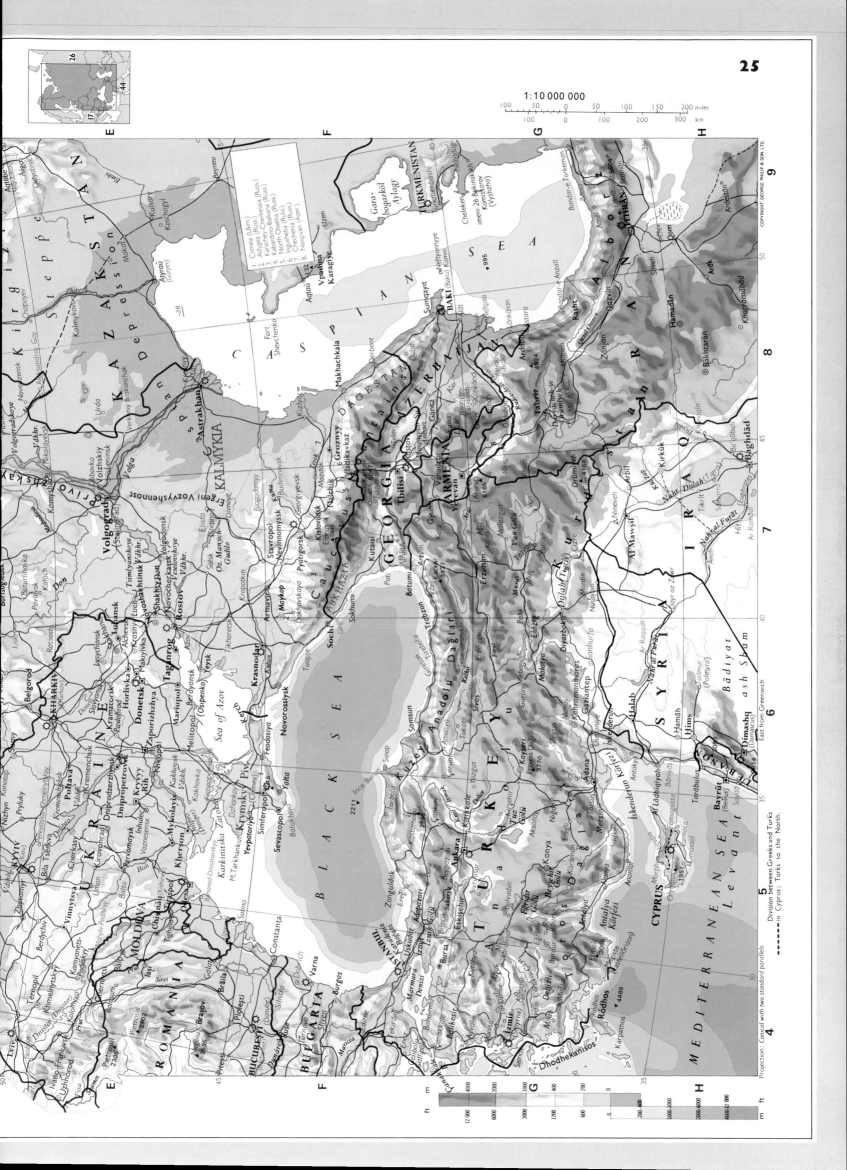

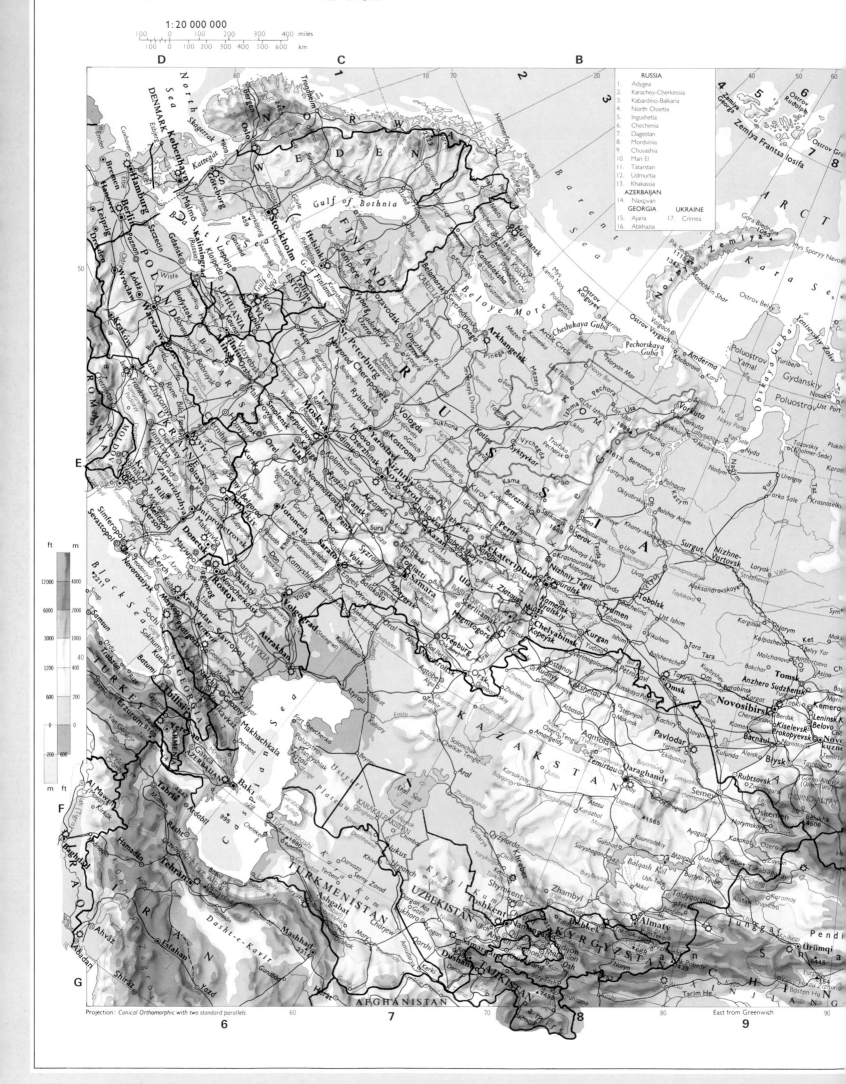

RUSSIA	
1.	Adygea
2.	Karachey-Cherkessia
3.	Kabardino-Balkaria
4.	North Ossetia
5.	Ingushetia
6.	Chechenia
7.	Dagestan
8.	Mordvinia
9.	Chuvashia
10.	Mari El
11.	Tatarstan
12.	Udmurtia
13.	Khakassia
AZERBAIJAN	
14.	Naxçivan
GEORGIA	**UKRAINE**
15.	Ajaria	17. Crimea
16.	Abkhazia	

Projection: Conical Orthomorphic with two standard parallels

East from Greenwich

Mys Dezhneva
(East C.)

Chukchi Sea

St. Lawrence I.
(U.S.A.)

60

Ostrov Vrangelya

Ostrov
Henrietta
Ostrova Delong

Ostrov
Bennett

Ostrov Zhokhova

Ostrov
Mevedzhi

Ostrov
Medvezhi

Novosibirskiye Ostrova

Ostrov Faddeyevskiy

Ostrov
Novaya Sibir

Bering
Sea

OCEAN

Mys Arkticheskiy

Ostrov
Shmidta

Ostrov
Kamsomolets

Ostrov
Pioner

Ostrov Oktyabrskoy
Revolyutsii

965

Severnaya
Zemlya

Ostrov Bolshevik

Proliv Vilkitskogo

Ostrova Ostrov Belkovskiy

Lyakhovskiye Ostrova

Proliv Dmitriya Lapteva

D

Poluostrov
Gory Byrranga 1146

Taymyr

L a p t e v

S e a

Ostrov Bolshoy
Begichev

Nordvik

Oz. Taymyr

E a s t   S i b e r i a n   S e a

Poluostrov
Kamchatka

Petropavlovsk-
Kamchatskiy

3456

Norilsk

Gory
Putorana
1701

962   Arctic Circle

S I B E R I A

Yakutsk

Sea of
Okhotsk

1780

Magadan

Okhotsk

Vilyuysk

Olekminsk

E

Bratsk

Krasnoyarsk

Kirensk

Vitim

Komsomolsk

Khabarovsk

Birobidzhan

Sakhalin

Yuzhno-Sakhalinsk

Sovetskaya Gavan

Chita

Ulan Ude

Irkutsk

Blagoveshchensk

Jiamusi

Vladivostok

Nakhodka

Ussuriysk

Hokkaido

Sapporo

Hakodate

40

Qiqihar

Harbin

Ulaanbaatar
(Ulan Bator)

M O N G O L I A

Jilin

Changchun

Chongjin

Honshū

1949

Siping

Fushun

Shenyang

Anshan

NORTH
KOREA

Wŏnsan

Sea of JAPAN

Niigata

Toyama

Kanazawa

F

3957

G O B I

Baotou Hohhot

Zhangjiakou

Beijing

Dalian

Pyongyang

Dandong

Sŏul
SOUTH KOREA

Inch'ŏn

Taejŏn

Taegu

Pusan

Boundaries of
Republics

COPYRIGHT. GEORGE PHILIP & SON. LTD.

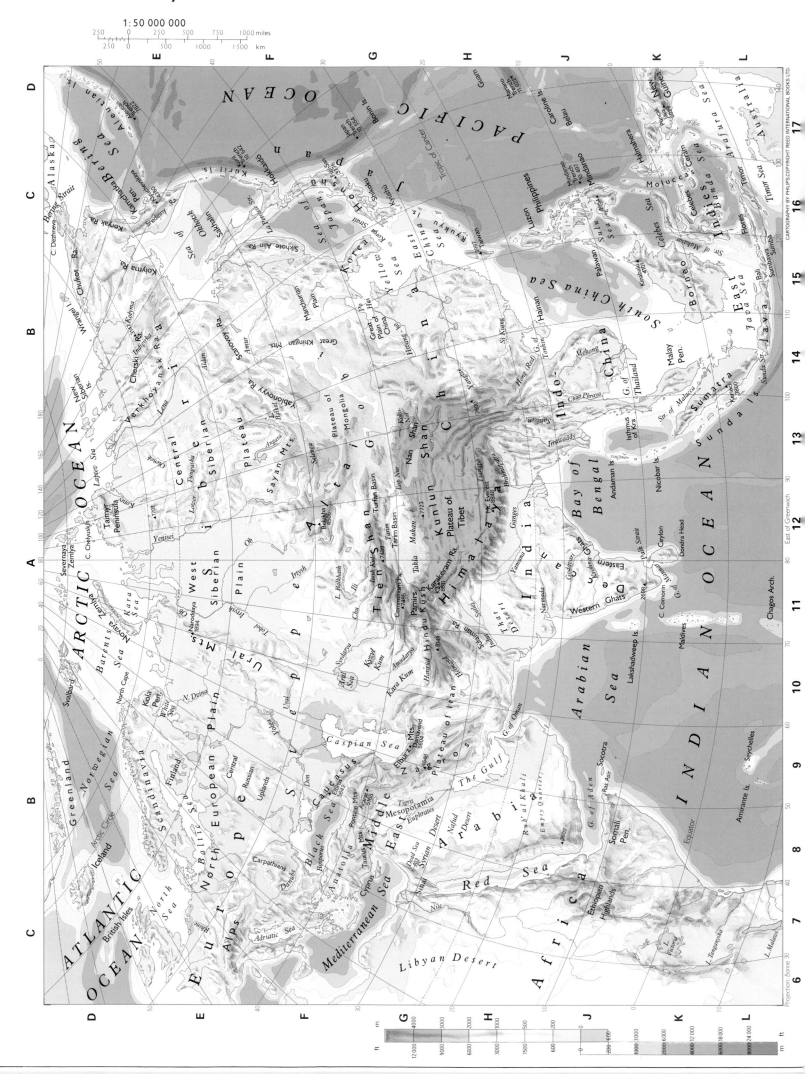

1 : 50 000 000

ASIA : Physical

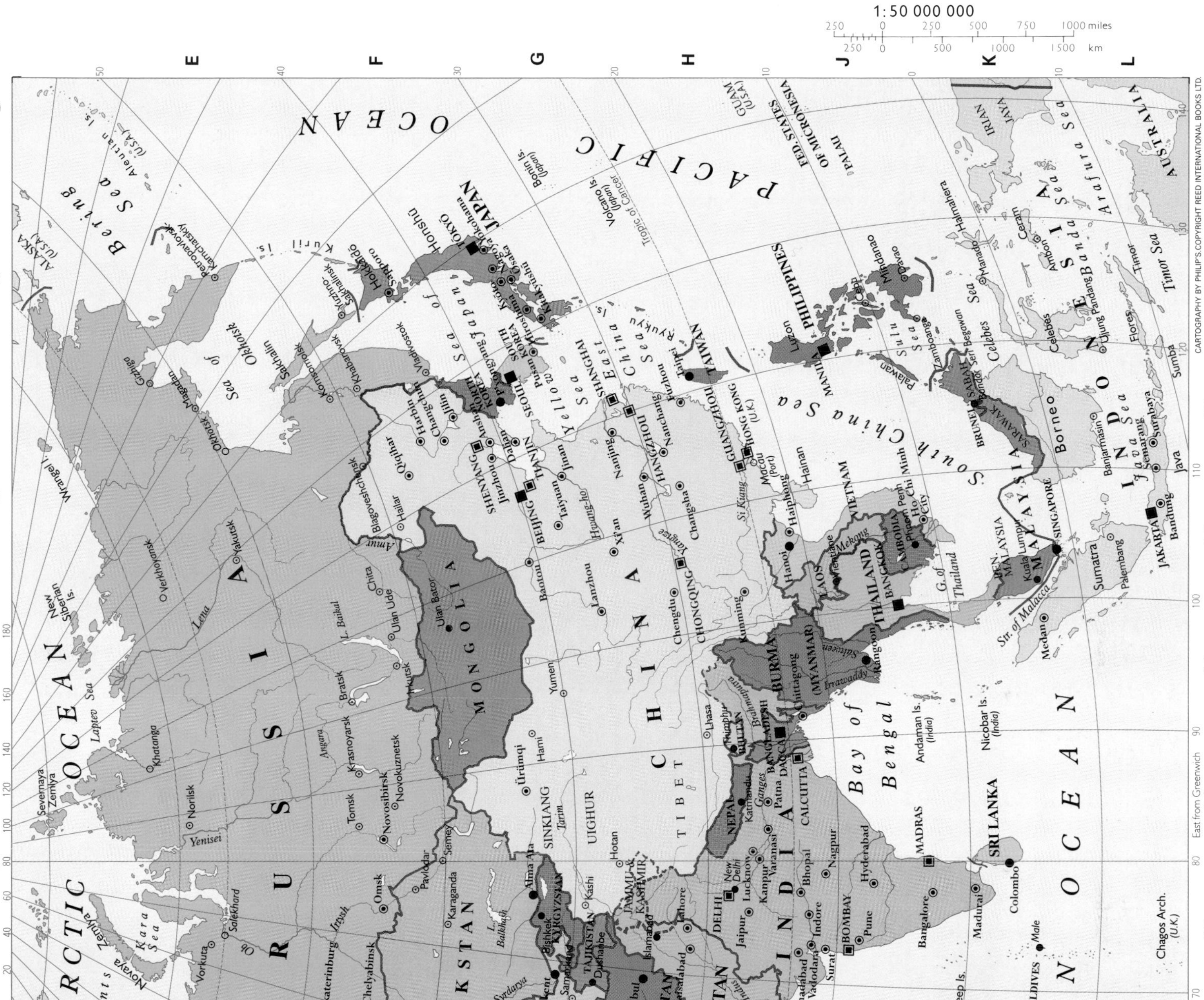

1:50 000 000

250   0   250   500   750   1000 miles
250   0   500   1000   1500 km

CARTOGRAPHY BY PHILIP'S COPYRIGHT REED INTERNATIONAL BOOKS LTD.

OCEAN

PACIFIC

FED. STATES
OF MICRONESIA

GUAM (USA)

PALAU

Tropic of Cancer

Volcano Is. (Japan)

JAPAN   Tokyo   Honshu   Hokkaido

Sea of Japan

Kyushu   Shikoku

SOUTH KOREA   SEOUL   Pusan
NORTH KOREA   Pyongyang

Ryukyu Is.

TAIWAN

PHILIPPINES   MANILA   Luzon   Mindanao

Sulu Sea

BRUNEI   SABAH   SARAWAK

MALAYSIA   KUALA LUMPUR   SINGAPORE

I N D O N E S I A

Sumatra   Borneo   Celebes   Ceram   Halmahera

Java Sea   Flores Sea   Banda Sea   Arafura Sea   Timor Sea

Java   Bandung   JAKARTA   Surabaya   Semarang

Bali   Sumba   Sumbawa   Flores   Timor

AUSTRALIA

Bering Sea

ALASKA (USA)

ARCTIC OCEAN

Wrangel I.
New Siberian Is.
Severnaya Zemlya
Novaya Zemlya
Svalbard

Laptev Sea   Kara Sea   Barents Sea

R U S S I A

Yenisei   Lena   Ob   Angara   Amur

Yakutsk   Norilsk   Khatanga   Tomsk   Krasnoyarsk   Novokuznetsk   Novosibirsk   Omsk   Irkutsk   Bratsk   Chita   Ulan Ude

Verkhoyansk   Oymyakon   Magadan   Okhotsk   Vladivostok   Khabarovsk

Sea of Okhotsk   Kamchatka   Kuril Is.   Sakhalin

MONGOLIA   Ulan Bator

C H I N A   BEIJING   SHENYANG   TIANJIN   NANJING   SHANGHAI   WUHAN   GUANGZHOU   HANGZHOU   CHONGQING   Chengdu   Lanzhou   Baotou   Xi'an   Taiyuan   Jinan   Dalian   Harbin   Changchun   Jilin   Qiqihar

Yellow Sea   East China Sea   South China Sea

HONG KONG (U.K.)   Macau (Port.)   Hainan

SINKIANG   UIGHUR   Tarim   Ürümqi   Hami   Kashi   Hotan

T I B E T   Lhasa

KAZAKSTAN   Alma Ata   Karaganda   Semey   Pavlodar   Aqtöbe

Ekaterinburg   Chelyabinsk   Perm   Ufa   Kazan   Samara   Saratov   Volgograd   Astrakhan   Rostov

MOSCOW   ST. PETERSBURG   Nizhniy Novgorod   Murmansk   Arkhangelsk

FINLAND   SWEDEN   NORWAY

White Sea

UKRAINE   Kiev   Odessa   Don   Volga

E u r o p e

ICELAND   GREENLAND   Arctic Circle

UNITED KINGDOM   LONDON   PARIS   FRANCE   GERMANY   Berlin   ITALY   Rome   Athens   Belgrade   Warsaw   Budapest   Bucharest

ATLANTIC OCEAN   North Sea

UZBEKISTAN   Tashkent   Samarkand
TURKMENISTAN   Ashkhabad   Mashhad
TAJIKISTAN   Dushanbe
KYRGYZSTAN   Bishkek
Aral Sea   Syrdarya   Amudarya   L. Balkhash

AFGHANISTAN   Kābul   Qandahār   Herat

PAKISTAN   Islamabad   Lahore   KARACHI

JAMMU & KASHMIR

I N D I A   New Delhi   DELHI   Jaipur   Kanpur   Lucknow   Varanasi   BOMBAY   CALCUTTA   MADRAS   Hyderabad   Bangalore   Nagpur   Bhopal   Indore   Ahmadabad   Vadodara   Surat   Pune   Madurai

NEPAL   Kathmandu   BHUTAN   Thimphu
BANGLADESH   DACCA   Chittagong
Ganges   Brahmaputra

BURMA (MYANMAR)   Rangoon   Mandalay   Irrawaddy

SRI LANKA   Colombo

MALDIVES   Male

Andaman Is. (India)   Nicobar Is. (India)   Lakshadweep Is. (India)

Chagos Arch. (U.K.)

Bay of Bengal   Arabian Sea   INDIAN OCEAN

IRAN   TEHRĀN   Esfahan   Shiraz   Tabriz   Mashhad   Zahedan

IRAQ   Baghdad   Basra   Mosul   Euphrates   Tigris

GEORGIA   ARMENIA   AZERBAIJAN   Baku   Yerevan   Tbilisi
Caspian Sea   Black Sea

TURKEY   Ankara   ISTANBUL   Izmir   Adana   Bursa

CYPRUS   LEBANON   Beirut   SYRIA   Damascus   ISRAEL   Jerusalem   Amman   JORDAN   Nicosia

SAUDI ARABIA   Riyadh   Mecca   Medina   Jedda

KUWAIT   BAHRAIN   QATAR   Doha   UNITED ARAB EMIRATES   Abu Dhabi   Dubai   OMAN   Muscat
The Gulf   G. of Oman

YEMEN   Aden   Sana
Red Sea   G. of Aden   Socotra (Yemen)

EGYPT   CAIRO   Nile   Aswân   Alexandria   Suez

LIBYA   SUDAN   Khartoum   Port Sudan

ETHIOPIA   Addis Ababa   ERITREA   DJIBOUTI   SOMALI REP.   Mogadishu

KENYA   Nairobi   Mombasa   UGANDA   TANZANIA   Dar es Salaam   ZAIRE   ZAMBIA   MALAWI   L. Victoria   L. Tanganyika   Equator

SEYCHELLES   Victoria   Amirante Is. (Seychelles)   Aldabra Is. (Seychelles)

Mediterranean Sea

A f r i c a

Hanoi ● Capital Cities

Str. of Malacca

VIETNAM   Hanoi   Haiphong   Ho Chi Minh City   Mekong
LAOS   Vientiane
CAMBODIA   Phnom Penh
THAILAND   BANGKOK   G. of Thailand

East from Greenwich

Projection: Bonne

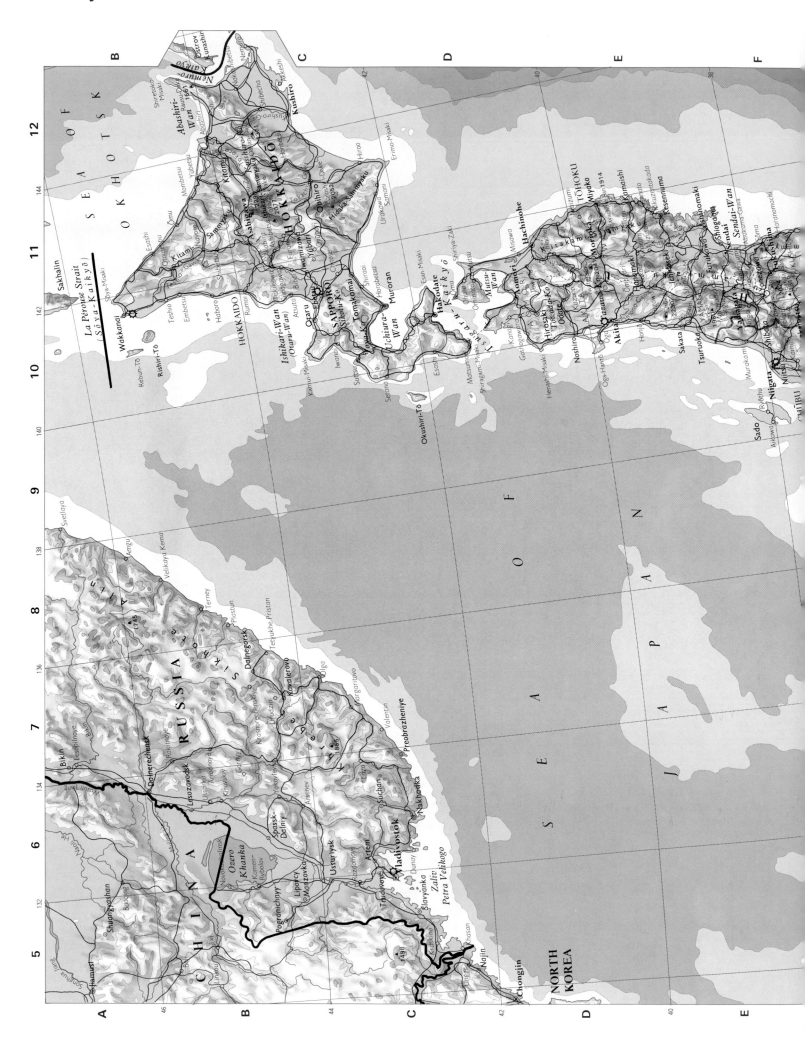

La Pérouse Strait
(Sōya-Kaikyō)

SEA OF OKHOTSK

RUSSIA

CHINA

NORTH KOREA

HOKKAIDO

SAPPORO

SEA OF JAPAN

TŌHOKU

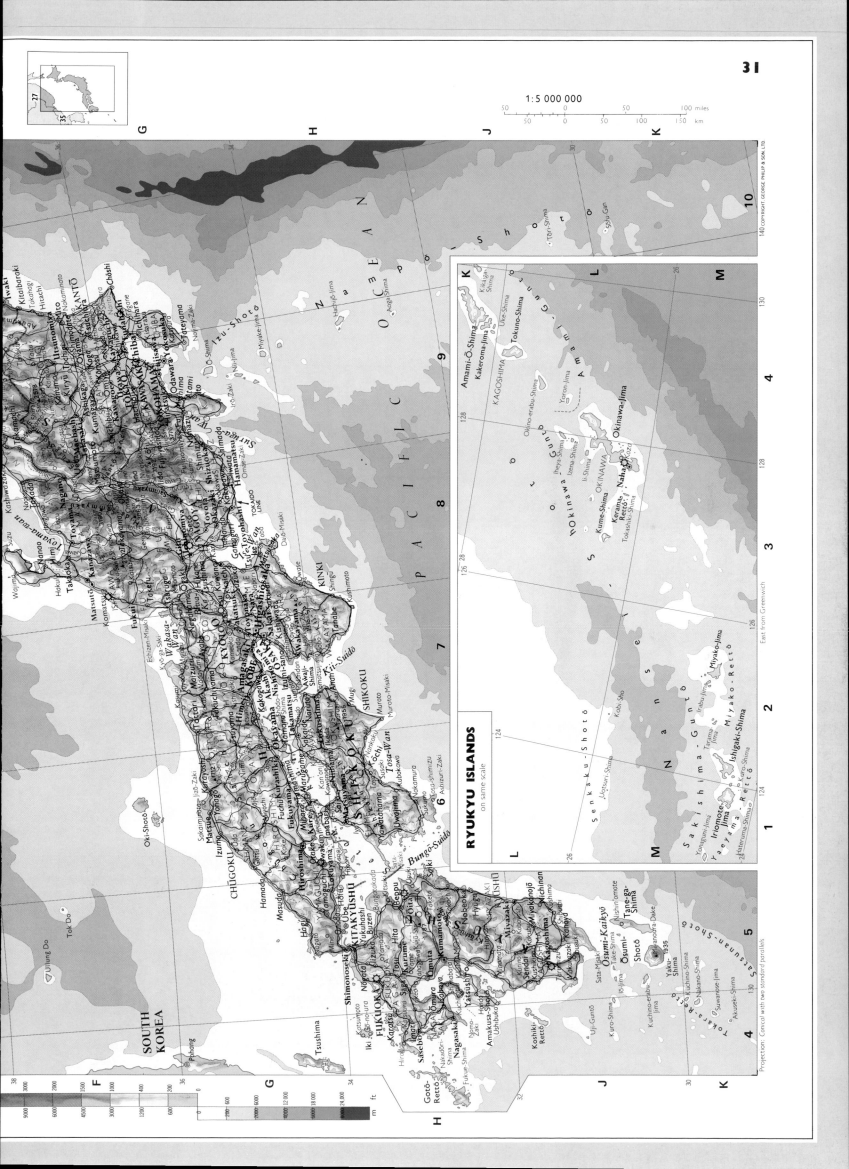

1:5 000 000

50   0   50   100 miles

50   0   50   100   150 km

RYUKYU ISLANDS

on same scale

SOUTH KOREA

PACIFIC OCEAN

East from Greenwich

Projection: Conical with two standard parallels

140 COPYRIGHT GEORGE PHILIP & SON, LTD

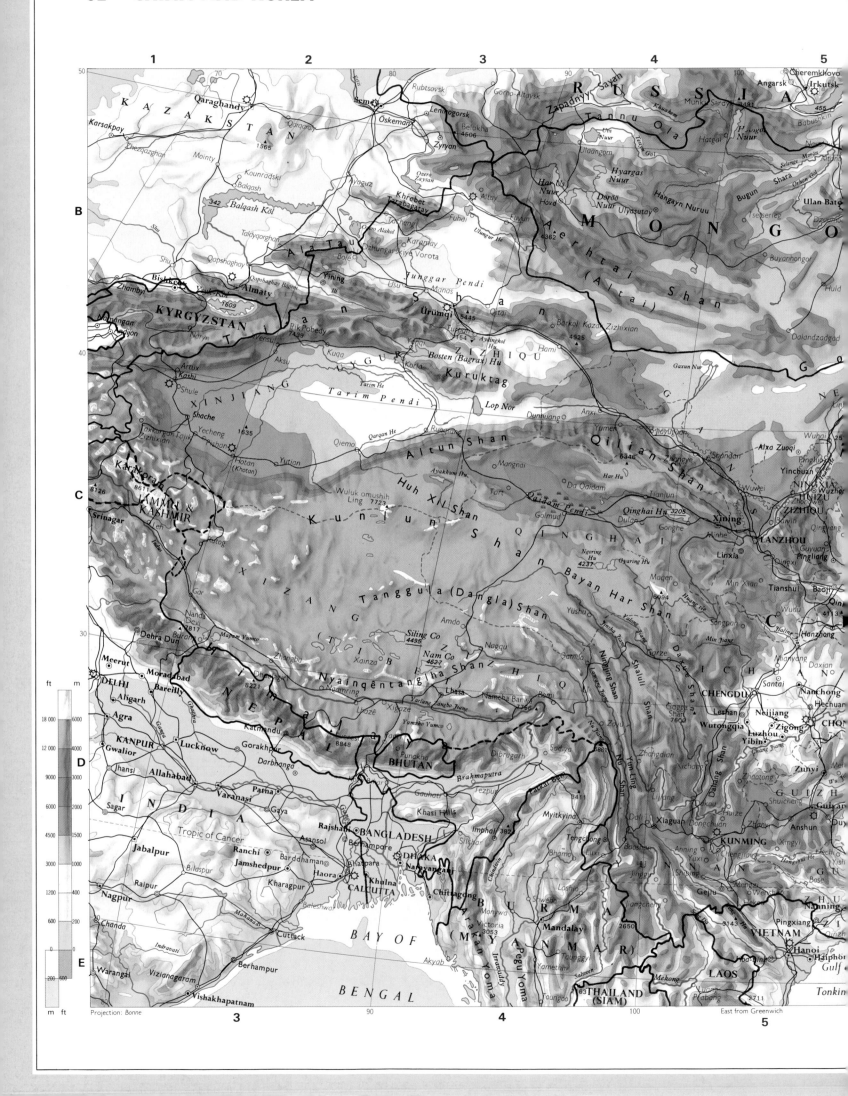

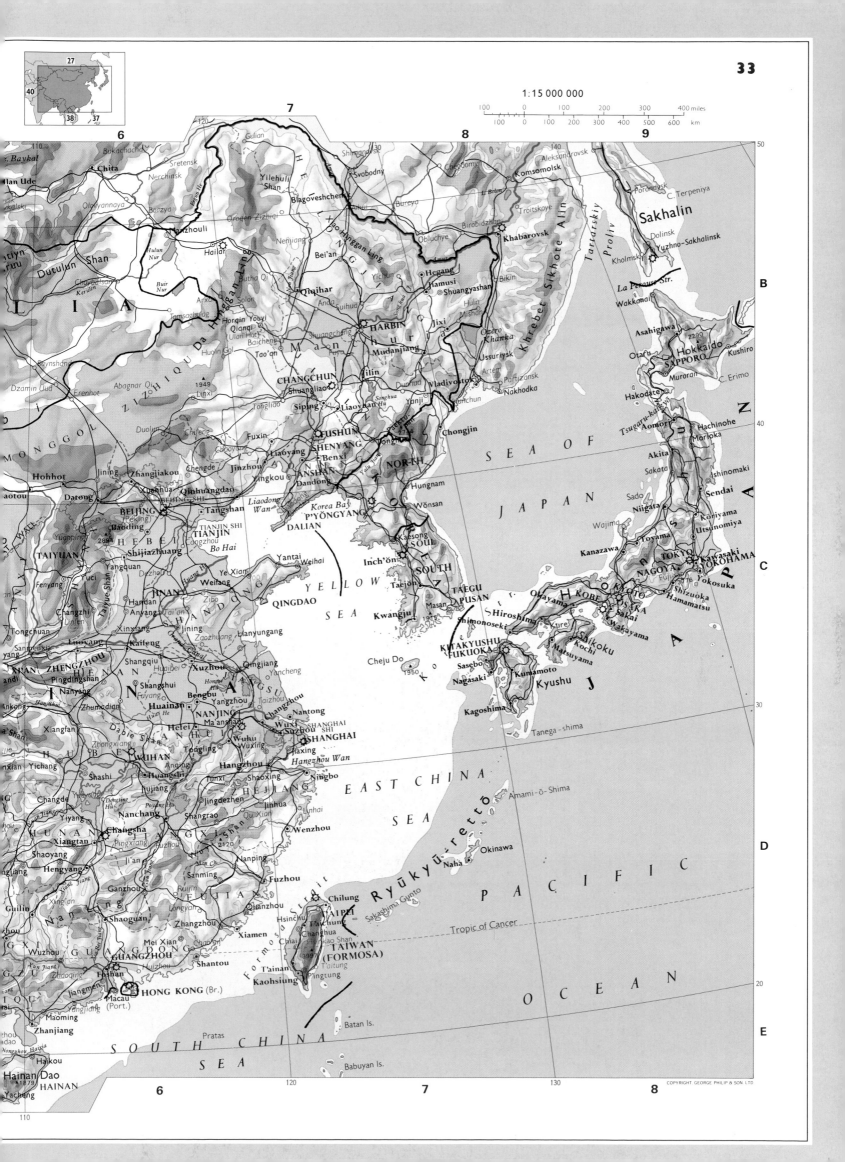

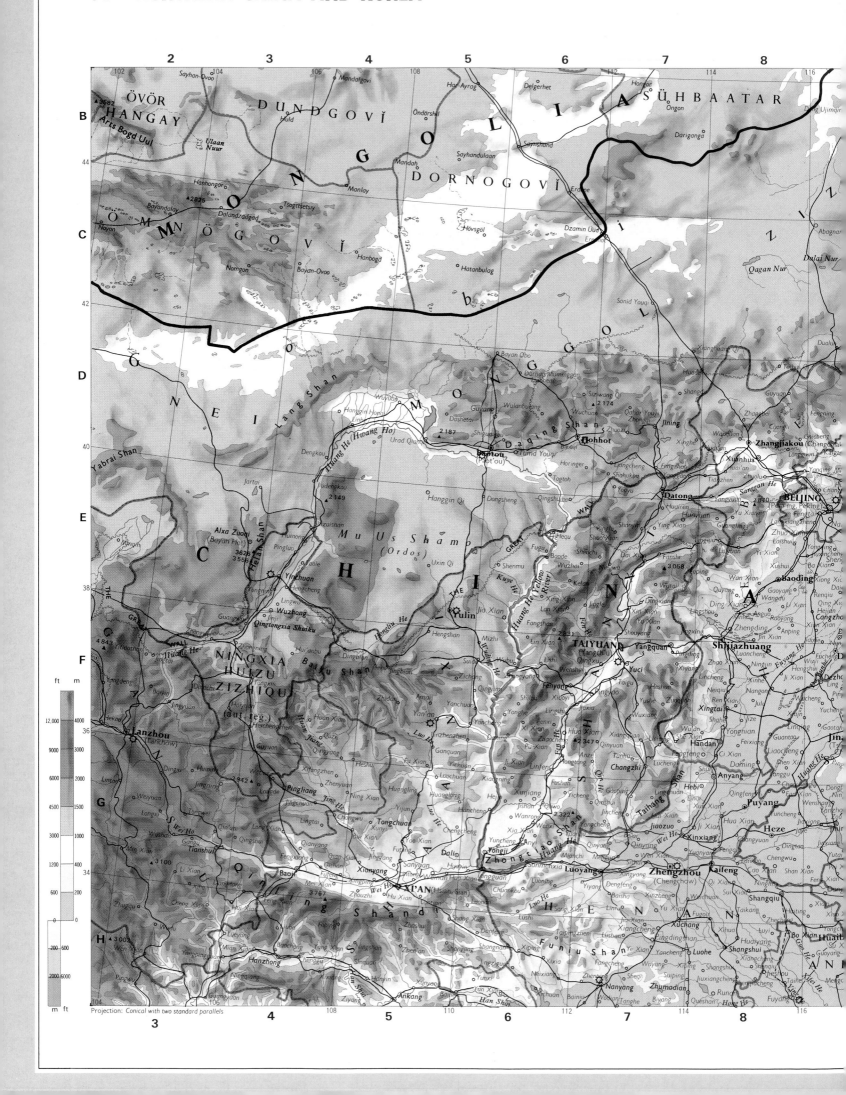

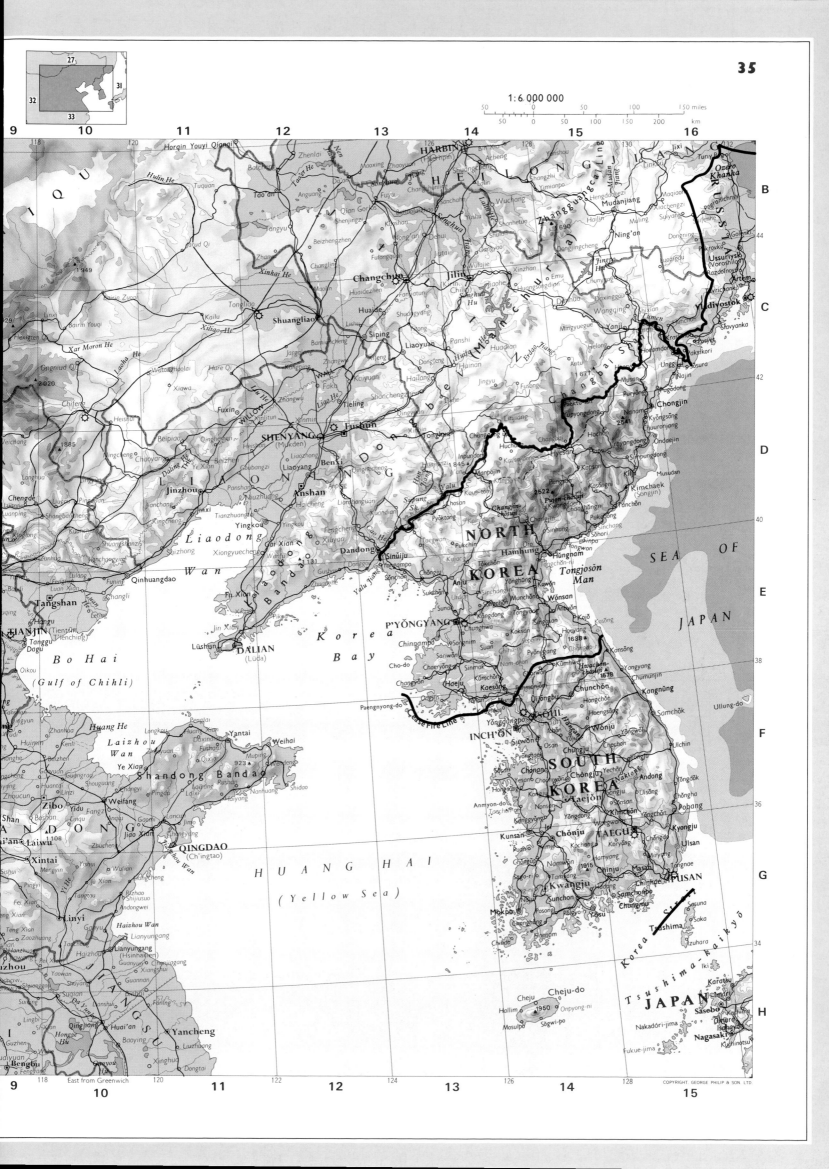

1:6 000 000

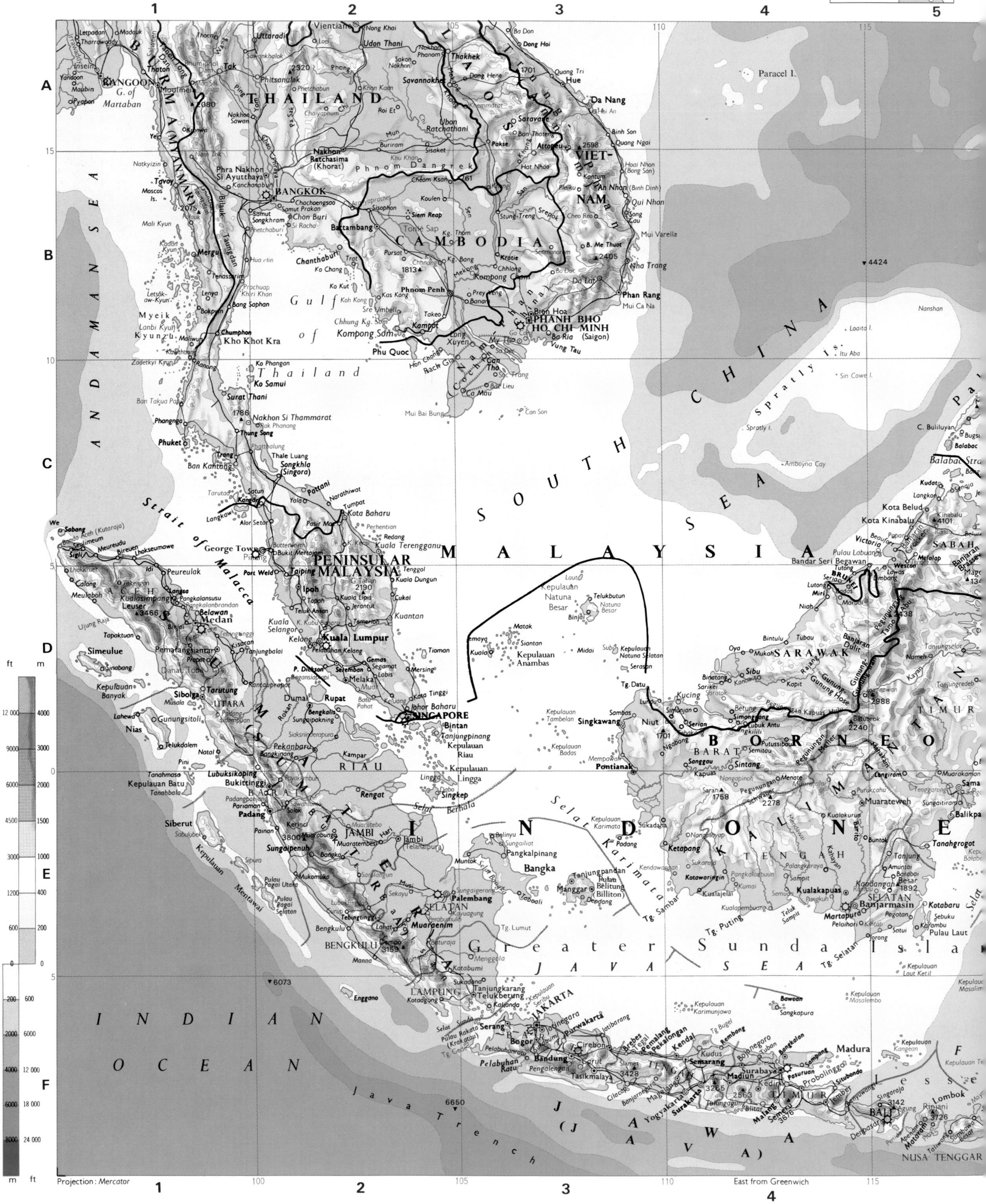

32 33
58
60 62

Map Labels

Seas and Oceans:
- ANDAMAN SEA
- SOUTH CHINA SEA
- INDIAN OCEAN
- Gulf of Thailand
- Strait of Malacca
- Selat Karimata
- Selat Berhala
- JAVA SEA
- Greater Sunda Islands
- Java Trench

Countries / Regions:
- BURMA (MYANMAR)
- THAILAND
- CAMBODIA
- VIET-NAM
- PENINSULAR MALAYSIA
- MALAYSIA
- SUMATERA
- KALIMANTAN
- BORNEO
- SARAWAK
- SABAH
- BRUNEI
- INDONESIA
- RIAU
- BARAT
- TENGAH
- SELATAN
- UTARA
- TIMUR

Selected cities and places:
- Rangoon, Moulmein, G. of Martaban, Tavoy, Mergui, Tenasserim
- Bangkok, Nakhon Ratchasima (Khorat), Phra Nakhon Si Ayutthaya, Kanchanaburi, Chon Buri, Si Racha, Phetchaburi
- Vientiane, Nong Khai, Udon Thani, Savannakhet, Thakhek
- Hue, Da Nang, Qui Nhon, Nha Trang, Phan Rang, Phan Thiet
- PHANH BHO HO CHI MINH (Saigon), Bien Hoa, Vung Tau
- Phnom Penh, Battambang, Siem Reap, Kompong Cham, Kompong Som
- Phnom Dangrek
- Tonle Sap
- Paracel I.
- Spratly Is., Spratly I., Itu Aba, Sin Cowe I., Loaita I., Amboyna Cay
- George Town, Pinang, Butterworth, Taiping, Ipoh, Kuala Lumpur, Melaka, Johor Baharu
- SINGAPORE, Bintan, Tanjungpinang
- Kepulauan Natuna Besar, Kepulauan Anambas, Kepulauan Natuna Selatan
- Medan, Belawan, Pematangsiantar, Sibolga, Tarutung, Padang, Bukittinggi, Pekanbaru, Jambi, Palembang, Bengkulu, Lampung, Tanjungkarang, Telukbetung
- Kota Kinabalu, Kota Belud, Kudat, Bandar Seri Begawan, Miri, Bintulu, Kuching, Sibu, Pontianak, Singkawang, Sintang, Banjarmasin, Balikpapan, Kotabaru
- JAKARTA, Bogor, Bandung, Cirebon, Pekalongan, Semarang, Surabaya, Yogyakarta, Surakarta, Madiun, Malang, Probolinggo
- Madura, BALI, NUSA TENGGARA, LOMBOK
- Enggano, Nias, Simeulue, Siberut
- Danau Toba

Elevation scale (left):
ft / m
- 12 000 / 4000
- 9000 / 3000
- 6000 / 2000
- 4500 / 1500
- 3000 / 1000
- 1200 / 400
- 600 / 200
- 0 / 0
- 200 / 600
- 2000 / 6000
- 4000 / 12 000
- 6000 / 18 000
- 8000 / 24 000
m / ft

1:12 500 000

100   100   0   100   200   300   miles
100   0   100   200   300   400   500   km

6   11   12   13   14   15   16

JAVA AND MADURA

1:7 500 000

50   0   50   100   150   200 miles
50   0   50   100   150   200   250   300   km

11   12   13   14   15   16

JAKARTA

Kepulauan
Karimunjawa

B A R A T   T E N G A H   Madura
Bandung   Semarang   Bangkalan   Sumenep
Surabaya   Selat Madura
Surakarta   Madjun   Gresik
Jogyakarta   Kediri   Probolinggo
T I M U R
Malang   Bali

Nusa
Kambangan   Nusa Barung

7   8   9   FEDERATED STATES   10   B

OF MICRONESIA
Yap Islands   8597   Ulithi Atoll

Ngulu Atoll
8527   Soral Atoll

P A C I F I C   PALAU   Babelthuap
Koror   8138
Angaur   C a r o l i n e   I s l a n d s   C

Sonsorol
Islands
O C E A N   Pulo-Anna
Merir   5798

Tobi   Helen Atoll   D

LUZON

MANILA

Equator   0   E

I R I A N   J A Y A
PAPUA NEW GUINEA

SULAWESI
(CELEBES)

B A N D A   S E A   MALUKU

A R A F U R A
S E A

5   7   130   8   135   9   10

COPYRIGHT GEORGE PHILIP & SON LTD

6

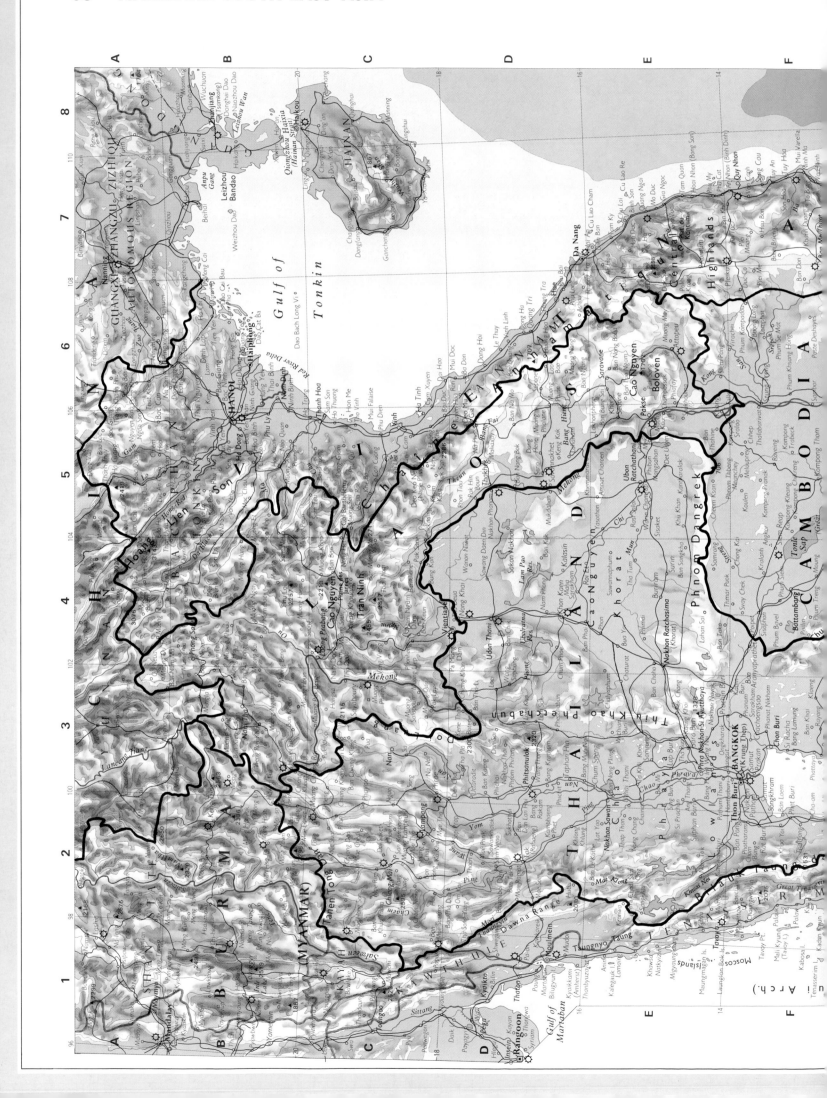

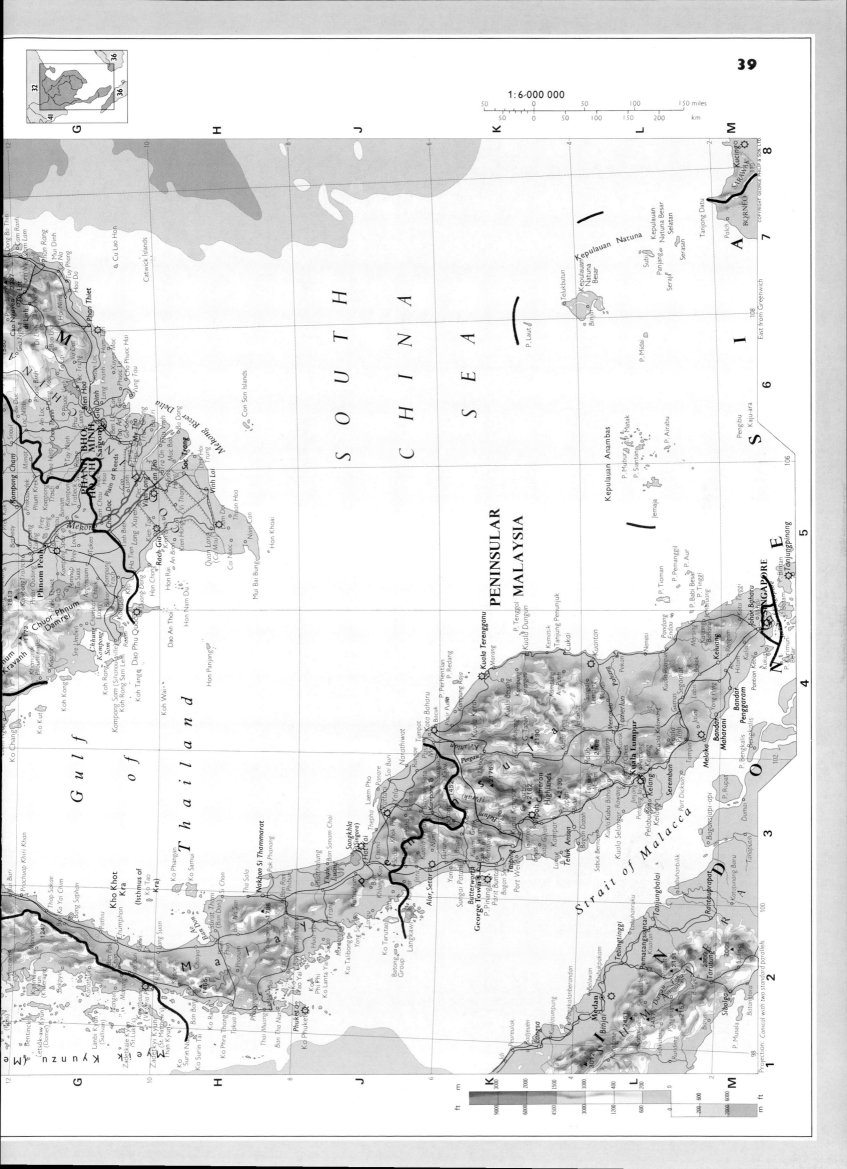

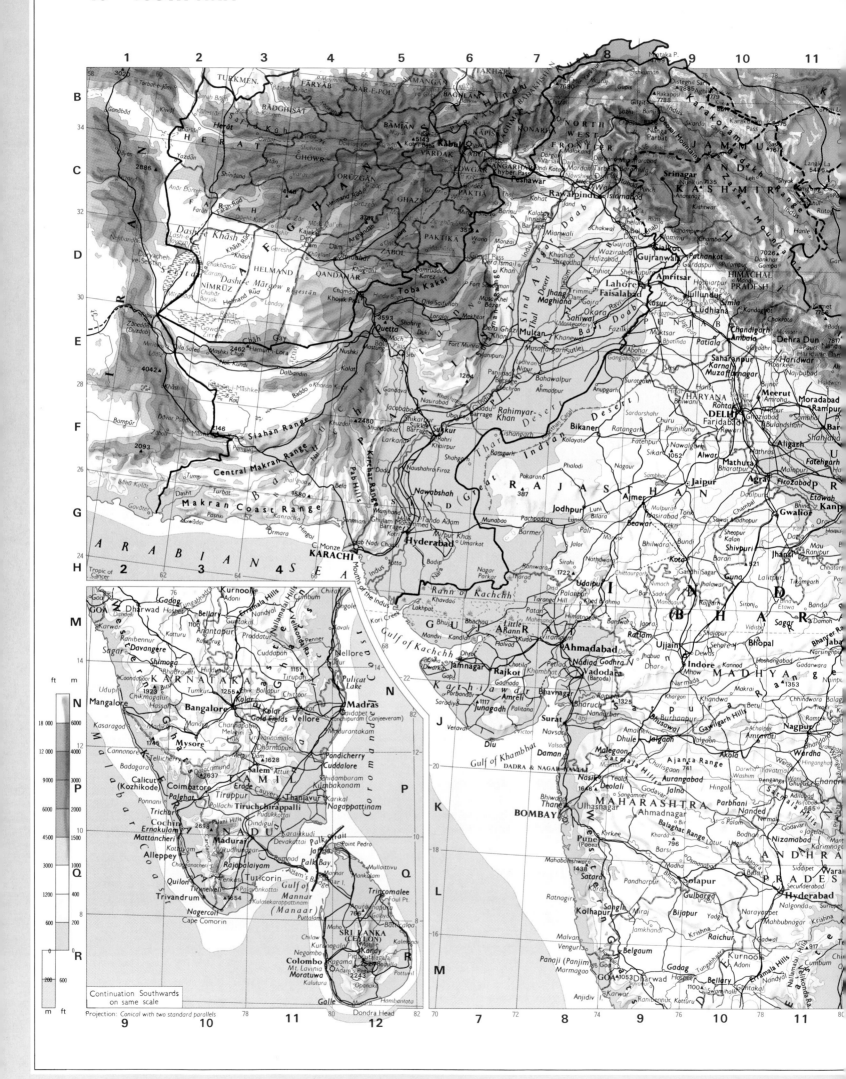

Projection: Conical with two standard parallels

Continuation Southwards on same scale

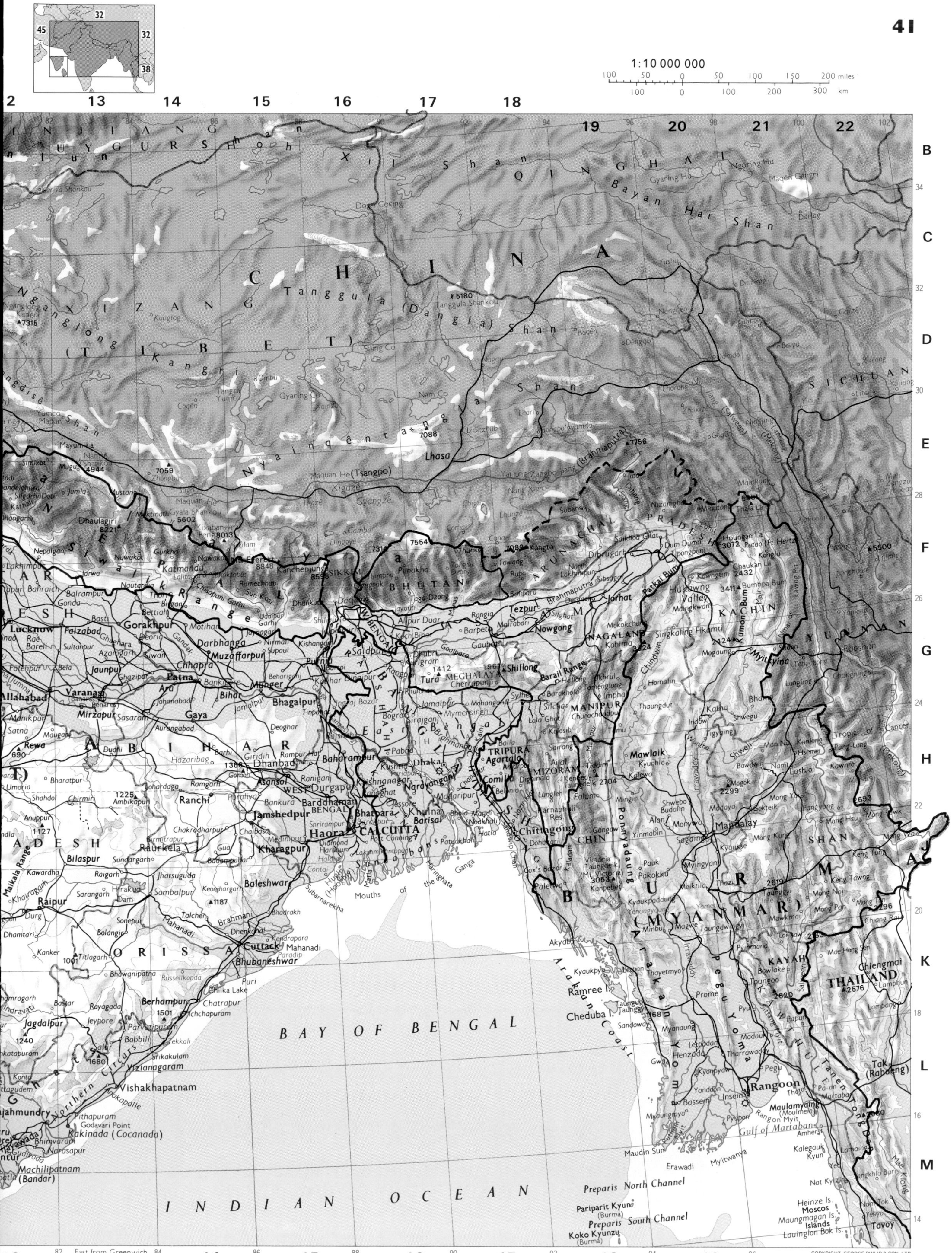

1:10 000 000

100 50 0 50 100 150 200 miles
100 0 100 200 300 km

BAY OF BENGAL

INDIAN OCEAN

CHINA

XIZANG (TIBET)

QINGHAI

SICHUAN

YUNNAN

BURMA (MYANMAR)

THAILAND

ORISSA

BIHAR

WEST BENGAL

NEPAL

BHUTAN

SIKKIM

ARUNACHAL PRADESH

NAGALAND

MANIPUR

MIZORAM

TRIPURA

MEGHALAYA

KACHIN

SHAN

KAYAH

Lhasa

CALCUTTA

Dhaka

Rangoon

Mandalay

Patna

Varanasi

Allahabad

Gorakhpur

Lucknow

Ranchi

Jamshedpur

Kharagpur

Haora

Cuttack

Bhubaneshwar

Berhampur

Vishakhapatnam

Chittagong

Agartala

Shillong

Imphal

Myitkyina

Lashio

Chiengmai

Tavoy

Bayan Har Shan

Tanggula (Danglia) Shan

Yarlung Zangbo Jiang (Brahmaputra)

Maquan He (Tsangpo)

Mouths of the Ganga

Gulf of Martaban

Preparis North Channel

Preparis South Channel

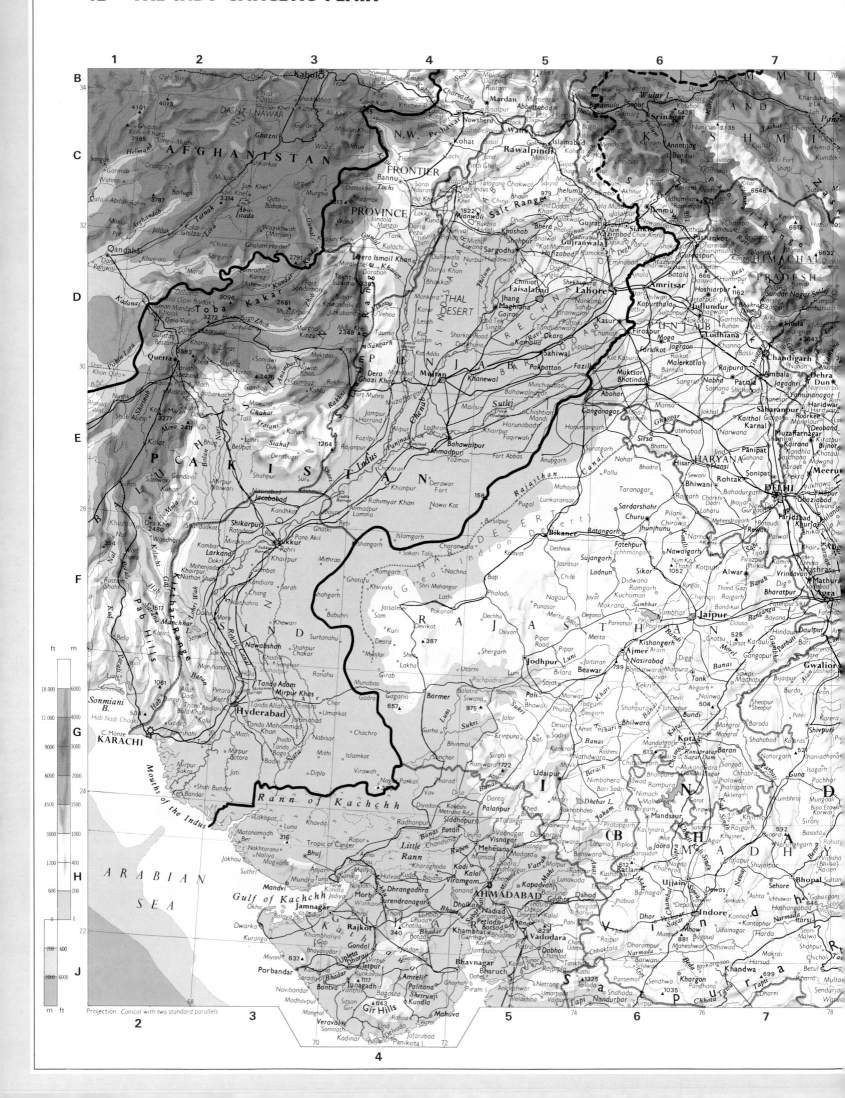

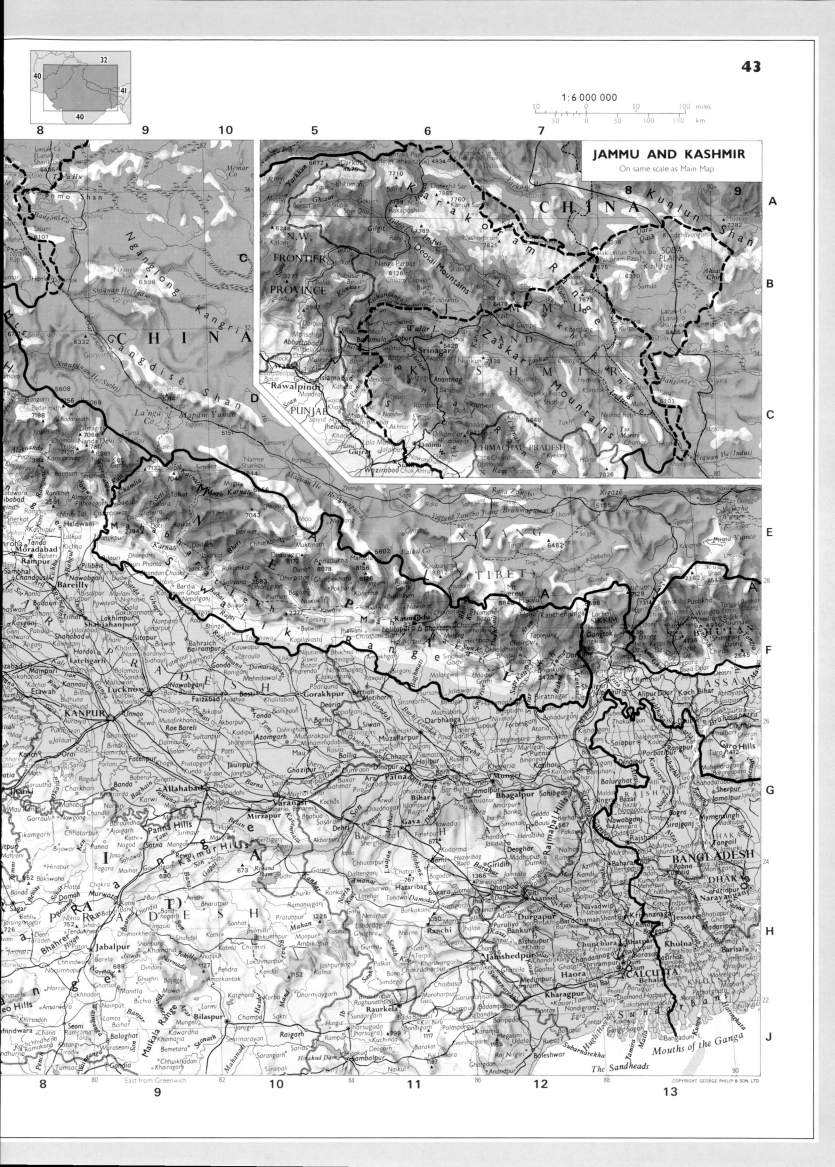

JAMMU AND KASHMIR
On same scale as Main Map

1:6 000 000

COPYRIGHT GEORGE PHILIP & SON LTD.

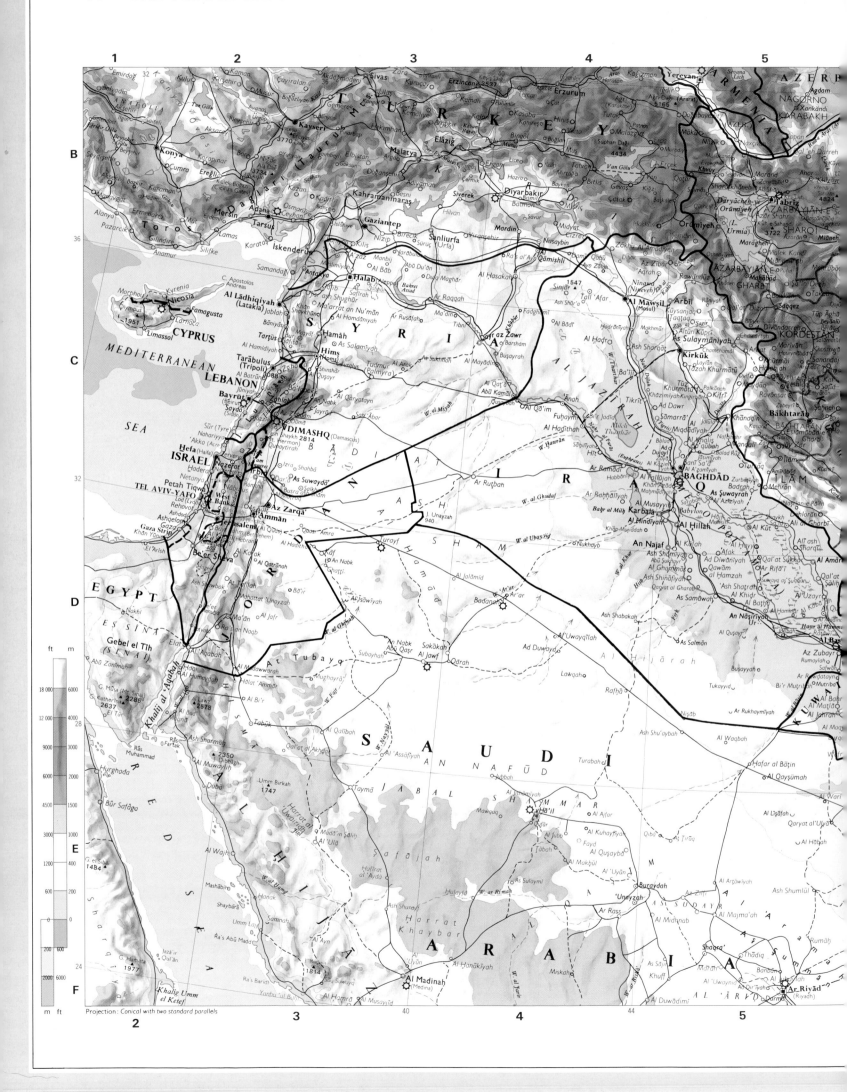

Projection : Conical with two standard parallels

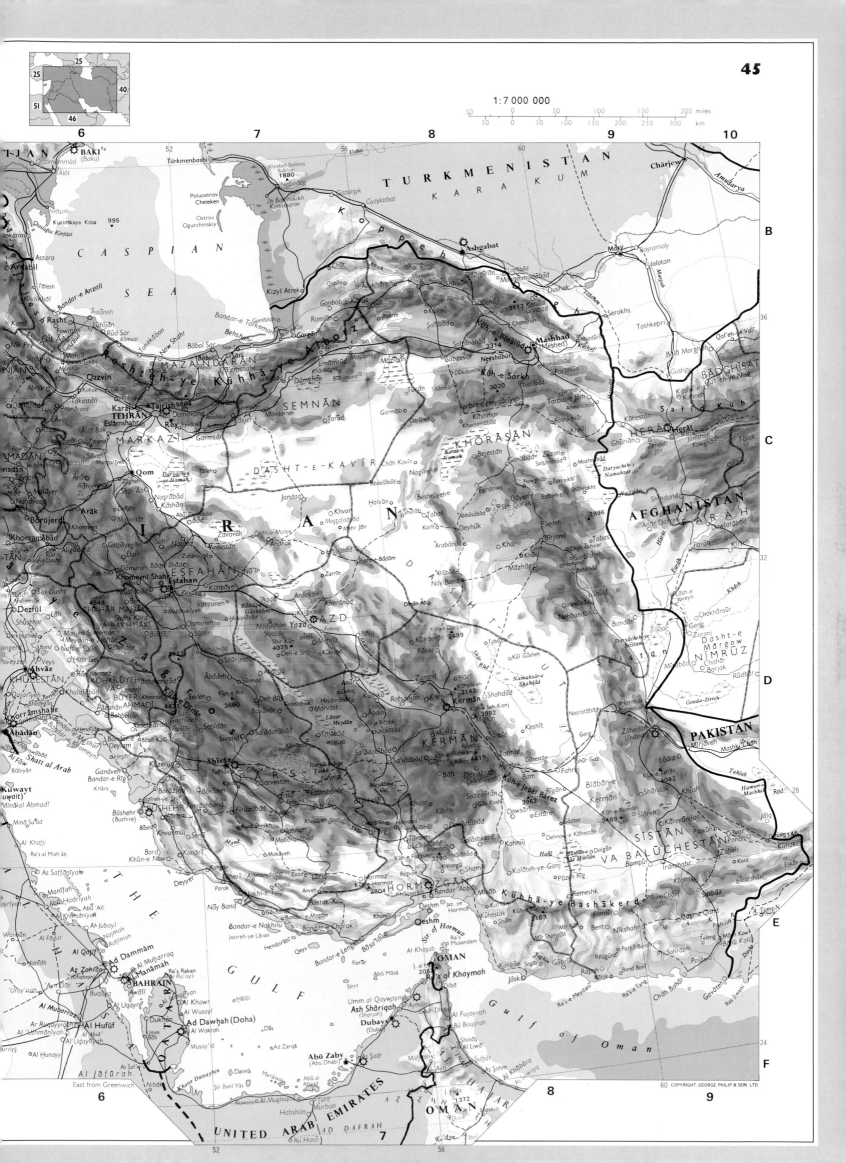

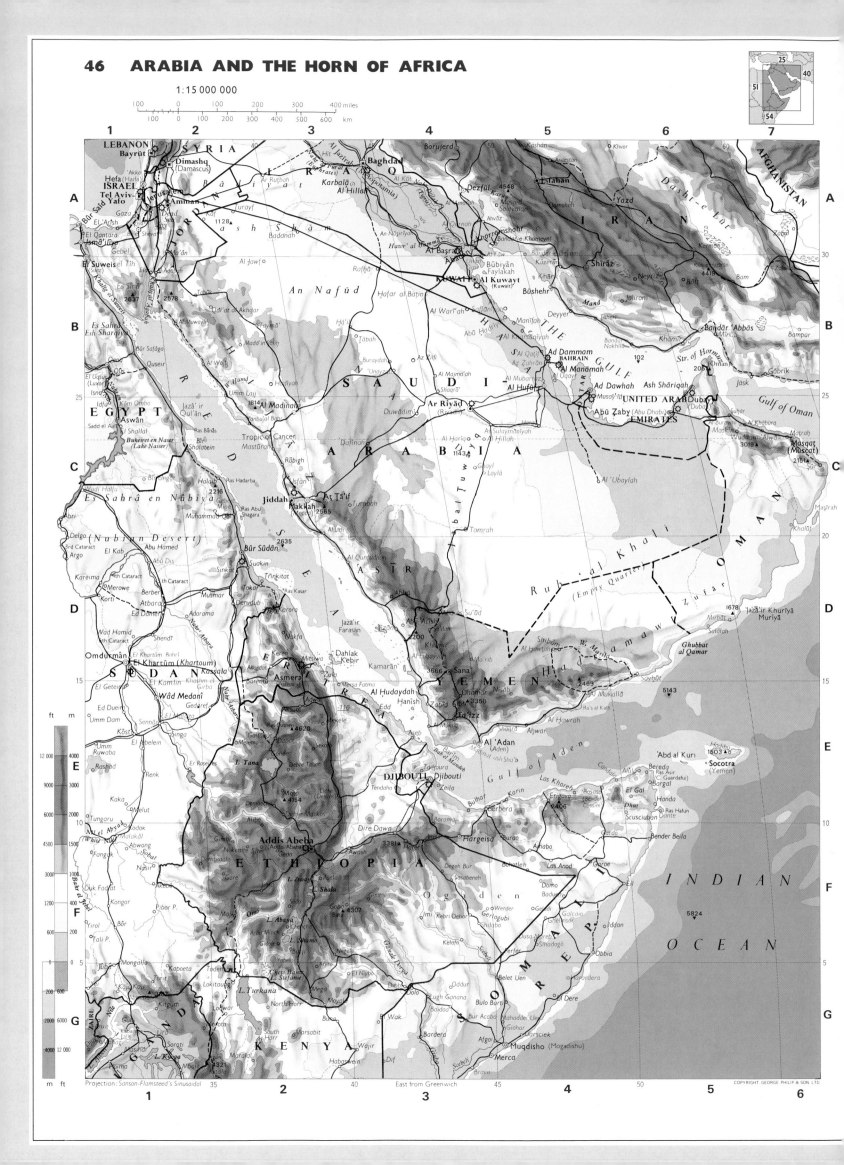

1:15 000 000

Projection: Sanson-Flamsteed's Sinusoidal

East from Greenwich

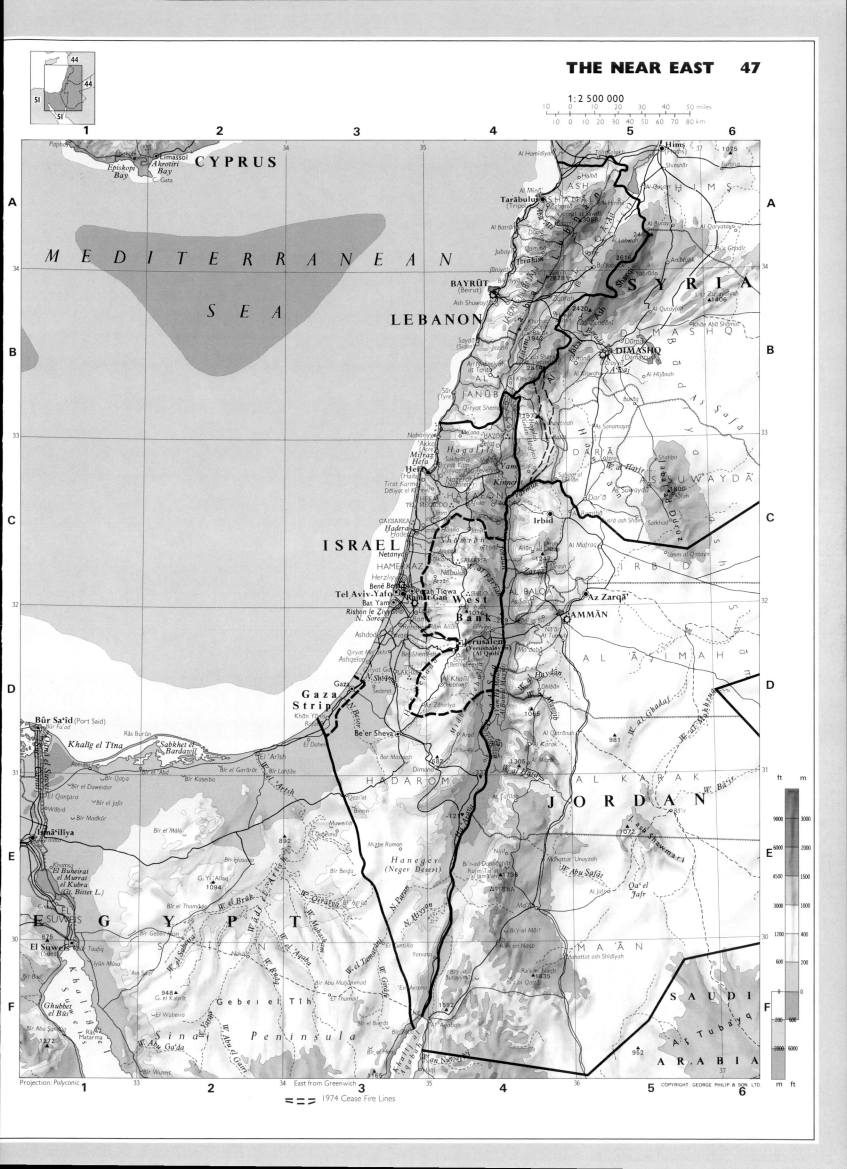

1:2 500 000

10 0 10 20 30 40 50 miles
10 0 10 20 30 40 50 60 70 80 km

MEDITERRANEAN

SEA

CYPRUS

Paphos
Limassol
Episkopi Bay
Akrotiri Bay
C. Gata

Al Hamīdīyah
Talli Kalakh
Hims (Homs)
1075
Furqlus
Halba
ASH SHAMĀL
Al Mīnā'
Tarābulus (Tripoli)
Al Qusayr
HIMS
Al Buraydī
Al Qaryatayn
Bī'r Ghadīr
Al Batrūn
3088
Qartaba
Ant Nabk
Jubayl
2616
Ibrahīm
2528
Bā Jabbūr
Jūniyah
Bilbrāyā
2420
BAYRŪT (Beirut)
Ash Shuwayfāt
Zahlah
Az Zubaydīyah
1406
LEBANON
Al Qutaylāh
Khān Abū Shāmat
Saydā (Sidon)
1942
Jazzīn
Ash Shaykh
DIMASHQ (Damascus)
Dūmā
AN NABŪB
An Nabaṭīyah at Tahtā
2814
Qaṭanā
Al Kiswah
Al Hijānah
Sūr (Tyre)
Qiryat Shemóna
Buṣq
JORDAN
SYRIA
DARʿĀ
AS SUWAYDĀ

ISRAEL

Nahariyya
HAZOR
Ḥagalil
Golan Heights
1197
Ḥamidīyah
Al Hartīrah
As Sanamayn
Akko (Acre)
Zefat
Meʿona
Sakhnin
Mifraẓ Ḥefa
Qiryat Yam
Qiryat Ata Tiberiya
Shabha
1800
Ḥefa (Haifa)
Nazerat (Nazareth)
Kinneret
Dārʿā
As Suwaydā
Tirat Karmel
Dāliyat el Karmel
HAZAFON
Yarmūk
Salkhad
TEL MEGIDDO
ʿAfula
Irbid
Al Ramthā
CAESAREA
Shōmrōn
Jenīn
Allūn ad Umm
Hadera
1247
SAMARIA
Az Zarqā
Al Mafraq
Netanya
Nāblus
W. al Fārīa
Jarash
HAMERKAZ
Herzliyya
SHILO
AL BALQĀ
IRBID
Benē Beraq
Petah Tiqwa
As Salt
Umm al Qittayn
Tel Aviv-Yafo
Ramlat Gan
AMMĀN
Bat Yam
West
Az Zarqā
Rishon le Ziyyon
N. Soreq
Bank
Naʿūr
Rehovot Ramla
Jerusalem (Yerushalayim)(Al Quds)
Ashdod
Bet Shemesh
Bayt Laḥm Bethlehem
Maʿīn
AL ʿĀSIMAH
Qiryat Malakhi
TEL LAKHISH
Al Khalīl (Hebron)
W. al Ḥuydān
Ashqelon
Dhibān
Gaza
N. Shiqma
Sederot
Az Zāhirīya
1065
W. al Mūjib
Gaza Strip
Khān Yūnis
Rafaḥ
Be'er Sheva
Al ʿArad
981
Bûr Saʿîd (Port Said)
Bûr Fuʾad
Rās Burûn
El Daheir
Al Karak
AL KARAK
Khalīg el Tîna
Sabkhet el Bardawîl
ʿEl ʿArîsh
Bor Mashash
W. al Ḥasā
Romani
Bîr el Garārât
Bîr Lahfān
Dimona
1305
Al Mazār
Bîr Qaṭia
Tar el Abd
882
At Tafīlah
JORDAN
El Qanṭara
Bîr el Duweidar
Bîr el Jafir
HADAROM
1072
Wāḥid
Qezīʿot
Bireīn
W. al Ghadaf
Ismâʾîliya
Bîr Madkūr
Bîr el Mālḥi
-12
W. al Bair
Ghalā
Al Qanṭara
W. el ʿArīsh
Muweilih
ʿEl Kuntilla
W. ʾab Shawmari
Khamsa
892
Bîr Ḥasana
Muḥaṭṭat Unayzah
El Buheirat el Murrat el Kubra (Gt. Bitter L.)
G. Yiʿllaq
1094
Mizpe Ramon
Ruim Talʿat al Jamāʿah
736
W. Abu Safir
Hanegev (Negev Desert)
Bi'n ad Dabbāghāt
Qaʿel Jafr
Bîr Beida
PETRA
Al Jafr
Bîr el Thamāda
N. Paran
Maʿān
MAʿĀN
Suweis
W. el Brūk
W. Qīrāṭra el ʿAgrūd
N. Ḥiyyon
El SUWEIS
875
Ghanim
EGYPT
Uyûn Mûsa
El Suweis (Suez)
ʿAin Sudr
W. el Ḥomaḥem
ʿEn Avrona
Ra's an Naqb
1435
Bi'r Mōri
Bîr Bad
Nakhl
W. el Aqaba
Yotvata
Ras an Naqb
Bîr el Butayḥin
Bîr el Qaṭṭār
Rās Abu Ṣanūlaq
948
G. el Kabrît
Gebel el Tîh
ʿEl Thamad
SAUDI
Ghubbet el Bûs
El Wabeira
1592
Aṭ Ṭubayq
1272
Ras Matarma
Sinai Peninsula
W. Abu Gaʿda
Bîr el Biarât
Aṭ Ṭubayq
ARABIA
952
Bîr Wuseret
1165
Khalīg el Aqaba

Projection: Polyconic   East from Greenwich   COPYRIGHT. GEORGE PHILIP & SON. LTD

— — — 1974 Cease Fire Lines

ft   m
9000   3000
6000   2000
4500   1500
3000   1000
1200   400
600   200
0   0
200   600
2000   6000
m   ft

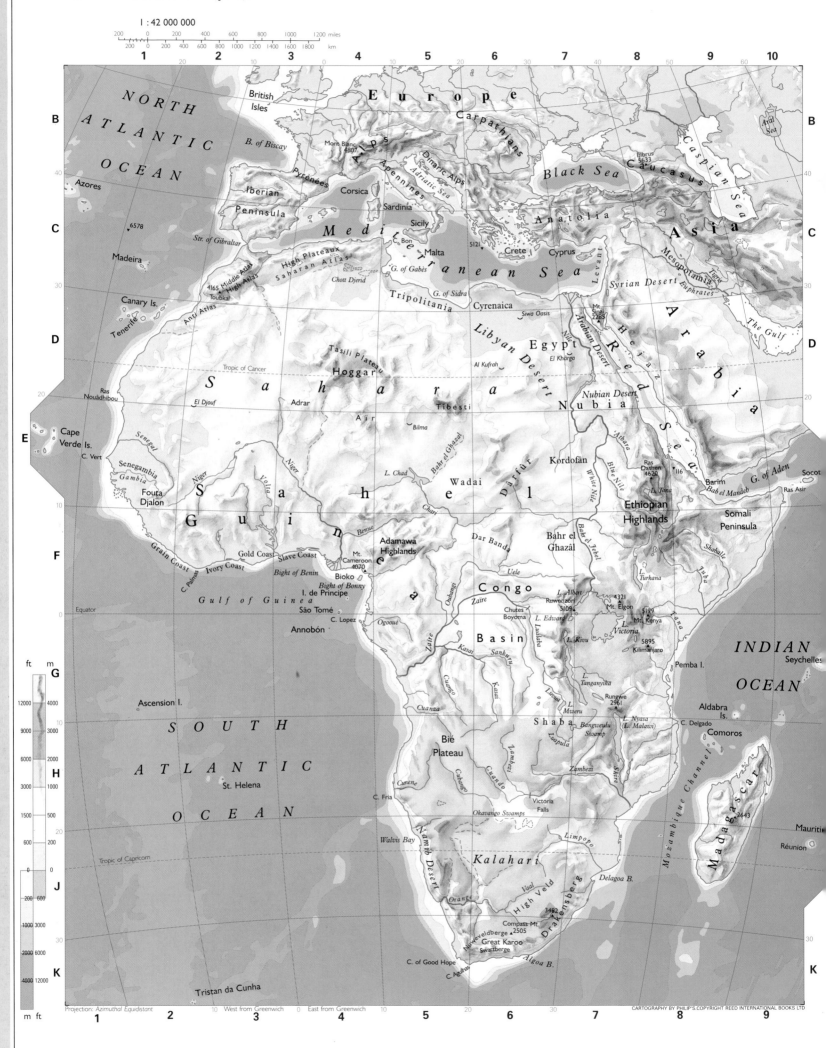

1 : 42 000 000

Projection: Azimuthal Equidistant   West from Greenwich   0   East from Greenwich   CARTOGRAPHY BY PHILIP'S. COPYRIGHT REED INTERNATIONAL BOOKS LTD

1 : 42 000 000

200 0 200 400 600 800 1000 1200 miles
200 0 200 400 600 800 1000 1200 1400 1600 1800 km

1 20 **2** 10 **3** 0 **4** 10 **5** 20 **6** 30 **7** 40 **8** 50 **9** 60 **10**

B

NORTH

ATLANTIC

OCEAN

B. of Biscay

UNITED KINGDOM
LONDON
NETH.
BELG.
GERMANY POLAND ○Kiev
Warsaw
RUSSIA
KAZAKSTAN
Aral Sea
PARIS ○Prague CZECH REP. UKRAINE ○Volgograd
FRANCE SWITZ. Vienna SLOVAK REP.
AUSTRIA HUNGARY
CROATIA ROMANIA ○Odessa
BOS. YUG. BULGARIA
HERZ. Black Sea GEORGIA
ITALY ALB. MAC. Ankara AZER. Baku
Corsica Rome GREECE TURKEY ARM.
40 Sardinia Athens CYPRUS Mosul TURKMEN.
SPAIN Madrid Sicily Crete SYRIA Tigris Baghdad Esfahan
Lisbon MALTA Aleppo LEB. Damascus IRAQ
PORTUGAL Algiers Tunis Tripoli Misratah Tel Aviv-Jaffa Euphrates Basra IRAN
Madeira Rabat Tetouan Fes Benghazi Alexandria Port Said ISRAEL Jerusalem Syrian Desert The Gulf
(Port.) Casablanca Constantine Sfax Jordan KUWAIT BAHRAIN
MOROCCO Marrakesh Chott Djerid Port Said Suez QATAR Riyadh
Canary Is. TUNISIA CAIRO SAUDI
(Sp.) El Aaiun El Faiyum
Dakhla WESTERN In Salah ALGERIA LIBYA EGYPT Asyut Medina ARABIA
SAHARA Tropic of Cancer Marzuq Aswan Mecca
Ras Fderik Al Jawf Jedda
Nouadhibou Sahara Wadi Halfa
MAURITANIA Port Sudan YEMEN
VERDE IS. Nouakchott NIGER CHAD Atbara Omdurman Khartoum ERITREA Mesewa Red Sea
Tombouctou Agades Wad Medani Asmera G. of Aden Socotra
St-Louis Senegal Abeche SUDAN El Obeid Blue Nile DJIBOUTI (Yemen)
C. Vert Niger L. Chad Ndjamena El Fasher Djibouti Ras Asir
Dakar SENEGAL MALI Niamey Kano White Nile Addis Ababa Harer Berbera
GAMBIA Bamako BURKINA Maiduguri Chari Malakal ETHIOPIA
GUINEA Banjul FASO Ouagadougou NIGERIA Wau Bahr el Jebel Shabelle
BISSAU GUINEA Bobo Dioulasso BENIN Abuja CENTRAL L. Turkana
Conakry SIERRA GHANA TOGO Ibadan AFRICAN REP. L. Albert
Freetown LEONE IVORY Kumasi Enugu Bangui UGANDA KENYA Mogadishu
COAST Bouake Lome Lagos CAMEROON Ubangi Kisangani Kampala
Monrovia Yamoussoukro Accra Porto Douala Yaounde Zaire L. Edward Kisumu Nairobi
LIBERIA Abidjan Novo Malabo Mbandaka RWANDA Victoria
Sekondi- Bight of Benin Port EQUATORIAL L. Kivu Kismayu
Takoradi Harcourt GUINEA ZAIRE BURUNDI
Gulf of Guinea SAO TOME & PRINCIPE Libreville CONGO Kasai Bujumbura Mombasa
Equator C. Lopez GABON Kananga TANZANIA Zanzibar INDIAN
Annobon Brazzaville Dodoma SEYCHELLES
Pointe Noire Kinshasa L. Tanganyika Dar es Salaam OCEAN
CABINDA Matadi Aldabra
(Angola) Is.
Ascension I. Luanda L. Mweru L. Malawi C. Delgado COMOROS
(U.K.) Likasi Lubumbashi Antsiranana
SOUTH Lobito ANGOLA Ndola MALAWI Mayotte
Huambo ZAMBIA Lilongwe (Fr.)
ATLANTIC Namibe Lusaka Blantyre Mocambique Mahajanga
St. Helena Zambezi MOZAMBIQUE
(U.K.) Livingstone Harare Beira Toamasina
OCEAN C. Fria ZIMBABWE Antananarivo
Bulawayo MADAGASCAR MAURITIUS
NAMIBIA BOTSWANA Limpopo
Tropic of Capricorn Windhoek Fianarantsoa Reunion
Gaborone (Fr.)
Johannesburg Pretoria Maputo
Mbabane SWAZ.
Orange Vaal LESOTHO Durban
SOUTH AFRICA Maseru
East London
Cape Town
C. of Good Hope Port Elizabeth
C. Agulhas
Tristan da Cunha
(U.K.)

Projection: Azimuthal Equidistant   West from Greenwich   East from Greenwich

1 10 **2** 0 **3** 10 **4** 20 **5** 30 **6** 40 **7** ● Dakar Capital Cities

CARTOGRAPHY BY PHILIP'S. COPYRIGHT REED INTERNATIONAL BOOKS LTD

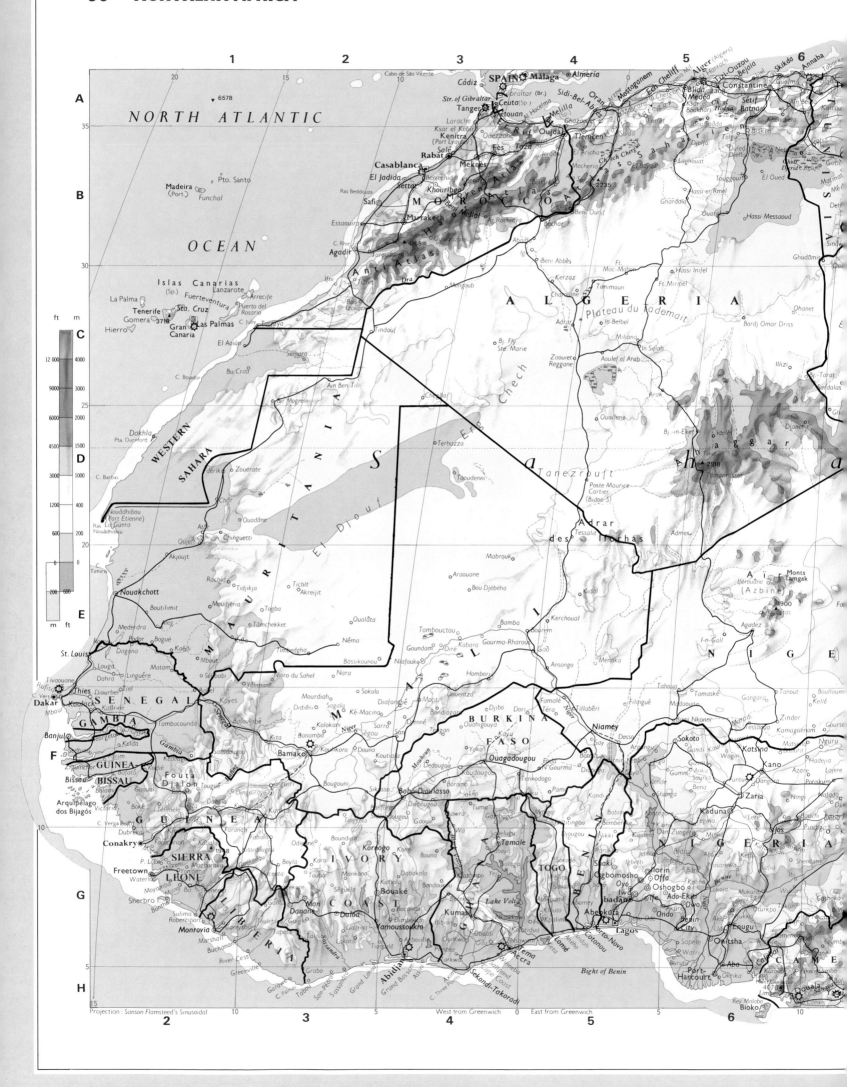

NORTH ATLANTIC

OCEAN

Projection: Sanson Flamsteed's Sinusoidal

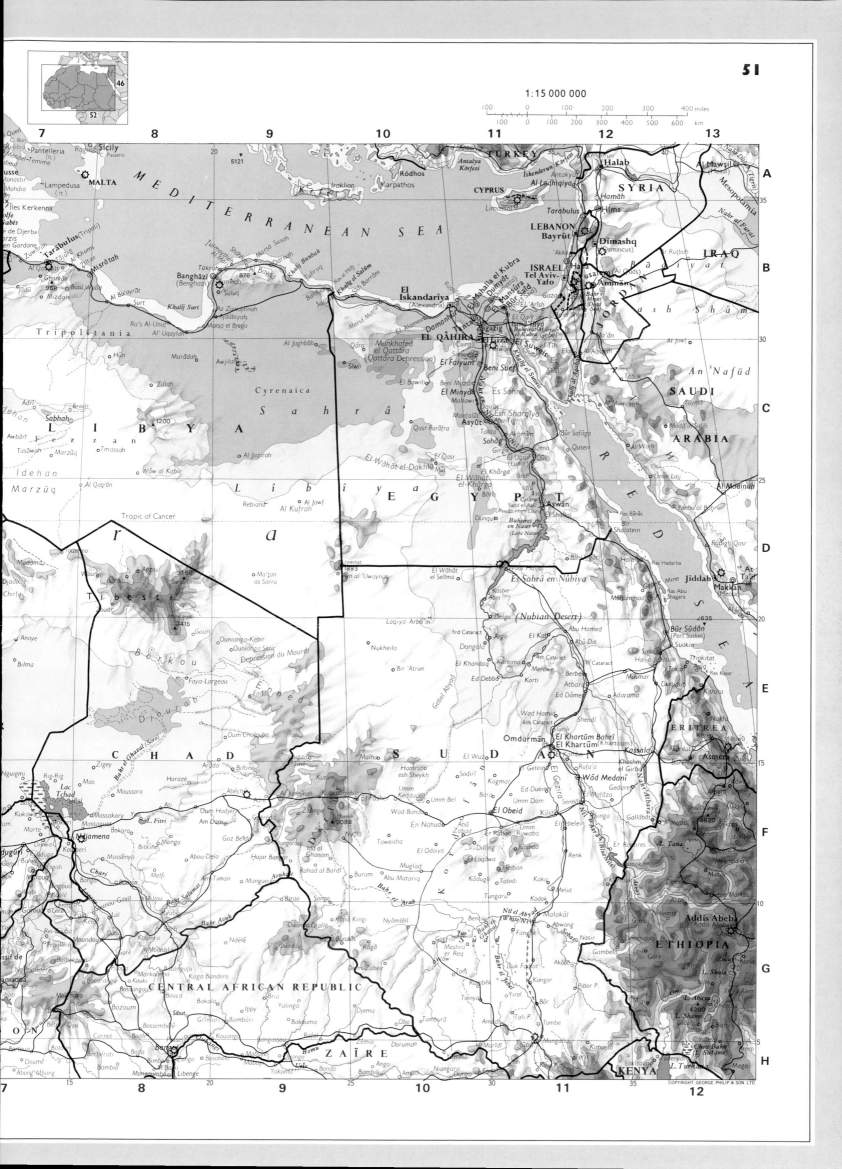

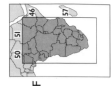

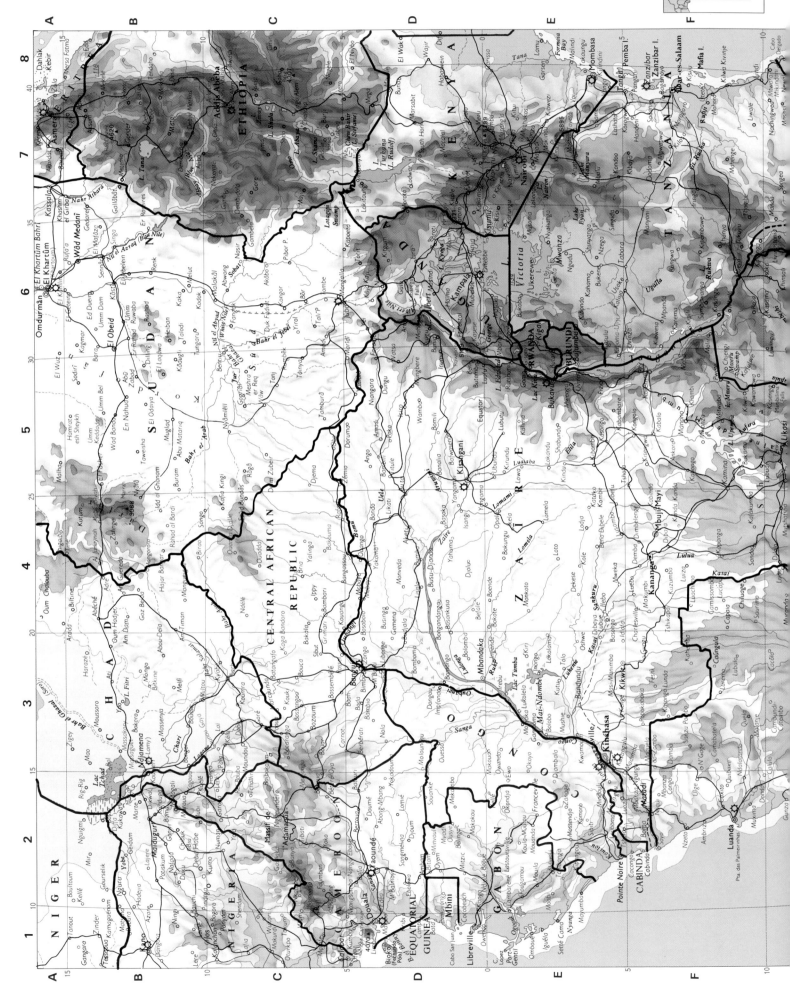

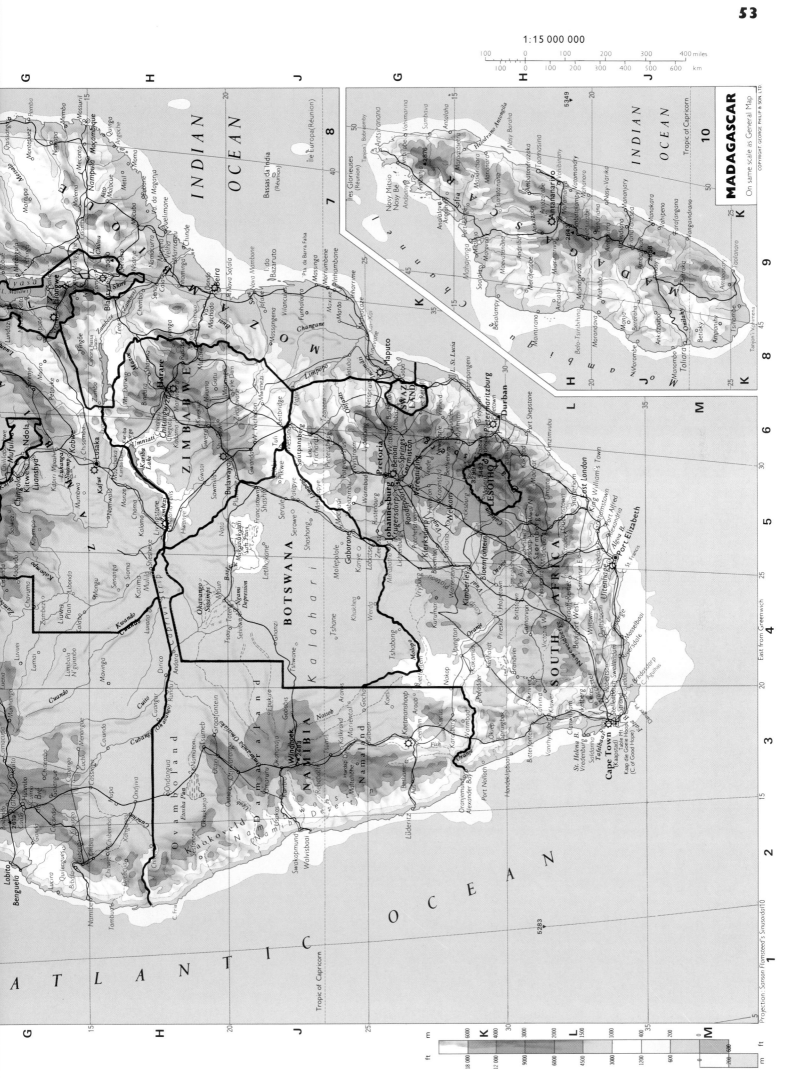

1:15 000 000

| 100 | 0 | 100 | 200 | 300 | 400 miles |

| 100 | 0 | 100 | 200 | 300 | 400 | 600 km |

MADAGASCAR
On same scale as General Map

COPYRIGHT GEORGE PHILIP & SON, LTD.

INDIAN OCEAN

Îles Glorieuses (Réunion)

Ile Europa (Réunion)

Bassas da India (Réunion)

ZIMBABWE

BOTSWANA

Kalahari

NAMIBIA

Namaland

SOUTH AFRICA

LESOTHO

SWAZILAND

ATLANTIC OCEAN

INDIAN OCEAN

Tropic of Capricorn

East from Greenwich

Projection: Sanson Flamsteed's Sinusoidal

m	ft
6000	18 000
4000	12 000
3000	9000
2000	6000
1500	4500
1000	3000
400	1200
200	600
0	0

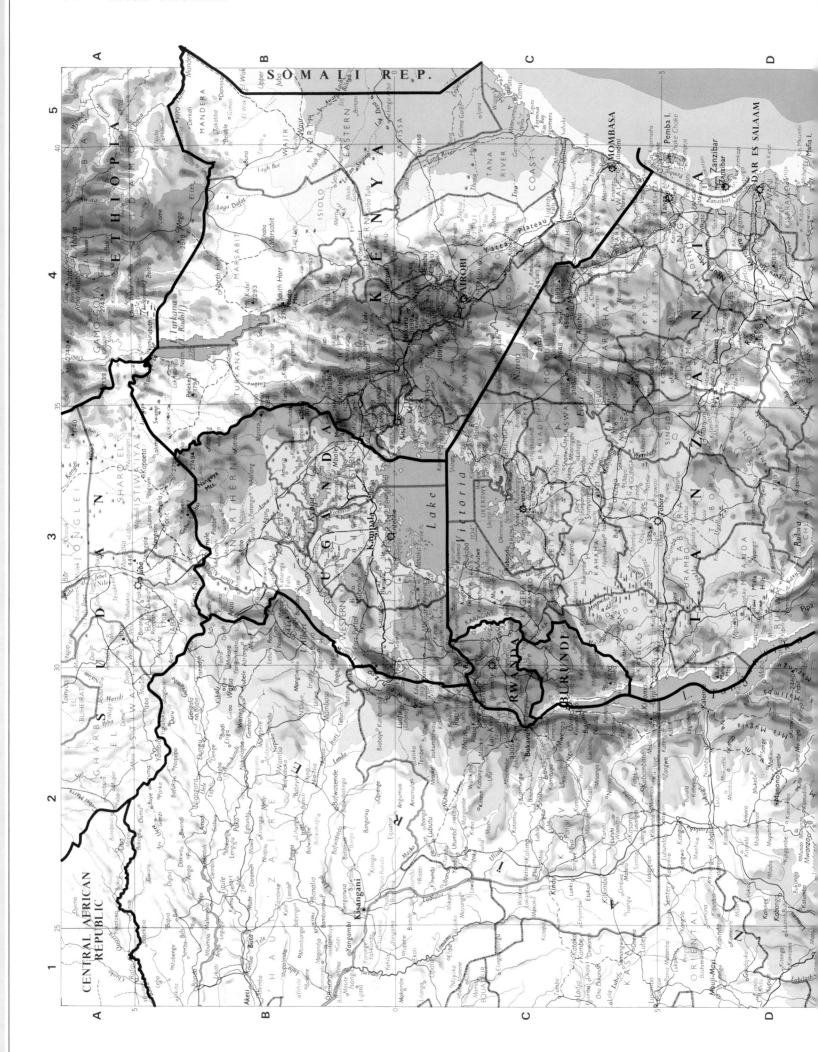

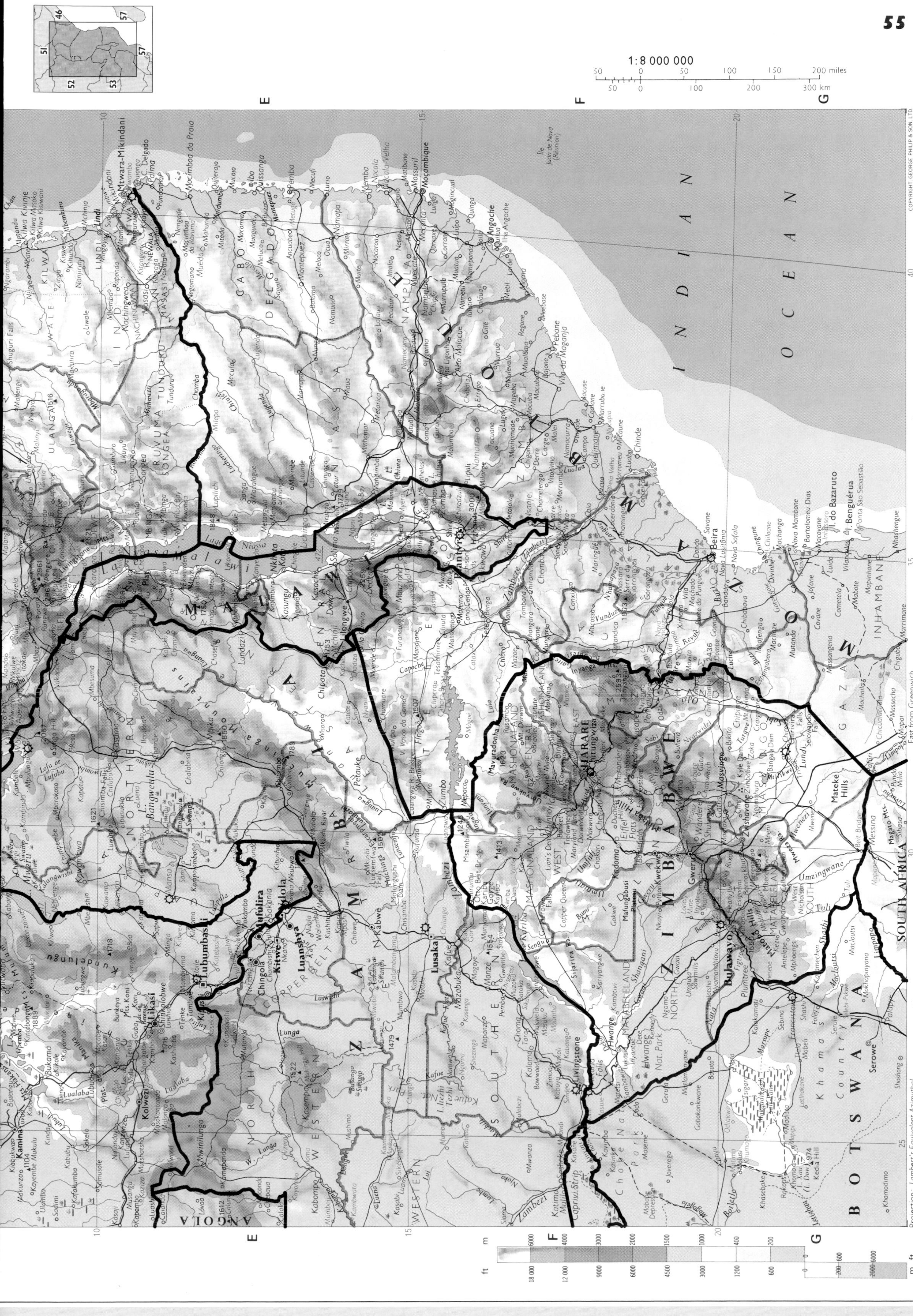

1:8 000 000

50   0   50   100   150   200 miles

50   0   100   200   300 km

COPYRIGHT GEORGE PHILIP & SON LTD

I N D I A N   O C E A N

M O Z A M B I Q U E

Z I M B A B W E

Z A M B I A

M A L A W I

A N G O L A

B O T S W A N A

SOUTH AFRICA

HARARE

Lusaka

Bulawayo

Beira

Livingstone

Lindi

Mtwara-Mikindani

CABO DELGADO

NAMPULA

NIASSA

RUVUMA

SONGEA

TUNDURU

ULANGA

GAZA

INHAMBANE

MANICALAND

MASHONALAND

MATABELELAND

SOUTH

NORTH

CENTRAL

WEST

EAST

NORTHERN

WESTERN

SOUTHERN

Kundelungu

Projection: Lambert's Equivalent Azimuthal

East from Greenwich

m   ft
6000   18 000
4000   12 000
3000   9000
2000   6000
1500   4500
1000   3000
400   1200
200   600
0
200   600
2000   6000
m   ft

ft

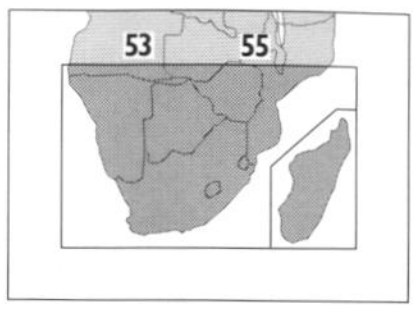

ANGOLA

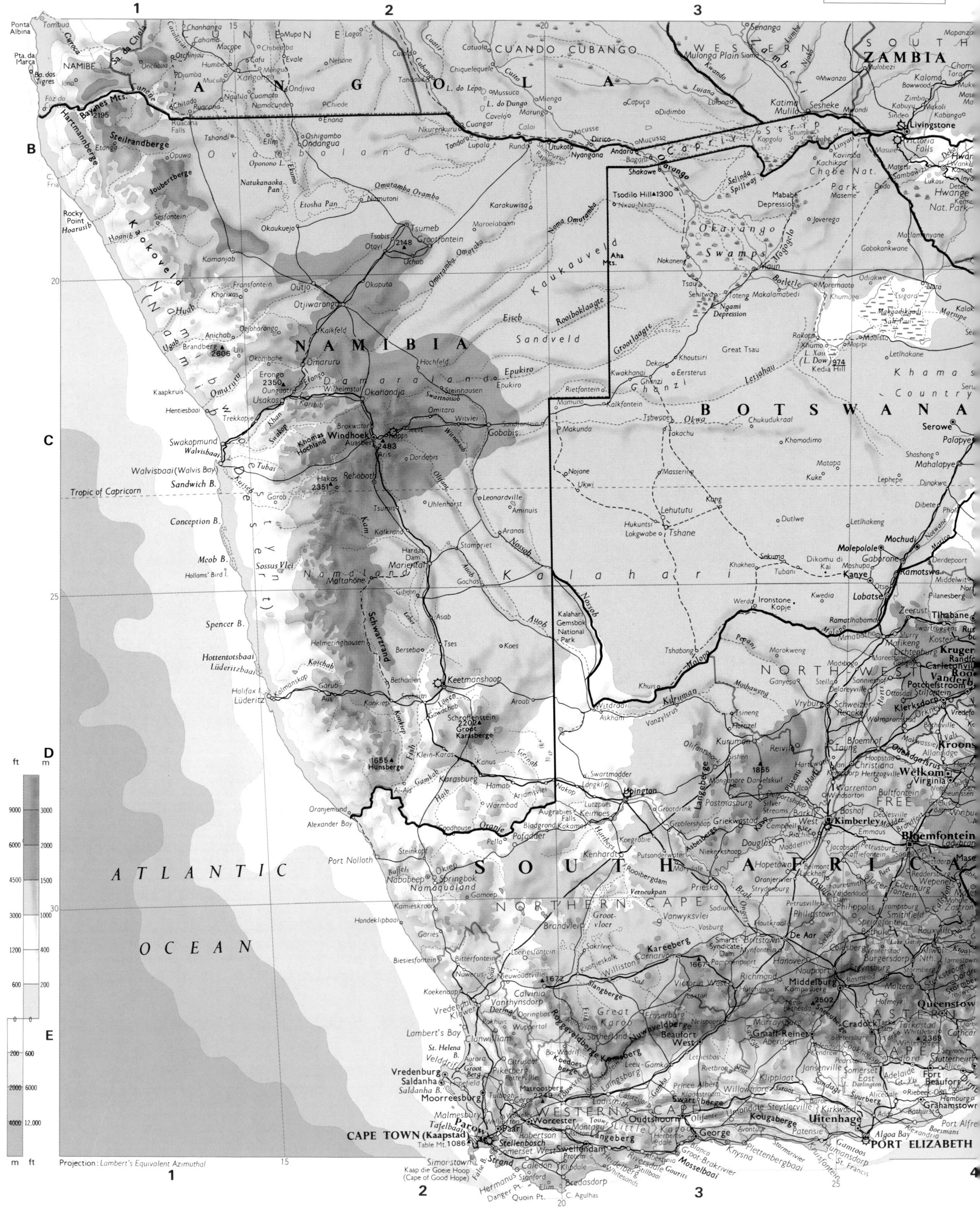

ZAMBIA

NAMIBIA

BOTSWANA

SOUTH AFRICA

ATLANTIC OCEAN

Tropic of Capricorn

CAPE TOWN (Kaapstad)

PORT ELIZABETH

Windhoek

Walvisbaai (Walvis Bay)

Keetmanshoop

Lüderitz

Kimberley

Bloemfontein

Welkom

Gaborone

NORTHERN CAPE

NORTH WEST

WESTERN CAPE

EASTERN CAPE

FREE STATE

Kalahari

Kalahari Gemsbok National Park

Okavango Swamps

Etosha Pan

Ovamboland

Kaokoveld

Namib Desert

Victoria Falls

Livingstone

Projection : Lambert's Equivalent Azimuthal

MADAGASCAR

On same scale as General Map

1 : 50 000 000

250   0   250   500   750   1000 miles
250   0   500   1000   1500   km

Physical map (top)

ft   m

12000   4000
9000   3000
6000   2000
3000   1000
1500   500
600   200
0   0
0   20
200   600
1000   3000
2000   6000
4000   12000
6000   18000
8000   24000
m ft

Malay Peninsula · Str. of Malacca · Sumatra · Borneo · Celebes Sea · Halmahera · Equator · Admiralty Is. · Nauru · Gilbert Is. · PACIFIC

Str. of Makassar · Celebes · Sula Is. · Ceram · G. of Sarera · Maoke Mts. · 5029 Puncak Jaya · New Ireland · Bismarck Arch. · New Britain · Bougainville · Solomon Is.

Java Sea · Buru · Ambon · Banda Sea · Aru Is. · New Guinea · 9103 · Malaita · Santa Cruz Is. · San Cristóbal · Ellice Is.

Flores Sea · Tanimbar Is. · Arafura Sea · Torres Strait · G. of Papua · Owen Stanley Ra. · D'Entrecasteaux · Guadalcanal · Espiritu Santo · Rotuma · Samoan I.

Timor Sea · Melville I. · Thursday I. · C. York · Great Barrier Reef · Coral Sea · Chesterfield Is. · Malakula · New Hebrides · Fiji Is. · Vanua Levu · Savai'i · Upol

Sumbawa · Sumba · Timor · Arnhem Land · C. Arnhem · Gulf of Carpentaria · Cape York Pen. · Viti Levu · Loyalty Is.

King Sd. · Victoria · Barkly Tableland · Flinders · Horner B. · Sandy C. · New Caledonia · Tonga Is. · Tongatapu

Fitzroy · Tanami Desert · Great Dividing Ra. · Australia · Darling Downs · C. Byron · New England Ra. · Norfolk I. · 10822

INDIAN OCEAN · North West C. · Mt. Bruce 1227 · L. Disappointment · Macdonnell Ras. · L. Mackay · L. Amadeus · Musgrave Ra. · L. Eyre · Cooper Cr. · Darling · Lachlan · Lord Howe I. · Kermadec Is. · 10047

6658 · Ashburton · Gascoyne · Shark Bay · Darling Ra. · Nullarbor Plain · L. Torrens · L. Gairdner · Eyre Pen. · Flinders Ras. · L. Frome · Murray · Botany Bay · Tasman Sea · North C.

Geographe Bay · C. Naturaliste · C. Leeuwin · Great Australian Bight · Spencer Gulf · Kangaroo I. · Encounter B. · Australian Alps · C. Howe · North I. · B. of Plenty · East C.

Tropic of Capricorn · P. Phillip B. · Bass Str. · Flinders I. · Ruapehu 2797 · L. Taupo · Hawke B. · King I. · South C. · Tasmania · South I. · Mt. Cook 3753 · Southern Alps · New Zealand · Stewart I.

Political map (bottom)

m ft

MALAYSIA · BRUNEI · PALAU · FEDERATED STATES OF MICRONESIA · MARSHALL IS.

Kuala Lumpur · SINGAPORE · Borneo · Sula Is. · Ceram · IRIAN JAYA · PAPUA NEW GUINEA · New Ireland · NAURU · KIRIBATI

Sumatra · Celebes · Buru · Ujung Pandang · INDONESIA · Aru Is. · New Guinea · Madang · Rabaul · New Britain · Bougainville I. · PACIFIC

Java Sea · Banda Sea · Tanimbar Is. · Lae · Choiseul · SOLOMON IS. · TUVALU

JAKARTA · Java · Flores · Kupang · Arafura Sea · Timor Sea · Torres Strait · Port Moresby · Honiara · Santa Isabel · Malaita · San Cristóbal · Funafuti

Sumbawa · Sumba · Timor · Darwin · Katherine · Gulf of Carpentaria · Guadalcanal · Santa Cruz Is.

CORAL SEA ISLANDS TERRITORY · Espiritu Santo · VANUATU · Rotuma · Is. Wallis & Futuna (Fr.) · WESTERN SAMOA · Apia

INDIAN OCEAN · Wyndham · Broome · NORTHERN · Cooktown · Cairns · Townsville · Chesterfield Is. · Port Vila · Viti Levu · Vanua Levu

Dampier · Onslow · WESTERN TERRITORY · QUEENSLAND · Charters Towers · Rockhampton · NEW CALEDONIA (Fr.) · Suva · FIJI · TONGA

AUSTRALIA · Mount Isa · Alice Springs · Longreach · Loyalty Is. · Nouméa

AUSTRALIA · Wiluna · SOUTH · Oodnadatta · Quilpie · Charleville · Toowoomba · Brisbane · OCEAN · Norfolk I. (Aust) · Nuku'alofa

Geraldton · Kalgoorlie-Boulder · AUSTRALIA · Cunnamulla · Warwick · Bourke · NEW SOUTH WALES

Perth · Fremantle · Esperance · Port Pirie · Broken Hill · Mildura · Newcastle · Lord Howe I. (Aust) · Kermadec Is. (N.Z.)

Albany · Great Australian Bight · Adelaide · A.C.T. · Sydney · Tasman Sea · North I. · NEW ZEALAND

VICTORIA · Canberra · Ballarat · Geelong · Melbourne · Auckland · New Plymouth · Hamilton · Napier

King I. · Bass Str. · Launceston · South I. · Wellington · Nelson · Greymouth

TASMANIA · Hobart · Invercargill · Dunedin · Christchurch · Chatham Is. (N.Z.)

International Date Line

Tropic of Capricorn

Projection: Bonne · 90 East from Greenwich · 100

CARTOGRAPHY BY PHILIP'S. COPYRIGHT REED INTERNATIONAL BOOKS LTD

● Canberra · Capital Cities

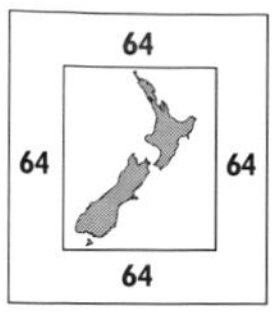

1 : 6 000 000

20 0 20 40 60 80 100 miles
20 0 40 80 120 160 km

KIRIBATI

TUVALU (Ellice Is.)
Tokelau Is. (N.Z.)
Tongareva (Penrhyn) I.
Rotuma
WESTERN SAMOA
Savaii Upolu
Tutuila
AMER. SAMOA (U.S.)
Rakahanga
Manihiki
Pukapuka
Nassau
Suwarrow
Northern Group
Cook Is. (N.Z.)
Îles de la Société
Wallis & Futuna (Fr.)
Vanua Levu
FIJI
Viti Levu
Lau or Eastern Group
TONGA (Friendly Is.)
Niue (N.Z.)
Palmerston
Atoll
Aitutaki
Lower Group
Mitiaro
Miuke
Rarotonga
Mangaia
FRENCH POLYNESIA
VAN-UATU
Tropic of Capricorn

PACIFIC OCEAN

Macauley
Raoul (Sunday)
Kermadec Is. (N.Z.)
Curtis
Three Kings Is.
Auckland
NORTH I.
Cook Strait
NEW ZEALAND
Wellington
Christchurch
Chatham Is.
Chatham I.
Pitt I.
Tasman Sea
SOUTH I.
Dunedin
Bounty Is.
Stewart I.
Snares
Antipodes Is.
Auckland Is.
Campbell I.
Macquarie I. (Austr.)
SOUTHERN OCEAN

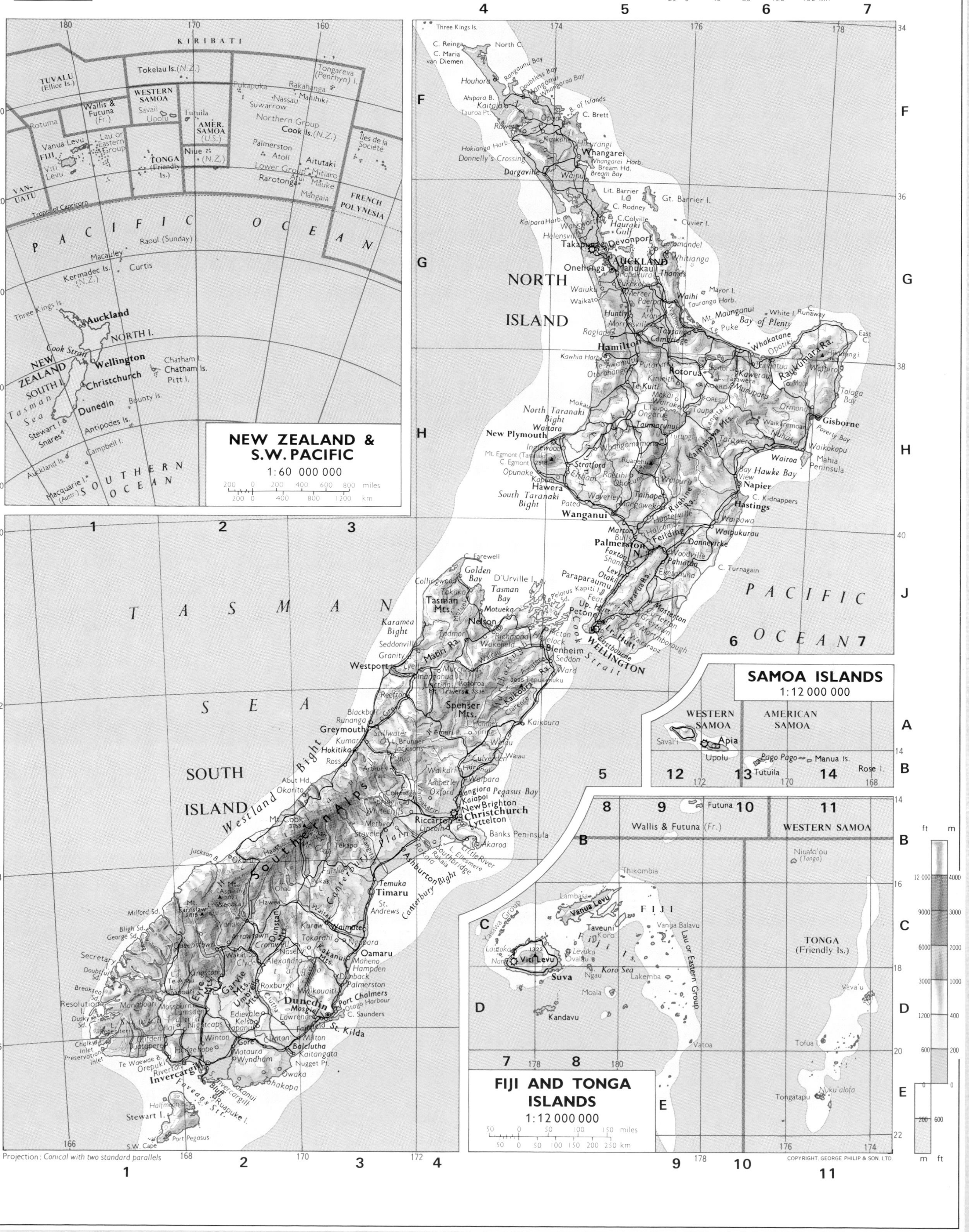

NEW ZEALAND & S.W. PACIFIC
1 : 60 000 000

200 0 200 400 600 800 miles
200 0 400 800 1200 km

NORTH ISLAND

Three Kings Is.
C. Reinga
North C.
C. Maria van Diemen
Houhora
Rangaunu Bay
Doubtless Bay
Ahipara B.
Whangaroa Bay
Kaitaia
B. of Islands
Tauroa Pt.
C. Brett
Rawene
Hokianga Harb.
Donnelly's Crossing
Hikurangi
Whangarei
Whangarei Harb.
Bream Hd.
Bream Bay
Dargaville
Waipu
Lit. Barrier I.
Gt. Barrier I.
C. Rodney
Cuvier I.
Kaipara Harb.
C. Colville
Helensville
Hauraki Gulf
Coromandel
Waiwera
Takapuna
Devonport
Whitianga
Onehunga
AUCKLAND
Manukau
Thames
Papakura
Mayor I.
Tauranga Harb.
Waiuku
Mercer
Paeroa
Waihi
NORTH
Waikato
Huntly
Paeroa
Tauranga
White I.
Runaway
ISLAND
Morrinsville
Mt. Maunganui
Bay of Plenty
Raglan
Taupiri
Cambridge
Whakatane
Opotiki
Kawhia Harb.
Hamilton
Te Puke
Raukumara Ra.
Otorohanga
Rotorua
Whangamomona
Te Kuiti
L. Rotorua
Tarawera
Murupara
Waihiro
Mokau
Kawerau
Ormond
Tolaga Bay
North Taranaki Bight
Waitara
Taumarunui
Raukumara
Kaimanawa Mts.
Waikaremoana
Gisborne
New Plymouth
Inglewood
L. Taupo
Tarawera
Poverty Bay
Mt. Egmont (Taranaki) 2518
Ongarue
Stratford
Ruapehu
Waiora
Waikokopu
Opunake
Eltham
Raetihi
Mahia Peninsula
Hawera
Waverley
Bay View
Napier
Ruahine Ra.
South Taranaki Bight
Talhape
Mangaweka
Hastings
C. Kidnappers
Patea
Wanganui
Waipukurau
Marton
Halcombe
Palmerston N.
Feilding
Dannevirke
Bulls
Foxton
Pahiatua
Woodville
Shannon
C. Turnagain
Levin
Eketahuna
Otaki
Eketahuna
Paraparaumu
Kapiti I.
Masterton
Up. Hutt
Carterton
Featherston
Greytown
Petone
Martinborough
WELLINGTON
Eastbourne

PACIFIC OCEAN

SOUTH ISLAND

C. Farewell
Collingwood
Golden Bay
D'Urville I.
Takaka
Tasman Bay
Tasman Mts.
Motueka
Nelson
Tadmor
Richmond
Wakefield
Picton
Cook Strait
Karamea Bight
Murchison
Havelock
Blenheim
Seddon
Ward
Westport
Lyell
Mt. Arthur
Inangahua Junction
L. Rotoroa
Reefton
Spenser Mts.
Kaikoura
Blackball
Runanga
Greymouth
Kumara
L. Brunner
Jacksons
Culverden
Waiau
Hokitika
Hanmer
Ross
Waikari
Hurunui
Abut Hd.
Okarito
Amberley
Oxford
Rangiora
Pegasus Bay
Kaiapoi
New Brighton
Christchurch
Riccarton
Lincoln
Lyttelton
Mt. Cook 3753
Whitecliffs
Methven
L. Ellesmere
Akaroa
Banks Peninsula
Jackson B.
Southern Alps
Rakaia
Rakaia River
Rakaia Bridge
Ashburton
Westland Bight
Canterbury Plain
Geraldine
Pukaki
Temuka
Timaru
Ohau
Canterbury Bight
Fairlie
St. Andrews
Milford Sd.
Tekapo
Kurow
Waimate
Bligh Sd.
Tokarahi
George Sd.
Cromwell
Naseby
Oamaru
Secretary I.
Queenstown
Clyde
Hampden
Alexandra
Dunback
Doubtful Sd.
Wanaka
Maheno
Palmerston
Roxburgh
Waikouaiti
Resolution I.
Manapouri
Port Chalmers
Breaksea Sd.
Lumsden
Dunedin
Otago Harbour
Dusky Sd.
Mosgiel
Lawrence
C. Saunders
Gore
Edievale
Kelso
St. Kilda
Chalky Inlet
Tapanui
Milton
Preservation Inlet
Wyndham
Mataura
Kaitangata
Balclutha
Te Waewae B.
Orepuki
Winton
Clinton
Nugget Pt.
Riverton
Owaka
Waiwera
Otakapa
Waikoikoi
Invercargill
Bluff
Foveaux Str.
Ruapuke I.
Halfmoon B.
Stewart I.
S.W. Cape
Port Pegasus

TASMAN SEA

Projection: Conical with two standard parallels

SAMOA ISLANDS
1 : 12 000 000

WESTERN SAMOA
AMERICAN SAMOA
Savai'i
Apia
Upolu
Pago Pago
Manua Is.
Tutuila
Rose I.

| 12 | 13 | 14 |

FIJI AND TONGA ISLANDS
1 : 12 000 000

Wallis & Futuna (Fr.)
Futuna
WESTERN SAMOA
Niuafo'ou (Tonga)
Thikombia
Lambasa
Vanua Levu
Vanua Balavu
FIJI
Taveuni
Kora
Tasawa Group
Loazoka
Nandi
Levuka
Ovalau
Lau or Eastern Group
Viti Levu 1323
Suva
Ngau
Lakemba
TONGA (Friendly Is.)
Koro Sea
Moala
Vava'u
Kandavu
Vatoa
Tofua
Niuku'alofa
Tongatapu

50 0 50 100 150 miles
50 0 50 100 150 200 250 km

| 7 | 8 | 9 | 10 | 11 |

COPYRIGHT. GEORGE PHILIP & SON. LTD.

ft m
12 000 4000
9000 3000
6000 2000
3000 1000
1200 400
600 200
0
200 600
m ft

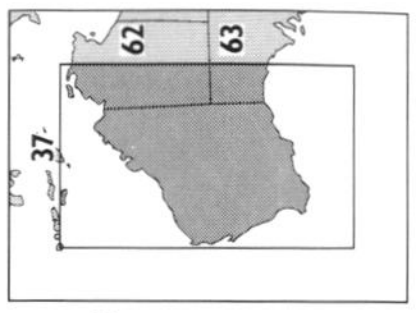

A · B · C · D

5 · 4 · 3 · 2

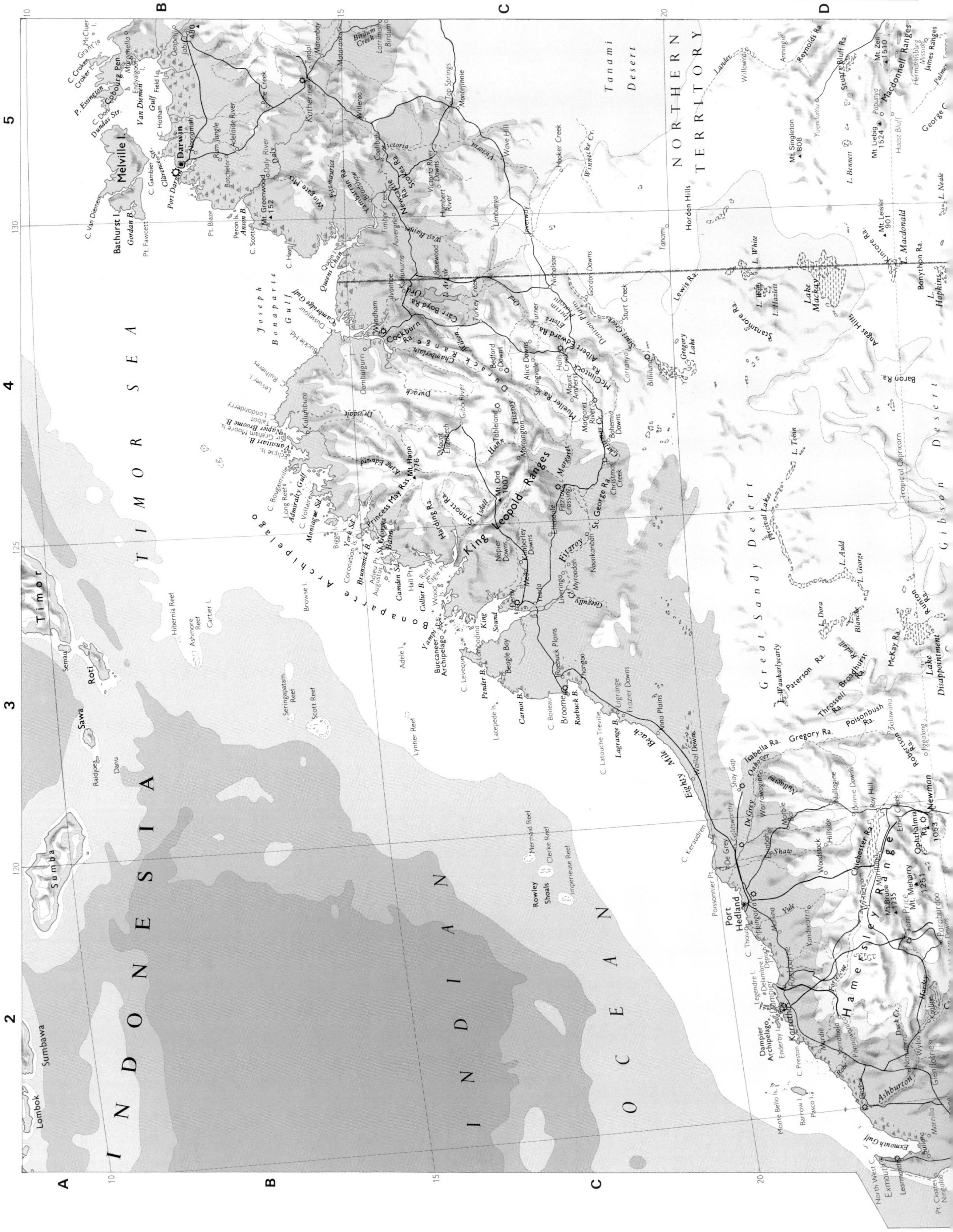

INDONESIA

TIMOR SEA

TIMOR

INDIAN OCEAN

NORTHERN TERRITORY

Tanami Desert

Great Sandy Desert

Gibson Desert

Joseph Bonaparte Gulf

Bonaparte Archipelago

Buccaneer Archipelago

King Leopold Ranges

Hamersley Range

Tropic of Capricorn

Darwin
Melville I.
Bathurst I.
Port Darwin
Katherine
Wyndham
Cockburn Ra.
Carr Boyd Ra.
Ord
Broome
Derby
Port Hedland
Karratha
Dampier Archipelago
Marble Bar
Newman
Lake Mackay
Lake Disappointment
MacDonnell Ranges
Macdonald
Tanami
Mt. Ord
Mt. Hann 776
Eighty Mile Beach
De Grey
Roebuck Plains
Fitzroy Crossing
Lagrange B.
Frazier Downs
Wallal Downs
Sawu
Sumba
Sumbawa
Lombok
Roti
Exmouth Gulf

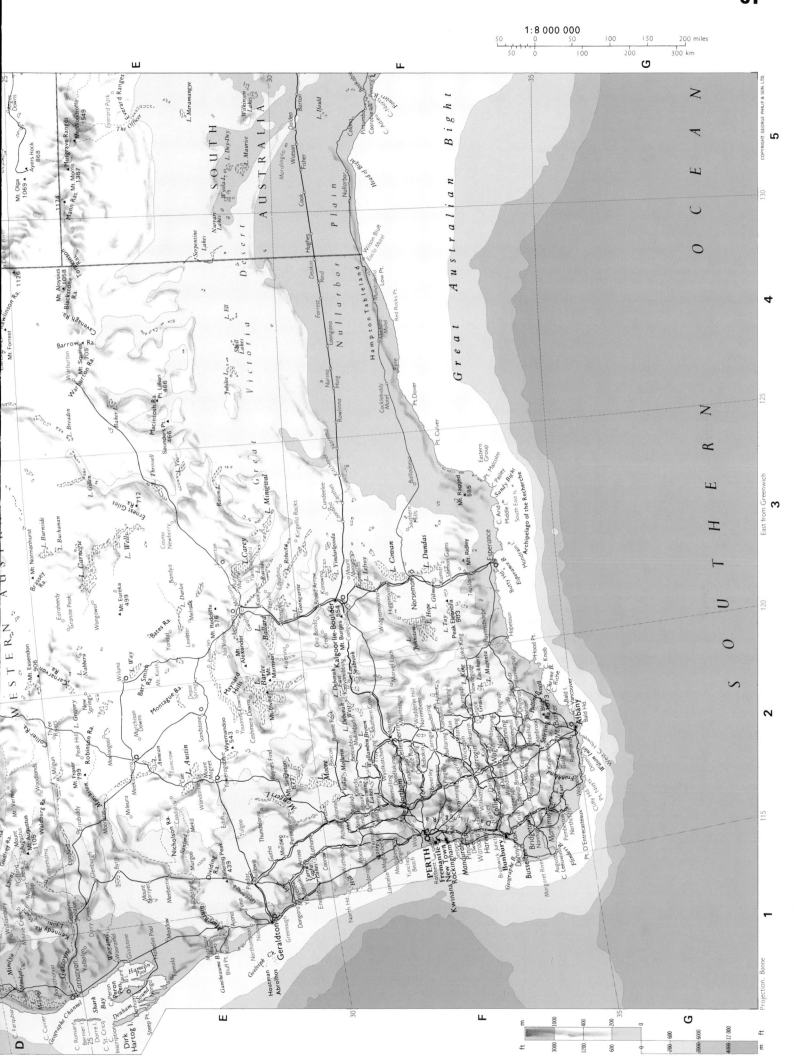

1:8 000 000

50   0   50   100   150   200 miles
50   0   100   200   300 km

D   E   F   G

S O U T H   A U S T R A L I A

W E S T E R N   A U S T R A L I A

Ayers Rock 868
Mt. Olga 1069
Mann Ras. Mt Morris 1387
Musgrave Ranges
Mt Woodroffe 1549
The Everard Ranges
Everard Park
Ayers Downs

L. Meramangye
Wilkinson Lakes
L. Dey-Dey
L. Maurice
Serpentine Lakes
Nurrari Lakes

L. Hould
Barton
Ooldea
Watson
Fisher
Cook
Hughes
Deakin
Forrest
Reid
Nurina
Haig
Nurung

Cook

Great   Australian   Bight

N U L L A R B O R   P L A I N
Nullarbor Plain
Hampton Tableland
Eucla Motel
Wilson Bluff
Madura Motel
Mundrabilla
Low Pt.
Eyre
Red Rocks Pt.

Cocklebiddy Motel
Rawlinna
Pt. Dover
Pt. Culver

S O U T H E R N   O C E A N

G i b s o n   D e s e r t

Warburton Ra.
Barrow Ra.
Mt Squires 705

Rawlinson Ra. 1126
Mt. Aloysius 1058
Blackstone Ra.
Cavenagh Ra.
Mt. Forrest

L. Breaden
L. Gillen
Carnegie
L. Carnegie
Ernest Giles Ra. 712

Mt Normanhurst
Brassey Ra.
Mt. Burnside
L. Buchanan
Eurobeedy
Granite Peak

G r e a t   V i c t o r i a   D e s e r t

Jubilee L.
Spill Lakes
L. Ell
L. Throssell
Macintosh Ra. Pt. Lillian 466
Saunders Pt. 466

Cosmo Newberry
Laverton
L. Wells
L. Minigwal

L. Raeside
Yamarna
Mt Eureka 499

Mt. Essendon 906
Carnarvon Ra.
Bates Ra.
Earaheedy

Wiluna
L. Way
Mt Keith
Nabberu

L. Carey
Murrin Murrin
Bandya
Mt Celia
Yeelirrie
Yundamindra
Yeo
L. Rason

Mt Remarkable
Laverton
Mt. Margaret
Mt. Weld
Mt Morgans
L. Marmion

Wongawol

Barr Smith Ra.
Depot Springs

Kaluwiri
Youanmi Downs
Cashmere Downs
Montague Ra.

Mt Sir Samuel
Leonora
Gwalia
Menzies

Mt Alexander
Mt Burges 554
Mt Redcliffe 576
Mt Monger
Bardoc
L. Ballard

Kalgoorlie-Boulder
Broad Arrow
Ora Banda
Credo
Coolgardie
Widgiemooltha
Norseman
L. Cowan
L. Dundas
L. Lefroy

Esperance
Archipelago of the Recherche
C. Arid
Middle I.
Pt. Malcolm
Eastern Group

Mt Ragged 585
Israelite B.
Cape Le Grand
Cape Arid
Wittenoom Hills
Southern Hills

Mt Ridley
Scaddan
Salmon Gums
Grass Patch
Gibson
Dundas

Peak Eleanora 503
L. King
Lake King
Mt Gilmour
L. Hope
L. Tay
Johnston
Ravensthorpe

Kambalda
Bonnie Vale

WESTERN AUSTRALIA

Murchison Downs
Cue
Mt Magnet
Sandstone

Wynyangoo 543

Youanmi
Sandstone

Paynes Find
Bulga Downs

Boorabbin
Southern Cross
Yellowdine
Bodallin
Westonia
Marvel Loch

L. Deborah
L. Deborah West
Koolyanobbing
Moorine Rock
Bullfinch

Mukinbudin
Bencubbin
Beacon
Nungarin
Koorda
Mt Marshall
Kalannie

Wialki
Dowerin
Wyalkatchem
Trayning
Kellerberrin
Merredin
Bruce Rock
Quairading
Corrigin

Gnowangerup
Nyabing
Pingrup
Lake Grace
Dumbleyung
Wagin
Katanning
Woodanilling
Broomehill
Tambellup
Cranbrook
Mt Barker
Kojonup

Narrogin
Wickepin
Kulin
Kondinin
Narembeen
Bruce Rock

Carnamah
Three Springs
Mingenew
Morawa
Perenjori
Mullewa
Wubin
Dalwallinu
Pithara
Ballidu
Wongan Hills
Goomalling

Moora
Watheroo
Coorow
Dandaragan
Gingin
Bindoon
Toodyay
Northam
York
Beverley
Brookton
Pingelly
Cuballing
Williams

PERTH
Fremantle
Rockingham
Kwinana
Armadale
Mandurah
Pinjarra
Waroona
Harvey
Collie
Bunbury
Busselton
Dunsborough
Margaret River
Augusta
C. Leeuwin
Pt. D'Entrecasteaux

Darkan
Boyup Brook
Bridgetown
Manjimup
Pemberton
Northcliffe
Nannup

Kojonup
Frankland
Rocky Gully
Denmark
Albany
Mt Barker
Stirling Ra. Bluff Knoll 1073
King George Sound
Cheyne B.
C. Riche
Bremer Bay
Hopetoun
Point Henry
Torbay

Houtman Abrolhos
Geraldton
Northampton
Greenough
Dongara
Port Denison
North Hd.
Jurien B.
Cervantes
Lancelin
Yanchep

Geographe Bay
C. Naturaliste
Cape Hamelin

Shark Bay
Dirk Hartog I.
Steep Pt.
Denham
Peron Pen.
Nanga
Hamelin Pool
C. Ronsard
Bernier I.
Dorre I.
C. Cuvier
C. St. Cricq
Inscription Pt.

Carnarvon
Gascoyne R.
Rocky Pool
Woodleigh
Wooramel
Meedo
Gladstone

Minilya
Williambury
Kennedy Ra.
Lyndon
Minnie Creek
Mooloo Downs
Gifford Cr.

Godfrey Ra.
Mt. Gould
Peak Hill
L. Nabberu
Mt. Vernon

Landor
Milgun
Mt Augustus 1106
Mt. Phillips
Waldburg Ra.
Ullawarra
Mt. Clere

Peak Hill
Meekatharra
Nannine
Mileura
Annean
L. Annean
Mount Magnet

Yalgoo
Paynesville
Mount Narryer
Murgoo
Pindar
Mullewa
Tardun
Morawa

Nerren Nerren
Meeberrie
Byro
Billabalong
Wooleen
Murchison

Galena
Northampton
Ajana
Yuna
Gutha

Tallering Peak 439
Mingenew
Mungari

Projection. Bonne.   East from Greenwich

115   1   120   2   3   125   4   130   5

30   30   35   35   25

ft   m
3000   1000
1200   400
600   200
0   0
m   ft
0   0
200   600
600   2000
4000   12 000

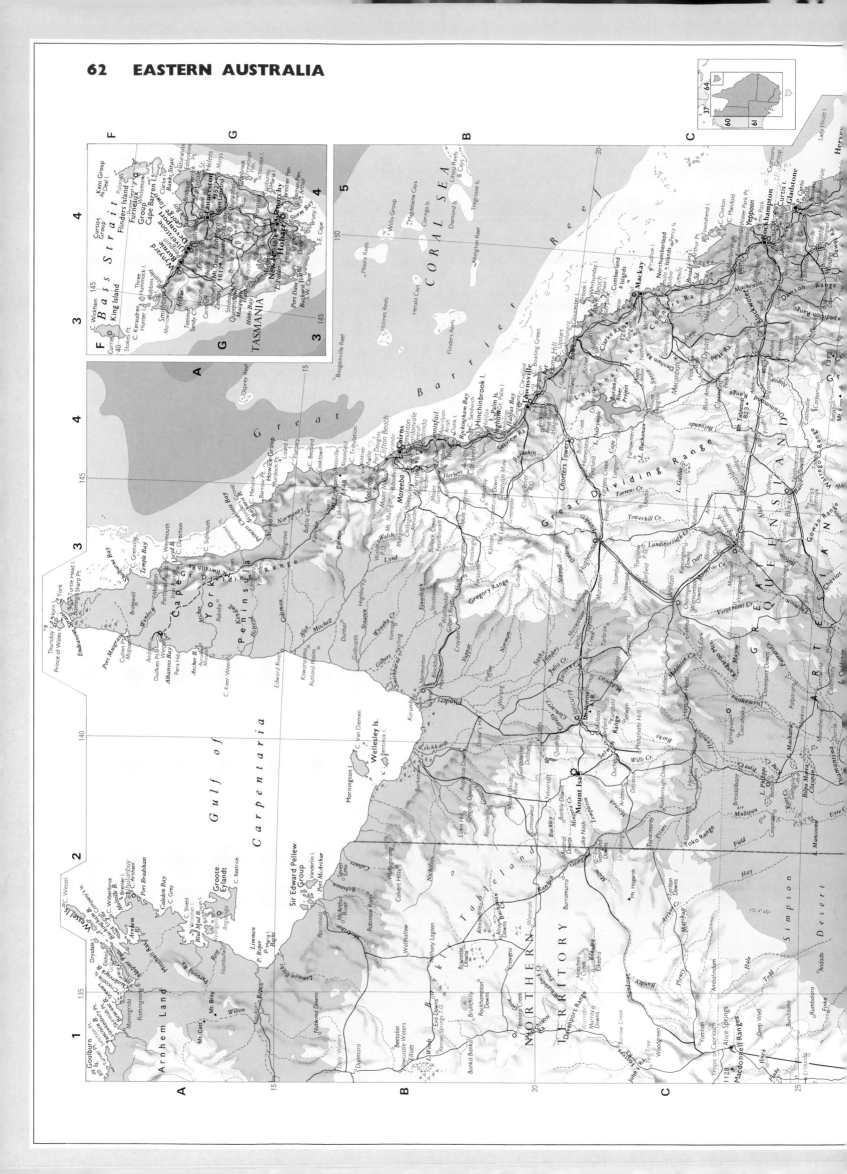

1 : 8 000 000

T A S M A N

S E A

Bonne

East from Greenwich

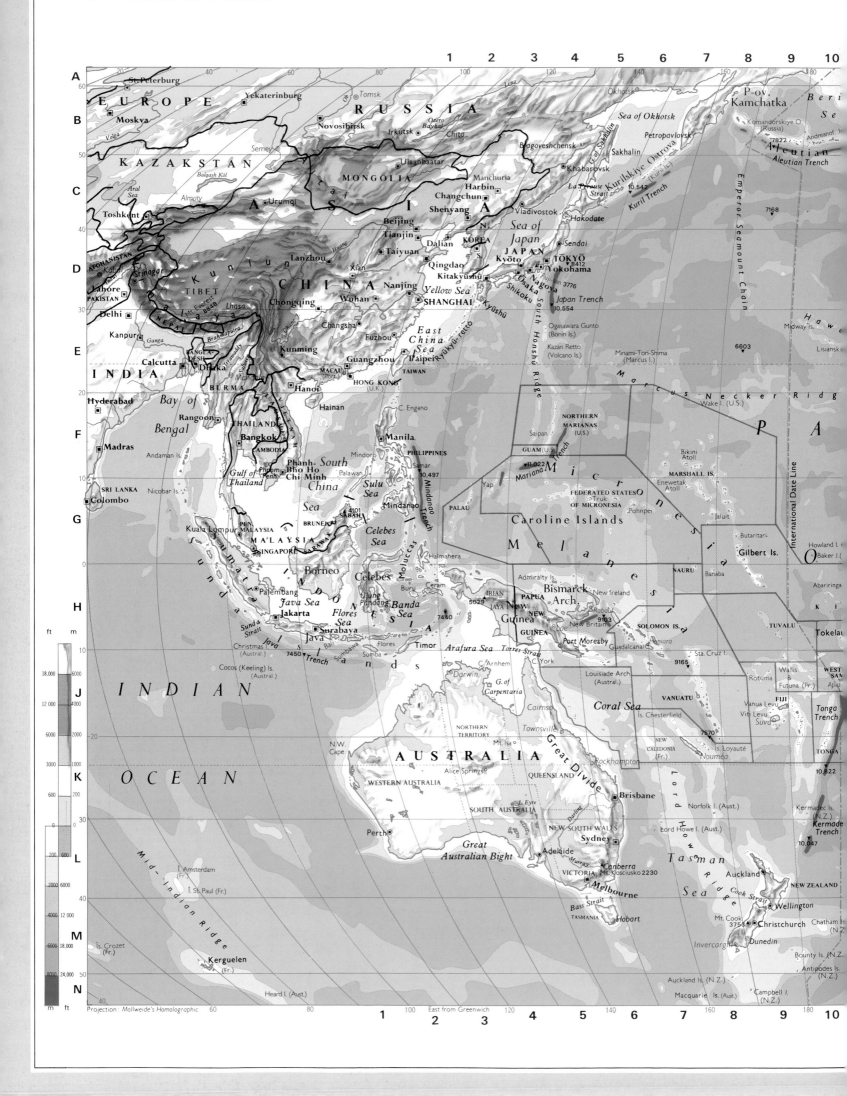

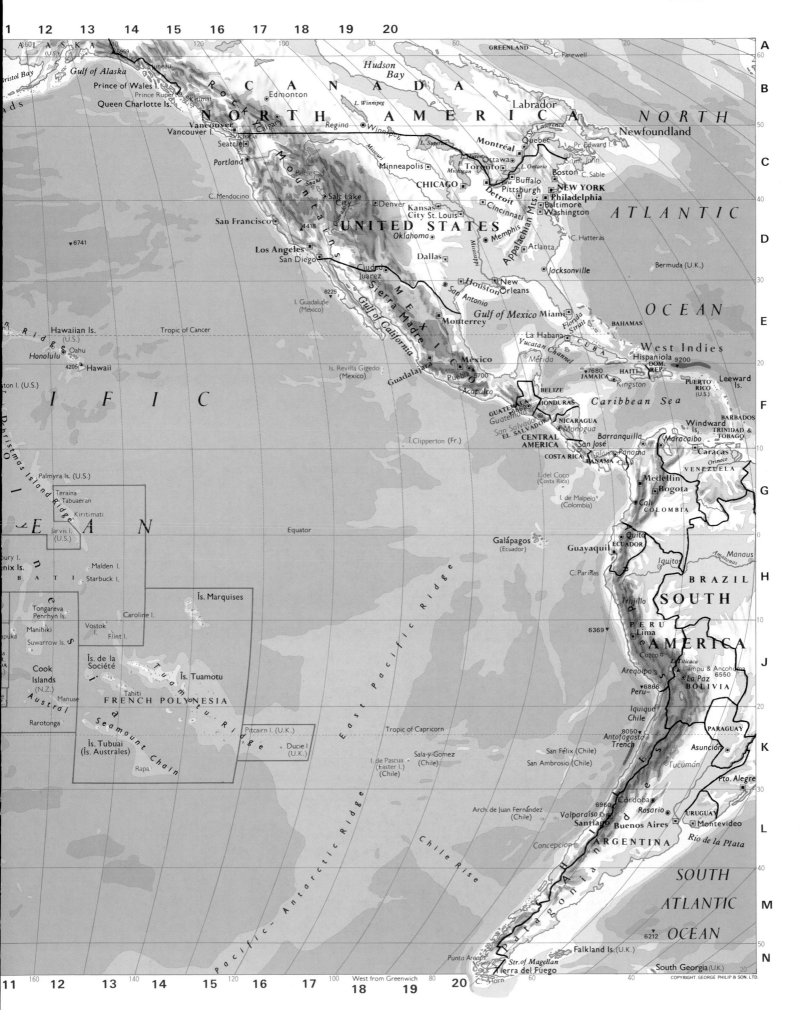

1:54 000 000

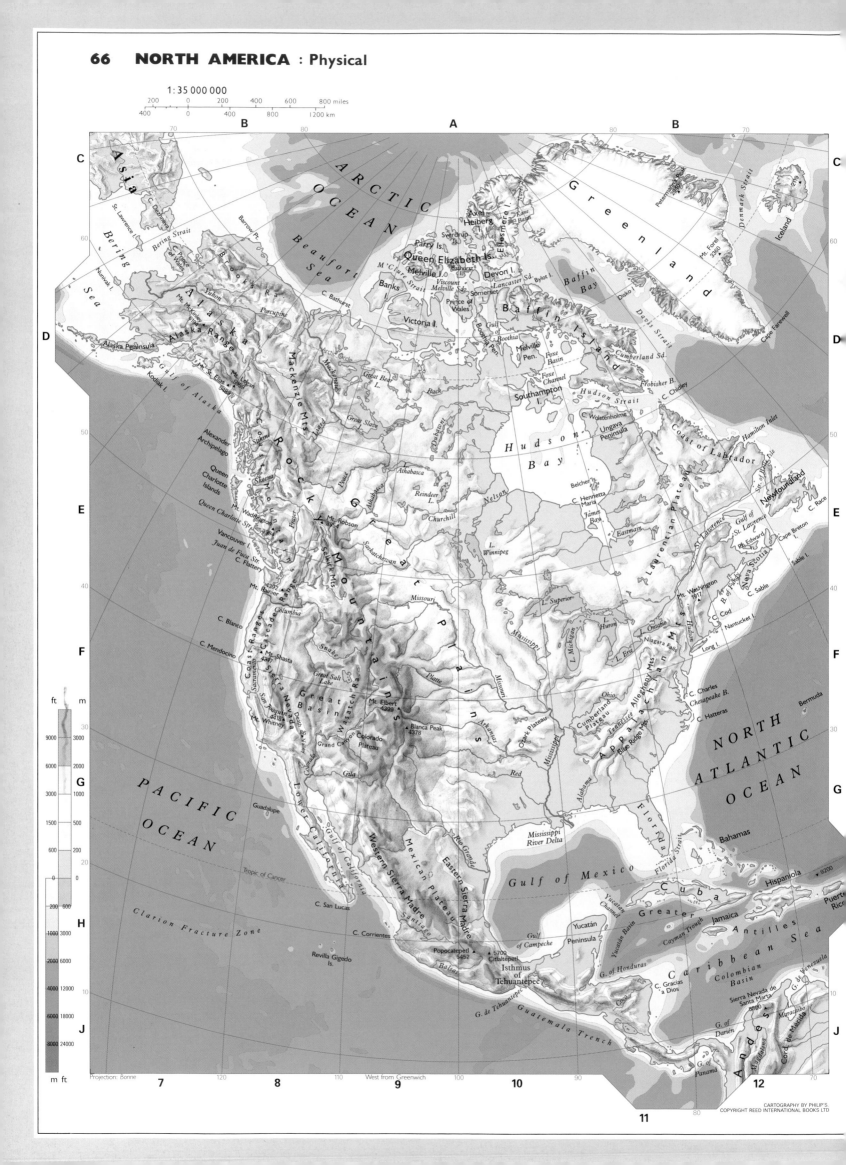

1 : 35 000 000

Projection: Bonne

CARTOGRAPHY BY PHILIP'S.
COPYRIGHT REED INTERNATIONAL BOOKS LTD

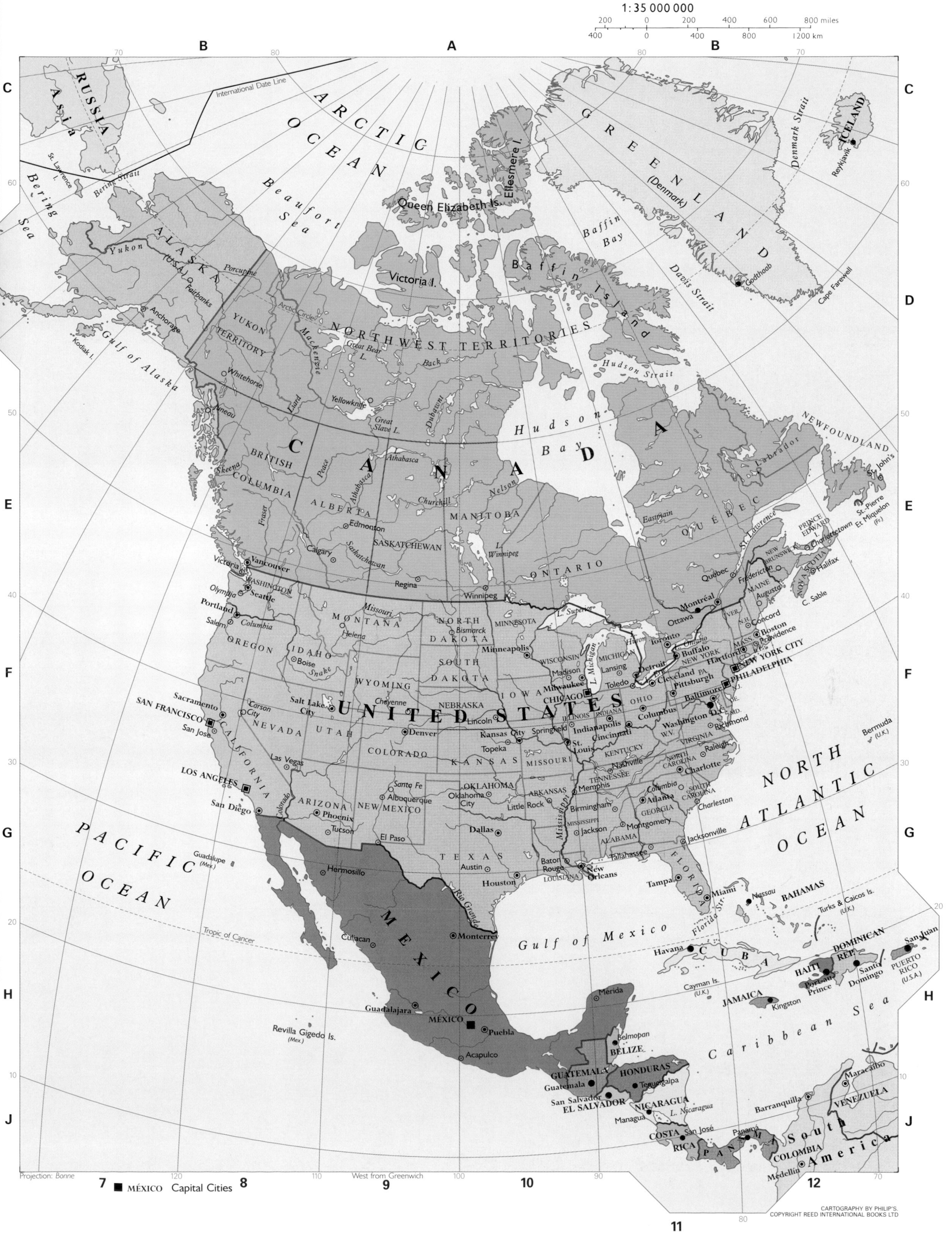

1 : 35 000 000

200   0   200   400   600   800 miles
400   0   400   800   1200 km

B   A   B

C   RUSSIA   Asia   International Date Line   ARCTIC   OCEAN   GREENLAND   (Denmark)   Denmark Strait   ICELAND   C

Bering Strait   Beaufort   Sea   Queen Elizabeth Is.   Ellesmere I.   Baffin   Bay   Reykjavik   Godthåb

St. Lawrence   Bering Sea   Yukon   ALASKA (U.S.A.)   Porcupine   Victoria I.   Baffin Island   Davis Strait   Cape Farewell

Fairbanks   Anchorage   YUKON TERRITORY   Arctic Circle   NORTHWEST TERRITORIES   Hudson Strait   D

Kodiak I.   Gulf of Alaska   Whitehorse   Mackenzie   Great Bear L.   Back   NEWFOUNDLAND

Juneau   Great Slave L.   Yellowknife   Dubawnt   Hudson   Bay   Labrador   50

E   CANADA   BRITISH COLUMBIA   ALBERTA   Edmonton   SASKATCHEWAN   Churchill   MANITOBA   Nelson   Eastmain   QUÉBEC   PRINCE EDWARD I.   St-Pierre Et Miquelon (Fr.)   St. John's   E

Skeena   Peace   Athabasca   Athabasca   L. Winnipeg   St. Lawrence   NEW BRUNSWICK   Charlottetown   NOVA SCOTIA   Halifax

Fraser   Calgary   Saskatchewan   Regina   ONTARIO   Québec   Fredericton   MAINE   Augusta   C. Sable

Victoria   Vancouver   Winnipeg   L. Superior   Montréal   Ottawa   N.H.   Concord   Boston   Providence

40   WASHINGTON   Seattle   Missouri   NORTH DAKOTA   Bismarck   MINNESOTA   Huron   Toronto   L. Ontario   NEW YORK   MASS.   Hartford   NEW YORK CITY   40

Olympia   Portland   Salem   Columbia   MONTANA   Helena   SOUTH DAKOTA   Minneapolis   WISCONSIN   Madison   L. Michigan   MICHIGAN   Lansing   Milwaukee   Detroit   Cleveland   PA   Pittsburgh   PHILADELPHIA   F

OREGON   IDAHO   Boise   Snake   WYOMING   Chicago   Toledo   OHIO   Baltimore

Sacramento   Salt Lake City   Cheyenne   NEBRASKA   IOWA   ILLINOIS   INDIANA   Columbus   W.V.   Washington D.C.   Richmond   Bermuda (U.K.)

SAN FRANCISCO   Carson City   NEVADA   UTAH   Denver   Lincoln   Springfield   Indianapolis   Cincinnati   KENTUCKY   VIRGINIA

San Jose   CALIFORNIA   Las Vegas   COLORADO   Topeka   Kansas City   St. Louis   Nashville   NORTH CAROLINA   Raleigh   30   NORTH

LOS ANGELES   Santa Fe   KANSAS   MISSOURI   TENNESSEE   Charlotte   ATLANTIC

San Diego   ARIZONA   NEW MEXICO   Albuquerque   Oklahoma City   OKLAHOMA   ARKANSAS   Memphis   Columbia   SOUTH CAROLINA   OCEAN

Colorado   Phoenix   Little Rock   MISSISSIPPI   Atlanta   Charleston

G   PACIFIC   Tucson   El Paso   Dallas   Birmingham   GEORGIA   G

Guadalupe (Mex.)   Hermosillo   Rio Grande   TEXAS   Jackson   ALABAMA   Montgomery   Jacksonville

OCEAN   Austin   Baton Rouge   LOUISIANA   Tallahassee   FLORIDA

Houston   New Orleans   Tampa   Miami   Nassau   BAHAMAS   Turks & Caicos Is. (U.K.)   20

Tropic of Cancer   Culiacán   MEXICO   Monterrey   Gulf of Mexico   Florida Str.   Havana   CUBA   DOMINICAN REP.   San Juan

H   MÉXICO   Cayman Is. (U.K.)   HAITI   Santo   PUERTO RICO (U.S.A.)   H

Revilla Gigedo Is. (Mex.)   Guadalajara   Mérida   Port-au-Prince   Domingo

MÉXICO   Puebla   Belmopan   JAMAICA   Kingston   Caribbean   Sea

Acapulco   BELIZE   Maracaibo

GUATEMALA   HONDURAS   Barranquilla   VENEZUELA

Guatemala   Tegucigalpa   South

San Salvador   EL SALVADOR   NICARAGUA

Managua   L. Nicaragua

J   COSTA   San José   Panamá   PANAMA   COLOMBIA   America   J

RICA   Medellín

Projection: Bonne

CARTOGRAPHY BY PHILIP'S.
COPYRIGHT REED INTERNATIONAL BOOKS LTD

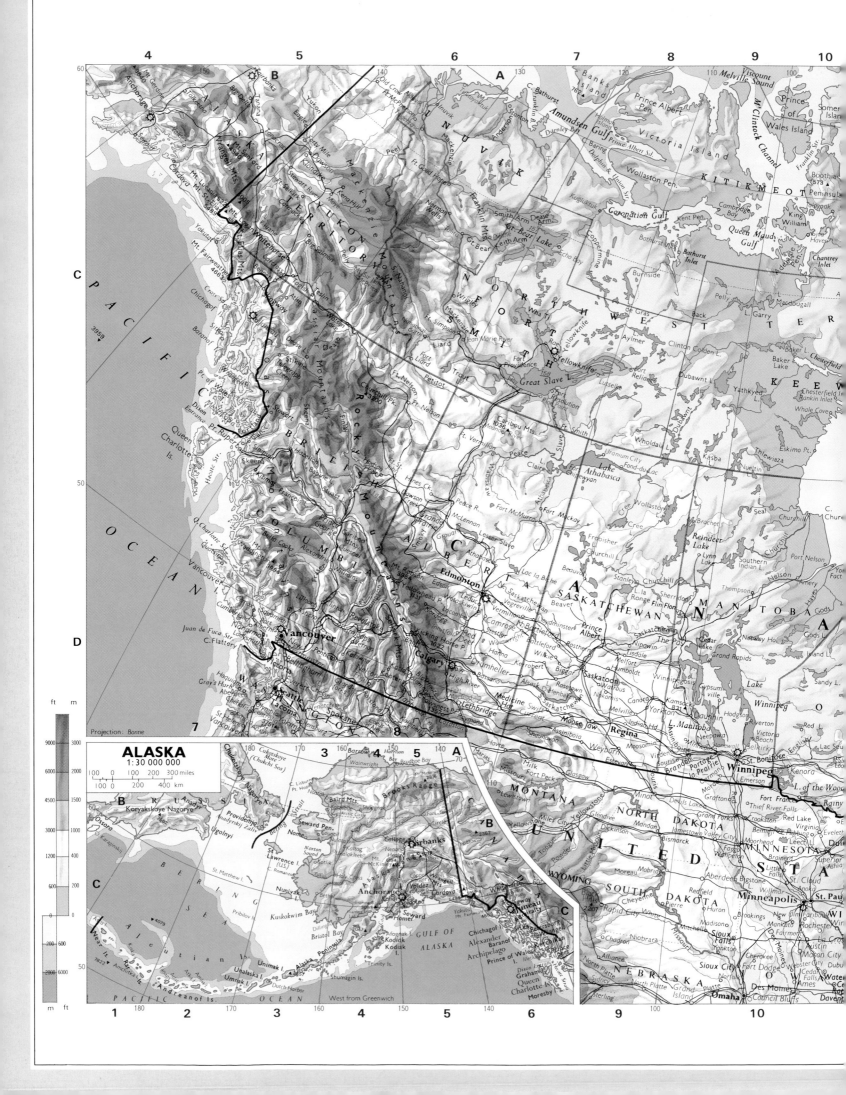

ALASKA
1:30 000 000

100 0   100 200 300 miles
100 0   200   400 km

Projection: Bonne

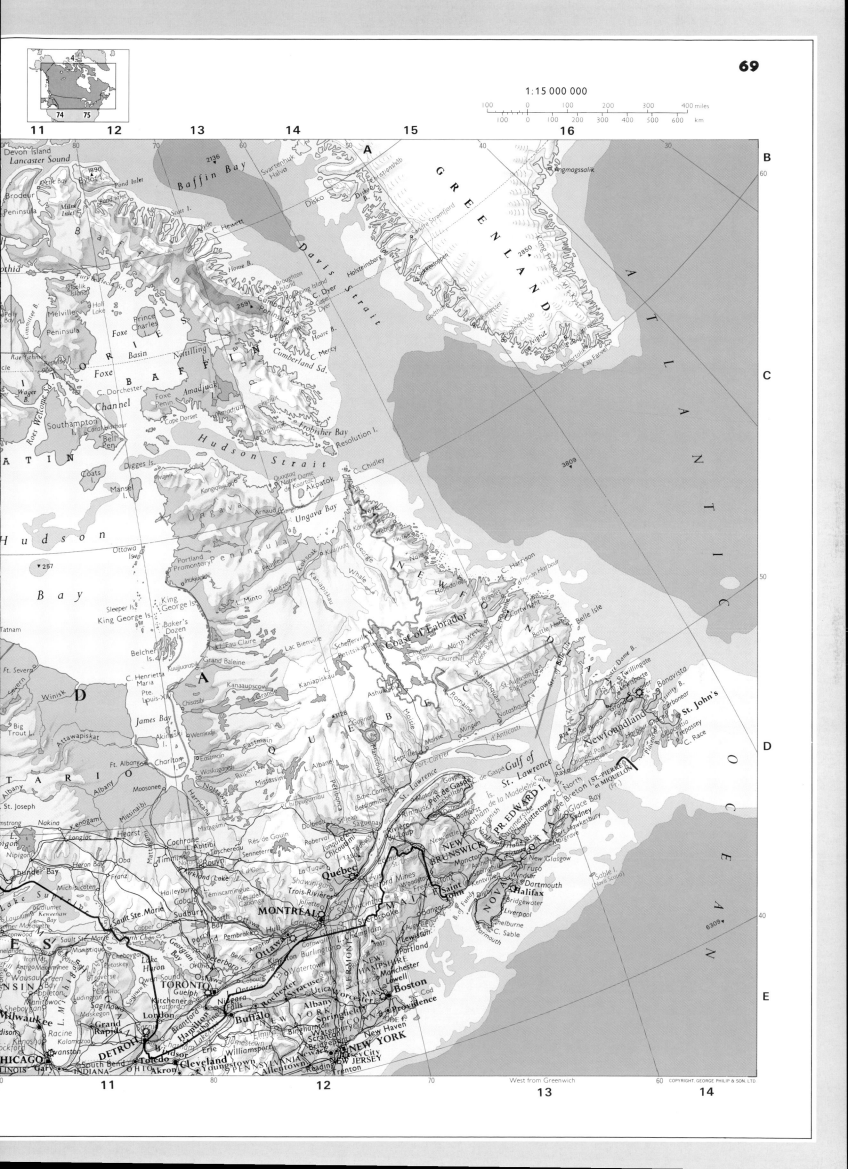

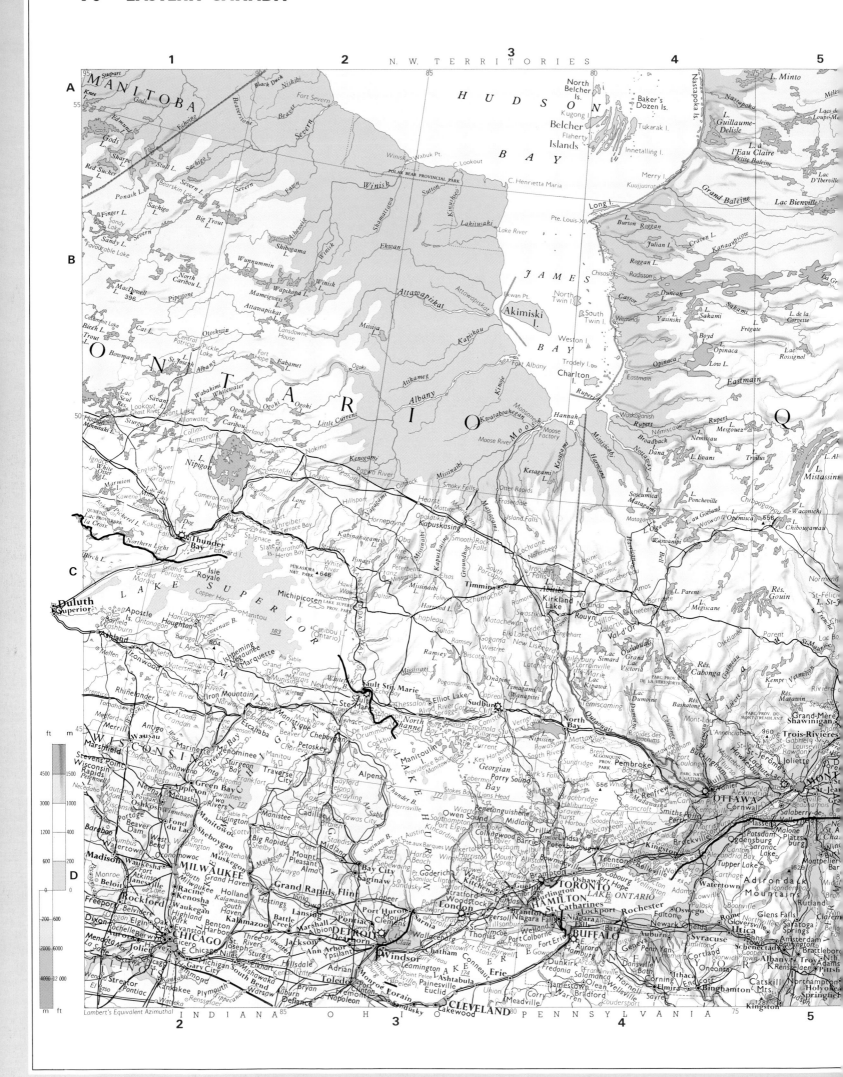

69
73
80
76

6   7   8   9

1:7 000 000

50   0   50   100   150   200 miles
50   0   50   100   150   200   250   300 km

A   55   50

NEW

South Aulatsivik I.
High I.
Paul I.
Voiseys B.
Nain
Davis Inlet
Nunaksaluk I.
Hopedale

COAST

Erlandson L.
Fort McKenzie
Nachicapau
Chakonipau L.
Otelnuk L. Whetle
Champdoré L.
Tudor
Whitegull L.
610
Mistastin L.

Kaniapiskau L.
Strigny

Harp L.

Big Bay
Kapokok B.
Allik
Mokkovik
Adlavik Is.
C. Harrison

OF

Néret
Kaniapiskau Lake
L. Bermen

Petitsikapau L.
Attikamagen L.
Herville
Woods L.
Kanairiktok
Nipishish L.

Nitchequon
Opiscoteo L.
Opiskotish L.
Shabogamo L.
Labrador City
Wabush

Ashuanipi L.
Lac Joseph
Atikonak L.

Naskaupi
Smallwood Res.
North-West River
Goose
Churchill Falls
Osokmanuan L.

Rigolet
Groswater B.
Holton
Indian Harbour

Happy Valley-Goose Bay
L. Melville
Mealy Mts.
1128

Cartwright
Sandwich B.
Island of Ponds

FOUNDLAND

LABRADOR

Separation Point
Square Islands

B

Winokapau L.
Grand L.
Minipi L.

Paradise
Eagle
Alexis

Battle Harbour
Mary's Harbour
St. Lewis

Red Bay
Belle I.

Burnt L.

Natashquan
Little Mecatina

St. Augustin
St. Paul

Bradore Bay
Fort
Blanc-Sablon
Str. of Belle Isle

St. Anthony
Cove
Hare B.

QUEBEC

1128

1048
Niptsou L.
L. Manitou

Res. Manicouagan
Petit Lac Manicouagan
Monte

Magpie L.
St-Jean L.
Romaine R.
Lac Allardz

Musquaro L.
Natashquan
Aguanus
Nabisipi

Olomane

St-Augustin Saguenay
Outer I.
Petit-Mécatina
Harrington Harbour

Groais I.
Conche
Englee
Bell I.

St-Paul

Roddickton
White B.
Horse Is.

50

Plétipi L.

Manouane L.

Betsiamites
Pipmuacan L.

Sheldrake
Mingan
Havre-St-Pierre

Aguanish
Gethemmu
Etamamu

Daniel's Harbour

Gros Morne Nat. Park
Trout River

Long Range Mts.
Deer L.
Howley
Springdale
South Brook
Botwood

La Scie
Notre Dame B.
Twillingate
Fogo I.

Wesleyville
Bonavista

Clarke City
Moisie
Sept-Îles
Walker L.
Port-Cartier
Rivière-Pentecôte

Pte. Ouest
Port-Menier
Î. d'Anticosti
Jupiter
Dét. de Jacques-Cartier
Heath Pt.

Bay of Islands
Long Pt.
Corner Brook
814
Buchans
Red Indian L.
Grand Falls
Bishop's Falls

Gander L.
Glenwood
Dark Cove
Gloverton
Trinity

C. Bonavista
C. Bonavista
Catalina

NEWFOUNDLAND

C

Baie-Trinité
Pte. des Monts
Baie-Comeau
Godbout
Franquelin
Forestville

1268
Grande-Vallée
Mont-Louis
Petit-Cap
d'Honguedo
Cloridorme

Port au Port B.
Port au Port
St. George's B.
St. George
Victoria L.
Grey Res.
Salmon Res.
Clarenville
Random I.
Content

Harbour Grace
Conception B.
Carbonear

St. Lau
Matane
Mt-Joli
Sayabec
Mts. Chic-Chocs
Pén. de Gaspé
Chandler
Gaspé
Douglastown

572

St. George's
St. David's
Long Range Mts.
South Branch
St. Alban's

GULF OF

St. Lawrence

Trinity B.
St. Mary's
Torbay
St. John's
Mt. Pearl
Petty Harbour
Bay Bulls

Rimouski
Trois-Pistoles
Bic
Causapscal
Amqui
Matapédia
Bonaventure
Bespébiac
New Richmond

Î. Brion
Grande-Entrée

C. St. George
Stephenville
Port aux Port
Barachois
Southern
Rose Blanche
C. Ray

White Bear Res.
Bay d'Espoir

Holyrood
Ferryland
Avalon Peninsula

Rivière-du-Loup
Cabano
Edmundston
Campbellton
Dalhousie
Chaleur Bay
Belledune
Bathurst

Les Îs. de la Madeleine
(Quebec)
Cap-aux-Meules
Havre-Aubert
C. North
St. Paul I.

Channel-Port aux Basques
Burgeo
Ramea
Fortune B.
Harbour Breton
Grand Bank
St. Lawrence

Placentia B.
St. Mary's B.
C. St. Mary's
C. Race
C. Pine

D

St-Pascal
St-Jean-Port-Joli
Montmagny
Lauzon
Lévis
QUEBEC

St. Leonard
Grand Falls
Plaster Rock
Van Buren
Caribou
NEW BRUNSWICK

819
Newcastle
Chatham
Blackville
Miramichi B.
North Pt.
Tignish
Alberton

Miquelon
Langlade
SAINT-PIERRE ET MIQUELON
(Fr.)
St-Pierre

Ste-Marie
Plessisville
Thetford Mines
Asbestos

Houlton
Presque Isle
Ashland
Island Falls
Chesuncook

Woodstock
Hartland
Stanley
Minto
Grand L.
Havelock

PRINCE EDWARD ISLAND
Summerside
Kensington
Charlottetown
Souris
East Pt.

Georgetown
Murray Hr.
Pictou

Sydney Mines
New Waterford
Glace Bay
Inverness
N. Sydney
Sydney
Cape Breton Island
Louisbourg

Sherbrooke
Coaticook
Lac-Mégantic
1606
Millinocket
Fredericton
Gagetown
Chipman
Sussex

Shediac
Moncton
Cape Tormentine
Amherst
Springhill
New Glasgow
Stellarton
Mulgrave
Chedabucto B.
Canso

Magog
Megantic
Mattawamkeag
Greenville
Lincoln
Old Town
Brewer
Bangor
Ellsworth

Saint John
Bay of Fundy
St. Martins
Minas Basin
Truro
Windsor
Stewiacke
Upper Musquodoboit
Sherbrooke

MAINE

East Angus
Bingham
Skowhegan
Waterville
Augusta

Blacks Hr.
St. Stephen
Calais
St. George
Kentville
Middleton
Annapolis Royal
Dartmouth
Musquodoboit Hr.
Sheet Hr.

ATLANTIC

Berlin
Bethel
Rumford
Mooselookmeguntic L.
Farmington
Auburn
Lewiston
Belfast

Grand Manan I.
Eastport
Machias
Jonesport
Digby
Mahone Bay
Lunenburg
Halifax

Bath
Brunswick
Bar Harbor
Mt. Desert I.
Freeport
Weymouth
St. Mary's B.
Bridgewater
Liverpool
Port Mouton

OCEAN

Sanford
Saco
Biddeford
Portland

Yarmouth
Wedgeport
Shelburne
Clark's Harbour
C. Sable

Sable I.
(Nova Scotia)

D

Rochester
Dover
Portsmouth
Haverhill
Lawrence
Lowell
Lynn
Waltham
BOSTON
Brockton

45

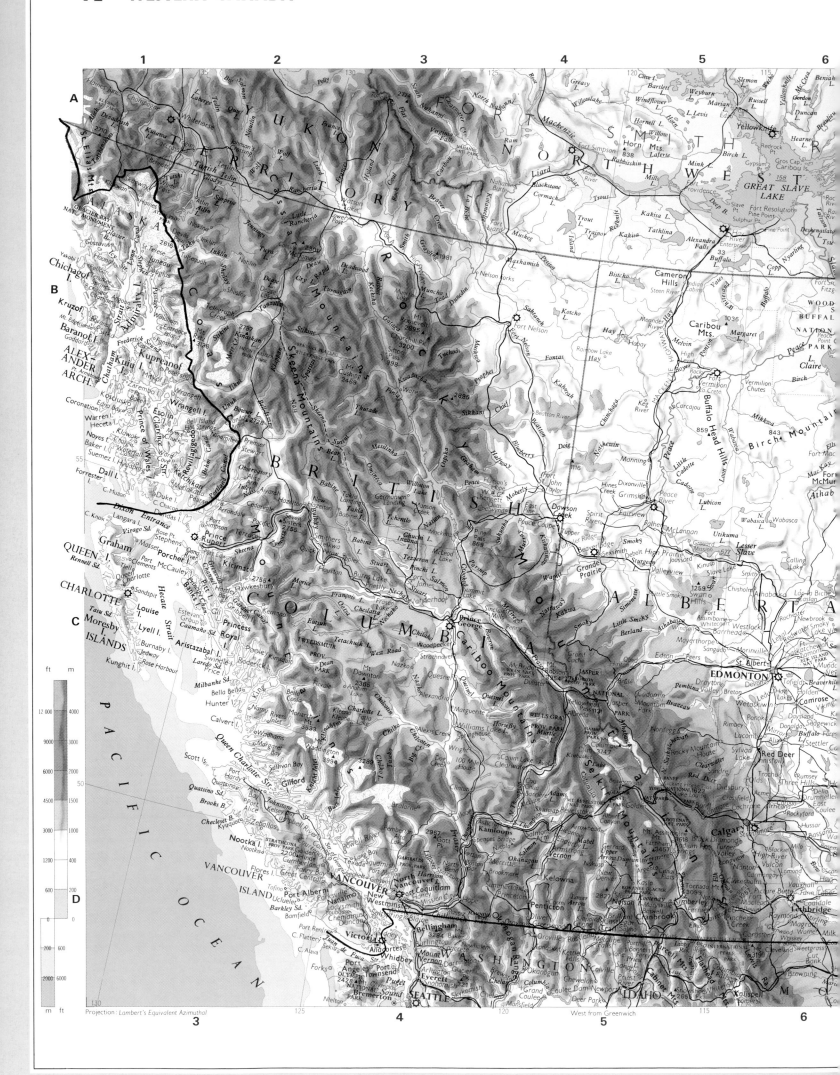

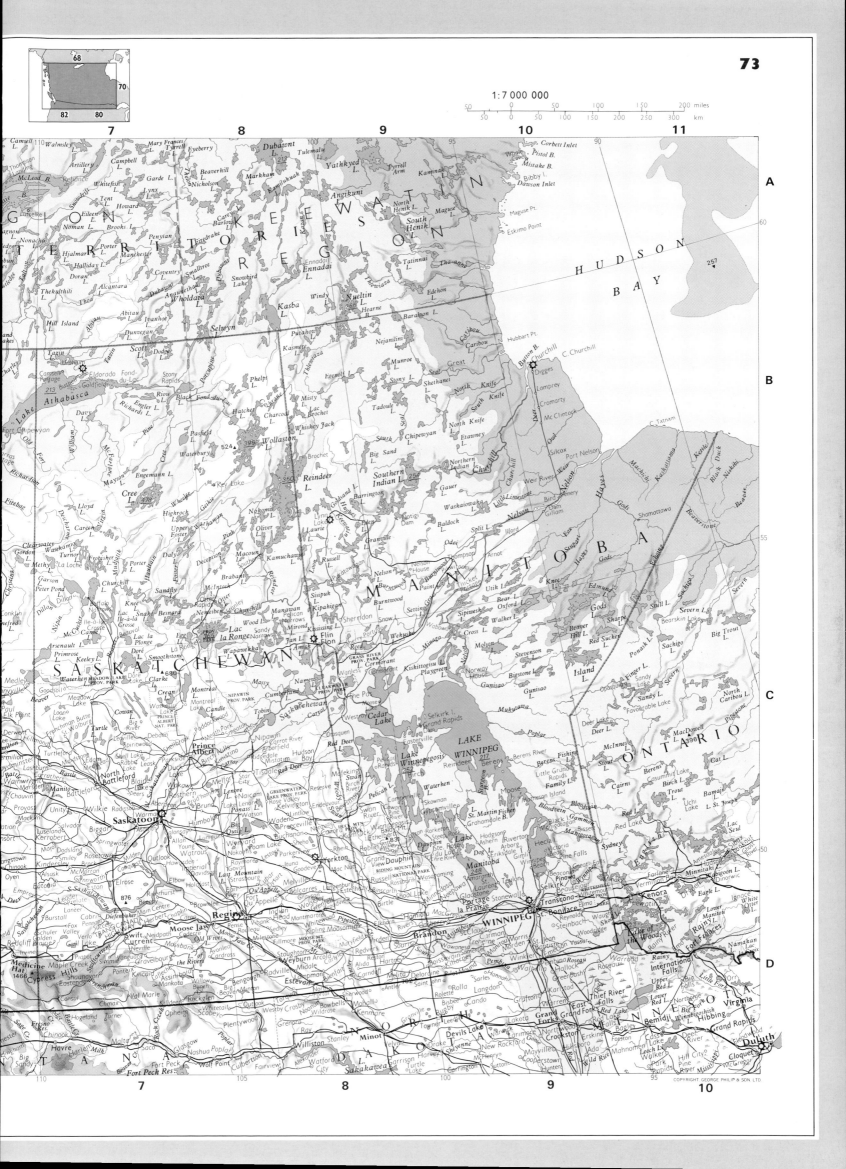

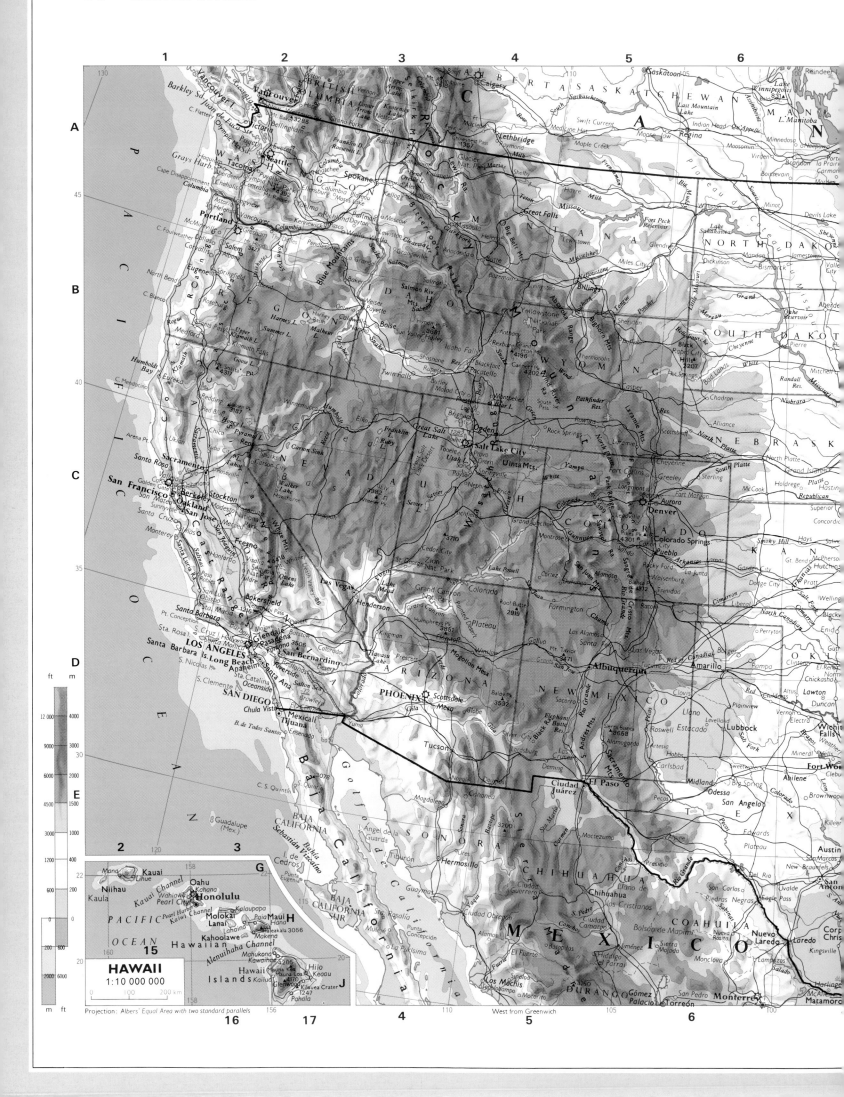

HAWAII
1:10 000 000

Projection: Albers' Equal Area with two standard parallels

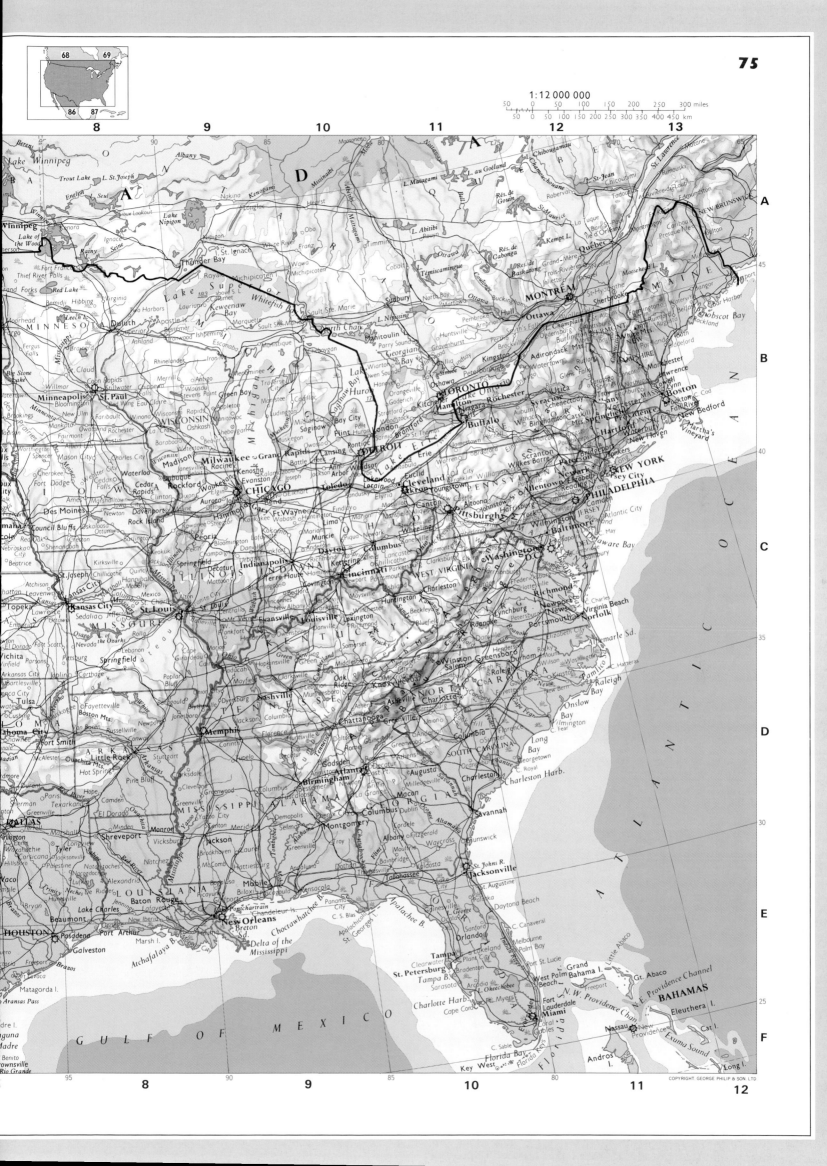

1:12 000 000

50   0   50   100   150   200   250   300 miles

50 0 50 100 150 200 250 300 350 400 450 km

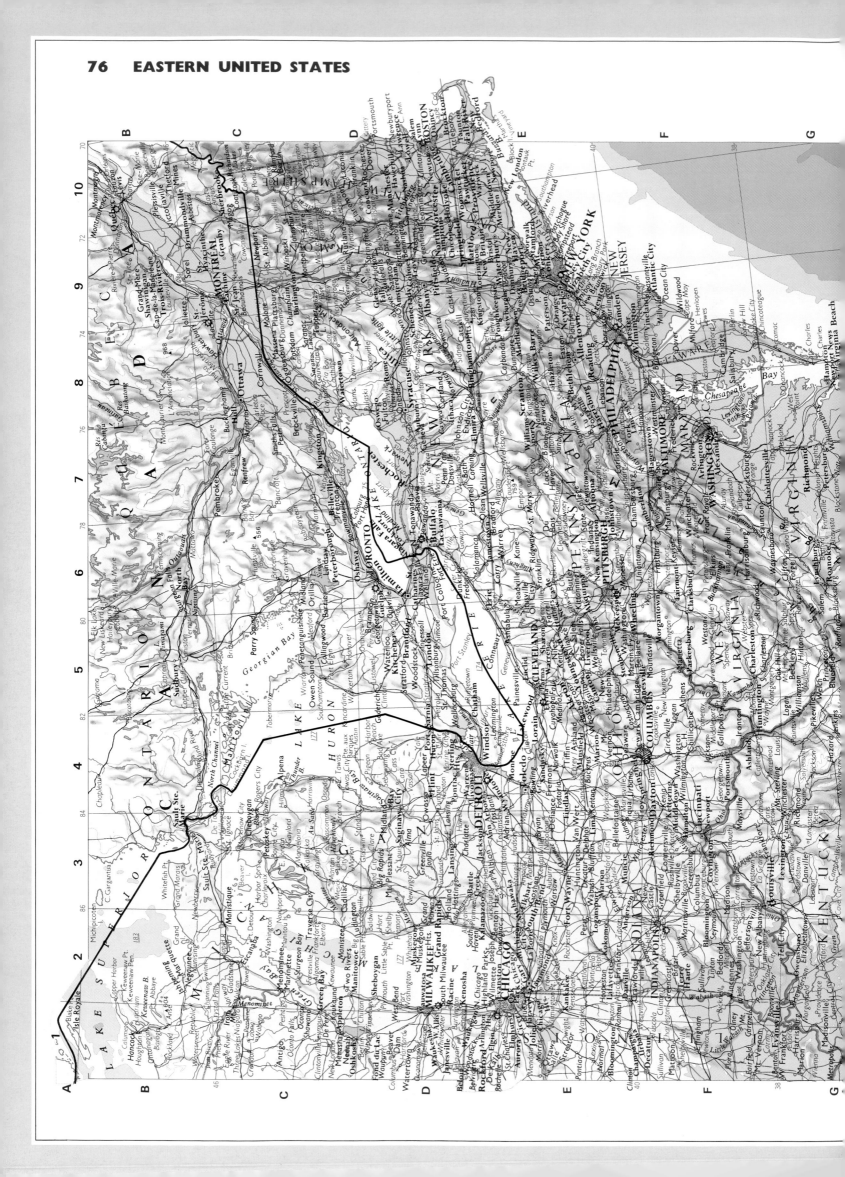

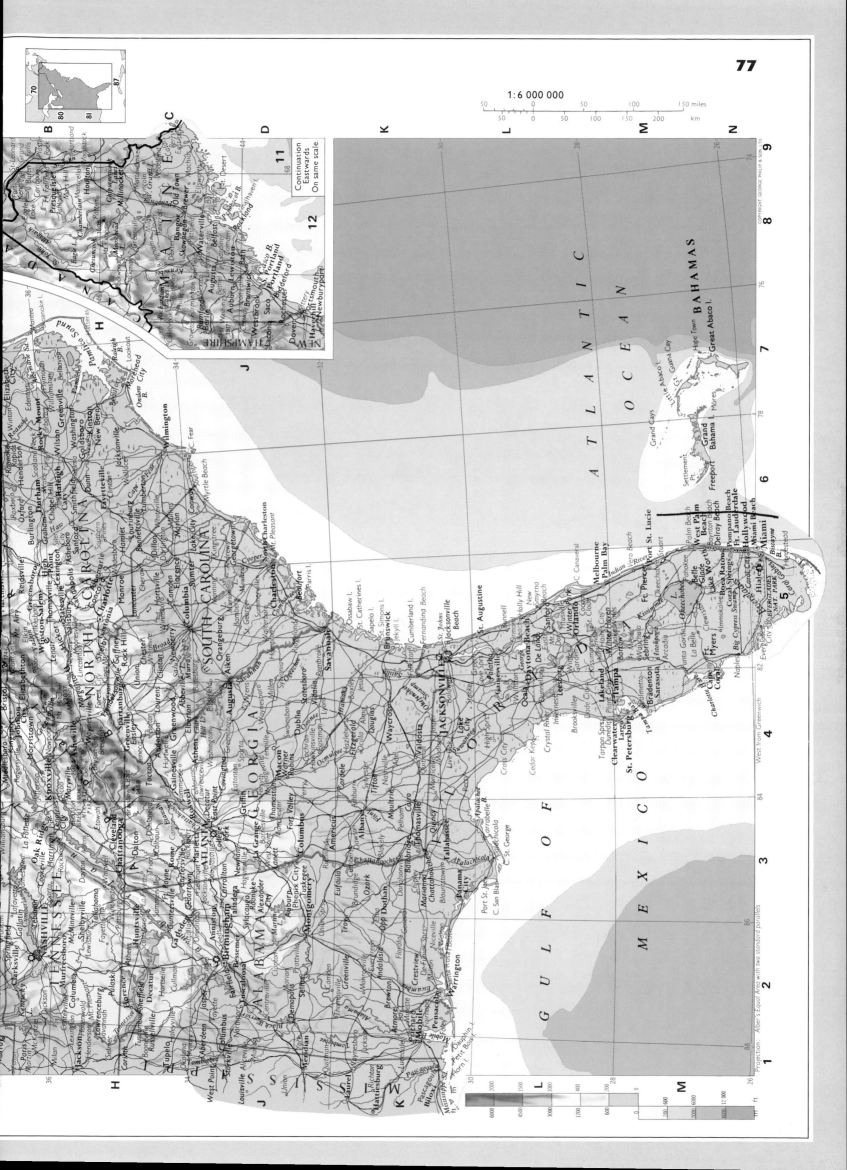

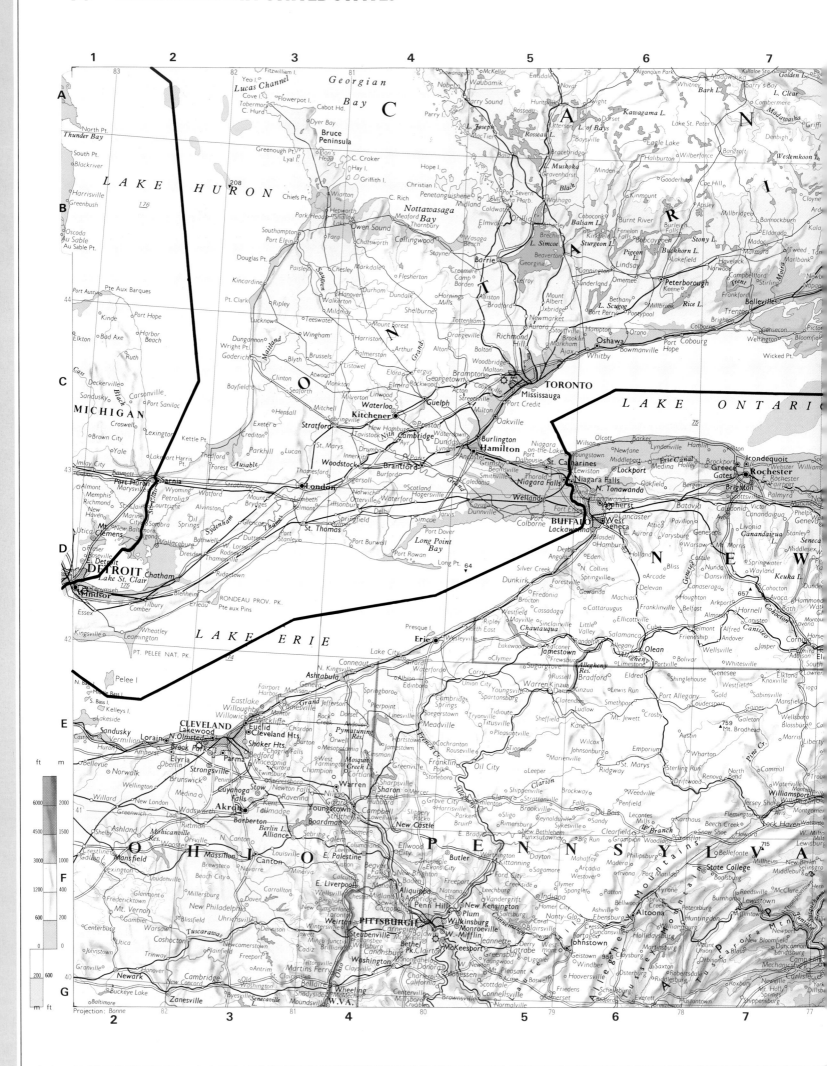

Projection: Bonne

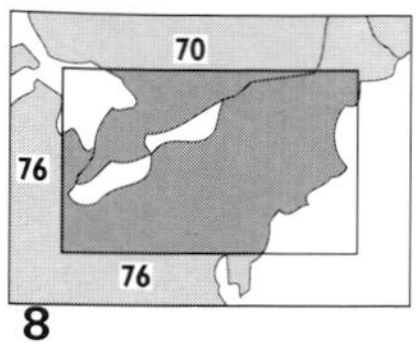

1:2 500 000

10 0 10 20 30 40 50 miles
10 0 10 20 30 40 50 60 70 80 km

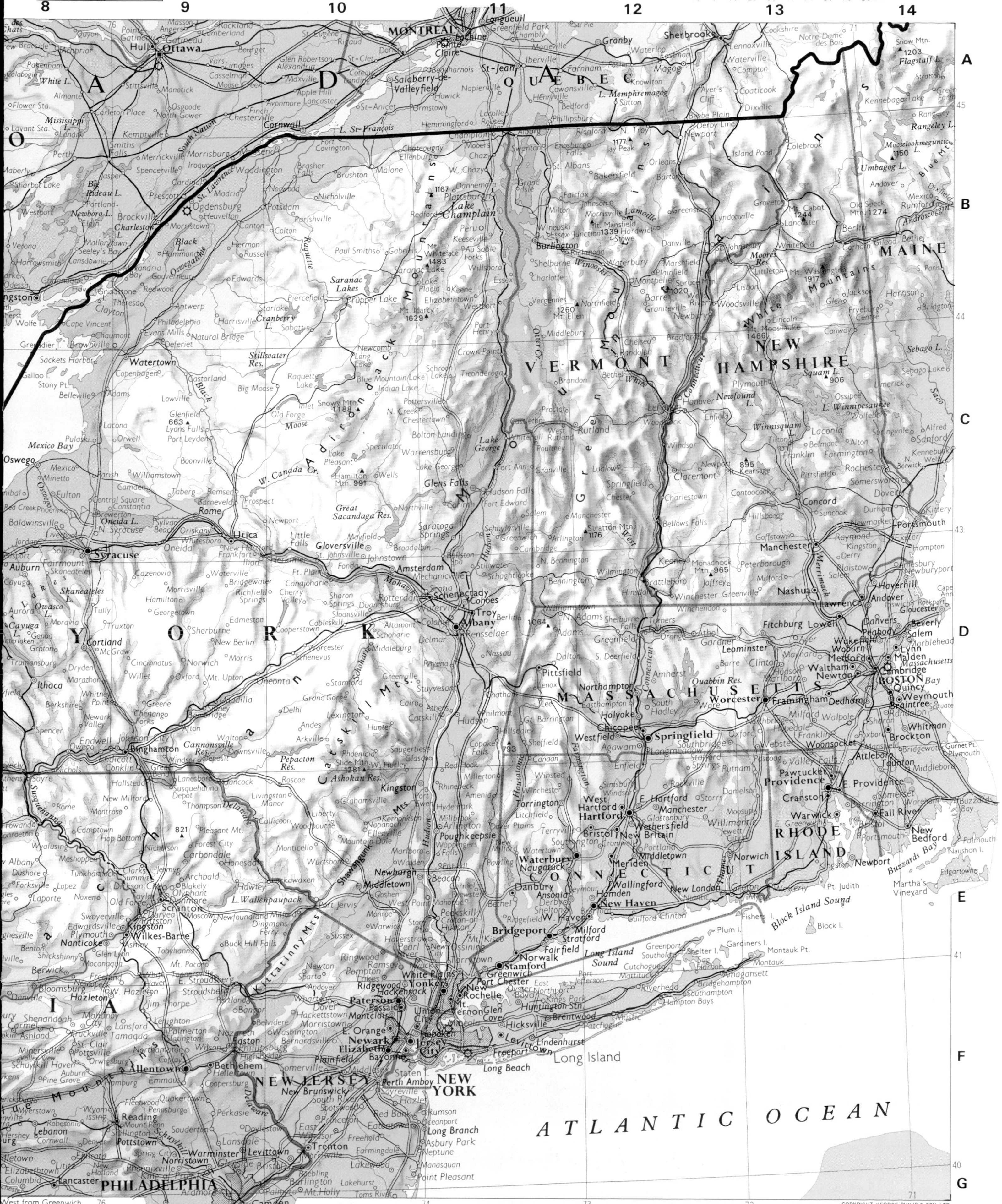

8 9 10 11 12 13 14

MONTREAL

QUEBEC

CANADA

Ottawa
Hull
Cornwall

Lake Champlain

VERMONT

NEW HAMPSHIRE

MAINE

Burlington
Montpelier

Watertown

Saratoga Springs

Glens Falls

Syracuse
Utica
Rome
Gloversville
Amsterdam
Schenectady
Troy
Albany
Rensselaer

YORK

Oneonta
Binghamton

Cortland
Ithaca

Pittsfield
Northampton
MASSACHUSETTS
Holyoke
Chicopee
Springfield
Worcester
Framingham
BOSTON
Cambridge
Quincy
Lynn
Salem

Concord
Manchester
Nashua
Lawrence
Lowell
Fitchburg
Leominster

Portsmouth

RHODE ISLAND
Providence
E. Providence
Cranston
Warwick
Pawtucket
Fall River
New Bedford
Newport

CONNECTICUT
Hartford
E. Hartford
New Britain
Bristol
Waterbury
Meriden
Middletown
New Haven
Bridgeport
Norwalk
Stamford
Danbury
Torrington
New London
Norwich

Kingston
Poughkeepsie
Newburgh
Middletown
Beacon

White Plains
Yonkers
New Rochelle
Mt. Vernon

Wilkes-Barre
Scranton
Hazleton

NEW JERSEY
Paterson
Passaic
Newark
E. Orange
Elizabeth
Jersey City
Hoboken
Bayonne
Perth Amboy
New Brunswick
Plainfield
Trenton

NEW YORK

Long Island

Long Beach

Asbury Park

Allentown
Bethlehem
Easton
Reading
Lancaster
Pottstown
Norristown
PHILADELPHIA
Camden

ATLANTIC OCEAN

West from Greenwich

COPYRIGHT. GEORGE PHILIP & SON LTD.

8 9 10 11 12 13 14

1:6 000 000

50   0   50   100   150 miles

50   0   50   100   150   200   km

CANADA

LAKE SUPERIOR

MICHIGAN

WISCONSIN

MINNESOTA

NORTH DAKOTA

SOUTH DAKOTA

MONTANA

WYOMING

NEBRASKA

IOWA

ILLINOIS

MISSOURI

KANSAS

COLORADO

LAKE MICHIGAN

MILWAUKEE

CHICAGO

ST. LOUIS

DENVER

Duluth

Minneapolis

St. Paul

Omaha

Kansas City

Lincoln

Bismarck

Rapid City

Sand Hills

Smoky Hills

Badlands

Laramie Mountains

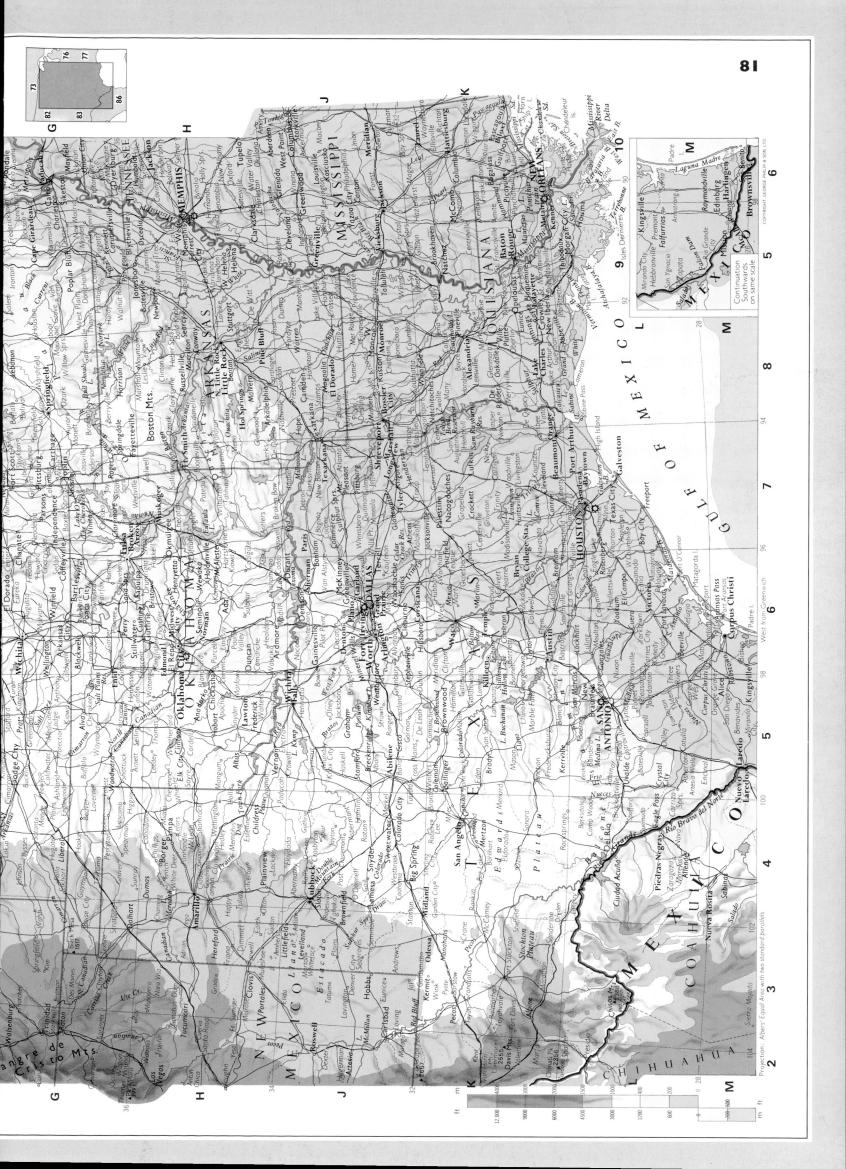

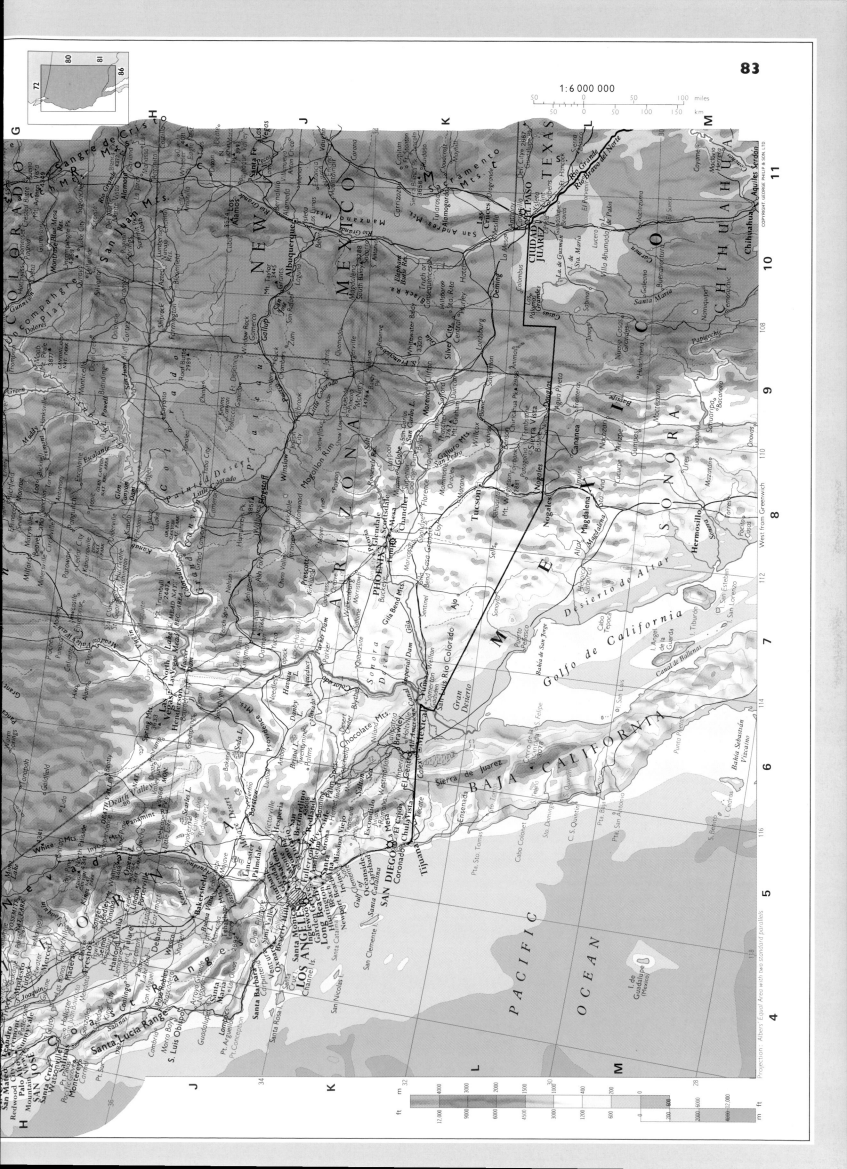

1:6 000 000

Projection: Albers' Equal Area with two standard parallels

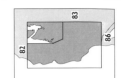

SEATTLE-PORTLAND REGION
On same scale

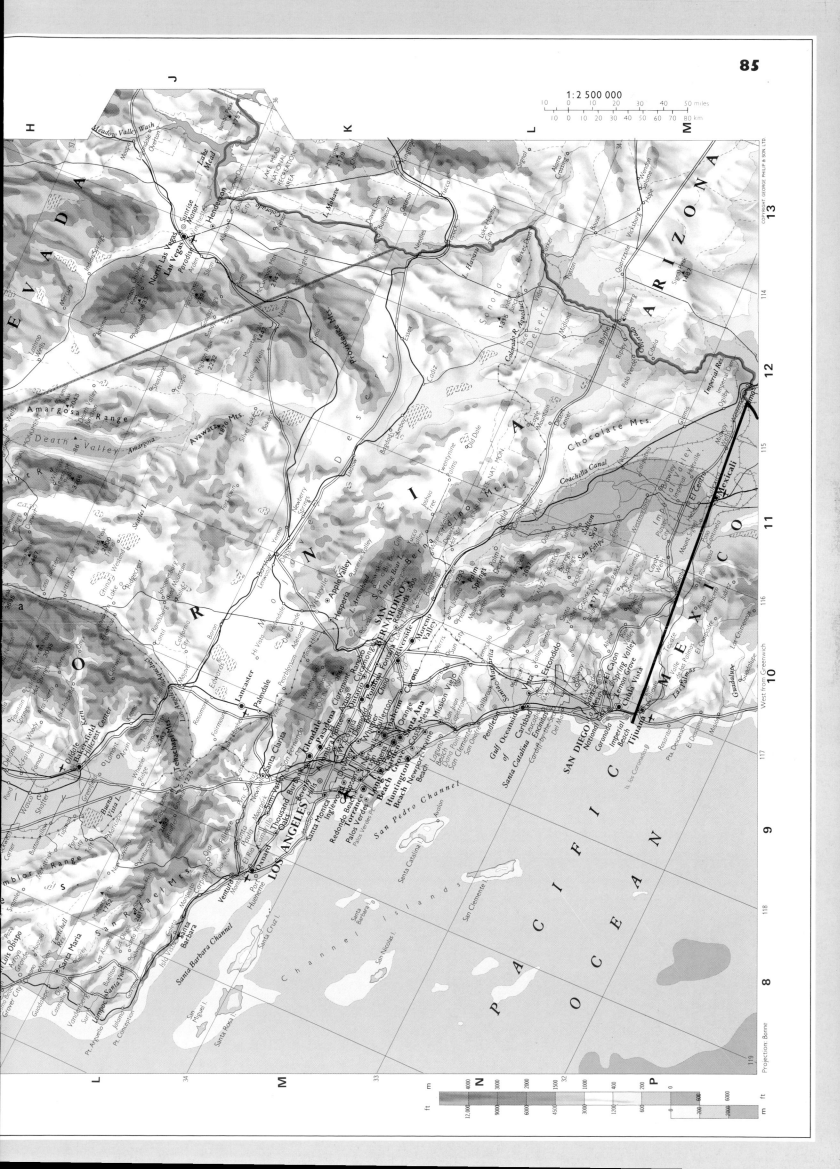

1 : 2 500 000

Projection: Bonne

COPYRIGHT GEORGE PHILIP & SON LTD.

West from Greenwich

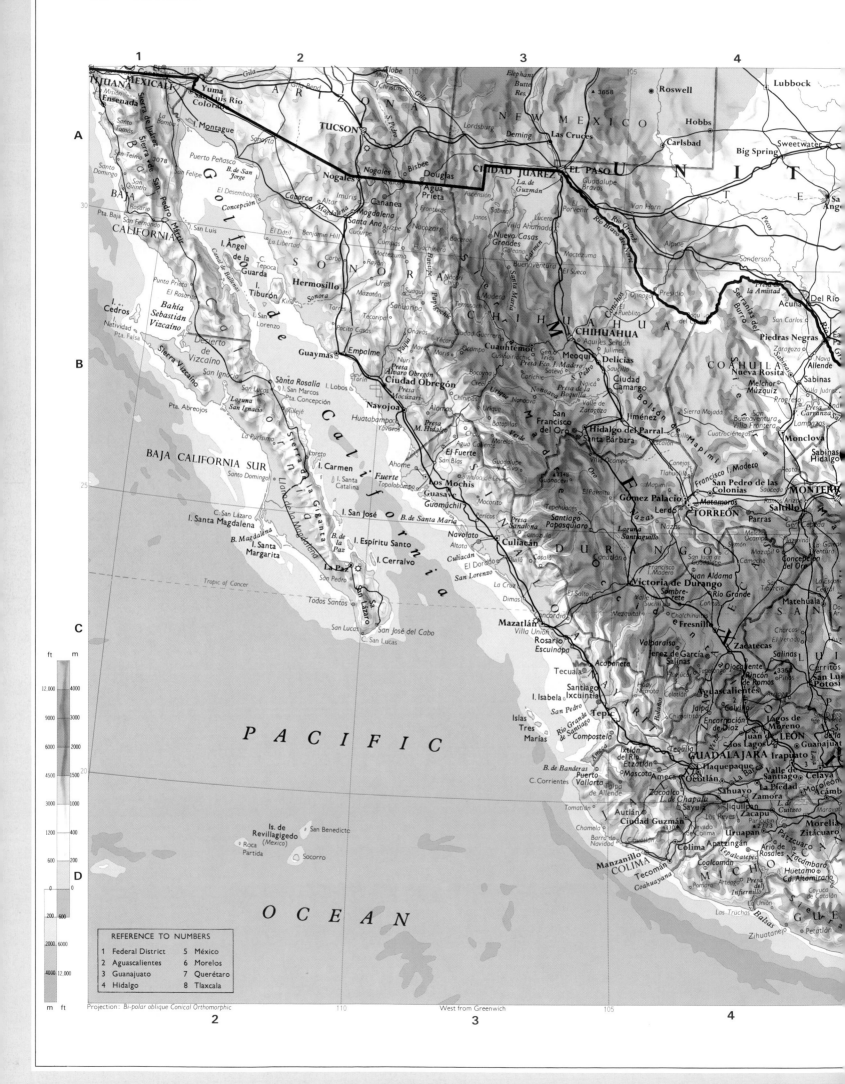

PACIFIC

OCEAN

REFERENCE TO NUMBERS

1	Federal District	5	México
2	Aguascalientes	6	Morelos
3	Guanajuato	7	Querétaro
4	Hidalgo	8	Tlaxcala

Projection: Bi-polar oblique Conical Orthomorphic

West from Greenwich

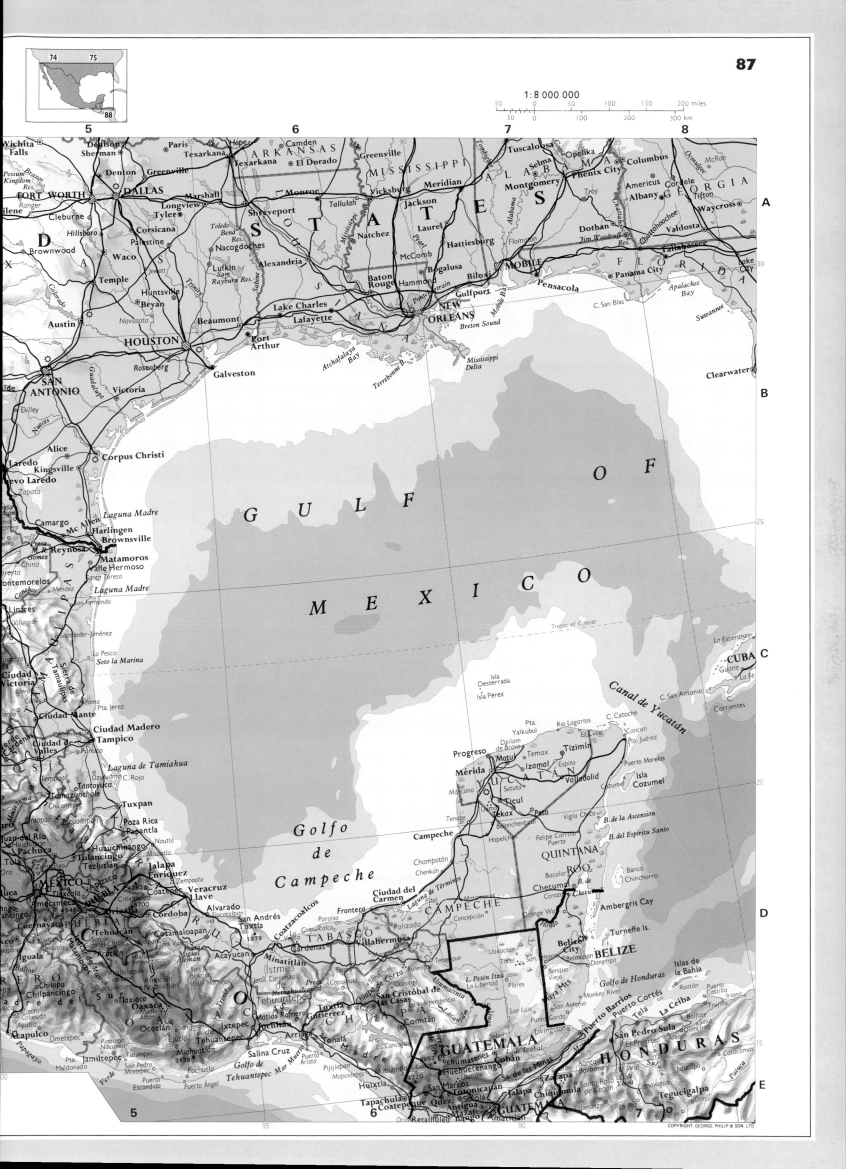

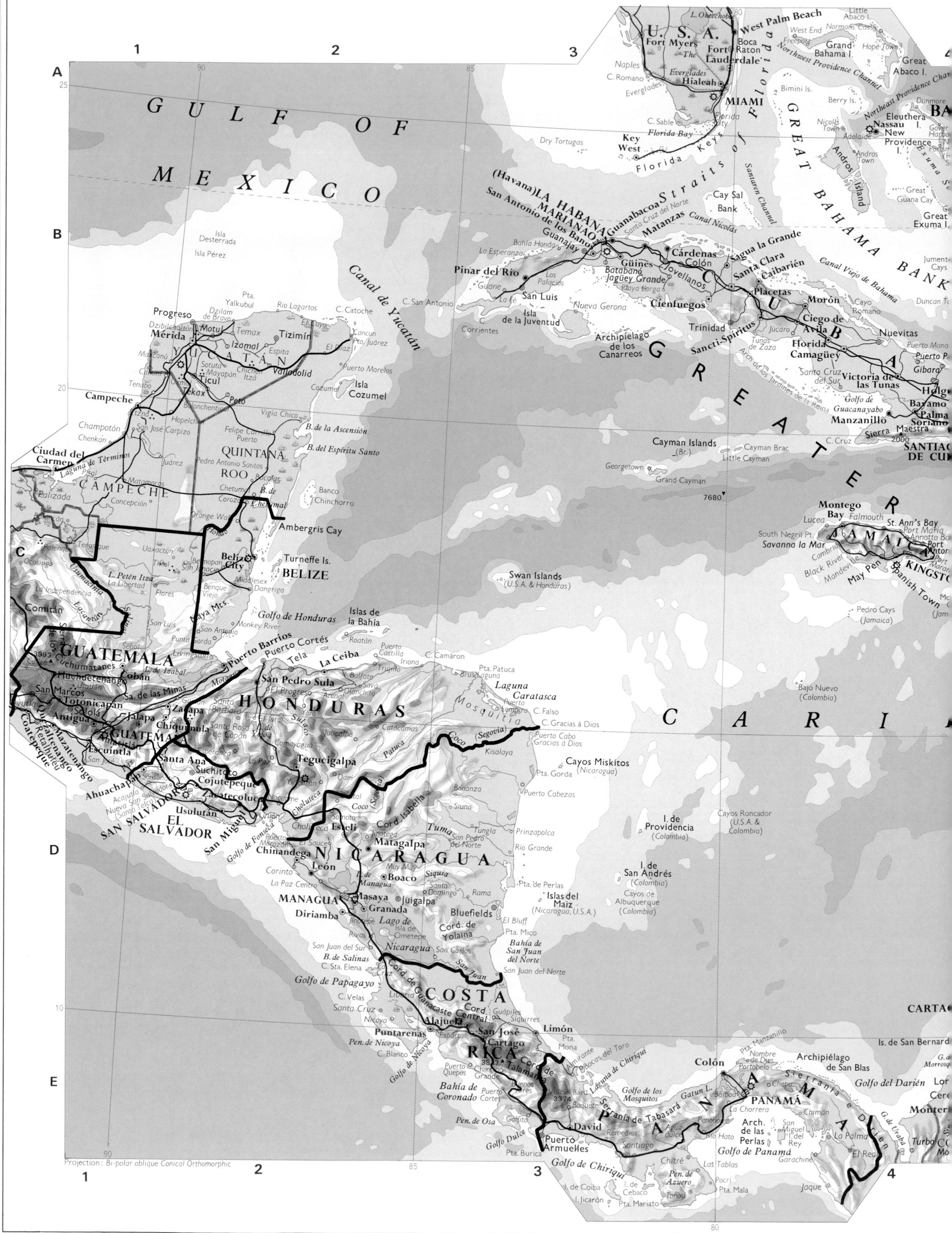

Projection: Bi-polar oblique Conical Orthomorphic

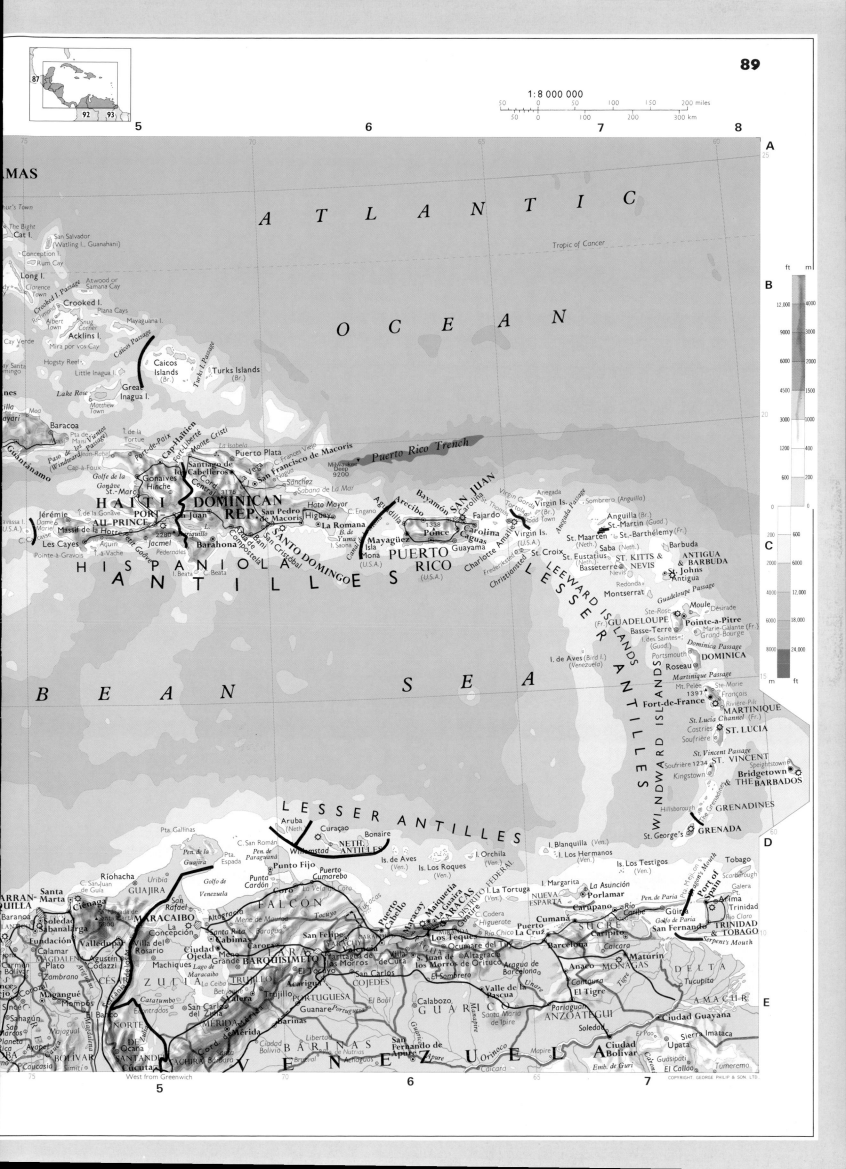

1 : 35 000 000

200 0 200 400 600 800 miles
400 0 400 800 1200 km

1 90 2 80 3 4 5 6 40 7

A

Tropic of Cancer

Yucatán Channel

Cuba

Turks & Caicos Is.

Greater Antilles

Gulf of Campeche

Yucatán Peninsula

Hispaniola

9200

Puerto Rico

NORTH

20

Isthmus of Tehuantepec

G. de Honduras

Jamaica

Guadeloupe
Dominica
Martinique

ATLANTIC

B

Guatemala Trench

C. Gracias a Dios

Cóco

Caribbean Sea

Lesser Antilles

St. Lucia
St. Vincent

Barbados

OCEAN

L. Nicaragua

Panama Canal

C. de la Aguja

5800

I. Margarita

Grenada

Tobago

Trinidad

Sierra Nevada de Santa Marta

Maracaibo

10

Panamá Canal

G. of Darién

Cord. de Merida

Orinoco

Guiana Highlands

C. Orange

C

Cordillera Occidental
Cordillera Central
Cordillera Oriental

Llanos

Meta

Mt. Roraima 2810

Sierra Pacaraima

Branco

Essequibo

Courantyne

Serra Tumucumaque

C. de San Francisco

Guaviare

Caquetá

Negro

Equator

Cotopaxi 6897

0

Galapagos Is.

Chimborazo 6267

Putumayo

Japurá

Amazon

Marajó I.

Tocantins

D

G. of Guayaquil

Napo

Marañón

Selvas

Juruá

Purus

Madeira

Amazon

Tapajós

Xingu

Araguaia

Parnaiba

C. de São Roque

Pta. Pariñas

Ucayali

Arinuaçá

Roosevelt

Teles Pires

Plat. of Borborema

Pta. Negra

Huascarán 6768

Madre de Dios

Guaporé

Mamoré

Arinos

São Francisco

Brazilian Highlands

10

Chincha Alta

L. Titicaca

Plateau of Mato Grosso

C

Nevada Ancohuma 6560

Bolivian Plateau

L. de Poopó

E

PACIFIC

Andes

Gran Chaco

Paraguay

Paraná

Abrolhos Bank

Serra da Mantiqueira 2890

20

Tropic of Capricorn

Atacama Desert

8050

Cerro Ojos del Salado 6863

Pilcomayo

Pico da Bandeira

C. Frio

San Félix

San Ambrosio

OCEAN

Salinas Grandes

Salado

Paraná

Iguaçu Falls

Uruguay

Serra do Mar

F

Mt. Aconcagua 6960

Sierra de Córdoba

L. Mar Chiquita

Entre Ríos

L. dos Patos

30

Arch. de Juan Fernández

Pampas

Río de la Plata

SOUTH

G

Chile Rise

Chiloé I.

Colorado

Bahía Blanca

ATLANTIC

Negro

G. San Matias

400

Valdés Peninsula

40

Chonos Archipelago

Chubut

Argentine

OCEAN

Taitao Peninsula

Mte. San Valentin 4058

Gulf of San Jorge

Basin

Gulf of Penas

Patagonia

6212

H

Wellington I.

Madre de Dios I.

West Falkland

Falkland Is.

Magellan's Str.

East Falkland

Santa Inés I.

Tierra del Fuego

Staten I.

South Georgia

Canal Cockburn

C. Horn

Canal Beagle

ft m

12000 4000

9000 3000

6000 2000

3000 1000

1500 500

600 200

0 0

200 600

1000 3000

2000 6000

4000 12000

6000 18000

8000 24000

m ft

Projection: Lambert's Azimuthal Equal Area

1 90 2 80 3 70 4 60 West from Greenwich 50 5 6 40 7 20

1 : 35 000 000

| 200 | 0 | 200 | 400 | 600 | 800 miles |
400 | 0 | 400 | 800 | 1200 km

1 **2** **3** **4** **5** **6** **7**

90 80 70 60 50 40

Tropic of Cancer

A

NORTH

Havana CUBA BAHAMAS
Turks & Caicos Is.
(U.K.)

ATLANTIC

Virgin Is.
DOMINICAN (U.K.)
HAITI REP. San Juan
Port-au-
Prince ST. KITTS-
JAMAICA Kingston PUERTO NEVIS ANTIGUA &
RICO BARBUDA
MEXICO (U.S.A.) Basse-Terre GUADELOUPE
BELIZE (Fr.)
DOMINICA
GUATEMALA HONDURAS Fort-de-France MARTINIQUE
Guatemala Tegucigalpa Castries (Fr.)
San Salvador ST. LUCIA
EL SALVADOR NICARAGUA ST. VINCENT BARBADOS
Managua Kingstown Bridgetown
COSTA San José GRENADA St. George's
RICA Port of TRINIDAD &
Panamá Spain TOBAGO

OCEAN

B

Caribbean Sea

C. de Aruba
la Aguja Curaçao
Barranquilla Caracas
Maracaibo
Cartagena Barquisimeto
Cúcuta Valencia
San Cristóbal Orinoco Ciudad Guayana
Bucaramanga Georgetown
Medellín VENEZUELA Paramaribo
Cali Bogotá GUYANA Cayenne
SURINAM C. Orange
COLOMBIA FRENCH
GUIANA
RORAIMA
AMAPÁ
Branco Essequibo
Equator

C

D

Galapagos Is. Quito
(Ecuador) ECUADOR Japurá Amazon Marajó Belém
Guayaquil Napo I.
G. of Guayaquil Putumayo Manaus Santarém
Marañón Iquitos
Juruá Amazon São Luís
AMAZONAS Madeira PARÁ Fortaleza
Chiclayo Purus MARANHÃO C. de
Trujillo Tocantins Teresina São Roque
ACRE CEARÁ Natal
Chimbote Pôrto Velho PIAUÍ RIO G.
PERÚ RONDÔNIA Parnaíba DO NORTE
Callao LIMA BRAZIL Campina Grande PARAÍBA
Cuzco TOCANTINS PERNAMBUCO Recife
L. MATO GROSSO ALAGOAS Maceió
Titicaca BAHÍA SERGIPE
Arequipa BOLIVIA Cuiabá GOIÁS São Francisco Aracaju
La Paz DIS. FED. Brasília Salvador
Cochabamba
Santa Cruz Goiânia
Sucre MINAS GERAIS
Iquique MATO GROSSO Belo
DO SUL Horizonte ESPÍRITO
Ribeirão SANTO
PACIFIC Paraná Prêto Juiz Vitória
Antofagasta Paraná de Fora Campos
PARAGUAY SÃO PAULO R. DE J.
Salta Campinas Niterói
PARANÁ SÃO RIO DE
San Miguel Asunción PAULO JANEIRO
de Tucumán Curitiba

E

F

Tropic of Capricorn

San Félix
(Chile)
San Ambrosio Resistencia SANTA CATARINA
(Chile) Corrientes
Uruguay RIO GRANDE
DO SUL
Córdoba Santa Fe Pôrto Alegre
Viña del Mar San Juan Paraná Pelotas
Arch. de Juan Fernández Valparaíso Mendoza Rosario URUGUAY
(Chile) SANTIAGO Montevideo
BUENOS AIRES
Talca La Plata Río de la Plata

G

OCEAN

Concepción Bahía
Blanca Mar del Plata
Colorado
Valdivia
Negro Viedma
Puerto Montt
Chubut

SOUTH

ATLANTIC

H

Gulf of Penas Comodoro Rivadavia
Gulf of San Jorge

OCEAN

West Falkland FALKLAND IS.
(U.K.)
Stanley
Magellan's Str. East Falkland
Punta Arenas Tierra del Fuego South Georgia
C. Horn (U.K.)

Projection: Lambert's Azimuthal Equal Area 30 CARTOGRAPHY BY PHILIP'S.
COPYRIGHT REED INTERNATIONAL BOOKS LTD

■ LIMA Capital Cities

1 **2** **3** **4** **5** **6** **7**

90 80 70 60 West from Greenwich 50 40

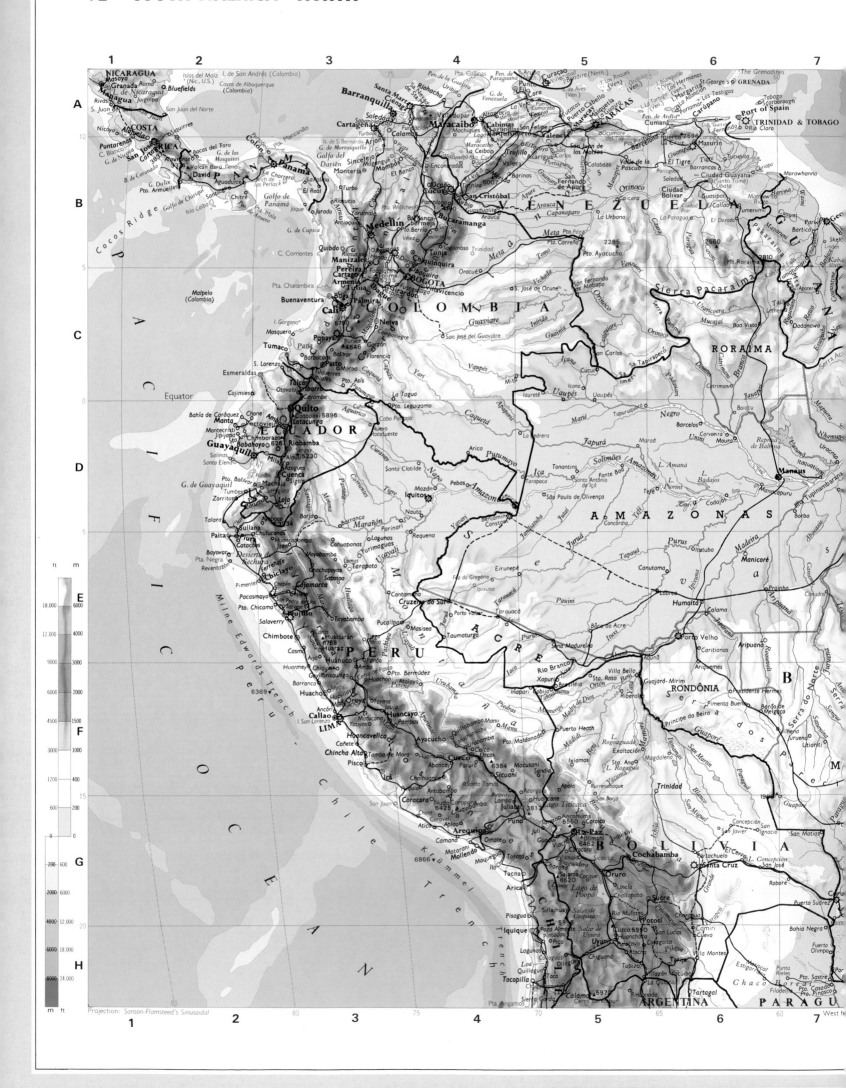

1:16 000 000

100 50 0 100 200 300 miles
100 0 100 200 300 400 km

8 9 10 11 12 13

A

B

C

ATLANTIC

Equator

D

E

6059

F

G

H

88 89
94 95

FR. GUIANA
Paramaribo
Nieuw Amsterdam
Cayenne
St. Laurent
C. Orange
St. Georges

AMAPÁ
Macapá
Mazagão
C. do Norte
Ilha de Maracá
Estuario do Rio Amazonas
Ilha Caviana
Ilha Mexiana
C. Maguarinho

PARÁ
Belém
Santarém
Óbidos
Almeirim
Pôrto de Moz
Monte Alegre
Altamira
Repr. de Tucuruí

Amazonas

MARANHÃO
São Luís
Imperatriz
Bacabal
Caxias
Grajaú
Barra do Corda
Pôrto Franco
Carolina

PIAUÍ
Teresina
Floriano
Parnaíba
Uruçuí
São João do Piauí
Paulistana

CEARÁ
Fortaleza
Sobral
Cascavel
Crateús
Iguatu
Crato
Juàzeiro do Norte

RIO GRANDE DO NORTE
Natal
Macau
Mossoró
C. de São Roque
Rocas

PARAÍBA
João Pessoa
Campina Grande
Cabedelo

PERNAMBUCO
RECIFE
Olinda
Caruaru
Garanhuns
Arcoverde
Petrolina
Juàzeiro

ALAGOAS
Maceió
Arapiraca
Paulo Afonso

SERGIPE
Aracaju
Propriá
Penedo
Estância

BAHIA
Salvador
Feira de Santana
Alagoinhas
Santo Amaro
Jacobina
Barreiras
Bom Jesus da Lapa
Vitória da Conquista
Ilhéus
Jequié
Itabuna
Canavieiras
Belmonte
Pôrto Seguro
Xique-Xique
Represa de Sobradinho

TOCANTINS
Pôrto Nacional
Palmas
Natividade

BRAZIL

GOIÁS
Goiânia
Anápolis
Catalão
Rio Verde

DIST. FEDERAL
Brasília
Formosa

MINAS GERAIS
Belo Horizonte
Uberlândia
Uberaba
Araguari
Montes Claros
Diamantina
Teófilo Otoni
Gov. Valadares
Ipatinga
Araxá
Divinópolis
Ouro Prêto
Juiz de Fora
Poços de Caldas

MATO GROSSO
Planalto do Mato Grosso
Serra do Roncador

MATO GROSSO DO SUL
Campo Grande
Aquidauana
Dourados

SÃO PAULO
Ribeirão Preto
São Carlos
Araraquara
Bauru
Marília
Piracicaba
Campinas
Botucatu

RIO DE JANEIRO
Niterói
Petrópolis
Campos
Cabo Frio
Volta Redonda
Nova Friburgo

ESPÍRITO SANTO
Vitória
Vila Velha
Cariacica
Linhares
São Mateus

Vitória

Fernando de Noronha (Braz.)

Trindade (Braz.)

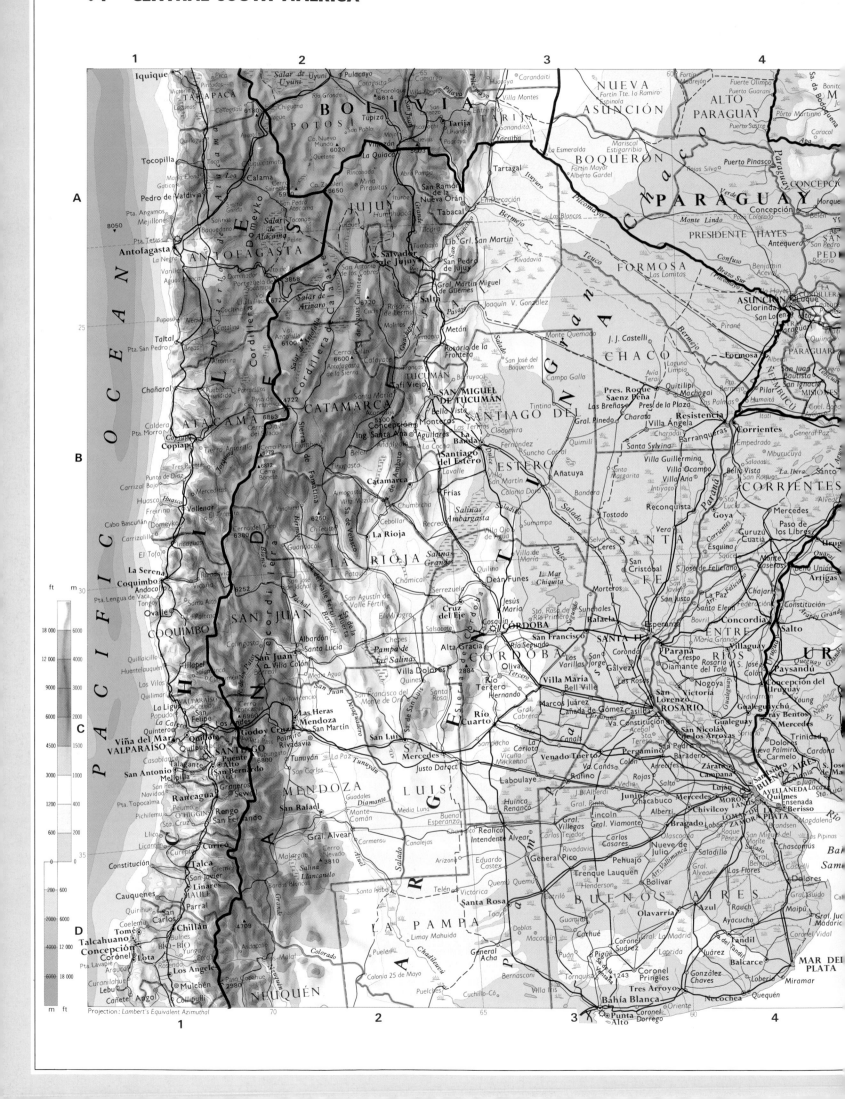

92 93
96

1:8 000 000

50 0 50 100 150 200 miles
50 0 100 200 300 km

ATLANTIC OCEAN

BRAZIL

MATO GROSSO DO SUL

SÃO PAULO

PARANÁ

SANTA CATARINA

RIO GRANDE DO SUL

MISIONES

RIO DE JANEIRO

Tropic of Capricorn

BELO HORIZONTE
Itabirito
Congonhas
Ouro Prêto
Ponte Nova
Vitória
Vila Velha
Guarapari
Cachoeiro de Itapemirim
Castelo
Itaquari
Oliveira
Campo Belo
Cons. Lafaiete
São João del Rei
Ubá
Carangola
Muriaé
Itaperuna
Alegre
Três Lagoas
Andradina
Mirassol
S. José do Rio Prêto
Olímpia
Passos
Batatais
São Seb. do Paraíso
Guaxupé
Três Pontas
Lavras
Barbacena
Juiz de Fora
Cataguases
Além Paraíba
Leopoldina
Guarus
CAMPOS
Cabo de São Tomé
Xavantina
Panorama
Pres. Epitácio
Adamantina
Birigui
Penápolis
Catanduva
Novo Horizonte
Jaboticabal
Mocóca
Casa Branca
Alfenas
Varginha
Três Corações
Pouso Alegre
Juatinga
Santos Dumont
Nova Friburgo
Macaé
Araçatuba
Lins
Tupã
Araraquara
São Carlos
Ribeirão Prêto
Taquaritinga
Pocos de Caldas
Itajubá
Volta Redonda
Barra do Pirai
DUQUE DE CAXIAS
SÃO GONÇALO
NITERÓI
RIO DE JANEIRO
Cabo Frio
L. de Araruama
Presidente Prudente
Martinópolis
Marília
Garça
Jaú
Bariri
Bauru
Rio Claro
São João da Boa Vista
Araras
Pinhal
Mogi-Mirim
Americana
Itajuba
Guaratinguetá
Cruzeiro
Mangaratiba
Mansa
Angra dos Reis
Nova Iguaçu
Paranavaí
Nova Esperança
Rancharia
Assis
Santa Cruz do Rio Pardo
Limeira
CAMPINAS
Ituí
Jundiaí
Taubaté
S. J. dos Campos
Jacareí
Pta. de Juatinga
Ilha Grande
Baía da Ilha Grande
Umuarama
Cianorte
Maringá
Apucarana
Arapongas
Ibaití
Itapetininga
Sorocaba
SÃO PAULO
São Bernardo del Campo
São Vicente
SANTO ANDRÉ
SANTOS
Guarujá
Ilha de São Sebastião
Pta. do Boi
Londrina
Cornélio Procópio
Jacarezinho
Itararé
Itapeva
Paranapiacaba
Registro
Iguape
Ilha Comprida
Ilha do Cardoso
Mandaguari
Campo Mourão
Joaquim Távora
Jaguariaiva
Castro
Itanhaém
Guaíra
Goio-Erê
Pitanga
Ponta Grossa
Palmeira
CURITIBA
Antonina
Paranaguá
Guaratuba
Foz do Iguaçu
Ciudad del Este
Guarapuava
União da Vitória
Irati
Lapa
Rio Negro
Mafra
São Francisco do Sul
Joinvile
Cascavel
Chopim
Pto. União
Palmas
Clevelândia
Caçador
Blumenau
Itajaí
Brusque
SANTA CATARINA
Campos Novos
Rio do Sul
Ilha de Santa Catarina
Florianópolis
Chapecó
Joaçaba
Erechim
Concórdia
Lajes
Passo Fundo
Carazinho
Vacaria
Tubarão
Laguna
Cabo Santa Marta Grande
Criciúma
Araranguá
Cruz Alta
Guaporé
Bento Gonçalves
Caxias do Sul
Santa Maria
Santa Cruz do Sul
Montenegro
Taquara
Nôvo Hamburgo
São Leopoldo
Canoas
Osorio
PORTO ALEGRE
Viamão
Santo Ângelo
São Luís Gonzaga
RIO GRANDE DO SUL
Cachoeira do Sul
Alegrete
São Gabriel
Dom Pedrito
Bagé
Camaquã
Mostardas
Lagoa dos Patos
Santiago
Santa Vitória do Palmar
Santana do Livramento
Rivera
Tacuarembó
Pelotas
Rio Grande
Melo
Jaguarão
Lagoa Mirim
Lagoa Mangueira
Treinta y Tres
Santa Clara de Olimar
Aigua
Rocha
San Carlos
Maldonado
MONTEVIDEO
Rio de la Plata

West from Greenwich

COPYRIGHT GEORGE PHILIP & SON, LTD.

A
B
C
D

5 6 7

55 50 45 40

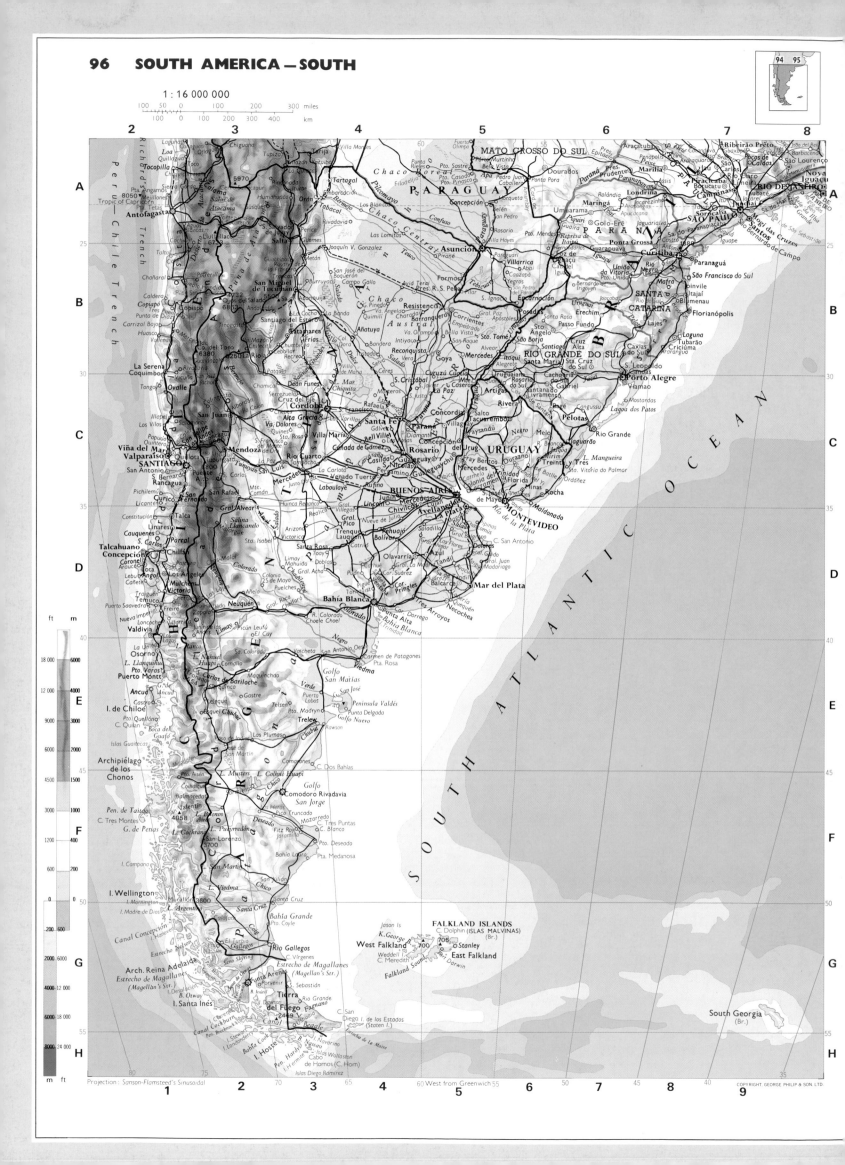

1 : 16 000 000

100 50 0 100 200 300 miles
100 0 100 200 300 400 km

94 95

A

Laguna
Chiguana
Loa
Quillagua
Tocopilla
Toco
Tropic of Capricorn
8050 Pta. Angamos
Antofagasta
Sierra Gorda
Calama
5970
Tupiza
Tarija
Villa Montes
Chaco Boreal
Pto. Sastre
Bela Vista
MATO GROSSO DO SUL
Araçatuba
Penápolis
RIBEIRÃO PRÊTO
Pôços de Caldas
São Carlos
Mogi das Cruzes
RIO DE JANEIRO
Santos

PARAGUAY

Tartagal
Embarcación
Orán
Concepción
Belém
Rosario
Umarama
Maringá
Londrina
PARANÁ
Ponta Grossa
Curitiba
Paranaguá
São Francisco do Sul

B

Copiapó
San Miguel de Tucumán
Santiago del Estero
Chaco
Resistencia
Corrientes
Posadas
Encarnación
RIO GRANDE DO SUL
SANTA CATARINA
Florianópolis
Lajes
Blumenau
Itajaí

C

La Serena
Coquimbo
Ovalle
San Juan
Córdoba
Santa Fe
Paraná
Rosario
URUGUAY
Concepción del Urug.
Porto Alegre
Pelotas
Rio Grande

D

Viña del Mar
Valparaíso
SANTIAGO
Mendoza
San Luis
BUENOS AIRES
Avellaneda
La Plata
MONTEVIDEO
Maldonado
Rocha

Talcahuano
Concepción
Los Angeles
Bahía Blanca
Mar del Plata
Necochea

E

Valdivia
Osorno
Puerto Montt
Ancud
I. de Chiloé
Neuquén
Viedma
Golfo San Matías
Península Valdés
Trelew
Rawson

F

Archipiélago de los Chonos
Comodoro Rivadavia
Golfo San Jorge
Pto. Deseado

G

Río Gallegos
Bahía Grande
Estrecho de Magallanes
(Magellan's Str.)
Punta Arenas
FALKLAND ISLANDS
(ISLAS MALVINAS) (Br.)
West Falkland
East Falkland
Stanley
South Georgia (Br.)

H

Tierra del Fuego
Islas Diego Ramírez
Cabo de Hornos (C. Horn)
Beagle

SOUTH ATLANTIC OCEAN

Projection: Sanson-Flamsteed's Sinusoidal

West from Greenwich

COPYRIGHT. GEORGE PHILIP & SON. LTD.

INDEX

The index contains the names of all the principal places and features shown on the World Maps. Each name is followed by an additional entry in italics giving the country or region within which it is located. The alphabetical order of names composed of two or more words is governed primarily by the first word and then by the second. This is an example of the rule:

Mīr Kūh, *Iran*	**45 E8**	26	22 N	58	55	E
Mīr Shahdād, *Iran*	**45 E8**	26	15 N	58	29	E
Miraj, *India*	**40 L9**	16	50 N	74	45	E
Miram Shah, *Pakistan*	**42 C4**	33	0 N	70	2	E
Miramar, *Mozam.*	**57 C6**	23	50 S	35	35	E

Physical features composed of a proper name (Erie) and a description (Lake) are positioned alphabetically by the proper name. The description is positioned after the proper name and is usually abbreviated:

Erie, L., *N. Amer.*	**78 D3**	42	15 N	81	0 W	

Where a description forms part of a settlement or administrative name, however, it is always written in full and put in its true alphabetic position:

Mount Morris, *U.S.A.*	**78 D7**	42	44 N	77	52 W	

Names beginning with M' and Mc are indexed as if they were spelled Mac. Names beginning St. are alphabetized under Saint, but Sankt, Sint, Sant', Santa and San are all spelled in full and are alphabetized accordingly. If the same place name occurs two or more times in the index and all are in the same country, each is followed by the name of the administrative subdivision in which it is located. The names are placed in the alphabetical order of the subdivisions. For example:

Jackson, *Ky., U.S.A.*	**76 G4**	37	33 N	83	23 W	
Jackson, *Mich., U.S.A.*	**76 D3**	42	15 N	84	24 W	
Jackson, *Minn., U.S.A.*	**80 D7**	43	37 N	95	1 W	

The number in bold type which follows each name in the index refers to the number of the map page where that feature or place will be found. This is usually the largest scale at which the place or feature appears.

The letter and figure which are in bold type immediately after the page number give the grid square on the map page, within which the feature is situated. The letter represents the latitude and the figure the longitude.

In some cases the feature itself may fall within the specified square, while the name is outside. This is usually the case only with features which are larger than a grid square.

For a more precise location the geographical coordinates which follow the letter/figure references give the latitude and the longitude of each place. The first set of figures represent the latitude which is the distance north or south of the Equator measured as an angle at the centre of the Earth. The Equator is latitude 0°, the North Pole is 90°N, and the South Pole 90°S.

The second set of figures represent the longitude, which is the distance East or West of the prime meridian, which runs through Greenwich, England. Longitude is also measured as an angle at the centre of the earth and is given East or West of the prime meridian, from 0° to 180° in either direction.

The unit of measurement for latitude and longitude is the degree, which is subdivided into 60 minutes. Each index entry states the position of a place in degrees and minutes, a space being left between the degrees and the minutes.

The latitude is followed by N(orth) or S(outh) and the longitude by E(ast) or W(est).

Rivers are indexed to their mouths or confluences, and carry the symbol → after their names. A solid square ■ follows the name of a country while, an open square □ refers to a first order administrative area.

Abbreviations used in the index

A.C.T. — Australian Capital Territory
Afghan. — Afghanistan
Ala. — Alabama
Alta. — Alberta
Amer. — America(n)
Arch. — Archipelago
Ariz. — Arizona
Ark. — Arkansas
Atl. Oc. — Atlantic Ocean
B. — Baie, Bahía, Bay, Bucht, Bugt
B.C. — British Columbia
Bangla. — Bangladesh
Barr. — Barrage
Bos. & H. — Bosnia and Herzegovina
C. — Cabo, Cap, Cape, Coast
C.A.R. — Central African Republic
C. Prov. — Cape Province
Calif. — California
Cent. — Central
Chan. — Channel
Colo. — Colorado
Conn. — Connecticut
Cord. — Cordillera
Cr. — Creek
Czech. — Czech Republic
D.C. — District of Columbia
Del. — Delaware
Dep. — Dependency
Des. — Desert
Dist. — District
Dj. — Djebel
Domin. — Dominica
Dom. Rep. — Dominican Republic
E. — East

El Salv. — El Salvador
Eq. Guin. — Equatorial Guinea
Fla. — Florida
Falk. Is. — Falkland Is.
G. — Golfe, Golfo, Gulf, Guba, Gebel
Ga. — Georgia
Gt. — Great, Greater
Guinea-Biss. — Guinea-Bissau
H.K. — Hong Kong
H.P. — Himachal Pradesh
Hants. — Hampshire
Harb. — Harbor, Harbour
Hd. — Head
Hts. — Heights
I.(s). — Île, Ilha, Insel, Isla, Island, Isle
Ill. — Illinois
Ind. — Indiana
Ind. Oc. — Indian Ocean
Ivory C. — Ivory Coast
J. — Jabal, Jebel, Jazira
Junc. — Junction
K. — Kap, Kapp
Kans. — Kansas
Kep. — Kepulauan
Ky. — Kentucky
L. — Lac, Lacul, Lago, Lagoa, Lake, Limni, Loch, Lough
La. — Louisiana
Liech. — Liechtenstein
Lux. — Luxembourg
Mad. P. — Madhya Pradesh
Madag. — Madagascar
Man. — Manitoba
Mass. — Massachusetts

Md. — Maryland
Me. — Maine
Medit. S. — Mediterranean Sea
Mich. — Michigan
Minn. — Minnesota
Miss. — Mississippi
Mo. — Missouri
Mont. — Montana
Mozam. — Mozambique
Mt.(e). — Mont, Monte, Monti, Montaña, Mountain
N. — Nord, Norte, North, Northern, Nouveau
N.B. — New Brunswick
N.C. — North Carolina
N. Cal. — New Caledonia
N. Dak. — North Dakota
N.H. — New Hampshire
N.I. — North Island
N.J. — New Jersey
N. Mex. — New Mexico
N.S. — Nova Scotia
N.S.W. — New South Wales
N.W.T. — North West Territory
N.Y. — New York
N.Z. — New Zealand
Nebr. — Nebraska
Neths. — Netherlands
Nev. — Nevada
Nfld. — Newfoundland
Nic. — Nicaragua
O. — Oued, Ouadi
Occ. — Occidentale
Okla. — Oklahoma
Ont. — Ontario
Or. — Orientale

Oreg. — Oregon
Os. — Ostrov
Oz. — Ozero
P. — Pass, Passo, Pasul, Pulau
P.E.I. — Prince Edward Island
Pa. — Pennsylvania
Pac. Oc. — Pacific Ocean
Papua N.G. — Papua New Guinea
Pass. — Passage
Pen. — Peninsula, Péninsule
Phil. — Philippines
Pk. — Park, Peak
Plat. — Plateau
P-ov. — Poluostrov
Prov. — Province, Provincial
Pt. — Point
Pta. — Ponta, Punta
Pte. — Pointe
Qué. — Québec
Queens. — Queensland
R. — Rio, River
R.I. — Rhode Island
Ra.(s). — Range(s)
Raj. — Rajasthan
Reg. — Region
Rep. — Republic
Res. — Reserve, Reservoir
S. — San, South, Sea
Si. Arabia — Saudi Arabia
S.C. — South Carolina
S. Dak. — South Dakota
S.I. — South Island
S. Leone — Sierra Leone
Sa. — Serra, Sierra
Sask. — Saskatchewan
Scot. — Scotland

Sd. — Sound
Sev. — Severnaya
Sib. — Siberia
Sprs. — Springs
St. — Saint, Sankt, Sint
Sta. — Santa, Station
Ste. — Sainte
Sto. — Santo
Str. — Strait, Stretto
Switz. — Switzerland
Tas. — Tasmania
Tenn. — Tennessee
Tex. — Texas
Tg. — Tanjung
Trin. & Tob. — Trinidad & Tobago
U.A.E. — United Arab Emirates
U.K. — United Kingdom
U.S.A. — United States of America
Ut. P. — Uttar Pradesh
Va. — Virginia
Vdkhr. — Vodokhranilishche
Vf. — Vîrful
Vic. — Victoria
Vol. — Volcano
Vt. — Vermont
W. — Wadi, West
W. Va. — West Virginia
Wash. — Washington
Wis. — Wisconsin
Wlkp. — Wielkopolski
Wyo. — Wyoming
Yorks. — Yorkshire

A Coruña

A

A Coruña = La Coruña, *Spain* **19 A1** 43 20N 8 25W
Aachen, *Germany* **16 C4** 50 45N 6 6 E
Aalborg = Ålborg, *Denmark* **9 H13** 57 2N 9 54 E
Aalen, *Germany* **16 D6** 48 51N 10 6 E
Aalsmeer, *Neths.* **15 B4** 52 17N 4 43 E
Aalst, *Belgium* **15 D4** 50 56N 4 2 E
Aalten, *Neths.* **15 C6** 51 56N 6 35 E
Äänekoski, *Finland* **9 E21** 62 36N 25 44 E
Aarau, *Switz.* **16 E5** 47 23N 8 4 E
Aare →, *Switz.* **16 E5** 47 33N 8 14 E
Aarhus = Århus, *Denmark* **9 H14** 56 8N 10 11 E
Aarschot, *Belgium* **15 D4** 50 59N 4 49 E
Aba, *Nigeria* **50 G6** 5 10N 7 19 E
Aba, *Zaïre* **54 B3** 3 58N 30 17 E
Ābādān, *Iran* **45 D6** 30 22N 48 20 E
Ābādeh, *Iran* **45 D7** 31 8N 52 40 E
Abadla, *Algeria* **50 B4** 31 2N 2 45W
Abaetetuba, *Brazil* **93 D9** 1 40S 48 50W
Abagnar Qi, *China* **34 C9** 43 52N 116 2 E
Abai, *Paraguay* **95 B4** 25 58S 55 54W
Abakan, *Russia* **27 D10** 53 40N 91 10 E
Abancay, *Peru* **92 F4** 13 35S 72 55W
Abariringa, *Kiribati* **64 H10** 2 50S 171 40W
Abarqū, *Iran* **45 D7** 31 10N 53 20 E
Abashiri, *Japan* **30 B12** 44 0N 144 15 E
Abashiri-Wan, *Japan* **30 B12** 44 0N 144 30 E
Abay, *Kazakstan* **26 E8** 49 38N 72 53 E
Abaya, L., *Ethiopia* **51 G12** 6 30N 37 50 E
Abaza, *Russia* **26 D10** 52 39N 90 6 E
'Abbāsābād, *Iran* **45 C8** 33 34N 58 23 E
Abbay = Nîl el Azraq →, *Sudan* **51 E11** 15 38N 32 31 E
Abbaye, Pt., *U.S.A.* **76 B1** 46 58N 88 8W
Abbeville, *France* **18 A4** 50 6N 1 49 E
Abbeville, *La., U.S.A.* **81 K8** 29 58N 92 8W
Abbeville, *S.C., U.S.A.* **77 H4** 34 11N 82 23W
Abbieglassie, *Australia* **63 D4** 27 15S 147 28 E
Abbot Ice Shelf, *Antarctica* **5 D16** 73 0S 92 0W
Abbotsford, *Canada* **72 D4** 49 5N 122 20W
Abbotsford, *U.S.A.* **80 C9** 44 57N 90 19W
Abbottabad, *Pakistan* **42 B5** 34 10N 73 15 E
Abd al Kūrī, *Ind. Oc.* **46 E5** 12 5N 52 20 E
Ābdar, *Iran* **45 D7** 30 16N 55 19 E
'Abdolābād, *Iran* **45 C8** 34 12N 56 30 E
Abéché, *Chad* **51 F9** 13 50N 20 35 E
Åbenrå, *Denmark* **9 J13** 55 3N 9 25 E
Abeokuta, *Nigeria* **50 G5** 7 3N 3 19 E
Aber, *Uganda* **54 B3** 2 12N 32 25 E
Aberaeron, *U.K.* **11 E3** 52 15N 4 15W
Aberayron = Aberaeron, *U.K.* **11 E3** 52 15N 4 15W
Aberconwy & Colwyn □, *U.K.* **10 D4** 53 10N 3 44W
Abercorn = Mbala, *Zambia* **55 D3** 8 46S 31 24 E
Abercorn, *Australia* **63 D5** 25 12S 151 5 E
Aberdare, *U.K.* **11 F4** 51 43N 3 27W
Aberdare Ra., *Kenya* **54 C4** 0 15S 36 50 E
Aberdeen, *Australia* **63 E5** 32 9S 150 56 E
Aberdeen, *Canada* **73 C7** 52 20N 106 8W
Aberdeen, *S. Africa* **56 E3** 32 28S 24 2 E
Aberdeen, *U.K.* **12 D6** 57 9N 2 5W
Aberdeen, *Ala., U.S.A.* **77 J1** 33 49N 88 33W
Aberdeen, *Idaho, U.S.A.* **82 E7** 42 57N 112 50W
Aberdeen, *S. Dak., U.S.A.* **80 C5** 45 28N 98 29W
Aberdeen, *Wash., U.S.A.* **84 D3** 46 59N 123 50W
Aberdeenshire □, *U.K.* **12 D6** 57 17N 2 36W
Aberdovey = Aberdyfi, *U.K.* **11 E3** 52 33N 4 3W
Aberdyfi, *U.K.* **11 E3** 52 33N 4 3W
Aberfeldy, *U.K.* **12 E5** 56 37N 3 51W
Abergavenny, *U.K.* **11 F4** 51 49N 3 1W
Abernathy, *U.S.A.* **81 J4** 33 50N 101 51W
Abert, L., *U.S.A.* **82 E3** 42 38N 120 14W
Aberystwyth, *U.K.* **11 E3** 52 25N 4 5W
Abhar, *Iran* **45 B6** 36 9N 49 13 E
Abhayapuri, *India* **43 F14** 26 24N 90 38 E
Abidjan, *Ivory C.* **50 G4** 5 26N 3 58W
Abilene, *Kans., U.S.A.* **80 F6** 38 55N 97 13W
Abilene, *Tex., U.S.A.* **81 J5** 32 28N 99 43W
Abingdon, *U.K.* **11 F6** 51 40N 1 17W
Abingdon, *Ill., U.S.A.* **80 E9** 40 48N 90 24W
Abingdon, *Va., U.S.A.* **77 G5** 36 43N 81 59W
Abington Reef, *Australia* **62 B4** 18 0S 149 35 E
Abitau →, *Canada* **73 B7** 59 53N 109 3W
Abitau L., *Canada* **73 A7** 60 27N 107 15W
Abitibi L., *Canada* **70 C4** 48 40N 79 40W
Abkhaz Republic □ = Abkhazia □, *Georgia* **25 F7** 43 12N 41 5 E
Abkhazia □, *Georgia* **25 F7** 43 12N 41 5 E
Abkit, *Russia* **27 C16** 64 10N 157 10 E
Abminga, *Australia* **63 D1** 26 8S 134 51 E
Åbo = Turku, *Finland* **9 F20** 60 30N 22 19 E
Abohar, *India* **42 D6** 30 10N 74 10 E
Abomey, *Benin* **50 G5** 7 10N 2 5 E
Abong-Mbang, *Cameroon* **52 D2** 4 0N 13 8 E
Abou-Deïa, *Chad* **51 F8** 11 20N 19 20 E
Aboyne, *U.K.* **12 D6** 57 4N 2 47W
Abra Pampa, *Argentina* **94 A2** 22 43S 65 42W
Abreojos, Pta., *Mexico* **86 B2** 26 50N 113 40W
Abri, *Sudan* **51 D11** 20 50N 30 27 E
Abrolhos, Banka, *Brazil* **93 G11** 18 0S 38 0W
Abrud, *Romania* **17 E12** 46 19N 23 5 E
Absaroka Range, *U.S.A.* **82 D9** 44 45N 109 50W
Abū al Khaşīb, *Iraq* **45 D6** 30 25N 48 0 E
Abū 'Alī, *Si. Arabia* **45 E6** 27 20N 49 27 E
Abū 'Alī →, *Lebanon* **47 A4** 34 25N 35 50 E
Abu 'Arīsh, *Si. Arabia* **46 D3** 16 53N 42 48 E
Abu Dhabi = Abū Ẓāby, *U.A.E.* **45 E7** 24 28N 54 22 E
Abû Dis, *Sudan* **51 E11** 19 12N 33 38 E
Abū Du'ān, *Syria* **44 B3** 36 25N 38 15 E
Abu el Gairi, W. →, *Egypt* **47 F2** 29 35N 33 30 E
Abu Ga'da, W. →, *Egypt* **47 F1** 29 15N 32 53 E
Abū Ḥadrīyah, *Si. Arabia* **45 E6** 27 20N 48 58 E
Abu Hamed, *Sudan* **51 E11** 19 32N 33 13 E
Abū Kamāl, *Syria* **44 C4** 34 30N 41 0 E
Abū Madd, Ra's, *Si. Arabia* **44 E3** 24 50N 37 7 E
Abu Matariq, *Sudan* **51 F10** 10 59N 26 9 E
Abu Şafāt, W. →, *Jordan* **47 E5** 30 24N 36 7 E
Abū Şukhayr, *Iraq* **44 D5** 31 54N 44 30 E
Abu Tig, *Egypt* **51 C11** 27 4N 31 15 E
Abû Zabad, *Sudan* **51 F10** 12 25N 29 10 E
Abū Ẓāby, *U.A.E.* **45 E7** 24 28N 54 22 E
Abū Zeydābād, *Iran* **45 C6** 33 54N 51 45 E
Abuja, *Nigeria* **50 G6** 9 16N 7 2 E
Abukuma-Gawa →, *Japan* **30 E10** 38 6N 140 52 E
Abukuma-Sammyaku, *Japan* **30 F10** 37 30N 140 45 E
Abunã, *Brazil* **92 E5** 9 40S 65 20W
Abunã →, *Brazil* **92 E5** 9 41S 65 20W
Aburo, *Zaïre* **54 B3** 2 4N 30 53 E
Abut Hd., *N.Z.* **59 K3** 43 7S 170 15 E
Abwong, *Sudan* **51 G11** 9 2N 32 14 E
Acajutla, *El Salv.* **88 D2** 13 36N 89 50W
Acámbaro, *Mexico* **86 C4** 20 0N 100 40W
Acaponeta, *Mexico* **86 C3** 22 30N 105 20W
Acapulco, *Mexico* **87 D5** 16 51N 99 56W
Acarigua, *Venezuela* **92 B5** 9 33N 69 12W
Acatlán, *Mexico* **87 D5** 18 10N 98 3W
Acayucan, *Mexico* **87 D6** 17 59N 94 58W
Accomac, *U.S.A.* **76 G8** 37 43N 75 40W
Accra, *Ghana* **50 G4** 5 35N 0 6W
Accrington, *U.K.* **10 D5** 53 45N 2 22W
Acebal, *Argentina* **94 C3** 33 20S 60 50W
Aceh □, *Indonesia* **36 D1** 4 15N 97 30 E
Achalpur, *India* **40 J10** 21 22N 77 32 E
Acheng, *China* **35 B14** 45 30N 126 58 E
Acher, *India* **42 H5** 23 10N 72 32 E
Achill, *Ireland* **13 C2** 53 56N 9 55W
Achill Hd., *Ireland* **13 C1** 53 58N 10 15W
Achill I., *Ireland* **13 C1** 53 58N 10 1W
Achill Sd., *Ireland* **13 C2** 53 54N 9 56W
Achinsk, *Russia* **27 D10** 56 20N 90 20 E
Acireale, *Italy* **20 F6** 37 37N 15 10 E
Ackerman, *U.S.A.* **81 J10** 33 19N 89 11W
Acklins I., *Bahamas* **89 B5** 22 30N 74 0W
Acme, *Canada* **72 C6** 51 33N 113 30W
Aconcagua, Cerro, *Argentina* **94 C2** 32 39S 70 0W
Aconquija, Mt., *Argentina* **94 B2** 27 0S 66 0W
Açores, Is. dos = Azores, *Atl. Oc.* **48 C1** 38 44N 29 0W
Acraman, L., *Australia* **63 E2** 32 2S 135 23 E
Acre = 'Akko, *Israel* **47 C4** 32 55N 35 4 E
Acre □, *Brazil* **92 E4** 9 1S 71 0W
Acre →, *Brazil* **92 E5** 8 45S 67 22W
Acton, *Canada* **78 C4** 43 38N 80 3W
Ad Dammām, *Si. Arabia* **45 E6** 26 20N 50 5 E
Ad Dawhah, *Qatar* **45 E6** 25 15N 51 35 E
Ad Dawr, *Iraq* **44 C4** 34 27N 43 47 E
Ad Dir'īyah, *Si. Arabia* **44 E5** 24 44N 46 35 E
Ad Dīwānīyah, *Iraq* **44 D5** 32 0N 45 0 E
Ad Dujayl, *Iraq* **44 C5** 33 51N 44 14 E
Ad Durūz, J., *Jordan* **47 C5** 32 35N 36 40 E
Ada, *Minn., U.S.A.* **80 B6** 47 18N 96 31W
Ada, *Okla., U.S.A.* **81 H6** 34 46N 96 41W
Adaja →, *Spain* **19 B3** 41 32N 4 52W
Adamaoua, Massif de l', *Cameroon* **51 G7** 7 20N 12 20 E
Adamawa Highlands = Adamaoua, Massif de l', *Cameroon* **51 G7** 7 20N 12 20 E
Adamello, Mte., *Italy* **20 A4** 46 9N 10 30 E
Adaminaby, *Australia* **63 F4** 36 0S 148 45 E
Adams, *Mass., U.S.A.* **79 D11** 42 38N 73 7W
Adams, *N.Y., U.S.A.* **79 C8** 43 49N 76 1W
Adams, *Wis., U.S.A.* **80 D10** 43 57N 89 49W
Adam's Bridge, *Sri Lanka* **40 Q11** 9 15N 79 40 E
Adams L., *Canada* **72 C5** 51 10N 119 40W
Adams Mt., *U.S.A.* **84 D5** 46 12N 121 30W
Adam's Peak, *Sri Lanka* **40 R12** 6 48N 80 30 E
Adana, *Turkey* **25 G6** 37 0N 35 16 E
Adapazarı, *Turkey* **25 F5** 40 48N 30 25 E
Adarama, *Sudan* **51 E11** 17 10N 34 52 E
Adare, C., *Antarctica* **5 D11** 71 0S 171 0 E
Adaut, *Indonesia* **37 F8** 8 8S 131 7 E
Adavale, *Australia* **63 D3** 25 52S 144 32 E
Adda →, *Italy* **20 B3** 45 8N 9 53 E
Addis Ababa = Addis Abeba, *Ethiopia* **51 G12** 9 2N 38 42 E
Addis Abeba, *Ethiopia* **51 G12** 9 2N 38 42 E
Addis Alem, *Ethiopia* **51 G12** 9 0N 38 17 E
Addison, *U.S.A.* **78 D7** 42 1N 77 14W
Addo, *S. Africa* **56 E4** 33 32S 25 45 E
Ādeh, *Iran* **44 B5** 37 42N 45 11 E
Adel, *U.S.A.* **77 K4** 31 8N 83 25W
Adelaide, *Australia* **63 E2** 34 52S 138 30 E
Adelaide, *Bahamas* **88 A4** 25 4N 77 31W
Adelaide, *S. Africa* **56 E4** 32 42S 26 20 E
Adelaide I., *Antarctica* **5 C17** 67 15S 68 30W
Adelaide Pen., *Canada* **68 B10** 68 15N 97 30W
Adelaide River, *Australia* **60 B5** 13 15S 131 7 E
Adelanto, *U.S.A.* **85 L9** 34 35N 117 22W
Adele I., *Australia* **60 C3** 15 32S 123 9 E
Adélie, Terre, *Antarctica* **5 C10** 68 0S 140 0 E
Adélie Land = Adélie, Terre, *Antarctica* **5 C10** 68 0S 140 0 E
Aden = Al 'Adan, *Yemen* **46 E4** 12 45N 45 0 E
Aden, G. of, *Asia* **46 E4** 12 30N 47 30 E
Adendorp, *S. Africa* **56 E3** 32 15S 24 30 E
Adh Dhayd, *U.A.E.* **45 E7** 25 17N 55 53 E
Adhoi, *India* **42 H4** 23 26N 70 32 E
Adi, *Indonesia* **37 E8** 4 15S 133 30 E
Adi Ugri, *Eritrea* **51 F12** 14 58N 38 48 E
Adieu, C., *Australia* **61 F5** 32 0S 132 10 E
Adieu Pt., *Australia* **60 C3** 15 14S 124 35 E
Adige →, *Italy* **20 B5** 45 9N 12 20 E
Adilabad, *India* **40 K11** 19 33N 78 20 E
Adin, *U.S.A.* **82 F3** 41 12N 120 57W
Adin Khel, *Afghan.* **40 C6** 32 45N 68 5 E
Adirondack Mts., *U.S.A.* **79 C10** 44 0N 74 0W
Adjumani, *Uganda* **54 B3** 3 20N 31 50 E
Adlavik Is., *Canada* **71 B8** 55 2N 57 45W
Admer, *Algeria* **50 D6** 20 21N 5 27 E
Admiralty G., *Australia* **60 B4** 14 20S 125 55 E
Admiralty I., *U.S.A.* **68 C6** 57 30N 134 30W
Admiralty Inlet, *U.S.A.* **82 C2** 48 8N 122 58W
Admiralty Is., *Papua N. G.* **64 H6** 2 0S 147 0 E
Ado-Ekiti, *Nigeria* **50 G6** 7 38N 5 12 E
Adonara, *Indonesia* **37 F6** 8 15S 123 5 E
Adoni, *India* **40 M10** 15 33N 77 18 E
Adour →, *France* **18 E3** 43 32N 1 32W
Adra, *India* **43 H12** 23 30N 86 42 E
Adra, *Spain* **19 D4** 36 43N 3 3W
Adrano, *Italy* **20 F6** 37 40N 14 50 E
Adrar, *Algeria* **50 C4** 27 51N 0 11W
Adré, *Chad* **51 F9** 13 40N 22 20 E
Adrī, *Libya* **51 C7** 27 32N 13 2 E
Adrian, *Mich., U.S.A.* **76 E3** 41 54N 84 2W
Adrian, *Tex., U.S.A.* **81 H3** 35 16N 102 40W
Adriatic Sea, *Medit. S.* **20 C6** 43 0N 16 0 E
Adua, *Indonesia* **37 E7** 1 45S 129 50 E
Adwa, *Ethiopia* **51 F12** 14 15N 38 52 E
Adzhar Republic □ = Ajaria □, *Georgia* **25 F7** 41 30N 42 0 E
Ægean Sea, *Medit. S.* **21 E11** 38 30N 25 0 E
Aerhtai Shan, *Mongolia* **32 B4** 46 40N 92 45 E
'Afak, *Iraq* **44 C5** 32 4N 45 15 E
Afándou, *Greece* **23 C10** 36 18N 28 12 E
Afghanistan ■, *Asia* **40 C4** 33 0N 65 0 E
Afgoi, *Somali Rep.* **46 G3** 2 7N 44 59 E
Afognak I., *U.S.A.* **68 C4** 58 15N 152 30W
'Afrīn, *Syria* **44 B3** 36 32N 36 50 E
Afton, *U.S.A.* **79 D9** 42 14N 75 32W
Afuá, *Brazil* **93 D8** 0 15S 50 20W
Afula, *Israel* **47 C4** 32 37N 35 17 E
Afyonkarahisar, *Turkey* **25 G5** 38 45N 30 33 E
Agadès = Agadez, *Niger* **50 E6** 16 58N 7 59 E
Agadez, *Niger* **50 E6** 16 58N 7 59 E
Agadir, *Morocco* **50 B3** 30 28N 9 55W
Agaete, *Canary Is.* **22 F4** 28 6N 15 43W
Agapa, *Russia* **27 B9** 71 27N 89 15 E
Agar, *India* **42 H7** 23 40N 76 2 E
Agartala, *India* **41 H17** 23 50N 91 23 E
Agassiz, *Canada* **72 D4** 49 14N 121 46W
Agats, *Indonesia* **37 F9** 5 33S 138 0 E
Agboville, *Ivory C.* **50 G4** 5 55N 4 15W
Agde, *France* **18 E5** 43 19N 3 28 E
Agen, *France* **18 D4** 44 12N 0 38 E
Āgh Kand, *Iran* **45 B6** 37 15N 48 4 E
Aginskoye, *Russia* **27 D12** 51 6N 114 32 E
Agra, *India* **42 F7** 27 17N 77 58 E
Agri →, *Italy* **20 D7** 40 13N 16 44 E
Ağrı Dağı, *Turkey* **25 G7** 39 50N 44 15 E
Ağrı Karakose, *Turkey* **25 G7** 39 44N 43 3 E
Agrigento, *Italy* **20 F5** 37 19N 13 34 E
Agrinion, *Greece* **21 E9** 38 37N 21 27 E
Agua Caliente, *Baja Calif., Mexico* **85 N10** 32 29N 116 59W
Agua Caliente, *Sinaloa, Mexico* **86 B3** 26 30N 108 20W
Agua Caliente Springs, *U.S.A.* **85 N10** 32 56N 116 19W
Água Clara, *Brazil* **93 H8** 20 25S 52 45W
Agua Hechicero, *Mexico* **85 N10** 32 26N 116 14W
Agua Prieta, *Mexico* **86 A3** 31 20N 109 32W
Aguadas, *Colombia* **92 B3** 5 40N 75 38W
Aguadilla, *Puerto Rico* **89 C6** 18 26N 67 10W
Aguadulce, *Panama* **88 E3** 8 15N 80 32W
Aguanga, *U.S.A.* **85 M10** 33 27N 116 51W
Aguanish, *Canada* **71 B7** 50 14N 62 2W
Aguanus →, *Canada* **71 B7** 50 13N 62 5W
Aguapey →, *Argentina* **94 B4** 29 7S 56 36W
Aguaray Guazú →, *Paraguay* **94 A4** 24 47S 57 19W
Aguarico →, *Ecuador* **92 D3** 0 59S 75 11W
Aguas Blancas, *Chile* **94 A2** 24 15S 69 55W
Aguas Calientes, Sierra de, *Argentina* **94 B2** 25 26S 66 40W
Aguascalientes, *Mexico* **86 C4** 21 53N 102 12W
Aguascalientes □, *Mexico* **86 C4** 22 0N 102 20W
Aguilares, *Argentina* **94 B2** 27 26S 65 35W
Aguilas, *Spain* **19 D5** 37 23N 1 35W
Agüimes, *Canary Is.* **22 G4** 27 58N 15 27W
Aguja, C. de la, *Colombia* **90 B3** 11 18N 74 12W
Agulhas, C., *S. Africa* **56 E3** 34 52S 20 0 E
Agulo, *Canary Is.* **22 F2** 28 11N 17 12W
Agung, *Indonesia* **36 F5** 8 20S 115 28 E
Agur, *Uganda* **54 B3** 2 28N 32 55 E
Agusan →, *Phil.* **37 C7** 9 0N 125 30 E
Aha Mts., *Botswana* **56 B3** 19 45S 21 0 E
Ahaggar, *Algeria* **50 D6** 23 0N 6 30 E
Ahar, *Iran* **44 B5** 38 35N 47 0 E
Ahipara B., *N.Z.* **59 F4** 35 5S 173 5 E
Ahiri, *India* **40 K12** 19 30N 80 0 E
Ahmad Wal, *Pakistan* **42 E1** 29 18N 65 58 E
Ahmadabad, *India* **42 H5** 23 0N 72 40 E
Aḥmadābād, *Khorāsān, Iran* **45 C9** 35 3N 60 50 E
Aḥmadābād, *Khorāsān, Iran* **45 C8** 35 49N 59 42 E
Aḥmadī, *Iran* **45 E8** 27 56N 56 42 E
Ahmadnagar, *India* **40 K9** 19 7N 74 46 E
Ahmadpur, *Pakistan* **42 E4** 29 12N 71 10 E
Ahmedabad = Ahmadabad, *India* **42 H5** 23 0N 72 40 E
Ahmednagar = Ahmadnagar, *India* **40 K9** 19 7N 74 46 E
Ahome, *Mexico* **86 B3** 25 55N 109 11W
Ahram, *Iran* **45 D6** 28 52N 51 16 E
Ahrax Pt., *Malta* **23 D1** 35 59N 14 22 E
Āhū, *Iran* **45 C6** 34 33N 50 2 E
Ahuachapán, *El Salv.* **88 D2** 13 54N 89 52W
Ahvāz, *Iran* **45 D6** 31 20N 48 40 E
Ahvenanmaa = Åland, *Finland* **9 F19** 60 15N 20 0 E
Aḥwar, *Yemen* **46 E4** 13 30N 46 40 E
Aichi □, *Japan* **31 G8** 35 0N 137 15 E
Aigua, *Uruguay* **95 C5** 34 13S 54 46W
Aigues-Mortes, *France* **18 E6** 43 35N 4 12 E
Aihui, *China* **33 A7** 50 10N 127 30 E
Aija, *Peru* **92 E3** 9 50S 77 45W
Aikawa, *Japan* **30 E9** 38 2N 138 15 E
Aiken, *U.S.A.* **77 J5** 33 34N 81 43W
Aillik, *Canada* **71 A8** 55 11N 59 18W
Ailsa Craig, *U.K.* **12 F3** 55 15N 5 6W
'Ailūn, *Jordan* **47 C4** 32 18N 35 47 E
Aim, *Russia* **27 D14** 59 0N 133 55 E
Aimere, *Indonesia* **37 F6** 8 45S 121 3 E
Aimogasta, *Argentina* **94 B2** 28 33S 66 50W
Aimorés, *Brazil* **93 G10** 19 30S 41 4W
Aïn Beïda, *Algeria* **50 A6** 35 50N 7 29 E
Aïn Ben Tili, *Mauritania* **50 C3** 25 59N 9 27W
Aïn-Sefra, *Algeria* **50 B4** 32 47N 0 37W
'Ain Sudr, *Egypt* **47 F2** 29 50N 33 6 E
Ainabo, *Somali Rep.* **46 F4** 9 0N 46 25 E
Ainaži, *Latvia* **9 H21** 57 50N 24 24 E
Ainsworth, *U.S.A.* **80 D5** 42 33N 99 52W
Aïr, *Niger* **50 E6** 18 30N 8 0 E
Air Hitam, *Malaysia* **39 M4** 1 55N 103 11 E
Airdrie, *U.K.* **12 F5** 55 52N 3 57W
Aire →, *U.K.* **10 D7** 53 43N 0 55W
Aire, I. del, *Spain* **22 B11** 39 48N 4 16 E
Airlie Beach, *Australia* **62 C4** 20 16S 148 43 E
Aisne →, *France* **18 B5** 49 26N 2 50 E
Aitkin, *U.S.A.* **80 B8** 46 32N 93 42W
Aiud, *Romania* **17 E12** 46 19N 23 44 E
Aix-en-Provence, *France* **18 E6** 43 32N 5 27 E
Aix-la-Chapelle = Aachen, *Germany* **16 C4** 50 45N 6 6 E
Aix-les-Bains, *France* **18 D6** 45 41N 5 53 E
Aiyansh, *Canada* **72 B3** 55 17N 129 2W
Aiyion, *Greece* **21 E10** 38 15N 22 5 E
Aizawl, *India* **41 H18** 23 40N 92 44 E
Aizkraukle, *Latvia* **9 H21** 56 36N 25 11 E
Aizpute, *Latvia* **9 H19** 56 43N 21 40 E
Aizuwakamatsu, *Japan* **30 F9** 37 30N 139 56 E
Ajaccio, *France* **18 F8** 41 55N 8 40 E
Ajalpan, *Mexico* **87 D5** 18 22N 97 15W
Ajanta Ra., *India* **40 J9** 20 28N 75 50 E
Ajari Rep. = Ajaria □, *Georgia* **25 F7** 41 30N 42 0 E
Ajaria □, *Georgia* **25 F7** 41 30N 42 0 E
Ajax, *Canada* **78 C5** 43 50N 79 1W
Ajdâbiyah, *Libya* **51 B9** 30 54N 20 4 E
Ajka, *Hungary* **17 E9** 47 4N 17 31 E
'Ajmān, *U.A.E.* **45 E7** 25 25N 55 30 E
Ajmer, *India* **42 F6** 26 28N 74 37 E
Ajo, *U.S.A.* **83 K7** 32 22N 112 52W
Ajo, C. de, *Spain* **19 A4** 43 31N 3 35W
Akabira, *Japan* **30 C11** 43 33N 142 5 E
Akamas □, *Cyprus* **23 D11** 35 3N 32 18 E
Akanthou, *Cyprus* **23 D12** 35 22N 33 45 E
Akaroa, *N.Z.* **59 K4** 43 49S 172 59 E
Akashi, *Japan* **31 G7** 34 45N 134 58 E
Akelamo, *Indonesia* **37 D7** 1 35N 129 40 E
Aketi, *Zaïre* **52 D4** 2 38N 23 47 E
Akharnaí, *Greece* **21 E10** 38 5N 23 44 E
Akhelóös →, *Greece* **21 E9** 38 19N 21 7 E
Akhisar, *Turkey* **21 E12** 38 56N 27 48 E
Akhmîm, *Egypt* **51 C11** 26 31N 31 47 E
Akhnur, *India* **43 C6** 32 52N 74 45 E
Aki, *Japan* **31 H6** 33 30N 133 54 E
Akimiski I., *Canada* **70 B3** 52 50N 81 30W
Akita, *Japan* **30 E10** 39 45N 140 7 E
Akita □, *Japan* **30 E10** 39 40N 140 30 E
Akjoujt, *Mauritania* **50 E2** 19 45N 14 15W
Akkeshi, *Japan* **30 C12** 43 2N 144 51 E
'Akko, *Israel* **47 C4** 32 55N 35 4 E
Akkol, *Kazakstan* **26 E8** 45 0N 75 39 E
Aklavik, *Canada* **68 B6** 68 12N 135 0W
Akmolinsk = Aqmola, *Kazakstan* **26 D8** 51 10N 71 30 E
Akō, *Japan* **31 G7** 34 45N 134 24 E
Akobo →, *Ethiopia* **51 G11** 7 48N 33 3 E
Akola, *India* **40 J10** 20 42N 77 2 E
Akordat, *Eritrea* **51 E12** 15 30N 37 40 E
Akpatok I., *Canada* **69 B13** 60 25N 68 8W
Åkrahamn, *Norway* **9 G11** 59 15N 5 10 E
Akranes, *Iceland* **8 D2** 64 19N 22 5W
Akreïjit, *Mauritania* **50 E3** 18 19N 9 11W
Akron, *Colo., U.S.A.* **80 E3** 40 10N 103 13W
Akron, *Ohio, U.S.A.* **78 E3** 41 5N 81 31W
Akrotiri, *Cyprus* **23 E11** 34 36N 32 57 E
Akrotiri Bay, *Cyprus* **23 E12** 34 35N 33 10 E
Aksai Chin, *India* **43 B8** 35 15N 79 55 E
Aksarka, *Russia* **26 C7** 66 31N 67 50 E
Aksay, *Kazakstan* **24 D9** 51 11N 53 0 E
Aksenovo Zilovskoye, *Russia* **27 D12** 53 20N 117 40 E
Aksu, *China* **32 B3** 41 5N 80 10 E
Aksum, *Ethiopia* **51 F12** 14 5N 38 40 E
Aktogay, *Kazakstan* **26 E8** 46 57N 79 40 E
Aktsyabrski, *Belarus* **17 B15** 52 38N 28 53 E
Aktyubinsk = Aqtöbe, *Kazakstan* **25 D10** 50 17N 57 10 E
Aku, *Nigeria* **50 G6** 6 40N 7 18 E
Akure, *Nigeria* **50 G6** 7 15N 5 5 E
Akureyri, *Iceland* **8 D4** 65 40N 18 6W
Akuseki-Shima, *Japan* **31 K4** 29 27N 129 37 E
Akyab = Sittwe, *Burma* **41 J18** 20 18N 92 45 E
Al 'Adan, *Yemen* **46 E4** 12 45N 45 0 E
Al Aḥsā, *Si. Arabia* **45 E6** 25 50N 49 0 E
Al Ajfar, *Si. Arabia* **44 E4** 27 26N 43 0 E
Al Amādīyah, *Iraq* **44 B4** 37 5N 43 30 E
Al Amārah, *Iraq* **44 D5** 31 55N 47 15 E
Al 'Aqabah, *Jordan* **47 F4** 29 31N 35 0 E
Al Arak, *Syria* **44 C3** 34 38N 38 35 E
Al 'Aramah, *Si. Arabia* **44 E5** 25 30N 46 0 E
Al Arṭāwīyah, *Si. Arabia* **44 E5** 26 31N 45 20 E
Al 'Āşimah □, *Jordan* **47 D5** 31 40N 36 30 E
Al' Assāfīyah, *Si. Arabia* **44 D3** 28 17N 38 59 E
Al 'Ayn, *Oman* **45 E7** 24 15N 55 45 E
Al 'Ayn, *Si. Arabia* **44 E3** 25 4N 38 6 E
Al A'ẓamīyah, *Iraq* **44 C5** 33 22N 44 22 E
Al 'Azīzīyah, *Iraq* **44 C5** 32 54N 45 4 E
Al Bāb, *Syria* **44 B3** 36 23N 37 29 E
Al Bad', *Si. Arabia* **44 D2** 28 28N 35 1 E
Al Bādī, *Iraq* **44 C4** 35 56N 41 32 E
Al Baḥrah, *Kuwait* **44 D5** 29 40N 47 52 E
Al Balqā' □, *Jordan* **47 C4** 32 5N 35 45 E
Al Bārūk, J., *Lebanon* **47 B4** 33 39N 35 40 E
Al Başrah, *Iraq* **44 D5** 30 30N 47 50 E
Al Baṭḥā, *Iraq* **44 D5** 31 6N 45 53 E
Al Batrūn, *Lebanon* **47 A4** 34 15N 35 40 E
Al Bayḍā, *Libya* **51 B9** 32 50N 21 44 E
Al Biqā □, *Lebanon* **47 A5** 34 10N 36 10 E
Al Bi'r, *Si. Arabia* **44 D3** 28 51N 36 16 E
Al Bu'ayrāt al Ḥasūn, *Libya* **51 B8** 31 24N 15 44 E
Al Burayj, *Syria* **47 A5** 34 15N 36 46 E
Al Fallūjah, *Iraq* **44 C4** 33 20N 43 55 E
Al Fāw, *Iraq* **45 D6** 30 0N 48 30 E
Al Fujayrah, *U.A.E.* **45 E8** 25 7N 56 18 E
Al Ghadaf, W. →, *Jordan* **47 D5** 31 26N 36 43 E
Al Ghammās, *Iraq* **44 D5** 31 45N 44 37 E

Amadi

Al Hābah, *Si. Arabia* **44 E5** 27 10N 47 0 E
Al Ḩadīthah, *Iraq* **44 C4** 34 0N 41 13 E
Al Ḩadīthah, *Si. Arabia* **44 D3** 31 28N 37 8 E
Al Hājānah, *Syria* **47 B5** 33 20N 36 33 E
Al Ḩāmad, *Si. Arabia* **44 D3** 31 30N 39 30 E
Al Hamdānīyah, *Syria* **44 C3** 35 25N 36 50 E
Al Hamīdīyah, *Syria* **47 A4** 34 42N 35 57 E
Al Ḩammār, *Iraq* **44 D5** 30 57N 46 51 E
Al Ḩarīr, W. →, *Syria* **47 C4** 32 44N 35 59 E
Al Ḩasā, W. →, *Jordan* **47 D4** 31 4N 35 29 E
Al Ḩasakah, *Syria* **44 B4** 36 35N 40 45 E
Al Ḩawrah, *Yemen* **46 E4** 13 50N 47 35 E
Al Haydān, W. →, *Jordan* **47 D4** 31 29N 35 34 E
Al Ḩayy, *Iraq* **44 C5** 32 5N 46 5 E
Al Ḩijāz, *Si. Arabia* **46 B2** 26 0N 37 30 E
Al Ḩillah, *Iraq* **44 C5** 32 30N 44 25 E
Al Ḩillah, *Si. Arabia* **46 C4** 23 35N 46 50 E
Al Hirmil, *Lebanon* **47 A5** 34 26N 36 24 E
Al Hoceïma, *Morocco* **50 A4** 35 8N 3 58W
Al Ḩudaydah, *Yemen* **46 E3** 14 50N 43 0 E
Al Hufūf, *Si. Arabia* **45 E6** 25 25N 49 45 E
Al Ḩumayḑah, *Si. Arabia* **44 D2** 29 14N 34 56 E
Al Ḩunayy, *Si. Arabia* **45 E6** 25 58N 48 45 E
Al Īsāwīyah, *Si. Arabia* **44 D3** 30 43N 37 59 E
Al Ittihad = Madīnat ash Sha'b, *Yemen* **46 E3** 12 50N 45 0 E
Al Jafr, *Jordan* **47 E5** 30 18N 36 14 E
Al Jaghbūb, *Libya* **51 C9** 29 42N 24 38 E
Al Jahrah, *Kuwait* **44 D5** 29 25N 47 40 E
Al Jalāmīd, *Si. Arabia* **44 D3** 31 20N 39 45 E
Al Jamalīyah, *Qatar* **45 E6** 25 37N 51 5 E
Al Janūb □, *Lebanon* **47 B4** 33 20N 35 20 E
Al Jawf, *Libya* **51 D9** 24 10N 23 24 E
Al Jawf, *Si. Arabia* **44 D3** 29 55N 39 40 E
Al Jazirah, *Iraq* **44 C5** 33 30N 44 0 E
Al Jazirah, *Libya* **51 C9** 26 10N 21 20 E
Al Jithāmīyah, *Si. Arabia* **44 E4** 27 41N 41 43 E
Al Jubayl, *Si. Arabia* **45 E6** 27 0N 49 50 E
Al Jubaylah, *Si. Arabia* **44 E5** 24 55N 46 25 E
Al Jubb, *Si. Arabia* **44 E4** 27 11N 42 17 E
Al Junaynah, *Sudan* **51 F9** 13 27N 22 45 E
Al Kabā'ish, *Iraq* **44 D5** 30 58N 47 0 E
Al Karak, *Jordan* **47 D4** 31 11N 35 42 E
Al Karak □, *Jordan* **47 E5** 31 0N 36 0 E
Al Kāzim Tyah, *Iraq* **44 C5** 33 22N 44 12 E
Al Khalīl, *West Bank* **47 D4** 31 32N 35 6 E
Al Khawr, *Qatar* **45 E6** 25 41N 51 30 E
Al Khiḑr, *Iraq* **44 D5** 31 12N 45 33 E
Al Khiyām, *Lebanon* **47 B4** 33 20N 35 36 E
Al Kiswah, *Syria* **47 B5** 33 23N 36 14 E
Al Kufrah, *Libya* **51 D9** 24 17N 23 15 E
Al Kuhayfiyah, *Si. Arabia* **44 E4** 27 12N 43 3 E
Al Kūt, *Iraq* **44 C5** 32 30N 46 0 E
Al Kuwayt, *Kuwait* **44 D5** 29 30N 48 0 E
Al Labwah, *Lebanon* **47 A5** 34 11N 36 20 E
Al Lādhiqīyah, *Syria* **44 C2** 35 30N 35 45 E
Al Liwā', *Oman* **45 E8** 24 31N 56 36 E
Al Luḩayyah, *Yemen* **46 D3** 15 45N 42 40 E
Al Madīnah, *Iraq* **44 D5** 30 57N 47 16 E
Al Madīnah, *Si. Arabia* **46 C2** 24 35N 39 52 E
Al-Mafraq, *Jordan* **47 C5** 32 17N 36 14 E
Al Maḩmūdīyah, *Iraq* **44 C5** 33 3N 44 21 E
Al Majma'ah, *Si. Arabia* **44 E5** 25 57N 45 22 E
Al Makhruq, W. →, *Jordan* **47 D6** 31 28N 37 0 E
Al Makḩūl, *Si. Arabia* **44 E4** 26 37N 42 39 E
Al Manāmah, *Bahrain* **45 E6** 26 10N 50 30 E
Al Maqwa', *Kuwait* **44 D5** 29 10N 47 59 E
Al Marj, *Libya* **51 B9** 32 25N 20 30 E
Al Maṭlā, *Kuwait* **44 D5** 29 24N 47 40 E
Al Mawjib, W. →, *Jordan* **47 D4** 31 28N 35 36 E
Al Mawşil, *Iraq* **44 B4** 36 15N 43 5 E
Al Mayādin, *Syria* **44 C4** 35 1N 40 27 E
Al Mazār, *Jordan* **47 D4** 31 4N 35 41 E
Al Midhnab, *Si. Arabia* **44 E5** 25 50N 44 18 E
Al Minā', *Lebanon* **47 A4** 34 24N 35 49 E
Al Miqdādīyah, *Iraq* **44 C5** 34 0N 45 0 E
Al Mubarraz, *Si. Arabia* **45 E6** 25 30N 49 40 E
Al Mughayrā', *U.A.E.* **45 E7** 24 5N 53 32 E
Al Muḩarraq, *Bahrain* **45 E6** 26 15N 50 40 E
Al Mukallā, *Yemen* **46 E4** 14 33N 49 2 E
Al Mukhā, *Yemen* **46 E3** 13 18N 43 15 E
Al Musayjīd, *Si. Arabia* **44 E3** 24 5N 39 5 E
Al Musayyib, *Iraq* **44 C5** 32 49N 44 20 E
Al Muwayliḩ, *Si. Arabia* **44 E2** 27 40N 35 30 E
Al Qā'im, *Iraq* **44 C4** 34 21N 41 7 E
Al Qalībah, *Si. Arabia* **44 D3** 28 24N 37 42 E
Al Qaryatayn, *Syria* **47 A6** 34 12N 37 13 E
Al Qaşabāt, *Libya* **51 B7** 32 39N 14 1 E
Al Qaṭ'ā, *Syria* **44 C4** 34 40N 40 48 E
Al Qaṭīf, *Si. Arabia* **45 E6** 26 35N 50 0 E
Al Qaṭrānah, *Jordan* **47 D5** 31 12N 36 6 E
Al Qaṭrūn, *Libya* **51 D8** 24 56N 15 3 E
Al Qayşūmah, *Si. Arabia* **44 D5** 28 20N 46 7 E
Al Quds = Jerusalem, *Israel* **47 D4** 31 47N 35 10 E
Al Qunaytirah, *Syria* **47 C4** 32 55N 35 45 E
Al Qurnah, *Iraq* **44 D5** 31 1N 47 25 E
Al Quşayr, *Iraq* **44 D5** 30 39N 45 50 E
Al Quşayr, *Syria* **47 A5** 34 31N 36 34 E
Al Qutayfah, *Syria* **47 B5** 33 44N 36 36 E
Al' Uḑaylīyah, *Si. Arabia* **45 E6** 25 8N 49 18 E
Al 'Ulā, *Si. Arabia* **44 E3** 26 35N 38 0 E
Al Uqaylah ash Sharqīgah, *Libya* **51 B8** 30 12N 19 10 E
Al Uqayr, *Si. Arabia* **45 E6** 25 40N 50 15 E
Al 'Uwaynid, *Si. Arabia* **44 E5** 24 50N 46 0 E
Al 'Uwayqīlah, *Si. Arabia* **44 D4** 30 30N 42 10 E
Al 'Uyūn, *Si. Arabia* **44 E4** 26 30N 43 50 E
Al 'Uyūn, *Si. Arabia* **44 E3** 24 33N 39 35 E
Al Wajh, *Si. Arabia* **44 E3** 26 10N 36 30 E
Al Wakrah, *Qatar* **45 E6** 25 10N 51 40 E
Al Wannān, *Si. Arabia* **45 E6** 26 55N 48 24 E
Al Waqbah, *Si. Arabia* **44 D5** 28 48N 45 33 E
Al Wari'āh, *Si. Arabia* **44 E5** 27 51N 47 25 E
Al Wusayl, *Qatar* **45 E6** 25 29N 51 29 E
Ala Tau Shankou = Dzhungarskiye Vorota, *Kazakstan* **32 B3** 45 0N 82 0 E
Alabama □, *U.S.A.* **77 J2** 33 0N 87 0W
Alabama →, *U.S.A.* **77 K2** 31 8N 87 57W
Alaçam Dağları, *Turkey* **21 E13** 39 18N 28 49 E
Alaérma, *Greece* **23 C9** 36 9N 27 57 E
Alagoa Grande, *Brazil* **93 E11** 7 3S 35 35W
Alagoas □, *Brazil* **93 E11** 9 0S 36 0W
Alagoinhas, *Brazil* **93 F11** 12 7S 38 20W
Alajero, *Canary Is.* **22 F2** 28 3N 17 13W
Alajuela, *Costa Rica* **88 D3** 10 2N 84 8W
Alakamisy, *Madag.* **57 C8** 21 19S 47 14 E
Alakurtti, *Russia* **24 A5** 67 0N 30 30 E
Alameda, *Calif., U.S.A.* **84 H4** 37 46N 122 15W
Alameda, *N. Mex., U.S.A.* **83 J10** 35 11N 106 37W
Alamo, *U.S.A.* **85 J11** 36 21N 115 10W
Alamo Crossing, *U.S.A.* **85 L13** 34 16N 113 33W
Alamogordo, *U.S.A.* **83 K11** 32 54N 105 57W
Alamos, *Mexico* **86 B3** 27 0N 109 0W
Alamosa, *U.S.A.* **83 H11** 37 28N 105 52W
Åland, *Finland* **9 F19** 60 15N 20 0 E
Ålands hav, *Sweden* **9 F18** 60 0N 19 30 E
Alandur, *India* **40 N12** 13 0N 80 15 E
Alania = North Ossetia □, *Russia* **25 F7** 43 30N 44 30 E
Alanya, *Turkey* **25 G5** 36 38N 32 0 E
Alaotra, Farihin', *Madag.* **57 B8** 17 30S 48 30 E
Alapayevsk, *Russia* **26 D7** 57 52N 61 42 E
Alaşehir, *Turkey* **21 E13** 38 23N 28 30 E
Alaska □, *U.S.A.* **68 B5** 64 0N 154 0W
Alaska, G. of, *Pac. Oc.* **68 C5** 58 0N 145 0W
Alaska Highway, *Canada* **72 B3** 60 0N 130 0W
Alaska Peninsula, *U.S.A.* **68 C4** 56 0N 159 0W
Alaska Range, *U.S.A.* **68 B4** 62 50N 151 0W
Älät, *Azerbaijan* **25 G8** 39 58N 49 25 E
Alatyr, *Russia* **24 D8** 54 55N 46 35 E
Alausi, *Ecuador* **92 D3** 2 0S 78 50W
Alava, C., *U.S.A.* **82 B1** 48 10N 124 44W
Alavus, *Finland* **9 E20** 62 35N 23 36 E
Alawoona, *Australia* **63 E3** 34 45S 140 30 E
'Alayh, *Lebanon* **47 B4** 33 46N 35 33 E
Alayor, *Spain* **22 B11** 39 57N 4 8 E
Alba, *Italy* **20 B3** 44 42N 8 2 E
Alba-Iulia, *Romania* **17 E12** 46 8N 23 39 E
Albacete, *Spain* **19 C5** 39 0N 1 50W
Albacutya, L., *Australia* **63 F3** 35 45S 141 58 E
Albania ■, *Europe* **21 D9** 41 0N 20 0 E
Albany, *Australia* **61 G2** 35 1S 117 58 E
Albany, *Ga., U.S.A.* **77 K3** 31 35N 84 10W
Albany, *Minn., U.S.A.* **80 C7** 45 38N 94 34W
Albany, *N.Y., U.S.A.* **79 D11** 42 39N 73 45W
Albany, *Oreg., U.S.A.* **82 D2** 44 38N 123 6W
Albany, *Tex., U.S.A.* **81 J5** 32 44N 99 18W
Albany →, *Canada* **70 B3** 52 17N 81 31W
Albardón, *Argentina* **94 C2** 31 20S 68 30W
Albatross B., *Australia* **62 A3** 12 45S 141 30 E
Albemarle, *U.S.A.* **77 H5** 35 21N 80 11W
Albemarle Sd., *U.S.A.* **77 H7** 36 5N 76 0W
Alberche →, *Spain* **19 C3** 39 58N 4 46W
Alberdi, *Paraguay* **94 B4** 26 14S 58 20W
Albert, L., *Australia* **63 F2** 35 30S 139 10 E
Albert Canyon, *Canada* **72 C5** 51 8N 117 41W
Albert Edward Ra., *Australia* **60 C4** 18 17S 127 57 E
Albert L., *Africa* **54 B3** 1 30N 31 0 E
Albert Lea, *U.S.A.* **80 D8** 43 39N 93 22W
Albert Nile →, *Uganda* **54 B3** 3 36N 32 2 E
Albert Town, *Bahamas* **89 B5** 22 37N 74 33W
Alberta □, *Canada* **72 C6** 54 40N 115 0W
Alberti, *Argentina* **94 D3** 35 1S 60 16W
Albertinia, *S. Africa* **56 E3** 34 11S 21 34 E
Alberton, *Canada* **71 C7** 46 50N 64 0W
Albertville = Kalemie, *Zaïre* **54 D2** 5 55S 29 9 E
Albertville, *France* **18 D7** 45 40N 6 22 E
Albi, *France* **18 E5** 43 56N 2 9 E
Albia, *U.S.A.* **80 E8** 41 2N 92 48W
Albina, *Surinam* **93 B8** 5 37N 54 15W
Albina, Ponta, *Angola* **56 B1** 15 52S 11 44 E
Albion, *Idaho, U.S.A.* **82 E7** 42 25N 113 35W
Albion, *Mich., U.S.A.* **76 D3** 42 15N 84 45W
Albion, *Nebr., U.S.A.* **80 E5** 41 42N 98 0W
Albion, *Pa., U.S.A.* **78 E4** 41 53N 80 22W
Alborán, *Medit. S.* **19 E4** 35 57N 3 0W
Ålborg, *Denmark* **9 H13** 57 2N 9 54 E
Alborz, Reshteh-ye Kūhhā-ye, *Iran* **45 C7** 36 0N 52 0 E
Albreda, *Canada* **72 C5** 52 35N 119 10W
Albuquerque, *U.S.A.* **83 J10** 35 5N 106 39W
Albuquerque, Cayos de, *Caribbean* **88 D3** 12 10N 81 50W
Alburg, *U.S.A.* **79 B11** 44 59N 73 18W
Albury, *Australia* **63 F4** 36 3S 146 56 E
Alcalá de Henares, *Spain* **19 B4** 40 28N 3 22W
Alcalá la Real, *Spain* **19 D4** 37 27N 3 57W
Alcamo, *Italy* **20 F5** 37 59N 12 55 E
Alcaniz, *Spain* **19 B5** 41 2N 0 8W
Alcântara, *Brazil* **93 D10** 2 20S 44 30W
Alcántara, Embalse de, *Spain* **19 C2** 39 44N 6 50W
Alcantara L., *Canada* **73 A7** 60 57N 108 9W
Alcantarilla, *Spain* **19 D5** 37 59N 1 12W
Alcaraz, Sierra de, *Spain* **19 C4** 38 40N 2 20W
Alcaudete, *Spain* **19 D3** 37 35N 4 5W
Alcázar de San Juan, *Spain* **19 C4** 39 24N 3 12W
Alchevsk, *Ukraine* **25 E6** 48 30N 38 45 E
Alcira, *Spain* **19 C5** 39 9N 0 30W
Alcoa, *U.S.A.* **77 H4** 35 48N 83 59W
Alcova, *U.S.A.* **82 E10** 42 34N 106 43W
Alcoy, *Spain* **19 C5** 38 43N 0 30W
Alcudia, *Spain* **22 B10** 39 51N 3 7 E
Alcudia, B. de, *Spain* **22 B10** 39 47N 3 15 E
Aldabra Is., *Seychelles* **49 G8** 9 22S 46 28 E
Aldama, *Mexico* **87 C5** 23 0N 98 4W
Aldan, *Russia* **27 D13** 58 40N 125 30 E
Aldan →, *Russia* **27 C13** 63 28N 129 35 E
Aldea, Pta. de la, *Canary Is.* **22 G4** 28 0N 15 50W
Aldeburgh, *U.K.* **11 E9** 52 10N 1 37 E
Alder, *U.S.A.* **82 D7** 45 19N 112 6W
Alder Pk., *U.S.A.* **84 K5** 35 53N 121 22W
Alderney, *U.K.* **11 H5** 49 42N 2 11W
Aldershot, *U.K.* **11 F7** 51 15N 0 44W
Aledo, *U.S.A.* **80 E9** 41 12N 90 45W
Aleg, *Mauritania* **50 E2** 17 3N 13 55W
Alegranza, *Canary Is.* **22 E6** 29 23N 13 32W
Alegranza, I., *Canary Is.* **22 E6** 29 23N 13 32W
Alegre, *Brazil* **95 A7** 20 50S 41 30W
Alegrete, *Brazil* **95 B4** 29 40S 56 0W
Aleisk, *Russia* **26 D9** 52 40N 83 0 E
Aleksandriya = Oleksandriya, *Ukraine* **17 C14** 50 37N 26 19 E
Aleksandrovsk-Sakhalinskiy, *Russia* **27 D15** 50 50N 142 20 E
Aleksandrovskiy Zavod, *Russia* **27 D12** 50 40N 117 50 E
Aleksandrovskoye, *Russia* **26 C8** 60 35N 77 50 E
Além Paraíba, *Brazil* **95 A7** 21 52S 42 41W
Alemania, *Argentina* **94 B2** 25 40S 65 30W
Alemania, *Chile* **94 B2** 25 10S 69 55W
Alençon, *France* **18 B4** 48 27N 0 4 E
Alenuihaha Channel, *U.S.A.* **74 H17** 20 30N 156 0W
Aleppo = Ḩalab, *Syria* **44 B3** 36 10N 37 15 E
Alert Bay, *Canada* **72 C3** 50 30N 126 55W
Alès, *France* **18 D6** 44 9N 4 5 E
Alessándria, *Italy* **20 B3** 44 54N 8 37 E
Ålesund, *Norway* **9 E12** 62 28N 6 12 E
Aleutian Is., *Pac. Oc.* **68 C2** 52 0N 175 0W
Aleutian Trench, *Pac. Oc.* **64 B10** 48 0N 180 0 E
Alexander, *U.S.A.* **80 B3** 47 51N 103 39W
Alexander, Mt., *Australia* **61 E3** 28 58S 120 16 E
Alexander Arch., *U.S.A.* **72 B2** 56 0N 136 0W
Alexander Bay, *S. Africa* **56 D2** 28 40S 16 30 E
Alexander City, *U.S.A.* **77 J3** 32 56N 85 58W
Alexander I., *Antarctica* **5 C17** 69 0S 70 0W
Alexandra, *Australia* **63 F4** 37 8S 145 40 E
Alexandra, *N.Z.* **59 L2** 45 14S 169 25 E
Alexandra Falls, *Canada* **72 A5** 60 29N 116 18W
Alexandria = El Iskandarîya, *Egypt* **51 B10** 31 13N 29 58 E
Alexandria, *Australia* **62 B2** 19 5S 136 40 E
Alexandria, *B.C., Canada* **72 C4** 52 35N 122 27W
Alexandria, *Ont., Canada* **70 C5** 45 19N 74 38W
Alexandria, *Romania* **17 G13** 43 57N 25 24 E
Alexandria, *S. Africa* **56 E4** 33 38S 26 28 E
Alexandria, *Ind., U.S.A.* **76 E3** 40 16N 85 41W
Alexandria, *La., U.S.A.* **81 K8** 31 18N 92 27W
Alexandria, *Minn., U.S.A.* **80 C7** 45 53N 95 22W
Alexandria, *S. Dak., U.S.A.* **80 D6** 43 39N 97 47W
Alexandria, *Va., U.S.A.* **76 F7** 38 48N 77 3W
Alexandria Bay, *U.S.A.* **79 B9** 44 20N 75 55W
Alexandrina, L., *Australia* **63 F2** 35 25S 139 10 E
Alexandroúpolis, *Greece* **21 D11** 40 50N 25 54 E
Alexis →, *Canada* **71 B8** 52 33N 56 8W
Alexis Creek, *Canada* **72 C4** 52 10N 123 20W
Alfabia, *Spain* **22 B9** 39 44N 2 44 E
Alfenas, *Brazil* **95 A6** 21 20S 46 10W
Alford, *U.K.* **12 D6** 57 14N 2 41W
Alfred, *Maine, U.S.A.* **79 C14** 43 29N 70 43W
Alfred, *N.Y., U.S.A.* **78 D7** 42 16N 77 48W
Alfreton, *U.K.* **10 D6** 53 6N 1 24W
Alga, *Kazakstan* **25 E10** 49 53N 57 20 E
Algaida, *Spain* **22 B9** 39 33N 2 53 E
Ålgård, *Norway* **9 G11** 58 46N 5 53 E
Algarve, *Portugal* **19 D1** 36 58N 8 20W
Algeciras, *Spain* **19 D3** 36 9N 5 28W
Algemesí, *Spain* **19 C5** 39 11N 0 27W
Alger, *Algeria* **50 A5** 36 42N 3 8 E
Algeria ■, *Africa* **50 C5** 28 30N 2 0 E
Alghero, *Italy* **20 D3** 40 33N 8 19 E
Algiers = Alger, *Algeria* **50 A5** 36 42N 3 8 E
Algoa B., *S. Africa* **56 E4** 33 50S 25 45 E
Algoma, *U.S.A.* **76 C2** 44 36N 87 26W
Algona, *U.S.A.* **80 D7** 43 4N 94 14W
Algonac, *U.S.A.* **78 D2** 42 37N 82 32W
Alhambra, *U.S.A.* **74 D3** 34 8N 118 6W
Alhucemas = Al Hoceïma, *Morocco* **50 A4** 35 8N 3 58W
'Alī al Gharbī, *Iraq* **44 C5** 32 30N 46 45 E
'Alī ash Sharqī, *Iraq* **44 C5** 32 7N 46 44 E
'Alī Khēl, *Afghan.* **42 C3** 33 57N 69 43 E
'Alī Shāh, *Iran* **44 B5** 38 9N 45 50 E
'Alīābād, *Khorāsān, Iran* **45 C8** 32 30N 57 30 E
'Alīābād, *Kordestān, Iran* **44 C5** 35 4N 46 58 E
'Alīābād, *Yazd, Iran* **45 D7** 31 41N 53 49 E
Aliağa, *Turkey* **21 E12** 38 47N 26 59 E
Aliákmon →, *Greece* **21 D10** 40 30N 22 36 E
Alibo, *Ethiopia* **51 G12** 9 52N 37 5 E
Alicante, *Spain* **19 C5** 38 23N 0 30W
Alice, *S. Africa* **56 E4** 32 48S 26 55 E
Alice, *U.S.A.* **81 M5** 27 45N 98 5W
Alice →, *Queens., Australia* **62 C3** 24 2S 144 50 E
Alice →, *Queens., Australia* **62 B3** 15 35S 142 20 E
Alice Arm, *Canada* **72 B3** 55 29N 129 31W
Alice Downs, *Australia* **60 C4** 17 45S 127 56 E
Alice Springs, *Australia* **62 C1** 23 40S 133 50 E
Alicedale, *S. Africa* **56 E4** 33 15S 26 4 E
Aliceville, *U.S.A.* **77 J1** 33 8N 88 9W
Alick Cr. →, *Australia* **62 C3** 20 55S 142 20 E
Alida, *Canada* **73 D8** 49 25N 101 55W
Aligarh, *Raj., India* **42 G7** 25 55N 76 15 E
Aligarh, *Ut. P., India* **42 F8** 27 55N 78 10 E
Alīgūdarz, *Iran* **45 C6** 33 25N 49 45 E
Alimnía, *Greece* **23 C9** 36 16N 27 43 E
Alingsås, *Sweden* **9 H15** 57 56N 12 31 E
Alipur, *Pakistan* **42 E4** 29 25N 70 55 E
Alipur Duar, *India* **41 F16** 26 30N 89 35 E
Aliquippa, *U.S.A.* **78 F4** 40 37N 80 15W
Alitus = Alytus, *Lithuania* **9 J21** 54 24N 24 3 E
Aliwal North, *S. Africa* **56 E4** 30 45S 26 45 E
Alix, *Canada* **72 C6** 52 24N 113 11W
Aljustrel, *Portugal* **19 D1** 37 55N 8 10W
Alkmaar, *Neths.* **15 B4** 52 37N 4 45 E
All American Canal, *U.S.A.* **83 K6** 32 45N 115 15W
Allah Dad, *Pakistan* **42 G2** 25 38N 67 34 E
Allahabad, *India* **43 G9** 25 25N 81 58 E
Allakh-Yun, *Russia* **27 C14** 60 50N 137 5 E
Allan, *Canada* **73 C7** 51 53N 106 4W
Allanmyo, *Burma* **41 K19** 19 30N 95 17 E
Allanridge, *S. Africa* **56 D4** 27 45S 26 40 E
Allanwater, *Canada* **70 B1** 50 14N 90 10W
Allegan, *U.S.A.* **76 D3** 42 32N 85 51W
Allegany, *U.S.A.* **78 D6** 42 6N 78 30W
Allegheny →, *U.S.A.* **78 F5** 40 27N 80 1W
Allegheny Mts., *U.S.A.* **76 G6** 38 15N 80 10W
Allegheny Plateau, *U.S.A.* **76 G6** 38 0N 80 0W
Allegheny Reservoir, *U.S.A.* **78 E6** 41 50N 79 0W
Allen, Bog of, *Ireland* **13 C4** 53 15N 7 0W
Allen, L., *Ireland* **13 B3** 54 8N 8 4W
Allende, *Mexico* **86 B4** 28 20N 100 50W
Allentown, *U.S.A.* **79 F9** 40 37N 75 29W
Alleppey, *India* **40 Q10** 9 30N 76 28 E
Aller →, *Germany* **16 B5** 52 56N 9 12 E
Alliance, *Nebr., U.S.A.* **80 D3** 42 6N 102 52W
Alliance, *Ohio, U.S.A.* **78 F3** 40 55N 81 6W
Allier →, *France* **18 C5** 46 57N 3 4 E
Alliston, *Canada* **70 D4** 44 9N 79 52W
Alloa, *U.K.* **12 E5** 56 7N 3 47W
Allora, *Australia* **63 D5** 28 2S 152 0 E
Alluitsup Paa = Sydprøven, *Greenland* **4 C5** 60 30N 45 35W
Alma, *Canada* **71 C5** 48 35N 71 40W
Alma, *Ga., U.S.A.* **77 K4** 31 33N 82 28W
Alma, *Kans., U.S.A.* **80 F6** 39 1N 96 17W
Alma, *Mich., U.S.A.* **76 D3** 43 23N 84 39W
Alma, *Nebr., U.S.A.* **80 E5** 40 6N 99 22W
Alma, *Wis., U.S.A.* **80 C9** 44 20N 91 55W
Alma Ata = Almaty, *Kazakstan* **26 E8** 43 15N 76 57 E
Almada, *Portugal* **19 C1** 38 40N 9 9W
Almaden, *Australia* **62 B3** 17 22S 144 40 E
Almadén, *Spain* **19 C3** 38 49N 4 52W
Almanor, L., *U.S.A.* **82 F3** 40 14N 121 9W
Almansa, *Spain* **19 C5** 38 51N 1 5W
Almanzor, Pico del Moro, *Spain* **19 B3** 40 15N 5 18W
Almanzora →, *Spain* **19 D5** 37 14N 1 46W
Almaty, *Kazakstan* **26 E8** 43 15N 76 57 E
Almazán, *Spain* **19 B4** 41 30N 2 30W
Almeirim, *Brazil* **93 D8** 1 30S 52 34W
Almelo, *Neths.* **15 B6** 52 22N 6 42 E
Almendralejo, *Spain* **19 C2** 38 41N 6 26W
Almería, *Spain* **19 D4** 36 52N 2 27W
Almirante, *Panama* **88 E3** 9 10N 82 30W
Almiroú, Kólpos, *Greece* **23 D6** 35 23N 24 20 E
Almont, *U.S.A.* **78 D1** 42 55N 83 3W
Almonte, *Canada* **79 A8** 45 14N 76 12W
Almora, *India* **43 E8** 29 38N 79 40 E
Alnwick, *U.K.* **10 B6** 55 24N 1 42W
Aloi, *Uganda* **54 B3** 2 16N 33 10 E
Alon, *Burma* **41 H19** 22 12N 95 5 E
Alor, *Indonesia* **37 F6** 8 15S 124 30 E
Alor Setar, *Malaysia* **39 J3** 6 7N 100 22 E
Aloysius, Mt., *Australia* **61 E4** 26 0S 128 38 E
Alpaugh, *U.S.A.* **84 K7** 35 53N 119 29W
Alpena, *U.S.A.* **76 C4** 45 4N 83 27W
Alpha, *Australia* **62 C4** 23 39S 146 37 E
Alpine, *Ariz., U.S.A.* **83 K9** 33 51N 109 9W
Alpine, *Calif., U.S.A.* **85 N10** 32 50N 116 46W
Alpine, *Tex., U.S.A.* **81 K3** 30 22N 103 40W
Alps, *Europe* **16 E5** 46 30N 9 30 E
Alroy Downs, *Australia* **62 B2** 19 20S 136 5 E
Alsace, *France* **18 B7** 48 15N 7 25 E
Alsask, *Canada* **73 C7** 51 21N 109 59W
Alsásua, *Spain* **19 A4** 42 54N 2 10W
Alsten, *Norway* **8 D15** 65 58N 12 40 E
Alta, *Norway* **8 B20** 69 57N 23 10 E
Alta Gracia, *Argentina* **94 C3** 31 40S 64 30W
Alta Lake, *Canada* **72 C4** 50 10N 123 0W
Alta Sierra, *U.S.A.* **85 K8** 35 42N 118 33W
Altaelva →, *Norway* **8 B20** 69 54N 23 17 E
Altafjorden, *Norway* **8 A20** 70 5N 23 5 E
Altagracia, *Venezuela* **92 A4** 10 45N 71 30W
Altai = Aerhtai Shan, *Mongolia* **32 B4** 46 40N 92 45 E
Altamaha →, *U.S.A.* **77 K5** 31 20N 81 20W
Altamira, *Brazil* **93 D8** 3 12S 52 10W
Altamira, *Chile* **94 B2** 25 47S 69 51W
Altamira, *Mexico* **87 C5** 22 24N 97 55W
Altamont, *U.S.A.* **79 D10** 42 43N 74 3W
Altamura, *Italy* **20 D7** 40 49N 16 33 E
Altanbulag, *Mongolia* **32 A5** 50 16N 106 30 E
Altar, *Mexico* **86 A2** 30 40N 111 50W
Altata, *Mexico* **86 C3** 24 30N 108 0W
Altavista, *U.S.A.* **76 G6** 37 6N 79 17W
Altay, *China* **32 B3** 47 48N 88 10 E
Altea, *Spain* **19 C5** 38 38N 0 2W
Alto Araguaia, *Brazil* **93 G8** 17 15S 53 20W
Alto Cuchumatanes = Cuchumatanes, Sierra de los, *Guatemala* **88 C1** 15 35N 91 25W
Alto del Inca, *Chile* **94 A2** 24 10S 68 10W
Alto Ligonha, *Mozam.* **55 F4** 15 30S 38 11 E
Alto Molocue, *Mozam.* **55 F4** 15 50S 37 35 E
Alto Paraguay □, *Paraguay* **94 A4** 21 0S 58 30W
Alto Paraná □, *Paraguay* **95 B5** 25 30S 54 50W
Alton, *Canada* **78 C4** 43 54N 80 5W
Alton, *U.S.A.* **80 F9** 38 53N 90 11W
Alton Downs, *Australia* **63 D2** 26 7S 138 57 E
Altoona, *U.S.A.* **78 F6** 40 31N 78 24W
Altūn Kūprī, *Iraq* **44 C5** 35 45N 44 9 E
Altun Shan, *China* **32 C3** 38 30N 88 0 E
Alturas, *U.S.A.* **82 F3** 41 29N 120 32W
Altus, *U.S.A.* **81 H5** 34 38N 99 20W
Alūksne, *Latvia* **9 H22** 57 24N 27 3 E
Alùla, *Somali Rep.* **46 E5** 11 50N 50 45 E
Alunite, *U.S.A.* **85 K12** 35 59N 114 55W
Alusi, *Indonesia* **37 F8** 7 35S 131 40 E
Al'Uzayr, *Iraq* **44 D5** 31 19N 47 25 E
Alva, *U.S.A.* **81 G5** 36 48N 98 40W
Alvarado, *Mexico* **87 D5** 18 40N 95 50W
Alvarado, *U.S.A.* **81 J6** 32 24N 97 13W
Alvaro Obregón, Presa, *Mexico* **86 B3** 27 55N 109 52W
Alvear, *Argentina* **94 B4** 29 5S 56 30W
Alvesta, *Sweden* **9 H16** 56 54N 14 35 E
Alvie, *Australia* **63 F3** 38 14S 143 30 E
Alvin, *U.S.A.* **81 L7** 29 26N 95 15W
Alvinston, *Canada* **78 D3** 42 49N 81 52W
Älvkarleby, *Sweden* **9 F17** 60 34N 17 26 E
Älvsbyn, *Sweden* **8 D19** 65 40N 21 0 E
Alwar, *India* **42 F7** 27 38N 76 34 E
Alxa Zuoqi, *China* **34 E3** 38 50N 105 40 E
Alyaskitovyy, *Russia* **27 C15** 64 45N 141 30 E
Alyata = Älät, *Azerbaijan* **25 G8** 39 58N 49 25 E
Alyth, *U.K.* **12 E5** 56 38N 3 13W
Alytus, *Lithuania* **9 J21** 54 24N 24 3 E
Alzada, *U.S.A.* **80 C2** 45 2N 104 25W
Am Dam, *Chad* **51 F9** 12 40N 20 35 E
Am-Timan, *Chad* **51 F9** 11 0N 20 10 E
Amadeus, L., *Australia* **61 D5** 24 54S 131 0 E
Amâdi, *Sudan* **51 G11** 5 29N 30 25 E
Amadi, *Zaïre* **54 B2** 3 40N 26 40 E

Amadjuak

Amadjuak, *Canada* **69 B12** 64 0N 72 39W
Amadjuak L., *Canada* ... **69 B12** 65 0N 71 8W
Amagasaki, *Japan* ...... **31 G7** 34 42N 135 20 E
Amakusa-Shotō, *Japan* .. **31 H5** 32 15N 130 10 E
Åmål, *Sweden* .... **9 G15** 59 3N 12 42 E
Amaliás, *Greece* .... **21 F9** 37 47N 21 22 E
Amalner, *India* .... **40 J9** 21 5N 75 5 E
Amambaí, *Brazil* **95 A4** 23 5S 55 13W
Amambaí →, *Brazil* **95 A5** 23 22S 53 56W
Amambay □, *Paraguay* .. **95 A4** 23 0S 56 0W
Amambay, Cordillera de,
S. Amer. **95 A4** 23 0S 55 45W
Amami-Guntō, *Japan* ... **31 L4** 27 16N 129 21 E
Amami-Ō-Shima, *Japan* . **31 L4** 28 0N 129 0 E
Amanda Park, *U.S.A.* **84 C3** 47 28N 123 55W
Amangeldy, *Kazakstan* .. **26 D7** 50 10N 65 10 E
Amapá, *Brazil* **93 C8** 2 5N 50 50W
Amapá □, *Brazil* **93 C8** 1 40N 52 0W
Amarante, *Brazil* **93 E10** 6 14S 42 50W
Amaranth, *Canada* **73 C9** 50 36N 98 43W
Amargosa, *Brazil* **93 F11** 13 2S 39 36W
Amargosa →, *U.S.A.* **85 J10** 36 14N 116 51W
Amargosa Range, *U.S.A.* **85 J10** 36 20N 116 45W
Amári, *Greece* .... **23 D6** 35 13N 24 40 E
Amarillo, *U.S.A.* **81 H4** 35 13N 101 50W
Amaro, Mte., *Italy* ...... **20 C6** 42 5N 14 5 E
Amarpur, *India* .... **43 G12** 25 5N 87 0 E
Amatikulu, *S. Africa* .... **57 D5** 29 3S 31 33 E
Amatitlán, *Guatemala* ... **88 D1** 14 29N 90 38W
Amazon = Amazonas →,
S. Amer. **93 C9** 0 5S 50 0W
Amazonas □, *Brazil* **92 E6** 5 0S 65 0W
Amazonas →, *S. Amer.* **93 C9** 0 5S 50 0W
Ambahakily, *Madag.* .... **57 C7** 21 36S 43 41 E
Ambala, *India* .... **42 D7** 30 23N 76 56 E
Ambalavao, *Madag.* .... **57 C8** 21 50S 46 56 E
Ambalindum, *Australia* .. **62 C2** 23 23S 135 0 E
Ambam, *Cameroon* ..... **52 D2** 2 20N 11 15 E
Ambanja, *Madag.* ...... **57 A8** 13 40S 48 27 E
Ambarchik, *Russia* ...... **27 C17** 69 40N 162 20 E
Ambarijeby, *Madag.* .... **57 A8** 14 56S 47 41 E
Ambaro, Helodranon',
Madag. .... **57 A8** 13 23S 48 38 E
Ambartsevo, *Russia* ..... **26 D9** 57 30N 83 52 E
Ambato, *Ecuador* **92 D3** 1 5S 78 42W
Ambato, Sierra de,
Argentina **94 B2** 28 25S 66 10W
Ambato Boeny, *Madag.* . **57 B8** 16 28S 46 43 E
Ambatofinandrahana,
Madag. .... **57 C8** 20 33S 46 48 E
Ambatolampy, *Madag.* .. **57 B8** 19 20S 47 35 E
Ambatondrazaka, *Madag.* **57 B8** 17 55S 48 28 E
Ambatosoratra, *Madag.* . **57 B8** 17 37S 48 31 E
Ambenja, *Madag.* ...... **57 B8** 15 17S 46 58 E
Amberg, *Germany* ...... **16 D6** 49 26N 11 52 E
Ambergris Cay, *Belize* ... **87 D7** 18 0N 88 0W
Amberley, *N.Z.* .... **59 K4** 43 9S 172 44 E
Ambikapur, *India* .... **43 H10** 23 15N 83 15 E
Ambilobé, *Madag.* ...... **57 A8** 13 10S 49 3 E
Ambinanindrano, *Madag.* **57 C8** 20 5S 48 23 E
Ambleside, *U.K.* **10 C5** 54 26N 2 58W
Ambo, *Peru* **92 F3** 10 5S 76 10W
Ambodifototra, *Madag.* .. **57 B8** 16 59S 49 52 E
Ambodilazana, *Madag.* .. **57 B8** 18 6S 49 10 E
Ambohimahasoa, *Madag.* **57 C8** 21 7S 47 13 E
Ambohimanga, *Madag.* . **57 C8** 20 52S 47 36 E
Ambohitra, *Madag.* ..... **57 A8** 12 30S 49 10 E
Amboise, *France* .... **18 C4** 47 24N 1 2 E
Ambon, *Indonesia* ...... **37 E7** 3 35S 128 20 E
Amboseli L., *Kenya* ..... **54 C4** 2 40S 37 10 E
Ambositra, *Madag.* ..... **57 C8** 20 31S 47 25 E
Ambovombé, *Madag.* .... **57 D8** 25 11S 46 5 E
Amboy, *U.S.A.* **85 L11** 34 33N 115 45W
Amboyna Cay,
S. China Sea .... **36 C4** 7 50N 112 50 E
Ambridge, *U.S.A.* **78 F4** 40 36N 80 14W
Ambriz, *Angola* .... **52 F2** 7 48S 13 8 E
Amby, *Australia* .... **63 D4** 26 30S 148 11 E
Amchitka I., *U.S.A.* ..... **68 C1** 51 32N 179 0 E
Amderma, *Russia* ...... **26 C7** 69 45N 61 30 E
Ameca, *Mexico* **86 C4** 20 30N 104 0W
Ameca →, *Mexico* **86 C3** 20 40N 105 15W
Amecameca, *Mexico* **87 D5** 19 7N 98 46W
Ameland, *Neths.* .... **15 A5** 53 27N 5 45 E
Amen, *Russia* .... **27 C18** 68 45N 180 0 E
American Falls, *U.S.A.* .. **82 E7** 42 47N 112 51W
American Falls Reservoir,
U.S.A. **82 E7** 42 47N 112 52W
American Highland,
Antarctica .... **5 D6** 73 0S 75 0 E
American Samoa ■,
Pac. Oc. **59 B13** 14 20S 170 40W
Americana, *Brazil* **95 A6** 22 45S 47 20W
Americus, *U.S.A.* **77 J3** 32 4N 84 14W
Amersfoort, *Neths.* ..... **15 B5** 52 9N 5 23 E
Amersfoort, *S. Africa* ... **57 D4** 26 59S 29 53 E
Amery, *Australia* .... **61 F2** 31 9S 117 5 E
Amery, *Canada* **73 B10** 56 34N 94 3W
Amery Ice Shelf,
Antarctica .... **5 C6** 69 30S 72 0 E
Ames, *U.S.A.* **80 E8** 42 2N 93 37W
Amesbury, *U.S.A.* **79 D14** 42 51N 70 56W
Amga, *Russia* .... **27 C14** 60 50N 132 0 E
Amga →, *Russia* ...... **27 C14** 62 38N 134 32 E
Amgu, *Russia* .... **27 E14** 45 45N 137 15 E
Amgun →, *Russia* ..... **27 D14** 52 56N 139 38 E
Amherst, *Burma* .... **41 L20** 16 2N 97 20 E
Amherst, *Canada* **71 C7** 45 48N 64 8W
Amherst, *Mass., U.S.A.* . **79 D12** 42 23N 72 31W
Amherst, *N.Y., U.S.A.* ... **78 D6** 42 59N 78 48W
Amherst, *Ohio, U.S.A.* ... **78 E2** 41 24N 82 14W
Amherst, *Tex., U.S.A.* ... **81 H3** 34 1N 102 25W
Amherst I., *Canada* **79 B8** 44 8N 76 43W
Amherstburg, *Canada* ... **70 D3** 42 6N 83 6W
Amiata, Mte., *Italy* ...... **20 C4** 42 53N 11 37 E
Amiens, *France* .... **18 B5** 49 54N 2 16 E
Amīrābād, *Iran* .... **44 C5** 33 20N 46 16 E
Amirante Is., *Seychelles* . **28 K9** 6 0S 53 0 E
Amisk L., *Canada* **73 C8** 54 35N 102 15W
Amistad, Presa de la,
Mexico **86 B4** 29 24N 101 0W
Amite, *U.S.A.* **81 K9** 30 44N 90 30W
Amlwch, *U.K.* **10 D3** 53 24N 4 20W
'Ammān, *Jordan* .... **47 D4** 31 57N 35 52 E
Ammanford, *U.K.* **11 F3** 51 48N 3 59W
Ammassalik =
Angmagssalik,
Greenland **4 C6** 65 40N 37 20W
Amnat Charoen, *Thailand* **38 E5** 15 51N 104 38 E
Āmol, *Iran* .... **45 B7** 36 23N 52 20 E
Amorgós, *Greece* .... **21 F11** 36 50N 25 57 E
Amory, *U.S.A.* **77 J1** 33 59N 88 29W
Amos, *Canada* **70 C4** 48 35N 78 5W
Åmot, *Norway* .... **9 G13** 59 57N 9 54 E
Amoy = Xiamen, *China* . **33 D6** 24 25N 118 4 E
Ampang, *Malaysia* ...... **39 L3** 3 8N 101 45 E
Ampanihy, *Madag.* ..... **57 C7** 24 40S 44 45 E
Ampasindava,
Helodranon', *Madag.* .. **57 A8** 13 40S 48 15 E
Ampasindava, Saikanosy,
Madag. .... **57 A8** 13 42S 47 55 E
Ampenan, *Indonesia* .... **36 F5** 8 35S 116 13 E
Amper →, *Germany* .... **16 D6** 48 29N 11 35 E
Ampotaka, *Madag.* ..... **57 D7** 25 3S 44 41 E
Ampoza, *Madag.* .... **57 C7** 22 20S 44 44 E
Amqui, *Canada* **71 C6** 48 28N 67 27W
Amravati, *India* .... **40 J10** 20 55N 77 45 E
Amreli, *India* .... **42 J4** 21 35N 71 17 E
Amritsar, *India* .... **42 D6** 31 35N 74 57 E
Amroha, *India* .... **43 E8** 28 53N 78 30 E
Amsterdam, *Neths.* ..... **15 B4** 52 23N 4 54 E
Amsterdam, *U.S.A.* **79 D10** 42 56N 74 11W
Amsterdam, I., *Ind. Oc.* .. **3 F13** 38 30S 77 30 E
Amstetten, *Austria* ..... **16 D8** 48 7N 14 51 E
Amudarya →, *Uzbekistan* **26 E6** 43 58N 59 34 E
Amundsen Gulf, *Canada* . **68 A7** 71 0N 124 0W
Amundsen Sea, *Antarctica* **5 D15** 72 0S 115 0W
Amuntai, *Indonesia* ..... **36 E5** 2 28S 115 25 E
Amur →, *Russia* .... **27 D15** 52 56N 141 10 E
Amurang, *Indonesia* .... **37 D6** 1 5N 124 40 E
Amuri Pass, *N.Z.* .... **59 K4** 42 31S 172 11 E
Amursk, *Russia* .... **27 D14** 50 14N 136 54 E
Amurzet, *Russia* .... **27 E14** 47 50N 131 5 E
Amyderya =
Amudarya →,
Uzbekistan .... **26 E6** 43 58N 59 34 E
An Bien, *Vietnam* ...... **39 H5** 9 45N 105 0 E
An Hoa, *Vietnam* ...... **38 E7** 15 40N 108 5 E
An Khe, *Vietnam* ...... **38 F7** 13 57N 108 39 E
An Nabatīyah at Tahta,
Lebanon .... **47 B4** 33 23N 35 27 E
An Nabk, *Si. Arabia* .... **44 D3** 31 20N 37 20 E
An Nabk, *Syria* .... **47 A5** 34 2N 36 44 E
An Nabk Abū Qaşr,
Si. Arabia .... **44 D3** 30 21N 38 34 E
An Nafūd, *Si. Arabia* .... **44 D4** 28 15N 41 0 E
An Najaf, *Iraq* .... **44 C5** 32 3N 44 15 E
An Nāşirīyah, *Iraq* ..... **44 D5** 31 0N 46 15 E
An Nhon, *Vietnam* ..... **38 F7** 13 55N 109 7 E
An Nu'ayrīyah, *Si. Arabia* **45 E6** 27 30N 48 30 E
An Nuwayb'ī, W. →,
Si. Arabia .... **47 F3** 29 18N 34 57 E
An Thoi, Dao, *Vietnam* .. **39 H4** 9 58N 104 0 E
An Uaimh, *Ireland* **13 C5** 53 39N 6 41W
Anabar →, *Russia* ..... **27 B12** 73 8N 113 36 E
'Anabtā, *West Bank* ..... **47 C4** 32 19N 35 7 E
Anaconda, *U.S.A.* **82 C7** 46 8N 112 57W
Anacortes, *U.S.A.* **84 B4** 48 30N 122 37W
Anadarko, *U.S.A.* **81 H5** 35 4N 98 15W
Anadolu, *Turkey* .... **25 G5** 39 0N 30 0 E
Anadyr, *Russia* .... **27 C18** 64 35N 177 20 E
Anadyr →, *Russia* ..... **27 C18** 64 55N 176 5 E
Anadyrskiy Zaliv, *Russia* . **27 C19** 64 0N 180 0 E
Anaga, Pta. de, *Canary Is.* **22 F3** 28 34N 16 9W
'Ānah, *Iraq* .... **44 C4** 34 25N 42 0 E
Anaheim, *U.S.A.* **85 M9** 33 50N 117 55W
Anahim Lake, *Canada* ... **72 C3** 52 28N 125 18W
Anáhuac, *Mexico* **86 B4** 27 14N 100 9W
Anakapalle, *India* ...... **41 L13** 17 42N 83 6 E
Anakie, *Australia* ...... **62 C4** 23 32S 147 45 E
Analalava, *Madag.* ..... **57 A8** 14 35S 48 0 E
Análipsis, *Greece* ...... **23 A3** 39 36N 19 55 E
Anambar →, *Pakistan* .. **42 D3** 30 15N 68 50 E
Anambas, Kepulauan,
Indonesia .... **36 D3** 3 20N 106 30 E
Anambas Is. = Anambas,
Kepulauan, *Indonesia* . **36 D3** 3 20N 106 30 E
Anamoose, *U.S.A.* **80 B4** 47 53N 100 15W
Anamosa, *U.S.A.* **80 D9** 42 7N 91 17W
Anamur, *Turkey* .... **25 G5** 36 8N 32 58 E
Anan, *Japan* .... **31 H7** 33 54N 134 40 E
Anand, *India* .... **42 H5** 22 32N 72 59 E
Anantnag, *India* .... **43 C6** 33 45N 75 10 E
Ananyiv, *Ukraine* ...... **17 E15** 47 44N 29 58 E
Anapodháris →, *Greece* **23 E7** 34 59N 25 20 E
Anápolis, *Brazil* **93 G9** 16 15S 48 50W
Anār, *Iran* .... **45 D7** 30 55N 55 13 E
Anārak, *Iran* .... **45 C7** 33 25N 53 40 E
Anatolia = Anadolu,
Turkey .... **25 G5** 39 0N 30 0 E
Anatone, *U.S.A.* **82 C5** 46 8N 117 8W
Anatsogno, *Madag.* .... **57 C7** 23 33S 43 46 E
Añatuya, *Argentina* **94 B3** 28 20S 62 50W
Anaunethad L., *Canada* .. **73 A8** 60 55N 104 25W
Anaye, *Niger* .... **51 E7** 19 15N 12 50 E
Anbyŏn, *N. Korea* ...... **35 E14** 39 1N 127 35 E
Anchor Bay, *U.S.A.* **84 G3** 38 48N 123 34W
Anchorage, *U.S.A.* **68 B5** 61 13N 149 54W
Anci, *China* .... **34 E9** 39 20N 116 40 E
Ancohuma, Nevada,
Bolivia **92 G5** 16 0S 68 50W
Ancón, *Peru* **92 F3** 11 50S 77 10W
Ancona, *Italy* .... **20 C5** 43 38N 13 30 E
Ancud, *Chile* **96 E2** 42 0S 73 50W
Ancud, G. de, *Chile* **96 E2** 42 0S 73 0W
Anda, *China* .... **33 B7** 46 24N 125 19 E
Andacollo, *Argentina* ... **94 D1** 37 10S 70 42W
Andacollo, *Chile* **94 C1** 30 5S 71 10W
Andado, *Australia* ...... **62 D2** 25 25S 135 15 E
Andalgalá, *Argentina* ... **94 B2** 27 40S 66 30W
Åndalsnes, *Norway* .... **9 E12** 62 35N 7 43 E
Andalucía □, *Spain* **19 D3** 37 35N 5 0W
Andalusia, *U.S.A.* **77 K2** 31 18N 86 29W
Andalusia □ =
Andalucía □, *Spain* ... **19 D3** 37 35N 5 0W
Andaman Is., *Ind. Oc.* ... **28 H13** 12 30N 92 30 E
Andaman Sea, *Ind. Oc.* .. **36 B1** 13 0N 96 0 E
Andara, *Namibia* .... **56 B3** 18 2S 21 9 E
Andenes, *Norway* ...... **8 B17** 69 19N 16 18 E
Andenne, *Belgium* ...... **15 D5** 50 28N 5 5 E
Anderson, *Calif., U.S.A.* . **82 F2** 40 27N 122 18W
Anderson, *Ind., U.S.A.* ... **76 E3** 40 10N 85 41W
Anderson, *Mo., U.S.A.* .. **81 G7** 36 39N 94 27W
Anderson, *S.C., U.S.A.* .. **77 H4** 34 31N 82 39W
Anderson →, *Canada* .. **68 B7** 69 42N 129 0W
Andes = Andes, Cord. de
los, *S. Amer.* **92 F4** 20 0S 68 0W
Andes, *S. Amer.* **92 F3** 10 0S 75 53W
Andes, Cord. de los,
S. Amer. **92 F4** 20 0S 68 0W
Andfjorden, *Norway* .... **8 B17** 69 10N 16 20 E
Andhra Pradesh □, *India* **40 L11** 18 0N 79 0 E
Andijon, *Uzbekistan* .... **26 E8** 41 10N 72 15 E
Andikíthira, *Greece* ..... **21 G10** 35 52N 23 15 E
Andīmeshk, *Iran* .... **45 C6** 32 27N 48 21 E
Andizhan = Andijon,
Uzbekistan .... **26 E8** 41 10N 72 15 E
Andoany, *Madag.* ...... **57 A8** 13 25S 48 16 E
Andong, *S. Korea* ...... **35 F15** 36 40N 128 43 E
Andongwei, *China* ..... **35 G10** 35 6N 119 20 E
Andorra ■, *Europe* ..... **19 A6** 42 30N 1 30 E
Andorra La Vella, *Andorra* **19 A6** 42 31N 1 32 E
Andover, *U.K.* **11 F6** 51 12N 1 29W
Andover, *Mass., U.S.A.* .. **79 D13** 42 40N 71 8W
Andover, *N.Y., U.S.A.* ... **78 D7** 42 10N 77 48W
Andover, *Ohio, U.S.A.* ... **78 E4** 41 36N 80 34W
Andøya, *Norway* .... **8 B16** 69 10N 15 50 E
Andrahary, Mt., *Madag.* . **57 A8** 13 37S 49 17 E
Andraitx, *Spain* .... **22 B9** 39 39N 2 25 E
Andramasina, *Madag.* ... **57 B8** 19 11S 47 35 E
Andranopasy, *Madag.* ... **57 C7** 21 17S 43 44 E
Andreanof Is., *U.S.A.* ... **68 C2** 52 0N 178 0W
Andrewilla, *Australia* .... **63 D2** 26 31S 139 17 E
Andrews, *S.C., U.S.A.* ... **77 J6** 33 27N 79 34W
Andrews, *Tex., U.S.A.* ... **81 J3** 32 19N 102 33W
Ándria, *Italy* .... **20 D7** 41 13N 16 17 E
Andriba, *Madag.* .... **57 B8** 17 30S 46 58 E
Androka, *Madag.* ...... **57 C7** 24 58S 44 2 E
Andropov = Rybinsk,
Russia .... **24 C6** 58 5N 38 50 E
Ándros, *Greece* .... **21 F11** 37 50N 24 57 E
Andros I., *Bahamas* **88 B4** 24 30N 78 0W
Andros Town, *Bahamas* . **88 B4** 24 43N 77 47W
Andselv, *Norway* .... **8 B18** 69 4N 18 34 E
Andújar, *Spain* **19 C3** 38 3N 4 5W
Andulo, *Angola* .... **52 G3** 11 25S 16 45 E
Anegada I., *Virgin Is.* **89 C7** 18 45N 64 20W
Anegada Passage,
W. Indies **89 C7** 18 15N 63 45W
Aného, *Togo* .... **50 G5** 6 12N 1 34 E
Aneto, Pico de, *Spain* ... **19 A6** 42 37N 0 40 E
Ang Thong, *Thailand* .... **38 E3** 14 35N 100 31 E
Angamos, Punta, *Chile* .. **94 A1** 23 1S 70 32W
Angara →, *Russia* ..... **27 D10** 58 5N 94 20 E
Angarsk, *Russia* .... **27 D11** 52 30N 104 0 E
Angas Downs, *Australia* . **61 E5** 25 2S 132 14 E
Angas Hills, *Australia* ... **60 D4** 23 0S 127 50 E
Angaston, *Australia* ..... **63 E2** 34 30S 139 8 E
Ånge, *Sweden* .... **9 E16** 62 31N 15 35 E
Ángel de la Guarda, I.,
Mexico **86 B2** 29 30N 113 30W
Angeles, *Phil.* .... **37 A6** 15 9N 120 33 E
Ängelholm, *Sweden* .... **9 H15** 56 15N 12 58 E
Angellala, *Australia* ..... **63 D4** 26 24S 146 54 E
Angels Camp, *U.S.A.* ... **83 G3** 38 4N 120 32W
Ångermanälven →,
Sweden .... **8 E17** 62 40N 18 0 E
Ångermanland, *Sweden* . **8 E18** 63 36N 17 45 E
Angers, *Canada* **79 A9** 45 31N 75 29W
Angers, *France* **18 C3** 47 30N 0 35W
Ängesån →, *Sweden* ... **8 C20** 66 16N 22 47 E
Angikuni L., *Canada* **73 A9** 62 0N 100 0W
Angkor, *Cambodia* ...... **38 F4** 13 22N 103 50 E
Anglesey, *U.K.* **10 D3** 53 17N 4 20W
Anglesey □, *U.K.* **10 D3** 53 16N 4 18W
Angleton, *U.S.A.* **81 L7** 29 10N 95 26W
Anglisidhes, *Cyprus* .... **23 E12** 34 51N 33 27 E
Angmagssalik, *Greenland* **4 C6** 65 40N 37 20W
Ango, *Zaïre* .... **54 B2** 4 10N 26 5 E
Angoche, *Mozam.* ...... **55 F4** 16 8S 39 55 E
Angoche, I., *Mozam.* .... **55 F4** 16 20S 39 50 E
Angol, *Chile* **94 D1** 37 56S 72 45W
Angola, *Ind., U.S.A.* **76 E3** 41 38N 85 0W
Angola, *N.Y., U.S.A.* ... **78 D5** 42 38N 79 2W
Angola ■, *Africa* ...... **53 G3** 12 0S 18 0 E
Angoon, *U.S.A.* **72 B2** 57 30N 134 35W
Angoulême, *France* .... **18 D4** 45 39N 0 10 E
Angoumois, *France* .... **18 D3** 45 50N 0 25 E
Angra dos Reis, *Brazil* ... **95 A7** 23 0S 44 10W
Angren, *Uzbekistan* .... **26 E8** 41 1N 70 12 E
Angtassom, *Cambodia* .. **39 G5** 11 1N 104 41 E
Angu, *Zaïre* .... **54 B1** 3 25N 24 28 E
Anguang, *China* .... **35 B12** 45 15N 123 45 E
Anguilla ■, *W. Indies* **89 C7** 18 14N 63 5W
Anguo, *China* .... **34 E8** 38 28N 115 15 E
Angurugu, *Australia* .... **62 A2** 14 0S 136 25 E
Angus □, *U.K.* **12 E6** 56 46N 2 56W
Angus, Braes of, *U.K.* ... **12 E5** 56 51N 3 10W
Anhanduí →, *Brazil* **95 A5** 21 46S 52 9W
Anholt, *Denmark* ...... **9 H14** 56 42N 11 33 E
Anhui □, *China* .... **33 C6** 32 0N 117 0 E
Anhwei □ = Anhui □,
China .... **33 C6** 32 0N 117 0 E
Anichab, *Namibia* ...... **56 C1** 21 0S 14 46 E
Animas, *U.S.A.* **83 L9** 31 57N 108 48W
Anivorano, *Madag.* ..... **57 B8** 18 44S 48 58 E
Anjalankoski, *Finland* ... **9 F22** 60 45N 26 51 E
Anjar, *India* .... **42 H4** 23 6N 70 10 E
Anjidiv I., *India* .... **40 M9** 14 40N 74 10 E
Anjou, *France* **18 C3** 47 20N 0 15W
Anjozorobe, *Madag.* .... **57 B8** 18 22S 47 52 E
Anju, *N. Korea* .... **35 E13** 39 36N 125 40 E
Anka, *Nigeria* .... **50 F6** 12 13N 5 58 E
Ankaboa, Tanjona, *Madag.* **57 C7** 21 58S 43 20 E
Ankang, *China* .... **34 H5** 32 40N 109 1 E
Ankara, *Turkey* .... **25 G5** 39 57N 32 54 E
Ankaramena, *Madag.* ... **57 C8** 21 57S 46 39 E
Ankazoabo, *Madag.* .... **57 C7** 22 18S 44 31 E
Ankazobe, *Madag.* ..... **57 B8** 18 20S 47 10 E
Ankisabe, *Madag.* ..... **57 B8** 19 17S 46 29 E
Ankoro, *Zaïre* .... **54 D2** 6 45S 26 55 E
Anmyŏn-do, *S. Korea* ... **35 F14** 36 25N 126 25 E
Ann, C., *U.S.A.* **79 D14** 42 38N 70 35W
Ann Arbor, *U.S.A.* **76 D4** 42 17N 83 45W
Anna, *U.S.A.* **81 G10** 37 28N 89 15W
Anna Plains, *Australia* ... **60 C3** 19 17S 121 37 E
Annaba, *Algeria* .... **50 A6** 36 50N 7 46 E
Annalee →, *Ireland* **13 B4** 54 2N 7 24W
Annam = Trung-Phan,
Vietnam .... **38 E7** 16 0N 108 0 E
Annamitique, Chaîne, *Asia* **38 D6** 17 0N 106 0 E
Annan, *U.K.* **12 G5** 54 59N 3 16W
Annan →, *U.K.* **12 G5** 54 58N 3 16W
Annapolis, *U.S.A.* **76 F7** 38 59N 76 30W
Annapolis Royal, *Canada* **71 D6** 44 44N 65 32W
Annapurna, *Nepal* ...... **43 E10** 28 34N 83 50 E
Annean, L., *Australia* .... **61 E2** 26 54S 118 14 E
Annecy, *France* .... **18 D7** 45 55N 6 8 E
Anning, *China* .... **32 D5** 24 55N 102 26 E
Anningie, *Australia* ..... **60 D5** 21 50S 133 7 E
Anniston, *U.S.A.* **77 J3** 33 39N 85 50W
Annobón, *Atl. Oc.* ...... **49 G4** 1 25S 5 36 E
Annotto Bay, *Jamaica* ... **88 C4** 18 17N 76 45W
Annuello, *Australia* ..... **63 E3** 34 53S 142 55 E
Annville, *U.S.A.* **79 F8** 40 20N 76 31W
Áno Viánnos, *Greece* .... **23 D7** 35 2N 25 21 E
Anoka, *U.S.A.* **75 A8** 45 12N 93 23W
Anorotsangana, *Madag.* . **57 A8** 13 56S 47 55 E
Anóyia, *Greece* .... **23 D6** 35 16N 24 52 E
Anping, *Hebei, China* ... **34 E8** 38 15N 115 30 E
Anping, *Liaoning, China* . **35 D12** 41 5N 123 30 E
Anqing, *China* .... **33 C6** 30 30N 117 3 E
Anqiu, *China* .... **35 F10** 36 25N 119 10 E
Ansai, *China* .... **34 F5** 36 50N 109 20 E
Ansbach, *Germany* ..... **16 D6** 49 28N 10 34 E
Anshan, *China* .... **35 D12** 41 5N 122 58 E
Anshun, *China* .... **32 D5** 26 18N 105 57 E
Ansirabe, *Madag.* ...... **57 B8** 19 55S 47 2 E
Ansley, *U.S.A.* **80 E5** 41 18N 99 23W
Anson, *U.S.A.* **81 J5** 32 45N 99 54W
Anson B., *Australia* ..... **60 B5** 13 20S 130 6 E
Ansongo, *Mali* .... **50 E5** 15 25N 0 35 E
Ansonia, *U.S.A.* **79 E11** 41 21N 73 5W
Anstruther, *U.K.* **12 E6** 56 14N 2 41W
Ansudu, *Indonesia* ..... **37 E9** 2 11S 139 22 E
Antabamba, *Peru* **92 F4** 14 40S 73 0W
Antakya, *Turkey* .... **25 G6** 36 14N 36 10 E
Antalaha, *Madag.* ...... **57 A9** 14 57S 50 20 E
Antalya, *Turkey* .... **25 G5** 36 52N 30 45 E
Antalya Körfezi, *Turkey* .. **25 G5** 36 15N 31 30 E
Antananarivo, *Madag.* ... **57 B8** 18 55S 47 31 E
Antananarivo □, *Madag.* . **57 B8** 19 0S 47 0 E
Antanimbaribe, *Madag.* .. **57 C7** 21 30S 44 48 E
Antarctic Pen., *Antarctica* **5 C18** 67 0S 60 0W
Antarctica .... **5 E3** 90 0S 0 0 E
Antelope, *Zimbabwe* .... **55 G2** 21 2S 28 31 E
Antequera, *Paraguay* ... **94 A4** 24 8S 57 7W
Antequera, *Spain* **19 D3** 37 5N 4 33W
Antero, Mt., *U.S.A.* **83 G10** 38 41N 106 15W
Anthony, *Kans., U.S.A.* .. **81 G5** 37 9N 98 2W
Anthony, *N. Mex., U.S.A.* **83 K10** 32 0N 106 36W
Anthony Lagoon, *Australia* **62 B2** 18 0S 135 30 E
Anti Atlas, *Morocco* **50 C3** 30 0N 8 30W
Anti-Lebanon = Ash
Sharqi, Al Jabal,
Lebanon .... **47 B5** 33 40N 36 10 E
Antibes, *France* .... **18 E7** 43 34N 7 6 E
Anticosti, I. d', *Canada* .. **71 C7** 49 30N 63 0W
Antigo, *U.S.A.* **80 C10** 45 9N 89 9W
Antigonish, *Canada* **71 C7** 45 38N 61 58W
Antigua, *Canary Is.* **22 F5** 28 24N 14 1W
Antigua, *Guatemala* **88 D1** 14 34N 90 41W
Antigua, *W. Indies* **89 C7** 17 0N 61 50W
Antigua & Barbuda ■,
W. Indies **89 C7** 17 20N 61 48W
Antilla, *Cuba* **88 B4** 20 40N 75 50W
Antimony, *U.S.A.* **83 G8** 38 7N 112 0W
Antioch, *U.S.A.* **84 G5** 38 1N 121 48W
Antioquia, *Colombia* **92 B3** 6 40N 75 55W
Antipodes Is., *Pac. Oc.* .. **64 M9** 49 45S 178 40 E
Antler, *U.S.A.* **80 A4** 48 59N 101 17W
Antler →, *Canada* **73 D8** 49 8N 101 0W
Antlers, *U.S.A.* **81 H7** 34 14N 95 37W
Antofagasta, *Chile* **94 A1** 23 50S 70 30W
Antofagasta □, *Chile* ... **94 A2** 24 0S 69 0W
Antofagasta de la Sierra,
Argentina **94 B2** 26 5S 67 20W
Antofalla, *Argentina* **94 B2** 25 30S 68 5W
Antofalla, Salar de,
Argentina **94 B2** 25 40S 67 45W
Anton, *U.S.A.* **81 J3** 33 49N 102 10W
Anton Chico, *U.S.A.* **83 J11** 35 12N 105 9W
Antongila, Helodrano,
Madag. .... **57 B8** 15 30S 49 50 E
Antonibé, *Madag.* ...... **57 B8** 15 7S 47 24 E
Antonibé, Presqu'île d',
Madag. .... **57 A8** 14 55S 47 20 E
Antonina, *Brazil* **95 B6** 25 26S 48 42W
Antonito, *U.S.A.* **83 H10** 37 5N 106 0W
Antrim, *U.K.* **13 B5** 54 43N 6 14W
Antrim □, *U.K.* **13 B5** 54 56N 6 25W
Antrim, Mts. of, *U.K.* **13 B5** 55 3N 6 14W
Antrim Plateau, *Australia* **60 C4** 18 8S 128 20 E
Antsalova, *Madag.* ..... **57 B7** 18 40S 44 37 E
Antsiranana, *Madag.* .... **57 A8** 12 25S 49 20 E
Antsohihy, *Madag.* ..... **57 A8** 14 50S 47 59 E
Antsohimbondrona
Seranana, *Madag.* .... **57 A8** 13 7S 48 48 E
Antu, *China* .... **35 C15** 42 30N 128 20 E
Antwerp = Antwerpen,
Belgium .... **15 C4** 51 13N 4 25 E
Antwerp, *U.S.A.* **79 B9** 44 12N 75 37W
Antwerpen, *Belgium* .... **15 C4** 51 13N 4 25 E
Antwerpen □, *Belgium* .. **15 C4** 51 15N 4 40 E
Anupgarh, *India* .... **42 E5** 29 10N 73 10 E
Anuradhapura, *Sri Lanka* **40 Q12** 8 22N 80 28 E
Anveh, *Iran* .... **45 E7** 27 23N 54 11 E
Anvers = Antwerpen,
Belgium .... **15 C4** 51 13N 4 25 E
Anvers I., *Antarctica* **5 C17** 64 30S 63 40W
Anxi, *China* .... **32 B4** 40 30N 95 43 E
Anxious B., *Australia* ... **63 E1** 33 24S 134 45 E
Anyang, *China* .... **34 F8** 36 5N 114 21 E
Anyi, *China* .... **34 G6** 35 2N 111 2 E
Anza, *U.S.A.* **85 M10** 33 35N 116 39W
Anze, *China* .... **34 F7** 36 10N 112 12 E

Asike

Anzhero-Sudzhensk, *Russia* **26 D9** 56 10N 86 0 E
Ánzio, *Italy* **20 D5** 41 27N 12 37 E
Aoga-Shima, *Japan* **31 H9** 32 28N 139 46 E
Aomori, *Japan* **30 D10** 40 45N 140 45 E
Aomori □, *Japan* **30 D10** 40 45N 140 40 E
Aonla, *India* **43 E8** 28 16N 79 11 E
Aosta, *Italy* **20 B2** 45 45N 7 20 E
Aoudéras, *Niger* **50 E6** 17 45N 8 20 E
Aoulef el Arab, *Algeria* **50 C5** 26 55N 1 2 E
Apa →, *S. Amer.* **94 A4** 22 6S 58 2W
Apache, *U.S.A.* **81 H5** 34 54N 98 22W
Apalachee B., *U.S.A.* **77 L3** 30 0N 84 0W
Apalachicola, *U.S.A.* **77 L3** 29 43N 84 59W
Apalachicola →, *U.S.A.* **77 L3** 29 43N 84 58W
Apaporis →, *Colombia* **92 D5** 1 23S 69 25W
Aparri, *Phil.* **37 A6** 18 22N 121 38 E
Apátity, *Russia* **24 A5** 67 34N 33 22 E
Apatzingán, *Mexico* **86 D4** 19 0N 102 20W
Apeldoorn, *Neths.* **15 B5** 52 13N 5 57 E
Apennines = Appennini, *Italy* **20 B4** 44 0N 10 0 E
Apia, *W. Samoa* **59 A13** 13 50S 171 50W
Apiacás, Serra dos, *Brazil* **92 E7** 9 50S 57 0W
Apizaco, *Mexico* **87 D5** 19 26N 98 9W
Aplao, *Peru* **92 G4** 16 0S 72 40W
Apo, Mt., *Phil.* **37 C7** 6 53N 125 14 E
Apolakkiá, *Greece* **23 C9** 36 5N 27 48 E
Apolakkiá, Órmos, *Greece* **23 C9** 36 5N 27 45 E
Apollonia = Marsá Susah, *Libya* **51 B9** 32 52N 21 59 E
Apolo, *Bolivia* **92 F5** 14 30S 68 30W
Apostle Is., *U.S.A.* **80 B9** 47 0N 90 40W
Apóstoles, *Argentina* **95 B4** 28 0S 56 0W
Apostolos Andreas, C., *Cyprus* **23 D13** 35 42N 34 35 E
Apoteri, *Guyana* **92 C7** 4 2N 58 32W
Appalachian Mts., *U.S.A.* **76 G6** 38 0N 80 0W
Appennini, *Italy* **20 B4** 44 0N 10 0 E
Apple Hill, *Canada* **79 A10** 45 13N 74 46W
Apple Valley, *U.S.A.* **85 L9** 34 32N 117 14W
Appleby-in-Westmorland, *U.K.* **10 C5** 54 35N 2 29W
Appleton, *U.S.A.* **76 C1** 44 16N 88 25W
Approuague, *Fr. Guiana* **93 C8** 4 20N 52 0W
Aprília, *Italy* **20 D5** 41 36N 12 39 E
Apucarana, *Brazil* **95 A5** 23 55S 51 33W
Apure →, *Venezuela* **92 B5** 7 37N 66 25W
Apurimac →, *Peru* **92 F4** 12 17S 73 56W
Aqabah = Al 'Aqabah, *Jordan* **47 F4** 29 31N 35 0 E
'Aqabah, Khalīj al, *Red Sea* **44 D2** 28 15N 33 20 E
'Aqdā, *Iran* **45 C7** 32 26N 53 37 E
Aqīq, *Sudan* **51 E12** 18 14N 38 12 E
Aqmola, *Kazakstan* **26 D8** 51 10N 71 30 E
Aqrah, *Iraq* **44 B4** 36 46N 43 45 E
Aqtöbe, *Kazakstan* **25 D10** 50 17N 57 10 E
Aquidauana, *Brazil* **93 H7** 20 30S 55 50W
Aquiles Serdán, *Mexico* **86 B3** 28 37N 105 54W
Aquin, *Haiti* **89 C5** 18 16N 73 24W
Aquitain, Bassin, *France* **18 D3** 44 0N 0 30W
Ar Rachidiya, *Morocco* **50 B4** 31 58N 4 20W
Ar Rafid, *Syria* **47 C4** 32 57N 35 52 E
Ar Raḥḥālīyah, *Iraq* **44 C4** 32 44N 43 23 E
Ar Ramādī, *Iraq* **44 C4** 33 25N 43 20 E
Ar Ramthā, *Jordan* **47 C5** 32 34N 36 0 E
Ar Raqqah, *Syria* **44 C3** 35 59N 39 8 E
Ar Rass, *Si. Arabia* **44 E4** 25 50N 43 40 E
Ar Rifā'ī, *Iraq* **44 D5** 31 50N 46 10 E
Ar Riyāḍ, *Si. Arabia* **46 C4** 24 41N 46 42 E
Ar Ru'ays, *Qatar* **45 E6** 26 8N 51 12 E
Ar Rukhaymīyah, *Iraq* **44 D5** 29 22N 45 38 E
Ar Ruqayyidah, *Si. Arabia* **45 E6** 25 21N 49 34 E
Ar Ruṣāfah, *Syria* **44 C3** 35 45N 38 49 E
Ar Ruṭbah, *Iraq* **44 C4** 33 0N 40 15 E
Ara, *India* **43 G11** 25 35N 84 32 E
'Arab, Bahr el →, *Sudan* **51 G10** 9 0N 29 30 E
'Arabābād, *Iran* **45 C8** 33 2N 57 41 E
Arabia, *Asia* **46 C4** 25 0N 45 0 E
Arabian Desert = Es Sahrâ' Esh Sharqîya, *Egypt* **51 C11** 27 30N 32 30 E
Arabian Gulf = Gulf, The, *Asia* **45 E6** 27 0N 50 0 E
Arabian Sea, *Ind. Oc.* **29 H10** 16 0N 65 0 E
Aracaju, *Brazil* **93 F11** 10 55S 37 4W
Aracataca, *Colombia* **92 A4** 10 38N 74 9W
Aracati, *Brazil* **93 D11** 4 30S 37 44W
Araçatuba, *Brazil* **95 A5** 21 10S 50 30W
Aracena, *Spain* **19 D2** 37 53N 6 38W
Araçuai, *Brazil* **93 G10** 16 52S 42 4W
'Arad, *Israel* **47 D4** 31 15N 35 12 E
Arad, *Romania* **17 E11** 46 10N 21 20 E
Arada, *Chad* **51 F9** 15 0N 20 20 E
Aradhippou, *Cyprus* **23 E12** 34 57N 33 36 E
Arafura Sea, *E. Indies* **37 F8** 9 0S 135 0 E
Aragón □, *Spain* **19 B5** 41 25N 0 40W
Aragón →, *Spain* **19 A5** 42 13N 1 44W
Araguacema, *Brazil* **93 E9** 8 50S 49 20W
Araguaia →, *Brazil* **93 E9** 5 21S 48 41W
Araguari, *Brazil* **93 G9** 18 38S 48 11W
Araguari →, *Brazil* **93 C9** 1 15N 49 55W
Arak, *Algeria* **50 C5** 25 20N 3 45 E
Arāk, *Iran* **45 C6** 34 0N 49 40 E
Arakan Coast, *Burma* **41 K19** 19 0N 94 0 E
Arakan Yoma, *Burma* **41 K19** 20 0N 94 40 E
Araks = Aras, Rūd-e →, *Azerbaijan* **44 B5** 40 5N 48 29 E
Aral, *Kazakstan* **26 E7** 46 41N 61 45 E
Aral Sea, *Asia* **26 E7** 44 30N 60 0 E
Aral Tengizi = Aral Sea, *Asia* **26 E7** 44 30N 60 0 E
Aralsk = Aral, *Kazakstan* **26 E7** 46 41N 61 45 E
Aralskoye More = Aral Sea, *Asia* **26 E7** 44 30N 60 0 E
Aramac, *Australia* **62 C4** 22 58S 145 14 E
Arambag, *India* **43 H12** 22 53N 87 48 E
Aran I., *Ireland* **13 B3** 55 0N 8 30W
Aran Is., *Ireland* **13 C2** 53 6N 9 38W
Aranda de Duero, *Spain* **19 B4** 41 39N 3 42W
Arandān, *Iran* **44 C5** 35 23N 46 55 E
Aranjuez, *Spain* **19 B4** 40 1N 3 40W
Aranos, *Namibia* **56 C2** 24 9S 19 7 E
Aransas Pass, *U.S.A.* **81 M6** 27 55N 97 9W
Araouane, *Mali* **50 E4** 18 55N 3 30W
Arapahoe, *U.S.A.* **80 E5** 40 18N 99 54W
Arapey Grande →, *Uruguay* **94 C4** 30 55S 57 49W
Arapiraca, *Brazil* **93 E11** 9 45S 36 39W
Arapongas, *Brazil* **95 A5** 23 29S 51 28W
Ar'ar, *Si. Arabia* **44 D4** 30 59N 41 2 E
Araranguá, *Brazil* **95 B6** 29 0S 49 30W
Araraquara, *Brazil* **93 H9** 21 50S 48 0W
Ararás, Serra das, *Brazil* **95 B5** 25 0S 53 10W
Ararat, *Australia* **63 F3** 37 16S 143 0 E
Ararat, Mt. = Ağrı Dağı, *Turkey* **25 G7** 39 50N 44 15 E
Araria, *India* **43 F12** 26 9N 87 33 E
Araripe, Chapada do, *Brazil* **93 E11** 7 20S 40 0W
Araruama, L. de, *Brazil* **95 A7** 22 53S 42 12W
Aras, Rūd-e →, *Azerbaijan* **44 B5** 40 5N 48 29 E
Arauca, *Colombia* **92 B4** 7 0N 70 40W
Arauca →, *Venezuela* **92 B5** 7 24N 66 35W
Arauco, *Chile* **94 D1** 37 16S 73 25W
Arauco □, *Chile* **94 D1** 37 40S 73 25W
Araxá, *Brazil* **93 G9** 19 35S 46 55W
Araya, Pen. de, *Venezuela* **92 A6** 10 40N 64 0W
Arbat, *Iraq* **44 C5** 35 25N 45 35 E
Arbatax, *Italy* **20 E3** 39 56N 9 42 E
Arbīl, *Iraq* **44 B5** 36 15N 44 5 E
Arborfield, *Canada* **73 C8** 53 6N 103 39W
Arborg, *Canada* **73 C9** 50 54N 97 13W
Arbroath, *U.K.* **12 E6** 56 34N 2 35W
Arbuckle, *U.S.A.* **84 F4** 39 1N 122 3W
Arcachon, *France* **18 D3** 44 40N 1 10W
Arcade, *U.S.A.* **78 D6** 42 32N 78 25W
Arcadia, *Fla., U.S.A.* **77 M5** 27 13N 81 52W
Arcadia, *La., U.S.A.* **81 J8** 32 33N 92 55W
Arcadia, *Nebr., U.S.A.* **80 E5** 41 25N 99 8W
Arcadia, *Pa., U.S.A.* **78 F6** 40 47N 78 51W
Arcadia, *Wis., U.S.A.* **80 C9** 44 15N 91 30W
Arcata, *U.S.A.* **82 F1** 40 52N 124 5W
Archangel = Arkhangelsk, *Russia* **24 B7** 64 38N 40 36 E
Archbald, *U.S.A.* **79 E9** 41 30N 75 32W
Archer →, *Australia* **62 A3** 13 28S 141 41 E
Archer B., *Australia* **62 A3** 13 20S 141 30 E
Archers Post, *Kenya* **54 B4** 0 35N 37 35 E
Arcila = Asilah, *Morocco* **50 A3** 35 29N 6 0W
Arckaringa, *Australia* **63 D1** 27 56S 134 45 E
Arckaringa Cr. →, *Australia* **63 D2** 28 10S 135 22 E
Arco, *U.S.A.* **82 E7** 43 38N 113 18W
Arcola, *Canada* **73 D8** 49 40N 102 30W
Arcos de la Frontera, *Spain* **19 D3** 36 45N 5 49W
Arcot, *India* **40 N11** 12 53N 79 20 E
Arcoverde, *Brazil* **93 E11** 8 25S 37 4W
Arctic Bay, *Canada* **69 A11** 73 1N 85 7W
Arctic Ocean, *Arctic* **4 B18** 78 0N 160 0W
Arctic Red River, *Canada* **68 B6** 67 15N 134 0W
Arda →, *Bulgaria* **21 D12** 41 40N 26 29 E
Ardabīl, *Iran* **45 B6** 38 15N 48 18 E
Ardakān = Sepīdān, *Iran* **45 D7** 30 20N 52 5 E
Ardee, *Ireland* **13 C5** 53 52N 6 33W
Arden, *Canada* **78 B8** 44 43N 76 56W
Arden, *Calif., U.S.A.* **84 G5** 38 36N 121 33W
Arden, *Nev., U.S.A.* **85 J11** 36 1N 115 14W
Ardenne, *Belgium* **15 E5** 49 50N 5 5 E
Ardennes = Ardenne, *Belgium* **15 E5** 49 50N 5 5 E
Ardestān, *Iran* **45 C7** 33 20N 52 25 E
Ardgour, *U.K.* **12 E3** 56 45N 5 25W
Ardlethan, *Australia* **63 E4** 34 22S 146 53 E
Ardmore, *Australia* **62 C2** 21 39S 139 11 E
Ardmore, *Okla., U.S.A.* **81 H6** 34 10N 97 8W
Ardmore, *Pa., U.S.A.* **79 G9** 39 58N 75 18W
Ardmore, *S. Dak., U.S.A.* **80 D3** 43 1N 103 40W
Ardnacrusha, *Ireland* **13 D3** 52 43N 8 38W
Ardnamurchan, Pt. of, *U.K.* **12 E2** 56 43N 6 14W
Ardrossan, *Australia* **63 E2** 34 26S 137 53 E
Ardrossan, *U.K.* **12 F4** 55 39N 4 49W
Ards □, *U.K.* **13 B6** 54 35N 5 30W
Ards Pen., *U.K.* **13 B6** 54 33N 5 34W
Arecibo, *Puerto Rico* **89 C6** 18 29N 66 43W
Areia Branca, *Brazil* **93 D11** 5 0S 37 0W
Arena, Pt., *U.S.A.* **84 G3** 38 57N 123 44W
Arendal, *Norway* **9 G13** 58 28N 8 46 E
Arequipa, *Peru* **92 G4** 16 20S 71 30W
Arero, *Ethiopia* **51 H12** 4 41N 38 50 E
Arévalo, *Spain* **19 B3** 41 3N 4 43W
Arezzo, *Italy* **20 C4** 43 25N 11 53 E
Argamakmur, *Indonesia* **36 E2** 3 35S 102 0 E
Arganda, *Spain* **19 B4** 40 19N 3 26W
Argentan, *France* **18 B3** 48 45N 0 1W
Argentário, Mte., *Italy* **20 C4** 42 24N 11 9 E
Argentia, *Canada* **71 C9** 47 18N 53 58W
Argentina ■, *S. Amer.* **96 D3** 35 0S 66 0W
Argentina Is., *Antarctica* **5 C17** 66 0S 64 0W
Argentino, L., *Argentina* **96 G2** 50 10S 73 0W
Argeș →, *Romania* **17 F14** 44 11N 26 25 E
Arghandab →, *Afghan.* **42 D1** 31 30N 64 15 E
Argo, *Sudan* **51 E11** 19 28N 30 30 E
Argolikós Kólpos, *Greece* **21 F10** 37 20N 22 52 E
Árgos, *Greece* **21 F10** 37 40N 22 43 E
Argostólion, *Greece* **21 E9** 38 12N 20 33 E
Arguello, Pt., *U.S.A.* **85 L6** 34 35N 120 39W
Arguineguín, *Canary Is.* **22 G4** 27 46N 15 41W
Argun →, *Russia* **27 D13** 53 20N 121 28 E
Argungu, *Nigeria* **50 F5** 12 40N 4 31 E
Argus Pk., *U.S.A.* **85 K9** 35 52N 117 26W
Argyle, *U.S.A.* **80 A6** 48 20N 96 49W
Argyle, L., *Australia* **60 C4** 16 20S 128 40 E
Argyll & Bute □, *U.K.* **12 E3** 56 13N 5 28W
Århus, *Denmark* **9 H14** 56 8N 10 11 E
Ariadnoye, *Russia* **30 B7** 45 8N 134 25 E
Ariamsvlei, *Namibia* **56 D2** 28 9S 19 51 E
Arica, *Chile* **92 G4** 18 32S 70 20W
Arica, *Colombia* **92 D4** 2 0S 71 50W
Arico, *Canary Is.* **22 F3** 28 9N 16 29W
Arid, C., *Australia* **61 F3** 34 1S 123 10 E
Arida, *Japan* **31 G7** 34 5N 135 8 E
Arīḥā, *Syria* **44 C3** 35 49N 36 35 E
Arílla, Ákra, *Greece* **23 A3** 39 43N 19 39 E
Arima, *Trin. & Tob.* **89 D7** 10 38N 61 17W
Arinos →, *Brazil* **92 F7** 10 25S 58 20W
Ario de Rosales, *Mexico* **86 D4** 19 12N 102 0W
Aripuanã, *Brazil* **92 E6** 9 25S 60 30W
Aripuanã →, *Brazil* **92 E6** 5 7S 60 25W
Ariquemes, *Brazil* **92 E6** 9 55S 63 6W
Arisaig, *U.K.* **12 E3** 56 55N 5 51W
Aristazabal I., *Canada* **72 C3** 52 40N 129 10W
Arivaca, *U.S.A.* **83 L8** 31 37N 111 25W
Arivonimamo, *Madag.* **57 B8** 19 1S 47 11 E
Arizaro, Salar de, *Argentina* **94 A2** 24 40S 67 50W
Arizona, *Argentina* **94 D2** 35 45S 65 25W
Arizona □, *U.S.A.* **83 J8** 34 0N 112 0W
Arizpe, *Mexico* **86 A2** 30 20N 110 11W
Arjeplog, *Sweden* **8 D18** 66 3N 18 2 E
Arjona, *Colombia* **92 A3** 10 14N 75 22W
Arjuno, *Indonesia* **37 G15** 7 49S 112 34 E
Arka, *Russia* **27 C15** 60 15N 142 0 E
Arkadelphia, *U.S.A.* **81 H8** 34 7N 93 4W
Arkaig, L., *U.K.* **12 E3** 56 59N 5 10W
Arkalyk = Arqalyk, *Kazakstan* **26 D7** 50 13N 66 50 E
Arkansas □, *U.S.A.* **81 H8** 35 0N 92 30W
Arkansas →, *U.S.A.* **81 J9** 33 47N 91 4W
Arkansas City, *U.S.A.* **81 G6** 37 4N 97 2W
Arkhángelos, *Greece* **23 C10** 36 13N 28 7 E
Arkhangelsk, *Russia* **24 B7** 64 38N 40 36 E
Arklow, *Ireland* **13 D5** 52 48N 6 10W
Arkticheskiy, Mys, *Russia* **27 A10** 81 10N 95 0 E
Arlanzón →, *Spain* **19 A3** 42 3N 4 17W
Arlberg P., *Austria* **16 E6** 47 9N 10 12 E
Arlee, *U.S.A.* **82 C6** 47 10N 114 5W
Arles, *France* **18 E6** 43 41N 4 40 E
Arlington, *S. Africa* **57 D4** 28 1S 27 53 E
Arlington, *Oreg., U.S.A.* **82 D3** 45 43N 120 12W
Arlington, *S. Dak., U.S.A.* **80 C6** 44 22N 97 8W
Arlington, *Va., U.S.A.* **76 F7** 38 53N 77 7W
Arlington, *Wash., U.S.A.* **84 B4** 48 12N 122 8W
Arlington Heights, *U.S.A.* **76 D2** 42 5N 87 59W
Arlon, *Belgium* **15 E5** 49 42N 5 49 E
Armagh, *U.K.* **13 B5** 54 21N 6 39W
Armagh □, *U.K.* **13 B5** 54 18N 6 37W
Armavir, *Russia* **25 E7** 45 2N 41 7 E
Armenia, *Colombia* **92 C3** 4 35N 75 45W
Armenia ■, *Asia* **25 F7** 40 20N 45 0 E
Armenistís, Ákra, *Greece* **23 C9** 36 8N 27 42 E
Armidale, *Australia* **63 E5** 30 30S 151 40 E
Armour, *U.S.A.* **80 D5** 43 19N 98 21W
Armstrong, *B.C., Canada* **72 C5** 50 25N 119 10W
Armstrong, *Ont., Canada* **70 B2** 50 18N 89 4W
Armstrong, *U.S.A.* **81 M6** 26 56N 97 47W
Armstrong →, *Australia* **60 C5** 16 35S 131 40 E
Arnarfjörður, *Iceland* **8 D2** 65 48N 23 40W
Arnaud →, *Canada* **69 B12** 60 0N 70 0W
Arnauti, C., *Cyprus* **23 D11** 35 6N 32 17 E
Arnett, *U.S.A.* **81 G5** 36 8N 99 46W
Arnhem, *Neths.* **15 C5** 51 58N 5 55 E
Arnhem, C., *Australia* **62 A2** 12 20S 137 30 E
Arnhem B., *Australia* **62 A2** 12 20S 136 10 E
Arnhem Land, *Australia* **62 A1** 13 10S 134 30 E
Arno →, *Italy* **20 C4** 43 41N 10 17 E
Arno Bay, *Australia* **63 E2** 33 54S 136 34 E
Arnold, *Calif., U.S.A.* **84 G6** 38 15N 120 20W
Arnold, *Nebr., U.S.A.* **80 E4** 41 26N 100 12W
Arnot, *Canada* **73 B9** 55 56N 96 41W
Arnøy, *Norway* **8 A19** 70 9N 20 40 E
Arnprior, *Canada* **70 C4** 45 26N 76 21W
Arnsberg, *Germany* **16 C5** 51 24N 8 5 E
Aroab, *Namibia* **56 D2** 26 41S 19 39 E
Arqalyk, *Kazakstan* **26 D7** 50 13N 66 50 E
Arrabury, *Australia* **63 D3** 26 45S 141 0 E
Arrah = Ara, *India* **43 G11** 25 35N 84 32 E
Arran, *U.K.* **12 F3** 55 34N 5 12W
Arrandale, *Canada* **72 C3** 54 57N 130 0W
Arras, *France* **18 A5** 50 17N 2 46 E
Arrecife, *Canary Is.* **22 F6** 28 57N 13 37W
Arrecifes, *Argentina* **94 C3** 34 6S 60 9W
Arrée, Mts. d', *France* **18 B2** 48 26N 3 55W
Arriaga, *Chiapas, Mexico* **87 D6** 16 15N 93 52W
Arriaga, *San Luis Potosí, Mexico* **86 C4** 21 55N 101 23W
Arrilalah P.O., *Australia* **62 C3** 23 43S 143 54 E
Arrino, *Australia* **61 E2** 29 30S 115 40 E
Arrow, L., *Ireland* **13 B3** 54 3N 8 19W
Arrow Rock Res., *U.S.A.* **82 E6** 43 45N 115 50W
Arrowhead, *Canada* **72 C5** 50 40N 117 55W
Arrowhead, L., *U.S.A.* **85 L9** 34 16N 117 10W
Arrowtown, *N.Z.* **59 L2** 44 57S 168 50 E
Arroyo Grande, *U.S.A.* **85 K6** 35 7N 120 35W
Ars, *Iran* **44 B5** 37 9N 47 46 E
Arsenault L., *Canada* **73 B7** 55 6N 108 32W
Arsenev, *Russia* **30 B6** 44 10N 133 15 E
Árta, *Greece* **21 E9** 39 8N 21 2 E
Artá, *Spain* **22 B10** 39 41N 3 21 E
Arteaga, *Mexico* **86 D4** 18 50N 102 20W
Artem, *Russia* **30 C6** 43 22N 132 13 E
Artemovsk, *Russia* **27 D10** 54 45N 93 35 E
Artesia = Mosomane, *Botswana* **56 C4** 24 2S 26 19 E
Artesia, *U.S.A.* **81 J2** 32 51N 104 24W
Artesia Wells, *U.S.A.* **81 L5** 28 17N 99 17W
Artesian, *U.S.A.* **80 C6** 44 1N 97 55W
Arthur →, *Australia* **62 G3** 41 2S 144 40 E
Arthur Cr. →, *Australia* **62 C2** 22 30S 136 25 E
Arthur Pt., *Australia* **62 C5** 22 7S 150 3 E
Arthur's Pass, *N.Z.* **59 K3** 42 54S 171 35 E
Arthur's Town, *Bahamas* **89 B4** 24 38N 75 42W
Artigas, *Uruguay* **94 C4** 30 20S 56 30W
Artillery L., *Canada* **73 A7** 63 9N 107 52W
Artois, *France* **18 A5** 50 20N 2 30 E
Artsyz, *Ukraine* **17 E15** 46 4N 29 26 E
Artvin, *Turkey* **25 F7** 41 14N 41 44 E
Aru, Kepulauan, *Indonesia* **37 F8** 6 0S 134 30 E
Aru Is. = Aru, Kepulauan, *Indonesia* **37 F8** 6 0S 134 30 E
Aru Meru □, *Tanzania* **54 C4** 3 20S 36 50 E
Arua, *Uganda* **54 B3** 3 1N 30 58 E
Aruanã, *Brazil* **93 F8** 14 54S 51 10W
Aruba ■, *W. Indies* **89 D6** 12 30N 70 0W
Arucas, *Canary Is.* **22 F4** 28 7N 15 32W
Arumpo, *Australia* **63 E3** 33 48S 142 55 E
Arun →, *Nepal* **43 F12** 26 55N 87 10 E
Arunachal Pradesh □, *India* **41 E19** 28 0N 95 0 E
Arusha, *Tanzania* **54 C4** 3 20S 36 40 E
Arusha □, *Tanzania* **54 C4** 4 0S 36 30 E
Arusha Chini, *Tanzania* **54 C4** 3 32S 37 20 E
Aruwimi →, *Zaïre* **54 B1** 1 13N 23 36 E
Arvada, *U.S.A.* **82 D10** 44 39N 106 8W
Árvi, *Greece* **23 E7** 34 59N 25 28 E
Arvida, *Canada* **71 C5** 48 25N 71 14W
Arvidsjaur, *Sweden* **8 D18** 65 35N 19 10 E
Arvika, *Sweden* **9 G15** 59 40N 12 36 E
Arvin, *U.S.A.* **85 K8** 35 12N 118 50W
Arxan, *China* **33 B6** 47 11N 119 57 E
Aryirádhes, *Greece* **23 B3** 39 27N 19 58 E
Aryiroúpolis, *Greece* **23 D6** 35 17N 24 20 E
Arys, *Kazakstan* **26 E7** 42 26N 68 48 E
Arzamas, *Russia* **24 C7** 55 27N 43 55 E
Arzew, *Algeria* **50 A4** 35 50N 0 23W
Aş Şadr, *U.A.E.* **45 E7** 24 40N 54 41 E
Aş Şafā, *Syria* **47 B6** 33 10N 37 0 E
'As Saffānīyah, *Si. Arabia* **45 D6** 28 5N 48 50 E
As Safīrah, *Syria* **44 B3** 36 5N 37 21 E
Aş Şahm, *Oman* **45 E8** 24 10N 56 53 E
As Sājir, *Si. Arabia* **44 E5** 25 11N 44 36 E
As Salamīyah, *Syria* **44 C3** 35 1N 37 2 E
As Salṭ, *Jordan* **47 C4** 32 2N 35 43 E
As Sal'w'a, *Qatar* **45 E6** 24 23N 50 50 E
As Samāwah, *Iraq* **44 D5** 31 15N 45 15 E
As Sanamayn, *Syria* **47 B5** 33 3N 36 10 E
As Sukhnah, *Syria* **44 C3** 34 52N 38 52 E
As Sulaymānīyah, *Iraq* **44 C5** 35 35N 45 29 E
As Sulaymī, *Si. Arabia* **44 E4** 26 17N 41 21 E
As Summān, *Si. Arabia* **44 E5** 25 0N 47 0 E
As Suwaydā', *Syria* **47 C5** 32 40N 36 30 E
As Suwaydā' □, *Syria* **47 C5** 32 45N 36 45 E
As Şuwayrah, *Iraq* **44 C5** 32 55N 45 0 E
Asab, *Namibia* **56 D2** 25 30S 18 0 E
Asahi-Gawa →, *Japan* **31 G6** 34 36N 133 58 E
Asahigawa, *Japan* **30 C11** 43 46N 142 22 E
Asansol, *India* **43 H12** 23 40N 87 1 E
Asbesberge, *S. Africa* **56 D3** 29 0S 23 0 E
Asbestos, *Canada* **71 C5** 45 47N 71 58W
Asbury Park, *U.S.A.* **79 F10** 40 13N 74 1W
Ascensión, *Mexico* **86 A3** 31 6N 107 59W
Ascensión, B. de la, *Mexico* **87 D7** 19 50N 87 20W
Ascension I., *Atl. Oc.* **49 G2** 8 0S 14 15W
Aschaffenburg, *Germany* **16 D5** 49 58N 9 6 E
Aschersleben, *Germany* **16 C6** 51 45N 11 29 E
Áscoli Piceno, *Italy* **20 C5** 42 51N 13 34 E
Ascope, *Peru* **92 E3** 7 46S 79 8W
Ascotán, *Chile* **94 A2** 21 45S 68 17W
Aseb, *Eritrea* **46 E3** 13 0N 42 40 E
Asela, *Ethiopia* **51 G12** 8 0N 39 0 E
Asenovgrad, *Bulgaria* **21 C11** 42 1N 24 51 E
Asgata, *Cyprus* **23 E12** 34 46N 33 15 E
Ash Fork, *U.S.A.* **83 J7** 35 13N 112 29W
Ash Grove, *U.S.A.* **81 G8** 37 19N 93 35W
Ash Shām, Bādiyat, *Asia* **28 F7** 32 0N 40 0 E
Ash Shamāl □, *Lebanon* **47 A5** 34 25N 36 0 E
Ash Shāmīyah, *Iraq* **44 D5** 31 55N 44 35 E
Ash Shāriqah, *U.A.E.* **45 E7** 25 23N 55 26 E
Ash Sharmah, *Si. Arabia* **44 D2** 28 1N 35 16 E
Ash Sharqāt, *Iraq* **44 C4** 35 27N 43 16 E
Ash Sharqi, Al Jabal, *Lebanon* **47 B5** 33 40N 36 10 E
Ash Shaṭrah, *Iraq* **44 D5** 31 30N 46 10 E
Ash Shawbak, *Jordan* **44 D2** 30 32N 35 34 E
Ash Shawmari, J., *Jordan* **47 E5** 30 35N 36 35 E
Ash Shaykh, J., *Lebanon* **47 B4** 33 25N 35 50 E
Ash Shināfiyah, *Iraq* **44 D5** 31 35N 44 39 E
Ash Shu'aybah, *Si. Arabia* **44 E5** 27 53N 44 43 E
Ash Shumlūl, *Si. Arabia* **44 E5** 26 31N 47 20 E
Ash Shūr'a, *Iraq* **44 C4** 35 58N 43 13 E
Ash Shurayf, *Si. Arabia* **44 E3** 25 43N 39 14 E
Ash Shuwayfāt, *Lebanon* **47 B4** 33 45N 35 30 E
Asha, *Russia* **24 D10** 55 0N 57 16 E
Ashau, *Vietnam* **38 D6** 16 6N 107 22 E
Ashburn, *U.S.A.* **77 K4** 31 43N 83 39W
Ashburton, *N.Z.* **59 K3** 43 53S 171 48 E
Ashburton →, *Australia* **60 D1** 21 40S 114 56 E
Ashburton Downs, *Australia* **60 D2** 23 25S 117 4 E
Ashby de la Zouch, *U.K.* **10 E6** 52 46N 1 29W
Ashcroft, *Canada* **72 C4** 50 40N 121 20W
Ashdod, *Israel* **47 D3** 31 49N 34 35 E
Asheboro, *U.S.A.* **77 H6** 35 43N 79 49W
Asherton, *U.S.A.* **81 L5** 28 27N 99 46W
Asheville, *U.S.A.* **77 H4** 35 36N 82 33W
Asheweig →, *Canada* **70 B2** 54 17N 87 12W
Ashford, *Australia* **63 D5** 29 15S 151 3 E
Ashford, *U.K.* **11 F8** 51 8N 0 53 E
Ashford, *U.S.A.* **82 C2** 46 46N 122 2W
Ashgabat, *Turkmenistan* **26 F6** 38 0N 57 50 E
Ashibetsu, *Japan* **30 C11** 43 31N 142 11 E
Ashikaga, *Japan* **31 F9** 36 28N 139 29 E
Ashizuri-Zaki, *Japan* **31 H6** 32 44N 133 0 E
Ashkarkot, *Afghan.* **42 C2** 33 3N 67 58 E
Ashkhabad = Ashgabat, *Turkmenistan* **26 F6** 38 0N 57 50 E
Ashland, *Kans., U.S.A.* **81 G5** 37 11N 99 46W
Ashland, *Ky., U.S.A.* **76 F4** 38 28N 82 38W
Ashland, *Maine, U.S.A.* **71 C6** 46 38N 68 24W
Ashland, *Mont., U.S.A.* **82 D10** 45 36N 106 16W
Ashland, *Nebr., U.S.A.* **80 E6** 41 3N 96 23W
Ashland, *Ohio, U.S.A.* **78 F2** 40 52N 82 19W
Ashland, *Oreg., U.S.A.* **82 E2** 42 12N 122 43W
Ashland, *Pa., U.S.A.* **79 F8** 40 45N 76 22W
Ashland, *Va., U.S.A.* **76 G7** 37 46N 77 29W
Ashland, *Wis., U.S.A.* **80 B9** 46 35N 90 53W
Ashley, *N. Dak., U.S.A.* **80 B5** 46 2N 99 22W
Ashley, *Pa., U.S.A.* **79 E9** 41 12N 75 55W
Ashmont, *Canada* **72 C6** 54 7N 111 35W
Ashmore Reef, *Australia* **60 B3** 12 14S 123 5 E
Ashmyany, *Belarus* **9 J21** 54 26N 25 52 E
Ashqelon, *Israel* **47 D3** 31 42N 34 35 E
Ashtabula, *U.S.A.* **78 E4** 41 52N 80 47W
Ashton, *S. Africa* **56 E3** 33 50S 20 5 E
Ashton, *U.S.A.* **82 D8** 44 4N 111 27W
Ashton under Lyne, *U.K.* **10 D5** 53 29N 2 6W
Ashuanipi, L., *Canada* **71 B6** 52 45N 66 15W
Asia, Kepulauan, *Indonesia* **37 D8** 1 0N 131 13 E
Āsīā Bak, *Iran* **45 C6** 35 19N 50 30 E
Asifabad, *India* **40 K11** 19 20N 79 24 E
Asike, *Indonesia* **37 F10** 6 39S 140 24 E

B

Bareilly

Bahía Blanca, Argentina 94 D3 38 35S 62 13W
Bahía de Caráquez, Ecuador 92 D2 0 40S 80 27W
Bahía Honda, Cuba 88 B3 22 54N 83 10W
Bahía Laura, Argentina 96 F3 48 10S 66 30W
Bahía Negra, Paraguay 92 H7 20 5S 58 5W
Bahmanzād, Iran 45 D6 31 15N 51 47 E
Bahr Aouk →, C.A.R. 52 C3 8 40N 19 0 E
Bahr el Ghazâl □, Sudan 48 F6 7 0N 28 0 E
Bahr Salamat →, Chad 51 G8 9 20N 18 0 E
Bahraich, India 43 F9 27 38N 81 37 E
Bahrain ■, Asia 45 E6 26 0N 50 35 E
Bahror, India 42 F7 27 51N 76 20 E
Bāhū Kalāt, Iran 45 E9 25 43N 61 25 E
Bai Bung, Mui, Vietnam 39 H5 8 38N 104 44 E
Bai Duc, Vietnam 38 C5 18 3N 105 49 E
Bai Thuong, Vietnam 38 C5 19 54N 105 23 E
Baia Mare, Romania 17 E12 47 40N 23 35 E
Baïbokoum, Chad 51 G8 7 46N 15 43 E
Baicheng, China 35 B12 45 38N 122 42 E
Baidoa, Somali Rep. 46 G3 3 8N 43 30 E
Baie Comeau, Canada 71 C6 49 12N 68 10W
Baie-St-Paul, Canada 71 C5 47 28N 70 32W
Baie Trinité, Canada 71 C6 49 25N 67 20W
Baie Verte, Canada 71 C8 49 55N 56 12W
Baihe, China 34 H6 32 50N 110 5 E
Ba'ījī, Iraq 44 C4 35 0N 43 30 E
Baikal, L. = Baykal, Oz., Russia 27 D11 53 0N 108 0 E
Baile Atha Cliath = Dublin, Ireland 13 C5 53 21N 6 15W
Băileşti, Romania 17 F12 44 1N 23 20 E
Bailundo, Angola 53 G3 12 10S 15 50 E
Bainbridge, Ga., U.S.A. 77 K3 30 55N 84 35W
Bainbridge, N.Y., U.S.A. 79 D9 42 18N 75 29W
Baing, Indonesia 37 F6 10 14S 120 34 E
Bainiu, China 34 H7 32 50N 112 15 E
Bainville, U.S.A. 80 A2 48 8N 104 13W
Bā'ir, Jordan 47 E5 30 45N 36 55 E
Baird, U.S.A. 81 J5 32 24N 99 24W
Baird Mts., U.S.A. 68 B3 67 0N 160 0W
Bairin Youqi, China 35 C10 43 30N 118 35 E
Bairin Zuoqi, China 35 C10 43 58N 119 15 E
Bairnsdale, Australia 63 F4 37 48S 147 36 E
Baisha, China 34 G7 34 20N 112 32 E
Baitadi, Nepal 43 E9 29 35N 80 25 E
Baiyin, China 34 F3 36 45N 104 14 E
Baiyu Shan, China 34 F4 37 15N 107 30 E
Baj Baj, India 43 H13 22 30N 88 5 E
Baja, Hungary 17 E10 46 12N 18 59 E
Baja, Pta., Mexico 86 B1 29 50N 116 0W
Baja California, Mexico 86 A1 31 10N 115 12W
Baja California □, Mexico 86 B2 30 0N 115 0W
Baja California Sur □, Mexico 86 B2 25 50N 111 50W
Bajamar, Canary Is. 22 F3 28 33N 16 20W
Bajana, India 42 H4 23 7N 71 49 E
Bājgīrān, Iran 45 B8 37 36N 58 24 E
Bajimba, Mt., Australia 63 D5 29 17S 152 6 E
Bajo Nuevo, Caribbean 88 C4 15 40N 78 50W
Bajool, Australia 62 C5 23 40S 150 35 E
Bakala, C.A.R. 51 G9 6 15N 20 20 E
Bakchar, Russia 26 D9 57 1N 82 5 E
Bakel, Senegal 50 F2 14 56N 12 20W
Baker, Calif., U.S.A. 85 K10 35 16N 116 4W
Baker, Mont., U.S.A. 80 B2 46 22N 104 17W
Baker, Oreg., U.S.A. 82 D5 44 47N 117 50W
Baker, L., Canada 68 B10 64 0N 96 0W
Baker I., Pac. Oc. 64 G10 0 10N 176 35W
Baker L., Australia 61 E4 26 54S 126 5 E
Baker Lake, Canada 68 B10 64 20N 96 3W
Baker Mt., U.S.A. 82 B3 48 50N 121 49W
Bakers Creek, Australia 62 C4 21 13S 149 7 E
Baker's Dozen Is., Canada 70 A4 56 45N 78 45W
Bakersfield, Calif., U.S.A. 85 K7 35 23N 119 1W
Bakersfield, Vt., U.S.A. 79 B12 44 45N 72 48W
Bākhtarān, Iran 44 C5 34 23N 47 0 E
Bākhtarān □, Iran 44 C5 34 0N 46 30 E
Bakı, Azerbaijan 25 F8 40 29N 49 56 E
Bakkafjörður, Iceland 8 C6 66 2N 14 48W
Bakony Forest = Bakony Hegyseg, Hungary 17 E9 47 10N 17 30 E
Bakony Hegyseg, Hungary 17 E9 47 10N 17 30 E
Bakouma, C.A.R. 51 G9 5 40N 22 56 E
Baku = Bakı, Azerbaijan 25 F8 40 29N 49 56 E
Bakutis Coast, Antarctica 5 D15 74 0S 120 0W
Baky = Bakı, Azerbaijan 25 F8 40 29N 49 56 E
Bala, Canada 78 A5 45 1N 79 37W
Bala, L., U.K. 10 E4 52 53N 3 37W
Balabac I., Phil. 36 C5 8 0N 117 0 E
Balabac Str., E. Indies 36 C5 7 53N 117 5 E
Balabagh, Afghan. 42 B4 34 25N 70 12 E
Ba'labakk, Lebanon 47 A5 34 0N 36 10 E
Balabalangan, Kepulauan, Indonesia 36 E5 2 20S 117 30 E
Balad, Iraq 44 C5 34 1N 44 9 E
Balad Rūz, Iraq 44 C5 33 42N 45 5 E
Bālādeh, Fārs, Iran 45 D6 29 17N 51 56 E
Bālādeh, Māzandaran, Iran 45 B6 36 12N 51 48 E
Balaghat, India 40 J12 21 49N 80 12 E
Balaghat Ra., India 40 K10 18 50N 76 30 E
Balaguer, Spain 19 B6 41 50N 0 50 E
Balaklava, Australia 63 E2 34 7S 138 22 E
Balaklava, Ukraine 25 F5 44 30N 33 30 E
Balakovo, Russia 24 D8 52 4N 47 55 E
Balancán, Mexico 87 D6 17 48N 91 32W
Balashov, Russia 24 D7 51 30N 43 10 E
Balasinor, India 42 H5 22 57N 73 23 E
Balasore = Baleshwar, India 41 J15 21 35N 87 3 E
Balaton, Hungary 17 E9 46 50N 17 40 E
Balbina, Reprêsa de, Brazil 92 D7 2 0S 59 30W
Balboa, Panama 88 E4 8 57N 79 34W
Balbriggan, Ireland 13 C5 53 37N 6 11W
Balcarce, Argentina 94 D4 38 0S 58 10W
Balcarres, Canada 73 C8 50 50N 103 35W
Balchik, Bulgaria 21 C13 43 28N 28 11 E
Balclutha, N.Z. 59 M2 46 15S 169 45 E
Bald Hd., Australia 61 G2 35 6S 118 1 E
Bald I., Australia 61 F2 34 57S 118 27 E
Bald Knob, U.S.A. 81 H9 35 19N 91 34W
Baldock L., Canada 73 B9 56 33N 97 57W
Baldwin, Fla., U.S.A. 77 K4 30 18N 81 59W
Baldwin, Mich., U.S.A. 76 D3 43 54N 85 51W
Baldwinsville, U.S.A. 79 C8 43 10N 76 20W
Baldy Peak, U.S.A. 83 K9 33 54N 109 34W
Baleares, Is., Spain 22 B10 39 30N 3 0 E
Balearic Is. = Baleares, Is., Spain 22 B10 39 30N 3 0 E
Baler, Phil. 37 A6 15 46N 121 34 E
Baleshwar, India 41 J15 21 35N 87 3 E
Balfate, Honduras 88 C2 15 48N 86 25W
Balfe's Creek, Australia 62 C4 20 12S 145 55 E
Bali, Cameroon 50 G7 5 54N 10 0 E
Balí, Greece 23 D6 35 25N 24 47 E
Bali, Indonesia 36 F5 8 20S 115 0 E
Bali □, Indonesia 36 F5 8 20S 115 0 E
Bali, Selat, Indonesia 37 H16 8 18S 114 25 E
Balikeşir, Turkey 21 E12 39 35N 27 58 E
Balikpapan, Indonesia 36 E5 1 10S 116 55 E
Balimbing, Phil. 37 C5 5 5N 119 58 E
Baling, Malaysia 39 K3 5 41N 100 55 E
Balipara, India 41 F18 26 50N 92 45 E
Baliza, Brazil 93 G8 16 0S 52 20W
Balkan Mts. = Stara Planina, Bulgaria 21 C10 43 15N 23 0 E
Balkhash = Balqash, Kazakstan 26 E8 46 50N 74 50 E
Balkhash, Ozero = Balqash Köl, Kazakstan 26 E8 46 0N 74 50 E
Balla, Bangla. 41 G17 24 10N 91 35 E
Ballachulish, U.K. 12 E3 56 41N 5 8W
Balladonia, Australia 61 F3 32 27S 123 51 E
Ballarat, Australia 63 F3 37 33S 143 50 E
Ballard, L., Australia 61 E3 29 20S 120 40 E
Ballater, U.K. 12 D5 57 3N 3 3W
Ballenas, Canal de, Mexico 86 B2 29 10N 113 45W
Balleny Is., Antarctica 5 C11 66 30S 163 0 E
Ballia, India 43 G11 25 46N 84 12 E
Ballidu, Australia 61 F2 30 35S 116 45 E
Ballina, Australia 63 D5 28 50S 153 31 E
Ballina, Mayo, Ireland 13 B2 54 7N 9 9W
Ballina, Tipp., Ireland 13 D3 52 49N 8 26W
Ballinasloe, Ireland 13 C3 53 20N 8 13W
Ballinger, U.S.A. 81 K5 31 45N 99 57W
Ballinrobe, Ireland 13 C2 53 38N 9 13W
Ballinskelligs B., Ireland 13 E1 51 48N 10 13W
Ballycastle, U.K. 13 A5 55 12N 6 15W
Ballymena, U.K. 13 B5 54 52N 6 17W
Ballymena □, U.K. 13 B5 54 53N 6 18W
Ballymoney, U.K. 13 A5 55 5N 6 31W
Ballymoney □, U.K. 13 A5 55 5N 6 23W
Ballyshannon, Ireland 13 B3 54 30N 8 11W
Balmaceda, Chile 96 F2 46 0S 71 50W
Balmoral, Australia 63 F3 37 15S 141 48 E
Balmoral, U.K. 12 D5 57 3N 3 13W
Balmorhea, U.S.A. 81 K3 30 59N 103 45W
Balonne →, Australia 63 D4 28 47S 147 56 E
Balqash, Kazakstan 26 E8 46 50N 74 50 E
Balqash Köl, Kazakstan 26 E8 46 0N 74 50 E
Balrampur, India 43 F10 27 30N 82 20 E
Balranald, Australia 63 E3 34 38S 143 33 E
Balsas, Mexico 87 D5 18 0N 99 40W
Balsas →, Mexico 86 D4 17 55N 102 10W
Balston Spa, U.S.A. 79 D11 43 0N 73 52W
Balta, Ukraine 17 D15 48 2N 29 45 E
Balta, U.S.A. 80 A4 48 10N 100 2W
Bălţi, Moldova 17 E14 47 48N 28 0 E
Baltic Sea, Europe 9 H18 57 0N 19 0 E
Baltimore, Ireland 13 E2 51 29N 9 22W
Baltimore, U.S.A. 76 F7 39 17N 76 37W
Baltit, Pakistan 43 A6 36 15N 74 40 E
Baltiysk, Russia 9 J18 54 41N 19 58 E
Baluchistan □, Pakistan 40 F4 27 30N 65 0 E
Balurghat, India 43 G13 25 15N 88 44 E
Balvi, Latvia 9 H22 57 8N 27 15 E
Balya, Turkey 21 E12 39 44N 27 35 E
Balygychan, Russia 27 C16 63 56N 154 12 E
Bam, Iran 45 D8 29 7N 58 14 E
Bama, Nigeria 51 F7 11 33N 13 41 E
Bamako, Mali 50 F3 12 34N 7 55W
Bamba, Mali 50 E4 17 5N 1 24W
Bambari, C.A.R. 51 G9 5 40N 20 35 E
Bambaroo, Australia 62 B4 18 50S 146 10 E
Bamberg, Germany 16 D6 49 54N 10 54 E
Bamberg, U.S.A. 77 J5 33 18N 81 2W
Bambili, Zaïre 54 B2 3 40N 26 0 E
Bamenda, Cameroon 50 G7 5 57N 10 11 E
Bamfield, Canada 72 D3 48 45N 125 10W
Bāmīān □, Afghan. 40 B5 35 0N 67 0 E
Bamiancheng, China 35 C13 43 15N 124 2 E
Bampūr, Iran 45 E9 27 15N 60 21 E
Ban Aranyaprathet, Thailand 38 F4 13 41N 102 30 E
Ban Ban, Laos 38 C4 19 31N 103 30 E
Ban Bang Hin, Thailand 39 H2 9 32N 98 35 E
Ban Chiang Klang, Thailand 38 C3 19 25N 100 55 E
Ban Chik, Laos 38 D4 17 15N 102 22 E
Ban Choho, Thailand 38 E4 15 2N 102 9 E
Ban Dan Lan Hoi, Thailand 38 D2 17 0N 99 35 E
Ban Don = Surat Thani, Thailand 39 H2 9 6N 99 20 E
Ban Don, Vietnam 38 F6 12 53N 107 48 E
Ban Don, Ao, Thailand 39 H2 9 20N 99 25 E
Ban Dong, Thailand 38 C3 19 30N 100 59 E
Ban Hong, Thailand 38 C2 18 18N 98 50 E
Ban Kaeng, Thailand 38 D3 17 29N 100 7 E
Ban Keun, Laos 38 C4 18 22N 102 35 E
Ban Khai, Thailand 38 F3 12 46N 101 18 E
Ban Kheun, Laos 38 B3 20 13N 101 7 E
Ban Khlong Kua, Thailand 39 J3 6 57N 100 8 E
Ban Khuan Mao, Thailand 39 J2 7 50N 99 37 E
Ban Khun Yuam, Thailand 38 C1 18 49N 97 57 E
Ban Ko Yai Chim, Thailand 39 G2 11 17N 99 26 E
Ban Kok, Thailand 38 D4 16 40N 103 40 E
Ban Laem, Thailand 38 F2 13 13N 99 59 E
Ban Lao Ngam, Laos 38 E6 15 28N 106 10 E
Ban Le Kathe, Thailand 38 E2 15 49N 98 53 E
Ban Mae Chedi, Thailand 38 C2 19 11N 99 31 E
Ban Mae Laeng, Thailand 38 B2 20 1N 99 17 E
Ban Mae Sariang, Thailand 38 C1 18 10N 97 56 E
Ban Mê Thuôt = Buon Me Thuot, Vietnam 38 F7 12 40N 108 3 E
Ban Mi, Thailand 38 E3 15 3N 100 32 E
Ban Muong Mo, Laos 38 C4 19 4N 103 58 E
Ban Na Mo, Laos 38 D5 17 7N 105 40 E
Ban Na San, Thailand 39 H2 8 53N 99 52 E
Ban Na Tong, Laos 38 B3 20 56N 101 47 E
Ban Nam Bac, Laos 38 B4 20 38N 102 20 E
Ban Nam Ma, Laos 38 A3 22 2N 101 37 E
Ban Ngang, Laos 38 E6 15 59N 106 11 E
Ban Nong Bok, Laos 38 D5 17 5N 104 48 E
Ban Nong Boua, Laos 38 E6 15 40N 106 33 E
Ban Nong Pling, Thailand 38 E3 15 40N 100 10 E
Ban Pak Chan, Thailand 39 G2 10 32N 98 51 E
Ban Phai, Thailand 38 D4 16 4N 102 44 E
Ban Pong, Thailand 38 F2 13 50N 99 55 E
Ban Ron Phibun, Thailand 39 H2 8 9N 99 51 E
Ban Sanam Chai, Thailand 39 J3 7 33N 100 25 E
Ban Sangkha, Thailand 38 E4 14 37N 103 52 E
Ban Tak, Thailand 38 D2 17 2N 99 4 E
Ban Tako, Thailand 38 E4 14 5N 102 40 E
Ban Tha Dua, Thailand 38 D2 17 59N 98 39 E
Ban Tha Li, Thailand 38 D3 17 37N 101 25 E
Ban Tha Nun, Thailand 39 H2 8 12N 98 18 E
Ban Thahine, Laos 38 E5 14 12N 105 33 E
Ban Xien Kok, Laos 38 B3 20 54N 100 39 E
Ban Yen Nhan, Vietnam 38 B6 20 57N 106 2 E
Banaba, Kiribati 64 H8 0 45S 169 50 E
Bañalbufar, Spain 22 B9 39 42N 2 31 E
Banalia, Zaïre 54 B2 1 32N 25 5 E
Banam, Cambodia 39 G5 11 20N 105 17 E
Banamba, Mali 50 F3 13 29N 7 22W
Banana, Australia 62 C5 24 28S 150 8 E
Bananal, I. do, Brazil 93 F8 11 30S 50 30W
Banaras = Varanasi, India 43 G10 25 22N 83 0 E
Banas →, Gujarat, India 42 H4 23 45N 71 25 E
Banas →, Mad. P., India 43 G9 24 15N 81 30 E
Banbān, Si. Arabia 44 E5 25 1N 46 35 E
Banbridge, U.K. 13 B5 54 22N 6 16W
Banbridge □, U.K. 13 B5 54 21N 6 16W
Banbury, U.K. 11 E6 52 4N 1 20W
Banchory, U.K. 12 D6 57 3N 2 29W
Bancroft, Canada 70 C4 45 3N 77 51W
Band Bonī, Iran 45 E8 25 30N 59 33 E
Band Qīr, Iran 45 D6 31 39N 48 53 E
Banda, India 43 G9 25 30N 80 26 E
Banda, Kepulauan, Indonesia 37 E7 4 37S 129 50 E
Banda Aceh, Indonesia 36 C1 5 35N 95 20 E
Banda Banda, Mt., Australia 63 E5 31 10S 152 28 E
Banda Elat, Indonesia 37 F8 5 40S 133 5 E
Banda Is. = Banda, Kepulauan, Indonesia 37 E7 4 37S 129 50 E
Banda Sea, Indonesia 37 F7 6 0S 130 0 E
Bandai-San, Japan 30 F10 37 36N 140 4 E
Bandān, Iran 45 D9 31 23N 60 44 E
Bandanaira, Indonesia 37 E7 4 32S 129 54 E
Bandanwara, India 42 F6 26 9N 74 38 E
Bandar = Machilipatnam, India 41 L12 16 12N 81 8 E
Bandār 'Abbās, Iran 45 E8 27 15N 56 15 E
Bandar-e Anzalī, Iran 45 B6 37 30N 49 30 E
Bandar-e Bushehr = Būshehr, Iran 45 D6 28 55N 50 55 E
Bandar-e Chārak, Iran 45 E7 26 45N 54 20 E
Bandar-e Deylam, Iran 45 D6 30 5N 50 10 E
Bandar-e Khomeynı, Iran 45 D6 30 30N 49 5 E
Bandar-e Lengeh, Iran 45 E7 26 35N 54 58 E
Bandar-e Maqām, Iran 45 E7 26 56N 53 29 E
Bandar-e Ma'shur, Iran 45 D6 30 35N 49 10 E
Bandar-e Nakhīlū, Iran 45 E7 26 58N 53 30 E
Bandar-e Rīg, Iran 45 D6 29 29N 50 38 E
Bandar-e Torkeman, Iran 45 B7 37 0N 54 10 E
Bandar Maharani = Muar, Malaysia 39 L4 2 3N 102 34 E
Bandar Penggaram = Batu Pahat, Malaysia 39 M4 1 50N 102 56 E
Bandar Seri Begawan, Brunei 36 C4 4 52N 115 0 E
Bandawe, Malawi 55 E3 11 58S 34 5 E
Bandeira, Pico da, Brazil 95 A7 20 26S 41 47W
Bandera, Argentina 94 B3 28 55S 62 20W
Bandera, U.S.A. 81 L5 29 44N 99 5W
Banderas, B. de, Mexico 86 C3 20 40N 105 30W
Bandiagara, Mali 50 F4 14 12N 3 29W
Bandırma, Turkey 21 D13 40 20N 28 0 E
Bandon, Ireland 13 E3 51 44N 8 44W
Bandon →, Ireland 13 E3 51 43N 8 37W
Bandula, Mozam. 55 F3 19 0S 33 7 E
Bandundu, Zaïre 52 E3 3 15S 17 22 E
Bandung, Indonesia 37 G12 6 54S 107 36 E
Bandya, Australia 61 E3 27 40S 122 5 E
Bāneh, Iran 44 C5 35 59N 45 53 E
Banes, Cuba 89 B4 21 0N 75 42W
Banff, Canada 72 C5 51 10N 115 34W
Banff, U.K. 12 D6 57 40N 2 33W
Banff Nat. Park, Canada 72 C5 51 30N 116 15W
Banfora, Burkina Faso 50 F4 10 40N 4 40W
Bang Fai →, Laos 38 D5 16 57N 104 45 E
Bang Hieng →, Laos 38 D5 16 10N 105 10 E
Bang Krathum, Thailand 38 D3 16 34N 100 18 E
Bang Lamung, Thailand 38 F3 13 3N 100 56 E
Bang Mun Nak, Thailand 38 D3 16 2N 100 23 E
Bang Pa In, Thailand 38 E3 14 14N 100 35 E
Bang Rakam, Thailand 38 D3 16 45N 100 7 E
Bang Saphan, Thailand 39 G2 11 14N 99 28 E
Bangala Dam, Zimbabwe 55 G3 21 7S 31 25 E
Bangalore, India 40 N10 12 59N 77 40 E
Bangaon, India 43 H13 23 0N 88 47 E
Bangassou, C.A.R. 52 D4 4 55N 23 7 E
Banggai, Kepulauan, Indonesia 37 E6 1 40S 123 30 E
Banggi, P., Malaysia 36 C5 7 17N 117 12 E
Banghāzī, Libya 51 B9 32 11N 20 3 E
Bangil, Indonesia 37 G15 7 36S 112 50 E
Bangka, P., Sulawesi, Indonesia 37 D7 1 50N 125 5 E
Bangka, P., Sumatera, Indonesia 36 E3 2 0S 105 50 E
Bangka, Selat, Indonesia 36 E3 2 30S 105 30 E
Bangkalan, Indonesia 37 G15 7 2S 112 46 E
Bangkinang, Indonesia 36 D2 0 18N 101 5 E
Bangko, Indonesia 36 E2 2 5S 102 9 E
Bangkok, Thailand 38 F3 13 45N 100 35 E
Bangladesh ■, Asia 41 H17 24 0N 90 0 E
Bangong Co, India 43 B8 35 50N 79 20 E
Bangor, Down, U.K. 13 B6 54 40N 5 40W
Bangor, Gwynedd, U.K. 10 D3 53 14N 4 8W
Bangor, Maine, U.S.A. 71 D6 44 48N 68 46W
Bangor, Pa., U.S.A. 79 F9 40 52N 75 13W
Bangued, Phil. 37 A6 17 40N 120 37 E
Bangui, C.A.R. 52 D3 4 23N 18 35 E
Banguru, Zaïre 54 B2 0 30N 27 10 E
Bangweulu, L., Zambia 55 E3 11 0S 30 0 E
Bangweulu Swamp, Zambia 55 E3 11 20S 30 15 E
Bani, Dom. Rep. 89 C5 18 16N 70 22W
Banī Sa'd, Iraq 44 C5 33 34N 44 32 E
Banī Walīd, Libya 51 B7 31 36N 13 53 E
Banihal Pass, India 43 C6 33 30N 75 12 E
Banīnah, Libya 51 B9 32 0N 20 12 E
Bāniyās, Syria 44 C3 35 10N 36 0 E
Banja Luka, Bos.-H. 20 B7 44 49N 17 11 E
Banjar, Indonesia 37 G13 7 24S 108 30 E
Banjarmasin, Indonesia 36 E4 3 20S 114 35 E
Banjarnegara, Indonesia 37 G13 7 24S 109 42 E
Banjul, Gambia 50 F1 13 28N 16 40W
Banka Banka, Australia 62 B1 18 50S 134 0 E
Banket, Zimbabwe 55 F3 17 27S 30 19 E
Bankipore, India 43 G11 25 35N 85 10 E
Banks I., B.C., Canada 72 C3 53 20N 130 0W
Banks I., N.W.T., Canada 68 A7 73 15N 121 30W
Banks Pen., N.Z. 59 K4 43 45S 173 15 E
Banks Str., Australia 62 G4 40 40S 148 10 E
Bankura, India 43 H12 23 11N 87 18 E
Bann →, Arm., U.K. 13 B5 54 30N 6 31W
Bann →, L'derry., U.K. 13 A5 55 8N 6 41W
Bannang Sata, Thailand 39 J3 6 16N 101 16 E
Banning, U.S.A. 85 M10 33 56N 116 53W
Banningville = Bandundu, Zaïre 52 E3 3 15S 17 22 E
Bannockburn, Canada 78 B7 44 39N 77 33W
Bannockburn, U.K. 12 E5 56 5N 3 55W
Bannockburn, Zimbabwe 55 G2 20 17S 29 48 E
Bannu, Pakistan 40 C7 33 0N 70 18 E
Banská Bystrica, Slovak Rep. 17 D10 48 46N 19 14 E
Banswara, India 42 H6 23 32N 74 24 E
Banten, Indonesia 37 G12 6 5S 106 8 E
Bantry, Ireland 13 E2 51 41N 9 27W
Bantry B., Ireland 13 E2 51 37N 9 44W
Bantul, Indonesia 37 G14 7 55S 110 19 E
Bantva, India 42 J4 21 29N 70 12 E
Banu, Afghan. 40 B6 35 35N 69 5 E
Banyak, Kepulauan, Indonesia 36 D1 2 10N 97 10 E
Banyo, Cameroon 50 G7 6 52N 11 45 E
Banyumas, Indonesia 37 G13 7 32S 109 18 E
Banyuwangi, Indonesia 37 H16 8 13S 114 21 E
Banzare Coast, Antarctica 5 C9 68 0S 125 0 E
Banzyville = Mobayi, Zaïre 52 D4 4 15N 21 8 E
Bao Ha, Vietnam 38 A5 22 11N 104 21 E
Bao Lac, Vietnam 38 A5 22 57N 105 40 E
Bao Loc, Vietnam 39 G6 11 32N 107 48 E
Baocheng, China 34 H4 33 12N 106 56 E
Baode, China 34 E6 39 1N 111 5 E
Baodi, China 35 E9 39 38N 117 20 E
Baoding, China 34 E8 38 50N 115 28 E
Baoji, China 34 G4 34 20N 107 5 E
Baoshan, China 32 D4 25 10N 99 5 E
Baotou, China 34 D6 40 32N 110 2 E
Baoying, China 35 H10 33 17N 119 20 E
Bap, India 42 F5 27 23N 72 18 E
Bapatla, India 41 M12 15 55N 80 30 E
Bāqerābād, Iran 45 C6 33 2N 51 58 E
Ba'qūbah, Iraq 44 C5 33 45N 44 50 E
Baquedano, Chile 94 A2 23 20S 69 52W
Bar, Montenegro, Yug. 21 C8 42 8N 19 8 E
Bar, Ukraine 17 D14 49 4N 27 40 E
Bar Bigha, India 43 G11 25 21N 85 47 E
Bar Harbor, U.S.A. 71 D6 44 23N 68 13W
Bar-le-Duc, France 18 B6 48 47N 5 10 E
Barabai, Indonesia 36 E5 2 32S 115 34 E
Barabinsk, Russia 26 D8 55 20N 78 20 E
Baraboo, U.S.A. 80 D10 43 28N 89 45W
Baracaldo, Spain 19 A4 43 18N 2 59W
Baracoa, Cuba 89 B5 20 20N 74 30W
Baradero, Argentina 94 C4 33 52S 59 29W
Baraga, U.S.A. 80 B10 46 47N 88 30W
Barahona, Dom. Rep. 89 C5 18 13N 71 7W
Barail Range, India 41 G18 25 15N 93 20 E
Barakhola, India 41 G18 25 0N 92 45 E
Barakot, India 43 J11 21 33N 84 59 E
Barakpur, India 43 H13 22 44N 88 30 E
Barakula, Australia 63 D5 26 30S 150 33 E
Baralaba, Australia 62 C4 24 13S 149 50 E
Baralzon L., Canada 73 B9 60 0N 98 3W
Baramula, India 43 B6 34 15N 74 20 E
Baran, India 42 G7 25 9N 76 40 E
Baranavichy, Belarus 17 B14 53 10N 26 0 E
Baranof I., U.S.A. 72 B1 57 0N 135 0W
Barão de Melgaço, Brazil 92 F6 11 50S 60 45W
Barapasi, Indonesia 37 E9 2 15S 137 5 E
Barasat, India 43 H13 22 46N 88 31 E
Barat Daya, Kepulauan, Indonesia 37 F7 7 30S 128 0 E
Barataria B., U.S.A. 81 L10 29 20N 89 55W
Baraut, India 42 E7 29 13N 77 7 E
Barbacena, Brazil 95 A7 21 15S 43 56W
Barbacoas, Colombia 92 C3 1 45N 78 0W
Barbados ■, W. Indies 89 D8 13 10N 59 30W
Barbastro, Spain 19 A6 42 2N 0 5 E
Barberton, S. Africa 57 D5 25 42S 31 2 E
Barberton, U.S.A. 78 E3 41 0N 81 39W
Barbourville, U.S.A. 77 G4 36 52N 83 53W
Barbuda, W. Indies 89 C7 17 30N 61 40W
Barcaldine, Australia 62 C4 23 43S 145 6 E
Barcellona Pozzo di Gotto, Italy 20 E6 38 9N 15 13 E
Barcelona, Spain 19 B7 41 21N 2 10 E
Barcelona, Venezuela 92 A6 10 10N 64 40W
Barcelos, Brazil 92 D6 1 0S 63 0W
Barcoo →, Australia 62 D3 25 30S 142 50 E
Bardai, Chad 51 D8 21 25N 17 0 E
Bardas Blancas, Argentina 94 D2 35 49S 69 45W
Barddhaman, India 43 H12 23 14N 87 39 E
Bardejov, Slovak Rep. 17 D11 49 18N 21 15 E
Bardera, Somali Rep. 46 G3 2 20N 42 27 E
Bardīyah, Libya 51 B9 31 45N 25 5 E
Bardsey I., U.K. 10 E3 52 45N 4 47W
Bardstown, U.S.A. 76 G3 37 49N 85 28W
Bareilly, India 43 E8 28 22N 79 27 E

Bihar

Belgorod, *Russia* 25 D6 50 35N 36 35 E
Belgorod-Dnestrovskiy = Bilhorod-Dnistrovskyy, *Ukraine* 25 E5 46 11N 30 23 E
Belgrade = Beograd, *Serbia, Yug.* 21 B9 44 50N 20 37 E
Belgrade, *U.S.A.* 82 D8 45 47N 111 11W
Belhaven, *U.S.A.* 77 H7 35 33N 76 37W
Beli Drim →, *Europe* 21 C9 42 6N 20 25 E
Belinga, *Gabon* 52 D2 1 10N 13 2 E
Belinyu, *Indonesia* 36 E3 1 35S 105 50 E
Beliton Is. = Belitung, *Indonesia* 36 E3 3 10S 107 50 E
Belitung, *Indonesia* 36 E3 3 10S 107 50 E
Belize ■, *Cent. Amer.* 87 D7 17 0N 88 30W
Belize City, *Belize* 87 D7 17 25N 88 0W
Belkovskiy, Ostrov, *Russia* 27 B14 75 32N 135 44 E
Bell →, *Canada* 70 C4 49 48N 77 38W
Bell Bay, *Australia* 62 G4 41 6S 146 53 E
Bell I., *Canada* 71 B8 50 46N 55 35W
Bell-Irving →, *Canada* 72 B3 56 12N 129 5W
Bell Peninsula, *Canada* 69 B11 63 50N 82 0W
Bell Ville, *Argentina* 94 C3 32 40S 62 40W
Bella Bella, *Canada* 72 C3 52 10N 128 10W
Bella Coola, *Canada* 72 C3 52 25N 126 40W
Bella Unión, *Uruguay* 94 C4 30 15S 57 40W
Bella Vista, *Corrientes, Argentina* 94 B4 28 33S 59 0W
Bella Vista, *Tucuman, Argentina* 94 B2 27 10S 65 25W
Bellaire, *U.S.A.* 78 F4 40 1N 80 45W
Bellary, *India* 40 M10 15 10N 76 56 E
Bellata, *Australia* 63 D4 29 53S 149 46 E
Belle Fourche, *U.S.A.* 80 C3 44 40N 103 51W
Belle Fourche →, *U.S.A.* 80 C3 44 26N 102 18W
Belle Glade, *U.S.A.* 77 M5 26 41N 80 40W
Belle-Ile, *France* 18 C2 47 20N 3 10W
Belle Isle, *Canada* 71 B8 51 57N 55 25W
Belle Isle, Str. of, *Canada* 71 B8 51 30N 56 30W
Belle Plaine, *Iowa, U.S.A.* 80 E8 41 54N 92 17W
Belle Plaine, *Minn., U.S.A.* 80 C8 44 37N 93 46W
Belledune, *Canada* 71 C6 47 55N 65 50W
Bellefontaine, *U.S.A.* 76 E4 40 22N 83 46W
Bellefonte, *U.S.A.* 78 F7 40 55N 77 47W
Belleoram, *Canada* 71 C8 47 31N 55 25W
Belleville, *Canada* 70 D4 44 10N 77 23W
Belleville, *Ill., U.S.A.* 80 F10 38 31N 89 59W
Belleville, *Kans., U.S.A.* 80 F6 39 50N 97 38W
Belleville, *N.Y., U.S.A.* 79 C8 43 46N 76 10W
Bellevue, *Canada* 72 D6 49 35N 114 22W
Bellevue, *Idaho, U.S.A.* 82 E6 43 28N 114 16W
Bellevue, *Ohio, U.S.A.* 78 E2 41 17N 82 51W
Bellevue, *Wash., U.S.A.* 84 C4 47 37N 122 12W
Bellin = Kangirsuk, *Canada* 69 B13 60 0N 70 0W
Bellingen, *Australia* 63 E5 30 25S 152 50 E
Bellingham, *U.S.A.* 84 B4 48 46N 122 29W
Bellingshausen Sea, *Antarctica* 5 C17 66 0S 80 0W
Bellinzona, *Switz.* 16 E5 46 11N 9 1 E
Bellows Falls, *U.S.A.* 79 C12 43 8N 72 27W
Bellpat, *Pakistan* 42 E3 29 0N 68 5 E
Belluno, *Italy* 20 A5 46 9N 12 13 E
Bellville, *U.S.A.* 81 L6 29 57N 96 15W
Bellwood, *U.S.A.* 78 F6 40 36N 78 20W
Belmont, *Australia* 63 E5 33 4S 151 42 E
Belmont, *Canada* 78 D3 42 53N 81 5W
Belmont, *S. Africa* 56 D3 29 28S 24 22 E
Belmont, *U.S.A.* 78 D6 42 14N 78 2W
Belmonte, *Brazil* 93 G11 16 0S 39 0W
Belmopan, *Belize* 87 D7 17 18N 88 30W
Belmullet, *Ireland* 13 B2 54 14N 9 58W
Belo Horizonte, *Brazil* 93 G10 19 55S 43 56W
Belo-sur-Mer, *Madag.* 57 C7 20 42S 44 0 E
Belo-Tsiribihina, *Madag.* 57 B7 19 40S 44 30 E
Belogorsk, *Russia* 27 D13 51 0N 128 20 E
Beloha, *Madag.* 57 D8 25 10S 45 3 E
Beloit, *Kans., U.S.A.* 80 F5 39 28N 98 6W
Beloit, *Wis., U.S.A.* 80 D10 42 31N 89 2W
Belokorovichi, *Ukraine* 17 C15 51 7N 28 2 E
Belomorsk, *Russia* 24 B5 64 35N 34 54 E
Belonia, *India* 41 H17 23 15N 91 30 E
Beloretsk, *Russia* 24 D10 53 58N 58 24 E
Belorussia ■ = Belarus ■, *Europe* 17 B14 53 30N 27 0 E
Belovo, *Russia* 26 D9 54 30N 86 0 E
Beloye, Ozero, *Russia* 24 B6 60 10N 37 35 E
Beloye More, *Russia* 24 A6 66 30N 38 0 E
Belozersk, *Russia* 24 B6 60 1N 37 45 E
Beltana, *Australia* 63 E2 30 48S 138 25 E
Belterra, *Brazil* 93 D8 2 45S 55 0W
Belton, *S.C., U.S.A.* 77 H4 34 31N 82 30W
Belton, *Tex., U.S.A.* 81 K6 31 3N 97 28W
Belton Res., *U.S.A.* 81 K6 31 8N 97 32W
Beltsy = Bălţi, *Moldova* 17 E14 47 48N 28 0 E
Belturbet, *Ireland* 13 B4 54 6N 7 26W
Belukha, *Russia* 26 E9 49 50N 86 50 E
Beluran, *Malaysia* 36 C5 5 48N 117 35 E
Belvidere, *Ill., U.S.A.* 80 D10 42 15N 88 50W
Belvidere, *N.J., U.S.A.* 79 F9 40 50N 75 5W
Belyando →, *Australia* 62 C4 21 38S 146 50 E
Belyy, Ostrov, *Russia* 26 B8 73 30N 71 0 E
Belyy Yar, *Russia* 26 D9 58 26N 84 39 E
Belzoni, *U.S.A.* 81 J9 33 11N 90 29W
Bemaraha, Lembalemban' i, *Madag.* 57 B7 18 40S 44 45 E
Bemarivo, *Madag.* 57 C7 21 45S 44 45 E
Bemarivo →, *Madag.* 57 B8 15 27S 47 40 E
Bemavo, *Madag.* 57 C8 21 33S 45 25 E
Bembéréke, *Benin* 50 F5 10 11N 2 43 E
Bembesi, *Zimbabwe* 55 F2 20 0S 28 58 E
Bembesi →, *Zimbabwe* 55 F2 18 57S 27 47 E
Bemidji, *U.S.A.* 80 B7 47 28N 94 53W
Ben, *Iran* 45 C6 32 32N 50 45 E
Ben Cruachan, *U.K.* 12 E3 56 26N 5 8W
Ben Dearg, *U.K.* 12 D4 57 47N 4 56W
Ben Gardane, *Tunisia* 51 B7 33 11N 11 11 E
Ben Hope, *U.K.* 12 C4 58 25N 4 36W
Ben Lawers, *U.K.* 12 E4 56 32N 4 14W
Ben Lomond, *N.S.W., Australia* 63 E5 30 1S 151 43 E
Ben Lomond, *Tas., Australia* 62 G4 41 38S 147 42 E
Ben Lomond, *U.K.* 12 E4 56 11N 4 38W
Ben Luc, *Vietnam* 39 G6 10 39N 106 29 E
Ben Macdhui, *U.K.* 12 D5 57 4N 3 40W
Ben Mhor, *U.K.* 12 D1 57 15N 7 18W
Ben More, *Arg. & Bute, U.K.* 12 E2 56 26N 6 1W
Ben More, *Stirl., U.K.* 12 E4 56 23N 4 32W
Ben More Assynt, *U.K.* 12 C4 58 8N 4 52W
Ben Nevis, *U.K.* 12 E4 56 48N 5 1W
Ben Quang, *Vietnam* 38 D6 17 3N 106 55 E
Ben Tre, *Vietnam* 39 G6 10 3N 106 36 E
Ben Vorlich, *U.K.* 12 E4 56 21N 4 14W
Ben Wyvis, *U.K.* 12 D4 57 40N 4 35W
Bena, *Nigeria* 50 F6 11 20N 5 50 E
Bena Dibele, *Zaïre* 52 E4 4 4S 22 50 E
Benagerie, *Australia* 63 E3 31 25S 140 22 E
Benalla, *Australia* 63 F4 36 30S 146 0 E
Benambra, Mt., *Australia* 63 F4 36 31S 147 34 E
Benares = Varanasi, *India* 43 G10 25 22N 83 0 E
Benavente, *Spain* 19 A3 42 2N 5 43W
Benavides, *U.S.A.* 81 M5 27 36N 98 25W
Benbecula, *U.K.* 12 D1 57 26N 7 21W
Benbonyathe, *Australia* 63 E2 30 25S 139 11 E
Bencubbin, *Australia* 61 F2 30 48S 117 52 E
Bend, *U.S.A.* 82 D3 44 4N 121 19W
Bender Beila, *Somali Rep.* 46 F5 9 30N 50 48 E
Bendering, *Australia* 61 F2 32 23S 118 18 E
Bendery = Tighina, *Moldova* 17 E15 46 50N 29 30 E
Bendigo, *Australia* 63 F3 36 40S 144 15 E
Benē Beraq, *Israel* 47 C3 32 6N 34 51 E
Benenitra, *Madag.* 57 C8 23 27S 45 5 E
Benevento, *Italy* 20 D6 41 8N 14 45 E
Benga, *Mozam.* 55 F3 16 11S 33 40 E
Bengal, Bay of, *Ind. Oc.* 41 K16 15 0N 90 0 E
Bengbu, *China* 35 H9 32 58N 117 20 E
Benghazi = Banghāzī, *Libya* 51 B9 32 11N 20 3 E
Bengkalis, *Indonesia* 36 D2 1 30N 102 10 E
Bengkulu, *Indonesia* 36 E2 3 50S 102 12 E
Bengkulu □, *Indonesia* 36 E2 3 48S 102 16 E
Bengough, *Canada* 73 D7 49 25N 105 10W
Benguela, *Angola* 53 G2 12 37S 13 25 E
Benguérua, I., *Mozam.* 57 C6 21 58S 35 28 E
Beni, *Zaïre* 54 B2 0 30N 29 27 E
Beni →, *Bolivia* 92 F5 10 23S 65 24W
Beni Abbès, *Algeria* 50 B4 30 5N 2 5W
Beni Mazâr, *Egypt* 51 C11 28 32N 30 44 E
Beni Mellal, *Morocco* 50 B3 32 21N 6 21W
Beni Ounif, *Algeria* 50 B4 32 0N 1 10W
Beni Suef, *Egypt* 51 C11 29 5N 31 6 E
Beniah L., *Canada* 72 A6 63 23N 112 17W
Benicia, *U.S.A.* 84 G4 38 3N 122 9W
Benidorm, *Spain* 19 C5 38 33N 0 9W
Benin ■, *Africa* 50 G5 10 0N 2 0 E
Benin, Bight of, *W. Afr.* 50 H5 5 0N 3 0 E
Benin City, *Nigeria* 50 G6 6 20N 5 31 E
Benitses, *Greece* 23 A3 39 32N 19 55 E
Benjamin Aceval, *Paraguay* 94 A4 24 58S 57 34W
Benjamin Constant, *Brazil* 92 D4 4 40S 70 15W
Benjamin Hill, *Mexico* 86 A2 30 10N 111 10W
Benkelman, *U.S.A.* 80 E4 40 3N 101 32W
Benlidi, *Australia* 62 C3 24 35S 144 50 E
Bennett, *Canada* 72 B2 59 56N 134 53W
Bennett, L., *Australia* 60 D5 22 50S 131 2 E
Bennett, Ostrov, *Russia* 27 B15 76 21N 148 56 E
Bennettsville, *U.S.A.* 77 H6 34 37N 79 41W
Bennington, *U.S.A.* 79 D11 43 0N 71 55W
Benoni, *S. Africa* 57 D4 26 11S 28 18 E
Benque Viejo, *Belize* 87 D7 17 5N 89 8W
Benson, *U.S.A.* 83 L8 31 58N 110 18W
Bent, *Iran* 45 E8 26 20N 59 31 E
Benteng, *Indonesia* 37 F6 6 10S 120 30 E
Bentinck I., *Australia* 62 B2 17 3S 139 35 E
Bento Gonçalves, *Brazil* 95 B5 29 10S 51 31W
Benton, *Ark., U.S.A.* 81 H8 34 34N 92 35W
Benton, *Calif., U.S.A.* 84 H8 37 48N 118 32W
Benton, *Ill., U.S.A.* 80 F10 38 0N 88 55W
Benton Harbor, *U.S.A.* 76 D2 42 6N 86 27W
Bentung, *Malaysia* 39 L3 3 31N 101 55 E
Benue →, *Nigeria* 50 G6 7 48N 6 46 E
Benxi, *China* 35 D12 41 20N 123 48 E
Beo, *Indonesia* 37 D7 4 25N 126 50 E
Beograd, *Serbia, Yug.* 21 B9 44 50N 20 37 E
Beowawe, *U.S.A.* 82 F5 40 35N 116 29W
Beppu, *Japan* 31 H5 33 15N 131 30 E
Beqaa Valley = Al Biqā □, *Lebanon* 47 A5 34 10N 36 10 E
Berati, *Albania* 21 D8 40 43N 19 59 E
Berau, Teluk, *Indonesia* 37 E8 2 30S 132 30 E
Berber, *Sudan* 51 E11 18 0N 34 0 E
Berbera, *Somali Rep.* 46 E4 10 30N 45 2 E
Berbérati, *C.A.R.* 52 D3 4 15N 15 40 E
Berberia, C. del, *Spain* 22 C7 38 39N 1 24 E
Berbice →, *Guyana* 92 B7 6 20N 57 32W
Berdichev = Berdychiv, *Ukraine* 17 D15 49 57N 28 30 E
Berdsk, *Russia* 26 D9 54 47N 83 2 E
Berdyansk, *Ukraine* 25 E6 46 45N 36 50 E
Berdychiv, *Ukraine* 17 D15 49 57N 28 30 E
Berea, *U.S.A.* 76 G3 37 34N 84 17W
Berebere, *Indonesia* 37 D7 2 25N 128 45 E
Bereda, *Somali Rep.* 46 E5 11 45N 51 0 E
Berehove, *Ukraine* 17 D12 48 15N 22 35 E
Berekum, *Ghana* 50 G4 7 29N 2 34W
Berens →, *Canada* 73 C9 52 25N 97 2W
Berens I., *Canada* 73 C9 52 18N 97 18W
Berens River, *Canada* 73 C9 52 25N 97 0W
Berestechko, *Ukraine* 17 C13 50 22N 25 5 E
Berevo, *Mahajanga, Madag.* 57 B7 17 14S 44 17 E
Berevo, *Toliara, Madag.* 57 B7 19 44S 44 58 E
Bereza, *Belarus* 17 B13 52 31N 24 51 E
Berezhany, *Ukraine* 17 D13 49 26N 24 58 E
Berezina = Byarezina →, *Belarus* 17 B16 52 33N 30 14 E
Berezniki, *Russia* 26 D6 59 24N 56 46 E
Berezovo, *Russia* 24 B11 64 0N 65 0 E
Berga, *Spain* 19 A6 42 6N 1 48 E
Bergama, *Turkey* 21 E12 39 8N 27 15 E
Bérgamo, *Italy* 20 B3 45 41N 9 43 E
Bergen, *Neths.* 15 B4 52 40N 4 43 E
Bergen, *Norway* 9 F11 60 20N 5 20 E
Bergen, *U.S.A.* 78 C7 43 5N 77 57W
Bergen-op-Zoom, *Neths.* 15 C4 51 28N 4 18 E
Bergerac, *France* 18 D4 44 51N 0 30 E
Bergum, *Neths.* 15 A5 53 13N 5 59 E
Bergville, *S. Africa* 57 D4 28 52S 29 18 E
Berhala, Selat, *Indonesia* 36 E2 1 0S 104 15 E
Berhampore = Baharampur, *India* 43 G13 24 2N 88 27 E
Berhampur, *India* 41 K14 19 15N 84 54 E
Bering Sea, *Pac. Oc.* 68 C1 58 0N 171 0 E
Bering Strait, *U.S.A.* 68 B3 65 30N 169 0W
Beringen, *Belgium* 15 C5 51 3N 5 14 E
Beringovskiy, *Russia* 27 C18 63 3N 179 19 E
Berisso, *Argentina* 94 C4 34 56S 57 50W
Berja, *Spain* 19 D4 36 50N 2 56W
Berkeley, *U.K.* 11 F5 51 41N 2 27W
Berkeley, *U.S.A.* 84 H4 37 52N 122 16W
Berkeley Springs, *U.S.A.* 76 F6 39 38N 78 14W
Berkner I., *Antarctica* 5 D18 79 30S 50 0W
Berkshire □, *U.K.* 11 F6 51 25N 1 17W
Berland →, *Canada* 72 C5 54 0N 116 50W
Berlin, *Germany* 16 B7 52 30N 13 25 E
Berlin, *Md., U.S.A.* 76 F8 38 20N 75 13W
Berlin, *N.H., U.S.A.* 79 B13 44 28N 71 11W
Berlin, *Wis., U.S.A.* 76 D1 43 58N 88 57W
Bermejo →, *Formosa, Argentina* 94 B4 26 51S 58 23W
Bermejo →, *San Juan, Argentina* 94 C2 32 30S 67 30W
Bermuda ■, *Atl. Oc.* 66 F13 32 45N 65 0W
Bern, *Switz.* 16 E4 46 57N 7 28 E
Bernado, *U.S.A.* 83 J10 34 30N 106 53W
Bernalillo, *U.S.A.* 83 J10 35 18N 106 33W
Bernardo de Irigoyen, *Argentina* 95 B5 26 15S 53 40W
Bernardo O'Higgins □, *Chile* 94 C1 34 15S 70 45W
Bernasconi, *Argentina* 94 D3 37 55S 63 44W
Bernburg, *Germany* 16 C6 51 47N 11 44 E
Berne = Bern, *Switz.* 16 E4 46 57N 7 28 E
Bernier I., *Australia* 61 D1 24 50S 113 12 E
Bernina, Piz, *Switz.* 16 E5 46 20N 9 54 E
Beroroha, *Madag.* 57 C8 21 40S 45 10 E
Beroun, *Czech.* 16 D8 49 57N 14 5 E
Berrechid, *Morocco* 50 B3 33 18N 7 36W
Berri, *Australia* 63 E3 34 14S 140 35 E
Berry, *Australia* 63 E5 34 46S 150 43 E
Berry, *France* 18 C5 46 50N 2 0 E
Berry Is., *Bahamas* 88 A4 25 40N 77 50W
Berryessa L., *U.S.A.* 84 G4 38 31N 122 6W
Berryville, *U.S.A.* 81 G8 36 22N 93 34W
Bershad, *Ukraine* 17 D15 48 22N 29 31 E
Berthold, *U.S.A.* 80 A4 48 19N 101 44W
Berthoud, *U.S.A.* 80 E2 40 19N 105 5W
Bertoua, *Cameroon* 52 D2 4 30N 13 45 E
Bertrand, *U.S.A.* 80 E5 40 32N 99 38W
Berwick, *U.S.A.* 79 E8 41 3N 76 14W
Berwick-upon-Tweed, *U.K.* 10 B6 55 46N 2 0W
Berwyn Mts., *U.K.* 10 E4 52 54N 3 26W
Besal, *Pakistan* 43 B5 35 4N 73 56 E
Besalampy, *Madag.* 57 B7 16 43S 44 29 E
Besançon, *France* 18 C7 47 15N 6 2 E
Besar, *Indonesia* 36 E5 2 40S 116 0 E
Besnard L., *Canada* 73 B7 55 25N 106 0W
Besor, N. →, *Egypt* 47 D3 31 28N 34 22 E
Bessarabiya, *Moldova* 17 E15 47 0N 28 10 E
Bessarabka = Basarabeasca, *Moldova* 17 E15 46 21N 28 58 E
Bessemer, *Ala., U.S.A.* 77 J2 33 24N 86 58W
Bessemer, *Mich., U.S.A.* 80 B9 46 29N 90 3W
Bet She'an, *Israel* 47 C4 32 30N 35 30 E
Bet Shemesh, *Israel* 47 D3 31 44N 35 0 E
Betafo, *Madag.* 57 B8 19 50S 46 51 E
Betancuria, *Canary Is.* 22 F5 28 25N 14 3W
Betanzos, *Spain* 19 A1 43 15N 8 12W
Bétaré Oya, *Cameroon* 52 C2 5 40N 14 5 E
Bethal, *S. Africa* 57 D4 26 27S 29 28 E
Bethanien, *Namibia* 56 D2 26 31S 17 8 E
Bethany, *U.S.A.* 80 E7 40 16N 94 2W
Bethel, *Alaska, U.S.A.* 68 B3 60 48N 161 45W
Bethel, *Vt., U.S.A.* 79 C12 43 50N 72 38W
Bethel Park, *U.S.A.* 78 F4 40 20N 80 1W
Bethlehem = Bayt Lahm, *West Bank* 47 D4 31 43N 35 12 E
Bethlehem, *S. Africa* 57 D4 28 14S 28 18 E
Bethlehem, *U.S.A.* 79 F9 40 37N 75 23W
Bethulie, *S. Africa* 56 E4 30 30S 25 59 E
Béthune, *France* 18 A5 50 30N 2 38 E
Bethungra, *Australia* 63 E4 34 45S 147 51 E
Betioky, *Madag.* 57 C7 23 48S 44 20 E
Betong, *Thailand* 39 K3 5 45N 101 5 E
Betoota, *Australia* 62 D3 25 45S 140 42 E
Betroka, *Madag.* 57 C8 23 16S 46 0 E
Betsiamites, *Canada* 71 C6 48 56N 68 40W
Betsiamites →, *Canada* 71 C6 48 56N 68 38W
Betsiboka →, *Madag.* 57 B8 16 3S 46 36 E
Bettiah, *India* 43 F11 26 48N 84 33 E
Betul, *India* 40 J10 21 58N 77 59 E
Betung, *Malaysia* 36 D4 1 24N 111 31 E
Beulah, *U.S.A.* 80 B4 47 16N 101 47W
Beverley, *Australia* 61 F2 32 9S 116 56 E
Beverley, *U.K.* 10 D7 53 51N 0 26W
Beverly, *Mass., U.S.A.* 79 D14 42 33N 70 53W
Beverly, *Wash., U.S.A.* 82 C4 46 50N 119 56W
Beverly Hills, *U.S.A.* 85 L8 34 4N 118 25W
Beverwijk, *Neths.* 15 B4 52 28N 4 38 E
Beya, *Russia* 27 D10 52 40N 92 30 E
Beyānlū, *Iran* 44 C5 36 0N 47 51 E
Beyla, *Guinea* 50 G3 8 30N 8 38W
Beyneu, *Kazakstan* 25 E10 45 18N 55 9 E
Beypazan, *Turkey* 25 F5 40 10N 31 56 E
Beyşehir Gölü, *Turkey* 25 G5 37 41N 31 33 E
Bezhitsa, *Russia* 24 D5 53 19N 34 17 E
Béziers, *France* 18 E5 43 20N 3 12 E
Bezwada = Vijayawada, *India* 41 L12 16 31N 80 39 E
Bhachau, *India* 40 H7 23 20N 70 16 E
Bhadarwah, *India* 43 C6 32 58N 75 46 E
Bhadrakh, *India* 41 J15 21 10N 86 30 E
Bhadravati, *India* 40 N9 13 49N 75 40 E
Bhagalpur, *India* 43 G12 25 10N 87 0 E
Bhakkar, *Pakistan* 42 D4 31 40N 71 5 E
Bhakra Dam, *India* 42 D7 31 30N 76 45 E
Bhamo, *Burma* 41 G20 24 15N 97 15 E
Bhandara, *India* 40 J11 21 5N 79 42 E
Bhanrer Ra., *India* 42 H8 23 40N 79 45 E
Bharat = India ■, *Asia* 40 K11 20 0N 78 0 E
Bharatpur, *India* 42 F7 27 15N 77 30 E
Bhatinda, *India* 42 D6 30 15N 74 57 E
Bhatpara, *India* 43 H13 22 50N 88 25 E
Bhaun, *Pakistan* 42 C5 32 55N 72 40 E
Bhaunagar = Bhavnagar, *India* 42 J5 21 45N 72 10 E
Bhavnagar, *India* 42 J5 21 45N 72 10 E
Bhawanipatna, *India* 41 K12 19 55N 80 10 E
Bhera, *Pakistan* 42 C5 32 29N 72 57 E
Bhilsa = Vidisha, *India* 42 H7 23 28N 77 53 E
Bhilwara, *India* 42 G6 25 25N 74 38 E
Bhima →, *India* 40 L10 16 25N 77 17 E
Bhimavaram, *India* 41 L12 16 30N 81 30 E
Bhimbar, *Pakistan* 43 C6 32 59N 74 3 E
Bhind, *India* 43 F8 26 30N 78 46 E
Bhiwandi, *India* 40 K8 19 20N 73 0 E
Bhiwani, *India* 42 E7 28 50N 76 9 E
Bhola, *Bangla.* 41 H17 22 45N 90 35 E
Bhopal, *India* 42 H7 23 20N 77 30 E
Bhubaneshwar, *India* 41 J14 20 15N 85 50 E
Bhuj, *India* 42 H3 23 15N 69 49 E
Bhumiphol Dam = Phumiphon, Khuan, *Thailand* 38 D2 17 15N 98 58 E
Bhusaval, *India* 40 J9 21 3N 75 46 E
Bhutan ■, *Asia* 41 F17 27 25N 90 30 E
Biafra, B. of = Bonny, Bight of, *Africa* 52 D1 3 30N 9 20 E
Biak, *Indonesia* 37 E9 1 10S 136 6 E
Biała Podlaska, *Poland* 17 B12 52 4N 23 6 E
Białogard, *Poland* 16 A8 54 2N 15 58 E
Białystok, *Poland* 17 B12 53 10N 23 10 E
Bīārjmand, *Iran* 45 B7 36 6N 55 53 E
Biaro, *Indonesia* 37 D7 2 5N 125 26 E
Biarritz, *France* 18 E3 43 29N 1 33W
Bibai, *Japan* 30 C10 43 19N 141 52 E
Bibala, *Angola* 53 G2 14 44S 13 24 E
Bibby I., *Canada* 73 A10 61 55N 93 0W
Biberach, *Germany* 16 D5 48 5N 9 47 E
Bibiani, *Ghana* 50 G4 6 30N 2 8W
Biboohra, *Australia* 62 B4 16 56S 145 25 E
Bibungwa, *Zaïre* 54 C2 2 40S 28 15 E
Bic, *Canada* 71 C6 48 20N 68 41W
Bickerton I., *Australia* 62 A2 13 45S 136 10 E
Bicknell, *Ind., U.S.A.* 76 F2 38 47N 87 19W
Bicknell, *Utah, U.S.A.* 83 G8 38 20N 111 33W
Bida, *Nigeria* 50 G6 9 3N 5 58 E
Bidar, *India* 40 L10 17 55N 77 35 E
Biddeford, *U.S.A.* 71 D5 43 30N 70 28W
Bideford, *U.K.* 11 F3 51 1N 4 13W
Bidon 5 = Poste Maurice Cortier, *Algeria* 50 D5 22 14N 1 2 E
Bidor, *Malaysia* 39 K3 4 6N 101 15 E
Bié, Planalto de, *Angola* 53 G3 12 0S 16 0 E
Bieber, *U.S.A.* 82 F3 41 7N 121 8W
Biel, *Switz.* 16 E4 47 8N 7 14 E
Bielé Karpaty, *Europe* 17 D9 49 5N 18 0 E
Bielefeld, *Germany* 16 B5 52 1N 8 33 E
Biella, *Italy* 20 B3 45 34N 8 3 E
Bielsk Podlaski, *Poland* 17 B12 52 47N 23 12 E
Bielsko-Biała, *Poland* 17 D10 49 50N 19 2 E
Bien Hoa, *Vietnam* 39 G6 10 57N 106 49 E
Bienfait, *Canada* 73 D8 49 10N 102 50W
Bienne = Biel, *Switz.* 16 E4 47 8N 7 14 E
Bienville, L., *Canada* 70 A5 55 5N 72 40W
Biesiesfontein, *S. Africa* 56 E2 30 57S 17 58 E
Big →, *Canada* 71 B8 54 50N 58 55W
Big B., *Canada* 71 A7 55 43N 60 35W
Big Bear City, *U.S.A.* 85 L10 34 16N 116 51W
Big Bear Lake, *U.S.A.* 85 L10 34 15N 116 56W
Big Beaver, *Canada* 73 D7 49 10N 105 10W
Big Belt Mts., *U.S.A.* 82 C8 46 30N 111 25W
Big Bend, *Swaziland* 57 D5 26 50S 31 58 E
Big Bend National Park, *U.S.A.* 81 L3 29 20N 103 5W
Big Black →, *U.S.A.* 81 J9 32 3N 91 4W
Big Blue →, *U.S.A.* 80 F6 39 35N 96 34W
Big Cr. →, *Canada* 72 C4 51 42N 122 41W
Big Creek, *U.S.A.* 84 H7 37 11N 119 14W
Big Cypress Swamp, *U.S.A.* 77 M5 26 12N 81 10W
Big Falls, *U.S.A.* 80 A8 48 12N 93 48W
Big Fork →, *U.S.A.* 80 A8 48 31N 93 43W
Big Horn Mts. = Bighorn Mts., *U.S.A.* 82 D10 44 30N 107 30W
Big Lake, *U.S.A.* 81 K4 31 12N 101 28W
Big Moose, *U.S.A.* 79 C10 43 49N 74 58W
Big Muddy Cr. →, *U.S.A.* 80 A2 48 8N 104 36W
Big Pine, *U.S.A.* 83 H4 37 10N 118 17W
Big Piney, *U.S.A.* 82 E8 42 32N 110 7W
Big Quill L., *Canada* 73 C8 51 55N 104 50W
Big Rapids, *U.S.A.* 76 D3 43 42N 85 29W
Big River, *Canada* 73 C7 53 50N 107 0W
Big Run, *U.S.A.* 78 F6 40 57N 78 55W
Big Sable Pt., *U.S.A.* 76 C2 44 3N 86 1W
Big Sand L., *Canada* 73 B9 57 45N 99 45W
Big Sandy, *U.S.A.* 82 B8 48 11N 110 7W
Big Sandy Cr. →, *U.S.A.* 80 F3 38 7N 102 29W
Big Sioux →, *U.S.A.* 80 D6 42 29N 96 27W
Big Spring, *U.S.A.* 81 J4 32 15N 101 28W
Big Springs, *U.S.A.* 80 E3 41 4N 102 5W
Big Stone City, *U.S.A.* 80 C6 45 18N 96 28W
Big Stone Gap, *U.S.A.* 77 G4 36 52N 82 47W
Big Stone L., *U.S.A.* 80 C6 45 30N 96 35W
Big Sur, *U.S.A.* 84 J5 36 15N 121 48W
Big Timber, *U.S.A.* 82 D9 45 50N 109 57W
Big Trout L., *Canada* 70 B1 53 40N 90 0W
Biğa, *Turkey* 21 D12 40 13N 27 14 E
Bigadiç, *Turkey* 21 E13 39 22N 28 7 E
Bigfork, *U.S.A.* 82 B6 48 4N 114 4W
Biggar, *Canada* 73 C7 52 4N 108 0W
Biggar, *U.K.* 12 F5 55 38N 3 32W
Bigge I., *Australia* 60 B4 14 35S 125 10 E
Biggenden, *Australia* 63 D5 25 31S 152 4 E
Biggs, *U.S.A.* 84 F5 39 25N 121 43W
Bighorn, *U.S.A.* 82 C10 46 10N 107 27W
Bighorn →, *U.S.A.* 82 C10 46 10N 107 28W
Bighorn Mts., *U.S.A.* 82 D10 44 30N 107 30W
Bigstone L., *Canada* 73 C9 53 42N 95 44W
Bigwa, *Tanzania* 54 D4 7 10S 39 10 E
Bihać, *Bos.-H.* 16 F8 44 49N 15 57 E
Bihar, *India* 43 G11 25 5N 85 40 E

Bihar

106

Bristol L.

Bolshoy Begichev, Ostrov, *Russia* . . . 27 B12 74 20N 112 30 E
Bolshoy Lyakhovskiy, Ostrov, *Russia* . . . 27 B15 73 35N 142 0 E
Bolshoy Tyuters, Ostrov, *Russia* . . . 9 G22 59 51N 27 13 E
Bolsward, *Neths.* . . . 15 A5 53 3N 5 32 E
Bolton, *Canada* . . . 78 C5 43 54N 79 45W
Bolton, *U.K.* . . . 10 D5 53 35N 2 26W
Bolu, *Turkey* . . . 25 F5 40 45N 31 35 E
Bolungavík, *Iceland* . . . 8 C2 66 9N 23 15W
Bolvadin, *Turkey* . . . 25 G5 38 45N 31 4 E
Bolzano, *Italy* . . . 20 A4 46 31N 11 22 E
Bom Despacho, *Brazil* . . . 93 G9 19 43S 45 15W
Bom Jesus da Lapa, *Brazil* 93 F10 13 15S 43 25W
Boma, *Zaïre* . . . 52 F2 5 50S 13 4 E
Bomaderry, *Australia* . . . 63 E5 34 52S 150 37 E
Bombala, *Australia* . . . 63 F4 36 56S 149 15 E
Bombay, *India* . . . 40 K8 18 55N 72 50 E
Bomboma, *Zaïre* . . . 52 D3 2 25N 18 55 E
Bombombwa, *Zaïre* . . . 54 B2 1 40N 25 40 E
Bomili, *Zaïre* . . . 54 B2 1 45N 27 5 E
Bømlo, *Norway* . . . 9 G11 59 37N 5 13 E
Bomokandi →, *Zaïre* . . . 54 B2 3 39N 26 8 E
Bomongo, *Zaïre* . . . 52 D3 1 27N 18 21 E
Bomu →, *C.A.R.* . . . 52 D4 4 40N 22 30 E
Bon, C., *Tunisia* . . . 51 A7 37 1N 11 2 E
Bon Sar Pa, *Vietnam* . . . 38 F6 12 24N 107 35 E
Bonaire, *Neth. Ant.* . . . 89 D6 12 10N 68 15W
Bonang, *Australia* . . . 63 F4 37 11S 148 41 E
Bonanza, *Nic.* . . . 88 D3 13 54N 84 35W
Bonaparte Arch., *Australia* 60 B3 14 0S 124 30 E
Bonaventure, *Canada* . . . 71 C6 48 5N 65 32W
Bonavista, *Canada* . . . 71 C9 48 40N 53 5W
Bonavista, C., *Canada* . . . 71 C9 48 42N 53 5W
Bondo, *Zaïre* . . . 54 B1 3 55N 23 53 E
Bondoukou, *Ivory C.* . . . 50 G4 8 2N 2 47W
Bondowoso, *Indonesia* . . . 37 G15 7 55S 113 49 E
Bone, Teluk, *Indonesia* . . . 37 E6 4 10S 120 50 E
Bonerate, *Indonesia* . . . 37 F6 7 25S 121 5 E
Bonerate, Kepulauan, *Indonesia* . . . 37 F6 6 30S 121 10 E
Bo'ness, *U.K.* . . . 12 E5 56 1N 3 37W
Bonete, Cerro, *Argentina* 94 B2 27 55S 68 40W
Bong Son = Hoai Nhon, *Vietnam* . . . 38 E7 14 28N 109 1 E
Bongandanga, *Zaïre* . . . 52 D4 1 24N 21 3 E
Bongor, *Chad* . . . 51 F8 10 35N 15 20 E
Bonham, *U.S.A.* . . . 81 J6 33 35N 96 11W
Bonifacio, *France* . . . 18 F8 41 24N 9 10 E
Bonin Is. = Ogasawara Gunto, *Pac. Oc.* . . . 28 G18 27 0N 142 0 E
Bonn, *Germany* . . . 16 C4 50 46N 7 6 E
Bonne Terre, *U.S.A.* . . . 81 G9 37 55N 90 33W
Bonners Ferry, *U.S.A.* . . . 82 B5 48 42N 116 19W
Bonney, L., *Australia* . . . 63 F3 37 50S 140 20 E
Bonnie Downs, *Australia* 62 C3 22 7S 143 50 E
Bonnie Rock, *Australia* . . . 61 F2 30 29S 118 22 E
Bonny, Bight of, *Africa* . . . 52 D1 3 30N 9 20 E
Bonnyville, *Canada* . . . 73 C6 54 20N 110 45W
Bonoi, *Indonesia* . . . 37 E9 1 45S 137 41 E
Bonsall, *U.S.A.* . . . 85 M9 33 16N 117 14W
Bontang, *Indonesia* . . . 36 D5 0 10N 117 30 E
Bonthain, *Indonesia* . . . 37 F5 5 34S 119 56 E
Bonthe, *S. Leone* . . . 50 G2 7 30N 12 33W
Bontoc, *Phil.* . . . 37 A6 17 7N 120 58 E
Bonython Ra., *Australia* . . . 60 D4 23 40S 128 45 E
Bookabie, *Australia* . . . 61 F5 31 50S 132 41 E
Booker, *U.S.A.* . . . 81 G4 36 27N 100 32W
Boolaboolka L., *Australia* 63 E3 32 38S 143 10 E
Booligal, *Australia* . . . 63 E3 33 58S 144 53 E
Boom, *Belgium* . . . 15 C4 51 6N 4 20 E
Boonah, *Australia* . . . 63 D5 27 58S 152 41 E
Boone, *Iowa, U.S.A.* . . . 80 D8 42 4N 93 53W
Boone, *N.C., U.S.A.* . . . 77 G5 36 13N 81 41W
Booneville, *Ark., U.S.A.* . . . 81 H8 35 8N 93 55W
Booneville, *Miss., U.S.A.* . . . 77 H1 34 39N 88 34W
Boonville, *Calif., U.S.A.* . . . 84 F3 39 1N 123 22W
Boonville, *Ind., U.S.A.* . . . 76 F2 38 3N 87 16W
Boonville, *Mo., U.S.A.* . . . 80 F8 38 58N 92 44W
Boonville, *N.Y., U.S.A.* . . . 79 C9 43 29N 75 20W
Boorindal, *Australia* . . . 63 E4 30 22S 146 11 E
Boorowa, *Australia* . . . 63 E4 34 28S 148 44 E
Boothia, Gulf of, *Canada* . . . 69 A11 71 0N 90 0W
Boothia Pen., *Canada* . . . 68 A10 71 0N 94 0W
Bootle, *U.K.* . . . 10 D4 53 28N 3 1W
Booué, *Gabon* . . . 52 E2 0 5S 11 55 E
Boquete, *Panama* . . . 88 E3 8 46N 82 27W
Boquilla, Presa de la, *Mexico* . . . 86 B3 27 40N 105 30W
Boquillas del Carmen, *Mexico* . . . 86 B4 29 17N 102 53W
Bor, *Serbia, Yug.* . . . 21 B10 44 5N 22 7 E
Bôr, *Sudan* . . . 51 G11 6 10N 31 40 E
Bor Mashash, *Israel* . . . 47 D3 31 7N 34 50 E
Boradā →, *Syria* . . . 47 B5 33 33N 36 34 E
Borah Peak, *U.S.A.* . . . 82 D7 44 8N 113 47W
Borama, *Somali Rep.* . . . 46 F3 9 55N 43 7 E
Borås, *Sweden* . . . 9 H15 57 43N 12 56 E
Borāzjān, *Iran* . . . 45 D6 29 22N 51 10 E
Borba, *Brazil* . . . 92 D7 4 12S 59 34W
Borborema, Planalto da, *Brazil* . . . 90 D7 7 0S 37 0W
Bord Khūn-e Now, *Iran* . . . 45 D6 28 3N 51 28 E
Borda, C., *Australia* . . . 63 F2 35 45S 136 34 E
Bordeaux, *France* . . . 18 D3 44 50N 0 36W
Borden, *Australia* . . . 61 F2 34 3S 118 12 E
Borden, *Canada* . . . 71 C7 46 18N 63 47W
Borden I., *Canada* . . . 4 B2 78 30N 111 30W
Borders □, *U.K.* . . . 12 F6 55 35N 2 50W
Bordertown, *Australia* . . . 63 F3 36 19S 140 45 E
Borðeyri, *Iceland* . . . 8 D3 65 12N 21 6W
Bordj Fly Ste. Marie, *Algeria* . . . 50 C4 27 19N 2 32W
Bordj-in-Eker, *Algeria* . . . 50 D6 24 9N 5 3 E
Bordj Omar Driss, *Algeria* 50 C6 28 10N 6 40 E
Bordj-Tarat, *Algeria* . . . 50 C6 25 55N 9 3 E
Borgå = Porvoo, *Finland* 9 F21 60 24N 25 40 E
Borgarfjörður, *Iceland* . . . 8 D7 65 31N 13 49W
Borgarnes, *Iceland* . . . 8 D3 64 32N 21 55W
Børgefjellet, *Norway* . . . 8 D15 65 20N 13 45 E
Borger, *Neths.* . . . 15 B6 52 54N 6 44 E
Borger, *U.S.A.* . . . 81 H4 35 39N 101 24W
Borgholm, *Sweden* . . . 9 H17 56 52N 16 39 E
Borikhane, *Laos* . . . 38 C4 18 33N 103 43 E
Borisoglebsk, *Russia* . . . 25 D7 51 27N 42 5 E
Borisov = Barysaw, *Belarus* . . . 17 A15 54 17N 28 28 E
Borja, *Peru* . . . 92 D3 4 20S 77 40W
Borkou, *Chad* . . . 51 E8 18 15N 18 50 E
Borkum, *Germany* . . . 16 B4 53 34N 6 40 E
Borlänge, *Sweden* . . . 9 F16 60 29N 15 26 E
Borley, C., *Antarctica* . . . 5 C5 66 15S 52 30 E
Borneo, *E. Indies* . . . 36 D5 1 0N 115 0 E
Bornholm, *Denmark* . . . 9 J16 55 10N 15 0 E
Borobudur, *Indonesia* . . . 37 G14 7 36S 110 13 E
Borogontsy, *Russia* . . . 27 C14 62 42N 131 8 E
Boromo, *Burkina Faso* . . . 50 F4 11 45N 2 58W
Boron, *U.S.A.* . . . 85 L9 35 0N 117 39W
Borongan, *Phil.* . . . 37 B7 11 37N 125 26 E
Bororen, *Australia* . . . 62 C5 24 13S 151 33 E
Borovichi, *Russia* . . . 24 C5 58 25N 33 55 E
Borrego Springs, *U.S.A.* . . . 85 M10 33 15N 116 23W
Borroloola, *Australia* . . . 62 B2 16 4S 136 17 E
Borşa, *Romania* . . . 17 E13 47 41N 24 50 E
Borth, *U.K.* . . . 11 E3 52 29N 4 2W
Borūjerd, *Iran* . . . 45 C6 33 55N 48 50 E
Boryslav, *Ukraine* . . . 17 D12 49 18N 23 28 E
Borzya, *Russia* . . . 27 D12 50 24N 116 31 E
Bosa, *Italy* . . . 20 D3 40 18N 8 30 E
Bosanska Gradiška, *Bos.-H.* . . . 20 B7 45 10N 17 15 E
Bosaso, *Somali Rep.* . . . 46 E4 11 12N 49 18 E
Boscastle, *U.K.* . . . 11 G3 50 41N 4 42W
Boshan, *China* . . . 35 F9 36 28N 117 49 E
Boshof, *S. Africa* . . . 56 D4 28 31S 25 13 E
Boshrūyeh, *Iran* . . . 45 C8 33 50N 57 30 E
Bosna →, *Bos.-H.* . . . 21 B8 45 4N 18 29 E
Bosna i Hercegovina = Bosnia-Herzegovina ■, *Europe* . . . 20 B7 44 0N 17 0 E
Bosnia-Herzegovina ■, *Europe* . . . 20 B7 44 0N 17 0 E
Bosnik, *Indonesia* . . . 37 E9 1 5S 136 10 E
Bosobolo, *Zaïre* . . . 52 D3 4 15N 19 50 E
Bosporus = Karadeniz Boğazı, *Turkey* . . . 21 D13 41 10N 29 10 E
Bossangoa, *C.A.R.* . . . 51 G8 6 35N 17 30 E
Bossembélé, *C.A.R.* . . . 51 G8 5 25N 17 40 E
Bossier City, *U.S.A.* . . . 81 J8 32 31N 93 44W
Bosso, *Niger* . . . 51 F7 13 43N 13 19 E
Bostānābād, *Iran* . . . 44 B5 37 50N 46 50 E
Bosten Hu, *China* . . . 32 B3 41 55N 87 40 E
Boston, *U.K.* . . . 10 E7 52 59N 0 2W
Boston, *U.S.A.* . . . 79 D13 42 22N 71 4W
Boston Bar, *Canada* . . . 72 D4 49 52N 121 30W
Boswell, *Canada* . . . 72 D5 49 28N 116 45W
Boswell, *Okla., U.S.A.* . . . 81 H7 34 2N 95 52W
Boswell, *Pa., U.S.A.* . . . 78 F5 40 10N 79 2W
Botad, *India* . . . 42 H4 22 15N 71 40 E
Botany B., *Australia* . . . 63 E5 34 0S 151 14 E
Botene, *Laos* . . . 38 D3 17 35N 101 12 E
Bothaville, *S. Africa* . . . 56 D4 27 23S 26 34 E
Bothnia, G. of, *Europe* . . . 8 E19 63 0N 20 15 E
Bothwell, *Australia* . . . 62 G4 42 20S 147 1 E
Bothwell, *Canada* . . . 78 D3 42 38N 81 52W
Botletle →, *Botswana* . . . 56 C3 20 10S 23 15 E
Botoşani, *Romania* . . . 17 E14 47 42N 26 41 E
Botswana ■, *Africa* . . . 56 C3 22 0S 24 0 E
Bottineau, *U.S.A.* . . . 80 A4 48 50N 100 27W
Bottrop, *Germany* . . . 15 C6 51 31N 6 58 E
Botucatu, *Brazil* . . . 95 A6 22 55S 48 30W
Botwood, *Canada* . . . 71 C8 49 6N 55 23W
Bou Djébéha, *Mali* . . . 50 E4 18 25N 2 45W
Bou Izakarn, *Morocco* . . . 50 C3 29 12N 9 46W
Bouaké, *Ivory C.* . . . 50 G3 7 40N 5 2W
Bouar, *C.A.R.* . . . 52 C3 6 0N 15 40 E
Bouârfa, *Morocco* . . . 50 B4 32 32N 1 58W
Bouca, *C.A.R.* . . . 51 G8 6 45N 18 25 E
Boucaut B., *Australia* . . . 62 A1 12 0S 134 25 E
Bougainville, C., *Australia* 60 B4 13 57S 126 4 E
Bougainville Reef, *Australia* . . . 62 B4 15 30S 147 5 E
Bougie = Bejaia, *Algeria* . . . 50 A6 36 42N 5 2 E
Bougouni, *Mali* . . . 50 F3 11 30N 7 20W
Bouillon, *Belgium* . . . 15 E5 49 44N 5 3 E
Boulder, *Colo., U.S.A.* . . . 80 E2 40 1N 105 17W
Boulder, *Mont., U.S.A.* . . . 82 C7 46 14N 112 7W
Boulder City, *U.S.A.* . . . 85 K12 35 59N 114 50W
Boulder Creek, *U.S.A.* . . . 84 H4 37 7N 122 7W
Boulder Dam = Hoover Dam, *U.S.A.* . . . 85 K12 36 1N 114 44W
Boulia, *Australia* . . . 62 C2 22 52S 139 51 E
Boulogne-sur-Mer, *France* 18 A4 50 42N 1 36 E
Boultoum, *Niger* . . . 50 F7 14 45N 10 25 E
Boun Neua, *Laos* . . . 38 B3 21 38N 101 54 E
Boun Tai, *Laos* . . . 38 B3 21 23N 101 58 E
Bouna, *Ivory C.* . . . 50 G4 9 10N 3 0W
Boundary Peak, *U.S.A.* . . . 84 H8 37 51N 118 21W
Boundiali, *Ivory C.* . . . 50 G3 9 30N 6 20W
Bountiful, *U.S.A.* . . . 82 F8 40 53N 111 53W
Bounty Is., *Pac. Oc.* . . . 64 M9 48 0S 178 30 E
Bourbonnais, *France* . . . 18 C5 46 28N 3 0 E
Bourem, *Mali* . . . 50 E4 17 0N 0 24W
Bourg-en-Bresse, *France* . . . 18 C6 46 13N 5 12 E
Bourg-St.-Maurice, *France* 18 D7 45 35N 6 46 E
Bourges, *France* . . . 18 C5 47 9N 2 25 E
Bourget, *Canada* . . . 79 A9 45 26N 75 9W
Bourgogne, *France* . . . 18 C6 47 0N 4 50 E
Bourke, *Australia* . . . 63 E4 30 8S 145 55 E
Bournemouth, *U.K.* . . . 11 G6 50 43N 1 52W
Bouse, *U.S.A.* . . . 85 M13 33 56N 114 0W
Bousso, *Chad* . . . 51 F8 10 34N 16 52 E
Boutilimit, *Mauritania* . . . 50 E2 17 45N 14 40W
Bouvet I. = Bouvetøya, *Antarctica* . . . 3 G10 54 26S 3 24 E
Bouvetøya, *Antarctica* . . . 3 G10 54 26S 3 24 E
Bovigny, *Belgium* . . . 15 D5 50 12N 5 55 E
Bovill, *U.S.A.* . . . 82 C5 46 51N 116 24W
Bow Island, *Canada* . . . 72 D6 49 50N 111 23W
Bowbells, *U.S.A.* . . . 80 A3 48 48N 102 15W
Bowdle, *U.S.A.* . . . 80 C5 45 27N 99 39W
Bowelling, *Australia* . . . 61 F2 33 25S 116 30 E
Bowen, *Australia* . . . 62 C4 20 0S 148 16 E
Bowen Mts., *Australia* . . . 63 F4 37 0S 147 50 E
Bowie, *Ariz., U.S.A.* . . . 83 K9 32 19N 109 29W
Bowie, *Tex., U.S.A.* . . . 81 J6 33 34N 97 51W
Bowkān, *Iran* . . . 44 B5 36 31N 46 12 E
Bowland, Forest of, *U.K.* . . . 10 D5 54 0N 2 30W
Bowling Green, *Ky., U.S.A.* 76 G2 36 59N 86 27W
Bowling Green, *Ohio, U.S.A.* . . . 76 E4 41 23N 83 39W
Bowling Green, C., *Australia* . . . 62 B4 19 19S 147 25 E
Bowman, *U.S.A.* . . . 80 B3 46 11N 103 24W
Bowman I., *Antarctica* . . . 5 C8 65 0S 104 0 E
Bowmans, *Australia* . . . 63 E2 34 10S 138 17 E
Bowmanville, *Canada* . . . 70 D4 43 55N 78 41W
Bowmore, *U.K.* . . . 12 F2 55 45N 6 17W
Bowral, *Australia* . . . 63 E5 34 26S 150 27 E
Bowraville, *Australia* . . . 63 E5 30 37S 152 52 E
Bowron →, *Canada* . . . 72 C4 54 3N 121 50W
Bowser L., *Canada* . . . 72 B3 56 30N 129 30W
Bowsman, *Canada* . . . 73 C8 52 14N 101 12W
Bowwood, *Zambia* . . . 55 F2 17 5S 26 20 E
Boxtel, *Neths.* . . . 15 C5 51 36N 5 20 E
Boyce, *U.S.A.* . . . 81 K8 31 23N 92 40W
Boyer →, *Canada* . . . 72 B5 58 27N 115 57W
Boyle, *Ireland* . . . 13 C3 53 59N 8 18W
Boyne →, *Ireland* . . . 13 C5 53 43N 6 15W
Boyne City, *U.S.A.* . . . 76 C3 45 13N 85 1W
Boynton Beach, *U.S.A.* . . . 77 M5 26 32N 80 4W
Boyoma, Chutes, *Zaïre* . . . 54 B2 0 35N 25 23 E
Boyup Brook, *Australia* . . . 61 F2 33 50S 116 23 E
Boz Dağlan, *Turkey* . . . 21 E13 38 20N 28 0 E
Bozburun, *Turkey* . . . 21 F13 36 43N 28 8 E
Bozcaada, *Turkey* . . . 21 E12 39 49N 26 3 E
Bozdoğan, *Turkey* . . . 21 F13 37 40N 28 17 E
Bozeman, *U.S.A.* . . . 82 D8 45 41N 111 2W
Bozen = Bolzano, *Italy* . . . 20 A4 46 31N 11 22 E
Bozoum, *C.A.R.* . . . 51 G8 6 25N 16 35 E
Bra, *Italy* . . . 20 B2 44 42N 7 51 E
Brabant □, *Belgium* . . . 15 D4 50 46N 4 30 E
Brabant L., *Canada* . . . 73 B8 55 58N 103 43W
Brač, *Croatia* . . . 20 C7 43 20N 16 40 E
Bracadale, L., *U.K.* . . . 12 D2 57 20N 6 30W
Bracciano, L. di, *Italy* . . . 20 C5 42 7N 12 14 E
Bracebridge, *Canada* . . . 70 C4 45 2N 79 19W
Brach, *Libya* . . . 51 C7 27 31N 14 20 E
Bräcke, *Sweden* . . . 9 E16 62 45N 15 26 E
Brackettville, *U.S.A.* . . . 81 L4 29 19N 100 25W
Brad, *Romania* . . . 17 E12 46 10N 22 50 E
Bradenton, *U.S.A.* . . . 77 M4 27 30N 82 34W
Bradford, *Canada* . . . 78 B5 44 7N 79 34W
Bradford, *U.K.* . . . 10 D6 53 47N 1 45W
Bradford, *Pa., U.S.A.* . . . 78 E6 41 58N 78 38W
Bradford, *Vt., U.S.A.* . . . 79 C12 43 59N 72 9W
Bradley, *Ark., U.S.A.* . . . 81 J8 33 6N 93 39W
Bradley, *Calif., U.S.A.* . . . 84 K6 35 52N 120 48W
Bradley, *S. Dak., U.S.A.* . . . 80 C6 45 5N 97 39W
Bradley Institute, *Zimbabwe* . . . 55 F3 17 7S 31 25 E
Bradore Bay, *Canada* . . . 71 B8 51 27N 57 18W
Bradshaw, *Australia* . . . 60 C5 15 21S 130 16 E
Brady, *U.S.A.* . . . 81 K5 31 9N 99 20W
Braemar, *Australia* . . . 63 E2 33 12S 139 35 E
Braeside, *Canada* . . . 79 A8 45 28N 76 24W
Braga, *Portugal* . . . 19 B1 41 35N 8 25W
Bragado, *Argentina* . . . 94 D3 35 2S 60 27W
Bragança, *Brazil* . . . 93 D9 1 0S 47 2W
Bragança, *Portugal* . . . 19 B2 41 48N 6 50W
Bragança Paulista, *Brazil* . . . 95 A6 22 55S 46 32W
Brahmanbaria, *Bangla.* . . . 41 H17 23 58N 91 15 E
Brahmani →, *India* . . . 41 J15 20 39N 86 46 E
Brahmaputra →, *India* . . . 43 G13 23 58N 89 50 E
Braich-y-pwll, *U.K.* . . . 10 E3 52 47N 4 46W
Braidwood, *Australia* . . . 63 F4 35 27S 149 49 E
Brăila, *Romania* . . . 17 F14 45 19N 27 59 E
Brainerd, *U.S.A.* . . . 80 B7 46 22N 94 12W
Braintree, *U.K.* . . . 11 F8 51 53N 0 34 E
Braintree, *U.S.A.* . . . 79 D14 42 13N 71 0W
Brak →, *S. Africa* . . . 56 D3 29 35S 22 55 E
Brakwater, *Namibia* . . . 56 C2 22 28S 17 3 E
Bralorne, *Canada* . . . 72 C4 50 50N 122 50W
Brampton, *Canada* . . . 70 D4 43 45N 79 45W
Bramwell, *Australia* . . . 62 A3 12 8S 142 37 E
Branco →, *Brazil* . . . 92 D6 1 20S 61 50W
Brandenburg = Neubrandenburg, *Germany* . . . 16 B7 53 33N 13 15 E
Brandenburg, *Germany* . . . 16 B7 52 25N 12 33 E
Brandenburg □, *Germany* 16 B6 52 50N 13 0 E
Brandfort, *S. Africa* . . . 56 D4 28 40S 26 30 E
Brandon, *Canada* . . . 73 D9 49 50N 99 57W
Brandon, *U.S.A.* . . . 79 C11 43 48N 73 4W
Brandon B., *Ireland* . . . 13 D1 52 17N 10 8W
Brandon Mt., *Ireland* . . . 13 D1 52 15N 10 15W
Brandsen, *Argentina* . . . 94 D4 35 10S 58 15W
Brandvlei, *S. Africa* . . . 56 E3 30 25S 20 30 E
Branford, *U.S.A.* . . . 79 E12 41 17N 72 49W
Braniewo, *Poland* . . . 17 A10 54 25N 19 50 E
Bransfield Str., *Antarctica* 5 C18 63 0S 59 0W
Branson, *Colo., U.S.A.* . . . 81 G3 37 1N 103 53W
Branson, *Mo., U.S.A.* . . . 81 G8 36 39N 93 13W
Brantford, *Canada* . . . 70 D3 43 10N 80 15W
Branxholme, *Australia* . . . 63 F3 37 52S 141 49 E
Bras d'Or, L., *Canada* . . . 71 C7 45 50N 60 50W
Brasil, Planalto, *Brazil* . . . 90 E6 18 0S 46 30W
Brasiléia, *Brazil* . . . 92 F5 11 0S 68 45W
Brasília, *Brazil* . . . 93 G9 15 47S 47 55W
Braslaw, *Belarus* . . . 9 J22 55 38N 27 0 E
Braşov, *Romania* . . . 17 F13 45 38N 25 35 E
Brasschaat, *Belgium* . . . 15 C4 51 19N 4 27 E
Brassey, Banjaran, *Malaysia* . . . 36 D5 5 0N 117 15 E
Brassey Ra., *Australia* . . . 61 E3 25 8S 122 15 E
Brasstown Bald, *U.S.A.* . . . 77 H4 34 53N 83 49W
Brastad, *Sweden* . . . 9 G14 58 23N 11 30 E
Bratislava, *Slovak Rep.* . . . 17 D9 48 10N 17 7 E
Bratsk, *Russia* . . . 27 D11 56 10N 101 30 E
Brattleboro, *U.S.A.* . . . 79 D12 42 51N 72 34W
Braunau, *Austria* . . . 16 D7 48 15N 13 3 E
Braunschweig, *Germany* . . . 16 B6 52 15N 10 31 E
Braunton, *U.K.* . . . 11 F3 51 7N 4 10W
Brava, *Somali Rep.* . . . 46 G3 1 20N 44 8 E
Bravo del Norte →, *Mexico* . . . 86 B5 25 57N 97 9W
Bravo del Norte, R. → = Grande, Rio →, *U.S.A.* 81 N6 25 58N 97 9W
Brawley, *U.S.A.* . . . 85 N11 32 59N 115 31W
Bray, *Ireland* . . . 13 C5 53 13N 6 7W
Bray, Mt., *Australia* . . . 62 A1 14 0S 134 30 E
Bray, Pays de, *France* . . . 18 B4 49 46N 1 26 E
Brazeau →, *Canada* . . . 72 C5 52 55N 115 14W
Brazil, *U.S.A.* . . . 76 F2 39 32N 87 8W
Brazil ■, *S. Amer.* . . . 93 F9 12 0S 50 0W
Brazilian Highlands = Brasil, Planalto, *Brazil* . 90 E6 18 0S 46 30W
Brazo Sur →, *S. Amer.* . . . 94 B4 25 21S 57 42W
Brazos →, *U.S.A.* . . . 81 L7 28 53N 95 23W
Brazzaville, *Congo* . . . 52 E3 4 9S 15 12 E
Brčko, *Bos.-H.* . . . 21 B8 44 54N 18 46 E
Breadalbane, *Australia* . . . 62 C2 23 50S 139 35 E
Breadalbane, *U.K.* . . . 12 E4 56 30N 4 15W
Breaden, L., *Australia* . . . 61 E4 25 51S 125 28 E
Breaksea Sd., *N.Z.* . . . 59 L1 45 35S 166 35 E
Bream B., *N.Z.* . . . 59 F5 35 56S 174 28 E
Bream Hd., *N.Z.* . . . 59 F5 35 51S 174 36 E
Breas, *Chile* . . . 94 B1 25 29S 70 24W
Brebes, *Indonesia* . . . 37 G13 6 52S 109 3 E
Brechin, *Canada* . . . 78 B5 44 32N 79 10W
Brechin, *U.K.* . . . 12 E6 56 44N 2 39W
Breckenridge, *Colo., U.S.A.* . . . 82 G10 39 29N 106 3W
Breckenridge, *Minn., U.S.A.* . . . 80 B6 46 16N 96 35W
Breckenridge, *Tex., U.S.A.* 81 J5 32 45N 98 54W
Breckland, *U.K.* . . . 11 E8 52 30N 0 40 E
Brecon, *U.K.* . . . 11 F4 51 57N 3 23W
Brecon Beacons, *U.K.* . . . 11 F4 51 53N 3 26W
Breda, *Neths.* . . . 15 C4 51 35N 4 45 E
Bredasdorp, *S. Africa* . . . 56 E3 34 33S 20 2 E
Bredbo, *Australia* . . . 63 F4 35 58S 149 10 E
Bregenz, *Austria* . . . 16 E5 47 30N 9 45 E
Breiðafjörður, *Iceland* . . . 8 D2 65 15N 23 15W
Brejo, *Brazil* . . . 93 D10 3 41S 42 47W
Bremen, *Germany* . . . 16 B5 53 4N 8 47 E
Bremer I., *Australia* . . . 62 A2 12 5S 136 45 E
Bremerhaven, *Germany* . . . 16 B5 53 33N 8 36 E
Bremerton, *U.S.A.* . . . 84 C4 47 34N 122 38W
Brenham, *U.S.A.* . . . 81 K6 30 10N 96 24W
Brenner P., *Austria* . . . 16 E6 47 2N 11 30 E
Brent, *Canada* . . . 70 C4 46 2N 78 29W
Brent, *U.K.* . . . 11 F7 51 33N 0 16W
Brentwood, *U.K.* . . . 11 F8 51 37N 0 19 E
Brentwood, *U.S.A.* . . . 79 F11 40 47N 73 15W
Bréscia, *Italy* . . . 20 B4 45 33N 10 15 E
Breskens, *Neths.* . . . 15 C3 51 23N 3 33 E
Breslau = Wrocław, *Poland* . . . 17 C9 51 5N 17 5 E
Bressanone, *Italy* . . . 20 A4 46 43N 11 39 E
Bressay, *U.K.* . . . 12 A7 60 9N 1 6W
Brest, *Belarus* . . . 17 B12 52 10N 23 40 E
Brest, *France* . . . 18 B1 48 24N 4 31W
Brest-Litovsk = Brest, *Belarus* . . . 17 B12 52 10N 23 40 E
Bretagne, *France* . . . 18 B2 48 10N 3 0W
Breton, *Canada* . . . 72 C6 53 7N 114 28W
Breton Sd., *U.S.A.* . . . 81 L10 29 35N 89 15W
Brett, C., *N.Z.* . . . 59 F5 35 10S 174 20 E
Brevard, *U.S.A.* . . . 77 H4 35 14N 82 44W
Brewarrina, *Australia* . . . 63 D4 30 0S 146 51 E
Brewer, *U.S.A.* . . . 71 D6 44 48N 68 46W
Brewer, Mt., *U.S.A.* . . . 84 J8 36 44N 118 28W
Brewster, *N.Y., U.S.A.* . . . 79 E11 41 23N 73 37W
Brewster, *Wash., U.S.A.* . 82 B4 48 6N 119 47W
Brewster, Kap, *Greenland* 4 B6 70 7N 22 0W
Brewton, *U.S.A.* . . . 77 K2 31 7N 87 4W
Breyten, *S. Africa* . . . 57 D4 26 16S 30 0 E
Brezhnev = Naberezhnyye Chelny, *Russia* . . . 24 C9 55 42N 52 19 E
Bria, *C.A.R.* . . . 51 G9 6 30N 21 58 E
Briançon, *France* . . . 18 D7 44 54N 6 39 E
Bribie I., *Australia* . . . 63 D5 27 0S 153 10 E
Bridgehampton, *U.S.A.* . . . 79 F12 40 56N 72 19W
Bridgend, *U.K.* . . . 11 F4 51 30N 3 34W
Bridgend □, *U.K.* . . . 11 F4 51 36N 3 36W
Bridgeport, *Calif., U.S.A.* 83 G4 38 15N 119 14W
Bridgeport, *Conn., U.S.A.* 79 E11 41 11N 73 12W
Bridgeport, *Nebr., U.S.A.* 80 E3 41 40N 103 6W
Bridgeport, *Tex., U.S.A.* . 81 J6 33 13N 97 45W
Bridger, *U.S.A.* . . . 82 D9 45 18N 108 55W
Bridgeton, *U.S.A.* . . . 76 F8 39 26N 75 14W
Bridgetown, *Australia* . . . 61 F2 33 58S 116 7 E
Bridgetown, *Barbados* . . . 89 D8 13 5N 59 30W
Bridgetown, *Canada* . . . 71 D6 44 55N 65 18W
Bridgewater, *Canada* . . . 71 D7 44 25N 64 31W
Bridgewater, *Mass., U.S.A.* 79 E14 41 59N 70 58W
Bridgewater, *S. Dak., U.S.A.* . . . 80 D6 43 33N 97 30W
Bridgewater, C., *Australia* 63 F3 38 23S 141 23 E
Bridgnorth, *U.K.* . . . 11 E5 52 32N 2 25W
Bridgton, *U.S.A.* . . . 79 B14 44 3N 70 42W
Bridgwater, *U.K.* . . . 11 F4 51 8N 2 59W
Bridlington, *U.K.* . . . 10 C7 54 5N 0 12W
Bridport, *Australia* . . . 62 G4 40 59S 147 23 E
Bridport, *U.K.* . . . 11 G5 50 44N 2 45W
Brig, *Switz.* . . . 16 E4 46 18N 7 59 E
Brigg, *U.K.* . . . 10 D7 53 34N 0 28W
Briggsdale, *U.S.A.* . . . 80 E2 40 38N 104 20W
Brigham City, *U.S.A.* . . . 82 F7 41 31N 112 1W
Bright, *Australia* . . . 63 F4 36 42S 146 56 E
Brighton, *Australia* . . . 63 F2 35 5S 138 30 E
Brighton, *Canada* . . . 70 D4 44 2N 77 44W
Brighton, *U.K.* . . . 11 G7 50 49N 0 7W
Brighton, *U.S.A.* . . . 80 F2 39 59N 104 49W
Brilliant, *Canada* . . . 72 D5 49 19N 117 38W
Brilliant, *U.S.A.* . . . 78 F4 40 15N 80 39W
Bríndisi, *Italy* . . . 21 D7 40 39N 17 55 E
Brinkley, *U.S.A.* . . . 81 H9 34 53N 91 12W
Brinkworth, *Australia* . . . 63 E2 33 42S 138 26 E
Brinnon, *U.S.A.* . . . 84 C4 47 41N 122 54W
Brion, I., *Canada* . . . 71 C7 47 46N 61 26W
Brisbane, *Australia* . . . 63 D5 27 25S 153 2 E
Brisbane →, *Australia* . . . 63 D5 27 24S 153 9 E
Bristol, *U.K.* . . . 11 F5 51 26N 2 35W
Bristol, *Conn., U.S.A.* . . . 79 E12 41 40N 72 57W
Bristol, *Pa., U.S.A.* . . . 79 F10 40 6N 74 51W
Bristol, *R.I., U.S.A.* . . . 79 E13 41 40N 71 16W
Bristol, *S. Dak., U.S.A.* . . . 80 C6 45 21N 97 45W
Bristol, *Tenn., U.S.A.* . . . 77 G4 36 36N 82 11W
Bristol □, *U.K.* . . . 11 F5 51 27N 2 36W
Bristol B., *U.S.A.* . . . 68 C4 58 0N 160 0W
Bristol Channel, *U.K.* . . . 11 F3 51 18N 4 30W
Bristol I., *Antarctica* . . . 5 B1 58 45S 28 0W
Bristol L., *U.S.A.* . . . 83 J5 34 23N 116 50W

Chilko, L.

Chadan, Russia 27 D10 51 17N 91 35 E
Chadileuvú →, Argentina 94 D2 37 46S 66 0W
Chadiza, Zambia 55 E3 14 45S 32 27 E
Chadron, U.S.A. 80 D3 42 50N 103 0W
Chadyr-Lunga = Ceadâr-Lunga, Moldova 17 E15 46 3N 28 51 E
Chae Hom, Thailand 38 C2 18 43N 99 35 E
Chaem →, Thailand 38 C2 18 11N 98 38 E
Chaeryŏng, N. Korea 35 E13 38 24N 125 36 E
Chagai Hills, Afghan. 40 E3 29 30N 63 0 E
Chagda, Russia 27 D14 58 45N 130 38 E
Chagos Arch., Ind. Oc. 29 K11 6 0S 72 0 E
Chāh Ākhvor, Iran 45 C8 32 41N 59 40 E
Chāh Bahār, Iran 45 E9 25 20N 60 40 E
Chāh-e-Malek, Iran 45 D8 28 35N 59 7 E
Chāh Kavīr, Iran 45 D7 31 45N 54 52 E
Chahar Burjak, Afghan. 40 D3 30 15N 62 0 E
Chaibasa, India 41 H14 22 42N 85 49 E
Chainat, Thailand 38 E3 15 11N 100 8 E
Chaiya, Thailand 39 H2 9 23N 99 14 E
Chaj Doab, Pakistan 42 C5 32 15N 73 0 E
Chajari, Argentina 94 C4 30 42S 58 0W
Chake Chake, Tanzania 54 D4 5 15S 39 45 E
Chakhānsūr, Afghan. 40 D3 31 10N 62 0 E
Chakonipau, L., Canada 71 A6 56 18N 68 30W
Chakradharpur, India 43 H11 22 45N 85 40 E
Chakwal, Pakistan 42 C5 32 56N 72 53 E
Chala, Peru 92 G4 15 48S 74 20W
Chalchihuites, Mexico 86 C4 23 29N 103 53W
Chalcis = Khalkís, Greece 21 E10 38 27N 23 42 E
Chaleur B., Canada 71 C6 47 55N 65 30W
Chalfant, U.S.A. 84 H8 37 32N 118 21W
Chalhuanca, Peru 92 F4 14 15S 73 15W
Chalisgaon, India 40 J9 20 30N 75 10 E
Chalky Inlet, N.Z. 59 M1 46 3S 166 31 E
Challapata, Bolivia 92 G5 18 53S 66 50W
Challis, U.S.A. 82 D6 44 30N 114 14W
Chalna, India 43 H13 22 36N 89 35 E
Chalon-sur-Saône, France 18 C6 46 48N 4 50 E
Châlons-en-Champagne, France 18 B6 48 58N 4 20 E
Chalyaphum, Thailand 38 E4 15 48N 102 2 E
Cham, Cu Lao, Vietnam 38 E7 15 57N 108 30 E
Chama, U.S.A. 83 H10 36 54N 106 35W
Chaman, Pakistan 40 D5 30 58N 66 25 E
Chamba, India 42 C7 32 35N 76 10 E
Chamba, Tanzania 55 E4 11 37S 37 0 E
Chambal →, India 43 F8 26 29N 79 15 E
Chamberlain, U.S.A. 80 D5 43 49N 99 20W
Chamberlain →, Australia 60 C4 15 30S 127 54 E
Chambers, U.S.A. 83 J9 35 11N 109 26W
Chambersburg, U.S.A. 76 F7 39 56N 77 40W
Chambéry, France 18 D6 45 34N 5 55 E
Chambly, Canada 79 A11 45 27N 73 17W
Chambord, Canada 71 C5 48 25N 72 6W
Chamchamal, Iraq 44 C5 35 32N 44 50 E
Chamela, Mexico 86 D3 19 32N 105 5W
Chamical, Argentina 94 C2 30 22S 66 27W
Chamkar Luong, Cambodia 39 G4 11 0N 103 45 E
Chamonix-Mont Blanc, France 18 D7 45 55N 6 51 E
Champa, India 43 H10 22 2N 82 43 E
Champagne, Canada 72 A1 60 49N 136 30W
Champagne, France 18 B6 48 40N 4 20 E
Champaign, U.S.A. 76 E1 40 7N 88 15W
Champassak, Laos 38 E5 14 53N 105 52 E
Champlain, Canada 76 B9 46 27N 72 24W
Champlain, U.S.A. 79 B11 44 59N 73 27W
Champlain, L., U.S.A. 79 B11 44 40N 73 20W
Champotón, Mexico 87 D6 19 20N 90 50W
Chana, Thailand 39 J3 6 55N 100 44 E
Chañaral, Chile 94 B1 26 23S 70 40W
Chanārān, Iran 45 B8 36 39N 59 6 E
Chanasma, India 42 H5 23 44N 72 5 E
Chandannagar, India 43 H13 22 52N 88 24 E
Chandausi, India 43 E8 28 27N 78 49 E
Chandeleur Is., U.S.A. 81 L10 29 55N 88 57W
Chandeleur Sd., U.S.A. 81 L10 29 55N 89 0W
Chandigarh, India 42 D7 30 43N 76 47 E
Chandler, Australia 63 D1 27 0S 133 19 E
Chandler, Canada 71 C7 48 18N 64 46W
Chandler, Ariz., U.S.A. 83 K8 33 18N 111 50W
Chandler, Okla., U.S.A. 81 H6 35 42N 96 53W
Chandpur, Bangla. 41 H17 23 8N 90 45 E
Chandpur, India 42 E8 29 8N 78 19 E
Chandrapur, India 40 K11 19 57N 79 25 E
Chānf, Iran 45 E9 26 38N 60 29 E
Chang, Pakistan 42 F3 26 59N 68 30 E
Chang, Ko, Thailand 39 F4 12 0N 102 23 E
Ch'ang Chiang = Chang Jiang →, China 33 C7 31 48N 121 10 E
Chang Jiang →, China 33 C7 31 48N 121 10 E
Changa, India 43 C7 33 53N 77 35 E
Changanacheri, India 40 Q10 9 25N 76 31 E
Changane →, Mozam. 57 C5 24 30S 33 30 E
Changbai, China 35 D15 41 25N 128 5 E
Changbai Shan, China 35 C15 42 20N 129 0 E
Changchiak'ou = Zhangjiakou, China 34 D8 40 48N 114 55 E
Ch'angchou = Changzhou, China 33 C6 31 47N 119 58 E
Changchun, China 35 C13 43 57N 125 17 E
Changchunling, China 35 B13 45 18N 125 27 E
Changde, China 33 D6 29 4N 111 35 E
Changdo-ri, N. Korea 35 E14 38 30N 127 40 E
Changhai = Shanghai, China 33 C7 31 15N 121 26 E
Changhua, Taiwan 33 D7 24 2N 120 30 E
Changhŭng, S. Korea 35 G14 34 41N 126 52 E
Changhŭngni, N. Korea 35 D15 40 24N 128 19 E
Changjiang, China 38 C7 19 20N 108 55 E
Changjin, N. Korea 35 D14 40 23N 127 15 E
Changjin-chŏsuji, N. Korea 35 D14 40 30N 127 15 E
Changli, China 35 E10 39 40N 119 13 E
Changling, China 35 B12 44 20N 123 58 E
Changlun, Malaysia 39 J3 6 25N 100 26 E
Changping, China 34 D9 40 14N 116 12 E
Changsha, China 33 D6 28 12N 113 0 E
Changwu, China 34 G4 35 10N 107 45 E
Changyi, China 35 F10 36 40N 119 30 E
Changyŏn, N. Korea 35 E13 38 15N 125 6 E
Changyuan, China 34 G8 35 15N 114 42 E
Changzhi, China 34 F7 36 10N 113 6 E
Changzhou, China 33 C6 31 47N 119 58 E
Chanhanga, Angola 56 B1 16 0S 14 8 E
Channapatna, India 40 N10 12 40N 77 15 E
Channel Is., U.K. 11 H5 49 19N 2 24W
Channel Is., U.S.A. 85 M7 33 40N 119 15W
Channel-Port aux Basques, Canada 71 C8 47 30N 59 9W
Channing, Mich., U.S.A. 76 B1 46 9N 88 5W
Channing, Tex., U.S.A. 81 H3 35 41N 102 20W
Chantada, Spain 19 A2 42 36N 7 46W
Chanthaburi, Thailand 38 F4 12 38N 102 12 E
Chantrey Inlet, Canada 68 B10 67 48N 96 20W
Chanute, U.S.A. 81 G7 37 41N 95 27W
Chao Phraya →, Thailand 38 F3 13 32N 100 36 E
Chao Phraya Lowlands, Thailand 38 E3 15 30N 100 0 E
Chao'an, China 33 D6 23 42N 116 32 E
Chaocheng, China 34 F8 36 4N 115 37 E
Chaoyang, China 35 D11 41 35N 120 22 E
Chapala, Mozam. 55 F4 15 50S 37 35 E
Chapala, L. de, Mexico 86 C4 20 10N 103 20W
Chapayev, Kazakstan 25 D9 50 25N 51 10 E
Chapayevsk, Russia 24 D8 53 0N 49 40 E
Chapecó, Brazil 95 B5 27 14S 52 41W
Chapel Hill, U.S.A. 77 H6 35 55N 79 4W
Chapleau, Canada 70 C3 47 50N 83 24W
Chaplin, Canada 73 C7 50 28N 106 40W
Chapra = Chhapra, India 43 G11 25 48N 84 44 E
Châr, Mauritania 50 D2 21 32N 12 45W
Chara, Russia 27 D12 56 54N 118 20 E
Charadai, Argentina 94 B4 27 35S 59 55W
Charagua, Bolivia 92 G6 19 45S 63 10W
Charaña, Bolivia 92 G5 17 30S 69 25W
Charata, Argentina 94 B3 27 13S 61 14W
Charcas, Mexico 86 C4 23 10N 101 20W
Charcoal L., Canada 73 B8 58 49N 102 22W
Chard, U.K. 11 G5 50 52N 2 58W
Chardara, Kazakstan 26 E7 41 16N 67 59 E
Chardon, U.S.A. 78 E3 41 35N 81 12W
Chardzhou = Chärjew, Turkmenistan 26 F7 39 6N 63 34 E
Charente →, France 18 D3 45 57N 1 5W
Chari →, Chad 51 F7 12 58N 14 31 E
Chārīkār, Afghan. 40 B6 35 0N 69 10 E
Chariton →, U.S.A. 80 F8 39 19N 92 58W
Chärjew, Turkmenistan 26 F7 39 6N 63 34 E
Charkhari, India 43 G8 25 24N 79 45 E
Charkhi Dadri, India 42 E7 28 37N 76 17 E
Charleroi, Belgium 15 D4 50 24N 4 27 E
Charleroi, U.S.A. 78 F5 40 9N 79 57W
Charles, C., U.S.A. 76 G8 37 7N 75 58W
Charles City, U.S.A. 80 D8 43 4N 92 41W
Charles L., Canada 73 B6 59 50N 110 33W
Charles Town, U.S.A. 76 F7 39 17N 77 52W
Charleston, Ill., U.S.A. 76 F1 39 30N 88 10W
Charleston, Miss., U.S.A. 81 H9 34 1N 90 4W
Charleston, Mo., U.S.A. 81 G10 36 55N 89 21W
Charleston, S.C., U.S.A. 77 J6 32 46N 79 56W
Charleston, W. Va., U.S.A. 76 F5 38 21N 81 38W
Charleston Peak, U.S.A. 85 J11 36 16N 115 42W
Charlestown, S. Africa 57 D4 27 26S 29 53 E
Charlestown, U.S.A. 76 F3 38 27N 85 40W
Charlesville, Zaïre 52 F4 5 27S 20 59 E
Charleville = Rath Luirc, Ireland 13 D3 52 21N 8 40W
Charleville, Australia 63 D4 26 24S 146 15 E
Charleville-Mézières, France 18 B6 49 44N 4 40 E
Charlevoix, U.S.A. 76 C3 45 19N 85 16W
Charlotte, Mich., U.S.A. 76 D3 42 34N 84 50W
Charlotte, N.C., U.S.A. 77 H5 35 13N 80 51W
Charlotte Amalie, Virgin Is. 89 C7 18 21N 64 56W
Charlotte Harbor, U.S.A. 77 M4 26 50N 82 10W
Charlottesville, U.S.A. 76 F6 38 2N 78 30W
Charlottetown, Canada 71 C7 46 14N 63 8W
Charlton, Australia 63 F3 36 16S 143 24 E
Charlton, U.S.A. 80 E8 40 59N 93 20W
Charlton I., Canada 70 B4 52 0N 79 20W
Charny, Canada 71 C5 46 43N 71 15W
Charolles, France 18 C6 46 27N 4 16 E
Charouine, Algeria 50 C4 29 0N 0 15W
Charre, Mozam. 55 F4 17 13S 35 10 E
Charsadda, Pakistan 42 B4 34 7N 71 45 E
Charters Towers, Australia 62 C4 20 5S 146 13 E
Chartres, France 18 B4 48 29N 1 30 E
Chascomús, Argentina 94 D4 35 30S 58 0W
Chasefu, Zambia 55 E3 11 55S 33 8 E
Chasovnya-Uchurskaya, Russia 27 D14 57 15N 132 50 E
Chāt, Iran 45 B7 37 59N 55 16 E
Châteaubriant, France 18 C3 47 43N 1 23W
Châteaulin, France 18 B1 48 11N 4 8W
Châteauroux, France 18 C4 46 50N 1 40 E
Châtellerault, France 18 C4 46 50N 0 30 E
Chatfield, U.S.A. 80 D9 43 51N 92 11W
Chatham, N.B., Canada 71 C6 47 2N 65 28W
Chatham, Ont., Canada 70 D3 42 24N 82 11W
Chatham, U.K. 11 F8 51 22N 0 32 E
Chatham, La., U.S.A. 81 J8 32 18N 92 27W
Chatham, N.Y., U.S.A. 79 D11 42 21N 73 36W
Chatham Is., Pac. Oc. 64 M10 44 0S 176 40W
Chatham Str., U.S.A. 72 B2 57 0N 134 40W
Chatmohar, Bangla. 43 G13 24 15N 89 15 E
Chatra, India 43 G11 24 12N 84 56 E
Chatrapur, India 41 K14 19 22N 85 2 E
Chats, L. des, Canada 79 A8 45 30N 76 20W
Chatsworth, Canada 78 B4 44 27N 80 54W
Chatsworth, Zimbabwe 55 F3 19 38S 31 13 E
Chattahoochee →, U.S.A. 77 K3 30 54N 84 57W
Chattanooga, U.S.A. 77 H3 35 3N 85 19W
Chaturat, Thailand 38 E3 15 40N 101 51 E
Chau Doc, Vietnam 39 G5 10 42N 105 7 E
Chauk, Burma 41 J19 20 53N 94 49 E
Chaukan La, Burma 41 F20 27 0N 97 15 E
Chaumont, France 18 B6 48 7N 5 8 E
Chaumont, U.S.A. 79 B8 44 4N 76 8W
Chautauqua L., U.S.A. 78 D5 42 10N 79 24W
Chauvin, Canada 73 C6 52 45N 110 10W
Chaves, Brazil 93 D9 0 15S 49 55W
Chaves, Portugal 19 B2 41 45N 7 32W
Chavuma, Zambia 53 G4 13 4S 22 40 E
Chawang, Thailand 39 H2 8 25N 99 30 E
Chaykovskiy, Russia 24 C9 56 47N 54 9 E
Chazy, U.S.A. 79 B11 44 53N 73 26W
Cheb, Czech. 16 C7 50 9N 12 28 E
Cheboksary, Russia 24 C8 56 8N 47 12 E
Cheboygan, U.S.A. 76 C3 45 39N 84 29W
Chech, Erg, Africa 50 D4 25 0N 2 15W
Chechenia □, Russia 25 F8 43 30N 45 29 E
Checheno-Ingush Republic = Chechenia □, Russia 25 F8 43 30N 45 29 E
Chechnya = Chechenia □, Russia 25 F8 43 30N 45 29 E
Chechon, S. Korea 35 F15 37 8N 128 12 E
Checleset B., Canada 72 C3 50 5N 127 35W
Checotah, U.S.A. 81 H7 35 28N 95 31W
Chedabucto B., Canada 71 C7 45 25N 61 8W
Cheduba I., Burma 41 K18 18 45N 93 40 E
Cheepie, Australia 63 D4 26 33S 145 1 E
Chegdomyn, Russia 27 D14 51 7N 133 1 E
Chegga, Mauritania 50 C3 25 27N 5 40W
Chegutu, Zimbabwe 55 F3 18 10S 30 14 E
Chehalis, U.S.A. 84 D4 46 40N 122 58W
Cheju Do, S. Korea 35 H14 33 29N 126 34 E
Chekiang = Zhejiang □, China 33 D7 29 0N 120 0 E
Chela, Sa. da, Angola 56 B1 16 20S 13 20 E
Chelan, U.S.A. 82 C4 47 51N 120 1W
Chelan, L., U.S.A. 82 C3 48 11N 120 30W
Cheleken, Turkmenistan 25 G9 39 34N 53 16 E
Chelforó, Argentina 96 D3 39 0S 66 33W
Chelkar = Shalqar, Kazakstan 26 E6 47 48N 59 39 E
Chelkar Tengiz, Solonchak, Kazakstan 26 E7 48 5N 63 7 E
Chełm, Poland 17 C12 51 8N 23 30 E
Chełmno, Poland 17 B10 53 20N 18 30 E
Chelmsford, U.K. 11 F8 51 44N 0 29 E
Chelsea, Okla., U.S.A. 81 G7 36 32N 95 26W
Chelsea, Vt., U.S.A. 79 C12 43 59N 72 27W
Cheltenham, U.K. 11 F5 51 54N 2 4W
Chelyabinsk, Russia 26 D7 55 10N 61 24 E
Chelyuskin, C., Russia 28 B14 77 30N 103 0 E
Chemainus, Canada 72 D4 48 55N 123 42W
Chemnitz, Germany 16 C7 50 51N 12 54 E
Chemult, U.S.A. 82 E3 43 14N 121 47W
Chen, Gora, Russia 27 C15 65 16N 141 50 E
Chenab →, Pakistan 42 D4 30 23N 71 2 E
Chenango Forks, U.S.A. 79 D9 42 15N 75 51W
Chencha, Ethiopia 51 G12 6 15N 37 32 E
Cheney, U.S.A. 82 C5 47 30N 117 35W
Cheng Xian, China 34 H3 33 43N 105 42 E
Chengcheng, China 34 G5 35 8N 109 56 E
Chengchou = Zhengzhou, China 34 G7 34 45N 113 34 E
Chengde, China 35 D9 40 59N 117 58 E
Chengdu, China 32 C5 30 38N 104 2 E
Chenggu, China 34 H4 33 10N 107 21 E
Chengjiang, China 32 D5 24 39N 103 0 E
Ch'engtu = Chengdu, China 32 C5 30 38N 104 2 E
Chengwu, China 34 G8 34 58N 115 50 E
Chengyang, China 35 F11 36 18N 120 21 E
Chenjiagang, China 35 G10 34 23N 119 47 E
Chenkán, Mexico 87 D6 19 8N 90 58W
Cheo Reo, Vietnam 38 F7 13 25N 108 28 E
Cheom Ksan, Cambodia 38 E5 14 13N 104 56 E
Chepén, Peru 92 E3 7 15S 79 23W
Chepes, Argentina 94 C2 31 20S 66 35W
Chepo, Panama 88 E4 9 10N 79 6W
Cheptulil, Mt., Kenya 54 B4 1 25N 35 35 E
Chequamegon B., U.S.A. 80 B9 46 40N 90 30W
Cher →, France 18 C4 47 21N 0 29 E
Cheraw, U.S.A. 77 H6 34 42N 79 53W
Cherbourg, France 18 B3 49 39N 1 40W
Cherchell, Algeria 50 A5 36 35N 2 12 E
Cherdyn, Russia 24 B10 60 24N 56 29 E
Cheremkhovo, Russia 27 D11 53 8N 103 1 E
Cherepanovo, Russia 26 D9 54 15N 83 30 E
Cherepovets, Russia 24 C6 59 5N 37 55 E
Chergui, Chott ech, Algeria 50 B5 34 21N 0 25 E
Cherikov = Cherykaw, Belarus 17 B16 53 32N 31 20 E
Cherkasy, Ukraine 25 E5 49 27N 32 4 E
Cherlak, Russia 26 D8 54 15N 74 55 E
Chernaya, Russia 27 B9 70 30N 89 10 E
Chernigov = Chernihiv, Ukraine 24 D5 51 28N 31 20 E
Chernihiv, Ukraine 24 D5 51 28N 31 20 E
Chernikovsk, Russia 24 D10 54 48N 56 8 E
Chernivtsi, Ukraine 17 D13 48 15N 25 52 E
Chernobyl = Chornobyl, Ukraine 17 C16 51 20N 30 15 E
Chernogorsk, Russia 27 D10 53 49N 91 18 E
Chernovtsy = Chernivtsi, Ukraine 17 D13 48 15N 25 52 E
Chernyakhovsk, Russia 9 J19 54 36N 21 48 E
Chernyshovskiy, Russia 27 C12 63 0N 112 30 E
Cherokee, Iowa, U.S.A. 80 D7 42 45N 95 33W
Cherokee, Okla., U.S.A. 81 G5 36 45N 98 21W
Cherokees, Lake O' The, U.S.A. 81 G7 36 28N 95 2W
Cherquenco, Chile 96 D2 38 35S 72 0W
Cherrapunji, India 41 G17 25 17N 91 47 E
Cherry Creek, U.S.A. 82 G6 39 54N 114 53W
Cherry Valley, U.S.A. 85 M10 33 59N 116 57W
Cherryvale, U.S.A. 81 G7 37 16N 95 33W
Cherskiy, Russia 27 C17 68 45N 161 18 E
Cherskogo Khrebet, Russia 27 C15 65 0N 143 0 E
Cherven, Belarus 17 B15 53 45N 28 28 E
Chervonohrad, Ukraine 17 C13 50 25N 24 10 E
Cherwell →, U.K. 11 F6 51 44N 1 14W
Cherykaw, Belarus 17 B16 53 32N 31 20 E
Chesapeake, U.S.A. 76 G7 36 50N 76 17W
Chesapeake B., U.S.A. 76 F7 38 0N 76 10W
Cheshire □, U.K. 10 D5 53 14N 2 30W
Cheshskaya Guba, Russia 24 A8 67 20N 47 0 E
Cheslatta L., Canada 72 C3 53 49N 125 20W
Chesley, Canada 78 B3 44 17N 81 5W
Chester, U.K. 10 D5 53 12N 2 53W
Chester, Calif., U.S.A. 82 F3 40 19N 121 14W
Chester, Ill., U.S.A. 81 G10 37 55N 89 49W
Chester, Mont., U.S.A. 82 B8 48 31N 110 58W
Chester, Pa., U.S.A. 76 F8 39 51N 75 22W
Chester, S.C., U.S.A. 77 H5 34 43N 81 12W
Chesterfield, U.K. 10 D6 53 15N 1 25W
Chesterfield, Is., N. Cal. 64 J7 19 52S 158 15 E
Chesterfield Inlet, Canada 68 B10 63 30N 90 45W
Chesterton Ra., Australia 63 D4 25 30S 147 27 E
Chesterville, Canada 79 A9 45 6N 75 14W
Chesuncook L., U.S.A. 71 C6 46 0N 69 21W
Chéticamp, Canada 71 C7 46 37N 60 59W
Chetumal, B. de, Mexico 87 D7 18 40N 88 10W
Chetwynd, Canada 72 B4 55 45N 121 36W
Cheviot, The, U.K. 10 B5 55 29N 2 9W
Cheviot Hills, U.K. 10 B5 55 20N 2 30W
Cheviot Ra., Australia 62 D3 25 20S 143 45 E
Chew Bahir, Ethiopia 51 H12 4 40N 36 50 E
Chewelah, U.S.A. 82 B5 48 17N 117 43W
Cheyenne, Okla., U.S.A. 81 H5 35 37N 99 40W
Cheyenne, Wyo., U.S.A. 80 E2 41 8N 104 49W
Cheyenne →, U.S.A. 80 C4 44 41N 101 18W
Cheyenne Wells, U.S.A. 80 F3 38 49N 102 21W
Cheyne B., Australia 61 F2 34 35S 118 50 E
Chhabra, India 42 G7 24 40N 76 54 E
Chhapra, India 43 G11 25 48N 84 44 E
Chhata, India 42 F7 27 42N 77 30 E
Chhatarpur, India 43 G8 24 55N 79 35 E
Chhep, Cambodia 38 F5 13 45N 105 24 E
Chhindwara, India 43 H8 22 2N 78 59 E
Chhlong, Cambodia 39 F5 12 15N 105 58 E
Chhuk, Cambodia 39 G5 10 46N 104 28 E
Chi →, Thailand 38 E5 15 11N 104 43 E
Chiai, Taiwan 33 D7 23 29N 120 25 E
Chiamis, Indonesia 37 G13 7 20S 108 21 E
Chiamussu = Jiamusi, China 33 B8 46 40N 130 26 E
Chiang Dao, Thailand 38 C2 19 22N 98 58 E
Chiang Kham, Thailand 38 C3 19 32N 100 18 E
Chiang Khan, Thailand 38 D3 17 52N 101 36 E
Chiang Khong, Thailand 38 B3 20 17N 100 24 E
Chiang Mai, Thailand 38 C2 18 47N 98 59 E
Chiang Saen, Thailand 38 B3 20 16N 100 5 E
Chiange, Angola 53 H2 15 35S 13 40 E
Chiapa →, Mexico 87 D6 16 42N 93 0W
Chiapa de Corzo, Mexico 87 D6 16 42N 93 0W
Chiapas □, Mexico 87 D6 17 0N 92 45W
Chiautla, Mexico 87 D5 18 18N 98 34W
Chiávari, Italy 20 B3 44 19N 9 19 E
Chiavenna, Italy 20 A3 46 19N 9 24 E
Chiba, Japan 31 G10 35 30N 140 7 E
Chibabava, Mozam. 57 C5 20 17S 33 35 E
Chibatu, Indonesia 37 G12 7 6S 107 59 E
Chibemba, Cunene, Angola 53 H2 15 48S 14 8 E
Chibemba, Huila, Angola 56 B2 16 20S 15 20 E
Chibia, Angola 53 H2 15 10S 13 42 E
Chibougamau, Canada 70 C5 49 56N 74 24W
Chibougamau L., Canada 70 C5 49 50N 74 20W
Chibuk, Nigeria 51 F7 10 52N 12 50 E
Chic-Chocs, Mts., Canada 71 C6 48 55N 66 0W
Chicacole = Srikakulam, India 41 K13 18 14N 83 58 E
Chicago, U.S.A. 76 E2 41 53N 87 38W
Chicago Heights, U.S.A. 76 E2 41 30N 87 38W
Chichagof I., U.S.A. 72 B1 57 30N 135 30W
Chicheng, China 34 D8 40 55N 115 55 E
Chichester, U.K. 11 G7 50 50N 0 47W
Chichibu, Japan 31 F9 36 5N 139 10 E
Ch'ich'ihaerh = Qiqihar, China 27 E13 47 26N 124 0 E
Chickasha, U.S.A. 81 H5 35 3N 97 58W
Chiclana de la Frontera, Spain 19 D2 36 26N 6 9W
Chiclayo, Peru 92 E3 6 42S 79 50W
Chico, U.S.A. 84 F5 39 44N 121 50W
Chico →, Chubut, Argentina 96 E3 44 0S 67 0W
Chico →, Santa Cruz, Argentina 96 G3 50 0S 68 30W
Chicomo, Mozam. 57 C5 24 31S 34 6 E
Chicontepec, Mexico 87 C5 20 58N 98 10W
Chicopee, U.S.A. 79 D12 42 9N 72 37W
Chicoutimi, Canada 71 C5 48 28N 71 5W
Chicualacuala, Mozam. 57 C5 22 6S 31 42 E
Chidambaram, India 40 P11 11 20N 79 45 E
Chidenguele, Mozam. 57 C5 24 55S 34 11 E
Chidley, C., Canada 69 B13 60 23N 64 26W
Chiede, Angola 56 B2 17 15S 16 22 E
Chiefs Pt., Canada 78 B3 44 41N 81 18W
Chiem Hoa, Vietnam 38 A5 22 12N 105 17 E
Chiemsee, Germany 16 E7 47 53N 12 28 E
Chiengi, Zambia 55 D2 8 45S 29 10 E
Chiengmai = Chiang Mai, Thailand 38 C2 18 47N 98 59 E
Chiese →, Italy 20 B4 45 8N 10 25 E
Chieti, Italy 20 C6 42 21N 14 10 E
Chifeng, China 35 C10 42 18N 118 58 E
Chignecto B., Canada 71 C7 45 30N 64 40W
Chiguana, Bolivia 94 A2 21 0S 67 58W
Chiha-ri, N. Korea 35 E14 38 40N 126 30 E
Chihli, G. of = Bo Hai, China 35 E10 39 0N 119 0 E
Chihli, G. of = Po Hai, China 28 F15 38 30N 119 0 E
Chihuahua, Mexico 86 B3 28 40N 106 3W
Chihuahua □, Mexico 86 B3 28 40N 106 3W
Chiili, Kazakstan 26 E7 44 20N 66 15 E
Chik Bollapur, India 40 N10 13 25N 77 45 E
Chikmagalur, India 40 N9 13 15N 75 45 E
Chikwawa, Malawi 55 F3 16 2S 34 50 E
Chilac, Mexico 87 D5 18 20N 97 24W
Chilako →, Canada 72 C4 53 53N 122 57W
Chilam Chavki, Pakistan 43 B6 35 5N 75 5 E
Chilanga, Zambia 55 F2 15 33S 28 16 E
Chilapa, Mexico 87 D5 17 40N 99 11W
Chilas, Pakistan 43 B6 35 25N 74 5 E
Chilaw, Sri Lanka 40 R11 7 30N 79 50 E
Chilcotin →, Canada 72 C4 51 44N 122 23W
Childers, Australia 63 D5 25 15S 152 17 E
Childress, U.S.A. 81 H4 34 25N 100 13W
Chile ■, S. Amer. 96 D2 35 0S 72 0W
Chile Rise, Pac. Oc. 65 L18 38 0S 92 0W
Chilecito, Argentina 94 B2 29 10S 67 30W
Chilete, Peru 92 E3 7 10S 78 50W
Chililabombwe, Zambia 55 E2 12 18S 27 43 E
Chilin = Jilin, China 35 C14 43 44N 126 30 E
Chilka L., India 41 K14 19 40N 85 25 E
Chilko →, Canada 72 C4 52 0N 123 40W
Chilko, L., Canada 72 C4 51 20N 124 10W

Chillagoe

Corinth, G. of

Corinth, G. of = Korinthiakós Kólpos, Greece 21 E10 38 16N 22 30 E
Corinto, Brazil 93 G10 18 20S 44 30W
Corinto, Nic. 88 D2 12 30N 87 10W
Cork, Ireland 13 E3 51 54N 8 29W
Cork □, Ireland 13 E3 51 57N 8 40W
Cork Harbour, Ireland 13 E3 51 47N 8 16W
Çorlu, Turkey 21 D12 41 11N 27 49 E
Cormack L., Canada 72 A4 60 56N 121 37W
Cormorant, Canada 73 C8 54 14N 100 35W
Cormorant L., Canada 73 C8 54 15N 100 50W
Corn Is. = Maíz, Is. del, Nic. 88 D3 12 15N 83 4W
Cornélio Procópio, Brazil 95 A5 23 7S 50 40W
Cornell, U.S.A. 80 C9 45 10N 91 9W
Corner Brook, Canada 71 C8 48 57N 57 58W
Corneşti, Moldova 17 E15 47 21N 28 1 E
Corning, Ark., U.S.A. 81 G9 36 25N 90 35W
Corning, Calif., U.S.A. 82 G2 39 56N 122 11W
Corning, Iowa, U.S.A. 80 E7 40 59N 94 44W
Corning, N.Y., U.S.A. 78 D7 42 9N 77 3W
Cornwall, Canada 70 C5 45 2N 74 44W
Cornwall □, U.K. 11 G3 50 26N 4 40W
Corny Pt., Australia 63 E2 34 55S 137 0 E
Coro, Venezuela 92 A5 11 25N 69 41W
Coroatá, Brazil 93 D10 4 8S 44 0W
Corocoro, Bolivia 92 G5 17 15S 68 28W
Coroico, Bolivia 92 G5 16 0S 67 50W
Coromandel, N.Z. 59 G5 36 45S 175 31 E
Coromandel Coast, India 40 N12 12 30N 81 0 E
Corona, Australia 63 E3 31 16S 141 24 E
Corona, Calif., U.S.A. 85 M9 33 53N 117 34W
Corona, N. Mex., U.S.A. 83 J11 34 15N 105 36W
Coronado, U.S.A. 85 N9 32 41N 117 11W
Coronado, B. de, Costa Rica 88 E3 9 0N 83 40W
Coronados, Is. los, U.S.A. 85 N9 32 25N 117 15W
Coronation, Canada 72 C6 52 5N 111 27W
Coronation Gulf, Canada 68 B8 68 25N 110 0W
Coronation I., Antarctica 5 C18 60 45S 46 0W
Coronation I., U.S.A. 72 B2 55 52N 134 20W
Coronation Is., Australia 60 B3 14 57S 124 55 E
Coronda, Argentina 94 C3 31 58S 60 56W
Coronel, Chile 94 D1 37 0S 73 10W
Coronel Bogado, Paraguay 94 B4 27 11S 56 18W
Coronel Dorrego, Argentina 94 D3 38 40S 61 10W
Coronel Oviedo, Paraguay 94 B4 25 24S 56 30W
Coronel Pringles, Argentina 94 D3 38 0S 61 30W
Coronel Suárez, Argentina 94 D3 37 30S 61 52W
Coronel Vidal, Argentina 94 D4 37 28S 57 45W
Corowa, Australia 63 F4 35 58S 146 21 E
Corozal, Belize 87 D7 18 23N 88 23W
Corpus, Argentina 95 B4 27 10S 55 30W
Corpus Christi, U.S.A. 81 M6 27 47N 97 24W
Corpus Christi, L., U.S.A. 81 L6 28 2N 97 52W
Corque, Bolivia 92 G5 18 20S 67 41W
Corralejo, Canary Is. 22 F6 28 43N 13 53W
Correntes, C. das, Mozam. 57 C6 24 6S 35 34 E
Corrib, L., Ireland 13 C2 53 27N 9 16W
Corrientes, Argentina 94 B4 27 30S 58 45W
Corrientes □, Argentina 94 B4 28 0S 57 0W
Corrientes →, Argentina 94 C4 30 42S 59 38W
Corrientes →, Peru 92 D4 3 43S 74 35W
Corrientes, C., Colombia 92 B3 5 30N 77 34W
Corrientes, C., Cuba 88 B3 21 43N 84 30W
Corrientes, C., Mexico 86 C3 20 25N 105 42W
Corrigan, U.S.A. 81 K7 31 0N 94 52W
Corrigin, Australia 61 F2 32 20S 117 53 E
Corry, U.S.A. 78 E5 41 55N 79 39W
Corse, France 18 F8 42 0N 9 0 E
Corse, C., France 18 E8 43 1N 9 25 E
Corsica = Corse, France 18 F8 42 0N 9 0 E
Corsicana, U.S.A. 81 J6 32 6N 96 28W
Corte, France 18 E8 42 19N 9 11 E
Cortez, U.S.A. 83 H9 37 21N 108 35W
Cortland, U.S.A. 79 D8 42 36N 76 11W
Çorum, Turkey 25 F5 40 30N 34 57 E
Corumbá, Brazil 92 G7 19 0S 57 30W
Corumbá de Goiás, Brazil 93 G9 16 0S 48 50W
Corunna = La Coruña, Spain 19 A1 43 20N 8 25W
Corvallis, U.S.A. 82 D2 44 34N 123 16W
Corvette, L. de la, Canada 70 B5 53 25N 74 3W
Corydon, U.S.A. 80 E8 40 46N 93 19W
Cosalá, Mexico 86 C3 24 28N 106 40W
Cosamaloapan, Mexico 87 D5 18 23N 95 50W
Cosenza, Italy 20 E7 39 18N 16 15 E
Coshocton, U.S.A. 78 F3 40 16N 81 51W
Cosmo Newberry, Australia 61 E3 28 0S 122 54 E
Coso Junction, U.S.A. 85 J9 36 3N 117 57W
Coso Pk., U.S.A. 85 J9 36 13N 117 44W
Cosquín, Argentina 94 C3 31 15S 64 30W
Costa Blanca, Spain 19 C5 38 25N 0 10W
Costa Brava, Spain 19 B7 41 30N 3 0 E
Costa del Sol, Spain 19 D3 36 30N 4 30W
Costa Dorada, Spain 19 B6 41 12N 1 15 E
Costa Mesa, U.S.A. 85 M9 33 38N 117 55W
Costa Rica ■, Cent. Amer. 88 D3 10 0N 84 0W
Costilla, U.S.A. 83 H11 36 59N 105 32W
Cosumnes →, U.S.A. 84 G5 38 16N 121 26W
Cotabato, Phil. 37 C6 7 14N 124 15 E
Cotagaita, Bolivia 94 A2 20 45S 65 40W
Côte d'Azur, France 18 E7 43 25N 7 10 E
Côte-d'Ivoire ■ = Ivory Coast ■, Africa 50 G3 7 30N 5 0W
Coteau des Prairies, U.S.A. 80 C6 45 20N 97 50W
Coteau du Missouri, U.S.A. 80 B4 47 0N 100 0W
Coteau Landing, Canada 79 A10 45 15N 74 13W
Cotentin, France 18 B3 49 15N 1 30W
Cotillo, Canary Is. 22 F5 28 41N 14 1W
Cotonou, Benin 50 G5 6 20N 2 25 E
Cotopaxi, Ecuador 92 D3 0 40S 78 30W
Cotswold Hills, U.K. 11 F5 51 42N 2 10W
Cottage Grove, U.S.A. 82 E2 43 48N 123 3W
Cottbus, Germany 16 C8 51 45N 14 20 E
Cottingham, U.K. 10 C5 53 47N 0 23W
Cottonwood, U.S.A. 83 J7 34 45N 112 1W
Cotulla, U.S.A. 81 L5 28 26N 99 14W
Coudersport, U.S.A. 78 E6 41 46N 78 1W
Couedic, C. du, Australia 63 F2 36 5S 136 40 E
Coulee City, U.S.A. 82 C4 47 37N 119 17W
Coulman I., Antarctica 5 D11 73 35S 170 0 E
Coulonge →, Canada 70 C4 45 52N 76 46W
Coulterville, U.S.A. 84 H6 37 43N 120 12W
Council, Alaska, U.S.A. 68 B3 64 55N 163 45W
Council, Idaho, U.S.A. 82 D5 44 44N 116 26W
Council Bluffs, U.S.A. 80 E7 41 16N 95 52W
Council Grove, U.S.A. 80 F6 38 40N 96 29W
Coupeville, U.S.A. 84 B4 48 13N 122 41W
Courantyne →, S. Amer. 92 B7 5 55N 57 5W
Courtenay, Canada 72 D3 49 45N 125 0W
Courtland, U.S.A. 84 G5 38 20N 121 34W
Courtrai = Kortrijk, Belgium 15 D3 50 50N 3 17 E
Courtright, Canada 78 D2 42 49N 82 28W
Coushatta, U.S.A. 81 J8 32 1N 93 21W
Coutts, Canada 72 D6 49 0N 111 57W
Coventry, U.K. 11 E6 52 25N 1 28W
Coventry L., Canada 73 A7 61 15N 106 15W
Covilhã, Portugal 19 B2 40 17N 7 31W
Covington, Ga., U.S.A. 77 J4 33 36N 83 51W
Covington, Ky., U.S.A. 76 F3 39 5N 84 31W
Covington, Okla., U.S.A. 81 G6 36 18N 97 35W
Covington, Tenn., U.S.A. 81 H10 35 34N 89 39W
Cowal, L., Australia 63 E4 33 40S 147 25 E
Cowan, Canada 73 C8 52 5N 100 45W
Cowan, L., Australia 61 F3 31 45S 121 45 E
Cowan L., Canada 73 C7 54 0N 107 15W
Cowangie, Australia 63 F3 35 12S 141 26 E
Cowansville, Canada 79 A12 45 14N 72 46W
Cowarie, Australia 63 D2 27 45S 138 15 E
Cowcowing Lakes, Australia 61 F2 30 55S 117 20 E
Cowdenbeath, U.K. 12 E5 56 7N 3 21W
Cowell, Australia 63 E2 33 39S 136 56 E
Cowes, U.K. 11 G6 50 45N 1 18W
Cowlitz →, U.S.A. 84 D4 46 6N 122 55W
Cowra, Australia 63 E4 33 49S 148 42 E
Coxilha Grande, Brazil 95 B5 28 18S 51 30W
Coxim, Brazil 93 G8 18 30S 54 55W
Cox's Bazar, Bangla. 41 J17 21 26N 91 59 E
Cox's Cove, Canada 71 C8 49 7N 58 5W
Coyame, Mexico 86 B3 29 28N 105 6W
Coyote Wells, U.S.A. 85 N11 32 44N 115 58W
Coyuca de Benítez, Mexico 87 D4 17 1N 100 8W
Coyuca de Catalan, Mexico 86 D4 18 18N 100 41W
Cozad, U.S.A. 80 E5 40 52N 99 59W
Cozumel, Mexico 87 C7 20 31N 86 55W
Cozumel, I. de, Mexico 87 C7 20 30N 86 40W
Craboon, Australia 63 E4 32 3S 149 30 E
Cracow = Kraków, Poland 17 C10 50 4N 19 57 E
Cracow, Australia 63 D5 25 17S 150 17 E
Cradock, S. Africa 56 E4 32 8S 25 36 E
Craig, Alaska, U.S.A. 72 B2 55 29N 133 9W
Craig, Colo., U.S.A. 82 F10 40 31N 107 33W
Craigavon, U.K. 13 B5 54 27N 6 23W
Craigmore, Zimbabwe 55 G3 20 28S 32 50 E
Crailsheim, Germany 16 D6 49 8N 10 5 E
Craiova, Romania 17 F12 44 21N 23 48 E
Cramsie, Australia 62 C3 23 20S 144 15 E
Cranberry Portage, Canada 73 C8 54 35N 101 23W
Cranbrook, Tas., Australia 62 G4 42 0S 148 5 E
Cranbrook, W. Austral., Australia 61 F2 34 18S 117 33 E
Cranbrook, Canada 72 D5 49 30N 115 46W
Crandon, U.S.A. 80 C10 45 34N 88 54W
Crane, Oreg., U.S.A. 82 E4 43 25N 118 35W
Crane, Tex., U.S.A. 81 K3 31 24N 102 21W
Cranston, U.S.A. 79 E13 41 47N 71 26W
Crater L., U.S.A. 82 E2 42 56N 122 6W
Crateús, Brazil 93 E10 5 10S 40 39W
Crato, Brazil 93 E11 7 10S 39 25W
Crawford, U.S.A. 80 D3 42 41N 103 25W
Crawfordsville, U.S.A. 76 E2 40 2N 86 54W
Crawley, U.K. 11 F7 51 7N 0 11W
Crazy Mts., U.S.A. 82 C8 46 12N 110 20W
Crean L., Canada 73 C7 54 5N 106 9W
Crediton, Canada 78 C3 43 17N 81 33W
Credo, Australia 61 F3 30 28S 120 45 E
Cree →, Canada 73 B7 58 57N 105 47W
Cree →, U.K. 12 G4 54 55N 4 25W
Cree L., Canada 73 B7 57 30N 106 30W
Creede, U.S.A. 83 H10 37 51N 106 56W
Creel, Mexico 86 B3 27 45N 107 38W
Creighton, U.S.A. 80 D6 42 28N 97 54W
Crema, Italy 20 B3 45 22N 9 41 E
Cremona, Italy 20 B4 45 7N 10 2 E
Cres, Croatia 16 F8 44 58N 14 25 E
Cresbard, U.S.A. 80 C5 45 10N 98 57W
Crescent, Okla., U.S.A. 81 H6 35 57N 97 36W
Crescent, Oreg., U.S.A. 82 E3 43 28N 121 42W
Crescent City, U.S.A. 82 F1 41 45N 124 12W
Crespo, Argentina 94 C3 32 2S 60 19W
Cressy, Australia 63 F3 38 2S 143 40 E
Crested Butte, U.S.A. 83 G10 38 52N 106 59W
Crestline, Calif., U.S.A. 85 L9 34 14N 117 18W
Crestline, Ohio, U.S.A. 78 F2 40 47N 82 44W
Creston, Canada 72 D5 49 10N 116 31W
Creston, Calif., U.S.A. 84 K6 35 32N 120 33W
Creston, Iowa, U.S.A. 80 E7 41 4N 94 22W
Creston, Wash., U.S.A. 82 C4 47 46N 118 31W
Crestview, Calif., U.S.A. 84 H8 37 46N 118 58W
Crestview, Fla., U.S.A. 77 K2 30 46N 86 34W
Crete = Kríti, Greece 23 D7 35 15N 25 0 E
Crete, U.S.A. 80 E6 40 38N 96 58W
Créteil, France 18 B5 48 47N 2 28 E
Creus, C. de, Spain 19 A7 42 20N 3 19 E
Creuse →, France 18 C4 47 0N 0 34 E
Crewe, U.K. 10 D5 53 6N 2 26W
Criciúma, Brazil 95 B6 28 40S 49 23W
Crieff, U.K. 12 E5 56 22N 3 50W
Crimean Pen. = Krymskyy Pivostriv, Ukraine 25 E5 45 0N 34 0 E
Crişul Alb →, Romania 17 E11 46 42N 21 17 E
Crişul Negru →, Romania 17 E11 46 42N 21 16 E
Crna Gora = Montenegro □, Yugoslavia 21 C8 42 40N 19 20 E
Crna Gora, Serbia, Yug. 21 C9 42 10N 21 30 E
Crna Reka →, Macedonia 21 D9 41 33N 21 59 E
Croagh Patrick, Ireland 13 C2 53 46N 9 40W
Croatia ■, Europe 16 F9 45 20N 16 0 E
Crocker, Banjaran, Malaysia 36 C5 5 40N 116 30 E
Crockett, U.S.A. 81 K7 31 19N 95 27W
Crocodile = Krokodil →, Mozam. 57 D5 25 14S 32 18 E
Crocodile Is., Australia 62 A1 12 3S 134 58 E
Croix, L. La, Canada 70 C1 48 20N 92 15W
Croker, C., Australia 60 B5 10 58S 132 35 E
Croker I., Australia 60 B5 11 12S 132 32 E
Cromarty, Canada 73 B10 58 3N 94 9W
Cromarty, U.K. 12 D4 57 40N 4 2W
Cromer, U.K. 10 E9 52 56N 1 17 E
Cromwell, N.Z. 59 L2 45 3S 169 14 E
Cronulla, Australia 63 E5 34 3S 151 8 E
Crooked →, Canada 72 C4 54 50N 122 54W
Crooked →, U.S.A. 82 D3 44 32N 121 16W
Crooked I., Bahamas 89 B5 22 50N 74 10W
Crooked Island Passage, Bahamas 89 B5 23 0N 74 30W
Crookston, Minn., U.S.A. 80 B6 47 47N 96 37W
Crookston, Nebr., U.S.A. 80 D4 42 56N 100 45W
Crooksville, U.S.A. 76 F4 39 46N 82 6W
Crookwell, Australia 63 E4 34 28S 149 24 E
Crosby, Minn., U.S.A. 80 B8 46 29N 93 58W
Crosby, N. Dak., U.S.A. 73 D8 48 55N 103 18W
Crosby, Pa., U.S.A. 78 E6 41 45N 78 23W
Crosbyton, U.S.A. 81 J4 33 40N 101 14W
Cross City, U.S.A. 77 L4 29 38N 83 7W
Cross Fell, U.K. 10 C5 54 43N 2 28W
Cross L., Canada 73 C9 54 45N 97 30W
Cross Plains, U.S.A. 81 J5 32 8N 99 11W
Cross Sound, U.S.A. 68 C6 58 0N 135 0W
Crossett, U.S.A. 81 J9 33 8N 91 58W
Crossfield, Canada 72 C6 51 25N 114 0W
Crosshaven, Ireland 13 E3 51 47N 8 17W
Croton-on-Hudson, U.S.A. 79 E11 41 12N 73 55W
Crotone, Italy 20 E7 39 5N 17 8 E
Crow →, Canada 72 B4 59 41N 124 20W
Crow Agency, U.S.A. 82 D10 45 36N 107 28W
Crow Hd., Ireland 13 E1 51 35N 10 9W
Crowell, U.S.A. 81 J5 33 59N 99 43W
Crowley, U.S.A. 81 K8 30 13N 92 22W
Crowley, L., U.S.A. 84 H8 37 35N 118 42W
Crown Point, U.S.A. 76 E2 41 25N 87 22W
Crows Landing, U.S.A. 84 H5 37 23N 121 6W
Crows Nest, Australia 63 D5 27 16S 152 4 E
Crowsnest Pass, Canada 72 D6 49 40N 114 40W
Croydon, Australia 62 B3 18 13S 142 14 E
Croydon, U.K. 11 F7 51 22N 0 5W
Crozet Is., Ind. Oc. 3 G12 46 27S 52 0 E
Cruz, C., Cuba 88 C4 19 50N 77 50W
Cruz Alta, Brazil 95 B5 28 45S 53 40W
Cruz del Eje, Argentina 94 C3 30 45S 64 50W
Cruzeiro, Brazil 95 A7 22 33S 45 0W
Cruzeiro do Oeste, Brazil 95 A5 23 46S 53 4W
Cruzeiro do Sul, Brazil 92 E4 7 35S 72 35W
Cry L., Canada 72 B3 58 45N 129 0W
Crystal Bay, U.S.A. 84 F7 39 15N 120 0W
Crystal Brook, Australia 63 E2 33 21S 138 12 E
Crystal City, Mo., U.S.A. 80 F9 38 13N 90 23W
Crystal City, Tex., U.S.A. 81 L5 28 41N 99 50W
Crystal Falls, U.S.A. 76 B1 46 5N 88 20W
Crystal River, U.S.A. 77 L4 28 54N 82 35W
Crystal Springs, U.S.A. 81 K9 31 59N 90 21W
Csongrád, Hungary 17 E11 46 43N 20 12 E
Cu Lao Hon, Vietnam 39 G7 10 54N 108 18 E
Cua Rao, Vietnam 38 C5 19 16N 104 27 E
Cuácua →, Mozam. 55 F4 17 54S 37 0 E
Cuamato, Angola 56 B2 17 2S 15 7 E
Cuamba, Mozam. 55 E4 14 45S 36 22 E
Cuando →, Angola 53 H4 17 30S 23 15 E
Cuando Cubango □, Angola 56 B3 16 25S 20 0 E
Cuangar, Angola 56 B2 17 36S 18 39 E
Cuanza →, Angola 48 G5 9 2S 13 30 E
Cuarto →, Argentina 94 C3 33 25S 63 2W
Cuatrociénegas, Mexico 86 B4 26 59N 102 5W
Cuauhtémoc, Mexico 86 B3 28 25N 106 52W
Cuba, N. Mex., U.S.A. 83 J10 36 1N 107 4W
Cuba, N.Y., U.S.A. 78 D6 42 13N 78 17W
Cuba ■, W. Indies 88 B4 22 0N 79 0W
Cuballing, Australia 61 F2 32 50S 117 10 E
Cubango →, Africa 56 B3 18 50S 22 25 E
Cuchi, Angola 53 G3 14 37S 16 58 E
Cuchumatanes, Sierra de los, Guatemala 88 C1 15 35N 91 25W
Cucurpe, Mexico 86 A2 30 20N 110 43W
Cúcuta, Colombia 92 B4 7 54N 72 31W
Cuddalore, India 40 P11 11 46N 79 45 E
Cuddapah, India 40 M11 14 30N 78 47 E
Cuddapan, L., Australia 62 D3 25 45S 141 26 E
Cudgewa, Australia 63 F4 36 10S 147 42 E
Cue, Australia 61 E2 27 25S 117 54 E
Cuenca, Ecuador 92 D3 2 50S 79 9W
Cuenca, Spain 19 B4 40 5N 2 10W
Cuenca, Serranía de, Spain 19 C5 39 55N 1 50W
Cuernavaca, Mexico 87 D5 18 55N 99 15W
Cuero, U.S.A. 81 L6 29 6N 97 17W
Cuervo, U.S.A. 81 H2 35 2N 104 25W
Cuevas del Almanzora, Spain 19 D5 37 18N 1 58W
Cuevo, Bolivia 92 H6 20 15S 63 30W
Cuiabá, Brazil 93 G7 15 30S 56 0W
Cuiabá →, Brazil 93 G7 17 5S 56 36W
Cuilco, Guatemala 88 C1 15 24N 91 58W
Cuillin Hills, U.K. 12 D2 57 13N 6 15W
Cuillin Sd., U.K. 12 D2 57 4N 6 20W
Cuima, Angola 53 G3 13 25S 15 45 E
Cuito →, Angola 56 B3 18 1S 20 48 E
Cuitzeo, L. de, Mexico 86 D4 19 55N 101 5W
Cukai, Malaysia 39 K4 4 13N 103 25 E
Culbertson, U.S.A. 80 A2 48 9N 104 31W
Culcairn, Australia 63 F4 35 41S 147 3 E
Culgoa →, Australia 63 D4 29 56S 146 20 E
Culiacán, Mexico 86 C3 24 50N 107 23W
Culiacán →, Mexico 86 C3 24 30N 107 42W
Culion, Phil. 37 B6 11 54N 120 1 E
Cullarin Ra., Australia 63 E4 34 30S 149 30 E
Cullen, U.K. 12 D6 57 45N 2 49W
Cullen Pt., Australia 62 A3 11 57S 141 54 E
Cullera, Spain 19 C5 39 9N 0 17W
Cullman, U.S.A. 77 H2 34 11N 86 51W
Culloden, U.K. 12 D4 57 30N 4 9W
Culpeper, U.S.A. 76 F7 38 30N 78 0W
Culuene →, Brazil 93 F8 12 56S 52 51W
Culver, Pt., Australia 61 F3 32 54S 124 43 E
Culverden, N.Z. 59 K4 42 47S 172 49 E
Cumaná, Venezuela 92 A6 10 30N 64 5W
Cumberland, Canada 72 D3 49 40N 125 0W
Cumberland, Md., U.S.A. 76 F6 39 39N 78 46W
Cumberland, Wis., U.S.A. 80 C8 45 32N 92 1W
Cumberland →, U.S.A. 77 G2 36 15N 87 0W
Cumberland I., U.S.A. 77 K5 30 50N 81 25W
Cumberland Is., Australia 62 C4 20 35S 149 10 E
Cumberland L., Canada 73 C8 54 3N 102 18W
Cumberland Pen., Canada 69 B13 67 0N 64 0W
Cumberland Plateau, U.S.A. 77 H3 36 0N 85 0W
Cumberland Sd., Canada 69 B13 65 30N 66 0W
Cumborah, Australia 63 D4 29 40S 147 45 E
Cumbria □, U.K. 10 C5 54 42N 2 52W
Cumbrian Mts., U.K. 10 C4 54 30N 3 0W
Cumbum, India 40 M11 15 40N 79 10 E
Cummings Mt., U.S.A. 85 K8 35 2N 118 34W
Cummins, Australia 63 E2 34 16S 135 43 E
Cumnock, Australia 63 E4 32 59S 148 46 E
Cumnock, U.K. 12 F4 55 28N 4 17W
Cumpas, Mexico 86 A3 30 0N 109 48W
Cumplida, Pta., Canary Is. 22 F2 28 50N 17 48W
Cuncumén, Chile 94 C1 31 53S 70 38W
Cundeelee, Australia 61 F3 30 43S 123 26 E
Cunderdin, Australia 61 F2 31 37S 117 12 E
Cunene →, Angola 56 B1 17 20S 11 50 E
Cúneo, Italy 20 B2 44 23N 7 32 E
Cunillera, I., Spain 22 C7 38 59N 1 13 E
Cunnamulla, Australia 63 D4 28 2S 145 38 E
Cupar, Canada 73 C8 50 57N 104 10W
Cupar, U.K. 12 E5 56 19N 3 1W
Cupica, G. de, Colombia 92 B3 6 25N 77 30W
Curaçao, Neth. Ant. 89 D6 12 10N 69 0W
Curanilahue, Chile 94 D1 37 29S 73 28W
Curaray →, Peru 92 D4 2 20S 74 5W
Curepto, Chile 94 D1 35 8S 72 1W
Curiapo, Venezuela 92 B6 8 33N 61 5W
Curicó, Chile 94 C1 34 55S 71 20W
Curicó □, Chile 94 C1 34 50S 71 15W
Curitiba, Brazil 95 B6 25 20S 49 10W
Currabubula, Australia 63 E5 31 16S 150 44 E
Currais Novos, Brazil 93 E11 6 13S 36 30W
Curralinho, Brazil 93 D9 1 45S 49 46W
Currant, U.S.A. 82 G6 38 51N 115 32W
Curraweena, Australia 63 E4 30 47S 145 54 E
Currawilla, Australia 62 D3 25 10S 141 20 E
Current →, U.S.A. 81 G9 36 15N 90 55W
Currie, Australia 62 F3 39 56S 143 53 E
Currie, U.S.A. 82 F6 40 16N 114 45W
Currituck Sd., U.S.A. 77 G8 36 20N 75 52W
Curtea de Argeş, Romania 17 F13 45 12N 24 42 E
Curtis, U.S.A. 80 E4 40 38N 100 31W
Curtis Group, Australia 62 F4 39 30S 146 37 E
Curtis I., Australia 62 C5 23 35S 151 10 E
Curuápanema →, Brazil 93 D7 2 25S 55 2W
Curuçá, Brazil 93 D9 0 43S 47 50W
Curuguaty, Paraguay 95 A4 24 31S 55 42W
Çürüksu Çayi →, Turkey 25 G4 37 27N 27 11 E
Curup, Indonesia 36 E2 4 26S 102 13 E
Cururupu, Brazil 93 D10 1 50S 44 50W
Curuzú Cuatiá, Argentina 94 B4 29 50S 58 5W
Cushing, U.S.A. 81 H6 35 59N 96 46W
Cushing, Mt., Canada 72 B3 57 35N 126 57W
Cusihuiriáchic, Mexico 86 B3 28 10N 106 50W
Custer, U.S.A. 80 D3 43 46N 103 36W
Cut Bank, U.S.A. 82 B7 48 38N 112 20W
Cuthbert, U.S.A. 77 K3 31 46N 84 48W
Cutler, U.S.A. 84 J7 36 31N 119 17W
Cuttaburra →, Australia 63 D3 29 43S 144 22 E
Cuttack, India 41 J14 20 25N 85 57 E
Cuvier, C., Australia 61 D1 23 14S 113 22 E
Cuvier I., N.Z. 59 G5 36 27S 175 50 E
Cuxhaven, Germany 16 B5 53 51N 8 41 E
Cuyahoga Falls, U.S.A. 78 E3 41 8N 81 29W
Cuyo, Phil. 37 B6 10 50N 121 5 E
Cuzco, Bolivia 92 H5 20 0S 66 50W
Cuzco, Peru 92 F4 13 32S 72 0W
Cwmbran, U.K. 11 F4 51 39N 3 2W
Cyangugu, Rwanda 54 C2 2 29S 28 54 E
Cyclades = Kikládhes, Greece 21 F11 37 20N 24 30 E
Cygnet, Australia 62 G4 43 8S 147 1 E
Cynthiana, U.S.A. 76 F3 38 23N 84 18W
Cypress Hills, Canada 73 D7 49 40N 109 30W
Cyprus ■, Asia 23 E12 35 0N 33 0 E
Cyrenaica, Libya 51 C9 27 0N 23 0 E
Cyrene = Shaḥḥāt, Libya 51 B9 32 48N 21 54 E
Czar, Canada 73 C6 52 27N 110 50W
Czech Rep. ■, Europe 16 D8 50 0N 15 0 E
Częstochowa, Poland 17 C10 50 49N 19 7 E

D

Da →, Vietnam 38 B5 21 15N 105 20 E
Da Hinggan Ling, China 33 B7 48 0N 121 0 E
Da Lat, Vietnam 39 G7 11 56N 108 25 E
Da Nang, Vietnam 38 D7 16 4N 108 13 E
Da Qaidam, China 32 C4 37 50N 95 15 E
Da Yunhe →, China 35 G11 34 25N 120 5 E
Da'an, China 35 B13 45 30N 124 7 E
Daba Shan, China 33 C5 32 0N 109 0 E
Dabakala, Ivory C. 50 G4 8 15N 4 20W
Dabhoi, India 42 H5 22 10N 73 20 E
Dabo, Indonesia 36 E2 0 30S 104 33 E
Dabola, Guinea 50 F2 10 50N 11 5W
Daboya, Ghana 50 G4 9 30N 1 20W
Dabung, Malaysia 39 K4 5 23N 102 1 E
Dacca = Dhaka, Bangla. 43 H14 23 43N 90 26 E
Dacca = Dhaka □, Bangla. 43 G14 24 25N 90 25 E
Dachau, Germany 16 D6 48 15N 11 26 E
Dadanawa, Guyana 92 C7 2 50N 59 30W
Dade City, U.S.A. 77 L4 28 22N 82 11W
Dadra and Nagar Haveli □, India 40 J8 20 5N 73 0 E

Dera Ghazi Khan

Dadri = Charkhi Dadri, India 42 E7 28 37N 76 17 E
Dadu, Pakistan 42 F2 26 45N 67 45 E
Daet, Phil. 37 B6 14 2N 122 55 E
Dagana, Senegal 50 E1 16 30N 15 35W
Dagestan □, Russia 25 F8 42 30N 47 0 E
Daggett, U.S.A. 85 L10 34 52N 116 52W
Daghestan Republic = Dagestan □, Russia 25 F8 42 30N 47 0 E
Dagö = Hiiumaa, Estonia 9 G20 58 50N 22 45 E
Dagu, China 35 E9 38 59N 117 40 E
Dagupan, Phil. 37 A6 16 3N 120 20 E
Dahlak Kebir, Eritrea 46 D3 15 50N 40 10 E
Dahlonega, U.S.A. 77 H4 34 32N 83 59W
Dahod, India 42 H6 22 50N 74 15 E
Dahomey = Benin ■, Africa 50 G5 10 0N 2 0 E
Dahra, Senegal 50 E1 15 22N 15 30W
Dai Hao, Vietnam 38 C6 18 1N 106 25 E
Dai-Sen, Japan 31 G6 35 22N 133 32 E
Dai Xian, China 34 E7 39 4N 112 58 E
Daicheng, China 34 E9 38 42N 116 38 E
Daingean, Ireland 13 C4 53 18N 7 17W
Daintree, Australia 62 B4 16 20S 145 20 E
Daiō-Misaki, Japan 31 G8 34 15N 136 45 E
Dairût, Egypt 51 C11 27 34N 30 43 E
Daisetsu-Zan, Japan 30 C11 43 30N 142 57 E
Dajarra, Australia 62 C2 21 42S 139 30 E
Dak Dam, Cambodia 38 F6 12 20N 107 21 E
Dak Nhe, Vietnam 38 E6 15 28N 107 48 E
Dak Pek, Vietnam 38 E6 15 4N 107 44 E
Dak Song, Vietnam 39 F6 12 19N 107 35 E
Dak Sui, Vietnam 38 E6 14 55N 107 43 E
Dakar, Senegal 50 F1 14 34N 17 29W
Dakhla, W. Sahara 50 D1 23 50N 15 53W
Dakhla, El Wâhât el-, Egypt 51 C10 25 30N 28 50 E
Dakhovskaya, Russia 25 F7 44 13N 40 13 E
Dakor, India 42 H5 22 45N 73 11 E
Dakota City, U.S.A. 80 D6 42 25N 96 25W
Đakovica, Serbia, Yug. 21 C9 42 22N 20 26 E
Dalachi, China 34 F3 36 48N 105 0 E
Dalai Nur, China 34 C9 43 20N 116 45 E
Dālakī, Iran 45 D6 29 26N 51 17 E
Dalälven, Sweden 9 F17 60 12N 16 43 E
Dalaman →, Turkey 21 F13 36 41N 28 43 E
Dalandzadgad, Mongolia 34 C3 43 27N 104 30 E
Dalarna, Sweden 9 F16 61 0N 14 0 E
Dālbandīn, Pakistan 40 E4 29 0N 64 23 E
Dalbeattie, U.K. 12 G5 54 56N 3 50W
Dalby, Australia 63 D5 27 10S 151 17 E
Dalgān, Iran 45 E8 27 31N 59 19 E
Dalhart, U.S.A. 81 G3 36 4N 102 31W
Dalhousie, Canada 71 C6 48 5N 66 26W
Dalhousie, India 42 C6 32 38N 75 58 E
Dali, Shaanxi, China 34 G5 34 48N 109 58 E
Dali, Yunnan, China 32 D5 25 40N 100 10 E
Dalian, China 35 E11 38 50N 121 40 E
Daliang Shan, China 32 D5 28 0N 102 45 E
Daling He →, China 35 D11 40 55N 121 40 E
Dāliyat el Karmel, Israel 47 C4 32 43N 35 2 E
Dalkeith, U.K. 12 F5 55 54N 3 4W
Dall I., U.S.A. 72 C2 54 59N 133 25W
Dallarnil, Australia 63 D5 25 19S 152 2 E
Dallas, Oreg., U.S.A. 82 D2 44 55N 123 19W
Dallas, Tex., U.S.A. 81 J6 32 47N 96 49W
Dalmacija, Croatia 20 C7 43 20N 17 0 E
Dalmatia = Dalmacija, Croatia 20 C7 43 20N 17 0 E
Dalmellington, U.K. 12 F4 55 19N 4 23W
Dalnegorsk, Russia 27 E14 44 32N 135 33 E
Dalnerechensk, Russia 27 E14 45 50N 133 40 E
Daloa, Ivory C. 50 G3 7 0N 6 30W
Dalsland, Sweden 9 G14 58 50N 12 15 E
Daltenganj, India 43 G11 24 0N 84 4 E
Dalton, Canada 70 C3 48 11N 84 1W
Dalton, Ga., U.S.A. 77 H3 34 46N 84 58W
Dalton, Mass., U.S.A. 79 D11 42 28N 73 11W
Dalton, Nebr., U.S.A. 80 E3 41 25N 102 58W
Dalton Iceberg Tongue, Antarctica 5 C9 66 15S 121 30 E
Dalvík, Iceland 8 D4 65 58N 18 32W
Daly →, Australia 60 B5 13 35S 130 19 E
Daly City, U.S.A. 84 H4 37 42N 122 28W
Daly L., Canada 73 B7 56 32N 105 39W
Daly Waters, Australia 62 B1 16 15S 133 24 E
Dam Doi, Vietnam 39 H5 8 50N 105 12 E
Dam Ha, Vietnam 38 B6 21 21N 107 36 E
Daman, India 40 J8 20 25N 72 57 E
Dāmaneh, Iran 45 C6 33 1N 50 29 E
Damanhûr, Egypt 51 B11 31 0N 30 30 E
Damanzhuang, China 34 E9 38 5N 116 35 E
Damar, Indonesia 37 F7 7 7S 128 40 E
Damaraland, Namibia 56 C2 21 0S 17 0 E
Damascus = Dimashq, Syria 47 B5 33 30N 36 18 E
Damāvand, Iran 45 C7 35 47N 52 0 E
Damāvand, Qolleh-ye, Iran 45 C7 35 56N 52 10 E
Damba, Angola 52 F3 6 44S 15 20 E
Dame Marie, Haiti 89 C5 18 36N 74 26W
Dāmghān, Iran 45 B7 36 10N 54 17 E
Damiel, Spain 19 C4 39 4N 3 37W
Damietta = Dumyât, Egypt 51 B11 31 24N 31 48 E
Daming, China 34 F8 36 15N 115 6 E
Damīr Qābū, Syria 44 B4 36 58N 41 51 E
Dammam = Ad Dammām, Si. Arabia 45 E6 26 20N 50 5 E
Damodar →, India 43 H12 23 17N 87 35 E
Damoh, India 43 H8 23 50N 79 28 E
Dampier, Australia 60 D2 20 41S 116 42 E
Dampier, Selat, Indonesia 37 E8 0 40S 131 0 E
Dampier Arch., Australia 60 D2 20 38S 116 32 E
Damrei, Chuor Phnum, Cambodia 39 G4 11 30N 103 0 E
Dana, Indonesia 37 F6 11 0S 122 52 E
Dana, L., Canada 70 B4 50 53N 77 20W
Dana, Mt., U.S.A. 84 H7 37 54N 119 12W
Danbury, U.S.A. 79 E11 41 24N 73 28W
Danby L., U.S.A. 83 J6 34 13N 115 5W
Dand, Afghan. 42 D1 31 28N 65 32 E
Dandaragan, Australia 61 F2 30 40S 115 40 E
Dandeldhura, Nepal 43 E9 29 20N 80 35 E
Dandeli, India 40 M9 15 5N 74 30 E
Dandenong, Australia 63 F4 38 0S 145 15 E
Dandong, China 35 D13 40 10N 124 20 E
Danfeng, China 34 H6 33 45N 110 25 E
Danforth, U.S.A. 71 C6 45 40N 67 52W
Danger Is. = Pukapuka, Cook Is. 65 J11 10 53S 165 49W
Danger Pt., S. Africa 56 E2 34 40S 19 17 E
Dangora, Nigeria 50 F6 11 30N 8 7 E
Dangrek, Phnom, Thailand 38 E5 14 15N 105 0 E
Dangriga, Belize 87 D7 17 0N 88 13W
Dangshan, China 34 G9 34 27N 116 22 E
Daniel, U.S.A. 82 E8 42 52N 110 4W
Daniel's Harbour, Canada 71 B8 50 13N 57 35W
Danielskuil, S. Africa 56 D3 28 11S 23 33 E
Danielson, U.S.A. 79 E13 41 48N 71 53W
Danilov, Russia 24 C7 58 16N 40 13 E
Daning, China 34 F6 36 28N 110 45 E
Danissa, Kenya 54 B5 3 15N 40 58 E
Dankhar Gompa, India 40 C11 32 10N 78 10 E
Danlí, Honduras 88 D2 14 4N 86 35W
Dannemora, U.S.A. 79 B11 44 43N 73 44W
Dannevirke, N.Z. 59 J6 40 12S 176 8 E
Dannhauser, S. Africa 57 D5 28 0S 30 3 E
Dansville, U.S.A. 78 D7 42 34N 77 42W
Dantan, India 43 J12 21 57N 87 20 E
Dante, Somali Rep. 46 E5 10 25N 51 16 E
Danube = Dunărea →, Europe 17 F15 45 20N 29 40 E
Danube →, Europe 6 F11 45 20N 29 40 E
Danvers, U.S.A. 79 D14 42 34N 70 56W
Danville, Ill., U.S.A. 76 E2 40 8N 87 37W
Danville, Ky., U.S.A. 76 G3 37 39N 84 46W
Danville, Va., U.S.A. 77 G6 36 36N 79 23W
Danzig = Gdańsk, Poland 17 A10 54 22N 18 40 E
Dao, Phil. 37 B6 10 30N 121 57 E
Daoud = Aïn Beïda, Algeria 50 A6 35 50N 7 29 E
Daqing Shan, China 34 D6 40 40N 111 0 E
Dar Banda, Africa 48 F6 8 0N 23 0 E
Dar el Beida = Casablanca, Morocco 50 B3 33 36N 7 36W
Dar es Salaam, Tanzania 54 D4 6 50S 39 12 E
Dar Mazār, Iran 45 D8 29 14N 57 20 E
Dar'ā, Syria 47 C5 32 36N 36 7 E
Dar'ā □, Syria 47 C5 32 55N 36 10 E
Dārāb, Iran 45 D7 28 50N 54 30 E
Daraj, Libya 50 B7 30 10N 10 28 E
Dārān, Iran 45 C6 32 59N 50 24 E
Dārayyā, Syria 47 B5 33 28N 36 15 E
Darband, Pakistan 42 B5 34 20N 72 50 E
Darband, Kūh-e, Iran 45 D8 31 34N 57 8 E
Darbhanga, India 43 F11 26 15N 85 55 E
Darby, U.S.A. 82 C6 46 1N 114 11W
Dardanelle, Ark., U.S.A. 81 H8 35 13N 93 9W
Dardanelle, Calif., U.S.A. 84 G7 38 20N 119 50W
Dardanelles = Çanakkale Boğazı, Turkey 21 D12 40 17N 26 32 E
Dārestān, Iran 45 D8 29 9N 58 42 E
Dârfûr, Sudan 51 F9 13 40N 24 0 E
Dargai, Pakistan 42 B4 34 25N 71 55 E
Dargan Ata, Uzbekistan 26 E7 40 29N 62 10 E
Dargaville, N.Z. 59 F4 35 57S 173 52 E
Darhan Muminggan Lianheqi, China 34 D6 41 40N 110 28 E
Darıca, Turkey 21 D13 40 45N 29 23 E
Darién, G. del, Colombia 92 B3 9 0N 77 0W
Dariganga, Mongolia 34 B7 45 21N 113 45 E
Darjeeling = Darjiling, India 43 F13 27 3N 88 18 E
Darjiling, India 43 F13 27 3N 88 18 E
Dark Cove, Canada 71 C9 48 47N 54 13W
Darkan, Australia 61 F2 33 20S 116 43 E
Darkhazīneh, Iran 45 D6 31 54N 48 39 E
Darkot Pass, Pakistan 43 A5 36 45N 73 26 E
Darling →, Australia 63 E3 34 4S 141 54 E
Darling Downs, Australia 63 D5 27 30S 150 30 E
Darling Ra., Australia 61 F2 32 30S 116 0 E
Darlington, U.K. 10 C6 54 32N 1 33W
Darlington, S.C., U.S.A. 77 H6 34 18N 79 52W
Darlington, Wis., U.S.A. 80 D9 42 41N 90 7W
Darlington, L., S. Africa 56 E4 33 10S 25 9 E
Darlot, L., Australia 61 E3 27 48S 121 35 E
Darłowo, Poland 16 A9 54 25N 16 25 E
Darmstadt, Germany 16 D5 49 51N 8 39 E
Darnah, Libya 51 B9 32 45N 22 45 E
Darnall, S. Africa 57 D5 29 23S 31 18 E
Darnley, C., Antarctica 5 C6 68 0S 69 0 E
Darnley B., Canada 68 B7 69 30N 123 30W
Darr, Australia 62 C3 23 13S 144 7 E
Darr →, Australia 62 C3 23 39S 143 50 E
Darrington, U.S.A. 82 B3 48 15N 121 36W
Dart →, U.K. 11 G4 50 24N 3 39W
Dart, C., Antarctica 5 D14 73 6S 126 20W
Dartmoor, U.K. 11 G4 50 38N 3 57W
Dartmouth, Australia 62 C3 23 31S 144 44 E
Dartmouth, Canada 71 D7 44 40N 63 30W
Dartmouth, U.K. 11 G4 50 21N 3 36W
Dartmouth, L., Australia 63 D4 26 4S 145 18 E
Dartuch, C., Spain 22 B10 39 55N 3 49 E
Darvaza, Turkmenistan 26 E6 40 11N 58 24 E
Darvel, Teluk, Malaysia 37 D5 4 50N 118 20 E
Darwha, India 40 J10 20 15N 77 45 E
Darwin, Australia 60 B5 12 25S 130 51 E
Darwin, U.S.A. 85 J9 36 15N 117 35W
Darwin River, Australia 60 B5 12 50S 130 58 E
Daryoi Amu = Amudarya →, Uzbekistan 26 E6 43 58N 59 34 E
Dās, U.A.E. 45 E7 25 20N 53 30 E
Dashetai, China 34 D5 41 0N 109 5 E
Dashhowuz, Turkmenistan 26 E6 41 49N 59 58 E
Dasht, Iran 45 B8 37 17N 56 7 E
Dasht →, Pakistan 40 G2 25 10N 61 40 E
Dasht-e Mārgow, Afghan. 40 D3 30 40N 62 30 E
Dasht-i-Nawar, Afghan. 42 C3 33 52N 68 0 E
Daska, Pakistan 42 C6 32 20N 74 20 E
Datça, Turkey 21 F12 36 46N 27 40 E
Datia, India 43 G8 25 39N 78 27 E
Datong, China 34 D7 40 6N 113 18 E
Datu, Tanjung, Indonesia 36 D3 2 5N 109 39 E
Datu Piang, Phil. 37 C6 7 2N 124 30 E
Daugava →, Latvia 9 H21 57 4N 24 3 E
Daugavpils, Latvia 9 J22 55 53N 26 32 E
Daulpur, India 42 F7 26 45N 77 59 E
Dauphin, Canada 73 C8 51 9N 100 5W
Dauphin I., U.S.A. 77 K1 30 15N 88 11W
Dauphin L., Canada 73 C9 51 20N 99 45W
Dauphiné, France 18 D6 45 15N 5 25 E
Dausa, India 42 F7 26 52N 76 20 E
Davangere, India 40 M9 14 25N 75 55 E
Davao, Phil. 37 C7 7 0N 125 40 E
Davao, G. of, Phil. 37 C7 6 30N 125 48 E
Dāvar Panāh, Iran 45 E9 27 25N 62 15 E
Davenport, Calif., U.S.A. 84 H4 37 1N 122 12W
Davenport, Iowa, U.S.A. 80 E9 41 32N 90 35W
Davenport, Wash., U.S.A. 82 C4 47 39N 118 9W
Davenport Downs, Australia 62 C3 24 8S 141 7 E
Davenport Ra., Australia 62 C1 20 28S 134 0 E
David, Panama 88 E3 8 30N 82 30W
David City, U.S.A. 80 E6 41 15N 97 8W
David Gorodok = Davyd Haradok, Belarus 17 B14 52 4N 27 8 E
Davidson, Canada 73 C7 51 16N 105 59W
Davis, U.S.A. 84 G5 38 33N 121 44W
Davis Dam, U.S.A. 85 K12 35 11N 114 34W
Davis Inlet, Canada 71 A7 55 50N 60 59W
Davis Mts., U.S.A. 81 K2 30 50N 103 55W
Davis Sea, Antarctica 5 C7 66 0S 92 0 E
Davis Str., N. Amer. 69 B14 65 0N 58 0W
Davos, Switz. 16 E5 46 48N 9 49 E
Davy L., Canada 73 B7 58 53N 108 18W
Davyd Haradok, Belarus 17 B14 52 4N 27 8 E
Dawes Ra., Australia 62 C5 24 40S 150 40 E
Dawson, Canada 68 B6 64 10N 139 30W
Dawson, Ga., U.S.A. 77 K3 31 46N 84 27W
Dawson, N. Dak., U.S.A. 80 B5 46 52N 99 45W
Dawson, I., Chile 96 G2 53 50S 70 50W
Dawson Creek, Canada 72 B4 55 45N 120 15W
Dawson Inlet, Canada 73 A10 61 50N 93 25W
Dawson Ra., Australia 62 C4 24 30S 149 48 E
Dax, France 18 E3 43 44N 1 3W
Daxian, China 32 C5 31 15N 107 23 E
Daxindian, China 35 F11 37 30N 120 50 E
Daxinggou, China 35 C15 43 25N 129 40 E
Daxue Shan, China 32 C5 30 30N 101 30 E
Daylesford, Australia 63 F3 37 21S 144 9 E
Dayr az Zawr, Syria 44 C4 35 20N 40 5 E
Daysland, Canada 72 C6 52 50N 112 20W
Dayton, Nev., U.S.A. 84 F7 39 14N 119 36W
Dayton, Ohio, U.S.A. 76 F3 39 45N 84 12W
Dayton, Pa., U.S.A. 78 F5 40 53N 79 15W
Dayton, Tenn., U.S.A. 77 H3 35 30N 85 1W
Dayton, Wash., U.S.A. 82 C4 46 19N 117 59W
Daytona Beach, U.S.A. 77 L5 29 13N 81 1W
Dayville, U.S.A. 82 D4 44 28N 119 32W
De Aar, S. Africa 56 E3 30 39S 24 0 E
De Funiak Springs, U.S.A. 77 K2 30 43N 86 7W
De Grey, Australia 60 D2 20 12S 119 12 E
De Grey →, Australia 60 D2 20 12S 119 13 E
De Kalb, U.S.A. 80 E10 41 56N 88 46W
De Land, U.S.A. 77 L5 29 2N 81 18W
De Leon, U.S.A. 81 J5 32 7N 98 32W
De Pere, U.S.A. 76 C1 44 27N 88 4W
De Queen, U.S.A. 81 H7 34 2N 94 21W
De Quincy, U.S.A. 81 K8 30 27N 93 26W
De Ridder, U.S.A. 81 K8 30 51N 93 17W
De Smet, U.S.A. 80 C6 44 23N 97 33W
De Soto, U.S.A. 80 F9 38 8N 90 34W
De Tour Village, U.S.A. 76 C4 46 0N 83 56W
De Witt, U.S.A. 81 H9 34 18N 91 20W
Dead Sea, Asia 47 D4 31 30N 35 30 E
Deadwood, U.S.A. 80 C3 44 23N 103 44W
Deadwood L., Canada 72 B3 59 10N 128 30W
Deakin, Australia 61 F4 30 46S 128 58 E
Deal, U.K. 11 F9 51 13N 1 25 E
Deal I., Australia 62 F4 39 30S 147 20 E
Dealesville, S. Africa 56 D4 28 41S 25 44 E
Dean, Forest of, U.K. 11 F5 51 45N 2 33W
Deán Funes, Argentina 94 C3 30 20S 64 20W
Dearborn, U.S.A. 70 D3 42 19N 83 11W
Dease →, Canada 72 B3 59 56N 128 32W
Dease L., Canada 72 B2 58 40N 130 5W
Dease Lake, Canada 72 B2 58 25N 130 6W
Death Valley, U.S.A. 85 J10 36 15N 116 50W
Death Valley Junction, U.S.A. 85 J10 36 20N 116 25W
Death Valley National Monument, U.S.A. 85 J10 36 45N 117 15W
Deba Habe, Nigeria 50 F7 10 14N 11 20 E
Debar, Macedonia 21 D9 41 31N 20 30 E
Debden, Canada 73 C7 53 30N 106 50W
Dębica, Poland 17 C11 50 2N 21 25 E
Debolt, Canada 72 B5 55 12N 118 1W
Deborah East, L., Australia 61 F2 30 45S 119 0 E
Deborah West, L., Australia 61 F2 30 45S 118 50 E
Debre Markos, Ethiopia 51 F12 10 20N 37 40 E
Debre Tabor, Ethiopia 51 F12 11 50N 38 26 E
Debrecen, Hungary 17 E11 47 33N 21 42 E
Decatur, Ala., U.S.A. 77 H2 34 36N 86 59W
Decatur, Ga., U.S.A. 77 J3 33 47N 84 18W
Decatur, Ill., U.S.A. 80 F10 39 51N 88 57W
Decatur, Ind., U.S.A. 76 E3 40 50N 84 56W
Decatur, Tex., U.S.A. 81 J6 33 14N 97 35W
Deccan, India 40 M10 18 0N 79 0 E
Deception L., Canada 73 B8 56 33N 104 13W
Děčín, Czech. 16 C8 50 47N 14 12 E
Deckerville, U.S.A. 78 C2 43 32N 82 44W
Decorah, U.S.A. 80 D9 43 18N 91 48W
Dedéagach = Alexandroúpolis, Greece 21 D11 40 50N 25 54 E
Dedham, U.S.A. 79 D13 42 15N 71 10W
Dédougou, Burkina Faso 50 F4 12 30N 3 25W
Dedza, Malawi 55 E3 14 20S 34 20 E
Dee →, C. of Aberd., U.K. 12 D6 57 9N 2 5W
Dee →, Wales, U.K. 10 D4 53 22N 3 17W
Deep B., Canada 72 A5 61 15N 116 35W
Deep Well, Australia 62 C1 24 20S 134 0 E
Deepwater, Australia 63 D5 29 25S 151 51 E
Deer →, Canada 73 B10 58 23N 94 13W
Deer Lake, Nfld., Canada 71 C8 49 11N 57 27W
Deer Lake, Ont., Canada 73 C10 52 36N 94 20W
Deer Lodge, U.S.A. 82 C7 46 24N 112 44W
Deer Park, U.S.A. 82 C5 47 57N 117 28W
Deer River, U.S.A. 80 B8 47 20N 93 48W
Deeral, Australia 62 B4 17 14S 145 55 E
Deerdepoort, S. Africa 56 C4 24 37S 26 27 E
Deferiet, U.S.A. 79 B9 44 2N 75 41W
Defiance, U.S.A. 76 E3 41 17N 84 22W
Degeh Bur, Ethiopia 46 F3 8 11N 43 31 E
Deggendorf, Germany 16 D7 48 50N 12 57 E
Deh Bīd, Iran 45 D7 30 39N 53 11 E
Deh-e Shīr, Iran 45 D7 31 29N 53 45 E
Dehaj, Iran 45 D7 30 42N 54 53 E
Dehdez, Iran 45 D6 31 43N 50 17 E
Dehestān, Iran 45 D7 28 30N 55 35 E
Dehgolān, Iran 44 C5 35 17N 47 25 E
Dehi Titan, Afghan. 40 C3 33 45N 63 50 E
Dehibat, Tunisia 50 B7 32 0N 10 47 E
Dehlorān, Iran 44 C5 32 41N 47 16 E
Dehnow-e Kūhestān, Iran 45 E8 27 58N 58 32 E
Dehra Dun, India 42 D8 30 20N 78 4 E
Dehri, India 43 G11 24 50N 84 15 E
Dehui, China 35 B13 44 30N 125 40 E
Deinze, Belgium 15 D3 50 59N 3 32 E
Dej, Romania 17 E12 47 10N 23 52 E
Dekese, Zaïre 52 E4 3 24S 21 24 E
Del Mar, U.S.A. 85 N9 32 58N 117 16W
Del Norte, U.S.A. 83 H10 37 41N 106 21W
Del Rio, U.S.A. 81 L4 29 22N 100 54W
Delano, U.S.A. 85 K7 35 46N 119 15W
Delareyville, S. Africa 56 D4 26 41S 25 26 E
Delavan, U.S.A. 80 D10 42 38N 88 39W
Delaware, U.S.A. 76 E4 40 18N 83 4W
Delaware □, U.S.A. 76 F8 39 0N 75 20W
Delaware →, U.S.A. 76 F8 39 15N 75 20W
Delaware B., U.S.A. 75 C12 39 0N 75 10W
Delegate, Australia 63 F4 37 4S 148 56 E
Delft, Neths. 15 B4 52 1N 4 22 E
Delfzijl, Neths. 15 A6 53 20N 6 55 E
Delgado, C., Mozam. 55 E5 10 45S 40 40 E
Delgerhet, Mongolia 34 B6 45 50N 110 30 E
Delgo, Sudan 51 D11 20 6N 30 40 E
Delhi, Canada 78 D4 42 51N 80 30W
Delhi, India 42 E7 28 38N 77 17 E
Delhi, U.S.A. 79 D10 42 17N 74 55W
Delia, Canada 72 C6 51 38N 112 23W
Delice →, Turkey 25 G5 39 45N 34 15 E
Delicias, Mexico 86 B3 28 10N 105 30W
Delījān, Iran 45 C6 33 59N 50 40 E
Déline, Canada 68 B7 65 10N 123 30W
Dell City, U.S.A. 83 L11 31 56N 105 12W
Dell Rapids, U.S.A. 80 D6 43 50N 96 43W
Delmar, U.S.A. 79 D11 42 37N 73 47W
Delmenhorst, Germany 16 B5 53 3N 8 37 E
Delmiro Gouveia, Brazil 93 E11 9 24S 38 6W
Delong, Ostrova, Russia 27 B15 76 40N 149 20 E
Deloraine, Australia 62 G4 41 30S 146 40 E
Deloraine, Canada 73 D8 49 15N 100 29W
Delphi, U.S.A. 76 E2 40 36N 86 41W
Delphos, U.S.A. 76 E3 40 51N 84 21W
Delportshoop, S. Africa 56 D3 28 22S 24 20 E
Delray Beach, U.S.A. 77 M5 26 28N 80 4W
Delta, Colo., U.S.A. 83 G9 38 44N 108 4W
Delta, Utah, U.S.A. 82 G7 39 21N 112 35W
Delungra, Australia 63 D5 29 39S 150 51 E
Delvinë, Albania 21 E9 39 59N 20 4 E
Demanda, Sierra de la, Spain 19 A4 42 15N 3 0W
Demavand = Damāvand, Iran 45 C7 35 47N 52 0 E
Demba, Zaïre 52 F4 5 28S 22 15 E
Dembecha, Ethiopia 51 F12 10 32N 37 30 E
Dembia, Zaïre 54 B2 3 33N 25 48 E
Dembidolo, Ethiopia 51 G11 8 34N 34 50 E
Demer →, Belgium 15 D4 50 57N 4 42 E
Deming, N. Mex., U.S.A. 83 K10 32 16N 107 46W
Deming, Wash., U.S.A. 84 B4 48 50N 122 13W
Demini →, Brazil 92 D6 0 46S 62 56W
Demirci, Turkey 21 E13 39 2N 28 38 E
Demirköy, Turkey 21 D12 41 49N 27 45 E
Demopolis, U.S.A. 77 J2 32 31N 87 50W
Dempo, Indonesia 36 E2 4 2S 103 15 E
Den Burg, Neths. 15 A4 53 3N 4 47 E
Den Chai, Thailand 38 D3 17 59N 100 4 E
Den Haag = 's-Gravenhage, Neths. 15 B4 52 7N 4 17 E
Den Helder, Neths. 15 B4 52 57N 4 45 E
Den Oever, Neths. 15 B5 52 56N 5 2 E
Denain, France 15 D3 50 20N 3 22 E
Denair, U.S.A. 84 H6 37 32N 120 48W
Denau, Uzbekistan 26 F7 38 16N 67 54 E
Denbigh, U.K. 10 D4 53 12N 3 25W
Denbighshire □, U.K. 10 D4 53 8N 3 22W
Dendang, Indonesia 36 E3 3 7S 107 56 E
Dendermonde, Belgium 15 C4 51 2N 4 5 E
Dengfeng, China 34 G7 34 25N 113 2 E
Dengkou, China 34 D4 40 18N 106 55 E
Denham, Australia 61 E1 25 56S 113 31 E
Denham Ra., Australia 62 C4 21 55S 147 46 E
Denham Sd., Australia 61 E1 25 45S 113 15 E
Denia, Spain 19 C6 38 49N 0 8 E
Denial B., Australia 63 E1 32 14S 133 32 E
Deniliquin, Australia 63 F3 35 30S 144 58 E
Denison, Iowa, U.S.A. 80 D7 42 1N 95 21W
Denison, Tex., U.S.A. 81 J6 33 45N 96 33W
Denison Plains, Australia 60 C4 18 35S 128 0 E
Denizli, Turkey 25 G4 37 42N 29 2 E
Denman Glacier, Antarctica 5 C7 66 45S 99 25 E
Denmark, Australia 61 F2 34 59S 117 25 E
Denmark ■, Europe 9 J13 55 30N 9 0 E
Denmark Str., Atl. Oc. 4 C6 66 0N 30 0W
Dennison, U.S.A. 78 F3 40 24N 81 19W
Denpasar, Indonesia 36 F5 8 45S 115 14 E
Denton, Mont., U.S.A. 82 C9 47 19N 109 57W
Denton, Tex., U.S.A. 81 J6 33 13N 97 8W
D'Entrecasteaux, Pt., Australia 61 F2 34 50S 115 57 E
Denver, U.S.A. 80 F2 39 44N 104 59W
Denver City, U.S.A. 81 J3 32 58N 102 50W
Deoband, India 42 E7 29 42N 77 43 E
Deoghar, India 43 G12 24 30N 86 42 E
Deolali, India 40 K8 19 58N 73 50 E
Deoli = Devli, India 42 G6 25 50N 75 20 E
Deoria, India 43 F10 26 31N 83 48 E
Deosai Mts., Pakistan 43 B6 35 40N 75 0 E
Deping, China 35 F9 37 25N 116 58 E
Deposit, U.S.A. 79 D9 42 4N 75 25W
Depot Springs, Australia 61 E3 27 55S 120 3 E
Deputatskiy, Russia 27 C14 69 18N 139 54 E
Dera Ghazi Khan, Pakistan 42 D4 30 5N 70 43 E

E

Eastsound

Eastsound, *U.S.A.* 84 B4 48 42N 122 55W
Eaton, *U.S.A.* 80 E2 40 32N 104 42W
Eatonia, *Canada* 73 C7 51 13N 109 25W
Eatonton, *U.S.A.* 77 J4 33 20N 83 23W
Eatontown, *U.S.A.* 79 F10 40 19N 74 4W
Eatonville, *U.S.A.* 84 D4 46 52N 122 16W
Eau Claire, *U.S.A.* 80 C9 44 49N 91 30W
Ebagoola, *Australia* 62 A3 14 15S 143 12 E
Ebbw Vale, *U.K.* 11 F4 51 46N 3 12W
Ebeltoft, *Denmark* 9 H14 56 12N 10 41 E
Ebensburg, *U.S.A.* 78 F6 40 29N 78 44W
Eberswalde-Finow, *Germany* 16 B7 52 50N 13 49 E
Ebetsu, *Japan* 30 C10 43 7N 141 34 E
Ebolowa, *Cameroon* 52 D2 2 55N 11 10 E
Ebro →, *Spain* 19 B6 40 43N 0 54 E
Eceabat, *Turkey* 21 D12 40 11N 26 21 E
Ech Cheliff, *Algeria* 50 A5 36 10N 1 20 E
Echigo-Sammyaku, *Japan* 31 F9 36 50N 139 50 E
Echizen-Misaki, *Japan* 31 G7 35 59N 135 57 E
Echo Bay, *N.W.T., Canada* 68 B8 66 5N 117 55W
Echo Bay, *Ont., Canada* 70 C3 46 29N 84 4W
Echoing →, *Canada* 73 B10 55 51N 92 5W
Echternach, *Lux.* 15 E6 49 49N 6 25 E
Echuca, *Australia* 63 F3 36 10S 144 20 E
Ecija, *Spain* 19 D3 37 30N 5 10W
Eclipse Is., *Australia* 60 B4 13 54S 126 19 E
Ecuador ■, *S. Amer.* 92 D3 2 0S 78 0W
Ed Dâmer, *Sudan* 51 E11 17 27N 34 0 E
Ed Debba, *Sudan* 51 E11 18 0N 30 51 E
Ed Dueim, *Sudan* 51 F11 14 0N 32 10 E
Edah, *Australia* 61 E2 28 16S 117 10 E
Edam, *Canada* 73 C7 53 11N 108 46W
Edam, *Neths.* 15 B5 52 31N 5 3 E
Eday, *U.K.* 12 B6 59 11N 2 47W
Edd, *Eritrea* 46 E3 14 0N 41 38 E
Eddrachillis B., *U.K.* 12 C3 58 17N 5 14W
Eddystone, *U.K.* 11 G3 50 11N 4 16W
Eddystone Pt., *Australia* 62 G4 40 59S 148 20 E
Ede, *Neths.* 15 B5 52 4N 5 40 E
Édea, *Cameroon* 50 H7 3 51N 10 9 E
Edehon L., *Canada* 73 A9 60 25N 97 15W
Eden, *Australia* 63 F4 37 3S 149 55 E
Eden, *N.C., U.S.A.* 77 G6 36 29N 79 53W
Eden, *N.Y., U.S.A.* 78 D6 42 39N 78 55W
Eden, *Tex., U.S.A.* 81 K5 31 13N 99 51W
Eden, *Wyo., U.S.A.* 82 E9 42 3N 109 26W
Eden →, *U.K.* 10 C4 54 57N 3 1W
Eden L., *Canada* 73 B8 56 38N 100 15W
Edenburg, *S. Africa* 56 D4 29 43S 25 58 E
Edendale, *S. Africa* 57 D5 29 39S 30 18 E
Edenderry, *Ireland* 13 C4 53 21N 7 4W
Edenton, *U.S.A.* 77 G7 36 4N 76 39W
Edenville, *S. Africa* 57 D4 27 37S 27 34 E
Eder →, *Germany* 16 C5 51 12N 9 28 E
Edgar, *U.S.A.* 80 E5 40 22N 97 58W
Edgartown, *U.S.A.* 79 E14 41 23N 70 31W
Edge Hill, *U.K.* 11 E6 52 8N 1 26W
Edgefield, *U.S.A.* 77 J5 33 47N 81 56W
Edgeley, *U.S.A.* 80 B5 46 22N 98 43W
Edgemont, *U.S.A.* 80 D3 43 18N 103 50W
Edgeøya, *Svalbard* 4 B9 77 45N 22 30 E
Édhessa, *Greece* 21 D10 40 48N 22 5 E
Edievale, *N.Z.* 59 L2 45 49S 169 22 E
Edina, *U.S.A.* 80 E8 40 10N 92 11W
Edinburg, *U.S.A.* 81 M5 26 18N 98 10W
Edinburgh, *U.K.* 12 F5 55 57N 3 13W
Edinița, *Moldova* 17 D14 48 9N 27 18 E
Edirne, *Turkey* 21 D12 41 40N 26 34 E
Edison, *U.S.A.* 84 B4 48 33N 122 27W
Edithburgh, *Australia* 63 F2 35 5S 137 43 E
Edjudina, *Australia* 61 E3 29 48S 122 23 E
Edmeston, *U.S.A.* 79 D9 42 42N 75 15W
Edmond, *U.S.A.* 81 H6 35 39N 97 29W
Edmonds, *U.S.A.* 84 C4 47 49N 122 23W
Edmonton, *Australia* 62 B4 17 2S 145 46 E
Edmonton, *Canada* 72 C6 53 30N 113 30W
Edmund L., *Canada* 73 C10 54 45N 93 17W
Edmundston, *Canada* 71 C6 47 23N 68 20W
Edna, *U.S.A.* 81 L6 28 59N 96 39W
Edna Bay, *U.S.A.* 72 B2 55 55N 133 40W
Edremit, *Turkey* 21 E12 39 34N 27 0 E
Edremit Körfezi, *Turkey* 21 E12 39 30N 26 45 E
Edson, *Canada* 72 C5 53 35N 116 28W
Eduardo Castex, *Argentina* 94 D3 35 50S 64 18W
Edward →, *Australia* 63 F3 35 5S 143 30 E
Edward, L., *Africa* 54 C2 0 25S 29 40 E
Edward I., *Canada* 70 C2 48 22N 88 37W
Edward River, *Australia* 62 A3 14 59S 141 26 E
Edward VII Land, *Antarctica* 5 E13 80 0S 150 0W
Edwards, *U.S.A.* 85 L9 34 55N 117 51W
Edwards Plateau, *U.S.A.* 81 K4 30 45N 101 20W
Edwardsville, *U.S.A.* 79 E9 41 15N 75 56W
Edzo, *Canada* 72 A5 62 49N 116 4W
Eekloo, *Belgium* 15 C3 51 11N 3 33 E
Effingham, *U.S.A.* 76 F1 39 7N 88 33W
Égadi, Ísole, *Italy* 20 F5 37 55N 12 16 E
Eganville, *Canada* 70 C4 45 32N 77 5W
Egeland, *U.S.A.* 80 A5 48 38N 99 6W
Egenolf L., *Canada* 73 B9 59 3N 100 0W
Eger = Cheb, *Czech.* 16 C7 50 9N 12 28 E
Eger, *Hungary* 17 E11 47 53N 20 27 E
Egersund, *Norway* 9 G12 58 26N 6 1 E
Egg L., *Canada* 73 B7 55 5N 105 30W
Eginbah, *Australia* 60 D2 20 53S 119 47 E
Egmont, C., *N.Z.* 59 H4 39 16S 173 45 E
Egmont, Mt., *N.Z.* 59 H5 39 17S 174 5 E
Eğridir, *Turkey* 25 G5 37 52N 30 51 E
Eğridir Gölü, *Turkey* 25 G5 37 53N 30 50 E
Egvekinot, *Russia* 27 C19 66 19N 179 50W
Egypt ■, *Africa* 51 C11 28 0N 31 0 E
Ehime □, *Japan* 31 H6 33 30N 132 40 E
Ehrenberg, *U.S.A.* 85 M12 33 36N 114 31W
Eibar, *Spain* 19 A4 43 11N 2 28W
Eidsvold, *Australia* 63 D5 25 25S 151 12 E
Eidsvoll, *Norway* 9 F14 60 19N 11 14 E
Eifel, *Germany* 16 C4 50 15N 6 50 E
Eiffel Flats, *Zimbabwe* 55 F3 18 20S 30 0 E
Eigg, *U.K.* 12 E2 56 54N 6 10W
Eighty Mile Beach, *Australia* 60 C3 19 30S 120 40 E
Eil, *Somali Rep.* 46 F4 8 0N 49 50 E
Eil, L., *U.K.* 12 E3 56 51N 5 16W
Eildon, L., *Australia* 63 F4 37 10S 146 0 E
Eileen L., *Canada* 73 A7 62 16N 107 37W
Einasleigh, *Australia* 62 B3 18 32S 144 5 E
Einasleigh →, *Australia* 62 B3 17 30S 142 17 E
Eindhoven, *Neths.* 15 C5 51 26N 5 28 E
Eire = Ireland ■, *Europe* 13 D4 53 50N 7 52W
Eiríksjökull, *Iceland* 8 D3 64 46N 20 24W
Eirunepé, *Brazil* 92 E5 6 35S 69 53W
Eisenach, *Germany* 16 C6 50 58N 10 19 E
Eisenerz, *Austria* 16 E8 47 32N 14 54 E
Eivissa = Ibiza, *Spain* 22 C7 38 54N 1 26 E
Ejutla, *Mexico* 87 D5 16 34N 96 44W
Ekalaka, *U.S.A.* 80 C2 45 53N 104 33W
Eketahuna, *N.Z.* 59 J5 40 38S 175 43 E
Ekibastuz, *Kazakstan* 26 D8 51 50N 75 10 E
Ekimchan, *Russia* 27 D14 53 0N 133 0 E
Ekoli, *Zaïre* 54 C1 0 23S 24 13 E
Eksjö, *Sweden* 9 H16 57 40N 14 58 E
Ekwan →, *Canada* 70 B3 53 12N 82 15W
Ekwan Pt., *Canada* 70 B3 53 16N 82 7W
El Aaiún, *W. Sahara* 50 C2 27 9N 13 12W
El 'Agrûd, *Egypt* 47 E3 30 14N 34 24 E
El Alamein, *Egypt* 51 B10 30 48N 28 58 E
El 'Aqaba, W. →, *Egypt* 47 E2 30 7N 33 54 E
El Arenal, *Spain* 22 B9 39 30N 2 45 E
El Aricha, *Algeria* 50 B4 34 13N 1 10W
El Arīhā, *West Bank* 47 D4 31 52N 35 27 E
El Arish, *Australia* 62 B4 17 35S 146 1 E
El 'Arîsh, *Egypt* 47 D2 31 8N 33 50 E
El 'Arîsh, W. →, *Egypt* 47 D2 31 8N 33 47 E
El Asnam = Ech Cheliff, *Algeria* 50 A5 36 10N 1 20 E
El Bawiti, *Egypt* 51 C10 28 25N 28 45 E
El Bayadh, *Algeria* 50 B5 33 40N 1 1 E
El Bluff, *Nic.* 88 D3 11 59N 83 40W
El Brûk, W. →, *Egypt* 47 E2 30 15N 33 50 E
El Cajon, *U.S.A.* 85 N10 32 48N 116 58W
El Callao, *Venezuela* 92 B6 7 18N 61 50W
El Campo, *U.S.A.* 81 L6 29 12N 96 16W
El Centro, *U.S.A.* 85 N11 32 48N 115 34W
El Cerro, *Bolivia* 92 G6 17 30S 61 40W
El Compadre, *Mexico* 85 N10 32 20N 116 14W
El Cuy, *Argentina* 96 D3 39 55S 68 25W
El Cuyo, *Mexico* 87 C7 21 30N 87 40W
El Daheir, *Egypt* 47 D3 31 13N 34 10 E
El Dere, *Somali Rep.* 46 G4 3 50N 47 8 E
El Descanso, *Mexico* 85 N10 32 12N 116 58W
El Desemboque, *Mexico* 86 A2 30 30N 112 57W
El Diviso, *Colombia* 92 C3 1 22N 78 14W
El Djouf, *Mauritania* 50 E3 20 0N 9 0W
El Dorado, *Ark., U.S.A.* 81 J8 33 12N 92 40W
El Dorado, *Kans., U.S.A.* 81 G6 37 49N 96 52W
El Dorado, *Venezuela* 92 B6 6 55N 61 37W
El Escorial, *Spain* 19 B3 40 35N 4 7W
El Faiyûm, *Egypt* 51 C11 29 19N 30 50 E
El Fâsher, *Sudan* 51 F10 13 33N 25 26 E
El Ferrol, *Spain* 19 A1 43 29N 8 15W
El Fuerte, *Mexico* 86 B3 26 30N 108 40W
El Gal, *Somali Rep.* 46 E5 10 58N 50 20 E
El Geneina = Al Junaynah, *Sudan* 51 F9 13 27N 22 45 E
El Geteina, *Sudan* 51 F11 14 50N 32 27 E
El Gîza, *Egypt* 51 C11 30 0N 31 10 E
El Iskandarîya, *Egypt* 51 B10 31 13N 29 58 E
El Jadida, *Morocco* 50 B3 33 11N 8 17W
El Jebelein, *Sudan* 51 F11 12 40N 32 55 E
El Kab, *Sudan* 51 E11 19 27N 32 46 E
El Kabrît, G., *Egypt* 47 F2 29 42N 33 16 E
El Kala, *Algeria* 50 A6 36 50N 8 30 E
El Kamlin, *Sudan* 51 E11 15 3N 33 11 E
El Kef, *Tunisia* 50 A6 36 12N 8 47 E
El Khandaq, *Sudan* 51 E11 18 30N 30 30 E
El Khârga, *Egypt* 51 C11 25 30N 30 33 E
El Khartûm, *Sudan* 51 E11 15 31N 32 35 E
El Khartûm Bahrî, *Sudan* 51 E11 15 40N 32 31 E
El Kuntilla, *Egypt* 47 E3 30 1N 34 45 E
El Laqâwa, *Sudan* 51 F10 11 25N 29 1 E
El Mafâza, *Sudan* 51 F11 13 38N 34 30 E
El Mahalla el Kubra, *Egypt* 51 B11 31 0N 31 0 E
El Mansûra, *Egypt* 51 B11 31 0N 31 19 E
El Medano, *Canary Is.* 22 F3 28 3N 16 32W
El Milagro, *Argentina* 94 C2 30 59S 65 59W
El Minyâ, *Egypt* 51 C11 28 7N 30 33 E
El Monte, *U.S.A.* 85 L8 34 4N 118 1W
El Obeid, *Sudan* 51 F11 13 8N 30 10 E
El Odaiya, *Sudan* 51 F10 12 8N 28 12 E
El Oro, *Mexico* 87 D4 19 48N 100 8W
El Oued, *Algeria* 50 B6 33 20N 6 58 E
El Palmito, Presa, *Mexico* 86 B3 25 40N 105 30W
El Paso, *U.S.A.* 83 L10 31 45N 106 29W
El Paso Robles, *U.S.A.* 84 K6 35 38N 120 41W
El Portal, *U.S.A.* 83 H4 37 41N 119 47W
El Porvenir, *Mexico* 86 A3 31 15N 105 51W
El Prat de Llobregat, *Spain* 19 B7 41 18N 2 3 E
El Progreso, *Honduras* 88 C2 15 26N 87 51W
El Pueblito, *Mexico* 86 B3 29 3N 105 4W
El Pueblo, *Canary Is.* 22 F2 28 36N 17 47W
El Puerto de Santa María, *Spain* 19 D2 36 36N 6 13W
El Qâhira, *Egypt* 51 B11 30 1N 31 14 E
El Qantara, *Egypt* 47 E1 30 51N 32 20 E
El Qasr, *Egypt* 51 C10 25 44N 28 42 E
El Quseima, *Egypt* 47 E3 30 40N 34 15 E
El Reno, *U.S.A.* 81 H6 35 32N 97 57W
El Rio, *U.S.A.* 85 L7 34 14N 119 10W
El Roque, Pta., *Canary Is.* 22 F4 28 10N 15 25W
El Rosarito, *Mexico* 86 B2 28 38N 114 4W
El Saheira, W. →, *Egypt* 47 E2 30 5N 33 25 E
El Salto, *Mexico* 86 C3 23 47N 105 22W
El Salvador ■, *Cent. Amer.* 88 D2 13 50N 89 0W
El Sauce, *Nic.* 88 D2 13 0N 86 40W
El Shallal, *Egypt* 51 D11 24 0N 32 53 E
El Suweis, *Egypt* 51 C11 29 58N 32 31 E
El Tamarâni, W. →, *Egypt* 47 E3 30 7N 34 43 E
El Thamad, *Egypt* 47 F3 29 40N 34 28 E
El Tigre, *Venezuela* 92 B6 8 44N 64 15W
El Tîh, G., *Egypt* 47 F2 29 40N 33 50 E
El Tîna, Khalîg, *Egypt* 47 D1 31 10N 32 40 E
El Tocuyo, *Venezuela* 92 B5 9 47N 69 48W
El Tofo, *Chile* 94 B1 29 22S 71 18W
El Tránsito, *Chile* 94 B1 28 52S 70 17W
El Turbio, *Argentina* 96 G2 51 45S 72 5W
El Uqsur, *Egypt* 51 C11 25 41N 32 38 E
El Venado, *Mexico* 86 C4 22 56N 101 10W
El Vigía, *Venezuela* 92 B4 8 38N 71 39W
El Wabeira, *Egypt* 47 F2 29 34N 33 6 E
El Wak, *Kenya* 54 B5 2 49N 40 56 E
El Wuz, *Sudan* 51 E11 15 5N 30 7 E
Elat, *Israel* 47 F3 29 30N 34 56 E
Elâzığ, *Turkey* 25 G6 38 37N 39 14 E
Elba, *Italy* 20 C4 42 46N 10 17 E
Elba, *U.S.A.* 77 K2 31 25N 86 4W
Elbasani, *Albania* 21 D9 41 9N 20 9 E
Elbe, *U.S.A.* 84 D4 46 45N 122 10W
Elbe →, *Europe* 16 B5 53 50N 9 0 E
Elbert, Mt., *U.S.A.* 83 G10 39 7N 106 27W
Elberta, *U.S.A.* 76 C2 44 37N 86 14W
Elberton, *U.S.A.* 77 H4 34 7N 82 52W
Elbeuf, *France* 18 B4 49 17N 1 2 E
Elbing = Elbląg, *Poland* 17 A10 54 10N 19 25 E
Elbląg, *Poland* 17 A10 54 10N 19 25 E
Elbow, *Canada* 73 C7 51 7N 106 35W
Elbrus, *Asia* 25 F7 43 21N 42 30 E
Elburg, *Neths.* 15 B5 52 26N 5 50 E
Elburz Mts. = Alborz, Reshteh-ye Kūhhā-ye, *Iran* 45 C7 36 0N 52 0 E
Elche, *Spain* 19 C5 38 15N 0 42W
Elcho I., *Australia* 62 A2 11 55S 135 45 E
Elda, *Spain* 19 C5 38 29N 0 47W
Elde →, *Germany* 16 B6 53 7N 11 15 E
Eldon, *Mo., U.S.A.* 80 F8 38 21N 92 35W
Eldon, *Wash., U.S.A.* 84 C3 47 33N 123 3W
Eldora, *U.S.A.* 80 D8 42 22N 93 5W
Eldorado, *Argentina* 95 B5 26 28S 54 43W
Eldorado, *Canada* 73 B7 59 35N 108 30W
Eldorado, *Mexico* 86 C3 24 20N 107 22W
Eldorado, *Ill., U.S.A.* 76 G1 37 49N 88 26W
Eldorado, *Tex., U.S.A.* 81 K4 30 52N 100 36W
Eldorado Springs, *U.S.A.* 81 G8 37 52N 94 1W
Eldoret, *Kenya* 54 B4 0 30N 35 17 E
Eldred, *U.S.A.* 78 E6 41 58N 78 23W
Elea, C., *Cyprus* 23 D13 35 19N 34 4 E
Electra, *U.S.A.* 81 H5 34 2N 98 55W
Elefantes →, *Mozam.* 57 C5 24 10S 32 40 E
Elektrostal, *Russia* 24 C6 55 41N 38 32 E
Elephant Butte Reservoir, *U.S.A.* 83 K10 33 9N 107 11W
Elephant I., *Antarctica* 5 C18 61 0S 55 0W
Eleuthera, *Bahamas* 88 A4 25 0N 76 20W
Elgeyo-Marakwet □, *Kenya* 54 B4 0 45N 35 30 E
Elgin, *N.B., Canada* 71 C6 45 48N 65 10W
Elgin, *Ont., Canada* 79 B8 44 36N 76 13W
Elgin, *U.K.* 12 D5 57 39N 3 19W
Elgin, *Ill., U.S.A.* 76 D1 42 2N 88 17W
Elgin, *N. Dak., U.S.A.* 80 B4 46 24N 101 51W
Elgin, *Nebr., U.S.A.* 80 E5 41 59N 98 5W
Elgin, *Nev., U.S.A.* 83 H6 37 21N 114 32W
Elgin, *Oreg., U.S.A.* 82 D5 45 34N 117 55W
Elgin, *Tex., U.S.A.* 81 K6 30 21N 97 22W
Elgon, Mt., *Africa* 54 B3 1 10N 34 30 E
Eliase, *Indonesia* 37 F8 8 21S 130 48 E
Elida, *U.S.A.* 81 J3 33 57N 103 39W
Elim, *S. Africa* 56 E2 34 35S 19 45 E
Elisabethville = Lubumbashi, *Zaïre* 55 E2 11 40S 27 28 E
Elista, *Russia* 25 E7 46 16N 44 14 E
Elizabeth, *Australia* 63 E2 34 42S 138 41 E
Elizabeth, *U.S.A.* 79 F10 40 40N 74 13W
Elizabeth City, *U.S.A.* 77 G7 36 18N 76 14W
Elizabethton, *U.S.A.* 77 G4 36 21N 82 13W
Elizabethtown, *Ky., U.S.A.* 76 G3 37 42N 85 52W
Elizabethtown, *N.Y., U.S.A.* 79 B11 44 13N 73 36W
Elizabethtown, *Pa., U.S.A.* 79 F8 40 9N 76 36W
Ełk, *Poland* 17 B12 53 50N 22 21 E
Elk City, *U.S.A.* 81 H5 35 25N 99 25W
Elk Creek, *U.S.A.* 84 F4 39 36N 122 32W
Elk Grove, *U.S.A.* 84 G5 38 25N 121 22W
Elk Island Nat. Park, *Canada* 72 C6 53 35N 112 59W
Elk Lake, *Canada* 70 C3 47 40N 80 25W
Elk Point, *Canada* 73 C6 53 54N 110 55W
Elk River, *Idaho, U.S.A.* 82 C5 46 47N 116 11W
Elk River, *Minn., U.S.A.* 80 C8 45 18N 93 35W
Elkedra, *Australia* 62 C2 21 9S 135 33 E
Elkedra →, *Australia* 62 C2 21 8S 136 22 E
Elkhart, *Ind., U.S.A.* 76 E3 41 41N 85 58W
Elkhart, *Kans., U.S.A.* 81 G4 37 0N 101 54W
Elkhorn, *Canada* 73 D8 49 59N 101 14W
Elkhorn →, *U.S.A.* 80 E6 41 8N 96 19W
Elkhovo, *Bulgaria* 21 C12 42 10N 26 40 E
Elkin, *U.S.A.* 77 G5 36 15N 80 51W
Elkins, *U.S.A.* 76 F6 38 55N 79 51W
Elko, *Canada* 72 D5 49 20N 115 10W
Elko, *U.S.A.* 82 F6 40 50N 115 46W
Ell, L., *Australia* 61 E4 29 13S 127 46 E
Ellef Ringnes I., *Canada* 4 B2 78 30N 102 2W
Ellendale, *Australia* 60 C3 17 56S 124 48 E
Ellendale, *U.S.A.* 80 B5 46 0N 98 32W
Ellensburg, *U.S.A.* 82 C3 46 59N 120 34W
Ellenville, *U.S.A.* 79 E10 41 43N 74 24W
Ellery, Mt., *Australia* 63 F4 37 28S 148 47 E
Ellesmere, L., *N.Z.* 59 M4 47 47S 172 28 E
Ellesmere I., *Canada* 4 B4 79 30N 80 0W
Ellesmere Port, *U.K.* 10 D5 53 17N 2 54W
Ellice Is. = Tuvalu ■, *Pac. Oc.* 64 H9 8 0S 178 0 E
Ellinwood, *U.S.A.* 80 F5 38 21N 98 35W
Elliot, *Australia* 62 B1 17 33S 133 32 E
Elliot, *S. Africa* 57 E4 31 22S 27 48 E
Elliot Lake, *Canada* 70 C3 46 25N 82 35W
Elliotdale = Xhora, *S. Africa* 57 E4 31 55S 28 38 E
Ellis, *U.S.A.* 80 F5 38 56N 99 34W
Elliston, *Australia* 63 E1 33 39S 134 53 E
Ellisville, *U.S.A.* 81 K10 31 36N 89 12W
Ellon, *U.K.* 12 D6 57 22N 2 4W
Ellore = Eluru, *India* 41 L12 16 48N 81 8 E
Ells →, *Canada* 72 B6 57 18N 111 40W
Ellsworth, *U.S.A.* 80 F5 38 44N 98 14W
Ellsworth Land, *Antarctica* 5 D16 76 0S 89 0W
Ellsworth Mts., *Antarctica* 5 D16 78 30S 85 0W
Ellwood City, *U.S.A.* 78 F4 40 52N 80 17W
Elma, *Canada* 73 D9 49 52N 95 55W
Elma, *U.S.A.* 84 D3 47 0N 123 25W
Elmalı, *Turkey* 25 G4 36 44N 29 56 E
Elmhurst, *U.S.A.* 76 E2 41 53N 87 56W
Elmira, *Canada* 78 C4 43 36N 80 33W
Elmira, *U.S.A.* 78 D8 42 6N 76 48W
Elmore, *Australia* 63 F3 36 30S 144 37 E
Elmore, *U.S.A.* 85 M11 33 7N 115 49W
Elmshorn, *Germany* 16 B5 53 43N 9 40 E
Elmvale, *Canada* 78 B5 44 35N 79 52W
Elora, *Canada* 78 C4 43 41N 80 26W
Eloúnda, *Greece* 23 D7 35 16N 25 42 E
Eloy, *U.S.A.* 83 K8 32 45N 111 33W
Elrose, *Canada* 73 C7 51 12N 108 0W
Elsas, *Canada* 70 C3 48 32N 82 55W
Elsie, *U.S.A.* 84 E3 45 52N 123 36W
Elsinore = Helsingør, *Denmark* 9 H15 56 2N 12 35 E
Elsinore, *U.S.A.* 83 G7 38 41N 112 9W
Eltham, *N.Z.* 59 H5 39 26S 174 19 E
Eluru, *India* 41 L12 16 48N 81 8 E
Elvas, *Portugal* 19 C2 38 50N 7 10W
Elverum, *Norway* 9 F14 60 53N 11 34 E
Elvire →, *Australia* 60 C4 17 51S 128 11 E
Elwood, *Ind., U.S.A.* 76 E3 40 17N 85 50W
Elwood, *Nebr., U.S.A.* 80 E5 40 36N 99 52W
Elx = Elche, *Spain* 19 C5 38 15N 0 42W
Ely, *U.K.* 11 E8 52 24N 0 16 E
Ely, *Minn., U.S.A.* 80 B9 47 55N 91 51W
Ely, *Nev., U.S.A.* 82 G6 39 15N 114 54W
Elyria, *U.S.A.* 78 E2 41 22N 82 7W
Emāmrūd, *Iran* 45 B7 36 30N 55 0 E
Emba = Embi, *Kazakstan* 26 E6 48 50N 58 8 E
Emba = Embi →, *Kazakstan* 25 E9 46 55N 53 28 E
Embarcación, *Argentina* 94 A3 23 10S 64 0W
Embarras Portage, *Canada* 73 B6 58 27N 111 28W
Embetsu, *Japan* 30 B10 44 44N 141 47 E
Embi, *Kazakstan* 26 E6 48 50N 58 8 E
Embi →, *Kazakstan* 25 E9 46 55N 53 28 E
Embóna, *Greece* 23 C9 36 13N 27 51 E
Embrun, *France* 18 D7 44 34N 6 30 E
Embu, *Kenya* 54 C4 0 32S 37 38 E
Embu □, *Kenya* 54 C4 0 30S 37 35 E
Emden, *Germany* 16 B4 53 21N 7 12 E
Emerald, *Australia* 62 C4 23 32S 148 10 E
Emerson, *Canada* 73 D9 49 0N 97 10W
Emery, *U.S.A.* 83 G8 38 55N 111 15W
Emet, *Turkey* 21 E13 39 20N 29 15 E
Emi Koussi, *Chad* 51 E8 19 45N 18 55 E
Eminabad, *Pakistan* 42 C6 32 2N 74 8 E
Emine, Nos, *Bulgaria* 21 C12 42 40N 27 56 E
Emlenton, *U.S.A.* 78 E5 41 11N 79 43W
Emmeloord, *Neths.* 15 B5 52 44N 5 46 E
Emmen, *Neths.* 15 B6 52 48N 6 57 E
Emmet, *Australia* 62 C3 24 45S 144 30 E
Emmetsburg, *U.S.A.* 80 D7 43 7N 94 41W
Emmett, *U.S.A.* 82 E5 43 52N 116 30W
Empalme, *Mexico* 86 B2 28 1N 110 49W
Empangeni, *S. Africa* 57 D5 28 50S 31 52 E
Empedrado, *Argentina* 94 B4 28 0S 58 46W
Emperor Seamount Chain, *Pac. Oc.* 64 D9 40 0N 170 0 E
Emporia, *Kans., U.S.A.* 80 F6 38 25N 96 11W
Emporia, *Va., U.S.A.* 77 G7 36 42N 77 32W
Emporium, *U.S.A.* 78 E6 41 31N 78 14W
Empress, *Canada* 73 C6 50 57N 110 0W
Empty Quarter = Rub' al Khali, *Si. Arabia* 46 D4 18 0N 48 0 E
Ems →, *Germany* 16 B4 53 20N 7 12 E
Emsdale, *Canada* 78 A5 45 32N 79 19W
Emu, *China* 35 C15 43 40N 128 6 E
Emu Park, *Australia* 62 C5 23 13S 150 50 E
'En 'Avrona, *Israel* 47 F3 29 43N 35 0 E
En Nahud, *Sudan* 51 F10 12 45N 28 25 E
Ena, *Japan* 31 G8 35 25N 137 25 E
Enana, *Namibia* 56 B2 17 30S 16 23 E
Enaratoli, *Indonesia* 37 E9 3 55S 136 21 E
Enard B., *U.K.* 12 C3 58 5N 5 20W
Enare = Inarijärvi, *Finland* 8 B22 69 0N 28 0 E
Encantadas, Serra, *Brazil* 95 C5 30 40S 53 0W
Encanto, C., *Phil.* 37 A6 15 45N 121 38 E
Encarnación, *Paraguay* 95 B4 27 15S 55 50W
Encarnación de Diaz, *Mexico* 86 C4 21 30N 102 13W
Encinal, *U.S.A.* 81 L5 28 2N 99 21W
Encinitas, *U.S.A.* 85 M9 33 3N 117 17W
Encino, *U.S.A.* 83 J11 34 39N 105 28W
Encounter B., *Australia* 63 F2 35 45S 138 45 E
Ende, *Indonesia* 37 F6 8 45S 121 40 E
Endeavour, *Canada* 73 C8 52 10N 102 39W
Endeavour Str., *Australia* 62 A3 10 45S 142 0 E
Enderbury I., *Kiribati* 64 H10 3 8S 171 5W
Enderby, *Canada* 72 C5 50 35N 119 10W
Enderby I., *Australia* 60 D2 20 35S 116 30 E
Enderby Land, *Antarctica* 5 C5 66 0S 53 0 E
Enderlin, *U.S.A.* 80 B6 46 38N 97 36W
Endicott, *N.Y., U.S.A.* 79 D8 42 6N 76 4W
Endicott, *Wash., U.S.A.* 82 C5 46 56N 117 41W
Endyalgout I., *Australia* 60 B5 11 40S 132 35 E
Enewetak Atoll, *Pac. Oc.* 64 F8 11 30N 162 15 E
Enez, *Turkey* 21 D12 40 45N 26 5 E
Enfield, *U.K.* 11 F7 51 38N 0 5W
Engadin, *Switz.* 16 E6 46 45N 10 10 E
Engaño, C., *Dom. Rep.* 89 C6 18 30N 68 20W
Engaño, C., *Phil.* 37 A6 18 35N 122 23 E
Engcobo, *S. Africa* 57 E4 31 37S 28 0 E
Engels, *Russia* 24 D8 51 28N 46 6 E
Engemann L., *Canada* 73 B7 58 0N 106 55W
Enggano, *Indonesia* 36 F2 5 20S 102 40 E
Enghien, *Belgium* 15 D4 50 37N 4 2 E
Engkilili, *Malaysia* 36 D4 1 3N 111 42 E
England, *U.S.A.* 81 H9 34 33N 91 58W
England □, *U.K.* 7 E5 53 0N 2 0W
Englee, *Canada* 71 B8 50 45N 56 5W
Englehart, *Canada* 70 C4 47 49N 79 52W
Engler L., *Canada* 73 B7 59 8N 106 52W
Englewood, *Colo., U.S.A.* 80 F2 39 39N 104 59W
Englewood, *Kans., U.S.A.* 81 G5 37 2N 99 59W
English →, *Canada* 73 C10 50 35N 93 30W
English Bazar = Ingraj Bazar, *India* 43 G13 24 58N 88 10 E
English Channel, *Europe* 18 A3 50 0N 2 0W
English River, *Canada* 70 C1 49 14N 91 0W
Enid, *U.S.A.* 81 G6 36 24N 97 53W

Farsund

Enkhuizen, Neths. 15 B5 52 42N 5 17 E
Enna, Italy 20 F6 37 34N 14 16 E
Ennadai, Canada 73 A8 61 8N 100 53W
Ennadai L., Canada 73 A8 61 0N 101 0W
Ennedi, Chad 51 E9 17 15N 22 0 E
Enngonia, Australia 63 D4 29 21S 145 50 E
Ennis, Ireland 13 D3 52 51N 8 59W
Ennis, Mont., U.S.A. 82 D8 45 21N 111 44W
Ennis, Tex., U.S.A. 81 J6 32 20N 96 38W
Enniscorthy, Ireland 13 D5 52 30N 6 34W
Enniskillen, U.K. 13 B4 54 21N 7 39W
Ennistimon, Ireland 13 D2 52 57N 9 17W
Enns →, Austria 16 D8 48 14N 14 32 E
Enontekiö, Finland 8 B20 68 23N 23 37 E
Enriquillo, L., Dom. Rep. 89 C5 18 20N 72 5W
Enschede, Neths. 15 B6 52 13N 6 53 E
Ensenada, Argentina 94 C4 34 55S 57 55W
Ensenada, Mexico 86 A1 31 50N 116 50W
Ensiola, Pta., Spain 22 B9 39 7N 2 55 E
Entebbe, Uganda 54 B3 0 4N 32 28 E
Enterprise, Canada 72 A5 60 47N 115 45W
Enterprise, Oreg., U.S.A. 82 D5 45 25N 117 17W
Enterprise, Utah, U.S.A. 83 H7 37 34N 113 43W
Entre Ríos, Bolivia 94 A3 21 30S 64 25W
Entre Ríos □, Argentina 94 C4 30 30S 58 30W
Entroncamento, Portugal 19 C1 39 28N 8 28W
Enugu, Nigeria 50 G6 6 20N 7 30 E
Enugu Ezike, Nigeria 50 G6 7 0N 7 29 E
Enumclaw, U.S.A. 84 C5 47 12N 121 59W
Éolie, Ís., Italy 20 E6 38 30N 14 57 E
Epe, Neths. 15 B5 52 21N 5 59 E
Épernay, France 18 B5 49 3N 3 56 E
Ephesus, Turkey 21 F12 37 55N 27 22 E
Ephraim, U.S.A. 82 G8 39 22N 111 35W
Ephrata, U.S.A. 82 C4 47 19N 119 33W
Épinal, France 18 B7 48 10N 6 27 E
Episkopi, Cyprus 23 E11 34 40N 32 54 E
Episkopí, Greece 23 D6 35 20N 24 20 E
Episkopi Bay, Cyprus 23 E11 34 35N 32 50 E
Epping, U.K. 11 F8 51 41N 0 7 E
Epukiro, Namibia 56 C2 21 40S 19 9 E
Equatorial Guinea ■, Africa 52 D1 2 0N 8 0 E
Er Rahad, Sudan 51 F11 12 45N 30 32 E
Er Rif, Morocco 50 A4 35 1N 4 1W
Er Roseires, Sudan 51 F11 11 55N 34 30 E
Erāwadī Myit = Irrawaddy →, Burma 41 M19 15 50N 95 6 E
Erbil = Arbīl, Iraq 44 B5 36 15N 44 5 E
Erciyaş Dağı, Turkey 25 G6 38 30N 35 30 E
Érd, Hungary 17 E10 47 22N 18 56 E
Erdao Jiang →, China 35 C14 43 0N 127 0 E
Erdek, Turkey 21 D12 40 23N 27 47 E
Erdene, Mongolia 34 B6 44 13N 111 10 E
Erebus, Mt., Antarctica 5 D11 77 35S 167 0 E
Erechim, Brazil 95 B5 27 35S 52 15W
Ereğli, Konya, Turkey 25 G5 37 31N 34 4 E
Ereğli, Zonguldak, Turkey 25 F5 41 15N 31 24 E
Erenhot, China 34 C7 43 48N 112 2 E
Eresma →, Spain 19 B3 41 26N 4 45W
Erewadi Myitwanya, Burma 41 M19 15 30N 95 0 E
Erfenisdam, S. Africa 56 D4 28 30S 26 50 E
Erfurt, Germany 16 C6 50 58N 11 2 E
Ergeni Vozvyshennost, Russia 25 E7 47 0N 44 0 E
Ērgli, Latvia 9 H21 56 54N 25 38 E
Eriboll, L., U.K. 12 C4 58 30N 4 42W
Érice, Italy 20 E5 38 2N 12 35 E
Erie, U.S.A. 78 D4 42 8N 80 5W
Erie, L., N. Amer. 78 D3 42 15N 81 0W
Erie Canal, U.S.A. 78 C6 43 5N 78 43W
Erieau, Canada 78 D3 42 16N 81 57W
Erigavo, Somali Rep. 46 E4 10 35N 47 20 E
Erikoúsa, Greece 23 A3 39 53N 19 34 E
Eriksdale, Canada 73 C9 50 52N 98 7W
Erímanthos, Greece 21 F9 37 57N 21 50 E
Erimo-misaki, Japan 30 D11 41 50N 143 15 E
Eritrea ■, Africa 51 F12 14 0N 38 30 E
Erlangen, Germany 16 D6 49 36N 11 0 E
Erldunda, Australia 62 D1 25 14S 133 12 E
Ermelo, Neths. 15 B5 52 18N 5 35 E
Ermelo, S. Africa 57 D4 26 31S 29 59 E
Ermones, Greece 23 A3 39 37N 19 46 E
Ermoúpolis = Síros, Greece 21 F11 37 28N 24 57 E
Ernakulam = Cochin, India 40 Q10 9 59N 76 22 E
Erne →, Ireland 13 B3 54 30N 8 16W
Erne, Lower L., U.K. 13 B4 54 28N 7 47W
Erne, Upper L., U.K. 13 B4 54 14N 7 32W
Ernest Giles Ra., Australia 61 E3 27 0S 123 45 E
Erode, India 40 P10 11 24N 77 45 E
Eromanga, Australia 63 D3 26 40S 143 11 E
Erongo, Namibia 56 C2 21 39S 15 58 E
Errabiddy, Australia 61 E2 25 25S 117 5 E
Erramala Hills, India 40 M11 15 30N 78 15 E
Errigal, Ireland 13 A3 55 2N 8 6W
Erris Hd., Ireland 13 B1 54 19N 10 0W
Erskine, U.S.A. 80 B7 47 40N 96 0W
Ertis → = Irtysh →, Russia 26 C7 61 4N 68 52 E
Erwin, U.S.A. 77 G4 36 9N 82 25W
Erzgebirge, Germany 16 C7 50 27N 12 55 E
Erzin, Russia 27 D10 50 15N 95 10 E
Erzincan, Turkey 25 G6 39 46N 39 30 E
Erzurum, Turkey 25 G7 39 57N 41 15 E
Es Caló, Spain 22 C8 38 40N 1 30 E
Es Canã, Spain 22 B8 39 2N 1 36 E
Es Sahrâ' Esh Sharqîya, Egypt 51 C11 27 30N 32 30 E
Es Sînâ', Egypt 51 C11 29 0N 34 0 E
Esambo, Zaïre 54 C1 3 48S 23 30 E
Esan-Misaki, Japan 30 D10 41 40N 141 10 E
Esashi, Hokkaidō, Japan 30 B11 44 56N 142 35 E
Esashi, Hokkaidō, Japan 30 D10 41 52N 140 7 E
Esbjerg, Denmark 9 J13 55 29N 8 29 E
Escalante, U.S.A. 83 H8 37 47N 111 36W
Escalante →, U.S.A. 83 H8 37 24N 110 57W
Escalón, Mexico 86 B4 26 46N 104 20W
Escambia →, U.S.A. 77 K2 30 32N 87 11W
Escanaba, U.S.A. 76 C2 45 45N 87 4W
Esch-sur-Alzette, Lux. 18 B6 49 32N 6 0 E
Escondido, U.S.A. 85 M9 33 7N 117 5W
Escuinapa, Mexico 86 C3 22 50N 105 50W
Escuintla, Guatemala 88 D1 14 20N 90 48W
Esenguly, Turkmenistan 26 F6 37 37N 53 59 E
Eşfahān, Iran 45 C6 32 39N 51 43 E
Esfideh, Iran 45 C8 33 39N 59 46 E
Esh Sham = Dimashq, Syria 47 B5 33 30N 36 18 E
Eshowe, S. Africa 57 D5 28 50S 31 30 E
Esil → = Ishim →, Russia 26 D8 57 45N 71 10 E
Esk →, Cumb., U.K. 12 G5 54 58N 3 2W
Esk →, N. Yorks., U.K. 10 C7 54 30N 0 37W
Eskifjörður, Iceland 8 D7 65 3N 13 55W
Eskilstuna, Sweden 9 G17 59 22N 16 32 E
Eskimo Pt., Canada 73 A10 61 10N 94 15W
Eskişehir, Turkey 25 G5 39 50N 30 35 E
Esla →, Spain 19 B2 41 29N 6 3W
Eslāmābād-e Gharb, Iran 44 C5 34 10N 46 30 E
Eşme, Turkey 21 E13 38 23N 28 58 E
Esmeraldas, Ecuador 92 C3 1 0N 79 40W
Espalmador, I., Spain 22 C7 38 47N 1 26 E
Espanola, Canada 70 C3 46 15N 81 46W
Espardell, I. del, Spain 22 C7 38 48N 1 29 E
Esparta, Costa Rica 88 E3 9 59N 84 40W
Esperance, Australia 61 F3 33 45S 121 55 E
Esperance B., Australia 61 F3 33 48S 121 55 E
Esperanza, Argentina 94 C3 31 29S 61 3W
Espichel, C., Portugal 19 C1 38 22N 9 16W
Espigão, Serra do, Brazil 95 B5 26 35S 50 30W
Espinal, Colombia 92 C4 4 9N 74 53W
Espinazo, Sierra del = Espinhaço, Serra do, Brazil 93 G10 17 30S 43 30W
Espinhaço, Serra do, Brazil 93 G10 17 30S 43 30W
Espinilho, Serra do, Brazil 95 B5 28 30S 55 0W
Espírito Santo □, Brazil 93 G10 20 0S 40 45W
Espíritu Santo, B. del, Mexico 87 D7 19 15N 87 0W
Espíritu Santo, I., Mexico 86 C2 24 30N 110 23W
Espita, Mexico 87 C7 21 1N 88 19W
Espoo, Finland 9 F21 60 12N 24 40 E
Espungabera, Mozam. 57 C5 20 29S 32 45 E
Esquel, Argentina 96 E2 42 55S 71 20W
Esquina, Argentina 94 B4 30 0S 59 30W
Essaouira, Morocco 50 B3 31 32N 9 42W
Essebie, Zaïre 54 B3 2 58N 30 40 E
Essen, Belgium 15 C4 51 28N 4 28 E
Essen, Germany 16 C4 51 28N 7 0 E
Essendon, Mt., Australia 61 E3 25 0S 120 29 E
Essequibo →, Guyana 92 B7 6 50N 58 30W
Essex, Canada 78 D2 42 10N 82 49W
Essex, Calif., U.S.A. 85 L11 34 44N 115 15W
Essex, N.Y., U.S.A. 79 B11 44 19N 73 21W
Essex □, U.K. 11 F8 51 54N 0 27 E
Esslingen, Germany 16 D5 48 44N 9 18 E
Estados, I. de Los, Argentina 96 G4 54 40S 64 30W
Eşţahbānāt, Iran 45 D7 29 8N 54 4 E
Estallenchs, Spain 22 B9 39 39N 2 29 E
Estância, Brazil 93 F11 11 16S 37 26W
Estancia, U.S.A. 83 J10 34 46N 106 4W
Estārm, Iran 45 D8 28 21N 58 21 E
Estcourt, S. Africa 57 D4 29 0S 29 53 E
Estelí, Nic. 88 D2 13 9N 86 22W
Estelline, S. Dak., U.S.A. 80 C6 44 35N 96 54W
Estelline, Tex., U.S.A. 81 H4 34 33N 100 26W
Esterhazy, Canada 73 C8 50 37N 102 5W
Estevan, Canada 73 D8 49 10N 102 59W
Estevan Group, Canada 72 C3 53 3N 129 38W
Estherville, U.S.A. 80 D7 43 24N 94 50W
Eston, Canada 73 C7 51 8N 108 40W
Estonia ■, Europe 9 G21 58 30N 25 30 E
Estrêla, Serra da, Portugal 19 B2 40 10N 7 45W
Estremoz, Portugal 19 C2 38 51N 7 39W
Estrondo, Serra do, Brazil 93 E9 7 20S 48 0W
Esztergom, Hungary 17 E10 47 47N 18 44 E
Etadunna, Australia 63 D2 28 43S 138 38 E
Etah, India 43 F8 27 35N 78 40 E
Etamamu, Canada 71 B8 50 18N 59 59W
Étampes, France 18 B5 48 26N 2 10 E
Etanga, Namibia 56 B1 17 55S 13 0 E
Etawah, India 43 F8 26 48N 79 6 E
Etawah →, U.S.A. 77 H3 34 20N 84 15W
Etawney L., Canada 73 B9 57 50N 96 50W
Ethel, U.S.A. 84 D4 46 32N 122 46W
Ethel Creek, Australia 60 D3 22 55S 120 11 E
Ethelbert, Canada 73 C8 51 32N 100 25W
Ethiopia ■, Africa 46 F3 8 0N 40 0 E
Ethiopian Highlands, Ethiopia 28 J7 10 0N 37 0 E
Etive, L., U.K. 12 E3 56 29N 5 10W
Etna, Italy 20 F6 37 50N 14 55 E
Etoile, Zaïre 55 E2 11 33S 27 30 E
Etolin I., U.S.A. 72 B2 56 5N 132 20W
Etosha Pan, Namibia 56 B2 18 40S 16 30 E
Etowah, U.S.A. 77 H3 35 20N 84 32W
Ettrick Water →, U.K. 12 F6 55 31N 2 55W
Etuku, Zaïre 54 C2 3 42S 25 45 E
Etzatlán, Mexico 86 C4 20 48N 104 5W
Euboea = Évvoia, Greece 21 E11 38 30N 24 0 E
Eucla Motel, Australia 61 F4 31 41S 128 52 E
Euclid, U.S.A. 78 E3 41 34N 81 32W
Eucumbene, L., Australia 63 F4 36 2S 148 40 E
Eudora, U.S.A. 81 J9 33 7N 91 16W
Eufaula, Ala., U.S.A. 77 K3 31 54N 85 9W
Eufaula, Okla., U.S.A. 81 H7 35 17N 95 35W
Eufaula L., U.S.A. 81 H7 35 18N 95 21W
Eugene, U.S.A. 82 E2 44 5N 123 4W
Eugowra, Australia 63 E4 33 22S 148 24 E
Eulo, Australia 63 D4 28 10S 145 3 E
Eunice, La., U.S.A. 81 K8 30 30N 92 25W
Eunice, N. Mex., U.S.A. 81 J3 32 26N 103 10W
Eupen, Belgium 15 D6 50 37N 6 3 E
Euphrates = Furāt, Nahr al →, Asia 44 D5 31 0N 47 25 E
Eureka, Canada 4 B3 80 0N 85 56W
Eureka, Calif., U.S.A. 82 F1 40 47N 124 9W
Eureka, Kans., U.S.A. 81 G6 37 49N 96 17W
Eureka, Mont., U.S.A. 82 B6 48 53N 115 3W
Eureka, Nev., U.S.A. 82 G5 39 31N 115 58W
Eureka, S. Dak., U.S.A. 80 C5 45 46N 99 38W
Eureka, Utah, U.S.A. 82 G7 39 58N 112 7W
Eureka, Mt., Australia 61 E3 26 35S 121 35 E
Euroa, Australia 63 F4 36 44S 145 35 E
Europa, I., Ind. Oc. 53 J8 22 20S 40 22 E
Europa, Picos de, Spain 19 A3 43 10N 4 49W
Europa, Pta. de, Gib. 19 D3 36 3N 5 21W
Europa Pt. = Europa, Pta. de, Gib. 19 D3 36 3N 5 21W
Europoort, Neths. 15 C4 51 57N 4 10 E
Eustis, U.S.A. 77 L5 28 51N 81 41W
Eutsuk L., Canada 72 C3 53 20N 126 45W
Eva Downs, Australia 62 B1 18 1S 134 52 E
Evale, Angola 56 B2 16 33S 15 44 E
Evans, U.S.A. 80 E2 40 23N 104 41W
Evans Head, Australia 63 D5 29 7S 153 27 E
Evans L., Canada 70 B4 50 50N 77 0W
Evans Mills, U.S.A. 79 B9 44 6N 75 48W
Evanston, Ill., U.S.A. 76 D2 42 3N 87 41W
Evanston, Wyo., U.S.A. 82 F8 41 16N 110 58W
Evansville, Ind., U.S.A. 76 F2 37 58N 87 35W
Evansville, Wis., U.S.A. 80 D10 42 47N 89 18W
Evaz, Iran 45 E7 27 46N 53 59 E
Eveleth, U.S.A. 80 B8 47 28N 92 32W
Evensk, Russia 27 C16 62 12N 159 30 E
Everard, L., Australia 63 E1 31 30S 135 0 E
Everard Park, Australia 61 E5 27 1S 132 43 E
Everard Ras., Australia 61 E5 27 5S 132 28 E
Everest, Mt., Nepal 43 E12 28 5N 86 58 E
Everett, Pa., U.S.A. 78 F6 40 1N 78 23W
Everett, Wash., U.S.A. 84 C4 47 59N 122 12W
Everglades, The, U.S.A. 77 N5 25 50N 81 0W
Everglades City, U.S.A. 77 N5 25 52N 81 23W
Everglades National Park, U.S.A. 77 N5 25 30N 81 0W
Evergreen, U.S.A. 77 K2 31 26N 86 57W
Everson, U.S.A. 82 B2 48 57N 122 22W
Evesham, U.K. 11 E6 52 6N 1 56W
Evinayong, Eq. Guin. 52 D2 1 26N 10 35 E
Evje, Norway 9 G12 58 36N 7 51 E
Évora, Portugal 19 C2 38 33N 7 57W
Evowghlī, Iran 44 B5 38 43N 45 13 E
Évreux, France 18 B4 49 3N 1 8 E
Évros →, Bulgaria 21 D12 41 40N 26 34 E
Evry, France 18 B5 48 38N 2 27 E
Évvoia, Greece 21 E11 38 30N 24 0 E
Ewe, L., U.K. 12 D3 57 49N 5 38W
Ewing, U.S.A. 80 D5 42 16N 98 21W
Ewo, Congo 52 E2 0 48S 14 45 E
Exaltación, Bolivia 92 F5 13 10S 65 20W
Excelsior Springs, U.S.A. 80 F7 39 20N 94 13W
Exe →, U.K. 11 G4 50 41N 3 29W
Exeter, Canada 78 C3 43 21N 81 29W
Exeter, U.K. 11 G4 50 43N 3 31W
Exeter, Calif., U.S.A. 83 H4 36 18N 119 9W
Exeter, N.H., U.S.A. 79 D14 42 59N 70 57W
Exeter, Nebr., U.S.A. 80 E6 40 39N 97 27W
Exmoor, U.K. 11 F4 51 12N 3 45W
Exmouth, Australia 60 D1 21 54S 114 10 E
Exmouth, U.K. 11 G4 50 37N 3 25W
Exmouth G., Australia 60 D1 22 15S 114 15 E
Expedition Ra., Australia 62 C4 24 30S 149 12 E
Extremadura □, Spain 19 C2 39 30N 6 5W
Exuma Sound, Bahamas 88 B4 24 30N 76 20W
Eyasi, L., Tanzania 54 C4 3 30S 35 0 E
Eyeberry L., Canada 73 A8 63 8N 104 43W
Eyemouth, U.K. 12 F6 55 52N 2 5W
Eyjafjörður, Iceland 8 C4 66 15N 18 30W
Eyre, Australia 61 F4 32 15S 126 18 E
Eyre (North), L., Australia 63 D2 28 30S 137 20 E
Eyre (South), L., Australia 63 D2 29 18S 137 25 E
Eyre Cr. →, Australia 63 D2 26 40S 139 0 E
Eyre Mts., N.Z. 59 L2 45 25S 168 25 E
Eyre Pen., Australia 63 E2 33 30S 136 17 E
Eysturoy, Færoe Is. 8 E9 62 13N 6 54W
Eyvānkī, Iran 45 C6 35 24N 51 56 E
Ezine, Turkey 21 E12 39 48N 26 20 E
Ezouza →, Cyprus 23 E11 34 44N 32 27 E

F

F.Y.R.O.M. = Macedonia ■, Europe 21 D9 41 53N 21 40 E
Fabens, U.S.A. 83 L10 31 30N 106 10W
Fabriano, Italy 20 C5 43 20N 12 54 E
Facatativá, Colombia 92 C4 4 49N 74 22W
Fachi, Niger 50 E7 18 6N 11 34 E
Fada, Chad 51 E9 17 13N 21 34 E
Fada-n-Gourma, Burkina Faso 50 F5 12 10N 0 30 E
Faddeyevskiy, Ostrov, Russia 27 B15 76 0N 144 0 E
Fadghāmī, Syria 44 C4 35 53N 40 52 E
Faenza, Italy 20 B4 44 17N 11 53 E
Færoe Is. = Føroyar, Atl. Oc. 8 F9 62 0N 7 0W
Făgăras, Romania 17 F13 45 48N 24 58 E
Fagersta, Sweden 9 F16 60 1N 15 46 E
Fagnano, L., Argentina 96 G3 54 30S 68 0W
Fahliān, Iran 45 D6 30 11N 51 28 E
Fahraj, Kermān, Iran 45 D8 29 0N 59 0 E
Fahraj, Yazd, Iran 45 D7 31 46N 54 36 E
Faial, Madeira 22 D3 32 47N 16 53W
Fair Hd., U.K. 13 A5 55 14N 6 9W
Fair Oaks, U.S.A. 84 G5 38 39N 121 16W
Fairbank, U.S.A. 83 L8 31 43N 110 11W
Fairbanks, U.S.A. 68 B5 64 51N 147 43W
Fairbury, U.S.A. 80 E6 40 8N 97 11W
Fairfax, U.S.A. 81 G6 36 34N 96 42W
Fairfield, Ala., U.S.A. 77 J2 33 29N 86 55W
Fairfield, Calif., U.S.A. 84 G4 38 15N 122 3W
Fairfield, Conn., U.S.A. 79 E11 41 9N 73 16W
Fairfield, Idaho, U.S.A. 82 E6 43 21N 114 44W
Fairfield, Ill., U.S.A. 76 F1 38 23N 88 22W
Fairfield, Iowa, U.S.A. 80 E9 40 56N 91 57W
Fairfield, Mont., U.S.A. 82 C8 47 37N 111 59W
Fairfield, Tex., U.S.A. 81 K7 31 44N 96 10W
Fairford, Canada 73 C9 51 37N 98 38W
Fairhope, U.S.A. 77 K2 30 31N 87 54W
Fairlie, N.Z. 59 L3 44 5S 170 49 E
Fairmead, U.S.A. 84 H6 37 5N 120 10W
Fairmont, Minn., U.S.A. 80 D7 43 39N 94 28W
Fairmont, W. Va., U.S.A. 76 F5 39 29N 80 9W
Fairmount, U.S.A. 85 L8 34 45N 118 26W
Fairplay, U.S.A. 83 G11 39 15N 106 2W
Fairport, U.S.A. 78 C7 43 6N 77 27W
Fairport Harbor, U.S.A. 78 E3 41 45N 81 17W
Fairview, Australia 62 B3 15 31S 144 17 E
Fairview, Canada 72 B5 56 5N 118 25W
Fairview, Mont., U.S.A. 80 B2 47 51N 104 3W
Fairview, Okla., U.S.A. 81 G5 36 16N 98 29W
Fairview, Utah, U.S.A. 82 G8 39 50N 111 0W
Fairweather, Mt., U.S.A. 68 C6 58 55N 137 32W
Faisalabad, Pakistan 42 D5 31 30N 73 5 E
Faith, U.S.A. 80 C3 45 2N 102 2W
Faizabad, India 43 F10 26 45N 82 10 E
Fajardo, Puerto Rico 89 C6 18 20N 65 39W
Fakfak, Indonesia 37 E8 3 0S 132 15 E
Faku, China 35 C12 42 32N 123 21 E
Falaise, France 18 B3 48 54N 0 12W
Falaise, Mui, Vietnam 38 C5 19 6N 105 45 E
Falam, Burma 41 H18 23 0N 93 45 E
Falcón, C., Spain 22 C7 38 50N 1 23 E
Falcon Dam, U.S.A. 81 M5 26 50N 99 20W
Falconara Marittima, Italy 20 C5 43 37N 13 24 E
Falcone, C., Italy 20 D3 40 58N 8 12 E
Falconer, U.S.A. 78 D5 42 7N 79 13W
Faleshty = Fălești, Moldova 17 E14 47 32N 27 44 E
Fălești, Moldova 17 E14 47 32N 27 44 E
Falfurrias, U.S.A. 81 M5 27 14N 98 9W
Falher, Canada 72 B5 55 44N 117 15W
Faliraki, Greece 23 C10 36 22N 28 12 E
Falkenberg, Sweden 9 H15 56 54N 12 30 E
Falkirk, U.K. 12 F5 56 0N 3 47W
Falkirk □, U.K. 12 F5 55 58N 3 49W
Falkland Is. □, Atl. Oc. 96 G5 51 30S 59 0W
Falkland Sd., Falk. Is. 96 G5 52 0S 60 0W
Falköping, Sweden 9 G15 58 12N 13 33 E
Fall River, U.S.A. 79 E13 41 43N 71 10W
Fall River Mills, U.S.A. 82 F3 41 3N 121 26W
Fallbrook, U.S.A. 83 K5 33 25N 117 12W
Fallbrook, Calif., U.S.A. 85 M9 33 23N 117 15W
Fallon, Mont., U.S.A. 80 B2 46 50N 105 8W
Fallon, Nev., U.S.A. 82 G4 39 28N 118 47W
Falls City, Nebr., U.S.A. 80 E7 40 3N 95 36W
Falls City, Oreg., U.S.A. 82 D2 44 52N 123 26W
Falls Creek, U.S.A. 78 E6 41 9N 78 48W
Falmouth, Jamaica 88 C4 18 30N 77 40W
Falmouth, U.K. 11 G2 50 9N 5 5W
Falmouth, U.S.A. 76 F3 38 41N 84 20W
False B., S. Africa 56 E2 34 15S 18 40 E
Falso, C., Honduras 88 C3 15 12N 83 21W
Falster, Denmark 9 J14 54 45N 11 55 E
Falsterbo, Sweden 9 J15 55 23N 12 50 E
Fălticeni, Romania 17 E14 47 21N 26 20 E
Falun, Sweden 9 F16 60 37N 15 37 E
Famagusta, Cyprus 23 D12 35 8N 33 55 E
Famagusta Bay, Cyprus 23 D13 35 15N 34 0 E
Famatina, Sierra de, Argentina 94 B2 27 30S 68 0W
Family L., Canada 73 C9 51 54N 95 27W
Famoso, U.S.A. 85 K7 35 37N 119 12W
Fan Xian, China 34 G8 35 55N 115 38 E
Fandriana, Madag. 57 C8 20 14S 47 21 E
Fang, Thailand 38 C2 19 55N 99 13 E
Fangcheng, China 34 H7 33 18N 112 59 E
Fangshan, China 34 E6 38 3N 111 25 E
Fangzi, China 35 F10 36 33N 119 10 E
Fanjiatun, China 35 C13 43 40N 125 15 E
Fannich, L., U.K. 12 D4 57 38N 4 59W
Fannūj, Iran 45 E8 26 35N 59 38 E
Fanny Bay, Canada 72 D4 49 37N 124 48W
Fanø, Denmark 9 J13 55 25N 8 25 E
Fano, Italy 20 C5 43 50N 13 1 E
Fanshaw, U.S.A. 72 B2 57 11N 133 30W
Fanshi, China 34 E7 39 12N 113 20 E
Fao = Al Fāw, Iraq 45 D6 30 0N 48 30 E
Faqirwali, Pakistan 42 E5 29 27N 73 0 E
Faradje, Zaïre 54 B2 3 50N 29 45 E
Farafangana, Madag. 57 C8 22 49S 47 50 E
Farāh, Afghan. 40 C3 32 20N 62 7 E
Farāh □, Afghan. 40 C3 32 25N 62 10 E
Farahalana, Madag. 57 A9 14 26S 50 10 E
Faranah, Guinea 50 F2 10 3N 10 45W
Farasān, Jazā'ir, Si. Arabia 46 D3 16 45N 41 55 E
Farasan Is. = Farasān, Jazā'ir, Si. Arabia 46 D3 16 45N 41 55 E
Faratsiho, Madag. 57 B8 19 24S 46 57 E
Fareham, U.K. 11 G6 50 51N 1 11W
Farewell, C., N.Z. 59 J4 40 29S 172 43 E
Farewell C. = Farvel, Kap, Greenland 4 D5 59 48N 43 55W
Farghona, Uzbekistan 26 E8 40 23N 71 19 E
Fargo, U.S.A. 80 B6 46 53N 96 48W
Fār'iah, W. al →, West Bank 47 C4 32 12N 35 27 E
Faribault, U.S.A. 80 C8 44 18N 93 16W
Faridkot, India 42 D6 30 44N 74 45 E
Faridpur, Bangla. 43 H13 23 15N 89 55 E
Farim, Guinea-Biss. 50 F1 12 27N 15 9W
Farīmān, Iran 45 C8 35 40N 59 49 E
Farina, Australia 63 E2 30 3S 138 15 E
Fariones, Pta., Canary Is. 22 E6 29 13N 13 28W
Farmerville, U.S.A. 81 J8 32 47N 92 24W
Farmington, Calif., U.S.A. 84 H6 37 55N 120 59W
Farmington, N.H., U.S.A. 79 C13 43 24N 71 4W
Farmington, N. Mex., U.S.A. 83 H9 36 44N 108 12W
Farmington, Utah, U.S.A. 82 F8 41 0N 111 12W
Farmington →, U.S.A. 79 E12 41 51N 72 38W
Farmville, U.S.A. 76 G6 37 18N 78 24W
Farnborough, U.K. 11 F7 51 16N 0 45W
Farne Is., U.K. 10 B6 55 38N 1 37W
Farnham, Canada 79 A12 45 17N 72 59W
Faro, Brazil 93 D7 2 10S 56 39W
Faro, Portugal 19 D2 37 2N 7 55W
Fårö, Sweden 9 H18 57 55N 19 5 E
Farquhar, C., Australia 61 D1 23 50S 113 36 E
Farrars Cr. →, Australia 62 D3 25 35S 140 43 E
Farrāshband, Iran 45 D7 28 57N 52 5 E
Farrell, U.S.A. 78 E4 41 13N 80 30W
Farrell Flat, Australia 63 E2 33 48S 138 48 E
Farrokhī, Iran 45 C8 33 50N 59 31 E
Farruch, C., Spain 22 B10 39 47N 3 21 E
Farrukhabad-cum-Fatehgarh, India 43 F8 27 30N 79 32 E
Fārs □, Iran 45 D7 29 30N 55 0 E
Fársala, Greece 21 E10 39 17N 22 23 E
Farsund, Norway 9 G12 58 5N 6 55 E

Fartak, Râs

Fartak, Râs, *Si. Arabia* 44 D2 28 5N 34 34 E
Fartura, Serra da, *Brazil* 95 B5 26 21S 52 52W
Fārūj, *Iran* 45 B8 37 14N 58 14 E
Farvel, Kap, *Greenland* 4 D5 59 48N 43 55W
Farwell, *U.S.A.* 81 H3 34 23N 103 2W
Fasā, *Iran* 45 D7 29 0N 53 39 E
Fasano, *Italy* 20 D7 40 50N 17 22 E
Fastiv, *Ukraine* 17 C15 50 7N 29 57 E
Fastnet Rock, *Ireland* 13 E2 51 22N 9 37W
Fastov = Fastiv, *Ukraine* 17 C15 50 7N 29 57 E
Fatagar, Tanjung, *Indonesia* 37 E8 2 46S 131 57 E
Fatehgarh, *India* 43 F8 27 25N 79 35 E
Fatehpur, *Raj., India* 42 F6 28 0N 74 40 E
Fatehpur, *Ut. P., India* 43 G9 25 56N 81 13 E
Fatima, *Canada* 71 C7 47 24N 61 53W
Faulkton, *U.S.A.* 80 C5 45 2N 99 8W
Faure I., *Australia* 61 E1 25 52S 113 50 E
Fauresmith, *S. Africa* 56 D4 29 44S 25 17 E
Fauske, *Norway* 8 C16 67 17N 15 25 E
Favara, *Italy* 20 F5 37 19N 13 39 E
Favaritx, C., *Spain* 22 A11 40 0N 4 15 E
Favignana, *Italy* 20 F5 37 56N 12 20 E
Favourable Lake, *Canada* 70 B1 52 50N 93 39W
Fawn →, *Canada* 70 A2 55 20N 87 35W
Fawnskin, *U.S.A.* 85 L10 34 16N 116 56W
Faxaflói, *Iceland* 8 D2 64 29N 23 0W
Faya-Largeau, *Chad* 51 E8 17 58N 19 6 E
Fayd, *Si. Arabia* 44 E4 27 1N 42 52 E
Fayette, *Ala., U.S.A.* 77 J2 33 41N 87 50W
Fayette, *Mo., U.S.A.* 80 F8 39 9N 92 41W
Fayetteville, *Ark., U.S.A.* 81 G7 36 4N 94 10W
Fayetteville, *N.C., U.S.A.* 77 H6 35 3N 78 53W
Fayetteville, *Tenn., U.S.A.* 77 H2 35 9N 86 34W
Fazilka, *India* 42 D6 30 27N 74 2 E
Fazilpur, *Pakistan* 42 E4 29 18N 70 29 E
Fdérik, *Mauritania* 50 D2 22 40N 12 45W
Feale →, *Ireland* 13 D2 52 27N 9 37W
Fear, C., *U.S.A.* 77 J7 33 50N 77 58W
Feather →, *U.S.A.* 82 G3 38 47N 121 36W
Feather Falls, *U.S.A.* 84 F5 39 36N 121 16W
Featherston, *N.Z.* 59 J5 41 6S 175 20 E
Featherstone, *Zimbabwe* 55 F3 18 42S 30 55 E
Fécamp, *France* 18 B4 49 45N 0 22 E
Federación, *Argentina* 94 C4 31 0S 57 55W
Fedeshkūh, *Iran* 45 D7 28 49N 53 50 E
Fehmarn, *Germany* 16 A6 54 27N 11 7 E
Fehmarn Bælt, *Europe* 9 J14 54 35N 11 20 E
Fei Xian, *China* 35 G9 35 18N 117 59 E
Feilding, *N.Z.* 59 J5 40 13S 175 35 E
Feira de Santana, *Brazil* 93 F11 12 15S 38 57W
Feixiang, *China* 34 F8 36 30N 114 45 E
Felanitx, *Spain* 22 B10 39 28N 3 9 E
Feldkirch, *Austria* 16 E5 47 15N 9 37 E
Felipe Carrillo Puerto, *Mexico* 87 D7 19 38N 88 3W
Felixstowe, *U.K.* 11 F9 51 58N 1 23 E
Felton, *U.K.* 10 B6 55 18N 1 42W
Felton, *U.S.A.* 84 H4 37 3N 122 4W
Femunden, *Norway* 9 E14 62 10N 11 53 E
Fen He →, *China* 34 G6 35 36N 110 42 E
Fenelon Falls, *Canada* 78 B6 44 32N 78 45W
Feng Xian, *Jiangsu, China* 34 G9 34 43N 116 35 E
Feng Xian, *Shaanxi, China* 34 H4 33 54N 106 40 E
Fengcheng, *China* 35 D13 40 28N 124 5 E
Fengfeng, *China* 34 F8 36 28N 114 8 E
Fengjie, *China* 33 C5 31 5N 109 36 E
Fengning, *China* 34 D9 41 10N 116 33 E
Fengqiu, *China* 34 G8 35 2N 114 25 E
Fengrun, *China* 35 E10 39 48N 118 8 E
Fengtai, *China* 34 E9 39 50N 116 18 E
Fengxiang, *China* 34 G4 34 29N 107 25 E
Fengyang, *China* 35 H9 32 51N 117 29 E
Fengzhen, *China* 34 D7 40 25N 113 2 E
Fenit, *Ireland* 13 D2 52 17N 9 51W
Fennimore, *U.S.A.* 80 D9 42 59N 90 39W
Fenoarivo Afovoany, *Madag.* 57 B8 18 26S 46 34 E
Fenoarivo Atsinanana, *Madag.* 57 B8 17 22S 49 25 E
Fens, The, *U.K.* 10 E8 52 38N 0 2W
Fenton, *U.S.A.* 76 D4 42 48N 83 42W
Fenxi, *China* 34 F6 36 40N 111 31 E
Fenyang, *China* 34 F6 37 18N 111 48 E
Feodosiya, *Ukraine* 25 E6 45 2N 35 16 E
Ferdows, *Iran* 45 C8 33 58N 58 2 E
Ferfer, *Somali Rep.* 46 F4 5 4N 45 9 E
Fergana = Farghona, *Uzbekistan* 26 E8 40 23N 71 19 E
Fergus, *Canada* 70 D3 43 43N 80 24W
Fergus Falls, *U.S.A.* 80 B6 46 17N 96 4W
Ferland, *Canada* 70 B2 50 19N 88 27W
Fermanagh □, *U.K.* 13 B4 54 21N 7 40W
Fermo, *Italy* 20 C5 43 9N 13 43 E
Fermoy, *Ireland* 13 D3 52 9N 8 16W
Fernández, *Argentina* 94 B3 27 55S 63 50W
Fernandina Beach, *U.S.A.* 77 K5 30 40N 81 27W
Fernando de Noronha, *Brazil* 93 D12 4 0S 33 10W
Fernando Póo = Bioko, *Eq. Guin.* 50 H6 3 30N 8 40 E
Ferndale, *Calif., U.S.A.* 82 F1 40 35N 124 16W
Ferndale, *Wash., U.S.A.* 84 B4 48 51N 122 36W
Fernie, *Canada* 72 D5 49 30N 115 5W
Fernlees, *Australia* 62 C4 23 51S 148 7 E
Fernley, *U.S.A.* 82 G4 39 36N 119 15W
Ferozepore = Firozpur, *India* 42 D6 30 55N 74 40 E
Ferrara, *Italy* 20 B4 44 50N 11 35 E
Ferreñafe, *Peru* 92 E3 6 42S 79 50W
Ferrerías, *Spain* 22 B11 39 59N 4 1 E
Ferret, C., *France* 18 D3 44 38N 1 15W
Ferriday, *U.S.A.* 81 K9 31 38N 91 33W
Ferrol = El Ferrol, *Spain* 19 A1 43 29N 8 15W
Ferron, *U.S.A.* 83 G8 39 5N 111 8W
Ferryland, *Canada* 71 C9 47 2N 52 53W
Fertile, *U.S.A.* 80 B6 47 32N 96 17W
Fès, *Morocco* 50 B4 34 0N 5 0W
Feshi, *Zaïre* 52 F3 6 8S 18 10 E
Fessenden, *U.S.A.* 80 B5 47 39N 99 38W
Feteşti, *Romania* 17 F14 44 22N 27 51 E
Fetlar, *U.K.* 12 A8 60 36N 0 52W
Feuilles →, *Canada* 69 C12 58 47N 70 4W
Fezzan, *Libya* 51 C8 27 0N 15 0 E
Ffestiniog, *U.K.* 10 E4 52 57N 3 55W
Fiambalá, *Argentina* 94 B2 27 45S 67 37W
Fianarantsoa, *Madag.* 57 C8 21 26S 47 5 E
Fianarantsoa □, *Madag.* 57 B8 19 30S 47 0 E
Fianga, *Cameroon* 51 G8 9 55N 15 9 E
Ficksburg, *S. Africa* 57 D4 28 51S 27 53 E
Field, *Canada* 70 C3 46 31N 80 1W
Field →, *Australia* 62 C2 23 48S 138 0 E
Field I., *Australia* 60 B5 12 5S 132 23 E
Fieri, *Albania* 21 D8 40 43N 19 33 E
Fife □, *U.K.* 12 E5 56 16N 3 1W
Fife Ness, *U.K.* 12 E6 56 17N 2 35W
Figeac, *France* 18 D5 44 37N 2 2 E
Figtree, *Zimbabwe* 55 G2 20 22S 28 20 E
Figueira da Foz, *Portugal* 19 B1 40 7N 8 54W
Figueras, *Spain* 19 A7 42 18N 2 58 E
Figuig, *Morocco* 50 B4 32 5N 1 11W
Fihaonana, *Madag.* 57 B8 18 36S 47 12 E
Fiherenana, *Madag.* 57 B8 18 29S 48 24 E
Fiherenana →, *Madag.* 57 C7 23 19S 43 37 E
Fiji ■, *Pac. Oc.* 59 C8 17 20S 179 0 E
Filer, *U.S.A.* 82 E6 42 34N 114 37W
Filey, *U.K.* 10 C7 54 12N 0 18W
Filfla, *Malta* 23 D1 35 47N 14 24 E
Filiatrá, *Greece* 21 F9 37 9N 21 35 E
Filipstad, *Sweden* 9 G16 59 43N 14 9 E
Fillmore, *Canada* 73 D8 49 50N 103 25W
Fillmore, *Calif., U.S.A.* 85 L8 34 24N 118 55W
Fillmore, *Utah, U.S.A.* 83 G7 38 58N 112 20W
Finch, *Canada* 79 A9 45 11N 75 7W
Findhorn →, *U.K.* 12 D5 57 38N 3 38W
Findlay, *U.S.A.* 76 E4 41 2N 83 39W
Finger L., *Canada* 73 C10 53 33N 93 30W
Fingõe, *Mozam.* 55 E3 14 55S 31 50 E
Finisterre, C., *Spain* 19 A1 42 50N 9 19W
Finke, *Australia* 62 D1 25 34S 134 35 E
Finke →, *Australia* 63 D2 27 0S 136 10 E
Finland ■, *Europe* 8 E22 63 0N 27 0 E
Finland, G. of, *Europe* 9 G21 60 0N 26 0 E
Finlay →, *Canada* 72 B3 57 0N 125 10W
Finley, *Australia* 63 F4 35 38S 145 35 E
Finley, *U.S.A.* 80 B6 47 31N 97 50W
Finn →, *Ireland* 13 B4 54 51N 7 28W
Finnigan, Mt., *Australia* 62 B4 15 49S 145 17 E
Finniss, C., *Australia* 63 E1 33 8S 134 51 E
Finnmark, *Norway* 8 B20 69 37N 23 57 E
Finnsnes, *Norway* 8 B18 69 14N 18 0 E
Finspång, *Sweden* 9 G16 58 43N 15 47 E
Fiora →, *Italy* 20 C4 42 20N 11 34 E
Fiq, *Syria* 47 C4 32 46N 35 41 E
Firat = Furāt, Nahr al →, *Asia* 44 D5 31 0N 47 25 E
Fire River, *Canada* 70 C3 48 47N 83 21W
Firebag →, *Canada* 73 B6 57 45N 111 21W
Firebaugh, *U.S.A.* 84 J6 36 52N 120 27W
Firedrake L., *Canada* 73 A8 61 25N 104 30W
Firenze, *Italy* 20 C4 43 46N 11 15 E
Firk →, *Iraq* 44 D5 30 59N 44 34 E
Firozabad, *India* 43 F8 27 10N 78 25 E
Firozpur, *India* 42 D6 30 55N 74 40 E
Fīrūzābād, *Iran* 45 D7 28 52N 52 35 E
Fīrūzkūh, *Iran* 45 C7 35 50N 52 50 E
Firvale, *Canada* 72 C3 52 27N 126 13W
Fish →, *Namibia* 56 D2 28 7S 17 10 E
Fish →, *S. Africa* 56 E3 31 30S 20 16 E
Fisher, *Australia* 61 F5 30 30S 131 0 E
Fisher B., *Canada* 73 C9 51 35N 97 13W
Fishguard, *U.K.* 11 F3 52 0N 5 0W
Fishing L., *Canada* 73 C9 52 10N 95 24W
Fitchburg, *U.S.A.* 79 D13 42 35N 71 48W
Fitri, L., *Chad* 51 F8 12 50N 17 28 E
Fitz Roy, *Argentina* 96 F3 47 0S 67 0W
Fitzgerald, *Canada* 72 B6 59 51N 111 36W
Fitzgerald, *U.S.A.* 77 K4 31 43N 83 15W
Fitzmaurice →, *Australia* 60 B5 14 45S 130 5 E
Fitzroy →, *Queens., Australia* 62 C5 23 32S 150 52 E
Fitzroy →, *W. Austral., Australia* 60 C3 17 31S 123 35 E
Fitzroy Crossing, *Australia* 60 C4 18 9S 125 38 E
Fitzwilliam I., *Canada* 78 A3 45 30N 81 45W
Fiume = Rijeka, *Croatia* 16 F8 45 20N 14 21 E
Five Points, *U.S.A.* 84 J6 36 26N 120 6W
Fizi, *Zaïre* 54 C2 4 17S 28 55 E
Flagler, *U.S.A.* 80 F3 39 18N 103 4W
Flagstaff, *U.S.A.* 83 J8 35 12N 111 39W
Flaherty I., *Canada* 70 A4 56 15N 79 15W
Flåm, *Norway* 9 F12 60 50N 7 7 E
Flambeau →, *U.S.A.* 80 C9 45 18N 91 14W
Flamborough Hd., *U.K.* 10 C7 54 7N 0 5W
Flaming Gorge Dam, *U.S.A.* 82 F9 40 55N 109 25W
Flaming Gorge Reservoir, *U.S.A.* 82 F9 41 10N 109 25W
Flamingo, Teluk, *Indonesia* 37 F9 5 30S 138 0 E
Flanders = West-Vlaanderen □, *Belgium* 15 D3 51 0N 3 0 E
Flandre, *Europe* 16 C2 51 0N 3 0 E
Flandre Occidentale = West-Vlaanderen □, *Belgium* 15 D3 51 0N 3 0 E
Flandre Orientale = Oost-Vlaanderen □, *Belgium* 15 C3 51 5N 3 50 E
Flandreau, *U.S.A.* 80 C6 44 3N 96 36W
Flanigan, *U.S.A.* 84 E7 40 10N 119 53W
Flannan Is., *U.K.* 12 C1 58 9N 7 52W
Flåsjön, *Sweden* 8 D16 64 5N 15 40 E
Flat →, *Canada* 72 A3 61 33N 125 18W
Flat River, *U.S.A.* 81 G9 37 51N 90 31W
Flathead L., *U.S.A.* 82 C6 47 51N 114 8W
Flattery, C., *Australia* 62 A4 14 58S 145 21 E
Flattery, C., *U.S.A.* 84 B2 48 23N 124 29W
Flaxton, *U.S.A.* 80 A3 48 54N 102 24W
Fleetwood, *U.K.* 10 D4 53 55N 3 1W
Flekkefjord, *Norway* 9 G12 58 18N 6 39 E
Flemington, *U.S.A.* 78 E7 41 7N 77 28W
Flensburg, *Germany* 16 A5 54 47N 9 27 E
Flers, *France* 18 B3 48 47N 0 33W
Flesherton, *Canada* 78 B4 44 16N 80 33W
Flesko, Tanjung, *Indonesia* 37 D6 0 29N 124 30 E
Flevoland □, *Neths.* 15 B5 52 30N 5 30 E
Flin Flon, *Canada* 73 C8 54 46N 101 53W
Flinders →, *Australia* 62 B3 17 36S 140 36 E
Flinders B., *Australia* 61 F2 34 19S 115 19 E
Flinders Group, *Australia* 62 A3 14 11S 144 15 E
Flinders I., *Australia* 62 F4 40 0S 148 0 E
Flinders Ranges, *Australia* 63 E2 31 30S 138 30 E
Flinders Reefs, *Australia* 62 B4 17 37S 148 31 E
Flint, *U.K.* 10 D4 53 15N 3 9W
Flint, *U.S.A.* 76 D4 43 1N 83 41W
Flint →, *U.S.A.* 77 K3 30 57N 84 34W
Flint I., *Kiribati* 65 J12 11 26S 151 48W
Flinton, *Australia* 63 D4 27 55S 149 32 E
Flintshire □, *U.K.* 10 D4 53 17N 3 17W
Flodden, *U.K.* 10 B5 55 37N 2 8W
Floodwood, *U.S.A.* 80 B8 46 55N 92 55W
Flora, *U.S.A.* 76 F1 38 40N 88 29W
Florala, *U.S.A.* 77 K2 31 0N 86 20W
Florence = Firenze, *Italy* 20 C4 43 46N 11 15 E
Florence, *Ala., U.S.A.* 77 H2 34 48N 87 41W
Florence, *Ariz., U.S.A.* 83 K8 33 2N 111 23W
Florence, *Colo., U.S.A.* 80 F2 38 23N 105 8W
Florence, *Oreg., U.S.A.* 82 E1 43 58N 124 7W
Florence, *S.C., U.S.A.* 77 H6 34 12N 79 46W
Florence, L., *Australia* 63 D2 28 53S 138 9 E
Florennes, *Belgium* 15 D4 50 15N 4 35 E
Florenville, *Belgium* 15 E5 49 40N 5 19 E
Flores, *Guatemala* 88 C2 16 59N 89 50W
Flores, *Indonesia* 37 F6 8 35S 121 0 E
Flores I., *Canada* 72 D3 49 20N 126 10W
Flores Sea, *Indonesia* 37 F6 6 30S 120 0 E
Floreşti, *Moldova* 17 E15 47 53N 28 17 E
Floresville, *U.S.A.* 81 L5 29 8N 98 10W
Floriano, *Brazil* 93 E10 6 50S 43 0W
Florianópolis, *Brazil* 95 B6 27 30S 48 30W
Florida, *Cuba* 88 B4 21 32N 78 14W
Florida, *Uruguay* 95 C4 34 7S 56 10W
Florida □, *U.S.A.* 77 L5 28 0N 82 0W
Florida, Straits of, *U.S.A.* 88 B3 25 0N 80 0W
Florida B., *U.S.A.* 88 A3 25 0N 80 45W
Florida Keys, *U.S.A.* 75 F10 24 40N 81 0W
Flórina, *Greece* 21 D9 40 48N 21 26 E
Florø, *Norway* 9 F11 61 35N 5 1 E
Flower Station, *Canada* 79 A8 45 10N 76 41W
Flower's Cove, *Canada* 71 B8 51 14N 56 46W
Floydada, *U.S.A.* 81 J4 33 59N 101 20W
Fluk, *Indonesia* 37 E7 1 42S 127 44 E
Flushing = Vlissingen, *Neths.* 15 C3 51 26N 3 34 E
Flying Fish, C., *Antarctica* 5 D15 72 6S 102 29W
Foam Lake, *Canada* 73 C8 51 40N 103 32W
Foça, *Turkey* 21 E12 38 39N 26 46 E
Focşani, *Romania* 17 F14 45 41N 27 15 E
Fóggia, *Italy* 20 D6 41 27N 15 34 E
Fogo, *Canada* 71 C9 49 43N 54 17W
Fogo I., *Canada* 71 C9 49 40N 54 5W
Föhr, *Germany* 16 A5 54 43N 8 30 E
Foix, *France* 18 E4 42 58N 1 38 E
Folda, *Nord-Trøndelag, Norway* 8 D14 64 32N 10 30 E
Folda, *Nordland, Norway* 8 C16 67 38N 14 50 E
Foleyet, *Canada* 70 C3 48 15N 82 25W
Folgefonni, *Norway* 9 F12 60 3N 6 23 E
Foligno, *Italy* 20 C5 42 57N 12 42 E
Folkestone, *U.K.* 11 F9 51 5N 1 12 E
Folkston, *U.S.A.* 77 K5 30 50N 82 0W
Follett, *U.S.A.* 81 G4 36 26N 100 8W
Folsom Res., *U.S.A.* 84 G5 38 42N 121 9W
Fond-du-Lac, *Canada* 73 B7 59 19N 107 12W
Fond du Lac, *U.S.A.* 80 D10 43 47N 88 27W
Fond-du-Lac →, *Canada* 73 B7 59 17N 106 0W
Fonda, *U.S.A.* 79 D10 42 57N 74 22W
Fondi, *Italy* 20 D5 41 21N 13 25 E
Fonsagrada, *Spain* 19 A2 43 8N 7 4W
Fonseca, G. de, *Cent. Amer.* 88 D2 13 10N 87 40W
Fontainebleau, *France* 18 B5 48 24N 2 40 E
Fontana, *U.S.A.* 85 L9 34 6N 117 26W
Fontas →, *Canada* 72 B4 58 14N 121 48W
Fonte Boa, *Brazil* 92 D5 2 33S 66 0W
Fontenay-le-Comte, *France* 18 C3 46 28N 0 48W
Fontur, *Iceland* 8 C6 66 23N 14 32W
Foochow = Fuzhou, *China* 33 D6 26 5N 119 16 E
Foping, *China* 34 H4 33 41N 108 0 E
Forbes, *Australia* 63 E4 33 22S 148 0 E
Forbesganj, *India* 43 F12 26 17N 87 18 E
Ford City, *Calif., U.S.A.* 85 K7 35 9N 119 27W
Ford City, *Pa., U.S.A.* 78 F5 40 46N 79 32W
Førde, *Norway* 9 F11 61 27N 5 53 E
Ford's Bridge, *Australia* 63 D4 29 41S 145 29 E
Fordyce, *U.S.A.* 81 J8 33 49N 92 25W
Forécariah, *Guinea* 50 G2 9 28N 13 10W
Forel, Mt., *Greenland* 4 C6 66 52N 36 55W
Foremost, *Canada* 72 D6 49 26N 111 34W
Forest, *Canada* 78 C3 43 6N 82 0W
Forest, *U.S.A.* 81 J10 32 22N 89 29W
Forest City, *Iowa, U.S.A.* 80 D8 43 16N 93 39W
Forest City, *N.C., U.S.A.* 77 H5 35 20N 81 52W
Forest City, *Pa., U.S.A.* 79 E9 41 39N 75 28W
Forest Grove, *U.S.A.* 84 E3 45 31N 123 7W
Forestburg, *Canada* 72 C6 52 35N 112 1W
Foresthill, *U.S.A.* 84 F6 39 1N 120 49W
Forestier Pen., *Australia* 62 G4 43 0S 148 0 E
Forestville, *Canada* 71 C6 48 48N 69 2W
Forestville, *Calif., U.S.A.* 84 G4 38 28N 122 54W
Forestville, *Wis., U.S.A.* 76 C2 44 41N 87 29W
Forfar, *U.K.* 12 E6 56 39N 2 53W
Forks, *U.S.A.* 84 C2 47 57N 124 23W
Forlì, *Italy* 20 B5 44 13N 12 3 E
Forman, *U.S.A.* 80 B6 46 7N 97 38W
Formby Pt., *U.K.* 10 D4 53 33N 3 6W
Formentera, *Spain* 22 C7 38 43N 1 27 E
Formentor, C. de, *Spain* 22 B10 39 58N 3 13 E
Former Yugoslav Republic of Macedonia = Macedonia ■, *Europe* 21 D9 41 53N 21 40 E
Fórmia, *Italy* 20 D5 41 15N 13 37 E
Formosa = Taiwan ■, *Asia* 33 D7 23 30N 121 0 E
Formosa, *Argentina* 94 B4 26 15S 58 10W
Formosa □, *Argentina* 94 B3 25 0S 60 0W
Formosa, Serra, *Brazil* 93 F8 12 0S 55 0W
Formosa Bay, *Kenya* 54 C5 2 40S 40 20 E
Fornells, *Spain* 22 A11 40 3N 4 7 E
Føroyar, *Atl. Oc.* 8 F9 62 0N 7 0W
Forres, *U.K.* 12 D5 57 37N 3 37W
Forrest, *Vic., Australia* 63 F3 38 33S 143 47 E
Forrest, *W. Austral., Australia* 61 F4 30 51S 128 6 E
Forrest, Mt., *Australia* 61 D4 24 48S 127 45 E
Forrest City, *U.S.A.* 81 H9 35 1N 90 47W
Forsayth, *Australia* 62 B3 18 33S 143 34 E
Forssa, *Finland* 9 F20 60 49N 23 38 E
Forst, *Germany* 16 C8 51 45N 14 37 E
Forster, *Australia* 63 E5 32 12S 152 31 E
Forsyth, *Ga., U.S.A.* 77 J4 33 2N 83 56W
Forsyth, *Mont., U.S.A.* 82 C10 46 16N 106 41W
Fort Albany, *Canada* 70 B3 52 15N 81 35W
Fort Apache, *U.S.A.* 83 K9 33 50N 110 0W
Fort Assiniboine, *Canada* 72 C6 54 20N 114 45W
Fort Augustus, *U.K.* 12 D4 57 9N 4 42W
Fort Beaufort, *S. Africa* 56 E4 32 46S 26 40 E
Fort Benton, *U.S.A.* 82 C8 47 49N 110 40W
Fort Bragg, *U.S.A.* 82 G2 39 26N 123 48W
Fort Bridger, *U.S.A.* 82 F8 41 19N 110 23W
Fort Chipewyan, *Canada* 73 B6 58 42N 111 8W
Fort Collins, *U.S.A.* 80 E2 40 35N 105 5W
Fort-Coulonge, *Canada* 70 C4 45 50N 76 45W
Fort Davis, *U.S.A.* 81 K3 30 35N 103 54W
Fort-de-France, *Martinique* 89 D7 14 36N 61 2W
Fort de Possel = Possel, *C.A.R.* 52 C3 5 5N 19 10 E
Fort Defiance, *U.S.A.* 83 J9 35 45N 109 5W
Fort Dodge, *U.S.A.* 80 D7 42 30N 94 11W
Fort Edward, *U.S.A.* 79 C11 43 16N 73 35W
Fort Frances, *Canada* 73 D10 48 36N 93 24W
Fort Garland, *U.S.A.* 83 H11 37 26N 105 26W
Fort George = Chisasibi, *Canada* 70 B4 53 50N 79 0W
Fort Good-Hope, *Canada* 68 B7 66 14N 128 40W
Fort Hancock, *U.S.A.* 83 L11 31 18N 105 51W
Fort Hertz = Putao, *Burma* 41 F20 27 28N 97 30 E
Fort Hope, *Canada* 70 B2 51 30N 88 0W
Fort Irwin, *U.S.A.* 85 K10 35 16N 116 34W
Fort Jameson = Chipata, *Zambia* 55 E3 13 38S 32 28 E
Fort Kent, *U.S.A.* 71 C6 47 15N 68 36W
Fort Klamath, *U.S.A.* 82 E3 42 42N 122 0W
Fort-Lamy = Ndjamena, *Chad* 51 F7 12 10N 14 59 E
Fort Laramie, *U.S.A.* 80 D2 42 13N 104 31W
Fort Lauderdale, *U.S.A.* 77 M5 26 7N 80 8W
Fort Liard, *Canada* 72 A4 60 14N 123 30W
Fort Liberté, *Haiti* 89 C5 19 42N 71 51W
Fort Lupton, *U.S.A.* 80 E2 40 5N 104 49W
Fort Mackay, *Canada* 72 B6 57 12N 111 41W
Fort McKenzie, *Canada* 71 A6 57 20N 69 0W
Fort Macleod, *Canada* 72 D6 49 45N 113 30W
Fort MacMahon, *Algeria* 50 C5 29 43N 1 45 E
Fort McMurray, *Canada* 72 B6 56 44N 111 7W
Fort McPherson, *Canada* 68 B6 67 30N 134 55W
Fort Madison, *U.S.A.* 80 E9 40 38N 91 27W
Fort Meade, *U.S.A.* 77 M5 27 45N 81 48W
Fort Miribel, *Algeria* 50 C5 29 25N 2 55 E
Fort Morgan, *U.S.A.* 80 E3 40 15N 103 48W
Fort Myers, *U.S.A.* 77 M5 26 39N 81 52W
Fort Nelson, *Canada* 72 B4 58 50N 122 44W
Fort Nelson →, *Canada* 72 B4 59 32N 124 0W
Fort Norman = Tulita, *Canada* 68 B7 64 57N 125 30W
Fort Payne, *U.S.A.* 77 H3 34 26N 85 43W
Fort Peck, *U.S.A.* 82 B10 48 1N 106 27W
Fort Peck Dam, *U.S.A.* 82 C10 48 0N 106 26W
Fort Peck L., *U.S.A.* 82 C10 48 0N 106 26W
Fort Pierce, *U.S.A.* 77 M5 27 27N 80 20W
Fort Pierre, *U.S.A.* 80 C4 44 21N 100 22W
Fort Plain, *U.S.A.* 79 D10 42 56N 74 37W
Fort Portal, *Uganda* 54 B3 0 40N 30 20 E
Fort Providence, *Canada* 72 A5 61 3N 117 40W
Fort Qu'Appelle, *Canada* 73 C8 50 45N 103 50W
Fort Resolution, *Canada* 72 A6 61 10N 113 40W
Fort Rixon, *Zimbabwe* 55 G2 20 2S 29 17 E
Fort Rosebery = Mansa, *Zambia* 55 E2 11 13S 28 55 E
Fort Ross, *U.S.A.* 84 G3 38 32N 123 13W
Fort Rupert = Waskaganish, *Canada* 70 B4 51 30N 78 40W
Fort St. James, *Canada* 72 C4 54 30N 124 10W
Fort St. John, *Canada* 72 B4 56 15N 120 50W
Fort Sandeman, *Pakistan* 42 D3 31 20N 69 31 E
Fort Saskatchewan, *Canada* 72 C6 53 40N 113 15W
Fort Scott, *U.S.A.* 81 G7 37 50N 94 42W
Fort Severn, *Canada* 70 A2 56 0N 87 40W
Fort Shevchenko, *Kazakstan* 25 F9 44 35N 50 23 E
Fort Simpson, *Canada* 72 A4 61 45N 121 15W
Fort Smith, *Canada* 72 B6 60 0N 111 51W
Fort Smith, *U.S.A.* 81 H7 35 23N 94 25W
Fort Stanton, *U.S.A.* 83 K11 33 30N 105 31W
Fort Stockton, *U.S.A.* 81 K3 30 53N 102 53W
Fort Sumner, *U.S.A.* 81 H2 34 28N 104 15W
Fort Trinquet = Bir Mogrein, *Mauritania* 50 C2 25 10N 11 25W
Fort Valley, *U.S.A.* 77 J4 32 33N 83 53W
Fort Vermilion, *Canada* 72 B5 58 24N 116 0W
Fort Walton Beach, *U.S.A.* 77 K2 30 25N 86 36W
Fort Wayne, *U.S.A.* 76 E3 41 4N 85 9W
Fort William, *U.K.* 12 E3 56 49N 5 7W
Fort Worth, *U.S.A.* 81 J6 32 45N 97 18W
Fort Yates, *U.S.A.* 80 B4 46 5N 100 38W
Fort Yukon, *U.S.A.* 68 B5 66 34N 145 16W
Fortaleza, *Brazil* 93 D11 3 45S 38 35W
Forteau, *Canada* 71 B8 51 28N 56 58W
Forth →, *U.K.* 12 E5 56 9N 3 50W
Forth, Firth of, *U.K.* 12 E6 56 5N 2 55W
Fortrose, *U.K.* 12 D4 57 35N 4 9W
Fortuna, *Calif., U.S.A.* 82 F1 40 36N 124 9W
Fortuna, *N. Dak., U.S.A.* 80 A3 48 55N 103 47W
Fortune B., *Canada* 71 C8 47 30N 55 22W
Foshan, *China* 33 D6 23 4N 113 5 E
Fosna, *Norway* 8 E14 63 50N 10 20 E
Fosnavåg, *Norway* 9 E11 62 22N 5 38 E
Fossano, *Italy* 20 B2 44 33N 7 43 E
Fossil, *U.S.A.* 82 D3 45 0N 120 9W
Fossilbrook, *Australia* 62 B3 17 47S 144 29 E
Fosston, *U.S.A.* 80 B7 47 35N 95 45W
Foster, *Canada* 79 A12 45 17N 72 30W
Foster →, *Canada* 73 B7 55 47N 105 49W
Fosters Ra., *Australia* 62 C1 21 35S 133 48 E
Fostoria, *U.S.A.* 76 E4 41 10N 83 25W

Garmāb

Garmāb, *Iran* **45 C8** 35 25N 56 45 E
Garmisch-Partenkirchen, *Germany* **16 E6** 47 30N 11 6 E
Garmsār, *Iran* **45 C7** 35 20N 52 25 E
Garner, *U.S.A.* **80 D8** 43 6N 93 36W
Garnett, *U.S.A.* **80 F7** 38 17N 95 14W
Garo Hills, *India* **43 G14** 25 30N 90 30 E
Garoe, *Somali Rep.* **46 F4** 8 25N 48 33 E
Garonne →, *France* **18 D3** 45 2N 0 36W
Garoua, *Cameroon* **51 G7** 9 19N 13 21 E
Garrison, *Mont., U.S.A.* **82 C7** 46 31N 112 49W
Garrison, *N. Dak., U.S.A.* **80 B4** 47 40N 101 25W
Garrison, *Tex., U.S.A.* **81 K7** 31 49N 94 30W
Garrison Res. = Sakakawea, L., *U.S.A.* **80 B3** 47 30N 101 25W
Garry →, *U.K.* **12 E5** 56 44N 3 47W
Garry, L., *Canada* **68 B9** 65 58N 100 18W
Garsen, *Kenya* **54 C5** 2 20S 40 5 E
Garson L., *Canada* **73 B6** 56 19N 110 2W
Garub, *Namibia* **56 D2** 26 37S 16 0 E
Garut, *Indonesia* **37 G12** 7 14S 107 53 E
Garvie Mts., *N.Z.* **59 L2** 45 30S 168 50 E
Garwa = Garoua, *Cameroon* **51 G7** 9 19N 13 21 E
Garwa, *India* **43 G10** 24 11N 83 47 E
Gary, *U.S.A.* **76 E2** 41 36N 87 20W
Garzê, *China* **32 C5** 31 38N 100 1 E
Garzón, *Colombia* **92 C3** 2 10N 75 40W
Gas-San, *Japan* **30 E10** 38 32N 140 1 E
Gasan Kuli = Esenguly, *Turkmenistan* **26 F6** 37 37N 53 59 E
Gascogne, *France* **18 E4** 43 45N 0 20 E
Gascogne, G. de, *Europe* **18 D2** 44 0N 2 0W
Gascony = Gascogne, *France* **18 E4** 43 45N 0 20 E
Gascoyne →, *Australia* **61 D1** 24 52S 113 37 E
Gascoyne Junc. T.O., *Australia* **61 E2** 25 2S 115 17 E
Gashaka, *Nigeria* **50 G7** 7 20N 11 29 E
Gasherbrum, *Pakistan* **43 B7** 35 40N 76 40 E
Gaspé, *Canada* **71 C7** 48 52N 64 30W
Gaspé, C. de, *Canada* **71 C7** 48 48N 64 7W
Gaspé, Pén. de, *Canada* **71 C6** 48 45N 65 40W
Gaspésie, Parc Prov. de la, *Canada* **71 C6** 48 55N 65 50W
Gassaway, *U.S.A.* **76 F5** 38 41N 80 47W
Gasteiz = Vitoria, *Spain* **19 A4** 42 50N 2 41W
Gastonia, *U.S.A.* **77 H5** 35 16N 81 11W
Gastre, *Argentina* **96 E3** 42 20S 69 15W
Gata, C., *Cyprus* **23 E12** 34 34N 33 2 E
Gata, C. de, *Spain* **19 D4** 36 41N 2 13W
Gata, Sierra de, *Spain* **19 B2** 40 20N 6 45W
Gataga →, *Canada* **72 B3** 58 35N 126 59W
Gates, *U.S.A.* **78 C7** 43 9N 77 42W
Gateshead, *U.K.* **10 C6** 54 57N 1 35W
Gatesville, *U.S.A.* **81 K6** 31 26N 97 45W
Gaths, *Zimbabwe* **55 G3** 20 2S 30 32 E
Gatico, *Chile* **94 A1** 22 29S 70 20W
Gatineau →, *Canada* **70 C4** 45 27N 75 42W
Gatineau, Parc de la, *Canada* **70 C4** 45 40N 76 0W
Gatun, L., *Panama* **88 E4** 9 7N 79 56W
Gatyana, *S. Africa* **57 E4** 32 16S 28 31 E
Gau, *Fiji* **59 D8** 18 2S 179 18 E
Gauer L., *Canada* **73 B9** 57 0N 97 50W
Gauhati, *India* **43 F14** 26 10N 91 45 E
Gauja →, *Latvia* **9 H21** 57 10N 24 16 E
Gaula →, *Norway* **8 E14** 63 21N 10 14 E
Gausta, *Norway* **9 G13** 59 48N 8 40 E
Gauteng □, *S. Africa* **57 D4** 26 0S 28 0 E
Gāv Koshī, *Iran* **45 D8** 28 38N 57 12 E
Gāvakān, *Iran* **45 D7** 29 37N 53 10 E
Gavāter, *Iran* **45 E9** 25 10N 61 31 E
Gāvbandī, *Iran* **45 E7** 27 12N 53 4 E
Gavdhopoúla, *Greece* **23 E6** 34 56N 24 0 E
Gávdhos, *Greece* **23 E6** 34 50N 24 5 E
Gaviota, *U.S.A.* **85 L6** 34 29N 120 13W
Gävle, *Sweden* **9 F17** 60 40N 17 9 E
Gawachab, *Namibia* **56 D2** 27 4S 17 55 E
Gawilgarh Hills, *India* **40 J10** 21 15N 76 45 E
Gawler, *Australia* **63 E2** 34 30S 138 42 E
Gaxun Nur, *China* **32 B5** 42 22N 100 30 E
Gay, *Russia* **24 D10** 51 27N 58 27 E
Gaya, *India* **43 G11** 24 47N 85 4 E
Gaya, *Niger* **50 F5** 11 52N 3 28 E
Gaylord, *U.S.A.* **76 C3** 45 2N 84 41W
Gayndah, *Australia* **63 D5** 25 35S 151 32 E
Gaysin = Haysyn, *Ukraine* **17 D15** 48 57N 29 25 E
Gayvoron = Hayvoron, *Ukraine* **17 D15** 48 22N 29 52 E
Gaza, *Gaza Strip* **47 D3** 31 30N 34 28 E
Gaza □, *Mozam.* **57 C5** 23 10S 32 45 E
Gaza Strip □, *Asia* **47 D3** 31 29N 34 25 E
Gāzbor, *Iran* **45 D8** 28 5N 58 51 E
Gazi, *Zaïre* **54 B1** 1 3N 24 30 E
Gaziantep, *Turkey* **25 G6** 37 6N 37 23 E
Gazli, *Uzbekistan* **26 E7** 40 14N 63 24 E
Gcuwa, *S. Africa* **57 E4** 32 20S 28 11 E
Gdańsk, *Poland* **17 A10** 54 22N 18 40 E
Gdańska, Zatoka, *Poland* **17 A10** 54 30N 19 20 E
Gdov, *Russia* **9 G22** 58 48N 27 55 E
Gdynia, *Poland* **17 A10** 54 35N 18 33 E
Gebe, *Indonesia* **37 D7** 0 5N 129 25 E
Gebeit Mine, *Sudan* **51 D12** 21 3N 36 29 E
Gebze, *Turkey* **21 D13** 40 47N 29 25 E
Gedaref, *Sudan* **51 F12** 14 2N 35 28 E
Gede, Tanjung, *Indonesia* **36 F3** 6 46S 105 12 E
Gediz →, *Turkey* **21 E12** 38 35N 26 48 E
Gedser, *Denmark* **9 J14** 54 35N 11 55 E
Geegully Cr. →, *Australia* **60 C3** 18 32S 123 41 E
Geelong, *Australia* **63 F3** 38 10S 144 22 E
Geelvink Chan., *Australia* **61 E1** 28 30S 114 0 E
Geesthacht, *Germany* **16 B6** 53 26N 10 22 E
Geidam, *Nigeria* **51 F7** 12 57N 11 57 E
Geikie →, *Canada* **73 B8** 57 45N 103 52W
Geili, *Sudan* **51 E11** 16 1N 32 37 E
Geita, *Tanzania* **54 C3** 2 48S 32 12 E
Geita □, *Tanzania* **54 C3** 2 50S 32 10 E
Gejiu, *China* **32 D5** 23 20N 103 10 E
Gela, *Italy* **20 F6** 37 4N 14 15 E
Geladi, *Ethiopia* **46 F4** 6 59N 46 30 E
Gelderland □, *Neths.* **15 B6** 52 5N 6 10 E
Geldermalsen, *Neths.* **15 C5** 51 53N 5 17 E
Geldrop, *Neths.* **15 C5** 51 25N 5 32 E
Geleen, *Neths.* **15 D5** 50 57N 5 49 E
Gelehun, *S. Leone* **50 G2** 8 20N 11 40W
Gelibolu, *Turkey* **21 D12** 40 28N 26 43 E
Gelsenkirchen, *Germany* **16 C4** 51 32N 7 1 E
Gemas, *Malaysia* **39 L4** 2 37N 102 36 E
Gembloux, *Belgium* **15 D4** 50 34N 4 43 E
Gemena, *Zaïre* **52 D3** 3 13N 19 48 E
Gemlik, *Turkey* **21 D13** 40 26N 29 9 E
Gendringen, *Neths.* **15 C6** 51 52N 6 21 E
General Acha, *Argentina* **94 D3** 37 20S 64 38W
General Alvear, *Buenos Aires, Argentina* **94 D3** 36 0S 60 0W
General Alvear, *Mendoza, Argentina* **94 D2** 35 0S 67 40W
General Artigas, *Paraguay* **94 B4** 26 52S 56 16W
General Belgrano, *Argentina* **94 D4** 36 35S 58 47W
General Cabrera, *Argentina* **94 C3** 32 53S 63 52W
General Cepeda, *Mexico* **86 B4** 25 23N 101 27W
General Guido, *Argentina* **94 D4** 36 40S 57 50W
General Juan Madariaga, *Argentina* **94 D4** 37 0S 57 0W
General La Madrid, *Argentina* **94 D3** 37 17S 61 20W
General MacArthur, *Phil.* **37 B7** 11 18N 125 28 E
General Martin Miguel de Güemes, *Argentina* **94 A3** 24 50S 65 0W
General Paz, *Argentina* **94 B4** 27 45S 57 36W
General Pico, *Argentina* **94 D3** 35 45S 63 50W
General Pinedo, *Argentina* **94 B3** 27 15S 61 20W
General Pinto, *Argentina* **94 C3** 34 45S 61 50W
General Santos, *Phil.* **37 C7** 6 5N 125 14 E
General Trevino, *Mexico* **87 B5** 26 14N 99 29W
General Trías, *Mexico* **86 B3** 28 21N 106 22W
General Viamonte, *Argentina* **94 D3** 35 1S 61 3W
General Villegas, *Argentina* **94 D3** 35 5S 63 0W
Genesee, *Idaho, U.S.A.* **82 C5** 46 33N 116 56W
Genesee, *Pa., U.S.A.* **78 E7** 41 59N 77 54W
Genesee →, *U.S.A.* **78 C7** 43 16N 77 36W
Geneseo, *Ill., U.S.A.* **80 E9** 41 27N 90 9W
Geneseo, *Kans., U.S.A.* **80 F5** 38 31N 98 10W
Geneseo, *N.Y., U.S.A.* **78 D7** 42 48N 77 49W
Geneva = Genève, *Switz.* **16 E4** 46 12N 6 9 E
Geneva, *Ala., U.S.A.* **77 K3** 31 2N 85 52W
Geneva, *N.Y., U.S.A.* **78 D7** 42 52N 76 59W
Geneva, *Nebr., U.S.A.* **80 E6** 40 32N 97 36W
Geneva, *Ohio, U.S.A.* **78 E4** 41 48N 80 57W
Geneva, L. = Léman, L., *Europe* **16 E4** 46 26N 6 30 E
Geneva, L., *U.S.A.* **76 D1** 42 38N 88 30W
Genève, *Switz.* **16 E4** 46 12N 6 9 E
Genil →, *Spain* **19 D3** 37 42N 5 19W
Genk, *Belgium* **15 D5** 50 58N 5 32 E
Gennargentu, Mti. del, *Italy* **20 D3** 40 1N 9 19 E
Gennep, *Neths.* **15 C5** 51 41N 5 59 E
Genoa = Génova, *Italy* **20 B3** 44 25N 8 57 E
Genoa, *Australia* **63 F4** 37 29S 149 35 E
Genoa, *N.Y., U.S.A.* **79 D8** 42 40N 76 32W
Genoa, *Nebr., U.S.A.* **80 E6** 41 27N 97 44W
Genoa, *Nev., U.S.A.* **84 F7** 39 2N 119 50W
Génova, *Italy* **20 B3** 44 25N 8 57 E
Génova, G. di, *Italy* **20 C3** 44 0N 9 0 E
Gent, *Belgium* **15 C3** 51 2N 3 42 E
Geographe B., *Australia* **61 F2** 33 30S 115 15 E
Geographe Chan., *Australia* **61 D1** 24 30S 113 0 E
Georga, Zemlya, *Russia* **26 A5** 80 30N 49 0 E
George, *S. Africa* **56 E3** 33 58S 22 29 E
George →, *Canada* **71 A6** 58 49N 66 10W
George, L., *N.S.W., Australia* **63 F4** 35 10S 149 25 E
George, L., *S. Austral., Australia* **63 F3** 37 25S 140 0 E
George, L., *W. Austral., Australia* **60 D3** 22 45S 123 40 E
George, L., *Uganda* **54 B3** 0 5N 30 10 E
George, L., *Fla., U.S.A.* **77 L5** 29 17N 81 36W
George, L., *N.Y., U.S.A.* **79 C11** 43 37N 73 33W
George Gill Ra., *Australia* **60 D5** 24 22S 131 45 E
George River = Kangiqsualujjuaq, *Canada* **69 C13** 58 30N 65 59W
George Sound, *N.Z.* **59 L1** 44 52S 167 25 E
George Town, *Bahamas* **88 B4** 23 33N 75 47W
George Town, *Malaysia* **39 K3** 5 25N 100 15 E
George V Land, *Antarctica* **5 C10** 69 0S 148 0 E
George VI Sound, *Antarctica* **5 D17** 71 0S 68 0W
George West, *U.S.A.* **81 L5** 28 20N 98 7W
Georgetown, *Australia* **62 B3** 18 17S 143 33 E
Georgetown, *Ont., Canada* **70 D4** 43 40N 79 56W
Georgetown, *P.E.I., Canada* **71 C7** 46 13N 62 24W
Georgetown, *Cayman Is.* **88 C3** 19 20N 81 24W
Georgetown, *Gambia* **50 F2** 13 30N 14 47W
Georgetown, *Guyana* **92 B7** 6 50N 58 12W
Georgetown, *Calif., U.S.A.* **84 G6** 38 54N 120 50W
Georgetown, *Colo., U.S.A.* **82 G11** 39 42N 105 42W
Georgetown, *Ky., U.S.A.* **76 F3** 38 13N 84 33W
Georgetown, *S.C., U.S.A.* **77 J6** 33 23N 79 17W
Georgetown, *Tex., U.S.A.* **81 K6** 30 38N 97 41W
Georgia □, *U.S.A.* **77 J4** 32 50N 83 15W
Georgia ■, *Asia* **25 F7** 42 0N 43 0 E
Georgia, Str. of, *Canada* **72 D4** 49 25N 124 0W
Georgian B., *Canada* **70 C3** 45 15N 81 0W
Georgina →, *Australia* **62 C2** 23 30S 139 47 E
Georgina Downs, *Australia* **62 C2** 21 10S 137 40 E
Georgiu-Dezh = Liski, *Russia* **25 D6** 51 3N 39 30 E
Georgiyevsk, *Russia* **25 F7** 44 12N 43 28 E
Gera, *Germany* **16 C7** 50 53N 12 4 E
Geraardsbergen, *Belgium* **15 D3** 50 45N 3 53 E
Geral, Serra, *Brazil* **95 B6** 26 25S 50 0W
Geral de Goiás, Serra, *Brazil* **93 F9** 12 0S 46 0W
Geraldine, *U.S.A.* **82 C8** 47 36N 110 16W
Geraldton, *Australia* **61 E1** 28 48S 114 32 E
Geraldton, *Canada* **70 C2** 49 44N 86 59W
Gereshk, *Afghan.* **40 D4** 31 47N 64 35 E
Gerik, *Malaysia* **39 K3** 5 50N 101 15 E
Gering, *U.S.A.* **80 E3** 41 50N 103 40W
Gerlach, *U.S.A.* **82 F4** 40 39N 119 21W
Gerlogubi, *Ethiopia* **46 F4** 6 53N 45 3 E
Germansen Landing, *Canada* **72 B4** 55 43N 124 40W
Germany ■, *Europe* **16 C6** 51 0N 10 0 E
Germiston, *S. Africa* **57 D4** 26 15S 28 10 E
Gero, *Japan* **31 G8** 35 48N 137 14 E
Gerona, *Spain* **19 B7** 41 58N 2 46 E
Gerrard, *Canada* **72 C5** 50 30N 117 17W
Geser, *Indonesia* **37 E8** 3 50S 130 54 E
Getafe, *Spain* **19 B4** 40 18N 3 44W
Gethsémani, *Canada* **71 B7** 50 13N 60 40W
Gettysburg, *Pa., U.S.A.* **76 F7** 39 50N 77 14W
Gettysburg, *S. Dak., U.S.A.* **80 C5** 45 1N 99 57W
Getz Ice Shelf, *Antarctica* **5 D14** 75 0S 130 0W
Geyser, *U.S.A.* **82 C8** 47 16N 110 30W
Geyserville, *U.S.A.* **84 G4** 38 42N 122 54W
Ghaghara →, *India* **43 G11** 25 45N 84 40 E
Ghana ■, *W. Afr.* **50 G4** 8 0N 1 0W
Ghansor, *India* **43 H9** 22 39N 80 1 E
Ghanzi, *Botswana* **56 C3** 21 50S 21 34 E
Ghanzi □, *Botswana* **56 C3** 21 50S 21 45 E
Ghardaïa, *Algeria* **50 B5** 32 20N 3 37 E
Gharyān, *Libya* **51 B7** 32 10N 13 0 E
Ghat, *Libya* **50 D7** 24 59N 10 11 E
Ghatal, *India* **43 H12** 22 40N 87 46 E
Ghatampur, *India* **43 F9** 26 8N 80 13 E
Ghaṭṭī, *Si. Arabia* **44 D3** 31 16N 37 31 E
Ghawdex = Gozo, *Malta* **23 C1** 36 3N 14 13 E
Ghazal, Bahr el →, *Chad* **51 F8** 13 0N 15 47 E
Ghazâl, Bahr el →, *Sudan* **51 G11** 9 31N 30 25 E
Ghazaouet, *Algeria* **50 A4** 35 8N 1 50W
Ghaziabad, *India* **42 E7** 28 42N 77 26 E
Ghazipur, *India* **43 G10** 25 38N 83 35 E
Ghaznī, *Afghan.* **42 C3** 33 30N 68 28 E
Ghaznī □, *Afghan.* **40 C6** 32 10N 68 20 E
Ghèlinsor, *Somali Rep.* **46 F4** 6 28N 46 39 E
Ghent = Gent, *Belgium* **15 C3** 51 2N 3 42 E
Ghizao, *Afghan.* **42 C1** 33 20N 65 44 E
Ghizar →, *Pakistan* **43 A5** 36 15N 73 43 E
Ghogha, *India* **42 J5** 21 40N 72 20 E
Ghotaru, *India* **42 F4** 27 20N 70 1 E
Ghotki, *Pakistan* **42 E3** 28 5N 69 21 E
Ghowr □, *Afghan.* **40 C4** 34 0N 64 20 E
Ghudaf, W. al →, *Iraq* **44 C4** 32 56N 43 30 E
Ghudāmis, *Libya* **49 C4** 30 11N 9 29 E
Ghughri, *India* **43 H9** 22 39N 80 41 E
Ghugus, *India* **40 K11** 19 58N 79 12 E
Ghulam Mohammad Barrage, *Pakistan* **42 G3** 25 30N 68 20 E
Ghūrīān, *Afghan.* **40 B2** 34 17N 61 25 E
Gia Dinh, *Vietnam* **39 G6** 10 49N 106 42 E
Gia Lai = Pleiku, *Vietnam* **38 F7** 13 57N 108 0 E
Gia Nghia, *Vietnam* **39 G6** 11 58N 107 42 E
Gia Ngoc, *Vietnam* **38 E7** 14 50N 108 58 E
Gia Vuc, *Vietnam* **38 E7** 14 42N 108 34 E
Gian, *Phil.* **37 C7** 5 45N 125 20 E
Giant Forest, *U.S.A.* **84 J8** 36 36N 118 43W
Giants Causeway, *U.K.* **13 A5** 55 16N 6 29W
Giarabub = Al Jaghbūb, *Libya* **51 C9** 29 42N 24 38 E
Giarre, *Italy* **20 F6** 37 43N 15 11 E
Gibara, *Cuba* **88 B4** 21 9N 76 11W
Gibb River, *Australia* **60 C4** 16 26S 126 26 E
Gibbon, *U.S.A.* **80 E5** 40 45N 98 51W
Gibraltar ■, *Europe* **19 D3** 36 7N 5 22W
Gibraltar, Str. of, *Medit. S.* **19 E3** 35 55N 5 40W
Gibson Desert, *Australia* **60 D4** 24 0S 126 0 E
Gibsons, *Canada* **72 D4** 49 24N 123 32W
Gibsonville, *U.S.A.* **84 F6** 39 46N 120 54W
Giddings, *U.S.A.* **81 K6** 30 11N 96 56W
Gidole, *Ethiopia* **51 G12** 5 40N 37 25 E
Giessen, *Germany* **16 C5** 50 34N 8 41 E
Gīfān, *Iran* **45 B8** 37 54N 57 28 E
Gifford Creek, *Australia* **60 D2** 24 3S 116 16 E
Gifu, *Japan* **31 G8** 35 30N 136 45 E
Gifu □, *Japan* **31 G8** 35 40N 137 0 E
Giganta, Sa. de la, *Mexico* **86 B2** 25 30N 111 30W
Gigha, *U.K.* **12 F3** 55 42N 5 44W
Giglio, *Italy* **20 C4** 42 20N 10 52 E
Gijón, *Spain* **19 A3** 43 32N 5 42W
Gil I., *Canada* **72 C3** 53 12N 129 15W
Gila →, *U.S.A.* **83 K6** 32 43N 114 33W
Gila Bend, *U.S.A.* **83 K7** 32 57N 112 43W
Gila Bend Mts., *U.S.A.* **83 K7** 33 10N 113 0W
Gīlān □, *Iran* **45 B6** 37 0N 50 0 E
Gilbert →, *Australia* **62 B3** 16 35S 141 15 E
Gilbert Is., *Kiribati* **64 G9** 1 0N 172 0 E
Gilbert Plains, *Canada* **73 C8** 51 9N 100 28W
Gilbert River, *Australia* **62 B3** 18 9S 142 52 E
Gilberton, *Australia* **62 B3** 19 16S 143 35 E
Gilford I., *Canada* **72 C3** 50 40N 126 30W
Gilgandra, *Australia* **63 E4** 31 43S 148 39 E
Gilgil, *Kenya* **54 C4** 0 30S 36 20 E
Gilgit, *India* **43 B6** 35 50N 74 15 E
Gilgit →, *Pakistan* **43 B6** 35 44N 74 37 E
Gillam, *Canada* **73 B10** 56 20N 94 40W
Gillen, L., *Australia* **61 E3** 26 11S 124 38 E
Gilles, L., *Australia* **63 E2** 32 50S 136 45 E
Gillette, *U.S.A.* **80 C2** 44 18N 105 30W
Gilliat, *Australia* **62 C3** 20 40S 141 28 E
Gillingham, *U.K.* **11 F8** 51 23N 0 33 E
Gilmer, *U.S.A.* **81 J7** 32 44N 94 57W
Gilmore, *Australia* **63 F4** 35 20S 148 12 E
Gilmore, L., *Australia* **61 F3** 32 29S 121 37 E
Gilmour, *Canada* **70 D4** 44 48N 77 37W
Gilroy, *U.S.A.* **83 H3** 37 1N 121 34W
Gimbi, *Ethiopia* **51 G12** 9 3N 35 42 E
Gimli, *Canada* **73 C9** 50 40N 97 0W
Gin Gin, *Australia* **63 D5** 25 0S 151 58 E
Gindie, *Australia* **62 C4** 23 44S 148 8 E
Gingin, *Australia* **61 F2** 31 22S 115 54 E
Ginir, *Ethiopia* **46 F3** 7 6N 40 40 E
Giohar, *Somali Rep.* **46 G4** 2 48N 45 30 E
Gióna, Óros, *Greece* **21 E10** 38 38N 22 14 E
Gir Hills, *India* **42 J4** 21 0N 71 0 E
Girab, *India* **42 F4** 26 2N 70 38 E
Girâfi, W. →, *Egypt* **47 F3** 29 58N 34 39 E
Girard, *Kans., U.S.A.* **81 G7** 37 31N 94 51W
Girard, *Ohio, U.S.A.* **78 E4** 41 9N 80 42W
Girard, *Pa., U.S.A.* **78 D4** 42 0N 80 19W
Girardot, *Colombia* **92 C4** 4 18N 74 48W
Girdle Ness, *U.K.* **12 D6** 57 9N 2 3W
Giresun, *Turkey* **25 F6** 40 55N 38 30 E
Girga, *Egypt* **51 C11** 26 17N 31 55 E
Giridih, *India* **43 G12** 24 10N 86 21 E
Girilambone, *Australia* **63 E4** 31 16S 146 57 E
Girne = Kyrenia, *Cyprus* **23 D12** 35 20N 33 20 E
Girona = Gerona, *Spain* **19 B7** 41 58N 2 46 E
Gironde →, *France* **18 D3** 45 32N 1 7W
Giru, *Australia* **62 B4** 19 30S 147 5 E
Girvan, *U.K.* **12 F4** 55 14N 4 51W
Gisborne, *N.Z.* **59 H7** 38 39S 178 5 E
Gisenyi, *Rwanda* **54 C2** 1 41S 29 15 E
Gislaved, *Sweden* **9 H15** 57 19N 13 32 E
Gitega, *Burundi* **54 C2** 3 26S 29 56 E
Giuba →, *Somali Rep.* **46 G3** 1 30N 42 35 E
Giurgiu, *Romania* **17 G13** 43 52N 25 57 E
Giza = El Gîza, *Egypt* **51 C11** 30 0N 31 10 E
Gizhiga, *Russia* **27 C17** 62 3N 160 30 E
Gizhiginskaya Guba, *Russia* **27 C16** 61 0N 158 0 E
Giżycko, *Poland* **17 A11** 54 2N 21 48 E
Gjirokastra, *Albania* **21 D9** 40 7N 20 10 E
Gjoa Haven, *Canada* **68 B10** 68 20N 96 8W
Gjøvik, *Norway* **9 F14** 60 47N 10 43 E
Glace Bay, *Canada* **71 C8** 46 11N 59 58W
Glacier Bay, *U.S.A.* **72 B1** 58 40N 136 0W
Glacier Nat. Park, *Canada* **72 C5** 51 15N 117 30W
Glacier Park, *U.S.A.* **82 B7** 48 30N 113 18W
Glacier Peak, *U.S.A.* **82 B3** 48 7N 121 7W
Gladewater, *U.S.A.* **81 J7** 32 33N 94 56W
Gladstone, *Queens., Australia* **62 C5** 23 52S 151 16 E
Gladstone, *S. Austral., Australia* **63 E2** 33 15S 138 22 E
Gladstone, *W. Austral., Australia* **61 E1** 25 57S 114 17 E
Gladstone, *Canada* **73 C9** 50 13N 98 57W
Gladstone, *U.S.A.* **76 C2** 45 51N 87 1W
Gladwin, *U.S.A.* **76 D3** 43 59N 84 29W
Gladys L., *Canada* **72 B2** 59 50N 133 0W
Glåma = Glomma →, *Norway* **9 G14** 59 12N 10 57 E
Gláma, *Iceland* **8 D2** 65 48N 23 0W
Glamis, *U.S.A.* **85 N11** 32 55N 115 5W
Glasco, *Kans., U.S.A.* **80 F6** 39 22N 97 50W
Glasco, *N.Y., U.S.A.* **79 D11** 42 3N 73 57W
Glasgow, *U.K.* **12 F4** 55 51N 4 15W
Glasgow, *Ky., U.S.A.* **76 G3** 37 0N 85 55W
Glasgow, *Mont., U.S.A.* **82 B10** 48 12N 106 38W
Glastonbury, *U.K.* **11 F5** 51 9N 2 43W
Glastonbury, *U.S.A.* **79 E12** 41 43N 72 37W
Glazov, *Russia* **24 C9** 58 9N 52 40 E
Gleiwitz = Gliwice, *Poland* **17 C10** 50 22N 18 41 E
Glen, *U.S.A.* **79 B13** 44 7N 71 11W
Glen Affric, *U.K.* **12 D4** 57 15N 5 1W
Glen Canyon Dam, *U.S.A.* **83 H8** 36 57N 111 29W
Glen Canyon National Recreation Area, *U.S.A.* **83 H8** 37 15N 111 0W
Glen Coe, *U.K.* **12 E4** 56 40N 5 0W
Glen Cove, *U.S.A.* **79 F11** 40 52N 73 38W
Glen Garry, *U.K.* **12 D3** 57 3N 5 7W
Glen Innes, *Australia* **63 D5** 29 44S 151 44 E
Glen Lyon, *U.S.A.* **79 E8** 41 10N 76 5W
Glen Mor, *U.K.* **12 D4** 57 9N 4 37W
Glen Moriston, *U.K.* **12 D4** 57 11N 4 52W
Glen Orchy, *U.K.* **12 E4** 56 27N 4 52W
Glen Spean, *U.K.* **12 E4** 56 53N 4 40W
Glen Ullin, *U.S.A.* **80 B4** 46 49N 101 50W
Glenburgh, *Australia* **61 E2** 25 26S 116 6 E
Glencoe, *Canada* **78 D3** 42 45N 81 43W
Glencoe, *S. Africa* **57 D5** 28 11S 30 11 E
Glencoe, *U.S.A.* **80 C7** 44 46N 94 9W
Glendale, *Ariz., U.S.A.* **83 K7** 33 32N 112 11W
Glendale, *Calif., U.S.A.* **85 L8** 34 9N 118 15W
Glendale, *Oreg., U.S.A.* **82 E2** 42 44N 123 26W
Glendale, *Zimbabwe* **55 F3** 17 22S 31 5 E
Glendive, *U.S.A.* **80 B2** 47 7N 104 43W
Glendo, *U.S.A.* **80 D2** 42 30N 105 2W
Glenelg, *Australia* **63 E2** 34 58S 138 31 E
Glenelg →, *Australia* **63 F3** 38 4S 140 59 E
Glenflorrie, *Australia* **60 D2** 22 55S 115 59 E
Glengarriff, *Ireland* **13 E2** 51 45N 9 34W
Glengyle, *Australia* **62 C2** 24 48S 139 37 E
Glenmora, *U.S.A.* **81 K8** 30 59N 92 35W
Glenmorgan, *Australia* **63 D4** 27 14S 149 42 E
Glenn, *U.S.A.* **84 F4** 39 31N 122 1W
Glenns Ferry, *U.S.A.* **82 E6** 42 57N 115 18W
Glenorchy, *Australia* **62 G4** 42 49S 147 18 E
Glenore, *Australia* **62 B3** 17 50S 141 12 E
Glenormiston, *Australia* **62 C2** 22 55S 138 50 E
Glenreagh, *Australia* **63 E5** 30 2S 153 1 E
Glenrock, *U.S.A.* **82 E11** 42 52N 105 52W
Glenrothes, *U.K.* **12 E5** 56 12N 3 10W
Glens Falls, *U.S.A.* **79 C11** 43 19N 73 39W
Glenties, *Ireland* **13 B3** 54 49N 8 16W
Glenville, *U.S.A.* **76 F5** 38 56N 80 50W
Glenwood, *Alta., Canada* **72 D6** 49 21N 113 31W
Glenwood, *Nfld., Canada* **71 C9** 49 0N 54 58W
Glenwood, *Ark., U.S.A.* **81 H8** 34 20N 93 33W
Glenwood, *Hawaii, U.S.A.* **74 J17** 19 29N 155 9W
Glenwood, *Iowa, U.S.A.* **80 E7** 41 3N 95 45W
Glenwood, *Minn., U.S.A.* **80 C7** 45 39N 95 23W
Glenwood, *Wash., U.S.A.* **84 D5** 46 1N 121 17W
Glenwood Springs, *U.S.A.* **82 G10** 39 33N 107 19W
Glettinganes, *Iceland* **8 D7** 65 30N 13 37W
Gliwice, *Poland* **17 C10** 50 22N 18 41 E
Globe, *U.S.A.* **83 K8** 33 24N 110 47W
Głogów, *Poland* **16 C9** 51 37N 16 5 E
Glomma →, *Norway* **9 G14** 59 12N 10 57 E
Glorieuses, Is., *Ind. Oc.* **57 A8** 11 30S 47 20 E
Glossop, *U.K.* **10 D6** 53 27N 1 56W
Gloucester, *Australia* **63 E5** 32 0S 151 59 E
Gloucester, *U.K.* **11 F5** 51 53N 2 15W
Gloucester, *U.S.A.* **79 D14** 42 37N 70 40W
Gloucester I., *Australia* **62 B4** 20 0S 148 30 E
Gloucestershire □, *U.K.* **11 F5** 51 46N 2 15W
Gloversville, *U.S.A.* **79 C10** 43 3N 74 21W
Glovertown, *Canada* **71 C9** 48 40N 54 3W
Glusk, *Belarus* **17 B15** 52 53N 28 41 E
Gmünd, *Austria* **16 D8** 48 45N 15 0 E
Gmunden, *Austria* **16 E7** 47 55N 13 48 E
Gniezno, *Poland* **17 B9** 52 30N 17 35 E
Gnowangerup, *Australia* **61 F2** 33 58S 117 59 E
Go Cong, *Vietnam* **39 G6** 10 22N 106 40 E

Greece

Gô-no-ura, *Japan* **31 H4** 33 44N 129 40 E
Go Quao, *Vietnam* **39 H5** 9 43N 105 17 E
Goa, *India* **40 M8** 15 33N 73 59 E
Goa □, *India* **40 M8** 15 33N 73 59 E
Goalen Hd., *Australia* **63 F5** 36 33S 150 4 E
Goalpara, *India* **41 F17** 26 10N 90 40 E
Goalundo Ghat, *Bangla.* **43 H13** 23 50N 89 47 E
Goat Fell, *U.K.* **12 F3** 55 38N 5 11W
Goba, *Ethiopia* **46 F2** 7 1N 39 59 E
Goba, *Mozam.* **57 D5** 26 15S 32 13 E
Gobabis, *Namibia* **56 C2** 22 30S 19 0 E
Gobi, *Asia* **34 C5** 44 0N 111 0 E
Gobō, *Japan* **31 H7** 33 53N 135 10 E
Gochas, *Namibia* **56 C2** 24 59S 18 55 E
Godavari →, *India* **41 L13** 16 25N 82 18 E
Godavari Point, *India* **41 L13** 17 0N 82 20 E
Godbout, *Canada* **71 C6** 49 20N 67 38W
Godda, *India* **43 G12** 24 50N 87 13 E
Goderich, *Canada* **70 D3** 43 45N 81 41W
Godhavn, *Greenland* **4 C5** 69 15N 53 38W
Godhra, *India* **42 H5** 22 49N 73 40 E
Godoy Cruz, *Argentina* **94 C2** 32 56S 68 52W
Gods →, *Canada* **73 B10** 56 22N 92 51W
Gods L., *Canada* **73 C10** 54 40N 94 15W
Godthåb, *Greenland* **69 B14** 64 10N 51 35W
Godwin Austen = K2, *Pakistan* **43 B7** 35 58N 76 32 E
Goeie Hoop, Kaap die = Good Hope, C. of, *S. Africa* **56 E2** 34 24S 18 30 E
Goéland, L. au, *Canada* **70 C4** 49 50N 76 48W
Goeree, *Neths.* **15 C3** 51 50N 4 0 E
Goes, *Neths.* **15 C3** 51 30N 3 55 E
Gogama, *Canada* **70 C3** 47 35N 81 43W
Gogango, *Australia* **62 C5** 23 40S 150 2 E
Gogebic, L., *U.S.A.* **80 B10** 46 30N 89 35W
Gogra = Ghaghara →, *India* **43 G11** 25 45N 84 40 E
Goiânia, *Brazil* **93 G9** 16 43S 49 20W
Goiás, *Brazil* **93 G8** 15 55S 50 10W
Goiás □, *Brazil* **93 F9** 12 10S 48 0W
Goio-Ere, *Brazil* **95 A5** 24 12S 53 1W
Gojō, *Japan* **31 G7** 34 21N 135 42 E
Gojra, *Pakistan* **42 D5** 31 10N 72 40 E
Gokarannath, *India* **43 F9** 27 57N 80 39 E
Gökçeada, *Turkey* **21 D11** 40 10N 25 50 E
Gokteik, *Burma* **41 H20** 22 26N 97 0 E
Gokurt, *Pakistan* **42 E2** 29 40N 67 26 E
Gola, *India* **43 E9** 28 3N 80 32 E
Golakganj, *India* **43 F13** 26 8N 89 52 E
Golan Heights = Hagolan, *Syria* **47 B4** 33 0N 35 45 E
Golāshkerd, *Iran* **45 E8** 27 59N 57 16 E
Golchikha, *Russia* **4 B12** 71 45N 83 30 E
Golconda, *U.S.A.* **82 F5** 40 58N 117 30W
Gold Beach, *U.S.A.* **82 E1** 42 25N 124 25W
Gold Coast, *Australia* **63 D5** 28 0S 153 25 E
Gold Coast, *W. Afr.* **48 F3** 4 0N 1 40W
Gold Hill, *U.S.A.* **82 E2** 42 26N 123 3W
Golden, *Canada* **72 C5** 51 20N 116 59W
Golden, *U.S.A.* **80 F2** 39 42N 105 15W
Golden B., *N.Z.* **59 J4** 40 40S 172 50 E
Golden Gate, *U.S.A.* **82 H2** 37 54N 122 30W
Golden Hinde, *Canada* **72 D3** 49 40N 125 44W
Golden Lake, *Canada* **78 A7** 45 34N 77 21W
Golden Prairie, *Canada* **73 C7** 50 13N 109 37W
Golden Vale, *Ireland* **13 D3** 52 33N 8 17W
Goldendale, *U.S.A.* **82 D3** 45 49N 120 50W
Goldfield, *U.S.A.* **83 H5** 37 42N 117 14W
Goldfields, *Canada* **73 B7** 59 28N 108 29W
Goldsand L., *Canada* **73 B8** 57 2N 101 8W
Goldsboro, *U.S.A.* **77 H7** 35 23N 77 59W
Goldsmith, *U.S.A.* **81 K3** 31 59N 102 37W
Goldsworthy, *Australia* **60 D2** 20 21S 119 30 E
Goldthwaite, *U.S.A.* **81 K5** 31 27N 98 34W
Golęniów, *Poland* **16 B8** 53 35N 14 50 E
Golestānak, *Iran* **45 D7** 30 36N 54 14 E
Goleta, *U.S.A.* **85 L7** 34 27N 119 50W
Golfito, *Costa Rica* **88 E3** 8 41N 83 5W
Golfo Aranci, *Italy* **20 D3** 40 59N 9 38 E
Goliad, *U.S.A.* **81 L6** 28 40N 97 23W
Golpāyegān, *Iran* **45 C6** 33 27N 50 18 E
Golra, *Pakistan* **42 C5** 33 37N 72 56 E
Golspie, *U.K.* **12 D5** 57 58N 3 59W
Goma, *Rwanda* **54 C2** 2 11S 29 18 E
Goma, *Zaïre* **54 C2** 1 37S 29 10 E
Gomati →, *India* **43 G10** 25 32N 83 11 E
Gombari, *Zaïre* **54 B2** 2 45N 29 3 E
Gombe →, *Tanzania* **54 C3** 4 38S 31 40 E
Gomel = Homyel, *Belarus* **17 B16** 52 28N 31 0 E
Gomera, *Canary Is.* **22 F2** 28 7N 17 14W
Gómez Palacio, *Mexico* **86 B4** 25 40N 104 0W
Gomīshān, *Iran* **45 B7** 37 4N 54 6 E
Gomogomo, *Indonesia* **37 F8** 6 39S 134 43 E
Gomoh, *India* **41 H15** 23 52N 86 10 E
Gompa = Ganta, *Liberia* **50 G3** 7 15N 8 59W
Gonābād, *Iran* **45 C8** 34 15N 58 45 E
Gonaïves, *Haiti* **89 C5** 19 20N 72 42W
Gonâve, G. de la, *Haiti* **89 C5** 19 29N 72 42W
Gonâve, I. de la, *Haiti* **89 C5** 18 45N 73 0W
Gonbab-e Kāvūs, *Iran* **45 B7** 37 20N 55 25 E
Gonda, *India* **43 F9** 27 9N 81 58 E
Gondal, *India* **42 J4** 21 58N 70 52 E
Gonder, *Ethiopia* **51 F12** 12 39N 37 30 E
Gondia, *India* **40 J12** 21 23N 80 10 E
Gondola, *Mozam.* **55 F3** 19 10S 33 37 E
Gönen, *Turkey* **21 D12** 40 6N 27 39 E
Gonghe, *China* **32 C5** 36 18N 100 32 E
Gongolgon, *Australia* **63 E4** 30 21S 146 54 E
Goniri, *Nigeria* **51 F7** 11 30N 12 15 E
Gonzales, *Calif., U.S.A.* **83 H3** 36 30N 121 26W
Gonzales, *Tex., U.S.A.* **81 L6** 29 30N 97 27W
González Chaves, *Argentina* **94 D3** 38 2S 60 5W
Good Hope, C. of, *S. Africa* **56 E2** 34 24S 18 30 E
Gooderham, *Canada* **70 D4** 44 54N 78 21W
Goodeve, *Canada* **73 C8** 51 4N 103 10W
Gooding, *U.S.A.* **82 E6** 42 56N 114 43W
Goodland, *U.S.A.* **80 F4** 39 21N 101 43W
Goodnight, *U.S.A.* **81 H4** 35 2N 101 11W
Goodooga, *Australia* **63 D4** 29 3S 147 28 E
Goodsoil, *Canada* **73 C7** 54 24N 109 13W
Goodsprings, *U.S.A.* **83 J6** 35 50N 115 26W
Goole, *U.K.* **10 D7** 53 42N 0 53W
Goolgowi, *Australia* **63 E4** 33 58S 145 41 E
Goomalling, *Australia* **61 F2** 31 15S 116 49 E
Goombalie, *Australia* **63 D4** 29 59S 145 26 E
Goonda, *Mozam.* **55 F3** 19 48S 33 57 E
Goondiwindi, *Australia* **63 D5** 28 30S 150 21 E
Goongarrie, L., *Australia* **61 F3** 30 3S 121 9 E
Goonyella, *Australia* **62 C4** 21 47S 147 58 E
Goor, *Neths.* **15 B6** 52 13N 6 33 E
Gooray, *Australia* **63 D5** 28 25S 150 2 E
Goose →, *Canada* **71 B7** 53 20N 60 35W
Goose L., *U.S.A.* **82 F3** 41 56N 120 26W
Gop, *India* **40 H6** 22 5N 69 50 E
Gopalganj, *India* **43 F11** 26 28N 84 30 E
Göppingen, *Germany* **16 D5** 48 42N 9 39 E
Gorakhpur, *India* **43 F10** 26 47N 83 23 E
Goražde, *Bos.-H.* **21 C8** 43 38N 18 58 E
Gorda, *U.S.A.* **84 K5** 35 53N 121 26W
Gorda, Pta., *Canary Is.* **22 F2** 28 45N 18 0W
Gorda, Pta., *Nic.* **88 D3** 14 20N 83 10W
Gordan B., *Australia* **60 B5** 11 35S 130 10 E
Gordon, *U.S.A.* **80 D3** 42 48N 102 12W
Gordon →, *Australia* **62 G4** 42 27S 145 30 E
Gordon Downs, *Australia* **60 C4** 18 48S 128 33 E
Gordon L., *Alta., Canada* **73 B6** 56 30N 110 25W
Gordon L., *N.W.T., Canada* **72 A6** 63 5N 113 11W
Gordonvale, *Australia* **62 B4** 17 5S 145 50 E
Gore, *Australia* **63 D5** 28 17S 151 30 E
Goré, *Chad* **51 G8** 7 59N 16 31 E
Gore, *Ethiopia* **51 G12** 8 12N 35 32 E
Gore, *N.Z.* **59 M2** 46 5S 168 58 E
Gore Bay, *Canada* **70 C3** 45 57N 82 28W
Gorey, *Ireland* **13 D5** 52 41N 6 18W
Gorg, *Iran* **45 D8** 29 29N 59 43 E
Gorgān, *Iran* **45 B7** 36 50N 54 29 E
Gorgona, I., *Colombia* **92 C3** 3 0N 78 10W
Gorham, *U.S.A.* **79 B13** 44 23N 71 10W
Gorinchem, *Neths.* **15 C4** 51 50N 4 59 E
Gorízia, *Italy* **20 B5** 45 56N 13 37 E
Gorki = Nizhniy Novgorod, *Russia* **24 C7** 56 20N 44 0 E
Gorkiy = Nizhniy Novgorod, *Russia* **24 C7** 56 20N 44 0 E
Gorkovskoye Vdkhr., *Russia* **24 C7** 57 2N 43 4 E
Görlitz, *Germany* **16 C8** 51 9N 14 58 E
Gorlovka = Horlivka, *Ukraine* **25 E6** 48 19N 38 5 E
Gorman, *Calif., U.S.A.* **85 L8** 34 47N 118 51W
Gorman, *Tex., U.S.A.* **81 J5** 32 12N 98 41W
Gorna Dzhumayo = Blagoevgrad, *Bulgaria* **21 C10** 42 2N 23 5 E
Gorna Oryakhovitsa, *Bulgaria* **21 C11** 43 7N 25 40 E
Gorno-Altay □, *Russia* **26 D9** 51 0N 86 0 E
Gorno-Altaysk, *Russia* **26 D9** 51 50N 86 5 E
Gorno Slinkino = Gornopravdinsk, *Russia* **26 C8** 60 5N 70 0 E
Gornopravdinsk, *Russia* **26 C8** 60 5N 70 0 E
Gornyatski, *Russia* **24 A11** 67 32N 64 3 E
Gornyi, *Russia* **30 B6** 44 57N 133 59 E
Gorodenka = Horodenka, *Ukraine* **17 D13** 48 41N 25 29 E
Gorodok = Horodok, *Ukraine* **17 D12** 49 46N 23 32 E
Gorokhov = Horokhiv, *Ukraine* **17 C13** 50 30N 24 45 E
Goromonzi, *Zimbabwe* **55 F3** 17 52S 31 22 E
Gorongose →, *Mozam.* **57 C5** 20 30S 34 40 E
Gorongoza, *Mozam.* **55 F3** 18 44S 34 2 E
Gorongoza, Sa. da, *Mozam.* **55 F3** 18 27S 34 2 E
Gorontalo, *Indonesia* **37 D6** 0 35N 123 5 E
Gort, *Ireland* **13 C3** 53 3N 8 49W
Gortis, *Greece* **23 D6** 35 4N 24 58 E
Gorzów Wielkopolski, *Poland* **16 B8** 52 43N 15 15 E
Gosford, *Australia* **63 E5** 33 23S 151 18 E
Goshen, *Calif., U.S.A.* **84 J7** 36 21N 119 25W
Goshen, *Ind., U.S.A.* **76 E3** 41 35N 85 50W
Goshen, *N.Y., U.S.A.* **79 E10** 41 24N 74 20W
Goshogawara, *Japan* **30 D10** 40 48N 140 27 E
Goslar, *Germany* **16 C6** 51 54N 10 25 E
Gospič, *Croatia* **16 F8** 44 35N 15 23 E
Gosport, *U.K.* **11 G6** 50 48N 1 9W
Gosse →, *Australia* **62 B1** 19 32S 134 37 E
Göta älv →, *Sweden* **9 H14** 57 42N 11 54 E
Göta kanal, *Sweden* **9 G16** 58 30N 15 58 E
Götaland, *Sweden* **9 G15** 57 30N 14 30 E
Göteborg, *Sweden* **9 H14** 57 43N 11 59 E
Gotha, *Germany* **16 C6** 50 56N 10 42 E
Gothenburg = Göteborg, *Sweden* **9 H14** 57 43N 11 59 E
Gothenburg, *U.S.A.* **80 E4** 40 56N 100 10W
Gotland, *Sweden* **9 H18** 57 30N 18 33 E
Gotska Sandön, *Sweden* **9 G18** 58 24N 19 15 E
Gōtsu, *Japan* **31 G6** 35 0N 132 14 E
Göttingen, *Germany* **16 C5** 51 31N 9 55 E
Gottwaldov = Zlin, *Czech.* **17 D9** 49 14N 17 40 E
Goubangzi, *China* **35 D11** 41 20N 121 52 E
Gouda, *Neths.* **15 B4** 52 1N 4 42 E
Goúdhoura, Ákra, *Greece* **23 E8** 34 59N 26 6 E
Gough I., *Atl. Oc.* **2 G9** 40 10S 9 45W
Gouin, Rés., *Canada* **70 C5** 48 35N 74 40W
Goulburn, *Australia* **63 E4** 34 44S 149 44 E
Goulburn Is., *Australia* **62 A1** 11 40S 133 20 E
Gounou-Gaya, *Chad* **51 G8** 9 38N 15 31 E
Gouri, *Chad* **51 E8** 19 36N 19 36 E
Gourits →, *S. Africa* **56 E3** 34 21S 21 52 E
Gourma Rharous, *Mali* **50 E4** 16 55N 1 50W
Goúrnais, *Greece* **23 D7** 35 19N 25 16 E
Gourock Ra., *Australia* **63 F4** 36 0S 149 25 E
Gouverneur, *U.S.A.* **79 B9** 44 20N 75 28W
Gouviá, *Greece* **23 A3** 39 39N 19 50 E
Govan, *Canada* **73 C8** 51 20N 105 0W
Governador Valadares, *Brazil* **93 G10** 18 15S 41 57W
Governor's Harbour, *Bahamas* **88 A4** 25 10N 76 14W
Gowan Ra., *Australia* **62 C4** 25 0S 145 0 E
Gowanda, *U.S.A.* **78 D6** 42 28N 78 56W
Gowd-e Zirreh, *Afghan.* **40 E3** 29 45N 62 0 E
Gower, *U.K.* **11 F3** 51 35N 4 10W
Gowna, L., *Ireland* **13 C4** 53 51N 7 34W
Goya, *Argentina* **94 B4** 29 10S 59 10W
Goyder Lagoon, *Australia* **63 D2** 27 3S 138 58 E
Goyllarisquisga, *Peru* **92 F3** 10 31S 76 24W
Goz Beïda, *Chad* **51 F9** 12 10N 21 20 E
Gozo, *Malta* **23 C1** 36 3N 14 13 E
Graaff-Reinet, *S. Africa* **56 E3** 32 13S 24 32 E
Gračac, *Croatia* **16 F8** 44 18N 15 57 E
Grace, *U.S.A.* **82 E8** 42 35N 111 44W
Graceville, *U.S.A.* **80 C6** 45 34N 96 26W
Gracias a Dios, C., *Honduras* **88 C3** 15 0N 83 10W
Graciosa, I., *Canary Is.* **22 E6** 29 15N 13 32W
Grado, *Spain* **19 A2** 43 23N 6 4W
Gradule, *Australia* **63 D4** 28 32S 149 15 E
Grady, *U.S.A.* **81 H3** 34 49N 103 19W
Grafton, *Australia* **63 D5** 29 38S 152 58 E
Grafton, *U.S.A.* **80 A6** 48 25N 97 25W
Graham, *Canada* **70 C1** 49 20N 90 30W
Graham, *N.C., U.S.A.* **77 G6** 36 5N 79 25W
Graham, *Tex., U.S.A.* **81 J5** 33 6N 98 35W
Graham →, *Canada* **72 B4** 56 31N 122 17W
Graham, Mt., *U.S.A.* **83 K9** 32 42N 109 52W
Graham Bell, Os., *Russia* **26 A7** 81 0N 62 0 E
Graham I., *Canada* **72 C2** 53 40N 132 30W
Graham Land, *Antarctica* **5 C17** 65 0S 64 0W
Grahamdale, *Canada* **73 C9** 51 23N 98 30W
Grahamstown, *S. Africa* **56 E4** 33 19S 26 31 E
Grain Coast, *W. Afr.* **48 F2** 4 20N 10 0W
Grajaú, *Brazil* **93 E9** 5 50S 46 4W
Grajaú →, *Brazil* **93 D10** 3 41S 44 48W
Grampian Highlands = Grampian Mts., *U.K.* **12 E5** 56 50N 4 0W
Grampian Mts., *U.K.* **12 E5** 56 50N 4 0W
Gran Canaria, *Canary Is.* **22 F4** 27 55N 15 35W
Gran Chaco, *S. Amer.* **94 B3** 25 0S 61 0W
Gran Paradiso, *Italy* **20 B2** 45 33N 7 17 E
Gran Sasso d'Italia, *Italy* **20 C5** 42 27N 13 42 E
Granada, *Nic.* **88 D2** 11 58N 86 0W
Granada, *Spain* **19 D4** 37 10N 3 35W
Granada, *U.S.A.* **81 F3** 38 4N 102 19W
Granadilla de Abona, *Canary Is.* **22 F3** 28 7N 16 33W
Granard, *Ireland* **13 C4** 53 47N 7 30W
Granbury, *U.S.A.* **81 J6** 32 27N 97 47W
Granby, *Canada* **70 C5** 45 25N 72 45W
Grand →, *Mo., U.S.A.* **80 F8** 39 23N 93 7W
Grand →, *S. Dak., U.S.A.* **80 C4** 45 40N 100 45W
Grand Bahama, *Bahamas* **88 A4** 26 40N 78 30W
Grand Bank, *Canada* **71 C8** 47 6N 55 48W
Grand Bassam, *Ivory C.* **50 G4** 5 10N 3 49W
Grand-Bourg, *Guadeloupe* **89 C7** 15 53N 61 19W
Grand Canal = Yun Ho →, *China* **35 E9** 39 10N 117 10 E
Grand Canyon, *U.S.A.* **83 H7** 36 3N 112 9W
Grand Canyon National Park, *U.S.A.* **83 H7** 36 15N 112 30W
Grand Cayman, *Cayman Is.* **88 C3** 19 20N 81 20W
Grand Coulee, *U.S.A.* **82 C4** 47 57N 119 0W
Grand Coulee Dam, *U.S.A.* **82 C4** 47 57N 118 59W
Grand Falls, *Canada* **71 C8** 48 56N 55 40W
Grand Forks, *Canada* **72 D5** 49 0N 118 30W
Grand Forks, *U.S.A.* **80 B6** 47 55N 97 3W
Grand Haven, *U.S.A.* **76 D2** 43 4N 86 13W
Grand I., *U.S.A.* **76 B2** 46 31N 86 40W
Grand Island, *U.S.A.* **80 E5** 40 55N 98 21W
Grand Isle, *U.S.A.* **81 L10** 29 14N 90 0W
Grand Junction, *U.S.A.* **83 G9** 39 4N 108 33W
Grand L., *N.B., Canada* **71 C6** 45 57N 66 7W
Grand L., *Nfld., Canada* **71 C8** 49 0N 57 30W
Grand L., *Nfld., Canada* **71 B7** 53 40N 60 30W
Grand L., *U.S.A.* **81 L8** 29 55N 92 47W
Grand Lac Victoria, *Canada* **70 C4** 47 35N 77 35W
Grand Lahou, *Ivory C.* **50 G3** 5 10N 5 5W
Grand Lake, *U.S.A.* **82 F11** 40 15N 105 49W
Grand Manan I., *Canada* **71 D6** 44 45N 66 52W
Grand Marais, *Canada* **80 B9** 47 45N 90 25W
Grand Marais, *U.S.A.* **76 B3** 46 40N 85 59W
Grand-Mère, *Canada* **70 C5** 46 36N 72 40W
Grand Portage, *U.S.A.* **70 C2** 47 58N 89 41W
Grand Prairie, *U.S.A.* **81 J6** 32 47N 97 0W
Grand Rapids, *Canada* **73 C9** 53 12N 99 19W
Grand Rapids, *Mich., U.S.A.* **76 D2** 42 58N 85 40W
Grand Rapids, *Minn., U.S.A.* **80 B8** 47 14N 93 31W
Grand St.-Bernard, Col du, *Europe* **16 F4** 45 50N 7 10 E
Grand Teton, *U.S.A.* **82 E8** 43 54N 111 50W
Grand Valley, *U.S.A.* **82 G9** 39 27N 108 3W
Grand View, *Canada* **73 C8** 51 10N 100 42W
Grande →, *Jujuy, Argentina* **94 A2** 24 20S 65 2W
Grande →, *Mendoza, Argentina* **94 D2** 36 52S 69 45W
Grande →, *Bolivia* **92 G6** 15 51S 64 39W
Grande →, *Bahia, Brazil* **93 F10** 11 30S 44 30W
Grande →, *Minas Gerais, Brazil* **93 H8** 20 6S 51 4W
Grande, B., *Argentina* **96 G3** 50 30S 68 20W
Grande, Rio →, *U.S.A.* **81 N6** 25 58N 97 9W
Grande Baie, *Canada* **71 C5** 48 19N 70 52W
Grande Baleine, R. de la →, *Canada* **70 A4** 55 16N 77 47W
Grande Cache, *Canada* **72 C5** 53 53N 119 8W
Grande de Santiago →, *Mexico* **86 C3** 21 36N 105 26W
Grande-Entrée, *Canada* **71 C7** 47 30N 61 40W
Grande Prairie, *Canada* **72 B5** 55 10N 118 50W
Grande-Rivière, *Canada* **71 C7** 48 26N 64 30W
Grande-Vallée, *Canada* **71 C6** 49 14N 65 8W
Grandes-Bergeronnes, *Canada* **71 C6** 48 16N 69 35W
Grandfalls, *U.S.A.* **81 K3** 31 20N 102 51W
Grandoe Mines, *Canada* **72 B3** 56 29N 129 54W
Grandview, *U.S.A.* **82 C4** 46 15N 119 54W
Graneros, *Chile* **94 C1** 34 5S 70 45W
Grangemouth, *U.K.* **12 E5** 56 1N 3 42W
Granger, *Wash., U.S.A.* **82 C3** 46 21N 120 11W
Granger, *Wyo., U.S.A.* **82 F9** 41 35N 109 58W
Grangeville, *U.S.A.* **82 D5** 45 56N 116 7W
Granite City, *U.S.A.* **80 F9** 38 42N 90 9W
Granite Falls, *U.S.A.* **80 C7** 44 49N 95 33W
Granite Mt., *U.S.A.* **85 M10** 33 5N 116 28W
Granite Peak, *Australia* **61 E3** 25 40S 121 20 E
Granite Peak, *U.S.A.* **82 D9** 45 10N 109 48W
Granity, *N.Z.* **59 J3** 41 39S 171 51 E
Granja, *Brazil* **93 D10** 3 7S 40 50W
Granollers, *Spain* **19 B7** 41 39N 2 18 E
Grant, *U.S.A.* **80 E4** 40 53N 101 42W
Grant, Mt., *U.S.A.* **82 G4** 38 34N 118 48W
Grant City, *U.S.A.* **80 E7** 40 29N 94 25W
Grant I., *Australia* **60 B5** 11 10S 132 52 E
Grant Range, *U.S.A.* **83 G6** 38 30N 115 25W
Grantham, *U.K.* **10 E7** 52 55N 0 38W
Grantown-on-Spey, *U.K.* **12 D5** 57 20N 3 36W
Grants, *U.S.A.* **83 J10** 35 9N 107 52W
Grants Pass, *U.S.A.* **82 E2** 42 26N 123 19W
Grantsburg, *U.S.A.* **80 C8** 45 47N 92 41W
Grantsville, *U.S.A.* **82 F7** 40 36N 112 28W
Granville, *France* **18 B3** 48 50N 1 35W
Granville, *N. Dak., U.S.A.* **80 A4** 48 16N 100 47W
Granville, *N.Y., U.S.A.* **76 D9** 43 24N 73 16W
Granville L., *Canada* **73 B8** 56 18N 100 30W
Grapeland, *U.S.A.* **81 K7** 31 30N 95 29W
Gras, L. de, *Canada* **68 B8** 64 30N 110 30W
Graskop, *S. Africa* **57 C5** 24 56S 30 49 E
Grass →, *Canada* **73 B9** 56 3N 96 33W
Grass Range, *U.S.A.* **82 C9** 47 0N 109 0W
Grass River Prov. Park, *Canada* **73 C8** 54 40N 100 50W
Grass Valley, *Calif., U.S.A.* **84 F6** 39 13N 121 4W
Grass Valley, *Oreg., U.S.A.* **82 D3** 45 22N 120 47W
Grasse, *France* **18 E7** 43 38N 6 56 E
Grassmere, *Australia* **63 E3** 31 24S 142 38 E
Graulhet, *France* **18 E4** 43 45N 1 59 E
Gravelbourg, *Canada* **73 D7** 49 50N 106 35W
's-Gravenhage, *Neths.* **15 B4** 52 7N 4 17 E
Gravenhurst, *Canada* **78 B5** 44 52N 79 20W
Gravesend, *Australia* **63 D5** 29 35S 150 20 E
Gravesend, *U.K.* **11 F8** 51 26N 0 22 E
Gravois, Pointe-à-, *Haiti* **89 C5** 18 15N 73 56W
Grayling, *U.S.A.* **76 C3** 44 40N 84 43W
Grayling →, *Canada* **72 B3** 59 21N 125 0W
Grays Harbor, *U.S.A.* **82 C1** 46 59N 124 1W
Grays L., *U.S.A.* **82 E8** 43 4N 111 26W
Grays River, *U.S.A.* **84 D3** 46 21N 123 37W
Grayson, *Canada* **73 C8** 50 45N 102 40W
Graz, *Austria* **16 E8** 47 4N 15 27 E
Greasy L., *Canada* **72 A4** 62 55N 122 12W
Great Abaco I., *Bahamas* **88 A4** 26 25N 77 10W
Great Artesian Basin, *Australia* **62 C3** 23 0S 144 0 E
Great Australian Bight, *Australia* **61 F5** 33 30S 130 0 E
Great Bahama Bank, *Bahamas* **88 B4** 23 15N 78 0W
Great Barrier I., *N.Z.* **59 G5** 36 11S 175 25 E
Great Barrier Reef, *Australia* **62 B4** 18 0S 146 50 E
Great Barrington, *U.S.A.* **79 D11** 42 12N 73 22W
Great Basin, *U.S.A.* **82 G5** 40 0N 117 0W
Great Bear →, *Canada* **68 B7** 65 0N 124 0W
Great Bear L., *Canada* **68 B7** 65 30N 120 0W
Great Belt = Store Bælt, *Denmark* **9 J14** 55 20N 11 0 E
Great Bend, *Kans., U.S.A.* **80 F5** 38 22N 98 46W
Great Bend, *Pa., U.S.A.* **79 E9** 41 58N 75 45W
Great Blasket I., *Ireland* **13 D1** 52 6N 10 32W
Great Britain, *Europe* **6 E5** 54 0N 2 15W
Great Central, *Canada* **72 D3** 49 20N 125 10W
Great Dividing Ra., *Australia* **62 C4** 23 0S 146 0 E
Great Driffield = Driffield, *U.K.* **10 C7** 54 0N 0 26W
Great Exuma I., *Bahamas* **88 B4** 23 30N 75 50W
Great Falls, *Canada* **73 C9** 50 27N 96 1W
Great Falls, *U.S.A.* **82 C8** 47 30N 111 17W
Great Fish = Groot Vis →, *S. Africa* **56 E4** 33 28S 27 5 E
Great Guana Cay, *Bahamas* **88 B4** 24 0N 76 20W
Great Harbour Deep, *Canada* **71 B8** 50 25N 56 32W
Great I., *Canada* **73 B9** 58 53N 96 35W
Great Inagua I., *Bahamas* **89 B5** 21 0N 73 20W
Great Indian Desert = Thar Desert, *India* **42 F4** 28 0N 72 0 E
Great Karoo, *S. Africa* **56 E3** 31 55S 21 0 E
Great Lake, *Australia* **62 G4** 41 50S 146 40 E
Great Malvern, *U.K.* **11 E5** 52 7N 2 18W
Great Ormes Head, *U.K.* **10 D4** 53 20N 3 52W
Great Ouse →, *U.K.* **10 E8** 52 48N 0 21 E
Great Palm I., *Australia* **62 B4** 18 45S 146 40 E
Great Plains, *N. Amer.* **74 A6** 47 0N 105 0W
Great Ruaha →, *Tanzania* **54 D4** 7 56S 37 52 E
Great Saint Bernard P. = Grand St.-Bernard, Col du, *Europe* **16 F4** 45 50N 7 10 E
Great Salt L., *U.S.A.* **82 F7** 41 15N 112 40W
Great Salt Lake Desert, *U.S.A.* **82 F7** 40 50N 113 30W
Great Salt Plains L., *U.S.A.* **81 G5** 36 45N 98 8W
Great Sandy Desert, *Australia* **60 D3** 21 0S 124 0 E
Great Sangi = Sangihe, P., *Indonesia* **37 D7** 3 45N 125 30 E
Great Slave L., *Canada* **72 A5** 61 23N 115 38W
Great Smoky Mts. Nat. Pk., *U.S.A.* **77 H4** 35 40N 83 40W
Great Stour = Stour →, *U.K.* **11 F9** 51 18N 1 22 E
Great Victoria Desert, *Australia* **61 E4** 29 30S 126 30 E
Great Wall, *China* **34 E5** 38 30N 109 30 E
Great Whernside, *U.K.* **10 C6** 54 10N 1 58W
Great Yarmouth, *U.K.* **10 E9** 52 37N 1 44 E
Greater Antilles, *W. Indies* **89 C5** 17 40N 74 0W
Greater London □, *U.K.* **11 F7** 51 31N 0 6W
Greater Manchester □, *U.K.* **10 D5** 53 30N 2 15W
Greater Sunda Is., *Indonesia* **36 F4** 7 0S 112 0 E
Greco, C., *Cyprus* **23 E13** 34 57N 34 5 E
Gredos, Sierra de, *Spain* **19 B3** 40 20N 5 0W
Greece, *U.S.A.* **78 C7** 43 13N 77 41W
Greece ■, *Europe* **21 E9** 40 0N 23 0 E

I

127

Juan de Fuca Str.

J

Jabal Lubnān, Lebanon . . 47 B4 33 45N 35 40 E
Jabalpur, India . . . . 43 H8 23 9N 79 58 E
Jabbūl, Syria . . . . 44 B3 36 4N 37 30 E
Jablah, Syria . . . . 44 C3 35 20N 36 0 E
Jablanica, Macedonia . . . 21 D9 41 15N 20 30 E
Jablonec, Czech. . . . . 16 C8 50 43N 15 10 E
Jaboatão, Brazil 93 E11 8 7S 35 1W
Jaboticabal, Brazil 95 A6 21 15S 48 17W
Jaburu, Brazil 92 E6 5 30S 64 0W
Jaca, Spain 19 A5 42 35N 0 33W
Jacareí, Brazil 95 A6 23 20S 46 0W
Jacarèzinho, Brazil 95 A6 23 5S 49 58W
Jackman, U.S.A. 71 C5 45 35N 70 17W
Jacksboro, U.S.A. 81 J5 33 14N 98 15W
Jackson, Australia . . . . . . 63 D4 26 39S 149 39 E
Jackson, Ala., U.S.A. 77 K2 31 31N 87 53W
Jackson, Calif., U.S.A. . . . 84 G6 38 21N 120 46W
Jackson, Ky., U.S.A. 76 G4 37 33N 83 23W
Jackson, Mich., U.S.A. . . 76 D3 42 15N 84 24W
Jackson, Minn., U.S.A. . . 80 D7 43 37N 95 1W
Jackson, Miss., U.S.A. . . . 81 J9 32 18N 90 12W
Jackson, Mo., U.S.A. 81 G10 37 23N 89 40W
Jackson, Ohio, U.S.A. . . . 76 F4 39 3N 82 39W
Jackson, Tenn., U.S.A. . . 77 H1 35 37N 88 49W
Jackson, Wyo., U.S.A. . . . 82 E8 43 29N 110 46W
Jackson B., N.Z. . . . . 59 K2 43 58S 168 42 E
Jackson L., U.S.A. 82 E8 43 52N 110 36W
Jacksons, N.Z. . . . . 59 K3 42 46S 171 32 E
Jacksonville, Ala., U.S.A. 77 J3 33 49N 85 46W
Jacksonville, Calif., U.S.A. 84 H6 37 52N 120 24W
Jacksonville, Fla., U.S.A. . 77 K5 30 20N 81 39W
Jacksonville, Ill., U.S.A. . . 80 F9 39 44N 90 14W
Jacksonville, N.C., U.S.A. 77 H7 34 45N 77 26W
Jacksonville, Oreg., U.S.A. 82 E2 42 19N 122 57W
Jacksonville, Tex., U.S.A. 81 K7 31 58N 95 17W
Jacksonville Beach, U.S.A. 77 K5 30 17N 81 24W
Jacmel, Haiti 89 C5 18 14N 72 32W
Jacob Lake, U.S.A. 83 H7 36 43N 112 13W
Jacobabad, Pakistan . . . . 42 E3 28 20N 68 29 E
Jacobina, Brazil 93 F10 11 11S 40 30W
Jacques-Cartier, Mt., Canada 71 C6 48 57N 66 0W
Jacuí →, Brazil 95 C5 30 2S 51 15W
Jacumba, U.S.A. 85 N10 32 37N 116 11W
Jacundá →, Brazil 93 D8 1 57S 50 26W
Jadotville = Likasi, Zaïre 55 E2 10 55S 26 48 E
Jādū, Libya . . . . 51 B7 32 0N 12 0 E
Jaén, Peru 92 E3 5 25S 78 40W
Jaén, Spain 19 D4 37 44N 3 43W
Jaffa = Tel Aviv-Yafo, Israel . . . . 47 C3 32 4N 34 48 E
Jaffa, C., Australia . . . . . . 63 F2 36 58S 139 40 E
Jaffna, Sri Lanka . . . . 40 Q12 9 45N 80 2 E
Jagadhri, India . . . . 42 D7 30 10N 77 20 E
Jagadishpur, India . . . . . . 43 G11 25 30N 84 21 E
Jagdalpur, India . . . . 41 K12 19 3N 82 0 E
Jagersfontein, S. Africa . . 56 D4 29 44S 25 27 E
Jagraon, India . . . . 40 D9 30 50N 75 25 E
Jagtial, India . . . . 40 K11 18 50N 79 0 E
Jaguariaíva, Brazil 95 A6 24 10S 49 50W
Jaguaribe →, Brazil 93 D11 4 25S 37 45W
Jagüey Grande, Cuba . . . 88 B3 22 35N 81 7W
Jahangirabad, India . . . . 42 E8 28 19N 78 4 E
Jahrom, Iran . . . . 45 D7 28 30N 53 31 E
Jailolo, Indonesia . . . . . . 37 D7 1 5N 127 30 E
Jailolo, Selat, Indonesia . 37 D7 0 5N 129 5 E
Jaipur, India . . . . 42 F6 27 0N 75 50 E
Jājarm, Iran . . . . 45 B8 36 58N 56 27 E
Jakarta, Indonesia . . . . . . 37 G12 6 9S 106 49 E
Jakobstad = Pietarsaari, Finland . . . . 8 E20 63 40N 22 43 E
Jal, U.S.A. 81 J3 32 7N 103 12W
Jalalabad, Afghan. . . . . . . 42 B4 34 30N 70 29 E
Jalalabad, India . . . . 43 F8 27 41N 79 42 E
Jalalpur Jattan, Pakistan . 42 C6 32 38N 74 11 E
Jalama, U.S.A. 85 L6 34 29N 120 29W
Jalapa, Guatemala 88 D2 14 39N 89 59W
Jalapa Enríquez, Mexico . 87 D5 19 32N 96 55W
Jalasjärvi, Finland . . . . . . 9 E20 62 29N 22 47 E
Jalaun, India . . . . 43 F8 26 8N 79 25 E
Jaleswar, Nepal . . . . 43 F11 26 38N 85 48 E
Jalgaon, Maharashtra, India . . . . 40 J10 21 2N 76 31 E
Jalgaon, Maharashtra, India . . . . 40 J9 21 0N 75 42 E
Jalībah, Iraq . . . . 44 D5 30 35N 46 32 E
Jalisco □, Mexico 86 C4 20 0N 104 0W
Jalkot, Pakistan . . . . 43 B5 35 14N 73 24 E
Jalna, India . . . . 40 K9 19 48N 75 38 E
Jalón →, Spain 19 B5 41 47N 1 4W
Jalpa, Mexico 86 C4 21 38N 102 58W
Jalpaiguri, India . . . . 41 F16 26 32N 88 46 E
Jaluit I., Pac. Oc. . . . . 64 G8 6 0N 169 30 E
Jalūlā, Iraq . . . . 44 C5 34 16N 45 10 E
Jamaica ■, W. Indies . . . 88 C4 18 10N 77 30W
Jamalpur, Bangla. . . . . . . 41 G16 24 52N 89 56 E
Jamalpur, India . . . . 43 G12 25 18N 86 28 E
Jamalpurganj, India . . . . . 43 H13 23 2N 88 1 E
Jamanxim →, Brazil 93 D7 4 43S 56 18W
Jambe, Indonesia . . . . 37 E8 1 15S 132 10 E
Jambi, Indonesia . . . . 36 E2 1 38S 103 30 E
Jambi □, Indonesia . . . . . 36 E2 1 30S 102 30 E
Jambusar, India . . . . 42 H5 22 3N 72 51 E
James →, U.S.A. 80 D6 42 52N 97 18W
James B., Canada 69 C11 51 30N 80 0W
James Ras., Australia . . . 60 D5 24 10S 132 30 E
James Ross I., Antarctica 5 C18 63 58S 57 50W
Jamestown, Australia . . . . 63 E2 33 10S 138 32 E
Jamestown, S. Africa . . . 56 E4 31 6S 26 45 E
Jamestown, Ky., U.S.A. . . 76 G3 36 59N 85 4W
Jamestown, N. Dak., U.S.A. 80 B5 46 54N 98 42W
Jamestown, N.Y., U.S.A. . 78 D5 42 6N 79 14W
Jamestown, Pa., U.S.A. . . 78 E4 41 29N 80 27W
Jamestown, Tenn., U.S.A. 77 G3 36 26N 84 56W
Jamīlābād, Iran . . . . 45 C6 34 24N 48 28 E
Jamiltepec, Mexico 87 D5 16 17N 97 49W
Jamkhandi, India . . . . 40 L9 16 30N 75 15 E
Jammu, India . . . . 42 C6 32 43N 74 54 E
Jammu & Kashmir □, India . . . . 43 B7 34 25N 77 0 E
Jamnagar, India . . . . 42 H4 22 30N 70 6 E
Jampur, Pakistan . . . . 42 E4 29 39N 70 40 E
Jamrud, Pakistan . . . . 42 C4 33 59N 71 24 E
Jämsä, Finland . . . . 9 F21 61 53N 25 10 E
Jamshedpur, India . . . . . . 43 H12 22 44N 86 12 E
Jamtara, India . . . . 43 H12 23 59N 86 49 E
Jämtland, Sweden . . . . . . 8 E15 63 31N 14 0 E
Jan L., Canada 73 C8 54 56N 102 55W
Jan Mayen, Arctic 4 B7 71 0N 9 0W
Janakkala, Finland . . . . . . 9 F21 60 54N 24 36 E
Jand, Pakistan . . . . 42 C5 33 30N 72 6 E
Jandaq, Iran . . . . 45 C7 34 3N 54 22 E
Jandia, Canary Is. 22 F5 28 6N 14 21W
Jandia, Pta. de, Canary Is. 22 F5 28 3N 14 31W
Jandola, Pakistan . . . . . . 42 C4 32 20N 70 9 E
Jandowae, Australia . . . . 63 D5 26 45S 151 7 E
Janesville, U.S.A. 80 D10 42 41N 89 1W
Janīn, West Bank . . . . 47 C4 32 28N 35 18 E
Janos, Mexico 86 A3 30 45N 108 10W
Januária, Brazil 93 G10 15 25S 44 25W
Janubio, Canary Is. 22 F6 28 56N 13 50W
Jaora, India . . . . 42 H6 23 40N 75 10 E
Japan ■, Asia . . . . 31 G8 36 0N 136 0 E
Japan, Sea of, Asia . . . . . 30 E7 40 0N 135 0 E
Japan Trench, Pac. Oc. . . 28 F18 32 0N 142 0 E
Japen = Yapen, Indonesia 37 E9 1 50S 136 0 E
Japurá →, Brazil 92 D5 3 8S 65 46W
Jaque, Panama 92 B3 7 27N 78 8W
Jarābulus, Syria . . . . 44 B3 36 49N 38 1 E
Jarama →, Spain 19 B4 40 24N 3 32W
Jaranwala, Pakistan . . . . 42 D5 31 15N 73 26 E
Jarash, Jordan . . . . 47 C4 32 17N 35 54 E
Jardim, Brazil 94 A4 21 28S 56 2W
Jardines de la Reina, Is., Cuba 88 B4 20 50N 78 50W
Jargalang, China . . . . 35 C12 43 5N 122 55 E
Jargalant = Hovd, Mongolia . . . . 32 B4 48 2N 91 37 E
Jarīr, W. al →, Si. Arabia 44 E4 25 38N 42 30 E
Jarosław, Poland . . . . 17 C12 50 2N 22 42 E
Jarrahdale, Australia . . . . 61 F2 32 24S 116 5 E
Jarres, Plaine des, Laos . 38 C4 19 27N 103 10 E
Jarso, Ethiopia . . . . 51 G12 5 15N 37 30 E
Jartai, China . . . . 34 E3 39 45N 105 48 E
Jarud Qi, China . . . . 35 B11 44 28N 120 50 E
Järvenpää, Finland . . . . . 9 F21 60 29N 25 5 E
Jarvis, Canada 78 D4 42 53N 80 6W
Jarvis I., Pac. Oc. 65 H12 0 15S 159 55W
Jarwa, India . . . . 43 F10 27 38N 82 30 E
Jāsimīyah, Iraq . . . . 44 C5 33 45N 44 41 E
Jasin, Malaysia . . . . 39 L4 2 20N 102 26 E
Jāsk, Iran . . . . 45 E8 25 38N 57 45 E
Jasło, Poland . . . . 17 D11 49 45N 21 30 E
Jasper, Alta., Canada 72 C5 52 55N 118 5W
Jasper, Ont., Canada 79 B9 44 52N 75 57W
Jasper, Ala., U.S.A. 77 J2 33 50N 87 17W
Jasper, Fla., U.S.A. 77 K4 30 31N 82 57W
Jasper, Minn., U.S.A. . . . 80 D6 43 51N 96 24W
Jasper, Tex., U.S.A. 81 K8 30 56N 94 1W
Jasper Nat. Park, Canada 72 C5 52 50N 118 8W
Jászberény, Hungary . . . . 17 E10 47 30N 19 55 E
Jataí, Brazil 93 G8 17 58S 51 48W
Jati, Pakistan . . . . 42 G3 24 20N 68 19 E
Jatibarang, Indonesia . . . 37 G13 6 28S 108 18 E
Jatinegara, Indonesia . . . 37 G12 6 13S 106 52 E
Játiva, Spain 19 C5 39 0N 0 32W
Jaú, Brazil 95 A6 22 10S 48 30W
Jauja, Peru 92 F3 11 45S 75 15W
Jaunpur, India . . . . 43 G10 25 46N 82 44 E
Java = Jawa, Indonesia . . 37 G14 7 0S 110 0 E
Java Sea, Indonesia . . . . 36 E3 4 35S 107 15 E
Java Trench, Ind. Oc. . . . 64 H2 9 0S 105 0 E
Javhlant = Ulyasutay, Mongolia . . . . 32 B4 47 56N 97 28 E
Jawa, Indonesia . . . . 37 G14 7 0S 110 0 E
Jay, U.S.A. 81 G7 36 25N 94 48W
Jaya, Puncak, Indonesia . 37 E9 3 57S 137 17 E
Jayanti, India . . . . 41 F16 26 45N 89 40 E
Jayapura, Indonesia . . . . 37 E10 2 28S 140 38 E
Jayawijaya, Pegunungan, Indonesia . . . . 37 E9 5 0S 139 0 E
Jaynagar, India . . . . 41 F15 26 43N 86 9 E
Jayrūd, Syria . . . . 44 C3 33 49N 36 44 E
Jayton, U.S.A. 81 J4 33 15N 100 34W
Jazīreh-ye Shīf, Iran . . . . 45 D6 29 4N 50 54 E
Jazminal, Mexico 86 C4 24 56N 101 25W
Jazzīn, Lebanon . . . . 47 B4 33 31N 35 35 E
Jean, U.S.A. 85 K11 35 47N 115 20W
Jean Marie River, Canada 72 A4 61 32N 120 38W
Jean Rabel, Haiti 89 C5 19 50N 73 5W
Jeanerette, U.S.A. 81 L9 29 55N 91 40W
Jeanette, Ostrov, Russia . 27 B16 76 43N 158 0 E
Jeannette, U.S.A. 78 F5 40 20N 79 36W
Jebba, Nigeria . . . . 50 G5 9 9N 4 48 E
Jebel, Bahr el →, Sudan 51 G11 9 30N 30 25 E
Jedburgh, U.K. 12 F6 55 29N 2 33W
Jedda = Jiddah, Si. Arabia . . . . 46 C2 21 29N 39 10 E
Jędrzejów, Poland . . . . . . 17 C11 50 35N 20 15 E
Jedway, Canada 72 C2 52 17N 131 14W
Jefferson, Iowa, U.S.A. . . 80 D7 42 1N 94 23W
Jefferson, Ohio, U.S.A. . . 78 E4 41 44N 80 46W
Jefferson, Tex., U.S.A. . . 81 J7 32 46N 94 21W
Jefferson, Wis., U.S.A. . . 80 D10 43 0N 88 48W
Jefferson, Mt., Nev., U.S.A. 82 G5 38 51N 117 0W
Jefferson, Mt., Oreg., U.S.A. 82 D3 44 41N 121 48W
Jefferson City, Mo., U.S.A. 80 F8 38 34N 92 10W
Jefferson City, Tenn., U.S.A. 77 G4 36 7N 83 30W
Jeffersonville, U.S.A. . . . 76 F3 38 17N 85 44W
Jega, Nigeria . . . . 50 F5 12 15N 4 23 E
Jēkabpils, Latvia . . . . 9 H21 56 29N 25 57 E
Jelenia Góra, Poland . . . . 16 C8 50 50N 15 45 E
Jelgava, Latvia . . . . 9 H20 56 41N 23 49 E
Jellicoe, Canada 70 C2 49 40N 87 30W
Jemaja, Indonesia . . . . . . 36 D3 3 5N 105 45 E
Jemaluang, Malaysia . . . . 39 L4 2 16N 103 52 E
Jember, Indonesia . . . . . . 37 H15 8 11S 113 41 E
Jembongan, Malaysia . . . 36 C5 6 45N 117 20 E
Jemeppe, Belgium . . . . . . 15 D5 50 37N 5 30 E
Jena, Germany . . . . 16 C6 50 54N 11 35 E
Jena, U.S.A. 81 K8 31 41N 92 8W
Jenkins, U.S.A. 76 G4 37 10N 82 38W
Jenner, U.S.A. 84 G3 38 27N 123 7W
Jennings, U.S.A. 81 K8 30 13N 92 40W
Jennings →, Canada . . . 72 B2 59 38N 132 5W
Jeparit, Australia . . . . 63 F3 36 8S 142 1 E
Jequié, Brazil 93 F10 13 51S 40 5W
Jequitinhonha, Brazil 93 G10 16 30S 41 0W
Jequitinhonha →, Brazil 93 G11 15 51S 38 53W
Jerada, Morocco 50 B4 34 17N 2 10W
Jerantut, Malaysia . . . . . . 39 L4 3 56N 102 22 E
Jérémie, Haiti 89 C5 18 40N 74 10W
Jerez, Punta, Mexico 87 C5 22 58N 97 40W
Jerez de García Salinas, Mexico 86 C4 22 39N 103 0W
Jerez de la Frontera, Spain 19 D2 36 41N 6 7W
Jerez de los Caballeros, Spain 19 C2 38 20N 6 45W
Jericho = Arīḥā, Syria . . 44 C3 35 49N 36 35 E
Jericho = El Arīḥā, West Bank . . . . 47 D4 31 52N 35 27 E
Jericho, Australia . . . . 62 C4 23 38S 146 6 E
Jerilderie, Australia . . . . . 63 F4 35 20S 145 41 E
Jermyn, U.S.A. 79 E9 41 31N 75 31W
Jerome, U.S.A. 83 J8 34 45N 112 7W
Jersey, U.K. 11 H5 49 11N 2 7W
Jersey City, U.S.A. 79 F10 40 44N 74 4W
Jersey Shore, U.S.A. 78 E7 41 12N 77 15W
Jerseyville, U.S.A. 80 F9 39 7N 90 20W
Jerusalem, Israel . . . . 47 D4 31 47N 35 10 E
Jervis B., Australia . . . . . 63 F5 35 8S 150 46 E
Jesselton = Kota Kinabalu, Malaysia . . . . 36 C5 6 0N 116 4 E
Jessore, Bangla. . . . . 41 H16 23 10N 89 10 E
Jesup, U.S.A. 77 K5 31 36N 81 53W
Jesús Carranza, Mexico . 87 D5 17 28N 95 1W
Jesús María, Argentina . . 94 C3 30 59S 64 5W
Jetmore, U.S.A. 81 F5 38 4N 99 54W
Jetpur, India . . . . 42 J4 21 45N 70 10 E
Jevnaker, Norway . . . . . . 9 F14 60 15N 10 26 E
Jewett, Ohio, U.S.A. 78 F3 40 22N 81 2W
Jewett, Tex., U.S.A. 81 K6 31 22N 96 9W
Jewett City, U.S.A. 79 E13 41 36N 72 0W
Jeyḥūnābād, Iran . . . . 45 C6 34 58N 48 59 E
Jeypore, India . . . . 41 K13 18 50N 82 38 E
Jhajjar, India . . . . 42 E7 28 37N 76 42 E
Jhal Jhao, Pakistan . . . . . 40 F4 26 20N 65 35 E
Jhalawar, India . . . . 42 G7 24 40N 76 10 E
Jhang Maghiana, Pakistan 42 D5 31 15N 72 22 E
Jhansi, India . . . . 43 G8 25 30N 78 36 E
Jharia, India . . . . 43 H12 23 45N 86 26 E
Jharsuguda, India . . . . . . 41 J14 21 56N 84 5 E
Jhelum, Pakistan . . . . 42 C5 33 0N 73 45 E
Jhelum →, Pakistan . . . 42 D5 31 20N 72 10 E
Jhunjhunu, India . . . . 42 E6 28 10N 75 30 E
Ji Xian, Hebei, China . . . . 34 F8 37 35N 115 30 E
Ji Xian, Henan, China . . . 34 G8 35 22N 114 5 E
Ji Xian, Shanxi, China . . . 34 F6 36 7N 110 40 E
Jia Xian, Henan, China . . . 34 H7 33 59N 113 12 E
Jia Xian, Shaanxi, China . 34 E6 38 12N 110 28 E
Jiamusi, China . . . . 33 B8 46 40N 130 26 E
Ji'an, Jiangxi, China . . . . 33 D6 27 6N 114 59 E
Ji'an, Jilin, China . . . . . . 35 D14 41 5N 126 10 E
Jianchang, China . . . . 35 D11 40 55N 120 35 E
Jianchangying, China . . . 35 D10 40 10N 118 50 E
Jiangcheng, China . . . . . . 32 D5 22 36N 101 52 E
Jiangmen, China . . . . 33 D6 22 32N 113 0 E
Jiangsu □, China . . . . 35 H10 33 0N 120 0 E
Jiangxi □, China . . . . 33 D6 27 30N 116 0 E
Jiao Xian, China . . . . 35 F11 36 18N 120 1 E
Jiaohe, Hebei, China . . . . 34 E9 38 2N 116 20 E
Jiaohe, Jilin, China . . . . . 35 C14 43 40N 127 22 E
Jiaozhou Wan, China . . . . 35 F11 36 5N 120 10 E
Jiaozuo, China . . . . 34 G7 35 16N 113 12 E
Jiawang, China . . . . 35 G9 34 28N 117 26 E
Jiaxiang, China . . . . 34 G9 35 25N 116 20 E
Jiaxing, China . . . . 33 C7 30 49N 120 45 E
Jiayi = Chiai, Taiwan . . . 33 D7 23 29N 120 25 E
Jibuti = Djibouti ■, Africa 46 E3 12 0N 43 0 E
Jicarón, I., Panama 88 E3 7 10N 81 50W
Jiddah, Si. Arabia . . . . . . 46 C2 21 29N 39 10 E
Jido, India . . . . 41 E19 29 2N 94 58 E
Jieshou, China . . . . 34 H8 33 18N 115 22 E
Jiexiu, China . . . . 34 F6 37 2N 111 55 E
Jiggalong, Australia . . . . 60 D3 23 21S 120 47 E
Jihlava, Czech. . . . . 16 D8 49 28N 15 35 E
Jihlava →, Czech. . . . . . 17 D9 48 55N 16 36 E
Jijel, Algeria . . . . 50 A6 36 52N 5 50 E
Jijiga, Ethiopia . . . . 46 F3 9 20N 42 50 E
Jilin, China . . . . 35 C14 43 44N 126 30 E
Jilin □, China . . . . 35 C13 44 0N 127 0 E
Jilong = Chilung, Taiwan 33 D7 25 3N 121 45 E
Jima, Ethiopia . . . . 51 G12 7 40N 36 47 E
Jiménez, Mexico 86 B4 27 10N 104 54W
Jimo, China . . . . 35 F11 36 23N 120 30 E
Jin Xian, Hebei, China . . . 34 E8 38 2N 115 2 E
Jin Xian, Liaoning, China 35 E11 38 55N 121 42 E
Jinan, China . . . . 34 F9 36 38N 117 1 E
Jincheng, China . . . . 34 G7 35 29N 112 50 E
Jind, India . . . . 42 E7 29 19N 76 22 E
Jindabyne, Australia . . . . 63 F4 36 25S 148 35 E
Jindrichuv Hradeç, Czech. 16 D8 49 10N 15 2 E
Jing He →, China . . . . . 34 G5 34 27N 109 4 E
Jingbian, China . . . . 34 F5 37 20N 108 30 E
Jingchuan, China . . . . 34 G4 35 20N 107 20 E
Jingdezhen, China . . . . . . 33 D6 29 20N 117 11 E
Jinggu, China . . . . 32 D5 23 35N 100 41 E
Jinghai, China . . . . 34 E9 38 55N 116 55 E
Jingle, China . . . . 34 E6 38 20N 111 55 E
Jingning, China . . . . 34 G3 35 30N 105 43 E
Jingpo Hu, China . . . . 35 C15 43 55N 128 55 E
Jingtai, China . . . . 34 F3 37 10N 104 6 E
Jingxing, China . . . . 34 E8 38 2N 114 8 E
Jingyang, China . . . . 34 G5 34 30N 108 50 E
Jingyu, China . . . . 35 C14 42 25N 126 45 E
Jingyuan, China . . . . 34 F3 36 30N 104 40 E
Jingziguan, China . . . . . . 34 H6 33 15N 111 0 E
Jinhua, China . . . . 33 D6 29 8N 119 38 E
Jining, Nei Mongol Zizhiqu, China . . . . 34 D7 41 5N 113 0 E
Jining, Shandong, China . 34 G9 35 22N 116 34 E
Jinja, Uganda . . . . 54 B3 0 25N 33 12 E
Jinjang, Malaysia . . . . 39 L3 3 13N 101 39 E
Jinji, China . . . . 34 F4 37 58N 106 8 E
Jinnah Barrage, Pakistan 40 C7 32 58N 71 33 E
Jinotega, Nic. 88 D2 13 6N 85 59W
Jinotepe, Nic. 88 D2 11 50N 86 10W
Jinsha Jiang →, China . 32 D5 28 50N 104 36 E
Jinxi, China . . . . 35 D11 40 52N 120 50 E
Jinxiang, China . . . . 34 G9 35 5N 116 22 E
Jinzhou, China . . . . 35 D11 41 5N 121 3 E
Jiparaná →, Brazil 92 E6 8 3S 62 52W
Jipijapa, Ecuador 92 D2 1 0S 80 40W
Jiquilpan, Mexico 86 D4 19 57N 102 42W
Jishan, China . . . . 34 G6 35 34N 110 58 E
Jisr ash Shughūr, Syria . 44 C3 35 49N 36 18 E
Jitarning, Australia . . . . . 61 F2 32 48S 117 57 E
Jitra, Malaysia . . . . 39 J3 6 16N 100 25 E
Jiu →, Romania . . . . 17 F12 43 47N 23 48 E
Jiudengkou, China . . . . . . 34 E4 39 56N 106 40 E
Jiujiang, China . . . . 33 D6 29 42N 115 58 E
Jiutai, China . . . . 35 B13 44 10N 125 50 E
Jiuxiangcheng, China . . . 34 H8 33 12N 114 50 E
Jiuxincheng, China . . . . . 34 E8 39 17N 115 59 E
Jixi, China . . . . 35 B16 45 20N 130 50 E
Jiyang, China . . . . 35 F9 37 0N 117 12 E
Jīzān, Si. Arabia . . . . 46 D3 17 0N 42 20 E
Jize, China . . . . 34 F8 36 54N 114 56 E
Jizō-Zaki, Japan . . . . 31 G6 35 34N 133 20 E
Jizzakh, Uzbekistan . . . . . 26 E7 40 6N 67 50 E
Joaçaba, Brazil 95 B5 27 5S 51 31W
João Pessoa, Brazil 93 E12 7 10S 34 52W
Joaquín V. González, Argentina 94 B3 25 10S 64 0W
Jodhpur, India . . . . 42 F5 26 23N 73 8 E
Joensuu, Finland . . . . 24 B4 62 37N 29 49 E
Jofane, Mozam. . . . . 57 C5 21 15S 34 18 E
Jõgeva, Estonia . . . . 9 G22 58 45N 26 24 E
Joggins, Canada 71 C7 45 42N 64 27W
Jogjakarta = Yogyakarta, Indonesia . . . . 37 G14 7 49S 110 22 E
Johannesburg, S. Africa . 57 D4 26 10S 28 2 E
Johannesburg, U.S.A. . . . 85 K9 35 22N 117 38W
John Day, U.S.A. 82 D4 44 25N 118 57W
John Day →, U.S.A. 82 D3 45 44N 120 39W
John H. Kerr Reservoir, U.S.A. 77 G6 36 36N 78 18W
John o' Groats, U.K. 12 C5 58 38N 3 4W
Johnnie, U.S.A. 85 J10 36 25N 116 5W
John's Ra., Australia . . . 62 C1 21 55S 133 23 E
Johnson, U.S.A. 81 G4 37 34N 101 45W
Johnson City, N.Y., U.S.A. 79 D9 42 7N 75 58W
Johnson City, Tenn., U.S.A. 77 G4 36 19N 82 21W
Johnson City, Tex., U.S.A. 81 K5 30 17N 98 25W
Johnsonburg, U.S.A. 78 E6 41 29N 78 41W
Johnsondale, U.S.A. 85 K8 35 58N 118 32W
Johnson's Crossing, Canada 72 A2 60 29N 133 18W
Johnston, L., Australia . . 61 F3 32 25S 120 30 E
Johnston Falls = Mambilima Falls, Zambia . . . . 55 E2 10 31S 28 45 E
Johnston I., Pac. Oc. . . . 65 F11 17 10N 169 8W
Johnstone Str., Canada . . 72 C3 50 28N 126 0W
Johnstown, N.Y., U.S.A. . 79 C10 43 0N 74 22W
Johnstown, Pa., U.S.A. . . 78 F6 40 20N 78 55W
Johor Baharu, Malaysia . 39 M4 1 28N 103 46 E
Jõhvi, Estonia . . . . 9 G22 59 22N 27 27 E
Joinvile, Brazil 95 B6 26 15S 48 55W
Joinville I., Antarctica . . 5 C18 65 0S 55 30W
Jojutla, Mexico 87 D5 18 37N 99 11W
Jokkmokk, Sweden . . . . . 8 C18 66 35N 19 50 E
Jökulsá á Bru →, Iceland 8 D6 65 40N 14 16W
Jökulsá á Fjöllum →, Iceland 8 C5 66 10N 16 30W
Jolfā, Āzarbājān-e Sharqī, Iran . . . . 44 B5 38 57N 45 38 E
Jolfā, Eşfahan, Iran . . . . 45 C6 32 58N 51 37 E
Joliet, U.S.A. 76 E1 41 32N 88 5W
Joliette, Canada 70 C5 46 3N 73 24W
Jolo, Phil. . . . . 37 C6 6 0N 121 0 E
Jolon, U.S.A. 84 K5 35 58N 121 9W
Jombang, Indonesia . . . . 37 G15 7 33S 112 14 E
Jome, Indonesia . . . . 37 E7 1 16S 127 30 E
Jonava, Lithuania . . . . . . 9 J21 55 8N 24 12 E
Jones Sound, Canada . . . 4 B3 76 0N 85 0W
Jonesboro, Ark., U.S.A. . . 81 H9 35 50N 90 42W
Jonesboro, Ill., U.S.A. . . . 81 G10 37 27N 89 16W
Jonesboro, La., U.S.A. . . 81 J8 32 15N 92 43W
Jonesport, U.S.A. 71 D6 44 32N 67 37W
Joniškis, Lithuania . . . . . 9 H20 56 13N 23 35 E
Jönköping, Sweden . . . . . 9 H16 57 45N 14 10 E
Jonquière, Canada 71 C5 48 27N 71 14W
Joplin, U.S.A. 81 G7 37 6N 94 31W
Jordan, U.S.A. 82 C10 47 19N 106 55W
Jordan ■, Asia . . . . 47 E5 31 0N 36 0 E
Jordan →, Asia . . . . 47 D4 31 48N 35 32 E
Jordan Valley, U.S.A. . . . 82 E5 42 59N 117 3W
Jorhat, India . . . . 41 F19 26 45N 94 12 E
Jörn, Sweden . . . . 8 D19 65 4N 20 1 E
Jorong, Indonesia . . . . . . 36 E4 3 58S 114 56 E
Jørpeland, Norway . . . . . 9 G11 59 3N 6 1 E
Jorquera →, Chile 94 B2 28 3S 69 58W
Jos, Nigeria . . . . 50 G6 9 53N 8 51 E
José Batlle y Ordóñez, Uruguay 95 C4 33 20S 55 10W
Joseph, U.S.A. 82 D5 45 21N 117 14W
Joseph, L., Nfld., Canada 71 B6 52 45N 65 18W
Joseph, L., Ont., Canada . 78 A5 45 10N 79 44W
Joseph Bonaparte G., Australia . . . . 60 B4 14 35S 128 50 E
Joseph City, U.S.A. 83 J8 34 57N 110 20W
Joshua Tree, U.S.A. 85 L10 34 8N 116 19W
Joshua Tree National Monument, U.S.A. 85 M10 33 55N 116 0W
Jostedalsbreen, Norway . 9 F12 61 40N 6 59 E
Jotunheimen, Norway . . . 9 F13 61 35N 8 25 E
Jourdanton, U.S.A. 81 L5 28 55N 98 33W
Joussard, Canada 72 B5 55 22N 115 50W
Jovellanos, Cuba 88 B3 22 40N 81 10W
Ju Xian, China . . . . 35 F10 36 35N 118 20 E
Juan Aldama, Mexico 86 C4 24 20N 103 23W
Juan Bautista Alberdi, Argentina 94 C3 34 26S 61 48W
Juan de Fuca Str., Canada 84 B2 48 15N 124 0W

Kenner

Kankendy = Xankändi, Azerbaijan 25 G8 39 52N 46 49 E
Kanker, India 41 J12 20 10N 81 40 E
Kankunskiy, Russia 27 D13 57 37N 126 8 E
Kannapolis, U.S.A. 77 H5 35 30N 80 37W
Kannauj, India 43 F8 27 3N 79 56 E
Kannod, India 40 H10 22 45N 76 40 E
Kano, Nigeria 50 F6 12 2N 8 30 E
Kan'onji, Japan 31 G6 34 7N 133 39 E
Kanowit, Malaysia 36 D4 2 14N 112 20 E
Kanowna, Australia 61 F3 30 32S 121 31 E
Kanoya, Japan 31 J5 31 25N 130 50 E
Kanpetlet, Burma 41 J18 21 10N 93 59 E
Kanpur, India 43 F9 26 28N 80 20 E
Kansas □, U.S.A. 80 F6 38 30N 99 0W
Kansas ➝, U.S.A. 80 F7 39 7N 94 37W
Kansas City, Kans., U.S.A. 80 F7 39 7N 94 38W
Kansas City, Mo., U.S.A. 80 F7 39 6N 94 35W
Kansenia, Zaïre 55 E2 10 20S 26 0 E
Kansk, Russia 27 D10 56 20N 95 37 E
Kansŏng, S. Korea 35 E15 38 24N 128 30 E
Kansu = Gansu □, China 34 G3 36 0N 104 0 E
Kantang, Thailand 39 J2 7 25N 99 31 E
Kantharalak, Thailand 38 E5 14 39N 104 39 E
Kantō □, Japan 31 F9 36 15N 139 30 E
Kantō-Sanchi, Japan 31 G9 35 59N 138 50 E
Kanturk, Ireland 13 D3 52 11N 8 54W
Kanuma, Japan 31 F9 36 34N 139 42 E
Kanus, Namibia 56 D2 27 50S 18 39 E
Kanye, Botswana 56 C4 24 55S 25 28 E
Kanzenze, Zaïre 55 E2 10 30S 25 12 E
Kanzi, Ras, Tanzania 54 D4 7 1S 39 33 E
Kaohsiung, Taiwan 33 D7 22 35N 120 16 E
Kaokoveld, Namibia 56 B1 19 15S 14 30 E
Kaolack, Senegal 50 F1 14 5N 16 8W
Kaoshan, China 35 B13 44 38N 124 50 E
Kapadvanj, India 42 H5 23 5N 73 0 E
Kapan, Armenia 25 G8 39 18N 46 27 E
Kapanga, Zaïre 52 F4 8 30S 22 40 E
Kapchagai = Qapshaghay, Kazakstan 26 E8 43 51N 77 14 E
Kapema, Zaïre 55 E2 10 45S 28 22 E
Kapfenberg, Austria 16 E8 47 26N 15 18 E
Kapiri Mposhi, Zambia 55 E2 13 59S 28 43 E
Kapiskau ➝, Canada 70 B3 52 47N 81 55W
Kapit, Malaysia 36 D4 2 0N 112 55 E
Kapiti I., N.Z. 59 J5 40 50S 174 56 E
Kapoe, Thailand 39 H2 9 34N 98 32 E
Kapoeta, Sudan 51 H11 4 50N 33 35 E
Kaposvár, Hungary 17 E9 46 25N 17 47 E
Kapowsin, U.S.A. 84 D4 46 59N 122 13W
Kapps, Namibia 56 C2 22 32S 17 18 E
Kapsan, N. Korea 35 D15 41 4N 128 19 E
Kapsukas = Marijampole, Lithuania 9 J20 54 33N 23 19 E
Kapuas ➝, Indonesia 36 E3 0 25S 109 20 E
Kapuas Hulu, Pegunungan, Malaysia 36 D4 1 30N 113 30 E
Kapuas Hulu Ra. = Kapuas Hulu, Pegunungan, Malaysia 36 D4 1 30N 113 30 E
Kapulo, Zaïre 55 D2 8 18S 29 15 E
Kapunda, Australia 63 E2 34 20S 138 56 E
Kapuni, N.Z. 59 H5 39 29S 174 8 E
Kapurthala, India 42 D6 31 23N 75 25 E
Kapuskasing, Canada 70 C3 49 25N 82 30W
Kapuskasing ➝, Canada 70 C3 49 49N 82 0W
Kaputar, Australia 63 E5 30 15S 150 10 E
Kaputir, Kenya 54 B4 2 5N 35 28 E
Kara, Russia 26 C7 69 10N 65 0 E
Kara Bogaz Gol, Zaliv = Garabogazköl Aylagy, Turkmenistan 25 F9 41 0N 53 30 E
Kara Kalpak Republic □ = Karakalpakstan □, Uzbekistan 26 E6 43 0N 58 0 E
Kara Kum, Turkmenistan 26 F6 39 30N 60 0 E
Kara Sea, Russia 26 B7 75 0N 70 0 E
Karabiğa, Turkey 21 D12 40 24N 27 18 E
Karaburun, Turkey 21 E12 38 41N 26 28 E
Karabutak = Qarabutaq, Kazakstan 26 E7 49 59N 60 14 E
Karacabey, Turkey 21 D13 40 12N 28 21 E
Karacasu, Turkey 21 F13 37 43N 28 35 E
Karachi, Pakistan 42 G2 24 53N 67 0 E
Karad, India 40 L9 17 15N 74 10 E
Karadeniz Boğazı, Turkey 21 D13 41 10N 29 10 E
Karaganda = Qaraghandy, Kazakstan 26 E8 49 50N 73 10 E
Karagayly, Kazakstan 26 E8 49 26N 76 0 E
Karaginskiy, Ostrov, Russia 27 D17 58 45N 164 0 E
Karagiye, Vpadina, Kazakstan 25 F9 43 27N 51 45 E
Karagiye Depression = Karagiye, Vpadina, Kazakstan 25 F9 43 27N 51 45 E
Karagwe □, Tanzania 54 C3 2 0S 31 0 E
Karaikal, India 40 P11 10 59N 79 50 E
Karaikkudi, India 40 P11 10 5N 78 45 E
Karaj, Iran 45 C6 35 48N 51 0 E
Karak, Malaysia 39 L4 3 25N 102 2 E
Karakalpakstan □, Uzbekistan 26 E6 43 0N 58 0 E
Karakas, Kazakstan 26 E9 48 20N 83 30 E
Karakelong, Indonesia 37 D7 4 35N 126 50 E
Karakitang, Indonesia 37 D7 3 14N 125 28 E
Karaklis = Vanadzor, Armenia 25 F7 40 48N 44 30 E
Karakoram Pass, Pakistan 43 B7 35 33N 77 50 E
Karakoram Ra., Pakistan 43 B7 35 30N 77 0 E
Karalon, Russia 27 D12 57 5N 115 50 E
Karaman, Turkey 25 G5 37 14N 33 13 E
Karamay, China 32 B3 45 30N 84 58 E
Karambu, Indonesia 36 E5 3 53S 116 6 E
Karamea Bight, N.Z. 59 J3 41 22S 171 40 E
Karamsad, India 42 H5 22 35N 72 50 E
Karand, Iran 44 C5 34 16N 46 15 E
Karanganyar, Indonesia 37 G13 7 38S 109 37 E
Karasburg, Namibia 56 D2 28 0S 18 44 E
Karasino, Russia 26 C9 66 50N 86 50 E
Karasjok, Norway 8 B21 69 27N 25 30 E
Karasuk, Russia 26 D8 53 44N 78 2 E
Karasuyama, Japan 31 F10 36 39N 140 9 E
Karatau = Qaratau, Kazakstan 26 E8 43 10N 70 28 E
Karatau, Khrebet, Kazakstan 26 E7 43 30N 69 30 E
Karauli, India 42 F7 26 30N 77 4 E
Karavostasi, Cyprus 23 D11 35 8N 32 50 E
Karawang, Indonesia 37 G12 6 30S 107 15 E
Karawanken, Europe 16 E8 46 30N 14 40 E
Karazhal, Kazakstan 26 E8 48 2N 70 49 E
Karbalā, Iraq 44 C5 32 36N 44 3 E
Karcag, Hungary 17 E11 47 19N 20 57 E
Karcha ➝, Pakistan 43 B7 34 45N 76 10 E
Karda, Russia 27 D11 55 0N 103 16 E
Kardhítsa, Greece 21 E9 39 23N 21 54 E
Kärdla, Estonia 9 G20 58 50N 22 40 E
Kareeberge, S. Africa 56 E3 30 59S 21 50 E
Karelia □, Russia 24 A5 65 30N 32 30 E
Karelian Republic □ = Karelia □, Russia 24 A5 65 30N 32 30 E
Kārevāndar, Iran 45 E9 27 53N 60 44 E
Kargasok, Russia 26 D9 59 3N 80 53 E
Kargat, Russia 26 D9 55 10N 80 15 E
Kargil, India 43 B7 34 32N 76 12 E
Kargopol, Russia 24 B6 61 30N 38 58 E
Karīān, Iran 45 E8 26 57N 57 14 E
Kariba, Zimbabwe 55 F2 16 28S 28 50 E
Kariba, L., Zimbabwe 55 F2 16 40S 28 25 E
Kariba Dam, Zimbabwe 55 F2 16 30S 28 35 E
Kariba Gorge, Zambia 55 F2 16 30S 28 50 E
Karibib, Namibia 56 C2 22 0S 15 56 E
Karimata, Kepulauan, Indonesia 36 E3 1 25S 109 0 E
Karimata, Selat, Indonesia 36 E3 2 0S 108 40 E
Karimata Is. = Karimata, Kepulauan, Indonesia 36 E3 1 25S 109 0 E
Karimnagar, India 40 K11 18 26N 79 10 E
Karimunjawa, Kepulauan, Indonesia 36 F4 5 50S 110 30 E
Karin, Somali Rep. 46 E4 10 50N 45 52 E
Karīt, Iran 45 C8 33 29N 56 55 E
Kariya, Japan 31 G8 34 58N 137 1 E
Karkaralinsk = Qarqaraly, Kazakstan 26 E8 49 26N 75 30 E
Karkinitska Zatoka, Ukraine 25 E5 45 56N 33 0 E
Karkinitskiy Zaliv = Karkinitska Zatoka, Ukraine 25 E5 45 56N 33 0 E
Karl-Marx-Stadt = Chemnitz, Germany 16 C7 50 51N 12 54 E
Karlovac, Croatia 16 F8 45 31N 15 36 E
Karlovo, Bulgaria 21 C11 42 38N 24 47 E
Karlovy Vary, Czech. 16 C7 50 13N 12 51 E
Karlsbad = Karlovy Vary, Czech. 16 C7 50 13N 12 51 E
Karlsborg, Sweden 9 G16 58 33N 14 33 E
Karlshamn, Sweden 9 H16 56 10N 14 51 E
Karlskoga, Sweden 9 G16 59 22N 14 33 E
Karlskrona, Sweden 9 H16 56 10N 15 35 E
Karlsruhe, Germany 16 D5 49 0N 8 23 E
Karlstad, Sweden 9 G15 59 23N 13 30 E
Karlstad, U.S.A. 80 A6 48 35N 96 31W
Karnal, India 42 E7 29 42N 77 2 E
Karnali ➝, Nepal 43 E9 28 45N 81 16 E
Karnaphuli Res., Bangla. 41 H18 22 40N 92 20 E
Karnataka □, India 40 N10 13 15N 77 0 E
Karnes City, U.S.A. 81 L6 28 53N 97 54W
Karnische Alpen, Europe 16 E7 46 36N 13 0 E
Kärnten □, Austria 16 E8 46 52N 13 30 E
Karoi, Zimbabwe 55 F2 16 48S 29 45 E
Karonga, Malawi 55 D3 9 57S 33 55 E
Karoonda, Australia 63 F2 35 1S 139 59 E
Karora, Sudan 51 E12 17 44N 38 15 E
Karpasia □, Cyprus 23 D13 35 32N 34 15 E
Kárpathos, Greece 21 G12 35 37N 27 10 E
Karpinsk, Russia 24 C11 59 45N 60 1 E
Karpogory, Russia 24 B7 64 0N 44 27 E
Karpuz Burnu = Apostolos Andreas, C., Cyprus 23 D13 35 42N 34 35 E
Kars, Turkey 25 F7 40 40N 43 5 E
Karsakpay, Kazakstan 26 E7 47 55N 66 40 E
Karshi = Qarshi, Uzbekistan 26 F7 38 53N 65 48 E
Karsiyang, India 43 F13 26 56N 88 18 E
Karsun, Russia 24 D8 54 14N 46 57 E
Kartaly, Russia 26 D7 53 3N 60 40 E
Kartapur, India 42 D6 31 27N 75 32 E
Karthaus, U.S.A. 78 E6 41 8N 78 9W
Karufa, Indonesia 37 E8 3 50S 133 20 E
Karumba, Australia 62 B3 17 31S 140 50 E
Karumo, Tanzania 54 C3 2 25S 32 50 E
Karumwa, Tanzania 54 C3 3 12S 32 38 E
Karungu, Kenya 54 C3 0 50S 34 10 E
Karviná, Czech. 17 D10 49 53N 18 25 E
Karwar, India 40 M9 14 55N 74 13 E
Karwi, India 43 G9 25 12N 80 57 E
Kasache, Malawi 55 E3 13 25S 34 20 E
Kasai ➝, Zaïre 52 E3 3 30S 16 10 E
Kasai Oriental □, Zaïre 54 C1 5 0S 24 30 E
Kasaji, Zaïre 55 E1 10 25S 23 27 E
Kasama, Zambia 55 E3 10 16S 31 9 E
Kasan-dong, N. Korea 35 D14 41 18N 126 55 E
Kasane, Namibia 56 B3 17 34S 24 50 E
Kasanga, Tanzania 55 D3 8 30S 31 10 E
Kasangulu, Zaïre 52 E3 4 33S 15 15 E
Kasaragod, India 40 N9 12 30N 74 58 E
Kasba L., Canada 73 A8 60 20N 102 10W
Kāseh Garān, Iran 44 C5 34 5N 46 2 E
Kasempa, Zambia 55 E2 13 30S 25 44 E
Kasenga, Zaïre 55 E2 10 20S 28 45 E
Kasese, Uganda 54 B3 0 13N 30 3 E
Kasewa, Zambia 55 E2 14 28S 28 53 E
Kasganj, India 43 F8 27 48N 78 42 E
Kashabowie, Canada 70 C1 48 40N 90 26W
Kāshān, Iran 45 C6 34 5N 51 30 E
Kashi, China 32 C2 39 30N 76 2 E
Kashimbo, Zaïre 55 E2 11 12S 26 19 E
Kashipur, India 43 E8 29 15N 79 0 E
Kashiwazaki, Japan 31 F9 37 22N 138 33 E
Kashk-e Kohneh, Afghan. 40 B3 34 55N 62 30 E
Kāshmar, Iran 45 C8 35 16N 58 26 E
Kashmir, Asia 43 C7 34 0N 76 0 E
Kashmor, Pakistan 42 E3 28 28N 69 32 E
Kashun Noerh = Gaxun Nur, China 32 B5 42 22N 100 30 E
Kasimov, Russia 24 D7 54 55N 41 20 E
Kasinge, Zaïre 54 D2 6 15S 26 58 E
Kasiruta, Indonesia 37 E7 0 25S 127 12 E
Kaskaskia ➝, U.S.A. 80 G10 37 58N 89 57W
Kaskattama ➝, Canada 73 B10 57 3N 90 4W
Kaskinen, Finland 9 E19 62 22N 21 15 E
Kaslo, Canada 72 D5 49 55N 116 55W
Kasmere L., Canada 73 B8 59 34N 101 10W
Kasongo, Zaïre 54 C2 4 30S 26 33 E
Kasongo Lunda, Zaïre 52 F3 6 35S 16 49 E
Kásos, Greece 21 G12 35 20N 26 55 E
Kassalâ, Sudan 51 E12 15 30N 36 0 E
Kassel, Germany 16 C5 51 18N 9 26 E
Kassiópi, Greece 23 A3 39 48N 19 53 E
Kassue, Indonesia 37 F9 6 58S 139 21 E
Kastamonu, Turkey 25 F5 41 25N 33 43 E
Kastélli, Greece 23 D5 35 29N 23 38 E
Kastéllion, Greece 23 D7 35 12N 25 20 E
Kastoria, Greece 21 D9 40 30N 21 19 E
Kasulu, Tanzania 54 C3 4 37S 30 5 E
Kasulu □, Tanzania 54 C3 4 37S 30 5 E
Kasumi, Japan 31 G7 35 38N 134 38 E
Kasungu, Malawi 55 E3 13 0S 33 29 E
Kasur, Pakistan 42 D6 31 5N 74 25 E
Kata, Russia 27 D11 58 46N 102 40 E
Kataba, Zambia 55 F2 16 5S 25 10 E
Katako Kombe, Zaïre 54 C1 3 25S 24 20 E
Katale, Tanzania 54 C3 4 52S 31 7 E
Katamatite, Australia 63 F4 36 6S 145 41 E
Katanda, Kivu, Zaïre 54 C2 0 55S 29 21 E
Katanda, Shaba, Zaïre 54 D1 7 52S 24 13 E
Katanga = Shaba □, Zaïre 54 D2 8 0S 25 0 E
Katangi, India 40 J11 21 56N 79 50 E
Katangli, Russia 27 D15 51 42N 143 14 E
Katavi Swamp, Tanzania 54 D3 6 50S 31 10 E
Kateríni, Greece 21 D10 40 18N 22 37 E
Katha, Burma 41 G20 24 10N 96 30 E
Katherine, Australia 60 B5 14 27S 132 20 E
Kathiawar, India 42 H4 22 20N 71 0 E
Kathikas, Cyprus 23 E11 34 55N 32 25 E
Katihar, India 43 G12 25 34N 87 36 E
Katima Mulilo, Zambia 56 B3 17 28S 24 13 E
Katimbira, Malawi 55 E3 12 40S 34 0 E
Katingan = Mendawai ➝, Indonesia 36 E4 3 30S 113 0 E
Katiola, Ivory C. 50 G3 8 10N 5 10W
Katmandu, Nepal 43 F11 27 45N 85 20 E
Káto Arkhánai, Greece 23 D7 35 15N 25 10 E
Káto Khorió, Greece 23 D7 35 3N 25 47 E
Kato Pyrgos, Cyprus 23 D11 35 11N 32 41 E
Katompe, Zaïre 54 D2 6 2S 26 23 E
Katonga ➝, Uganda 54 B3 0 34N 31 50 E
Katoomba, Australia 63 E5 33 41S 150 19 E
Katowice, Poland 17 C10 50 17N 19 5 E
Katrine, L., U.K. 12 E4 56 15N 4 30W
Katrineholm, Sweden 9 G17 59 9N 16 12 E
Katsepe, Madag. 57 B8 15 45S 46 15 E
Katsina, Nigeria 50 F6 13 0N 7 32 E
Katsumoto, Japan 31 H4 33 51N 129 42 E
Katsuura, Japan 31 G10 35 10N 140 20 E
Katsuyama, Japan 31 F8 36 3N 136 30 E
Kattaviá, Greece 23 D9 35 57N 27 46 E
Kattegat, Denmark 9 H14 57 0N 11 20 E
Katumba, Zaïre 54 D2 7 40S 25 17 E
Katungu, Kenya 54 C5 2 55S 40 3 E
Katwa, India 43 H13 23 30N 88 5 E
Katwijk-aan-Zee, Neths. 15 B4 52 12N 4 24 E
Kauai, U.S.A. 74 H15 22 3N 159 30W
Kauai Channel, U.S.A. 74 H15 21 45N 158 50W
Kaufman, U.S.A. 81 J6 32 35N 96 19W
Kauhajoki, Finland 9 E20 62 25N 22 10 E
Kaukauna, U.S.A. 76 C1 44 17N 88 17W
Kaukauveld, Namibia 56 C3 20 0S 20 15 E
Kaunas, Lithuania 9 J20 54 54N 23 54 E
Kaura Namoda, Nigeria 50 F6 12 37N 6 33 E
Kautokeino, Norway 8 B20 69 0N 23 4 E
Kavacha, Russia 27 C17 60 16N 169 51 E
Kavalerovo, Russia 30 B7 44 15N 135 4 E
Kavali, India 40 M12 14 55N 80 1 E
Kavála, Greece 21 D11 40 57N 24 28 E
Kavār, Iran 45 D7 29 11N 52 44 E
Kavos, Greece 23 B4 39 23N 20 3 E
Kaw, Fr. Guiana 93 C8 4 30N 52 15W
Kawagama L., Canada 78 A6 45 18N 78 45W
Kawagoe, Japan 31 G9 35 55N 139 29 E
Kawaguchi, Japan 31 G9 35 52N 139 45 E
Kawaihae, U.S.A. 74 H17 20 3N 155 50W
Kawambwa, Zambia 55 D2 9 48S 29 3 E
Kawanoe, Japan 31 G6 34 1N 133 34 E
Kawardha, India 43 J9 22 0N 81 17 E
Kawasaki, Japan 31 G9 35 35N 139 42 E
Kawene, Canada 70 C1 48 45N 91 15W
Kawerau, N.Z. 59 H6 38 7S 176 42 E
Kawhia Harbour, N.Z. 59 H5 38 5S 174 51 E
Kawio, Kepulauan, Indonesia 37 D7 4 30N 125 30 E
Kawnro, Burma 41 H21 22 48N 99 8 E
Kawthoolei = Kawthule □, Burma 41 L20 18 0N 97 30 E
Kawthule □, Burma 41 L20 18 0N 97 30 E
Kaya, Burkina Faso 50 F4 13 4N 1 10W
Kayah □, Burma 41 K20 19 15N 97 15 E
Kayan ➝, Indonesia 36 D5 2 55N 117 35 E
Kaycee, U.S.A. 82 E10 43 43N 106 38W
Kayeli, Indonesia 37 E7 3 20S 127 10 E
Kayenta, U.S.A. 83 H8 36 44N 110 15W
Kayes, Mali 50 F2 14 25N 11 30W
Kayoa, Indonesia 37 D7 0 1N 127 28 E
Kayomba, Zambia 55 E1 13 11S 24 2 E
Kayrunnera, Australia 63 E3 30 40S 142 30 E
Kayseri, Turkey 25 G6 38 45N 35 30 E
Kaysville, U.S.A. 82 F8 41 2N 111 56W
Kayuagung, Indonesia 36 E2 3 24S 104 50 E
Kazachye, Russia 27 B14 70 52N 135 58 E
Kazakstan ■, Asia 26 E7 50 0N 70 0 E
Kazan, Russia 24 C8 55 50N 49 10 E
Kazan-Rettō, Pac. Oc. 64 E6 25 0N 141 0 E
Kazanlŭk, Bulgaria 21 C11 42 38N 25 20 E
Kazatin = Kozyatyn, Ukraine 17 D15 49 45N 28 50 E
Kāzerūn, Iran 45 D6 29 38N 51 40 E
Kazumba, Zaïre 52 F4 6 25S 22 5 E
Kazuno, Japan 30 D10 40 10N 140 45 E
Kazym ➝, Russia 26 C7 63 54N 65 50 E
Ké-Macina, Mali 50 F3 13 58N 5 22W
Kéa, Greece 21 F11 37 35N 24 22 E
Keams Canyon, U.S.A. 83 J8 35 49N 110 12W
Kearney, U.S.A. 80 E5 40 42N 99 5W
Keban, Turkey 25 G6 38 50N 38 50 E
Kebnekaise, Sweden 8 C18 67 53N 18 33 E
Kebri Dehar, Ethiopia 46 F3 6 45N 44 17 E
Kebumen, Indonesia 37 G13 7 42S 109 40 E
Kechika ➝, Canada 72 B3 59 41N 127 12W
Kecskemét, Hungary 17 E10 46 57N 19 42 E
Kedgwick, Canada 71 C6 47 40N 67 20W
Kédhros Óros, Greece 23 D6 35 11N 24 37 E
Kedia Hill, Botswana 56 C3 21 28S 24 37 E
Kediniai, Lithuania 9 J21 55 15N 24 2 E
Kediri, Indonesia 37 G15 7 51S 112 1 E
Kédougou, Senegal 50 F2 12 35N 12 10W
Keeler, U.S.A. 84 J9 36 29N 117 52W
Keeley L., Canada 73 C7 54 54N 108 8W
Keeling Is. = Cocos Is., Ind. Oc. 64 J1 12 10S 96 55 E
Keene, Calif., U.S.A. 85 K8 35 13N 118 33W
Keene, N.H., U.S.A. 79 D12 42 56N 72 17W
Keeper Hill, Ireland 13 D3 52 45N 8 16W
Keer-Weer, C., Australia 62 A3 14 0S 141 32 E
Keeseville, U.S.A. 79 B11 44 29N 73 30W
Keetmanshoop, Namibia 56 D2 26 35S 18 8 E
Keewatin, U.S.A. 80 B8 47 24N 93 5W
Keewatin □, Canada 73 A9 63 20N 95 0W
Keewatin ➝, Canada 73 B8 56 29N 100 46W
Kefallinía, Greece 21 E9 38 20N 20 30 E
Kefamenanu, Indonesia 37 F6 9 28S 124 29 E
Keffi, Nigeria 50 G6 8 55N 7 43 E
Keflavík, Iceland 8 D2 64 2N 22 35W
Keg River, Canada 72 B5 57 54N 117 55W
Kegaska, Canada 71 B7 50 9N 61 18W
Keighley, U.K. 10 D6 53 52N 1 54W
Keila, Estonia 9 G21 59 18N 24 25 E
Keimoes, S. Africa 56 D3 28 41S 20 59 E
Keitele, Finland 8 E22 63 10N 26 20 E
Keith, Australia 63 F3 36 6S 140 20 E
Keith, U.K. 12 D6 57 32N 2 57W
Keith Arm, Canada 68 B7 64 20N 122 15W
Kejser Franz Joseph Fjord = Kong Franz Joseph Fd., Greenland 4 B6 73 30N 24 30W
Kekri, India 42 G6 26 0N 75 10 E
Kël, Russia 27 C13 69 30N 124 10 E
Kelan, China 34 E6 38 43N 111 31 E
Kelang, Malaysia 39 L3 3 2N 101 26 E
Kelantan ➝, Malaysia 39 J4 6 13N 102 14 E
Kelibia, Tunisia 51 A7 36 50N 11 3 E
Kellé, Congo 52 E2 0 8S 14 38 E
Keller, U.S.A. 82 B4 48 5N 118 41W
Kellerberrin, Australia 61 F2 31 36S 117 38 E
Kellett, C., Canada 4 B1 72 0N 126 0W
Kelleys I., U.S.A. 78 E2 41 36N 82 42W
Kellogg, U.S.A. 82 C5 47 32N 116 7W
Kells = Ceanannus Mor, Ireland 13 C5 53 44N 6 53W
Kélo, Chad 51 G8 9 10N 15 45 E
Kelokedhara, Cyprus 23 E11 34 48N 32 39 E
Kelowna, Canada 72 D5 49 50N 119 25W
Kelsey Bay, Canada 72 C3 50 25N 126 0W
Kelseyville, U.S.A. 84 G4 38 59N 122 50W
Kelso, N.Z. 59 L2 45 54S 169 15 E
Kelso, U.K. 12 F6 55 36N 2 26W
Kelso, U.S.A. 84 D4 46 9N 122 54W
Keluang, Malaysia 39 L4 2 3N 103 18 E
Kelvington, Canada 73 C8 52 10N 103 30W
Kem, Russia 24 B5 65 0N 34 38 E
Kem ➝, Russia 24 B5 64 57N 34 41 E
Kema, Indonesia 37 D7 1 22N 125 8 E
Kemano, Canada 72 C3 53 35N 128 0W
Kemasik, Malaysia 39 K4 4 25N 103 27 E
Kemerovo, Russia 26 D9 55 20N 86 5 E
Kemi, Finland 8 D21 65 44N 24 34 E
Kemi älv = Kemijoki ➝, Finland 8 D21 65 47N 24 32 E
Kemijärvi, Finland 8 C22 66 43N 27 22 E
Kemijoki ➝, Finland 8 D21 65 47N 24 32 E
Kemmerer, U.S.A. 82 F8 41 48N 110 32W
Kemmuna = Comino, Malta 23 C1 36 2N 14 20 E
Kemp, L., U.S.A. 81 J5 33 46N 99 9W
Kemp Land, Antarctica 5 C5 69 0S 55 0 E
Kempsey, Australia 63 E5 31 1S 152 50 E
Kempt, L., Canada 70 C5 47 25N 74 22W
Kempten, Germany 16 E6 47 45N 10 17 E
Kemptville, Canada 70 C4 45 0N 75 38W
Kendal, Indonesia 36 F4 6 56S 110 14 E
Kendal, U.K. 10 C5 54 20N 2 44W
Kendall, Australia 63 E5 31 35S 152 44 E
Kendall ➝, Australia 62 A3 14 4S 141 35 E
Kendallville, U.S.A. 76 E3 41 27N 85 16W
Kendari, Indonesia 37 E6 3 50S 122 30 E
Kendawangan, Indonesia 36 E4 2 32S 110 17 E
Kende, Nigeria 50 F5 11 30N 4 12 E
Kendenup, Australia 61 F2 34 30S 117 38 E
Kendrapara, India 41 J15 20 35N 86 30 E
Kendrew, S. Africa 56 E3 32 32S 24 30 E
Kendrick, U.S.A. 82 C5 46 37N 116 39W
Kene Thao, Laos 38 D3 17 44N 101 10 E
Kenedy, U.S.A. 81 L6 28 49N 97 51W
Kenema, S. Leone 50 G2 7 50N 11 14W
Keng Kok, Laos 38 D5 16 26N 105 12 E
Keng Tawng, Burma 41 J21 20 45N 98 18 E
Keng Tung, Burma 41 J21 21 0N 99 30 E
Kenge, Zaïre 52 E3 4 50S 17 4 E
Kengeja, Tanzania 54 D4 5 26S 39 45 E
Kenhardt, S. Africa 56 D3 29 19S 21 12 E
Kenitra, Morocco 50 B3 34 15N 6 40W
Kenli, China 35 F10 37 30N 118 20 E
Kenmare, Ireland 13 E2 51 53N 9 36W
Kenmare, U.S.A. 80 A3 48 41N 102 5W
Kenmare ➝, Ireland 13 E2 51 48N 9 51W
Kennebec, U.S.A. 80 D5 43 54N 99 52W
Kennedy, Zimbabwe 55 F2 18 52S 27 10 E
Kennedy Ra., Australia 61 D2 24 45S 115 10 E
Kennedy Taungdeik, Burma 41 H18 23 15N 93 45 E
Kenner, U.S.A. 81 L9 29 59N 90 15W

Korea Bay

Korea Bay, *Korea* **35 E13** 39 0N 124 0 E
Korea Strait, *Asia* **35 G15** 34 0N 129 30 E
Korets, *Ukraine* **17 C14** 50 40N 27 5 E
Korhogo, *Ivory C.* **50 G3** 9 29N 5 28W
Korim, *Indonesia* **37 E9** 0 58S 136 10 E
Korinthiakós Kólpos, *Greece* **21 E10** 38 16N 22 30 E
Kórinthos, *Greece* **21 F10** 37 56N 22 55 E
Korissa, Límni, *Greece* **23 B3** 39 27N 19 53 E
Kōriyama, *Japan* **30 F10** 37 24N 140 23 E
Korla, *China* **32 B3** 41 45N 86 4 E
Kormakiti, C., *Cyprus* **23 D11** 35 23N 32 56 E
Korneshty = Corneşti, *Moldova* **17 E15** 47 21N 28 1 E
Koro, *Fiji* **59 C8** 17 19S 179 23 E
Koro, *Ivory C.* **50 G3** 8 32N 7 30W
Koro, *Mali* **50 F4** 14 1N 2 58W
Koro Sea, *Fiji* **59 C9** 17 30S 179 45W
Korogwe, *Tanzania* **54 D4** 5 5S 38 25 E
Korogwe □, *Tanzania* **54 D4** 5 0S 38 20 E
Koroit, *Australia* **63 F3** 38 18S 142 24 E
Koror, *Pac. Oc.* **37 C8** 7 20N 134 28 E
Körös ⟶, *Hungary* **17 E11** 46 43N 20 12 E
Korosten, *Ukraine* **17 C15** 50 54N 28 36 E
Korostyshev, *Ukraine* **17 C15** 50 19N 29 4 E
Korraraika, Helodranon' i, *Madag.* **57 B7** 17 45S 43 57 E
Korsakov, *Russia* **27 E15** 46 36N 142 42 E
Korshunovo, *Russia* **27 D12** 58 37N 110 10 E
Korsør, *Denmark* **9 J14** 55 20N 11 9 E
Korti, *Sudan* **51 E11** 18 6N 31 33 E
Kortrijk, *Belgium* **15 D3** 50 50N 3 17 E
Korwai, *India* **42 G8** 24 7N 78 5 E
Koryakskoye Nagorye, *Russia* **27 C18** 61 0N 171 0 E
Koryŏng, *S. Korea* **35 G15** 35 44N 128 15 E
Kos, *Greece* **21 F12** 36 50N 27 15 E
Koschagyl, *Kazakstan* **25 E9** 46 40N 54 0 E
Kościan, *Poland* **17 B9** 52 5N 16 40 E
Kosciusko, *U.S.A.* **81 J10** 33 4N 89 35W
Kosciusko, Mt., *Australia* **63 F4** 36 27S 148 16 E
Kosciusko I., *U.S.A.* **72 B2** 56 0N 133 40W
Kosha, *Sudan* **51 D11** 20 50N 30 30 E
K'oshih = Kashi, *China* **32 C2** 39 30N 76 2 E
Koshiki-Rettō, *Japan* **31 J4** 31 45N 129 49 E
Kosi, *India* **42 F7** 27 48N 77 29 E
Košice, *Slovak Rep.* **17 D11** 48 42N 21 15 E
Koskhinoú, *Greece* **23 C10** 36 23N 28 13 E
Koslan, *Russia* **24 B8** 63 34N 49 14 E
Kosŏng, *N. Korea* **35 E15** 38 40N 128 22 E
Kosovo □, *Serbia, Yug.* **21 C9** 42 30N 21 0 E
Kosovska-Mitrovica = Titova-Mitrovica, *Serbia, Yug.* **21 C9** 42 54N 20 52 E
Kostamuksa, *Russia* **24 B5** 62 34N 32 44 E
Koster, *S. Africa* **56 D4** 25 52S 26 54 E
Kôstî, *Sudan* **51 F11** 13 8N 32 43 E
Kostopil, *Ukraine* **17 C14** 50 51N 26 22 E
Kostroma, *Russia* **24 C7** 57 50N 40 58 E
Kostrzyn, *Poland* **16 B8** 52 35N 14 39 E
Koszalin, *Poland* **16 A9** 54 11N 16 8 E
Kot Addu, *Pakistan* **42 D4** 30 30N 71 0 E
Kot Moman, *Pakistan* **42 C5** 32 13N 73 0 E
Kota, *India* **42 G6** 25 14N 75 49 E
Kota Baharu, *Malaysia* **39 J4** 6 7N 102 14 E
Kota Belud, *Malaysia* **36 C5** 6 21N 116 26 E
Kota Kinabalu, *Malaysia* **36 C5** 6 0N 116 4 E
Kota Tinggi, *Malaysia* **39 M4** 1 44N 103 53 E
Kotaagung, *Indonesia* **36 F2** 5 38S 104 29 E
Kotabaru, *Indonesia* **36 E5** 3 20S 116 20 E
Kotabumi, *Indonesia* **36 E2** 4 49S 104 54 E
Kotagede, *Indonesia* **37 G14** 7 54S 110 26 E
Kotamobagu, *Indonesia* **37 D6** 0 57N 124 31 E
Kotaneelee ⟶, *Canada* **72 A4** 60 11N 123 42W
Kotawaringin, *Indonesia* **36 E4** 2 28S 111 27 E
Kotcho L., *Canada* **72 B4** 59 7N 121 12W
Kotelnich, *Russia* **24 C8** 58 22N 48 24 E
Kotelnikovo, *Russia* **25 E7** 47 38N 43 8 E
Kotelnyy, Ostrov, *Russia* **27 B14** 75 10N 139 0 E
Kothi, *India* **43 G9** 24 45N 80 40 E
Kotiro, *Pakistan* **42 F2** 26 17N 67 13 E
Kotka, *Finland* **9 F22** 60 28N 26 58 E
Kotlas, *Russia* **24 B8** 61 17N 46 43 E
Kotli, *Pakistan* **42 C5** 33 30N 73 55 E
Kotmul, *Pakistan* **43 B6** 35 32N 75 10 E
Kotor, *Montenegro, Yug.* **21 C8** 42 25N 18 47 E
Kotovsk, *Ukraine* **17 E15** 47 45N 29 35 E
Kotputli, *India* **42 F7** 27 43N 76 12 E
Kotri, *Pakistan* **42 G3** 25 22N 68 22 E
Kottayam, *India* **40 Q10** 9 35N 76 33 E
Kotturu, *India* **40 M10** 14 45N 76 10 E
Kotuy ⟶, *Russia* **27 B11** 71 54N 102 6 E
Kotzebue, *U.S.A.* **68 B3** 66 53N 162 39W
Kouango, *C.A.R.* **52 C4** 5 0N 20 10 E
Koudougou, *Burkina Faso* **50 F4** 12 10N 2 20W
Koufonísi, *Greece* **23 E8** 34 56N 26 8 E
Kougaberge, *S. Africa* **56 E3** 33 48S 23 50 E
Kouilou ⟶, *Congo* **52 E2** 4 10S 12 5 E
Kouki, *C.A.R.* **52 C3** 7 22N 17 3 E
Koula Moutou, *Gabon* **52 E2** 1 15S 12 25 E
Koulen, *Cambodia* **38 F5** 13 50N 104 40 E
Koulikoro, *Mali* **50 F3** 12 40N 7 50W
Kouloúra, *Greece* **23 A3** 39 42N 19 54 E
Koúm-bournoú, Ákra, *Greece* **23 C10** 36 15N 28 11 E
Koumala, *Australia* **62 C4** 21 38S 149 15 E
Koumra, *Chad* **51 G8** 8 50N 17 35 E
Kounradskiy, *Kazakstan* **26 E8** 46 59N 75 0 E
Kountze, *U.S.A.* **81 K7** 30 22N 94 19W
Kouris ⟶, *Cyprus* **23 E11** 34 38N 32 54 E
Kouroussa, *Guinea* **50 F3** 10 45N 9 45W
Kousseri, *Cameroon* **51 F7** 12 0N 14 55 E
Koutiala, *Mali* **50 F3** 12 25N 5 23W
Kouvola, *Finland* **9 F22** 60 52N 26 43 E
Kovdor, *Russia* **24 A5** 67 34N 30 24 E
Kovel, *Ukraine* **17 C13** 51 11N 24 38 E
Kovrov, *Russia* **24 C7** 56 25N 41 25 E
Kowanyama, *Australia* **62 B3** 15 29S 141 44 E
Kowkash, *Canada* **70 B2** 50 20N 87 12W
Kowŏn, *N. Korea* **35 E14** 39 26N 127 14 E
Köyceğiz, *Turkey* **21 F13** 36 57N 28 40 E
Koyuk, *U.S.A.* **68 B3** 64 56N 161 9W
Koyukuk ⟶, *U.S.A.* **68 B4** 64 55N 157 32W
Koza, *Japan* **31 L3** 26 19N 127 46 E
Kozáni, *Greece* **21 D9** 40 19N 21 47 E
Kozhikode = Calicut, *India* **40 P9** 11 15N 75 43 E
Kozhva, *Russia* **24 A10** 65 10N 57 0 E
Kozyatyn, *Ukraine* **17 D15** 49 45N 28 50 E
Kpalimé, *Togo* **50 G5** 6 57N 0 44 E
Kra, Isthmus of = Kra, Kho Khot, *Thailand* **39 G2** 10 15N 99 30 E
Kra, Kho Khot, *Thailand* **39 G2** 10 15N 99 30 E
Kra Buri, *Thailand* **39 G2** 10 22N 98 46 E
Krabi, *Thailand* **39 H2** 8 4N 98 55 E
Kragan, *Indonesia* **37 G14** 6 43S 111 38 E
Kragerø, *Norway* **9 G13** 58 52N 9 25 E
Kragujevac, *Serbia, Yug.* **21 B9** 44 2N 20 56 E
Krajina, *Bos.-H.* **20 B7** 44 45N 16 35 E
Krakatau = Rakata, Pulau, *Indonesia* **36 F3** 6 10S 105 20 E
Krakor, *Cambodia* **38 F5** 12 32N 104 12 E
Kraków, *Poland* **17 C10** 50 4N 19 57 E
Kraksaan, *Indonesia* **37 G15** 7 43S 113 23 E
Kralanh, *Cambodia* **38 F4** 13 35N 103 25 E
Kraljevo, *Serbia, Yug.* **21 C9** 43 44N 20 41 E
Kramatorsk, *Ukraine* **25 E6** 48 50N 37 30 E
Kramfors, *Sweden* **9 E17** 62 55N 17 48 E
Kranj, *Slovenia* **16 E8** 46 16N 14 22 E
Krankskop, *S. Africa* **57 D5** 28 0S 30 47 E
Krasavino, *Russia* **24 B8** 60 58N 46 29 E
Kraskino, *Russia* **27 E14** 42 44N 130 48 E
Kraśnik, *Poland* **17 C12** 50 55N 22 5 E
Krasnoarmeysk, *Russia* **26 D5** 51 0N 45 42 E
Krasnodar, *Russia* **25 E6** 45 5N 39 0 E
Krasnokamsk, *Russia* **24 C10** 58 4N 55 48 E
Krasnoperekopsk, *Ukraine* **25 E5** 46 0N 33 54 E
Krasnorechenskiy, *Russia* **30 B7** 44 41N 135 14 E
Krasnoselkupsk, *Russia* **26 C9** 65 20N 82 10 E
Krasnoturinsk, *Russia* **24 C11** 59 46N 60 12 E
Krasnoufimsk, *Russia* **24 C10** 56 36N 57 38 E
Krasnouralsk, *Russia* **24 C11** 58 21N 60 3 E
Krasnovishersk, *Russia* **24 B10** 60 23N 57 3 E
Krasnovodsk = Türkmenbashi, *Turkmenistan* **25 F9** 40 5N 53 5 E
Krasnoyarsk, *Russia* **27 D10** 56 8N 93 0 E
Krasnyy Luch, *Ukraine* **25 E6** 48 13N 39 0 E
Krasnyy Yar, *Russia* **25 E8** 46 43N 48 23 E
Kratie, *Cambodia* **38 F6** 12 32N 106 10 E
Krau, *Indonesia* **37 E10** 3 19S 140 5 E
Kravanh, Chuor Phnum, *Cambodia* **39 G4** 12 0N 103 32 E
Krefeld, *Germany* **16 C4** 51 20N 6 33 E
Kremen, *Croatia* **16 F8** 44 28N 15 53 E
Kremenchug = Kremenchuk, *Ukraine* **25 E5** 49 5N 33 25 E
Kremenchuk, *Ukraine* **25 E5** 49 5N 33 25 E
Kremenchuksk Vdskh., *Ukraine* **25 E5** 49 20N 32 30 E
Kremenets, *Ukraine* **17 C13** 50 8N 25 43 E
Kremmling, *U.S.A.* **82 F10** 40 4N 106 24W
Krems, *Austria* **16 D8** 48 25N 15 36 E
Kretinga, *Lithuania* **9 J19** 55 53N 21 15 E
Kribi, *Cameroon* **52 D1** 2 57N 9 56 E
Krichev = Krychaw, *Belarus* **17 B16** 53 40N 31 41 E
Kriós, Ákra, *Greece* **23 D5** 35 13N 23 34 E
Krishna ⟶, *India* **41 M12** 15 57N 80 59 E
Krishnanagar, *India* **43 H13** 23 24N 88 33 E
Kristiansand, *Norway* **9 G13** 58 8N 8 1 E
Kristianstad, *Sweden* **9 H16** 56 2N 14 9 E
Kristiansund, *Norway* **8 E12** 63 7N 7 45 E
Kristiinankaupunki, *Finland* **9 E19** 62 16N 21 21 E
Kristinehamn, *Sweden* **9 G16** 59 18N 14 13 E
Kristinestad = Kristiinankaupunki, *Finland* **9 E19** 62 16N 21 21 E
Kríti, *Greece* **23 D7** 35 15N 25 0 E
Kritsá, *Greece* **23 D7** 35 10N 25 41 E
Krivoy Rog = Kryvyy Rih, *Ukraine* **25 E5** 47 51N 33 20 E
Krk, *Croatia* **16 F8** 45 8N 14 40 E
Krokodil ⟶, *Mozam.* **57 D5** 25 14S 32 18 E
Kronprins Olav Kyst, *Antarctica* **5 C5** 69 0S 42 0 E
Kronshtadt, *Russia* **24 B4** 59 57N 29 51 E
Kroonstad, *S. Africa* **56 D4** 27 43S 27 19 E
Kropotkin, *Irkutsk, Russia* **27 D12** 59 0N 115 30 E
Kropotkin, *Krasnodar, Russia* **25 E7** 45 28N 40 28 E
Krosno, *Poland* **17 D11** 49 42N 21 46 E
Krotoszyn, *Poland* **17 C9** 51 42N 17 23 E
Kroussón, *Greece* **23 D6** 35 13N 24 59 E
Kruger Nat. Park, *S. Africa* **57 C5** 23 30S 31 40 E
Krugersdorp, *S. Africa* **57 D4** 26 5S 27 46 E
Kruisfontein, *S. Africa* **56 E3** 33 59S 24 43 E
Krung Thep = Bangkok, *Thailand* **38 F3** 13 45N 100 35 E
Krupki, *Belarus* **17 A15** 54 19N 29 8 E
Kruševac, *Serbia, Yug.* **21 C9** 43 35N 21 28 E
Kruzof I., *U.S.A.* **72 B1** 57 10N 135 40W
Krychaw, *Belarus* **17 B16** 53 40N 31 41 E
Krymskiy Poluostrov = Krymskyy Pivostriv, *Ukraine* **25 E5** 45 0N 34 0 E
Krymskyy Pivostriv, *Ukraine* **25 E5** 45 0N 34 0 E
Kryvyy Rih, *Ukraine* **25 E5** 47 51N 33 20 E
Ksar el Boukhari, *Algeria* **50 A5** 35 51N 2 52 E
Ksar el Kebir, *Morocco* **50 B3** 35 0N 6 0W
Ksar es Souk = Ar Rachidiya, *Morocco* **50 B4** 31 58N 4 20W
Kuala, *Indonesia* **36 D3** 2 55N 105 47 E
Kuala Berang, *Malaysia* **39 K4** 5 5N 103 1 E
Kuala Dungun, *Malaysia* **39 K4** 4 45N 103 25 E
Kuala Kangsar, *Malaysia* **39 K3** 4 46N 100 56 E
Kuala Kelawang, *Malaysia* **39 L4** 2 56N 102 5 E
Kuala Kerai, *Malaysia* **39 K4** 5 30N 102 12 E
Kuala Kubu Baharu, *Malaysia* **39 L3** 3 34N 101 39 E
Kuala Lipis, *Malaysia* **39 K4** 4 10N 102 3 E
Kuala Lumpur, *Malaysia* **39 L3** 3 9N 101 41 E
Kuala Nerang, *Malaysia* **39 J3** 6 16N 100 37 E
Kuala Pilah, *Malaysia* **39 L4** 2 45N 102 15 E
Kuala Rompin, *Malaysia* **39 L4** 2 49N 103 29 E
Kuala Selangor, *Malaysia* **39 L3** 3 20N 101 15 E
Kuala Terengganu, *Malaysia* **39 K4** 5 20N 103 8 E
Kualajelai, *Indonesia* **36 E4** 2 58S 110 46 E
Kualakapuas, *Indonesia* **36 E4** 2 55S 114 20 E
Kualakurun, *Indonesia* **36 E4** 1 10S 113 50 E
Kualapembuang, *Indonesia* **36 E4** 3 14S 112 38 E
Kualasimpang, *Indonesia* **36 D1** 4 17N 98 3 E
Kuancheng, *China* **35 D10** 40 37N 118 30 E
Kuandang, *Indonesia* **37 D6** 0 56N 123 1 E
Kuandian, *China* **35 D13** 40 45N 124 45 E
Kuangchou = Guangzhou, *China* **33 D6** 23 5N 113 10 E
Kuantan, *Malaysia* **39 L4** 3 49N 103 20 E
Kuba = Quba, *Azerbaijan* **25 F8** 41 21N 48 32 E
Kuban ⟶, *Russia* **25 E6** 45 20N 37 30 E
Kubokawa, *Japan* **31 H6** 33 12N 133 8 E
Kucha Gompa, *India* **43 B7** 34 25N 76 56 E
Kuchaman, *India* **42 F6** 27 13N 74 47 E
Kuchino-eruba-Jima, *Japan* **31 J5** 30 28N 130 12 E
Kuchino-Shima, *Japan* **31 K4** 29 57N 129 55 E
Kuchinotsu, *Japan* **31 H5** 32 36N 130 11 E
Kucing, *Malaysia* **36 D4** 1 33N 110 25 E
Kud ⟶, *Pakistan* **42 F2** 26 5N 66 20 E
Kuda, *India* **40 H7** 23 10N 71 15 E
Kudat, *Malaysia* **36 C5** 6 55N 116 55 E
Kudus, *Indonesia* **37 G14** 6 48S 110 51 E
Kudymkar, *Russia* **26 D6** 59 1N 54 39 E
Kueiyang = Guiyang, *China* **32 D5** 26 32N 106 40 E
Kufra Oasis = Al Kufrah, *Libya* **51 D9** 24 17N 23 15 E
Kufstein, *Austria* **16 E7** 47 35N 12 11 E
Kugluktuk, *Canada* **68 B8** 67 50N 115 5W
Kugong I., *Canada* **70 A4** 56 18N 79 50W
Kūh-e-Hazārām, *Iran* **45 D8** 29 35N 57 20 E
Kūhak, *Iran* **40 F3** 27 12N 63 10 E
Kūhbonān, *Iran* **45 D8** 31 23N 56 19 E
Kūhestak, *Iran* **45 E8** 26 47N 57 2 E
Kūhīn, *Iran* **45 C6** 35 13N 48 25 E
Kūhīrī, *Iran* **45 E9** 26 55N 61 2 E
Kūhpāyeh, *Eşfahan, Iran* **45 C7** 32 44N 52 20 E
Kūhpāyeh, *Kermān, Iran* **45 D8** 30 35N 57 15 E
Kui Buri, *Thailand* **39 F2** 12 3N 99 52 E
Kuito, *Angola* **53 G3** 12 22S 16 55 E
Kujang, *N. Korea* **35 E14** 39 57N 126 1 E
Kuji, *Japan* **30 D10** 40 11N 141 46 E
Kujū-San, *Japan* **31 H5** 33 5N 131 15 E
Kukawa, *Nigeria* **51 F7** 12 58N 13 27 E
Kukerin, *Australia* **61 F2** 33 13S 118 0 E
Kukësi, *Albania* **21 C9** 42 5N 20 20 E
Kukup, *Malaysia* **39 M4** 1 20N 103 27 E
Kula, *Turkey* **21 E13** 38 32N 28 40 E
Kulai, *Malaysia* **39 M4** 1 44N 103 35 E
Kulal, Mt., *Kenya* **54 B4** 2 42N 36 57 E
Kulasekarappattinam, *India* **40 Q11** 8 20N 78 5 E
Kuldiga, *Latvia* **9 H19** 56 58N 21 59 E
Kuldja = Yining, *China* **26 E9** 43 58N 81 10 E
Kulgam, *India* **43 C6** 33 36N 75 2 E
Kulim, *Malaysia* **39 K3** 5 22N 100 34 E
Kulin, *Australia* **61 F2** 32 40S 118 2 E
Kulja, *Australia* **61 F2** 30 28S 117 18 E
Kulm, *U.S.A.* **80 B5** 46 18N 98 57W
Kŭlob, *Tajikistan* **26 F7** 37 55N 69 50 E
Kulsary, *Kazakstan* **25 E9** 46 59N 54 1 E
Kulti, *India* **43 H12** 23 43N 86 50 E
Kulumbura, *Australia* **60 B4** 13 55S 126 35 E
Kulunda, *Russia* **26 D8** 52 35N 78 57 E
Kulungar, *Afghan.* **42 C3** 34 0N 69 2 E
Kūlvand, *Iran* **45 D7** 31 21N 54 35 E
Kulwin, *Australia* **63 F3** 35 0S 142 42 E
Kulyab = Kŭlob, *Tajikistan* **26 F7** 37 55N 69 50 E
Kum Tekei, *Kazakstan* **26 E8** 43 10N 79 30 E
Kuma ⟶, *Russia* **25 F8** 44 55N 47 0 E
Kumagaya, *Japan* **31 F9** 36 9N 139 22 E
Kumai, *Indonesia* **36 E4** 2 44S 111 43 E
Kumamba, Kepulauan, *Indonesia* **37 E9** 1 36S 138 45 E
Kumamoto, *Japan* **31 H5** 32 45N 130 45 E
Kumamoto □, *Japan* **31 H5** 32 55N 130 55 E
Kumanovo, *Macedonia* **21 C9** 42 9N 21 42 E
Kumara, *N.Z.* **59 K3** 42 37S 171 12 E
Kumarl, *Australia* **61 F3** 32 47S 121 33 E
Kumasi, *Ghana* **50 G4** 6 41N 1 38W
Kumayri = Gyumri, *Armenia* **25 F7** 40 47N 43 50 E
Kumba, *Cameroon* **50 H6** 4 36N 9 24 E
Kumbakonam, *India* **40 P11** 10 58N 79 25 E
Kumbarilla, *Australia* **63 D5** 27 15S 150 55 E
Kŭmchŏn, *N. Korea* **35 E14** 38 10N 126 29 E
Kumdok, *India* **43 C8** 33 32N 78 10 E
Kume-Shima, *Japan* **31 L3** 26 20N 126 47 E
Kumertau, *Russia* **24 D10** 52 45N 55 57 E
Kŭmhwa, *S. Korea* **35 E14** 38 17N 127 28 E
Kumi, *Uganda* **54 B3** 1 30N 33 58 E
Kumla, *Sweden* **9 G16** 59 8N 15 10 E
Kumo, *Nigeria* **50 F7** 10 1N 11 12 E
Kumon Bum, *Burma* **41 F20** 26 30N 97 15 E
Kunama, *Australia* **63 F4** 35 35S 148 4 E
Kunashir, Ostrov, *Russia* **27 E15** 44 0N 146 0 E
Kunda, *Estonia* **9 G22** 59 30N 26 34 E
Kundla, *India* **42 J4** 21 21N 71 25 E
Kungala, *Australia* **63 D5** 29 58S 153 7 E
Kunghit I., *Canada* **72 C2** 52 6N 131 3W
Kungrad = Qŭnghirot, *Uzbekistan* **26 E6** 43 6N 58 54 E
Kungsbacka, *Sweden* **9 H15** 57 30N 12 5 E
Kungur, *Russia* **24 C10** 57 25N 56 57 E
Kungurri, *Australia* **62 C4** 21 3S 148 46 E
Kunhar ⟶, *Pakistan* **43 B5** 34 20N 73 30 E
Kuningan, *Indonesia* **37 G13** 6 59S 108 29 E
Kunlong, *Burma* **41 H21** 23 20N 98 50 E
Kunlun Shan, *Asia* **32 C3** 36 0N 86 30 E
Kunming, *China* **32 D5** 25 1N 102 41 E
Kunsan, *S. Korea* **35 G14** 35 59N 126 45 E
Kununurra, *Australia* **60 C4** 15 40S 128 50 E
Kunwarara, *Australia* **62 C5** 22 55S 150 9 E
Kunya-Urgench = Köneürgench, *Turkmenistan* **26 E6** 42 19N 59 10 E
Kuopio, *Finland* **8 E22** 62 53N 27 35 E
Kupa ⟶, *Croatia* **16 F9** 45 28N 16 24 E
Kupang, *Indonesia* **37 F6** 10 19S 123 39 E
Kupyansk, *Ukraine* **26 E4** 49 52N 37 35 E
Kuqa, *China* **32 B3** 41 35N 82 30 E
Kür ⟶, *Azerbaijan* **25 G8** 39 29N 49 15 E
Kura = Kür ⟶, *Azerbaijan* **25 G8** 39 29N 49 15 E
Kuranda, *Australia* **62 B4** 16 48S 145 35 E
Kurashiki, *Japan* **31 G6** 34 40N 133 50 E
Kurayoshi, *Japan* **31 G6** 35 26N 133 50 E
Kŭrdzhali, *Bulgaria* **21 D11** 41 38N 25 21 E
Kure, *Japan* **31 G6** 34 14N 132 32 E
Kuressaare, *Estonia* **9 G20** 58 15N 22 30 E
Kurgaldzhinskiy, *Kazakstan* **26 D8** 50 35N 70 20 E
Kurgan, *Russia* **26 D7** 55 26N 65 18 E
Kuria Maria Is. = Khūrīyā Mūrīyā, Jazā 'ir, *Oman* **46 D6** 17 30N 55 58 E
Kuridala, *Australia* **62 C3** 21 16S 140 29 E
Kurigram, *Bangla.* **41 G16** 25 49N 89 39 E
Kurikka, *Finland* **9 E20** 62 36N 22 24 E
Kuril Is. = Kurilskiye Ostrova, *Russia* **27 E15** 45 0N 150 0 E
Kuril Trench, *Pac. Oc.* **28 E19** 44 0N 153 0 E
Kurilsk, *Russia* **27 E15** 45 14N 147 53 E
Kurilskiye Ostrova, *Russia* **27 E15** 45 0N 150 0 E
Kurino, *Japan* **31 J5** 31 57N 130 43 E
Kurmuk, *Sudan* **51 F11** 10 33N 34 21 E
Kurnool, *India* **40 M10** 15 45N 78 0 E
Kuro-Shima, *Kagoshima, Japan* **31 J4** 30 50N 129 57 E
Kuro-Shima, *Okinawa, Japan* **31 M2** 24 14N 124 1 E
Kurow, *N.Z.* **59 L3** 44 44S 170 29 E
Kurrajong, *Australia* **63 E5** 33 33S 150 42 E
Kurram ⟶, *Pakistan* **42 C4** 32 36N 71 20 E
Kurri Kurri, *Australia* **63 E5** 32 50S 151 28 E
Kurshskiy Zaliv, *Russia* **9 J19** 55 9N 21 6 E
Kursk, *Russia* **24 D6** 51 42N 36 11 E
Kuruktag, *China* **32 B3** 41 0N 89 0 E
Kuruman, *S. Africa* **56 D3** 27 28S 23 28 E
Kuruman ⟶, *S. Africa* **56 D3** 26 56S 20 39 E
Kurume, *Japan* **31 H5** 33 15N 130 30 E
Kurunegala, *Sri Lanka* **40 R12** 7 30N 80 23 E
Kurya, *Russia* **27 C11** 61 15N 108 10 E
Kus Gölü, *Turkey* **21 D12** 40 10N 27 55 E
Kuşadası, *Turkey* **21 F12** 37 52N 27 15 E
Kusatsu, *Japan* **31 F9** 36 37N 138 36 E
Kusawa L., *Canada* **72 A1** 60 20N 136 13W
Kushikino, *Japan* **31 J5** 31 44N 130 16 E
Kushima, *Japan* **31 J5** 31 29N 131 14 E
Kushimoto, *Japan* **31 H7** 33 28N 135 47 E
Kushiro, *Japan* **30 C12** 43 0N 144 25 E
Kushiro ⟶, *Japan* **30 C12** 42 59N 144 23 E
Kūshk, *Iran* **45 D8** 28 46N 56 51 E
Kushka = Gushgy, *Turkmenistan* **26 F7** 35 20N 62 18 E
Kūshkī, *Īlām, Iran* **44 C5** 33 31N 47 13 E
Kūshkī, *Khorāsān, Iran* **45 B8** 37 2N 57 26 E
Kūshkū, *Iran* **45 E7** 27 19N 53 28 E
Kushol, *India* **43 C7** 33 40N 76 36 E
Kushtia, *Bangla.* **41 H16** 23 55N 89 5 E
Kushva, *Russia* **24 C10** 58 18N 59 45 E
Kuskokwim ⟶, *U.S.A.* **68 B3** 60 5N 162 25W
Kuskokwim B., *U.S.A.* **68 C3** 59 45N 162 25W
Kussharo-Ko, *Japan* **30 C12** 43 38N 144 21 E
Kustanay = Qostanay, *Kazakstan* **26 D7** 53 10N 63 35 E
Kut, Ko, *Thailand* **39 G4** 11 40N 102 35 E
Kütahya, *Turkey* **25 G5** 39 30N 30 2 E
Kutaisi, *Georgia* **25 F7** 42 19N 42 40 E
Kutaraja = Banda Aceh, *Indonesia* **36 C1** 5 35N 95 20 E
Kutch, Gulf of = Kachchh, Gulf of, *India* **42 H3** 22 50N 69 15 E
Kutch, Rann of = Kachchh, Rann of, *India* **42 G4** 24 0N 70 0 E
Kutiyana, *India* **42 J4** 21 36N 70 2 E
Kutno, *Poland* **17 B10** 52 15N 19 23 E
Kuttabul, *Australia* **62 C4** 21 5S 148 48 E
Kutu, *Zaïre* **52 E3** 2 40S 18 11 E
Kutum, *Sudan* **51 F9** 14 10N 24 40 E
Kuujjuaq, *Canada* **69 C13** 58 6N 68 15W
Kuŭp-tong, *N. Korea* **35 D14** 40 45N 126 1 E
Kuusamo, *Finland* **8 D23** 65 57N 29 8 E
Kuusankoski, *Finland* **9 F22** 60 55N 26 38 E
Kuwait = Al Kuwayt, *Kuwait* **44 D5** 29 30N 48 0 E
Kuwait ■, *Asia* **44 D5** 29 30N 47 30 E
Kuwana, *Japan* **31 G8** 35 5N 136 43 E
Kuybyshev = Samara, *Russia* **24 D9** 53 8N 50 6 E
Kuybyshev, *Russia* **26 D8** 55 27N 78 19 E
Kuybyshevskoye Vdkhr., *Russia* **24 C8** 55 2N 49 30 E
Kuye He ⟶, *China* **34 E6** 38 23N 110 46 E
Kūyeh, *Iran* **44 B5** 38 45N 47 57 E
Kūysanjaq, *Iraq* **44 B5** 36 5N 44 38 E
Kuyto, Ozero, *Russia* **24 B5** 65 6N 31 20 E
Kuyumba, *Russia* **27 C10** 60 58N 96 59 E
Kuzey Anadolu Dağlan, *Turkey* **25 F6** 41 30N 35 0 E
Kuznetsk, *Russia* **24 D8** 53 12N 46 40 E
Kuzomen, *Russia* **24 A6** 66 22N 36 50 E
Kvænangen, *Norway* **8 A19** 70 5N 21 15 E
Kvaløy, *Norway* **8 B18** 69 40N 18 30 E
Kvarner, *Croatia* **16 F8** 44 50N 14 10 E
Kvarnerič, *Croatia* **16 F8** 44 43N 14 37 E
Kwabhaca, *S. Africa* **57 E4** 30 51S 29 0 E
Kwadacha ⟶, *Canada* **72 B3** 57 28N 125 38W
Kwakhanai, *Botswana* **56 C3** 21 39S 21 16 E
Kwakoegron, *Surinam* **93 B7** 5 12N 55 25W
Kwale, *Kenya* **54 C4** 4 15S 39 31 E
Kwale □, *Kenya* **54 C4** 4 15S 39 10 E
KwaMashu, *S. Africa* **57 D5** 29 45S 30 58 E
Kwamouth, *Zaïre* **52 E3** 3 9S 16 12 E
Kwando ⟶, *Africa* **56 B3** 18 27S 23 32 E
Kwangdaeri, *N. Korea* **35 D14** 40 31N 127 32 E
Kwangju, *S. Korea* **35 G14** 35 9N 126 54 E
Kwango ⟶, *Zaïre* **49 G5** 3 14S 17 22 E
Kwangsi-Chuang = Guangxi Zhuangzu Zizhiqu □, *China* **33 D5** 24 0N 109 0 E
Kwangtung = Guangdong □, *China* **33 D6** 23 0N 113 0 E

135

Longlac

Longlac, *Canada* **70 C2** 49 45N 86 25W
Longmont, *U.S.A.* **80 E2** 40 10N 105 6W
Longnawan, *Indonesia* **36 D4** 1 51N 114 55 E
Longreach, *Australia* **62 C3** 23 28S 144 14 E
Longton, *Australia* **62 C4** 20 58S 145 55 E
Longtown, *U.K.* **11 F5** 51 58N 2 59W
Longueuil, *Canada* **79 A11** 45 32N 73 28W
Longview, *Canada* **72 C6** 50 32N 114 10W
Longview, *Tex., U.S.A.* **81 J7** 32 30N 94 44W
Longview, *Wash., U.S.A.* **84 D4** 46 8N 122 57W
Longxi, *China* **34 G3** 34 53N 104 40 E
Lonoke, *U.S.A.* **81 H9** 34 47N 91 54W
Lons-le-Saunier, *France* **18 C6** 46 40N 5 31 E
Lookout, C., *Canada* **70 A3** 55 18N 83 56W
Lookout, C., *U.S.A.* **77 H7** 34 35N 76 32W
Loolmalasin, *Tanzania* **54 C4** 3 0S 35 53 E
Loon →, *Alta., Canada* **72 B5** 57 8N 115 3W
Loon →, *Man., Canada* **73 B8** 55 53N 101 59W
Loon Lake, *Canada* **73 C7** 54 2N 109 10W
Loongana, *Australia* **61 F4** 30 52S 127 5 E
Loop Hd., *Ireland* **13 D2** 52 34N 9 56W
Lop Buri, *Thailand* **38 E3** 14 48N 100 37 E
Lop Nor = Lop Nur, *China* **32 B4** 40 20N 90 10 E
Lop Nur, *China* **32 B4** 40 20N 90 10 E
Lopatina, G., *Russia* **27 D15** 50 47N 143 10 E
Lopez, C., *Gabon* **52 E1** 0 47S 8 40 E
Lopphavet, *Norway* **8 A19** 70 27N 21 15 E
Lora →, *Afghan.* **40 D4** 31 35N 65 50 E
Lora, Hamun-i-, *Pakistan* **40 E4** 29 38N 64 58 E
Lora Cr. →, *Australia* **63 D2** 28 10S 135 22 E
Lora del Río, *Spain* **19 D3** 37 39N 5 33W
Lorain, *U.S.A.* **78 E2** 41 28N 82 11W
Loralai, *Pakistan* **42 D3** 30 20N 68 41 E
Lorca, *Spain* **19 D5** 37 41N 1 42W
Lord Howe I., *Pac. Oc.* **64 L7** 31 33S 159 6 E
Lord Howe Ridge, *Pac. Oc.* **64 L8** 30 0S 162 30 E
Lordsburg, *U.S.A.* **83 K9** 32 21N 108 43W
Loreto, *Brazil* **93 E9** 7 5S 45 10W
Loreto, *Mexico* **86 B2** 26 1N 111 21W
Lorient, *France* **18 C2** 47 45N 3 23W
Lorn, *U.K.* **12 E3** 56 26N 5 10W
Lorn, Firth of, *U.K.* **12 E3** 56 20N 5 40W
Lorne, *Australia* **63 F3** 38 33S 143 59 E
Lorovouno, *Cyprus* **23 D11** 35 8N 32 36 E
Lorraine, *France* **18 B7** 48 53N 6 0 E
Lorrainville, *Canada* **70 C4** 47 21N 79 23W
Los Alamos, *Calif., U.S.A.* **85 L6** 34 44N 120 17W
Los Alamos, *N. Mex., U.S.A.* **83 J10** 35 53N 106 19W
Los Altos, *U.S.A.* **84 H4** 37 23N 122 7W
Los Andes, *Chile* **94 C1** 32 50S 70 40W
Los Angeles, *Chile* **94 D1** 37 28S 72 23W
Los Angeles, *U.S.A.* **85 L8** 34 4N 118 15W
Los Angeles Aqueduct, *U.S.A.* **85 K9** 35 22N 118 5W
Los Banos, *U.S.A.* **83 H3** 37 4N 120 51W
Los Blancos, *Argentina* **94 A3** 23 40S 62 30W
Los Cristianos, *Canary Is.* **22 F3** 28 3N 16 42W
Los Gatos, *U.S.A.* **84 H5** 37 14N 121 59W
Los Hermanos, *Venezuela* **89 D7** 11 45N 64 25W
Los Islotes, *Canary Is.* **22 E6** 29 4N 13 44W
Los Llanos de Aridane, *Canary Is.* **22 F2** 28 38N 17 54W
Los Lunas, *U.S.A.* **83 J10** 34 48N 106 44W
Los Mochis, *Mexico* **86 B3** 25 45N 108 57W
Los Olivos, *U.S.A.* **85 L6** 34 40N 120 7W
Los Palacios, *Cuba* **88 B3** 22 35N 83 15W
Los Reyes, *Mexico* **86 D4** 19 34N 102 30W
Los Roques, *Venezuela* **92 A5** 11 50N 66 45W
Los Testigos, *Venezuela* **92 A6** 11 23N 63 6W
Los Vilos, *Chile* **94 C1** 32 10S 71 30W
Loshkalakh, *Russia* **27 C15** 62 45N 147 20 E
Lošinj, *Croatia* **16 F8** 44 30N 14 30 E
Lossiemouth, *U.K.* **12 D5** 57 42N 3 17W
Lot →, *France* **18 D4** 44 18N 0 20 E
Lota, *Chile* **94 D1** 37 5S 73 10W
Loṭfābād, *Iran* **45 B8** 37 32N 59 20 E
Lothair, *S. Africa* **57 D5** 26 22S 30 27 E
Loubomo, *Congo* **52 E2** 4 9S 12 47 E
Loudon, *U.S.A.* **77 H3** 35 45N 84 20W
Loudonville, *U.S.A.* **78 F2** 40 38N 82 14W
Louga, *Senegal* **50 E1** 15 45N 16 5W
Loughborough, *U.K.* **10 E6** 52 47N 1 11W
Loughrea, *Ireland* **13 C3** 53 12N 8 33W
Loughros More B., *Ireland* **13 B3** 54 48N 8 32W
Louis Trichardt, *S. Africa* **57 C4** 23 1S 29 43 E
Louis XIV, Pte., *Canada* **70 B4** 54 37N 79 45W
Louisa, *U.S.A.* **76 F4** 38 7N 82 36W
Louisbourg, *Canada* **71 C8** 45 55N 60 0W
Louise I., *Canada* **72 C2** 52 55N 131 50W
Louiseville, *Canada* **70 C5** 46 20N 72 56W
Louisiade Arch., *Papua N. G.* **64 J7** 11 10S 153 0 E
Louisiana, *U.S.A.* **80 F9** 39 27N 91 3W
Louisiana □, *U.S.A.* **81 K9** 30 50N 92 0W
Louisville, *Ky., U.S.A.* **76 F3** 38 15N 85 46W
Louisville, *Miss., U.S.A.* **81 J10** 33 7N 89 3W
Loulé, *Portugal* **19 D1** 37 9N 8 0W
Loup City, *U.S.A.* **80 E5** 41 17N 98 58W
Lourdes, *France* **18 E3** 43 6N 0 3W
Lourdes-du-Blanc-Sablon, *Canada* **71 B8** 51 24N 57 12W
Lourenço-Marques = Maputo, *Mozam.* **57 D5** 25 58S 32 32 E
Louth, *Australia* **63 E4** 30 30S 145 8 E
Louth, *Ireland* **13 C5** 53 58N 6 32W
Louth, *U.K.* **10 D7** 53 22N 0 1W
Louth □, *Ireland* **13 C5** 53 56N 6 34W
Louvain = Leuven, *Belgium* **15 D4** 50 52N 4 42 E
Louwsburg, *S. Africa* **57 D5** 27 37S 31 7 E
Love, *Canada* **73 C8** 53 29N 104 10W
Lovech, *Bulgaria* **21 C11** 43 8N 24 42 E
Loveland, *U.S.A.* **80 E2** 40 24N 105 5W
Lovell, *U.S.A.* **82 D9** 44 50N 108 24W
Lovelock, *U.S.A.* **82 F4** 40 11N 118 28W
Loviisa, *Finland* **9 F22** 60 28N 26 12 E
Loving, *U.S.A.* **81 J2** 32 17N 104 6W
Lovington, *U.S.A.* **81 J3** 32 57N 103 21W
Lovisa = Loviisa, *Finland* **9 F22** 60 28N 26 12 E
Low Pt., *Australia* **61 F4** 32 25S 127 25 E
Low Tatra = Nízké Tatry, *Slovak Rep.* **17 D10** 48 55N 19 30 E
Lowa, *Zaïre* **54 C2** 1 25S 25 47 E
Lowa →, *Zaïre* **54 C2** 1 24S 25 51 E
Lowell, *U.S.A.* **79 D13** 42 38N 71 19W
Lower Arrow L., *Canada* **72 D5** 49 40N 118 5W
Lower California = Baja California, *Mexico* **86 A1** 31 10N 115 12W
Lower Hutt, *N.Z.* **59 J5** 41 10S 174 55 E
Lower L., *U.S.A.* **82 F3** 41 16N 120 2W
Lower Lake, *U.S.A.* **84 G4** 38 55N 122 37W
Lower Post, *Canada* **72 B3** 59 58N 128 30W
Lower Red L., *U.S.A.* **80 B7** 47 58N 95 0W
Lower Saxony = Niedersachsen □, *Germany* **16 B5** 53 8N 9 0 E
Lower Tunguska = Tunguska, Nizhnyaya →, *Russia* **27 C9** 65 48N 88 4 E
Lowestoft, *U.K.* **11 E9** 52 29N 1 45 E
Łowicz, *Poland* **17 B10** 52 6N 19 55 E
Lowville, *U.S.A.* **79 C9** 43 47N 75 29W
Loxton, *Australia* **63 E3** 34 28S 140 31 E
Loxton, *S. Africa* **56 E3** 31 30S 22 22 E
Loyalton, *U.S.A.* **84 F6** 39 41N 120 14W
Loyalty Is. = Loyauté, Is., *N. Cal.* **64 K8** 20 50S 166 30 E
Loyang = Luoyang, *China* **34 G7** 34 40N 112 26 E
Loyauté, Is., *N. Cal.* **64 K8** 20 50S 166 30 E
Loyev = Loyew, *Belarus* **17 C16** 51 56N 30 46 E
Loyew, *Belarus* **17 C16** 51 56N 30 46 E
Loyoro, *Uganda* **54 B3** 3 22N 34 14 E
Luachimo, *Angola* **52 F4** 7 23S 20 48 E
Luacono, *Angola* **52 G4** 11 15S 21 37 E
Lualaba →, *Zaïre* **54 B5** 0 26N 25 20 E
Luampa, *Zambia* **55 F1** 15 4S 24 20 E
Luan Chau, *Vietnam* **38 B4** 21 38N 103 24 E
Luan He →, *China* **35 E10** 39 20N 119 5 E
Luan Xian, *China* **35 E10** 39 40N 118 40 E
Luancheng, *China* **34 F8** 37 53N 114 40 E
Luanda, *Angola* **52 F2** 8 50S 13 15 E
Luang Prabang, *Laos* **38 C4** 19 52N 102 10 E
Luang Thale, *Thailand* **39 J3** 7 30N 100 15 E
Luangwa, *Zambia* **55 F3** 15 35S 30 16 E
Luangwa →, *Zambia* **55 E3** 14 25S 30 25 E
Luangwa Valley, *Zambia* **55 E3** 13 30S 31 30 E
Luanne, *China* **35 D9** 40 55N 117 40 E
Luanping, *China* **35 D9** 40 53N 117 23 E
Luanshya, *Zambia* **55 E2** 13 3S 28 28 E
Luapula □, *Zambia* **55 E2** 11 0S 29 0 E
Luapula →, *Africa* **55 D2** 9 26S 28 33 E
Luarca, *Spain* **19 A2** 43 32N 6 32W
Luashi, *Zaïre* **55 E1** 10 50S 23 36 E
Luau, *Angola* **52 G4** 10 40S 22 10 E
Lubalo, *Angola* **52 F3** 9 10S 19 15 E
Lubana, Ozero = Lubānas Ezers, *Latvia* **9 H22** 56 45N 27 0 E
Lubānas Ezers, *Latvia* **9 H22** 56 45N 27 0 E
Lubang Is., *Phil.* **37 B6** 13 50N 120 12 E
Lubbock, *U.S.A.* **81 J4** 33 35N 101 51W
Lübeck, *Germany* **16 B6** 53 52N 10 40 E
Lubefu, *Zaïre* **54 C1** 4 47S 24 27 E
Lubefu →, *Zaïre* **54 C1** 4 10S 23 0 E
Lubero = Luofu, *Zaïre* **54 C2** 0 10S 29 15 E
Lubicon L., *Canada* **72 B5** 56 23N 115 56W
Lubin, *Poland* **16 C9** 51 24N 16 11 E
Lublin, *Poland* **17 C12** 51 12N 22 38 E
Lubnān, J., *Lebanon* **47 B4** 33 50N 35 45 E
Lubny, *Ukraine* **26 D4** 50 3N 32 58 E
Lubongola, *Zaïre* **54 C2** 2 35S 27 50 E
Lubuagan, *Phil.* **37 A6** 17 21N 121 10 E
Lubudi →, *Zaïre* **55 D2** 9 0S 25 35 E
Lubuk Antu, *Malaysia* **36 D4** 1 3N 111 50 E
Lubuklinggau, *Indonesia* **36 E2** 3 15S 102 55 E
Lubuksikaping, *Indonesia* **36 D2** 0 10N 100 15 E
Lubumbashi, *Zaïre* **55 E2** 11 40S 27 28 E
Lubunda, *Zaïre* **54 D2** 5 12S 26 41 E
Lubungu, *Zambia* **55 E2** 14 35S 26 24 E
Lubutu, *Zaïre* **54 C2** 0 45S 26 30 E
Luc An Chau, *Vietnam* **38 A5** 22 6N 104 43 E
Lucan, *Canada* **78 C3** 43 11N 81 24W
Lucca, *Italy* **20 C4** 43 50N 10 29 E
Luce Bay, *U.K.* **12 G4** 54 45N 4 48W
Lucea, *Jamaica* **88 C4** 18 25N 78 10W
Lucedale, *U.S.A.* **77 K1** 30 56N 88 35W
Lucena, *Phil.* **37 B6** 13 56N 121 37 E
Lucena, *Spain* **19 D3** 37 27N 4 31W
Lučenec, *Slovak Rep.* **17 D10** 48 18N 19 42 E
Lucerne = Luzern, *Switz.* **16 E5** 47 3N 8 18 E
Lucerne, *U.S.A.* **84 F4** 39 6N 122 48W
Lucerne Valley, *U.S.A.* **85 L10** 34 27N 116 57W
Lucero, *Mexico* **86 A3** 30 49N 106 30W
Lucheng, *China* **34 F7** 36 20N 113 11 E
Lucheringo →, *Mozam.* **55 E4** 11 43S 36 17 E
Lucira, *Angola* **53 G2** 14 0S 12 35 E
Luckenwalde, *Germany* **16 B7** 52 5N 13 10 E
Lucknow, *India* **43 F9** 26 50N 81 0 E
Lüda = Dalian, *China* **35 E11** 38 50N 121 40 E
Lüderitz, *Namibia* **56 D2** 26 41S 15 8 E
Ludewe □, *Tanzania* **55 D3** 10 0S 34 50 E
Ludhiana, *India* **42 D6** 30 57N 75 56 E
Ludington, *U.S.A.* **76 D2** 43 57N 86 27W
Ludlow, *U.K.* **11 E5** 52 22N 2 42W
Ludlow, *Calif., U.S.A.* **85 L10** 34 43N 116 10W
Ludlow, *Vt., U.S.A.* **79 C12** 43 24N 72 42W
Ludvika, *Sweden* **9 F16** 60 8N 15 14 E
Ludwigsburg, *Germany* **16 D5** 48 53N 9 11 E
Ludwigshafen, *Germany* **16 D5** 49 29N 8 26 E
Luebo, *Zaïre* **52 F4** 5 21S 21 23 E
Lueki, *Zaïre* **54 C2** 3 20S 25 48 E
Luena, *Zaïre* **55 D2** 9 28S 25 43 E
Luena, *Zambia* **55 E3** 10 40S 30 25 E
Lüeyang, *China* **34 H4** 33 22N 106 10 E
Lufira →, *Zaïre* **55 D2** 9 30S 27 0 E
Lufkin, *U.S.A.* **81 K7** 31 21N 94 44W
Lufupa, *Zaïre* **55 E1** 10 37S 24 56 E
Luga, *Russia* **24 C4** 58 40N 29 55 E
Lugano, *Switz.* **16 E5** 46 0N 8 57 E
Lugansk = Luhansk, *Ukraine* **25 E6** 48 38N 39 15 E
Lugard's Falls, *Kenya* **54 C4** 3 6S 38 41 E
Lugela, *Mozam.* **55 F4** 16 25S 36 43 E
Lugenda →, *Mozam.* **55 E4** 11 25S 38 33 E
Lugh Ganana, *Somali Rep.* **46 G3** 3 48N 42 34 E
Lugnaquilla, *Ireland* **13 D5** 52 58N 6 28W
Lugo, *Italy* **20 B4** 44 25N 11 54 E
Lugo, *Spain* **19 A2** 43 2N 7 35W
Lugoj, *Romania* **17 F11** 45 42N 21 57 E
Lugovoy, *Kazakstan* **26 E8** 42 55N 72 43 E
Luhansk, *Ukraine* **25 E6** 48 38N 39 15 E
Luiana, *Angola* **56 B3** 17 25S 22 59 E
Luimneach = Limerick, *Ireland* **13 D3** 52 40N 8 37W
Luís Correia, *Brazil* **93 D10** 3 0S 41 35W
Luitpold Coast, *Antarctica* **5 D1** 78 30S 32 0W
Luiza, *Zaïre* **52 F4** 7 40S 22 30 E
Luizi, *Zaïre* **54 D2** 6 0S 27 25 E
Luján, *Argentina* **94 C4** 34 45S 59 5W
Lukanga Swamp, *Zambia* **55 E2** 14 30S 27 40 E
Lukenie →, *Zaïre* **52 E3** 3 0S 18 50 E
Lukhisaral, *India* **43 G12** 25 11N 86 5 E
Lukolela, *Equateur, Zaïre* **52 E3** 1 10S 17 12 E
Lukolela, *Kasai Or., Zaïre* **54 D1** 5 23S 24 32 E
Lukosi, *Zimbabwe* **55 F2** 18 30S 26 30 E
Łuków, *Poland* **17 C12** 51 55N 22 23 E
Lule älv →, *Sweden* **8 D19** 65 35N 22 10 E
Luleå, *Sweden* **8 D20** 65 35N 22 10 E
Lüleburgaz, *Turkey* **21 D12** 41 23N 27 22 E
Luling, *U.S.A.* **81 L6** 29 41N 97 39W
Lulong, *China* **35 E10** 39 53N 118 51 E
Lulonga →, *Zaïre* **52 D3** 1 0N 18 10 E
Lulua →, *Zaïre* **52 E4** 4 30S 20 30 E
Luluabourg = Kananga, *Zaïre* **52 F4** 5 55S 22 18 E
Lumai, *Angola* **53 G4** 13 13S 21 25 E
Lumajang, *Indonesia* **37 H15** 8 8S 113 13 E
Lumbala N'guimbo, *Angola* **53 G4** 14 18S 21 18 E
Lumberton, *Miss., U.S.A.* **81 K10** 31 0N 89 27W
Lumberton, *N.C., U.S.A.* **77 H6** 34 37N 79 0W
Lumberton, *N. Mex., U.S.A.* **83 H10** 36 56N 106 56W
Lumbwa, *Kenya* **54 C4** 0 12S 35 28 E
Lumsden, *N.Z.* **59 L2** 45 44S 168 27 E
Lumut, *Malaysia* **39 K3** 4 13N 100 37 E
Lumut, Tg., *Indonesia* **36 E3** 3 50S 105 58 E
Lunavada, *India* **42 H5** 23 8N 73 37 E
Lund, *Sweden* **9 J15** 55 44N 13 12 E
Lund, *U.S.A.* **82 G6** 38 52N 115 0W
Lundazi, *Zambia* **55 E3** 12 20S 33 7 E
Lundi →, *Zimbabwe* **55 G3** 21 43S 32 34 E
Lundu, *Malaysia* **36 D3** 1 40N 109 50 E
Lundy, *U.K.* **11 F3** 51 10N 4 41W
Lune →, *U.K.* **10 C5** 54 0N 2 51W
Lüneburg, *Germany* **16 B6** 53 15N 10 24 E
Lüneburg Heath = Lüneburger Heide, *Germany* **16 B6** 53 10N 10 12 E
Lüneburger Heide, *Germany* **16 B6** 53 10N 10 12 E
Lunenburg, *Canada* **71 D7** 44 22N 64 18W
Lunéville, *France* **18 B7** 48 36N 6 30 E
Lunga →, *Zambia* **55 E2** 14 34S 26 25 E
Lunglei, *India* **41 H18** 22 55N 92 45 E
Luni, *India* **42 F5** 26 0N 73 6 E
Luni →, *India* **42 G4** 24 41N 71 14 E
Luninets = Luninyets, *Belarus* **17 B14** 52 15N 26 50 E
Luning, *U.S.A.* **82 G4** 38 30N 118 11W
Luninyets, *Belarus* **17 B14** 52 15N 26 50 E
Lunsemfwa →, *Zambia* **55 E3** 14 54S 30 12 E
Lunsemfwa Falls, *Zambia* **55 E2** 14 30S 29 6 E
Luo He →, *China* **34 G6** 34 35N 110 20 E
Luochuan, *China* **34 G5** 35 45N 109 26 E
Luofu, *Zaïre* **54 C2** 0 10S 29 15 E
Luohe, *China* **34 H8** 33 32N 114 2 E
Luonan, *China* **34 G6** 34 5N 110 10 E
Luoning, *China* **34 G6** 34 35N 111 40 E
Luoyang, *China* **34 G7** 34 40N 112 26 E
Luozi, *Zaïre* **52 E2** 4 54S 14 0 E
Luozigou, *China* **35 C16** 43 42N 130 18 E
Lupanshui, *China* **32 D5** 26 38N 104 48 E
Lupilichi, *Mozam.* **55 E4** 11 47S 35 13 E
Luque, *Paraguay* **94 B4** 25 19S 57 25W
Luray, *U.S.A.* **76 F6** 38 40N 78 28W
Luremo, *Angola* **52 F3** 8 30S 17 50 E
Lurgan, *U.K.* **13 B5** 54 28N 6 19W
Lusaka, *Zambia* **55 F2** 15 28S 28 16 E
Lusambo, *Zaïre* **54 C1** 4 58S 23 28 E
Lusangaye, *Zaïre* **54 C2** 4 54S 26 0 E
Luseland, *Canada* **73 C7** 52 5N 109 24W
Lushan, *China* **34 H7** 33 45N 112 55 E
Lushi, *China* **34 G6** 34 3N 111 3 E
Lushnja, *Albania* **21 D8** 40 55N 19 41 E
Lushoto, *Tanzania* **54 C4** 4 47S 38 20 E
Lushoto □, *Tanzania* **54 C4** 4 45S 38 20 E
Lüshun, *China* **35 E11** 38 45N 121 15 E
Lusk, *U.S.A.* **80 D2** 42 46N 104 27W
Luta = Dalian, *China* **35 E11** 38 50N 121 40 E
Luton, *U.K.* **11 F7** 51 53N 0 24W
Lutong, *Malaysia* **36 D4** 4 28N 114 0 E
Lutselke, *Canada* **73 A6** 62 24N 110 44W
Lutsk, *Ukraine* **17 C13** 50 50N 25 15 E
Lützow Holmbukta, *Antarctica* **5 C4** 69 10S 37 30 E
Lutzputs, *S. Africa* **56 D3** 28 3S 20 40 E
Luverne, *U.S.A.* **80 D6** 43 39N 96 13W
Luvua, *Zaïre* **55 D2** 8 48S 25 17 E
Luvua →, *Zaïre* **54 D2** 6 50S 27 30 E
Luwegu →, *Tanzania* **55 D4** 8 31S 37 23 E
Luwuk, *Indonesia* **37 E6** 0 56S 122 47 E
Luxembourg, *Lux.* **18 B7** 49 37N 6 9 E
Luxembourg □, *Belgium* **15 E5** 49 58N 5 30 E
Luxembourg ■, *Europe* **18 B7** 49 45N 6 0 E
Luxi, *China* **32 D4** 24 27N 98 36 E
Luxor = El Uqsur, *Egypt* **51 C11** 25 41N 32 38 E
Luyi, *China* **34 H8** 33 50N 115 35 E
Luza, *Russia* **24 B8** 60 39N 47 10 E
Luzern, *Switz.* **16 E5** 47 3N 8 18 E
Luzhou, *China* **32 D5** 28 52N 105 20 E
Luziânia, *Brazil* **93 G9** 16 20S 48 0W
Luzon, *Phil.* **37 A6** 16 0N 121 0 E
Lviv, *Ukraine* **17 D13** 49 50N 24 0 E
Lvov = Lviv, *Ukraine* **17 D13** 49 50N 24 0 E
Lyakhavichy, *Belarus* **17 B14** 53 2N 26 32 E
Lyakhovskiye, Ostrova, *Russia* **27 B15** 73 40N 141 0 E
Lyallpur = Faisalabad, *Pakistan* **42 D5** 31 30N 73 5 E
Lycksele, *Sweden* **8 D18** 64 38N 18 40 E
Lydda = Lod, *Israel* **47 D3** 31 57N 34 54 E
Lydenburg, *S. Africa* **57 D5** 25 10S 30 29 E
Lydia, *Turkey* **21 E13** 38 48N 28 19 E
Lyell, *N.Z.* **59 J4** 41 48S 172 4 E
Lyell I., *Canada* **72 C2** 52 40N 131 35W
Lyepyel, *Belarus* **24 D4** 54 50N 28 40 E
Lyman, *U.S.A.* **82 F8** 41 20N 110 18W
Lyme Regis, *U.K.* **11 G5** 50 43N 2 57W
Lymington, *U.K.* **11 G6** 50 45N 1 32W
Łyna →, *Poland* **9 J19** 54 37N 21 14 E
Lynchburg, *U.S.A.* **76 G6** 37 25N 79 9W
Lynd →, *Australia* **62 B3** 16 28S 143 18 E
Lynd Ra., *Australia* **63 D4** 25 30S 149 20 E
Lynden, *Canada* **78 C4** 43 14N 80 9W
Lynden, *U.S.A.* **84 B4** 48 57N 122 27W
Lyndhurst, *Queens., Australia* **62 B3** 19 12S 144 20 E
Lyndhurst, *S. Austral., Australia* **63 E2** 30 15S 138 18 E
Lyndon →, *Australia* **61 D1** 23 29S 114 6 E
Lyndonville, *N.Y., U.S.A.* **78 C6** 43 20N 78 23W
Lyndonville, *Vt., U.S.A.* **79 B12** 44 31N 72 1W
Lyngen, *Norway* **8 B19** 69 45N 20 30 E
Lynher Reef, *Australia* **60 C3** 15 27S 121 55 E
Lynn, *U.S.A.* **79 D14** 42 28N 70 57W
Lynn Canal, *U.S.A.* **72 B1** 58 50N 135 15W
Lynn Lake, *Canada* **73 B8** 56 51N 101 3W
Lynnwood, *U.S.A.* **84 C4** 47 49N 122 19W
Lynton, *U.K.* **11 F4** 51 13N 3 50W
Lyntupy, *Belarus* **9 J22** 55 4N 26 23 E
Lynx L., *Canada* **73 A7** 62 25N 106 15W
Lyon, *France* **18 D6** 45 46N 4 50 E
Lyonnais, *France* **18 D6** 45 45N 4 15 E
Lyons = Lyon, *France* **18 D6** 45 46N 4 50 E
Lyons, *Colo., U.S.A.* **80 E2** 40 14N 105 16W
Lyons, *Ga., U.S.A.* **77 J4** 32 12N 82 19W
Lyons, *Kans., U.S.A.* **80 F5** 38 21N 98 12W
Lyons, *N.Y., U.S.A.* **78 C8** 43 5N 77 0W
Lys = Leie →, *Belgium* **15 C3** 51 2N 3 45 E
Lysva, *Russia* **24 C10** 58 7N 57 49 E
Lysychansk, *Ukraine* **25 E6** 48 55N 38 30 E
Lytle, *U.S.A.* **81 L5** 29 14N 98 48W
Lyttelton, *N.Z.* **59 K4** 43 35S 172 44 E
Lytton, *Canada* **72 C4** 50 13N 121 31W
Lyubertsy, *Russia* **24 C6** 55 39N 37 50 E
Lyuboml, *Ukraine* **17 C13** 51 11N 24 4 E

M

Ma →, *Vietnam* **38 C5** 19 47N 105 56 E
Ma'adaba, *Jordan* **47 E4** 30 43N 35 47 E
Maamba, *Zambia* **56 B4** 17 17S 26 28 E
Ma'ān, *Jordan* **47 E4** 30 12N 35 44 E
Ma'ān □, *Jordan* **47 F5** 30 0N 36 0 E
Maanselkä, *Finland* **8 C23** 63 52N 28 32 E
Ma'anshan, *China* **33 C6** 31 44N 118 29 E
Maarianhamina, *Finland* **9 F18** 60 5N 19 55 E
Ma'arrat an Nu'mān, *Syria* **44 C3** 35 43N 36 43 E
Maas →, *Neths.* **15 C4** 51 45N 4 32 E
Maaseik, *Belgium* **15 C5** 51 6N 5 45 E
Maassluis, *Neths.* **15 C4** 51 56N 4 16 E
Maastricht, *Neths.* **18 A6** 50 50N 5 40 E
Maave, *Mozam.* **57 C5** 21 4S 34 47 E
Mabel L., *Canada* **72 C5** 50 35N 118 43W
Mabenge, *Zaïre* **54 B1** 4 15N 24 12 E
Mablethorpe, *U.K.* **10 D8** 53 20N 0 15 E
Maboma, *Zaïre* **54 B2** 2 30N 28 10 E
Mabrouk, *Mali* **50 E4** 19 29N 1 15W
Mabton, *U.S.A.* **82 C3** 46 13N 120 0W
Mac Bac, *Vietnam* **39 H6** 9 46N 106 7 E
Macachín, *Argentina* **94 D3** 37 10S 63 43W
Macaé, *Brazil* **95 A7** 22 20S 41 43W
McAlester, *U.S.A.* **81 H7** 34 56N 95 46W
McAllen, *U.S.A.* **81 M5** 26 12N 98 14W
Macamic, *Canada* **70 C4** 48 45N 79 0W
Macao = Macau ■, *China* **33 D6** 22 16N 113 35 E
Macapá, *Brazil* **93 C8** 0 5N 51 4W
McArthur →, *Australia* **62 B2** 15 54S 136 40 E
McArthur, Port, *Australia* **62 B2** 16 4S 136 23 E
McArthur River, *Australia* **62 B2** 16 27S 136 7 E
Macau, *Brazil* **93 E11** 5 15S 36 40W
Macau ■, *China* **33 D6** 22 16N 113 35 E
McBride, *Canada* **72 C4** 53 20N 120 19W
McCall, *U.S.A.* **82 D5** 44 55N 116 6W
McCamey, *U.S.A.* **81 K3** 31 8N 102 14W
McCammon, *U.S.A.* **82 E7** 42 39N 112 12W
McCauley I., *Canada* **72 C2** 53 40N 130 15W
McCleary, *U.S.A.* **84 C3** 47 3N 123 16W
Macclesfield, *U.K.* **10 D5** 53 15N 2 8W
McClintock, *Canada* **73 B10** 57 50N 94 10W
M'Clintock Chan., *Canada* **68 A9** 72 0N 102 0W
McClintock Ra., *Australia* **60 C4** 18 44S 127 38 E
McCloud, *U.S.A.* **82 F2** 41 15N 122 8W
McCluer I., *Australia* **60 B5** 11 5S 133 0 E
McClure, *U.S.A.* **78 F7** 40 42N 77 19W
McClure, L., *U.S.A.* **84 H6** 37 35N 120 16W
M'Clure Str., *Canada* **4 B2** 75 0N 119 0W
McClusky, *U.S.A.* **80 B4** 47 29N 100 27W
McComb, *U.S.A.* **81 K9** 31 15N 90 27W
McConaughy, L., *U.S.A.* **80 E4** 41 14N 101 40W
McCook, *U.S.A.* **80 E4** 40 12N 100 38W
McCullough Mt., *U.S.A.* **85 K11** 35 35N 115 13W
McCusker →, *Canada* **73 B7** 55 32N 108 39W
McDame, *Canada* **72 B3** 59 44N 128 59W
McDermitt, *U.S.A.* **82 F5** 41 59N 117 43W
Macdonald, L., *Australia* **60 D4** 23 30S 129 0 E
McDonald Is., *Ind. Oc.* **3 G13** 53 0S 73 0 E
Macdonnell Ranges, *Australia* **60 D5** 23 40S 133 0 E
McDouall Peak, *Australia* **63 D1** 29 51S 134 55 E
Macdougall L., *Canada* **68 B10** 66 0N 98 27W
MacDowell L., *Canada* **70 B1** 52 15N 92 45W
Macduff, *U.K.* **12 D6** 57 40N 2 31W
Macedonia = Makedhonia □, *Greece* **21 D10** 40 39N 22 0 E
Macedonia ■, *Europe* **21 D9** 41 53N 21 40 E
Maceió, *Brazil* **93 E11** 9 40S 35 41W
Macenta, *Guinea* **50 G3** 8 35N 9 32W
Macerata, *Italy* **20 C5** 43 19N 13 27 E
McFarland, *U.S.A.* **85 K7** 35 41N 119 14W
McFarlane →, *Canada* **73 B7** 59 12N 107 58W
Macfarlane, L., *Australia* **63 E2** 32 0S 136 40 E

Maluku

McGehee, U.S.A. 81 J9 33 38N 91 24W
McGill, U.S.A. 82 G6 39 23N 114 47W
Macgillycuddy's Reeks, Ireland 13 D2 51 58N 9 45W
MacGregor, Canada 73 D9 49 57N 98 48W
McGregor, U.S.A. 80 D9 43 1N 91 11W
McGregor →, Canada 72 B4 55 10N 122 0W
McGregor Ra., Australia 63 D3 27 0S 142 45 E
Mach, Pakistan 40 E5 29 50N 67 20 E
Māch Kowr, Iran 45 E9 25 48N 61 28 E
Machado = Jiparaná →, Brazil 92 E6 8 3S 62 52W
Machagai, Argentina 94 B3 26 56S 60 2W
Machakos, Kenya 54 C4 1 30S 37 15 E
Machakos □, Kenya 54 C4 1 30S 37 15 E
Machala, Ecuador 92 D3 3 20S 79 57W
Machanga, Mozam. 57 C6 20 59S 35 0 E
Machattie, L., Australia 62 C2 24 50S 139 48 E
Machava, Mozam. 57 D5 25 54S 32 28 E
Machece, Mozam. 55 F4 19 15S 35 32 E
Machevna, Russia 27 C18 61 20N 172 20 E
Machias, U.S.A. 71 D6 44 43N 67 28W
Machichi →, Canada 73 B10 57 3N 92 6W
Machico, Madeira 22 D3 32 43N 16 44W
Machilipatnam, India 41 L12 16 12N 81 8 E
Machiques, Venezuela 92 A4 10 4N 72 34W
Machupicchu, Peru 92 F4 13 8S 72 30W
Machynlleth, U.K. 11 E4 52 35N 3 50W
McIlwraith Ra., Australia 62 A3 13 50S 143 20 E
McIntosh, U.S.A. 80 C4 45 55N 101 21W
McIntosh L., Canada 73 B8 55 45N 105 0W
Macintosh Ra., Australia 61 E4 27 39S 125 32 E
Macintyre →, Australia 63 D5 28 37S 150 47 E
Mackay, Australia 62 C4 21 8S 149 11 E
Mackay, U.S.A. 82 E7 43 55N 113 37W
MacKay →, Canada 72 B6 57 10N 111 38W
Mackay, L., Australia 60 D4 22 30S 129 0 E
McKay Ra., Australia 60 D3 23 0S 122 30 E
McKeesport, U.S.A. 78 F5 40 21N 79 52W
McKenna, U.S.A. 84 D4 46 56N 122 33W
Mackenzie, Canada 72 B4 55 20N 123 5W
McKenzie, U.S.A. 77 G1 36 8N 88 31W
Mackenzie →, Australia 62 C4 23 38S 149 46 E
Mackenzie →, Canada 68 B6 69 10N 134 20W
McKenzie →, U.S.A. 82 D2 44 7N 123 6W
Mackenzie Bay, Canada 4 B1 69 0N 137 30W
Mackenzie City = Linden, Guyana 92 B7 6 0N 58 10W
Mackenzie Highway, Canada 72 B5 58 0N 117 15W
Mackenzie Mts., Canada 68 B6 64 0N 130 0W
Mackinaw City, U.S.A. 76 C3 45 47N 84 44W
McKinlay, Australia 62 C3 21 16S 141 18 E
McKinlay →, Australia 62 C3 20 50S 141 28 E
McKinley, Mt., U.S.A. 68 B4 63 4N 151 0W
McKinley Sea, Arctic 4 A7 82 0N 0 0 E
McKinney, U.S.A. 81 J6 33 12N 96 37W
Mackinnon Road, Kenya 54 C4 3 40S 39 1 E
Macksville, Australia 63 E5 30 40S 152 56 E
McLaughlin, U.S.A. 80 C4 45 49N 100 49W
Maclean, Australia 63 D5 29 26S 153 16 E
McLean, U.S.A. 81 H4 35 14N 100 36W
McLeansboro, U.S.A. 80 F10 38 6N 88 32W
Maclear, S. Africa 57 E4 31 2S 28 23 E
Macleay →, Australia 63 E5 30 56S 153 0 E
McLennan, Canada 72 B5 55 42N 116 50W
MacLeod, B., Canada 73 A7 62 53N 110 0W
McLeod, L., Australia 61 D1 24 9S 113 47 E
MacLeod Lake, Canada 72 C4 54 58N 123 0W
McLoughlin, Mt., U.S.A. 82 E2 42 27N 122 19W
McLure, Canada 72 C4 51 2N 120 13W
McMechen, U.S.A. 78 G4 39 57N 80 44W
McMillan, L., U.S.A. 81 J2 32 36N 104 21W
McMinnville, Oreg., U.S.A. 82 D2 45 13N 123 12W
McMinnville, Tenn., U.S.A. 77 H3 35 41N 85 46W
McMorran, Canada 73 C7 51 19N 108 42W
McMurdo Sd., Antarctica 5 D11 77 0S 170 0 E
McMurray = Fort McMurray, Canada 72 B6 56 44N 111 7W
McMurray, U.S.A. 84 B4 48 19N 122 14W
McNary, U.S.A. 83 J9 34 4N 109 51W
MacNutt, Canada 73 C8 51 5N 101 36W
Macodoene, Mozam. 57 C6 23 32S 35 5 E
Macomb, U.S.A. 80 E9 40 27N 90 40W
Mâcon, France 18 C6 46 19N 4 50 E
Macon, Ga., U.S.A. 77 J4 32 51N 83 38W
Macon, Miss., U.S.A. 77 J1 33 7N 88 34W
Macon, Mo., U.S.A. 80 F8 39 44N 92 28W
Macondo, Angola 53 G4 12 37S 23 46 E
Macossa, Mozam. 55 F3 17 55S 33 56 E
Macoun L., Canada 73 B8 56 32N 103 40W
Macovane, Mozam. 57 C6 21 30S 35 2 E
McPherson, U.S.A. 80 F6 38 22N 97 40W
McPherson Pk., U.S.A. 85 L7 34 53N 119 53W
McPherson Ra., Australia 63 D5 28 15S 153 15 E
Macquarie Harbour, Australia 62 G4 42 15S 145 23 E
Macquarie Is., Pac. Oc. 64 N7 54 36S 158 55 E
MacRobertson Land, Antarctica 5 D6 71 0S 64 0 E
Macroom, Ireland 13 E3 51 54N 8 57W
Macroy, Australia 60 D2 20 53S 118 2 E
MacTier, Canada 78 A5 45 9N 79 46W
Macubela, Mozam. 55 F4 16 53S 37 49 E
Macuiza, Mozam. 55 F3 18 7S 34 29 E
Macuse, Mozam. 55 F4 17 45S 37 10 E
Macuspana, Mexico 87 D6 17 46N 92 36W
Macusse, Angola 56 B3 17 48S 20 23 E
McVille, U.S.A. 80 B5 47 46N 98 11W
Madadeni, S. Africa 57 D5 27 43S 30 3 E
Madagali, Nigeria 51 F7 10 56N 13 33 E
Madagascar ■, Africa 57 C8 20 0S 47 0 E
Madā'in Sālih, Si. Arabia 44 E3 26 46N 37 57 E
Madama, Niger 51 D7 22 0N 13 40 E
Madame I., Canada 71 C7 45 30N 60 58W
Madaoua, Niger 50 F6 14 5N 6 27 E
Madaripur, Bangla. 41 H17 23 19N 90 15 E
Madauk, Burma 41 L20 17 56N 96 52 E
Madawaska, Canada 78 A7 45 30N 78 0W
Madawaska →, Canada 78 A8 45 27N 76 21W
Madaya, Burma 41 H20 22 12N 96 10 E
Maddalena, Italy 20 D3 41 16N 9 23 E
Madeira, Atl. Oc. 22 D3 32 50N 17 0W
Madeira →, Brazil 92 D7 3 22S 58 45W
Madeleine, Is. de la, Canada 71 C7 47 30N 61 40W
Madera, U.S.A. 83 H3 36 57N 120 3W
Madha, India 40 L9 18 0N 75 30 E
Madhubani, India 43 F12 26 21N 86 7 E
Madhya Pradesh □, India 42 J7 22 50N 78 0 E
Madikeri, India 40 N9 12 30N 75 45 E
Madill, U.S.A. 81 H6 34 6N 96 46W
Madimba, Zaïre 52 E3 4 58S 15 5 E
Ma'din, Syria 44 C3 35 45N 39 36 E
Madīnat ash Sha'b, Yemen 46 E3 12 50N 45 0 E
Madingou, Congo 52 E2 4 10S 13 33 E
Madirovalo, Madag. 57 B8 16 26S 46 32 E
Madison, Calif., U.S.A. 84 G5 38 41N 121 59W
Madison, Fla., U.S.A. 77 K4 30 28N 83 25W
Madison, Ind., U.S.A. 76 F3 38 44N 85 23W
Madison, Nebr., U.S.A. 80 E6 41 50N 97 27W
Madison, Ohio, U.S.A. 78 E3 41 46N 81 3W
Madison, S. Dak., U.S.A. 80 D6 44 0N 97 7W
Madison, Wis., U.S.A. 80 D10 43 4N 89 24W
Madison →, U.S.A. 82 D8 45 56N 111 31W
Madisonville, Ky., U.S.A. 76 G2 37 20N 87 30W
Madisonville, Tex., U.S.A. 81 K7 30 57N 95 55W
Madista, Botswana 56 C4 21 15S 25 6 E
Madiun, Indonesia 37 G14 7 38S 111 32 E
Madley, U.K. 11 E5 52 2N 2 51W
Madona, Latvia 9 H22 56 53N 26 5 E
Madras = Tamil Nadu □, India 40 P10 11 0N 77 0 E
Madras, India 40 N12 13 8N 80 19 E
Madras, U.S.A. 82 D3 44 38N 121 8W
Madre, L., Mexico 87 B5 25 0N 97 30W
Madre, Laguna, U.S.A. 81 M6 27 0N 97 30W
Madre, Sierra, Phil. 37 A6 17 0N 122 0 E
Madre de Dios →, Bolivia 92 F5 10 59S 66 8W
Madre de Dios, I., Chile 96 G1 50 20S 75 10W
Madre del Sur, Sierra, Mexico 87 D5 17 30N 100 0W
Madre Occidental, Sierra, Mexico 86 B3 27 0N 107 0W
Madre Oriental, Sierra, Mexico 86 C4 25 0N 100 0W
Madri, India 42 G5 24 16N 73 32 E
Madrid, Spain 19 B4 40 25N 3 45W
Madura, Selat, Indonesia 37 G15 7 30S 113 20 E
Madura Motel, Australia 61 F4 31 55S 127 0 E
Madurai, India 40 Q11 9 55N 78 10 E
Madurantakam, India 40 N11 12 30N 79 50 E
Mae Chan, Thailand 38 B2 20 9N 99 52 E
Mae Hong Son, Thailand 38 C2 19 16N 98 1 E
Mae Khlong →, Thailand 38 F3 13 24N 100 0 E
Mae Phrik, Thailand 38 D2 17 27N 99 7 E
Mae Ramat, Thailand 38 D2 16 58N 98 31 E
Mae Rim, Thailand 38 C2 18 54N 98 57 E
Mae Sot, Thailand 38 D2 16 43N 98 34 E
Mae Suai, Thailand 38 C2 19 39N 99 33 E
Mae Tha, Thailand 38 C2 18 28N 99 8 E
Maebashi, Japan 31 F9 36 24N 139 4 E
Maesteg, U.K. 11 F4 51 36N 3 40W
Maestra, Sierra, Cuba 88 B4 20 15N 77 0W
Maestrazgo, Mts. del, Spain 19 B5 40 30N 0 25W
Maevatanana, Madag. 57 B8 16 56S 46 49 E
Mafeking = Mafikeng, S. Africa 56 D4 25 50S 25 38 E
Mafeking, Canada 73 C8 52 40N 101 10W
Mafeteng, Lesotho 56 D4 29 51S 27 15 E
Maffra, Australia 63 F4 37 53S 146 58 E
Mafia I., Tanzania 54 D4 7 45S 39 50 E
Mafikeng, S. Africa 56 D4 25 50S 25 38 E
Mafra, Brazil 95 B6 26 10S 49 55W
Mafra, Portugal 19 C1 38 55N 9 20W
Mafungabusi Plateau, Zimbabwe 55 F2 18 30S 29 8 E
Magadan, Russia 27 D16 59 38N 150 50 E
Magadi, Kenya 54 C4 1 54S 36 19 E
Magadi, L., Kenya 54 C4 1 54S 36 19 E
Magaliesburg, S. Africa 57 D4 26 0S 27 32 E
Magallanes, Estrecho de, Chile 96 G2 52 30S 75 0W
Magangué, Colombia 92 B4 9 14N 74 45W
Magburaka, S. Leone 50 G2 8 47N 12 0W
Magdalen Is. = Madeleine, Is. de la, Canada 71 C7 47 30N 61 40W
Magdalena, Argentina 94 D4 35 5S 57 30W
Magdalena, Bolivia 92 F6 13 13S 63 57W
Magdalena, Malaysia 36 D5 4 25N 117 55 E
Magdalena, Mexico 86 A2 30 50N 112 0W
Magdalena, U.S.A. 83 J10 34 7N 107 15W
Magdalena →, Colombia 92 A4 11 6N 74 51W
Magdalena →, Mexico 86 A2 30 40N 112 25W
Magdalena, B., Mexico 86 C2 24 30N 112 10W
Magdalena, Llano de la, Mexico 86 C2 25 0N 111 30W
Magdeburg, Germany 16 B6 52 7N 11 38 E
Magdelaine Cays, Australia 62 B5 16 33S 150 18 E
Magee, U.S.A. 81 K10 31 52N 89 44W
Magee, I., U.K. 13 B6 54 48N 5 43W
Magelang, Indonesia 37 G14 7 29S 110 13 E
Magellan's Str. = Magallanes, Estrecho de, Chile 96 G2 52 30S 75 0W
Magenta, L., Australia 61 F2 33 30S 119 2 E
Magerøya, Norway 8 A21 71 3N 25 40 E
Maggiore, L., Italy 20 B3 45 57N 8 39 E
Magherafelt, U.K. 13 B5 54 45N 6 37W
Magistralnyy, Russia 27 D11 56 16N 107 36 E
Magnetic Pole (North) = North Magnetic Pole, Canada 4 B2 77 58N 102 8W
Magnetic Pole (South) = South Magnetic Pole, Antarctica 5 C9 64 8S 138 8 E
Magnitogorsk, Russia 24 D10 53 27N 59 4 E
Magnolia, Ark., U.S.A. 81 J8 33 16N 93 14W
Magnolia, Miss., U.S.A. 81 K9 31 9N 90 28W
Magog, Canada 71 C5 45 18N 72 9W
Magoro, Uganda 54 B3 1 45N 34 12 E
Magosa = Famagusta, Cyprus 23 D12 35 8N 33 55 E
Magouládhes, Greece 23 A3 39 45N 19 42 E
Magoye, Zambia 55 F2 16 1S 27 30 E
Magpie L., Canada 71 B7 51 0N 64 41W
Magrath, Canada 72 D6 49 25N 112 50W
Magu □, Tanzania 54 C3 2 31S 33 28 E
Maguarinho, C., Brazil 93 D9 0 15S 48 30W
Mağusa = Famagusta, Cyprus 23 D12 35 8N 33 55 E
Maguse L., Canada 73 A9 61 40N 95 10W
Maguse Pt., Canada 73 A10 61 20N 93 50W
Magwe, Burma 41 J19 20 10N 95 0 E
Maha Sarakham, Thailand 38 D4 16 12N 103 16 E
Mahābād, Iran 44 B5 36 50N 45 45 E
Mahabharat Lekh, Nepal 43 E9 28 30N 82 0 E
Mahabo, Madag. 57 C7 20 23S 44 40 E
Mahadeo Hills, India 42 H8 22 20N 78 30 E
Mahagi, Zaïre 54 B3 2 20N 31 0 E
Mahajamba →, Madag. 57 B8 15 33S 47 8 E
Mahajamba, Helodranon' i, Madag. 57 B8 15 24S 47 5 E
Mahajan, India 42 E5 28 48N 73 56 E
Mahajanga, Madag. 57 B8 15 40S 46 25 E
Mahajanga □, Madag. 57 B8 17 0S 47 0 E
Mahajilo →, Madag. 57 B8 19 42S 45 22 E
Mahakam →, Indonesia 36 E5 0 35S 117 17 E
Mahalapye, Botswana 56 C4 23 1S 26 51 E
Maḩallāt, Iran 45 C6 33 55N 50 30 E
Māhān, Iran 45 D8 30 5N 57 18 E
Mahanadi →, India 41 J15 20 20N 86 25 E
Mahanoro, Madag. 57 B8 19 54S 48 48 E
Mahanoy City, U.S.A. 79 F8 40 49N 76 9W
Maharashtra □, India 40 J9 20 30N 75 30 E
Mahari Mts., Tanzania 54 D2 6 20S 30 0 E
Mahasham, W. →, Egypt 47 E3 30 15N 34 10 E
Mahasolo, Madag. 57 B8 19 7S 46 22 E
Mahattat ash Shīdīyah, Jordan 47 F4 29 55N 35 55 E
Mahattat 'Unayzah, Jordan 47 E4 30 30N 35 47 E
Mahaxay, Laos 38 D5 17 22N 105 12 E
Mahbubnagar, India 40 L10 16 45N 77 59 E
Maḩḑah, Oman 45 E7 24 24N 55 59 E
Mahdia, Tunisia 51 A7 35 28N 11 0 E
Mahe, India 43 C8 33 10N 78 32 E
Mahenge, Tanzania 55 D4 8 45S 36 41 E
Maheno, N.Z. 59 L3 45 10S 170 50 E
Mahesana, India 42 H5 23 39N 72 26 E
Mahia Pen., N.Z. 59 H6 39 9S 177 55 E
Mahilyow, Belarus 17 B16 53 55N 30 18 E
Mahmud Kot, Pakistan 42 D4 30 16N 71 0 E
Mahnomen, U.S.A. 80 B7 47 19N 95 58W
Mahoba, India 43 G8 25 15N 79 55 E
Mahón, Spain 22 B11 39 53N 4 16 E
Mahone Bay, Canada 71 D7 44 30N 64 20W
Mai-Ndombe, L., Zaïre 52 E3 2 0S 18 20 E
Mai-Sai, Thailand 38 B2 20 20N 99 55 E
Maicurú →, Brazil 93 D8 2 14S 54 17W
Maidan Khula, Afghan. 42 C3 33 36N 69 50 E
Maidenhead, U.K. 11 F7 51 31N 0 42W
Maidstone, Canada 73 C7 53 5N 109 20W
Maidstone, U.K. 11 F8 51 16N 0 32 E
Maiduguri, Nigeria 51 F7 12 0N 13 20 E
Maijdi, Bangla. 41 H17 22 48N 91 10 E
Maikala Ra., India 41 J12 22 0N 81 0 E
Mailsi, Pakistan 42 E5 29 48N 72 15 E
Main →, Germany 16 C5 50 0N 8 18 E
Main →, U.K. 13 B5 54 48N 6 18W
Main Centre, Canada 73 C7 50 35N 107 21W
Maine, France 18 C3 47 55N 0 25W
Maine □, U.S.A. 71 C6 45 20N 69 0W
Maine →, Ireland 13 D2 52 9N 9 45W
Maingkwan, Burma 41 F20 26 15N 96 37 E
Mainit, L., Phil. 37 C7 9 31N 125 30 E
Mainland, Orkney, U.K. 12 C5 58 59N 3 8W
Mainland, Shet., U.K. 12 A7 60 15N 1 22W
Mainpuri, India 43 F8 27 18N 79 4 E
Maintirano, Madag. 57 B7 18 3S 44 1 E
Mainz, Germany 16 C5 50 1N 8 14 E
Maipú, Argentina 94 D4 36 52S 57 50W
Maiquetía, Venezuela 92 A5 10 36N 66 57W
Mairabari, India 41 F18 26 30N 92 22 E
Maisí, Cuba 89 B5 20 17N 74 9W
Maisi, Pta. de, Cuba 89 B5 20 10N 74 10W
Maitland, N.S.W., Australia 63 E5 32 33S 151 36 E
Maitland, S. Austral., Australia 63 E2 34 23S 137 40 E
Maitland →, Canada 78 C3 43 45N 81 43W
Maiz, Is. del, Nic. 88 D3 12 15N 83 4W
Maizuru, Japan 31 G7 35 25N 135 22 E
Majalengka, Indonesia 37 G13 6 50S 108 13 E
Majene, Indonesia 37 E5 3 38S 118 57 E
Maji, Ethiopia 51 G12 6 12N 35 30 E
Major, Canada 73 C7 51 52N 109 37W
Majorca = Mallorca, Spain 22 B10 39 30N 3 0 E
Maka, Senegal 50 F2 13 40N 14 10W
Makale, Indonesia 37 E5 3 6S 119 51 E
Makamba, Burundi 54 C2 4 8S 29 49 E
Makari, Cameroon 52 B2 12 35N 14 28 E
Makarikari = Makgadikgadi Salt Pans, Botswana 56 C4 20 40S 25 45 E
Makarovo, Russia 27 D11 57 40N 107 45 E
Makasar = Ujung Pandang, Indonesia 37 F5 5 10S 119 20 E
Makasar, Selat, Indonesia 37 E5 1 0S 118 20 E
Makasar, Str. of = Makasar, Selat, Indonesia 37 E5 1 0S 118 20 E
Makat, Kazakstan 25 E9 47 39N 53 19 E
Makedhonía □, Greece 21 D10 40 39N 22 0 E
Makedonija = Macedonia ■, Europe 21 D9 41 53N 21 40 E
Makena, U.S.A. 74 H16 20 39N 156 27W
Makeni, S. Leone 50 G2 8 55N 12 5W
Makeyevka = Makiyivka, Ukraine 25 E6 48 0N 38 0 E
Makgadikgadi Salt Pans, Botswana 56 C4 20 40S 25 45 E
Makhachkala, Russia 25 F8 43 0N 47 30 E
Makhmūr, Iraq 44 C4 35 46N 43 35 E
Makian, Indonesia 37 D7 0 20N 127 20 E
Makindu, Kenya 54 C4 2 18S 37 50 E
Makinsk, Kazakstan 26 D8 52 37N 70 26 E
Makiyivka, Ukraine 25 E6 48 0N 38 0 E
Makkah, Si. Arabia 46 C2 21 30N 39 54 E
Makkovik, Canada 71 A8 55 10N 59 10W
Makó, Hungary 17 E11 46 14N 20 33 E
Makokou, Gabon 52 D2 0 40N 12 50 E
Makongo, Zaïre 54 B2 3 25N 26 17 E
Makoro, Zaïre 54 B2 3 10N 29 59 E
Makoua, Congo 52 E3 0 5S 15 50 E
Makrai, India 40 H10 22 2N 77 0 E
Makran Coast Range, Pakistan 40 G4 25 40N 64 0 E
Makrana, India 42 F6 27 2N 74 46 E
Makriyialos, Greece 23 D7 35 2N 25 59 E
Maksimkin Yar, Russia 26 D9 58 42N 86 50 E
Mākū, Iran 44 B5 39 15N 44 31 E
Makumbi, Zaïre 52 F4 5 50S 20 43 E
Makunda, Botswana 56 C3 22 30S 20 7 E
Makurazaki, Japan 31 J5 31 15N 130 20 E
Makurdi, Nigeria 50 G6 7 43N 8 35 E
Makūyeh, Iran 45 D7 28 7N 53 9 E
Makwassie, S. Africa 56 D4 27 17S 26 0 E
Mal B., Ireland 13 D2 52 50N 9 30W
Mala, Pta., Panama 88 E3 7 28N 80 2W
Malabang, Phil. 37 C6 7 36N 124 3 E
Malabar Coast, India 40 P9 11 0N 75 0 E
Malabo = Rey Malabo, Eq. Guin. 50 H6 3 45N 8 50 E
Malacca, Str. of, Indonesia 39 L3 3 0N 101 0 E
Malad City, U.S.A. 82 E7 42 12N 112 15W
Maladzyechna, Belarus 17 A14 54 20N 26 50 E
Málaga, Spain 19 D3 36 43N 4 23W
Malaga, U.S.A. 81 J2 32 14N 104 4W
Malagarasi, Tanzania 54 D3 5 5S 30 50 E
Malagarasi →, Tanzania 54 D2 5 12S 29 47 E
Malaimbandy, Madag. 57 C8 20 20S 45 36 E
Malakâl, Sudan 51 G11 9 33N 31 40 E
Malakand, Pakistan 42 B4 34 40N 71 55 E
Malakoff, U.S.A. 81 J7 32 10N 96 1W
Malamyzh, Russia 27 E14 49 50N 136 50 E
Malang, Indonesia 37 G15 7 59S 112 45 E
Malangen, Norway 8 B18 69 24N 18 37 E
Malanje, Angola 52 F3 9 36S 16 17 E
Mälaren, Sweden 9 G17 59 30N 17 10 E
Malargüe, Argentina 94 D2 35 32S 69 30W
Malartic, Canada 70 C4 48 9N 78 9W
Malaryta, Belarus 17 C13 51 50N 24 3 E
Malatya, Turkey 25 G6 38 25N 38 20 E
Malawi ■, Africa 55 E3 11 55S 34 0 E
Malawi, L., Africa 55 E3 12 30S 34 30 E
Malay Pen., Asia 39 J3 7 25N 100 0 E
Malaybalay, Phil. 37 C7 8 5N 125 7 E
Malāyer, Iran 45 C6 34 19N 48 51 E
Malaysia ■, Asia 36 D4 5 0N 110 0 E
Malazgirt, Turkey 25 G7 39 10N 42 33 E
Malbon, Australia 62 C3 21 5S 140 17 E
Malbooma, Australia 63 E1 30 41S 134 11 E
Malbork, Poland 17 B10 54 3N 19 1 E
Malcolm, Australia 61 E3 28 51S 121 25 E
Malcolm, Pt., Australia 61 F3 33 48S 123 45 E
Maldegem, Belgium 15 C3 51 14N 3 26 E
Malden, Mass., U.S.A. 79 D13 42 26N 71 4W
Malden, Mo., U.S.A. 81 G10 36 34N 89 57W
Malden I., Kiribati 65 H12 4 3S 155 1W
Maldives ■, Ind. Oc. 29 J11 5 0N 73 0 E
Maldonado, Uruguay 95 C5 34 59S 55 0W
Maldonado, Punta, Mexico 87 D5 16 19N 98 35W
Malé Karpaty, Slovak Rep. 17 D9 48 30N 17 20 E
Maléa, Ákra, Greece 21 F10 36 28N 23 7 E
Malegaon, India 40 J9 20 30N 74 38 E
Malei, Mozam. 55 F4 17 12S 36 58 E
Malek Kandī, Iran 44 B5 37 9N 46 6 E
Malela, Zaïre 54 C2 4 22S 26 8 E
Malema, Mozam. 55 E4 14 57S 37 20 E
Máleme, Greece 23 D5 35 31N 23 49 E
Malerkotla, India 42 D6 30 32N 75 58 E
Máles, Greece 23 D7 35 6N 25 35 E
Malgomaj, Sweden 8 D17 64 40N 16 30 E
Malha, Sudan 51 E10 15 8N 25 10 E
Malheur →, U.S.A. 82 D5 44 4N 116 59W
Malheur L., U.S.A. 82 E4 43 20N 118 48W
Mali ■, Africa 50 E4 17 0N 3 0W
Mali →, Burma 41 G20 25 40N 97 40 E
Malibu, U.S.A. 85 L8 34 2N 118 41W
Malik, Indonesia 37 E6 0 39S 123 16 E
Malili, Indonesia 37 E6 2 42S 121 6 E
Malimba, Mts., Zaïre 54 D2 7 30S 29 30 E
Malin Hd., Ireland 13 A4 55 23N 7 23W
Malindi, Kenya 54 C5 3 12S 40 5 E
Malines = Mechelen, Belgium 15 C4 51 2N 4 29 E
Malino, Indonesia 37 D6 1 0N 121 0 E
Malinyi, Tanzania 55 D4 8 56S 36 0 E
Malita, Phil. 37 C7 6 19N 125 39 E
Malkara, Turkey 21 D12 40 53N 26 53 E
Mallacoota, Australia 63 F4 37 40S 149 40 E
Mallacoota Inlet, Australia 63 F4 37 34S 149 40 E
Mallaig, U.K. 12 E3 57 0N 5 50W
Mallawan, India 43 F9 27 4N 80 12 E
Mallawi, Egypt 51 C11 27 44N 30 44 E
Mállia, Greece 23 D7 35 17N 25 27 E
Mallión, Kólpos, Greece 23 D7 35 19N 25 27 E
Mallorca, Spain 22 B10 39 30N 3 0 E
Mallorytown, Canada 79 B9 44 29N 75 53W
Mallow, Ireland 13 D3 52 8N 8 39W
Malmberget, Sweden 8 C19 67 11N 20 40 E
Malmédy, Belgium 15 D6 50 25N 6 2 E
Malmesbury, S. Africa 56 E2 33 28S 18 41 E
Malmö, Sweden 9 J15 55 36N 12 59 E
Malolos, Phil. 37 B6 14 50N 120 49 E
Malombe L., Malawi 55 E4 14 40S 35 15 E
Malone, U.S.A. 79 B10 44 51N 74 18W
Måløy, Norway 9 F11 61 57N 5 6 E
Malozemelskaya Tundra, Russia 24 A9 67 0N 50 0 E
Malpaso, Canary Is. 22 G1 27 43N 18 3W
Malpelo, Colombia 92 C2 4 3N 81 35W
Malta, Idaho, U.S.A. 82 E7 42 18N 113 22W
Malta, Mont., U.S.A. 82 B10 48 21N 107 52W
Malta ■, Europe 23 D1 35 50N 14 30 E
Maltahöhe, Namibia 56 C2 24 55S 17 0 E
Malton, Canada 78 C5 43 42N 79 38W
Malton, U.K. 10 C7 54 9N 0 49W
Maluku, Indonesia 37 E7 1 0S 127 0 E
Maluku □, Indonesia 37 E7 3 0S 128 0 E

Maluku Sea

Maluku Sea = Molucca Sea, Indonesia 37 E6 2 0S 124 0 E
Malvan, India 40 L8 16 2N 73 30 E
Malvern, U.S.A. 81 H8 34 22N 92 49W
Malvern Hills, U.K. 11 E5 52 0N 2 19W
Malvinas, Is. = Falkland Is. □, Atl. Oc. 96 G5 51 30S 59 0W
Malya, Tanzania 54 C3 3 5S 33 38 E
Malyn, Ukraine 17 C15 50 46N 29 3 E
Malyy Lyakhovskiy, Ostrov, Russia 27 B15 74 7N 140 36 E
Malyy Nimnyr, Russia 27 D13 57 50N 125 10 E
Mama, Russia 27 D12 58 18N 112 54 E
Mamanguape, Brazil 93 E11 6 50S 35 4W
Mamasa, Indonesia 37 E5 2 55S 119 20 E
Mambasa, Zaïre 54 B2 1 22N 29 3 E
Mamberamo →, Indonesia 37 E9 2 0S 137 50 E
Mambilima Falls, Zambia 55 E2 10 31S 28 45 E
Mambirima, Zaïre 55 E2 11 25S 27 33 E
Mambo, Tanzania 54 C4 4 52S 38 22 E
Mambrui, Kenya 54 C5 3 5S 40 5 E
Mamburao, Phil. 37 B6 13 13N 120 39 E
Mameigwess L., Canada 70 B2 52 35N 87 50W
Mamfe, Cameroon 50 G6 5 50N 9 15 E
Mammoth, U.S.A. 83 K8 32 43N 110 39W
Mamoré →, Bolivia 92 F5 10 23S 65 53W
Mamou, Guinea 50 F2 10 15N 12 0W
Mamuju, Indonesia 37 E5 2 41S 118 50 E
Man, Ivory C. 50 G3 7 30N 7 40W
Man, I. of, U.K. 10 C3 54 15N 4 30W
Man Na, Burma 41 H20 23 27N 97 19 E
Mana, Fr. Guiana 93 B8 5 45N 53 55W
Manaar, G. of = Mannar, G. of, Asia 40 Q11 8 30N 79 0 E
Manacapuru, Brazil 92 D6 3 16S 60 37W
Manacor, Spain 22 B10 39 34N 3 13 E
Manado, Indonesia 37 D6 1 29N 124 51 E
Managua, Nic. 88 D2 12 6N 86 20W
Managua, L., Nic. 88 D2 12 20N 86 30W
Manakara, Madag. 57 C8 22 8S 48 1 E
Manama = Al Manāmah, Bahrain 45 E6 26 10N 50 30 E
Manambao →, Madag. 57 B7 17 35S 44 0 E
Manambato, Madag. 57 A8 13 43S 49 7 E
Manambolo →, Madag. 57 B7 19 18S 44 22 E
Manambolosy, Madag. 57 B8 16 2S 49 40 E
Mananara, Madag. 57 B8 16 10S 49 46 E
Mananara →, Madag. 57 C8 23 21S 47 42 E
Mananjary, Madag. 57 C8 21 13S 48 20 E
Manantenina, Madag. 57 C8 24 17S 47 19 E
Manaos = Manaus, Brazil 92 D7 3 0S 60 0W
Manapouri, N.Z. 59 L1 45 34S 167 39 E
Manapouri, L., N.Z. 59 L1 45 32S 167 32 E
Manas, China 32 B3 44 17N 85 56 E
Manas →, India 41 F17 26 12N 90 40 E
Manaslu, Nepal 43 E11 28 33N 84 33 E
Manasquan, U.S.A. 79 F10 40 8N 74 3W
Manassa, U.S.A. 83 H11 37 11N 105 56W
Manaung, Burma 41 K18 18 45N 93 40 E
Manaus, Brazil 92 D7 3 0S 60 0W
Manawan L., Canada 73 B8 55 24N 103 14W
Manay, Phil. 37 C7 7 17N 126 33 E
Manbij, Syria 44 B3 36 31N 37 57 E
Mancelona, U.S.A. 76 C3 44 54N 85 4W
Manchester, U.K. 10 D5 53 29N 2 12W
Manchester, Calif., U.S.A. 84 G3 38 58N 123 41W
Manchester, Conn., U.S.A. 79 E12 41 47N 72 31W
Manchester, Ga., U.S.A. 77 J3 32 51N 84 37W
Manchester, Iowa, U.S.A. 80 D9 42 29N 91 27W
Manchester, Ky., U.S.A. 76 G4 37 9N 83 46W
Manchester, N.H., U.S.A. 79 D13 42 59N 71 28W
Manchester, N.Y., U.S.A. 78 D7 42 56N 77 16W
Manchester, Vt., U.S.A. 79 C11 43 10N 73 5W
Manchester L., Canada 73 A7 61 28N 107 29W
Manchuria = Dongbei, China 35 D13 42 0N 125 0 E
Manchurian Plain, China 28 E16 47 0N 124 0 E
Mand →, Iran 45 D7 28 20N 52 30 E
Manda, Chunya, Tanzania 54 D3 6 51S 32 29 E
Manda, Ludewe, Tanzania 55 E3 10 30S 34 40 E
Mandabé, Madag. 57 C7 21 0S 44 55 E
Mandaguari, Brazil 95 A5 23 32S 51 42W
Mandah, Mongolia 34 B5 44 27N 108 2 E
Mandal, Norway 9 G12 58 2N 7 25 E
Mandalay, Burma 41 J20 22 0N 96 4 E
Mandale = Mandalay, Burma 41 J20 22 0N 96 4 E
Mandalgovi, Mongolia 34 B4 45 45N 106 10 E
Mandalī, Iraq 44 C5 33 43N 45 28 E
Mandan, U.S.A. 80 B4 46 50N 100 54W
Mandar, Teluk, Indonesia 37 E5 3 35S 119 15 E
Mandaue, Phil. 37 B6 10 20N 123 56 E
Mandera, Kenya 54 B5 3 55N 41 53 E
Mandera □, Kenya 54 B5 3 30N 41 0 E
Mandi, India 42 D7 31 39N 76 58 E
Mandimba, Mozam. 55 E4 14 20S 35 40 E
Mandioli, Indonesia 37 E7 0 40S 127 20 E
Mandla, India 43 H9 22 39N 80 30 E
Mandoto, Madag. 57 B8 19 34S 46 17 E
Mandra, Pakistan 42 C5 33 23N 73 12 E
Mandrare →, Madag. 57 D8 25 10S 46 30 E
Mandritsara, Madag. 57 B8 15 50S 48 49 E
Mandsaur, India 42 G6 24 3N 75 8 E
Mandurah, Australia 61 F2 32 36S 115 48 E
Mandvi, India 42 H3 22 51N 69 22 E
Mandya, India 40 N10 12 30N 77 0 E
Mandzai, Pakistan 42 D2 30 55N 67 6 E
Maneh, Iran 45 B8 37 39N 57 7 E
Maneroo, Australia 62 C3 23 22S 143 53 E
Maneroo Cr. →, Australia 62 C3 23 21S 143 53 E
Manfalût, Egypt 51 C11 27 20N 30 52 E
Manfred, Australia 63 E3 33 19S 143 45 E
Manfredónia, Italy 20 D6 41 38N 15 55 E
Mangalia, Romania 17 G15 43 50N 28 35 E
Mangalore, India 40 N9 12 55N 74 47 E
Mangaweka, N.Z. 59 H5 39 48S 175 47 E
Manggar, Indonesia 36 E3 2 50S 108 10 E
Manggawitu, Indonesia 37 E8 4 8S 133 32 E
Mangkalihat, Tanjung, Indonesia 37 D5 1 2N 118 59 E
Mangla Dam, Pakistan 43 C5 33 9N 73 44 E
Manglaur, India 42 E7 29 44N 77 49 E
Mangnai, China 32 C4 37 52N 91 43 E
Mango, Togo 50 F5 10 20N 0 30 E
Mangoche, Malawi 55 E4 14 25S 35 16 E
Mangoky →, Madag. 57 C7 21 29S 43 41 E
Mangole, Indonesia 37 E7 1 50S 125 55 E
Mangombe, Zaïre 54 C2 1 20S 26 48 E
Mangonui, N.Z. 59 F4 35 1S 173 32 E
Mangueigne, Chad 51 F9 10 30N 21 15 E
Mangueira, L. da, Brazil 95 C5 33 0S 52 50W
Mangum, U.S.A. 81 H5 34 53N 99 30W
Mangyshlak Poluostrov, Kazakstan 26 E6 44 30N 52 30 E
Manhattan, U.S.A. 80 F6 39 11N 96 35W
Manhiça, Mozam. 57 D5 25 23S 32 49 E
Manhuaçu, Brazil 93 H10 20 15S 42 2W
Mania →, Madag. 57 B8 19 42S 45 22 E
Manica, Mozam. 57 B5 18 58S 32 59 E
Manica e Sofala □, Mozam. 57 B5 19 10S 33 45 E
Manicaland □, Zimbabwe 55 F3 19 0S 32 30 E
Manicoré, Brazil 92 E6 5 48S 61 16W
Manicouagan →, Canada 71 C6 49 30N 68 30W
Manīfah, Si. Arabia 45 E6 27 44N 49 0 E
Manifold, Australia 62 C5 22 41S 150 40 E
Manifold, C., Australia 62 C5 22 41S 150 50 E
Manigotagan, Canada 73 C9 51 6N 96 18W
Manihiki, Cook Is. 65 J11 10 24S 161 1W
Manika, Plateau de la, Zaïre 55 E2 10 0S 25 5 E
Manila, Phil. 37 B6 14 40N 121 3 E
Manila, U.S.A. 82 F9 40 59N 109 43W
Manila B., Phil. 37 B6 14 40N 120 35 E
Manilla, Australia 63 E5 30 45S 150 43 E
Maningrida, Australia 62 A1 12 3S 134 13 E
Manipur □, India 41 G18 25 0N 94 0 E
Manipur →, Burma 41 H19 23 45N 94 20 E
Manisa, Turkey 21 E12 38 38N 27 30 E
Manistee, U.S.A. 76 C2 44 15N 86 19W
Manistee →, U.S.A. 76 C2 44 15N 86 21W
Manistique, U.S.A. 76 C2 45 57N 86 15W
Manito L., Canada 73 C7 52 43N 109 43W
Manitoba □, Canada 73 B9 55 30N 97 0W
Manitoba, L., Canada 73 C9 51 0N 98 45W
Manitou, Canada 73 D9 49 15N 98 32W
Manitou I., U.S.A. 70 C2 47 25N 87 37W
Manitou Is., U.S.A. 76 C2 45 8N 86 0W
Manitou L., Canada 71 B6 50 55N 65 17W
Manitou Springs, U.S.A. 80 F2 38 52N 104 55W
Manitoulin I., Canada 70 C3 45 40N 82 30W
Manitowaning, Canada 70 C3 45 46N 81 49W
Manitowoc, U.S.A. 76 C2 44 5N 87 40W
Manizales, Colombia 92 B3 5 5N 75 32W
Manja, Madag. 57 C7 21 26S 44 20 E
Manjacaze, Mozam. 57 C5 24 45S 34 0 E
Manjakandriana, Madag. 57 B8 18 55S 47 47 E
Manjhand, Pakistan 42 G3 25 50N 68 10 E
Manjil, Iran 45 B6 36 46N 49 30 E
Manjimup, Australia 61 F2 34 15S 116 6 E
Manjra →, India 40 K10 18 49N 77 52 E
Mankato, Kans., U.S.A. 80 F5 39 47N 98 13W
Mankato, Minn., U.S.A. 80 C8 44 10N 94 0W
Mankayane, Swaziland 57 D5 26 40S 31 4 E
Mankono, Ivory C. 50 G3 8 1N 6 10W
Mankota, Canada 73 D7 49 25N 107 5W
Manlay, Mongolia 34 B4 44 9N 107 0 E
Manly, Australia 63 E5 33 48S 151 17 E
Manmad, India 40 J9 20 18N 74 28 E
Mann Ras., Australia 61 E5 26 6S 130 5 E
Manna, Indonesia 36 E2 4 25S 102 55 E
Mannahill, Australia 63 E3 32 25S 140 0 E
Mannar, Sri Lanka 40 Q11 9 1N 79 54 E
Mannar, G. of, Asia 40 Q11 8 30N 79 0 E
Mannar I., Sri Lanka 40 Q11 9 5N 79 45 E
Mannheim, Germany 16 D5 49 29N 8 29 E
Manning, Canada 72 B5 56 53N 117 39W
Manning, Oreg., U.S.A. 84 E3 45 45N 123 13W
Manning, S.C., U.S.A. 77 J5 33 42N 80 13W
Manning Prov. Park, Canada 72 D4 49 5N 120 45W
Mannington, U.S.A. 76 F5 39 32N 80 21W
Mannum, Australia 63 E2 34 50S 139 20 E
Mano, S. Leone 50 G2 8 3N 12 2W
Manokwari, Indonesia 37 E8 0 54S 134 0 E
Manombo, Madag. 57 C7 22 57S 43 28 E
Manono, Zaïre 54 D2 7 15S 27 25 E
Manosque, France 18 E6 43 49N 5 47 E
Manouane, L., Canada 71 B5 50 45N 70 45W
Manpojin, N. Korea 35 D14 41 6N 126 24 E
Manresa, Spain 19 B6 41 48N 1 50 E
Mansa, Gujarat, India 42 H5 23 27N 72 45 E
Mansa, Punjab, India 42 E6 30 0N 75 27 E
Mansa, Zambia 55 E2 11 13S 28 55 E
Mansehra, Pakistan 42 B5 34 20N 73 15 E
Mansel I., Canada 69 B11 62 0N 80 0W
Mansfield, Australia 63 F4 37 4S 146 6 E
Mansfield, U.K. 10 D6 53 9N 1 11W
Mansfield, La., U.S.A. 81 J8 32 2N 93 43W
Mansfield, Mass., U.S.A. 79 D13 42 2N 71 13W
Mansfield, Ohio, U.S.A. 78 F2 40 45N 82 31W
Mansfield, Pa., U.S.A. 78 E7 41 48N 77 5W
Mansfield, Wash., U.S.A. 82 C4 47 49N 119 38W
Manson Creek, Canada 72 B4 55 37N 124 32W
Manta, Ecuador 92 D2 1 0S 80 40W
Mantalingajan, Mt., Phil. 36 C5 8 55N 117 45 E
Mantare, Tanzania 54 C3 2 42S 33 13 E
Manteca, U.S.A. 83 H3 37 48N 121 13W
Manteo, U.S.A. 77 H8 35 55N 75 40W
Mantes-la-Jolie, France 18 B4 48 58N 1 41 E
Manthani, India 40 K11 18 40N 79 35 E
Manti, U.S.A. 82 G8 39 16N 111 38W
Mantiqueira, Serra da, Brazil 95 A7 22 0S 44 0W
Manton, U.S.A. 76 C3 44 25N 85 24W
Mántova, Italy 20 B4 45 9N 10 48 E
Mänttä, Finland 9 E21 62 0N 24 40 E
Mantua = Mántova, Italy 20 B4 45 9N 10 48 E
Manu, Peru 92 F4 12 10S 70 51W
Manua Is., Amer. Samoa 59 B14 14 13S 169 35W
Manuae, Cook Is. 65 J12 19 30S 159 0W
Manuel Alves →, Brazil 93 F9 11 19S 48 28W
Manui, Indonesia 37 E6 3 35S 123 5 E
Manville, U.S.A. 80 D2 42 47N 104 37W
Many, U.S.A. 81 K8 31 34N 93 29W
Manyara, L., Tanzania 54 C4 3 40S 35 50 E
Manych-Gudilo, Ozero, Russia 25 E7 46 24N 42 38 E
Manyonga →, Tanzania 54 C3 4 10S 34 15 E
Manyoni, Tanzania 54 D3 5 45S 34 55 E
Manyoni □, Tanzania 54 D3 6 30S 34 30 E
Manzai, Pakistan 42 C4 32 12N 70 15 E
Manzanares, Spain 19 C4 39 2N 3 22W
Manzanillo, Cuba 88 B4 20 20N 77 31W
Manzanillo, Mexico 86 D4 19 0N 104 20W
Manzanillo, Pta., Panama 88 E4 9 30N 79 40W
Manzano Mts., U.S.A. 83 J10 34 40N 106 20W
Manzarīyeh, Iran 45 C6 34 53N 50 50 E
Manzhouli, China 33 B6 49 35N 117 25 E
Manzini, Swaziland 57 D5 26 30S 31 25 E
Mao, Chad 51 F8 14 4N 15 19 E
Maoke, Pegunungan, Indonesia 37 E9 3 40S 137 30 E
Maolin, China 35 C12 43 58N 123 30 E
Maoming, China 33 D6 21 50N 110 54 E
Maoxing, China 35 B13 45 28N 124 40 E
Mapam Yumco, China 32 C3 30 45N 81 28 E
Mapastepec, Mexico 87 D6 15 26N 92 54W
Mapia, Kepulauan, Indonesia 37 D8 0 50N 134 20 E
Mapimí, Mexico 86 B4 25 50N 103 50W
Mapimí, Bolsón de, Mexico 86 B4 27 30N 104 15W
Mapinga, Tanzania 54 D4 6 40S 39 12 E
Mapinhane, Mozam. 57 C6 22 20S 35 0 E
Maple Creek, Canada 73 D7 49 55N 109 29W
Maple Valley, U.S.A. 84 C4 47 25N 122 3W
Mapleton, U.S.A. 82 D2 44 2N 123 52W
Mapuera →, Brazil 92 D7 1 5S 57 2W
Maputo, Mozam. 57 D5 25 58S 32 32 E
Maputo, B. de, Mozam. 57 D5 25 50S 32 45 E
Maqiaohe, China 35 B16 44 40N 130 30 E
Maqnā, Si. Arabia 44 D2 28 25N 34 50 E
Maquela do Zombo, Angola 52 F3 6 0S 15 15 E
Maquinchao, Argentina 96 E3 41 15S 68 50W
Maquoketa, U.S.A. 80 D9 42 4N 90 40W
Mar, Serra do, Brazil 95 B6 25 30S 49 0W
Mar Chiquita, L., Argentina 94 C3 30 40S 62 50W
Mar del Plata, Argentina 94 D4 38 0S 57 30W
Mar Menor, Spain 19 D5 37 40N 0 45W
Mara, Tanzania 54 C3 1 30S 34 32 E
Mara □, Tanzania 54 C3 1 45S 34 20 E
Maraã, Brazil 92 D5 1 52S 65 25W
Marabá, Brazil 93 E9 5 20S 49 5W
Maracá, I. de, Brazil 93 C8 2 10N 50 30W
Maracaibo, Venezuela 92 A4 10 40N 71 37W
Maracaibo, L. de, Venezuela 92 B4 9 40N 71 30W
Maracaju, Brazil 95 A4 21 38S 55 9W
Maracay, Venezuela 92 A5 10 15N 67 28W
Marādah, Libya 51 C8 29 15N 19 15 E
Maradi, Niger 50 F6 13 29N 7 20 E
Marāgheh, Iran 44 B5 37 30N 46 12 E
Marāh, Si. Arabia 44 E5 25 0N 45 35 E
Marajó, I. de, Brazil 93 D9 1 0S 49 30W
Marākand, Iran 44 B5 38 51N 45 16 E
Maralal, Kenya 54 B4 1 0N 36 38 E
Maralinga, Australia 61 F5 30 13S 131 32 E
Marama, Australia 63 F3 35 10S 140 10 E
Marampa, S. Leone 50 G2 8 45N 12 28W
Maran, Malaysia 39 L4 3 35N 102 45 E
Marana, U.S.A. 83 K8 32 27N 111 13W
Maranboy, Australia 60 B5 14 40S 132 39 E
Marand, Iran 44 B5 38 30N 45 45 E
Marang, Malaysia 39 K4 5 12N 103 13 E
Maranguape, Brazil 93 D11 3 55S 38 50W
Maranhão = São Luís, Brazil 93 D10 2 39S 44 15W
Maranhão □, Brazil 93 E9 5 0S 46 0W
Maranoa →, Australia 63 D4 27 50S 148 37 E
Marañón →, Peru 92 D4 4 30S 73 35W
Marão, Mozam. 57 C5 24 18S 34 2 E
Maraş = Kahramanmaraş, Turkey 25 G6 37 37N 36 53 E
Marathasa □, Cyprus 23 E11 34 59N 32 51 E
Marathon, Australia 62 C3 20 51S 143 32 E
Marathon, Canada 70 C2 48 44N 86 23W
Marathon, N.Y., U.S.A. 79 D8 42 27N 76 2W
Marathon, Tex., U.S.A. 81 K3 30 12N 103 15W
Marathóvouno, Cyprus 23 D12 35 13N 33 37 E
Maratua, Indonesia 37 D5 2 10N 118 35 E
Maravatío, Mexico 86 D4 19 51N 100 25W
Marāwih, U.A.E. 45 E7 24 18N 53 18 E
Marbella, Spain 19 D3 36 30N 4 57W
Marble Bar, Australia 60 D2 21 9S 119 44 E
Marble Falls, U.S.A. 81 K5 30 35N 98 16W
Marblehead, U.S.A. 79 D14 42 30N 70 51W
Marburg, Germany 16 C5 50 47N 8 46 E
March, U.K. 11 E8 52 33N 0 5 E
Marche, France 18 C4 46 5N 1 20 E
Marche-en-Famenne, Belgium 15 D5 50 14N 5 19 E
Marchena, Spain 19 D3 37 18N 5 23W
Marcos Juárez, Argentina 94 C3 32 42S 62 5W
Marcus I. = Minami-Tori-Shima, Pac. Oc. 64 E7 24 0N 153 45 E
Marcus Necker Ridge, Pac. Oc. 64 F9 20 0N 175 0 E
Marcy, Mt., U.S.A. 79 B11 44 7N 73 56W
Mardan, Pakistan 42 B5 34 20N 72 0 E
Mardie, Australia 60 D2 21 12S 115 59 E
Mardin, Turkey 25 G7 37 20N 40 43 E
Maree, L., U.K. 12 D3 57 40N 5 26W
Mareeba, Australia 62 B4 16 59S 145 28 E
Marek = Stanke Dimitrov, Bulgaria 21 C10 42 17N 23 9 E
Marek, Indonesia 37 E6 4 41S 120 24 E
Marengo, U.S.A. 80 E8 41 48N 92 4W
Marenyi, Kenya 54 C4 4 22S 39 8 E
Marerano, Madag. 57 C7 21 23S 44 52 E
Marfa, U.S.A. 81 K2 30 19N 104 1W
Marfa Pt., Malta 23 D1 35 59N 14 19 E
Margaret →, Australia 60 C4 18 9S 125 41 E
Margaret Bay, Canada 72 C3 51 20N 127 35W
Margaret L., Canada 72 B5 58 56N 115 25W
Margaret River, Australia 60 C4 18 38S 126 52 E
Margarita, I. de, Venezuela 92 A6 11 0N 64 0W
Margaritovo, Russia 30 C7 43 25N 134 45 E
Margate, S. Africa 57 E5 30 50S 30 20 E
Margate, U.K. 11 F9 51 23N 1 23 E
Margelan = Marghilon, Uzbekistan 26 E8 40 27N 71 42 E
Marghilon, Uzbekistan 26 E8 40 27N 71 42 E
Marguerite, Canada 72 C4 52 30N 122 25W
Mari El □, Russia 24 C8 56 30N 48 0 E
Mari Republic □ = Mari El □, Russia 24 C8 56 30N 48 0 E
María Elena, Chile 94 A2 22 18S 69 40W
María Grande, Argentina 94 C4 31 45S 59 55W
Maria I., N. Terr., Australia 62 A2 14 52S 135 45 E
Maria I., Tas., Australia 62 G4 42 35S 148 0 E
Maria van Diemen, C., N.Z. 59 F4 34 29S 172 40 E
Mariakani, Kenya 54 C4 3 50S 39 27 E
Marian L., Canada 72 A5 63 0N 116 15W
Mariana Trench, Pac. Oc. 28 H18 13 0N 145 0 E
Marianao, Cuba 88 B3 23 8N 82 24W
Marianna, Ark., U.S.A. 81 H9 34 46N 90 46W
Marianna, Fla., U.S.A. 77 K3 30 46N 85 14W
Marias →, U.S.A. 82 C8 47 56N 110 30W
Mariato, Punta, Panama 88 E3 7 12N 80 52W
Ma'rib, Yemen 46 D4 15 25N 45 21 E
Maribor, Slovenia 16 E8 46 36N 15 40 E
Marico →, Africa 56 C4 23 35S 26 57 E
Maricopa, Ariz., U.S.A. 83 K7 33 4N 112 3W
Maricopa, Calif., U.S.A. 85 K7 35 4N 119 24W
Maricourt, Canada 69 C12 56 34N 70 49W
Marîdî, Sudan 51 H10 4 55N 29 25 E
Marie Byrd Land, Antarctica 5 D14 79 30S 125 0W
Marie-Galante, Guadeloupe 89 C7 15 56N 61 16W
Mariecourt = Kangiqsujuaq, Canada 69 B12 61 30N 72 0W
Marienberg, Neths. 15 B6 52 2N 6 35 E
Marienbourg, Belgium 15 D4 50 6N 4 31 E
Mariental, Namibia 56 C2 24 36S 18 0 E
Marienville, U.S.A. 78 E5 41 28N 79 8W
Mariestad, Sweden 9 G15 58 43N 13 50 E
Marietta, Ga., U.S.A. 77 J3 33 57N 84 33W
Marietta, Ohio, U.S.A. 76 F5 39 25N 81 27W
Marieville, Canada 79 A11 45 26N 73 10W
Mariinsk, Russia 26 D9 56 10N 87 20 E
Marijampolė, Lithuania 9 J20 54 33N 23 19 E
Marília, Brazil 95 A5 22 13S 50 0W
Marillana, Australia 60 D2 22 37S 119 16 E
Marín, Spain 19 A1 42 23N 8 42W
Marina, U.S.A. 84 J5 36 41N 121 48W
Marina Plains, Australia 62 A3 14 37S 143 57 E
Marinduque, Phil. 37 B6 13 25N 122 0 E
Marine City, U.S.A. 76 D4 42 43N 82 30W
Marinette, U.S.A. 76 C2 45 6N 87 38W
Maringá, Brazil 95 A5 23 26S 52 2W
Marion, Ala., U.S.A. 77 J2 32 38N 87 19W
Marion, Ill., U.S.A. 81 G10 37 44N 88 56W
Marion, Ind., U.S.A. 76 E3 40 32N 85 40W
Marion, Iowa, U.S.A. 80 D9 42 2N 91 36W
Marion, Kans., U.S.A. 80 F6 38 21N 97 1W
Marion, Mich., U.S.A. 76 C3 44 6N 85 9W
Marion, N.C., U.S.A. 77 H4 35 41N 82 1W
Marion, Ohio, U.S.A. 76 E4 40 35N 83 8W
Marion, S.C., U.S.A. 77 H6 34 11N 79 24W
Marion, Va., U.S.A. 77 G5 36 50N 81 31W
Marion, L., U.S.A. 77 J5 33 28N 80 10W
Mariposa, U.S.A. 83 H4 37 29N 119 58W
Mariscal Estigarribia, Paraguay 94 A3 22 3S 60 40W
Maritime Alps = Maritimes, Alpes, Europe 16 F4 44 10N 7 10 E
Maritimes, Alpes, Europe 16 F4 44 10N 7 10 E
Maritsa = Évros →, Bulgaria 21 D12 41 40N 26 34 E
Maritsa, Greece 23 C10 36 22N 28 10 E
Mariupol, Ukraine 25 E6 47 5N 37 31 E
Marīvān, Iran 44 C5 35 30N 46 25 E
Markazī □, Iran 45 C6 35 0N 49 30 E
Markdale, Canada 78 B4 44 19N 80 39W
Marked Tree, U.S.A. 81 H9 35 32N 90 25W
Marken, Neths. 15 B5 52 26N 5 12 E
Market Drayton, U.K. 10 E5 52 54N 2 29W
Market Harborough, U.K. 11 E7 52 29N 0 55W
Markham, Canada 78 C5 43 52N 79 16W
Markham, Mt., Antarctica 5 E11 83 0S 164 0 E
Markham L., Canada 73 A8 62 30N 102 35W
Markleeville, U.S.A. 84 G7 38 42N 119 47W
Markovo, Russia 27 C17 64 40N 169 40 E
Marks, Russia 24 D8 51 45N 46 50 E
Marksville, U.S.A. 81 K8 31 8N 92 4W
Marla, Australia 63 D1 27 19S 133 33 E
Marlboro, U.S.A. 79 D13 42 19N 71 33W
Marlborough, Australia 62 C4 22 46S 149 52 E
Marlborough Downs, U.K. 11 F6 51 27N 1 53W
Marlin, U.S.A. 81 K6 31 18N 96 54W
Marlow, U.S.A. 81 H6 34 39N 97 58W
Marmagao, India 40 M8 15 25N 73 56 E
Marmara, Turkey 21 D12 40 35N 27 38 E
Marmara, Sea of = Marmara Denizi, Turkey 21 D13 40 45N 28 15 E
Marmara Denizi, Turkey 21 D13 40 45N 28 15 E
Marmaris, Turkey 21 F13 36 50N 28 14 E
Marmarth, U.S.A. 80 B3 46 18N 103 54W
Marmion, Mt., Australia 61 E2 29 16S 119 50 E
Marmion L., Canada 70 C1 48 55N 91 20W
Marmolada, Mte., Italy 20 A4 46 26N 11 51 E
Marmora, Canada 70 D4 44 28N 77 41W
Marne →, France 18 B5 48 48N 2 24 E
Maroala, Madag. 57 B8 15 23S 47 59 E
Maroantsetra, Madag. 57 B8 15 26S 49 44 E
Maromandia, Madag. 57 A8 14 13S 48 5 E
Marondera, Zimbabwe 55 F3 18 5S 31 42 E
Maroni →, Fr. Guiana 93 B8 5 30N 54 0W
Maroochydore, Australia 63 D5 26 29S 153 5 E
Maroona, Australia 63 F3 37 27S 142 54 E
Marosakoa, Madag. 57 B8 15 26S 46 38 E
Maroua, Cameroon 51 F7 10 40N 14 20 E
Marovoay, Madag. 57 B8 16 6S 46 39 E
Marquard, S. Africa 56 D4 28 40S 27 28 E
Marquesas Is. = Marquises, Is., Pac. Oc. 65 H14 9 30S 140 0W
Marquette, U.S.A. 76 B2 46 33N 87 24W
Marquises, Is., Pac. Oc. 65 H14 9 30S 140 0W

Meknès

Meknès, Morocco **50 B3** 33 57N 5 33W
Mekong →, Asia **39 H6** 9 30N 106 15 E
Mekongga, Indonesia **37 E6** 3 39S 121 15 E
Mekvari = Kür →, Azerbaijan **25 G8** 39 29N 49 15 E
Melagiri Hills, India **40 N10** 12 20N 77 30 E
Melaka, Malaysia **39 L4** 2 15N 102 15 E
Melalap, Malaysia **36 C5** 5 10N 116 5 E
Mélambes, Greece **23 D6** 35 8N 24 40 E
Melanesia, Pac. Oc. **64 H7** 4 0S 155 0 E
Melbourne, Australia **63 F3** 37 50S 145 0 E
Melbourne, U.S.A. **77 L5** 28 5N 80 37W
Melchor Múzquiz, Mexico **86 B4** 27 50N 101 30W
Melchor Ocampo, Mexico **86 C4** 24 52N 101 40W
Mélèzes →, Canada **69 C12** 57 30N 71 0W
Melfi, Chad **51 F8** 11 0N 17 59 E
Melfort, Canada **73 C8** 52 50N 104 37W
Melfort, Zimbabwe **55 F3** 18 0S 31 25 E
Melhus, Norway **8 E14** 63 17N 10 18 E
Melilla, N. Afr. **19 E4** 35 21N 2 57W
Melipilla, Chile **94 C1** 33 42S 71 15W
Mélissa, Ákra, Greece **23 D6** 35 6N 24 33 E
Melita, Canada **73 D8** 49 15N 101 0W
Melitopol, Ukraine **25 E6** 46 50N 35 22 E
Melk, Austria **16 D8** 48 13N 15 20 E
Mellansel, Sweden **8 E18** 63 25N 18 17 E
Mellen, U.S.A. **80 B9** 46 20N 90 40W
Mellerud, Sweden **9 G15** 58 41N 12 28 E
Mellette, U.S.A. **80 C5** 45 9N 98 30W
Mellieha, Malta **23 D1** 35 57N 14 21 E
Melo, Uruguay **95 C5** 32 20S 54 10W
Melolo, Indonesia **37 F6** 9 53S 120 40 E
Melouprey, Cambodia **38 F5** 13 48N 105 16 E
Melrose, N.S.W., Australia **63 E4** 32 42S 146 57 E
Melrose, W. Austral., Australia **61 E3** 27 50S 121 15 E
Melrose, U.K. **12 F6** 55 36N 2 43W
Melrose, U.S.A. **81 H3** 34 26N 103 38W
Melstone, U.S.A. **82 C10** 46 36N 107 52W
Melton Mowbray, U.K. **10 E7** 52 47N 0 54W
Melun, France **18 B5** 48 32N 2 39 E
Melut, Sudan **51 F11** 10 30N 32 13 E
Melville, Canada **73 C8** 50 55N 102 50W
Melville, C., Australia **62 A3** 14 11S 144 30 E
Melville, L., Canada **71 B8** 53 30N 60 0W
Melville B., Australia **62 A2** 12 0S 136 45 E
Melville I., Australia **60 B5** 11 30S 131 0 E
Melville I., Canada **4 B2** 75 30N 112 0W
Melville Pen., Canada **69 B11** 68 0N 84 0W
Melvin →, Canada **72 B5** 59 11N 117 31W
Memba, Mozam. **55 E5** 14 11S 40 30 E
Memboro, Indonesia **37 F5** 9 30S 119 30 E
Memel = Klaipeda, Lithuania **9 J19** 55 43N 21 10 E
Memel, S. Africa **57 D4** 27 38S 29 36 E
Memmingen, Germany **16 E6** 47 58N 10 10 E
Mempawah, Indonesia **36 D3** 0 30N 109 5 E
Memphis, Tenn., U.S.A. **81 H10** 35 8N 90 3W
Memphis, Tex., U.S.A. **81 H4** 34 44N 100 33W
Mena, U.S.A. **81 H7** 34 35N 94 15W
Menai Strait, U.K. **10 D3** 53 11N 4 13W
Ménaka, Mali **50 E5** 15 59N 2 18 E
Menam = Chao Phraya →, Thailand **38 F3** 13 32N 100 36 E
Menarandra →, Madag. **57 D7** 25 17S 44 30 E
Menard, U.S.A. **81 K5** 30 55N 99 47W
Menasha, U.S.A. **76 C1** 44 13N 88 26W
Menate, Indonesia **36 E4** 0 12S 113 3 E
Mendawai →, Indonesia **36 E4** 3 30S 113 0 E
Mende, France **18 D5** 44 31N 3 30 E
Mendez, Mexico **87 B5** 25 7N 98 34W
Mendhar, India **43 C6** 33 35N 74 10 E
Mendip Hills, U.K. **11 F5** 51 17N 2 40W
Mendocino, U.S.A. **82 G2** 39 19N 123 48W
Mendocino, C., U.S.A. **82 F1** 40 26N 124 25W
Mendota, Calif., U.S.A. **83 H3** 36 45N 120 23W
Mendota, Ill., U.S.A. **80 E10** 41 33N 89 7W
Mendoza, Argentina **94 C2** 32 50S 68 52W
Mendoza □, Argentina **94 C2** 33 0S 69 0W
Mene Grande, Venezuela **92 B4** 9 49N 70 56W
Menemen, Turkey **21 E12** 38 34N 27 3 E
Menen, Belgium **15 D3** 50 47N 3 7 E
Menggala, Indonesia **36 E3** 4 30S 105 15 E
Mengjin, China **34 G7** 34 55N 112 45 E
Mengyin, China **35 G9** 35 40N 117 58 E
Mengzi, China **32 D5** 23 20N 103 22 E
Menihek L., Canada **71 B6** 54 0N 67 0W
Menin = Menen, Belgium **15 D3** 50 47N 3 7 E
Menindee, Australia **63 E3** 32 20S 142 25 E
Menindee L., Australia **63 E3** 32 20S 142 25 E
Meningie, Australia **63 F2** 35 50S 139 18 E
Menlo Park, U.S.A. **84 H4** 37 27N 122 12W
Menominee, U.S.A. **76 C2** 45 6N 87 37W
Menominee →, U.S.A. **76 C2** 45 6N 87 36W
Menomonie, U.S.A. **80 C9** 44 53N 91 55W
Menongue, Angola **53 G3** 14 48S 17 52 E
Menorca, Spain **22 B11** 40 0N 4 0 E
Mentakab, Malaysia **39 L4** 3 29N 102 21 E
Mentawai, Kepulauan, Indonesia **36 E1** 2 0S 99 0 E
Menton, France **18 E7** 43 50N 7 29 E
Mentor, U.S.A. **78 E3** 41 40N 81 21W
Menzelinsk, Russia **24 C9** 55 47N 53 11 E
Menzies, Australia **61 E3** 29 40S 121 2 E
Me'ona, Israel **47 B4** 33 1N 35 15 E
Meoqui, Mexico **86 B3** 28 17N 105 29W
Mepaco, Mozam. **55 F3** 15 57S 30 48 E
Meppel, Neths. **15 B6** 52 42N 6 12 E
Mer Rouge, U.S.A. **81 J9** 32 47N 91 48W
Merabéllou, Kólpos, Greece **23 D7** 35 10N 25 50 E
Meramangye, L., Australia **61 E5** 28 25S 132 13 E
Meran = Merano, Italy **20 A4** 46 40N 11 9 E
Merano, Italy **20 A4** 46 40N 11 9 E
Merauke, Indonesia **37 F10** 8 29S 140 24 E
Merbabu, Indonesia **37 G14** 7 30S 110 40 E
Merbein, Australia **63 E3** 34 10S 142 2 E
Merca, Somali Rep. **46 G3** 1 48N 44 50 E
Mercadal, Spain **22 B11** 39 59N 4 5 E
Merced, U.S.A. **83 H3** 37 18N 120 29W
Merced Pk., U.S.A. **84 H7** 37 36N 119 24W
Mercedes, Buenos Aires, Argentina **94 C4** 34 40S 59 30W
Mercedes, Corrientes, Argentina **94 B4** 29 10S 58 5W
Mercedes, San Luis, Argentina **94 C2** 33 40S 65 21W
Mercedes, Uruguay **94 C4** 33 12S 58 0W
Merceditas, Chile **94 B1** 28 20S 70 35W
Mercer, N.Z. **59 G5** 37 16S 175 5 E
Mercer, U.S.A. **78 E4** 41 14N 80 15W
Mercury, U.S.A. **85 J11** 36 40N 115 58W
Mercy C., Canada **69 B13** 65 0N 63 30W
Meredith, C., Falk. Is. **96 G4** 52 15S 60 40W
Meredith, L., U.S.A. **81 H4** 35 43N 101 33W
Merga = Nukheila, Sudan **51 E10** 19 1N 26 21 E
Mergui Arch. = Myeik Kyunzu, Burma **39 G1** 11 30N 97 30 E
Mérida, Mexico **87 C7** 20 58N 89 37W
Mérida, Spain **19 C2** 38 55N 6 25W
Mérida, Venezuela **92 B4** 8 24N 71 8W
Mérida, Cord. de, Venezuela **90 C3** 9 0N 71 0W
Meriden, U.S.A. **79 E12** 41 32N 72 48W
Meridian, Calif., U.S.A. **84 F5** 39 9N 121 55W
Meridian, Idaho, U.S.A. **82 E5** 43 37N 116 24W
Meridian, Miss., U.S.A. **77 J1** 32 22N 88 42W
Meridian, Tex., U.S.A. **81 K6** 31 56N 97 39W
Meriruma, Brazil **93 C8** 1 15N 54 50W
Merkel, U.S.A. **81 J4** 32 28N 100 1W
Merksem, Belgium **15 C4** 51 16N 4 25 E
Mermaid Reef, Australia **60 C2** 17 6S 119 36 E
Merowe, Sudan **51 E11** 18 29N 31 46 E
Merredin, Australia **61 F2** 31 28S 118 18 E
Merrick, U.K. **12 F4** 55 8N 4 28W
Merrickville, Canada **79 B9** 44 55N 75 50W
Merrill, Oreg., U.S.A. **82 E3** 42 1N 121 36W
Merrill, Wis., U.S.A. **80 C10** 45 11N 89 41W
Merriman, U.S.A. **80 D4** 42 55N 101 42W
Merritt, Canada **72 C4** 50 10N 120 45W
Merriwa, Australia **63 E5** 32 6S 150 22 E
Merriwagga, Australia **63 E4** 33 47S 145 43 E
Merry I., Canada **70 A4** 55 29N 77 31W
Merrygoen, Australia **63 E4** 31 51S 149 12 E
Merryville, U.S.A. **81 K8** 30 45N 93 33W
Mersa Fatma, Eritrea **46 E3** 14 57N 40 17 E
Mersch, Lux. **15 E6** 49 44N 6 7 E
Merseburg, Germany **16 C6** 51 22N 11 59 E
Mersey →, U.K. **10 D5** 53 25N 3 1W
Merseyside □, U.K. **10 D5** 53 31N 3 2W
Mersin, Turkey **25 G5** 36 51N 34 36 E
Mersing, Malaysia **39 L4** 2 25N 103 50 E
Merta, India **42 F6** 26 39N 74 4 E
Merthyr Tydfil, U.K. **11 F4** 51 45N 3 22W
Merthyr Tydfil □, U.K. **11 F4** 51 46N 3 21W
Mértola, Portugal **19 D2** 37 40N 7 40W
Mertzon, U.S.A. **81 K4** 31 16N 100 49W
Meru, Kenya **54 B4** 0 3N 37 40 E
Meru, Tanzania **54 C4** 3 15S 36 46 E
Meru □, Kenya **54 B4** 0 3N 37 46 E
Mesa, U.S.A. **83 K8** 33 25N 111 50W
Mesanagrós, Greece **23 C9** 36 1N 27 49 E
Mesaoría □, Cyprus **23 D12** 35 12N 33 14 E
Mesarás, Kólpos, Greece **23 D6** 35 6N 24 47 E
Mesgouez, L., Canada **70 B4** 51 20N 75 0W
Meshed = Mashhad, Iran **45 B8** 36 20N 59 35 E
Meshoppen, U.S.A. **79 E8** 41 36N 76 3W
Meshra er Req, Sudan **51 G10** 8 25N 29 18 E
Mesick, U.S.A. **76 C3** 44 24N 85 43W
Mesilinka →, Canada **72 B4** 56 6N 124 30W
Mesilla, U.S.A. **83 K10** 32 16N 106 48W
Mesolóngion, Greece **21 E9** 38 21N 21 28 E
Mesopotamia = Al Jazirah, Iraq **44 C5** 33 30N 44 0 E
Mesquite, U.S.A. **83 H6** 36 47N 114 6W
Mess Cr. →, Canada **72 B2** 57 55N 131 14W
Messalo →, Mozam. **55 E4** 12 25S 39 15 E
Messina, Italy **20 E6** 38 11N 15 34 E
Messina, S. Africa **57 C5** 22 20S 30 5 E
Messina, Str. di, Italy **20 F6** 38 15N 15 35 E
Messíni, Greece **21 F10** 37 4N 22 1 E
Messiniakós Kólpos, Greece **21 F10** 36 45N 22 5 E
Messonghi, Greece **23 B3** 39 29N 19 56 E
Mesta →, Bulgaria **21 D11** 40 54N 24 49 E
Meta →, S. Amer. **92 B5** 6 12N 67 28W
Metairie, U.S.A. **81 L9** 29 58N 90 10W
Metaline Falls, U.S.A. **82 B5** 48 52N 117 22W
Metán, Argentina **94 B3** 25 30S 65 0W
Metangula, Mozam. **55 E3** 12 40S 34 50 E
Metema, Ethiopia **51 F12** 12 56N 36 13 E
Metengobalame, Mozam. **55 E3** 14 49S 34 30 E
Methven, N.Z. **59 K3** 43 38S 171 40 E
Methy L., Canada **73 B7** 56 28N 109 30W
Metil, Mozam. **55 F4** 16 24S 39 0 E
Metlakatla, U.S.A. **72 B2** 55 8N 131 35W
Metropolis, U.S.A. **81 G10** 37 9N 88 44W
Mettur Dam, India **40 P10** 11 45N 77 45 E
Metz, France **18 B7** 49 8N 6 10 E
Meulaboh, Indonesia **36 D1** 4 11N 96 3 E
Meureudu, Indonesia **36 C1** 5 19N 96 10 E
Meuse →, Europe **18 A6** 50 45N 5 41 E
Mexborough, U.K. **10 D6** 53 30N 1 15W
Mexia, U.S.A. **81 K6** 31 41N 96 29W
Mexiana, I., Brazil **93 C9** 0 0 49 30W
Mexicali, Mexico **86 A1** 32 40N 115 30W
Mexican Plateau, Mexico **66 G9** 25 0N 104 0W
México, Mexico **87 D5** 19 20N 99 10W
Mexico, Maine, U.S.A. **79 B14** 44 34N 70 33W
Mexico, Mo., U.S.A. **80 F9** 39 10N 91 53W
México □, Mexico **86 D5** 19 20N 99 10W
Mexico ■, Cent. Amer. **86 C4** 25 0N 105 0W
Mexico, G. of, Cent. Amer. **87 C7** 25 0N 90 0W
Meymaneh, Afghan. **40 B4** 35 53N 64 38 E
Mezen, Russia **24 A7** 65 50N 44 20 E
Mezen →, Russia **24 A7** 65 44N 44 22 E
Mézene, France **18 D6** 44 54N 4 11 E
Mezőkövesd, Hungary **17 E11** 47 49N 20 35 E
Mezőtúr, Hungary **17 E11** 46 58N 20 41 E
Mezquital, Mexico **86 C4** 23 29N 104 23W
Mgeta, Tanzania **55 D4** 8 22S 36 6 E
Mhlaba Hills, Zimbabwe **55 F3** 18 30S 30 30 E
Mhow, India **42 H6** 22 33N 75 50 E
Miahuatlán, Mexico **87 D5** 16 21N 96 36W
Miallo, Australia **62 B4** 16 28S 145 22 E
Miami, Ariz., U.S.A. **83 K8** 33 24N 110 52W
Miami, Fla., U.S.A. **77 N5** 25 47N 80 11W
Miami, Tex., U.S.A. **81 H4** 35 42N 100 38W
Miami →, U.S.A. **76 F3** 39 20N 84 40W
Miami Beach, U.S.A. **77 N5** 25 47N 80 8W
Mian Xian, China **34 H4** 33 10N 106 32 E
Mianchi, China **34 G6** 34 48N 111 48 E
Mīāndowāb, Iran **44 B5** 37 0N 46 5 E
Miandrivazo, Madag. **57 B8** 19 31S 45 29 E
Mīāneh, Iran **44 B5** 37 30N 47 40 E
Mianwali, Pakistan **42 C4** 32 38N 71 28 E
Miarinarivo, Madag. **57 B8** 18 57S 46 55 E
Miass, Russia **24 D11** 54 59N 60 6 E
Michalovce, Slovak Rep. **17 D11** 48 47N 21 58 E
Michigan □, U.S.A. **76 C3** 44 0N 85 0W
Michigan, L., U.S.A. **76 C2** 44 0N 87 0W
Michigan City, U.S.A. **76 E2** 41 43N 86 54W
Michikamau L., Canada **71 B7** 54 20N 63 10W
Michipicoten, Canada **70 C3** 47 55N 84 55W
Michipicoten I., Canada **70 C2** 47 40N 85 40W
Michoacan □, Mexico **86 D4** 19 0N 102 0W
Michurin, Bulgaria **21 C12** 42 9N 27 51 E
Michurinsk, Russia **24 D7** 52 58N 40 27 E
Miclere, Australia **62 C4** 22 34S 147 32 E
Mico, Pta., Nic. **88 D3** 12 0N 83 30W
Micronesia, Federated States of ■, Pac. Oc. **64 G7** 9 0N 150 0 E
Midai, P., Indonesia **39 L6** 3 0N 107 47 E
Midale, Canada **73 D8** 49 25N 103 20W
Middelburg, Neths. **15 C3** 51 30N 3 36 E
Middelburg, Eastern Cape, S. Africa **56 E3** 31 30S 25 0 E
Middelburg, Mpumalanga, S. Africa **57 D4** 25 49S 29 28 E
Middelwit, S. Africa **56 C4** 24 51S 27 3 E
Middle Alkali L., U.S.A. **82 F3** 41 27N 120 5W
Middle Fork Feather →, U.S.A. **84 F5** 38 33N 121 30W
Middle I., Australia **61 F3** 34 6S 123 11 E
Middle Loup →, U.S.A. **80 E5** 41 17N 98 24W
Middleboro, U.S.A. **79 E14** 41 54N 70 55W
Middleburg, N.Y., U.S.A. **79 D10** 42 36N 74 20W
Middleburg, Pa., U.S.A. **78 F7** 40 47N 77 3W
Middlebury, U.S.A. **79 B11** 44 1N 73 10W
Middleport, U.S.A. **76 F4** 39 0N 82 3W
Middlesboro, U.S.A. **77 G4** 36 36N 83 43W
Middlesbrough, U.K. **10 C6** 54 35N 1 13W
Middlesbrough □, U.K. **10 C6** 54 28N 1 13W
Middlesex, Belize **88 C2** 17 2N 88 31W
Middlesex, U.S.A. **79 F10** 40 36N 74 30W
Middleton, Australia **62 C3** 22 22S 141 32 E
Middleton, Canada **71 D6** 44 57N 65 4W
Middletown, Calif., U.S.A. **84 G4** 38 45N 122 37W
Middletown, Conn., U.S.A. **79 E12** 41 34N 72 39W
Middletown, N.Y., U.S.A. **79 E10** 41 27N 74 25W
Middletown, Ohio, U.S.A. **76 F3** 39 31N 84 24W
Middletown, Pa., U.S.A. **79 F8** 40 12N 76 44W
Midi, Canal du →, France **18 E4** 43 45N 1 21 E
Midland, Canada **70 D4** 44 45N 79 50W
Midland, Calif., U.S.A. **85 M12** 33 52N 114 48W
Midland, Mich., U.S.A. **76 D3** 43 37N 84 14W
Midland, Pa., U.S.A. **78 F4** 40 39N 80 27W
Midland, Tex., U.S.A. **81 K3** 32 0N 102 3W
Midlands □, Zimbabwe **55 F2** 19 40S 29 0 E
Midleton, Ireland **13 E3** 51 55N 8 10W
Midlothian, U.S.A. **81 J6** 32 30N 97 0W
Midlothian □, U.K. **12 F5** 55 51N 3 5W
Midongy, Tangorombohitr' i, Madag. **57 C8** 23 30S 47 0 E
Midongy Atsimo, Madag. **57 C8** 23 35S 47 1 E
Midway Is., Pac. Oc. **64 E10** 28 13N 177 22W
Midway Wells, U.S.A. **85 N11** 32 41N 115 7W
Midwest, U.S.A. **75 B9** 42 0N 90 0W
Midwest, Wyo., U.S.A. **82 E10** 43 25N 106 16W
Midwest City, U.S.A. **81 H6** 35 27N 97 24W
Midžor, Bulgaria **21 C10** 43 24N 22 40 E
Mie □, Japan **31 G8** 34 30N 136 10 E
Międzychód, Poland **16 B8** 52 35N 15 53 E
Międzyrzec Podlaski, Poland **17 C12** 51 58N 22 45 E
Mielec, Poland **17 C11** 50 15N 21 25 E
Mienga, Angola **56 B2** 17 12S 19 48 E
Miercurea Ciuc, Romania **17 E13** 46 21N 25 48 E
Mieres, Spain **19 A3** 43 18N 5 48W
Mifflintown, U.S.A. **78 F7** 40 34N 77 24W
Mifraz Hefa, Israel **47 C4** 32 52N 35 0 E
Migdāl, Israel **47 C4** 32 51N 35 30 E
Miguel Alemán, Presa, Mexico **87 D5** 18 15N 96 40W
Miguel Alves, Brazil **93 D10** 4 11S 42 55W
Mihara, Japan **31 G6** 34 24N 133 5 E
Mikese, Tanzania **54 D4** 6 48S 37 55 E
Mikhaylovgrad, Bulgaria **21 C10** 43 27N 23 16 E
Mikkeli, Finland **9 F22** 61 43N 27 15 E
Mikkwa →, Canada **72 B6** 58 25N 114 46W
Míkonos, Greece **21 F11** 37 30N 25 25 E
Mikumi, Tanzania **54 D4** 7 26S 37 0 E
Mikun, Russia **24 B9** 62 20N 50 0 E
Milaca, U.S.A. **80 C8** 45 45N 93 39W
Milagro, Ecuador **92 D3** 2 11S 79 36W
Milan = Milano, Italy **20 B3** 45 28N 9 12 E
Milan, Mo., U.S.A. **80 E8** 40 12N 93 7W
Milan, Tenn., U.S.A. **77 H1** 35 55N 88 46W
Milang, Australia **63 E2** 32 2S 139 10 E
Milange, Mozam. **55 F4** 16 3S 35 45 E
Milano, Italy **20 B3** 45 28N 9 12 E
Milâs, Turkey **21 F12** 37 20N 27 50 E
Milatos, Greece **23 D7** 35 18N 25 34 E
Milazzo, Italy **20 E6** 38 13N 15 15 E
Milbank, U.S.A. **80 C6** 45 13N 96 38W
Milden, Canada **73 C7** 51 29N 107 32W
Mildmay, Canada **78 B3** 44 3N 81 7W
Mildura, Australia **63 E3** 34 13S 142 9 E
Miles, Australia **63 D5** 26 40S 150 9 E
Miles, U.S.A. **81 K4** 31 36N 100 11W
Miles City, U.S.A. **80 B2** 46 25N 105 51W
Milestone, Canada **73 D8** 49 59N 104 31W
Miletus, Turkey **21 F12** 37 30N 27 18 E
Mileura, Australia **61 E2** 26 22S 117 20 E
Milford, Calif., U.S.A. **84 E6** 40 10N 120 22W
Milford, Conn., U.S.A. **79 E11** 41 14N 73 3W
Milford, Del., U.S.A. **76 F8** 38 55N 75 26W
Milford, Mass., U.S.A. **79 D13** 42 8N 71 31W
Milford, Pa., U.S.A. **79 E10** 41 19N 74 48W
Milford, Utah, U.S.A. **83 G7** 38 24N 113 1W
Milford Haven, U.K. **11 F2** 51 42N 5 7W
Milford Sd., N.Z. **59 L1** 44 41S 167 47 E
Milgun, Australia **61 D2** 24 56S 118 18 E
Milḥ, Baḥr al, Iraq **44 C4** 32 40N 43 35 E
Miliana, Algeria **50 C5** 27 20N 2 32 E
Miling, Australia **61 F2** 30 30S 116 17 E
Milk →, U.S.A. **82 B10** 48 4N 106 19W
Milk River, Canada **72 D6** 49 10N 112 5W
Mill City, U.S.A. **82 D2** 44 45N 122 29W
Mill I., Antarctica **5 C8** 66 0S 101 30 E
Mill Valley, U.S.A. **84 H4** 37 54N 122 32W
Millau, France **18 D5** 44 8N 3 4 E
Millbridge, Canada **78 B7** 44 41N 77 36W
Millbrook, Canada **78 B6** 44 10N 78 29W
Mille Lacs, L. des, Canada **70 C1** 48 45N 90 35W
Mille Lacs L., U.S.A. **80 B8** 46 15N 93 39W
Milledgeville, U.S.A. **77 J4** 33 5N 83 14W
Millen, U.S.A. **77 J5** 32 48N 81 57W
Miller, U.S.A. **80 C5** 44 31N 98 59W
Millersburg, Ohio, U.S.A. **78 F3** 40 33N 81 55W
Millersburg, Pa., U.S.A. **78 F8** 40 32N 76 58W
Millerton, U.S.A. **79 E11** 41 57N 73 31W
Millerton L., U.S.A. **84 J7** 37 1N 119 41W
Millicent, Australia **63 F3** 37 34S 140 21 E
Millinocket, U.S.A. **71 C6** 45 39N 68 43W
Millmerran, Australia **63 D5** 27 53S 151 16 E
Mills L., Canada **72 A5** 61 30N 118 20W
Millsboro, U.S.A. **78 G4** 40 0N 80 0W
Milltown Malbay, Ireland **13 D2** 52 52N 9 24W
Millville, U.S.A. **76 F8** 39 24N 75 2W
Millwood L., U.S.A. **81 J8** 33 42N 93 58W
Milne →, Australia **62 C2** 21 10S 137 33 E
Milne Inlet, Canada **69 A11** 72 30N 80 0W
Milnor, U.S.A. **80 B6** 46 16N 97 27W
Milo, Canada **72 C6** 50 34N 112 53W
Milos, Greece **21 F11** 36 44N 24 25 E
Milparinka P.O., Australia **63 D3** 29 46S 141 57 E
Milton, Canada **78 C5** 43 31N 79 53W
Milton, N.Z. **59 M2** 46 7S 169 59 E
Milton, U.K. **12 D4** 57 18N 4 32W
Milton, Calif., U.S.A. **84 G6** 38 3N 120 51W
Milton, Fla., U.S.A. **77 K2** 30 38N 87 3W
Milton, Pa., U.S.A. **78 F8** 41 1N 76 51W
Milton-Freewater, U.S.A. **82 D4** 45 56N 118 23W
Milton Keynes, U.K. **11 E7** 52 1N 0 44W
Miltou, Chad **51 F8** 10 14N 17 26 E
Milverton, Canada **78 C4** 43 34N 80 55W
Milwaukee, U.S.A. **76 D2** 43 2N 87 55W
Milwaukee Deep, Atl. Oc. **89 C6** 19 50N 68 0W
Milwaukie, U.S.A. **84 E4** 45 27N 122 38W
Min Chiang →, China **33 D6** 26 0N 119 35 E
Min Jiang →, China **32 D5** 28 45N 104 40 E
Min Xian, China **34 G3** 34 25N 104 5 E
Mina, U.S.A. **83 G4** 38 24N 118 7W
Mina Pirquitas, Argentina **94 A2** 22 40S 66 30W
Mīnā Su'ud, Si. Arabia **45 D6** 28 45N 48 28 E
Mīnā'al Aḥmadī, Kuwait **45 D6** 29 5N 48 10 E
Mīnāb, Iran **45 E8** 27 10N 57 1 E
Minago →, Canada **73 C9** 54 33N 98 59W
Minaki, Canada **73 D10** 49 59N 94 40W
Minamata, Japan **31 H5** 32 10N 130 30 E
Minami-Tori-Shima, Pac. Oc. **64 E7** 24 0N 153 45 E
Minas, Uruguay **95 C4** 34 20S 55 10W
Minas, Sierra de las, Guatemala **88 C2** 15 9N 89 31W
Minas Basin, Canada **71 C7** 45 20N 64 12W
Minas Gerais □, Brazil **93 G9** 18 50S 46 0W
Minatitlán, Mexico **87 D6** 17 59N 94 31W
Minbu, Burma **41 J19** 20 10N 94 52 E
Mindanao, Phil. **37 C6** 8 0N 125 0 E
Mindanao Sea = Bohol Sea, Phil. **37 C6** 9 0N 124 0 E
Mindanao Trench, Pac. Oc. **37 B7** 12 0N 126 6 E
Minden, Canada **78 B6** 44 55N 78 43W
Minden, Germany **16 B5** 52 17N 8 55 E
Minden, La., U.S.A. **81 J8** 32 37N 93 17W
Minden, Nev., U.S.A. **84 G7** 38 57N 119 46W
Mindiptana, Indonesia **37 F10** 5 55S 140 22 E
Mindoro, Phil. **37 B6** 13 0N 121 0 E
Mindoro Str., Phil. **37 B6** 12 30N 120 30 E
Mindouli, Congo **52 E2** 4 12S 14 28 E
Mine, Japan **31 G5** 34 12N 131 7 E
Minehead, U.K. **11 F4** 51 12N 3 29W
Mineola, U.S.A. **81 J7** 32 40N 95 29W
Mineral King, U.S.A. **84 J8** 36 27N 118 36W
Mineral Wells, U.S.A. **81 J5** 32 48N 98 7W
Minersville, Pa., U.S.A. **79 F8** 40 41N 76 16W
Minersville, Utah, U.S.A. **83 G7** 38 13N 112 56W
Minerva, U.S.A. **78 F3** 40 44N 81 6W
Minetto, U.S.A. **79 C8** 43 24N 76 28W
Mingäçevir Su Anban, Azerbaijan **25 F8** 40 57N 46 50 E
Mingan, Canada **71 B7** 50 20N 64 0W
Mingechaurskoye Vdkhr. = Mingäçevir Su Anbarı, Azerbaijan **25 F8** 40 57N 46 50 E
Mingela, Australia **62 B4** 19 52S 146 38 E
Mingenew, Australia **61 E2** 29 12S 115 21 E
Mingera Cr. →, Australia **62 C2** 20 38S 137 45 E
Mingin, Burma **41 H19** 22 50N 94 30 E
Mingt'iehkaitafan = Mintaka Pass, Pakistan **43 A6** 37 0N 74 58 E
Mingyuegue, China **35 C15** 43 2N 128 50 E
Minho = Miño →, Spain **19 A2** 41 52N 8 40W
Minho, Portugal **19 B1** 41 25N 8 20W
Minidoka, U.S.A. **82 E7** 42 45N 113 29W
Minigwal, L., Australia **61 E3** 29 31S 123 14 E
Minilya, Australia **61 D1** 23 55S 114 0 E
Minilya →, Australia **61 D1** 23 45S 114 0 E
Minipi, L., Canada **71 B7** 52 25N 60 45W
Mink L., Canada **72 A5** 61 54N 117 40W
Minna, Nigeria **50 G6** 9 37N 6 30 E
Minneapolis, Kans., U.S.A. **80 F6** 39 8N 97 42W
Minneapolis, Minn., U.S.A. **80 C8** 44 59N 93 16W
Minnedosa, Canada **73 C9** 50 14N 99 50W
Minnesota □, U.S.A. **80 B7** 46 0N 94 15W
Minnie Creek, Australia **61 D2** 24 3S 115 42 E
Minnipa, Australia **63 E2** 32 51S 135 9 E
Minnitaki L., Canada **70 C1** 49 57N 92 10W
Mino, Japan **31 G8** 35 32N 136 55 E
Miño →, Spain **19 A2** 41 52N 8 40W
Minorca = Menorca, Spain **22 B11** 40 0N 4 0 E

Moonie

Minore, Australia 63 E4 32 14S 148 27 E
Minot, U.S.A. 80 A4 48 14N 101 18W
Minqin, China 34 E2 38 38N 103 20 E
Minsk, Belarus 17 B14 53 52N 27 30 E
Mińsk Mazowiecki, Poland 17 B11 52 10N 21 33 E
Mintaka Pass, Pakistan 43 A6 37 0N 74 58 E
Minto, U.S.A. 68 B5 64 53N 149 11W
Minton, Canada 73 D8 49 10N 104 35W
Minturn, U.S.A. 82 G10 39 35N 106 26W
Minusinsk, Russia 27 D10 53 50N 91 20 E
Minutang, India 41 E20 28 15N 96 30 E
Minvoul, Gabon 52 D2 2 9N 12 8 E
Mir, Niger 51 F7 14 5N 11 59 E
Mīr Kūh, Iran 45 E8 26 22N 58 55 E
Mīr Shahdād, Iran 45 E8 26 15N 58 29 E
Mira, Italy 20 B5 45 26N 12 8 E
Mira por vos Cay, Bahamas 89 B5 22 9N 74 30W
Miraj, India 40 L9 16 50N 74 45 E
Miram Shah, Pakistan 42 C4 33 0N 70 2 E
Miramar, Argentina 94 D4 38 15S 57 50W
Miramar, Mozam. 57 C6 23 50S 35 35 E
Miramichi B., Canada 71 C7 47 15N 65 0W
Miranda, Brazil 93 H7 20 10S 56 15W
Miranda de Ebro, Spain 19 A4 42 41N 2 57W
Miranda do Douro, Portugal 19 B2 41 30N 6 16W
Mirando City, U.S.A. 81 M5 27 26N 99 0W
Mirandópolis, Brazil 95 A5 21 9S 51 6W
Mirango, Malawi 55 E3 13 32S 34 58 E
Mirani, Australia 62 C4 21 9S 148 53 E
Mirassol, Brazil 95 A6 20 46S 49 28W
Mirbāţ, Oman 46 D5 17 0N 54 45 E
Miri, Malaysia 36 D4 4 23N 113 59 E
Miriam Vale, Australia 62 C5 24 20S 151 33 E
Mirim, L., S. Amer. 95 C5 32 45S 52 50W
Mirnyy, Russia 27 C12 62 33N 113 53 E
Mirond L., Canada 73 B8 55 6N 102 47W
Mirpur, Pakistan 43 C5 33 32N 73 56 E
Mirpur Bibiwari, Pakistan 42 E2 28 33N 67 44 E
Mirpur Khas, Pakistan 42 G3 25 30N 69 0 E
Mirpur Sakro, Pakistan 42 G2 24 33N 67 41 E
Mirror, Canada 72 C6 52 30N 113 7W
Miryang, S. Korea 35 G15 35 31N 128 44 E
Mirzapur, India 43 G10 25 10N 82 34 E
Mirzapur-cum-Vindhyachal = Mirzapur, India 43 G10 25 10N 82 34 E
Misantla, Mexico 87 D5 19 56N 96 50W
Misawa, Japan 30 D10 40 41N 141 24 E
Miscou I., Canada 71 C7 47 57N 64 31W
Mish'āb, Ra'as al, Si. Arabia 45 D6 28 15N 48 43 E
Mishan, China 33 B8 45 37N 131 48 E
Mishawaka, U.S.A. 76 E2 41 40N 86 11W
Mishima, Japan 31 G9 35 10N 138 52 E
Misión, Mexico 85 N10 32 6N 116 53W
Misiones □, Argentina 95 B5 27 0S 55 0W
Misiones □, Paraguay 94 B4 27 0S 56 0W
Miskah, Si. Arabia 44 E4 24 49N 42 56 E
Miskitos, Cayos, Nic. 88 D3 14 26N 82 50W
Miskolc, Hungary 17 D11 48 7N 20 50 E
Misoke, Zaïre 54 C2 0 42S 28 2 E
Misool, Indonesia 37 E8 1 52S 130 10 E
Misrātah, Libya 51 B8 32 24N 15 3 E
Missanabie, Canada 70 C3 48 20N 84 6W
Missinaibi →, Canada 70 B3 50 43N 81 29W
Missinaibi L., Canada 70 C3 48 23N 83 40W
Mission, S. Dak., U.S.A. 80 D4 43 18N 100 39W
Mission, Tex., U.S.A. 81 M5 26 13N 98 20W
Mission City, Canada 72 D4 49 10N 122 15W
Mission Viejo, U.S.A. 85 M9 33 36N 117 40W
Missisa L., Canada 70 B2 52 20N 85 7W
Mississagi →, Canada 70 C3 46 15N 83 9W
Mississippi □, U.S.A. 81 J10 33 0N 90 0W
Mississippi →, U.S.A. 81 L10 29 9N 89 15W
Mississippi L., Canada 79 A8 45 5N 76 10W
Mississippi River Delta, U.S.A. 81 L9 29 10N 89 15W
Mississippi Sd., U.S.A. 81 K10 30 20N 89 0W
Missoula, U.S.A. 82 C6 46 52N 114 1W
Missouri □, U.S.A. 80 F8 38 25N 92 30W
Missouri →, U.S.A. 80 F9 38 49N 90 7W
Missouri Valley, U.S.A. 80 E7 41 34N 95 53W
Mist, U.S.A. 84 E3 45 59N 123 15W
Mistake B., Canada 73 A10 62 8N 93 0W
Mistassini →, Canada 71 C5 48 42N 72 20W
Mistassini L., Canada 70 B5 51 0N 73 30W
Mistastin L., Canada 71 A7 55 57N 63 20W
Mistatim, Canada 73 C8 52 52N 103 22W
Misty L., Canada 73 B8 58 53N 101 40W
Misurata = Misrātah, Libya 51 B8 32 24N 15 3 E
Mitchell, Australia 63 D4 26 29S 147 58 E
Mitchell, Canada 78 C3 43 28N 81 12W
Mitchell, Ind., U.S.A. 76 F2 38 44N 86 28W
Mitchell, Nebr., U.S.A. 80 E3 41 57N 103 49W
Mitchell, Oreg., U.S.A. 82 D3 44 34N 120 9W
Mitchell, S. Dak., U.S.A. 80 D5 43 43N 98 2W
Mitchell →, Australia 62 B3 15 12S 141 35 E
Mitchell, Mt., U.S.A. 77 H4 35 46N 82 16W
Mitchell Ras., Australia 62 A2 12 49S 135 36 E
Mitchelstown, Ireland 13 D3 52 15N 8 16W
Mitha Tiwana, Pakistan 42 C5 32 13N 72 6 E
Mitilíni, Greece 21 E12 39 6N 26 35 E
Mito, Japan 31 F10 36 20N 140 30 E
Mitrovica = Titova-Mitrovica, Serbia, Yug. 21 C9 42 54N 20 52 E
Mitsinjo, Madag. 57 B8 16 1S 45 52 E
Mitsiwa, Eritrea 51 E12 15 35N 39 25 E
Mitsukaidō, Japan 31 F9 36 1N 139 59 E
Mittagong, Australia 63 E5 34 28S 150 29 E
Mitú, Colombia 92 C4 1 8N 70 3W
Mitumba, Tanzania 54 D3 7 8S 31 2 E
Mitumba, Chaîne des, Zaïre 54 D2 7 0S 27 30 E
Mitumba Mts. = Mitumba, Chaîne des, Zaïre 54 D2 7 0S 27 30 E
Mitwaba, Zaïre 55 D2 8 2S 27 17 E
Mityana, Uganda 54 B3 0 23N 32 2 E
Mitzic, Gabon 52 D2 0 45N 11 40 E
Mixteco →, Mexico 87 D5 18 11N 98 30W
Miyagi □, Japan 30 E10 38 15N 140 45 E
Miyāh, W. el →, Syria 44 C3 34 44N 39 57 E
Miyake-Jima, Japan 31 G9 34 5N 139 30 E
Miyako, Japan 30 E10 39 40N 141 59 E
Miyako-Jima, Japan 31 M2 24 45N 125 20 E
Miyako-Rettō, Japan 31 M2 24 24N 125 0 E
Miyakonojō, Japan 31 J5 31 40N 131 5 E
Miyanoura-Dake, Japan 31 J5 30 20N 130 31 E
Miyazaki, Japan 31 J5 31 56N 131 30 E
Miyazaki □, Japan 31 H5 32 30N 131 30 E
Miyazu, Japan 31 G7 35 35N 135 10 E
Miyet, Bahr el = Dead Sea, Asia 47 D4 31 30N 35 30 E
Miyoshi, Japan 31 G6 34 48N 132 51 E
Miyun, China 34 D9 40 28N 116 50 E
Miyun Shuiku, China 35 D9 40 30N 117 0 E
Mizdah, Libya 51 B7 31 30N 13 0 E
Mizen Hd., Cork, Ireland 13 E2 51 27N 9 50W
Mizen Hd., Wick., Ireland 13 D5 52 51N 6 4W
Mizhi, China 34 F6 37 47N 110 12 E
Mizoram □, India 41 H18 23 30N 92 40 E
Mizpe Ramon, Israel 47 E3 30 34N 34 49 E
Mizusawa, Japan 30 E10 39 8N 141 8 E
Mjölby, Sweden 9 G16 58 20N 15 10 E
Mjøsa, Norway 9 F14 60 40N 11 0 E
Mkata, Tanzania 54 D4 5 45S 38 20 E
Mkokotoni, Tanzania 54 D4 5 55S 39 15 E
Mkomazi, Tanzania 54 C4 4 40S 38 7 E
Mkomazi →, S. Africa 57 E5 30 12S 30 50 E
Mkulwe, Tanzania 55 D3 8 37S 32 20 E
Mkumbi, Ras, Tanzania 54 D4 7 38S 39 55 E
Mkushi, Zambia 55 E2 14 25S 29 15 E
Mkushi River, Zambia 55 E2 13 32S 29 45 E
Mkuze, S. Africa 57 D5 27 10S 32 0 E
Mladá Boleslav, Czech. 16 C8 50 27N 14 53 E
Mlala Hills, Tanzania 54 D3 6 50S 31 40 E
Mlange, Malawi 55 F4 16 2S 35 33 E
Mława, Poland 17 B11 53 9N 20 25 E
Mljet, Croatia 20 C7 42 43N 17 30 E
Mmabatho, S. Africa 56 D4 25 49S 25 30 E
Mo i Rana, Norway 8 C16 66 20N 14 7 E
Moa, Indonesia 37 F7 8 0S 128 0 E
Moab, U.S.A. 83 G9 38 35N 109 33W
Moabi, Gabon 52 E2 2 24S 10 59 E
Moala, Fiji 59 D8 18 36S 179 53 E
Moalie Park, Australia 63 D3 29 42S 143 3 E
Moba, Zaïre 54 D2 7 0S 29 48 E
Mobārakābād, Iran 45 D7 28 24N 53 20 E
Mobārakīyeh, Iran 45 C6 32 23N 51 37 E
Mobaye, C.A.R. 52 D4 4 25N 21 5 E
Mobayi, Zaïre 52 D4 4 15N 21 8 E
Moberly, U.S.A. 80 F8 39 25N 92 26W
Moberly →, Canada 72 B4 56 12N 120 55W
Mobile, U.S.A. 77 K1 30 41N 88 3W
Mobile B., U.S.A. 77 K2 30 30N 88 0W
Mobridge, U.S.A. 80 C4 45 32N 100 26W
Mobutu Sese Seko, L. = Albert L., Africa 54 B3 1 30N 31 0 E
Moc Chau, Vietnam 38 B5 20 50N 104 38 E
Moc Hoa, Vietnam 39 G5 10 46N 105 56 E
Mocabe Kasari, Zaïre 55 D2 9 58S 26 12 E
Moçambique, Mozam. 55 F5 15 3S 40 42 E
Moçâmedes = Namibe, Angola 53 H2 15 7S 12 11 E
Mochudi, Botswana 56 C4 24 27S 26 7 E
Mocimboa da Praia, Mozam. 55 E5 11 25S 40 20 E
Moclips, U.S.A. 84 C2 47 14N 124 13W
Mocoa, Colombia 92 C3 1 7N 76 35W
Mococa, Brazil 95 A6 21 28S 47 0W
Mocorito, Mexico 86 B3 25 30N 107 53W
Moctezuma, Mexico 86 B3 29 50N 109 0W
Moctezuma →, Mexico 87 C5 21 59N 98 34W
Mocuba, Mozam. 55 F4 16 54S 36 57 E
Mocúzari, Presa, Mexico 86 B3 27 10N 109 10W
Modane, France 18 D7 45 12N 6 40 E
Modasa, India 42 H5 23 30N 73 21 E
Modder →, S. Africa 56 D3 29 2S 24 37 E
Modderrivier, S. Africa 56 D3 29 2S 24 38 E
Módena, Italy 20 B4 44 40N 10 55 E
Modena, U.S.A. 83 H7 37 48N 113 56W
Modesto, U.S.A. 83 H3 37 39N 121 0W
Módica, Italy 20 F6 36 52N 14 46 E
Moe, Australia 63 F4 38 12S 146 19 E
Moebase, Mozam. 55 F4 17 3S 38 41 E
Moengo, Surinam 93 B8 5 45N 54 20W
Moffat, U.K. 12 F5 55 21N 3 27W
Moga, India 42 D6 30 48N 75 8 E
Mogadishu = Muqdisho, Somali Rep. 46 G4 2 2N 45 25 E
Mogador = Essaouira, Morocco 50 B3 31 32N 9 42W
Mogalakwena →, S. Africa 57 C4 22 38S 28 40 E
Mogami →, Japan 30 E10 38 45N 140 0 E
Mogán, Canary Is. 22 G4 27 53N 15 43W
Mogaung, Burma 41 G20 25 20N 97 0 E
Mogi das Cruzes, Brazil 95 A6 23 31S 46 11W
Mogi-Guaçu →, Brazil 95 A6 20 53S 48 10W
Mogi-Mirim, Brazil 95 A6 22 29S 47 0W
Mogilev = Mahilyow, Belarus 17 B16 53 55N 30 18 E
Mogilev-Podolskiy = Mohyliv-Podilskyy, Ukraine 17 D14 48 26N 27 48 E
Mogincual, Mozam. 55 F5 15 35S 40 25 E
Mogocha, Russia 27 D12 53 40N 119 50 E
Mogoi, Indonesia 37 E8 1 55S 133 10 E
Mogok, Burma 41 H20 23 0N 96 40 E
Mogumber, Australia 61 F2 31 2S 116 3 E
Mohács, Hungary 17 F10 45 58N 18 41 E
Mohales Hoek, Lesotho 56 E4 30 7S 27 26 E
Mohall, U.S.A. 80 A4 48 46N 101 31W
Moḩammadābād, Iran 45 B8 37 52N 59 5 E
Mohave, L., U.S.A. 85 K12 35 12N 114 34W
Mohawk →, U.S.A. 79 D11 42 47N 73 41W
Mohoro, Tanzania 54 D4 8 6S 39 8 E
Mohyliv-Podilskyy, Ukraine 17 D14 48 26N 27 48 E
Moidart, L., U.K. 12 E3 56 47N 5 52W
Moires, Greece 23 D6 35 4N 24 56 E
Moisaküla, Estonia 9 G21 58 3N 25 12 E
Moisie, Canada 71 B6 50 12N 66 1W
Moisie →, Canada 71 B6 50 14N 66 5W
Moïssala, Chad 51 G8 8 21N 17 46 E
Mojave, U.S.A. 85 K8 35 3N 118 10W
Mojave Desert, U.S.A. 85 L10 35 0N 116 30W
Mojo, Bolivia 94 A2 21 48S 65 33W
Mojokerto, Indonesia 37 G15 7 28S 112 26 E
Mokai, N.Z. 59 H5 38 32S 175 56 E
Mokambo, Zaïre 55 E2 12 25S 28 20 E
Mokameh, India 43 G11 25 24N 85 55 E
Mokelumne →, U.S.A. 84 G5 38 13N 121 28W
Mokelumne Hill, U.S.A. 84 G6 38 18N 120 43W
Mokhós, Greece 23 D7 35 16N 25 27 E
Mokhotlong, Lesotho 57 D4 29 22S 29 2 E
Mokokchung, India 41 F19 26 15N 94 30 E
Mokra Gora, Serbia, Yug. 21 C9 42 50N 20 30 E
Mol, Belgium 15 C5 51 11N 5 5 E
Molchanovo, Russia 26 D9 57 40N 83 50 E
Mold, U.K. 10 D4 53 9N 3 8W
Moldavia ■ = Moldova ■, Europe 17 E15 47 0N 28 0 E
Molde, Norway 8 E12 62 45N 7 9 E
Moldova ■, Europe 17 E15 47 0N 28 0 E
Moldoveana, Romania 17 F13 45 36N 24 45 E
Molepolole, Botswana 56 C4 24 28S 25 28 E
Molfetta, Italy 20 D7 41 12N 16 36 E
Moline, U.S.A. 80 E9 41 30N 90 31W
Molinos, Argentina 94 B2 25 28S 66 15W
Moliro, Zaïre 54 D3 8 12S 30 30 E
Mollahat, Bangla. 43 H13 22 56N 89 48 E
Mollendo, Peru 92 G4 17 0S 72 0W
Mollerin, L., Australia 61 F2 30 30S 117 35 E
Mölndal, Sweden 9 H15 57 40N 12 3 E
Molodechno = Maladzyechna, Belarus 17 A14 54 20N 26 50 E
Molokai, U.S.A. 74 H16 21 8N 157 0W
Molong, Australia 63 E4 33 5S 148 54 E
Molopo →, Africa 56 D3 27 30S 20 13 E
Molotov = Perm, Russia 24 C10 58 0N 56 10 E
Moloundou, Cameroon 52 D3 2 8N 15 15 E
Molson L., Canada 73 C9 54 22N 96 40W
Molteno, S. Africa 56 E4 31 22S 26 22 E
Molu, Indonesia 37 F8 6 45S 131 40 E
Molucca Sea, Indonesia 37 E6 2 0S 124 0 E
Moluccas = Maluku, Indonesia 37 E7 1 0S 127 0 E
Moma, Mozam. 55 F4 16 47S 39 4 E
Moma, Zaïre 54 C1 1 35S 23 52 E
Mombasa, Kenya 54 C4 4 2S 39 43 E
Mombetsu, Japan 30 B11 44 21N 143 22 E
Momchilgrad, Bulgaria 21 D11 41 33N 25 23 E
Momi, Zaïre 54 C2 1 42S 27 0 E
Mompós, Colombia 92 B4 9 14N 74 26W
Møn, Denmark 9 J15 54 57N 12 15 E
Mon →, Burma 41 J19 20 25N 94 30 E
Mona, Canal de la, W. Indies 89 C6 18 30N 67 45W
Mona, Isla, Puerto Rico 89 C6 18 5N 67 54W
Mona, Pta., Costa Rica 88 E3 9 37N 82 36W
Monach Is., U.K. 12 D1 57 32N 7 40W
Monaco ■, Europe 18 E7 43 46N 7 23 E
Monadhliath Mts., U.K. 12 D4 57 10N 4 4W
Monaghan, Ireland 13 B5 54 15N 6 57W
Monaghan □, Ireland 13 B5 54 11N 6 56W
Monahans, U.S.A. 81 K3 31 36N 102 54W
Monapo, Mozam. 55 E5 14 56S 40 19 E
Monarch Mt., Canada 72 C3 51 55N 125 57W
Monastir = Bitola, Macedonia 21 D9 41 5N 21 10 E
Monastir, Tunisia 51 A7 35 50N 10 49 E
Moncayo, Sierra del, Spain 19 B5 41 48N 1 50W
Monchegorsk, Russia 24 A5 67 54N 32 58 E
Mönchengladbach, Germany 16 C4 51 11N 6 27 E
Monchique, Portugal 19 D1 37 19N 8 38W
Monclova, Mexico 86 B4 26 50N 101 30W
Moncton, Canada 71 C7 46 7N 64 51W
Mondego →, Portugal 19 B1 40 9N 8 52W
Mondeodo, Indonesia 37 E6 3 34S 122 9 E
Mondovì, Italy 20 B2 44 23N 7 49 E
Mondovi, U.S.A. 80 C9 44 34N 91 40W
Mondrain I., Australia 61 F3 34 9S 122 14 E
Monduli □, Tanzania 54 C4 3 0S 36 0 E
Monessen, U.S.A. 78 F5 40 9N 79 54W
Monett, U.S.A. 81 G8 36 55N 93 55W
Monforte de Lemos, Spain 19 A2 42 31N 7 33W
Mong Hsu, Burma 41 J21 21 54N 98 30 E
Mong Kung, Burma 41 J20 21 35N 97 35 E
Mong Nai, Burma 41 J20 20 32N 97 46 E
Mong Pawk, Burma 41 H21 22 4N 99 16 E
Mong Ton, Burma 41 J21 20 17N 98 45 E
Mong Wa, Burma 41 J22 21 26N 100 27 E
Mong Yai, Burma 41 H21 22 21N 98 3 E
Mongalla, Sudan 51 G11 5 8N 31 42 E
Mongers, L., Australia 61 E2 29 25S 117 5 E
Monghyr = Munger, India 43 G12 25 23N 86 30 E
Mongibello = Etna, Italy 20 F6 37 50N 14 55 E
Mongo, Chad 51 F8 12 14N 18 43 E
Mongolia ■, Asia 27 E10 47 0N 103 0 E
Mongororo, Chad 51 F9 12 3N 22 26 E
Mongu, Zambia 53 H4 15 16S 23 12 E
Mônguá, Angola 56 B2 16 43S 15 20 E
Monkey Bay, Malawi 55 E4 14 7S 35 1 E
Monkey River, Belize 87 D7 16 22N 88 29W
Monkira, Australia 62 C3 24 46S 140 30 E
Monkoto, Zaïre 52 E4 1 38S 20 35 E
Monmouth, U.K. 11 F5 51 48N 2 42W
Monmouth, U.S.A. 80 E9 40 55N 90 39W
Monmouthshire □, U.K. 11 F5 51 48N 2 54W
Mono L., U.S.A. 83 H4 38 1N 119 1W
Monolith, U.S.A. 85 K8 35 7N 118 22W
Monólithos, Greece 23 C9 36 7N 27 45 E
Monongahela, U.S.A. 78 F5 40 12N 79 56W
Monópoli, Italy 20 D7 40 57N 17 18 E
Monqoumba, C.A.R. 52 D3 3 33N 18 40 E
Monroe, Ga., U.S.A. 77 J4 33 47N 83 43W
Monroe, La., U.S.A. 81 J8 32 30N 92 7W
Monroe, Mich., U.S.A. 76 E4 41 55N 83 24W
Monroe, N.C., U.S.A. 77 H5 34 59N 80 33W
Monroe, N.Y., U.S.A. 79 E10 41 20N 74 11W
Monroe, Utah, U.S.A. 83 G7 38 38N 112 7W
Monroe, Wash., U.S.A. 84 C5 47 51N 121 58W
Monroe, Wis., U.S.A. 80 D10 42 36N 89 38W
Monroe City, U.S.A. 80 F9 39 39N 91 44W
Monroeville, Ala., U.S.A. 77 K2 31 31N 87 20W
Monroeville, Pa., U.S.A. 78 F5 40 26N 79 45W
Monrovia, Liberia 50 G2 6 18N 10 47W
Mons, Belgium 15 D3 50 27N 3 58 E
Monse, Indonesia 37 E6 4 0S 123 10 E
Mont-de-Marsan, France 18 E3 43 54N 0 31W
Mont-Joli, Canada 71 C6 48 37N 68 10W
Mont-Laurier, Canada 70 C4 46 35N 75 30W
Mont-St.-Michel, Le = Le Mont-St.-Michel, France 18 B3 48 40N 1 30W
Mont Tremblant Prov. Park, Canada 70 C5 46 30N 74 30W
Montagu, S. Africa 56 E3 33 45S 20 8 E
Montagu I., Antarctica 5 B1 58 25S 26 20W
Montague, Canada 71 C7 46 10N 62 39W
Montague, U.S.A. 82 F2 41 44N 122 32W
Montague, I., Mexico 86 A2 31 40N 114 56W
Montague Ra., Australia 61 E2 27 15S 119 30 E
Montague Sd., Australia 60 B4 14 28S 125 20 E
Montalbán, Spain 19 B5 40 50N 0 45W
Montalvo, U.S.A. 85 L7 34 15N 119 12W
Montaña, Peru 92 E4 6 0S 73 0W
Montana □, U.S.A. 82 C9 47 0N 110 0W
Montaña Clara, I., Canary Is. 22 E6 29 17N 13 33W
Montargis, France 18 C5 47 59N 2 43 E
Montauban, France 18 D4 44 2N 1 21 E
Montauk, U.S.A. 79 E13 41 3N 71 57W
Montauk Pt., U.S.A. 79 E13 41 4N 71 52W
Montbéliard, France 18 C7 47 31N 6 48 E
Montceau-les-Mines, France 18 C6 46 40N 4 23 E
Montclair, U.S.A. 79 F10 40 49N 74 13W
Monte Albán, Mexico 87 D5 17 2N 96 45W
Monte Alegre, Brazil 93 D8 2 0S 54 0W
Monte Azul, Brazil 93 G10 15 9S 42 53W
Monte Bello Is., Australia 60 D2 20 30S 115 45 E
Monte-Carlo, Monaco 16 G4 43 46N 7 23 E
Monte Caseros, Argentina 94 C4 30 10S 57 50W
Monte Comán, Argentina 94 C2 34 40S 67 53W
Monte Cristi, Dom. Rep. 89 C5 19 52N 71 39W
Monte Lindo →, Paraguay 94 A4 23 56S 57 12W
Monte Quemado, Argentina 94 B3 25 53S 62 41W
Monte Rio, U.S.A. 84 G4 38 28N 123 0W
Monte Santu, C. di, Italy 20 D3 40 5N 9 44 E
Monte Vista, U.S.A. 83 H10 37 35N 106 9W
Monteagudo, Argentina 95 B5 27 14S 54 8W
Montebello, Canada 70 C5 45 40N 74 55W
Montecito, U.S.A. 85 L7 34 26N 119 40W
Montecristi, Ecuador 92 D2 1 0S 80 40W
Montecristo, Italy 20 C4 42 20N 10 19 E
Montego Bay, Jamaica 88 C4 18 30N 78 0W
Montejinnie, Australia 60 C5 16 40S 131 38 E
Montélimar, France 18 D6 44 33N 4 45 E
Montello, U.S.A. 80 D10 43 48N 89 20W
Montemorelos, Mexico 87 B5 25 11N 99 42W
Montenegro, Brazil 95 B5 29 39S 51 29W
Montenegro □, Yugoslavia 21 C8 42 40N 19 20 E
Montepuez, Mozam. 55 E4 13 8S 38 59 E
Montepuez →, Mozam. 55 E5 12 32S 40 27 E
Monterey, U.S.A. 83 H3 36 37N 121 55W
Monterey B., U.S.A. 84 J5 36 45N 122 0W
Montería, Colombia 92 B3 8 46N 75 53W
Monteros, Argentina 94 B2 27 11S 65 30W
Monterrey, Mexico 86 B4 25 40N 100 30W
Montes Claros, Brazil 93 G10 16 30S 43 50W
Montesano, U.S.A. 84 D3 46 59N 123 36W
Montesilvano Marina, Italy 20 C6 42 29N 14 8 E
Montevideo, Uruguay 95 C4 34 50S 56 11W
Montevideo, U.S.A. 80 C7 44 57N 95 43W
Montezuma, U.S.A. 80 E8 41 35N 92 32W
Montgomery = Sahiwal, Pakistan 42 D5 30 45N 73 8 E
Montgomery, U.K. 11 E4 52 34N 3 8W
Montgomery, Ala., U.S.A. 77 J2 32 23N 86 19W
Montgomery, W. Va., U.S.A. 76 F5 38 11N 81 19W
Monticello, Ark., U.S.A. 81 J9 33 38N 91 47W
Monticello, Fla., U.S.A. 77 K4 30 33N 83 52W
Monticello, Ind., U.S.A. 76 E2 40 45N 86 46W
Monticello, Iowa, U.S.A. 80 D9 42 15N 91 12W
Monticello, Ky., U.S.A. 77 G3 36 50N 84 51W
Monticello, Minn., U.S.A. 80 C8 45 18N 93 48W
Monticello, Miss., U.S.A. 81 K9 31 33N 90 7W
Monticello, N.Y., U.S.A. 79 E10 41 39N 74 42W
Monticello, Utah, U.S.A. 83 H9 37 52N 109 21W
Montijo, Portugal 19 C1 38 41N 8 54W
Montilla, Spain 19 D3 37 36N 4 40W
Montluçon, France 18 C5 46 22N 2 36 E
Montmagny, Canada 71 C5 46 58N 70 34W
Montmartre, Canada 73 C8 50 14N 103 27W
Montmorency, Canada 71 C5 46 53N 71 11W
Montmorillon, France 18 C4 46 26N 0 50 E
Monto, Australia 62 C5 24 52S 151 6 E
Montoro, Spain 19 C3 38 1N 4 27W
Montour Falls, U.S.A. 78 D8 42 21N 76 51W
Montpelier, Idaho, U.S.A. 82 E8 42 19N 111 18W
Montpelier, Ohio, U.S.A. 76 E3 41 35N 84 37W
Montpelier, Vt., U.S.A. 79 B12 44 16N 72 35W
Montpellier, France 18 E5 43 37N 3 52 E
Montréal, Canada 70 C5 45 31N 73 34W
Montreal L., Canada 73 C7 54 20N 105 45W
Montreal Lake, Canada 73 C7 54 3N 105 46W
Montreux, Switz. 16 E4 46 26N 6 55 E
Montrose, U.K. 12 E6 56 44N 2 27W
Montrose, Colo., U.S.A. 83 G10 38 29N 107 53W
Montrose, Pa., U.S.A. 79 E9 41 50N 75 53W
Monts, Pte. des, Canada 71 C6 49 20N 67 12W
Montserrat ■, W. Indies 89 C7 16 40N 62 10W
Montuiri, Spain 22 B9 39 34N 2 59 E
Monveda, Zaïre 52 D4 2 52N 21 30 E
Monywa, Burma 41 H19 22 7N 95 11 E
Monza, Italy 20 B3 45 35N 9 16 E
Monze, Zambia 55 F2 16 17S 27 29 E
Monze, C., Pakistan 42 G2 24 47N 66 37 E
Monzón, Spain 19 B6 41 52N 0 10 E
Mooi River, S. Africa 57 D4 29 13S 29 50 E
Moolawatana, Australia 63 D2 29 55S 139 45 E
Mooliabeenee, Australia 61 F2 31 20S 116 2 E
Mooloogool, Australia 61 E2 26 2S 119 5 E
Moomin Cr. →, Australia 63 D4 29 44S 149 20 E
Moonah →, Australia 62 C2 22 3S 138 33 E
Moonbeam, Canada 70 C3 49 20N 82 10W
Moonda, L., Australia 62 D3 25 52S 140 25 E
Moonie, Australia 63 D5 27 46S 150 20 E
Moonie →, Australia 63 D4 29 19S 148 43 E

North Las Vegas

North Las Vegas, U.S.A. 85 J11 36 12N 115 7W
North Lincolnshire □, U.K. 10 D7 53 36N 0 30W
North Little Rock, U.S.A. 81 H8 34 45N 92 16W
North Loup →, U.S.A. 80 E5 41 17N 98 24W
North Magnetic Pole, Canada 4 B2 77 58N 102 8W
North Minch, U.K. 12 C3 58 5N 5 55W
North Nahanni →, Canada 72 A4 62 15N 123 20W
North Olmsted, U.S.A. 78 E3 41 25N 81 56W
North Ossetia □, Russia 25 F7 43 30N 44 30 E
North Pagai, I. = Pagai Utara, Indonesia 36 E2 2 35S 100 0 E
North Palisade, U.S.A. 83 H4 37 6N 118 31W
North Platte, U.S.A. 80 E4 41 8N 100 46W
North Platte →, U.S.A. 80 E4 41 7N 100 42W
North Pole, Arctic 4 A 90 0N 0 0 E
North Portal, Canada 73 D8 49 0N 102 33W
North Powder, U.S.A. 82 D5 45 2N 117 55W
North Pt., Canada 71 C7 47 5N 64 0W
North Rhine Westphalia □ = Nordrhein-Westfalen □, Germany 16 C4 51 45N 7 30 E
North Ronaldsay, U.K. 12 B6 59 22N 2 26W
North Saskatchewan →, Canada 73 C7 53 15N 105 5W
North Sea, Europe 6 D6 56 0N 4 0 E
North Somerset □, U.K. 11 F5 51 24N 2 45W
North Sporades = Voríai Sporádhes, Greece 21 E10 39 15N 23 30 E
North Sydney, Canada 71 C7 46 12N 60 15W
North Taranaki Bight, N.Z. 59 H5 38 50S 174 15 E
North Thompson →, Canada 72 C4 50 40N 120 20W
North Tonawanda, U.S.A. 78 C6 43 2N 78 53W
North Troy, U.S.A. 79 B12 45 0N 72 24W
North Truchas Pk., U.S.A. 83 J11 36 0N 105 30W
North Twin I., Canada 70 B3 53 20N 80 0W
North Tyne →, U.K. 10 C5 55 0N 2 8W
North Uist, U.K. 12 D1 57 40N 7 15W
North Vancouver, Canada 72 D4 49 25N 123 3W
North Vernon, U.S.A. 76 F3 39 0N 85 38W
North Wabasca L., Canada 72 B6 56 0N 113 55W
North Walsham, U.K. 10 E9 52 50N 1 22 E
North-West □, S. Africa 56 D4 27 0S 25 0 E
North West C., Australia 60 D1 21 45S 114 9 E
North West Christmas I. Ridge, Pac. Oc. 65 G11 6 30N 165 0W
North West Frontier □, Pakistan 42 C4 34 0N 72 0 E
North West Highlands, U.K. 12 D3 57 33N 4 58W
North West Providence Channel, W. Indies 88 A4 26 0N 78 0W
North West River, Canada 71 B7 53 30N 60 10W
North West Territories □, Canada 68 B9 67 0N 110 0W
North Western □, Zambia 55 E2 13 30S 25 30 E
North York Moors, U.K. 10 C7 54 23N 0 53W
North Yorkshire □, U.K. 10 C6 54 15N 1 25W
Northallerton, U.K. 10 C6 54 20N 1 26W
Northam, S. Africa 56 C4 24 56S 27 18 E
Northampton, Australia 61 E1 28 27S 114 33 E
Northampton, U.K. 11 E7 52 15N 0 53W
Northampton, Mass., U.S.A. 79 D12 42 19N 72 38W
Northampton, Pa., U.S.A. 79 F9 40 41N 75 30W
Northampton Downs, Australia 62 C4 24 35S 145 48 E
Northamptonshire □, U.K. 11 E7 52 16N 0 55W
Northbridge, U.S.A. 79 D13 42 9N 71 39W
Northcliffe, Australia 61 F2 34 39S 116 7 E
Northern □, Malawi 55 E3 11 0S 34 0 E
Northern □, Uganda 54 B3 3 5N 32 30 E
Northern □, Zambia 55 E3 10 30S 31 0 E
Northern Cape □, S. Africa 56 D3 30 0S 20 0 E
Northern Circars, India 41 L13 17 30N 82 30 E
Northern Indian L., Canada 73 B9 57 20N 97 20W
Northern Ireland □, U.K. 13 B5 54 45N 7 0W
Northern Light, L., Canada 70 C1 48 15N 90 39W
Northern Marianas ■, Pac. Oc. 64 F6 17 0N 145 0 E
Northern Territory □, Australia 60 D5 20 0S 133 0 E
Northern Transvaal □, S. Africa 57 C4 24 0S 29 0 E
Northfield, U.S.A. 80 C8 44 27N 93 9W
Northland □, N.Z. 59 F4 35 30S 173 30 E
Northome, U.S.A. 80 B7 47 52N 94 17W
Northport, Ala., U.S.A. 77 J2 33 14N 87 35W
Northport, Mich., U.S.A. 76 C3 45 8N 85 37W
Northport, Wash., U.S.A. 82 B5 48 55N 117 48W
Northumberland □, U.K. 10 B5 55 12N 2 0W
Northumberland, C., Australia 63 F3 38 5S 140 40 E
Northumberland Is., Australia 62 C4 21 30S 149 50 E
Northumberland Str., Canada 71 C7 46 20N 64 0W
Northwich, U.K. 10 D5 53 15N 2 31W
Northwood, Iowa, U.S.A. 80 D8 43 27N 93 13W
Northwood, N. Dak., U.S.A. 80 B6 47 44N 97 34W
Norton, U.S.A. 80 F5 39 50N 99 53W
Norton, Zimbabwe 55 F3 17 52S 30 40 E
Norton Sd., U.S.A. 68 B3 63 50N 164 0W
Norwalk, Calif., U.S.A. 85 M8 33 54N 118 5W
Norwalk, Conn., U.S.A. 79 E11 41 7N 73 22W
Norwalk, Ohio, U.S.A. 78 E2 41 15N 82 37W
Norway, U.S.A. 76 C2 45 47N 87 55W
Norway ■, Europe 8 E14 63 0N 11 0 E
Norway House, Canada 73 C9 53 59N 97 50W
Norwegian Sea, Atl. Oc. 4 C8 66 0N 1 0 E
Norwich, Canada 78 D4 42 59N 80 36W
Norwich, U.K. 10 E9 52 38N 1 18 E
Norwich, Conn., U.S.A. 79 E12 41 31N 72 5W
Norwich, N.Y., U.S.A. 79 D9 42 32N 75 32W
Norwood, Canada 78 B7 44 23N 77 59W
Noshiro, Japan 30 D10 40 12N 140 0 E
Nosok, Russia 26 B9 70 10N 82 20 E
Noss Hd., U.K. 12 C5 58 28N 3 3W
Nossob →, S. Africa 56 D3 26 55S 20 45 E
Nosy Bé, Madag. 53 G9 13 25S 48 15 E
Nosy Boraha, Madag. 57 B8 16 50S 49 55 E
Nosy Mitsio, Madag. 53 G9 12 54S 48 36 E
Nosy Varika, Madag. 57 C8 20 35S 48 32 E
Noteć →, Poland 16 B8 52 44N 15 26 E
Notigi Dam, Canada 73 B9 56 40N 99 10W
Notikewin →, Canada 72 B5 57 2N 117 38W
Notodden, Norway 9 G13 59 35N 9 17 E
Notre-Dame, Canada 71 C7 46 18N 64 46W
Notre Dame B., Canada 71 C8 49 45N 55 30W
Notre Dame de Koartac = Quaqtaq, Canada 69 B13 60 55N 69 40W
Notre Dame d'Ivugivic = Ivujivik, Canada 69 B12 62 24N 77 55W
Nottaway →, Canada 70 B4 51 22N 78 55W
Nottingham, U.K. 10 E6 52 58N 1 10W
Nottinghamshire □, U.K. 10 D7 53 10N 1 3W
Nottoway →, U.S.A. 76 G7 36 33N 76 55W
Notwane →, Botswana 56 C4 23 35S 26 58 E
Nouâdhibou, Mauritania 50 D1 20 54N 17 0W
Nouâdhibou, Ras, Mauritania 50 D1 20 50N 17 0W
Nouakchott, Mauritania 50 E1 18 9N 15 58W
Nouméa, N. Cal. 64 K8 22 17S 166 30 E
Noupoort, S. Africa 56 E3 31 10S 24 57 E
Nouveau Comptoir = Wemindji, Canada 70 B4 53 0N 78 49W
Nouvelle-Calédonie = New Caledonia ■, Pac. Oc. 64 K8 21 0S 165 0 E
Nova Casa Nova, Brazil 93 E10 9 25S 41 5W
Nova Cruz, Brazil 93 E11 6 28S 35 25W
Nova Esperança, Brazil 95 A5 23 8S 52 24W
Nova Friburgo, Brazil 95 A7 22 16S 42 30W
Nova Gaia = Cambundi-Catembo, Angola 52 G3 10 10S 17 35 E
Nova Iguaçu, Brazil 95 A7 22 45S 43 28W
Nova Iorque, Brazil 93 E10 7 0S 44 5W
Nova Lima, Brazil 95 A7 19 59S 43 51W
Nova Lisboa = Huambo, Angola 53 G3 12 42S 15 54 E
Nova Lusitânia, Mozam. 55 F3 19 50S 34 34 E
Nova Mambone, Mozam. 57 C6 21 0S 35 3 E
Nova Scotia □, Canada 71 C7 45 10N 63 0W
Nova Sofala, Mozam. 57 C5 20 7S 34 42 E
Nova Venécia, Brazil 93 G10 18 45S 40 24W
Nova Zagora, Bulgaria 21 C11 42 32N 25 59 E
Novara, Italy 20 B3 45 28N 8 38 E
Novato, U.S.A. 84 G4 38 6N 122 35W
Novaya Ladoga, Russia 24 B5 60 7N 32 16 E
Novaya Lyalya, Russia 26 D7 59 4N 60 45 E
Novaya Sibir, Ostrov, Russia 27 B16 75 10N 150 0 E
Novaya Zemlya, Russia 26 B6 75 0N 56 0 E
Nové Zámky, Slovak Rep. 17 D10 48 2N 18 8 E
Novgorod, Russia 24 C5 58 30N 31 25 E
Novgorod-Severskiy = Novhorod-Siverskyy, Ukraine 24 D5 52 2N 33 10 E
Novhorod-Siverskyy, Ukraine 24 D5 52 2N 33 10 E
Novi Ligure, Italy 20 B3 44 46N 8 47 E
Novi Pazar, Serbia, Yug. 21 C9 43 12N 20 28 E
Novi Sad, Serbia, Yug. 21 B8 45 18N 19 52 E
Nôvo Hamburgo, Brazil 95 B5 29 37S 51 7W
Novo Mesto, Slovenia 16 F8 45 48N 15 10 E
Novo Remanso, Brazil 93 E10 9 41S 42 4W
Novoataysk, Russia 26 D9 53 30N 84 0 E
Novocherkassk, Russia 25 E7 47 27N 40 15 E
Novogrudok = Navahrudak, Belarus 17 B13 53 40N 25 50 E
Novohrad-Volynskyy, Ukraine 17 C14 50 34N 27 35 E
Novokachalinsk, Russia 30 B6 45 5N 132 0 E
Novokazalinsk = Zhangaqazaly, Kazakstan 26 E7 45 48N 62 6 E
Novokuybyshevsk, Russia 24 D8 53 7N 49 58 E
Novokuznetsk, Russia 26 D9 53 45N 87 10 E
Novomoskovsk, Russia 24 D6 54 5N 38 15 E
Novorossiysk, Russia 25 F6 44 43N 37 46 E
Novorybnoye, Russia 27 B11 72 50N 105 50 E
Novoselytsya, Ukraine 17 D14 48 14N 26 15 E
Novoshakhtinsk, Russia 25 E6 47 46N 39 58 E
Novosibirsk, Russia 26 D9 55 0N 83 5 E
Novosibirskiye Ostrova, Russia 27 B15 75 0N 142 0 E
Novotroitsk, Russia 26 D6 51 10N 58 15 E
Novouzensk, Russia 25 D8 50 32N 48 17 E
Novovolynsk, Ukraine 17 C13 50 45N 24 4 E
Novska, Croatia 20 B7 45 19N 17 0 E
Novyy Port, Russia 26 C8 67 40N 72 30 E
Now Shahr, Iran 45 B6 36 40N 51 30 E
Nowa Sól, Poland 16 C8 51 48N 15 44 E
Nowbarān, Iran 45 C6 35 8N 49 42 E
Nowghāb, Iran 45 C8 33 53N 59 4 E
Nowgong, India 41 F18 26 20N 92 50 E
Nowra, Australia 63 E5 34 53S 150 35 E
Nowshera, Pakistan 40 B8 34 0N 72 0 E
Nowy Sącz, Poland 17 D11 49 40N 20 41 E
Nowy Targ, Poland 17 D11 49 29N 20 2 E
Nowy Tomyśl, Poland 16 B9 52 19N 16 10 E
Noxen, U.S.A. 79 E8 41 25N 76 4W
Noxon, U.S.A. 82 C6 48 0N 115 43W
Noyes I., U.S.A. 72 B2 55 30N 133 40W
Noyon, France 18 B5 49 34N 2 59 E
Noyon, Mongolia 34 C2 43 2N 102 4 E
Nsanje, Malawi 55 F4 16 55S 35 12 E
Nsawam, Ghana 50 G4 5 50N 0 24W
Nsomba, Zambia 55 E2 10 45S 29 51 E
Nsukka, Nigeria 50 G6 6 51N 7 29 E
Nu Jiang →, China 32 D4 29 58N 97 25 E
Nu Shan, China 32 D4 26 0N 99 20 E
Nubia, Africa 48 D7 21 0N 32 0 E
Nubian Desert = Nûbîya, Es Sahrâ En, Sudan 51 D11 21 30N 33 30 E
Nûbîya, Es Sahrâ En, Sudan 51 D11 21 30N 33 30 E
Ñuble □, Chile 94 D1 37 0S 72 0W
Nuboai, Indonesia 37 E9 2 10S 136 30 E
Nubra →, India 43 B7 34 35N 77 35 E
Nueces →, U.S.A. 81 M6 27 51N 97 30W
Nueltin L., Canada 73 A9 60 30N 99 30W
Nueva Asunción □, Paraguay 94 A3 21 0S 61 0W
Nueva Gerona, Cuba 88 B3 21 53N 82 49W
Nueva Imperial, Chile 96 D2 38 45S 72 58W
Nueva Palmira, Uruguay 94 C4 33 52S 58 20W
Nueva Rosita, Mexico 86 B4 28 0N 101 11W
Nueva San Salvador, El Salv. 88 D2 13 40N 89 18W
Nuéve de Julio, Argentina 94 D3 35 30S 61 0W
Nuevitas, Cuba 88 B4 21 30N 77 20W
Nuevo, G., Argentina 96 E4 43 0S 64 30W
Nuevo Guerrero, Mexico 87 B5 26 34N 99 15W
Nuevo Laredo, Mexico 87 B5 27 30N 99 30W
Nuevo León □, Mexico 86 C4 25 0N 100 0W
Nugget Pt., N.Z. 59 M2 46 27S 169 50 E
Nuhaka, N.Z. 59 H6 39 3S 177 45 E
Nukey Bluff, Australia 63 E2 32 26S 135 29 E
Nukheila, Sudan 51 E10 19 1N 26 21 E
Nuku'alofa, Tonga 59 E11 21 10S 174 0W
Nukus, Uzbekistan 26 E6 42 27N 59 41 E
Nulato, U.S.A. 68 B4 64 43N 158 6W
Nullagine →, Australia 60 D3 21 20S 120 20 E
Nullarbor, Australia 61 F5 31 28S 130 55 E
Nullarbor Plain, Australia 61 F4 31 10S 129 0 E
Numalla, L., Australia 63 D3 28 43S 144 20 E
Numan, Nigeria 51 G7 9 29N 12 3 E
Numata, Japan 31 F9 36 45N 139 4 E
Numazu, Japan 31 G9 35 7N 138 51 E
Numbulwar, Australia 62 A2 14 15S 135 45 E
Numfoor, Indonesia 37 E8 1 0S 134 50 E
Numurkah, Australia 63 F4 36 5S 145 26 E
Nunaksaluk I., Canada 71 A7 55 49N 60 20W
Nuneaton, U.K. 11 E6 52 32N 1 27W
Nungo, Mozam. 55 E4 13 23S 37 43 E
Nungwe, Tanzania 54 C3 2 48S 32 2 E
Nunivak I., U.S.A. 68 B3 60 10N 166 30W
Nunkun, India 43 C7 33 57N 76 2 E
Nunspeet, Neths. 15 B5 52 21N 5 45 E
Nùoro, Italy 20 D3 40 20N 9 20 E
Nūrābād, Iran 45 E8 27 47N 57 12 E
Nuremberg = Nürnberg, Germany 16 D6 49 27N 11 3 E
Nuri, Mexico 86 B3 28 2N 109 22W
Nurina, Australia 61 F4 30 56S 126 33 E
Nuriootpa, Australia 63 E2 34 27S 139 0 E
Nurmes, Finland 8 E23 63 33N 29 10 E
Nürnberg, Germany 16 D6 49 27N 11 3 E
Nurran, L. = Terewah, L., Australia 63 D4 29 52S 147 35 E
Nurrari Lakes, Australia 61 E5 29 1S 130 5 E
Nusa Barung, Indonesia 37 H15 8 10S 113 30 E
Nusa Kambangan, Indonesia 37 G13 7 40S 108 10 E
Nusa Tenggara Barat □, Indonesia 36 F5 8 50S 117 30 E
Nusa Tenggara Timur □, Indonesia 37 F6 9 30S 122 0 E
Nusaybin, Turkey 25 G7 37 3N 41 10 E
Nushki, Pakistan 42 E2 29 35N 66 0 E
Nutak, Canada 69 C13 57 28N 61 59W
Nutwood Downs, Australia 62 B1 15 49S 134 10 E
Nuuk = Godthåb, Greenland 69 B14 64 10N 51 35W
Nuwakot, Nepal 43 E10 28 10N 83 55 E
Nuweveldberge, S. Africa 56 E3 32 10S 21 45 E
Nuyts, C., Australia 61 F5 32 2S 132 21 E
Nuyts Arch., Australia 63 E1 32 35S 133 20 E
Nxau-Nxau, Botswana 56 B3 18 57S 21 4 E
Nyack, U.S.A. 79 E11 41 5N 73 55W
Nyah West, Australia 63 F3 35 16S 143 21 E
Nyahanga, Tanzania 54 C3 2 20S 33 37 E
Nyahua, Tanzania 54 D3 5 25S 33 23 E
Nyahururu, Kenya 54 B4 0 2N 36 27 E
Nyainqentanglha Shan, China 32 D3 30 0N 90 0 E
Nyakanazi, Tanzania 54 C3 3 2S 31 10 E
Nyâlâ, Sudan 51 F9 12 2N 24 58 E
Nyamandhlovu, Zimbabwe 55 F2 19 55S 28 16 E
Nyambiti, Tanzania 54 C3 2 48S 33 27 E
Nyamwaga, Tanzania 54 C3 1 27S 34 33 E
Nyandekwa, Tanzania 54 C3 3 57S 32 32 E
Nyandoma, Russia 24 B7 61 40N 40 12 E
Nyangana, Namibia 56 B3 18 0S 20 40 E
Nyanguge, Tanzania 54 C3 2 30S 33 12 E
Nyanza, Burundi 54 C2 4 21S 29 36 E
Nyanza, Rwanda 54 C2 2 20S 29 42 E
Nyanza □, Kenya 54 C3 0 10S 34 15 E
Nyarling →, Canada 72 A6 60 41N 113 23W
Nyasa, L. = Malawi, L., Africa 55 E3 12 30S 34 30 E
Nyasvizh, Belarus 17 B14 53 14N 26 38 E
Nyazepetrovsk, Russia 24 C10 56 3N 59 36 E
Nyazura, Zimbabwe 55 F3 18 40S 32 16 E
Nyazwidzi →, Zimbabwe 55 F3 20 0S 31 17 E
Nybro, Sweden 9 H16 56 44N 15 55 E
Nyda, Russia 26 C8 66 40N 72 58 E
Nyeri, Kenya 54 C4 0 23S 36 56 E
Nyíregyháza, Hungary 17 E11 47 58N 21 47 E
Nykøbing, Storstrøm, Denmark 9 J14 54 56N 11 52 E
Nykøbing, Vestsjælland, Denmark 9 J14 55 55N 11 40 E
Nykøbing, Viborg, Denmark 9 H13 56 48N 8 51 E
Nyköping, Sweden 9 G17 58 45N 17 0 E
Nylstroom, S. Africa 57 C4 24 42S 28 22 E
Nymagee, Australia 63 E4 32 7S 146 20 E
Nynäshamn, Sweden 9 G17 58 54N 17 57 E
Nyngan, Australia 63 E4 31 30S 147 8 E
Nyoman = Neman →, Lithuania 9 J19 55 25N 21 10 E
Nysa, Poland 17 C9 50 30N 17 22 E
Nysa →, Europe 16 B8 52 4N 14 46 E
Nyssa, U.S.A. 82 E5 43 53N 117 0W
Nyunzu, Zaïre 54 D2 5 57S 27 58 E
Nyurbe, Russia 27 C12 63 17N 118 28 E
Nzega, Tanzania 54 C3 4 10S 33 12 E
Nzega □, Tanzania 54 C3 4 10S 33 10 E
N'Zérékoré, Guinea 50 G3 7 49N 8 48W
Nzeto, Angola 52 F2 7 10S 12 52 E
Nzilo, Chutes de, Zaïre 55 E2 10 18S 25 27 E
Nzubuka, Tanzania 54 C3 4 45S 32 50 E

O

Ō-Shima, Nagasaki, Japan 31 G4 34 29N 129 33 E
Ō-Shima, Shizuoka, Japan 31 G9 34 44N 139 24 E
Oacoma, U.S.A. 80 D5 43 48N 99 24W
Oahe, L., U.S.A. 80 C4 44 27N 100 24W
Oahe Dam, U.S.A. 80 C4 44 27N 100 24W
Oahu, U.S.A. 74 H16 21 28N 157 58W
Oak Creek, U.S.A. 82 F10 40 16N 106 57W
Oak Harbor, U.S.A. 84 B4 48 18N 122 39W
Oak Hill, U.S.A. 76 G5 37 59N 81 9W
Oak Park, U.S.A. 76 E2 41 53N 87 47W
Oak Ridge, U.S.A. 77 G3 36 1N 84 16W
Oak View, U.S.A. 85 L7 34 24N 119 18W
Oakan-Dake, Japan 30 C12 43 27N 144 10 E
Oakbank, Australia 63 E3 33 4S 140 33 E
Oakdale, Calif., U.S.A. 83 H3 37 46N 120 51W
Oakdale, La., U.S.A. 81 K8 30 49N 92 40W
Oakengates, U.K. 10 E5 52 41N 2 26W
Oakes, U.S.A. 80 B5 46 8N 98 6W
Oakesdale, U.S.A. 82 C5 47 8N 117 15W
Oakey, Australia 63 D5 27 25S 151 43 E
Oakham, U.K. 10 E7 52 40N 0 43W
Oakhurst, U.S.A. 84 H7 37 19N 119 40W
Oakland, Calif., U.S.A. 83 H2 37 49N 122 16W
Oakland, Oreg., U.S.A. 82 E2 43 25N 123 18W
Oakland City, U.S.A. 76 F2 38 20N 87 21W
Oakley, Idaho, U.S.A. 82 E7 42 15N 113 53W
Oakley, Kans., U.S.A. 80 F4 39 8N 100 51W
Oakover →, Australia 60 D3 21 0S 120 40 E
Oakridge, U.S.A. 82 E2 43 45N 122 28W
Oakville, U.S.A. 84 D3 46 51N 123 14W
Oamaru, N.Z. 59 L3 45 5S 170 59 E
Oasis, Calif., U.S.A. 85 M10 33 28N 116 6W
Oasis, Nev., U.S.A. 84 H9 37 29N 117 55W
Oates Land, Antarctica 5 C11 69 0S 160 0 E
Oatman, U.S.A. 85 K12 35 1N 114 19W
Oaxaca, Mexico 87 D5 17 2N 96 40W
Oaxaca □, Mexico 87 D5 17 0N 97 0W
Ob →, Russia 26 C7 66 45N 69 30 E
Oba, Canada 70 C3 49 4N 84 7W
Obama, Japan 31 G7 35 30N 135 45 E
Oban, U.K. 12 E3 56 25N 5 29W
Obbia, Somali Rep. 46 F4 5 25N 48 30 E
Obed, Canada 72 C5 53 30N 117 10W
Obera, Argentina 95 B4 27 21S 55 2W
Oberhausen, Germany 16 C4 51 28N 6 51 E
Oberlin, Kans., U.S.A. 80 F4 39 49N 100 32W
Oberlin, La., U.S.A. 81 K8 30 37N 92 46W
Oberlin, Ohio, U.S.A. 78 E2 41 18N 82 13W
Oberon, Australia 63 E4 33 45S 149 52 E
Obi, Kepulauan, Indonesia 37 E7 1 23S 127 45 E
Obi Is. = Obi, Kepulauan, Indonesia 37 E7 1 23S 127 45 E
Óbidos, Brazil 93 D7 1 50S 55 30W
Obihiro, Japan 30 C11 42 56N 143 12 E
Obilatu, Indonesia 37 E7 1 25S 127 20 E
Obluchye, Russia 27 E14 49 1N 131 4 E
Obo, C.A.R. 54 A2 5 20N 26 32 E
Oboa, Mt., Uganda 54 B3 1 45N 34 45 E
Oboyan, Russia 26 D4 51 15N 36 21 E
Obozerskaya = Obozerskiy, Russia 26 C5 63 34N 40 21 E
Obozerskiy, Russia 26 C5 63 34N 40 21 E
Observatory Inlet, Canada 72 B3 55 10N 129 54W
Obshchi Syrt, Russia 6 E16 52 0N 53 0 E
Obskaya Guba, Russia 26 C8 69 0N 73 0 E
Obuasi, Ghana 50 G4 6 17N 1 40W
Ocala, U.S.A. 77 L4 29 11N 82 8W
Ocampo, Mexico 86 B3 28 9N 108 24W
Ocaña, Spain 19 C4 39 55N 3 30W
Ocanomowoc, U.S.A. 80 D10 43 7N 88 30W
Ocate, U.S.A. 81 G2 36 11N 105 3W
Occidental, Cordillera, Colombia 92 C3 5 0N 76 0W
Ocean City, N.J., U.S.A. 76 F8 39 17N 74 35W
Ocean City, Wash., U.S.A. 84 C2 47 4N 124 10W
Ocean I. = Banaba, Kiribati 64 H8 0 45S 169 50 E
Ocean Park, U.S.A. 84 D2 46 30N 124 3W
Oceano, U.S.A. 85 K6 35 6N 120 37W
Oceanport, U.S.A. 79 F10 40 19N 74 3W
Oceanside, U.S.A. 85 M9 33 12N 117 23W
Ochil Hills, U.K. 12 E5 56 14N 3 40W
Ochre River, Canada 73 C9 51 4N 99 47W
Ocilla, U.S.A. 77 K4 31 36N 83 15W
Ocmulgee →, U.S.A. 77 K4 31 58N 82 33W
Ocniţa, Moldova 17 D14 48 25N 27 30 E
Oconee →, U.S.A. 77 K4 31 58N 82 33W
Oconto, U.S.A. 76 C2 44 53N 87 52W
Oconto Falls, U.S.A. 76 C1 44 52N 88 9W
Ocosingo, Mexico 87 D6 17 10N 92 15W
Ocotal, Nic. 88 D2 13 41N 86 31W
Ocotlán, Mexico 86 C4 20 21N 102 42W
Octave, U.S.A. 83 J7 34 10N 112 43W
Ocumare del Tuy, Venezuela 92 A5 10 7N 66 46W
Ōda, Japan 31 G6 35 11N 132 30 E
Ódáðahraun, Iceland 8 D5 65 5N 17 0W
Odate, Japan 30 D10 40 16N 140 34 E
Odawara, Japan 31 G9 35 20N 139 6 E
Odda, Norway 9 F12 60 3N 6 35 E
Oddur, Somali Rep. 46 G3 4 11N 43 52 E
Odei →, Canada 73 B9 56 6N 96 54W
Ödemiş, Turkey 21 E13 38 15N 28 0 E
Odendaalsrus, S. Africa 56 D4 27 48S 26 45 E
Odense, Denmark 9 J14 55 22N 10 23 E
Oder →, Germany 16 B8 53 33N 14 38 E
Odesa, Ukraine 25 E5 46 30N 30 45 E
Odessa = Odesa, Ukraine 25 E5 46 30N 30 45 E
Odessa, Canada 79 B8 44 17N 76 43W
Odessa, Tex., U.S.A. 81 K3 31 52N 102 23W
Odessa, Wash., U.S.A. 82 C4 47 20N 118 41W
Odiakwe, Botswana 56 C4 20 12S 25 17 E
Odienné, Ivory C. 50 G3 9 30N 7 34W
Odintsovo, Russia 24 C6 55 39N 37 15 E
O'Donnell, U.S.A. 81 J4 32 58N 101 50W
Odorheiu Secuiesc, Romania 17 E13 46 21N 25 21 E
Odra = Oder →, Germany 16 B8 53 33N 14 38 E

Oshmyany

Odzi, *Zimbabwe* **57 B5** 19 0S 32 20 E
Oeiras, *Brazil* **93 E10** 7 0S 42 8W
Oelrichs, *U.S.A.* **80 D3** 43 11N 103 14W
Oelwein, *U.S.A.* **80 D9** 42 41N 91 55W
Oenpelli, *Australia* **60 B5** 12 20S 133 4 E
Ofanto →, *Italy* **20 D7** 41 22N 16 13 E
Offa, *Nigeria* **50 G5** 8 13N 4 42 E
Offaly □, *Ireland* **13 C4** 53 15N 7 30W
Offenbach, *Germany* **16 C5** 50 6N 8 44 E
Offenburg, *Germany* **16 D4** 48 28N 7 56 E
Ofotfjorden, *Norway* **8 B17** 68 27N 17 0 E
Ōfunato, *Japan* **30 E10** 39 4N 141 43 E
Oga, *Japan* **30 E9** 39 55N 139 50 E
Oga-Hantō, *Japan* **30 E9** 39 58N 139 47 E
Ogahalla, *Canada* **70 B2** 50 6N 85 51W
Ōgaki, *Japan* **31 G8** 35 21N 136 37 E
Ogallala, *U.S.A.* **80 E4** 41 8N 101 43W
Ogasawara Gunto, *Pac. Oc.* **28 G18** 27 0N 142 0 E
Ogbomosho, *Nigeria* **50 G5** 8 1N 4 11 E
Ogden, *Iowa, U.S.A.* **80 D8** 42 2N 94 2W
Ogden, *Utah, U.S.A.* **82 F7** 41 13N 111 58W
Ogdensburg, *U.S.A.* **79 B9** 44 42N 75 30W
Ogeechee →, *U.S.A.* **77 K5** 31 50N 81 3W
Ogilby, *U.S.A.* **85 N12** 32 49N 114 50W
Oglio →, *Italy* **20 B4** 45 2N 10 39 E
Ogmore, *Australia* **62 C4** 22 37S 149 35 E
Ogoki →, *Canada* **70 B2** 51 38N 85 57W
Ogoki L., *Canada* **70 B2** 50 50N 87 10W
Ogoki Res., *Canada* **70 B2** 50 45N 88 15W
Ogooué →, *Gabon* **52 E1** 1 0S 9 0 E
Ogowe = Ogooué →, *Gabon* **52 E1** 1 0S 9 0 E
Ogre, *Latvia* **9 H21** 56 49N 24 36 E
Ohai, *N.Z.* **59 L2** 45 55S 168 0 E
Ohakune, *N.Z.* **59 H5** 39 24S 175 24 E
Ohanet, *Algeria* **50 C6** 28 44N 8 46 E
Ohata, *Japan* **30 D10** 41 24N 141 10 E
Ohau, L., *N.Z.* **59 L2** 44 15S 169 53 E
Ohey, *Belgium* **15 D5** 50 26N 5 8 E
Ohio □, *U.S.A.* **76 E3** 40 15N 82 45W
Ohio →, *U.S.A.* **76 G1** 36 59N 89 8W
Ohre →, *Czech.* **16 C8** 50 30N 14 10 E
Ohrid, *Macedonia* **21 D9** 41 8N 20 52 E
Ohridsko Jezero, *Macedonia* **21 D9** 41 8N 20 52 E
Ohrigstad, *S. Africa* **57 C5** 24 39S 30 36 E
Oikou, *China* **35 E9** 38 35N 117 42 E
Oil City, *U.S.A.* **78 E5** 41 26N 79 42W
Oildale, *U.S.A.* **85 K7** 35 25N 119 1W
Oise →, *France* **18 B5** 49 0N 2 4 E
Ōita, *Japan* **31 H5** 33 14N 131 36 E
Ōita □, *Japan* **31 H5** 33 15N 131 30 E
Oiticica, *Brazil* **93 E10** 5 3S 41 5W
Ojai, *U.S.A.* **85 L7** 34 27N 119 15W
Ojinaga, *Mexico* **86 B4** 29 34N 104 25W
Ojiya, *Japan* **31 F9** 37 18N 138 48 E
Ojos del Salado, Cerro, *Argentina* **94 B2** 27 0S 68 40W
Oka →, *Russia* **26 D5** 56 20N 43 59 E
Okaba, *Indonesia* **37 F9** 8 6S 139 42 E
Okahandja, *Namibia* **56 C2** 22 0S 16 59 E
Okahukura, *N.Z.* **59 H5** 38 48S 175 14 E
Okanagan L., *Canada* **72 C5** 50 0N 119 30W
Okandja, *Gabon* **52 E2** 0 35S 13 45 E
Okanogan, *U.S.A.* **82 B4** 48 22N 119 35W
Okanogan →, *U.S.A.* **82 B4** 48 6N 119 44W
Okaputa, *Namibia* **56 C2** 20 5S 17 0 E
Okara, *Pakistan* **42 D5** 30 50N 73 31 E
Okarito, *N.Z.* **59 K3** 43 15S 170 9 E
Okaukuejo, *Namibia* **56 B2** 19 10S 16 0 E
Okavango Swamps, *Botswana* **56 B3** 18 45S 22 45 E
Okaya, *Japan* **31 F9** 36 5N 138 10 E
Okayama, *Japan* **31 G6** 34 40N 133 54 E
Okayama □, *Japan* **31 G6** 35 0N 133 50 E
Okazaki, *Japan* **31 G8** 34 57N 137 10 E
Okeechobee, *U.S.A.* **77 M5** 27 15N 80 50W
Okeechobee, L., *U.S.A.* **77 M5** 27 0N 80 50W
Okefenokee Swamp, *U.S.A.* **77 K4** 30 40N 82 20W
Okehampton, *U.K.* **11 G3** 50 44N 4 0W
Okha, *Russia* **27 D15** 53 40N 143 0 E
Okhotsk, *Russia* **27 D15** 59 20N 143 10 E
Okhotsk, Sea of, *Asia* **27 D15** 55 0N 145 0 E
Okhotskiy Perevoz, *Russia* **27 C14** 61 52N 135 35 E
Oki-Shotō, *Japan* **31 F6** 36 5N 133 15 E
Okiep, *S. Africa* **56 D2** 29 39S 17 53 E
Okinawa □, *Japan* **31 L3** 26 40N 128 0 E
Okinawa-Guntō, *Japan* **31 L3** 26 40N 128 0 E
Okinawa-Jima, *Japan* **31 L4** 26 32N 128 0 E
Okino-erabu-Shima, *Japan* **31 L4** 27 21N 128 33 E
Oklahoma □, *U.S.A.* **81 H6** 35 20N 97 30W
Oklahoma City, *U.S.A.* **81 H6** 35 30N 97 30W
Okmulgee, *U.S.A.* **81 H7** 35 37N 95 58W
Oknitsa = Ocniţa, *Moldova* **17 D14** 48 25N 27 30 E
Okolo, *Uganda* **54 B3** 2 37N 31 8 E
Okolona, *U.S.A.* **81 H10** 34 0N 88 45W
Okrika, *Nigeria* **50 H6** 4 40N 7 10 E
Oksovskiy, *Russia* **24 B6** 62 33N 39 57 E
Oktabrsk = Oktyabrsk, *Kazakstan* **25 E10** 49 28N 57 25 E
Oktyabrsk, *Kazakstan* **25 E10** 49 28N 57 25 E
Oktyabrskiy = Aktsyabrski, *Belarus* **17 B15** 52 38N 28 53 E
Oktyabrskiy, *Russia* **24 D9** 54 28N 53 28 E
Oktyabrskoy Revolyutsii, Os., *Russia* **27 B10** 79 30N 97 0 E
Oktyabrskoye, *Russia* **26 C7** 62 28N 66 3 E
Okuru, *N.Z.* **59 K2** 43 55S 168 55 E
Okushiri-Tō, *Japan* **30 C9** 42 15N 139 30 E
Okwa →, *Botswana* **56 C3** 22 30S 23 0 E
Ola, *U.S.A.* **81 H8** 35 2N 93 13W
Ólafsfjörður, *Iceland* **8 C4** 66 4N 18 39W
Ólafsvík, *Iceland* **8 D2** 64 53N 23 43W
Olancha, *U.S.A.* **85 J8** 36 17N 118 1W
Olancha Pk., *U.S.A.* **85 J8** 36 15N 118 7W
Olanchito, *Honduras* **88 C2** 15 30N 86 30W
Öland, *Sweden* **9 H17** 56 45N 16 38 E
Olary, *Australia* **63 E3** 32 18S 140 19 E
Olascoaga, *Argentina* **94 D3** 35 15S 60 39W
Olathe, *U.S.A.* **80 F7** 38 53N 94 49W
Olavarría, *Argentina* **94 D3** 36 55S 60 20W
Oława, *Poland* **17 C9** 50 57N 17 20 E
Ólbia, *Italy* **20 D3** 40 55N 9 31 E
Old Bahama Chan. = Bahama, Canal Viejo de, *W. Indies* **88 B4** 22 10N 77 30W
Old Baldy Pk. = San Antonio, Mt., *U.S.A.* **85 L9** 34 17N 117 38W
Old Cork, *Australia* **62 C3** 22 57S 141 52 E
Old Crow, *Canada* **68 B6** 67 30N 139 55W
Old Dale, *U.S.A.* **85 L11** 34 8N 115 47W
Old Fletton, *U.K.* **11 E7** 52 33N 0 14W
Old Forge, *N.Y., U.S.A.* **79 C10** 43 43N 74 58W
Old Forge, *Pa., U.S.A.* **79 E9** 41 22N 75 45W
Old Fort →, *Canada* **73 B6** 58 36N 110 24W
Old Shinyanga, *Tanzania* **54 C3** 3 33S 33 27 E
Old Speck Mt., *U.S.A.* **79 B14** 44 34N 70 57W
Old Town, *U.S.A.* **71 D6** 44 56N 68 39W
Old Wives L., *Canada* **73 C7** 50 5N 106 0W
Oldbury, *U.K.* **11 F5** 51 38N 2 33W
Oldcastle, *Ireland* **13 C4** 53 46N 7 10W
Oldeani, *Tanzania* **54 C4** 3 22S 35 35 E
Oldenburg, *Germany* **16 B5** 53 9N 8 13 E
Oldenzaal, *Neths.* **15 B6** 52 19N 6 53 E
Oldham, *U.K.* **10 D5** 53 33N 2 7W
Oldman →, *Canada* **72 D6** 49 57N 111 42W
Olds, *Canada* **72 C6** 51 50N 114 10W
Olean, *U.S.A.* **78 D6** 42 5N 78 26W
Olekma →, *Russia* **27 C13** 60 22N 120 42 E
Olekminsk, *Russia* **27 C13** 60 25N 120 30 E
Oleksandriya, *Ukraine* **17 C14** 50 37N 26 19 E
Olema, *U.S.A.* **84 G4** 38 3N 122 47W
Olenegorsk, *Russia* **24 A5** 68 9N 33 18 E
Olenek, *Russia* **27 C12** 68 28N 112 18 E
Olenek →, *Russia* **27 B13** 73 0N 120 10 E
Oléron, I. d', *France* **18 D3** 45 55N 1 15W
Oleśnica, *Poland* **17 C9** 51 13N 17 22 E
Olevsk, *Ukraine* **17 C14** 51 12N 27 39 E
Olga, *Russia* **27 E14** 43 50N 135 14 E
Olga, L., *Canada* **70 C4** 49 47N 77 15W
Olga, Mt., *Australia* **61 E5** 25 20S 130 50 E
Olhão, *Portugal* **19 D2** 37 3N 7 48W
Olifants →, *Africa* **57 C5** 23 57S 31 58 E
Olifantshoek, *S. Africa* **56 D3** 27 57S 22 42 E
Ólimbos, Óros, *Greece* **21 D10** 40 6N 22 23 E
Olímpia, *Brazil* **95 A6** 20 44S 48 54W
Olinda, *Brazil* **93 E12** 8 1S 34 51W
Oliva, *Argentina* **94 C3** 32 0S 63 38W
Olivehurst, *U.S.A.* **84 F5** 39 6N 121 34W
Oliveira, *Brazil* **93 H10** 20 39S 44 50W
Olivenza, *Spain* **19 C2** 38 41N 7 9W
Oliver, *Canada* **72 D5** 49 13N 119 37W
Oliver L., *Canada* **73 B8** 56 56N 103 22W
Ollagüe, *Chile* **94 A2** 21 15S 68 10W
Olney, *Ill., U.S.A.* **76 F1** 38 44N 88 5W
Olney, *Tex., U.S.A.* **81 J5** 33 22N 98 45W
Olomane →, *Canada* **71 B7** 50 14N 60 37W
Olomouc, *Czech.* **17 D9** 49 38N 17 12 E
Olonets, *Russia* **24 B5** 61 0N 32 54 E
Olongapo, *Phil.* **37 B6** 14 50N 120 18 E
Olot, *Spain* **19 A7** 42 11N 2 30 E
Olovyannaya, *Russia* **27 D12** 50 58N 115 35 E
Oloy →, *Russia* **27 C16** 66 29N 159 29 E
Olsztyn, *Poland* **17 B11** 53 48N 20 29 E
Olt →, *Romania* **17 G13** 43 43N 24 51 E
Olteniţa, *Romania* **17 F14** 44 7N 26 42 E
Olton, *U.S.A.* **81 H3** 34 11N 102 8W
Olymbos, *Cyprus* **23 D12** 35 21N 33 45 E
Olympia, *Greece* **21 F9** 37 39N 21 39 E
Olympia, *U.S.A.* **84 D4** 47 3N 122 53W
Olympic Mts., *U.S.A.* **84 C3** 47 55N 123 45W
Olympic Nat. Park, *U.S.A.* **84 C3** 47 48N 123 30W
Olympus, *Cyprus* **23 E11** 34 56N 32 52 E
Olympus, Mt. = Ólimbos, Óros, *Greece* **21 D10** 40 6N 22 23 E
Olympus, Mt., *U.S.A.* **84 C3** 47 48N 123 43W
Olyphant, *U.S.A.* **79 E9** 41 27N 75 36W
Om →, *Russia* **26 D8** 54 59N 73 22 E
Om Koi, *Thailand* **38 D2** 17 48N 98 22 E
Ōma, *Japan* **30 D10** 41 45N 141 5 E
Ōmachi, *Japan* **31 F8** 36 30N 137 50 E
Omae-Zaki, *Japan* **31 G9** 34 36N 138 14 E
Ōmagari, *Japan* **30 E10** 39 27N 140 29 E
Omagh, *U.K.* **13 B4** 54 36N 7 19W
Omagh □, *U.K.* **13 B4** 54 35N 7 15W
Omaha, *U.S.A.* **80 E7** 41 17N 95 58W
Omak, *U.S.A.* **82 B4** 48 25N 119 31W
Omalos, *Greece* **23 D5** 35 19N 23 55 E
Oman ■, *Asia* **46 C6** 23 0N 58 0 E
Oman, G. of, *Asia* **45 E8** 24 30N 58 30 E
Omaruru, *Namibia* **56 C2** 21 26S 16 0 E
Omaruru →, *Namibia* **56 C1** 22 7S 14 15 E
Omate, *Peru* **92 G4** 16 45S 71 0W
Ombai, Selat, *Indonesia* **37 F6** 8 30S 124 50 E
Omboué, *Gabon* **52 E1** 1 35S 9 15 E
Ombrone →, *Italy* **20 C4** 42 42N 11 5 E
Omdurmân, *Sudan* **51 E11** 15 40N 32 28 E
Omeonga, *Zaïre* **54 C1** 3 40S 24 22 E
Ometepe, I. de, *Nic.* **88 D2** 11 32N 85 35W
Ometepec, *Mexico* **87 D5** 16 39N 98 23W
Ominato, *Japan* **30 D10** 41 17N 141 10 E
Omineca →, *Canada* **72 B4** 56 3N 124 16W
Omitara, *Namibia* **56 C2** 22 16S 18 2 E
Ōmiya, *Japan* **31 G9** 35 54N 139 38 E
Ommen, *Neths.* **15 B6** 52 31N 6 26 E
Ömnögovĭ □, *Mongolia* **34 C3** 43 15N 104 0 E
Omo →, *Ethiopia* **51 G12** 6 25N 36 10 E
Omodhos, *Cyprus* **23 E11** 34 51N 32 48 E
Omolon →, *Russia* **27 C16** 68 42N 158 36 E
Omono-Gawa →, *Japan* **30 E10** 39 46N 140 3 E
Omsk, *Russia* **26 D8** 55 0N 73 12 E
Omsukchan, *Russia* **27 C16** 62 32N 155 48 E
Ōmu, *Japan* **30 B11** 44 34N 142 58 E
Omul, Vf., *Romania* **17 F13** 45 27N 25 29 E
Ōmura, *Japan* **31 H4** 32 56N 129 57 E
Omuramba Omatako →, *Namibia* **53 H4** 17 45S 20 25 E
Ōmuta, *Japan* **31 H5** 33 5N 130 26 E
Onaga, *U.S.A.* **80 F6** 39 29N 96 10W
Onalaska, *U.S.A.* **80 D9** 43 53N 91 14W
Onamia, *U.S.A.* **80 B8** 46 4N 93 40W
Onancock, *U.S.A.* **76 G8** 37 43N 75 45W
Onang, *Indonesia* **37 E5** 3 2S 118 49 E
Onaping L., *Canada* **70 C3** 47 3N 81 30W
Onavas, *Mexico* **86 B3** 28 28N 109 30W
Onawa, *U.S.A.* **80 D6** 42 2N 96 6W
Onaway, *U.S.A.* **76 C3** 45 21N 84 14W
Oncócua, *Angola* **56 B1** 16 30S 13 25 E
Onda, *Spain* **19 C5** 39 55N 0 17W
Ondaejin, *N. Korea* **35 D15** 41 34N 129 40 E
Ondangua, *Namibia* **56 B2** 17 57S 16 4 E
Ondjiva, *Angola* **56 B2** 16 48S 15 50 E
Ondo, *Nigeria* **50 G5** 7 4N 4 47 E
Öndörshil, *Mongolia* **34 B5** 45 13N 108 5 E
Öndverðarnes, *Iceland* **8 D1** 64 52N 24 0W
Onega, *Russia* **24 B6** 64 0N 38 10 E
Onega →, *Russia* **24 B6** 63 58N 38 2 E
Onega, G. of = Onezhskaya Guba, *Russia* **24 B6** 64 24N 36 38 E
Onega, L. = Onezhskoye Ozero, *Russia* **24 B6** 61 44N 35 22 E
Onehunga, *N.Z.* **59 G5** 36 55S 174 48 E
Oneida, *U.S.A.* **79 C9** 43 6N 75 39W
Oneida L., *U.S.A.* **79 C9** 43 12N 75 54W
O'Neill, *U.S.A.* **80 D5** 42 27N 98 39W
Onekotan, Ostrov, *Russia* **27 E16** 49 25N 154 45 E
Onema, *Zaïre* **54 C1** 4 35S 24 30 E
Oneonta, *Ala., U.S.A.* **77 J2** 33 57N 86 28W
Oneonta, *N.Y., U.S.A.* **79 D9** 42 27N 75 4W
Oneşti, *Romania* **17 E14** 46 15N 26 45 E
Onezhskaya Guba, *Russia* **24 B6** 64 24N 36 38 E
Onezhskoye Ozero, *Russia* **24 B6** 61 44N 35 22 E
Ongarue, *N.Z.* **59 H5** 38 42S 175 19 E
Ongerup, *Australia* **61 F2** 33 58S 118 28 E
Ongjin, *N. Korea* **35 F13** 37 56N 125 21 E
Ongkharak, *Thailand* **38 E3** 14 8N 101 1 E
Ongniud Qi, *China* **35 C10** 43 0N 118 38 E
Ongoka, *Zaïre* **54 C2** 1 20S 26 0 E
Ongole, *India* **40 M12** 15 33N 80 2 E
Ongon, *Mongolia* **34 B7** 45 41N 113 5 E
Onguren, *Russia* **27 D11** 53 38N 107 36 E
Onida, *U.S.A.* **80 C4** 44 42N 100 4W
Onilahy →, *Madag.* **57 C7** 23 34S 43 45 E
Onitsha, *Nigeria* **50 G6** 6 6N 6 42 E
Onoda, *Japan* **31 G5** 34 2N 131 25 E
Onpyŏng-ni, *S. Korea* **35 H14** 33 25N 126 55 E
Onslow, *Australia* **60 D2** 21 40S 115 12 E
Onslow B., *U.S.A.* **77 H7** 34 20N 77 15W
Onstwedde, *Neths.* **15 A7** 53 2N 7 4 E
Ontake-San, *Japan* **31 G8** 35 53N 137 29 E
Ontario, *Calif., U.S.A.* **85 L9** 34 4N 117 39W
Ontario, *Oreg., U.S.A.* **82 D5** 44 2N 116 58W
Ontario □, *Canada* **70 B2** 48 0N 83 0W
Ontario, L., *U.S.A.* **70 D4** 43 20N 78 0W
Ontonagon, *U.S.A.* **80 B10** 46 52N 89 19W
Onyx, *U.S.A.* **85 K8** 35 41N 118 14W
Oodnadatta, *Australia* **63 D2** 27 33S 135 30 E
Ooldea, *Australia* **61 F5** 30 27S 131 50 E
Oombulgurri, *Australia* **60 C4** 15 15S 127 45 E
Oona River, *Canada* **72 C2** 53 57N 130 16W
Oorindi, *Australia* **62 C3** 20 40S 141 1 E
Oost-Vlaanderen □, *Belgium* **15 C3** 51 5N 3 50 E
Oostende, *Belgium* **15 C2** 51 15N 2 54 E
Oosterhout, *Neths.* **15 C4** 51 39N 4 47 E
Oosterschelde, *Neths.* **15 C4** 51 33N 4 0 E
Ootacamund, *India* **40 P10** 11 30N 76 44 E
Ootsa L., *Canada* **72 C3** 53 50N 126 2W
Opala, *Russia* **27 D16** 51 58N 156 30 E
Opala, *Zaïre* **54 C1** 0 40S 24 20 E
Opanake, *Sri Lanka* **40 R12** 6 35N 80 40 E
Opasatika, *Canada* **70 C3** 49 30N 82 50W
Opasquia, *Canada* **73 C10** 53 16N 93 34W
Opava, *Czech.* **17 D9** 49 57N 17 58 E
Opelousas, *U.S.A.* **81 K8** 30 32N 92 5W
Opémisca, L., *Canada* **70 C5** 49 56N 74 52W
Opheim, *U.S.A.* **82 B10** 48 51N 106 24W
Ophthalmia Ra., *Australia* **60 D2** 23 15S 119 30 E
Opinaca →, *Canada* **70 B4** 52 15N 78 2W
Opinaca L., *Canada* **70 B4** 52 39N 76 20W
Opiskotish, L., *Canada* **71 B6** 53 10N 67 50W
Opole, *Poland* **17 C9** 50 42N 17 58 E
Oporto = Porto, *Portugal* **19 B1** 41 8N 8 40W
Opotiki, *N.Z.* **59 H6** 38 1S 177 19 E
Opp, *U.S.A.* **77 K2** 31 17N 86 16W
Oppdal, *Norway* **9 E13** 62 35N 9 41 E
Opua, *N.Z.* **59 F5** 35 19S 174 9 E
Opunake, *N.Z.* **59 H4** 39 26S 173 52 E
Ora, *Cyprus* **23 E12** 34 51N 33 12 E
Ora Banda, *Australia* **61 F3** 30 20S 121 0 E
Oracle, *U.S.A.* **83 K8** 32 37N 110 46W
Oradea, *Romania* **17 E11** 47 2N 21 58 E
Öræfajökull, *Iceland* **8 D5** 64 2N 16 39W
Orai, *India* **43 G8** 25 58N 79 30 E
Oral = Zhayyq →, *Kazakstan* **25 E9** 47 0N 51 48 E
Oral, *Kazakstan* **24 D9** 51 20N 51 20 E
Oran, *Algeria* **50 A4** 35 45N 0 39W
Oran, *Argentina* **94 A3** 23 10S 64 20W
Orange = Oranje →, *S. Africa* **56 D2** 28 41S 16 28 E
Orange, *Australia* **63 E4** 33 15S 149 7 E
Orange, *France* **18 D6** 44 8N 4 47 E
Orange, *Calif., U.S.A.* **85 M9** 33 47N 117 51W
Orange, *Mass., U.S.A.* **79 D12** 42 35N 72 19W
Orange, *Tex., U.S.A.* **81 K8** 30 6N 93 44W
Orange, *Va., U.S.A.* **76 F6** 38 15N 78 7W
Orange, C., *Brazil* **93 C8** 4 20N 51 30W
Orange Cove, *U.S.A.* **84 J7** 36 38N 119 19W
Orange Free State □ = Free State □, *S. Africa* **56 D4** 28 30S 27 0 E
Orange Grove, *U.S.A.* **81 M6** 27 58N 97 56W
Orange Walk, *Belize* **87 D7** 18 6N 88 33W
Orangeburg, *U.S.A.* **77 J5** 33 30N 80 52W
Orangeville, *Canada* **70 D3** 43 55N 80 5W
Oranienburg, *Germany* **16 B7** 52 45N 13 14 E
Oranje →, *S. Africa* **56 D2** 28 41S 16 28 E
Oranje Vrystaat □ = Free State □, *S. Africa* **56 D4** 28 30S 27 0 E
Oranjemund, *Namibia* **56 D2** 28 38S 16 29 E
Oranjerivier, *S. Africa* **56 D3** 29 40S 24 12 E
Oras, *Phil.* **37 B7** 12 9N 125 28 E
Oraşul Stalin = Braşov, *Romania* **17 F13** 45 38N 25 35 E
Orbetello, *Italy* **20 C4** 42 27N 11 13 E
Orbost, *Australia* **63 F4** 37 40S 148 29 E
Orchila, I., *Venezuela* **92 A5** 11 48N 66 10W
Orcutt, *U.S.A.* **85 L6** 34 52N 120 27W
Ord →, *Australia* **60 C4** 15 33S 128 15 E
Ord, Mt., *Australia* **60 C4** 17 20S 125 34 E
Orderville, *U.S.A.* **83 H7** 37 17N 112 38W
Ordos = Mu Us Shamo, *China* **34 E5** 39 0N 109 0 E
Ordway, *U.S.A.* **80 F3** 38 13N 103 46W
Ordzhonikidze = Vladikavkaz, *Russia* **25 F7** 43 0N 44 35 E
Ore, *Zaïre* **54 B2** 3 17N 29 30 E
Ore Mts. = Erzgebirge, *Germany* **16 C7** 50 27N 12 55 E
Örebro, *Sweden* **9 G16** 59 20N 15 18 E
Oregon, *U.S.A.* **80 D10** 42 1N 89 20W
Oregon □, *U.S.A.* **82 E3** 44 0N 121 0W
Oregon City, *U.S.A.* **84 E4** 45 21N 122 36W
Orekhovo-Zuyevo, *Russia* **24 C6** 55 50N 38 55 E
Orel, *Russia* **24 D6** 52 57N 36 3 E
Orem, *U.S.A.* **82 F8** 40 19N 111 42W
Ören, *Turkey* **21 F12** 37 3N 27 57 E
Orenburg, *Russia* **24 D10** 51 45N 55 6 E
Orense, *Spain* **19 A2** 42 19N 7 55W
Orepuki, *N.Z.* **59 M1** 46 19S 167 46 E
Orestiás, *Greece* **21 D12** 41 30N 26 33 E
Orford Ness, *U.K.* **11 E9** 52 5N 1 35 E
Organos, Pta. de los, *Canary Is.* **22 F2** 28 12N 17 17W
Orgaz, *Spain* **19 C4** 39 39N 3 53W
Orgeyev = Orhei, *Moldova* **17 E15** 47 24N 28 50 E
Orhaneli, *Turkey* **21 E13** 39 54N 28 59 E
Orhangazi, *Turkey* **21 D13** 40 29N 29 18 E
Orhei, *Moldova* **17 E15** 47 24N 28 50 E
Orhon Gol →, *Mongolia* **32 A5** 50 21N 106 0 E
Orient, *Australia* **63 D3** 28 7S 142 50 E
Oriental, Cordillera, *Colombia* **92 B4** 6 0N 73 0W
Oriente, *Argentina* **94 D3** 38 44S 60 37W
Orihuela, *Spain* **19 C5** 38 7N 0 55W
Orinoco →, *Venezuela* **92 B6** 9 15N 61 30W
Orissa □, *India* **41 K14** 20 0N 84 0 E
Orissaare, *Estonia* **9 G20** 58 34N 23 5 E
Oristano, *Italy* **20 E3** 39 54N 8 36 E
Oristano, G. di, *Italy* **20 E3** 39 50N 8 29 E
Orizaba, *Mexico* **87 D5** 18 51N 97 6W
Orkanger, *Norway* **8 E13** 63 18N 9 52 E
Orkla →, *Norway* **8 E13** 63 18N 9 51 E
Orkney, *S. Africa* **56 D4** 26 58S 26 40 E
Orkney □, *U.K.* **12 C6** 59 2N 3 13W
Orkney Is., *U.K.* **12 C6** 59 0N 3 0W
Orland, *U.S.A.* **84 F4** 39 45N 122 12W
Orlando, *U.S.A.* **77 L5** 28 33N 81 23W
Orléanais, *France* **18 C5** 48 0N 2 0 E
Orléans, *France* **18 C4** 47 54N 1 52 E
Orleans, *U.S.A.* **79 B12** 44 49N 72 12W
Orléans, I. d', *Canada* **71 C5** 46 54N 70 58W
Ormara, *Pakistan* **40 G4** 25 16N 64 33 E
Ormoc, *Phil.* **37 B6** 11 0N 124 37 E
Ormond, *N.Z.* **59 H6** 38 33S 177 56 E
Ormond Beach, *U.S.A.* **77 L5** 29 17N 81 3W
Ormstown, *Canada* **79 A11** 45 8N 74 0W
Örnsköldsvik, *Sweden* **8 E18** 63 17N 18 40 E
Oro, *N. Korea* **35 D14** 40 1N 127 27 E
Oro →, *Mexico* **86 B3** 25 35N 105 2W
Oro Grande, *U.S.A.* **85 L9** 34 36N 117 20W
Orocué, *Colombia* **92 C4** 4 48N 71 20W
Orogrande, *U.S.A.* **83 K10** 32 24N 106 5W
Orol Dengizi = Aral Sea, *Asia* **26 E7** 44 30N 60 0 E
Oromocto, *Canada* **71 C6** 45 54N 66 29W
Orono, *Canada* **78 C6** 43 59N 78 37W
Oroqen Zizhiqi, *China* **33 A7** 50 34N 123 43 E
Oroquieta, *Phil.* **37 C6** 8 32N 123 44 E
Orós, *Brazil* **93 E11** 6 15S 38 55W
Orosháza, *Hungary* **17 E11** 46 32N 20 42 E
Orotukan, *Russia* **27 C16** 62 16N 151 42 E
Oroville, *Calif., U.S.A.* **84 F5** 39 31N 121 33W
Oroville, *Wash., U.S.A.* **82 B4** 48 56N 119 26W
Oroville, L., *U.S.A.* **84 F5** 39 33N 121 29W
Orroroo, *Australia* **63 E2** 32 43S 138 38 E
Orrville, *U.S.A.* **78 F3** 40 50N 81 46W
Orsha, *Belarus* **24 D5** 54 30N 30 25 E
Orsk, *Russia* **24 D10** 51 12N 58 34 E
Orşova, *Romania* **17 F12** 44 41N 22 25 E
Ortaca, *Turkey* **21 F13** 36 49N 28 45 E
Ortegal, C., *Spain* **19 A2** 43 43N 7 52W
Orthez, *France* **18 E3** 43 29N 0 48W
Ortigueira, *Spain* **19 A2** 43 40N 7 50W
Orting, *U.S.A.* **84 C4** 47 6N 122 12W
Ortles, *Italy* **20 A4** 46 31N 10 33 E
Ortón →, *Bolivia* **92 F5** 10 50S 67 0W
Orūmīyeh, *Iran* **44 B5** 37 40N 45 0 E
Orūmīyeh, Daryācheh-ye, *Iran* **44 B5** 37 50N 45 30 E
Oruro, *Bolivia* **92 G5** 18 0S 67 9W
Orust, *Sweden* **9 G14** 58 10N 11 40 E
Oruzgān □, *Afghan.* **40 C5** 33 30N 66 0 E
Orvieto, *Italy* **20 C5** 42 43N 12 7 E
Orwell, *U.S.A.* **78 E4** 41 32N 80 52W
Orwell →, *U.K.* **11 E9** 51 59N 1 18 E
Oryakhovo, *Bulgaria* **21 C10** 43 40N 23 57 E
Osa, *Russia* **24 C10** 57 17N 55 26 E
Osa, Pen. de, *Costa Rica* **88 E3** 8 0N 84 0W
Osage, *Iowa, U.S.A.* **80 D8** 43 17N 92 49W
Osage, *Wyo., U.S.A.* **80 D2** 43 59N 104 25W
Osage →, *U.S.A.* **80 F9** 38 35N 91 57W
Osage City, *U.S.A.* **80 F7** 38 38N 95 50W
Ōsaka, *Japan* **31 G7** 34 40N 135 30 E
Osan, *S. Korea* **35 F14** 37 11N 127 4 E
Osawatomie, *U.S.A.* **80 F7** 38 31N 94 57W
Osborne, *U.S.A.* **80 F5** 39 26N 98 42W
Osceola, *Ark., U.S.A.* **81 H10** 35 42N 89 58W
Osceola, *Iowa, U.S.A.* **80 E8** 41 2N 93 46W
Oscoda, *U.S.A.* **78 B1** 44 26N 83 20W
Ösel = Saaremaa, *Estonia* **9 G20** 58 30N 22 30 E
Osh, *Kyrgyzstan* **26 E8** 40 37N 72 49 E
Oshawa, *Canada* **70 D4** 43 50N 78 50W
Oshkosh, *Nebr., U.S.A.* **80 E3** 41 24N 102 21W
Oshkosh, *Wis., U.S.A.* **80 C10** 44 1N 88 33W
Oshmyany = Ashmyany, *Belarus* **9 J21** 54 26N 25 52 E

Oshnovīyeh

Oshnovīyeh, *Iran* 44 B5 37 2N 45 6 E
Oshogbo, *Nigeria* 50 G5 7 48N 4 37 E
Oshtorīnān, *Iran* 45 C6 34 1N 48 38 E
Oshwe, *Zaïre* 52 E3 3 25S 19 28 E
Osijek, *Croatia* 21 B8 45 34N 18 41 E
Osipenko = Berdyansk, *Ukraine* 25 E6 46 45N 36 50 E
Osipovichi = Asipovichy, *Belarus* 17 B15 53 19N 28 33 E
Osizweni, *S. Africa* 57 D5 27 49S 30 7 E
Oskaloosa, *U.S.A.* 80 E8 41 18N 92 39W
Oskarshamn, *Sweden* 9 H17 57 15N 16 27 E
Oskélanéo, *Canada* 70 C4 48 5N 75 15W
Öskemen, *Kazakstan* 26 E9 50 0N 82 36 E
Oslo, *Norway* 9 G14 59 55N 10 45 E
Oslob, *Phil.* 37 C6 9 31N 123 26 E
Oslofjorden, *Norway* 9 G14 59 20N 10 35 E
Osmanabad, *India* 40 K10 18 5N 76 10 E
Osmaniye, *Turkey* 25 G6 37 5N 36 10 E
Osnabrück, *Germany* 16 B5 52 17N 8 3 E
Osorio, *Brazil* 95 B5 29 53S 50 17W
Osorno, *Chile* 96 E2 40 25S 73 0W
Osoyoos, *Canada* 72 D5 49 0N 119 30W
Osøyri, *Norway* 9 F11 60 9N 5 30 E
Ospika →, *Canada* 72 B4 56 20N 124 0W
Osprey Reef, *Australia* 62 A4 13 52S 146 36 E
Oss, *Neths.* 15 C5 51 46N 5 32 E
Ossa, Mt., *Australia* 62 G4 41 52S 146 3 E
Óssa, Oros, *Greece* 21 E10 39 47N 22 42 E
Ossabaw I., *U.S.A.* 77 K5 31 50N 81 5W
Ossining, *U.S.A.* 79 E11 41 10N 73 55W
Ossipee, *U.S.A.* 79 C13 43 41N 71 7W
Ossokmanuan L., *Canada* 71 B7 53 25N 65 0W
Ossora, *Russia* 27 D17 59 20N 163 13 E
Ostend = Oostende, *Belgium* 15 C2 51 15N 2 54 E
Oster, *Ukraine* 17 C16 50 57N 30 53 E
Österdalälven, *Sweden* 9 F16 61 30N 13 45 E
Østerdalen, *Norway* 9 F14 61 40N 10 50 E
Östersund, *Sweden* 8 E16 63 10N 14 38 E
Ostfriesische Inseln, *Germany* 16 B4 53 42N 7 0 E
Ostrava, *Czech.* 17 D10 49 51N 18 18 E
Ostróda, *Poland* 17 B10 53 42N 19 58 E
Ostroh, *Ukraine* 17 C14 50 20N 26 30 E
Ostrołęka, *Poland* 17 B11 53 4N 21 32 E
Ostrów Mazowiecka, *Poland* 17 B11 52 50N 21 51 E
Ostrów Wielkopolski, *Poland* 17 C9 51 36N 17 44 E
Ostrowiec-Świętokrzyski, *Poland* 17 C11 50 55N 21 22 E
Ostuni, *Italy* 21 D7 40 44N 17 35 E
Ōsumi-Kaikyō, *Japan* 31 J5 30 55N 131 0 E
Ōsumi-Shotō, *Japan* 31 J5 30 30N 130 0 E
Osuna, *Spain* 19 D3 37 14N 5 8W
Oswego, *U.S.A.* 79 C8 43 27N 76 31W
Oswestry, *U.K.* 10 E4 52 52N 3 3W
Oświęcim, *Poland* 17 C10 50 2N 19 11 E
Otago □, *N.Z.* 59 L2 45 15S 170 0 E
Otago Harbour, *N.Z.* 59 L3 45 47S 170 42 E
Ōtake, *Japan* 31 G6 34 12N 132 13 E
Otaki, *N.Z.* 59 J5 40 45S 175 10 E
Otaru, *Japan* 30 C10 43 10N 141 0 E
Otaru-Wan = Ishikari-Wan, *Japan* 30 C10 43 25N 141 1 E
Otavalo, *Ecuador* 92 C3 0 13N 78 20W
Otavi, *Namibia* 56 B2 19 40S 17 24 E
Otchinjau, *Angola* 56 B1 16 30S 13 56 E
Othello, *U.S.A.* 82 C4 46 50N 119 10W
Otira Gorge, *N.Z.* 59 K3 42 53S 171 33 E
Otis, *U.S.A.* 80 E3 40 9N 102 58W
Otjiwarongo, *Namibia* 56 C2 20 30S 16 33 E
Otoineppu, *Japan* 30 B11 44 44N 142 16 E
Otorohanga, *N.Z.* 59 H5 38 12S 175 14 E
Otoskwin →, *Canada* 70 B2 52 13N 88 6W
Otosquen, *Canada* 73 C8 53 17N 102 1W
Otra →, *Norway* 9 G13 58 9N 8 1 E
Otranto, *Italy* 21 D8 40 9N 18 28 E
Otranto, C. d', *Italy* 21 D8 40 7N 18 30 E
Otranto, Str. of, *Italy* 21 D8 40 15N 18 40 E
Otse, *S. Africa* 56 D4 25 2S 25 45 E
Ōtsu, *Japan* 31 G7 35 0N 135 50 E
Ōtsuki, *Japan* 31 G9 35 36N 138 57 E
Ottawa = Outaouais →, *Canada* 70 C5 45 27N 74 8W
Ottawa, *Canada* 70 C4 45 27N 75 42W
Ottawa, *Ill., U.S.A.* 80 E10 41 21N 88 51W
Ottawa, *Kans., U.S.A.* 80 F7 38 37N 95 16W
Ottawa Is., *Canada* 69 C11 59 35N 80 10W
Otter L., *Canada* 73 B8 55 35N 104 39W
Otter Rapids, *Ont., Canada* 70 B3 50 11N 81 39W
Otter Rapids, *Sask., Canada* 73 B8 55 38N 104 44W
Otterville, *Canada* 78 D4 42 55N 80 36W
Otto Beit Bridge, *Zimbabwe* 55 F2 15 59S 28 56 E
Ottosdal, *S. Africa* 56 D4 26 46S 25 59 E
Ottumwa, *U.S.A.* 80 E8 41 1N 92 25W
Oturkpo, *Nigeria* 50 G6 7 16N 8 8 E
Otway, B., *Chile* 96 G2 53 30S 74 0W
Otway, C., *Australia* 63 F3 38 52S 143 30 E
Otwock, *Poland* 17 B11 52 5N 21 20 E
Ou →, *Laos* 38 B4 20 4N 102 13 E
Ou Neua, *Laos* 38 A3 22 18N 101 48 E
Ou-Sammyaku, *Japan* 30 E10 39 20N 140 35 E
Ouachita →, *U.S.A.* 81 K9 31 38N 91 49W
Ouachita, L., *U.S.A.* 81 H8 34 34N 93 12W
Ouachita Mts., *U.S.A.* 81 H7 34 40N 94 25W
Ouadâne, *Mauritania* 50 D2 20 50N 11 40W
Ouadda, *C.A.R.* 51 G9 8 15N 22 20 E
Ouagadougou, *Burkina Faso* 50 F4 12 25N 1 30W
Ouahran = Oran, *Algeria* 50 A4 35 45N 0 39W
Ouallene, *Algeria* 50 D5 24 41N 1 11 E
Ouanda Djallé, *C.A.R.* 51 G9 8 55N 22 53 E
Ouango, *C.A.R.* 52 D4 4 19N 22 30 E
Ouargla, *Algeria* 50 B6 31 59N 5 16 E
Ouarzazate, *Morocco* 50 B3 30 55N 6 50W
Oubangi →, *Zaïre* 52 E3 0 30S 17 50 E
Ouddorp, *Neths.* 15 C3 51 50N 3 57 E
Oude Rijn →, *Neths.* 15 B4 52 12N 4 24 E
Oudenaarde, *Belgium* 15 D3 50 50N 3 37 E
Oudtshoorn, *S. Africa* 56 E3 33 35S 22 14 E
Ouessant, I. d', *France* 18 B1 48 28N 5 6W
Ouesso, *Congo* 52 D3 1 37N 16 5 E
Ouest, Pte., *Canada* 71 C7 49 52N 64 40W
Ouezzane, *Morocco* 50 B3 34 51N 5 35W
Ouidah, *Benin* 50 G5 6 25N 2 0 E
Oujda, *Morocco* 50 B4 34 41N 1 55W
Oujeft, *Mauritania* 50 D2 20 2N 13 0W
Oulainen, *Finland* 8 D21 64 17N 24 47 E
Ouled Djellal, *Algeria* 50 B6 34 28N 5 2 E
Oulu, *Finland* 8 D21 65 1N 25 29 E
Oulujärvi, *Finland* 8 D22 64 25N 27 15 E
Oulujoki →, *Finland* 8 D21 65 1N 25 30 E
Oum Chalouba, *Chad* 51 E9 15 48N 20 46 E
Ounasjoki →, *Finland* 8 C21 66 31N 25 40 E
Ounguati, *Namibia* 56 C2 22 0S 15 46 E
Ounianga-Kébir, *Chad* 51 E9 19 4N 20 29 E
Ounianga Sérir, *Chad* 51 E9 18 54N 20 51 E
Our →, *Lux.* 15 E6 49 55N 6 5 E
Ouray, *U.S.A.* 83 G10 38 1N 107 40W
Ourense = Orense, *Spain* 19 A2 42 19N 7 55W
Ouricuri, *Brazil* 93 E10 7 53S 40 5W
Ourinhos, *Brazil* 95 A6 23 0S 49 54W
Ouro Fino, *Brazil* 95 A6 22 16S 46 25W
Ouro Prêto, *Brazil* 95 A7 20 20S 43 30W
Ourthe →, *Belgium* 15 D5 50 29N 5 35 E
Ouse, *Australia* 62 G4 42 38S 146 42 E
Ouse →, *E. Susx., U.K.* 11 G8 50 47N 0 4 E
Ouse →, *N. Yorks., U.K.* 10 C8 53 44N 0 55W
Outaouais →, *Canada* 70 C5 45 27N 74 8W
Outardes →, *Canada* 71 C6 49 24N 69 30W
Outer Hebrides, *U.K.* 12 D1 57 30N 7 40W
Outer I., *Canada* 71 B8 51 10N 58 35W
Outjo, *Namibia* 56 C2 20 5S 16 7 E
Outlook, *Canada* 73 C7 51 30N 107 0W
Outlook, *U.S.A.* 80 A2 48 53N 104 47W
Outokumpu, *Finland* 8 E23 62 43N 29 1 E
Ouyen, *Australia* 63 F3 35 1S 142 22 E
Ovalau, *Fiji* 59 C8 17 40S 178 48 E
Ovalle, *Chile* 94 C1 30 33S 71 18W
Ovamboland, *Namibia* 56 B2 18 30S 16 0 E
Overflakkee, *Neths.* 15 C4 51 44N 4 10 E
Overijssel □, *Neths.* 15 B6 52 25N 6 35 E
Overland Park, *U.S.A.* 80 F7 38 55N 94 50W
Overpelt, *Belgium* 15 C5 51 12N 5 20 E
Overton, *U.S.A.* 85 J12 36 33N 114 27W
Övertorneå, *Sweden* 8 C20 66 23N 23 38 E
Ovid, *U.S.A.* 80 E3 40 58N 102 23W
Oviedo, *Spain* 19 A3 43 25N 5 50W
Oviši, *Latvia* 9 H19 57 33N 21 44 E
Övör Hangay □, *Mongolia* 34 B2 45 0N 102 30 E
Øvre Årdal, *Norway* 9 F12 61 19N 7 48 E
Ovruch, *Ukraine* 17 C15 51 25N 28 45 E
Owaka, *N.Z.* 59 M2 46 27S 169 40 E
Owambo = Ovamboland, *Namibia* 56 B2 18 30S 16 0 E
Owase, *Japan* 31 G8 34 7N 136 12 E
Owatonna, *U.S.A.* 80 C8 44 5N 93 14W
Owbeh, *Afghan.* 40 B3 34 28N 63 10 E
Owego, *U.S.A.* 79 D8 42 6N 76 16W
Owen Falls Dam, *Uganda* 54 B3 0 30N 33 5 E
Owen Sound, *Canada* 70 D3 44 35N 80 55W
Owendo, *Gabon* 52 D1 0 17N 9 30 E
Owens →, *U.S.A.* 84 J9 36 32N 117 59W
Owens L., *U.S.A.* 85 J9 36 26N 117 57W
Owensboro, *U.S.A.* 76 G2 37 46N 87 7W
Owensville, *U.S.A.* 80 F9 38 21N 91 30W
Owl →, *Canada* 73 B10 57 51N 92 44W
Owo, *Nigeria* 50 G6 7 10N 5 39 E
Owosso, *U.S.A.* 76 D3 43 0N 84 10W
Owyhee, *U.S.A.* 82 F5 41 57N 116 6W
Owyhee →, *U.S.A.* 82 E5 43 49N 117 2W
Owyhee, L., *U.S.A.* 82 E5 43 38N 117 14W
Öxarfjörður, *Iceland* 8 C5 66 15N 16 45W
Oxelösund, *Sweden* 9 G17 58 43N 17 15 E
Oxford, *N.Z.* 59 K4 43 18S 172 11 E
Oxford, *U.K.* 11 F6 51 46N 1 15W
Oxford, *Miss., U.S.A.* 81 H10 34 22N 89 31W
Oxford, *N.C., U.S.A.* 77 G6 36 19N 78 35W
Oxford, *Ohio, U.S.A.* 76 F3 39 31N 84 45W
Oxford L., *Canada* 73 C9 54 51N 95 37W
Oxfordshire □, *U.K.* 11 F6 51 48N 1 16W
Oxley, *Australia* 63 E3 34 11S 144 6 E
Oxnard, *U.S.A.* 85 L7 34 12N 119 11W
Oxus = Amudarya →, *Uzbekistan* 26 E6 43 58N 59 34 E
Oya, *Malaysia* 36 D4 2 55N 111 55 E
Oyama, *Japan* 31 F9 36 18N 139 48 E
Oyem, *Gabon* 52 D2 1 34N 11 31 E
Oyen, *Canada* 73 C6 51 22N 110 28W
Oykel →, *U.K.* 12 D4 57 56N 4 26W
Oymyakon, *Russia* 27 C15 63 25N 142 44 E
Oyo, *Nigeria* 50 G5 7 46N 3 56 E
Oyster Bay, *U.S.A.* 79 F11 40 52N 73 32W
Ōyubari, *Japan* 30 C11 43 1N 142 5 E
Ozamiz, *Phil.* 37 C6 8 15N 123 50 E
Ozark, *Ala., U.S.A.* 77 K3 31 28N 85 39W
Ozark, *Ark., U.S.A.* 81 H8 35 29N 93 50W
Ozark, *Mo., U.S.A.* 81 G8 37 1N 93 12W
Ozark Plateau, *U.S.A.* 81 G9 37 20N 91 40W
Ozarks, L. of the, *U.S.A.* 80 F8 38 12N 92 38W
Ózd, *Hungary* 17 D11 48 14N 20 15 E
Ozette L., *U.S.A.* 84 B2 48 6N 124 38W
Ozona, *U.S.A.* 81 K4 30 43N 101 12W
Ozuluama, *Mexico* 87 C5 21 40N 97 50W

P

Pa-an, *Burma* 41 L20 16 51N 97 40 E
Pa Mong Dam, *Thailand* 38 D4 18 0N 102 22 E
Paamiut = Frederikshåb, *Greenland* 4 C5 62 0N 49 43W
Paarl, *S. Africa* 56 E2 33 45S 18 56 E
Paauilo, *U.S.A.* 74 H17 20 2N 155 22W
Pab Hills, *Pakistan* 42 F2 26 30N 66 45 E
Pabianice, *Poland* 17 C10 51 40N 19 20 E
Pabna, *Bangla.* 41 G16 24 1N 89 18 E
Pabo, *Uganda* 54 B3 3 1N 32 10 E
Pacaja →, *Brazil* 93 D8 1 56S 50 50W
Pacaraima, Sierra, *Venezuela* 92 C6 4 0N 62 30W
Pacasmayo, *Peru* 92 E3 7 20S 79 35W
Pachhar, *India* 42 G7 24 40N 77 42 E
Pachpadra, *India* 40 G8 25 58N 72 10 E
Pachuca, *Mexico* 87 C5 20 10N 98 40W
Pacific, *Canada* 72 C3 54 48N 128 28W
Pacific-Antarctic Ridge, *Pac. Oc.* 65 M16 43 0S 115 0W
Pacific Grove, *U.S.A.* 83 H3 36 38N 121 56W
Pacific Ocean, *Pac. Oc.* 65 G14 10 0N 140 0W
Pacifica, *U.S.A.* 84 H4 37 36N 122 30W
Pacitan, *Indonesia* 37 H14 8 12S 111 7 E
Packwood, *U.S.A.* 84 D5 46 36N 121 40W
Padaido, Kepulauan, *Indonesia* 37 E9 1 5S 138 0 E
Padang, *Indonesia* 36 E2 1 0S 100 20 E
Padangpanjang, *Indonesia* 36 E2 0 40S 100 20 E
Padangsidempuan, *Indonesia* 36 D1 1 30N 99 15 E
Paddockwood, *Canada* 73 C7 53 30N 105 30W
Paderborn, *Germany* 16 C5 51 42N 8 45 E
Padloping Island, *Canada* 69 B13 67 0N 62 50W
Pádova, *Italy* 20 B4 45 25N 11 53 E
Padra, *India* 42 H5 22 15N 73 7 E
Padrauna, *India* 43 F10 26 54N 83 59 E
Padre I., *U.S.A.* 81 M6 27 10N 97 25W
Padstow, *U.K.* 11 G3 50 33N 4 58W
Padua = Pádova, *Italy* 20 B4 45 25N 11 53 E
Paducah, *Ky., U.S.A.* 76 G1 37 5N 88 37W
Paducah, *Tex., U.S.A.* 81 H4 34 1N 100 18W
Paengnyong-do, *S. Korea* 35 F13 37 57N 124 40 E
Paeroa, *N.Z.* 59 G5 37 23S 175 41 E
Pafúri, *Mozam.* 57 C5 22 28S 31 17 E
Pag, *Croatia* 16 F8 44 25N 15 3 E
Pagadian, *Phil.* 37 C6 7 55N 123 30 E
Pagai Selatan, P., *Indonesia* 36 E2 3 0S 100 15 E
Pagai Utara, *Indonesia* 36 E2 2 35S 100 0 E
Pagalu = Annobón, *Atl. Oc.* 49 G4 1 25S 5 36 E
Pagastikós Kólpos, *Greece* 21 E10 39 15N 23 0 E
Pagatan, *Indonesia* 36 E5 3 33S 115 59 E
Page, *Ariz., U.S.A.* 83 H8 36 57N 111 27W
Page, *N. Dak., U.S.A.* 80 B6 47 10N 97 34W
Pago Pago, *Amer. Samoa* 59 B13 14 16S 170 43W
Pagosa Springs, *U.S.A.* 83 H10 37 16N 107 1W
Pagwa River, *Canada* 70 B2 50 2N 85 14W
Pahala, *U.S.A.* 74 J17 19 12N 155 29W
Pahang →, *Malaysia* 39 L4 3 30N 103 9 E
Pahiatua, *N.Z.* 59 J5 40 27S 175 50 E
Pahokee, *U.S.A.* 77 M5 26 50N 80 40W
Pahrump, *U.S.A.* 85 J11 36 12N 115 59W
Pahute Mesa, *U.S.A.* 84 H10 37 20N 116 45W
Pai, *Thailand* 38 C2 19 19N 98 27 E
Paia, *U.S.A.* 74 H16 20 54N 156 22W
Paicines, *U.S.A.* 84 J5 36 44N 121 17W
Paide, *Estonia* 9 G21 58 57N 25 31 E
Paignton, *U.K.* 11 G4 50 26N 3 35W
Päijänne, *Finland* 9 F21 61 30N 25 30 E
Painan, *Indonesia* 36 E2 1 21S 100 34 E
Painesville, *U.S.A.* 78 E3 41 43N 81 15W
Paint Hills = Wemindji, *Canada* 70 B4 53 0N 78 49W
Paint L., *Canada* 73 B9 55 28N 97 57W
Paint Rock, *U.S.A.* 81 K5 31 31N 99 55W
Painted Desert, *U.S.A.* 83 J8 36 0N 111 0W
Paintsville, *U.S.A.* 76 G4 37 49N 82 48W
País Vasco □, *Spain* 19 A4 42 50N 2 45W
Paisley, *Canada* 78 B3 44 18N 81 16W
Paisley, *U.K.* 12 F4 55 50N 4 25W
Paisley, *U.S.A.* 82 E3 42 42N 120 32W
Paita, *Peru* 92 E2 5 11S 81 9W
Pajares, Puerto de, *Spain* 19 A3 42 58N 5 46W
Pak Lay, *Laos* 38 C3 18 15N 101 27 E
Pak Phanang, *Thailand* 39 H3 8 21N 100 12 E
Pak Sane, *Laos* 38 C4 18 22N 103 39 E
Pak Song, *Laos* 38 E6 15 11N 106 14 E
Pak Suong, *Laos* 38 C4 19 58N 102 15 E
Pakaraima Mts., *Guyana* 92 B6 6 0N 60 0W
Pákhnes, *Greece* 23 D6 35 16N 24 4 E
Pakistan ■, *Asia* 42 E3 30 0N 70 0 E
Pakkading, *Laos* 38 C4 18 19N 103 59 E
Pakokku, *Burma* 41 J19 21 20N 95 0 E
Pakpattan, *Pakistan* 42 D5 30 25N 73 27 E
Pakse, *Laos* 38 E5 15 5N 105 52 E
Paktīā □, *Afghan.* 40 C6 33 0N 69 15 E
Pakwach, *Uganda* 54 B3 2 28N 31 27 E
Pala, *Chad* 51 G8 9 25N 15 5 E
Pala, *U.S.A.* 85 M9 33 22N 117 5W
Pala, *Zaïre* 54 D2 6 45S 29 30 E
Palabek, *Uganda* 54 B3 3 22N 32 33 E
Palacios, *U.S.A.* 81 L6 28 42N 96 13W
Palagruža, *Croatia* 20 C7 42 24N 16 15 E
Palaiókastron, *Greece* 23 D8 35 12N 26 15 E
Palaiokhóra, *Greece* 23 D5 35 16N 23 39 E
Palam, *India* 40 K10 19 0N 77 0 E
Palampur, *India* 42 C7 32 10N 76 30 E
Palana, *Australia* 62 F4 39 45S 147 55 E
Palana, *Russia* 27 D16 59 10N 159 59 E
Palanan, *Phil.* 37 A6 17 8N 122 29 E
Palanan Pt., *Phil.* 37 A6 17 17N 122 30 E
Palandri, *Pakistan* 43 C5 33 42N 73 40 E
Palanga, *Lithuania* 9 J19 55 58N 21 3 E
Palangkaraya, *Indonesia* 36 E4 2 16S 113 56 E
Palani Hills, *India* 40 P10 10 14N 77 33 E
Palanpur, *India* 42 G5 24 10N 72 25 E
Palanro, *Indonesia* 37 E5 3 21S 119 23 E
Palapye, *Botswana* 56 C4 22 30S 27 7 E
Palas, *Pakistan* 43 B5 35 4N 73 14 E
Palatka, *Russia* 27 C16 60 6N 150 54 E
Palatka, *U.S.A.* 77 L5 29 39N 81 38W
Palau ■, *Pac. Oc.* 28 J17 7 30N 134 30 E
Palawan, *Phil.* 36 C5 9 30N 118 30 E
Palayankottai, *India* 40 Q10 8 45N 77 45 E
Paldiski, *Estonia* 9 G21 59 23N 24 9 E
Paleleh, *Indonesia* 37 D6 1 10N 121 50 E
Palembang, *Indonesia* 36 E2 3 0S 104 50 E
Palencia, *Spain* 19 A3 42 1N 4 34W
Paleokastrítsa, *Greece* 23 A3 39 40N 19 41 E
Paleometokho, *Cyprus* 23 D12 35 7N 33 11 E
Palermo, *Italy* 20 E5 38 7N 13 22 E
Palermo, *U.S.A.* 82 G3 39 26N 121 33W
Palestine, *Asia* 47 D4 32 0N 35 0 E
Palestine, *U.S.A.* 81 K7 31 46N 95 38W
Paletwa, *Burma* 41 J18 21 10N 92 50 E
Palghat, *India* 40 P10 10 46N 76 42 E
Palgrave, Mt., *Australia* 60 D2 23 22S 115 58 E
Pali, *India* 42 G5 25 50N 73 20 E
Palioúrion, Ákra, *Greece* 21 E10 39 57N 23 45 E
Palisade, *U.S.A.* 80 E4 40 21N 101 7W
Palitana, *India* 42 J4 21 32N 71 49 E
Palizada, *Mexico* 87 D6 18 18N 92 8W
Palk Bay, *Asia* 40 Q11 9 30N 79 15 E
Palk Strait, *Asia* 40 Q11 10 0N 79 45 E
Palkānah, *Iraq* 44 C5 35 49N 44 26 E
Palla Road = Dinokwe, *Botswana* 56 C4 23 29S 26 37 E
Pallanza = Verbánia, *Italy* 20 B3 45 56N 8 33 E
Pallisa, *Uganda* 54 B3 1 12N 33 43 E
Pallu, *India* 42 E6 28 59N 74 14 E
Palm Bay, *U.S.A.* 77 L5 28 2N 80 35W
Palm Beach, *U.S.A.* 77 M6 26 43N 80 2W
Palm Desert, *U.S.A.* 85 M10 33 43N 116 22W
Palm Is., *Australia* 62 B4 18 40S 146 35 E
Palm Springs, *U.S.A.* 85 M10 33 50N 116 33W
Palma, *Mozam.* 55 E5 10 46S 40 29 E
Palma →, *Brazil* 93 F9 12 33S 47 52W
Palma, B. de, *Spain* 22 B9 39 30N 2 39 E
Palma de Mallorca, *Spain* 22 B9 39 35N 2 39 E
Palma Soriano, *Cuba* 88 B4 20 15N 76 0W
Palmares, *Brazil* 93 E11 8 41S 35 28W
Palmas, *Brazil* 95 B5 26 29S 52 0W
Palmas, C., *Liberia* 50 H3 4 27N 7 46W
Pálmas, G. di, *Italy* 20 E3 39 0N 8 30 E
Palmdale, *U.S.A.* 85 L8 34 35N 118 7W
Palmeira dos Índios, *Brazil* 93 E11 9 25S 36 37W
Palmeirinhas, Pta. das, *Angola* 52 F2 9 2S 12 57 E
Palmer, *U.S.A.* 68 B5 61 36N 149 7W
Palmer →, *Australia* 62 B3 16 0S 142 26 E
Palmer Arch., *Antarctica* 5 C17 64 15S 65 0W
Palmer Lake, *U.S.A.* 80 F2 39 7N 104 55W
Palmer Land, *Antarctica* 5 D18 73 0S 63 0W
Palmerston, *Canada* 78 C4 43 50N 80 51W
Palmerston, *N.Z.* 59 L3 45 29S 170 43 E
Palmerston North, *N.Z.* 59 J5 40 21S 175 39 E
Palmerton, *U.S.A.* 79 F9 40 48N 75 37W
Palmetto, *U.S.A.* 77 M4 27 31N 82 34W
Palmi, *Italy* 20 E6 38 21N 15 51 E
Palmira, *Argentina* 94 C2 32 59S 68 34W
Palmira, *Colombia* 92 C3 3 32N 76 16W
Palmyra = Tudmur, *Syria* 44 C3 34 36N 38 15 E
Palmyra, *Mo., U.S.A.* 80 F9 39 48N 91 32W
Palmyra, *N.Y., U.S.A.* 78 C7 43 5N 77 18W
Palmyra Is., *Pac. Oc.* 65 G11 5 52N 162 5W
Palo Alto, *U.S.A.* 83 H2 37 27N 122 10W
Palo Verde, *U.S.A.* 85 M12 33 26N 114 44W
Palopo, *Indonesia* 37 E6 3 0S 120 16 E
Palos, C. de, *Spain* 19 D5 37 38N 0 40W
Palos Verdes, *U.S.A.* 85 M8 33 48N 118 23W
Palos Verdes, Pt., *U.S.A.* 85 M8 33 43N 118 26W
Palouse, *U.S.A.* 82 C5 46 55N 117 4W
Palparara, *Australia* 62 C3 24 47S 141 28 E
Palu, *Indonesia* 37 E5 1 0S 119 52 E
Palu, *Turkey* 25 G7 38 45N 40 0 E
Paluan, *Phil.* 37 B6 13 26N 120 29 E
Palwal, *India* 42 E7 28 8N 77 19 E
Pama, *Burkina Faso* 50 F5 11 19N 0 44 E
Pamanukan, *Indonesia* 37 G12 6 16S 107 49 E
Pamekasan, *Indonesia* 37 G15 7 10S 113 28 E
Pamiers, *France* 18 E4 43 7N 1 39 E
Pamirs, *Tajikistan* 26 F8 37 40N 73 0 E
Pamlico →, *U.S.A.* 77 H7 35 20N 76 28W
Pamlico Sd., *U.S.A.* 77 H8 35 20N 76 0W
Pampa, *U.S.A.* 81 H4 35 32N 100 58W
Pampa de las Salinas, *Argentina* 94 C2 32 1S 66 58W
Pampanua, *Indonesia* 37 E6 4 16S 120 8 E
Pampas, *Argentina* 94 D3 35 0S 63 0W
Pampas, *Peru* 92 F4 12 20S 74 50W
Pamplona, *Colombia* 92 B4 7 23N 72 39W
Pamplona, *Spain* 19 A5 42 48N 1 38W
Pampoenpoort, *S. Africa* 56 E3 31 3S 22 40 E
Pana, *U.S.A.* 80 F10 39 23N 89 5W
Panaca, *U.S.A.* 83 H6 37 47N 114 23W
Panaitan, *Indonesia* 37 G11 6 36S 105 12 E
Panaji, *India* 40 M8 15 25N 73 50 E
Panamá, *Panama* 88 E4 9 0N 79 25W
Panama ■, *Cent. Amer.* 88 E4 8 48N 79 55W
Panamá, G. de, *Panama* 88 E4 8 4N 79 20W
Panama Canal, *Panama* 88 E4 9 10N 79 37W
Panama City, *U.S.A.* 77 K3 30 10N 85 40W
Panamint Range, *U.S.A.* 85 J9 36 20N 117 20W
Panamint Springs, *U.S.A.* 85 J9 36 20N 117 28W
Panão, *Peru* 92 E3 9 55S 75 55W
Panare, *Thailand* 39 J3 6 51N 101 30 E
Panarukan, *Indonesia* 37 G15 7 42S 113 56 E
Panay, *Phil.* 37 B6 11 10N 122 30 E
Panay, G., *Phil.* 37 B6 11 0N 122 30 E
Pancake Range, *U.S.A.* 83 G6 38 30N 115 50W
Pančevo, *Serbia, Yug.* 21 B9 44 52N 20 41 E
Pandan, *Phil.* 37 B6 11 45N 122 10 E
Pandegelang, *Indonesia* 37 G12 6 25S 106 5 E
Pandharpur, *India* 40 L9 17 41N 75 20 E
Pando, *Uruguay* 95 C4 34 44S 56 0W
Pando, L. = Hope, L., *Australia* 63 D2 28 24S 139 18 E
Pandokrátor, *Greece* 23 A3 39 45N 19 50 E
Pandora, *Costa Rica* 88 E3 9 43N 83 3W
Panevėžys, *Lithuania* 9 J21 55 42N 24 25 E
Panfilov, *Kazakstan* 26 E8 44 10N 80 0 E
Pang-Long, *Burma* 41 H21 23 11N 98 45 E
Pang-Yang, *Burma* 41 H21 22 7N 98 48 E
Panga, *Zaïre* 54 B2 1 52N 26 18 E
Pangalanes, Canal des, *Madag.* 57 C8 22 48S 47 50 E
Pangani, *Tanzania* 54 D4 5 25S 38 58 E
Pangani □, *Tanzania* 54 D4 5 25S 39 0 E
Pangani →, *Tanzania* 54 D4 5 26S 38 58 E
Pangfou = Bengbu, *China* 35 H9 32 58N 117 20 E
Pangil, *Zaïre* 54 C2 3 10S 26 35 E
Pangkah, Tanjung, *Indonesia* 37 G15 6 51S 112 33 E
Pangkajene, *Indonesia* 37 E5 4 46S 119 34 E
Pangkalanbrandan, *Indonesia* 36 D1 4 1N 98 20 E
Pangkalanbuun, *Indonesia* 36 E4 2 41S 111 37 E

Q

Ravena

Qasr 'Amra, Jordan 44 D3 31 48N 36 35 E
Qaşr-e Qand, Iran 45 E9 26 15N 60 45 E
Qasr Farâfra, Egypt 51 C10 27 0N 28 1 E
Qatanâ, Syria 47 B5 33 26N 36 4 E
Qatar ■, Asia 45 E6 25 30N 51 15 E
Qatlīsh, Iran 45 B8 37 50N 57 19 E
Qattâra, Munkhafed el, Egypt 51 C10 29 30N 27 30 E
Qattâra Depression = Qattâra, Munkhafed el, Egypt 51 C10 29 30N 27 30 E
Qawām al Ḩamzah, Iraq 44 D5 31 43N 44 58 E
Qāyen, Iran 45 C8 33 40N 59 10 E
Qazaqstan = Kazakstan ■, Asia 26 E7 50 0N 70 0 E
Qazvin, Iran 45 B6 36 15N 50 0 E
Qena, Egypt 51 C11 26 10N 32 43 E
Qeqertarsuaq = Disko, Greenland 4 C5 69 45N 53 30W
Qeqertarsuaq = Godhavn, Greenland 4 C5 69 15N 53 38W
Qeshlāq, Iran 44 C5 34 55N 46 28 E
Qeshm, Iran 45 E8 26 55N 56 10 E
Qezi'ot, Israel 47 E3 30 52N 34 26 E
Qi Xian, China 34 G8 34 40N 114 48 E
Qian Gorlos, China 35 B13 45 5N 124 42 E
Qian Xian, China 34 G5 34 31N 108 15 E
Qianyang, China 34 G4 34 40N 107 8 E
Qibā', Si. Arabia 44 E5 27 24N 44 20 E
Qila Safed, Pakistan 40 E2 29 0N 61 30 E
Qila Saifullāh, Pakistan 42 D3 30 45N 68 17 E
Qilian Shan, China 32 C4 38 30N 96 0 E
Qin He →, China 34 G7 35 1N 113 22 E
Qin Ling = Qinling Shandi, China 34 H5 33 50N 108 10 E
Qin'an, China 34 G3 34 48N 105 40 E
Qing Xian, China 34 E9 38 35N 116 45 E
Qingcheng, China 35 F9 37 15N 117 40 E
Qingdao, China 35 F11 36 5N 120 20 E
Qingfeng, China 34 G8 35 52N 115 8 E
Qinghai □, China 32 C4 36 0N 98 0 E
Qinghai Hu, China 32 C5 36 40N 100 10 E
Qinghecheng, China 35 D13 41 15N 124 30 E
Qinghemen, China 35 D11 41 48N 121 25 E
Qingjian, China 34 F6 37 8N 110 8 E
Qingjiang, China 35 H10 33 30N 119 2 E
Qingshui, China 34 G4 34 48N 106 8 E
Qingshuihe, China 34 E6 39 55N 111 35 E
Qingtongxia Shuiku, China 34 F3 37 50N 105 58 E
Qingxu, China 34 F7 37 34N 112 22 E
Qingyang, China 34 F4 36 2N 107 55 E
Qingyuan, China 35 C13 42 10N 124 55 E
Qingyun, China 35 F9 37 45N 117 20 E
Qinhuangdao, China 35 E10 39 56N 119 30 E
Qinling Shandi, China 34 H5 33 50N 108 10 E
Qinshui, China 34 G7 35 40N 112 8 E
Qinyang, China 34 G7 35 7N 112 57 E
Qinyuan, China 34 F7 36 29N 112 20 E
Qinzhou, China 32 D5 21 58N 108 38 E
Qionghai, China 38 C8 19 15N 110 26 E
Qiongshan, China 38 C8 19 51N 110 26 E
Qiongzhou Haixia, China 38 B8 20 10N 110 15 E
Qiqihar, China 27 E13 47 26N 124 0 E
Qiraîya, W. →, Egypt 47 E3 30 27N 34 0 E
Qiryat Ata, Israel 47 C4 32 47N 35 6 E
Qiryat Gat, Israel 47 D3 31 32N 34 46 E
Qiryat Mal'akhi, Israel 47 D3 31 44N 34 44 E
Qiryat Shemona, Israel 47 B4 33 13N 35 35 E
Qiryat Yam, Israel 47 C4 32 51N 35 4 E
Qishan, China 34 G4 34 25N 107 38 E
Qitai, China 32 B3 44 2N 89 35 E
Qixia, China 35 F11 37 17N 120 52 E
Qojūr, Iran 44 B5 36 12N 47 55 E
Qom, Iran 45 C6 34 40N 51 0 E
Qomsheh, Iran 45 D6 32 0N 51 55 E
Qostanay, Kazakstan 26 D7 53 10N 63 35 E
Qu Xian, China 33 D6 28 57N 118 54 E
Quairading, Australia 61 F2 32 0S 117 21 E
Quakertown, U.S.A. 79 F9 40 26N 75 21W
Qualeup, Australia 61 F2 33 48S 116 48 E
Quambatook, Australia 63 F3 35 49S 143 34 E
Quambone, Australia 63 E4 30 57S 147 53 E
Quamby, Australia 62 C3 20 22S 140 17 E
Quan Long, Vietnam 39 H5 9 7N 105 8 E
Quanah, U.S.A. 81 H5 34 18N 99 44W
Quandialla, Australia 63 E4 34 1S 147 47 E
Quang Ngai, Vietnam 38 E7 15 13N 108 58 E
Quang Yen, Vietnam 38 B6 20 56N 106 52 E
Quantock Hills, U.K. 11 F4 51 8N 3 10W
Quanzhou, China 33 D6 24 55N 118 34 E
Quaqtaq, Canada 69 B13 60 55N 69 40W
Quaraí, Brazil 94 C4 30 15S 56 20W
Quartu Sant'Elena, Italy 20 E3 39 15N 9 10 E
Quartzsite, U.S.A. 85 M12 33 40N 114 13W
Quatsino, Canada 72 C3 50 30N 127 40W
Quatsino Sd., Canada 72 C3 50 25N 127 58W
Quba, Azerbaijan 25 F8 41 21N 48 32 E
Qūchān, Iran 45 B8 37 10N 58 27 E
Queanbeyan, Australia 63 F4 35 17S 149 14 E
Québec, Canada 71 C5 46 52N 71 13W
Québec □, Canada 71 B6 48 0N 74 0W
Queen Alexandra Ra., Antarctica 5 E11 85 0S 170 0 E
Queen Charlotte, Canada 72 C2 53 15N 132 2W
Queen Charlotte Is., Canada 72 C2 53 20N 132 10W
Queen Charlotte Str., Canada 72 C3 51 0N 128 0W
Queen Elizabeth Is., Canada 66 B10 76 0N 95 0W
Queen Elizabeth Nat. Park, Uganda 54 C3 0 0 30 0 E
Queen Mary Land, Antarctica 5 D7 70 0S 95 0 E
Queen Maud G., Canada 68 B9 68 15N 102 30W
Queen Maud Land, Antarctica 5 D3 72 30S 12 0 E
Queen Maud Mts., Antarctica 5 E13 86 0S 160 0W
Queens Chan., Australia 60 C4 15 0S 129 30 E
Queenscliff, Australia 63 F3 38 16S 144 39 E
Queensland □, Australia 62 C3 22 0S 142 0 E
Queenstown, Australia 62 G4 42 4S 145 35 E
Queenstown, N.Z. 59 L2 45 1S 168 40 E
Queenstown, S. Africa 56 E4 31 52S 26 52 E
Queets, U.S.A. 84 C2 47 32N 124 20W
Queguay Grande →, Uruguay 94 C4 32 9S 58 9W
Queimadas, Brazil 93 F11 11 0S 39 38W
Quela, Angola 52 F3 9 10S 16 56 E
Quelimane, Mozam. 55 F4 17 53S 36 58 E
Quelpart = Cheju Do, S. Korea 35 H14 33 29N 126 34 E
Quemado, N. Mex., U.S.A. 83 J9 34 20N 108 30W
Quemado, Tex., U.S.A. 81 L4 28 58N 100 35W
Quemú-Quemú, Argentina 94 D3 36 3S 63 36W
Quequén, Argentina 94 D4 38 30S 58 30W
Querétaro, Mexico 86 C4 20 36N 100 23W
Querétaro □, Mexico 86 C5 20 30N 100 0W
Queshan, China 34 H8 32 55N 114 2 E
Quesnel, Canada 72 C4 53 0N 122 30W
Quesnel →, Canada 72 C4 52 58N 122 29W
Quesnel L., Canada 72 C4 52 30N 121 20W
Questa, U.S.A. 83 H11 36 42N 105 36W
Quetico Prov. Park, Canada 70 C1 48 30N 91 45W
Quetta, Pakistan 42 D2 30 15N 66 55 E
Quezaltenango, Guatemala 88 D1 14 50N 91 30W
Quezon City, Phil. 37 B6 14 38N 121 0 E
Qufār, Si. Arabia 44 E4 27 26N 41 37 E
Qui Nhon, Vietnam 38 F7 13 40N 109 13 E
Quibaxe, Angola 52 F2 8 24S 14 27 E
Quibdo, Colombia 92 B3 5 42N 76 40W
Quiberon, France 18 C2 47 29N 3 9W
Quick, Canada 72 C3 54 36N 126 54W
Quiet L., Canada 72 A2 61 5N 133 5W
Quiindy, Paraguay 94 B4 25 58S 57 14W
Quila, Mexico 86 C3 24 23N 107 13W
Quilán, C., Chile 96 E2 43 15S 74 30W
Quilcene, U.S.A. 84 C4 47 49N 122 53W
Quilengues, Angola 53 G2 14 12S 14 12 E
Quilimarí, Chile 94 C1 32 5S 71 30W
Quilino, Argentina 94 C3 30 14S 64 29W
Quillabamba, Peru 92 F4 12 50S 72 50W
Quillagua, Chile 94 A2 21 40S 69 40W
Quillaicillo, Chile 94 C1 31 17S 71 40W
Quillota, Chile 94 C1 32 54S 71 16W
Quilmes, Argentina 94 C4 34 43S 58 15W
Quilon, India 40 Q10 8 50N 76 38 E
Quilpie, Australia 63 D3 26 35S 144 11 E
Quilpué, Chile 94 C1 33 5S 71 33W
Quilua, Mozam. 55 F4 16 17S 39 54 E
Quimili, Argentina 94 B3 27 40S 62 30W
Quimper, France 18 B1 48 0N 4 9W
Quimperlé, France 18 C2 47 53N 3 33W
Quinault →, U.S.A. 84 C2 47 21N 124 18W
Quincy, Calif., U.S.A. 84 F6 39 56N 120 57W
Quincy, Fla., U.S.A. 77 K3 30 35N 84 34W
Quincy, Ill., U.S.A. 80 F9 39 56N 91 23W
Quincy, Mass., U.S.A. 79 D14 42 15N 71 0W
Quincy, Wash., U.S.A. 82 C4 47 22N 119 56W
Quines, Argentina 94 C2 32 13S 65 48W
Quinga, Mozam. 55 F5 15 49S 40 15 E
Quintana Roo □, Mexico 87 D7 19 0N 88 0W
Quintanar de la Orden, Spain 19 C4 39 36N 3 5W
Quintero, Chile 94 C1 32 45S 71 30W
Quinyambie, Australia 63 E3 30 15S 141 0 E
Quipungo, Angola 53 G2 14 37S 14 40 E
Quirihue, Chile 94 D1 36 15S 72 35W
Quirindi, Australia 63 E5 31 28S 150 40 E
Quissanga, Mozam. 55 E5 12 24S 40 28 E
Quitilipi, Argentina 94 B3 26 50S 60 13W
Quitman, Ga., U.S.A. 77 K4 30 47N 83 34W
Quitman, Miss., U.S.A. 77 J1 32 2N 88 44W
Quitman, Tex., U.S.A. 81 J7 32 48N 95 27W
Quito, Ecuador 92 D3 0 15S 78 35W
Quixadá, Brazil 93 D11 4 55S 39 0W
Quixaxe, Mozam. 55 F5 15 17S 40 4 E
Qumbu, S. Africa 57 E4 31 10S 28 48 E
Quneitra, Syria 47 B4 33 7N 35 48 E
Qŭnghirot, Uzbekistan 26 E6 43 6N 58 54 E
Quoin I., Australia 60 B4 14 54S 129 32 E
Quoin Pt., S. Africa 56 E2 34 46S 19 37 E
Quondong, Australia 63 E3 33 6S 140 18 E
Quorn, Australia 63 E2 32 25S 138 5 E
Qŭqon, Uzbekistan 26 E8 40 30N 70 57 E
Qurnat as Sawdā', Lebanon 47 A5 34 18N 36 6 E
Qûs, Egypt 51 C11 25 55N 32 50 E
Qusaybah, Iraq 44 C4 34 24N 40 59 E
Quseir, Egypt 51 C11 26 7N 34 16 E
Qūshchī, Iran 44 B5 37 59N 45 3 E
Quthing, Lesotho 57 E4 30 25S 27 36 E
Qūţīābād, Iran 45 C6 35 47N 48 30 E
Quwo, China 34 G6 35 38N 111 25 E
Quyang, China 34 E8 38 35N 114 40 E
Quynh Nhai, Vietnam 38 B4 21 49N 103 33 E
Quzi, China 34 F4 36 20N 107 20 E
Qyzylorda, Kazakstan 26 E7 44 48N 65 28 E

R

Ra, Ko, Thailand 39 H2 9 13N 98 16 E
Raahe, Finland 8 D21 64 40N 24 28 E
Raasay, U.K. 12 D2 57 25N 6 4W
Raasay, Sd. of, U.K. 12 D2 57 30N 6 8W
Raba, Indonesia 37 F5 8 36S 118 55 E
Rába →, Hungary 17 E9 47 38N 17 38 E
Rabai, Kenya 54 C4 3 50S 39 31 E
Rabat, Malta 23 D1 35 53N 14 25 E
Rabat, Morocco 50 B3 34 2N 6 48W
Rabaul, Papua N. G. 64 H7 4 24S 152 18 E
Rabbit →, Canada 72 B3 59 41N 127 12W
Rabbit Lake, Canada 73 C7 53 8N 107 46W
Rabbitskin →, Canada 72 A4 61 47N 120 42W
Rābor, Iran 45 D8 29 17N 56 55 E
Race, C., Canada 71 C9 46 40N 53 5W
Rach Gia, Vietnam 39 G5 10 5N 105 5 E
Racibórz, Poland 17 C10 50 7N 18 18 E
Racine, U.S.A. 76 D2 42 41N 87 51W
Rackerby, U.S.A. 84 F5 39 26N 121 22W
Radama, Nosy, Madag. 57 A8 14 0S 47 47 E
Radama, Saikanosy, Madag. 57 A8 14 16S 47 53 E
Rădăuţi, Romania 17 E13 47 50N 25 59 E
Radekhiv, Ukraine 17 C13 50 25N 24 32 E
Radekhov = Radekhiv, Ukraine 17 C13 50 25N 24 32 E
Radford, U.S.A. 76 G5 37 8N 80 34W
Radhanpur, India 42 H4 23 50N 71 38 E
Radisson, Canada 73 C7 52 30N 107 20W
Radium Hot Springs, Canada 72 C5 50 35N 116 2W
Radnor Forest, U.K. 11 E4 52 17N 3 10W
Radom, Poland 17 C11 51 23N 21 12 E
Radomsko, Poland 17 C10 51 5N 19 28 E
Radomyshl, Ukraine 17 C15 50 30N 29 12 E
Radstock, U.K. 11 F5 51 17N 2 26W
Radstock, C., Australia 63 E1 33 12S 134 20 E
Radviliškis, Lithuania 9 J20 55 49N 23 33 E
Radville, Canada 73 D8 49 30N 104 15W
Rae, Canada 72 A5 62 50N 116 3W
Rae Bareli, India 43 F9 26 18N 81 20 E
Rae Isthmus, Canada 69 B11 66 40N 87 30W
Raeren, Belgium 15 D6 50 41N 6 7 E
Raeside, L., Australia 61 E3 29 20S 122 0 E
Raetihi, N.Z. 59 H5 39 25S 175 17 E
Rafaela, Argentina 94 C3 31 10S 61 30W
Rafah, Gaza Strip 47 D3 31 18N 34 14 E
Rafai, C.A.R. 54 B1 4 59N 23 58 E
Rafḩā, Si. Arabia 44 D4 29 35N 43 35 E
Rafsanjān, Iran 45 D8 30 30N 56 5 E
Raft Pt., Australia 60 C3 16 4S 124 26 E
Ragachow, Belarus 17 B16 53 8N 30 5 E
Ragama, Sri Lanka 40 R11 7 0N 79 50 E
Ragged, Mt., Australia 61 F3 33 27S 123 25 E
Raglan, Australia 62 C5 23 42S 150 49 E
Raglan, N.Z. 59 G5 37 55S 174 55 E
Ragusa, Italy 20 F6 36 55N 14 44 E
Raha, Indonesia 37 E6 4 55S 123 0 E
Rahad al Bardī, Sudan 51 F9 11 20N 23 40 E
Rahaeng = Tak, Thailand 38 D2 16 52N 99 8 E
Raḩīmah, Si. Arabia 45 E6 26 42N 50 4 E
Rahimyar Khan, Pakistan 42 E4 28 30N 70 25 E
Rāhjerd, Iran 45 C6 34 22N 50 22 E
Raichur, India 40 L10 16 10N 77 20 E
Raiganj, India 43 G13 25 37N 88 10 E
Raigarh, India 41 J13 21 56N 83 25 E
Raijua, Indonesia 37 F6 10 37S 121 36 E
Railton, Australia 62 G4 41 25S 146 28 E
Rainbow Lake, Canada 72 B5 58 30N 119 23W
Rainier, U.S.A. 84 D4 46 53N 122 41W
Rainier, Mt., U.S.A. 84 D5 46 52N 121 46W
Rainy L., Canada 73 D10 48 42N 93 10W
Rainy River, Canada 73 D10 48 43N 94 29W
Raippaluoto, Finland 8 E19 63 13N 21 14 E
Raipur, India 41 J12 21 17N 81 45 E
Raisio, Finland 9 F20 60 28N 22 11 E
Raj Nandgaon, India 41 J12 21 5N 81 5 E
Raja, Ujung, Indonesia 36 D1 3 40N 96 25 E
Raja Ampat, Kepulauan, Indonesia 37 E7 0 30S 130 0 E
Rajahmundry, India 41 L12 17 1N 81 48 E
Rajang →, Malaysia 36 D4 2 30N 112 0 E
Rajapalaiyam, India 40 Q10 9 25N 77 35 E
Rajasthan □, India 42 F5 26 45N 73 30 E
Rajasthan Canal, India 42 E5 28 0N 72 0 E
Rajauri, India 43 C6 33 25N 74 21 E
Rajgarh, Mad. P., India 42 G7 24 2N 76 45 E
Rajgarh, Raj., India 42 E6 28 40N 75 25 E
Rajkot, India 42 H4 22 15N 70 56 E
Rajmahal Hills, India 43 G12 24 30N 87 30 E
Rajpipla, India 40 J8 21 50N 73 30 E
Rajpura, India 42 D7 30 25N 76 32 E
Rajshahi, Bangla. 41 G16 24 22N 88 39 E
Rajshahi □, Bangla. 43 G13 25 0N 89 0 E
Rakaia, N.Z. 59 K4 43 45S 172 1 E
Rakaia →, N.Z. 59 K4 43 36S 172 15 E
Rakan, Ra's, Qatar 45 E6 26 10N 51 20 E
Rakaposhi, Pakistan 43 A6 36 10N 74 25 E
Rakata, Pulau, Indonesia 36 F3 6 10S 105 20 E
Rakhiv, Ukraine 17 D13 48 3N 24 12 E
Rakhni, Pakistan 42 D3 30 4N 69 56 E
Rakitnoye, Russia 30 B7 45 36N 134 17 E
Rakops, Botswana 56 C3 21 1S 24 28 E
Rakvere, Estonia 9 G22 59 20N 26 25 E
Raleigh, U.S.A. 77 H6 35 47N 78 39W
Raleigh B., U.S.A. 77 H7 34 50N 76 15W
Ralls, U.S.A. 81 J4 33 41N 101 24W
Ram →, Canada 72 A4 62 1N 123 41W
Rām Allāh, West Bank 47 D4 31 55N 35 10 E
Ram Hd., Australia 63 F4 37 47S 149 30 E
Rama, Nic. 88 D3 12 9N 84 15W
Raman, Thailand 39 J3 6 29N 101 18 E
Ramanathapuram, India 40 Q11 9 25N 78 55 E
Ramanetaka, B. de, Madag. 57 A8 14 13S 47 52 E
Ramat Gan, Israel 47 C3 32 4N 34 48 E
Ramatlhabama, S. Africa 56 D4 25 37S 25 33 E
Ramban, India 43 C6 33 14N 75 12 E
Rambipuji, Indonesia 37 H15 8 12S 113 37 E
Ramea, Canada 71 C8 47 31N 57 23W
Ramechhap, Nepal 43 F12 27 25N 86 10 E
Ramelau, Indonesia 37 F7 8 55S 126 22 E
Ramgarh, Bihar, India 43 H11 23 40N 85 35 E
Ramgarh, Raj., India 42 F6 27 16N 75 14 E
Ramgarh, Raj., India 42 F4 27 30N 70 36 E
Rāmhormoz, Iran 45 D6 31 15N 49 35 E
Ramīān, Iran 45 B7 37 3N 55 16 E
Ramingining, Australia 62 A2 12 19S 135 3 E
Ramla, Israel 47 D3 31 55N 34 52 E
Ramnad = Ramanathapuram, India 40 Q11 9 25N 78 55 E
Ramnagar, India 43 C6 32 47N 75 18 E
Ramona, U.S.A. 85 M10 33 2N 116 52W
Ramore, Canada 70 C3 48 30N 80 25W
Ramotswa, Botswana 56 C4 24 50S 25 52 E
Rampur, H.P., India 42 D7 31 26N 77 43 E
Rampur, Mad. P., India 42 H5 23 25N 73 53 E
Rampur, Ut. P., India 43 E8 28 50N 79 5 E
Rampur Hat, India 43 G12 24 10N 87 50 E
Rampura, India 42 G6 24 30N 75 27 E
Ramree I. = Ramree Kyun, Burma 41 K18 19 0N 94 0 E
Ramree Kyun, Burma 41 K18 19 0N 94 0 E
Rāmsar, Iran 45 B6 36 53N 50 41 E
Ramsey, Canada 70 C3 47 25N 82 20W
Ramsey, U.K. 10 C3 54 20N 4 22W
Ramsgate, U.K. 11 F9 51 20N 1 25 E
Ramtek, India 40 J11 21 20N 79 15 E
Ranaghat, India 43 H13 23 15N 88 35 E
Ranahu, Pakistan 42 G3 25 55N 69 45 E
Ranau, Malaysia 36 C5 6 2N 116 40 E
Rancagua, Chile 94 C1 34 10S 70 50W
Rancheria →, Canada 72 A3 60 13N 129 7W
Ranchester, U.S.A. 82 D10 44 54N 107 10W
Ranchi, India 43 H11 23 19N 85 27 E
Rancho Cucamonga, U.S.A. 85 L9 34 10N 117 30W
Randers, Denmark 9 H14 56 29N 10 1 E
Randfontein, S. Africa 57 D4 26 8S 27 45 E
Randle, U.S.A. 84 D5 46 32N 121 57W
Randolph, Mass., U.S.A. 79 D13 42 10N 71 2W
Randolph, N.Y., U.S.A. 78 D6 42 10N 78 59W
Randolph, Utah, U.S.A. 82 F8 41 40N 111 11W
Randolph, Vt., U.S.A. 79 C12 43 55N 72 40W
Råne älv →, Sweden 8 D20 65 50N 22 20 E
Rangae, Thailand 39 J3 6 19N 101 44 E
Rangaunu B., N.Z. 59 F4 34 51S 173 15 E
Rangeley, U.S.A. 79 B14 44 58N 70 39W
Rangely, U.S.A. 82 F9 40 5N 108 48W
Ranger, U.S.A. 81 J5 32 28N 98 41W
Rangia, India 41 F17 26 28N 91 38 E
Rangiora, N.Z. 59 K4 43 19S 172 36 E
Rangitaiki →, N.Z. 59 G6 37 54S 176 49 E
Rangitata →, N.Z. 59 K3 43 45S 171 15 E
Rangkasbitung, Indonesia 37 G12 6 21S 106 15 E
Rangon →, Burma 41 L20 16 28N 96 40 E
Rangoon, Burma 41 L20 16 45N 96 20 E
Rangpur, Bangla. 41 G16 25 42N 89 22 E
Rangsit, Thailand 38 F3 13 59N 100 37 E
Ranibennur, India 40 M9 14 35N 75 30 E
Raniganj, India 43 H12 23 40N 87 5 E
Raniwara, India 40 G8 24 50N 72 10 E
Rāniyah, Iraq 44 B5 36 15N 44 53 E
Ranken →, Australia 62 C2 20 31S 137 36 E
Rankin, U.S.A. 81 K4 31 13N 101 56W
Rankin Inlet, Canada 68 B10 62 30N 93 0W
Rankins Springs, Australia 63 E4 33 49S 146 14 E
Rannoch, L., U.K. 12 E4 56 41N 4 20W
Rannoch Moor, U.K. 12 E4 56 38N 4 48W
Ranobe, Helodranon' i, Madag. 57 C7 23 3S 43 33 E
Ranohira, Madag. 57 C8 22 29S 45 24 E
Ranomafana, Toamasina, Madag. 57 B8 18 57S 48 50 E
Ranomafana, Toliara, Madag. 57 C8 24 34S 47 0 E
Ranong, Thailand 39 H2 9 56N 98 40 E
Rānsa, Iran 45 C6 33 39N 48 18 E
Ransiki, Indonesia 37 E8 1 30S 134 10 E
Rantau, Indonesia 36 E5 2 56S 115 9 E
Rantauprapat, Indonesia 36 D1 2 15N 99 50 E
Rantemario, Indonesia 37 E5 3 15S 119 57 E
Rantoul, U.S.A. 76 E1 40 19N 88 9W
Raoyang, China 34 E8 38 15N 115 45 E
Rapa, Pac. Oc. 65 K13 27 35S 144 20W
Rapallo, Italy 20 B3 44 21N 9 14 E
Rāpch, Iran 45 E8 25 40N 59 15 E
Rapid →, Canada 72 B3 59 15N 129 5W
Rapid City, U.S.A. 80 D3 44 5N 103 14W
Rapid River, U.S.A. 76 C2 45 55N 86 58W
Rapides des Joachims, Canada 70 C4 46 13N 77 43W
Rapla, Estonia 9 G21 59 1N 24 52 E
Rarotonga, Cook Is. 65 K12 21 30S 160 0W
Ra's al 'Ayn, Syria 44 B4 36 45N 40 12 E
Ra's al Khaymah, U.A.E. 45 E8 25 50N 56 5 E
Ra's al-Unuf, Libya 51 B8 30 46N 18 11 E
Ra's an Naqb, Jordan 47 F4 30 0N 35 29 E
Ras Bânâs, Egypt 51 D12 23 57N 35 59 E
Ras Dashen, Ethiopia 51 F12 13 8N 38 26 E
Râs Timirist, Mauritania 50 E1 19 21N 16 30W
Rasa, Punta, Argentina 96 E4 40 50S 62 15W
Rasca, Pta. de la, Canary Is. 22 G3 27 59N 16 41W
Raseiniai, Lithuania 9 J20 55 25N 23 5 E
Rashad, Sudan 51 F11 11 55N 31 0 E
Rashîd, Egypt 51 B11 31 21N 30 22 E
Rasht, Iran 45 B6 37 20N 49 40 E
Rasi Salai, Thailand 38 E5 15 20N 104 9 E
Rason L., Australia 61 E3 28 45S 124 25 E
Rasra, India 43 G10 25 50N 83 50 E
Rat Buri, Thailand 38 F2 13 30N 99 54 E
Rat Islands, U.S.A. 68 C1 52 0N 178 0 E
Rat River, Canada 72 A6 61 7N 112 36W
Ratangarh, India 42 E6 28 5N 74 35 E
Raţāwī, Iraq 44 D5 30 38N 47 13 E
Rath, India 43 G8 25 36N 79 37 E
Rath Luirc, Ireland 13 D3 52 21N 8 40W
Rathdrum, Ireland 13 D5 52 56N 6 14W
Rathenow, Germany 16 B7 52 37N 12 19 E
Rathkeale, Ireland 13 D3 52 32N 8 56W
Rathlin I., U.K. 13 A5 55 18N 6 14W
Rathlin O'Birne I., Ireland 13 B3 54 40N 8 49W
Ratibor = Racibórz, Poland 17 C10 50 7N 18 18 E
Ratlam, India 42 H6 23 20N 75 0 E
Ratnagiri, India 40 L8 16 57N 73 18 E
Raton, U.S.A. 81 G2 36 54N 104 24W
Rattaphum, Thailand 39 J3 7 8N 100 16 E
Rattray Hd., U.K. 12 D7 57 38N 1 50W
Ratz, Mt., Canada 72 B2 57 23N 132 12W
Raub, Malaysia 39 L3 3 47N 101 52 E
Rauch, Argentina 94 D4 36 45S 59 5W
Raufarhöfn, Iceland 8 C6 66 27N 15 57W
Raufoss, Norway 9 F14 60 44N 10 37 E
Raukumara Ra., N.Z. 59 H6 38 5S 177 55 E
Rauma, Finland 9 F19 61 10N 21 30 E
Raurkela, India 43 H11 22 14N 84 50 E
Rausu-Dake, Japan 30 B12 44 4N 145 7 E
Rava-Ruska, Ukraine 17 C12 50 15N 23 42 E
Rava Russkaya = Rava-Ruska, Ukraine 17 C12 50 15N 23 42 E
Ravänsar, Iran 44 C5 34 43N 46 40 E
Rāvar, Iran 45 D8 31 20N 56 51 E
Ravena, U.S.A. 79 D11 42 28N 73 49W

159

Shanchengzhen

Savanur, *India* . . . . 40 M9 14 59N 75 21 E
Savé, *Benin* . . . . 50 G5 8 2N 2 29 E
Save →, *Mozam.* . . . . . . 57 C5 21 16S 34 0 E
Sāveh, *Iran* . . . . 45 C6 35 2N 50 20 E
Savelugu, *Ghana* 50 G4 9 38N 0 54W
Savo, *Finland* . . . . 8 E22 62 45N 27 30 E
Savoie □, *France* . . . . 18 D7 45 26N 6 25 E
Savona, *Italy* . . . . 20 B3 44 17N 8 30 E
Savonlinna, *Finland* . . . . . 24 B4 61 52N 28 53 E
Sawahlunto, *Indonesia* . . 36 E2 0 40S 100 52 E
Sawai, *Indonesia* . . . . . . 37 E7 3 0S 129 5 E
Sawai Madhopur, *India* . . 42 F7 26 0N 76 25 E
Sawang Daen Din, *Thailand* . . . . 38 D4 17 28N 103 28 E
Sawankhalok, *Thailand* . . 38 D2 17 19N 99 50 E
Sawara, *Japan* . . . . 31 G10 35 55N 140 30 E
Sawatch Mts., *U.S.A.* 83 G10 38 30N 106 30W
Sawel Mt., *U.K.* 13 B4 54 50N 7 2W
Sawi, *Thailand* . . . . 39 G2 10 14N 99 5 E
Sawmills, *Zimbabwe* . . . . 55 F2 19 30S 28 2 E
Sawu, *Indonesia* . . . . 37 F6 9 35S 121 50 E
Sawu Sea, *Indonesia* . . . . 37 F6 9 30S 121 50 E
Saxby →, *Australia* . . . . 62 B3 18 25S 140 53 E
Saxony, Lower = Niedersachsen □, *Germany* . . . . 16 B5 53 8N 9 0 E
Saxton, *U.S.A.* 78 F6 40 13N 78 15W
Say, *Niger* . . . . 50 F5 13 8N 2 22 E
Sayabec, *Canada* 71 C6 48 35N 67 41W
Sayaboury, *Laos* . . . . 38 C3 19 15N 101 45 E
Sayán, *Peru* 92 F3 11 8S 77 12W
Sayan, Vostochnyy, *Russia* 27 D10 54 0N 96 0 E
Sayan, Zapadnyy, *Russia* 27 D10 52 30N 94 0 E
Saydā, *Lebanon* . . . . 47 B4 33 35N 35 25 E
Sayhan-Ovoo, *Mongolia* . 34 B2 45 27N 103 54 E
Sayhandulaan, *Mongolia* 34 B5 44 40N 109 1 E
Sayḩut, *Yemen* . . . . 46 D5 15 12N 51 10 E
Saynshand, *Mongolia* . . . 34 B6 44 55N 110 11 E
Sayre, *Okla., U.S.A.* 81 H5 35 18N 99 38W
Sayre, *Pa., U.S.A.* 79 E8 41 59N 76 32W
Sayula, *Mexico* 86 D4 19 50N 103 40W
Sazanit, *Albania* . . . . 21 D8 40 30N 19 20 E
Sázava →, *Czech.* . . . . . 16 D8 49 53N 14 24 E
Sazin, *Pakistan* . . . . 43 B5 35 35N 73 30 E
Scafell Pike, *U.K.* 10 C4 54 27N 3 14W
Scalpay, *U.K.* 12 D2 57 52N 6 40W
Scandia, *Canada* 72 C6 50 20N 112 0W
Scandicci, *Italy* . . . . 20 C4 43 45N 11 11 E
Scandinavia, *Europe* . . . . 6 C8 64 0N 12 0 E
Scapa Flow, *U.K.* 12 C5 58 53N 3 3W
Scappoose, *U.S.A.* 84 E4 45 45N 122 53W
Scarborough, *Trin. & Tob.* 89 D7 11 11N 60 42W
Scarborough, *U.K.* 10 C7 54 17N 0 24W
Scebeli, Wabi →, *Somali Rep.* . . . . 46 G3 2 0N 44 0 E
Scenic, *U.S.A.* 80 D3 43 47N 102 33W
Schaffhausen, *Switz.* . . . . 16 E5 47 42N 8 39 E
Schagen, *Neths.* . . . . 15 B4 52 49N 4 48 E
Schefferville, *Canada* 71 B6 54 48N 66 50W
Schelde →, *Belgium* . . . 15 C4 51 15N 4 16 E
Schell Creek Ra., *U.S.A.* . 82 G6 39 15N 114 30W
Schenectady, *U.S.A.* 79 D11 42 49N 73 57W
Scheveningen, *Neths.* . . . 15 B4 52 6N 4 16 E
Schiedam, *Neths.* . . . . 15 C4 51 55N 4 25 E
Schiermonnikoog, *Neths.* 15 A6 53 30N 6 15 E
Schio, *Italy* . . . . 20 B4 45 43N 11 21 E
Schleswig, *Germany* . . . . 16 A5 54 31N 9 34 E
Schleswig-Holstein □, *Germany* . . . . 16 A5 54 30N 9 30 E
Schofield, *U.S.A.* 80 C10 44 54N 89 36W
Scholls, *U.S.A.* 84 E4 45 24N 122 56W
Schouten I., *Australia* . . . 62 G4 42 20S 148 20 E
Schouten Is. = Supiori, *Indonesia* . . . . 37 E9 1 0S 136 0 E
Schouwen, *Neths.* . . . . . . 15 C3 51 43N 3 45 E
Schreiber, *Canada* 70 C2 48 45N 87 20W
Schuler, *Canada* 73 C6 50 20N 110 6W
Schumacher, *Canada* 70 C3 48 30N 81 16W
Schurz, *U.S.A.* 82 G4 38 57N 118 49W
Schuyler, *U.S.A.* 80 E6 41 27N 97 4W
Schuylkill Haven, *U.S.A.* . 79 F8 40 37N 76 11W
Schwäbische Alb, *Germany* . . . . 16 D5 48 20N 9 30 E
Schwaner, Pegunungan, *Indonesia* . . . . 36 E4 1 0S 112 30 E
Schwarzwald, *Germany* . 16 D5 48 30N 8 20 E
Schwedt, *Germany* . . . . . 16 B8 53 3N 14 16 E
Schweinfurt, *Germany* . . 16 C6 50 3N 10 14 E
Schweizer-Reneke, *S. Africa* . . . . 56 D4 27 11S 25 18 E
Schwenningen = Villingen-Schwenningen, *Germany* . . . . 16 D5 48 3N 8 26 E
Schwerin, *Germany* . . . . . 16 B6 53 36N 11 22 E
Schwyz, *Switz.* . . . . 16 E5 47 2N 8 39 E
Sciacca, *Italy* . . . . 20 F5 37 31N 13 3 E
Scilla, *Italy* . . . . 20 E6 38 15N 15 43 E
Scilly, Isles of, *U.K.* 11 H1 49 56N 6 22W
Scioto →, *U.S.A.* 76 F4 38 44N 83 1W
Scobey, *U.S.A.* 80 A2 48 47N 105 25W
Scone, *Australia* . . . . 63 E5 32 5S 150 52 E
Scoresbysund, *Greenland* 4 B6 70 20N 23 0W
Scotia, *Calif., U.S.A.* 82 F1 40 29N 124 6W
Scotia, *N.Y., U.S.A.* 79 D11 42 50N 73 58W
Scotia Sea, *Antarctica* . . . 5 B18 56 5S 56 0W
Scotland, *U.S.A.* 80 D6 43 9N 97 43W
Scotland □, *U.K.* 12 E5 57 0N 4 0W
Scotland Neck, *U.S.A.* . . . 77 G7 36 8N 77 25W
Scott, C., *Australia* . . . . . 60 B4 13 30S 129 49 E
Scott City, *U.S.A.* 80 F4 38 29N 100 54W
Scott Glacier, *Antarctica* . 5 C8 66 15S 100 5 E
Scott I., *Antarctica* . . . . . 5 C11 67 0S 179 0 E
Scott Inlet, *Canada* 69 A12 71 0N 71 0W
Scott Is., *Canada* 72 C3 50 48N 128 40W
Scott L., *Canada* 73 B7 59 55N 106 18W
Scott Reef, *Australia* . . . 60 B3 14 0S 121 50 E
Scottburgh, *S. Africa* . . . 57 E5 30 15S 30 47 E
Scottdale, *U.S.A.* 78 F5 40 6N 79 35W
Scottsbluff, *U.S.A.* 80 E3 41 52N 103 40W
Scottsboro, *U.S.A.* 77 H2 34 40N 86 2W
Scottsburg, *U.S.A.* 76 F3 38 41N 85 47W
Scottsdale, *Australia* . . . . 62 G4 41 9S 147 31 E
Scottsdale, *U.S.A.* 83 K7 33 29N 111 56W
Scottsville, *Ky., U.S.A.* . . . 77 G2 36 45N 86 11W
Scottsville, *N.Y., U.S.A.* . . 78 C7 43 2N 77 47W
Scottville, *U.S.A.* 76 D2 43 58N 86 17W
Scranton, *U.S.A.* 79 E9 41 25N 75 40W
Scugog, L., *Canada* 78 B6 44 10N 78 55W
Scunthorpe, *U.K.* 10 D7 53 36N 0 39W
Scusciuban, *Somali Rep.* 46 E5 10 18N 50 12 E
Scutari = Üsküdar, *Turkey* 25 F4 41 0N 29 5 E
Seabrook, L., *Australia* . . 61 F2 30 55S 119 40 E
Seaford, *U.S.A.* 76 F8 38 39N 75 37W
Seaforth, *Canada* 70 D3 43 35N 81 25W
Seagraves, *U.S.A.* 81 J3 32 57N 102 34W
Seal →, *Canada* 73 B10 59 4N 94 48W
Seal Cove, *Canada* 71 C8 49 57N 56 22W
Seal L., *Canada* 71 B7 54 20N 61 30W
Sealy, *U.S.A.* 81 L6 29 47N 96 9W
Searchlight, *U.S.A.* 85 K12 35 28N 114 55W
Searcy, *U.S.A.* 81 H9 35 15N 91 44W
Searles L., *U.S.A.* 85 K9 35 44N 117 21W
Seaside, *Calif., U.S.A.* . . . 84 J5 36 37N 121 50W
Seaside, *Oreg., U.S.A.* . . . 84 E3 46 0N 123 56W
Seaspray, *Australia* . . . . . 63 F4 38 25S 147 15 E
Seattle, *U.S.A.* 84 C4 47 36N 122 20W
Seaview Ra., *Australia* . . 62 B4 18 40S 145 45 E
Sebastián Vizcaino, B., *Mexico* 86 B2 28 0N 114 30W
Sebastopol = Sevastopol, *Ukraine* . . . . 25 F5 44 35N 33 30 E
Sebastopol, *U.S.A.* 84 G4 38 24N 122 49W
Sebewaing, *U.S.A.* 76 D4 43 44N 83 27W
Sebha = Sabhah, *Libya* . 51 C7 27 9N 14 29 E
Sebring, *Fla., U.S.A.* 77 M5 27 30N 81 27W
Sebring, *Ohio, U.S.A.* . . . 78 F3 40 55N 81 2W
Sebringville, *Canada* 78 C3 43 24N 81 4W
Sebta = Ceuta, *N. Afr.* . . 19 E3 35 52N 5 18W
Sebuku, *Indonesia* . . . . . . 36 E5 3 30S 116 25 E
Sebuku, Teluk, *Malaysia* . 36 D5 4 0N 118 10 E
Sechelt, *Canada* 72 D4 49 25N 123 42W
Sechura, Desierto de, *Peru* 92 E2 6 0S 80 30W
Secretary I., *N.Z.* . . . . 59 L1 45 15S 166 56 E
Secunderabad, *India* . . . . 40 L11 17 28N 78 30 E
Sedalia, *U.S.A.* 80 F8 38 42N 93 14W
Sedan, *Australia* . . . . 63 E2 34 34S 139 19 E
Sedan, *France* . . . . 18 B6 49 43N 4 57 E
Sedan, *U.S.A.* 81 G6 37 8N 96 11W
Seddon, *N.Z.* . . . . 59 J5 41 40S 174 7 E
Seddonville, *N.Z.* . . . . 59 J4 41 33S 172 1 E
Sedeh, *Fārs, Iran* . . . . 45 D7 30 45N 52 11 E
Sedeh, *Khorāsān, Iran* . . . 45 C8 33 20N 59 14 E
Sederot, *Israel* . . . . 47 D3 31 32N 34 37 E
Sedgewick, *Canada* 72 C6 52 48N 111 41W
Sedhiou, *Senegal* 50 F1 12 44N 15 30W
Sedley, *Canada* 73 C8 50 10N 104 0W
Sedova, Pik, *Russia* . . . . . 26 B6 73 29N 54 58 E
Sedro Woolley, *U.S.A.* . . . 84 B4 48 30N 122 14W
Seeheim, *Namibia* . . . . 56 D2 26 50S 17 45 E
Seekoei →, *S. Africa* . . . 56 E4 30 18S 25 1 E
Seferihisar, *Turkey* . . . . . 21 E12 38 10N 26 50 E
Seg-ozero, *Russia* . . . . . . 24 B5 63 20N 33 46 E
Segamat, *Malaysia* . . . . . . 39 L4 2 30N 102 50 E
Segesta, *Italy* . . . . 20 F5 37 56N 12 50 E
Seget, *Indonesia* . . . . 37 E8 1 24S 130 58 E
Segezha, *Russia* . . . . 24 B5 63 44N 34 19 E
Ségou, *Mali* 50 F3 13 30N 6 16W
Segovia = Coco →, *Cent. Amer.* 88 D3 15 0N 83 8W
Segovia, *Spain* 19 B3 40 57N 4 10W
Segre →, *Spain* . . . . 19 B6 41 40N 0 43 E
Séguéla, *Ivory C.* 50 G3 7 55N 6 40W
Seguin, *U.S.A.* 81 L6 29 34N 97 58W
Segundo →, *Argentina* . 94 C3 30 53S 62 44W
Segura →, *Spain* 19 C5 38 3N 0 44W
Seh Qal'eh, *Iran* . . . . 45 C8 33 40N 58 24 E
Sehitwa, *Botswana* . . . . . . 56 C3 20 30S 22 30 E
Sehore, *India* . . . . 42 H7 23 10N 77 5 E
Sehwan, *Pakistan* . . . . 42 F2 26 28N 67 53 E
Seiland, *Norway* . . . . 8 A20 70 25N 23 15 E
Seiling, *U.S.A.* 81 G5 36 9N 98 56W
Seinäjoki, *Finland* . . . . . . 9 E20 62 40N 22 51 E
Seine →, *France* . . . . 18 B4 49 26N 0 26 E
Seistan, *Iran* . . . . 45 D9 30 50N 61 0 E
Sekayu, *Indonesia* . . . . . . 36 E2 2 51S 103 51 E
Seke, *Tanzania* . . . . 54 C3 3 20S 33 31 E
Sekenke, *Tanzania* . . . . . . 54 C3 4 18S 34 11 E
Sekondi-Takoradi, *Ghana* 50 H4 4 58N 1 45W
Sekuma, *Botswana* . . . . . . 56 C3 24 36S 23 50 E
Selah, *U.S.A.* 82 C3 46 39N 120 32W
Selama, *Malaysia* . . . . 39 K3 5 12N 100 42 E
Selaru, *Indonesia* . . . . 37 F8 8 9S 131 0 E
Selby, *U.K.* 10 D6 53 47N 1 5W
Selby, *U.S.A.* 80 C4 45 31N 100 2W
Selçuk, *Turkey* . . . . 21 F12 37 56N 27 22 E
Selden, *U.S.A.* 80 F4 39 33N 100 34W
Sele →, *Italy* . . . . 20 D6 40 29N 14 56 E
Selemdzha →, *Russia* . . 27 D13 51 42N 128 53 E
Selenga = Selenge Mörön →, *Asia* . . . . . . 32 A5 52 16N 106 16 E
Selenge Mörön →, *Asia* 32 A5 52 16N 106 16 E
Seletan, Tg., *Indonesia* . . 36 E4 4 10S 114 40 E
Selfridge, *U.S.A.* 80 B4 46 2N 100 56W
Sélibabi, *Mauritania* 50 E2 15 10N 12 15W
Seligman, *U.S.A.* 83 J7 35 20N 112 53W
Selîma, El Wâhât el, *Sudan* . . . . 51 D10 21 22N 29 19 E
Selinda Spillway, *Botswana* . . . . 56 B3 18 35S 23 10 E
Selkirk, *Canada* 73 C9 50 10N 96 55W
Selkirk, *U.K.* 12 F6 55 33N 2 50W
Selkirk I., *Canada* 73 C9 53 20N 99 6W
Selkirk Mts., *Canada* 72 C5 51 15N 117 40W
Selliá, *Greece* . . . . 23 D6 35 12N 24 23 E
Sells, *U.S.A.* 83 L8 31 55N 111 53W
Selma, *Ala., U.S.A.* 77 J2 32 25N 87 1W
Selma, *Calif., U.S.A.* 83 H4 36 34N 119 37W
Selma, *N.C., U.S.A.* 77 H6 35 32N 78 17W
Selmer, *U.S.A.* 77 H1 35 10N 88 36W
Selowandoma Falls, *Zimbabwe* . . . . 55 G3 21 15S 31 50 E
Selpele, *Indonesia* . . . . . . 37 E8 0 1S 130 5 E
Selsey Bill, *U.K.* 11 G7 50 43N 0 47W
Selu, *Indonesia* . . . . 37 F8 7 32S 130 55 E
Selva, *Argentina* 94 B3 29 50S 62 0W
Selvas, *Brazil* 92 E5 6 30S 67 0W
Selwyn, *Australia* . . . . 62 C3 21 32S 140 30 E
Selwyn L., *Canada* 73 A8 60 0N 104 30W
Selwyn Ra., *Australia* . . . . 62 C3 21 10S 140 0 E
Semani →, *Albania* . . . . 21 D8 40 47N 19 30 E
Semarang, *Indonesia* . . . . 37 G14 7 0S 110 26 E
Semau, *Indonesia* . . . . 37 F6 10 13S 123 22 E
Sembabule, *Uganda* . . . . . 54 C3 0 4S 31 25 E
Semeru, *Indonesia* . . . . . . 37 H15 8 4S 112 55 E
Semey, *Kazakstan* . . . . . . 26 D9 50 30N 80 10 E
Seminoe Reservoir, *U.S.A.* 82 E10 42 9N 106 55W
Seminole, *Okla., U.S.A.* . . 81 H6 35 14N 96 41W
Seminole, *Tex., U.S.A.* . . . 81 J3 32 43N 102 39W
Semiozernoye, *Kazakstan* 26 D7 52 22N 64 8 E
Semipalatinsk = Semey, *Kazakstan* . . . . 26 D9 50 30N 80 10 E
Semirara Is., *Phil.* . . . . 37 B6 12 0N 121 20 E
Semisopochnoi I., *U.S.A.* 68 C2 51 55N 179 36 E
Semitau, *Indonesia* . . . . . . 36 D4 0 29N 111 57 E
Semiyarka, *Kazakstan* . . . . 26 D8 50 55N 78 23 E
Semiyarskoye = Semiyarka, *Kazakstan* . 26 D8 50 55N 78 23 E
Semmering P., *Austria* . . 16 E8 47 41N 15 45 E
Semnān, *Iran* . . . . 45 C7 35 40N 53 23 E
Semnān □, *Iran* . . . . 45 C7 36 0N 54 0 E
Semois →, *Europe* . . . . 15 E4 49 53N 4 44 E
Semporna, *Malaysia* . . . . 37 D5 4 30N 118 33 E
Semuda, *Indonesia* . . . . . 36 E4 2 51S 112 58 E
Senā, *Iran* . . . . 45 D6 28 27N 51 36 E
Sena, *Mozam.* . . . . 55 F3 17 25S 35 0 E
Sena Madureira, *Brazil* . . 92 E5 9 5S 68 45W
Senador Pompeu, *Brazil* . 93 E11 5 40S 39 20W
Senaja, *Malaysia* . . . . 36 C5 6 45N 117 3 E
Senanga, *Zambia* . . . . 56 B3 16 2S 23 14 E
Senatobia, *U.S.A.* 81 H10 34 37N 89 58W
Sendai, *Kagoshima, Japan* 31 J5 31 50N 130 20 E
Sendai, *Miyagi, Japan* . . . 30 E10 38 15N 140 53 E
Sendai-Wan, *Japan* . . . . . 30 E10 38 15N 141 0 E
Seneca, *Oreg., U.S.A.* . . . 82 D4 44 8N 118 58W
Seneca, *S.C., U.S.A.* 77 H4 34 41N 82 57W
Seneca Falls, *U.S.A.* 79 D8 42 55N 76 48W
Seneca L., *U.S.A.* 78 D8 42 40N 76 54W
Senegal ■, *W. Afr.* 50 F2 14 30N 14 30W
Senegal →, *W. Afr.* 50 E1 15 48N 16 32W
Senegambia, *Africa* 48 E2 12 45N 12 0W
Senekal, *S. Africa* . . . . . . 57 D4 28 20S 27 36 E
Senga Hill, *Zambia* . . . . . 55 D3 9 19S 31 11 E
Senge Khambab = Indus →, *Pakistan* . . . 42 G2 24 20N 67 47 E
Sengerema □, *Tanzania* . 54 C3 2 10S 32 20 E
Sengkang, *Indonesia* . . . . 37 E6 4 8S 120 1 E
Sengua →, *Zimbabwe* . . . 55 F2 17 7S 28 5 E
Senhor-do-Bonfim, *Brazil* 93 F10 10 30S 40 10W
Senigállia, *Italy* . . . . 20 C5 43 43N 13 13 E
Senj, *Croatia* . . . . 16 F8 45 0N 14 58 E
Senja, *Norway* . . . . 8 B17 69 25N 17 30 E
Senlis, *France* . . . . 18 B5 49 13N 2 35 E
Senmonorom, *Cambodia* . 38 F6 12 27N 107 12 E
Sennâr, *Sudan* . . . . 51 F11 13 30N 33 35 E
Senneterre, *Canada* 70 C4 48 25N 77 15W
Seno, *Laos* . . . . 38 D5 16 35N 104 50 E
Sens, *France* . . . . 18 B5 48 11N 3 15 E
Senta, *Serbia, Yug.* . . . . . 21 B9 45 55N 20 3 E
Sentani, *Indonesia* . . . . . . 37 E10 2 36S 140 37 E
Sentery, *Zaire* . . . . 54 D2 5 17S 25 42 E
Sentinel, *U.S.A.* 83 K7 32 52N 113 13W
Sentolo, *Indonesia* . . . . . . 37 G14 7 55S 110 13 E
Seo de Urgel, *Spain* . . . . 19 A6 42 22N 1 23 E
Seohara, *India* . . . . 43 E8 29 15N 78 33 E
Seoni, *India* . . . . 43 H8 22 5N 79 30 E
Seoul = Sŏul, *S. Korea* . . 35 F14 37 31N 126 58 E
Separation Point, *Canada* 71 B8 53 37N 57 25W
Sepīdān, *Iran* . . . . 45 D7 30 20N 52 5 E
Sepo-ri, *N. Korea* . . . . 35 E14 38 57N 127 25 E
Sepone, *Laos* . . . . 38 D6 16 45N 106 13 E
Sept-Îles, *Canada* 71 B6 50 13N 66 22W
Sequim, *U.S.A.* 84 B3 48 5N 123 6W
Sequoia National Park, *U.S.A.* 83 H4 36 30N 118 30W
Seraing, *Belgium* . . . . 15 D5 50 35N 5 32 E
Seraja, *Indonesia* . . . . . . 39 L7 2 41N 108 35 E
Serakhis →, *Cyprus* . . . . 23 D11 35 13N 32 55 E
Seram, *Indonesia* . . . . 37 E7 3 10S 129 0 E
Seram Laut, Kepulauan, *Indonesia* . . . . 37 E8 4 5S 131 25 E
Seram Sea, *Indonesia* . . . 37 E7 2 30S 128 30 E
Serang, *Indonesia* . . . . 37 G12 6 8S 106 10 E
Serasan, *Indonesia* . . . . . . 39 L7 2 29N 109 4 E
Serbia □, *Yugoslavia* . . . . 21 C9 43 30N 21 0 E
Serdobsk, *Russia* . . . . 24 D7 52 28N 44 10 E
Seremban, *Malaysia* . . . . . 39 L3 2 43N 101 53 E
Serengeti □, *Tanzania* . . . 54 C3 2 0S 34 30 E
Serengeti Plain, *Tanzania* 54 C3 2 40S 35 0 E
Serenje, *Zambia* . . . . 55 E3 13 14S 30 15 E
Sereth = Siret →, *Romania* . . . . 17 F14 45 24N 28 1 E
Sergipe □, *Brazil* 93 F11 10 30S 37 30W
Sergiyev Posad, *Russia* . . 24 C6 56 20N 38 10 E
Seria, *Brunei* . . . . 36 D4 4 37N 114 23 E
Serian, *Malaysia* . . . . 36 D4 1 10N 110 31 E
Seribu, Kepulauan, *Indonesia* . . . . 36 F3 5 36S 106 33 E
Sérifos, *Greece* . . . . 21 F11 37 9N 24 30 E
Seringapatam Reef, *Australia* . . . . 60 B3 13 38S 122 5 E
Sermata, *Indonesia* . . . . . . 37 F7 8 15S 128 50 E
Serny Zavod, *Turkmenistan* . . . . 26 F6 39 59N 58 50 E
Serov, *Russia* . . . . 24 C11 59 29N 60 35 E
Serowe, *Botswana* . . . . 56 C4 22 25S 26 43 E
Serpentine, *Australia* . . . . 61 F2 32 23S 115 58 E
Serpentine Lakes, *Australia* . . . . 61 E4 28 30S 129 10 E
Serpukhov, *Russia* . . . . . . 24 D6 54 55N 37 28 E
Sérrai, *Greece* . . . . 21 D10 41 5N 23 31 E
Serrezuela, *Argentina* . . . 94 C2 30 40S 65 20W
Serrinha, *Brazil* 93 F11 11 39S 39 0W
Sertânia, *Brazil* 93 E11 8 5S 37 20W
Sertanópolis, *Brazil* 95 A5 23 4S 51 2W
Serua, *Indonesia* . . . . 37 F8 6 18S 130 1 E
Serui, *Indonesia* . . . . 37 E9 1 53S 136 10 E
Serule, *Botswana* . . . . 56 C4 21 57S 27 20 E
Sese Is., *Uganda* . . . . 54 C3 0 20S 32 20 E
Sesepe, *Indonesia* . . . . 37 E7 1 30S 127 59 E
Sesfontein, *Namibia* . . . . 56 B1 19 7S 13 39 E
Sesheke, *Zambia* . . . . 56 B3 17 29S 24 13 E
S'estañol, *Spain* . . . . 22 B9 39 22N 2 54 E
Setana, *Japan* . . . . 30 C9 42 26N 139 51 E
Sète, *France* . . . . 18 E5 43 25N 3 42 E
Sete Lagôas, *Brazil* 93 G10 19 27S 44 16W
Sétif, *Algeria* . . . . 50 A6 36 9N 5 26 E
Seto, *Japan* . . . . 31 G8 35 14N 137 6 E
Setonaikai, *Japan* . . . . 31 G6 34 20N 133 30 E
Settat, *Morocco* 50 B3 33 0N 7 40W
Setté-Cama, *Gabon* . . . . . 52 E1 2 32S 9 45 E
Setting L., *Canada* 73 B9 55 0N 98 38W
Settle, *U.K.* 10 C5 54 5N 2 16W
Settlement Pt., *Bahamas* . 77 M6 26 40N 79 0W
Setúbal, *Portugal* 19 C1 38 30N 8 58W
Setúbal, B. de, *Portugal* . 19 C1 38 40N 8 56W
Seulimeum, *Indonesia* . . 36 C1 5 27N 95 15 E
Sevan, Ozero = Sevana Lich, *Armenia* . . . . 25 F8 40 30N 45 20 E
Sevana Lich, *Armenia* . . . 25 F8 40 30N 45 20 E
Sevastopol, *Ukraine* . . . . 25 F5 44 35N 33 30 E
Seven Emu, *Australia* . . . 62 B2 16 20S 137 8 E
Seven Sisters, *Canada* . . 72 C3 54 56N 128 10W
Severn →, *Canada* 70 A2 56 2N 87 36W
Severn →, *U.K.* 11 F5 51 35N 2 40W
Severn L., *Canada* 70 B1 53 54N 90 48W
Severnaya Zemlya, *Russia* 27 B10 79 0N 100 0 E
Severnyye Uvaly, *Russia* 24 C8 60 0N 50 0 E
Severo-Kurilsk, *Russia* . . . 27 D16 50 40N 156 8 E
Severo-Yeniseyskiy, *Russia* . . . . 27 C10 60 22N 93 1 E
Severodvinsk, *Russia* . . . 24 B6 64 27N 39 58 E
Severomorsk, *Russia* . . . . 24 A5 69 5N 33 27 E
Severouralsk, *Russia* . . . 24 B10 60 9N 59 57 E
Sevier, *U.S.A.* 83 G7 38 39N 112 11W
Sevier →, *U.S.A.* 83 G7 39 4N 113 6W
Sevier L., *U.S.A.* 82 G7 38 54N 113 9W
Sevilla, *Spain* 19 D2 37 23N 6 0W
Seville = Sevilla, *Spain* . . 19 D2 37 23N 6 0W
Sevlievo, *Bulgaria* . . . . . . 21 C11 43 2N 25 3 E
Seward, *Alaska, U.S.A.* . . 68 B5 60 7N 149 27W
Seward, *Nebr., U.S.A.* 80 E6 40 55N 97 6W
Seward Pen., *U.S.A.* 68 B3 65 0N 164 0W
Sewell, *Chile* 94 C1 34 10S 70 23W
Sewer, *Indonesia* . . . . 37 F8 5 53S 134 40 E
Sewickley, *U.S.A.* 78 F4 40 32N 80 12W
Sexsmith, *Canada* 72 B5 55 21N 118 47W
Seychelles ■, *Ind. Oc.* . . . 49 G9 5 0S 56 0 E
Seyðisfjörður, *Iceland* . . . 8 D6 65 16N 13 57W
Seydvān, *Iran* . . . . 44 B5 38 34N 45 2 E
Seymchan, *Russia* . . . . . . 27 C16 62 54N 152 30 E
Seymour, *Australia* . . . . . . 63 F4 37 0S 145 10 E
Seymour, *S. Africa* . . . . . . 57 E4 32 33S 26 46 E
Seymour, *Conn., U.S.A.* . . 79 E11 41 24N 73 4W
Seymour, *Ind., U.S.A.* 76 F3 38 58N 85 53W
Seymour, *Tex., U.S.A.* 81 J5 33 35N 99 16W
Seymour, *Wis., U.S.A.* . . . 76 C1 44 31N 88 20W
Sfax, *Tunisia* . . . . 51 B7 34 49N 10 48 E
Sfîntu Gheorghe, *Romania* 17 F13 45 52N 25 48 E
Shaanxi □, *China* . . . . 34 G5 35 0N 109 0 E
Shaba □, *Zaïre* . . . . 54 D2 8 0S 25 0 E
Shabunda, *Zaïre* . . . . 54 C2 2 40S 27 16 E
Shache, *China* . . . . 32 C2 38 20N 77 10 E
Shackleton Ice Shelf, *Antarctica* . . . . 5 C8 66 0S 100 0 E
Shackleton Inlet, *Antarctica* . . . . 5 E11 83 0S 160 0 E
Shādegān, *Iran* . . . . 45 D6 30 40N 48 38 E
Shadi, *India* . . . . 43 C7 33 24N 77 14 E
Shadrinsk, *Russia* . . . . 26 D7 56 5N 63 32 E
Shafter, *Calif., U.S.A.* 85 K7 35 30N 119 16W
Shafter, *Tex., U.S.A.* 81 L2 29 49N 104 18W
Shaftesbury, *U.K.* 11 F5 51 0N 2 11W
Shagram, *Pakistan* . . . . . . 43 A5 36 24N 72 20 E
Shah Bunder, *Pakistan* . . . 42 G2 24 13N 67 56 E
Shahabad, *Punjab, India* . . 42 D7 30 10N 76 55 E
Shahabad, *Raj., India* . . . . 42 G7 25 15N 77 11 E
Shahabad, *Ut. P., India* . . . 43 F8 27 36N 79 56 E
Shahadpur, *Pakistan* . . . . . 42 G3 25 55N 68 35 E
Shahba, *Syria* . . . . 47 C5 32 52N 36 38 E
Shahdād, *Iran* . . . . 45 D8 30 30N 57 40 E
Shahdadkot, *Pakistan* . . . . 42 F2 27 50N 67 55 E
Shahe, *China* . . . . 34 F8 37 0N 114 32 E
Shahganj, *India* . . . . 43 F10 26 3N 82 44 E
Shahgarh, *India* . . . . 40 F6 27 15N 69 50 E
Shaḩḩāt, *Libya* . . . . 51 B9 32 48N 21 54 E
Shahjahanpur, *India* . . . . . 43 F8 27 54N 79 57 E
Shahpur, *India* . . . . 42 H7 22 12N 77 58 E
Shahpur, *Pakistan* . . . . 42 E3 28 46N 68 27 E
Shahpura, *India* . . . . 43 H9 23 10N 80 45 E
Shahr Kord, *Iran* . . . . 45 C6 32 15N 50 55 E
Shāhrakht, *Iran* . . . . 45 C9 33 38N 60 16 E
Shahrig, *Pakistan* . . . . 42 D2 30 15N 67 40 E
Shahukou, *China* . . . . 34 D7 40 20N 112 18 E
Shaikhabad, *Afghan.* . . . . . 42 B3 34 2N 68 45 E
Shajapur, *India* . . . . 42 H7 23 27N 76 21 E
Shakargarh, *Pakistan* . . . . 42 C6 32 17N 75 10 E
Shakawe, *Botswana* . . . . . . 56 B3 18 28S 21 49 E
Shaker Heights, *U.S.A.* . . . 78 E3 41 29N 81 32W
Shakhty, *Russia* . . . . 25 E7 47 40N 40 16 E
Shakhunya, *Russia* . . . . . . 24 C8 57 40N 46 46 E
Shaki, *Nigeria* . . . . 50 G5 8 41N 3 21 E
Shala, L., *Ethiopia* . . . . . . 51 G12 7 30N 38 30 E
Shallow Lake, *Canada* 78 B3 44 36N 81 5W
Shalqar, *Kazakstan* . . . . . . 26 E6 47 48N 59 39 E
Shaluli Shan, *China* . . . . . . 32 C4 30 40N 99 55 E
Shām, *Iran* . . . . 45 E8 26 39N 57 21 E
Shamâl Kordofân □, *Sudan* . . . . 48 E6 15 0N 30 0 E
Shamanovo, *Russia* . . . . . . 27 C15 69 45N 147 20 E
Shamattawa, *Canada* 73 B10 55 51N 92 5W
Shamattawa →, *Canada* 70 A2 55 1N 85 23W
Shamīl, *Iran* . . . . 45 E8 27 30N 56 55 E
Shāmkūh, *Iran* . . . . 45 C8 35 47N 57 50 E
Shamli, *India* . . . . 42 E7 29 32N 77 18 E
Shamo = Gobi, *Asia* . . . . 34 C5 44 0N 111 0 E
Shamo, L., *Ethiopia* . . . . . 51 G12 5 45N 37 30 E
Shamokin, *U.S.A.* 79 F8 40 47N 76 34W
Shamrock, *U.S.A.* 81 H4 35 13N 100 15W
Shamva, *Zimbabwe* . . . . . . 55 F3 17 20S 31 32 E
Shan □, *Burma* . . . . 41 J21 21 30N 98 30 E
Shan Xian, *China* . . . . 34 G9 34 50N 116 5 E
Shanchengzhen, *China* . . . 35 C13 42 20N 125 20 E

Songnim

Sind □, *Pakistan* ...... **42 F3** 26 0N 69 0 E
Sind →, *India* .... **43 B6** 34 18N 74 45 E
Sind Sagar Doab, *Pakistan* **42 D4** 32 0N 71 30 E
Sindangan, *Phil.* .... **37 C6** 8 10N 123 5 E
Sindangbarang, *Indonesia* **37 G12** 7 27S 107 1 E
Sinde, *Zambia* .... **55 F2** 17 28S 25 51 E
Sines, *Portugal* **19 D1** 37 56N 8 51W
Sines, C. de, *Portugal* ... **19 D1** 37 58N 8 53W
Sineu, *Spain* .... **22 B10** 39 38N 3 1 E
Sing Buri, *Thailand* .... **38 E3** 14 53N 100 25 E
Singa, *Sudan* .... **51 F11** 13 10N 33 57 E
Singapore ■, *Asia* ..... **39 M4** 1 17N 103 51 E
Singapore, Straits of, *Asia* **39 M5** 1 15N 104 0 E
Singaraja, *Indonesia* ... **36 F5** 8 6S 115 10 E
Singida, *Tanzania* ..... **54 C3** 4 49S 34 48 E
Singida □, *Tanzania* ... **54 D3** 6 0S 34 30 E
Singitikós Kólpos, *Greece* **21 D11** 40 6N 24 0 E
Singkaling Hkamti, *Burma* **41 G19** 26 0N 95 39 E
Singkawang, *Indonesia* .. **36 D3** 1 0N 108 57 E
Singleton, *Australia* .... **63 E5** 32 33S 151 0 E
Singleton, Mt., *N. Terr., Australia* .... **60 D5** 22 0S 130 46 E
Singleton, Mt., *W. Austral., Australia* .. **61 E2** 29 27S 117 15 E
Singoli, *India* .... **42 G6** 25 0N 75 22 E
Singora = Songkhla, *Thailand* .... **39 J3** 7 13N 100 37 E
Singosan, *N. Korea* ..... **35 E14** 38 52N 127 25 E
Sinhung, *N. Korea* ..... **35 D14** 40 11N 127 34 E
Sînî □, *Egypt* .... **47 F2** 30 0N 34 0 E
Sinjai, *Indonesia* ...... **37 F6** 5 7S 120 20 E
Sinjār, *Iraq* .... **44 B4** 36 19N 41 52 E
Sinkat, *Sudan* .... **51 E12** 18 55N 36 49 E
Sinkiang Uighur = Xinjiang Uygur Zizhiqu □, *China* ..... **32 B3** 42 0N 86 0 E
Sinmak, *N. Korea* ...... **35 E14** 38 25N 126 14 E
Sinni →, *Italy* .... **20 D7** 40 8N 16 41 E
Sînnicolau Maré, *Romania* **17 E11** 46 5N 20 39 E
Sinnuris, *Egypt* .... **51 C11** 29 26N 30 31 E
Sinop, *Turkey* .... **25 F6** 42 1N 35 11 E
Sinpo, *N. Korea* .... **35 E15** 40 0N 128 13 E
Sinsk, *Russia* .... **27 C13** 61 8N 126 48 E
Sint Eustatius, I., *Neth. Ant.* **89 C7** 17 30N 62 59W
Sint Maarten, I., *W. Indies* **89 C7** 18 4N 63 4W
Sint Niklaas, *Belgium* .... **15 C4** 51 10N 4 9 E
Sint Truiden, *Belgium* .... **15 D5** 50 48N 5 10 E
Sintang, *Indonesia* ..... **36 D4** 0 5N 111 35 E
Sinton, *U.S.A.* **81 L6** 28 2N 97 31W
Sintra, *Portugal* **19 C1** 38 47N 9 25W
Sinŭiju, *N. Korea* ...... **35 D13** 40 5N 124 24 E
Siocon, *Phil.* .... **37 C6** 7 40N 122 10 E
Siófok, *Hungary* .... **17 E10** 46 54N 18 3 E
Sioma, *Zambia* .... **56 B3** 16 25S 23 28 E
Sion, *Switz.* .... **16 E4** 46 14N 7 20 E
Sioux City, *U.S.A.* **80 D6** 42 30N 96 24W
Sioux Falls, *U.S.A.* **80 D6** 43 33N 96 44W
Sioux Lookout, *Canada* .. **70 B1** 50 10N 91 50W
Siping, *China* .... **35 C13** 43 8N 124 21 E
Sipiwesk L., *Canada* **73 B9** 55 5N 97 35W
Sipura, *Indonesia* ...... **36 E1** 2 18S 99 40 E
Siquia →, *Nic.* **88 D3** 12 10N 84 20W
Siquijor, *Phil.* .... **37 C6** 9 12N 123 35 E
Siquirres, *Costa Rica* ... **88 D3** 10 6N 83 30W
Sir Edward Pellew Group, *Australia* .... **62 B2** 15 40S 137 10 E
Sir Graham Moore Is., *Australia* .... **60 B4** 13 53S 126 34 E
Sira →, *Norway* .... **9 G12** 58 23N 6 34 E
Siracusa, *Italy* .... **20 F6** 37 4N 15 17 E
Sirajganj, *Bangla.* ...... **43 G13** 24 25N 89 47 E
Sirdān, *Iran* .... **45 B6** 36 39N 49 12 E
Sirdaryo = Syrdarya →, *Kazakstan* .... **26 E7** 46 3N 61 0 E
Sirer, *Spain* .... **22 C7** 38 56N 1 22 E
Siret →, *Romania* ..... **17 F14** 45 24N 28 1 E
Sirohi, *India* .... **42 G5** 24 52N 72 53 E
Sironj, *India* .... **42 G7** 24 5N 77 39 E
Síros, *Greece* .... **21 F11** 37 28N 24 57 E
Sirretta Pk., *U.S.A.* **85 K8** 35 56N 118 19W
Sirsa, *India* .... **42 E6** 29 33N 75 4 E
Sisak, *Croatia* .... **16 F9** 45 30N 16 21 E
Sisaket, *Thailand* .... **38 E5** 15 8N 104 23 E
Sishen, *S. Africa* .... **56 D3** 27 47S 22 59 E
Sishui, *Henan, China* .... **34 G7** 34 48N 113 15 E
Sishui, *Shandong, China* . **35 G9** 35 42N 117 18 E
Sisipuk L., *Canada* **73 B8** 55 45N 101 50W
Sisophon, *Cambodia* .... **38 F4** 13 38N 102 59 E
Sisseton, *U.S.A.* **80 C6** 45 40N 97 3W
Sīstān va Balūchestān □, *Iran* .... **45 E9** 27 0N 62 0 E
Sisters, *U.S.A.* **82 D3** 44 18N 121 33W
Sitamarhi, *India* .... **43 F11** 26 37N 85 30 E
Sitapur, *India* .... **43 F9** 27 38N 80 45 E
Siteki, *Swaziland* .... **57 D5** 26 32S 31 58 E
Sitges, *Spain* .... **19 B6** 41 17N 1 47 E
Sitía, *Greece* .... **23 D8** 35 13N 26 6 E
Sitka, *U.S.A.* **68 C6** 57 3N 135 20W
Sitoti, *Botswana* .... **56 C3** 23 15S 23 40 E
Sittang Myit →, *Burma* . **41 L20** 17 20N 96 45 E
Sittard, *Neths.* .... **15 C5** 51 0N 5 52 E
Sittwe, *Burma* .... **41 J18** 20 18N 92 45 E
Siuna, *Nic.* **88 D3** 13 37N 84 45W
Siuri, *India* .... **43 H12** 23 50N 87 34 E
Sivana, *India* .... **42 E8** 28 37N 78 6 E
Sīvand, *Iran* .... **45 D7** 30 5N 52 55 E
Sivas, *Turkey* .... **25 G6** 39 43N 36 58 E
Sivomaskinskiy, *Russia* .. **24 A11** 66 40N 62 35 E
Sivrihisar, *Turkey* ...... **25 G5** 39 30N 31 35 E
Sîwa, *Egypt* .... **51 C10** 29 11N 25 31 E
Siwa Oasis, *Egypt* ..... **48 D6** 29 10N 25 30 E
Siwalik Range, *Nepal* ... **43 F10** 28 0N 83 0 E
Siwan, *India* .... **43 F11** 26 13N 84 21 E
Sizewell, *U.K.* .... **11 E9** 52 12N 1 37 E
Siziwang Qi, *China* ..... **34 D6** 41 25N 111 40 E
Sjælland, *Denmark* ..... **9 J14** 55 30N 11 30 E
Sjumen = Šumen, *Bulgaria* .... **21 C12** 43 18N 26 55 E
Skadarsko Jezero, *Montenegro, Yug.* .... **21 C8** 42 10N 19 20 E
Skaftafell, *Iceland* **8 D5** 64 1N 17 0W
Skagafjörður, *Iceland* ... **8 D4** 65 54N 19 35W
Skagastølstindane, *Norway* .... **9 F12** 61 28N 7 52 E
Skagaströnd, *Iceland* **8 D3** 65 50N 20 19W
Skagen, *Denmark* .... **9 H14** 57 43N 10 35 E
Skagerrak, *Denmark* .... **9 H13** 57 30N 9 0 E
Skagit →, *U.S.A.* **84 B4** 48 23N 122 22W
Skagway, *U.S.A.* **72 B1** 59 28N 135 19W
Skala-Podilska, *Ukraine* .. **17 D14** 48 50N 26 15 E
Skala Podolskaya = Skala-Podilska, *Ukraine* ..... **17 D14** 48 50N 26 15 E
Skalat, *Ukraine* .... **17 D13** 49 23N 25 55 E
Skåne, *Sweden* .... **9 J15** 55 59N 13 30 E
Skara, *Sweden* .... **9 G15** 58 25N 13 30 E
Skardu, *Pakistan* .... **43 B6** 35 20N 75 44 E
Skarzysko-Kamienna, *Poland* .... **17 C11** 51 7N 20 52 E
Skeena →, *Canada* **72 C2** 54 9N 130 5W
Skeena Mts., *Canada* **72 B3** 56 40N 128 30W
Skegness, *U.K.* .... **10 D8** 53 9N 0 20 E
Skeldon, *Guyana* **92 B7** 5 55N 57 20W
Skellefte älv →, *Sweden* **8 D19** 64 45N 21 10 E
Skellefteå, *Sweden* ..... **8 D19** 64 45N 20 50 E
Skelleftehamn, *Sweden* . **8 D19** 64 40N 21 9 E
Skerries, The, *U.K.* **10 D3** 53 25N 4 36W
Ski, *Norway* .... **9 G14** 59 43N 10 52 E
Skíathos, *Greece* .... **21 E10** 39 12N 23 30 E
Skibbereen, *Ireland* **13 E2** 51 33N 9 16W
Skiddaw, *U.K.* **10 C4** 54 39N 3 9W
Skien, *Norway* .... **9 G13** 59 12N 9 35 E
Skierniewice, *Poland* .... **17 C11** 51 58N 20 10 E
Skikda, *Algeria* .... **50 A6** 36 50N 6 58 E
Skilloura, *Cyprus* .... **23 D12** 35 14N 33 10 E
Skipton, *Australia* ...... **63 F3** 37 39S 143 40 E
Skipton, *U.K.* **10 D5** 53 58N 2 3W
Skirmish Pt., *Australia* ... **62 A1** 11 59S 134 17 E
Skíros, *Greece* .... **21 E11** 38 55N 24 34 E
Skive, *Denmark* .... **9 H13** 56 33N 9 2 E
Skjálfandafljót →, *Iceland* **8 D5** 65 59N 17 25W
Skjálfandi, *Iceland* **8 C5** 66 5N 17 30W
Skoghall, *Sweden* ...... **9 G15** 59 20N 13 30 E
Skole, *Ukraine* .... **17 D12** 49 3N 23 30 E
Skópelos, *Greece* ...... **21 E10** 39 9N 23 47 E
Skopí, *Greece* .... **23 D8** 35 11N 26 2 E
Skopje, *Macedonia* ..... **21 C9** 42 1N 21 32 E
Skövde, *Sweden* .... **9 G15** 58 24N 13 50 E
Skovorodino, *Russia* .... **27 D13** 54 0N 124 0 E
Skowhegan, *U.S.A.* **71 D6** 44 46N 69 43W
Skownan, *Canada* **73 C9** 51 58N 99 35W
Skull, *Ireland* **13 E2** 51 32N 9 34W
Skunk →, *U.S.A.* **80 E9** 40 42N 91 7W
Skuodas, *Lithuania* ..... **9 H19** 56 16N 21 33 E
Skvyra, *Ukraine* .... **17 D15** 49 44N 29 40 E
Skye, *U.K.* **12 D2** 57 15N 6 10W
Skykomish, *U.S.A.* **82 C3** 47 42N 121 22W
Skyros = Skíros, *Greece* . **21 E11** 38 55N 24 34 E
Slættaratindur, *Færoe Is.* **8 E9** 62 18N 7 1W
Slagelse, *Denmark* ..... **9 J14** 55 23N 11 19 E
Slamet, *Indonesia* ...... **36 F3** 7 16S 109 8 E
Slaney →, *Ireland* **13 D5** 52 26N 6 33W
Śląsk, *Poland* .... **16 C9** 51 0N 16 30 E
Slate Is., *Canada* **70 C2** 48 40N 87 0W
Slatina, *Romania* .... **17 F13** 44 28N 24 22 E
Slaton, *U.S.A.* **81 J4** 33 26N 101 39W
Slave →, *Canada* **72 A6** 61 18N 113 39W
Slave Coast, *W. Afr.* .... **48 F4** 6 0N 2 30 E
Slave Lake, *Canada* **72 B6** 55 17N 114 43W
Slave Pt., *Canada* **72 A5** 61 11N 115 56W
Slavgorod, *Russia* ...... **26 D8** 53 1N 78 37 E
Slavonski Brod, *Croatia* . **21 B8** 45 11N 18 0 E
Slavuta, *Ukraine* .... **17 C14** 50 15N 27 2 E
Slavyanka, *Russia* ...... **30 C5** 42 53N 131 21 E
Slavyansk = Slovyansk, *Ukraine* .... **25 E6** 48 55N 37 36 E
Slawharad, *Belarus* ..... **17 B16** 53 27N 31 0 E
Sleaford, *U.K.* **10 E7** 53 0N 0 24W
Sleaford B., *Australia* ... **63 E2** 34 55S 135 45 E
Sleat, Sd. of, *U.K.* **12 D3** 57 5N 5 47W
Sleeper Is., *Canada* **69 C11** 58 30N 81 0W
Sleepy Eye, *U.S.A.* **80 C7** 44 18N 94 43W
Sleman, *Indonesia* ...... **37 G14** 7 40S 110 20 E
Slemon L., *Canada* **72 A5** 63 13N 116 4W
Slidell, *U.S.A.* **81 K10** 30 17N 89 47W
Sliedrecht, *Neths.* ...... **15 C4** 51 50N 4 45 E
Sliema, *Malta* .... **23 D2** 35 54N 14 30 E
Slieve Aughty, *Ireland* ... **13 C3** 53 4N 8 30W
Slieve Bloom, *Ireland* ... **13 C4** 53 4N 7 40W
Slieve Donard, *U.K.* **13 B6** 54 11N 5 55W
Slieve Gullion, *U.K.* **13 B5** 54 7N 6 26W
Slieve Mish, *Ireland* **13 D2** 52 12N 9 50W
Slievenamon, *Ireland* ... **13 D4** 52 25N 7 34W
Sligeach = Sligo, *Ireland* **13 B3** 54 16N 8 28W
Sligo, *Ireland* **13 B3** 54 16N 8 28W
Sligo □, *Ireland* **13 B3** 54 8N 8 42W
Sligo B., *Ireland* **13 B3** 54 18N 8 40W
Slite, *Sweden* .... **9 H18** 57 42N 18 48 E
Sliven, *Bulgaria* .... **21 C12** 42 42N 26 19 E
Sloan, *U.S.A.* **85 K11** 35 57N 115 13W
Sloansville, *U.S.A.* **79 D10** 42 45N 74 22W
Slobodskoy, *Russia* .... **24 C9** 58 40N 50 6 E
Slobozia, *Romania* ...... **17 F14** 44 34N 27 23 E
Slocan, *Canada* **72 D5** 49 48N 117 28W
Slochteren, *Neths.* ..... **15 A6** 53 12N 6 48 E
Slonim, *Belarus* .... **17 B13** 53 4N 25 19 E
Slough, *U.K.* **11 F7** 51 30N 0 36W
Sloughhouse, *U.S.A.* **84 G5** 38 26N 121 12W
Slovak Rep. ■, *Europe* .. **17 D10** 48 30N 20 0 E
Slovakia = Slovak Rep. ■, *Europe* .... **17 D10** 48 30N 20 0 E
Slovakian Ore Mts. = Slovenské Rudohorie, *Slovak Rep.* .... **17 D10** 48 45N 20 0 E
Slovenia ■, *Europe* ..... **16 F8** 45 58N 14 30 E
Slovenija = Slovenia ■, *Europe* .... **16 F8** 45 58N 14 30 E
Slovenská Republika = Slovak Rep. ■, *Europe* **17 D10** 48 30N 20 0 E
Slovenské Rudohorie, *Slovak Rep.* .... **17 D10** 48 45N 20 0 E
Slovyansk, *Ukraine* ..... **25 E6** 48 55N 37 36 E
Sluch →, *Ukraine* ..... **17 C14** 51 37N 26 38 E
Sluis, *Neths.* .... **15 C3** 51 18N 3 23 E
Słupsk, *Poland* .... **17 A9** 54 30N 17 3 E
Slurry, *S. Africa* .... **56 D4** 25 49S 25 42 E
Slutsk, *Belarus* .... **17 B14** 53 2N 27 31 E
Slyne Hd., *Ireland* **13 C1** 53 25N 10 10W
Slyudyanka, *Russia* .... **27 D11** 51 40N 103 40 E
Småland, *Sweden* ...... **9 H16** 57 15N 15 25 E
Smalltree L., *Canada* ... **73 A7** 61 0N 105 0W
Smara, *Morocco* **50 B3** 32 9N 8 16W
Smarhon, *Belarus* ...... **17 A14** 54 20N 26 24 E
Smartt Syndicate Dam, *S. Africa* .... **56 E3** 30 45S 23 10 E
Smartville, *U.S.A.* **84 F5** 39 13N 121 18W
Smeaton, *Canada* **73 C8** 53 30N 104 49W
Smederevo, *Serbia, Yug.* **21 B9** 44 40N 20 57 E
Smethport, *U.S.A.* **78 E6** 41 49N 78 27W
Smidovich, *Russia* ..... **27 E14** 48 36N 133 49 E
Smiley, *Canada* **73 C7** 51 38N 109 29W
Smith, *Canada* **72 B6** 55 10N 114 0W
Smith →, *Canada* **72 B3** 59 34N 126 30W
Smith Arm, *Canada* **68 B7** 66 15N 123 0W
Smith Center, *U.S.A.* **80 F5** 39 47N 98 47W
Smith Sund, *Greenland* . **4 B4** 78 30N 74 0W
Smithburne →, *Australia* **62 B3** 17 3S 140 57 E
Smithers, *Canada* **72 C3** 54 45N 127 10W
Smithfield, *S. Africa* ..... **57 E4** 30 9S 26 30 E
Smithfield, *N.C., U.S.A.* .. **77 H6** 35 31N 78 21W
Smithfield, *Utah, U.S.A.* . **82 F8** 41 50N 111 50W
Smiths Falls, *Canada* **70 D4** 44 55N 76 0W
Smithton, *Australia* ..... **62 G4** 40 53S 145 6 E
Smithtown, *Australia* .... **63 E5** 30 58S 152 48 E
Smithville, *Canada* **78 C5** 43 6N 79 33W
Smithville, *U.S.A.* **81 K6** 30 1N 97 10W
Smoky →, *Canada* **72 B5** 56 10N 117 21W
Smoky Bay, *Australia* ... **63 E1** 32 22S 134 13 E
Smoky Falls, *Canada* **70 B3** 50 4N 82 10W
Smoky Hill →, *U.S.A.* .. **80 F6** 39 4N 96 48W
Smoky Lake, *Canada* **72 C6** 54 10N 112 30W
Smøla, *Norway* .... **8 E13** 63 23N 8 3 E
Smolensk, *Russia* ...... **24 D5** 54 45N 32 5 E
Smolikas, Óros, *Greece* .. **21 D9** 40 9N 20 58 E
Smolyan, *Bulgaria* ...... **21 D11** 41 36N 24 38 E
Smooth Rock Falls, *Canada* **70 C3** 49 17N 81 37W
Smoothstone L., *Canada* . **73 C7** 54 40N 106 50W
Smorgon = Smarhon, *Belarus* .... **17 A14** 54 20N 26 24 E
Smyrna = İzmir, *Turkey* . **21 E12** 38 25N 27 8 E
Snæfell, *Iceland* **8 D6** 64 48N 15 34W
Snaefell, *U.K.* **10 C3** 54 16N 4 27W
Snæfellsjökull, *Iceland* .. **8 D2** 64 49N 23 46W
Snake →, *U.S.A.* **82 C4** 46 12N 119 2W
Snake I., *Australia* ...... **63 F4** 38 47S 146 33 E
Snake L., *Canada* **73 B7** 55 32N 106 35W
Snake Range, *U.S.A.* **82 G6** 39 0N 114 20W
Snake River Plain, *U.S.A.* **82 E7** 42 50N 114 0W
Snåsavatnet, *Norway* .... **8 D14** 64 12N 12 0 E
Sneek, *Neths.* .... **15 A5** 53 2N 5 40 E
Sneeuberge, *S. Africa* ... **56 E3** 31 46S 24 20 E
Snelling, *U.S.A.* **84 H6** 37 31N 120 26W
Sněžka, *Europe* .... **16 C8** 50 41N 15 50 E
Snizort, L., *U.K.* **12 D2** 57 33N 6 28W
Snøhetta, *Norway* ...... **9 E13** 62 19N 9 16 E
Snohomish, *U.S.A.* **84 C4** 47 55N 122 6W
Snoul, *Cambodia* .... **39 F6** 12 4N 106 26 E
Snow Hill, *U.S.A.* **76 F8** 38 11N 75 24W
Snow Lake, *Canada* **73 C8** 54 52N 100 3W
Snow Mt., *U.S.A.* **84 F4** 39 23N 122 45W
Snowbird L., *Canada* **73 A8** 60 45N 103 0W
Snowdon, *U.K.* **10 D3** 53 4N 4 5W
Snowdrift →, *Canada* .. **73 A6** 62 24N 110 44W
Snowflake, *U.S.A.* **83 J8** 34 30N 110 5W
Snowshoe Pk., *U.S.A.* ... **82 B6** 48 13N 115 41W
Snowtown, *Australia* .... **63 E2** 33 46S 138 14 E
Snowville, *U.S.A.* **82 F7** 41 58N 112 43W
Snowy →, *Australia* .... **63 F4** 37 46S 148 30 E
Snowy Mts., *Australia* ... **63 F4** 36 30S 148 20 E
Snug Corner, *Bahamas* .. **89 B5** 22 33N 73 52W
Snyatyn, *Ukraine* .... **17 D13** 48 27N 25 38 E
Snyder, *Okla., U.S.A.* **81 H5** 34 40N 98 57W
Snyder, *Tex., U.S.A.* **81 J4** 32 44N 100 55W
Soahanina, *Madag.* ..... **57 B7** 18 42S 44 13 E
Soalala, *Madag.* .... **57 B8** 16 6S 45 20 E
Soan →, *Pakistan* ..... **42 C4** 33 1N 71 44 E
Soanierana-Ivongo, *Madag.* .... **57 B8** 16 55S 49 35 E
Soap Lake, *U.S.A.* **82 C4** 47 23N 119 29W
Sobat, Nahr →, *Sudan* . **51 G11** 9 22N 31 33 E
Sobhapur, *India* .... **42 H8** 22 47N 78 17 E
Sobolevo, *Russia* .... **27 D16** 54 20N 155 30 E
Sobradinho, Reprêsa de, *Brazil* .... **93 E10** 9 30S 42 0 E
Sobral, *Brazil* **93 D10** 3 50S 40 20W
Soc Giang, *Vietnam* ..... **38 A6** 22 54N 106 1 E
Soc Trang, *Vietnam* ..... **39 H5** 9 37N 105 50 E
Soch'e = Shache, *China* . **32 C2** 38 20N 77 10 E
Sochi, *Russia* .... **25 F6** 43 35N 39 40 E
Société, Is. de la, *Pac. Oc.* **65 J12** 17 0S 151 0W
Society Is. = Société, Is. de la, *Pac. Oc.* **65 J12** 17 0S 151 0W
Socompa, Portezuelo de, *Chile* **94 A2** 24 27S 68 18W
Socorro, *Colombia* **92 B4** 6 29N 73 16W
Socorro, *U.S.A.* **83 J10** 34 4N 106 54W
Socorro, I., *Mexico* **86 D2** 18 45N 110 58W
Socotra, *Ind. Oc.* .... **46 E5** 12 30N 54 0 E
Soda L., *U.S.A.* **83 J5** 35 10N 116 4W
Soda Plains, *India* ...... **43 B8** 35 30N 79 0 E
Soda Springs, *U.S.A.* **82 E8** 42 39N 111 36W
Sodankylä, *Finland* ..... **8 C22** 67 29N 26 40 E
Söderhamn, *Sweden* .... **9 F17** 61 18N 17 10 E
Söderköping, *Sweden* ... **9 G17** 58 31N 16 20 E
Södermanland, *Sweden* .. **9 G17** 58 56N 16 55 E
Södertälje, *Sweden* ..... **9 G17** 59 12N 17 39 E
Sodiri, *Sudan* .... **51 F10** 14 27N 29 0 E
Sodo, *Ethiopia* .... **51 G12** 7 0N 37 41 E
Sodus, *U.S.A.* **78 C7** 43 14N 77 4W
Soekmekaar, *S. Africa* ... **57 C4** 23 30S 29 55 E
Soest, *Neths.* .... **15 B5** 52 9N 5 19 E
Sofia = Sofiya, *Bulgaria* . **21 C10** 42 45N 23 20 E
Sofia →, *Madag.* ...... **57 B8** 15 27S 47 23 E
Sofiya, *Bulgaria* .... **21 C10** 42 45N 23 20 E
Sofiysk, *Russia* .... **27 D14** 52 15N 133 59 E
Sōfu-Gan, *Japan* .... **31 K10** 29 49N 140 21 E
Sogamoso, *Colombia* ... **92 B4** 5 43N 72 56W
Sogār, *Iran* .... **45 E8** 25 53N 58 6 E
Sogndalsfjøra, *Norway* .. **9 F12** 61 14N 7 5 E
Søgne, *Norway* .... **9 G12** 58 5N 7 48 E
Sognefjorden, *Norway* .. **9 F11** 61 10N 5 50 E
Sŏgwi-po, *S. Korea* ..... **35 H14** 33 13N 126 34 E
Soh, *Iran* .... **45 C6** 33 26N 51 27 E
Sohâg, *Egypt* .... **51 C11** 26 33N 31 43 E
Sŏhori, *N. Korea* .... **35 D15** 40 7N 128 23 E
Soignies, *Belgium* ...... **15 D4** 50 35N 4 5 E
Soissons, *France* .... **18 B5** 49 25N 3 19 E
Sōja, *Japan* .... **31 G6** 34 40N 133 45 E
Sojat, *India* .... **42 G5** 25 55N 73 45 E
Sokal, *Ukraine* .... **17 C13** 50 31N 24 15 E
Söke, *Turkey* .... **21 F12** 37 48N 27 28 E
Sokelo, *Zaïre* .... **55 D1** 9 55S 24 36 E
Sokhumi, *Georgia* ...... **25 F7** 43 0N 41 0 E
Sokodé, *Togo* .... **50 G5** 9 0N 1 11 E
Sokol, *Russia* .... **24 C7** 59 30N 40 5 E
Sokółka, *Poland* .... **17 B12** 53 25N 23 30 E
Sokolo, *Mali* **50 F3** 14 53N 6 8W
Sokołów Podlaski, *Poland* **17 B12** 52 25N 22 15 E
Sokoto, *Nigeria* .... **50 F6** 13 2N 5 16 E
Sol Iletsk, *Russia* ...... **24 D10** 51 10N 55 0 E
Solai, *Kenya* .... **54 B4** 0 2N 36 12 E
Solano, *Phil.* .... **37 A6** 16 31N 121 15 E
Solapur, *India* .... **40 L9** 17 43N 75 56 E
Soléa □, *Cyprus* .... **23 D12** 35 5N 33 4 E
Soledad, *U.S.A.* **83 H3** 36 26N 121 20W
Soledad, *Venezuela* **92 B6** 8 10N 63 34W
Solent, The, *U.K.* **11 G6** 50 45N 1 25W
Solfonn, *Norway* .... **9 F12** 60 2N 6 57 E
Soligalich, *Russia* ...... **24 C7** 59 5N 42 10 E
Soligorsk = Salihorsk, *Belarus* .... **17 B14** 52 51N 27 27 E
Solikamsk, *Russia* ...... **24 C10** 59 38N 56 50 E
Solila, *Madag.* .... **57 C8** 21 25S 46 37 E
Solimões = Amazonas →, *S. Amer.* **93 C9** 0 5S 50 0W
Solingen, *Germany* ..... **15 C7** 51 10N 7 5 E
Sollefteå, *Sweden* ...... **8 E17** 63 12N 17 20 E
Sóller, *Spain* .... **22 B9** 39 46N 2 43 E
Sologne, *France* .... **18 C4** 47 40N 1 45 E
Solok, *Indonesia* .... **36 E2** 0 45S 100 40 E
Sololá, *Guatemala* **88 D1** 14 49N 91 10W
Solomon, N. Fork →, *U.S.A.* **80 F5** 39 29N 98 26W
Solomon, S. Fork →, *U.S.A.* **80 F5** 39 25N 99 12W
Solomon Is. ■, *Pac. Oc.* . **64 H7** 6 0S 155 0 E
Solon, *China* .... **33 B7** 46 32N 121 10 E
Solon Springs, *U.S.A.* **80 B9** 46 22N 91 49W
Solor, *Indonesia* .... **37 F6** 8 27S 123 0 E
Solothurn, *Switz.* .... **16 E4** 47 13N 7 32 E
Šolta, *Croatia* .... **20 C7** 43 24N 16 15 E
Soltānābād, *Khorāsān, Iran* .... **45 C8** 34 13N 59 58 E
Soltānābād, *Khorāsān, Iran* .... **45 B8** 36 29N 58 5 E
Soltānābād, *Markazī, Iran* **45 C6** 35 31N 51 10 E
Solunska Glava, *Macedonia* .... **21 D9** 41 44N 21 31 E
Solvang, *U.S.A.* **85 L6** 34 36N 120 8W
Solvay, *U.S.A.* **79 C8** 43 3N 76 13W
Sölvesborg, *Sweden* .... **9 H16** 56 5N 14 35 E
Solvychegodsk, *Russia* .. **24 B8** 61 21N 46 56 E
Solway Firth, *U.K.* **10 C4** 54 49N 3 35W
Solwezi, *Zambia* .... **55 E2** 12 11S 26 21 E
Sōma, *Japan* .... **30 F10** 37 40N 140 50 E
Soma, *Turkey* .... **21 E12** 39 10N 27 35 E
Somali Pen., *Africa* ..... **48 F8** 7 0N 46 0 E
Somali Rep. ■, *Africa* .. **46 F4** 7 0N 47 0 E
Somalia = Somali Rep. ■, *Africa* .... **46 F4** 7 0N 47 0 E
Sombor, *Serbia, Yug.* ... **21 B8** 45 46N 19 9 E
Sombra, *Canada* **78 D2** 42 43N 82 29W
Sombrerete, *Mexico* **86 C4** 23 40N 103 40W
Sombrero, *Anguilla* **89 C7** 18 37N 63 30W
Somers, *U.S.A.* **82 B6** 48 5N 114 13W
Somerset, *Canada* **73 D9** 49 25N 98 39W
Somerset, *Colo., U.S.A.* . **83 G10** 38 56N 107 28W
Somerset, *Ky., U.S.A.* ... **76 G3** 37 5N 84 36W
Somerset, *Mass., U.S.A.* . **79 E13** 41 47N 71 8W
Somerset, *Pa., U.S.A.* ... **78 F5** 40 1N 79 5W
Somerset □, *U.K.* **11 F5** 51 9N 3 0W
Somerset East, *S. Africa* . **56 E4** 32 42S 25 35 E
Somerset I., *Canada* **68 A10** 73 30N 93 0W
Somerset West, *S. Africa* **56 E2** 34 8S 18 50 E
Somerton, *U.S.A.* **83 K6** 32 36N 114 43W
Somerville, *U.S.A.* **79 F10** 40 35N 74 38W
Someş →, *Romania* .... **17 D12** 47 49N 22 43 E
Sommariva, *Australia* ... **63 D4** 26 24S 146 36 E
Somme →, *France* ..... **18 A4** 50 11N 1 38 E
Somosierra, Puerto de, *Spain* **19 B4** 41 4N 3 35W
Somoto, *Nic.* **88 D2** 13 28N 86 37W
Somport, Puerto de, *Spain* **18 E3** 42 48N 0 31W
Son Ha, *Vietnam* .... **38 E7** 15 3N 108 34 E
Son Hoa, *Vietnam* .... **38 F7** 13 2N 108 58 E
Son La, *Vietnam* .... **38 B4** 21 20N 103 50 E
Son Tay, *Vietnam* .... **38 B5** 21 8N 105 30 E
Soná, *Panama* **88 E3** 8 0N 81 20W
Sonamarg, *India* .... **43 B6** 34 18N 75 21 E
Sonamukhi, *India* ...... **43 H12** 23 18N 87 27 E
Sŏnchŏn, *N. Korea* ..... **35 E13** 39 48N 124 55 E
Sondags →, *S. Africa* .. **56 E4** 33 44S 25 51 E
Sondar, *India* .... **43 C6** 33 28N 75 56 E
Sønderborg, *Denmark* ... **9 J13** 54 55N 9 49 E
Søndre Strømfjord, *Greenland* **69 B14** 66 59N 50 40W
Sóndrio, *Italy* .... **20 A3** 46 10N 9 52 E
Sone, *Mozam.* .... **55 F3** 17 23S 34 55 E
Sonepur, *India* .... **41 J13** 20 55N 83 50 E
Song, *Thailand* .... **38 C3** 18 28N 100 11 E
Song Cau, *Vietnam* ..... **38 F7** 13 27N 109 18 E
Song Xian, *China* .... **34 G7** 34 12N 112 8 E
Songchŏn, *N. Korea* .... **35 E14** 39 12N 126 15 E
Songea, *Tanzania* ...... **55 E4** 10 40S 35 40 E
Songea □, *Tanzania* .... **55 E4** 10 30S 36 0 E
Songhua Hu, *China* ..... **35 C14** 43 35N 126 50 E
Songhua Jiang →, *China* **33 B8** 47 45N 132 30 E
Songjin, *N. Korea* ...... **35 D15** 40 40N 129 10 E
Songjŏng-ni, *S. Korea* ... **35 G14** 35 8N 126 47 E
Songkhla, *Thailand* ..... **39 J3** 7 13N 100 37 E
Songnim, *N. Korea* ..... **35 E13** 38 45N 125 39 E

Sweetwater

Sweetwater →, U.S.A. 82 E10 42 31N 107 2W
Swellendam, S. Africa 56 E3 34 1S 20 26 E
Świdnica, Poland 17 C9 50 50N 16 30 E
Świdnik, Poland 17 C12 51 13N 22 39 E
Świebodzin, Poland 16 B8 52 15N 15 31 E
Świecie, Poland 17 B10 53 25N 18 30 E
Swift Current, Canada 73 C7 50 20N 107 45W
Swiftcurrent →, Canada 73 C7 50 38N 107 44W
Swilly, L., Ireland 13 A4 55 12N 7 33W
Swindle, I., Canada 72 C3 52 30N 128 35W
Swindon, U.K. 11 F6 51 34N 1 46W
Swinemünde = Świnoujście, Poland 16 B8 53 54N 14 16 E
Świnoujście, Poland 16 B8 53 54N 14 16 E
Switzerland ■, Europe 16 E5 46 30N 8 0 E
Swords, Ireland 13 C5 53 28N 6 13W
Sydney, Australia 63 E5 33 53S 151 10 E
Sydney, Canada 71 C7 46 7N 60 7W
Sydney Mines, Canada 71 C7 46 18N 60 15W
Sydprøven, Greenland 4 C5 60 30N 45 35W
Sydra, G. of = Surt, Khalīj, Libya 51 B8 31 40N 18 30 E
Syktyvkar, Russia 24 B9 61 45N 50 40 E
Sylacauga, U.S.A. 77 J2 33 10N 86 15W
Sylarna, Sweden 8 E15 63 2N 12 13 E
Sylhet, Bangla. 41 G17 24 54N 91 52 E
Sylt, Germany 16 A5 54 54N 8 22 E
Sylvan Lake, Canada 72 C6 52 20N 114 3W
Sylvania, U.S.A. 77 J5 32 45N 81 38W
Sylvester, U.S.A. 77 K4 31 32N 83 50W
Sym, Russia 26 C9 60 20N 88 18 E
Symón, Mexico 86 C4 24 42N 102 35W
Synnott Ra., Australia 60 C4 16 30S 125 20 E
Syracuse, Kans., U.S.A. 81 F4 37 59N 101 45W
Syracuse, N.Y., U.S.A. 79 C8 43 3N 76 9W
Syrdarya →, Kazakstan 26 E7 46 3N 61 0 E
Syria ■, Asia 44 C3 35 0N 38 0 E
Syrian Desert = Ash Shām, Bādiyat, Asia 28 F7 32 0N 40 0 E
Syul'dzhyukyor, Russia 27 C12 63 14N 113 32 E
Syzran, Russia 24 D8 53 12N 48 30 E
Szczecin, Poland 16 B8 53 27N 14 27 E
Szczecinek, Poland 17 B9 53 43N 16 41 E
Szczytno, Poland 17 B11 53 33N 21 0 E
Szechwan = Sichuan □, China 32 C5 31 0N 104 0 E
Szeged, Hungary 17 E11 46 16N 20 10 E
Székesfehérvár, Hungary 17 E10 47 15N 18 25 E
Szekszárd, Hungary 17 E10 46 22N 18 42 E
Szentes, Hungary 17 E11 46 39N 20 21 E
Szolnok, Hungary 17 E11 47 10N 20 15 E
Szombathely, Hungary 17 E9 47 14N 16 38 E

T

Ta Khli Khok, Thailand 38 E3 15 18N 100 20 E
Ta Lai, Vietnam 39 G6 11 24N 107 23 E
Tabacal, Argentina 94 A3 23 15S 64 15W
Tabaco, Phil. 37 B6 13 22N 123 44 E
Ṭābah, Si. Arabia 44 E4 26 55N 42 38 E
Tabarka, Tunisia 50 A6 36 56N 8 46 E
Ṭabas, Khorāsān, Iran 45 C9 32 48N 60 12 E
Ṭabas, Khorāsān, Iran 45 C8 33 35N 56 55 E
Tabasará, Serranía de, Panama 88 E3 8 35N 81 40W
Tabasco □, Mexico 87 D6 17 45N 93 30W
Tabatinga, Serra da, Brazil 93 F10 10 30S 44 0W
Tabāzīn, Iran 45 D8 31 12N 57 54 E
Taber, Canada 72 D6 49 47N 112 8W
Tablas, Phil. 37 B6 12 25N 122 2 E
Table B. = Tafelbaai, S. Africa 56 E2 33 35S 18 25 E
Table B., Canada 71 B8 53 40N 56 25W
Table Mt., S. Africa 56 E2 34 0S 18 22 E
Tableland, Australia 60 C4 17 16S 126 51 E
Tabletop, Mt., Australia 62 C4 23 24S 147 11 E
Tábor, Czech. 16 D8 49 25N 14 39 E
Tabora, Tanzania 54 D3 5 2S 32 50 E
Tabora □, Tanzania 54 D3 5 0S 33 0 E
Tabou, Ivory C. 50 H3 4 30N 7 20W
Tabrīz, Iran 44 B5 38 7N 46 20 E
Tabuaeran, Pac. Oc. 65 G12 3 51N 159 22W
Tabūk, Si. Arabia 44 D3 28 23N 36 36 E
Tacámbaro de Codallos, Mexico 86 D4 19 14N 101 28W
Tacheng, China 32 B3 46 40N 82 58 E
Tach'ing Shan = Daqing Shan, China 34 D6 40 40N 111 0 E
Tacloban, Phil. 37 B6 11 15N 124 58 E
Tacna, Peru 92 G4 18 0S 70 20W
Tacoma, U.S.A. 84 C4 47 14N 122 26W
Tacuarembó, Uruguay 95 C4 31 45S 56 0W
Tademaït, Plateau du, Algeria 50 C5 28 30N 2 30 E
Tadjoura, Djibouti 46 E3 11 50N 42 55 E
Tadmor, N.Z. 59 J4 41 27S 172 45 E
Tadoule, L., Canada 73 B9 58 36N 98 20W
Tadoussac, Canada 71 C6 48 11N 69 42W
Tadzhikistan = Tajikistan ■, Asia 26 F8 38 30N 70 0 E
Taechŏn-ni, S. Korea 35 F14 36 21N 126 36 E
Taegu, S. Korea 35 G15 35 50N 128 37 E
Taegwan, N. Korea 35 D13 40 13N 125 12 E
Taejŏn, S. Korea 35 F14 36 20N 127 28 E
Tafalla, Spain 19 A5 42 30N 1 41W
Tafelbaai, S. Africa 56 E2 33 35S 18 25 E
Tafermaar, Indonesia 37 F8 6 47S 134 10 E
Tafí Viejo, Argentina 94 B2 26 43S 65 17W
Tafīhān, Iran 45 D7 29 25N 52 39 E
Taft, Iran 45 D7 31 45N 54 14 E
Taft, Phil. 37 B7 11 57N 125 30 E
Taft, Calif., U.S.A. 85 K7 35 8N 119 28W
Taft, Tex., U.S.A. 81 M6 27 59N 97 24W
Taga Dzong, Bhutan 41 F16 27 5N 89 55 E
Taganrog, Russia 25 E6 47 12N 38 50 E
Tagbilaran, Phil. 37 C6 9 39N 123 51 E
Tagish, Canada 72 A2 60 19N 134 16W
Tagish L., Canada 72 A2 60 10N 134 20W
Tagliamento →, Italy 20 B5 45 38N 13 6 E
Tagomago, I. de, Spain 22 B8 39 2N 1 39 E
Taguatinga, Brazil 93 F10 12 16S 42 26W
Tagum, Phil. 37 C7 7 33N 125 53 E
Tagus = Tejo →, Europe 19 C1 38 40N 9 24W
Tahakopa, N.Z. 59 M2 46 30S 169 23 E
Tahan, Gunong, Malaysia 39 K4 4 34N 102 17 E
Tahat, Algeria 50 D6 23 18N 5 33 E
Tāheri, Iran 45 E7 27 43N 52 20 E
Tahiti, Pac. Oc. 65 J13 17 37S 149 27W
Tahoe, L., U.S.A. 84 G6 39 6N 120 2W
Tahoe City, U.S.A. 84 F6 39 10N 120 9W
Taholah, U.S.A. 84 C2 47 21N 124 17W
Tahoua, Niger 50 F6 14 57N 5 16 E
Tahta, Egypt 51 C11 26 44N 31 32 E
Tahulandang, Indonesia 37 D7 2 27N 125 23 E
Tahuna, Indonesia 37 D7 3 38N 125 30 E
Taï, Ivory C. 50 G3 5 55N 7 30W
Tai Shan, China 35 F9 36 25N 117 20 E
Tai'an, China 35 F9 36 12N 117 8 E
Taibei = T'aipei, Taiwan 33 D7 25 2N 121 30 E
Taibique, Canary Is. 22 G2 27 42N 17 58W
Taibus Qi, China 34 D8 41 54N 115 22 E
T'aichung, Taiwan 33 D7 24 9N 120 37 E
Taieri →, N.Z. 59 M3 46 3S 170 12 E
Taigu, China 34 F7 37 28N 112 30 E
Taihang Shan, China 34 G7 36 0N 113 30 E
Taihape, N.Z. 59 H5 39 41S 175 48 E
Taihe, China 34 H8 33 20N 115 42 E
Taikang, China 34 G8 34 5N 114 50 E
Tailem Bend, Australia 63 F2 35 12S 139 29 E
Taimyr Peninsula = Taymyr, Poluostrov, Russia 27 B11 75 0N 100 0 E
Tain, U.K. 12 D4 57 49N 4 4W
T'ainan, Taiwan 33 D7 23 0N 120 10 E
Tainaron, Ákra, Greece 21 F10 36 22N 22 27 E
T'aipei, Taiwan 33 D7 25 2N 121 30 E
Taiping, Malaysia 39 K3 4 51N 100 44 E
Taipingzhen, China 34 H6 33 35N 111 42 E
Tairbeart = Tarbert, U.K. 12 D2 57 54N 6 49W
Taita □, Kenya 54 C4 4 0S 38 30 E
Taita Hills, Kenya 54 C4 3 25S 38 15 E
Taitao, Pen. de, Chile 96 F2 46 30S 75 0W
T'aitung, Taiwan 33 D7 22 43N 121 4 E
Taivalkoski, Finland 8 D23 65 33N 28 12 E
Taiwan ■, Asia 33 D7 23 30N 121 0 E
Taïyetos Óros, Greece 21 F10 37 0N 22 23 E
Taiyiba, Israel 47 C4 32 36N 35 27 E
Taiyuan, China 34 F7 37 52N 112 33 E
Taizhong = T'aichung, Taiwan 33 D7 24 9N 120 37 E
Ta'izz, Yemen 46 E3 13 35N 44 2 E
Tājābād, Iran 45 D7 30 2N 54 24 E
Tajikistan ■, Asia 26 F8 38 30N 70 0 E
Tajima, Japan 31 F9 37 12N 139 46 E
Tajo = Tejo →, Europe 19 C1 38 40N 9 24W
Tajrīsh, Iran 45 C6 35 48N 51 25 E
Tājūrā, Libya 51 B7 32 51N 13 21 E
Tak, Thailand 38 D2 16 52N 99 8 E
Takāb, Iran 44 B5 36 24N 47 7 E
Takachiho, Japan 31 H5 32 42N 131 18 E
Takada, Japan 31 F9 37 7N 138 15 E
Takahagi, Japan 31 F10 36 43N 140 45 E
Takaka, N.Z. 59 J4 40 51S 172 50 E
Takamatsu, Japan 31 G7 34 20N 134 5 E
Takaoka, Japan 31 F8 36 47N 137 0 E
Takapuna, N.Z. 59 G5 36 47S 174 47 E
Takasaki, Japan 31 F9 36 20N 139 0 E
Takatsuki, Japan 31 G7 34 51N 135 37 E
Takaungu, Kenya 54 C4 3 38S 39 52 E
Takayama, Japan 31 F8 36 18N 137 11 E
Take-Shima, Japan 31 J5 30 49N 130 26 E
Takefu, Japan 31 G8 35 50N 136 10 E
Takengon, Indonesia 36 D1 4 45N 96 50 E
Takeo, Cambodia 39 G5 10 59N 104 47 E
Takeo, Japan 31 H5 33 12N 130 1 E
Tākestān, Iran 45 C6 36 0N 49 40 E
Taketa, Japan 31 H5 32 58N 131 24 E
Takh, India 43 C7 33 6N 77 32 E
Takhman, Cambodia 39 G5 11 29N 104 57 E
Takikawa, Japan 30 C10 43 33N 141 54 E
Takla L., Canada 72 B3 55 15N 125 45W
Takla Landing, Canada 72 B3 55 30N 125 50W
Takla Makan = Taklamakan Shamo, China 32 C3 38 0N 83 0 E
Taklamakan Shamo, China 32 C3 38 0N 83 0 E
Taku →, Canada 72 B2 58 30N 133 50W
Takum, Nigeria 50 G6 7 18N 9 36 E
Tal Halāl, Iran 45 D7 28 54N 55 1 E
Tala, Uruguay 95 C4 34 21S 55 46W
Talagante, Chile 94 C1 33 40S 70 50W
Talamanca, Cordillera de, Cent. Amer. 88 E3 9 20N 83 20W
Talara, Peru 92 D2 4 38S 81 18W
Talas, Kyrgyzstan 26 E8 42 30N 72 13 E
Talâta, Egypt 47 E1 30 36N 32 20 E
Talaud, Kepulauan, Indonesia 37 D7 4 30N 127 10 E
Talaud Is. = Talaud, Kepulauan, Indonesia 37 D7 4 30N 127 10 E
Talavera de la Reina, Spain 19 C3 39 55N 4 46W
Talawana, Australia 60 D3 22 51S 121 9 E
Talayan, Phil. 37 C6 6 52N 124 24 E
Talbot, C., Australia 60 B4 13 48S 126 43 E
Talbragar →, Australia 63 E4 32 12S 148 37 E
Talca, Chile 94 D1 35 28S 71 40W
Talca □, Chile 94 D1 35 20S 71 46W
Talcahuano, Chile 94 D1 36 40S 73 10W
Talcher, India 41 J14 21 0N 85 18 E
Taldy Kurgan = Taldyqorghan, Kazakstan 26 E8 45 10N 78 45 E
Taldyqorghan, Kazakstan 26 E8 45 10N 78 45 E
Tālesh, Iran 45 B6 37 58N 48 58 E
Ṭālesh, Kūhhā-ye, Iran 45 B6 37 42N 48 55 E
Tali Post, Sudan 51 G11 5 55N 30 44 E
Talibon, Phil. 37 B6 10 9N 124 20 E
Talibong, Ko, Thailand 39 J2 7 15N 99 23 E
Talihina, U.S.A. 81 H7 34 45N 95 3W
Taliwang, Indonesia 36 F5 8 50S 116 55 E
Tall 'Asūr, West Bank 47 D4 31 59N 35 17 E
Tall Kalakh, Syria 47 A5 34 41N 36 15 E
Talladega, U.S.A. 77 J2 33 26N 86 6W
Tallahassee, U.S.A. 77 K3 30 27N 84 17W
Tallangatta, Australia 63 F4 36 15S 147 19 E
Tallarook, Australia 63 F4 37 5S 145 6 E
Tallering Pk., Australia 61 E2 28 6S 115 37 E
Tallinn, Estonia 9 G21 59 22N 24 48 E
Tallulah, U.S.A. 81 J9 32 25N 91 11W
Talodi, Sudan 51 F11 10 35N 30 22 E
Taloyoak, Canada 68 B10 69 32N 93 32W
Talpa de Allende, Mexico 86 C4 20 23N 104 51W
Talsi, Latvia 9 H20 57 10N 22 30 E
Taltal, Chile 94 B1 25 23S 70 33W
Taltson →, Canada 72 A6 61 24N 112 46W
Talwood, Australia 63 D4 28 29S 149 29 E
Talyawalka Cr. →, Australia 63 E3 32 28S 142 22 E
Tam Chau, Vietnam 39 G5 10 48N 105 12 E
Tam Ky, Vietnam 38 E7 15 34N 108 29 E
Tam Quan, Vietnam 38 E7 14 35N 109 3 E
Tama, U.S.A. 80 E8 41 58N 92 35W
Tamala, Australia 61 E1 26 42S 113 47 E
Tamale, Ghana 50 G4 9 22N 0 50W
Tamano, Japan 31 G6 34 29N 133 59 E
Tamanrasset, Algeria 50 D6 22 50N 5 30 E
Tamaqua, U.S.A. 79 F9 40 48N 75 58W
Tamar →, U.K. 11 G3 50 27N 4 15W
Tamarang, Australia 63 E5 31 27S 150 5 E
Tamarinda, Spain 22 B10 39 55N 3 49 E
Tamashima, Japan 31 G6 34 32N 133 40 E
Tamaské, Niger 50 F6 14 49N 5 43 E
Tamaulipas □, Mexico 87 C5 24 0N 99 0W
Tamaulipas, Sierra de, Mexico 87 C5 23 30N 98 20W
Tamazula, Mexico 86 C3 24 55N 106 58W
Tamazunchale, Mexico 87 C5 21 16N 98 47W
Tambacounda, Senegal 50 F2 13 45N 13 40W
Tambelan, Kepulauan, Indonesia 36 D3 1 0N 107 30 E
Tambellup, Australia 61 F2 34 4S 117 37 E
Tambo, Australia 62 C4 24 54S 146 14 E
Tambo de Mora, Peru 92 F3 13 30S 76 8W
Tambohorano, Madag. 57 B7 17 30S 43 58 E
Tambora, Indonesia 36 F5 8 12S 118 5 E
Tambov, Russia 24 D7 52 45N 41 28 E
Tambuku, Indonesia 37 G15 7 8S 113 40 E
Tamburâ, Sudan 51 G10 5 40N 27 25 E
Tâmchekket, Mauritania 50 E2 17 25N 10 40W
Tamega →, Portugal 19 B1 41 5N 8 21W
Tamenglong, India 41 G18 25 0N 93 35 E
Tamgak, Mts., Niger 50 E6 19 12N 8 35 E
Tamiahua, L. de, Mexico 87 C5 21 30N 97 30W
Tamil Nadu □, India 40 P10 11 0N 77 0 E
Tamluk, India 43 H12 22 18N 87 58 E
Tammerfors = Tampere, Finland 9 F20 61 30N 23 50 E
Tammisaari, Finland 9 F20 60 0N 23 26 E
Tamo Abu, Pegunungan, Malaysia 36 D5 3 10N 115 5 E
Tampa, U.S.A. 77 M4 27 57N 82 27W
Tampa B., U.S.A. 77 M4 27 50N 82 30W
Tampere, Finland 9 F20 61 30N 23 50 E
Tampico, Mexico 87 C5 22 20N 97 50W
Tampin, Malaysia 39 L4 2 28N 102 13 E
Tamrida = Qādib, Yemen 46 E5 12 37N 53 57 E
Tamu, Burma 41 G19 24 13N 94 12 E
Tamworth, Australia 63 E5 31 7S 150 58 E
Tamworth, U.K. 11 E6 52 39N 1 41W
Tamyang, S. Korea 35 G14 35 19N 126 59 E
Tan An, Vietnam 39 G6 10 32N 106 25 E
Tana →, Kenya 54 C5 2 32S 40 31 E
Tana →, Norway 8 A23 70 30N 28 14 E
Tana, L., Ethiopia 51 F12 13 5N 37 30 E
Tana River, Kenya 54 C4 2 0S 39 30 E
Tanabe, Japan 31 H7 33 44N 135 22 E
Tanafjorden, Norway 8 A23 70 45N 28 25 E
Tanaga, Pta., Canary Is. 22 G1 27 42N 18 10W
Tanahbala, Indonesia 36 E1 0 30S 98 30 E
Tanahgrogot, Indonesia 36 E5 1 55S 116 15 E
Tanahjampea, Indonesia 37 F6 7 10S 120 35 E
Tanahmasa, Indonesia 36 E1 0 12S 98 39 E
Tanahmerah, Indonesia 37 F10 6 5S 140 16 E
Tanakura, Japan 31 F10 37 10N 140 20 E
Tanami, Australia 60 C4 19 59S 129 43 E
Tanami Desert, Australia 60 C5 18 50S 132 0 E
Tanana, U.S.A. 68 B4 65 10N 152 4W
Tanana →, U.S.A. 68 B4 65 10N 151 58W
Tananarive = Antananarivo, Madag. 57 B8 18 55S 47 31 E
Tánaro →, Italy 20 B3 44 55N 8 40 E
Tanbar, Australia 62 D3 25 51S 141 55 E
Tancheng, China 35 G10 34 25N 118 20 E
Tanchŏn, N. Korea 35 D15 40 27N 128 54 E
Tanda, Ut. P., India 43 F10 26 33N 82 35 E
Tanda, Ut. P., India 43 E8 28 57N 78 56 E
Tandag, Phil. 37 C7 9 4N 126 9 E
Tandaia, Tanzania 55 D3 9 25S 34 15 E
Tandaué, Angola 56 B2 16 58S 18 5 E
Tandil, Argentina 94 D4 37 15S 59 6W
Tandil, Sa. del, Argentina 94 D4 37 30S 59 0W
Tandlianwala, Pakistan 42 D5 31 3N 73 9 E
Tando Adam, Pakistan 42 G3 25 45N 68 40 E
Tandou L., Australia 63 E3 32 40S 142 5 E
Tane-ga-Shima, Japan 31 J5 30 30N 131 0 E
Taneatua, N.Z. 59 H6 38 4S 177 1 E
Tanen Tong Dan, Burma 38 D2 16 30N 98 30 E
Tanezrouft, Algeria 50 D5 23 9N 0 11 E
Tang, Koh, Cambodia 39 G4 10 16N 103 7 E
Tang Krasang, Cambodia 38 F5 12 34N 105 3 E
Tanga, Tanzania 54 D4 5 5S 39 2 E
Tanga □, Tanzania 54 D4 5 20S 38 0 E
Tanganyika, L., Africa 54 D2 6 40S 30 0 E
Tanger = Tangier, Morocco 50 A3 35 50N 5 49W
Tangerang, Indonesia 37 G12 6 11S 106 37 E
Tanggu, China 35 E9 39 2N 117 40 E
Tanggula Shan, China 32 C4 32 40N 92 10 E
Tanghe, China 34 H7 32 47N 112 50 E
Tangier, Morocco 50 A3 35 50N 5 49W
Tangorin P.O., Australia 62 C3 21 47S 144 12 E
Tangshan, China 35 E10 39 38N 118 10 E
Tangtou, China 35 G10 35 28N 118 30 E
Tanimbar, Kepulauan, Indonesia 37 F8 7 30S 131 30 E
Tanimbar Is. = Tanimbar, Kepulauan, Indonesia 37 F8 7 30S 131 30 E
Tanjay, Phil. 37 C6 9 30N 123 5 E
Tanjong Malim, Malaysia 39 L3 3 42N 101 31 E
Tanjore = Thanjavur, India 40 P11 10 48N 79 12 E
Tanjung, Indonesia 36 E5 2 10S 115 25 E
Tanjungbalai, Indonesia 36 D1 2 55N 99 44 E
Tanjungbatu, Indonesia 36 D5 2 23N 118 3 E
Tanjungkarang Telukbetung, Indonesia 36 F3 5 20S 105 10 E
Tanjungpandan, Indonesia 36 E3 2 43S 107 38 E
Tanjungpinang, Indonesia 36 D2 1 5N 104 30 E
Tanjungpriok, Indonesia 37 G12 6 8S 106 55 E
Tanjungredeb, Indonesia 36 D5 2 9N 117 29 E
Tanjungselor, Indonesia 36 D5 2 55N 117 25 E
Tank, Pakistan 42 C4 32 14N 70 25 E
Tannu-Ola, Russia 27 D10 51 0N 94 0 E
Tanout, Niger 50 F6 14 50N 8 55 E
Tanta, Egypt 51 B11 30 45N 30 57 E
Tantoyuca, Mexico 87 C5 21 21N 98 10W
Tantung = Dandong, China 35 D13 40 10N 124 20 E
Tanunda, Australia 63 E2 34 30S 139 0 E
Tanzania ■, Africa 54 D3 6 0S 34 0 E
Tanzilla →, Canada 72 B2 58 8N 130 43W
Tao Ko, Thailand 39 G2 10 5N 99 52 E
Tao'an, China 35 B12 45 22N 122 40 E
Tao'er He →, China 35 B13 45 45N 124 5 E
Taolanaro, Madag. 57 D8 25 2S 47 0 E
Taole, China 34 E4 38 48N 106 40 E
Taos, U.S.A. 83 H11 36 24N 105 35W
Taoudenni, Mali 50 D4 22 40N 3 55W
Taourirt, Morocco 50 B4 34 25N 2 53W
Tapa, Estonia 9 G21 59 15N 25 50 E
Tapa Shan = Daba Shan, China 33 C5 32 0N 109 0 E
Tapachula, Mexico 87 E6 14 54N 92 17W
Tapah, Malaysia 39 K3 4 12N 101 15 E
Tapajós →, Brazil 93 D8 2 24S 54 41W
Tapaktuan, Indonesia 36 D1 3 15N 97 10 E
Tapanui, N.Z. 59 L2 45 56S 169 18 E
Tapauá →, Brazil 92 E6 5 40S 64 21W
Tapeta, Liberia 50 G3 6 29N 8 52W
Taphan Hin, Thailand 38 D3 16 13N 100 26 E
Tapi →, India 40 J8 21 8N 72 41 E
Tapirapecó, Serra, Venezuela 92 C6 1 10N 65 0W
Tappahannock, U.S.A. 76 G7 37 56N 76 52W
Tapuaenuku, Mt., N.Z. 59 J4 42 0S 173 39 E
Tapul Group, Phil. 37 C6 5 35N 120 50 E
Taqīābād, Iran 45 C8 35 33N 59 11 E
Ṭaqṭaq, Iraq 44 C5 35 53N 44 35 E
Taquara, Brazil 95 B5 29 36S 50 46W
Taquari →, Brazil 92 G7 19 15S 57 17W
Tara, Australia 63 D5 27 17S 150 31 E
Tara, Canada 78 B3 44 28N 81 9W
Tara, Russia 26 D8 56 55N 74 24 E
Tara, Zambia 55 F2 16 58S 26 45 E
Tara →, Montenegro, Yug. 21 C8 43 21N 18 51 E
Tara →, Russia 26 D8 56 42N 74 36 E
Tarabagatay, Khrebet, Kazakstan 26 E9 48 0N 83 0 E
Tarābulus, Lebanon 47 A4 34 31N 35 50 E
Tarābulus, Libya 51 B7 32 49N 13 7 E
Tarajalejo, Canary Is. 22 F5 28 12N 14 7W
Tarakan, Indonesia 36 D5 3 20N 117 35 E
Tarakit, Mt., Kenya 54 B4 2 2N 35 10 E
Taralga, Australia 63 E4 34 26S 149 52 E
Tarama-Jima, Japan 31 M2 24 39N 124 42 E
Taran, Mys, Russia 9 J18 54 56N 19 59 E
Taranagar, India 42 E6 28 43N 74 50 E
Taranaki □, N.Z. 59 H5 39 25S 174 30 E
Tarancón, Spain 19 B4 40 1N 3 0W
Taranga, India 42 H5 23 56N 72 43 E
Taranga Hill, India 42 H5 24 0N 72 40 E
Táranto, Italy 20 D7 40 28N 17 14 E
Táranto, G. di, Italy 20 D7 40 8N 17 20 E
Tarapacá, Colombia 92 D5 2 56S 69 46W
Tarapacá □, Chile 94 A2 20 45S 69 30W
Tararua Ra., N.Z. 59 J5 40 45S 175 25 E
Tarashcha, Ukraine 17 D16 49 30N 30 31 E
Tarauacá, Brazil 92 E4 8 6S 70 48W
Tarauacá →, Brazil 92 E5 6 42S 69 48W
Tarawera, N.Z. 59 H6 39 2S 176 36 E
Tarawera L., N.Z. 59 H6 38 13S 176 27 E
Tarazona, Spain 19 B5 41 55N 1 43W
Tarbat Ness, U.K. 12 D5 57 52N 3 47W
Tarbela Dam, Pakistan 42 B5 34 8N 72 52 E
Tarbert, Arg. & Bute, U.K. 12 F3 55 52N 5 25W
Tarbert, W. Isles, U.K. 12 D2 57 54N 6 49W
Tarbes, France 18 E4 43 15N 0 3 E
Tarboro, U.S.A. 77 H7 35 54N 77 32W
Tarbrax, Australia 62 C3 21 7S 142 26 E
Tarcoola, Australia 63 E1 30 44S 134 36 E
Tarcoon, Australia 63 E4 30 15S 146 43 E
Taree, Australia 63 E5 31 50S 152 30 E
Tarfaya, Morocco 50 C2 27 55N 12 55W
Tarifa, Spain 19 D3 36 1N 5 36W
Tarija, Bolivia 94 A3 21 30S 64 40W
Tarija □, Bolivia 94 A3 21 30S 63 30W
Tariku →, Indonesia 37 E9 2 55S 138 26 E
Tarim Basin = Tarim Pendi, China 32 B3 40 0N 84 0 E
Tarim He →, China 32 C3 39 30N 88 30 E
Tarim Pendi, China 32 B3 40 0N 84 0 E
Tarime □, Tanzania 54 C3 1 15S 34 0 E
Taritatu →, Indonesia 37 E9 2 54S 138 27 E
Tarka →, S. Africa 56 E4 32 10S 26 0 E
Tarkastad, S. Africa 56 E4 32 0S 26 16 E
Tarkhankut, Mys, Ukraine 25 E5 45 25N 32 30 E
Tarko Sale, Russia 26 C8 64 55N 77 50 E
Tarkwa, Ghana 50 G4 5 20N 2 0W
Tarlac, Phil. 37 A6 15 29N 120 35 E
Tarlton Downs, Australia 62 C2 22 40S 136 45 E
Tarma, Peru 92 F3 11 25S 75 45W
Tarn →, France 18 E4 43 5N 1 6 E
Tarnobrzeg, Poland 17 C11 50 35N 21 41 E
Tarnów, Poland 17 C11 50 3N 21 0 E
Tarnowskie Góry, Poland 17 C10 50 27N 18 54 E
Taroom, Australia 63 D4 25 36S 149 48 E
Taroudannt, Morocco 50 B3 30 30N 8 52W
Tarpon Springs, U.S.A. 77 L4 28 9N 82 45W

Theunissen

Theunissen, S. Africa 56 D4 28 26S 26 43 E
Thevenard, Australia 63 E1 32 9S 133 38 E
Thibodaux, U.S.A. 81 L9 29 48N 90 49W
Thicket Portage, Canada 73 B9 55 19N 97 42W
Thief River Falls, U.S.A. 80 A6 48 7N 96 10W
Thiel Mts., Antarctica 5 E16 85 15S 91 0W
Thiers, France 18 D5 45 52N 3 33 E
Thies, Senegal 50 F1 14 50N 16 51W
Thika, Kenya 54 C4 1 1S 37 5 E
Thikombia, Fiji 59 B9 15 44S 179 55W
Thimphu, Bhutan 41 F16 27 31N 89 45 E
þingvallavatn, Iceland 8 D3 64 11N 21 9W
Thionville, France 18 B7 49 20N 6 10 E
Thira, Greece 21 F11 36 23N 25 27 E
Thirsk, U.K. 10 C6 54 14N 1 19W
Thisted, Denmark 9 H13 56 58N 8 40 E
Thistle I., Australia 63 F2 35 0S 136 8 E
Thívai, Greece 21 E10 38 19N 23 19 E
þjórsá →, Iceland 8 E3 63 47N 20 48W
Thlewiaza →, Man., Canada 73 B8 59 43N 100 5W
Thlewiaza →, N.W.T., Canada 73 A10 60 29N 94 40W
Thmar Puok, Cambodia 38 F4 13 57N 103 4 E
Tho Vinh, Vietnam 38 C5 19 16N 105 42 E
Thoa →, Canada 73 A7 60 31N 109 47W
Thoen, Thailand 38 D2 17 43N 99 12 E
Thoeng, Thailand 38 C3 19 41N 100 12 E
Tholdi, Pakistan 43 B7 35 5N 76 6 E
Thomas, Okla., U.S.A. 81 H5 35 45N 98 45W
Thomas, W. Va., U.S.A. 76 F6 39 9N 79 30W
Thomas, L., Australia 63 D2 26 4S 137 58 E
Thomaston, U.S.A. 77 J3 32 53N 84 20W
Thomasville, Ala., U.S.A. 77 K2 31 55N 87 44W
Thomasville, Ga., U.S.A. 77 K3 30 50N 83 59W
Thomasville, N.C., U.S.A. 77 H5 35 53N 80 5W
Thompson, Canada 73 B9 55 45N 97 52W
Thompson, U.S.A. 83 G9 38 58N 109 43W
Thompson →, Canada 72 C4 50 15N 121 24W
Thompson →, U.S.A. 80 F8 39 46N 93 37W
Thompson Falls, U.S.A. 82 C6 47 36N 115 21W
Thompson Landing, Canada 73 A6 62 56N 110 40W
Thompson Pk., U.S.A. 82 F2 41 0N 123 0W
Thomson's Falls = Nyahururu, Kenya 54 B4 0 2N 36 27 E
Thon Buri, Thailand 39 F3 13 43N 100 29 E
þórisvatn, Iceland 8 D4 64 20N 18 55W
Thornaby on Tees, U.K. 10 C6 54 33N 1 18W
Thornbury, Canada 78 B4 44 34N 80 26W
Thorold, Canada 78 C5 43 7N 79 12W
þórshöfn, Iceland 8 C6 66 12N 15 20W
Thouin, C., Australia 60 D2 20 20S 118 10 E
Thousand Oaks, U.S.A. 85 L8 34 10N 118 50W
Thrace, Turkey 21 D12 41 0N 27 0 E
Three Forks, U.S.A. 82 D8 45 54N 111 33W
Three Hills, Canada 72 C6 51 43N 113 15W
Three Hummock I., Australia 62 G3 40 25S 144 55 E
Three Lakes, U.S.A. 80 C10 45 48N 89 10W
Three Points, C., Ghana 50 H4 4 42N 2 6W
Three Rivers, Australia 61 E2 25 10S 119 5 E
Three Rivers, Calif., U.S.A. 84 J8 36 26N 118 54W
Three Rivers, Tex., U.S.A. 81 L5 28 28N 98 11W
Three Sisters, U.S.A. 82 D3 44 4N 121 51W
Throssell, L., Australia 61 E3 27 33S 124 10 E
Throssell Ra., Australia 60 D3 22 3S 121 43 E
Thuan Hoa, Vietnam 39 H5 8 58N 105 30 E
Thubun Lakes, Canada 73 A6 61 30N 112 0W
Thuin, Belgium 15 D4 50 20N 4 17 E
Thule, Greenland 4 B4 77 40N 69 0W
Thun, Switz. 16 E4 46 45N 7 38 E
Thundelarra, Australia 61 E2 28 53S 117 7 E
Thunder B., U.S.A. 78 B1 45 0N 83 20W
Thunder Bay, Canada 70 C2 48 20N 89 15W
Thung Song, Thailand 39 H2 8 10N 99 40 E
Thunkar, Bhutan 41 F17 27 55N 91 0 E
Thuong Tra, Vietnam 38 D6 16 2N 107 42 E
Thüringer Wald, Germany 16 C6 50 35N 11 0 E
Thurles, Ireland 13 D4 52 41N 7 49W
Thurloo Downs, Australia 63 D3 29 15S 143 30 E
Thursday I., Australia 62 A3 10 30S 142 3 E
Thurso, Canada 70 C4 45 36N 75 15W
Thurso, U.K. 12 C5 58 36N 3 32W
Thurston I., Antarctica 5 D16 72 0S 100 0W
Thutade L., Canada 72 B3 57 0N 126 55W
Thylungra, Australia 63 D3 26 4S 143 28 E
Thyolo, Malawi 55 F4 16 7S 35 5 E
Thysville = Mbanza Ngungu, Zaïre 52 F2 5 12S 14 53 E
Tia, Australia 63 E5 31 10S 151 50 E
Tian Shan, Asia 32 B3 42 0N 76 0 E
Tianjin, China 35 E9 39 8N 117 10 E
Tianshui, China 34 G3 34 32N 105 40 E
Tianzhen, China 34 D8 40 24N 114 5 E
Tianzhuangtai, China 35 D12 40 43N 122 5 E
Tiaret, Algeria 50 A5 35 20N 1 21 E
Tiassalé, Ivory C. 50 G4 5 58N 4 57W
Tibagi, Brazil 95 A5 24 30S 50 24W
Tibagi →, Brazil 95 A5 22 47S 51 1W
Tibati, Cameroon 51 G7 6 22N 12 30 E
Tiber = Tévere →, Italy 20 D5 41 44N 12 14 E
Tiber Reservoir, U.S.A. 82 B8 48 19N 111 6W
Tiberias = Teverya, Israel 47 C4 32 47N 35 32 E
Tiberias, L. = Yam Kinneret, Israel 47 C4 32 45N 35 35 E
Tibesti, Chad 51 D8 21 0N 17 30 E
Tibet = Xizang □, China 32 C3 32 0N 88 0 E
Tibet, Plateau of, Asia 28 F12 32 0N 86 0 E
Tibnī, Syria 44 C3 35 36N 39 50 E
Tibooburra, Australia 63 D3 29 26S 142 1 E
Tiburón, Mexico 86 B2 29 0N 112 30W
Tîchît, Mauritania 50 E3 18 21N 9 29W
Ticino →, Italy 20 B3 45 9N 9 14 E
Ticonderoga, U.S.A. 79 C11 43 51N 73 26W
Ticul, Mexico 87 C7 20 20N 89 31W
Tidaholm, Sweden 9 G15 58 12N 13 55 E
Tiddim, Burma 41 H18 23 28N 93 45 E
Tidjikja, Mauritania 50 E2 18 29N 11 35W
Tidore, Indonesia 37 D7 0 40N 127 25 E
Tiel, Neths. 15 C5 51 53N 5 26 E
Tiel, Senegal 50 F1 14 55N 15 5W
Tieling, China 35 C12 42 20N 123 55 E
Tielt, Belgium 15 D3 51 0N 3 20 E
Tien Shan = Tian Shan, Asia 32 B3 42 0N 76 0 E
Tien-tsin = Tianjin, China 35 E9 39 8N 117 10 E
Tien Yen, Vietnam 38 B6 21 20N 107 24 E
T'ienching = Tianjin, China 35 E9 39 8N 117 10 E
Tienen, Belgium 15 D4 50 48N 4 57 E
Tientsin = Tianjin, China 35 E9 39 8N 117 10 E
Tierra Amarilla, Chile 94 B1 27 28S 70 18W
Tierra Amarilla, U.S.A. 83 H10 36 42N 106 33W
Tierra Colorada, Mexico 87 D5 17 10N 99 35W
Tierra de Campos, Spain 19 A3 42 10N 4 50W
Tierra del Fuego, I. Gr. de, Argentina 96 G3 54 0S 69 0W
Tiétar →, Spain 19 C3 39 50N 6 1W
Tieté →, Brazil 95 A5 20 40S 51 35W
Tieyon, Australia 63 D1 26 12S 133 52 E
Tiffin, U.S.A. 76 E4 41 7N 83 11W
Tiflis = Tbilisi, Georgia 25 F7 41 43N 44 50 E
Tifton, U.S.A. 77 K4 31 27N 83 31W
Tifu, Indonesia 37 E7 3 39S 126 24 E
Tighina, Moldova 17 E15 46 50N 29 30 E
Tigil, Russia 27 D16 57 49N 158 40 E
Tignish, Canada 71 C7 46 58N 64 2W
Tigre →, Peru 92 D4 4 30S 74 10W
Tigris = Dijlah, Nahr →, Asia 44 D5 31 0N 47 25 E
Tigyaing, Burma 41 H20 23 45N 96 10 E
Tîh, Gebel el, Egypt 51 C11 29 32N 33 26 E
Tijuana, Mexico 85 N9 32 30N 117 10W
Tikal, Guatemala 88 C2 17 13N 89 24W
Tikamgarh, India 43 G8 24 44N 78 50 E
Tikhoretsk, Russia 25 E7 45 56N 40 5 E
Tikrīt, Iraq 44 C4 34 35N 43 37 E
Tiksi, Russia 27 B13 71 40N 128 45 E
Tilamuta, Indonesia 37 D6 0 32N 122 23 E
Tilburg, Neths. 15 C5 51 31N 5 6 E
Tilbury, Canada 70 D3 42 17N 82 23W
Tilbury, U.K. 11 F8 51 27N 0 22 E
Tilcara, Argentina 94 A2 23 36S 65 23W
Tilden, Nebr., U.S.A. 80 D6 42 3N 97 50W
Tilden, Tex., U.S.A. 81 L5 28 28N 98 33W
Tilhar, India 43 F8 28 0N 79 45 E
Tilichiki, Russia 27 C17 60 27N 166 5 E
Tílissos, Greece 23 D7 35 20N 25 1 E
Till →, U.K. 10 B5 55 35N 2 3W
Tillabéri, Niger 50 F5 14 28N 1 28 E
Tillamook, U.S.A. 82 D2 45 27N 123 51W
Tillsonburg, Canada 70 D3 42 53N 80 44W
Tillyeria □, Cyprus 23 D11 35 6N 32 40 E
Tílos, Greece 21 F12 36 27N 27 27 E
Tilpa, Australia 63 E3 30 57S 144 24 E
Tilsit = Sovetsk, Russia 9 J19 55 6N 21 50 E
Tilt →, U.K. 12 E5 56 46N 3 51W
Tilton, U.S.A. 79 C13 43 27N 71 36W
Timagami L., Canada 70 C3 47 0N 80 10W
Timanskiy Kryazh, Russia 24 A9 65 58N 50 5 E
Timaru, N.Z. 59 L3 44 23S 171 14 E
Timau, Kenya 54 B4 0 4N 37 15 E
Timbákion, Greece 23 D6 35 4N 24 45 E
Timbedgha, Mauritania 50 E3 16 17N 8 16W
Timber Lake, U.S.A. 80 C4 45 26N 101 5W
Timber Mt., U.S.A. 84 H10 37 6N 116 28W
Timboon, Australia 63 F3 38 30S 142 58 E
Timbuktu = Tombouctou, Mali 50 E4 16 50N 3 0W
Timi, Cyprus 23 E11 34 44N 32 31 E
Timimoun, Algeria 50 C5 29 14N 0 16 E
Timişoara, Romania 17 F11 45 43N 21 15 E
Timmins, Canada 70 C3 48 28N 81 25W
Timok →, Serbia, Yug. 21 B10 44 10N 22 40 E
Timon, Brazil 93 E10 5 8S 42 52W
Timor, Indonesia 37 F7 9 0S 125 0 E
Timor □, Indonesia 37 F7 9 0S 125 0 E
Timor Sea, Ind. Oc. 60 B4 12 0S 127 0 E
Tin Mt., U.S.A. 84 J9 36 50N 117 10W
Tinaca Pt., Phil. 37 C7 5 30N 125 25 E
Tinajo, Canary Is. 22 E6 29 4N 13 42W
Tindouf, Algeria 50 C3 27 42N 8 10W
Tinggi, Pulau, Malaysia 39 L5 2 18N 104 7 E
Tingo Maria, Peru 92 E3 9 10S 75 54W
Tinh Bien, Vietnam 39 G5 10 36N 104 57 E
Tinjoub, Algeria 50 C3 29 45N 5 40W
Tinkurrin, Australia 61 F2 32 59S 117 46 E
Tinnevelly = Tirunelveli, India 40 Q10 8 45N 77 45 E
Tinogasta, Argentina 94 B2 28 5S 67 32W
Tinos, Greece 21 F11 37 33N 25 8 E
Tintina, Argentina 94 B3 27 2S 62 45W
Tintinara, Australia 63 F3 35 48S 140 2 E
Tioga, U.S.A. 78 E7 41 55N 77 8W
Tioman, Pulau, Malaysia 39 L5 2 50N 104 10 E
Tionesta, U.S.A. 78 E5 41 30N 79 28W
Tipongpani, India 41 F19 27 20N 95 55 E
Tipperary, Ireland 13 D3 52 28N 8 10W
Tipperary □, Ireland 13 D4 52 37N 7 55W
Tipton, U.K. 11 E5 52 32N 2 4W
Tipton, Calif., U.S.A. 83 H4 36 4N 119 19W
Tipton, Ind., U.S.A. 76 E2 40 17N 86 2W
Tipton, Iowa, U.S.A. 80 E9 41 46N 91 8W
Tipton Mt., U.S.A. 85 K12 35 32N 114 12W
Tiptonville, U.S.A. 81 G10 36 23N 89 29W
Tīrān, Iran 45 C6 32 45N 51 8 E
Tirana, Albania 21 D8 41 18N 19 49 E
Tiranë = Tirana, Albania 21 D8 41 18N 19 49 E
Tiraspol, Moldova 17 E15 46 55N 29 35 E
Tirat Karmel, Israel 47 C3 32 46N 34 58 E
Tire, Turkey 21 E12 38 5N 27 50 E
Tirebolu, Turkey 25 F6 40 58N 38 45 E
Tiree, U.K. 12 E2 56 31N 6 55W
Tîrgovişte, Romania 17 F13 44 55N 25 27 E
Tîrgu-Jiu, Romania 17 F12 45 5N 23 19 E
Tîrgu Mureş, Romania 17 E13 46 31N 24 38 E
Tirich Mir, Pakistan 40 A7 36 15N 71 55 E
Tîrnăveni, Romania 17 E13 46 19N 24 13 E
Tírnavos, Greece 21 E10 39 45N 22 18 E
Tirodi, India 40 J11 21 40N 79 44 E
Tirol □, Austria 16 E6 47 3N 10 43 E
Tirso →, Italy 20 E3 39 53N 8 32 E
Tiruchchirappalli, India 40 P11 10 45N 78 45 E
Tirunelveli, India 40 Q10 8 45N 77 45 E
Tirupati, India 40 N11 13 39N 79 25 E
Tiruppur, India 40 P10 11 5N 77 22 E
Tiruvannamalai, India 40 N11 12 15N 79 5 E
Tisa →, Serbia, Yug. 21 B9 45 15N 20 17 E
Tisdale, Canada 73 C8 52 50N 104 0W
Tishomingo, U.S.A. 81 H6 34 14N 96 41W
Tisza = Tisa →, Serbia, Yug. 21 B9 45 15N 20 17 E
Tit-Ary, Russia 27 B13 71 55N 127 2 E
Tithwal, Pakistan 43 B5 34 21N 73 50 E
Titicaca, L., S. Amer. 92 G5 15 30S 69 30W
Titograd = Podgorica, Montenegro, Yug. 21 C8 42 30N 19 19 E
Titov Veles, Macedonia 21 D9 41 46N 21 47 E
Titova-Mitrovica, Serbia, Yug. 21 C9 42 54N 20 52 E
Titovo Užice, Serbia, Yug. 21 C8 43 55N 19 50 E
Titule, Zaïre 54 B2 3 15N 25 31 E
Titusville, Fla., U.S.A. 77 L5 28 37N 80 49W
Titusville, Pa., U.S.A. 78 E5 41 38N 79 41W
Tivaouane, Senegal 50 F1 14 56N 16 45W
Tiverton, U.K. 11 G4 50 54N 3 29W
Tívoli, Italy 20 D5 41 58N 12 45 E
Tizi-Ouzou, Algeria 50 A5 36 42N 4 3 E
Tizimín, Mexico 87 C7 21 0N 88 1W
Tiznit, Morocco 50 C3 29 48N 9 45W
Tjeggelvas, Sweden 8 C17 66 37N 17 45 E
Tjirebon = Cirebon, Indonesia 37 G13 6 45S 108 32 E
Tjörn, Sweden 9 G14 58 0N 11 35 E
Tlacotalpan, Mexico 87 D5 18 37N 95 40W
Tlahualilo, Mexico 86 B4 26 20N 103 30W
Tlaquepaque, Mexico 86 C4 20 39N 103 19W
Tlaxcala, Mexico 87 D5 19 20N 98 14W
Tlaxcala □, Mexico 87 D5 19 30N 98 20W
Tlaxiaco, Mexico 87 D5 17 18N 97 40W
Tlell, Canada 72 C2 53 34N 131 56W
Tlemcen, Algeria 50 B4 34 52N 1 21W
Tmassah, Libya 51 C8 26 19N 15 51 E
To Bong, Vietnam 38 F7 12 45N 109 16 E
Toad →, Canada 72 B4 59 25N 124 57W
Toamasina, Madag. 57 B8 18 10S 49 25 E
Toamasina □, Madag. 57 B8 18 0S 49 0 E
Toay, Argentina 94 D3 36 43S 64 38W
Toba, Japan 31 G8 34 30N 136 51 E
Toba Kakar, Pakistan 42 D3 31 30N 69 0 E
Toba Tek Singh, Pakistan 42 D5 30 55N 72 25 E
Tobago, W. Indies 89 D7 11 10N 60 30W
Tobelo, Indonesia 37 D7 1 45N 127 56 E
Tobermorey, Australia 62 C2 22 12S 138 0 E
Tobermory, Canada 70 C3 45 12N 81 40W
Tobermory, U.K. 12 E2 56 38N 6 5W
Tobin, U.S.A. 84 F5 39 55N 121 19W
Tobin, L., Australia 60 D4 21 45S 125 49 E
Tobin L., Canada 73 C8 53 35N 103 30W
Toboali, Indonesia 36 E3 3 0S 106 25 E
Tobol, Kazakstan 26 D7 52 40N 62 39 E
Tobol →, Russia 26 D7 58 10N 68 12 E
Toboli, Indonesia 37 E6 0 38S 120 5 E
Tobolsk, Russia 26 D7 58 15N 68 10 E
Tobruk = Tubruq, Libya 51 B9 32 7N 23 55 E
Tobyhanna, U.S.A. 79 E9 41 11N 75 25W
Tobyl = Tobol →, Russia 26 D7 58 10N 68 12 E
Tocantinópolis, Brazil 93 E9 6 20S 47 25W
Tocantins □, Brazil 93 F9 10 0S 48 0W
Tocantins →, Brazil 93 D9 1 45S 49 10W
Toccoa, U.S.A. 77 H4 34 35N 83 19W
Tochigi, Japan 31 F9 36 25N 139 45 E
Tochigi □, Japan 31 F9 36 45N 139 45 E
Tocopilla, Chile 94 A1 22 5S 70 10W
Tocumwal, Australia 63 F4 35 51S 145 31 E
Tocuyo →, Venezuela 92 A5 11 3N 68 23W
Todd →, Australia 62 C2 24 52S 135 48 E
Todeli, Indonesia 37 E6 1 38S 124 34 E
Todenyang, Kenya 54 B4 4 35N 35 56 E
Todos os Santos, B. de, Brazil 93 F11 12 48S 38 38W
Todos Santos, Mexico 86 C2 23 27N 110 13W
Tofield, Canada 72 C6 53 25N 112 40W
Tofino, Canada 72 D3 49 11N 125 55W
Tofua, Tonga 59 D11 19 45S 175 5W
Tōgane, Japan 31 G10 35 33N 140 22 E
Togba, Mauritania 50 E2 17 26N 10 12W
Togian, Kepulauan, Indonesia 37 E6 0 20S 121 50 E
Togliatti, Russia 24 D8 53 32N 49 24 E
Togo ■, W. Afr. 50 G5 8 30N 1 35 E
Togtoh, China 34 D6 40 15N 111 10 E
Tōhoku □, Japan 30 E10 39 50N 141 45 E
Toinya, Sudan 51 G10 6 17N 29 46 E
Tojikiston = Tajikistan ■, Asia 26 F8 38 30N 70 0 E
Tojo, Indonesia 37 E6 1 20S 121 15 E
Tōjō, Japan 31 G6 34 53N 133 16 E
Tokachi-Dake, Japan 30 C11 43 17N 142 5 E
Tokachi-Gawa →, Japan 30 C11 42 44N 143 42 E
Tokala, Indonesia 37 E6 1 30S 121 40 E
Tōkamachi, Japan 31 F9 37 8N 138 43 E
Tokanui, N.Z. 59 M2 46 34S 168 56 E
Tokar, Sudan 51 E12 18 27N 37 56 E
Tokara-Rettō, Japan 31 K4 29 37N 129 43 E
Tokarahi, N.Z. 59 L3 44 56S 170 39 E
Tokashiki-Shima, Japan 31 L3 26 11N 127 21 E
Tŏkchŏn, N. Korea 35 E14 39 45N 126 18 E
Tokeland, U.S.A. 84 D3 46 42N 123 59W
Tokelau Is., Pac. Oc. 64 H10 9 0S 171 45W
Tokmak, Kyrgyzstan 26 E8 42 49N 75 15 E
Toko Ra., Australia 62 C2 23 5S 138 20 E
Tokoro-Gawa →, Japan 30 B12 44 7N 144 5 E
Tokuno-Shima, Japan 31 L4 27 56N 128 55 E
Tokushima, Japan 31 G7 34 4N 134 34 E
Tokushima □, Japan 31 H7 33 55N 134 0 E
Tokuyama, Japan 31 G5 34 3N 131 50 E
Tōkyō, Japan 31 G9 35 45N 139 45 E
Tolaga Bay, N.Z. 59 H7 38 21S 178 20 E
Tolbukhin = Dobrich, Bulgaria 21 C12 43 37N 27 49 E
Toledo, Spain 19 C3 39 50N 4 2W
Toledo, Ohio, U.S.A. 76 E4 41 39N 83 33W
Toledo, Oreg., U.S.A. 82 D2 44 37N 123 56W
Toledo, Wash., U.S.A. 82 C2 46 26N 122 51W
Toledo, Montes de, Spain 19 C3 39 33N 4 20W
Tolga, Algeria 50 B6 34 40N 5 22 E
Toliara, Madag. 57 C7 23 21S 43 40 E
Toliara □, Madag. 57 C8 21 0S 45 0 E
Tolima, Colombia 92 C3 4 40N 75 19W
Tolitoli, Indonesia 37 D6 1 5N 120 50 E
Tollhouse, U.S.A. 84 H7 37 1N 119 24W
Tolo, Zaïre 52 E3 2 55S 18 34 E
Tolo, Teluk, Indonesia 37 E6 2 20S 122 10 E
Toluca, Mexico 87 D5 19 20N 99 40W
Tom Burke, S. Africa 57 C4 23 5S 28 0 E
Tom Price, Australia 60 D2 22 40S 117 48 E
Tomah, U.S.A. 80 D9 43 59N 90 30W
Tomahawk, U.S.A. 80 C10 45 28N 89 44W
Tomakomai, Japan 30 C10 42 38N 141 36 E
Tomales, U.S.A. 84 G4 38 15N 122 53W
Tomales B., U.S.A. 84 G3 38 15N 123 58W
Tomar, Portugal 19 C1 39 36N 8 25W
Tomaszów Mazowiecki, Poland 17 C10 51 30N 19 57 E
Tomatlán, Mexico 86 D3 19 56N 105 15W
Tombé, Sudan 51 G11 5 53N 31 40 E
Tombigbee →, U.S.A. 77 K2 31 8N 87 57W
Tombouctou, Mali 50 E4 16 50N 3 0W
Tombstone, U.S.A. 83 L8 31 43N 110 4W
Tombua, Angola 56 B1 15 55S 11 55 E
Tomé, Chile 94 D1 36 36S 72 57W
Tomelloso, Spain 19 C4 39 10N 3 2W
Tomingley, Australia 63 E4 32 26S 148 16 E
Tomini, Indonesia 37 D6 0 30N 120 30 E
Tomini, Teluk, Indonesia 37 E6 0 10S 122 0 E
Tomkinson Ras., Australia 61 E4 26 11S 129 5 E
Tommot, Russia 27 D13 59 4N 126 20 E
Tomnavoulin, U.K. 12 D5 57 19N 3 19W
Tomnop Ta Suos, Cambodia 39 G5 11 20N 104 15 E
Tomorit, Albania 21 D9 40 42N 20 11 E
Toms Place, U.S.A. 84 H8 37 34N 118 41W
Toms River, U.S.A. 79 G10 39 58N 74 12W
Tomsk, Russia 26 D9 56 30N 85 5 E
Tonalá, Mexico 87 D6 16 8N 93 41W
Tonalea, U.S.A. 83 H8 36 19N 110 56W
Tonantins, Brazil 92 D5 2 45S 67 45W
Tonasket, U.S.A. 82 B4 48 42N 119 26W
Tonawanda, U.S.A. 78 D6 43 1N 78 53W
Tonbridge, U.K. 11 F8 51 11N 0 17 E
Tondano, Indonesia 37 D6 1 35N 124 54 E
Tonekābon, Iran 45 B6 36 45N 51 12 E
Tong Xian, China 34 E9 39 55N 116 35 E
Tonga ■, Pac. Oc. 59 D11 19 50S 174 30W
Tonga Trench, Pac. Oc. 64 J10 18 0S 173 0W
Tongaat, S. Africa 57 D5 29 33S 31 9 E
Tongareva, Cook Is. 65 H12 9 0S 158 0W
Tongatapu, Tonga 59 E11 21 10S 174 0W
Tongchŏn-ni, N. Korea 35 E14 39 50N 127 25 E
Tongchuan, China 34 G5 35 6N 109 3 E
Tongeren, Belgium 15 D5 50 47N 5 28 E
Tongguan, China 34 G6 34 40N 110 25 E
Tonghua, China 35 D13 41 42N 125 58 E
Tongjosŏn Man, N. Korea 35 E14 39 30N 128 0 E
Tongking, G. of = Tonkin, G. of, Asia 32 E5 20 0N 108 0 E
Tongliao, China 35 C12 43 38N 122 18 E
Tongnae, S. Korea 35 G15 35 12N 129 5 E
Tongobory, Madag. 57 C7 23 32S 44 20 E
Tongoy, Chile 94 C1 30 16S 71 31W
Tongres = Tongeren, Belgium 15 D5 50 47N 5 28 E
Tongsa Dzong, Bhutan 41 F17 27 31N 90 31 E
Tongue, U.K. 12 C4 58 29N 4 25W
Tongue →, U.S.A. 80 B2 46 25N 105 52W
Tongwei, China 34 G3 35 0N 105 5 E
Tongxin, China 34 F3 36 59N 105 58 E
Tongyang, N. Korea 35 E14 39 9N 126 53 E
Tongyu, China 35 B12 44 45N 123 4 E
Tonk, India 42 F6 26 6N 75 54 E
Tonkawa, U.S.A. 81 G6 36 41N 97 18W
Tonkin = Bac Phan, Vietnam 38 B5 22 0N 105 0 E
Tonkin, G. of, Asia 32 E5 20 0N 108 0 E
Tonlé Sap, Cambodia 38 F4 13 0N 104 0 E
Tono, Japan 30 E10 39 19N 141 32 E
Tonopah, U.S.A. 83 G5 38 4N 117 14W
Tonosí, Panama 88 E3 7 20N 80 20W
Tønsberg, Norway 9 G14 59 19N 10 25 E
Tooele, U.S.A. 82 F7 40 32N 112 18W
Toompine, Australia 63 D3 27 15S 144 19 E
Toonpan, Australia 62 B4 19 28S 146 48 E
Toora, Australia 63 F4 38 39S 146 23 E
Toora-Khem, Russia 27 D10 52 28N 96 17 E
Toowoomba, Australia 63 D5 27 32S 151 56 E
Top-ozero, Russia 24 A5 65 35N 32 0 E
Topaz, U.S.A. 84 G7 38 41N 119 30W
Topeka, U.S.A. 80 F7 39 3N 95 40W
Topki, Russia 26 D9 55 20N 85 35 E
Topley, Canada 72 C3 54 49N 126 18W
Topocalma, Pta., Chile 94 C1 34 10S 72 2W
Topock, U.S.A. 85 L12 34 46N 114 29W
Topol'čany, Slovak Rep. 17 D10 48 35N 18 12 E
Topolobampo, Mexico 86 B3 25 40N 109 4W
Toppenish, U.S.A. 82 C3 46 23N 120 19W
Toraka Vestale, Madag. 57 B7 16 20S 43 58 E
Torata, Peru 92 G4 17 23S 70 1W
Torbalı, Turkey 21 E12 38 10N 27 21 E
Torbay, Canada 71 C9 47 40N 52 42W
Torbay, U.K. 11 G4 50 26N 3 31W
Tordesillas, Spain 19 B3 41 30N 5 0W
Torfaen □, U.K. 11 F4 51 43N 3 3W
Torgau, Germany 16 C7 51 34N 13 0 E
Torhout, Belgium 15 C3 51 5N 3 7 E
Tori-Shima, Japan 31 J10 30 29N 140 19 E
Torin, Mexico 86 B2 27 33N 110 15W
Torino, Italy 20 B2 45 3N 7 40 E
Torit, Sudan 51 H11 4 27N 32 31 E
Tormes →, Spain 19 B2 41 18N 6 29W
Tornado Mt., Canada 72 D6 49 55N 114 40W
Torne älv →, Sweden 8 D21 65 50N 24 12 E
Torneå = Tornio, Finland 8 D21 65 50N 24 12 E
Torneträsk, Sweden 8 B18 68 24N 19 15 E
Tornio, Finland 8 D21 65 50N 24 12 E
Tornionjoki →, Finland 8 D21 65 50N 24 12 E
Tornquist, Argentina 94 D3 38 8S 62 15W
Toro, Spain 22 B11 39 59N 4 8 E
Toro, Cerro del, Chile 94 B2 29 10S 69 50W
Toro Pk., U.S.A. 85 M10 33 34N 116 24W
Toroníios Kólpos, Greece 21 D10 40 5N 23 30 E

Toronto, *Australia* 63 E5 33 0S 151 30 E
Toronto, *Canada* 70 D4 43 39N 79 20W
Toronto, *U.S.A.* 78 F4 40 28N 80 36W
Toropets, *Russia* 24 C5 56 30N 31 40 E
Tororo, *Uganda* 54 B3 0 45N 34 12 E
Toros Dağlari, *Turkey* 25 G5 37 0N 32 30 E
Torquay, *Canada* 73 D8 49 9N 103 30W
Torquay, *U.K.* 11 G4 50 27N 3 32W
Torrance, *U.S.A.* 85 M8 33 50N 118 19W
Tôrre de Moncorvo, *Portugal* 19 B2 41 12N 7 8W
Torre del Greco, *Italy* 20 D6 40 47N 14 22 E
Torrejón de Ardoz, *Spain* 19 B4 40 27N 3 29W
Torrelavega, *Spain* 19 A3 43 20N 4 5W
Torremolinos, *Spain* 19 D3 36 38N 4 30W
Torrens, L., *Australia* 63 E2 31 0S 137 50 E
Torrens Cr. →, *Australia* 62 C4 22 23S 145 9 E
Torrens Creek, *Australia* 62 C4 20 48S 145 3 E
Torrente, *Spain* 19 C5 39 27N 0 28W
Torreón, *Mexico* 86 B4 25 33N 103 26W
Torres, *Mexico* 86 B2 28 46N 110 47W
Torres Strait, *Australia* 64 H6 9 50S 142 20 E
Torres Vedras, *Portugal* 19 C1 39 5N 9 15W
Torrevieja, *Spain* 19 D5 37 59N 0 42W
Torrey, *U.S.A.* 83 G8 38 18N 111 25W
Torridge →, *U.K.* 11 G3 51 0N 4 13W
Torridon, L., *U.K.* 12 D3 57 35N 5 50W
Torrington, *Conn., U.S.A.* 79 E11 41 48N 73 7W
Torrington, *Wyo., U.S.A.* 80 D2 42 4N 104 11W
Tórshavn, *Færoe Is.* 8 E9 62 5N 6 56W
Tortola, *Virgin Is.* 89 C7 18 19N 64 45W
Tortosa, *Spain* 19 B6 40 49N 0 31 E
Tortosa, C. de, *Spain* 19 B6 40 41N 0 52 E
Tortue, I. de la, *Haiti* 89 B5 20 5N 72 57W
Ţorūd, *Iran* 45 C7 35 25N 55 5 E
Toruń, *Poland* 17 B10 53 2N 18 39 E
Tory I., *Ireland* 13 A3 55 16N 8 14W
Tosa, *Japan* 31 H6 33 24N 133 23 E
Tosa-Shimizu, *Japan* 31 H6 32 52N 132 58 E
Tosa-Wan, *Japan* 31 H6 33 15N 133 30 E
Toscana □, *Italy* 20 C4 43 25N 11 0 E
Toshkent, *Uzbekistan* 26 E7 41 20N 69 10 E
Tostado, *Argentina* 94 B3 29 15S 61 50W
Tostón, Pta. de, *Canary Is.* 22 F5 28 42N 14 2W
Tosu, *Japan* 31 H5 33 22N 130 31 E
Toteng, *Botswana* 56 C3 20 22S 22 58 E
Totma, *Russia* 24 C7 60 0N 42 40 E
Totnes, *U.K.* 11 G4 50 26N 3 42W
Totonicapán, *Guatemala* 88 D1 14 58N 91 12W
Totten Glacier, *Antarctica* 5 C8 66 45S 116 10 E
Tottenham, *Australia* 63 E4 32 14S 147 21 E
Tottenham, *Canada* 78 B5 44 1N 79 49W
Tottori, *Japan* 31 G7 35 30N 134 15 E
Tottori □, *Japan* 31 G7 35 30N 134 12 E
Touba, *Ivory C.* 50 G3 8 22N 7 40W
Toubkal, Djebel, *Morocco* 50 B3 31 0N 8 0W
Tougan, *Burkina Faso* 50 F4 13 11N 2 58W
Touggourt, *Algeria* 50 B6 33 6N 6 4 E
Tougué, *Guinea* 50 F2 11 25N 11 50W
Toul, *France* 18 B6 48 40N 5 53 E
Toulepleu, *Ivory C.* 50 G3 6 32N 8 24W
Toulon, *France* 18 E6 43 10N 5 55 E
Toulouse, *France* 18 E4 43 37N 1 27 E
Toummo, *Niger* 51 D7 22 45N 14 8 E
Toungoo, *Burma* 41 K20 19 0N 96 30 E
Touraine, *France* 18 C4 47 20N 0 30 E
Tourane = Da Nang, *Vietnam* 38 D7 16 4N 108 13 E
Tourcoing, *France* 18 A5 50 42N 3 10 E
Touriñán, C., *Spain* 19 A1 43 3N 9 18W
Tournai, *Belgium* 15 D3 50 35N 3 25 E
Tournon, *France* 18 D6 45 4N 4 50 E
Tours, *France* 18 C4 47 22N 0 40 E
Touwsrivier, *S. Africa* 56 E3 33 20S 20 2 E
Towada, *Japan* 30 D10 40 37N 141 13 E
Towada-Ko, *Japan* 30 D10 40 28N 140 55 E
Towamba, *Australia* 63 F4 37 6S 149 43 E
Towanda, *U.S.A.* 79 E8 41 46N 76 27W
Towang, *India* 41 F17 27 37N 91 50 E
Tower, *U.S.A.* 80 B8 47 48N 92 17W
Towerhill Cr. →, *Australia* 62 C3 22 28S 144 35 E
Towner, *U.S.A.* 80 A4 48 21N 100 25W
Townsend, *U.S.A.* 82 C8 46 19N 111 31W
Townshend I., *Australia* 62 C5 22 10S 150 31 E
Townsville, *Australia* 62 B4 19 15S 146 45 E
Towson, *U.S.A.* 76 F7 39 24N 76 36W
Toya-Ko, *Japan* 30 C10 42 35N 140 51 E
Toyah, *U.S.A.* 81 K3 31 19N 103 48W
Toyahvale, *U.S.A.* 81 K3 30 57N 103 47W
Toyama, *Japan* 31 F8 36 40N 137 15 E
Toyama □, *Japan* 31 F8 36 45N 137 30 E
Toyama-Wan, *Japan* 31 F8 37 0N 137 30 E
Toyohashi, *Japan* 31 G8 34 45N 137 25 E
Toyokawa, *Japan* 31 G8 34 48N 137 27 E
Toyonaka, *Japan* 31 G7 34 50N 135 28 E
Toyooka, *Japan* 31 G7 35 35N 134 48 E
Toyota, *Japan* 31 G8 35 3N 137 7 E
Tozeur, *Tunisia* 50 B6 33 56N 8 8 E
Trá Li = Tralee, *Ireland* 13 D2 52 16N 9 42W
Tra On, *Vietnam* 39 H5 9 58N 105 55 E
Trabzon, *Turkey* 25 F6 41 0N 39 45 E
Tracadie, *Canada* 71 C7 47 30N 64 55W
Tracy, *Calif., U.S.A.* 83 H3 37 44N 121 26W
Tracy, *Minn., U.S.A.* 80 C7 44 14N 95 37W
Trafalgar, C., *Spain* 19 D2 36 10N 6 2W
Trail, *Canada* 72 D5 49 5N 117 40W
Trainor L., *Canada* 72 A4 60 24N 120 17W
Trákhonas, *Cyprus* 23 D12 35 12N 33 21 E
Tralee, *Ireland* 13 D2 52 16N 9 42W
Tralee B., *Ireland* 13 D2 52 17N 9 55W
Tramore, *Ireland* 13 D4 52 10N 7 10W
Tran Ninh, Cao Nguyen, *Laos* 38 C4 19 30N 103 10 E
Tranås, *Sweden* 9 G16 58 3N 14 59 E
Trancas, *Argentina* 94 B2 26 11S 65 20W
Trang, *Thailand* 39 J2 7 33N 99 38 E
Trangahy, *Madag.* 57 B7 19 7S 44 31 E
Trangan, *Indonesia* 37 F8 6 40S 134 20 E
Trangie, *Australia* 63 E4 32 4S 148 0 E
Trani, *Italy* 20 D7 41 17N 16 25 E
Tranoroa, *Madag.* 57 C8 24 42S 45 4 E
Tranqueras, *Uruguay* 95 C4 31 13S 55 45W
Trans Nzoia □, *Kenya* 54 B3 1 0N 35 0 E
Transantarctic Mts., *Antarctica* 5 E12 85 0S 170 0W
Transcaucasia = Zakavkazye, *Asia* 25 F7 42 0N 44 0 E
Transcona, *Canada* 73 D9 49 55N 97 0W
Transilvania, *Romania* 17 E12 45 19N 25 0 E
Transilvanian Alps = Carpaţii Meridionali, *Romania* 17 F13 45 30N 25 0 E
Transylvania = Transilvania, *Romania* 17 E12 45 19N 25 0 E
Trápani, *Italy* 20 E5 38 1N 12 29 E
Trapper Pk., *U.S.A.* 82 D6 45 54N 114 18W
Traralgon, *Australia* 63 F4 38 12S 146 34 E
Trasimeno, L., *Italy* 20 C5 43 8N 12 6 E
Trat, *Thailand* 39 F4 12 14N 102 33 E
Traun, *Austria* 16 D8 48 14N 14 15 E
Traveller's L., *Australia* 63 E3 33 20S 142 0 E
Travemünde, *Germany* 16 B6 53 57N 10 52 E
Travers, Mt., *N.Z.* 59 K4 42 1S 172 45 E
Traverse City, *U.S.A.* 76 C3 44 46N 85 38W
Travnik, *Bos.-H.* 21 B7 44 17N 17 39 E
Trayning, *Australia* 61 F2 31 7S 117 40 E
Trébbia →, *Italy* 20 B3 45 4N 9 41 E
Třebíč, *Czech.* 16 D8 49 14N 15 55 E
Trebinje, *Bos.-H.* 21 C8 42 44N 18 22 E
Tredegar, *U.K.* 11 F4 51 47N 3 14W
Tregaron, *U.K.* 11 E4 52 14N 3 56W
Tregrosse Is., *Australia* 62 B5 17 41S 150 43 E
Treherne, *Canada* 73 D9 49 38N 98 42W
Treinta y Tres, *Uruguay* 95 C5 33 16S 54 17W
Trelew, *Argentina* 96 E3 43 10S 65 20W
Trelleborg, *Sweden* 9 J15 55 20N 13 10 E
Tremonton, *U.S.A.* 82 F7 41 43N 112 10W
Tremp, *Spain* 19 A6 42 10N 0 52 E
Trenche →, *Canada* 70 C5 47 46N 72 53W
Trenčín, *Slovak Rep.* 17 D10 48 52N 18 4 E
Trenggalek, *Indonesia* 37 H14 8 3S 111 43 E
Trenque Lauquen, *Argentina* 94 D3 36 5S 62 45W
Trent →, *U.K.* 10 D7 53 41N 0 42W
Trento, *Italy* 20 A4 46 4N 11 8 E
Trenton, *Canada* 70 D4 44 10N 77 34W
Trenton, *Mo., U.S.A.* 80 E8 40 5N 93 37W
Trenton, *N.J., U.S.A.* 79 F10 40 14N 74 46W
Trenton, *Nebr., U.S.A.* 80 E4 40 11N 101 1W
Trenton, *Tenn., U.S.A.* 81 H10 35 59N 88 56W
Trepassey, *Canada* 71 C9 46 43N 53 25W
Tres Arroyos, *Argentina* 94 D3 38 26S 60 20W
Três Corações, *Brazil* 95 A6 21 44S 45 15W
Três Lagoas, *Brazil* 93 H8 20 50S 51 43W
Tres Marías, *Mexico* 86 C3 21 25N 106 28W
Tres Montes, C., *Chile* 96 F1 46 50S 75 30W
Tres Pinos, *U.S.A.* 84 J5 36 48N 121 19W
Três Pontas, *Brazil* 95 A6 21 23S 45 29W
Tres Puentes, *Chile* 94 B1 27 50S 70 15W
Tres Puntas, C., *Argentina* 96 F3 47 0S 66 0W
Três Rios, *Brazil* 95 A7 22 6S 43 15W
Tres Valles, *Mexico* 87 D5 18 15N 96 8W
Treviso, *Italy* 20 B5 45 40N 12 15 E
Triabunna, *Australia* 62 G4 42 30S 147 55 E
Triánda, *Greece* 23 C10 36 25N 28 10 E
Triang, *Malaysia* 39 L4 3 15N 102 26 E
Tribulation, C., *Australia* 62 B4 16 5S 145 29 E
Tribune, *U.S.A.* 80 F4 38 28N 101 45W
Trichinopoly = Tiruchchirappalli, *India* 40 P11 10 45N 78 45 E
Trichur, *India* 40 P10 10 30N 76 18 E
Trida, *Australia* 63 E4 33 1S 145 1 E
Trier, *Germany* 16 D4 49 45N 6 38 E
Trieste, *Italy* 20 B5 45 40N 13 46 E
Triglav, *Slovenia* 16 E7 46 21N 13 50 E
Trikkala, *Greece* 21 E9 39 34N 21 47 E
Trikomo, *Cyprus* 23 D12 35 17N 33 52 E
Trikora, Puncak, *Indonesia* 37 E9 4 15S 138 45 E
Trim, *Ireland* 13 C5 53 33N 6 48W
Trincomalee, *Sri Lanka* 40 Q12 8 38N 81 15 E
Trindade, I., *Atl. Oc.* 2 F8 20 20S 29 50W
Trinidad, *Bolivia* 92 F6 14 46S 64 50W
Trinidad, *Colombia* 92 B4 5 25N 71 40W
Trinidad, *Cuba* 88 B3 21 48N 80 0W
Trinidad, *Uruguay* 94 C4 33 30S 56 50W
Trinidad, *U.S.A.* 81 G2 37 10N 104 31W
Trinidad, *W. Indies* 89 D7 10 30N 61 15W
Trinidad →, *Mexico* 87 D5 17 49N 95 9W
Trinidad, I., *Argentina* 96 D4 39 10S 62 0W
Trinidad & Tobago ■, *W. Indies* 89 D7 10 30N 61 20W
Trinity, *Canada* 71 C9 48 59N 53 55W
Trinity, *U.S.A.* 81 K7 30 57N 95 22W
Trinity →, *Calif., U.S.A.* 82 F2 41 11N 123 42W
Trinity →, *Tex., U.S.A.* 81 L7 29 45N 94 43W
Trinity B., *Canada* 71 C9 48 20N 53 10W
Trinity Range, *U.S.A.* 82 F4 40 15N 118 45W
Trinkitat, *Sudan* 51 E12 18 45N 37 51 E
Trion, *U.S.A.* 77 H3 34 33N 85 19W
Tripoli = Tarābulus, *Lebanon* 47 A4 34 31N 35 50 E
Tripoli = Tarābulus, *Libya* 51 B7 32 49N 13 7 E
Tripolis, *Greece* 21 F10 37 31N 22 25 E
Tripolitania, *N. Afr.* 48 C5 31 0N 13 0 E
Tripp, *U.S.A.* 80 D6 43 13N 97 58W
Tripura □, *India* 41 H17 24 0N 92 0 E
Tripylos, *Cyprus* 23 E11 34 59N 32 41 E
Tristan da Cunha, *Atl. Oc.* 49 K2 37 6S 12 20W
Trivandrum, *India* 40 Q10 8 41N 77 0 E
Trnava, *Slovak Rep.* 17 D9 48 23N 17 35 E
Trochu, *Canada* 72 C6 51 50N 113 13W
Trodely I., *Canada* 70 B4 52 15N 79 26W
Troglav, *Croatia* 20 C7 43 56N 16 36 E
Troilus, L., *Canada* 70 B5 50 50N 74 35W
Trois-Pistoles, *Canada* 71 C6 48 5N 69 10W
Trois-Rivières, *Canada* 70 C5 46 25N 72 34W
Troitsk, *Russia* 26 D7 54 10N 61 35 E
Troitsko Pechorsk, *Russia* 24 B10 62 40N 56 10 E
Trölladyngja, *Iceland* 8 D5 64 54N 17 16W
Trollhättan, *Sweden* 9 G15 58 17N 12 20 E
Trollheimen, *Norway* 8 E13 62 46N 9 1 E
Tromsø, *Norway* 8 B18 69 40N 18 56 E
Trona, *U.S.A.* 85 K9 35 46N 117 23W
Tronador, *Argentina* 96 E2 41 10S 71 50W
Trøndelag, *Norway* 8 D14 64 17N 11 50 E
Trondheim, *Norway* 8 E14 63 36N 10 25 E
Trondheimsfjorden, *Norway* 8 E14 63 35N 10 30 E
Troodos, *Cyprus* 23 E11 34 55N 32 52 E
Troon, *U.K.* 12 F4 55 33N 4 39W
Tropic, *U.S.A.* 83 H7 37 37N 112 5W
Trossachs, The, *U.K.* 12 E4 56 14N 4 24W
Trostan, *U.K.* 13 A5 55 3N 6 10W
Trotternish, *U.K.* 12 D2 57 32N 6 15W
Troup, *U.S.A.* 81 J7 32 9N 95 7W
Trout →, *Canada* 72 A5 61 19N 119 51W
Trout L., *N.W.T., Canada* 72 A4 60 40N 121 14W
Trout L., *Ont., Canada* 73 C10 51 20N 93 15W
Trout Lake, *Mich., U.S.A.* 70 C2 46 12N 85 1W
Trout Lake, *Wash., U.S.A.* 84 E5 46 0N 121 32W
Trout River, *Canada* 71 C8 49 29N 58 8W
Trouville-sur-Mer, *France* 18 B4 49 21N 0 5 E
Trowbridge, *U.K.* 11 F5 51 18N 2 12W
Troy, *Turkey* 21 E12 39 57N 26 12 E
Troy, *Ala., U.S.A.* 77 K3 31 48N 85 58W
Troy, *Idaho, U.S.A.* 82 C5 46 44N 116 46W
Troy, *Kans., U.S.A.* 80 F7 39 47N 95 5W
Troy, *Mo., U.S.A.* 80 F9 38 59N 90 59W
Troy, *Mont., U.S.A.* 82 B6 48 28N 115 53W
Troy, *N.Y., U.S.A.* 79 D11 42 44N 73 41W
Troy, *Ohio, U.S.A.* 76 E3 40 2N 84 12W
Troyes, *France* 18 B6 48 19N 4 3 E
Trucial States = United Arab Emirates ■, *Asia* 45 F7 23 50N 54 0 E
Truckee, *U.S.A.* 84 F6 39 20N 120 11W
Trudovoye, *Russia* 30 C6 43 17N 132 5 E
Trujillo, *Honduras* 88 C2 16 0N 86 0W
Trujillo, *Peru* 92 E3 8 6S 79 0W
Trujillo, *Spain* 19 C3 39 28N 5 55W
Trujillo, *U.S.A.* 81 H2 35 32N 104 42W
Trujillo, *Venezuela* 92 B4 9 22N 70 38W
Truk, *Pac. Oc.* 64 G7 7 25N 151 46 E
Trumann, *U.S.A.* 81 H9 35 41N 90 31W
Trumbull, Mt., *U.S.A.* 83 H7 36 25N 113 8W
Trundle, *Australia* 63 E4 32 53S 147 35 E
Trung-Phan, *Vietnam* 38 E7 16 0N 108 0 E
Truro, *Canada* 71 C7 45 21N 63 14W
Truro, *U.K.* 11 G2 50 16N 5 4W
Truskavets, *Ukraine* 17 D12 49 17N 23 30 E
Truslove, *Australia* 61 F3 33 20S 121 45 E
Truth or Consequences, *U.S.A.* 83 K10 33 8N 107 15W
Trutnov, *Czech.* 16 C8 50 37N 15 54 E
Tryon, *U.S.A.* 77 H4 35 13N 82 14W
Tryonville, *U.S.A.* 78 E5 41 42N 79 48W
Tsaratanana, *Madag.* 57 B8 16 47S 47 39 E
Tsaratanana, Mt. de, *Madag.* 57 A8 14 0S 49 0 E
Tsarevo = Michurin, *Bulgaria* 21 C12 42 9N 27 51 E
Tsau, *Botswana* 56 C3 20 8S 22 22 E
Tselinograd = Aqmola, *Kazakstan* 26 D8 51 10N 71 30 E
Tsetserleg, *Mongolia* 32 B5 47 36N 101 32 E
Tshabong, *Botswana* 56 D3 26 2S 22 29 E
Tshane, *Botswana* 56 C3 24 5S 21 54 E
Tshela, *Zaïre* 52 E2 4 57S 13 4 E
Tshesebe, *Botswana* 57 C4 21 51S 27 32 E
Tshibeke, *Zaïre* 54 C2 2 40S 28 35 E
Tshibinda, *Zaïre* 54 C2 2 23S 28 43 E
Tshikapa, *Zaïre* 52 F4 6 28S 20 48 E
Tshilenge, *Zaïre* 54 D1 6 17S 23 48 E
Tshinsenda, *Zaïre* 55 E2 12 20S 28 0 E
Tshofa, *Zaïre* 54 D2 5 13S 25 16 E
Tshwane, *Botswana* 56 C3 22 24S 22 1 E
Tsigara, *Botswana* 56 C4 20 22S 25 54 E
Tsihombe, *Madag.* 57 D8 25 10S 45 41 E
Tsimlyansk Res. = Tsimlyanskoye Vdkhr., *Russia* 25 E7 48 0N 43 0 E
Tsimlyanskoye Vdkhr., *Russia* 25 E7 48 0N 43 0 E
Tsinan = Jinan, *China* 34 F9 36 38N 117 1 E
Tsineng, *S. Africa* 56 D3 27 5S 23 5 E
Tsinghai = Qinghai □, *China* 32 C4 36 0N 98 0 E
Tsingtao = Qingdao, *China* 35 F11 36 5N 120 20 E
Tsinjomitondraka, *Madag.* 57 B8 15 40S 47 8 E
Tsiroanomandidy, *Madag.* 57 B8 18 46S 46 2 E
Tsivory, *Madag.* 57 C8 24 4S 46 5 E
Tskhinvali, *Georgia* 25 F7 42 14N 44 1 E
Tsna →, *Russia* 24 D7 54 55N 41 58 E
Tso Moriri, L., *India* 43 C8 32 50N 78 20 E
Tsodilo Hill, *Botswana* 56 B3 18 49S 21 43 E
Tsogttsetsiy, *Mongolia* 34 C3 43 43N 105 35 E
Tsolo, *S. Africa* 57 E4 31 18S 28 37 E
Tsomo, *S. Africa* 57 E4 32 0S 27 42 E
Tsu, *Japan* 31 G8 34 45N 136 25 E
Tsu L., *Canada* 72 A6 60 40N 111 52W
Tsuchiura, *Japan* 31 F10 36 5N 140 15 E
Tsugaru-Kaikyō, *Japan* 30 D10 41 35N 141 0 E
Tsumeb, *Namibia* 56 B2 19 9S 17 44 E
Tsumis, *Namibia* 56 C2 23 39S 17 29 E
Tsuruga, *Japan* 31 G8 35 45N 136 2 E
Tsurugi-San, *Japan* 31 H7 33 51N 134 6 E
Tsuruoka, *Japan* 30 E9 38 44N 139 50 E
Tsushima, *Gifu, Japan* 31 G8 35 10N 136 43 E
Tsushima, *Nagasaki, Japan* 31 G4 34 20N 129 20 E
Tsyelyakhany, *Belarus* 17 B13 52 30N 25 46 E
Tual, *Indonesia* 37 F8 5 38S 132 44 E
Tuam, *Ireland* 13 C3 53 31N 8 51W
Tuamotu Arch. = Tuamotu Is., *Pac. Oc.* 65 J13 17 0S 144 0W
Tuamotu Is., *Pac. Oc.* 65 J13 17 0S 144 0W
Tuamotu Ridge, *Pac. Oc.* 65 K14 20 0S 138 0W
Tuao, *Phil.* 37 A6 17 55N 121 22 E
Tuapse, *Russia* 25 F6 44 5N 39 10 E
Tuatapere, *N.Z.* 59 M1 46 8S 167 41 E
Tuba City, *U.S.A.* 83 H8 36 8N 111 14W
Tuban, *Indonesia* 37 G15 6 54S 112 3 E
Tubarão, *Brazil* 95 B6 28 30S 49 0W
Tūbās, *West Bank* 47 C4 32 20N 35 22 E
Tubau, *Malaysia* 36 D4 3 10N 113 40 E
Tübingen, *Germany* 16 D5 48 31N 9 4 E
Tubruq, *Libya* 51 B9 32 7N 23 55 E
Tubuai Is., *Pac. Oc.* 65 K12 25 0S 150 0W
Tuc Trung, *Vietnam* 39 G6 11 1N 107 12 E
Tucacas, *Venezuela* 92 A5 10 48N 68 19W
Tuchodi →, *Canada* 72 B4 58 17N 123 42W
Tucson, *U.S.A.* 83 K8 32 13N 110 58W
Tucumán □, *Argentina* 94 B2 26 48S 66 2W
Tucumcari, *U.S.A.* 81 H3 35 10N 103 44W
Tucupita, *Venezuela* 92 B6 9 2N 62 3W
Tucuruí, *Brazil* 93 D9 3 42S 49 44W
Tucuruí, Represa de, *Brazil* 93 D9 4 0S 49 30W
Tudela, *Spain* 19 A5 42 4N 1 39W
Tudmur, *Syria* 44 C3 34 36N 38 15 E
Tudor, L., *Canada* 71 A6 55 50N 65 25W
Tuen, *Australia* 63 D4 28 33S 145 37 E
Tugela →, *S. Africa* 57 D5 29 14S 31 30 E
Tuguegarao, *Phil.* 37 A6 17 35N 121 42 E
Tugur, *Russia* 27 D14 53 44N 136 45 E
Tuineje, *Canary Is.* 22 F5 28 19N 14 3W
Tukangbesi, Kepulauan, *Indonesia* 37 F6 6 0S 124 0 E
Tukarak I., *Canada* 70 A4 56 15N 78 45W
Tukayyid, *Iraq* 44 D5 29 47N 45 36 E
Tūkrah, *Libya* 51 B9 32 30N 20 37 E
Tuktoyaktuk, *Canada* 68 B6 69 27N 133 2W
Tukums, *Latvia* 9 H20 57 2N 23 10 E
Tukuyu, *Tanzania* 55 D3 9 17S 33 35 E
Tula, *Hidalgo, Mexico* 87 C5 20 5N 99 20W
Tula, *Tamaulipas, Mexico* 87 C5 23 0N 99 40W
Tula, *Russia* 24 D6 54 13N 37 38 E
Tulancingo, *Mexico* 87 C5 20 5N 99 22W
Tulare, *U.S.A.* 83 H4 36 13N 119 21W
Tulare Lake Bed, *U.S.A.* 83 J4 36 0N 119 48W
Tularosa, *U.S.A.* 83 K10 33 5N 106 1W
Tulbagh, *S. Africa* 56 E2 33 16S 19 6 E
Tulcán, *Ecuador* 92 C3 0 48N 77 43W
Tulcea, *Romania* 17 F15 45 13N 28 46 E
Tulchyn, *Ukraine* 17 D15 48 41N 28 49 E
Tūleh, *Iran* 45 C7 34 35N 52 33 E
Tulemalu L., *Canada* 73 A9 62 58N 99 25W
Tuli, *Indonesia* 37 E6 1 24S 122 26 E
Tuli, *Zimbabwe* 55 G2 21 58S 29 13 E
Tulia, *U.S.A.* 81 H4 34 32N 101 46W
Tulita, *Canada* 68 B7 64 57N 125 30W
Ţūlkarm, *West Bank* 47 C4 32 19N 35 2 E
Tullahoma, *U.S.A.* 77 H2 35 22N 86 13W
Tullamore, *Australia* 63 E4 32 39S 147 36 E
Tullamore, *Ireland* 13 C4 53 16N 7 31W
Tulle, *France* 18 D4 45 16N 1 46 E
Tullibigeal, *Australia* 63 E4 33 25S 146 44 E
Tullow, *Ireland* 13 D4 52 49N 6 45W
Tully, *Australia* 62 B4 17 56S 145 55 E
Ţulmaythah, *Libya* 51 B9 32 40N 20 55 E
Tulmur, *Australia* 62 C3 22 40S 142 20 E
Tulsa, *U.S.A.* 81 G7 36 10N 95 55W
Tulsequah, *Canada* 72 B2 58 39N 133 35W
Tulua, *Colombia* 92 C3 4 6N 76 11W
Tulun, *Russia* 27 D11 54 32N 100 35 E
Tulungagung, *Indonesia* 36 F4 8 5S 111 54 E
Tum, *Indonesia* 37 E8 3 36S 130 21 E
Tuma →, *Nic.* 88 D3 13 6N 84 35W
Tumaco, *Colombia* 92 C3 1 50N 78 45W
Tumatumari, *Guyana* 92 B7 5 20N 58 55W
Tumba, *Sweden* 9 G17 59 12N 17 48 E
Tumba, L., *Zaïre* 52 E3 0 50S 18 0 E
Tumbarumba, *Australia* 63 F4 35 44S 148 0 E
Tumbaya, *Argentina* 94 A2 23 50S 65 26W
Tumbes, *Peru* 92 D2 3 37S 80 27W
Tumbwe, *Zaïre* 55 E2 11 25S 27 15 E
Tumby Bay, *Australia* 63 E2 34 21S 136 8 E
Tumd Youqi, *China* 34 D6 40 30N 110 30 E
Tumen, *China* 35 C15 43 0N 129 50 E
Tumen Jiang →, *China* 35 C16 42 20N 130 35 E
Tumeremo, *Venezuela* 92 B6 7 18N 61 30W
Tumkur, *India* 40 N10 13 18N 77 6 E
Tummel, L., *U.K.* 12 E5 56 43N 3 55W
Tump, *Pakistan* 40 F3 26 7N 62 16 E
Tumpat, *Malaysia* 39 J4 6 11N 102 10 E
Tumu, *Ghana* 50 F4 10 56N 1 56W
Tumucumaque, Serra, *Brazil* 93 C8 2 0N 55 0W
Tumut, *Australia* 63 F4 35 16S 148 13 E
Tumwater, *U.S.A.* 82 C2 47 1N 122 54W
Tunas de Zaza, *Cuba* 88 B4 21 39N 79 34W
Tunbridge Wells = Royal Tunbridge Wells, *U.K.* 11 F8 51 7N 0 16 E
Tuncurry, *Australia* 63 E5 32 17S 152 29 E
Tunduru, *Tanzania* 55 E4 11 8S 37 25 E
Tunduru □, *Tanzania* 55 E4 11 5S 37 22 E
Tundzha →, *Bulgaria* 21 C11 41 40N 26 35 E
Tunga Pass, *India* 41 E19 29 0N 94 14 E
Tungabhadra →, *India* 40 M11 15 57N 78 15 E
Tungaru, *Sudan* 51 F11 10 9N 30 52 E
Tungla, *Nic.* 88 D3 13 24N 84 21W
Tungsten, *Canada* 72 A3 61 57N 128 16W
Tunguska, Nizhnyaya →, *Russia* 27 C9 65 48N 88 4 E
Tunica, *U.S.A.* 81 H9 34 41N 90 23W
Tunis, *Tunisia* 50 A7 36 50N 10 11 E
Tunisia ■, *Africa* 50 B6 33 30N 9 10 E
Tunja, *Colombia* 92 B4 5 33N 73 25W
Tunkhannock, *U.S.A.* 79 E9 41 32N 75 57W
Tunliu, *China* 34 F7 36 13N 112 52 E
Tunnsjøen, *Norway* 8 D15 64 45N 13 25 E
Tunungayualok I., *Canada* 71 A7 56 0N 61 0W
Tunuyán, *Argentina* 94 C2 33 35S 69 0W
Tunuyán →, *Argentina* 94 C2 33 33S 67 30W
Tunxi, *China* 33 D6 29 42N 118 25 E
Tuolumne, *U.S.A.* 83 H3 37 58N 120 15W
Tuolumne →, *U.S.A.* 84 H5 37 36N 121 13W
Tuoy-Khaya, *Russia* 27 C12 62 32N 111 25 E
Tūp Āghāj, *Iran* 44 B5 36 3N 47 50 E
Tupã, *Brazil* 95 A5 21 57S 50 28W
Tupelo, *U.S.A.* 77 H1 34 16N 88 43W
Tupik, *Russia* 27 D12 54 26N 119 57 E
Tupinambaranas, *Brazil* 92 D7 3 0S 58 0W
Tupiza, *Bolivia* 94 A2 21 30S 65 40W
Tupman, *U.S.A.* 85 K7 35 18N 119 21W
Tupper, *Canada* 72 B4 55 32N 120 1W
Tupper Lake, *U.S.A.* 79 B10 44 14N 74 28W
Tupungato, Cerro, *S. Amer.* 94 C2 33 15S 69 50W
Tuquan, *China* 35 B11 45 18N 121 38 E
Túquerres, *Colombia* 92 C3 1 5N 77 37W
Tura, *Russia* 27 C11 64 20N 100 17 E

Turabah, Si. Arabia 44 D4 28 20N 43 15 E
Tūrān, Iran 45 C8 35 39N 56 42 E
Turan, Russia 27 D10 51 55N 95 0 E
Turayf, Si. Arabia 44 D3 31 41N 38 39 E
Turda, Romania 17 E12 46 34N 23 47 E
Turek, Poland 17 B10 52 3N 18 30 E
Turfan = Turpan, China 32 B3 43 58N 89 10 E
Turfan Depression = Turpan Hami, China 28 E12 42 40N 89 25 E
Tŭrgovishte, Bulgaria 21 C12 43 17N 26 38 E
Turgutlu, Turkey 21 E12 38 30N 27 48 E
Turia →, Spain 19 C5 39 27N 0 19W
Turiaçu, Brazil 93 D9 1 40S 45 19W
Turiaçu →, Brazil 93 D9 1 36S 45 19W
Turin = Torino, Italy 20 B2 45 3N 7 40 E
Turin, Canada 72 D6 49 58N 112 31W
Turkana □, Kenya 54 B4 3 0N 35 30 E
Turkana, L., Africa 54 B4 3 30N 36 5 E
Turkestan = Türkistan, Kazakstan 26 E7 43 17N 68 16 E
Turkey ■, Eurasia 25 G6 39 0N 36 0 E
Turkey Creek, Australia 60 C4 17 2S 128 12 E
Türkistan, Kazakstan 26 E7 43 17N 68 16 E
Türkmenbashi, Turkmenistan 25 F9 40 5N 53 5 E
Turkmenistan ■, Asia 26 F6 39 0N 59 0 E
Turks & Caicos Is. ■, W. Indies 89 B5 21 20N 71 20W
Turks Island Passage, W. Indies 89 B5 21 30N 71 30W
Turku, Finland 9 F20 60 30N 22 19 E
Turkwe →, Kenya 54 B4 3 6N 36 6 E
Turlock, U.S.A. 83 H3 37 30N 120 51W
Turnagain →, Canada 72 B3 59 12N 127 35W
Turnagain, C., N.Z. 59 J6 40 28S 176 38 E
Turneffe Is., Belize 87 D7 17 20N 87 50W
Turner, Australia 60 C4 17 52S 128 16 E
Turner, U.S.A. 82 B9 48 51N 108 24W
Turner Pt., Australia 62 A1 11 47S 133 32 E
Turner Valley, Canada 72 C6 50 40N 114 17W
Turners Falls, U.S.A. 79 D12 42 36N 72 33W
Turnhout, Belgium 15 C4 51 19N 4 57 E
Turnor L., Canada 73 B7 56 35N 108 35W
Tŭrnovo = Veliko Tŭrnovo, Bulgaria 21 C11 43 5N 25 41 E
Turnu Măgurele, Romania 17 G13 43 46N 24 56 E
Turnu Roşu, P., Romania 17 F13 45 33N 24 17 E
Turon, U.S.A. 81 G5 37 48N 98 26W
Turpan, China 32 B3 43 58N 89 10 E
Turpan Hami, China 28 E12 42 40N 89 25 E
Turriff, U.K. 12 D6 57 32N 2 27W
Tursāq, Iraq 44 C5 33 27N 45 47 E
Turtle Head I., Australia 62 A3 10 56S 142 37 E
Turtle L., Canada 73 C7 53 36N 108 38W
Turtle Lake, N. Dak., U.S.A. 80 B4 47 31N 100 53W
Turtle Lake, Wis., U.S.A. 80 C8 45 24N 92 8W
Turtleford, Canada 73 C7 53 23N 108 57W
Turukhansk, Russia 27 C9 65 21N 88 5 E
Tuscaloosa, U.S.A. 77 J2 33 12N 87 34W
Tuscany = Toscana □, Italy 20 C4 43 25N 11 0 E
Tuscola, Ill., U.S.A. 76 F1 39 48N 88 17W
Tuscola, Tex., U.S.A. 81 J5 32 12N 99 48W
Tuscumbia, U.S.A. 77 H2 34 44N 87 42W
Tuskar Rock, Ireland 13 D5 52 12N 6 10W
Tuskegee, U.S.A. 77 J3 32 25N 85 42W
Tustin, U.S.A. 85 M9 33 44N 117 49W
Tuticorin, India 40 Q11 8 50N 78 12 E
Tutóia, Brazil 93 D10 2 45S 42 20W
Tutong, Brunei 36 D4 4 47N 114 40 E
Tutrakan, Bulgaria 21 B12 44 2N 26 40 E
Tutshi L., Canada 72 B2 59 56N 134 30W
Tuttle, U.S.A. 80 B5 47 9N 100 0W
Tuttlingen, Germany 16 E5 47 58N 8 48 E
Tutuala, Indonesia 37 F7 8 25S 127 15 E
Tutuila, Amer. Samoa 59 B13 14 19S 170 50W
Tutuyepec, Mexico 87 D5 16 9N 97 38W
Tuva □, Russia 27 D10 51 30N 95 0 E
Tuvalu ■, Pac. Oc. 64 H9 8 0S 178 0 E
Tuxpan, Mexico 87 C5 20 58N 97 23W
Tuxtla Gutiérrez, Mexico 87 D6 16 50N 93 10W
Tuy, Spain 19 A1 42 3N 8 39W
Tuy An, Vietnam 38 F7 13 17N 109 16 E
Tuy Duc, Vietnam 39 F6 12 15N 107 27 E
Tuy Hoa, Vietnam 38 F7 13 5N 109 10 E
Tuy Phong, Vietnam 39 G7 11 14N 108 43 E
Tuya L., Canada 72 B2 59 7N 130 35W
Tuyen Hoa, Vietnam 38 D6 17 50N 106 10 E
Tuyen Quang, Vietnam 38 B5 21 50N 105 10 E
Tūysarkān, Iran 45 C6 34 33N 48 27 E
Tuz Gölü, Turkey 25 G5 38 42N 33 18 E
Ţūz Khurmātū, Iraq 44 C5 34 56N 44 38 E
Tuzla, Bos.-H. 21 B8 44 34N 18 41 E
Tver, Russia 24 C6 56 55N 35 55 E
Twain, U.S.A. 84 E5 40 1N 121 3W
Twain Harte, U.S.A. 84 G6 38 2N 120 14W
Tweed, Canada 78 B7 44 29N 77 19W
Tweed →, U.K. 12 F7 55 45N 2 0W
Tweed Heads, Australia 63 D5 28 10S 153 31 E
Tweedsmuir Prov. Park, Canada 72 C3 53 0N 126 20W
Twentynine Palms, U.S.A. 85 L10 34 8N 116 3W
Twillingate, Canada 71 C9 49 42N 54 45W
Twin Bridges, U.S.A. 82 D7 45 33N 112 20W
Twin Falls, U.S.A. 82 E6 42 34N 114 28W
Twin Valley, U.S.A. 80 B6 47 16N 96 16W
Twisp, U.S.A. 82 B3 48 22N 120 7W
Two Harbors, U.S.A. 80 B9 47 2N 91 40W
Two Hills, Canada 72 C6 53 43N 111 52W
Two Rivers, U.S.A. 76 C2 44 9N 87 34W
Twofold B., Australia 63 F4 37 8S 149 59 E
Tyachiv, Ukraine 17 D12 48 1N 23 35 E
Tychy, Poland 17 C10 50 9N 18 59 E
Tyler, U.S.A. 75 D7 32 18N 95 17W
Tyler, Minn., U.S.A. 80 C6 44 18N 96 8W
Tyler, Tex., U.S.A. 81 J7 32 21N 95 18W
Tynda, Russia 27 D13 55 10N 124 43 E
Tyne →, U.K. 10 C6 54 59N 1 32W
Tyne & Wear □, U.K. 10 C6 55 6N 1 17W
Tynemouth, U.K. 10 B6 55 1N 1 26W
Tyre = Sūr, Lebanon 47 B4 33 19N 35 16 E
Tyrifjorden, Norway 9 F14 60 2N 10 8 E
Tyrol = Tirol □, Austria 16 E6 47 3N 10 43 E
Tyrone, U.S.A. 78 F6 40 40N 78 14W
Tyrrell →, Australia 63 F3 35 26S 142 51 E
Tyrrell, L., Australia 63 F3 35 20S 142 50 E
Tyrrell Arm, Canada 73 A9 62 27N 97 30W
Tyrrell L., Canada 73 A7 63 7N 105 27W
Tyrrhenian Sea, Medit. S. 20 E5 40 0N 12 30 E
Tysfjorden, Norway 8 B17 68 7N 16 25 E
Tyulgan, Russia 24 D10 52 22N 56 12 E
Tyumen, Russia 26 D7 57 11N 65 29 E
Tywi →, U.K. 11 F3 51 48N 4 21W
Tywyn, U.K. 11 E3 52 35N 4 5W
Tzaneen, S. Africa 57 C5 23 47S 30 9 E
Tzermiádhes, Greece 23 D7 35 12N 25 29 E
Tzukong = Zigong, China 32 D5 29 15N 104 48 E

U

U Taphao, Thailand 38 F3 12 35N 101 0 E
U.S.A. = United States of America ■, N. Amer. 74 C7 37 0N 96 0W
Uanda, Australia 62 C3 21 37S 144 55 E
Uarsciek, Somali Rep. 46 G4 2 28N 45 55 E
Uasin □, Kenya 54 B4 0 30N 35 20 E
Uato-Udo, Indonesia 37 F7 9 7S 125 36 E
Uatumã →, Brazil 92 D7 2 26S 57 37W
Uaupés, Brazil 92 D5 0 8S 67 5W
Uaupés →, Brazil 92 C5 0 2N 67 16W
Uaxactún, Guatemala 88 C2 17 25N 89 29W
Ubá, Brazil 95 A7 21 8S 43 0W
Ubaitaba, Brazil 93 F11 14 18S 39 20W
Ubangi = Oubangi →, Zaïre 52 E3 0 30S 17 50 E
Ubauro, Pakistan 42 E3 28 15N 69 45 E
Ube, Japan 31 H5 33 56N 131 15 E
Ubeda, Spain 19 C4 38 3N 3 23W
Uberaba, Brazil 93 G9 19 50S 47 55W
Uberlândia, Brazil 93 G9 19 0S 48 20W
Ubolratna Res., Thailand 38 D4 16 45N 102 30 E
Ubombo, S. Africa 57 D5 27 31S 32 4 E
Ubon Ratchathani, Thailand 38 E5 15 15N 104 50 E
Ubondo, Zaïre 54 C2 0 55S 25 42 E
Ubort →, Belarus 17 B15 52 6N 28 30 E
Ubundu, Zaïre 54 C2 0 22S 25 30 E
Ucayali →, Peru 92 D4 4 30S 73 30W
Uchi Lake, Canada 73 C10 51 5N 92 35W
Uchiura-Wan, Japan 30 C10 42 25N 140 40 E
Uchur →, Russia 27 D14 58 48N 130 35 E
Ucluelet, Canada 72 D3 48 57N 125 32W
Uda →, Russia 27 D14 54 42N 135 14 E
Udaipur, India 42 G5 24 36N 73 44 E
Udaipur Garhi, Nepal 43 F12 27 0N 86 35 E
Uddevalla, Sweden 9 G14 58 21N 11 55 E
Uddjaur, Sweden 8 D17 65 56N 17 49 E
Udgir, India 40 K10 18 25N 77 5 E
Udhampur, India 43 C6 33 0N 75 5 E
Udi, Nigeria 50 G6 6 17N 7 21 E
Údine, Italy 20 A5 46 3N 13 14 E
Udmurtia □, Russia 24 C9 57 30N 52 30 E
Udon Thani, Thailand 38 D4 17 29N 102 46 E
Udupi, India 40 N9 13 25N 74 42 E
Udzungwa Range, Tanzania 55 D4 9 30S 35 10 E
Ueda, Japan 31 F9 36 24N 138 16 E
Uedineniya, Os., Russia 4 B12 78 0N 85 0 E
Uele →, Zaïre 52 D4 3 45N 24 45 E
Uelen, Russia 27 C19 66 10N 170 0W
Uelzen, Germany 16 B6 52 57N 10 32 E
Ufa, Russia 24 D10 54 45N 55 55 E
Ufa →, Russia 24 D10 54 40N 56 0 E
Ugab →, Namibia 56 C1 20 55S 13 30 E
Ugalla →, Tanzania 54 D3 5 8S 30 42 E
Uganda ■, Africa 54 B3 2 0N 32 0 E
Ugie, S. Africa 57 E4 31 10S 28 13 E
Uglegorsk, Russia 27 E15 49 5N 142 2 E
Ugljane, Croatia 16 F8 44 12N 14 56 E
Ugolyak, Russia 27 C13 64 33N 120 30 E
Ugûn Mûsa, Egypt 47 F1 29 53N 32 40 E
Uhrichsville, U.S.A. 78 F3 40 24N 81 21W
Uibhist a Deas = South Uist, U.K. 12 D1 57 20N 7 15W
Uibhist a Tuath = North Uist, U.K. 12 D1 57 40N 7 15W
Uíge, Angola 52 F2 7 30S 14 40 E
Uijŏngbu, S. Korea 35 F14 37 48N 127 0 E
Ŭiju, N. Korea 35 D13 40 15N 124 35 E
Uinta Mts., U.S.A. 82 F8 40 45N 110 30W
Uitenhage, S. Africa 56 E4 33 40S 25 28 E
Uithuizen, Neths. 15 A6 53 24N 6 41 E
Ujhani, India 43 F8 28 0N 79 6 E
Uji-guntō, Japan 31 J4 31 15N 129 25 E
Ujjain, India 42 H6 23 9N 75 43 E
Ujung Pandang, Indonesia 37 F5 5 10S 119 20 E
Uka, Russia 27 D17 57 50N 162 0 E
Ukara I., Tanzania 54 C3 1 50S 33 0 E
Uke-Shima, Japan 31 K4 28 2N 129 14 E
Ukerewe □, Tanzania 54 C3 2 0S 32 30 E
Ukerewe I., Tanzania 54 C3 2 0S 33 0 E
Ukhrul, India 41 G19 25 10N 94 25 E
Ukhta, Russia 24 B9 63 34N 53 41 E
Ukiah, U.S.A. 84 F3 39 9N 123 13W
Ukki Fort, India 43 C7 33 28N 76 54 E
Ukmerge, Lithuania 9 J21 55 15N 24 45 E
Ukraine ■, Europe 25 E5 49 0N 32 0 E
Ukwi, Botswana 56 C3 23 29S 20 30 E
Ulaanbaatar, Mongolia 27 E11 47 55N 106 53 E
Ulaangom, Mongolia 32 A4 50 5N 92 10 E
Ulamba, Zaïre 55 D1 9 3S 23 38 E
Ulan Bator = Ulaanbaatar, Mongolia 27 E11 47 55N 106 53 E
Ulan Ude, Russia 27 D11 51 45N 107 40 E
Ulanga □, Tanzania 55 D4 8 40S 36 50 E
Ulaya, Morogoro, Tanzania 54 D4 7 3S 36 55 E
Ulaya, Tabora, Tanzania 54 C3 4 25S 33 30 E
Ulcinj, Montenegro, Yug. 21 D8 41 58N 19 10 E
Ulco, S. Africa 56 D3 28 21S 24 15 E
Ulefoss, Norway 9 G13 59 17N 9 16 E
Ulhasnagar, India 40 K8 19 15N 73 10 E
Ulladulla, Australia 63 F5 35 21S 150 29 E
Ullapool, U.K. 12 D3 57 54N 5 9W
Ullswater, U.K. 10 C5 54 34N 2 52W
Ullung-do, S. Korea 35 F16 37 30N 130 30 E
Ulm, Germany 16 D5 48 23N 9 58 E
Ulmarra, Australia 63 D5 29 37S 153 4 E
Ulonguè, Mozam. 55 E3 14 37S 34 19 E
Ulricehamn, Sweden 9 H15 57 46N 13 26 E
Ulsan, S. Korea 35 G15 35 20N 129 15 E
Ulster □, U.K. 13 B5 54 35N 6 30W
Ulubaria, India 43 H13 22 31N 88 4 E
Ulubat Gölü, Turkey 21 D13 40 9N 28 35 E
Uludağ, Turkey 21 D13 40 4N 29 13 E
Uluguru Mts., Tanzania 54 D4 7 15S 37 40 E
Ulungur He →, China 32 B3 47 1N 87 24 E
Uluru = Ayers Rock, Australia 61 E5 25 23S 131 5 E
Ulutau, Kazakstan 26 E7 48 39N 67 1 E
Ulverston, U.K. 10 C4 54 13N 3 5W
Ulverstone, Australia 62 G4 41 11S 146 11 E
Ulya, Russia 27 D15 59 10N 142 0 E
Ulyanovsk = Simbirsk, Russia 24 D8 54 20N 48 25 E
Ulyasutay, Mongolia 32 B4 47 56N 97 28 E
Ulysses, U.S.A. 81 G4 37 35N 101 22W
Umala, Bolivia 92 G5 17 25S 68 5W
Uman, Ukraine 17 D16 48 40N 30 12 E
Umaria, India 41 H12 23 35N 80 50 E
Umarkot, Pakistan 40 G6 25 15N 69 40 E
Umatilla, U.S.A. 82 D4 45 55N 119 21W
Umba, Russia 24 A5 66 42N 34 11 E
Umbrella Mts., N.Z. 59 L2 45 35S 169 5 E
Ume älv →, Sweden 8 E19 63 45N 20 20 E
Umeå, Sweden 8 E19 63 45N 20 20 E
Umera, Indonesia 37 E7 0 12S 129 37 E
Umfuli →, Zimbabwe 55 F2 17 30S 29 23 E
Umgusa, Zimbabwe 55 F2 19 29S 27 52 E
Umkomaas, S. Africa 57 E5 30 13S 30 48 E
Umm ad Daraj, J., Jordan 47 C4 32 18N 35 48 E
Umm al Qaywayn, U.A.E. 45 E7 25 30N 55 35 E
Umm al Qittayn, Jordan 47 C5 32 18N 36 40 E
Umm Bāb, Qatar 45 E6 25 12N 50 48 E
Umm Bel, Sudan 51 F10 13 35N 28 0 E
Umm el Fahm, Israel 47 C4 32 31N 35 9 E
Umm Lajj, Si. Arabia 44 E3 25 0N 37 23 E
Umm Ruwaba, Sudan 51 F11 12 50N 31 20 E
Umnak I., U.S.A. 68 C3 53 15N 168 20W
Umniati →, Zimbabwe 55 F2 16 49S 28 45 E
Umpqua →, U.S.A. 82 E1 43 40N 124 12W
Umreth, India 42 H5 22 41N 73 4 E
Umtata, S. Africa 57 E4 31 36S 28 49 E
Umuarama, Brazil 95 A5 23 45S 53 20W
Umvukwe Ra., Zimbabwe 55 F3 16 45S 30 45 E
Umzimvubu = Port St. Johns, S. Africa 57 E4 31 38S 29 33 E
Umzingwane →, Zimbabwe 55 G2 22 12S 29 56 E
Umzinto, S. Africa 57 E5 30 15S 30 45 E
Una, India 42 J4 20 46N 71 8 E
Una →, Bos.-H. 16 F9 45 0N 16 20 E
Unadilla, U.S.A. 79 D9 42 20N 75 19W
Unalaska, U.S.A. 68 C3 53 53N 166 32W
Uncía, Bolivia 92 G5 18 25S 66 40W
Uncompahgre Peak, U.S.A. 83 G10 38 4N 107 28W
Underbool, Australia 63 F3 35 10S 141 51 E
Ungarie, Australia 63 E4 33 38S 146 56 E
Ungarra, Australia 63 E2 34 12S 136 2 E
Ungava B., Canada 69 C13 59 30N 67 30W
Ungava Pen., Canada 69 C12 60 0N 74 0W
Ungeny = Ungheni, Moldova 17 E14 47 11N 27 51 E
Unggi, N. Korea 35 C16 42 16N 130 28 E
Ungheni, Moldova 17 E14 47 11N 27 51 E
União da Vitória, Brazil 95 B5 26 13S 51 5W
Unimak I., U.S.A. 68 C3 54 45N 164 0W
Union, Miss., U.S.A. 81 J10 32 34N 89 7W
Union, Mo., U.S.A. 80 F9 38 27N 91 0W
Union, S.C., U.S.A. 77 H5 34 43N 81 37W
Union, Mt., U.S.A. 83 J7 34 34N 112 21W
Union City, Calif., U.S.A. 84 H4 37 36N 122 1W
Union City, N.J., U.S.A. 79 F10 40 45N 74 2W
Union City, Pa., U.S.A. 78 E5 41 54N 79 51W
Union City, Tenn., U.S.A. 81 G10 36 26N 89 3W
Union Gap, U.S.A. 82 C3 46 33N 120 28W
Union Springs, U.S.A. 77 J3 32 9N 85 43W
Uniondale, S. Africa 56 E3 33 39S 23 7 E
Uniontown, U.S.A. 76 F6 39 54N 79 44W
Unionville, U.S.A. 80 E8 40 29N 93 1W
United Arab Emirates ■, Asia 45 F7 23 50N 54 0 E
United Kingdom ■, Europe 7 E5 53 0N 2 0W
United States of America ■, N. Amer. 74 C7 37 0N 96 0W
Unity, Canada 73 C7 52 30N 109 5W
Unjha, India 42 H5 23 46N 72 24 E
Unnao, India 43 F9 26 35N 80 30 E
Unst, U.K. 12 A8 60 44N 0 53W
Unuk →, Canada 72 B2 56 5N 131 3W
Uozu, Japan 31 F8 36 48N 137 24 E
Upata, Venezuela 92 B6 8 1N 62 24W
Upemba, L., Zaïre 55 D2 8 30S 26 20 E
Upernavik, Greenland 4 B5 72 49N 56 20W
Upington, S. Africa 56 D3 28 25S 21 15 E
Upleta, India 42 J4 21 46N 70 16 E
Upolu, W. Samoa 59 A13 13 58S 172 0W
Upper Alkali Lake, U.S.A. 82 F3 41 47N 120 8W
Upper Arrow L., Canada 72 C5 50 30N 117 50W
Upper Foster L., Canada 73 B7 56 47N 105 20W
Upper Hutt, N.Z. 59 J5 41 8S 175 5 E
Upper Klamath L., U.S.A. 82 E3 42 25N 121 55W
Upper Lake, U.S.A. 84 F4 39 10N 122 54W
Upper Musquodoboit, Canada 71 C7 45 10N 62 58W
Upper Red L., U.S.A. 80 A7 48 8N 94 45W
Upper Sandusky, U.S.A. 76 E4 40 50N 83 17W
Upper Volta = Burkina Faso ■, Africa 50 F4 12 0N 1 0W
Uppland, Sweden 9 F17 59 59N 17 48 E
Uppsala, Sweden 9 G17 59 53N 17 38 E
Upshi, India 43 C7 33 48N 77 52 E
Upstart, C., Australia 62 B4 19 41S 147 45 E
Upton, U.S.A. 80 C2 44 6N 104 38W
Ur, Iraq 44 D5 30 55N 46 25 E
Uracara, Brazil 92 D7 2 20S 57 50W
Urad Qianqi, China 34 D5 40 40N 108 30 E
Urakawa, Japan 30 C11 42 9N 142 47 E
Ural = Zhayyq →, Kazakstan 25 E9 47 0N 51 48 E
Ural, Australia 63 E4 33 21S 146 12 E
Ural Mts. = Uralskie Gory, Eurasia 24 C10 60 0N 59 0 E
Uralla, Australia 63 E5 30 37S 151 29 E
Uralsk = Oral, Kazakstan 24 D9 51 20N 51 20 E
Uralskie Gory, Eurasia 24 C10 60 0N 59 0 E
Urambo, Tanzania 54 D3 5 4S 32 0 E
Urambo □, Tanzania 54 D3 5 0S 32 0 E
Urandangi, Australia 62 C2 21 32S 138 14 E
Uranium City, Canada 73 B7 59 34N 108 37W
Uranquinty, Australia 63 F4 35 10S 147 12 E
Urawa, Japan 31 G9 35 50N 139 40 E
Uray, Russia 26 C7 60 5N 65 15 E
'Uray'irah, Si. Arabia 45 E6 25 57N 48 53 E
Urbana, Ill., U.S.A. 76 E1 40 7N 88 12W
Urbana, Ohio, U.S.A. 76 E4 40 7N 83 45W
Urbino, Italy 20 C5 43 43N 12 38 E
Urbión, Picos de, Spain 19 A4 42 1N 2 52W
Urcos, Peru 92 F4 13 40S 71 38W
Urda, Kazakstan 25 E8 48 52N 47 23 E
Urdinarrain, Argentina 94 C4 32 37S 58 52W
Urdzhar, Kazakstan 26 E9 47 5N 81 38 E
Ure →, U.K. 10 C6 54 19N 1 31W
Ures, Mexico 86 B2 29 30N 110 30W
Urfa = Sanliurfa, Turkey 25 G6 37 12N 38 50 E
Urganch, Uzbekistan 26 E7 41 40N 60 41 E
Urgench = Urganch, Uzbekistan 26 E7 41 40N 60 41 E
Uri, India 43 B6 34 8N 74 2 E
Uribia, Colombia 92 A4 11 43N 72 16W
Uriondo, Bolivia 94 A3 21 41S 64 41W
Urique, Mexico 86 B3 27 13N 107 55W
Urique →, Mexico 86 B3 26 29N 107 58W
Urk, Neths. 15 B5 52 39N 5 36 E
Urla, Turkey 21 E12 38 20N 26 47 E
Urmia = Orūmīyeh, Iran 44 B5 37 40N 45 0 E
Urmia, L. = Orūmīyeh, Daryācheh-ye, Iran 44 B5 37 50N 45 30 E
Uroševac, Serbia, Yug. 21 C9 42 23N 21 10 E
Uruana, Brazil 93 G9 15 30S 49 41W
Uruapan, Mexico 86 D4 19 30N 102 0W
Urubamba, Peru 92 F4 13 20S 72 10W
Urubamba →, Peru 92 F4 10 43S 73 48W
Uruçuí, Brazil 93 E10 7 20S 44 28W
Uruguai →, Brazil 95 B5 26 0S 53 30W
Uruguaiana, Brazil 94 B4 29 50S 57 0W
Uruguay ■, S. Amer. 94 C4 32 30S 56 30W
Uruguay →, S. Amer. 94 C4 34 12S 58 18W
Urumchi = Ürümqi, China 26 E9 43 45N 87 45 E
Ürümqi, China 26 E9 43 45N 87 45 E
Urup, Os., Russia 27 E16 46 0N 151 0 E
Usa →, Russia 24 A10 66 16N 59 49 E
Uşak, Turkey 25 G4 38 43N 29 28 E
Usakos, Namibia 56 C2 21 54S 15 31 E
Usedom, Germany 16 B8 53 55N 14 2 E
Ush-Tobe, Kazakstan 26 E8 45 16N 78 0 E
Ushakova, Os., Russia 4 A12 82 0N 80 0 E
Ushant = Ouessant, I. d', France 18 B1 48 28N 5 6W
Ushashi, Tanzania 54 C3 1 59S 33 57 E
Ushibuka, Japan 31 H5 32 11N 130 1 E
Ushuaia, Argentina 96 G3 54 50S 68 23W
Ushumun, Russia 27 D13 52 47N 126 32 E
Usk →, U.K. 11 F5 51 33N 2 58W
Üsküdar, Turkey 25 F4 41 0N 29 5 E
Usman, Russia 24 D6 52 5N 39 48 E
Usoke, Tanzania 54 D3 5 8S 32 24 E
Usolye Sibirskoye, Russia 27 D11 52 48N 103 40 E
Uspallata, P. de, Argentina 94 C2 32 37S 69 22W
Uspenskiy, Kazakstan 26 E8 48 41N 72 43 E
Ussuri →, Asia 30 A7 48 27N 135 0 E
Ussuriysk, Russia 27 E14 43 48N 131 59 E
Ussurka, Russia 30 B6 45 12N 133 31 E
Ust-Aldan = Batamay, Russia 27 C13 63 30N 129 15 E
Ust Amginskoye = Khandyga, Russia 27 C14 62 42N 135 35 E
Ust-Bolsheretsk, Russia 27 D16 52 50N 156 15 E
Ust Chaun, Russia 27 C18 68 47N 170 30 E
Ust'-Ilga, Russia 27 D11 55 5N 104 55 E
Ust Ilimpeya = Yukti, Russia 27 C11 63 26N 105 42 E
Ust-Ilimsk, Russia 27 D11 58 3N 102 39 E
Ust Ishim, Russia 26 D8 57 45N 71 10 E
Ust-Kamchatsk, Russia 27 D17 56 10N 162 28 E
Ust-Kamenogorsk = Öskemen, Kazakstan 26 E9 50 0N 82 36 E
Ust-Karenga, Russia 27 D12 54 25N 116 30 E
Ust Khayryuzovo, Russia 27 D16 57 15N 156 45 E
Ust-Kut, Russia 27 D11 56 50N 105 42 E
Ust Kuyga, Russia 27 B14 70 1N 135 43 E
Ust Maya, Russia 27 C14 60 30N 134 28 E
Ust-Mil, Russia 27 D14 59 40N 133 11 E
Ust Muya, Russia 27 D12 56 27N 115 50 E
Ust-Nera, Russia 27 C15 64 35N 143 15 E
Ust-Nyukzha, Russia 27 D13 56 34N 121 37 E
Ust Olenek, Russia 27 B12 73 0N 120 5 E
Ust-Omchug, Russia 27 C15 61 9N 149 38 E
Ust Port, Russia 26 C9 69 40N 84 26 E
Ust Tsilma, Russia 24 A9 65 28N 52 11 E
Ust-Tungir, Russia 27 D13 55 25N 120 36 E
Ust Urt = Ustyurt, Plateau, Asia 26 E6 44 0N 55 0 E
Ust Usa, Russia 24 A10 66 2N 56 57 E
Ust Vorkuta, Russia 26 C7 67 24N 64 0 E
Ústí nad Labem, Czech. 16 C8 50 41N 14 3 E
Ustica, Italy 20 E5 38 42N 13 11 E
Ustinov = Izhevsk, Russia 24 C9 56 51N 53 14 E
Ustye, Russia 27 D10 57 46N 94 37 E
Ustyurt, Plateau, Asia 26 E6 44 0N 55 0 E
Usu, China 32 B3 44 27N 84 40 E
Usuki, Japan 31 H5 33 8N 131 49 E
Usulután, El Salv. 88 D2 13 25N 88 28W
Usumacinta →, Mexico 87 D6 17 0N 91 0W
Usumbura = Bujumbura, Burundi 54 C2 3 16S 29 18 E

Vienna

Usure, Tanzania 54 C3 4 40S 34 22 E
Uta, Indonesia 37 E9 4 33S 136 0 E
Utah □, U.S.A. 82 G8 39 20N 111 30W
Utah, L., U.S.A. 82 F8 40 10N 111 58W
Ute Creek →, U.S.A. 81 H3 35 21N 103 50W
Utena, Lithuania 9 J21 55 27N 25 40 E
Utete, Tanzania 54 D4 8 0S 38 45 E
Uthai Thani, Thailand 38 E3 15 22N 100 3 E
Uthal, Pakistan 42 G2 25 44N 66 40 E
Utiariti, Brazil 92 F7 13 0S 58 10W
Utica, N.Y., U.S.A. 79 C9 43 6N 75 14W
Utica, Ohio, U.S.A. 78 F2 40 14N 82 27W
Utik L., Canada 73 B9 55 15N 96 0W
Utikuma L., Canada 72 B5 55 50N 115 30W
Utrecht, Neths. 15 B5 52 5N 5 8 E
Utrecht, S. Africa 57 D5 27 38S 30 20 E
Utrecht □, Neths. 15 B5 52 6N 5 7 E
Utrera, Spain 19 D3 37 12N 5 48W
Utsjoki, Finland 8 B22 69 51N 26 59 E
Utsunomiya, Japan 31 F9 36 30N 139 50 E
Uttar Pradesh □, India 43 F9 27 0N 80 0 E
Uttaradit, Thailand 38 D3 17 36N 100 5 E
Uttoxeter, U.K. 10 E6 52 54N 1 52W
Uummannarsuaq = Farvel, Kap, Greenland 4 D5 59 48N 43 55W
Uusikaarlepyy, Finland 8 E20 63 32N 22 31 E
Uusikaupunki, Finland 9 F19 60 47N 21 25 E
Uva, Russia 24 C9 56 59N 52 13 E
Uvalde, U.S.A. 81 L5 29 13N 99 47W
Uvat, Russia 26 D7 59 5N 68 50 E
Uvinza, Tanzania 54 D3 5 5S 30 24 E
Uvira, Zaïre 54 C2 3 22S 29 3 E
Uvs Nuur, Mongolia 32 A4 50 20N 92 30 E
Uwajima, Japan 31 H6 33 10N 132 35 E
Uxbridge, Canada 78 B5 44 6N 79 7W
Uxin Qi, China 34 E5 38 50N 109 5 E
Uxmal, Mexico 87 C7 20 22N 89 46W
Uyandi, Russia 27 C15 69 19N 141 0 E
Uyuni, Bolivia 92 H5 20 28S 66 47W
Uzbekistan ■, Asia 26 E7 41 30N 65 0 E
Uzen, Kazakstan 25 F9 43 29N 52 54 E
Uzerche, France 18 D4 45 25N 1 34 E
Uzh →, Ukraine 17 C16 51 15N 30 12 E
Uzhgorod = Uzhhorod, Ukraine 17 D12 48 36N 22 18 E
Uzhhorod, Ukraine 17 D12 48 36N 22 18 E
Uzunköprü, Turkey 21 D12 41 16N 26 43 E

V

Vaal →, S. Africa 56 D3 29 4S 23 38 E
Vaal Dam, S. Africa 57 D4 27 0S 28 14 E
Vaalwater, S. Africa 57 C4 24 15S 28 8 E
Vaasa, Finland 8 E19 63 6N 21 38 E
Vác, Hungary 17 E10 47 49N 19 10 E
Vacaria, Brazil 95 B5 28 31S 50 52W
Vacaville, U.S.A. 84 G5 38 21N 121 59W
Vach → = Vakh →, Russia 26 C8 60 45N 76 45 E
Vache, Î.-à-, Haiti 89 C5 18 2N 73 35W
Vadnagar, India 42 H5 23 47N 72 40 E
Vadodara, India 42 H5 22 20N 73 10 E
Vadsø, Norway 8 A23 70 3N 29 50 E
Vaduz, Liech. 16 E5 47 8N 9 31 E
Værøy, Norway 8 C15 67 40N 12 40 E
Vágar, Færoe Is. 8 E9 62 5N 7 15W
Vågsfjorden, Norway 8 B17 68 50N 16 50 E
Váh →, Slovak Rep. 17 D9 47 43N 18 7 E
Vahsel B., Antarctica 5 D1 75 0S 35 0W
Váï, Greece 23 D8 35 15N 26 18 E
Vaigach, Russia 26 B6 70 10N 59 0 E
Vakh →, Russia 26 C8 60 45N 76 45 E
Val d'Or, Canada 70 C4 48 7N 77 47W
Val Marie, Canada 73 D7 49 15N 107 45W
Valahia, Romania 17 F13 44 35N 25 0 E
Valandovo, Macedonia 21 D10 41 19N 22 34 E
Valcheta, Argentina 96 E3 40 40S 66 8W
Valdayskaya Vozvyshennost, Russia 24 C5 57 0N 33 30 E
Valdepeñas, Spain 19 C4 38 43N 3 25W
Valdés, Pen., Argentina 96 E4 42 30S 63 45W
Valdez, U.S.A. 68 B5 61 7N 146 16W
Valdivia, Chile 96 D2 39 50S 73 14W
Valdosta, U.S.A. 77 K4 30 50N 83 17W
Valdres, Norway 9 F13 61 5N 9 5 E
Vale, U.S.A. 82 E5 43 59N 117 15W
Vale of Glamorgan □, U.K. 11 F4 51 28N 3 25W
Valença, Brazil 93 F11 13 20S 39 5W
Valença do Piauí, Brazil 93 E10 6 20S 41 45W
Valence, France 18 D6 44 57N 4 54 E
Valencia, Spain 19 C5 39 27N 0 23W
Valencia, Venezuela 92 A5 10 11N 68 0W
Valencia □, Spain 19 C5 39 20N 0 40W
Valencia, G. de, Spain 19 C6 39 30N 0 20 E
Valencia de Alcántara, Spain 19 C2 39 25N 7 14W
Valencia Harbour, Ireland 13 E1 51 56N 10 19W
Valencia I., Ireland 13 E1 51 54N 10 22W
Valenciennes, France 18 A5 50 20N 3 34 E
Valentim, Sa. do, Brazil 93 E10 6 0S 43 30W
Valentin, Russia 30 C7 43 8N 134 17 E
Valentine, Nebr., U.S.A. 80 D4 42 52N 100 33W
Valentine, Tex., U.S.A. 81 K2 30 35N 104 30W
Valera, Venezuela 92 B4 9 19N 70 37W
Valga, Estonia 9 H22 57 47N 26 2 E
Valier, U.S.A. 82 B7 48 18N 112 16W
Valjevo, Serbia, Yug. 21 B8 44 18N 19 53 E
Valka, Latvia 9 H21 57 42N 25 57 E
Valkeakoski, Finland 9 F20 61 16N 24 2 E
Valkenswaard, Neths. 15 C5 51 21N 5 29 E
Vall de Uxó, Spain 19 C5 39 49N 0 15W
Valladolid, Mexico 87 C7 20 40N 88 11W
Valladolid, Spain 19 B3 41 38N 4 43W
Valldemosa, Spain 22 B9 39 43N 2 37 E
Valle de la Pascua, Venezuela 92 B5 9 13N 66 0W
Valle de las Palmas, Mexico 85 N10 32 20N 116 43W
Valle de Santiago, Mexico 86 C4 20 25N 101 15W
Valle de Suchil, Mexico 86 C4 23 38N 103 55W
Valle de Zaragoza, Mexico 86 B3 27 28N 105 49W
Valle Fértil, Sierra del, Argentina 94 C2 30 20S 68 0W
Valle Hermoso, Mexico 87 B5 25 35N 97 40W
Valledupar, Colombia 92 A4 10 29N 73 15W
Vallehermoso, Canary Is. 22 F2 28 10N 17 15W
Vallejo, U.S.A. 84 G4 38 7N 122 14W
Vallenar, Chile 94 B1 28 30S 70 50W
Valletta, Malta 23 D2 35 54N 14 31 E
Valley Center, U.S.A. 85 M9 33 13N 117 2W
Valley City, U.S.A. 80 B6 46 55N 98 0W
Valley Falls, U.S.A. 82 E3 42 29N 120 17W
Valley Springs, U.S.A. 84 G6 38 12N 120 50W
Valley Wells, U.S.A. 85 K11 35 27N 115 46W
Valleyview, Canada 72 B5 55 5N 117 17W
Vallimanca, Arroyo, Argentina 94 D4 35 40S 59 10W
Valls, Spain 19 B6 41 18N 1 15 E
Valmiera, Latvia 9 H21 57 37N 25 29 E
Valognes, France 18 B3 49 30N 1 28W
Valona = Vlóra, Albania 21 D8 40 32N 19 28 E
Valozhyn, Belarus 17 A14 54 3N 26 30 E
Valparaíso, Chile 94 C1 33 2S 71 40W
Valparaíso, Mexico 86 C4 22 50N 103 32W
Valparaiso, U.S.A. 76 E2 41 28N 87 4W
Valparaíso □, Chile 94 C1 33 2S 71 40W
Vals →, S. Africa 56 D4 27 23S 26 30 E
Vals, Tanjung, Indonesia 37 F9 8 26S 137 25 E
Valsad, India 40 J8 20 40N 72 58 E
Valverde, Canary Is. 22 G2 27 48N 17 55W
Valverde del Camino, Spain 19 D2 37 35N 6 47W
Vammala, Finland 9 F20 61 20N 22 54 E
Vámos, Greece 23 D6 35 24N 24 13 E
Van, Turkey 25 G7 38 30N 43 20 E
Van, L. = Van Gölü, Turkey 25 G7 38 30N 43 0 E
Van Alstyne, U.S.A. 81 J6 33 25N 96 35W
Van Bruyssel, Canada 71 C5 47 56N 72 9W
Van Buren, Canada 71 C6 47 10N 67 55W
Van Buren, Ark., U.S.A. 81 H7 35 26N 94 21W
Van Buren, Maine, U.S.A. 77 B11 47 10N 67 58W
Van Buren, Mo., U.S.A. 81 G9 37 0N 91 1W
Van Canh, Vietnam 38 F7 13 37N 109 0 E
Van Diemen, C., N. Terr., Australia 60 B5 11 9S 130 24 E
Van Diemen, C., Queens., Australia 62 B2 16 30S 139 46 E
Van Diemen G., Australia 60 B5 11 45S 132 0 E
Van Gölü, Turkey 25 G7 38 30N 43 0 E
Van Horn, U.S.A. 81 K2 31 3N 104 50W
Van Ninh, Vietnam 38 F7 12 42N 109 14 E
Van Rees, Pegunungan, Indonesia 37 E9 2 35S 138 15 E
Van Tassell, U.S.A. 80 D2 42 40N 104 5W
Van Wert, U.S.A. 76 E3 40 52N 84 35W
Van Yen, Vietnam 38 B5 21 4N 104 42 E
Vanadzor, Armenia 25 F7 40 48N 44 30 E
Vanavara, Russia 27 C11 60 22N 102 16 E
Vancouver, Canada 72 D4 49 15N 123 10W
Vancouver, U.S.A. 84 E4 45 38N 122 40W
Vancouver, C., Australia 61 G2 35 2S 118 11 E
Vancouver I., Canada 72 D3 49 50N 126 0W
Vandalia, Ill., U.S.A. 80 F10 38 58N 89 6W
Vandalia, Mo., U.S.A. 80 F9 39 19N 91 29W
Vandenburg, U.S.A. 85 L6 34 35N 120 33W
Vanderbijlpark, S. Africa 57 D4 26 42S 27 54 E
Vandergrift, U.S.A. 78 F5 40 36N 79 34W
Vanderhoof, Canada 72 C4 54 0N 124 0W
Vanderkloof Dam, S. Africa 56 E3 30 4S 24 40 E
Vanderlin I., Australia 62 B2 15 44S 137 2 E
Vandyke, Australia 62 C4 24 10S 147 51 E
Vänern, Sweden 9 G15 58 47N 13 30 E
Vänersborg, Sweden 9 G15 58 26N 12 19 E
Vang Vieng, Laos 38 C4 18 58N 102 32 E
Vanga, Kenya 54 C4 4 35S 39 12 E
Vangaindrano, Madag. 57 C8 23 21S 47 36 E
Vanguard, Canada 73 D7 49 55N 107 20W
Vanier, Canada 70 C4 45 27N 75 40W
Vankleek Hill, Canada 70 C5 45 32N 74 40W
Vanna, Norway 8 A18 70 6N 19 50 E
Vännäs, Sweden 8 E18 63 58N 19 48 E
Vannes, France 18 C2 47 40N 2 47W
Vanrhynsdorp, S. Africa 56 E2 31 36S 18 44 E
Vanrook, Australia 62 B3 16 57S 141 57 E
Vansbro, Sweden 9 F16 60 32N 14 15 E
Vansittart B., Australia 60 B4 14 3S 126 17 E
Vantaa, Finland 9 F21 60 18N 24 58 E
Vanthli, India 42 J4 21 28N 70 25 E
Vanua Levu, Fiji 59 C8 16 33S 179 15 E
Vanua Mbalavu, Fiji 59 C9 17 40S 178 57W
Vanuatu ■, Pac. Oc. 64 J8 15 0S 168 0 E
Vanwyksvlei, S. Africa 56 E3 30 18S 21 49 E
Vanzylsrus, S. Africa 56 D3 26 52S 22 4 E
Vapnyarka, Ukraine 17 D15 48 32N 28 45 E
Varanasi, India 43 G10 25 22N 83 0 E
Varanger-halvøya, Norway 8 A23 70 25N 29 30 E
Varangerfjorden, Norway 8 A23 70 3N 29 25 E
Varaždin, Croatia 16 E9 46 20N 16 20 E
Varberg, Sweden 9 H15 57 6N 12 20 E
Vardar = Axiós →, Greece 21 D10 40 57N 22 35 E
Varde, Denmark 9 J13 55 38N 8 29 E
Vardø, Norway 8 A24 70 23N 31 5 E
Varella, Mui, Vietnam 38 F7 12 54N 109 26 E
Varėna, Lithuania 9 J21 54 12N 24 30 E
Varese, Italy 20 B3 45 48N 8 50 E
Varginha, Brazil 95 A6 21 33S 45 25W
Variadero, U.S.A. 81 H2 35 43N 104 17W
Varillas, Chile 94 A1 24 0S 70 10W
Varkaus, Finland 9 E22 62 19N 27 50 E
Varna, Bulgaria 21 C12 43 13N 27 56 E
Värnamo, Sweden 9 H16 57 10N 14 3 E
Vars, Canada 79 A9 45 21N 75 21W
Varzaneh, Iran 45 C7 32 25N 52 40 E
Vasa Barris →, Brazil 93 F11 11 10S 37 10W
Vascongadas = País Vasco □, Spain 19 A4 42 50N 2 45W
Vasht = Khāsh, Iran 40 E2 28 15N 61 15 E
Vasilevichi, Belarus 17 B15 52 15N 29 50 E
Vasilkov = Vasylkiv, Ukraine 17 C16 50 7N 30 15 E
Vaslui, Romania 17 E14 46 38N 27 42 E
Vassar, Canada 73 D9 49 10N 95 55W
Vassar, U.S.A. 76 D4 43 22N 83 35W
Västerås, Sweden 9 G17 59 37N 16 38 E
Västerbotten, Sweden 8 D18 64 36N 20 4 E
Västerdalälven →, Sweden 9 F16 60 30N 14 7 E
Västervik, Sweden 9 H17 57 43N 16 33 E
Västmanland, Sweden 9 G16 59 45N 16 20 E
Vasto, Italy 20 C6 42 8N 14 40 E
Vasylkiv, Ukraine 17 C16 50 7N 30 15 E
Vatican City ■, Europe 20 D5 41 54N 12 27 E
Vatili, Cyprus 23 D12 35 6N 33 40 E
Vatnajökull, Iceland 8 D5 64 30N 16 48W
Vatoa, Fiji 59 D9 19 50S 178 13W
Vatólakkos, Greece 23 D5 35 27N 23 53 E
Vatoloha, Madag. 57 B8 17 52S 47 48 E
Vatomandry, Madag. 57 B8 19 20S 48 59 E
Vatra-Dornei, Romania 17 E13 47 22N 25 22 E
Vättern, Sweden 9 G16 58 25N 14 30 E
Vaughn, Mont., U.S.A. 82 C8 47 33N 111 33W
Vaughn, N. Mex., U.S.A. 83 J11 34 36N 105 13W
Vaupés = Uaupés →, Brazil 92 C5 0 2N 67 16W
Vauxhall, Canada 72 C6 50 5N 112 9W
Vava'u, Tonga 59 D11 18 36S 174 0W
Vawkavysk, Belarus 17 B13 53 9N 24 30 E
Växjö, Sweden 9 H16 56 52N 14 50 E
Vaygach, Ostrov, Russia 26 C6 70 0N 60 0 E
Váyia, Ákra, Greece 23 C10 36 15N 28 11 E
Vechte →, Neths. 15 B6 52 34N 6 6 E
Vedea →, Romania 17 G13 43 53N 25 59 E
Vedia, Argentina 94 C3 34 30S 61 31W
Vedra, I. del, Spain 22 C7 38 52N 1 12 E
Veendam, Neths. 15 A6 53 5N 6 52 E
Veenendaal, Neths. 15 B5 52 2N 5 34 E
Vefsna →, Norway 8 D15 65 48N 13 10 E
Vega, Norway 8 D14 65 40N 11 55 E
Vega, U.S.A. 81 H3 35 15N 102 26W
Veghel, Neths. 15 C5 51 37N 5 32 E
Vegreville, Canada 72 C6 53 30N 112 5W
Vejer de la Frontera, Spain 19 D3 36 15N 5 59W
Vejle, Denmark 9 J13 55 43N 9 30 E
Velas, C., Costa Rica 88 D2 10 21N 85 52W
Velasco, Sierra de, Argentina 94 B2 29 20S 67 10W
Velddrif, S. Africa 56 E2 32 42S 18 11 E
Velebit Planina, Croatia 16 F8 44 50N 15 20 E
Vélez, Colombia 92 B4 6 1N 73 41W
Vélez Málaga, Spain 19 D3 36 48N 4 5W
Vélez Rubio, Spain 19 D4 37 41N 2 5W
Velhas →, Brazil 93 G10 17 13S 44 49W
Velika Kapela, Croatia 16 F8 45 10N 15 5 E
Velikaya →, Russia 24 C4 57 48N 28 10 E
Velikaya Kema, Russia 30 B8 45 30N 137 12 E
Veliki Ustyug, Russia 24 B8 60 47N 46 20 E
Velikiye Luki, Russia 24 C5 56 25N 30 32 E
Veliko Tŭrnovo, Bulgaria 21 C11 43 5N 25 41 E
Velikonda Range, India 40 M11 14 45N 79 10 E
Velletri, Italy 20 D5 41 41N 12 47 E
Vellore, India 40 N11 12 57N 79 10 E
Velsen-Noord, Neths. 15 B4 52 27N 4 40 E
Velsk, Russia 24 B7 61 10N 42 5 E
Velva, U.S.A. 80 A4 48 4N 100 56W
Venado Tuerto, Argentina 94 C3 33 50S 62 0W
Vendée □, France 18 C3 46 50N 1 35W
Vendôme, France 18 C4 47 47N 1 3 E
Venézia, Italy 20 B5 45 27N 12 21 E
Venézia, G. di, Italy 20 B5 45 15N 13 0 E
Venezuela ■, S. Amer. 92 B5 8 0N 66 0W
Venezuela, G. de, Venezuela 92 A4 11 30N 71 0W
Vengurla, India 40 M8 15 53N 73 45 E
Venice = Venézia, Italy 20 B5 45 27N 12 21 E
Venkatapuram, India 41 K12 18 20N 80 30 E
Venlo, Neths. 15 C6 51 22N 6 11 E
Vennesla, Norway 9 G12 58 15N 8 0 E
Venraij, Neths. 15 C5 51 31N 6 0 E
Ventana, Punta de la, Mexico 86 C3 24 4N 109 48W
Ventana, Sa. de la, Argentina 94 D3 38 0S 62 30W
Ventersburg, S. Africa 56 D4 28 7S 27 9 E
Venterstad, S. Africa 56 E4 30 47S 25 48 E
Ventnor, U.K. 11 G6 50 36N 1 12W
Ventotene, Italy 20 D5 40 47N 13 25 E
Ventoux, Mt., France 18 D6 44 10N 5 17 E
Ventspils, Latvia 9 H19 57 25N 21 32 E
Ventuari →, Venezuela 92 C5 3 58N 67 2W
Ventucopa, U.S.A. 85 L7 34 50N 119 29W
Ventura, U.S.A. 85 L7 34 17N 119 18W
Venus B., Australia 63 F4 38 40S 145 42 E
Vera, Argentina 94 B3 29 30S 60 20W
Vera, Spain 19 D5 37 15N 1 51W
Veracruz, Mexico 87 D5 19 10N 96 10W
Veracruz □, Mexico 87 D5 19 0N 96 15W
Veraval, India 42 J4 20 53N 70 27 E
Verbánia, Italy 20 B3 45 56N 8 33 E
Vercelli, Italy 20 B3 45 19N 8 25 E
Verdalsøra, Norway 8 E14 63 48N 11 30 E
Verde →, Argentina 96 E3 41 56S 65 5W
Verde →, Chihuahua, Mexico 86 B3 26 29N 107 58W
Verde →, Oaxaca, Mexico 87 D5 15 59N 97 50W
Verde →, Veracruz, Mexico 86 C4 21 10N 102 50W
Verde →, Paraguay 94 A4 23 9S 57 37W
Verde, Cay, Bahamas 88 B4 23 0N 75 5W
Verden, Germany 16 B5 52 55N 9 14 E
Verdi, U.S.A. 84 F7 39 31N 119 59W
Verdigre, U.S.A. 80 D5 42 36N 98 2W
Verdun, France 18 B6 49 9N 5 24 E
Vereeniging, S. Africa 57 D4 26 38S 27 57 E
Vérendrye, Parc Prov. de la, Canada 70 C4 47 20N 76 40W
Verga, C., Guinea 50 F2 10 30N 14 10W
Vergemont, Australia 62 C3 23 33S 143 1 E
Vergemont Cr. →, Australia 62 C3 24 16S 143 16 E
Vergennes, U.S.A. 79 B11 44 10N 73 15W
Verin, Spain 19 B2 41 57N 7 27W
Verkhnevilyuysk, Russia 27 C13 63 27N 120 18 E
Verkhneye Kalinino, Russia 27 D11 59 54N 108 8 E
Verkhniy Baskunchak, Russia 25 E8 48 14N 46 44 E
Verkhnyaya Amga, Russia 27 D13 59 50N 127 0 E
Verkhoyansk, Russia 27 C14 67 35N 133 25 E
Verkhoyansk Ra. = Verkhoyanskiy Khrebet, Russia 27 C13 66 0N 129 0 E
Verkhoyanskiy Khrebet, Russia 27 C13 66 0N 129 0 E
Verlo, Canada 73 C7 50 19N 108 35W
Vermilion, Canada 73 C6 53 20N 110 50W
Vermilion →, Alta., Canada 73 C6 53 22N 110 51W
Vermilion →, Qué., Canada 70 C5 47 38N 72 56W
Vermilion, B., U.S.A. 81 L9 29 45N 91 55W
Vermilion Bay, Canada 73 D10 49 51N 93 34W
Vermilion Chutes, Canada 72 B6 58 22N 114 51W
Vermilion L., U.S.A. 80 B8 47 53N 92 26W
Vermillion, U.S.A. 80 D6 42 47N 96 56W
Vermont □, U.S.A. 79 C12 44 0N 73 0W
Vernal, U.S.A. 82 F9 40 27N 109 32W
Vernalis, U.S.A. 84 H5 37 36N 121 17W
Verner, Canada 70 C3 46 25N 80 8W
Verneukpan, S. Africa 56 D3 30 0S 21 0 E
Vernon, Canada 72 C5 50 20N 119 15W
Vernon, U.S.A. 81 H5 34 9N 99 17W
Vernonia, U.S.A. 84 E3 45 52N 123 11W
Vero Beach, U.S.A. 77 M5 27 38N 80 24W
Véroia, Greece 21 D10 40 34N 22 12 E
Verona, Italy 20 B4 45 27N 11 0 E
Versailles, France 18 B5 48 48N 2 8 E
Vert, C., Senegal 50 F1 14 45N 17 30W
Verulam, S. Africa 57 D5 29 38S 31 2 E
Verviers, Belgium 15 D5 50 37N 5 52 E
Veselovskoye Vdkhr., Russia 25 E7 46 58N 41 25 E
Vesoul, France 18 C7 47 40N 6 11 E
Vesterålen, Norway 8 B16 68 45N 15 0 E
Vestfjorden, Norway 8 C15 67 55N 14 0 E
Vestmannaeyjar, Iceland 8 E3 63 27N 20 15W
Vestspitsbergen, Svalbard 4 B8 78 40N 17 0 E
Vestvågøy, Norway 8 B15 68 18N 13 50 E
Vesuvio, Italy 20 D6 40 49N 14 26 E
Vesuvius, Mt. = Vesuvio, Italy 20 D6 40 49N 14 26 E
Veszprém, Hungary 17 E9 47 8N 17 57 E
Vetlanda, Sweden 9 H16 57 24N 15 3 E
Vetlugu →, Russia 26 D5 56 36N 46 4 E
Vettore, Mte., Italy 20 C5 42 49N 13 16 E
Veurne, Belgium 15 C2 51 5N 2 40 E
Veys, Iran 45 D6 31 30N 49 0 E
Vezhen, Bulgaria 21 C11 42 50N 24 20 E
Vi Thanh, Vietnam 39 H5 9 42N 105 26 E
Viacha, Bolivia 92 G5 16 39S 68 18W
Viamão, Brazil 95 C5 30 5S 51 0W
Viana, Brazil 93 D10 3 13S 44 55W
Viana do Alentejo, Portugal 19 C2 38 17N 7 59W
Viana do Castelo, Portugal 19 B1 41 42N 8 50W
Vianópolis, Brazil 93 G9 16 40S 48 35W
Viaréggio, Italy 20 C4 43 52N 10 14 E
Vibank, Canada 73 C8 50 20N 103 56W
Vibo Valéntia, Italy 20 E7 38 40N 16 6 E
Viborg, Denmark 9 H13 56 27N 9 23 E
Vicenza, Italy 20 B4 45 33N 11 33 E
Vich, Spain 19 B7 41 58N 2 19 E
Vichy, France 18 C5 46 9N 3 26 E
Vicksburg, Ariz., U.S.A. 85 M13 33 45N 113 45W
Vicksburg, Mich., U.S.A. 76 D3 42 7N 85 32W
Vicksburg, Miss., U.S.A. 81 J9 32 21N 90 53W
Viçosa, Brazil 93 E11 9 28S 36 14W
Victor, India 42 J4 21 0N 71 30 E
Victor, Colo., U.S.A. 80 F2 38 43N 105 9W
Victor, N.Y., U.S.A. 78 D7 42 58N 77 24W
Victor Harbor, Australia 63 F2 35 30S 138 37 E
Victoria, Argentina 94 C3 32 40S 60 10W
Victoria, Canada 72 D4 48 30N 123 25W
Victoria, Chile 96 D2 38 13S 72 20W
Victoria, Guinea 50 F2 10 50N 14 32W
Victoria, Malaysia 36 C5 5 20N 115 14 E
Victoria, Malta 23 C1 36 2N 14 14 E
Victoria, Kans., U.S.A. 80 F5 38 52N 99 9W
Victoria, Tex., U.S.A. 81 L6 28 48N 97 0W
Victoria □, Australia 63 F3 37 0S 144 0 E
Victoria →, Australia 60 C4 15 10S 129 40 E
Victoria, Grand L., Canada 70 C4 47 31N 77 30W
Victoria, L., Africa 54 C3 1 0S 33 0 E
Victoria, L., Australia 63 E3 33 57S 141 15 E
Victoria Beach, Canada 73 C9 50 40N 96 35W
Victoria de Durango, Mexico 86 C4 24 3N 104 39W
Victoria de las Tunas, Cuba 88 B4 20 58N 76 59W
Victoria Falls, Zimbabwe 55 F2 17 58S 25 52 E
Victoria Harbour, Canada 70 D4 44 45N 79 45W
Victoria I., Canada 68 A8 71 0N 111 0W
Victoria Ld., Antarctica 5 D11 75 0S 160 0 E
Victoria Nile →, Uganda 54 B3 2 14N 31 26 E
Victoria Res., Canada 71 C8 48 20N 57 27W
Victoria River Downs, Australia 60 C5 16 25S 131 0 E
Victoria Taungdeik, Burma 41 J18 21 15N 93 55 E
Victoria West, S. Africa 56 E3 31 25S 23 4 E
Victoriaville, Canada 71 C5 46 4N 71 56W
Victorica, Argentina 94 D2 36 20S 65 30W
Victorville, U.S.A. 85 L9 34 32N 117 18W
Vicuña, Chile 94 C1 30 0S 70 50W
Vicuña Mackenna, Argentina 94 C3 33 53S 64 25W
Vidal, U.S.A. 85 L12 34 7N 114 31W
Vidal Junction, U.S.A. 85 L12 34 11N 114 34W
Vidalia, U.S.A. 77 J4 32 13N 82 25W
Vidho, Greece 23 A3 39 38N 19 55 E
Vidin, Bulgaria 21 C10 43 59N 22 50 E
Vidisha, India 42 H7 23 28N 77 53 E
Vidzy, Belarus 9 J22 55 23N 26 37 E
Viedma, Argentina 96 E4 40 50S 63 0W
Viedma, L., Argentina 96 F2 49 30S 72 30W
Vieng Pou Kha, Laos 38 B3 20 41N 101 4 E
Vienna = Wien, Austria 16 D9 48 12N 16 22 E

Vienna

Vienna, *U.S.A.* 81 G10 37 25N 88 54W
Vienne, *France* 18 D6 45 31N 4 53 E
Vienne →, *France* 18 C4 47 13N 0 5 E
Vientiane, *Laos* 38 D4 17 58N 102 36 E
Vientos, Paso de los, *Caribbean* 89 C5 20 0N 74 0W
Vierzon, *France* 18 C5 47 13N 2 5 E
Vietnam ■, *Asia* 38 C5 19 0N 106 0 E
Vigan, *Phil.* 37 A6 17 35N 120 28 E
Vigévano, *Italy* 20 B3 45 19N 8 51 E
Vigia, *Brazil* 93 D9 0 50S 48 5W
Vigía Chico, *Mexico* 87 D7 19 46N 87 35W
Víglas, Ákra, *Greece* 23 D9 35 54N 27 51 E
Vigo, *Spain* 19 A1 42 12N 8 41W
Vijayawada, *India* 41 L12 16 31N 80 39 E
Vík, *Iceland* 8 E4 63 25N 19 1W
Vikeke, *Indonesia* 37 F7 8 52S 126 23 E
Viking, *Canada* 72 C6 53 7N 111 50W
Vikna, *Norway* 8 D14 64 55N 10 58 E
Vikulovo, *Russia* 26 D8 56 50N 70 40 E
Vila da Maganja, *Mozam.* 55 F4 17 18S 37 30 E
Vila de João Belo = Xai-Xai, *Mozam.* 57 D5 25 6S 33 31 E
Vila do Bispo, *Portugal* 19 D1 37 5N 8 53W
Vila do Chibuto, *Mozam.* 57 C5 24 40S 33 33 E
Vila Franca de Xira, *Portugal* 19 C1 38 57N 8 59W
Vila Gamito, *Mozam.* 55 E3 14 12S 33 0 E
Vila Gomes da Costa, *Mozam.* 57 C5 24 20S 33 37 E
Vila Machado, *Mozam.* 55 F3 19 15S 34 14 E
Vila Mouzinho, *Mozam.* 55 E3 14 48S 34 25 E
Vila Nova de Gaia, *Portugal* 19 B1 41 8N 8 37W
Vila Real, *Portugal* 19 B2 41 17N 7 48W
Vila Real de Santo António, *Portugal* 19 D2 37 10N 7 28W
Vila Vasco da Gama, *Mozam.* 55 E3 14 54S 32 14 E
Vila Velha, *Brazil* 95 A7 20 20S 40 17W
Vilaine →, *France* 18 C2 47 30N 2 27W
Vilanandro, Tanjona, *Madag.* 57 B7 16 11S 44 27 E
Vilanculos, *Mozam.* 57 C6 22 1S 35 17 E
Vileyka, *Belarus* 17 A14 54 30N 26 53 E
Vilhelmina, *Sweden* 8 D17 64 35N 16 39 E
Vilhena, *Brazil* 92 F6 12 40S 60 5W
Viliga, *Russia* 27 C16 61 36N 156 56 E
Viliya →, *Lithuania* 9 J21 55 8N 24 16 E
Viljandi, *Estonia* 9 G21 58 28N 25 30 E
Vilkitskogo, Proliv, *Russia* 27 B11 78 0N 103 0 E
Vilkovo = Vylkove, *Ukraine* 17 F15 45 28N 29 32 E
Villa Abecia, *Bolivia* 94 A2 21 0S 68 18W
Villa Ahumada, *Mexico* 86 A3 30 38N 106 30W
Villa Ana, *Argentina* 94 B4 28 28S 59 40W
Villa Ángela, *Argentina* 94 B3 27 34S 60 45W
Villa Bella, *Bolivia* 92 F5 10 25S 65 22W
Villa Bens = Tarfaya, *Morocco* 50 C2 27 55N 12 55W
Villa Cañás, *Argentina* 94 C3 34 0S 61 35W
Villa Carlos, *Spain* 22 B11 39 53N 4 17 E
Villa Cisneros = Dakhla, *W. Sahara* 50 D1 23 50N 15 53W
Villa Colón, *Argentina* 94 C2 31 38S 68 20W
Villa Constitución, *Argentina* 94 C3 33 15S 60 20W
Villa de María, *Argentina* 94 B3 29 55S 63 43W
Villa Dolores, *Argentina* 94 C2 31 58S 65 15W
Villa Frontera, *Mexico* 86 B4 26 56N 101 27W
Villa Guillermina, *Argentina* 94 B4 28 15S 59 29W
Villa Hayes, *Paraguay* 94 B4 25 5S 57 20W
Villa Iris, *Argentina* 94 D3 38 12S 63 12W
Villa Juárez, *Mexico* 86 B4 27 37N 100 44W
Villa María, *Argentina* 94 C3 32 20S 63 10W
Villa Mazán, *Argentina* 94 B2 28 40S 66 30W
Villa Montes, *Bolivia* 94 A3 21 10S 63 30W
Villa Ocampo, *Argentina* 94 B4 28 30S 59 20W
Villa Ocampo, *Mexico* 86 B3 26 29N 105 30W
Villa Ojo de Agua, *Argentina* 94 B3 29 30S 63 44W
Villa San José, *Argentina* 94 C4 32 12S 58 15W
Villa San Martín, *Argentina* 94 B3 28 15S 64 9W
Villa Unión, *Mexico* 86 C3 23 12N 106 14W
Villacarrillo, *Spain* 19 C4 38 7N 3 3W
Villach, *Austria* 16 E7 46 37N 13 51 E
Villafranca de los Caballeros, *Spain* 22 B10 39 34N 3 25 E
Villagarcía de Arosa, *Spain* 19 A1 42 34N 8 46W
Villagrán, *Mexico* 87 C5 24 29N 99 29W
Villaguay, *Argentina* 94 C4 32 0S 59 0W
Villahermosa, *Mexico* 87 D6 17 59N 92 55W
Villajoyosa, *Spain* 19 C5 38 30N 0 12W
Villalba, *Spain* 19 A2 43 26N 7 40W
Villanueva, *U.S.A.* 83 J11 35 16N 105 22W
Villanueva de la Serena, *Spain* 19 C3 38 59N 5 50W
Villanueva y Geltrú, *Spain* 19 B6 41 13N 1 40 E
Villarreal, *Spain* 19 C5 39 55N 0 3W
Villarrica, *Chile* 96 D2 39 15S 72 15W
Villarrica, *Paraguay* 94 B4 25 40S 56 30W
Villarrobledo, *Spain* 19 C4 39 18N 2 36W
Villavicencio, *Argentina* 94 C2 32 28S 69 0W
Villavicencio, *Colombia* 92 C4 4 9N 73 37W
Villaviciosa, *Spain* 19 A3 43 32N 5 27W
Villazón, *Bolivia* 94 A2 22 0S 65 35W
Ville-Marie, *Canada* 70 C4 47 20N 79 30W
Ville Platte, *U.S.A.* 81 K8 30 41N 92 17W
Villena, *Spain* 19 C5 38 39N 0 52W
Villeneuve-d'Ascq, *France* 18 A5 50 38N 3 9 E
Villeneuve-sur-Lot, *France* 18 D4 44 24N 0 42 E
Villiers, *S. Africa* 57 D4 27 2S 28 36 E
Villingen-Schwenningen, *Germany* 16 D5 48 3N 8 26 E
Villisca, *U.S.A.* 80 E7 40 56N 94 59W
Vilna, *Canada* 72 C6 54 7N 111 55W
Vilnius, *Lithuania* 9 J21 54 38N 25 19 E
Vilvoorde, *Belgium* 15 D4 50 56N 4 26 E
Vilyuy →, *Russia* 27 C13 64 24N 126 26 E
Vilyuysk, *Russia* 27 C13 63 40N 121 35 E
Viña del Mar, *Chile* 94 C1 33 0S 71 30W
Vinaroz, *Spain* 19 B6 40 30N 0 27 E
Vincennes, *U.S.A.* 76 F2 38 41N 87 32W
Vincent, *U.S.A.* 85 L8 34 33N 118 11W
Vinchina, *Argentina* 94 B2 28 45S 68 15W
Vindelälven →, *Sweden* 8 E18 63 55N 19 50 E
Vindeln, *Sweden* 8 D18 64 12N 19 43 E
Vindhya Ra., *India* 42 H7 22 50N 77 0 E
Vineland, *U.S.A.* 76 F8 39 29N 75 2W
Vinh, *Vietnam* 38 C5 18 45N 105 38 E
Vinh Linh, *Vietnam* 38 D6 17 4N 107 2 E
Vinh Long, *Vietnam* 39 G5 10 16N 105 57 E
Vinh Yen, *Vietnam* 38 B5 21 21N 105 35 E
Vinita, *U.S.A.* 81 G7 36 39N 95 9W
Vinkovci, *Croatia* 21 B8 45 19N 18 48 E
Vinnitsa = Vinnytsya, *Ukraine* 17 D15 49 15N 28 30 E
Vinnytsya, *Ukraine* 17 D15 49 15N 28 30 E
Vinton, *Calif., U.S.A.* 84 F6 39 48N 120 10W
Vinton, *Iowa, U.S.A.* 80 D8 42 10N 92 1W
Vinton, *La., U.S.A.* 81 K8 30 11N 93 35W
Virac, *Phil.* 37 B6 13 30N 124 20 E
Virachei, *Cambodia* 38 F6 13 59N 106 49 E
Virago Sd., *Canada* 72 C2 54 0N 132 30W
Viramgam, *India* 42 H5 23 5N 72 0 E
Virden, *Canada* 73 D8 49 50N 100 56W
Vire, *France* 18 B3 48 50N 0 53W
Vírgenes, C., *Argentina* 96 G3 52 19S 68 21W
Virgin →, *Canada* 73 B7 57 2N 108 17W
Virgin →, *U.S.A.* 83 H6 36 28N 114 21W
Virgin Gorda, *Virgin Is.* 89 C7 18 30N 64 26W
Virgin Is. (British) ■, *W. Indies* 89 C7 18 30N 64 30W
Virgin Is. (U.S.) ■, *W. Indies* 89 C7 18 20N 65 0W
Virginia, *S. Africa* 56 D4 28 8S 26 55 E
Virginia, *U.S.A.* 80 B8 47 31N 92 32W
Virginia □, *U.S.A.* 76 G7 37 30N 78 45W
Virginia Beach, *U.S.A.* 76 G8 36 51N 75 59W
Virginia City, *Mont., U.S.A.* 82 D8 45 18N 111 56W
Virginia City, *Nev., U.S.A.* 84 F7 39 19N 119 39W
Virginia Falls, *Canada* 72 A3 61 38N 125 42W
Virginiatown, *Canada* 70 C4 48 9N 79 36W
Viroqua, *U.S.A.* 80 D9 43 34N 90 53W
Virovitica, *Croatia* 20 B7 45 51N 17 21 E
Virton, *Belgium* 15 E5 49 35N 5 32 E
Virudunagar, *India* 40 Q10 9 30N 77 58 E
Vis, *Croatia* 20 C7 43 4N 16 10 E
Visalia, *U.S.A.* 83 H4 36 20N 119 18W
Visayan Sea, *Phil.* 37 B6 11 30N 123 30 E
Visby, *Sweden* 9 H18 57 37N 18 18 E
Viscount Melville Sd., *Canada* 4 B2 74 10N 108 0W
Visé, *Belgium* 15 D5 50 44N 5 41 E
Višegrad, *Bos.-H.* 21 C8 43 47N 19 17 E
Viseu, *Brazil* 93 D9 1 10S 46 5W
Viseu, *Portugal* 19 B2 40 40N 7 55W
Vishakhapatnam, *India* 41 L13 17 45N 83 20 E
Visnagar, *India* 42 H5 23 45N 72 32 E
Viso, Mte., *Italy* 20 B2 44 38N 7 5 E
Visokoi I., *Antarctica* 5 B1 56 43S 27 15W
Vista, *U.S.A.* 85 M9 33 12N 117 14W
Vistula = Wisła →, *Poland* 17 A10 54 22N 18 55 E
Vitebsk = Vitsyebsk, *Belarus* 24 C5 55 10N 30 15 E
Viterbo, *Italy* 20 C5 42 25N 12 6 E
Viti Levu, *Fiji* 59 C7 17 30S 177 30 E
Vitigudino, *Spain* 19 B2 41 1N 6 26W
Vitim, *Russia* 27 D12 59 28N 112 35 E
Vitim →, *Russia* 27 D12 59 26N 112 34 E
Vitória, *Brazil* 93 H10 20 20S 40 22W
Vitoria, *Spain* 19 A4 42 50N 2 41W
Vitória da Conquista, *Brazil* 93 F10 14 51S 40 51W
Vitsyebsk, *Belarus* 24 C5 55 10N 30 15 E
Vittória, *Italy* 20 F6 36 57N 14 32 E
Vittório Véneto, *Italy* 20 B5 45 59N 12 18 E
Vivero, *Spain* 19 A2 43 39N 7 38W
Vizcaíno, Desierto de, *Mexico* 86 B2 27 40N 113 50W
Vizcaíno, Sierra, *Mexico* 86 B2 27 30N 114 0W
Vize, *Turkey* 21 D12 41 34N 27 45 E
Vizianagaram, *India* 41 K13 18 6N 83 30 E
Vjosa →, *Albania* 21 D8 40 37N 19 24 E
Vlaardingen, *Neths.* 15 C4 51 55N 4 21 E
Vladikavkaz, *Russia* 25 F7 43 0N 44 35 E
Vladimir, *Russia* 24 C7 56 15N 40 30 E
Vladimir Volynskiy = Volodymyr-Volynskyy, *Ukraine* 17 C13 50 50N 24 18 E
Vladivostok, *Russia* 27 E14 43 10N 131 53 E
Vlieland, *Neths.* 15 A4 53 16N 4 55 E
Vlissingen, *Neths.* 15 C3 51 26N 3 34 E
Vlóra, *Albania* 21 D8 40 32N 19 28 E
Vltava →, *Czech.* 16 D8 50 21N 14 30 E
Vo Dat, *Vietnam* 39 G6 11 9N 107 31 E
Vogelkop = Doberai, Jazirah, *Indonesia* 37 E8 1 25S 133 0 E
Vogelsberg, *Germany* 16 C5 50 31N 9 12 E
Voghera, *Italy* 20 B3 44 59N 9 1 E
Vohibinany, *Madag.* 57 B8 18 49S 49 4 E
Vohimarina, *Madag.* 57 A9 13 25S 50 0 E
Vohimena, Tanjon' i, *Madag.* 57 D8 25 36S 45 8 E
Vohipeno, *Madag.* 57 C8 22 22S 47 51 E
Voi, *Kenya* 54 C4 3 25S 38 32 E
Voiron, *France* 18 D6 45 22N 5 35 E
Voisey B., *Canada* 71 A7 56 15N 61 50W
Vojmsjön, *Sweden* 8 D17 64 55N 16 40 E
Vojvodina □, *Serbia, Yug.* 21 B9 45 20N 20 0 E
Volborg, *U.S.A.* 80 C2 45 51N 105 41W
Volcano Is. = Kazan-Rettō, *Pac. Oc.* 64 E6 25 0N 141 0 E
Volchayevka, *Russia* 27 E14 48 40N 134 30 E
Volda, *Norway* 9 E12 62 9N 6 5 E
Volga →, *Russia* 25 E8 46 0N 48 30 E
Volga Hts. = Privolzhskaya Vozvyshennost, *Russia* 25 D8 51 0N 46 0 E
Volgodonsk, *Russia* 25 E7 47 33N 42 5 E
Volgograd, *Russia* 25 E7 48 40N 44 25 E
Volgogradskoye Vdkhr., *Russia* 25 D8 50 0N 45 20 E
Volkhov →, *Russia* 24 B5 60 8N 32 20 E
Volkovysk = Vawkavysk, *Belarus* 17 B13 53 9N 24 30 E
Volksrust, *S. Africa* 57 D4 27 24S 29 53 E
Vollenhove, *Neths.* 15 B5 52 40N 5 58 E
Volochanka, *Russia* 27 B10 71 0N 94 28 E
Volodymyr-Volynskyy, *Ukraine* 17 C13 50 50N 24 18 E
Vologda, *Russia* 24 C6 59 10N 39 45 E
Vólos, *Greece* 21 E10 39 24N 22 59 E
Volovets, *Ukraine* 17 D12 48 43N 23 11 E
Volozhin = Valozhyn, *Belarus* 17 A14 54 3N 26 30 E
Volsk, *Russia* 24 D8 52 5N 47 22 E
Volta →, *Ghana* 50 5 46N 0 41 E
Volta, L., *Ghana* 50 G5 7 30N 0 15 E
Volta Redonda, *Brazil* 95 A7 22 31S 44 5W
Voltaire, C., *Australia* 60 B4 14 16S 125 35 E
Volterra, *Italy* 20 C4 43 24N 10 51 E
Volturno →, *Italy* 20 D5 41 1N 13 55 E
Volvo, *Australia* 63 E3 31 41S 143 57 E
Volzhskiy, *Russia* 25 E7 48 56N 44 46 E
Vondrozo, *Madag.* 57 C8 22 49S 47 20 E
Voorburg, *Neths.* 15 B4 52 5N 4 24 E
Vopnafjörður, *Iceland* 8 D6 65 45N 14 50W
Vorías Sporádhes, *Greece* 21 E10 39 15N 23 30 E
Vorkuta, *Russia* 24 A11 67 48N 64 20 E
Vormsi, *Estonia* 9 G20 59 1N 23 13 E
Voronezh, *Russia* 24 D6 51 40N 39 10 E
Voroshilovgrad = Luhansk, *Ukraine* 25 E6 48 38N 39 15 E
Voroshilovsk = Alchevsk, *Ukraine* 25 E6 48 30N 38 45 E
Vorovskoye, *Russia* 27 D16 54 30N 155 50 E
Võrts Järv, *Estonia* 9 G22 58 16N 26 3 E
Võru, *Estonia* 9 H22 57 48N 26 54 E
Vosges, *France* 18 B7 48 20N 7 10 E
Voss, *Norway* 9 F12 60 38N 6 26 E
Vostok I., *Kiribati* 65 J12 10 5S 152 23W
Votkinsk, *Russia* 24 C9 57 0N 53 55 E
Votkinskoye Vdkhr., *Russia* 24 C10 57 22N 55 12 E
Vouga →, *Portugal* 19 B1 40 41N 8 40W
Voúxa, Ákra, *Greece* 23 D5 35 37N 23 32 E
Vozhe Ozero, *Russia* 24 B6 60 45N 39 0 E
Voznesenka, *Russia* 27 D10 56 40N 95 3 E
Voznesensk, *Ukraine* 25 E5 47 35N 31 21 E
Voznesenye, *Russia* 24 B6 61 0N 35 28 E
Vrangelya, Ostrov, *Russia* 27 B19 71 0N 180 0 E
Vranje, *Serbia, Yug.* 21 C9 42 34N 21 54 E
Vratsa, *Bulgaria* 21 C10 43 13N 23 30 E
Vrbas →, *Bos.-H.* 20 B7 45 8N 17 29 E
Vrede, *S. Africa* 57 D4 27 24S 29 6 E
Vredefort, *S. Africa* 56 D4 27 0S 27 22 E
Vredenburg, *S. Africa* 56 E2 32 56S 18 0 E
Vredendal, *S. Africa* 56 E2 31 41S 18 35 E
Vrindavan, *India* 42 F7 27 37N 77 40 E
Vríses, *Greece* 23 D6 35 23N 24 13 E
Vršac, *Serbia, Yug.* 21 B9 45 8N 21 18 E
Vryburg, *S. Africa* 56 D3 26 55S 24 45 E
Vryheid, *S. Africa* 57 D5 27 45S 30 47 E
Vu Liet, *Vietnam* 38 C5 18 43N 105 23 E
Vught, *Neths.* 15 C5 51 38N 5 20 E
Vukovar, *Croatia* 21 B8 45 21N 18 59 E
Vulcan, *Canada* 72 C6 50 25N 113 15W
Vulcan, *Romania* 17 F12 45 23N 23 17 E
Vulcan, *U.S.A.* 76 C2 45 47N 87 53W
Vulcaneşti, *Moldova* 17 F15 45 35N 28 30 E
Vulcano, *Italy* 20 E6 38 24N 14 58 E
Vulkaneshty = Vulcaneşti, *Moldova* 17 F15 45 35N 28 30 E
Vunduzi →, *Mozam.* 55 F3 18 56S 34 1 E
Vung Tau, *Vietnam* 39 G6 10 21N 107 4 E
Vyatka = Kirov, *Russia* 24 C8 58 35N 49 40 E
Vyatka →, *Russia* 24 C9 55 37N 51 28 E
Vyatskiye Polyany, *Russia* 24 C9 56 14N 51 5 E
Vyazemskiy, *Russia* 27 E14 47 32N 134 45 E
Vyazma, *Russia* 24 C5 55 10N 34 15 E
Vyborg, *Russia* 24 B4 60 43N 28 47 E
Vychegda →, *Russia* 24 B8 61 18N 46 36 E
Vychodné Beskydy, *Europe* 17 D11 49 20N 22 0 E
Vyg-ozero, *Russia* 24 B5 63 47N 34 29 E
Vylkove, *Ukraine* 17 F15 45 28N 29 32 E
Vynohradiv, *Ukraine* 17 D12 48 9N 23 2 E
Vyrnwy, L., *U.K.* 10 E4 52 48N 3 31W
Vyshniy Volochek, *Russia* 24 C5 57 30N 34 30 E
Vyshzha = imeni 26 Bakinskikh Komissarov, *Turkmenistan* 25 G9 39 22N 54 10 E
Vyškov, *Czech.* 17 D9 49 17N 17 0 E
Vytegra, *Russia* 24 B6 61 0N 36 27 E

W

W.A.C. Bennett Dam, *Canada* 72 B4 56 2N 122 6W
Wa, *Ghana* 50 F4 10 7N 2 25W
Waal →, *Neths.* 15 C5 51 37N 5 0 E
Wabakimi L., *Canada* 70 B2 50 38N 89 45W
Wabana, *Canada* 71 C9 47 40N 53 0W
Wabasca, *Canada* 72 B6 55 57N 113 56W
Wabash, *U.S.A.* 76 E3 40 48N 85 49W
Wabash →, *U.S.A.* 76 G1 37 48N 88 2W
Wabeno, *U.S.A.* 76 C1 45 26N 88 39W
Wabigoon L., *Canada* 73 D10 49 44N 92 44W
Wabowden, *Canada* 73 C9 54 55N 98 38W
Wabuk Pt., *Canada* 70 A2 55 20N 85 5W
Wabush, *Canada* 71 B6 52 55N 66 52W
Wabuska, *U.S.A.* 82 G4 39 9N 119 11W
Waco, *U.S.A.* 81 K6 31 33N 97 9W
Waconichi, L., *Canada* 70 B5 50 8N 74 0W
Wad Banda, *Sudan* 51 F10 13 10N 27 56 E
Wad Hamid, *Sudan* 51 E11 16 30N 32 45 E
Wâd Medanî, *Sudan* 51 F11 14 28N 33 30 E
Wad Thana, *Pakistan* 42 F2 27 22N 66 23 E
Wadai, *Africa* 48 E5 12 0N 19 0 E
Wadayama, *Japan* 31 G7 35 19N 134 52 E
Waddeneilanden, *Neths.* 15 A5 53 25N 5 10 E
Waddenzee, *Neths.* 15 A5 53 6N 5 10 E
Wadderin Hill, *Australia* 61 F2 32 0S 118 25 E
Waddington, *U.S.A.* 79 B9 44 52N 75 12W
Waddington, Mt., *Canada* 72 C3 51 23N 125 15W
Waddy Pt., *Australia* 63 C5 24 58S 153 21 E
Wadena, *Canada* 73 C8 51 57N 103 47W
Wadena, *U.S.A.* 80 B7 46 26N 95 8W
Wadesboro, *U.S.A.* 77 H5 34 58N 80 5W
Wadhams, *Canada* 72 C3 51 30N 127 30W
Wādī as Sīr, *Jordan* 47 D4 31 56N 35 49 E
Wadi Halfa, *Sudan* 51 D11 21 53N 31 19 E
Wadsworth, *U.S.A.* 82 G4 39 38N 119 17W
Waegwan, *S. Korea* 35 G15 35 59N 128 23 E
Wafrah, *Si. Arabia* 44 D5 28 33N 47 56 E
Wageningen, *Neths.* 15 C5 51 58N 5 40 E
Wager B., *Canada* 69 B11 65 26N 88 40W
Wager Bay, *Canada* 69 B10 65 56N 90 49W
Wagga Wagga, *Australia* 63 F4 35 7S 147 24 E
Waghete, *Indonesia* 37 E9 4 10S 135 50 E
Wagin, *Australia* 61 F2 33 17S 117 25 E
Wagon Mound, *U.S.A.* 81 G2 36 1N 104 42W
Wagoner, *U.S.A.* 81 G7 35 58N 95 22W
Wah, *Pakistan* 42 C5 33 45N 72 40 E
Wahai, *Indonesia* 37 E7 2 48S 129 35 E
Wahiawa, *U.S.A.* 74 H15 21 30N 158 2W
Wâḥid, *Egypt* 47 E1 30 48N 32 21 E
Wahnai, *Afghan.* 42 C1 32 40N 65 50 E
Wahoo, *U.S.A.* 80 E6 41 13N 96 37W
Wahpeton, *U.S.A.* 80 B6 46 16N 96 36W
Wai, Koh, *Cambodia* 39 H4 9 55N 102 55 E
Waiau →, *N.Z.* 59 K4 42 47S 173 22 E
Waibeem, *Indonesia* 37 E8 0 30S 132 59 E
Waigeo, *Indonesia* 37 E8 0 20S 130 40 E
Waihi, *N.Z.* 59 G5 37 23S 175 52 E
Waihou →, *N.Z.* 59 G5 37 15S 175 40 E
Waika, *Zaïre* 54 C2 2 22S 25 42 E
Waikabubak, *Indonesia* 37 F5 9 45S 119 25 E
Waikari, *N.Z.* 59 K4 42 58S 172 41 E
Waikato →, *N.Z.* 59 G5 37 23S 174 43 E
Waikerie, *Australia* 63 E2 34 9S 140 0 E
Waikokopu, *N.Z.* 59 H6 39 3S 177 52 E
Waikouaiti, *N.Z.* 59 L3 45 36S 170 41 E
Waimakariri →, *N.Z.* 59 K4 43 24S 172 42 E
Waimate, *N.Z.* 59 L3 44 45S 171 3 E
Wainganga →, *India* 40 K11 18 50N 79 55 E
Waingapu, *Indonesia* 37 F6 9 35S 120 11 E
Wainwright, *Canada* 73 C6 52 50N 110 50W
Wainwright, *U.S.A.* 68 A3 70 38N 160 2W
Waiouru, *N.Z.* 59 H5 39 28S 175 41 E
Waipara, *N.Z.* 59 K4 43 3S 172 46 E
Waipawa, *N.Z.* 59 H6 39 56S 176 38 E
Waipiro, *N.Z.* 59 H7 38 2S 178 22 E
Waipu, *N.Z.* 59 F5 35 59S 174 29 E
Waipukurau, *N.Z.* 59 J6 40 1S 176 33 E
Wairakei, *N.Z.* 59 H6 38 37S 176 6 E
Wairarapa, L., *N.Z.* 59 J5 41 14S 175 15 E
Wairoa, *N.Z.* 59 H6 39 3S 177 25 E
Waitaki →, *N.Z.* 59 L3 44 56S 171 7 E
Waitara, *N.Z.* 59 H5 38 59S 174 15 E
Waitsburg, *U.S.A.* 82 C5 46 16N 118 9W
Waiuku, *N.Z.* 59 G5 37 15S 174 45 E
Wajima, *Japan* 31 F8 37 30N 137 0 E
Wajir, *Kenya* 54 B5 1 42N 40 5 E
Wajir □, *Kenya* 54 B5 1 42N 40 20 E
Wakasa, *Japan* 31 G7 35 20N 134 24 E
Wakasa-Wan, *Japan* 31 G7 35 40N 135 30 E
Wakatipu, L., *N.Z.* 59 L2 45 5S 168 33 E
Wakaw, *Canada* 73 C7 52 39N 105 44W
Wakayama, *Japan* 31 G7 34 15N 135 15 E
Wakayama-ken □, *Japan* 31 H7 33 50N 135 30 E
Wake Forest, *U.S.A.* 77 H6 35 59N 78 30W
Wake I., *Pac. Oc.* 64 F8 19 18N 166 36 E
Wakefield, *N.Z.* 59 J4 41 24S 173 5 E
Wakefield, *U.K.* 10 D6 53 41N 1 29W
Wakefield, *Mass., U.S.A.* 79 D13 42 30N 71 4W
Wakefield, *Mich., U.S.A.* 80 B10 46 29N 89 56W
Wakeham Bay = Maricourt, *Canada* 69 C12 56 34N 70 49W
Wakema, *Burma* 41 L19 16 30N 95 11 E
Wakkanai, *Japan* 30 B10 45 28N 141 35 E
Wakkerstroom, *S. Africa* 57 D5 27 24S 30 10 E
Wakool, *Australia* 63 F3 35 28S 144 23 E
Wakool →, *Australia* 63 F3 35 5S 143 33 E
Wakre, *Indonesia* 37 E8 0 19S 131 5 E
Wakuach L., *Canada* 71 A6 55 34N 67 32W
Walamba, *Zambia* 55 E2 13 30S 28 42 E
Wałbrzych, *Poland* 16 C9 50 45N 16 18 E
Walbury Hill, *U.K.* 11 F6 51 21N 1 28W
Walcha, *Australia* 63 E5 30 55S 151 31 E
Walcheren, *Neths.* 15 C3 51 30N 3 35 E
Walcott, *U.S.A.* 82 F10 41 46N 106 51W
Wałcz, *Poland* 16 B9 53 17N 16 27 E
Waldburg Ra., *Australia* 60 D2 24 40S 117 35 E
Walden, *Colo., U.S.A.* 82 F10 40 44N 106 17W
Walden, *N.Y., U.S.A.* 79 E10 41 34N 74 11W
Waldport, *U.S.A.* 82 D1 44 26N 124 4W
Waldron, *U.S.A.* 81 H7 34 54N 94 5W
Wales □, *U.K.* 11 E4 52 19N 4 43W
Walgett, *Australia* 63 E4 30 0S 148 5 E
Walgreen Coast, *Antarctica* 5 D15 75 15S 105 0W
Walhalla, *Australia* 63 F4 37 56S 146 29 E
Walhalla, *U.S.A.* 73 D9 48 55N 97 55W
Walker, *U.S.A.* 80 B7 47 6N 94 35W
Walker L., *Man., Canada* 73 C9 54 42N 95 57W
Walker L., *Qué., Canada* 71 B6 50 20N 67 11W
Walker L., *U.S.A.* 82 G4 38 42N 118 43W
Walkerston, *Australia* 62 C4 21 11S 149 8 E
Walkerton, *Canada* 78 B3 44 10N 81 10W
Wall, *U.S.A.* 80 C3 44 0N 102 8W
Walla Walla, *U.S.A.* 82 C4 46 4N 118 20W
Wallabadah, *Australia* 62 B3 17 57S 142 15 E
Wallace, *Idaho, U.S.A.* 82 C6 47 28N 115 56W
Wallace, *N.C., U.S.A.* 77 H7 34 44N 77 59W
Wallace, *Nebr., U.S.A.* 80 E4 40 50N 101 10W
Wallaceburg, *Canada* 70 D3 42 34N 82 23W
Wallachia = Valahia, *Romania* 17 F13 44 35N 25 0 E
Wallal, *Australia* 63 D4 26 32S 146 7 E
Wallal Downs, *Australia* 60 C3 19 47S 120 40 E
Wallambin, L., *Australia* 61 F2 30 57S 117 35 E
Wallaroo, *Australia* 63 E2 33 56S 137 39 E
Wallasey, *U.K.* 10 D4 53 25N 3 2W
Wallerawang, *Australia* 63 E5 33 25S 150 4 E
Wallhallow, *Australia* 62 B2 17 50S 135 50 E

Woodville, U.S.A. 81 K7 30 47N 94 25W
Woodward, U.S.A. 81 G5 36 26N 99 24W
Woody, U.S.A. 85 K8 35 42N 118 50W
Woolamai, C., Australia 63 F4 38 30S 145 23 E
Woolgoolga, Australia 63 E5 30 6S 153 11 E
Woombye, Australia 63 D5 26 40S 152 55 E
Woomera, Australia 63 E2 31 5S 136 50 E
Woonsocket, R.I., U.S.A. 79 D13 42 0N 71 31W
Woonsocket, S. Dak., U.S.A. 80 C5 44 3N 98 17W
Wooramel, Australia 61 E1 25 45S 114 17 E
Wooramel →, Australia 61 E1 25 47S 114 10 E
Wooroloo, Australia 61 F2 31 48S 116 18 E
Wooster, U.S.A. 78 F3 40 48N 81 56W
Worcester, S. Africa 56 E2 33 39S 19 27 E
Worcester, U.K. 11 E5 52 11N 2 12W
Worcester, Mass., U.S.A. 79 D13 42 16N 71 48W
Worcester, N.Y., U.S.A. 79 D10 42 36N 74 45W
Workington, U.K. 10 C4 54 39N 3 33W
Worksop, U.K. 10 D6 53 18N 1 7W
Workum, Neths. 15 B5 52 59N 5 26 E
Worland, U.S.A. 82 D10 44 1N 107 57W
Worms, Germany 16 D5 49 37N 8 21 E
Wortham, U.S.A. 81 K6 31 47N 96 28W
Worthing, U.K. 11 G7 50 49N 0 21W
Worthington, U.S.A. 80 D7 43 37N 95 36W
Wosi, Indonesia 37 E7 0 15S 128 0 E
Wou-han = Wuhan, China 33 C6 30 31N 114 18 E
Wour, Chad 51 D8 21 14N 16 0 E
Wousi = Wuxi, China 33 C7 31 33N 120 18 E
Wowoni, Indonesia 37 E6 4 5S 123 5 E
Woy Woy, Australia 63 E5 33 30S 151 19 E
Wrangel I. = Vrangelya, Ostrov, Russia 27 B19 71 0N 180 0 E
Wrangell, U.S.A. 68 C6 56 28N 132 23W
Wrangell I., U.S.A. 72 B2 56 16N 132 12W
Wrangell Mts., U.S.A. 68 B5 61 30N 142 0W
Wrath, C., U.K. 12 C3 58 38N 5 1W
Wray, U.S.A. 80 E3 40 5N 102 13W
Wrekin, The, U.K. 10 E5 52 41N 2 32W
Wrens, U.S.A. 77 J4 33 12N 82 23W
Wrexham, U.K. 10 D4 53 3N 3 0W
Wrexham □, U.K. 10 D5 53 1N 2 58W
Wright, Canada 72 C4 51 52N 121 40W
Wright, Phil. 37 B7 11 42N 125 2 E
Wrightson Mt., U.S.A. 83 L8 31 42N 110 51W
Wrightwood, U.S.A. 85 L9 34 21N 117 38W
Wrigley, Canada 68 B7 63 16N 123 37W
Wrocław, Poland 17 C9 51 5N 17 5 E
Września, Poland 17 B9 52 21N 17 36 E
Wu Jiang →, China 32 D5 29 40N 107 20 E
Wu'an, China 34 F8 36 40N 114 15 E
Wubin, Australia 61 F2 30 6S 116 37 E
Wubu, China 34 F6 37 28N 110 42 E
Wuchang, China 35 B14 44 55N 127 5 E
Wucheng, China 34 F9 37 12N 116 20 E
Wuchuan, China 34 D6 41 5N 111 28 E
Wudi, China 35 F9 37 40N 117 35 E
Wuding He →, China 34 F6 37 2N 110 23 E
Wudu, China 34 H3 33 22N 104 54 E
Wuhan, China 33 C6 30 31N 114 18 E
Wuhe, China 35 H9 33 10N 117 50 E
Wuhsi = Wuxi, China 33 C7 31 33N 120 18 E
Wuhu, China 33 C6 31 22N 118 21 E
Wukari, Nigeria 50 G6 7 51N 9 42 E
Wulajie, China 35 B14 44 6N 126 33 E
Wulanbulang, China 34 D6 41 5N 110 55 E
Wulian, China 35 G10 35 40N 119 12 E
Wuliaru, Indonesia 37 F8 7 27S 131 0 E
Wuluk'omushih Ling, China 32 C3 36 25N 87 25 E
Wulumuchi = Ürümqi, China 26 E9 43 45N 87 45 E
Wum, Cameroon 50 G7 6 24N 10 2 E
Wunnummin L., Canada 70 B2 52 55N 89 10W
Wuntho, Burma 41 H19 23 55N 95 45 E
Wuppertal, Germany 16 C4 51 16N 7 12 E
Wuppertal, S. Africa 56 E2 32 13S 19 12 E
Wuqing, China 35 E9 39 23N 117 4 E
Wurung, Australia 62 B3 19 13S 140 38 E
Würzburg, Germany 16 D5 49 46N 9 55 E
Wushan, China 34 G3 34 43N 104 53 E
Wusuli Jiang = Ussuri →, Asia 30 A7 48 27N 135 0 E
Wutai, China 34 E7 38 40N 113 12 E
Wuting = Huimin, China 35 F9 37 27N 117 28 E
Wutonghaolai, China 35 C11 42 50N 120 5 E
Wutongqiao, China 32 D5 29 22N 103 50 E
Wuwei, China 32 C5 37 57N 102 34 E
Wuxi, China 33 C7 31 33N 120 18 E
Wuxiang, China 34 F7 36 49N 112 50 E
Wuxing, China 33 C7 30 51N 120 8 E
Wuyang, China 34 H7 33 25N 113 35 E
Wuyi, China 34 F8 37 46N 115 56 E
Wuyi Shan, China 33 D6 27 0N 117 0 E
Wuyuan, China 34 D5 41 2N 108 20 E
Wuzhai, China 34 E6 38 54N 111 48 E
Wuzhi Shan, China 38 C7 18 45N 109 45 E
Wuzhong, China 34 E4 38 2N 106 12 E
Wuzhou, China 33 D6 23 30N 111 18 E
Wyaaba Cr. →, Australia 62 B3 16 27S 141 35 E
Wyalkatchem, Australia 61 F2 31 8S 117 22 E
Wyalusing, U.S.A. 79 E8 41 40N 76 16W
Wyandotte, U.S.A. 76 D4 42 12N 83 9W
Wyandra, Australia 63 D4 27 12S 145 56 E
Wyangala Res., Australia 63 E4 33 54S 149 0 E
Wyara, L., Australia 63 D3 28 42S 144 14 E
Wycheproof, Australia 63 F3 36 5S 143 17 E
Wye →, U.K. 11 F5 51 38N 2 40W
Wyemandoo, Australia 61 E2 28 28S 118 29 E
Wymondham, U.K. 11 E7 52 45N 0 43W
Wymore, U.S.A. 80 E6 40 7N 96 40W
Wynbring, Australia 63 E1 30 33S 133 32 E
Wyndham, Australia 60 C4 15 33S 128 3 E
Wyndham, N.Z. 59 M2 46 20S 168 51 E
Wyndmere, U.S.A. 80 B6 46 16N 97 8W
Wynne, U.S.A. 81 H9 35 14N 90 47W
Wynnum, Australia 63 D5 27 27S 153 9 E
Wynyard, Australia 62 G4 41 5S 145 44 E
Wynyard, Canada 73 C8 51 45N 104 10W
Wyola, L., Australia 61 E5 29 8S 130 17 E
Wyoming □, U.S.A. 82 E10 43 0N 107 30W
Wyong, Australia 63 E5 33 14S 151 24 E
Wytheville, U.S.A. 76 G5 36 57N 81 5W

X

Xai-Xai, Mozam. 57 D5 25 6S 33 31 E
Xainza, China 32 C3 30 58N 88 35 E
Xangongo, Angola 56 B2 16 45S 15 5 E
Xankändi, Azerbaijan 25 G8 39 52N 46 49 E
Xánthi, Greece 21 D11 41 10N 24 58 E
Xapuri, Brazil 92 F5 10 35S 68 35W
Xar Moron He →, China 35 C11 43 25N 120 35 E
Xau, L., Botswana 56 C3 21 15S 24 44 E
Xavantina, Brazil 95 A5 21 15S 52 48W
Xenia, U.S.A. 76 F4 39 41N 83 56W
Xeropotamos →, Cyprus 23 E11 34 42N 32 33 E
Xhora, S. Africa 57 E4 31 55S 28 38 E
Xhumo, Botswana 56 C3 21 7S 24 35 E
Xi Jiang →, China 33 D6 22 5N 113 20 E
Xi Xian, China 34 F6 36 41N 110 58 E
Xia Xian, China 34 G6 35 8N 111 12 E
Xiachengzi, China 35 B16 44 40N 130 18 E
Xiaguan, China 32 D5 25 32N 100 16 E
Xiajin, China 34 F8 36 56N 116 0 E
Xiamen, China 33 D6 24 25N 118 4 E
Xi'an, China 34 G5 34 15N 109 0 E
Xian Xian, China 34 E9 38 12N 116 6 E
Xiang Jiang →, China 33 D6 28 55N 112 50 E
Xiangcheng, Henan, China 34 H8 33 29N 114 52 E
Xiangcheng, Henan, China 34 H7 33 50N 113 27 E
Xiangfan, China 33 C6 32 2N 112 8 E
Xianghuang Qi, China 34 C7 42 2N 113 50 E
Xiangning, China 34 G6 35 58N 110 50 E
Xiangquan, China 34 F7 36 30N 113 1 E
Xiangshui, China 35 G10 34 12N 119 33 E
Xiangtan, China 33 D6 27 51N 112 54 E
Xianyang, China 34 G5 34 20N 108 40 E
Xiao Hinggan Ling, China 33 B7 49 0N 127 0 E
Xiao Xian, China 34 G9 34 15N 116 55 E
Xiaoyi, China 34 F6 37 8N 111 48 E
Xiawa, China 35 C11 42 35N 120 38 E
Xiayi, China 34 G9 34 15N 116 10 E
Xichang, China 32 D5 27 51N 102 19 E
Xichuan, China 34 H6 33 0N 111 30 E
Xieng Khouang, Laos 38 C4 19 17N 103 25 E
Xifei He →, China 34 H9 32 45N 116 40 E
Xifeng, China 35 C13 42 42N 124 45 E
Xifengzhen, China 34 G4 35 40N 107 40 E
Xigazê, China 32 D3 29 5N 88 45 E
Xihe, China 34 G3 34 2N 105 20 E
Xihua, China 34 H8 33 45N 114 30 E
Xiliao He →, China 35 C12 43 32N 123 35 E
Xin Xian, China 34 E7 38 22N 112 46 E
Xinavane, Mozam. 57 D5 25 2S 32 47 E
Xinbin, China 35 D13 41 40N 125 2 E
Xing Xian, China 34 E6 38 27N 111 7 E
Xing'an, China 33 D6 25 38N 110 40 E
Xingcheng, China 35 D11 40 40N 120 45 E
Xinghe, China 34 D7 40 55N 113 55 E
Xinghua, China 35 H10 32 58N 119 48 E
Xinglong, China 35 D9 40 25N 117 30 E
Xingping, China 34 G5 34 20N 108 28 E
Xingtai, China 34 F8 37 3N 114 32 E
Xingu →, Brazil 93 D8 1 30S 51 53W
Xingyang, China 34 G7 34 45N 112 52 E
Xinhe, China 34 F8 37 30N 115 15 E
Xining, China 32 C5 36 34N 101 40 E
Xinjiang, China 34 G6 35 34N 111 11 E
Xinjiang Uygur Zizhiqu □, China 32 B3 42 0N 86 0 E
Xinjin, China 35 E11 39 25N 121 58 E
Xinkai He →, China 35 C12 43 32N 123 35 E
Xinle, China 34 E8 38 25N 114 40 E
Xinlitun, China 35 D12 42 0N 122 8 E
Xinmin, China 35 D12 41 59N 122 50 E
Xintai, China 35 G9 35 55N 117 45 E
Xinxiang, China 34 G7 35 18N 113 50 E
Xinzhan, China 35 C14 43 50N 127 18 E
Xinzheng, China 34 G7 34 20N 113 45 E
Xiong Xian, China 34 E9 38 59N 116 8 E
Xiongyuecheng, China 35 D12 40 12N 122 5 E
Xiping, Henan, China 34 H8 33 22N 114 5 E
Xiping, Henan, China 34 H6 33 25N 111 8 E
Xique-Xique, Brazil 93 F10 10 50S 42 40W
Xisha Qundao = Paracel Is., S. China Sea 36 A4 15 50N 112 0 E
Xiuyan, China 35 D12 40 18N 123 11 E
Xixabangma Feng, China 41 E14 28 20N 85 40 E
Xixia, China 34 H6 33 25N 111 29 E
Xixiang, China 34 H4 33 0N 107 44 E
Xiyang, China 34 F7 37 38N 113 38 E
Xizang □, China 32 C3 32 0N 88 0 E
Xlendi, Malta 23 C1 36 1N 14 12 E
Xuan Loc, Vietnam 39 G6 10 56N 107 14 E
Xuanhua, China 34 D8 40 40N 115 2 E
Xuchang, China 34 G7 34 2N 113 48 E
Xun Xian, China 34 G8 35 42N 114 33 E
Xunyang, China 34 H5 32 48N 109 22 E
Xunyi, China 34 G5 35 8N 108 20 E
Xushui, China 34 E8 39 2N 115 40 E
Xuyen Moc, Vietnam 39 G6 10 34N 107 25 E
Xuzhou, China 35 G9 34 18N 117 10 E
Xylophagou, Cyprus 23 E12 34 54N 33 51 E

Y

Ya Xian, China 38 C7 18 14N 109 29 E
Yaamba, Australia 62 C5 23 8S 150 22 E
Yaapeet, Australia 63 F3 35 45S 142 3 E
Yabelo, Ethiopia 51 H12 4 50N 38 8 E
Yablonovy Ra. = Yablonovyy Khrebet, Russia 27 D12 53 0N 114 0 E
Yablonovyy Khrebet, Russia 27 D12 53 0N 114 0 E
Yabrai Shan, China 34 E2 39 40N 103 0 E
Yabrūd, Syria 47 B5 33 58N 36 39 E
Yacheng, China 33 E5 18 22N 109 6 E
Yacuiba, Bolivia 94 A3 22 0S 63 43W
Yadgir, India 40 L10 16 45N 77 5 E
Yadkin →, U.S.A. 77 H5 35 29N 80 9W
Yagodnoye, Russia 27 C15 62 33N 149 40 E
Yagoua, Cameroon 52 B3 10 20N 15 13 E
Yaha, Thailand 39 J3 6 29N 101 8 E
Yahila, Zaïre 54 B1 0 13N 24 28 E
Yahk, Canada 72 D5 49 6N 116 10W
Yahuma, Zaïre 52 D4 1 0N 23 10 E
Yaita, Japan 31 F9 36 48N 139 56 E
Yaiza, Canary Is. 22 F6 28 57N 13 46W
Yakima, U.S.A. 82 C3 46 36N 120 31W
Yakima →, U.S.A. 82 C3 47 0N 120 30W
Yakovlevka, Russia 30 B6 44 26N 133 28 E
Yaku-Shima, Japan 31 J5 30 20N 130 30 E
Yakutat, U.S.A. 68 C6 59 33N 139 44W
Yakutia = Sakha □, Russia 27 C13 62 0N 130 0 E
Yakutsk, Russia 27 C13 62 5N 129 50 E
Yala, Thailand 39 J3 6 33N 101 18 E
Yalbalgo, Australia 61 E1 25 10S 114 45 E
Yalboroo, Australia 62 C4 20 50S 148 40 E
Yale, U.S.A. 78 C2 43 8N 82 48W
Yalgoo, Australia 61 E2 28 16S 116 39 E
Yalinga, C.A.R. 51 G9 6 33N 23 10 E
Yalkubul, Punta, Mexico 87 C7 21 32N 88 37W
Yalleroi, Australia 62 C4 24 3S 145 42 E
Yalobusha →, U.S.A. 81 J9 33 33N 90 10W
Yalong Jiang →, China 32 D5 26 40N 101 55 E
Yalova, Turkey 21 D13 40 41N 29 15 E
Yalta, Ukraine 25 F5 44 30N 34 10 E
Yalu Jiang →, China 35 E13 40 0N 124 22 E
Yalutorovsk, Russia 26 D7 56 41N 66 12 E
Yam Ha Melaḥ = Dead Sea, Asia 47 D4 31 30N 35 30 E
Yam Kinneret, Israel 47 C4 32 45N 35 35 E
Yamada, Japan 31 H5 33 33N 130 49 E
Yamagata, Japan 30 E10 38 15N 140 15 E
Yamagata □, Japan 30 E10 38 30N 140 0 E
Yamaguchi, Japan 31 G5 34 10N 131 32 E
Yamaguchi □, Japan 31 G5 34 20N 131 40 E
Yamal, Poluostrov, Russia 26 B8 71 0N 70 0 E
Yamal Pen. = Yamal, Poluostrov, Russia 26 B8 71 0N 70 0 E
Yamanashi □, Japan 31 G9 35 40N 138 40 E
Yamantau, Gora, Russia 24 D10 54 15N 58 6 E
Yamba, N.S.W., Australia 63 D5 29 26S 153 23 E
Yamba, S. Austral., Australia 63 E3 34 10S 140 52 E
Yambah, Australia 62 C1 23 10S 133 50 E
Yambarran Ra., Australia 60 C5 15 10S 130 25 E
Yâmbiô, Sudan 51 H10 4 35N 28 16 E
Yambol, Bulgaria 21 C12 42 30N 26 36 E
Yamdena, Indonesia 37 F8 7 45S 131 20 E
Yame, Japan 31 H5 33 13N 130 35 E
Yamethin, Burma 41 J20 20 29N 96 18 E
Yamma-Yamma, L., Australia 63 D3 26 16S 141 20 E
Yamoussoukro, Ivory C. 50 G3 6 49N 5 17W
Yampa →, U.S.A. 82 F9 40 32N 108 59W
Yampi Sd., Australia 60 C3 16 8S 123 38 E
Yampil, Moldova 17 D15 48 15N 28 15 E
Yampol = Yampil, Moldova 17 D15 48 15N 28 15 E
Yamuna →, India 43 G9 25 30N 81 53 E
Yamzho Yumco, China 32 D4 28 48N 90 35 E
Yana →, Russia 27 B14 71 30N 136 0 E
Yanac, Australia 63 F3 36 8S 141 25 E
Yanagawa, Japan 31 H5 33 10N 130 24 E
Yanai, Japan 31 H6 33 58N 132 7 E
Yan'an, China 34 F5 36 35N 109 26 E
Yanaul, Russia 24 C10 56 25N 55 0 E
Yanbu 'al Baḥr, Si. Arabia 44 F3 24 0N 38 5 E
Yancannia, Australia 63 E3 30 12S 142 35 E
Yanchang, China 34 F6 36 43N 110 1 E
Yancheng, Henan, China 34 H7 33 35N 114 0 E
Yancheng, Jiangsu, China 35 H11 33 23N 120 8 E
Yanchi, China 34 F4 37 48N 107 20 E
Yanchuan, China 34 F6 36 51N 110 10 E
Yanco Cr. →, Australia 63 F4 35 14S 145 35 E
Yandal, Australia 61 E3 27 35S 121 10 E
Yandanooka, Australia 61 E2 29 18S 115 29 E
Yandaran, Australia 62 C5 24 43S 152 6 E
Yandoon, Burma 41 L19 17 0N 95 40 E
Yang Xian, China 34 H4 33 15N 107 30 E
Yangambi, Zaïre 54 B1 0 47N 24 20 E
Yangcheng, China 34 G7 35 28N 112 22 E
Yangch'ü = Taiyuan, China 34 F7 37 52N 112 33 E
Yanggao, China 34 D7 40 21N 113 55 E
Yanggu, China 34 F8 36 8N 115 43 E
Yangliuqing, China 35 E9 39 2N 117 5 E
Yangon = Rangoon, Burma 41 L20 16 45N 96 20 E
Yangpingguan, China 34 H4 32 58N 106 5 E
Yangquan, China 34 F7 37 58N 113 31 E
Yangtze Kiang = Chang Jiang →, China 33 C7 31 48N 121 10 E
Yangyang, S. Korea 35 E15 38 4N 128 38 E
Yangyuan, China 34 D8 40 1N 114 10 E
Yangzhou, China 33 C6 32 21N 119 26 E
Yanji, China 35 C15 42 59N 129 30 E
Yankton, U.S.A. 80 D6 42 53N 97 23W
Yanna, Australia 63 D4 26 58S 146 0 E
Yanonge, Zaïre 54 B1 0 35N 24 38 E
Yanqi, China 32 B3 42 5N 86 35 E
Yanqing, China 34 D8 40 30N 115 58 E
Yanshan, China 35 E9 38 4N 117 22 E
Yanshou, China 35 B15 45 28N 128 22 E
Yantabulla, Australia 63 D4 29 21S 145 0 E
Yantai, China 35 F11 37 34N 121 22 E
Yantykurgan, Kazakstan 26 E7 43 50N 68 48 E
Yanzhou, China 34 G9 35 35N 116 49 E
Yao, Chad 51 F8 12 56N 17 33 E
Yao Xian, China 34 G5 34 55N 108 59 E
Yao Yai, Ko, Thailand 39 J2 8 0N 98 35 E
Yaoundé, Cameroon 50 H7 3 50N 11 35 E
Yaowan, China 35 G10 34 15N 118 3 E
Yap I., Pac. Oc. 64 G5 9 30N 138 10 E
Yapen, Indonesia 37 E9 1 50S 136 0 E
Yapen, Selat, Indonesia 37 E9 1 20S 136 10 E
Yappar →, Australia 62 B3 18 22S 141 16 E
Yaqui →, Mexico 86 B2 27 37N 110 39W
Yar-Sale, Russia 26 C8 66 50N 70 50 E
Yaraka, Australia 62 C3 24 53S 144 3 E
Yaransk, Russia 24 C8 57 22N 47 49 E
Yardea P.O., Australia 63 E2 32 23S 135 32 E
Yare →, U.K. 11 E9 52 35N 1 38 E
Yaremcha, Ukraine 17 D13 48 27N 24 33 E
Yarensk, Russia 24 B8 62 11N 49 15 E
Yarí →, Colombia 92 D4 0 20S 72 20W
Yarkand = Shache, China 32 C2 38 20N 77 10 E
Yarker, Canada 79 B8 44 23N 76 46W
Yarkhun →, Pakistan 43 A5 36 17N 72 30 E
Yarmouth, Canada 71 D6 43 50N 66 7W
Yarmūk →, Syria 47 C4 32 42N 35 40 E
Yaroslavl, Russia 24 C6 57 35N 39 55 E
Yarqa, W. →, Egypt 47 F2 30 0N 33 49 E
Yarra Yarra Lakes, Australia 61 E2 29 40S 115 45 E
Yarraden, Australia 62 A3 14 17S 143 15 E
Yarraloola, Australia 60 D2 21 33S 115 52 E
Yarram, Australia 63 F4 38 29S 146 39 E
Yarraman, Australia 63 D5 26 50S 152 0 E
Yarranvale, Australia 63 D4 26 50S 145 20 E
Yarras, Australia 63 E5 31 25S 152 20 E
Yarrowmere, Australia 62 C4 21 27S 145 53 E
Yartsevo, Russia 27 C10 60 20N 90 0 E
Yasawa Group, Fiji 59 C7 17 0S 177 23 E
Yaselda, Belarus 17 B14 52 7N 26 28 E
Yasin, Pakistan 43 A5 36 24N 73 23 E
Yasinski, L., Canada 70 B4 53 16N 77 35W
Yasinya, Ukraine 17 D13 48 16N 24 21 E
Yasothon, Thailand 38 E5 15 50N 104 10 E
Yass, Australia 63 E4 34 49S 148 54 E
Yatağan, Turkey 21 F13 37 20N 28 10 E
Yates Center, U.S.A. 81 G7 37 53N 95 44W
Yathkyed L., Canada 73 A9 62 40N 98 0W
Yatsushiro, Japan 31 H5 32 30N 130 40 E
Yatta Plateau, Kenya 54 C4 2 0S 38 0 E
Yauyos, Peru 92 F3 12 19S 75 50W
Yavari →, Peru 92 D4 4 21S 70 2W
Yavatmal, India 40 J11 20 20N 78 15 E
Yavne, Israel 47 D3 31 52N 34 45 E
Yavoriv, Ukraine 17 D12 49 55N 23 20 E
Yavorov = Yavoriv, Ukraine 17 D12 49 55N 23 20 E
Yawatahama, Japan 31 H6 33 27N 132 24 E
Yayama-Rettō, Japan 31 M1 24 30N 123 40 E
Yazd, Iran 45 D7 31 55N 54 27 E
Yazd □, Iran 45 D7 32 0N 55 0 E
Yazoo →, U.S.A. 81 J9 32 22N 90 54W
Yazoo City, U.S.A. 81 J9 32 51N 90 25W
Yding Skovhøj, Denmark 9 J13 55 59N 9 46 E
Ye Xian, Henan, China 34 H7 33 35N 113 25 E
Ye Xian, Shandong, China 35 F10 37 8N 119 57 E
Yealering, Australia 61 F2 32 36S 117 36 E
Yebyu, Burma 41 M21 14 15N 98 13 E
Yechŏn, S. Korea 35 F15 36 39N 128 27 E
Yecla, Spain 19 C5 38 35N 1 5W
Yécora, Mexico 86 B3 28 20N 108 58W
Yedintsy = Edinița, Moldova 17 D14 48 9N 27 18 E
Yeeda, Australia 60 C3 17 31S 123 38 E
Yeelanna, Australia 63 E2 34 9S 135 45 E
Yegros, Paraguay 94 B4 26 20S 56 25W
Yehuda, Midbar, Israel 47 D4 31 35N 35 15 E
Yei, Sudan 51 H11 4 9N 30 40 E
Yekaterinburg, Russia 24 C11 56 50N 60 30 E
Yekaterinodar = Krasnodar, Russia 25 E6 45 5N 39 0 E
Yelanskoye, Russia 27 C13 61 25N 128 0 E
Yelarbon, Australia 63 D5 28 33S 150 38 E
Yelets, Russia 24 D6 52 40N 38 30 E
Yelizavetgrad = Kirovohrad, Ukraine 25 E5 48 35N 32 20 E
Yell, U.K. 12 A7 60 35N 1 5W
Yell Sd., U.K. 12 A7 60 33N 1 15W
Yellow Sea, China 35 G12 35 0N 123 0 E
Yellowhead Pass, Canada 72 C5 52 53N 118 25W
Yellowknife, Canada 72 A6 62 27N 114 29W
Yellowknife →, Canada 72 A6 62 31N 114 19W
Yellowstone →, U.S.A. 80 B3 47 59N 103 59W
Yellowstone L., U.S.A. 82 D8 44 27N 110 22W
Yellowstone National Park, U.S.A. 82 D8 44 40N 110 30W
Yellowtail Res., U.S.A. 82 D9 45 6N 108 8W
Yelsk, Belarus 17 C15 51 50N 29 10 E
Yelvertoft, Australia 62 C2 20 13S 138 45 E
Yemen ■, Asia 46 E3 15 0N 44 0 E
Yen Bai, Vietnam 38 B5 21 42N 104 52 E
Yenangyaung, Burma 41 J19 20 30N 95 0 E
Yenbo = Yanbu 'al Baḥr, Si. Arabia 44 F3 24 0N 38 5 E
Yenda, Australia 63 E4 34 13S 146 14 E
Yenice, Turkey 21 E12 39 55N 27 17 E
Yenisey →, Russia 26 B9 71 50N 82 40 E
Yeniseysk, Russia 27 D10 58 27N 92 13 E
Yeniseyskiy Zaliv, Russia 26 B9 72 20N 81 0 E
Yennádhi, Greece 23 C9 36 2N 27 56 E
Yenyuka, Russia 27 D13 57 57N 121 15 E
Yeo, L., Australia 61 E3 28 0S 124 30 E
Yeola, India 40 J9 20 2N 74 30 E
Yeoryioúpolis, Greece 23 D6 35 20N 24 15 E
Yeovil, U.K. 11 G5 50 57N 2 38W
Yeppoon, Australia 62 C5 23 5S 150 47 E
Yerbent, Turkmenistan 26 F6 39 30N 58 50 E
Yerbogachen, Russia 27 C11 61 16N 108 0 E
Yerevan, Armenia 25 F7 40 10N 44 31 E
Yerilla, Australia 61 E3 29 24S 121 47 E
Yermak, Kazakstan 26 D8 52 2N 76 55 E
Yermakovo, Russia 27 D13 52 25N 126 20 E
Yermo, U.S.A. 85 L10 34 54N 116 50W
Yerofey Pavlovich, Russia 27 D13 54 0N 122 0 E
Yerólakkos, Cyprus 23 D12 35 11N 33 15 E
Yeropol, Russia 27 C17 65 15N 168 40 E
Yeropótamos →, Greece 23 D6 35 3N 24 50 E
Yeroskipos, Cyprus 23 E11 34 46N 32 28 E
Yershov, Russia 25 D8 51 23N 48 27 E
Yerushalayim = Jerusalem, Israel 47 D4 31 47N 35 10 E
Yes Tor, U.K. 11 G4 50 41N 4 0W
Yesan, S. Korea 35 F14 36 41N 126 51 E
Yeso, U.S.A. 81 H2 34 26N 104 37W
Yessey, Russia 27 C11 68 29N 102 10 E
Yeu, I. d', France 18 C2 46 42N 2 20W
Yevpatoriya, Ukraine 25 E5 45 15N 33 20 E
Yeysk, Russia 25 E6 46 40N 38 12 E
Yezd = Yazd, Iran 45 D7 31 55N 54 27 E
Yhati, Paraguay 94 B4 25 45S 56 35W
Yhú, Paraguay 95 B4 25 0S 56 0W
Yi →, Uruguay 94 C4 33 7S 57 8W